Rand McNally
World Atlas

Rand McNally & Company
Chicago / New York / San Francisco

Contents

Using the Atlas ... 3A

The Planet Earth

The Origin and Destiny of
   the Solar System _____ 6A
The Solar System _____ 8A
Earth's Companion: The Moon _____ 10A
Anatomy of the Earth _____ 12A
The Evolution of Land and Sea _____ 14A
The Active Earth _____ 16A
Forces That Shape The Land _____ 18A
The Record in the Rocks _____ 20A
The Active Oceans _____ 22A
The Earth Under the Sea _____ 24A
The Atmosphere _____ 26A
The Structure of Weather Systems _____ 28A
Extremes of Weather _____ 30A

World Time Zones _____ 32A

The Political World in Maps

The World
Polar Map of the World _____ 1
The World _____ 2

Europe
Europe _____ 3
British Isles _____ 4
France and the Low Countries _____ 5
Germany, Austria and Switzerland _____ 6
Poland and Czechoslovakia _____ 7
Spain and Portugal _____ 8
Italy _____ 9
Yugoslavia, Hungary, Romania
   and Bulgaria _____ 10
Norway, Sweden and Finland _____ 11
Western Soviet Union _____ 12
Soviet Union _____ 13
Eastern Mediterranean _____ 14

Asia
Israel and Arabia _____ 15
Eurasia _____ 16
China, Mongolia, Korea, Japan and Taiwan _____ 17
Japan and Korea _____ 18
Indonesia and the Philippines _____ 19
India, Pakistan, Bangladesh, Burma
   and Sri Lanka _____ 20

Africa
Africa _____ 21
Northwestern Africa _____ 22
Northeastern Africa _____ 23
Central and Southern Africa _____ 24

Australia and New Zealand
Australia _____ 25
Southeastern Australia and New Zealand _____ 26

South America
South America _____ 27
Central and Southern Argentina and Chile _____ 28
Bolivia, Paraguay, Northern Argentina
   and Chile _____ 29
Uruguay and Southern Brazil _____ 30
Peru and Ecuador _____ 31
Colombia and Venezuela _____ 32

North America
North America _____ 33
Mexico _____ 34
West Indies _____ 35
Canada _____ 36
   British Columbia _____ 37
   Alberta _____ 38
   Saskatchewan _____ 39
   Manitoba _____ 40
   Ontario _____ 41
   Quebec _____ 42
   Maritime Provinces _____ 43
   Newfoundland _____ 44
United States _____ 45
   Alabama _____ 46
   Alaska _____ 47
   Arizona and New Mexico _____ 48
   Arkansas _____ 49
   California _____ 50
   Colorado _____ 51
   Connecticut and Rhode Island _____ 52
   Delaware and Maryland _____ 53
   Florida _____ 54
   Georgia _____ 55
   Hawaii _____ 56
   Idaho _____ 57
   Illinois _____ 58
   Indiana _____ 59
   Iowa _____ 60
   Kansas _____ 61
   Kentucky _____ 62
   Louisiana _____ 63
   Maine _____ 64
   Massachusetts _____ 65
   Michigan _____ 66
   Minnesota _____ 67
   Mississippi _____ 68
   Missouri _____ 69
   Montana _____ 70
   Nebraska _____ 71
   Nevada and Utah _____ 72
   New Hampshire and Vermont _____ 73
   New Jersey _____ 74
   New York _____ 75
   North Carolina _____ 76
   North Dakota and South Dakota _____ 77
   Ohio _____ 78
   Oklahoma _____ 79
   Oregon _____ 80
   Pennsylvania _____ 81
   South Carolina _____ 82
   Tennessee _____ 83
   Texas _____ 84
   Virginia _____ 85
   Washington _____ 86
   West Virginia _____ 87
   Wisconsin _____ 88
   Wyoming _____ 89

World Geographical Information

General; The Continents; Historical Populations;
   Largest Countries: Population;
   Largest Countries: Area _____ 90
Principal Mountains _____ 91
Oceans, Seas, and Gulfs;
   Principal Lakes; Principal Rivers;
   Principal Islands _____ 92
World Political Information _____ 93-96

Abbreviations _____ 97

Index _____ 98-172

United States Geographical Information

General; Territorial Acquisition
   and Population Movement;
   State Areas and Populations _____ 173
United States General Information _____ 174
United States Historical Populations _____ 175
United States Metropolitan Areas _____ 176

United States and World Populations

United States Populations and
   Zip Codes _____ 177-200
World Populations _____ 201-224

Maps and Atlases

Since ancient times, maps have played a unique role in presenting information about the world, and maps defining territory and ownership are almost as old as the human territorial instinct itself. Dating from the second and first millenia B.C., the rock-carving map of the Val Camonica, Italy, in figure 1 shows stepped square fields, paths, rivers, and houses. Elegant as well as useful maps have been produced by many cultures. In figure 2, the Mexican map of the Tepetlaoztoc Valley, drawn in 1583, marks hills with wavy lines and roads with footprints between parallel lines. The methods and materials used to create these maps were dependent upon the technology available, and their accuracy suffered considerably, whereas modern maps are highly accurate, benefiting from our ever-increasing technological knowledge. Satellite imagery, shown in figure 3, now furnishes current, highly precise material from which maps such as that in figure 4 may be created or updated.

In the 1500s Gerardus Mercator, a Flemish cartographer, coined the word *atlas* to describe

Using the Atlas

a collection of maps. The atlas is unique among reference publications because only it, with its maps, actually shows *where* things are located in the world. As a dictionary defines words, as an encyclopedia defines things, an atlas graphically defines the world. Only on a map can the countries, cities, roads, rivers, and lakes covering a vast area be simultaneously viewed in their relative locations. Routes between places can be traced, trips planned, boundaries of neighboring states and countries examined, distances between places measured, the meandering of streams and the sizes of lakes visualized—and remote places imagined.

This atlas brings together not only a variety of maps but also an assortment of tables and other reference material, with topics ranging from the world's size and population to the countries' political status. To get the most out of the atlas, it is necessary to have a general idea of the arrangement of the information.

Sequence of the Maps

The world is made up of seven major landmasses: the continents of Europe, Asia, Africa, Australia, South America, North America, and Antarctica (figure 5). To allow for the inclusion of detail, each continent is broken down into a series of maps, and this grouping is arranged so that as consecutive pages are turned, a continuous and successive part of the continent is shown. Larger-scale maps are used for regions of greater detail (having many cities, for example) or for areas of global significance.

The continental sequence of the maps is as follows: Europe (traditionally first in atlases), Asia (connected to Europe and forming the Eurasian landmass), Africa, Australia and Oceania, South America, and North America.

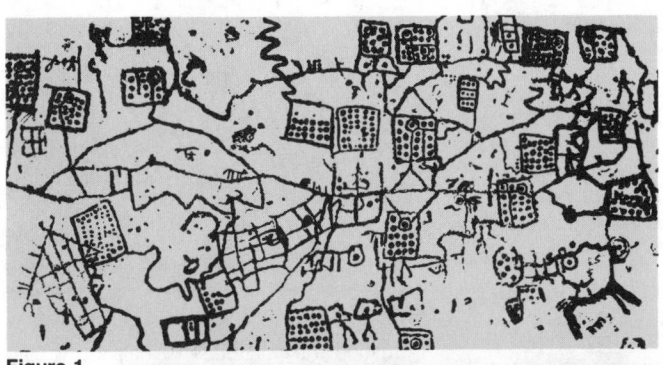
Figure 1

Figure 2

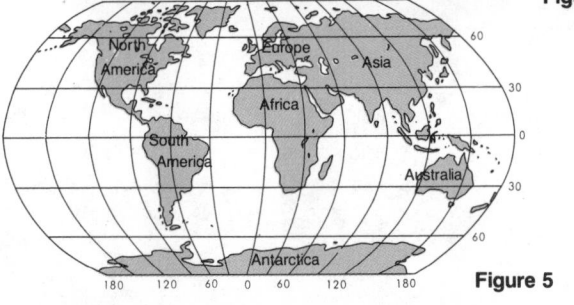
Figure 3

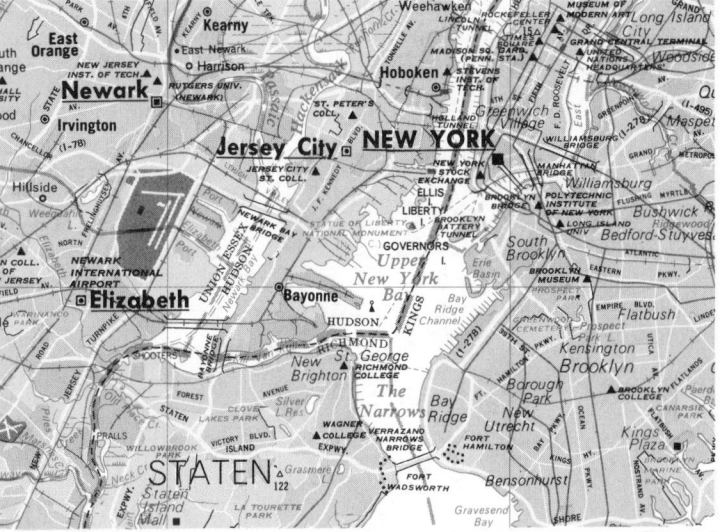
Figure 4

Figure 5

Getting the Information

An atlas can be used for many purposes, from planning a trip to finding hot spots in the news and supplementing world knowledge. But to realize the full potential of an atlas, the user must be able to:

1. Find places on the maps
2. Measure distances
3. Determine directions
4. Understand map symbols

Finding Places

One of the most common and important tasks facilitated by an atlas is finding the *location* of a place in the world. A river's name in a book, a city mentioned in the news, or a vacation spot may prompt your need to know where the place is located. The illustrations and text below explain how to find Benguela, Angola.

1. Look up the place-name in the index at the back of the atlas. Benguela, Angola, can be found on the map on page 24, and it can be located on the map by the letter-number key *C2* (figure 6).

Bay-Ber		155
Benewah, Idaho	B2	57
Benewah, co., Idaho	B2	57
Bengal, reg., Bngl., India	D8	20
Bengasi (Banghāzī), Libya	B2	23
Bengbu, China	E8	17
Bengkulu, Indon.	F2	19
Benguela, Ang.	C2	24
Benguela, dist., Ang.	C3	24
Benham, Ky.	D7	62
Ben Hill, co., Ga.	D3	55

Figure 6

2. Turn to the map of Central and Southern Africa on page 24. Note that the letters A through H and the numbers 1 through 10 appear in the margins of the maps.

3. To find Benguela on the map, place your left index finger on C and your right index finger on 2. Move your left finger across the map and your right finger down the map. Your fingers will meet in the area in which Benguela is located (figure 7).

Figure 7

Measuring Distances

In planning trips, determining the distance between two places is essential, and an atlas can help in travel preparation. For instance, to determine the approximate distance between Paris and Rouen, France, follow these three steps:

1. Lay a slip of paper on the map on page 5 so that its edge touches the two cities. Adjust the paper so one corner touches Rouen. Mark the paper directly at the spot where Paris is located (figure 8).

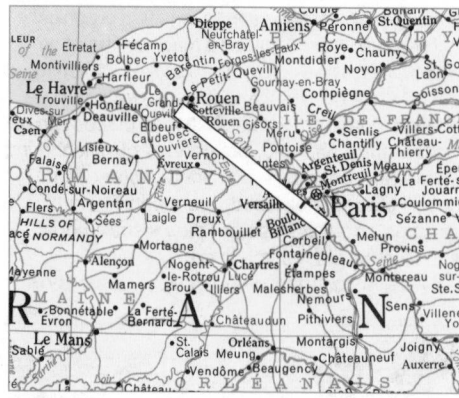

Figure 8

2. Place the paper along the scale of statute miles beneath the map. Position the corner at 0 and line up the edge of the paper along the scale. The pencil mark on the paper indicates Rouen is between 50 and 75 miles from Paris (figure 9).

Figure 9

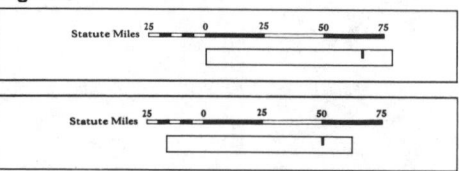

Figure 10

3. To find the exact distance, move the paper to the left so that the pencil mark is at 50 on the scale. The corner of the paper stands in the fourth 5-mile unit on the scale. This means that the two towns are 50 plus 15 plus 2, or 67 miles, apart (figure 10).

Determining Directions

Most of the maps in the atlas are drawn so that when oriented for normal reading north is at the top of the map, south is at the bottom, west is at the left, and east is at the right. Most maps have a series of lines drawn across them—the lines of latitude and longitude. Lines of latitude, or parallels of latitude, are drawn east and west.

Figure 11

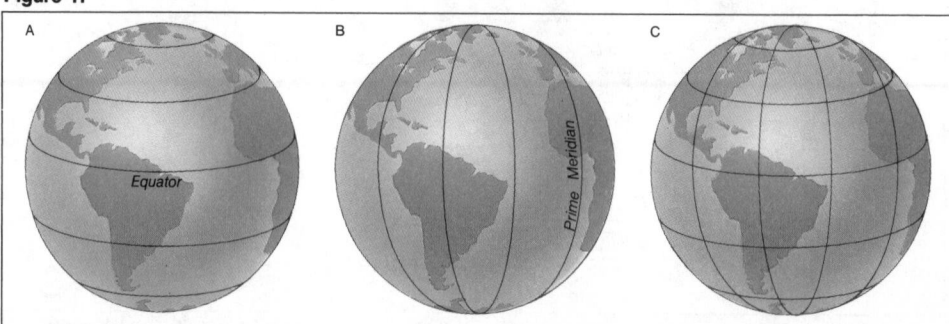

Lines of longitude, or meridians of longitude, are drawn north and south (figure 11).

Parallels and meridians appear as either curved or straight lines. For example, in the section of the map of Europe in figure 12, the parallels of latitude appear as curved lines. The meridians of longitude are straight lines that come together toward the top of the map.

Figure 12

Latitude and longitude lines help locate places on maps. Parallels of latitude are numbered in degrees north and south of the *Equator.* Meridians of longitude are numbered in degrees east and west of a line called the *Prime Meridian,* running through Greenwich, England, near London. Any place on earth can be located by the latitude and longitude lines running through it.

To determine directions or locations on maps, you must use the parallels and meridians. For example, suppose you want to know which city is farther north, Bergen, Norway, or Stockholm, Sweden. The map in figure 12 shows that Stockholm is south of the 60° parallel of latitude and Bergen is north of it. This means that Bergen is farther north than Stockholm. By looking at the meridians of longitude, you can determine which city is farther east. Bergen is approximately 5° east of the 0° meridian (Prime Meridian), and Stockholm is almost 20° east of it. This means that Stockholm is farther east than Bergen.

Map Symbols (Legend)
For maps pages 1–89

CULTURAL FEATURES

Political Boundaries

═══════ International

───────── Secondary (State, province, etc.)

· · · · · · County

Populated Places

Cities, towns, and villages

• • • • • ● ● Symbol size represents population of the place

Chicago
Gary
Racine
Glenview
Edgewood

Type size represents relative importance of the place

▨ Corporate area of large U.S. and Canadian cities and urban area of other foreign cities

Major Urban Area
Area of continuous commercial, industrial, and residential development in and around a major city

○ Community within a city

⊛ Capital of major political unit

☆ Capital of secondary political unit

◉ Capital of U.S. state or Canadian province

◦ County Seat

▲ Military Installation

⊙ Scientific Station

Miscellaneous

▨ National Park

▨ National Monument

▨ Provincial Park

▨ Indian Reservation

△ Point of Interest

∴ Ruins

■ ╢ Buildings

⬭ Race Track

───── Railroad

┼─┼─┼ Tunnel

────── Underground or Subway

⌂ Dam

⏀ Bridge

⏀ Dike

LAND FEATURES

Passes =)(

Point of Elevation above sea level + 8.520 FT

Figure 13

WATER FEATURES

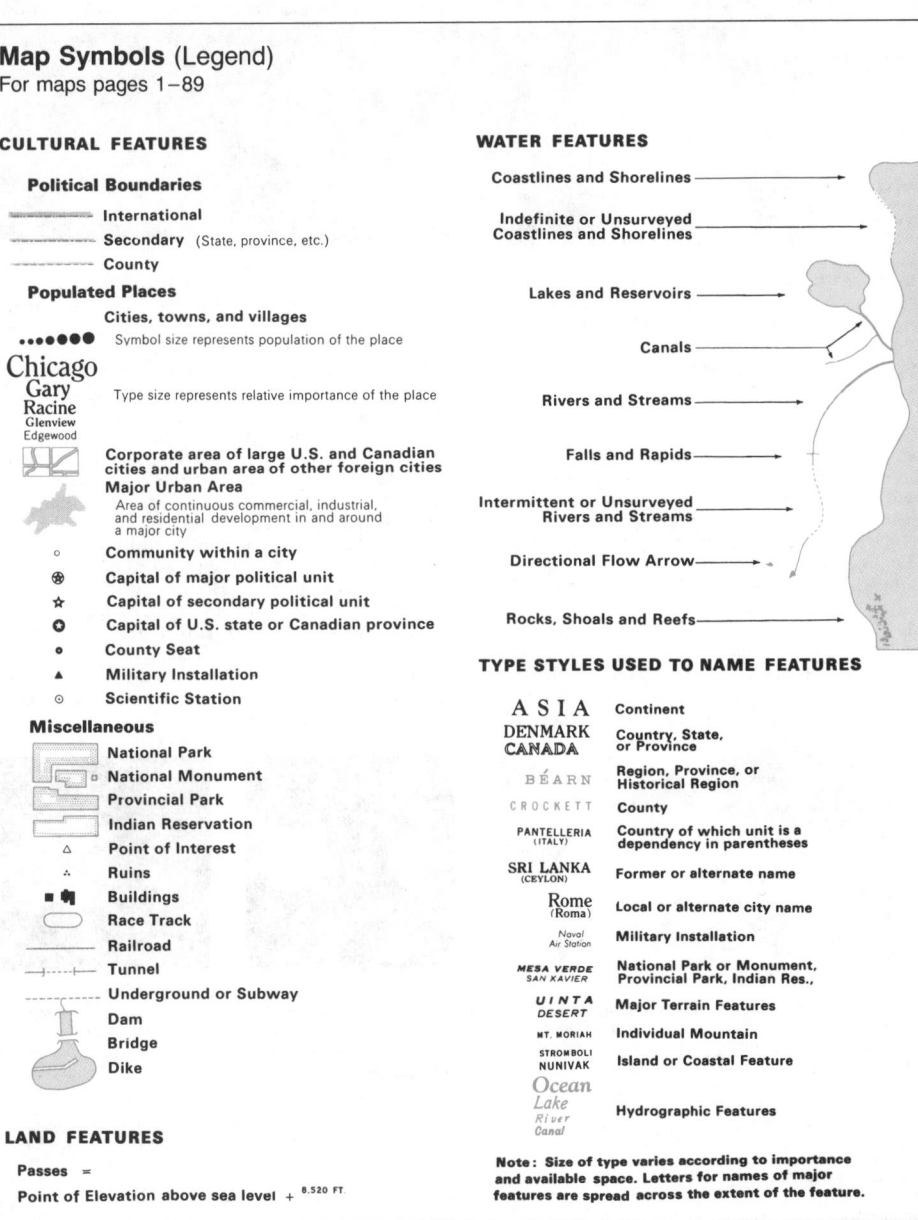

Coastlines and Shorelines

Indefinite or Unsurveyed Coastlines and Shorelines

Lakes and Reservoirs

Canals

Rivers and Streams

Falls and Rapids

Intermittent or Unsurveyed Rivers and Streams

Directional Flow Arrow

Rocks, Shoals and Reefs

TYPE STYLES USED TO NAME FEATURES

A S I A	Continent
DENMARK CANADA	Country, State, or Province
B É A R N	Region, Province, or Historical Region
C R O C K E T T	County
PANTELLERIA (ITALY)	Country of which unit is a dependency in parentheses
SRI LANKA (CEYLON)	Former or alternate name
Rome (Roma)	Local or alternate city name
Naval Air Station	Military Installation
MESA VERDE SAN XAVIER	National Park or Monument, Provincial Park, Indian Res.,
UINTA DESERT	Major Terrain Features
MT. MORIAH	Individual Mountain
STROMBOLI NUNIVAK	Island or Coastal Feature
Ocean Lake River Canal	Hydrographic Features

Note: Size of type varies according to importance and available space. Letters for names of major features are spread across the extent of the feature.

Figure 14

Figure 15

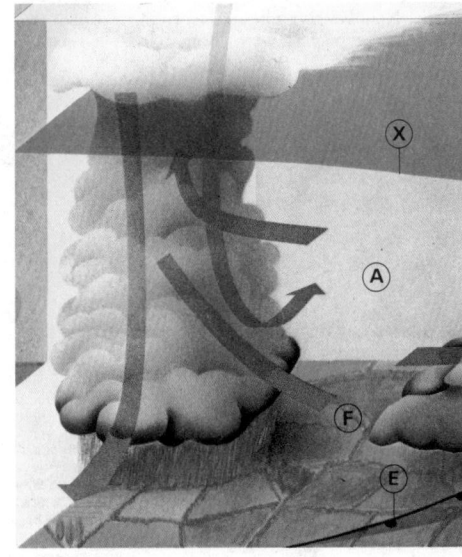

Understanding Map Symbols

In a very real sense, the whole map is a symbol, representing the world or a part of it. It is a reduced representation of the earth; each of the world's features — cities, rivers, etc. — is represented on the map by a symbol. Map symbols may take the form of points, such as dots or stars (often used for cities, capital cities, or points of interest), or lines (roads, rivers, railroads). Symbols may also occupy an area, showing extent of coverage (states, forests, deserts). They seldom look like the feature they represent and therefore must be identified and interpreted. For instance, the maps in this atlas show and differentiate political units (countries, states) with color. The political units are further defined by a heavy line depicting their boundaries. Neither the colors nor the boundary lines are actually found on the surface of the earth, but because countries and states are such important political components of the world, strong symbols are used to represent them.

The legend in figure 13 identifies the symbols used in this atlas.

The Planet Earth and Tables

The reference maps and index provide the source of much of the information in the atlas. Supplementing these are The Planet Earth Section and tables.

The Planet Earth

This special section illustrates the dynamic natural forces which have shaped the earth. Maps such as in figure 14, portraying the earth under the sea, and diagrams, as in figure 15, depicting a typical weather system, are used to show the processes which have created and continue to mold the varied landscapes in which we live.

The creation of the solar system, the evolving planet, and the weather and climate systems which affect us on a day to day basis are some of the topics treated in this section. The text accompanying the maps and illustrations concisely describes the major concepts needed to understand these basic natural phenomena. The section thus adds important knowledge of the earth to that conveyed by the reference maps and index.

Tables

The tables in the atlas supplement the information found on the maps, providing statistical data about the world.

For each political unit, the World Political Information Table specifies area in square miles, latest estimated population, population density, capital, largest city, and principal languages. In addition, the table describes form of government and political or administrative status. Another world table shows the population of major foreign cities and towns.

A table of United States cities and towns lists the latest estimated population and the ZIP code of major cities. Geographical and historical facts about the United States are also included in the tabular section.

The Origin and Destiny of the Solar System

1 According to the most widely accepted theory, (the 'accretion' theory) the solar system originally consisted only of a mass of tenuous gas, and dust. There was no true Sun, and there was no production of nuclear energy. The gas was made up chiefly of hydrogen, with occasional random condensations.

2 Gravitational forces now cause the cloud to shrink and assume a more regular shape. Its density and mass near the center increase, but there are still no nuclear processes.

3 The gas cloud begins to assume the form of a regular disk. The infant Sun begins to shine - by the energy from gravitational shrinkage.

4 Material is thrown off from the Sun to join that already in the solar cloud, whose condensations have become more noticeable.

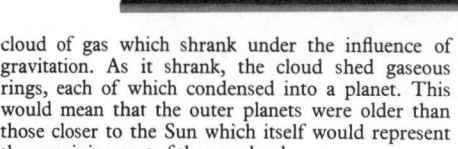

How did the Earth come into existence? This question has intrigued mankind for centuries, but it was not until the start of true science that plausible theories were advanced. Although some theories held sway for many years, they were eventually deposed by the discovery of some fatal flaw. Even today, it is impossible to be sure that the main problem has been solved, but at least some concrete facts exist as a guide. It is now reasonably certain that the age of the Earth is of the order of 4550-4700 million years. The other planets are presumably about the same age, since they were probably formed by the same process in the same epoch.

Several centuries ago Archbishop Ussher of Armagh maintained that the world had come into being at a definite moment in the year 4004 BC. This estimate was made on purely religious grounds, and it soon became clear that the Earth is much older. In 1796 the French astronomer Laplace put forward the famous Nebular Hypothesis, according to which the Sun and the planets were formed from a rotating cloud of gas which shrank under the influence of gravitation. As it shrank, the cloud shed gaseous rings, each of which condensed into a planet. This would mean that the outer planets were older than those closer to the Sun which itself would represent the remaining part of the gas cloud.

The Nebular Hypothesis was accepted for many years, but eventually serious mathematical weaknesses were found in it. Next came a number of tidal theories according to which the Earth and other planets were formed from a cigar-shaped tongue of matter torn from the Sun by the gravitational pull of a passing star. The first plausible theory of this kind came from the English astronomer Sir James Jeans, but this too was found to be mathematically untenable and the idea had to be given up.

Most modern theories assume that the planets were formed by accretion from a rotating solar cloud of gas and finely-dispersed dust. If the Sun were originally attended by such a cloud, this cloud would, over a sufficiently long period of time, become a flat disk.

If random concentration had become sufficiently massive, it would draw in extra material by virtue of its gravitational attraction, forming 'proto-planets'. When the Sun began to radiate strongly, part of the mass of each proto-planet would be driven off due to the high temperatures, leaving a solar system of the kind that exists today.

The fact that such an evolutionary sequence can be traced emphasizes that in talking about the origin of the Earth we are considering only a small part of a continuous story. What will become of the Earth in the far future? The Sun is radiating energy because of the nuclear process within it: hydrogen is being converted into helium causing mass to be lost with a resulting release of energy. However, when the supply of hydrogen begins to run low, the Sun must change radically. It will move towards a red giant stage swelling and engulfing the Earth. Fortunately, this will not happen for at least another 5000 to 6000 million years, but eventually the Sun, which sustains our planet, will finally destroy it.

Alternative theories

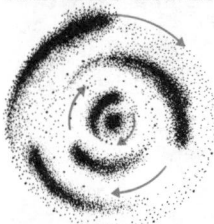

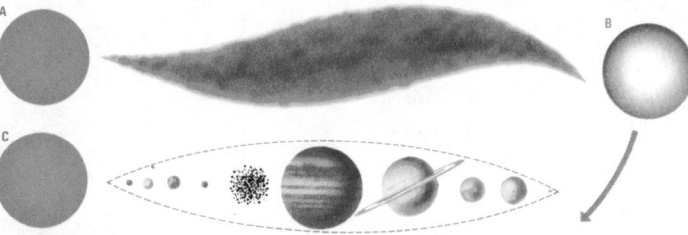

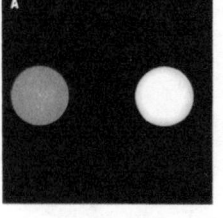

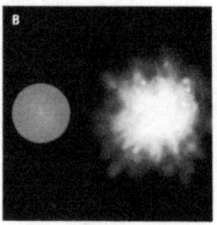

Contracting nebula *above*
Laplace suggested that a contracting nebula might shed gas which then condensed.

Tidal theories *above*
In 1917 Sir James Jeans postulated that Sun A was attracted to another star B which passed at close range. A cloud of matter was drawn off by their gravitational attraction. Star B moved on while the cloud condensed to form planets circling our Sun at C.

A violent beginning *above*
One of the theories of how the solar system came to be formed assumes that the Sun once had a binary companion star. This exploded as a supernova (above) and was blown off as a white dwarf

16 As the 'fuel' runs out, the radiation pressure falls, and under internal gravity the Sun will collapse inwards changing in only 50000 years from a red giant into a super-dense white dwarf.

17 As a white dwarf, the Sun will continue to radiate feebly for an immense period. At last all radiation must cease, and the Sun will remain as a dead, dark globe - a black dwarf.

15 By now all the inner planets will have long since been destroyed. The Sun will become unstable, reaching the most violent stage of its career as a red giant, with a vast, relatively cool surface and an intensely hot, dense core.

14 When the center of the Sun has reached another critical temperature, the helium will begin to 'burn' giving the so-called 'helium flash'. After a temporary contraction the Sun will then swell out to a diameter 400 times that at present.

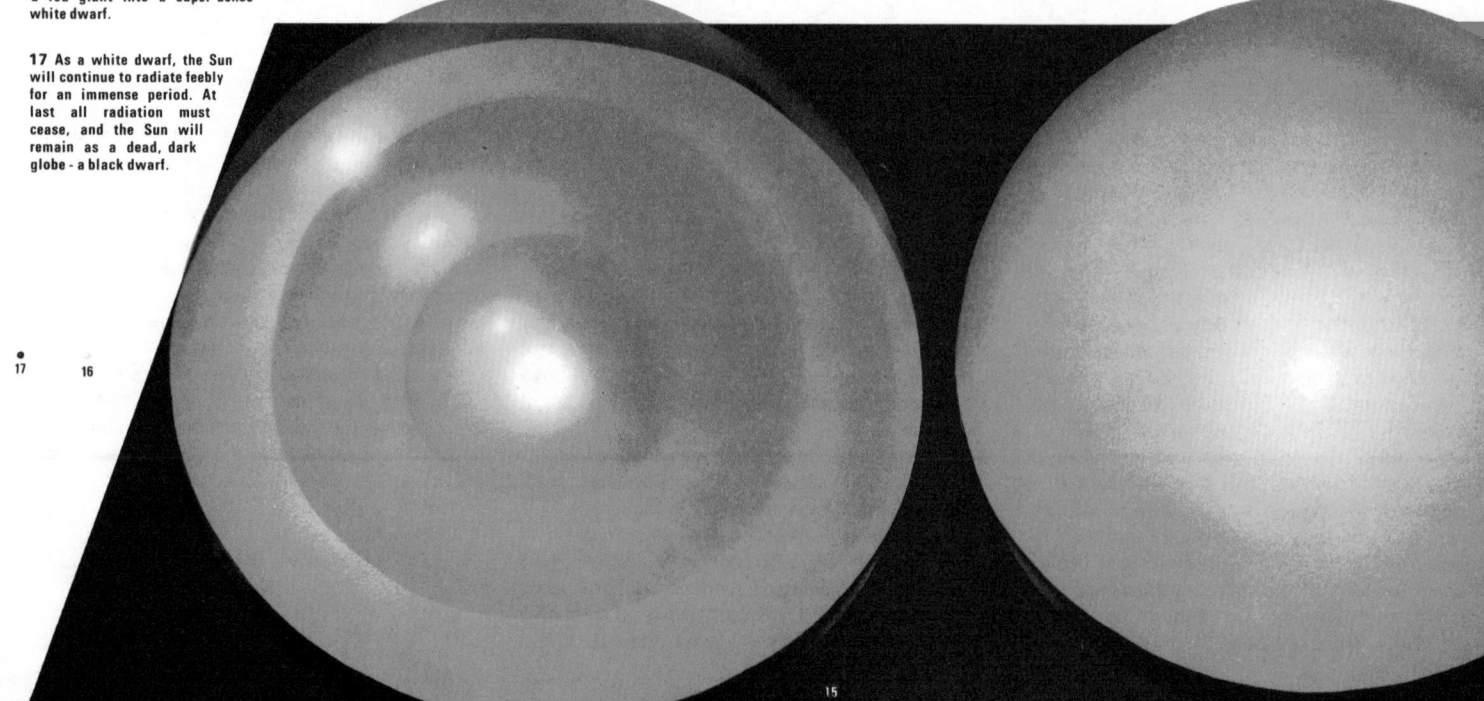

17 16

15

5 The Sun, still contracting, continues to radiate because of gravitational effects. More and more of the solar cloud collects into the condensations.

6 The Sun, surrounded by a system of regularly-shaped proto-planets, shrinks to about its present size, though its surface is only half as bright.

7 By now the solar system becomes recognizable, though the Sun is still orange and slowly contracting. Much of the material in the solar cloud has been absorbed.

8 The core of the Sun reaches the critical temperature to start the nuclear reaction that converts hydrogen into helium. There are relatively few proto-planets left.

9 As the Sun settles down to a period of stable radiation, the proto-planets assume a spherical shape. The four largest, Jupiter, Saturn, Uranus and Neptune, are over 400 million miles from the Sun.

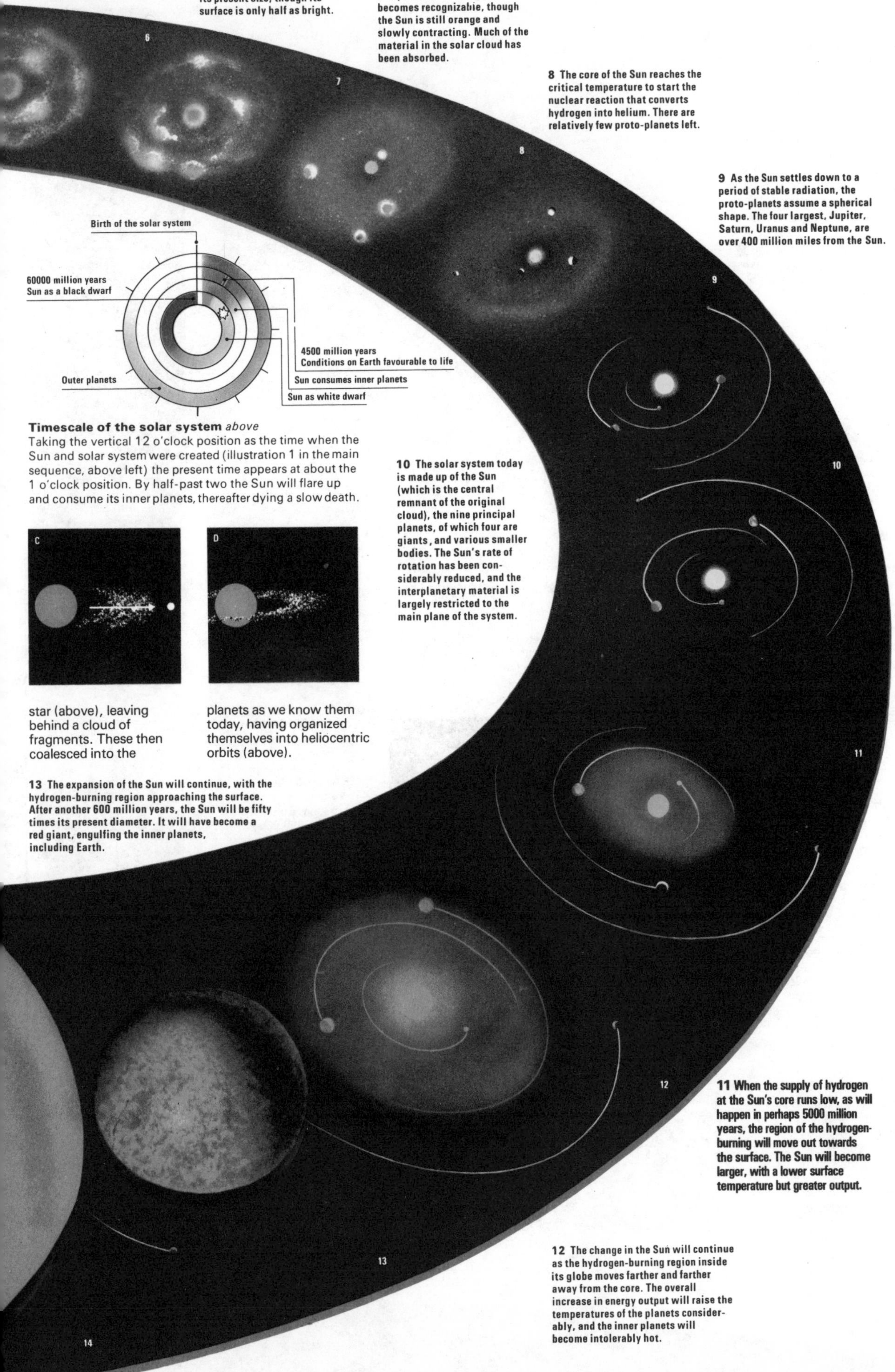

Birth of the solar system

60000 million years
Sun as a black dwarf

Outer planets

4500 million years
Conditions on Earth favourable to life

Sun consumes inner planets

Sun as white dwarf

Timescale of the solar system *above*
Taking the vertical 12 o'clock position as the time when the Sun and solar system were created (illustration 1 in the main sequence, above left) the present time appears at about the 1 o'clock position. By half-past two the Sun will flare up and consume its inner planets, thereafter dying a slow death.

C

D

star (above), leaving behind a cloud of fragments. These then coalesced into the

planets as we know them today, having organized themselves into heliocentric orbits (above).

13 The expansion of the Sun will continue, with the hydrogen-burning region approaching the surface. After another 600 million years, the Sun will be fifty times its present diameter. It will have become a red giant, engulfing the inner planets, including Earth.

10 The solar system today is made up of the Sun (which is the central remnant of the original cloud), the nine principal planets, of which four are giants, and various smaller bodies. The Sun's rate of rotation has been considerably reduced, and the interplanetary material is largely restricted to the main plane of the system.

11 When the supply of hydrogen at the Sun's core runs low, as will happen in perhaps 5000 million years, the region of the hydrogen-burning will move out towards the surface. The Sun will become larger, with a lower surface temperature but greater output.

12 The change in the Sun will continue as the hydrogen-burning region inside its globe moves farther and farther away from the core. The overall increase in energy output will raise the temperatures of the planets considerably, and the inner planets will become intolerably hot.

The lifespan of the Earth

The Earth was produced from the solar cloud (1-6 on main diagram). It had no regular form, but, as more and more material was drawn in, it began to assume a spherical shape (7-8)

When it had reached its present size (9), the Earth had a dense atmosphere; not the original hydrogen atmosphere but one produced by gas from the interior. Life had not started.

The Earth today (10), moving in a stable orbit, has an equable temperature and oxygen-rich atmosphere, so that it alone of all the planets in the solar system is suitable for life.

When the Sun nears the red giant stage (11-13), the Earth will be heated to an intolerable degree. The atmosphere will be driven off, the oceans will boil and life must come to an end.

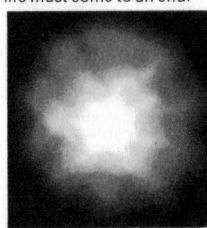

As the Sun reaches the peak of its violence (14-15) it will swell out until the Earth is engulfed. Its natural life is probably no more than 9000 million years. Its end is certain.

The Solar System

The Sun is the controlling body of the solar system and is far more massive than all its planets combined. Even Jupiter, much the largest of the planets, has a diameter only about one-tenth that of the Sun. The solar system is divided into two main parts. The inner region includes four relatively small, solid planets: Mercury, Venus, the Earth and Mars. Beyond the orbit of Mars comes a wide gap in which move many thousands of small minor planets or asteroids, some of which are little more than rocks. Further out come the four giants: Jupiter, Saturn, Uranus and Neptune. Pluto, on the fringe of the system, is a curious little planet; it appears to be in a class of its own, but at present very little is known about it and even its size is a matter for conjecture. Maps of the solar system can be misleading in that they tend to give a false idea about distance. The outer planets are very widely separated. For example, Saturn is further away from Uranus than it is from the Earth.

The contrasting planets

The inner, or terrestrial, planets have some points in common, but a greater number of differences. Mercury, the planet closest to the Sun, has almost no atmosphere and that of Mars is very thin; but Venus, strikingly similar to the Earth in size and mass, has a dense atmosphere made up chiefly of carbon dioxide, and a surface temperature of over 400°C. The giant planets are entirely different. At least in their outer layers they are made up of gas, like a star; but, unlike a star, they have no light of their own and shine only by reflecting the light of their star, the Sun. Several of the planets have moons. The Earth has one (or it may be our partner in a binary system), Jupiter has at least sixteen, Saturn twenty-three (discounting its rings), Uranus five, Neptune two and Pluto one. Mars also has two satellites, but these are less than 15 mi (24 km) in diameter and of a type different from the Earth's Moon. The Earth is unique in the solar system in having oceans on its surface and an atmosphere made up chiefly of nitrogen and oxygen. It is the only planet suited to life of a terrestrial type. It is not believed that highly evolved life can exist on any other planet in the Sun's family, although it is possible that if a life-form were placed on Mars, it could survive.

Observing the planets

Five of the planets, Mercury, Venus, Mars, Jupiter and Saturn, were known to the inhabitants of the Earth in very ancient times. They are starlike in aspect but easy to distinguish because, unlike the stars, they seem to wander slowly about the sky whereas the true stars appear to hold their position for century after century. The so-called proper motions of the stars are too slight to be noticed by the naked eye, but they can be measured by modern techniques. Mercury and Venus always appear to be in the same part of the sky as the Sun. Mercury is never prominent but Venus is dazzlingly bright, partly because its upper clouds are highly reflective and partly because it is close; it can come within 25,000,000 mi (40,200,000 km), only about 100 times as far as the Moon. Jupiter is generally very bright, as is Mars when it is well placed. Saturn is also conspicuous to the naked eye, but Uranus is only just visible and Neptune and Pluto are much fainter.

The Sun's active surface *right*

The structure of a star, such as the Sun, is immensely complex. The very concept of its surface is hard to define, and the size of the Sun depends on the wavelength of the light with which it is viewed. Using the 'hydrogen alpha' wavelength the bright surface of the Sun, known as the photosphere, appears as shown right, above. The surface, at about 5500 °C, is dotted with light and dark patches as a result of the violent upcurrents of hotter gas and cooler areas between them. Larger, darker regions are sunspots (right), temporary but very large disturbances.

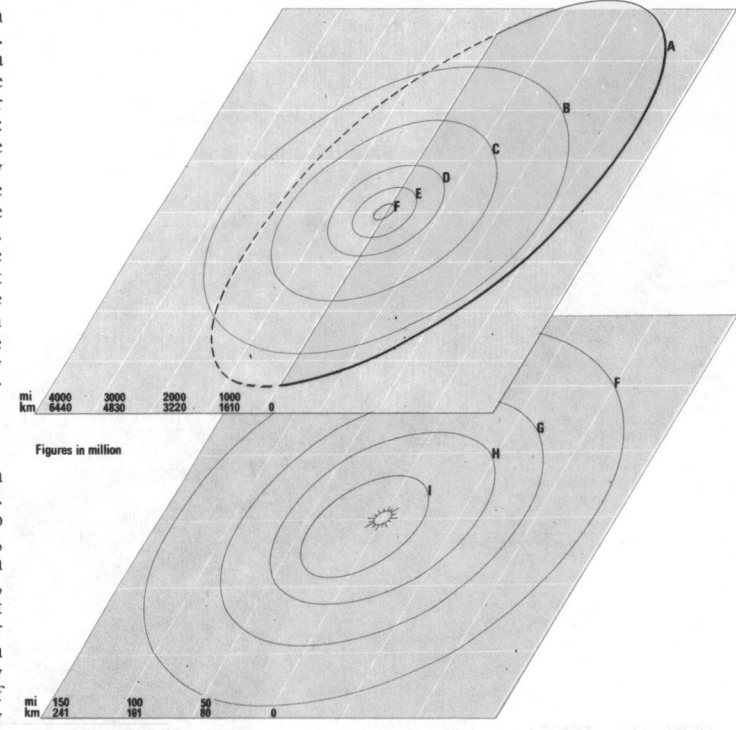

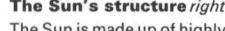

Orbits around the Sun *above*

The Sun's nine known planets, and the asteroids, describe heliocentric orbits in the same direction. But some planetary orbits are highly eccentric, while some asteroids are both eccentric and steeply inclined. The outermost planet, Pluto, passes within the orbit of Neptune, while one asteroid reaches almost to the radius of Saturn. Over 350 years ago Johannes Kepler showed that the planets do not move in perfect circles, and found that the line joining each planet to the Sun sweeps out a constant area in a given time. so that speed is greatest close to the Sun.

Figures in million

mi 4000 3000 2000 1000 0
km 6440 4830 3220 1610 0

mi 150 100 50 0
km 241 181 80 0

A	Pluto
B	Neptune
C	Uranus
D	Saturn
E	Jupiter
F	Mars
G	Earth
H	Venus
I	Mercury

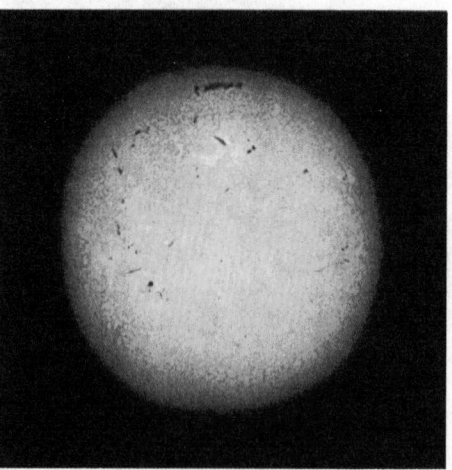

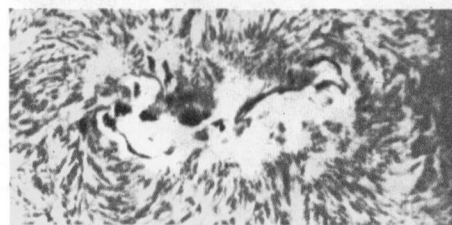

The Sun's structure *right*

The Sun is made up of highly dissimilar regions. This narrow sector includes the inner part of the corona (A) which, though very diffuse, has a temperature of some 1,000,000 °C. Into it leap solar prominences, 'flames' thousands of miles long which arch along the local magnetic field from the chromosphere (B), the outer layer of the Sun proper, which covers the visible photosphere with a layer of variable, highly mobile and rarefied gas about 6000 mi (10000 km) thick. Inside the Sun the outer layer (C) of gas is in constant movement and transfers heat from the interior. Inner region D is thought to transfer energy mainly by radiation. The innermost zone of all (E), the conditions of which can only be surmised but are thought to include a temperature of some 15,000,000 °C, sustains the energy of the Sun (and its planets) by continuous fusion of hydrogen into helium.

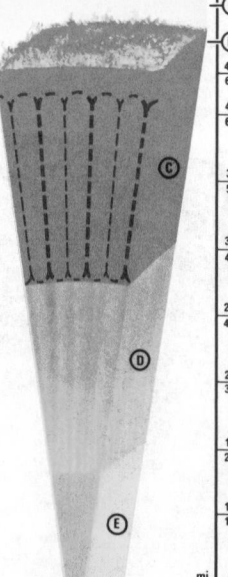

1,250,000
2,000,000

A
B
432,400
695,800
400,000
640,000
350,000
560,000
300,000
480,000
250,000
400,000
C
200,000
320,000
D
150,000
240,000
100,000
160,000
E
mi 50,000
km 80,000

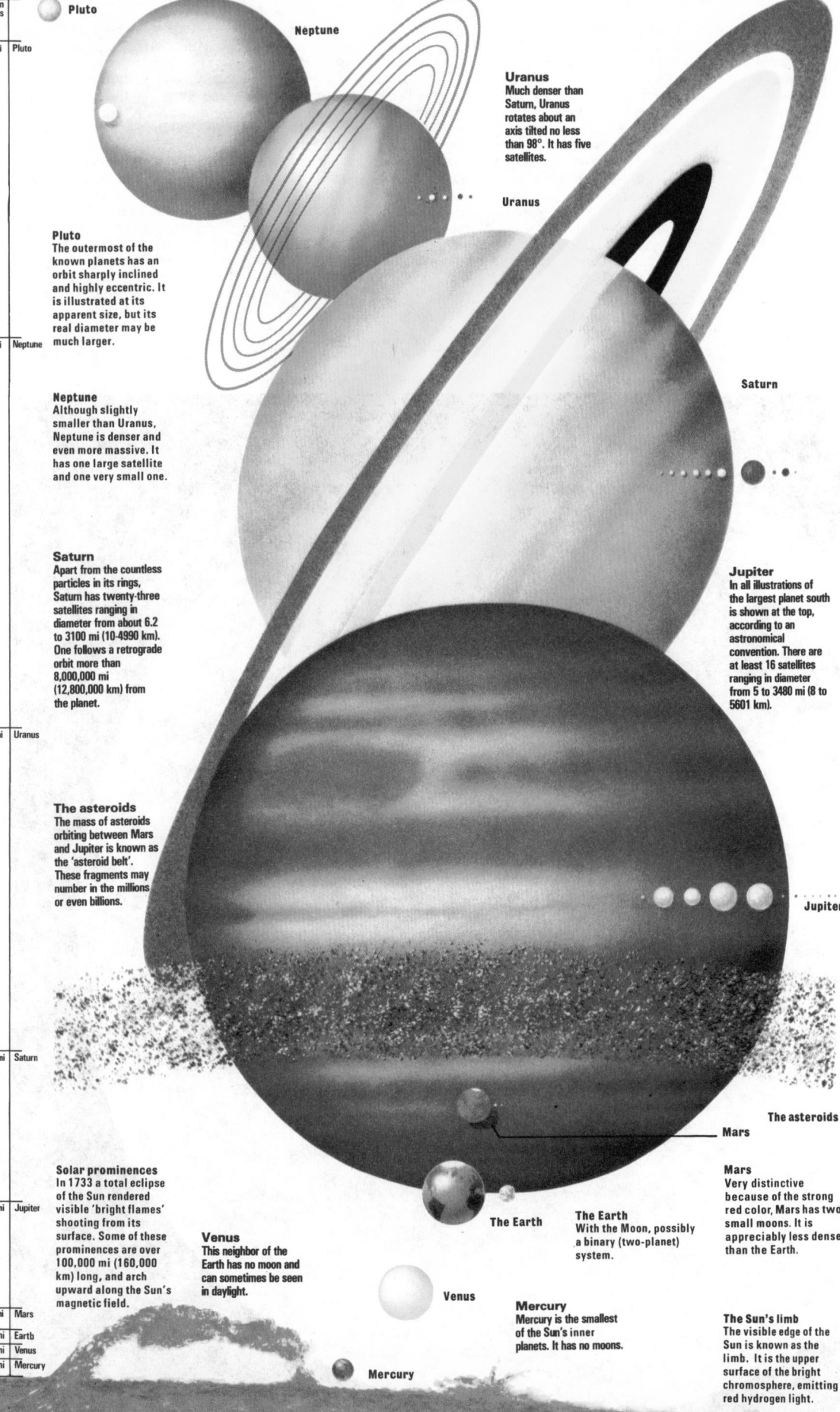

Pluto

Neptune

Uranus
Much denser than
Saturn, Uranus
rotates about an
axis tilted no less
than 98°. It has five
satellites.

Uranus

Pluto
The outermost of the
known planets has an
orbit sharply inclined
and highly eccentric. It
is illustrated at its
apparent size, but its
real diameter may be
much larger.

Saturn

Neptune
Although slightly
smaller than Uranus,
Neptune is denser and
even more massive. It
has one large satellite
and one very small one.

Saturn
Apart from the countless
particles in its rings,
Saturn has twenty-three
satellites ranging in
diameter from about 6.2
to 3100 mi (10-4990 km).
One follows a retrograde
orbit more than
8,000,000 mi
(12,800,000 km) from
the planet.

Jupiter
In all illustrations of
the largest planet south
is shown at the top,
according to an
astronomical
convention. There are
at least 16 satellites
ranging in diameter
from 5 to 3480 mi (8 to
5601 km).

The asteroids
The mass of asteroids
orbiting between Mars
and Jupiter is known as
the 'asteroid belt'.
These fragments may
number in the millions
or even billions.

Jupiter

The asteroids

Mars

Solar prominences
In 1733 a total eclipse
of the Sun rendered
visible 'bright flames'
shooting from its
surface. Some of these
prominences are over
100,000 mi (160,000
km) long, and arch
upward along the Sun's
magnetic field.

Venus
This neighbor of the
Earth has no moon and
can sometimes be seen
in daylight.

The Earth

The Earth
With the Moon, possibly
a binary (two-planet)
system.

Mars
Very distinctive
because of the strong
red color, Mars has two
small moons. It is
appreciably less dense
than the Earth.

Venus

Mercury
Mercury is the smallest
of the Sun's inner
planets. It has no moons.

The Sun's limb
The visible edge of the
Sun is known as the
limb. It is the upper
surface of the bright
chromosphere, emitting
red hydrogen light.

Mercury

The solar system *left*
The Sun is the major body in the solar
system. It lies 30000 light-years from
the center of our galaxy and takes about
200 million years to complete one
journey around it. There are nine planets
and their satellites in the system, as well
as comets and various minor bodies such
as meteoroids. The diagram on the
left shows the upper limb of the
Sun (bottom) and the main
constituent members of the solar
system very greatly condensed into a
smaller space. To indicate the amount of
the radial compression, the limb of the
Sun is drawn for a near-sphere of 5 ft
(1.52 m) diameter. On this scale the Earth
would be about 420 ft (127 m) away
and the outermost planet Pluto, no less
than 3 mi (4.9 km) distant.

Pluto, discovered in 1930, has a very
eccentric orbit, with a radius varying
between 2748 and 4571 million mi
(4423 and 7356 million kilometers).
Being so far from the Sun, it is
extremely cold.

Neptune, discovered in 1846, has a
diameter of 30200 mi (48600 km) and is
made up of gas, although little is known
of its interior. It orbits the Sun once in
164 3/4 years. Seen through binoculars
it is a small greenish disk.

Uranus, discovered in 1781, is
apparently similar to Neptune, but less
massive. Although faintly visible to
the naked eye, even large telescopes
show little detail upon its greenish surface.

Saturn is the second largest planet, its
equatorial diameter being 74600 mi
(120,000 km). Visually it is unlike any
other heavenly body, because of its
great number of rings, made up of
particles of various sizes. The planet itself
is less dense than water and at least its
outer layers are gaseous.

Jupiter, the largest planet, has an
equatorial diameter of 88700 mi
(142,700 km), but its rapid rotation,
once about every 10 hours, makes it
very flattened at the poles. It appears
to have cloud belts and various spots,
of which the Great Red Spot seems to
be permanent.

The asteroids, irregularly shaped
fragments of planetary material, vary
greatly in size. Most are in orbit
between Mars and Jupiter, although
some have eccentric orbits that
bring them near to Earth.

Mars is about 2400 mi (6790km) in
diameter. It has a thin atmosphere, mainly
of carbon dioxide, and its surface is
pitted with Moon-like craters. It is not
thought today that the planet contains
any life.

The Earth/Moon system is today
regarded as a double planet rather than a
planet and satellite. The Moon has an
average distance from Earth of
238,857 mi (384,403 km) and it is now
known that it has never contained life.

Venus is almost the twin of the Earth in
size and mass. It is too hot to contain
life, and its very dense atmosphere is
mainly carbon dioxide. It has a year of
225 Earth days, and it spins on its axis
once every 243 Earth days.

Mercury, the innermost planet, is only
about 3031 mi (4878 km) in diameter,
and has lost almost all of its atmosphere.
Like Venus it shows phases, but it is
always close to the Sun when viewed
from the Earth and cannot be seen clearly.

(scale, left margin)
res in
illions
60 mi Pluto
'88 mi Neptune
'81 mi Uranus
885 mi Saturn
484 mi Jupiter
142 mi Mars
93 mi Earth
67 mi Venus
36 mi Mercury

Earth's Companion: The Moon

The Moon is our companion in space. Its mean distance from the Earth is less than a quarter of a million miles—it varies between 221,456 miles (356,399 km) and 252,711 miles (406,699 km)—and it was the first world other than our Earth to come within the range of man's space probes. At first mere masses, these then became instrument packages and finally spacecraft carrying men. With their aid our knowledge of the Moon has been vastly increased in the past decade. Astronauts Neil Armstrong and Edwin Aldrin made the first human journey to the lunar surface in July 1969, and the Moon has since been subjected to detailed and direct investigation.

The mean diameter of the Moon is 2160 miles (3476 km), and its mass is 1/81st as much as that of the Earth. Despite this wide difference the ratio is much less than that between other planets and their moons, and the Earth/Moon system is now widely regarded as a double planet rather than as a planet and satellite. The Moon's mean density is less than that of the Earth, and it may lack a comparable heavy core. Escape velocity from the lunar surface is only 1.5 mi/sec (2.4 km/sec), and this is so low that the Moon has lost any atmosphere it may once have had. To Earth life it is therefore an extremely hostile world. Analysis of lunar rock brought back to Earth laboratories and investigated by Soviet probes on the Moon has so far revealed no trace of any life. The Moon appears to have always been sterile.

Much of the surface of the Moon comprises large grey plains, mis-called 'maria'(seas), but most of it is extremely rough. There are great ranges of mountains, isolated peaks and countless craters which range from tiny pits up to vast enclosures more than 150 miles (240 km) in diameter. Many of the craters have central mountains or mountain-groups. Some of the larger craters show signs of having been produced by volcanic action, while others appear to have resulted from the impacts of meteorites.

The Moon rotates slowly, performing one complete turn on its axis every 27 days, 7 hours, 43 minutes. It always presents the same face to the Earth. But in October 1959 the Soviet probe *Lunik 3* photographed the hidden rear hemisphere and it has since been mapped in detail. It contains no large 'seas'. The appearance of the lunar surface depends strongly on the angle at which it is viewed and the direction of solar illumination. In the photograph on the right, taken from a height of about 70 miles (115 km) with the Earth having once more come into full view ahead, the lunar surface looks deceptively smooth; in fact, there is practically no level ground any where in the field of vision. The lunar horizon is always sharply defined, because there is no atmosphere to cause blurring or distortion. For the same reason, the sky seen from the Moon is always jet black.

Full Moon *below*

This striking photograph was taken by the *Apollo 11* astronauts in July 1969. It shows parts of both the Earth-turned and far hemispheres. The dark plain near the center is the Mare Crisium.

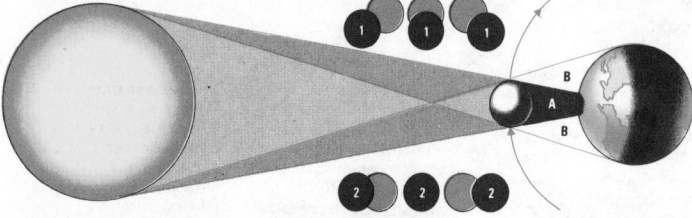

Earthrise *above*

This view of the Earth rising was visible to the crew of *Apollo 10* in May 1969 as they orbited the Moon 70 miles (112 km) above the surface. They had just come round from the Moon's rear hemisphere.

Eclipses

Once regarded as terrifying actions of angry gods, eclipses are today merely useful. They provide a different view of the Sun and Moon that opens up fresh information. In a lunar eclipse the Earth passes directly between the Sun and Moon; in a solar eclipse the Moon passes between Sun and Earth. Both the Earth and Moon constantly cast a shadow comprising a dark inner cone surrounded by a region to which part of the sunlight penetrates. A body passing through the outer shadow experiences a partial eclipse, while the inner cone causes a total eclipse in which all direct sunlight is cut off.

A total solar eclipse is magnificent. The bright star is blocked out by a black Moon, but around it the Sun's atmosphere flashes into view. The pearly corona of thin gas can be seen extending a million miles from the Sun. Closer to the surface huge 'prominences' of red hydrogen leap into space and curve back along the solar magnetic field. In a partial solar eclipse these things cannot be seen, while in a total eclipse caused by the Moon at its greatest distance from Earth a ring of the Sun is left visible. As the Moon's orbit is not in the same plane as the Earth's, total solar eclipses occur very rarely, on occasions when the tip of the Moon's dark shadow crosses the Earth as a spot 169 miles (272 km) wide.

Eclipses *left and below*

When the Moon passes in front of the Sun as in sequence 1 its shadow B causes a partial solar eclipse (below, left, taken 21 November 1966). But in the case of sequence 2, shadow cone A gives a total eclipse (below, right, 15 February 1961).

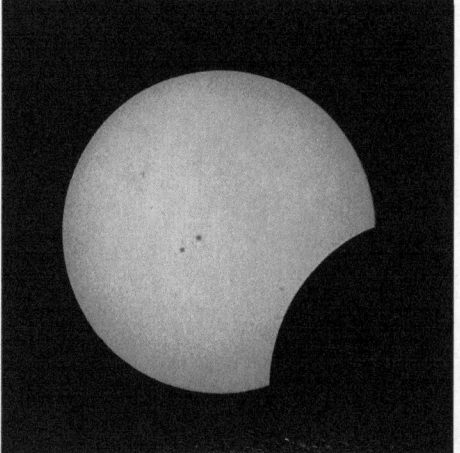

Anatomy of the Earth

A fundamental mystery that still confronts science even today is the detailed internal structure of the planet on which we live. Although Jules Verne's intrepid 'Professor Otto Lindenbrock was able to journey to the center of the Earth, this is one scientific fantasy that will never be achieved. The deepest boreholes and mines do little more than scratch the surface and so, deprived of direct observation, the geologist is forced to rely almost entirely on indirect evidence to construct his picture of the Earth's anatomy. In spite of these drawbacks, he can outline with some confidence the story of the planet's development from the time of its formation as a separate body in space some 4550 million years ago.

Since that time the Earth has been continuously evolving. The crust, mantle and inner core developed during its first 1000 million years, but there is only scant evidence of how they did so. Probably the original homogenous mass then partly or completely melted, whereupon gravitational attraction caused the densest material to form a part-liquid, part-solid central core overlaid by the less dense mantle. The extremely thin outermost layer of 'scum' began to form at an early stage and as long ago as 3500 million years parts of it had reached almost their present state. But most of the crust evolved in a complex way through long-term cyclic changes spanning immense periods of time. The evidence of today's rocks can be interpreted in different ways; for example, the core, mantle and crust could have separated out quickly at an early stage or gradually over a longer period.

Today's restless Earth

Many of the changes which have taken place in the Earth's structure and form have been very gradual. For example, although it may well be that our planet has been getting larger (as illustrated below), the rate of increase in radius has been no more rapid than 2½ inches (65 mm) per century. But this does not alter the fact that the Earth is very far from being a mere inert sphere of matter. Although it is not possible faithfully to portray it, almost the whole globe is at brilliant white heat. If the main drawing were true to life it would contain no color except for a thin band, about as thick as cardboard, around the outer crust in which the color would change from white through yellow and orange to red. With such high temperatures the interior of the Earth is able to flow under the influence of relatively small differences in density and stress. The result is to set up convection currents which are now believed to be the main driving force behind the formation of mountain ranges and the drifting apart of continents. But the fact remains that our knowledge of the interior of our planet is derived almost entirely from indirect evidence, such as the passage of earthquake shock waves through the mantle (page 13A). Direct exploration is confined to the surface and to boreholes which so far have never penetrated more than about five miles (8 km) into the crust. It is difficult to imagine how man could ever devise experiments that would greatly enhance and refine his knowledge of the Earth's interior. Indeed, he knows as much about the Moon and other much more distant heavenly bodies as he does about the Earth below a depth of a mere 20 miles (32 km).

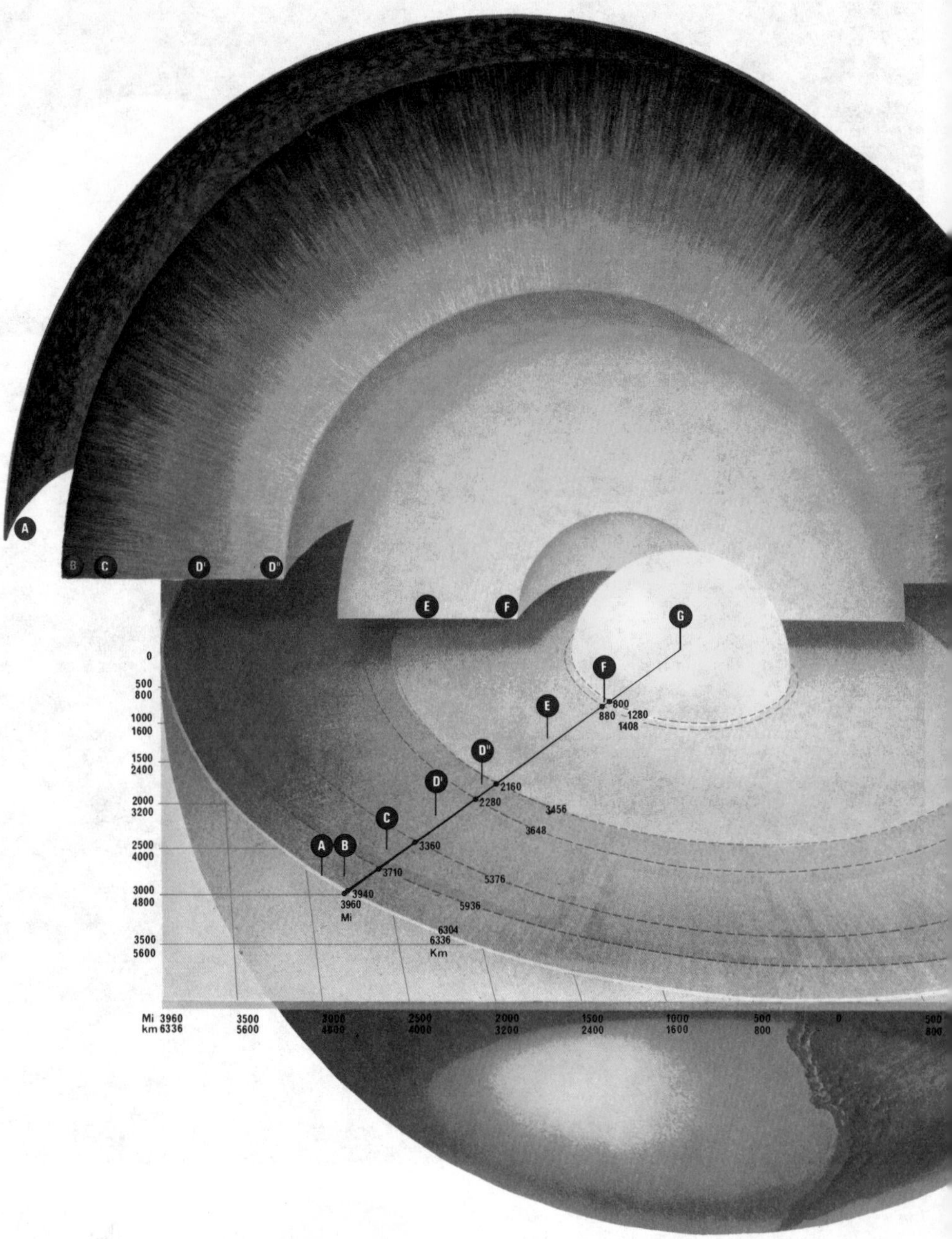

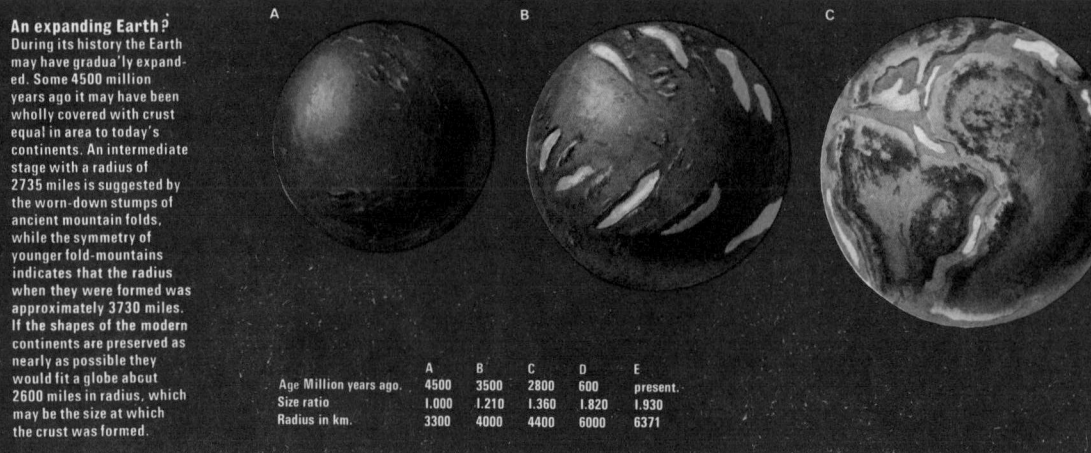

The crust (A)
This varies in thickness from 20 miles (32 km) in continental regions, where it is largely granitic, to 5 miles (8 km) under the oceans, where it is basaltic.

The upper mantle (B, C)
From the crust down to 375 miles (600 km), this layer is divided into upper and lower zones with differing P wave speeds (see page 39).

The lower mantle (D1, D2)
Made of peridotite, as is the upper mantle, this zone extends down to a depth of 1800 miles (2900 km). P wave speeds increase still further.

The outer core (E, F)
Largely iron and nickel, this molten zone reaches to 3200 miles (5120 km). Dynamo action of convection currents may cause the Earth's magnetic field.

Not a true sphere *below*
The Earth's shape is controlled by equilibrium between inward gravitational attraction and outward centrifugal force. This results in the average radius at the equator of 3963 miles (6378 km) slightly exceeding that at the poles of 3950 miles (6356 km).

An expanding Earth?
During its history the Earth may have gradually expanded. Some 4500 million years ago it may have been wholly covered with crust equal in area to today's continents. An intermediate stage with a radius of 2735 miles is suggested by the worn-down stumps of ancient mountain folds, while the symmetry of younger fold-mountains indicates that the radius when they were formed was approximately 3730 miles. If the shapes of the modern continents are preserved as nearly as possible they would fit a globe about 2600 miles in radius, which may be the size at which the crust was formed.

	A	B	C	D	E
Age Million years ago.	4500	3500	2800	600	present.
Size ratio	1.000	1.210	1.360	1.820	1.930
Radius in km.	3300	4000	4400	6000	6371

Temperature *left*
Temperature inside the Earth increases with depth, initially at a rate of 48°C per mile (30°C/km) so that 60 miles (100 km) down it is white hot. The rate of increase then falls, and the shaded area indicates how uncertain is man's knowledge of great depths.

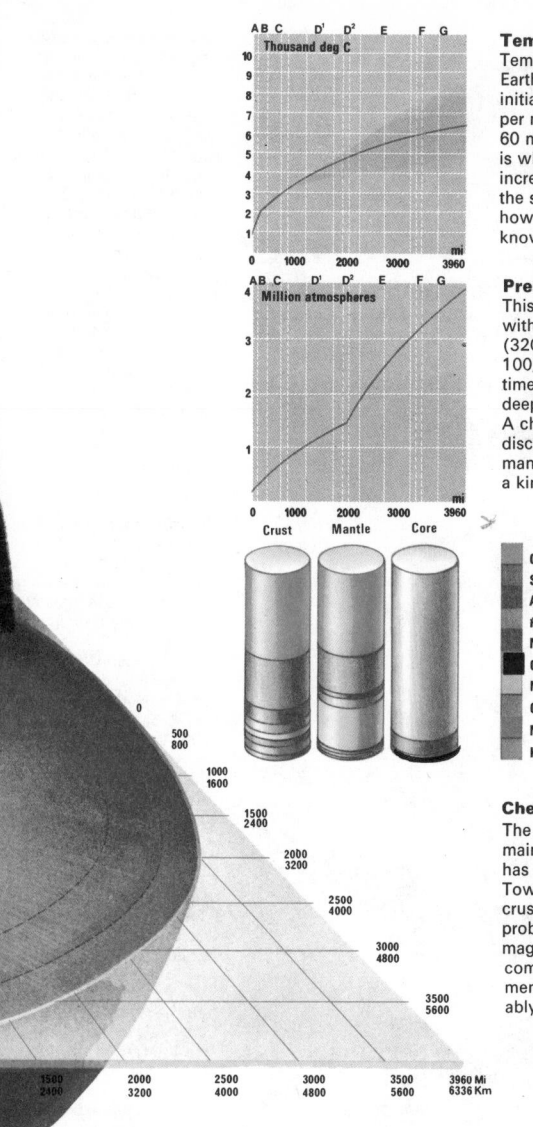

Pressure *left*
This likewise increases with depth. Only 200 miles (320 km) down it reaches 100,000 atmospheres, 1200 times the pressure at the deepest point in the ocean. A change of state at the discontinuity between the mantle and core shows as a kink on the graph.

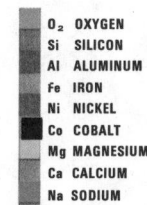

O_2	OXYGEN
Si	SILICON
Al	ALUMINUM
Fe	IRON
Ni	NICKEL
Co	COBALT
Mg	MAGNESIUM
Ca	CALCIUM
Na	SODIUM
K	POTASSIUM

Chemical composition *above*
The crust is made of mainly light elements and has relatively low density. Towards the base of the crust the composition is probably richer in iron and magnesium. The mantle is composed of heavier elements and the core is probably of iron and nickel.

The inner core (G)
The pressure of $3\frac{1}{2}$ million atmospheres (35000 kg/mm²) keeps this a solid ball of 800 miles (1300 km) radius. Its density varies from 14 to about 16.

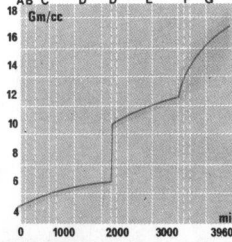

Density *left*
Virtually all man's knowledge of the interior of the Earth stems from measuring the transit of earthquake waves. The resulting data indicate sharp increases in density at the boundaries of both the outer core and the 'solid' inner core, with several intermediate zones.

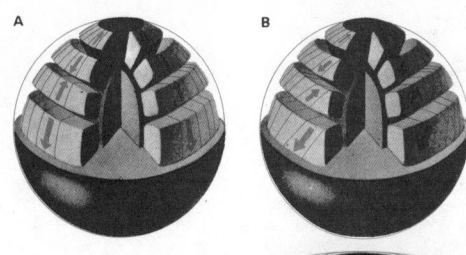

Convection currents
The fundamental pattern of movement in the mantle (A) is modified by the Earth's rotation (B) and also by friction between adjacent cells as shown in the main figure, below, in which core (X) and mantle (Y) are shown but crust (Z) is removed.

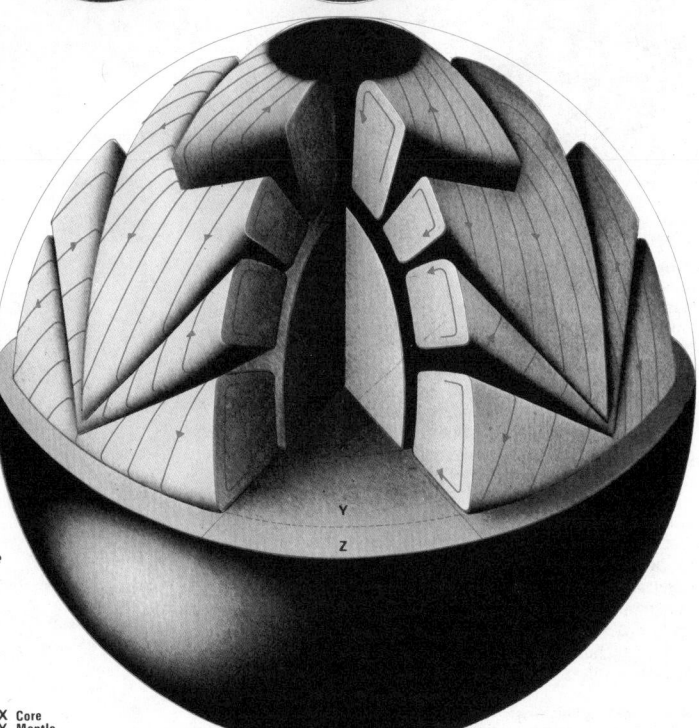

X Core
Y Mantle
Z Crust

Convection theory

Geologists and geophysicists are not unanimous on the question of whether there are convection currents present in the Earth's mantle or not, nor on the part these could play in providing the driving mechanism for major movements of the continents. Slow movement of 'solid' rocks can occur over long periods of time when the temperature is high and only relatively small density differences would be required to trigger them. Another matter for debate is whether convection is confined to the upper mantle or is continuous throughout the whole. It is not certain whether changes of physical state at different levels would constitute barriers to mantle-wide convection. The convection cells above are highly schematic but could largely explain the formation of some of the major geosynclinal fold mountains in the crust over the past thousand million years. Large-scale convection current systems in the mantle could also be the driving force for sea floor spreading and the associated continental drift.

The watery Earth *below*
Almost three-quarters of the Earth is covered by water. Basically the continents are rafts of relatively light crust 'floating' on generally denser oceanic crust. They comprise not only the visible land but also the adjacent continental shelves covered by shallow water. Oceanic crust underlies the deep sea platforms and ocean trenches. The areas of the major lands and seas (below, left) do not take into account the continental shelves but are the gross areas reckoned in terms of the land and water distribution at mean sea level. Extra area due to terrain is not included.

The watery Earth *right*
Key to numbered areas

Oceans	Area sq mi	km²
1 Arctic	3,662,000	9,485,100
2 Pacific	63,800,000	165,200,000
3 Atlantic	31,530,000	81,662,000
4 Indian	28,356,000	73,441,700

Landmasses		
5 Americas	16,289,000	42,189,000
6 Europe (excluding Soviet Union)	1,914,000	4,957,000
7 Asia (excluding Soviet Union)	10,617,000	27,498,000
8 Soviet Union	8,601,000	22,277,000
9 Africa	11,708,000	30,324,000
10 Oceania and Australia	3,287,000	8,513,000
11 Antarctica	5,100,000	13,209,000

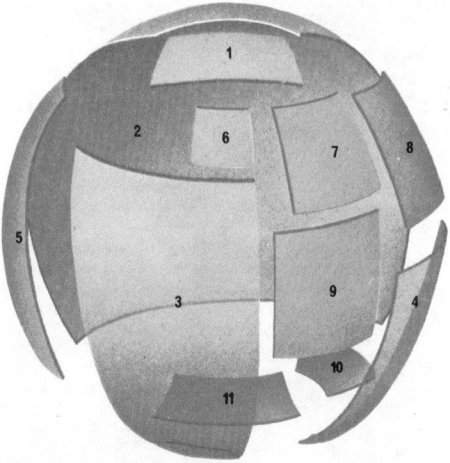

The Evolution of Land and Sea

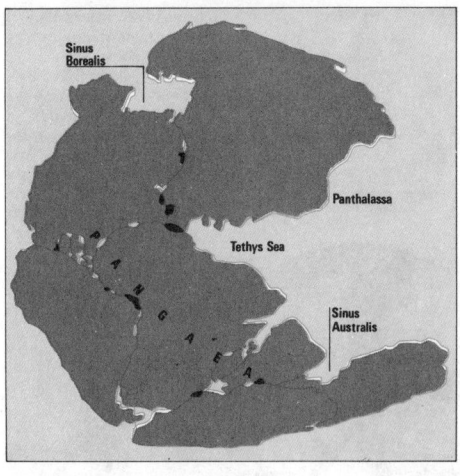

Pangaea *above*
About 200 million years ago there was only a single land mass on Earth, named Pangaea. The map shows how today's continents can be fitted together, with the aid of a computer, at the edge of the continental shelf at a depth of 1000 fathoms (6000 ft, 1830 m).

Although land and water first appeared on the Earth's surface several thousand million years before anyone could be there to watch, modern man has a very good idea of how it came about. The Earth's gravitational field caused the lighter, more volatile elements gradually to move outwards through the mantle and form a solid crust on the surface. By far the largest proportion of material newly added to the crust is basaltic volcanic rock derived from partial melting of the mantle beneath; in fact the oceanic crust which underlies the Earth's great water areas is made of almost nothing else. So the earliest crust to form was probably volcanic and of basaltic composition.

Air and water appear
The earliest records of the existence of an atmosphere of air and a hydrosphere of water are to be found in sediments laid down some 3300 million years ago from the residue of erosion of previously existing rocks. These sediments could not have been formed without atmospheric weathering, water transport and water deposition. The atmosphere was probably originally similar to the fumes which today issue from volcanoes and hot springs and which are about three-quarters water vapor. Once formed, the primitive atmosphere and oceans could erode the crust to produce vast layers of sediments of new chemical compositions. Gradually the oceans deepened and the land took on a more varied form. Convection in the mantle produced mountain ranges which in turn eroded to generate new sedimentary rocks. The ceaseless cycles of growth and decay had started, causing continually changing patterns of seas, mountains and plains. And in the past few years man has discovered how the continents and oceans have developed over the most recent 200 million years of geological time. The results of this research are to be seen in the maps on this page.

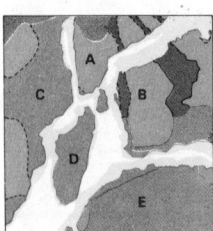

Another arrangement *left*
India (A) may have been separated by Australia (B) from East Antarctica (E) more than 200 million years ago on the evidence of today's geological deposition zones. Africa (C) and Madagascar (D) complete this convincing fit.

Migrant Australia *left*
By measuring the direction of magnetization of old Australian rocks it is possible to trace successive positions of that continent with respect to the Earth's magnetic pole. It appears to have moved across the world and back during the past 1000 million years.

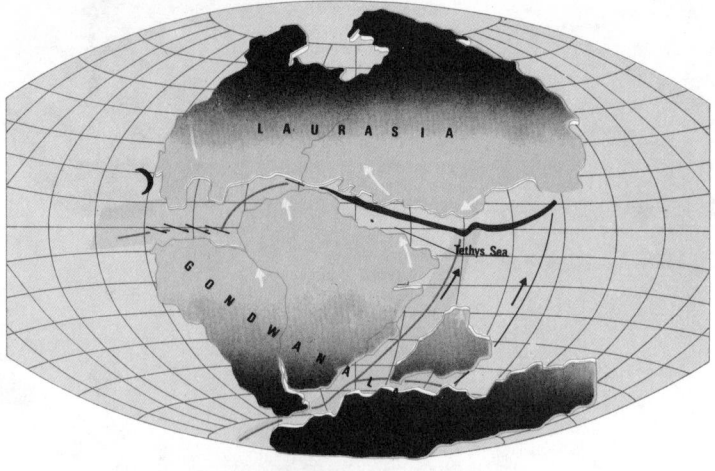

180 million years ago
At this time the original Pangaea land mass had just begun to break up. The continents first split along the lines of the North Atlantic and Indian Oceans. North America separated from Africa and so did India and Antarctica. The Tethys Sea, between Africa and Asia, closed somewhat, and the super continents of Laurasia to the north and Gondwanaland to the south became almost completely separated. In effect the Earth possessed three super landmasses, plus an India that had already begun to move strongly northward.

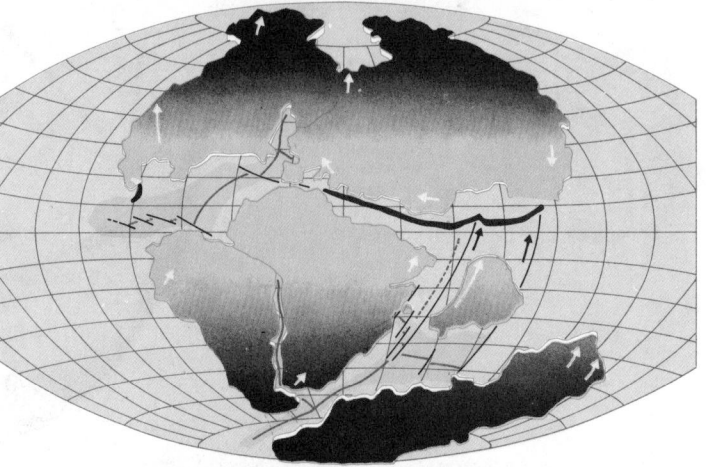

135 million years ago
After a further 45 million years of drifting, the world map had still not taken on a form that looks familiar today. But the two original splits, the North Atlantic and the Indian Ocean, have continued to open out. The North Atlantic is now about 600–650 miles (1000 km) wide. Rifting is extending towards the split which opened up the Labrador Sea and this will eventually separate Greenland from North America. India has firmly launched itself on its collision course with the southern coast of Asia, which is still 2000 miles (3200 km) away.

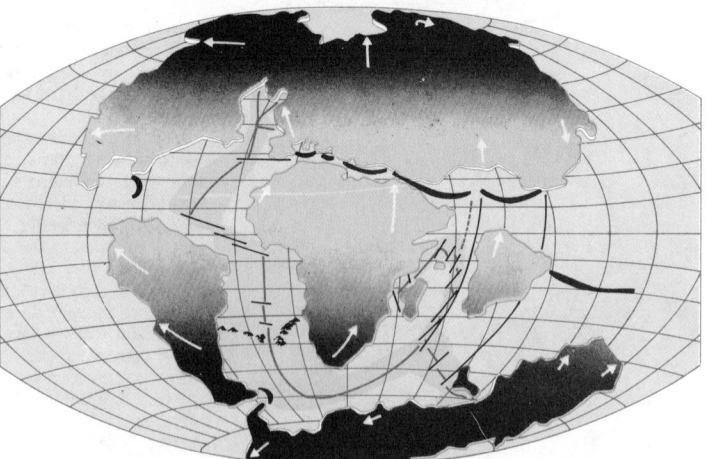

65 million years ago
Some 135 million years after the start of the drifting process the continents have begun to assume their present configuration. South America has at last separated from Africa and in Gondwanaland only Australia and Antarctica have yet to move apart. A continuation of the North Atlantic rifting will shortly bring about another big separation in Laurasia. Greenland will move apart from Europe and eventually North America will separate completely from the Eurasian landmass. The pink area (below) shows the extent of the crustal movements.

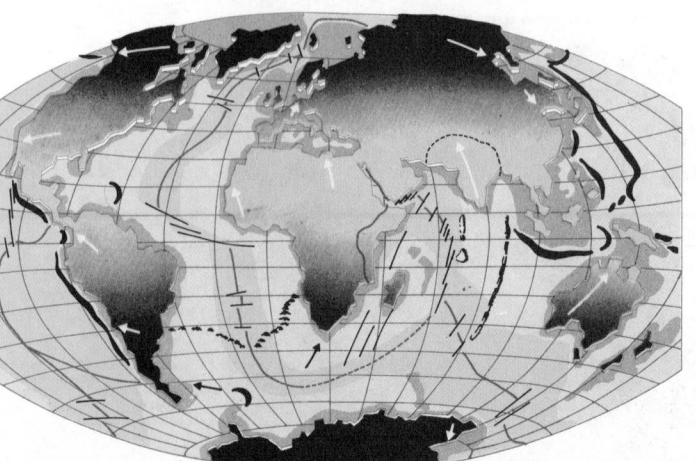

Today's positions
The Atlantic is now a wide ocean from Arctic to Antarctic, the Americas have joined and Australia has separated from Antarctica and moved far to the north. India has likewise moved northwards and its collision with Asia and continued movement has given rise to the extensive uplift of the Himalayas. All the continents which formerly made up the great land mass of Pangaea are now separated by wide oceans. Comparison of areas shows how much of India has been submerged by sliding underneath the crust of Asia (see facing page, far right).

Plate tectonics

This theory has revolutionized the way the Earth's crust – continents and oceans – is interpreted on a global scale. The crust is regarded as being made up of huge plates which converge or diverge along margins marked by earthquakes, volcanoes and other seismic activity. Major divergent margins are the mid-ocean ridges where molten lava forces its way upward and escapes. This causes vast regions of crust to move apart at a rate of an inch or two (some centimeters) per year. When sustained for up to 200 million years this means movements of thousands of miles or kilometers. The process can be seen in operation today in and around Iceland. Oceanic trenches are margins where the plates are moving together and the crust is consumed downward. The overall result is for the crustal plates to move as relatively rigid entities, carrying the continents along with them as if they were on a giant conveyor belt. Over further considerable periods of geologic time this will markedly change today's maps.

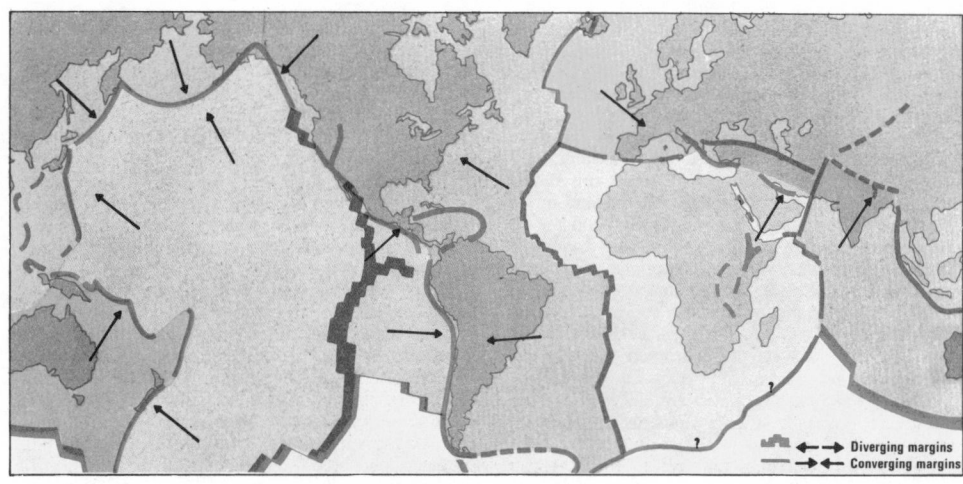

← → Diverging margins
→ ← Converging margins

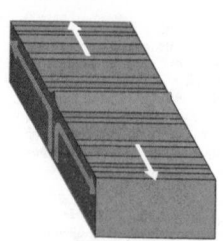

Sea-floor spreading *left*
Arrows show how the lava flows on the ocean bed spread out on each side of a mid-ocean ridge. Evidence for such movement is provided by the fact the rock is alternately magnetized in opposing directions (coloured stripes).

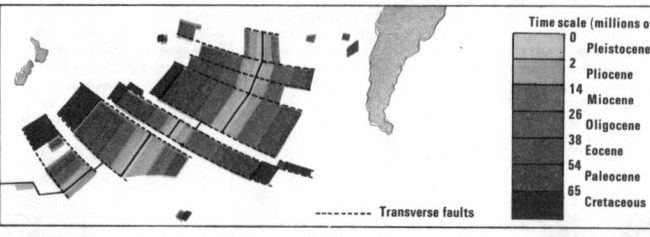

Time scale (millions of years)

0	Pleistocene
2	Pliocene
14	Miocene
26	Oligocene
38	Eocene
54	Paleocene
65	Cretaceous

--------- Transverse faults

Plate movements
above and left
The Earth's crust is a series of large plates 'floating' on the fluid mantle. At their edges the plates are either growing or disappearing. Magnetic measurements in the S. Pacific (left) show rock ages on each side of the mid-ocean ridges.

Plate movements in cross-section *above*
The basic mechanism of plate movements is illustrated above in simplified form with the vertical scale greatly exaggerated. This figure is explained in detail in both of the captions below.

Crustal divergence
above and right
The Earth's crust (1) behaves as a series of rigid plates which move on top of the fluid mantle (2). At their mating edges some of these plates are moving apart (3). This was the mechanism that separated North America (A) from Europe (B). The plates moved to the north and also away from each other under the influence of convection currents in the mantle (C). Between the land areas appeared an oceanic gap with a mid-ocean ridge (D) and lateral ridges (E). The movements continued for some 200 million years, fresh volcanoes being generated by igneous material escaping through the plate joint (F) to add to the lateral ridges which today cross the Atlantic (G). The volcanoes closest to the median line in mid-Atlantic are still young and active — whereas those nearer to the continents are old and extinct.

Crustal convergence
above and right
Diverging plate margins occur only in the centers of the major oceans (see map above) but plates are converging on both sea and land. Where an oceanic plate (4, above) is under-riding a continental plate (5) a deep ocean trench is the result (6). Such trenches extend around much of the Pacific; those around the northwest Pacific include the deepest on Earth where the sea bed is almost seven miles below the ocean surface. The continental margin is squeezed upward to form mountains such as the Andes or Rockies (7). If continental masses converge, such as India (A, right) and Asia (B), the convection in the mantle (C) pulls the plates together so hard that the upper crust crumples (D). Sedimentary deposits between the plates (E) are crushed and squeezed out upward (F), while the mantle on each side is turned downward, one side being forced under the other (G). Continued movement causes gross deformation at the point of collision. The static or slow-moving crust is crushed and tilted, and giant young mountains (the Himalayas, H) are thrust upward along the collision just behind the edge of the crumpled plate.

The Active Earth

When faced with the violence of an earthquake or the destructive and indiscriminate force of a volcano, even our sophisticated technological society is often helpless. These cataclysmic phenomena frequently occur along the same belts of instability in the Earth's crust and are often only different manifestations of the same fundamental processes. About 800 volcanoes are known to have been active in historical times, and many are extremely active today. All the mid-ocean ridges are volcanic in origin, and many underwater eruptions occur along these submarine mountain ranges. Spectacular volcanic eruptions sometimes break the ocean surface, such as during the formation in 1963 of the island of Surtsey, south of Iceland (photograph, right). Some islands, such as Iceland itself, are the products of continued outpourings of lava along the crest of the mid-ocean ridge.

Oceanic earthquakes caused by sudden sea-floor displacements may result in tsunamis or giant sea waves. About 80 per cent of the shallow earthquakes and almost all deep ones take place along the belt around the Pacific. Clear evidence of the large scale movements of the mantle are provided by the zones within which earthquake shocks are generated along some Pacific island arc systems. These zones plunge down from sea-floor level to depths as great as 400 miles (640 km) beneath the adjacent continents and mark the positions of downward flow of the mantle convection currents (page 11A). The corresponding upwelling regions lie along the mid-ocean ridges, where new basic volcanic material is continually being added to the ocean crust as outward movement takes place away from the ridges.

These sea-floor spreading movements act as 'conveyor belts' for the continents, and constitute the basic mechanism for the large displacements involved in continental drifting. Geological data confirm the former close fits of the reassembled continental jig-saw puzzle, and also corroborate the detailed paleomagnetic evidence visible in today's rocks of the movements of the continents relative to the geographic poles.

Geysers
Ground water and mud heated by volcanic activity can lie on the surface as puddles and hot springs, rendered colorful by dissolved minerals, or be pumped out in the form of geysers. The latter are connected to extensive underground reservoirs in which steam pressure builds up above the hot water. Intermittently the system discharges high into the air.

Fissure eruption
In this type of eruption freely flowing molten basaltic material exudes from apertures forced in the crust. The surface crack may be several miles in length and the more or less horizontal flow has on occasion covered more than 200 square miles (500 km²).

Hawaiian-type eruption
In this case large, shallow cones, often containing lakes of molten lava, generally release gas and vapor in a relatively passive way. But sometimes glowing lava is expelled as a fine spray which in a high wind can be drawn out into fine threads called Pelée's hair.

Emissions
Incandescent lava issues from the main cone or from side vents, while dense vapors pour from every crevice. Water vapor is the main gaseous component, but nitrogen and sulphur dioxide are also important.

Layering
Most volcanoes have a history extending back thousands or even millions of years. Over this time the main cone has built up in many stratified layers, sometimes of contrasting types of lava. Each fresh eruption produces at least one additional layer.

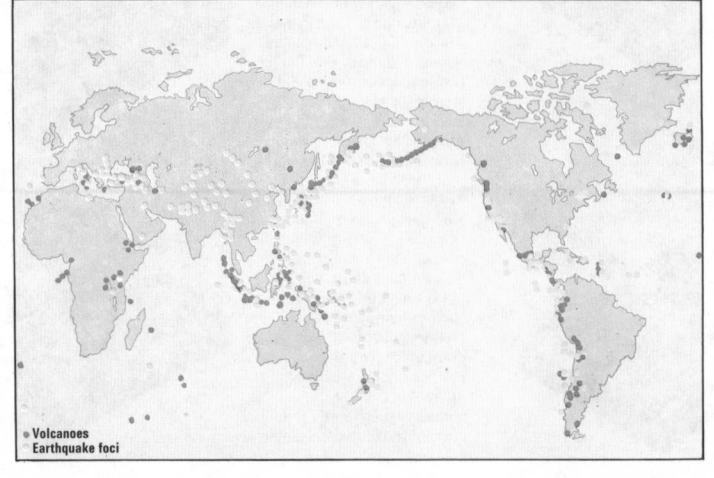

Underground water
Heated beyond normal boiling point, the pressurized water issues in a rush when pressure is relieved.

Magma chamber
Underlying every volcano is a volume of intensely hot fluid under high pressure.

Laccolith
Above the pipes and sills of the hot magma lies a giant lens-shaped intrusion of cold rock.

Metamorphic rock
The strata adjacent to the fiery magma are physically and chemically altered by the heat.

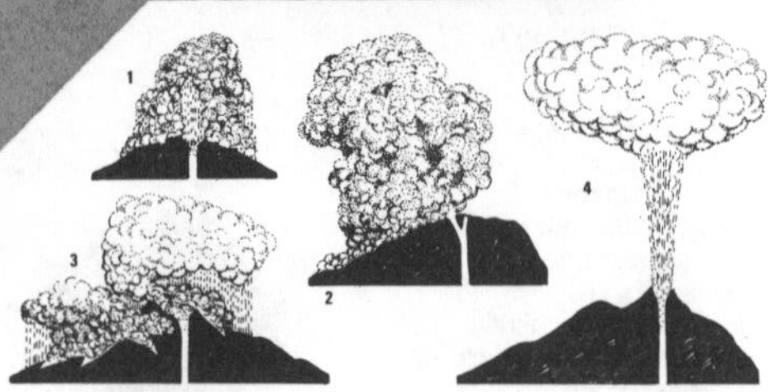

Where the Earth seems active *right*
Although we live on a white-hot globe with a thin cool crust, the fierce heat and energy of the interior is manifest only along fairly clearly defined belts. Around the Pacific, volcanoes and earthquakes are frequent. Another belt traverses the mountains from southeast Asia through the Middle East to the Mediterranean. Every site is an external expression of activity within the crust and upper mantle. The underlying cause is a slow flowing of the rocks of the mantle in response to changes in temperature and density.

• Volcanoes
• Earthquake foci

Types of eruption *above*
Volcanic cones differ in both shape and activity. The Strombolian (1) erupts every few minutes or hours; the Peléan form (2) gives a hot avalanche; the Vesuvian (3) is a fierce upward expulsion, while the Plinian (4) is the extreme form.

A caldera *left*
Expulsion of lava (A) from the magma chamber (B) may leave the central core (C) without support. A collapse results in a large, steep-sided caldera (D). The magma chamber may cool and solidify (E), and water may collect inside the caldera (F).

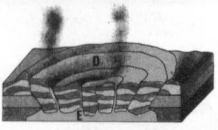
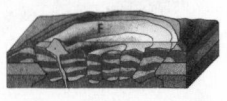

Earthquake *right*
Along lines of potential movement, such as fault planes, stresses may build up over many years until the breaking strength of some part of the rock is exceeded (A). A sudden break occurs and the two sides of the fault line move, generating shockwaves which travel outward in all directions from the focus at the point of rupture (B). The point on the surface directly above the focus is the epicenter (C). While the fault movement reaches its fullest extent, the shockwaves reach the surface (D). Far right the aftermath of an earthquake.

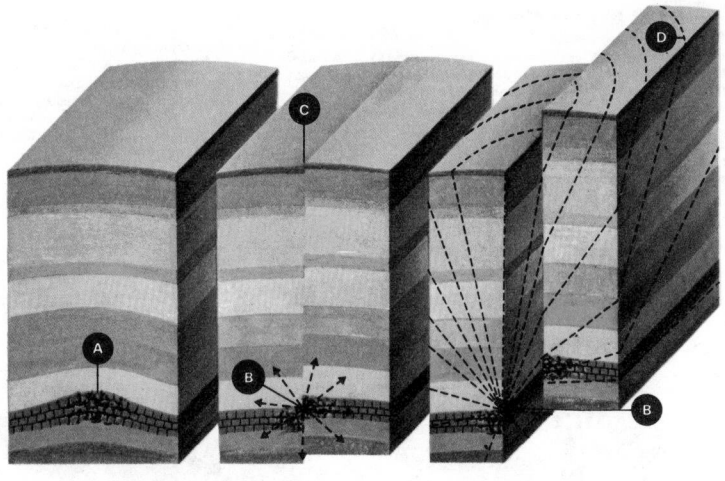

Destructive waves *right*
The Japanese, who have suffered severely from them, have given the name tsunami to the terrifying waves which follow earthquakes. Their character depends on the cause. In the case of a sudden rift and slump in the ocean bed (A) the wave at the surface is initially a trough, which travels away to both sides followed by a crest and subsequent smaller waves (B). A fault causing a sudden changed level of sea bed (C) can generate a tsunami that starts with a crest (D). Travelling at 400 miles (650 km) per hour or more the tsunami arrives at a beach as a series of waves up to 200 feet (60 m) high (E), the 'trough first' variety being heralded by a sudden withdrawal of the ocean from the shore. Warning stations ring the Pacific (far right) and the concentric rings show tsunamic travel time from an earthquake site to Hawaii at the center.

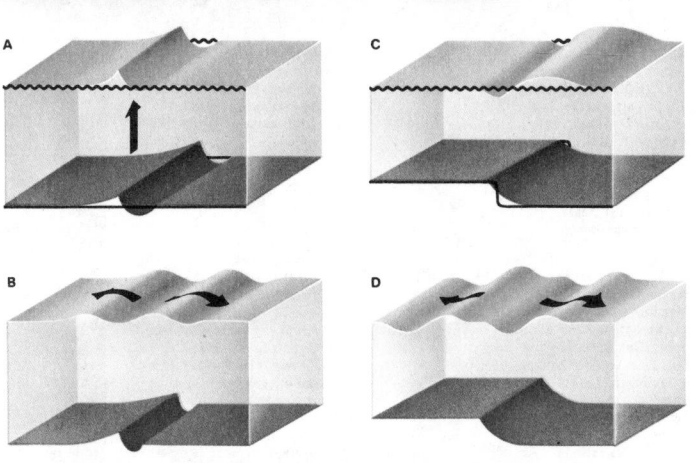

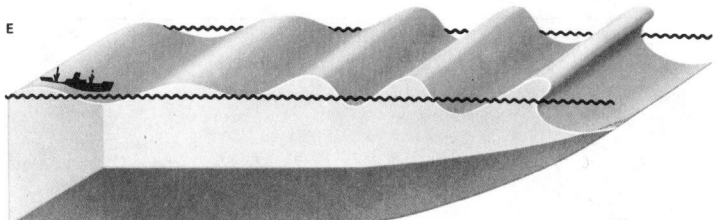

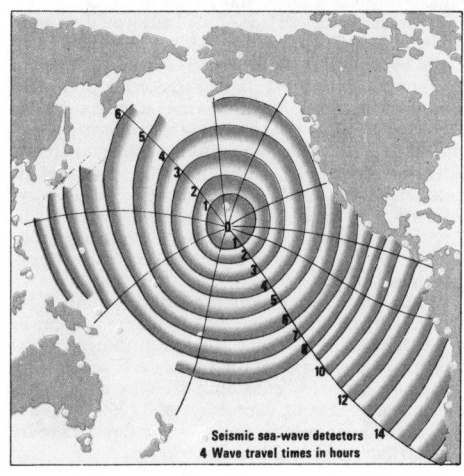

Tsunami warning *above*
Numerous seismographic warning stations around the earthquake belt of the Pacific Ocean maintain a continuous alert for earthquake shocks and for the tsunami waves that may follow it. Possible recipients of such waves plot a series of concentric rings, such as these centered on the Hawaiian Islands, which show the time in hours that would be taken for a tsunami to travel from any earthquake epicenter. Aircraft and satellites are increasingly helping to create a globally integrated life-saving system.

Seismic waves *right*
An earthquake caused by a sudden movement in the crust at the focus (A) sends out a pattern of shock waves radiating like ripples in a pond. These waves are of three kinds. Primary (P) waves (full lines) vibrate in the direction of propagation, and thus are a rapid succession of high and low pressures. Secondary (S) waves (broken lines), which travel only 60 per cent as fast, shake from side to side. Long waves (L) travel round the crust. In a belt around the world only waves of the L-type occur, giving rise to the concept of a shadow zone (B and shaded belt in inset at lower right). But intermittent records of P waves in this zone led seismologists to the belief that the Earth must have a very dense fluid core (D, lower drawing) capable of strongly refracting P waves like a lens. Seismic waves are almost man's only source of knowledge about the Earth's interior.

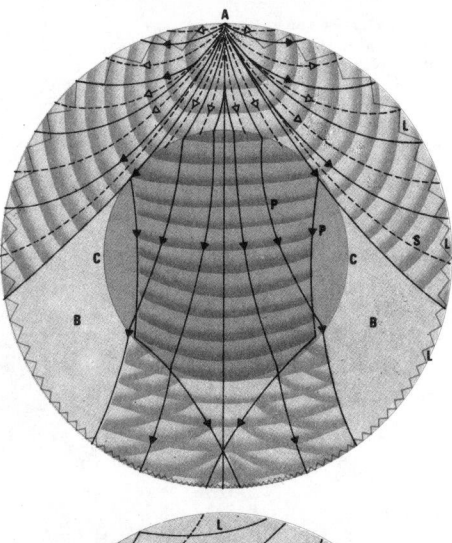

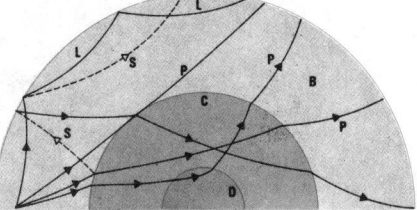

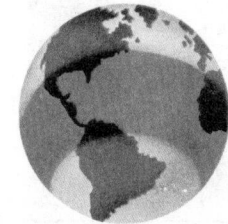

Seismology *right*
Seismic waves of all three types (P, S and L) are detected and recorded by seismographs. Usually these contain a sprung mass which, when an earthquake shock passes, stays still while the rest of the instrument moves. Some seismographs detect horizontal waves (A) while others detect vertical ones (B). The pen in the instrument leaves a distinctive trace (P-S-L). P (primary) waves are a succession of rarefactions and compressions, denoted by the packing of the dots; S (secondary) waves are a sideways shaking, shown here in plan view.

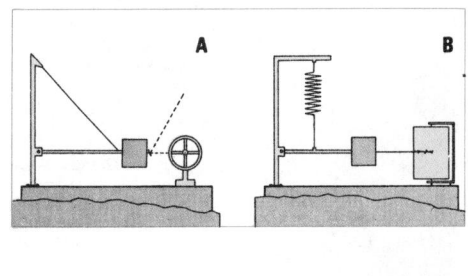

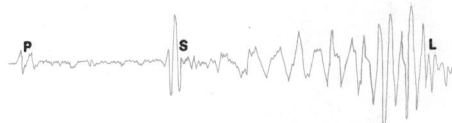

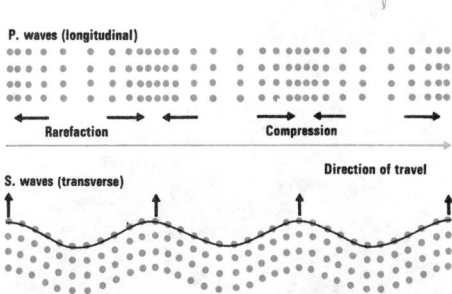

Forces That Shape The Land

Measured against the time standards of everyday life, the major forces that shape the face of the Earth seem to act almost unbelievably slowly. But in geological terms the erosion of rock formations by river, marine or ice action is in fact rather rapid. Indeed in isolated locations, on coasts or below waterfalls, visible erosion can take place in a period of months or even days.

Over large regions of the Earth the rates of river erosion, expressed as the mass of material removed from each unit of land area in a given time, range between 34 and 6720 short tons per square mile per year (12–2354 metric tons/km^2/year). The main factor determining the rate at any place is the climate. The average rate of erosion for Eurasia, Africa, the Americas and Australia, a land area of some 50 million sq. mi. (130 million km^2), has been calculated to be about 392 short tons per sq. mi. per year (137 metric tons/km^2/year). This corresponds to a general lowering of the surface of the land by about 40 inches (one meter) every 22000 years. At this rate these continents would be worn down to sea level in less than 20 million years, which in geological terms is a fairly short span of time.

In practice, the surface of the land would be most unlikely to suffer such a fate. Although isolated areas could be worn away, worldwide erosion on this scale and at a steady rate would be balanced or prevented by a number of factors, one of which is the continuing large-scale uplift of the land in other regions. Nevertheless long-term estimates do emphasize the cumulative effects of the apparently slow processes of erosion. Even man's own structures wear away. Already the portland stone of St. Paul's cathedral in London has lost half an inch (13 mm) overall in 250 years, aided by the additional force of atmospheric pollution.

Where do all the products of this erosion go? By far the largest accumulations of sediments occur in river deltas, and at many periods in the geological past great thicknesses of such deposits have been laid down in extensive subsiding troughs called geosynclines. A rate of deposition of 1/250 inch (0.1 millimeter) per year is enough to lay down 12 miles (20 km) of strata in 200 million years.

The cycle of rock change

The agents of weathering
Gross break-up of the Earth's surface rocks is caused by earthquakes, the ceaseless cycle of diurnal and annual heating and cooling, and by the freezing of water trapped in fissures and crevices. The water of the seas, rivers and rain dissolves some rocks and in others leaches out particular minerals. Water is especially powerful as a weathering agent when it contains dissolved acidic chemicals. Today's main sources are plants and animals (1), but in the primeval world such chemicals were evolved mainly by volcanoes (2).

Erosion of the land
Only the material exposed at the surface of the Earth by volcanic action (2) or uplift (3) is subjected to erosion, but this material is constantly changing. Chemical erosion is an extension of the weathering process, converting the surface material into different and usually physically degraded substances. Physical erosion (4) is effected by running water and the wind (in both cases accelerated by the presence of an abrasive load) and by ice action and frost shattering.

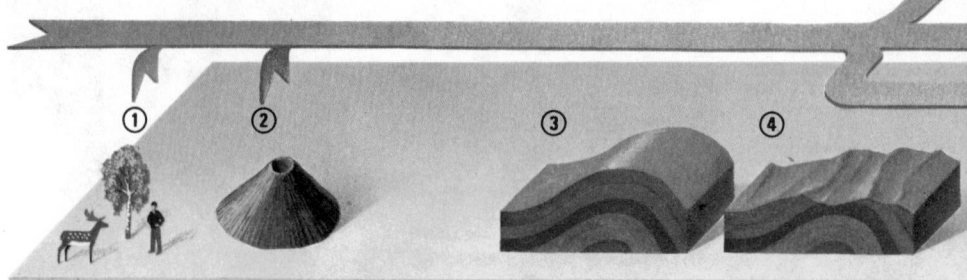

Extrusions
Most lavas are at a temperature of 900-1200°C. Acidic (granitic) lava is fairly viscous, but basic (basalt) lava flows relatively freely and when extruded from surface fissures or volcanoes can cover large areas (15). Lavas which have originated from partial melting of crustal rocks can also be erupted.

Basic magmas
Basic magma generated by partial melting in the mantle (14) may rise into and through the crust to be extruded from surface volcanoes. Basic magmas are the hottest, as well as the most freely flowing, and are often generated at very considerable depth. In their ascent they can intrude large areas of the crust and finally extrude through fissures in the surface.

Intrusions
Contact metamorphism is a form of baking and re-crystallization caused by the intrusion of hot magma into existing strata (13).

Granitic magmas
Partial melting deep in the crust generates new granitic magma—hot, rather viscous molten rock of an acidic nature which is able to migrate both upwards and laterally (12). This may then inject and mix with the surrounding rocks to form a migmatite complex.

Slow uplift
Strata can be slowly uplifted (11) until they once more appear at the surface; continued or violent uplift results in mountain-building. In either case, erosion begins afresh.

Deep metamorphism
If the strata are depressed far down, to depths up to about 25 miles (40 km), deep metamorphism at high pressures and high temperatures (10) results in complete re-crystallization. This gradually converts the original sediments into a complex of new rock types.

Erosion

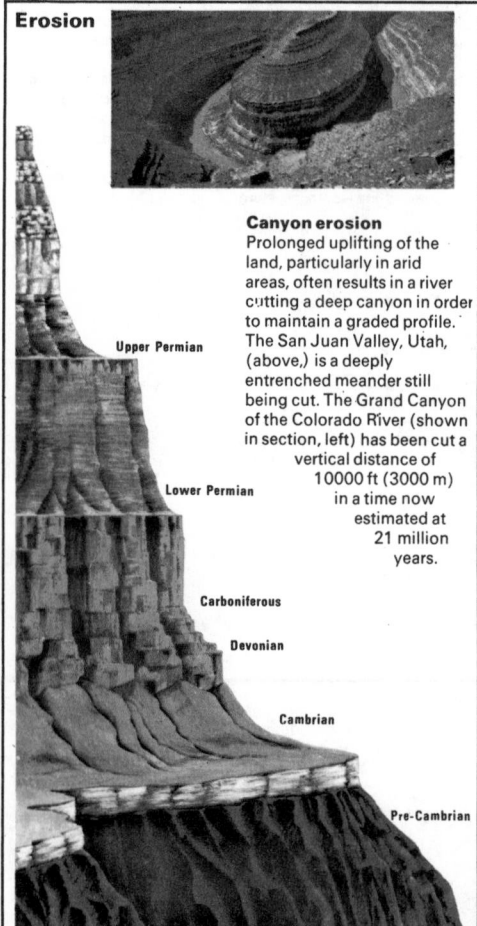

Canyon erosion
Prolonged uplifting of the land, particularly in arid areas, often results in a river cutting a deep canyon in order to maintain a graded profile. The San Juan Valley, Utah, (above,) is a deeply entrenched meander still being cut. The Grand Canyon of the Colorado River (shown in section, left) has been cut a vertical distance of 10000 ft (3000 m) in a time now estimated at 21 million years.

Upper Permian

Lower Permian

Carboniferous

Devonian

Cambrian

Pre-Cambrian

Wind erosion
Laden with grains of sand and other air-transportable debris, the wind exerts a powerful sculpturing effect. Rate of erosion varies with rock hardness, giving rise to odd effects (Mushroom Rock, Death Valley, California, left). Desert sand forms 'barchan' dunes (right), which slowly travel points-first.

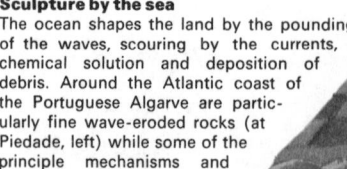

Sculpture by the sea
The ocean shapes the land by the pounding of the waves, scouring by the currents, chemical solution and deposition of debris. Around the Atlantic coast of the Portuguese Algarve are particularly fine wave-eroded rocks (at Piedade, left) while some of the principle mechanisms and coastal features are seen at right (key, far right).

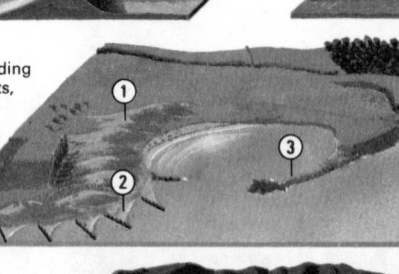

River development
The youthful river flows fast, eroding a narrow channel in an otherwise unchanged landscape. In maturity the channel is wider; flow is slower and some transported debris is deposited. The old river meanders across a broad flood plain (River Wye near Goodrich, left), some meanders becoming cut off as ox-bow lakes.

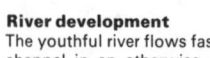

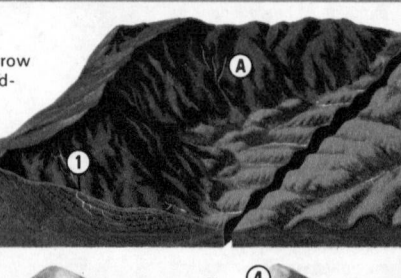

Glacial action
Briksdal Glacier, Norway (left), is a remnant of the Ice Ages, carving U-shaped valleys (2) in the pre-glacial rock (1). The bergschrund (3) forms close to the back wall, while other crevasses (4) form at gradient changes. Eroded rocks form a longitudinal moraine (5).

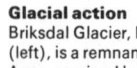

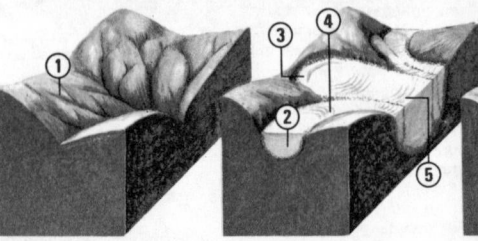

Transportation

As material is worn away from the surface rocks it is carried away by various processes. The most important transport system is flowing water (5), which can move sediments in suspension, in solution or carried along the beds of river channels. In open country, and especially over deserts, much solid debris is blown by the wind (6). Even slow-moving glaciers (7) perform a significant erosion and transport role by bearing heavy burdens of rock debris.

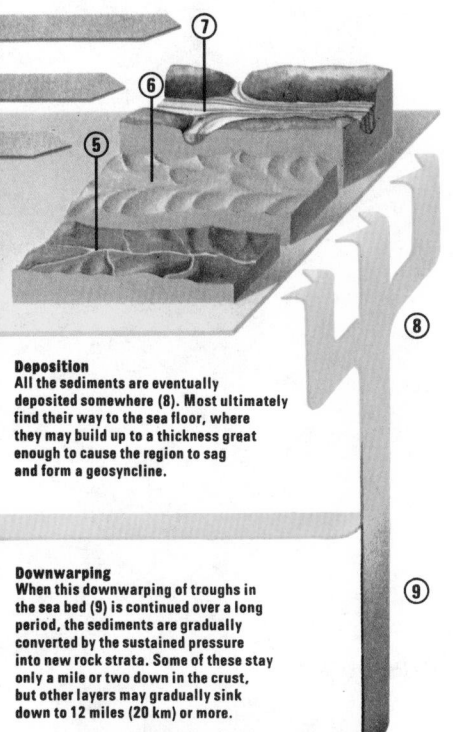

Deposition

All the sediments are eventually deposited somewhere (8). Most ultimately find their way to the sea floor, where they may build up to a thickness great enough to cause the region to sag and form a geosyncline.

Downwarping

When this downwarping of troughs in the sea bed (9) is continued over a long period, the sediments are gradually converted by the sustained pressure into new rock strata. Some of these stay only a mile or two down in the crust, but other layers may gradually sink down to 12 miles (20 km) or more.

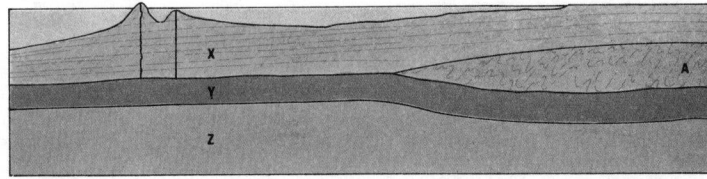

250 million years ago

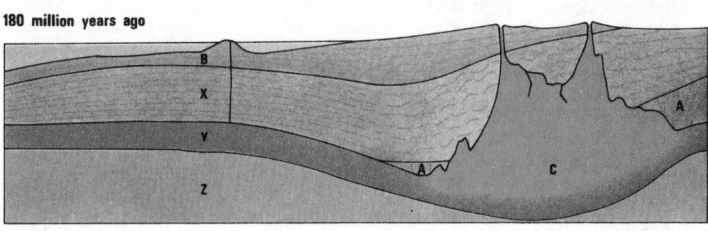

180 million years ago

130 million years ago

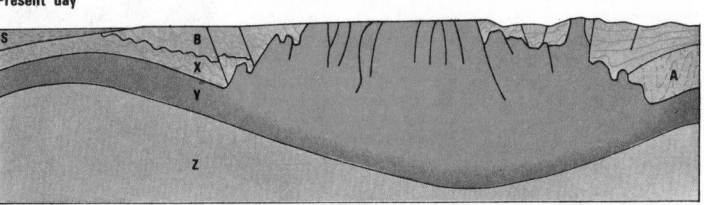

Present day

Late Paleozoic *left*
The formation of a geosyncline begins with the laying down of heavy sediments. In the creation of the Sierra Nevada range sediments X were deposited by the primeval ocean on top of Precambrian rock A, basalt crust Y and peridotite mantle Z.

Jurassic *left*
Downwarping of the crust causes the deposition of Mesozoic sediments B and carries the lower basalt crust and sediments into the zone of the mantle's influence. The bottom of the bulge is gradually converted into hot, fluid magma C.

Cretaceous *left*
In this period the geosynclinal process is in a mature stage. The inner rocks reach their maximum downward penetration into the mantle and are metamorphosed by high temperature and pressure. The deep metamorphism spreads (curved shading).

Present day *left*
Uplift and cooling opens the way to a new cycle of formation. The metamorphic rocks are exposed at the surface and subsequently eroded to yield today's complex landscape structure. Final withdrawal of the sea exposes marine sediments S.

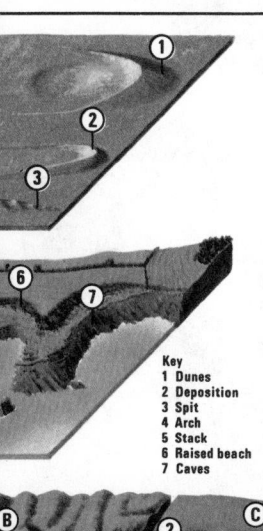

Wind-blown sand *left*
Sand deserts exhibit dunes of various forms. Unlike a barchan the parabolic blowout (1) travels with points trailing. In elongated form this becomes a parabolic hairpin (2), and a third form is the longitudinal ridge (3), known in the Sahara as a seif dune.

Emerging coastline *right*
Where the shoreline is rising, the continental shelf becomes exposed. River silt accumulates and forms an offshore bar, pierced by the river flow. Eventually infilling forms a tidal salt marsh through which the braided river reaches a new shore. Spain (far right) and Italy provide good examples.

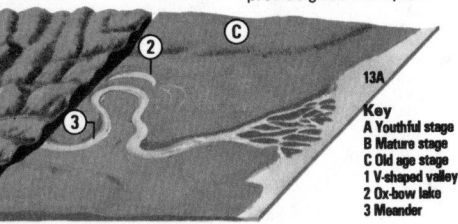

Key
1 Dunes
2 Deposition
3 Spit
4 Arch
5 Stack
6 Raised beach
7 Caves

Glaciated landscape *left*
The landscape shows evidence of former ice coverage. Broken rock debris forms valley-floor moraines (6), the peaks are sharp and knife-edged (7), and hanging valleys (8) mark the entry of the glacier's tributaries. Terminal moraines (9) are a characteristic feature.

Key
A Initial stage
B Late youth
C Early maturity
1 Cut-off
2 Spit
3 4 Bars
5 Lagoon

Key
A Initial stage
B Bar development
C Emergence complete

13A

Key
A Youthful stage
B Mature stage
C Old age stage
1 V-shaped valley
2 Ox-bow lake
3 Meander

Key
1 Esker
2 Recessional moraine
3 Drumlin
4 Lake
5 Terminal moraine
6 Outwash delta
7 Lake deposits
8 Kettle lake
9 Outwash plain
10 Kettle hole

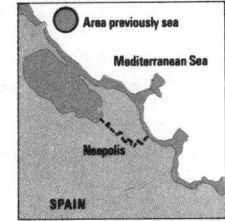

Subsiding coastline *left*
Most coastal regions undergoing submergence are highly irregular. Drowned hills are eroded by the waves to form cliff headlands, or cut-offs; spits and bars cross the submerged valleys, enclose them and form lagoons. Finally all these features wear back to a new shoreline.

○ Area previously sea

Mediterranean Sea

Neapolis

SPAIN

Glaciated landforms *left*
Throughout a vast area of the temperate lands evidence of past glacial action is abundant. A geomorphologist, studying the landscape shown in the larger illustration, would deduce the former glacial situation depicted in the inset. Weight and sculpture by the ice carved out characteristic depressions, some later filled with water. Subglacial streams left alluvial deposits in the form of eskers and an outwash fan or delta, while the limit of the glacier is suggested by rocks deposited as a terminal moraine. Kettle holes result from the melting of ice within moraine debris.

The Record in the Rocks

All the past history of the Earth since the original formation of the crust is there to be discovered in the rocks existing today if only the appropriate techniques are used to find it. Sedimentary, igneous and metamorphic – the three basic types of rock – all have an enormous amount of information stored within them on such diverse aspects of the Earth's history as, for example, the variations of past climates in space and in time, the incidence of ice ages and the positions of former mountain ranges. The migrations of the ancient geo-magnetic poles at different periods of time can be discovered by studying some sedimentary and igneous rocks, while other types can yield their ages of formation or metamorphism – their changed character over long periods. The prevailing wind directions over certain regions, the direction of stream flow in river deltas that have long since vanished, or the ways in which the ice flowed in some past ice age are all there to be discovered. So are the past distributions of land and sea, areas of deposition, periods of uplift and the raising of great mountain chains (see pages 12–13A and 18–19A). Even lightning strikes millions of years old can be clearly seen.

The first task of the geologist is to make a map showing the positions and relative ages of the various rock types in a region. It is around this basic information incorporated into the geological map that all else is built, whether it is to be studies of the geological history and evolution of the region, or detailed investigations of the flora and fauna, or any of many other lines of research – such as the disentangling of various periods of deformation which have affected the region during which the rocks may have been folded or faulted (foot of this page) or eroded down to sea level. Two of the most important methods of dating, by which the age of rock is determined, are the study of fossils and the use of radiometric methods in which age is calculated by analyzing radioactive minerals having a known half-life (opposite page). Using a combination of 'correlation' techniques and either method of dating it is possible for a skilled geologist to compare the relative time sequences of geological events in any regions in the world.

A geological map *below*

A geological map records the outcrop pattern and the structural features of each region as they are today, corresponding with the final stage of the reconstruction—right.

How the story unfolds
right

The complex 3500 million year story of the rocks is very far from being superficially obvious. Even a skilled geologist can do no more than study the land as it is today, plot a geological map and then try to think backward over periods of millions of years in an endeavor to determine the sequences which produced the present terrain. On the right is depicted such a sequence, which might reasonably be arrived at after studying the map below, left.
The history begins (A) with the landmass rising and the sea retreating, leaving behind 'off-lap' sediments. The landmass continues to rise and is folded by compressive forces, the fold tops then being eroded (B). Over a long period the landmass then subsides and tilts; the sea once more advances, laying down 'on-lap' sediments (C). Then a great upheaval causes the sea to retreat completely.
The landmass is strongly uplifted and faulted, and the higher mass is at once attacked by erosion (D). Continued erosion gradually reduces the region to a more or less common level. Rivers, formed at stage C, carry eroded materials away and deposit them at lower levels (left side of E). Finally, the northeast part of the region is invaded by an extrusive mass of volcanic material. Of course, the processes of change would continue even now.

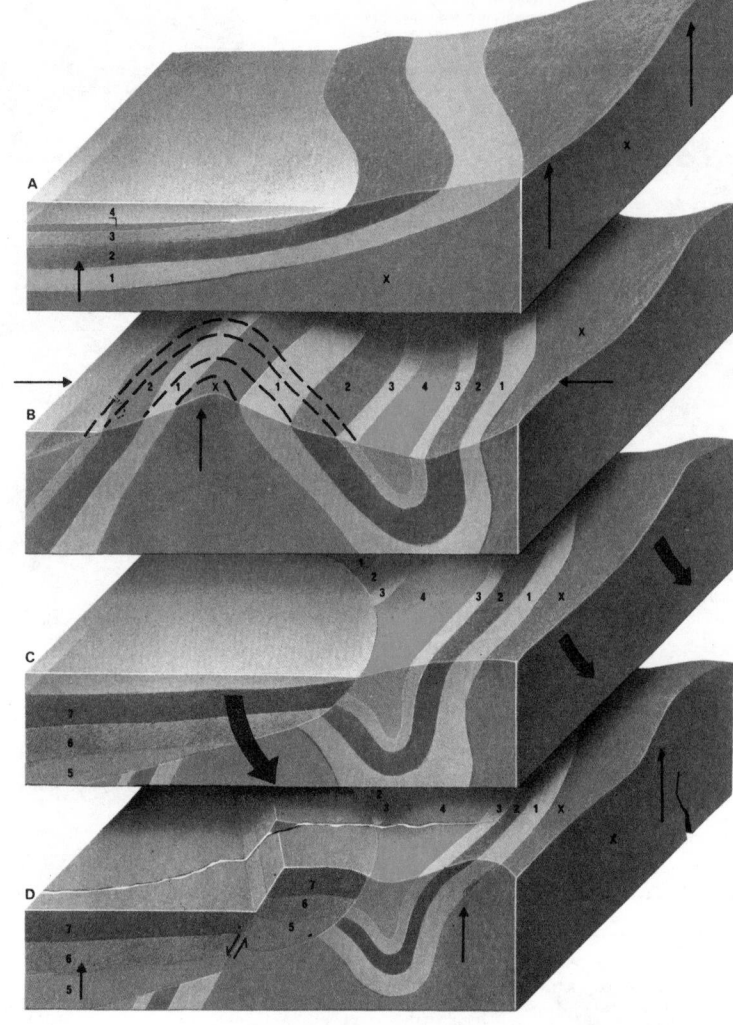

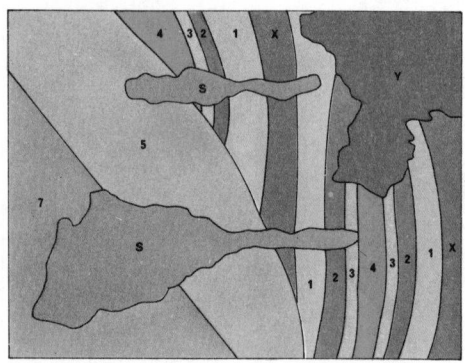

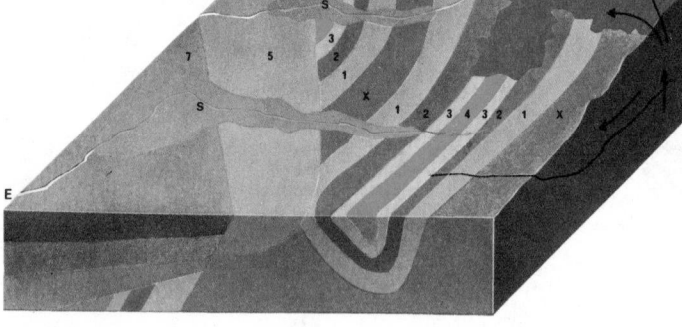

S	River sediments
V	Volcanic extrusion
7	
6	Later sedimentary sequence
5	
4	Period of erosion
3	
2	Early sedimentary sequence
1	
	Period of erosion
x	Older basement rocks

The language of geology

Plane of movement of a normal fault (1) displacing strata to right (downthrow side) relative to left (upthrow side).

Block of strata (2) dropped between two tensional faults forming a rift valley. Other strata are compressional.

Normal anticline (3) and syncline (4) with symmetrically dipping limbs on either side of the axial plane of the strata.

Positions of the axial planes (5, 6) passing through an asymmetrical anticline (5) and an asymmetrical syncline (6).

Compressional reversed fault (7). In this case the left side of the fault is over-riding basically horizontal strata on the right.

Monoclinal fold (8), with a relatively steep limb separating basically horizontal areas of strata at two levels.

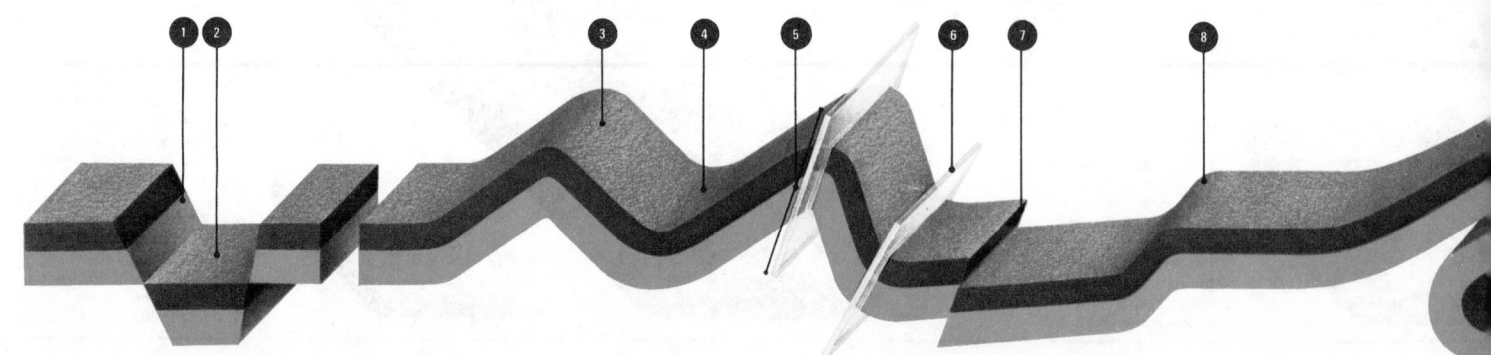

Geological dating

The relative dating of geological strata is found from the sequence in which the layers were deposited, the oldest being at the base of a local sequence and the youngest at the top. On this basis, together with correlations over wide areas based on the fossil evidence of the forms of life at different stages of the 'geological column', the main periods and sub-divisions can be worked out.

Prior to the Cambrian, the oldest epoch of the Paleozoic era (see scale at right), evidence of life is seldom found in the rocks. The extremely primitive earliest forms of life have generally not been preserved in the form of fossils, and so correlations by palaeontological methods cannot be applied to the Precambrian.

In recent years the progressive evolution of radio-carbon dating has enabled geologists to assign actual dates to the relative sequences of strata. This is done by measuring the amount of radioactive decay of an isotope of carbon, carbon-14, or C^{14}. This radio-isotope decays to form nitrogen, its half-life being about 5,730 years. After the death of a living organism, it no longer takes carbon dioxide into its body, so that the amount of carbon-14 that body contains is fixed as a known quantity in relation to its total weight. As time goes by, this amount lessens in accordance with radioactive decay. The precise amount that remains is determined by refined physical and chemical analysis. In this way the age of a specimen can be approximately determined, for even after millions of years no radioactive isotope is ever quite used up.

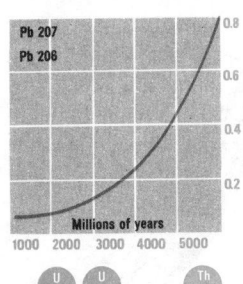

Half-life *left*
Radioactive materials decay according to a law. Each isotope has a characteristic half-life, the time required for the number of radioactive atoms to decay to half their original number. The half-life for each element is unalterable.

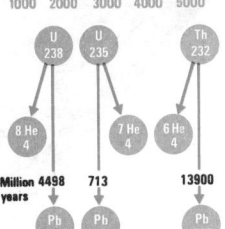

Degeneration
above and left
Some of the isotopes, shown above with their half-lives and end-products, can be used for dating over the whole age of the Earth. For more recent dating, radio-carbon with a half-life of 5570 years is used (left).

1 Neutron
2 Nitrogen 14
3 Proton
4 Carbon 14
5 Nitrogen 14
6 β particle

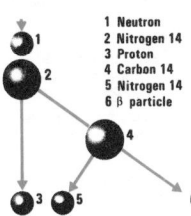

Overturned anticline (9) overlying an overturned syncline in a system distinguished by isoclinal (almost parallel) limbs.

Plane of thrusting (10) causes the overturned anticline (11) to ride over lower strata in form of a horizontally displaced 'nappe'.

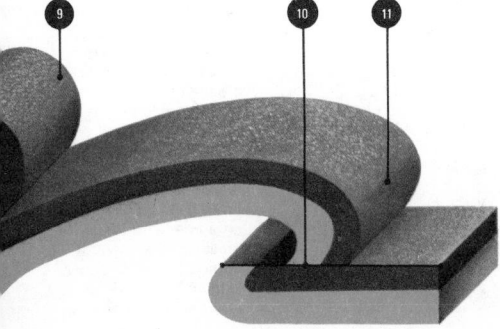

Quaternary
This most recent period of geological history leads up to the appearance of man and the present day. Changes of climate took place which brought on the great ice ages with glacial periods alternating with warmer sequences between them. And, of course, the period is still in progress.

Tertiary
A complex history of changes took place, each epoch of the Tertiary period from Paleocene to Pliocene showing a diverse sequence of volcanism and mountain-building in different regions. Shallow seas alternated with sub-tropical delta flats harboring the precursors of today's life.

Cretaceous
The Tethys Sea spread over large areas of the adjacent continents. Fossil evidence reveals a diverse flora and fauna. The South Atlantic reached a width of some 1900 miles (3000 km) and only Antarctica and Australia and the northern lands of the North Atlantic remained unseparated.

Jurassic
The North Atlantic had opened to a width of some 600 miles (1000 km). Sedimentary deposits formed marginal belts around the continents which had separated, and deeper-water sediments were deposited in the Tethys Sea. Extensive eruption of basalts accompanied the rifting of the South Atlantic.

Triassic
This was the period in which the continental drift began. The progressive opening of the North Atlantic was accompanied by rift-valley faulting and large outpourings of basalt along the eastern seaboard of what is today North America. Gondwanaland in the south began to break up.

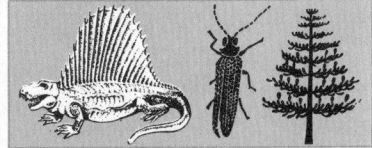

Permian
Many areas were characterized by arid or semi-arid climates, with frequent salt lakes giving rise to evaporite deposits and red desert sandstones. Much volcanic activity took place on a local scale. This was the last period in which Pangaea remained a single continental mass. New flora were abundant.

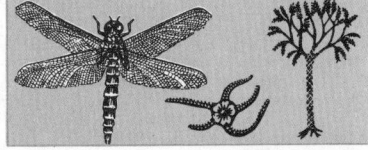

Carboniferous
Extensive forest and deltaic swamp conditions led to the eventual formation of coal basins in North America and Europe. Phases of folding and mountain formation occurred in many places. In Gondwanaland widespread glaciation occurred, with glaciers radiating from a great central ice-cap.

Devonian
Large areas of arid continental and sandstone deposits formed, partly as the products of erosion of the mountains formed previously. Intervening basins of shallow sea or lagoonal deposits occurred, with abundant fossil fish. Distinct faunal provinces have been recognized from this period.

Silurian
In this period further widespread basins of thick sedimentary deposits were laid down. Many of these are characterized by the abundance of marine fossils, including corals. The Caledonian mountains were formed in Laurasia in which enormous volumes of granitic rocks were later emplaced.

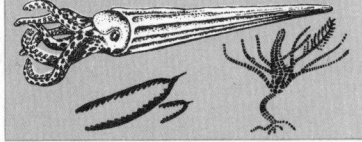

Ordovician
Graptolites and trilobites continued to be important forms of marine life. Thick marine sediments continued to be laid down, and there were extensive and widespread outbursts of volcanic activity. In some regions deformation and uplift of the rocks created major mountain ranges.

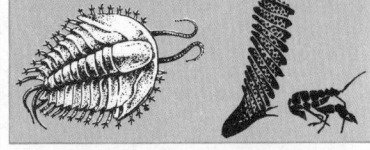

Cambrian
Rocks of this period contain the earliest fossilized remnants of more complex forms of life such as graptolites, brachiopods, trilobites and gastropods. In many regions the Cambrian period was characterized by the deposition of thick sequences of sedimentary rocks, usually on an eroded basement.

Precambrian
By far the longest period of geological time is included in the Precambrian. This encompasses a complex history of sedimentation, mountain-building, volcanism, and granitic intrusions. Precambrian rocks form basements to many sedimentary deposits, and make up the nuclei of continents.

Million years / Major periods

Cenozoic
Mesozoic
Paleozoic
Upper Proterozoic
Lower Proterozoic
Archaean
Katarchaean
Oldest known crust
formation of the earth

500
1000
1500
2000
2500
3000
3500
4000
4500

Period scale / Million years / Period

65
100
136
190
200
225
280
300
345
395
400
430
500
570
600

Pb 207
Pb 206

0.8
0.6
0.4
0.2

Millions of years
1000 2000 3000 4000 5000

U 238 → 8 He 4 → Pb 206 — Million years 4498
U 235 → 7 He 4 → Pb 207 — 713
Th 232 → 6 He 4 → Pb 208 — 13900
Rb 87 → Sr 87 — 50000
K 40 → A 40 — 11850
K 40 → Ca 40 — 1470

9 10 11

The Active Oceans

The surface of the oceans presents an infinite variety of contrasts ranging from glassy calm to terrifying storms with towering waves and wind-whipped wraiths of spray. But no part of the oceans is ever really still. Together the oceans comprise 300 million cubic miles (1250 million km³) of ever-active water. The whole mass ebbs and flows on a global scale with the tides. The surface is disturbed by winds into great patterns of waves which eventually break on the shores of the land. And the largest and most far-reaching movements of all are the ocean currents, some on or near the surface and others at great depths, which profoundly alter not only the oceans but also the weather.

Best known of all these currents is the Gulf Stream, which was discovered in late medieval times when early navigators found that their ships were consistently not in the place predicted by their calculations of course and estimated speed. Some 500 years ago it had become customary for Spanish captains voyaging to the New World to keep well south of the Gulf Stream on their outward journey and then use its swift four or five knot (8–9 km/hr) current to help them along on the return. The Gulf Stream brings mild weather to northwest Europe, and a corresponding role is played on the other side of the globe by the Kuroshio, a warm current which flows northeastward off Japan. Conversely, in the southeastern Pacific the Peru Current brings cold water from the sub-Antarctic region northward towards the equator. The surface flow is accompanied during most months of the year by an 'upwelling' of water rich in nutrients along the coast of Chile and Peru, and this, like many other cold currents elsewhere, supports great fisheries.

In coastal seas the water movements are often dominated by the currents that accompany the rise and fall of the tide. Because of the friction of the tides, the Moon is moving slowly further from the Earth.

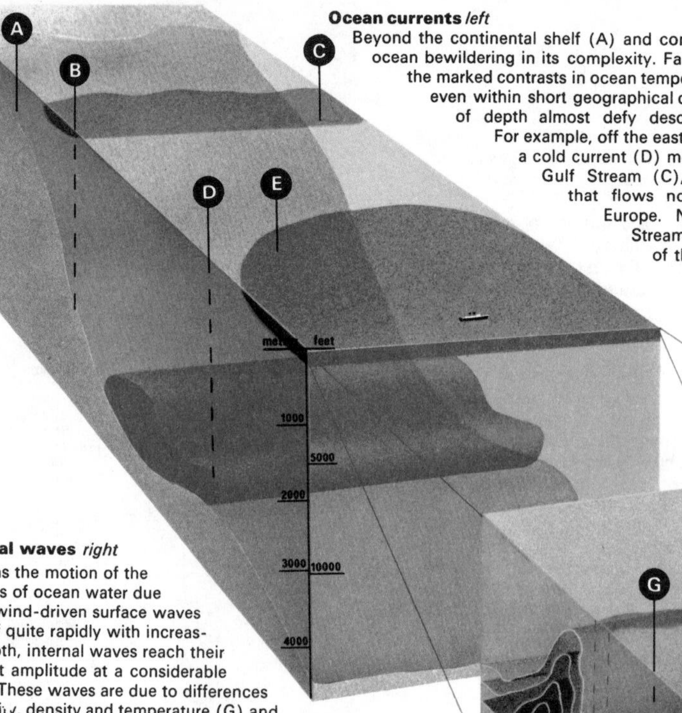

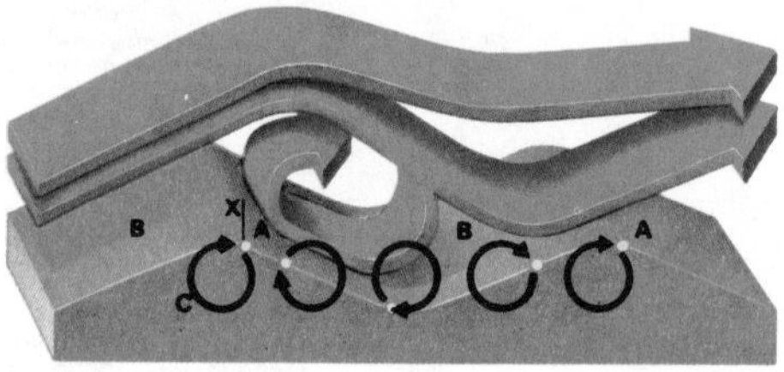

Wave generation *right*
Waves are generated on the surface by the wind. Once a slight undulation has been formed it will react on the air flow so that an eddying motion, with a reduced pressure, is produced on the lee side (A) of each crest. Combined with the wind pressure on the windward side (B), this causes the waves to grow in height. The wave travels forward in the direction of the wind, but the individual water particles (X) move in almost closed orbits (C).

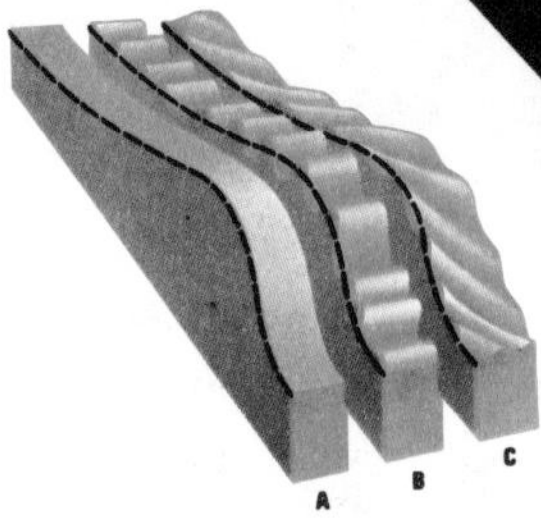

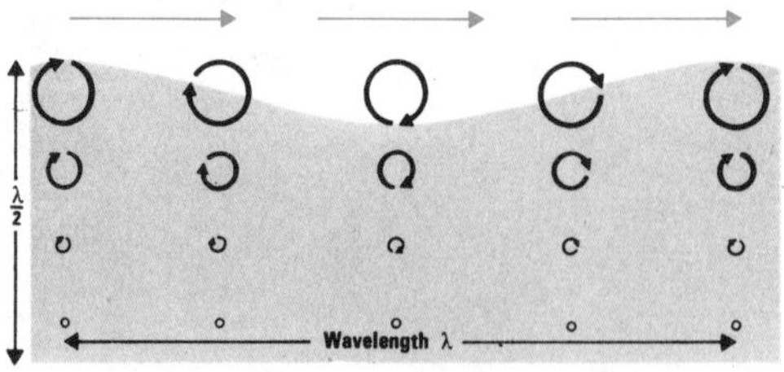

Internal motion *right*
On the surface of deep water these orbits are almost circular. Below the surface the radii of the orbits decrease with depth and become very small at a depth equal to half a wavelength. In shallow water the orbits are ellipses, becoming flatter towards the bottom.

Shore and rip currents *below*
In addition to its circular movement, each water particle slowly moves in the direction of propagation. When waves approach a coast water tends to pile up at the shoreline. This leads to a return flow seaward (X) which is concentrated in narrow, fast-flowing rip currents (Y). Beyond the breaker zone these spread out into a head and gradually disperse (Z).

Ocean currents *left*
Beyond the continental shelf (A) and continental slope (B) lies an ocean bewildering in its complexity. Far from being homogenous, the marked contrasts in ocean temperature, density and salinity even within short geographical distances or narrow ranges of depth almost defy description and measurement. For example, off the east coast of the United States a cold current (D) moves southward below the Gulf Stream (C), a warm surface current that flows northeast towards Western Europe. Near its source the Gulf Stream borders the western edge of the Sargasso Sea (E).

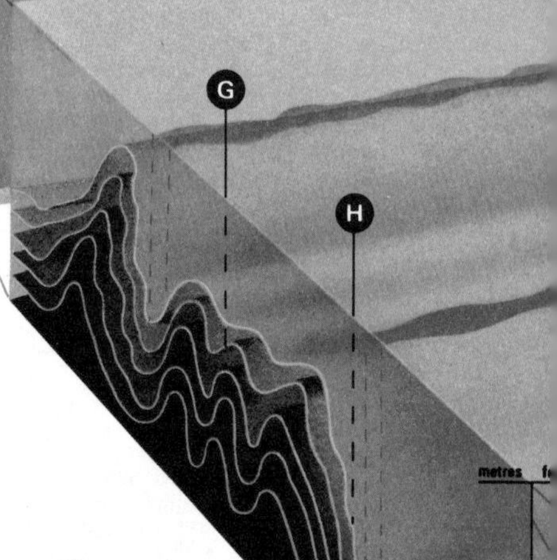

Internal waves *right*
Whereas the motion of the particles of ocean water due to the wind-driven surface waves falls off quite rapidly with increasing depth, internal waves reach their greatest amplitude at a considerable depth. These waves are due to differences in salinity, density and temperature (G) and are manifest in a motion similar to surface waves (H). They are most marked where there is a sharp transition — between, for example, warm water overlying cold, denser water. Their amplitude can exceed 100 feet (30 m) and their period can range from 30 minutes up to longer than the tidal period. Sometimes their presence is made evident by the appearance of banded slicks (J) on the surface of the sea lying directly over the troughs of the internal waves.

Waves and swell *above*
Ocean swell (A) is invariably present and travels hundreds of miles. On it the wind can superimpose small waves (B), which die out relatively rapidly. These smaller waves may be at any angle to the original swell (C).

Change of wave front *left, below*
When waves from the open sea pass into a region of shallow water where the depth is less than about half a wavelength their forward velocity is progressively reduced. One consequence of this is that the wave fronts are refracted so that they turn towards the shallower water, and the wave crests tend to line up parallel to the shore. In the diagram X-X is the original frontal axis of the waves coming in from the ocean. When the depth of water varies along a coast, waves tend to become focused on the shallower areas (Y) and to diverge from the deeper ones such as the head of a submarine valley or canyon (Z). For the same reason large waves can often be seen breaking on a headland while the breakers in an area of originally deeper water, leading to a bay, are relatively much smaller.

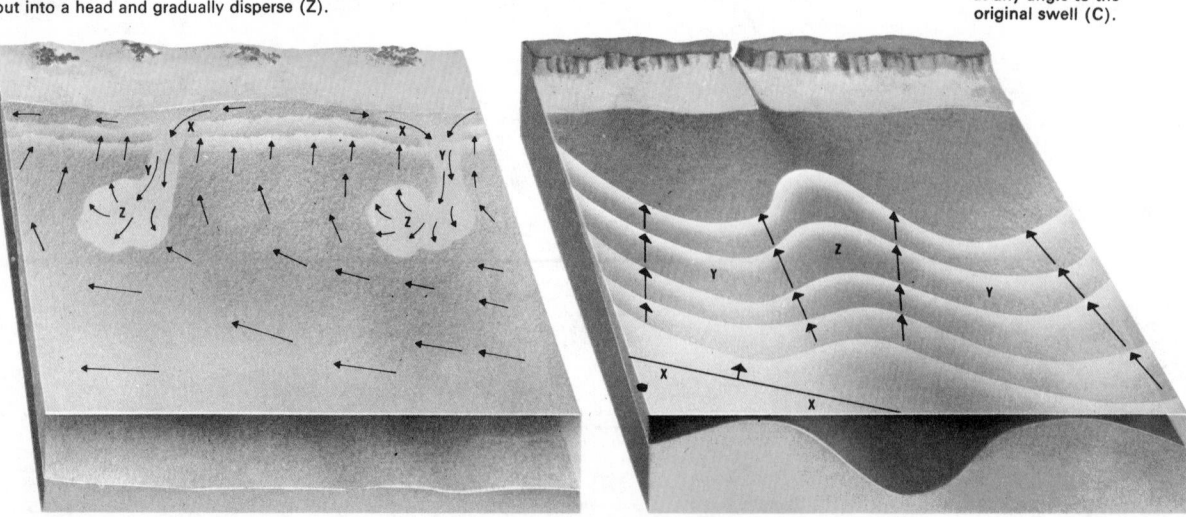

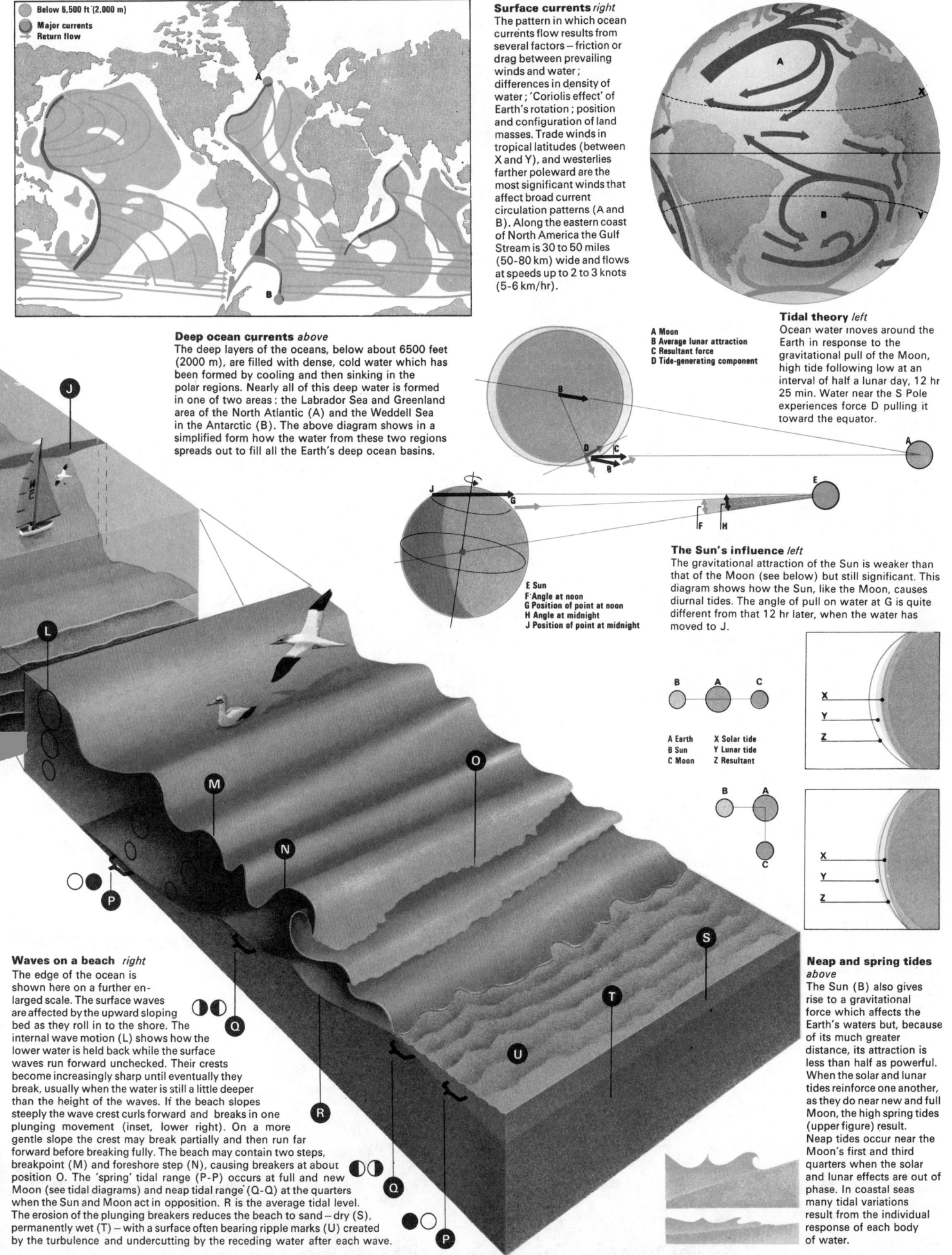

Below 6,500 ft (2,000 m)
Major currents
Return flow

Surface currents *right*
The pattern in which ocean currents flow results from several factors – friction or drag between prevailing winds and water; differences in density of water; 'Coriolis effect' of Earth's rotation; position and configuration of land masses. Trade winds in tropical latitudes (between X and Y), and westerlies farther poleward are the most significant winds that affect broad current circulation patterns (A and B). Along the eastern coast of North America the Gulf Stream is 30 to 50 miles (50-80 km) wide and flows at speeds up to 2 to 3 knots (5-6 km/hr).

Deep ocean currents *above*
The deep layers of the oceans, below about 6500 feet (2000 m), are filled with dense, cold water which has been formed by cooling and then sinking in the polar regions. Nearly all of this deep water is formed in one of two areas: the Labrador Sea and Greenland area of the North Atlantic (A) and the Weddell Sea in the Antarctic (B). The above diagram shows in a simplified form how the water from these two regions spreads out to fill all the Earth's deep ocean basins.

A Moon
B Average lunar attraction
C Resultant force
D Tide-generating component

Tidal theory *left*
Ocean water moves around the Earth in response to the gravitational pull of the Moon, high tide following low at an interval of half a lunar day, 12 hr 25 min. Water near the S Pole experiences force D pulling it toward the equator.

E Sun
F Angle at noon
G Position of point at noon
H Angle at midnight
J Position of point at midnight

The Sun's influence *left*
The gravitational attraction of the Sun is weaker than that of the Moon (see below) but still significant. This diagram shows how the Sun, like the Moon, causes diurnal tides. The angle of pull on water at G is quite different from that 12 hr later, when the water has moved to J.

A Earth   X Solar tide
B Sun   Y Lunar tide
C Moon   Z Resultant

Waves on a beach *right*
The edge of the ocean is shown here on a further en-larged scale. The surface waves are affected by the upward sloping bed as they roll in to the shore. The internal wave motion (L) shows how the lower water is held back while the surface waves run forward unchecked. Their crests become increasingly sharp until eventually they break, usually when the water is still a little deeper than the height of the waves. If the beach slopes steeply the wave crest curls forward and breaks in one plunging movement (inset, lower right). On a more gentle slope the crest may break partially and then run far forward before breaking fully. The beach may contain two steps, breakpoint (M) and foreshore step (N), causing breakers at about position O. The 'spring' tidal range (P-P) occurs at full and new Moon (see tidal diagrams) and neap tidal range' (Q-Q) at the quarters when the Sun and Moon act in opposition. R is the average tidal level. The erosion of the plunging breakers reduces the beach to sand – dry (S), permanently wet (T) – with a surface often bearing ripple marks (U) created by the turbulence and undercutting by the receding water after each wave.

Neap and spring tides *above*
The Sun (B) also gives rise to a gravitational force which affects the Earth's waters but, because of its much greater distance, its attraction is less than half as powerful. When the solar and lunar tides reinforce one another, as they do near new and full Moon, the high spring tides (upper figure) result. Neap tides occur near the Moon's first and third quarters when the solar and lunar effects are out of phase. In coastal seas many tidal variations result from the individual response of each body of water.

The Earth Under the Sea

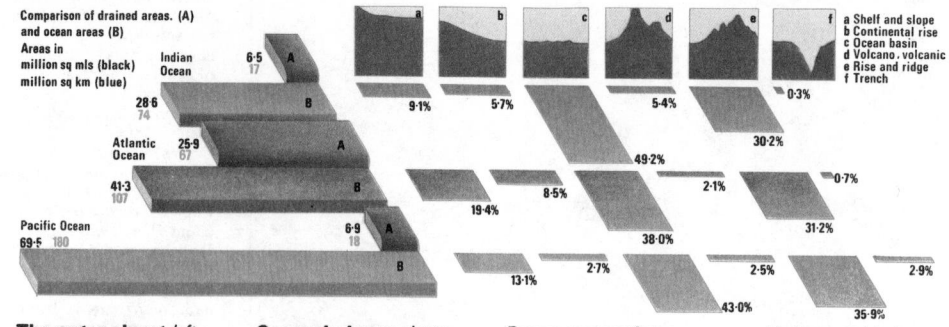

Comparison of drained areas. (A) and ocean areas (B)
Areas in million sq mls (black) million sq km (blue)

Indian Ocean	6·5 / 17	A
	28·6 / 74	B
Atlantic Ocean	25·9 / 67	A
	41·3 / 107	B
Pacific Ocean	6·9 / 18	A
69·5 / 180		B

a Shelf and slope
b Continental rise
c Ocean basin
d Volcano. volcanic ridge
e Rise and ridge
f Trench

a 9·1% b 5·7% d 5·4% e 30·2% f 0·3%
49·2% 8·5% 2·1% 0·7%
19·4% 38·0% 2·5% 31·2%
13·1% 2·7% 43·0% 2·9% 35·9%

The water planet *left*
From directly over Tahiti the Earth appears to be covered by water. The Pacific averages 2.5 miles (4 km) deep, with great mountains and trenches.

Ocean drainage *above*
The ratio between the areas of the oceans and the land they drain varies greatly. Many large rivers feed the Atlantic but few discharge into the Pacific.

Ocean proportions *above*
The major oceans show a similarity in the proportions of their submarine topography. By far the greatest areas contain deep plains

with rises and ridges. More prominent features, the mid-ocean volcanic ridges and trenches, occupy much smaller areas. About one tenth of each ocean is continental shelf.

At present the sea covers about 71 per cent of the Earth's surface. But if the continents could be sliced away and put into the deep oceans to make a perfectly uniform sphere the sea would have an average depth of about 8000 feet (2500 m) over the whole planet. In the distant past the level of the sea has fluctuated violently. The main cause has been the comings and goings of the ice ages. Glaciers and ice-caps lock up enormous volumes of water and the advance and recession of ice has alternately covered the continental shelves with shallow seas and revealed them as dry land. If the Earth's present polar ice-caps and glaciers were to melt, the mean sea level would rise by about 200 feet (60 m), which would submerge half the world's population. Average depth of the sea is more than 12000 feet (3600 m), five times the average height of the land above sea level.

The deep oceans
Below the level of the continental shelf lies the deep ocean floor with great topographical contrasts ranging from abyssal plains at a depth of about 13000 feet (4 km) to towering submarine mountain ranges of the mid-ocean ridges which reach far up toward the surface. Great advances have recently been made in exploring the ocean floors which were previously unknown. Most of the ocean area is abyssal plain which extends over about 78 million square miles (200 million km²). But a more remarkable feature of the deep ocean is the almost continuous mid-ocean mountain range which sweeps 40000 miles (64000 km) around the globe and occasionally – as at Iceland – is seen above sea level in the form of isolated volcanic islands. The basic symmetry of the oceans is the central ridge flanked by abyssal plain sloping up to the continental shelves. On the deep floor sediments accumulate at a rate of 30–35 feet (10 m) per million years; they also build up more slowly at the central ridges. No ocean sediments have been found older than 150 million years, which suggests that the material which now makes up the floors of the deep oceans was formed comparatively recently. Exploration and detailed mapping of the ocean bed is still in its infancy.

Submarine landscape
Principal features of the bed of the oceans can be grouped into a much smaller space than they would actually occupy. Although each ocean differs in detail, all tend to conform to the general layout of a central volcanic ridge (which can break the surface in places), broad abyssal plains with occasional deep trenches and shallow slopes and shelves bordering the continents.

Submarine relief *below*
The bottom of the sea is very far from being flat. If the ocean waters were removed a new landscape would become visible, with immense relief features.

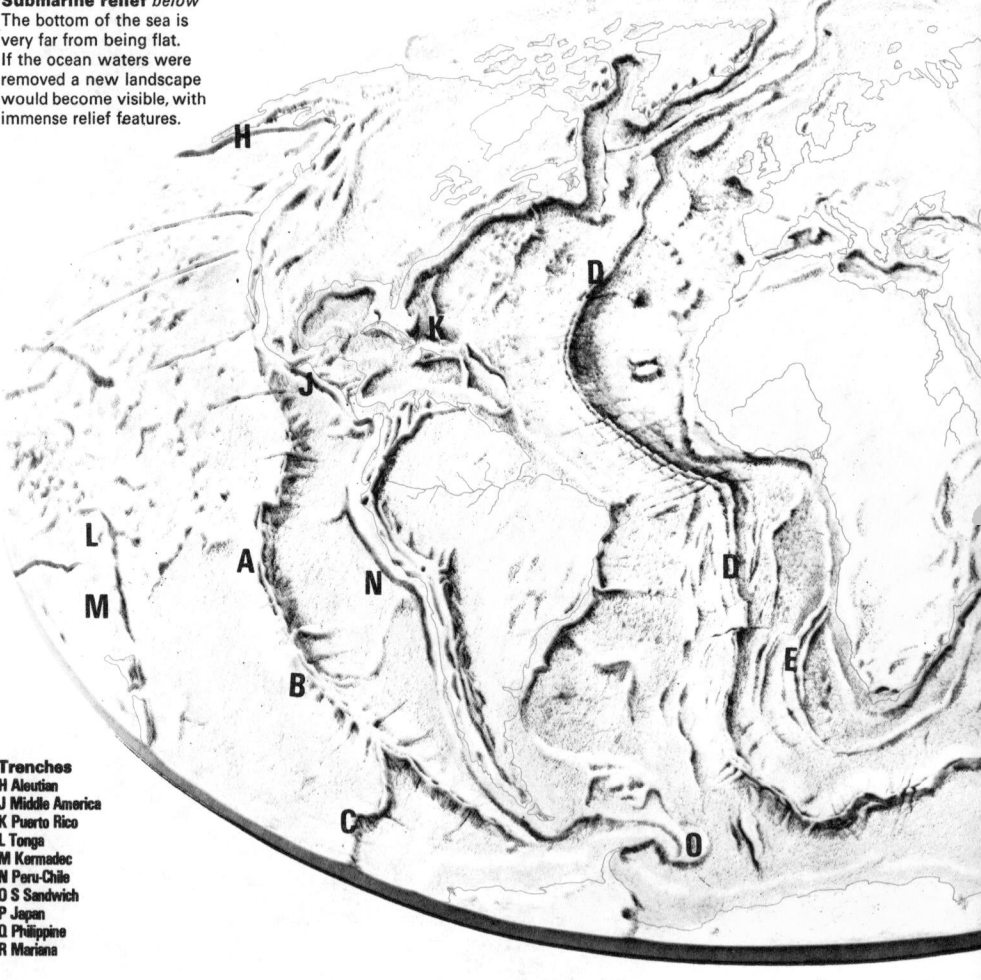

Trenches
H Aleutian
J Middle America
K Puerto Rico
L Tonga
M Kermadec
N Peru-Chile
O S Sandwich
P Japan
Q Philippine
R Mariana

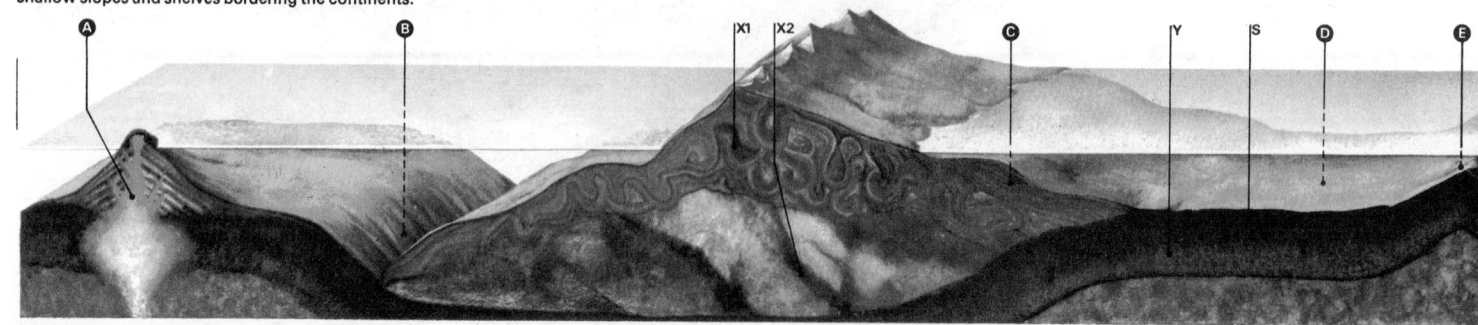

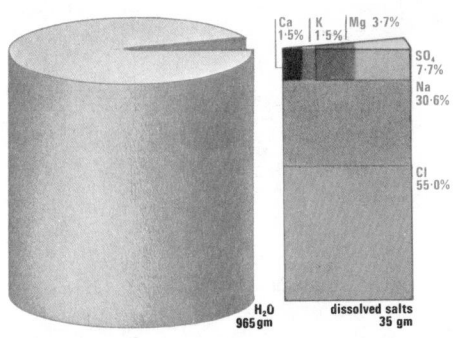

Composition of sea-water *above*
The water of the Earth's oceans is an exceedingly complex solution of many organic and inorganic salts, together with suspended solid matter. In a typical kilogram of sea-water there are 35 grams of chlorine, sodium, sulphates, magnesium, potassium and calcium.

Ca 1·5% | K 1·5% | Mg 3·7%
SO₄ 7·7%
Na 30·6%
Cl 55·0%
H₂O 965gm
dissolved salts 35 gm

Rises and Ridges
A-B E Pacific
C Pacific-Antarctic
D Mid-Atlantic
E Walvis
F SW Indian
G SE Indian

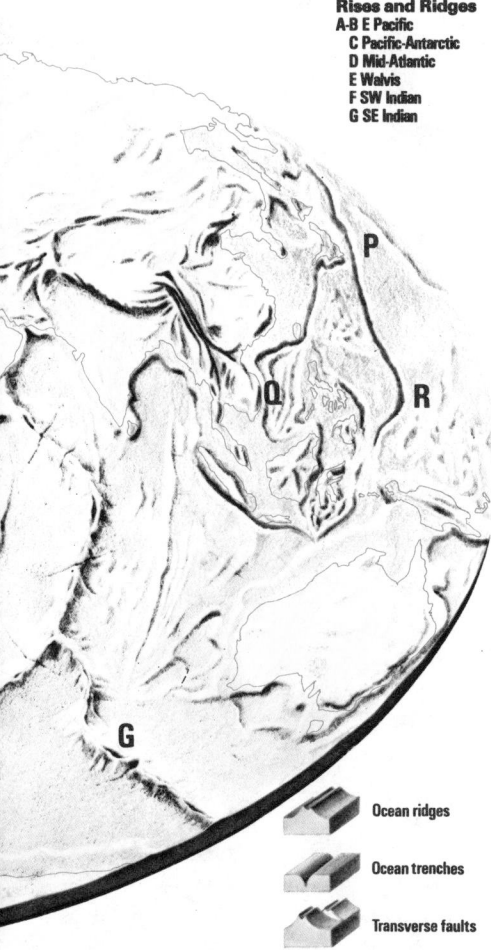

Ocean ridges

Ocean trenches

Transverse faults

A Volcano in mid-ocean ridge
B Deep oceanic trench
C Continental shelf
D Abyssal plain
E Mid-ocean ridge
F Guyots
G Oceanic islands
X1 Upper granitic crust and sediments
X2 Lower granitic crust
Y Basaltic crust
Z Mantle

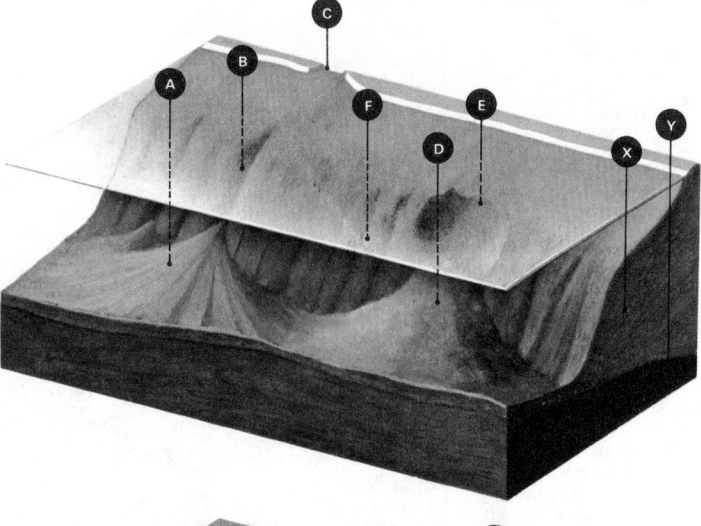

Continental shelf *left*
The submerged continental fringes lie at depths to about 450 feet (135 m) and have a total area of some 11 million square miles (28 million km²). The surface of the land is eroded and carried by rivers to form sedimentary deposits on the shelf. At its outer margin it slopes down to the abyssal plains of the deep ocean at about 2½ miles (4 km) below sea level.

A Scree fan
B Gully opposite river
C River delta
D Slump (turbidite) mass
E Scar left by (D)
F Continental slope
X Granite
Y Basalt

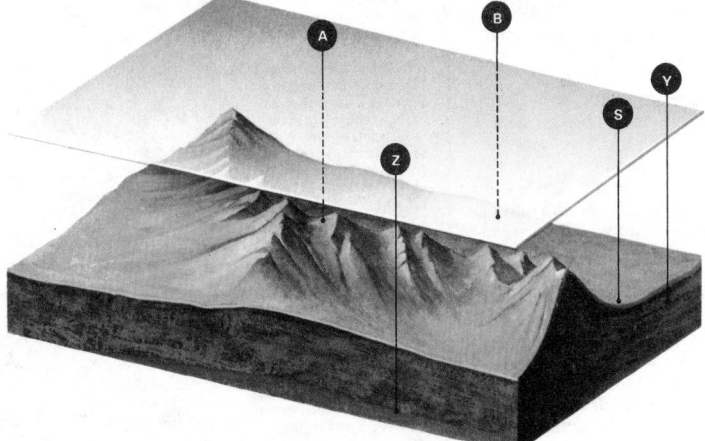

Mid-ocean ridge *left*
Well-marked ridges are found along the centers of the major oceans and form an extensive worldwide system. The central part of the ridge may have a double crest with an intervening deep trough forming a rift valley, or there may be several ridges. They are volcanic in nature and along them is generated new basaltic ocean crust. The volcanoes become progressively younger as the mid-ocean ridge is approached.

A Mid-ocean ridge
B Abyssal plain
S Ocean floor sediments
Y Basalt crust
Z Mantle

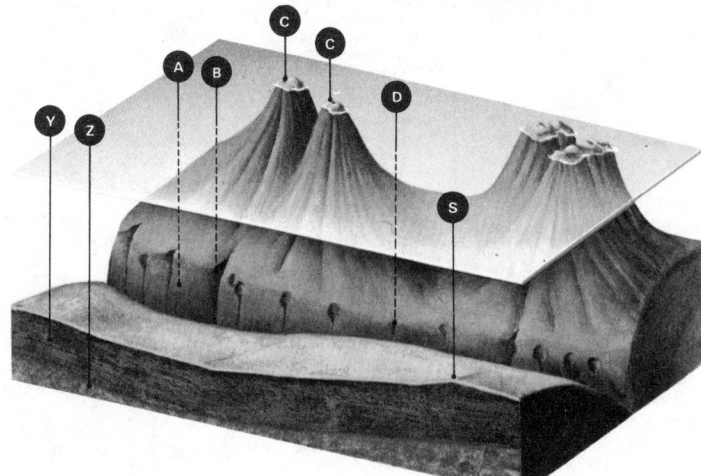

Oceanic trench *left*
These long and relatively narrow depressions are the deepest portions of the oceans, averaging over 30,000 feet (10 km) below sea level. Around the Pacific they lie close to the continental margins and in the western Pacific are often associated with chains of volcanic islands. Some trenches are slowly becoming narrower as the ocean floor plates on either side converge.

A Trench wall
B Canyon
C Island arc
D Trench
S Sediment
Y Basalt
Z Mantle

A sinking island *below*
A pre-requisite to the formation of a coral atoll is an island that is becoming submerged by the sea. Such islands are formed by the peaks of the volcanic mountains which are found on the flanks of the great mid-oceanic ridges.

Coral grows *below*
Millions of polyps, small marine animals, secrete a substance which forms the hard and often beautiful coral. The structure grows round the island in shallow water and extends above the sinking island to form an enclosed and shallow salt-water lagoon.

The mature atoll *below*
Continued submergence of the volcano results in the disappearance of the original island, but the upward growth of the coral continues unabated. The reef is then worn away by the sea and the coral debris fills in the central part of the lagoon.

A guyot *below*
Eventually the coral atoll itself begins to sink beneath the ocean surface. By this time the lagoon is likely to have become completely filled in by debris eroded from the reef, and the result is a submerged flat island, known as a guyot.

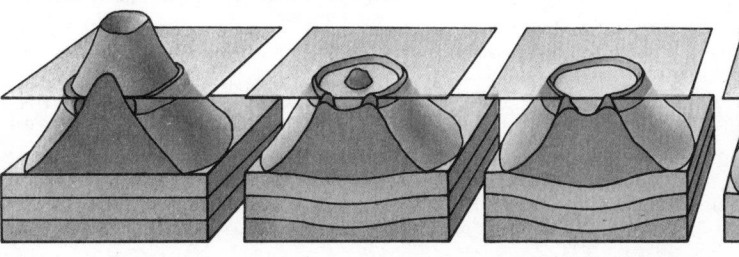

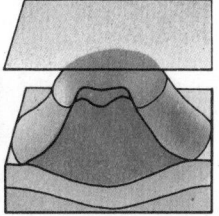

The Atmosphere

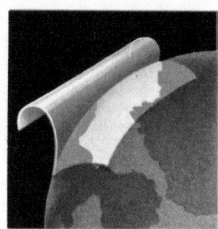

A thin coating *left*
The protective atmospheric shell around the Earth is proportionally no thicker than the skin of an apple. Gravity compresses the air so that half its mass lies within 3.5 miles (5.5 km) of the surface and all the weather within an average depth of 12 miles (20 km).

Space exploration has enabled man to stand back and take a fresh look at his Earth. Even though we, like all Earth life, have evolved to suit the Earth environment, we can see today as never before how miraculous that environment is. And by far the most important single factor in determining that environment is the atmosphere.

The Earth orbits round the Sun in a near-total vacuum. So rarefied is the interplanetary medium that it contains little heat energy, but the gas molecules that are present are vibrating so violently that their individual temperature is over 2000°C. And the surface of the Sun, at some 6000°C, would melt almost everything on the surface of the Earth, while the tenuous chromosphere around the Sun is as hot as 1,000,000°C. From the chromosphere, and from millions of other stars and heavenly objects, come radio waves. Various places in the universe, most of them far beyond the solar system, send us a penetrating kind of radiation known as cosmic rays. The Earth also receives gamma rays, X-rays and ultra-violet radiation, and from the asteroid belt in the solar system (see page 3A) comes a stream of solid material. Most of these are small micrometeorites, no more than flying specks, but the Earth also receives meteors and meteorites.

A meteorite is a substantial mass that strikes the Earth; fortunately, none has yet hit in a populous area. Apart from these extremely rare objects, every other influence from the environment that would be dangerous to life is filtered out by the atmosphere. Meteors burn up through friction as they plunge into the upper parts of the atmosphere. To avoid burning up in the same way, spacecraft designed to return to the Earth from lunar or interplanetary flight require a special re-entry shield.

Much of the ultraviolet radiation is arrested many miles above the Earth and creates ionized layers known as the ionosphere which man uses to reflect radio waves. Much of the infra-red (heat) radiation is likewise absorbed, lower down in the atmosphere, and most of the cosmic radiation is broken up by collisions far above the ground into such particles as 'mu-mesons'. Only a few cosmic rays, harmless radio waves and visible light penetrate the blanket of air to reach the planetary surface and its teeming life.

Credit for our vital atmosphere rests with the Earth's gravitational attraction, which both prevents the molecules and atoms in the atmosphere from escaping into space and also pulls them down tightly against the Earth. As a result nearly all the atmosphere's mass is concentrated in a very thin layer; three-quarters of it lies below 29000 feet (8840 m), the height of Mount Everest. The highest-flying aircraft, 22 miles (35 km) up, are above 90 per cent of the atmosphere. The total weight of the atmosphere is of the order of 5000 million million tons. In the lower parts are some 17 million million tons of water vapour.

The water vapor plays a great part in determining the weather on Earth, the only way in which the atmosphere consciously affects daily human life. All the weather is confined to the lower parts of the atmosphere below the tropopause. In this region, called the troposphere, temperature falls away sharply with increasing altitude. The Sun heats up the Earth's surface, water is evaporated from the surface of the oceans and an immensely complicated pattern of global and local weather systems is set up. Every part of the air in the troposphere is in motion. Sometimes the motion is so slow as to be barely perceptible, while on other occasions, or at the same time in other places, the air roars over the surface with terrifying force at speeds of 200 miles (320 km) per hour or more. It erodes the land, lashes the surface with rain and clogs cold regions with snow. Yet it is man's shield against dangers, an ocean of air without which we could not exist.

Characteristics of the atmosphere *right*
Basically the Earth's atmosphere consists of a layer of mixed gases covering the surface of the globe which, as a result of the Earth's gravitational attraction, increases in density as the surface is approached. But there is very much more to it than this. Temperature, composition and physical properties vary greatly through the depth of the atmosphere. The Earth's surface is assumed to lie along the bottom of the illustration, and the various major regions of the atmosphere—which imperceptibly merge into each other—are indicated by the numbers on the vertical scale on the facing page.

Thermosphere (1)
The thermosphere is the top layer of the Earth's atmosphere. It is made up of an upper and extremely rarefied region, called the *exosphere*, and a lower region called the *ionosphere*. The exosphere is taken to start at a height of some 400 miles (650 km) and to merge above into the interplanetary medium. Atomic oxygen exists up to 600 mi (1000 km); from there up to about 1500 mi (2400 km), helium and hydrogen are approximately equally abundant. The ionosphere contains electrically conducting layers capable of reflecting radio waves and thus of enabling radio signals to be received over great distances across the Earth. The major reflecting layers, designated D, E, F1 and F2, are at the approximate heights shown. Meteors burn up brightly at heights of around 100 mi (160 km).

Mesosphere (2)
The mesosphere lies between the thermosphere and the stratosphere. It extends from a distance of about 30 mi (48 km) to about 50 mi (80 km) above the Earth's surface. In the upper levels of this region the trails left by meteors become visible. The upper layer of the mesosphere is called the *mesopause*, and that is where the lowest temperatures in the atmosphere occur, dropping to about 135°F (−93°C).

Stratosphere (3)
This lies above the tropopause which varies in altitude from about 10 mi (16 km) over the equator to just below 7 mi (11 km) in temperate latitudes. The lower stratosphere has a constant temperature of −56°C up to 19 mi (30 km); higher still the 'mesosphere' becomes warmer again. One of the vital properties of the stratosphere is its minute ozone content which shields the Earth life from some harmful short-wave radiations which, before the Earth's atmosphere had developed, penetrated to the surface.

Troposphere (4)
Within this relatively very shallow layer is concentrated about 80 per cent of the total mass of the atmosphere, as well as all the weather and all the Earth's life. The upper boundary of the troposphere is the tropopause, which is about 36000 ft (11000 m) above the surface in temperate latitudes; over the tropics it is higher, and therefore colder, while it is at a lower altitude over the poles. Air temperature falls uniformly with increasing height until the tropopause is reached; thereafter it remains constant in the stratosphere. Composition of the troposphere is essentially constant, apart from the vital factor of clouds and humidity.

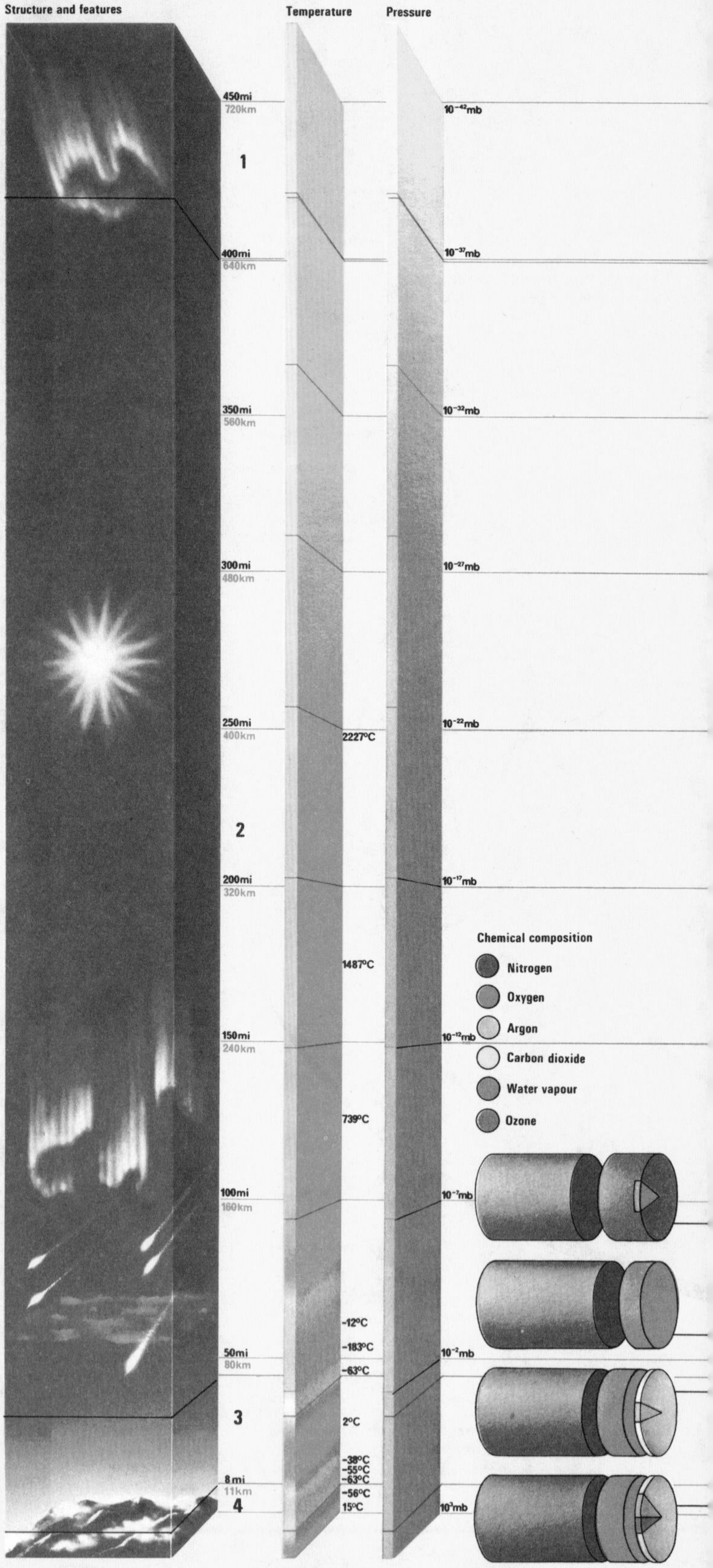

Structure and features

Temperature

Pressure

	Temperature	Pressure
450mi / 720km		10^{-42}mb
400mi / 640km		10^{-37}mb
350mi / 560km		10^{-33}mb
300mi / 480km		10^{-27}mb
250mi / 400km	2227°C	10^{-22}mb
200mi / 320km		10^{-17}mb
	1487°C	
150mi / 240km		10^{-10}mb
	739°C	
100mi / 160km		10^{-7}mb
50mi / 80km	−12°C / −183°C / −63°C	10^{-2}mb
	2°C	
8mi / 11km	−38°C / −55°C / −63°C / −56°C / 15°C	10^{3}mb

Chemical composition
- Nitrogen
- Oxygen
- Argon
- Carbon dioxide
- Water vapour
- Ozone

Temperature
The mean temperature at the Earth's surface is about 15°C. As height is gained the temperature falls swiftly, to −56°C at the tropopause. It remains at this value to 19 miles (30 km), becomes warmer again, and then falls to a very low value around 60 miles (100 km). It rises once again in space.

Pressure
At sea level the pressure is some 1000 millibars, or about 14.7 pounds per square inch. The total force acting on the surface of an adult human body is thus of the order of 20 tons. But only 10 miles (16 km) above the Earth the pressure, and the atmospheric density, have both fallen by some 90 per cent.

Composition
Chemical composition of the atmosphere varies considerably with altitude. In the troposphere the mixture of nitrogen, oxygen and other gases is supplemented by water vapor, which exerts a profound influence on the weather. Ozone in the stratosphere shields life from harmful ultraviolet rays.

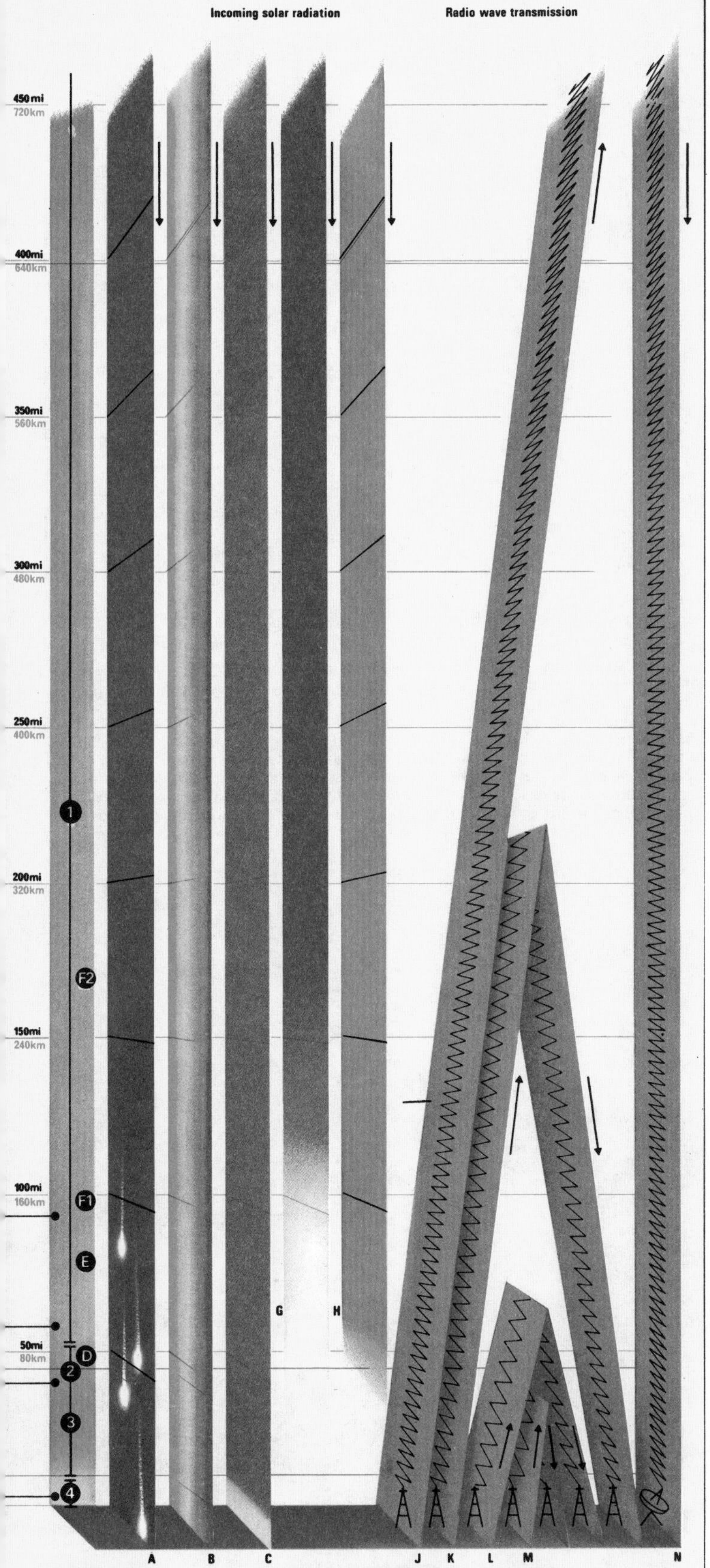

Incoming solar radiation   Radio wave transmission

450 mi
720 km

400 mi
640 km

350 mi
560 km

300 mi
480 km

250 mi
400 km

1

F2

200 mi
320 km

150 mi
240 km

100 mi
160 km   **F1**

E

50 mi
80 km   **D**
2

3

4

G   H

A   B   C   J K   L   M   N

A particle shield
The Earth is continuously bom-
barded with solid particles from
elsewhere in the solar system and
possibly from more distant parts
of the universe. Only the largest
meteors (A) reach the surface.
Small meteorites generally
burn up through friction caused
by passage through the thin air
more than 40 miles (65 km) up.

A radiation shield
Most of the Sun's visible light
(B) can penetrate the whole of
the atmosphere right down to
the Earth's surface, except where
cloud intervenes. But only some
of the infra-red radiation gets
through (C); the rest (G) is cut
off, along with the harmful
ultraviolet radiation (H), by
atmospheric gases.

Radio waves
Very-high-frequency radio waves
(VHF) can penetrate the whole
depth of the atmosphere (J), but
short-wave transmissions are reflected by the Appleton F2 layer
(K). Medium (L) and long waves
(M) are reflected at lower levels
by the D, E or F1 layers. Yet
radio waves from distant stellar
sources can be received (N).

The circulation of the atmosphere *left*
The atmosphere maintains
its equilibrium by
transferring heat, moisture
and momentum from low
levels at low latitudes to
high levels at high
latitudes where the
heat is radiated to space.
This circulation appears to
comprise three distinct
'cells' in each hemisphere.
In the tropical (A) and
polar (B) cells the
circulations are thermally
direct — warm air rises and
cold air sinks — but the
mid-latitude circulation,
the Ferrel cell (C), is
distorted by the polar front
as shown in greater detail
below.

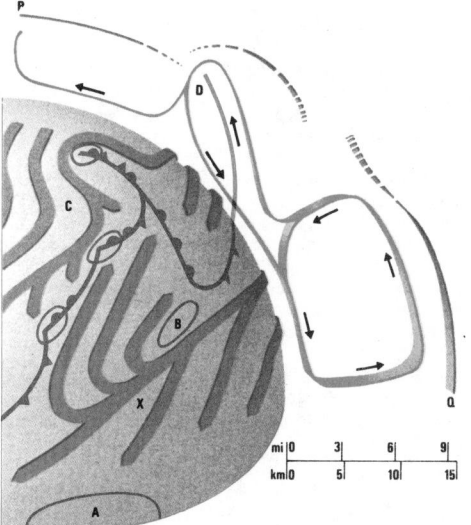

P

D

C

B

X

A

Q

| | mi | 0 | 3 | 6 | 9 |
| | km | 0 | 5 | 10 | 15 |

Warm front
Cold front

A Area of low pressure   D Polar front
B Area of high pressure   P Polar cell tropopause
C Area of low pressure   Q Tropical tropopause

Frontal systems *left*
Although the figure above
shows a true general
picture, the actual
circulation is more
complicated. A portion of
the Earth on a larger scale
shows how frontal systems
develop between the polar
and tropical air masses.
The tropopause, the
demarcation between the
troposphere in which
temperature falls with
height, and the strato-
sphere above, is much
higher in the tropics than
in the polar cell. Between
the cells the polar front
causes constant successions
of warm and cold fronts
and changeable weather.
Surface winds are shown,
together with areas of low
pressure and high pressure.
The scale along the bottom,
although exaggerated,
indicates the greater height
of the tropical tropopause
compared with that in polar
regions. Conventional
symbols indicate warm and
cold fronts.

Precipitation *left*
This map shows the mean
annual rain, hail and snow
over the Earth.

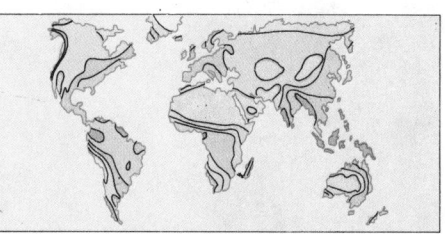

0	Cm per year
25	
50	
100	
200	

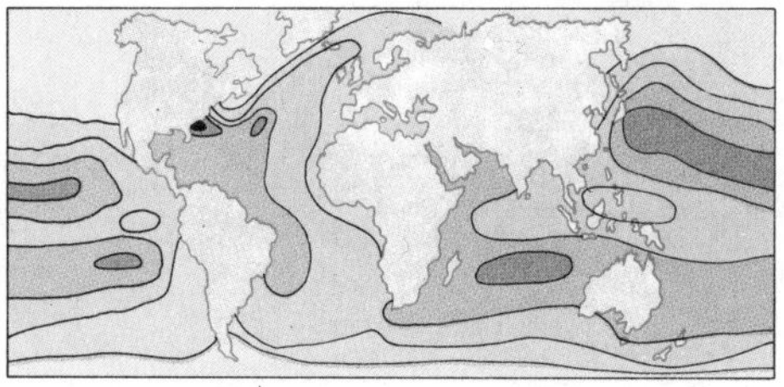

Evaporation *left*
Accurate estimates of
evaporation can be made
only over the oceans.

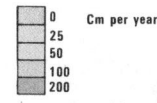

0	Cm per year
60	
100	
150	
200	
250	

Surface radiation *left*
Variations in heat output
over the Earth's surface affect
air and ocean circulations.

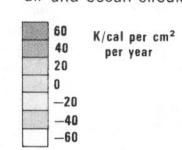

60	K/cal per cm²
40	per year
20	
0	
−20	
−40	
−60	

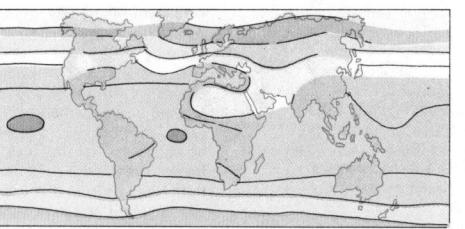

The Structure of Weather Systems

Until recently there were few scientists in the tropics or the polar regions, and the science of meteorology therefore evolved in the mid-latitudes. Likewise, the early concepts of meteorology were all based on observations of the mid-latitude atmosphere. Originally only two types of air mass were recognized: polar and tropical. Today a distinct equatorial air mass has been identified, as well as Arctic and Antarctic masses at latitudes even higher than the original polar ones. The concept of a 'front' between dissimilar air masses dates from as recently as 1919, and three years later the development of a cyclone – a large system of air rotating around an area of low pressure– was first described. Today satellite photographs have confirmed the validity of these early studies and enable the whole Earth's weather to be watched on daily computer processed photo-charts as it develops.

Why the weather varies

Anywhere in the Earth's mid-latitudes the climate is determined mainly by the frequency and intensity of the cyclones, with their frontal systems and contrasting air masses, which unceasingly alter the local temperature, wind velocity, air pressure and humidity. In turn, the frequency of the cyclonic visits is governed principally by the behavior of the long waves in the upper westerlies. When these waves change their shape and position the cyclonic depressions follow different paths. The major changes are seasonal, but significant variations also occur on a cycle of 5-6 weeks. It is still proving difficult to investigate the long wave variations. As a front passes, a fairly definite sequence of cloud, wind, humidity, temperature, precipitation and visibility can be seen. The most obvious change is the type of cloud, of which nine are shown opposite. Each cyclone contains numerous cloud types in its structure. Within these clouds several forms of precipitation can form; raindrops are the most common, but ice precipitation also forms, with snow in winter and hail in the summer when intense atmospheric instability produces towering cumulonimbus clouds topped by an 'anvil' of ice crystals.

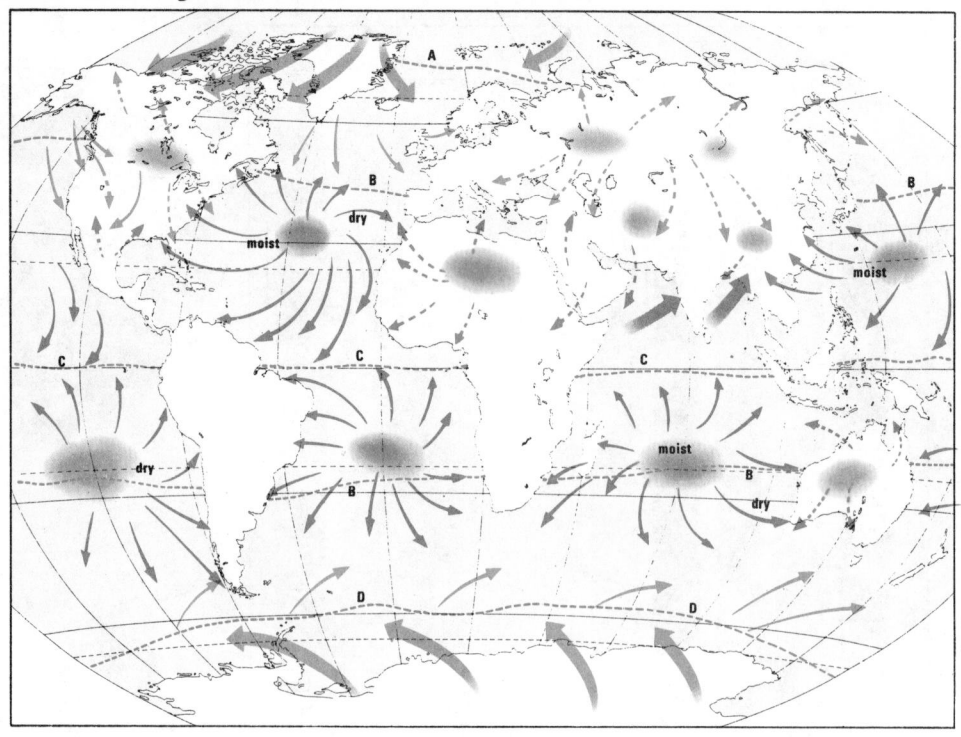

Air masses and convergences *above*

An air mass is an extensive portion of the atmosphere in which, at any given altitude, the moisture and temperature are almost uniform. Such a mass generally arises when the air rests for a time on a large area of land or water which has uniform surface conditions. There are some 20 source regions throughout the world. A second pre-requisite is large-scale subsidence and divergence over the source region. The boundary between air masses is a convergence or front. (A Arctic, B Polar, C Equatorial, D Antarctic.) The polar front is particularly important in governing much of the weather in mid-latitudes. The pattern depicted provides a raw framework for the world's weather. It is considerably modified by the air's vertical motion, by surface friction, land topography, the Earth's rotation and other factors.

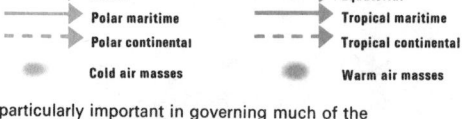

➡ Arctic	➡ Equatorial
⇢ Polar maritime	➡ Tropical maritime
-- Polar continental	-- Tropical continental
Cold air masses	Warm air masses

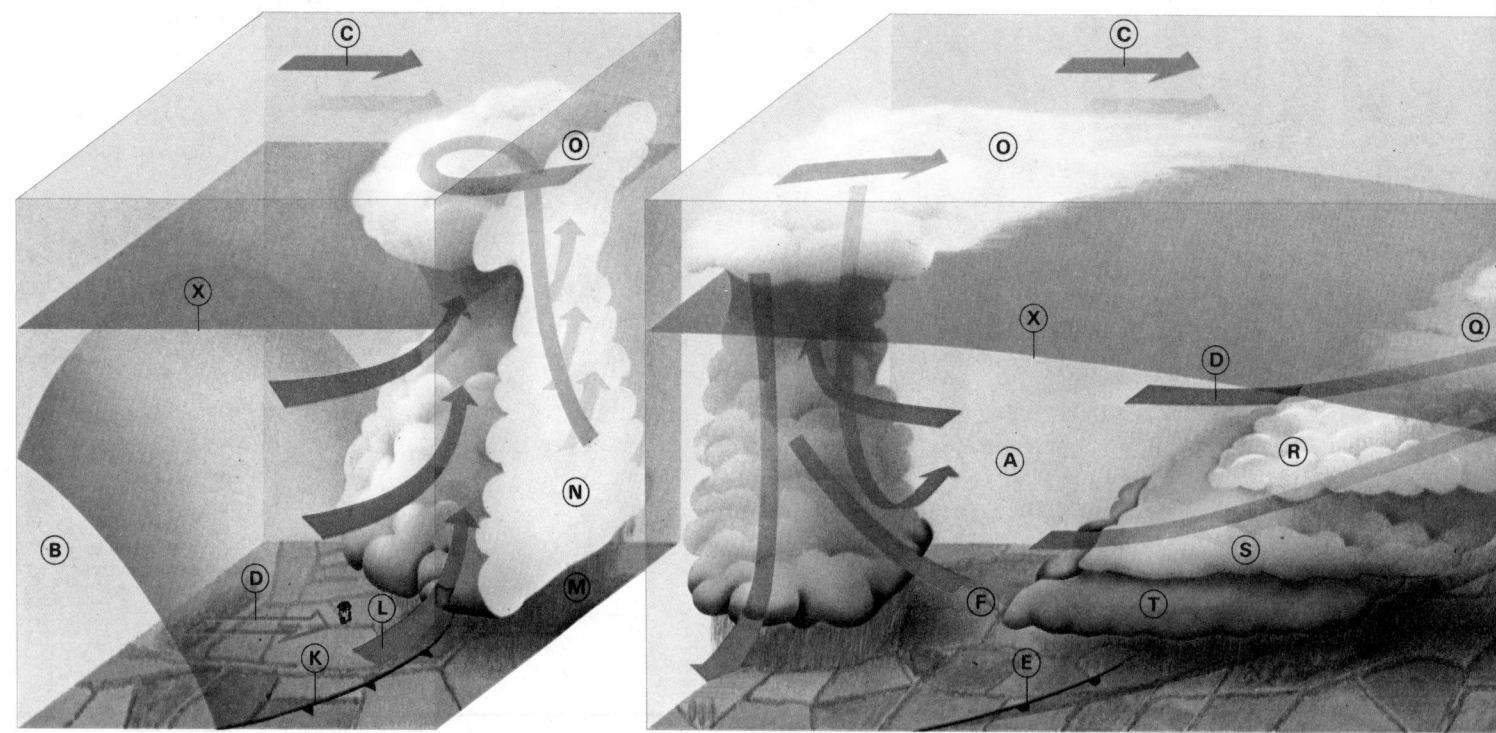

Anatomy of a depression

Seen in cross section, a mature mid-latitude cyclone forms a large system which always follows basically the same pattern. Essentially it comprises a wedge of warm air (A) riding over, and being undercut by; cold air masses (B). (Page 23A shows full development.) The entire cyclone is moving from left to right, and this is also the basic direction of the winds (C) and (D). To an observer on the ground the warm front (E) may take 12-24 hours to pass, followed by the warm sector (F) perhaps 180 miles (300 km) wide.

The cold front (K)

As this frontal zone, about one mile (1-2 km) wide, passes overhead the direction of the wind alters (L) and precipitation (M) pours from cumuliform clouds (N). If the air above the frontal surface is moving upwards then giant cumulonimbus (O) may grow, with heavy rain or hail. Cirrus clouds then form in air above the freezing level (X). Sometimes the front is weak with subsidence of air predominant on both sides of it. In this case there is little cloud development and near-zero surface precipitation.

The warm front (E)

The front is first heralded by cirrus clouds (P), followed by cirrostratus (Q), altocumulus (R), stratus (S) and finally nimbostratus (T). The descending layers are due partly to humidity distribution and partly to the warm air rising over the sloping frontal surface. Precipitation may be steady and last for hours. Alternatively some warm fronts have a predominantly subsident air motion, with the result that there is only a little thin cloud and negligible precipitation. Air temperature increases as the front passes.

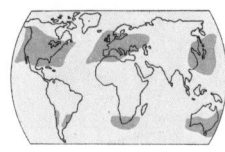

Development of a depression *right*

Most mid-latitude depressions (cyclones) develop on the polar front (map above). An initial disturbance along this front causes a fall in pressure and a confluence at the surface, deforming the front into a wave (1, right). The confluence and thermal structure accelerate the cyclonic spin into a fully developed depression (2). The depression comprises a warm sector bounded by a sharp cold front (A) and warm front (B). The fast-moving cold front overtakes the warm front and eventually the warm sector is lifted completely clear of the ground resulting in an occlusion (3). The continued overlapping of the two wedges of cold air eventually fills up the depression and causes it to weaken and disperse (4). By the time this occurs the warm sector has been lifted high in the atmosphere. In this way, depressions fulfil an essential role in transferring heat from low to high levels and from low to high latitudes.

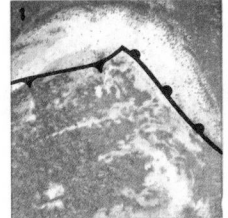
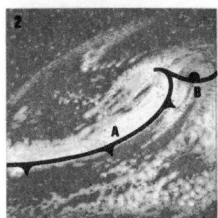
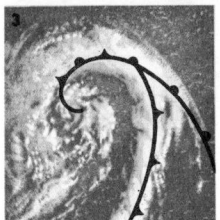
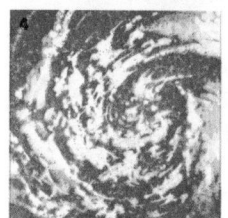

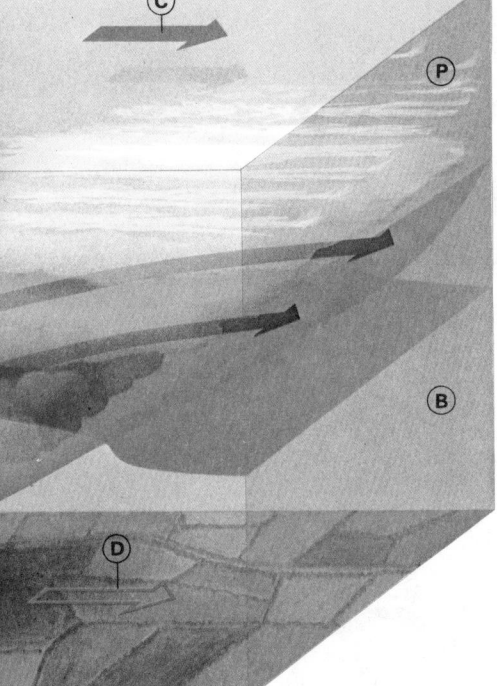

Plan view *left*

A developing cyclone will appear this way on the 'synoptic' weather chart. Lines of equal pressure (isobars) are nearly straight within the warm sector but curve sharply in the cold sector to enclose the low pressure focus of the system.

Examples of the three major cloud groups

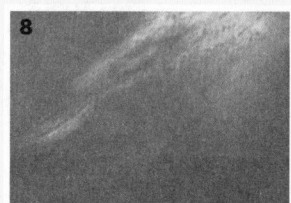

Low cloud *top*
Stratocumulus (1) is a grey or white layer of serried masses or rolls. Cumulus (2) is the familiar white cauliflower. It can develop into cumulonimbus (3), a large, threatening cloud, characterized by immense vertical development topped by an 'anvil' of ice crystals. These produce heavy rain or hail.

Medium cloud *left*
Nimbostratus (4) is a ragged grey layer producing drizzle or snow. Altocumulus (5) comprises rows of 'blobs' of ice and water forming a sheet at a height of 1.5-4.5 miles (2-7 km). Altostratus (6) occurs at similar heights but is a water/ice sheet either uniform, striated or fibrous in appearance.

High cloud *right*
Cirrus (7) is the highest cloud and appears as fine white ice filaments at 8–10 miles (13–16 km), often hair-like or silky. Cirro-cumulus (8) forms into thin white layers made up of very numerous icy globules or ripples. Cirrostratus (9) is a high-level veil of ice crystals often forming a halo round the Sun.

Four kinds of precipitation

Rain
Most rain results from the coalescence of microscopic droplets (1) which are condensed from vapor onto nuclei in the atmosphere. The repeated merging of small droplets eventually forms water droplets (2) which are too large to be kept up by the air currents. Rain drops may also form from melting of ice crystals in the atmosphere.

Sleet
In completely undisturbed air it is possible for water to remain liquid even at temperatures well below freezing point. So air above the freezing level (X) may contain large quantities of this 'supercooled water'. This can fall as rain and freeze on impact with objects, coating them with ice.

Dry snow
The origin of snow differs from that of rain in that the vapor droplets (1) settle on microscopic crystals of ice and freeze. The result is the growth of a white or translucent ice crystal having a basically hexagonal form (photomicrograph below). The crystals then agglomerate into flakes (2).

Hail
In cumulonimbus clouds raindrops (formed at 1,2) may encounter up-currents strong enough to lift them repeatedly back through a freezing level (X). On each pass (3) a fresh layer of ice is collected. The hailstone builds up like an onion until it is so heavy (4) that it falls to the ground.

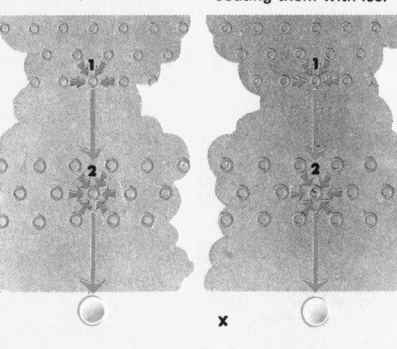
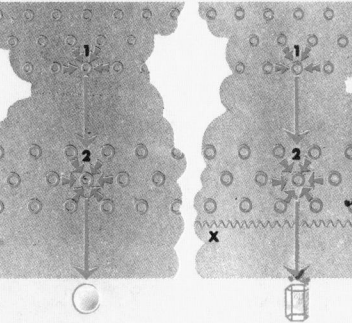
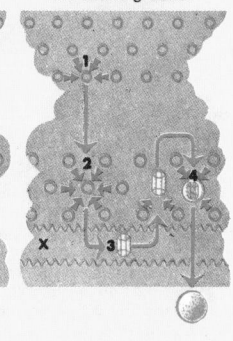

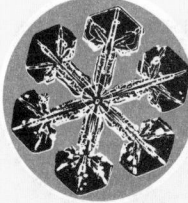
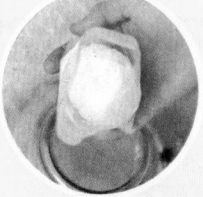

Extremes of Weather

Tropical weather, between the Tropic of Cancer at 23½°N and the Tropic of Capricorn at 23½°S, differs fundamentally from that at higher latitudes. Overall there is a considerable surplus of heat, giving high mean temperatures; and the 'Coriolis force' due to the Earth's rotation, which deflects air currents to the right in the northern hemisphere and to the left in the southern, is almost non-existent. As a result, tropical weather hardly ever contains distinct air masses, fronts and cyclones. Instead the region is occupied mainly by the tradewinds, which are laden with moisture and potentially unstable. Thunderstorms are frequent, especially over land, and the pattern of land and sea leads to local anomalies, such as the monsoon of southeast Asia. This particular anomaly, too big to be called local, changes the prevailing wind over a vast area. It is superimposed on the apparently simple global circulation near the Equator.

Polar weather

At very high latitudes the atmosphere radiates heat to space. The Arctic is essentially an ocean surrounded by land, whereas the Antarctic is land surrounded by ocean. The land around the Arctic quickly takes up solar heat but the southern oceans transfer heat to deeper water to make the Antarctic the coldest region on Earth. Because the air is so intensely cold it can hold very little moisture, so the south polar region is a freezing desert with exceptionally clean air.

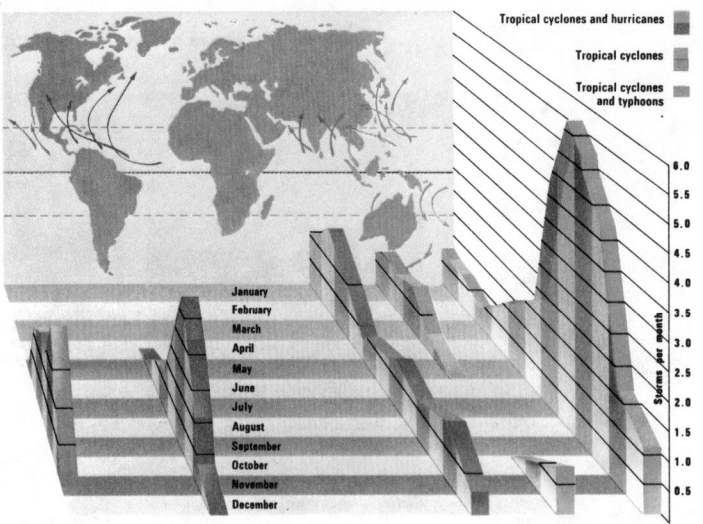

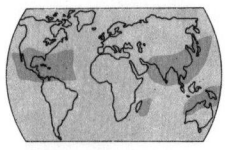

The afflicted areas *above*
Tropical cyclones build up over the warm oceans, and many of them—about half over the Caribbean and four-fifths over the western Pacific—develop into hurricanes. Precisely how a hurricane is triggered is still not fully known, but there is no doubt it is a thermodynamic engine on a giant scale which either misfires completely or runs with catastrophic effect.

Hurricanes *left*
These violent storms form over ocean warm enough (27°C) to maintain strong vertical circulation, except for the belt closest to the equator where lack of a Coriolis force prevents cyclonic spin from building up. Condensation of the moisture taken up from the ocean surface releases latent heat and thus provides energy to drive the storm. The daily energy can be equivalent to that released by several hundred H bombs. Despite their formidable power hurricanes are penetrated by specially equipped aircraft whose mission is both to provide early warning and to gather data enabling the storm's mechanism to be better understood.

Hurricane structure
A Spiral rainbands.
B High-altitude winds.
C Easterly tradewinds.

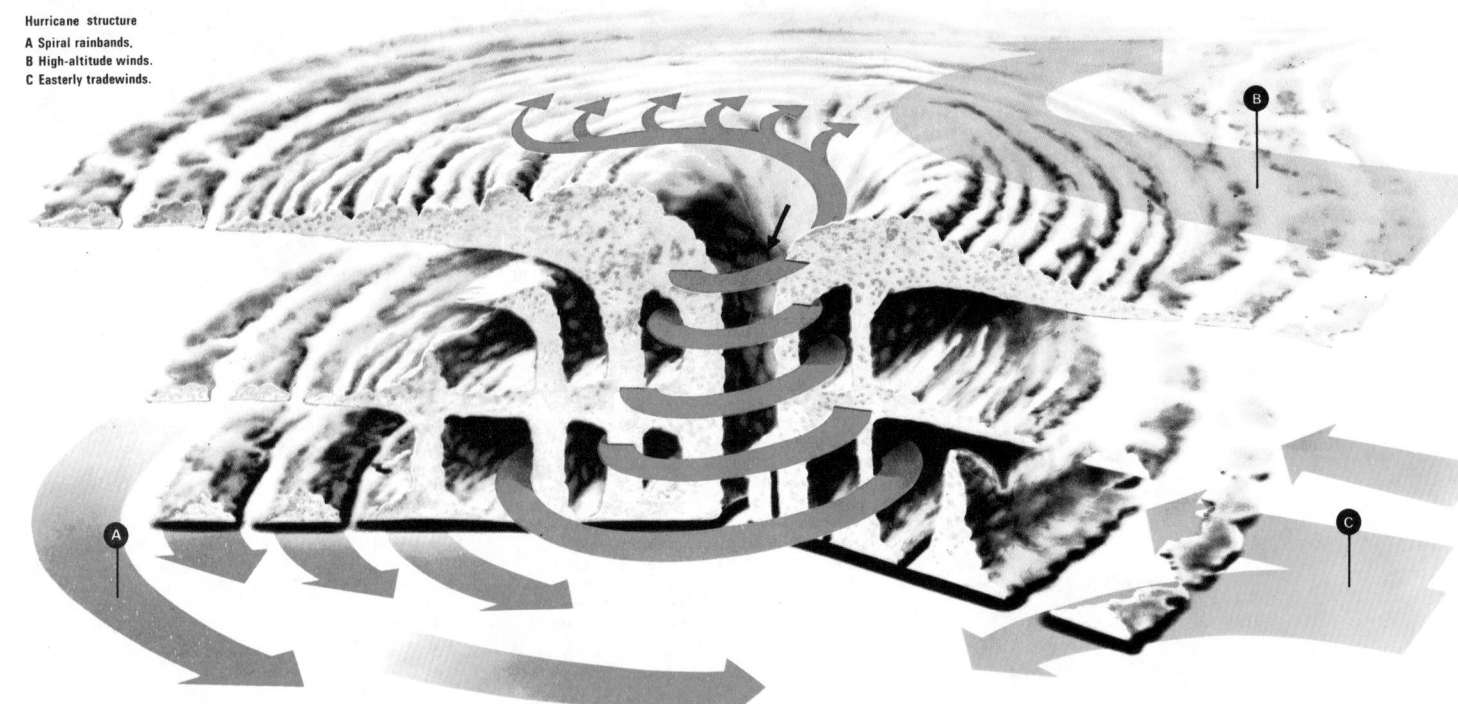

Structure of a hurricane *above*
A hurricane consists of a huge swirl of clouds rotating around a calm center known as the eye. This cyclonic circulation may be as much as 250 miles (400 km) in diameter, and it extends right through the troposphere which is about 9-12 miles (15-20 km) thick. The clouds, nearly all of the cumulonimbus type, are arranged in bands around the eye. The largest form the wall of the eye and it is here that precipitation is heaviest. The whole system is usually capped by streamers of cirrus. Wind speeds range from about 110 mph (180 kmh) at 20–25 miles (30–40 km) from the eye wall down to about 45 mph (72 kmh) at a distance of 90 miles (140 km). Warm, calm air in the eye is sucked downwards.

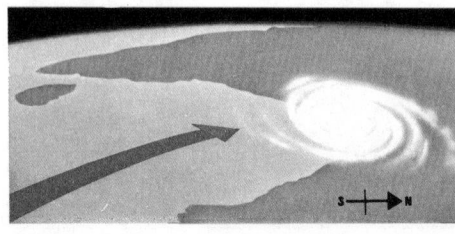

Nature's giant energy
left and above
A hurricane such as that which killed over half a million people in Bangladesh in November 1970 (left) dissipates thousands of millions of horsepower. The spiral structure is clearly visible from a satellite (above).

Hurricane development *below*

Birth of a storm.
Hurricanes usually have their origin in a low-pressure disturbance directing part of an easterly wind (A) to the north. The air rises to some 40,000 ft (12 km) where it releases heat and moisture (B) before descending.

The young hurricane
The Earth's rotation imparts a twist to the rising column which becomes a cylinder (C) spiralling round a relatively still core (D). Warm, moist air off the sea picks up speed and feeds energy at a very high rate to intensify the rising column.

Dying of starvation
The hurricane does not begin to die until it moves over colder water or over land (E). Then, cut off from its supply of energy, the speed of the spiralling winds falls away. The eye begins to fill with clouds, the hurricane expands (F) and dissipates.

The monsoon *right*

In principle the processes which give rise to the monsoon are the same as those causing a sea breeze but on a vastly larger scale in space and time. In southeast Asia each May and June warm, moist air streams in from the south causing heavy rain and occasional violent storms. In winter the circulation is reversed and winds come mainly from high pressure over Siberia. In detail the monsoon is considerably modified by the Himalayas and the positions of the waves in the westerlies in the atmosphere's upper levels, but its mechanism is not fully known.

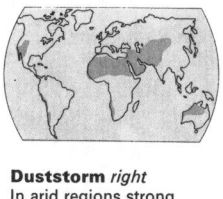

Duststorm *right*

In arid regions strong wind circulations can become filled with dust and extend over considerable areas. The storm typically arrives in the form of an advancing wall of dust possibly five miles (8 km) long and 1000 ft (300 m) high. The haboobs of the Sudan, a recurrent series of storms, are most frequent from May to September and can approach from almost any direction. They usually occur, after a few days of rising temperature and falling pressure, where the soil is very dry. Dust-devils, small local whirlwinds forming pillars of sand, can dot the land.

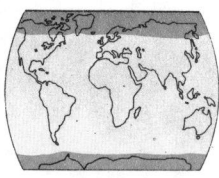

Nacreous cloud *right*

At high latitudes, when the Sun is below the horizon, these clouds sometimes come into view as fine filmy areas containing regions of bright spectral color. They look rather like a form of cirrus, but are far higher. Nacreous cloud in the Antarctic—such as that in the photograph, taken in Grahamland—has been measured at heights from 8.5 to 19 miles (13.5-30 km), and Scandinavian observations lie in the 20-30 km range. Despite their great altitude, nacreous clouds are undoubtedly formed as a result of air being lifted by passage across high mountains.

Flash flood *below*
In historic times floods have drowned millions. Even in a modern advanced country a major flood is a national disaster. The scene below is a flooded crossing on the road from Lake Grace to Dumbleyung, W Australia. It is a 'flash flood', caused by heavy rain and poor drainage.

The monsoon seasons *below*
In summer an intense low-pressure area over northwest India overcomes the equatorial low pressure region. In winter an intense high over central Asia blows cold, dry air in the reverse direction.

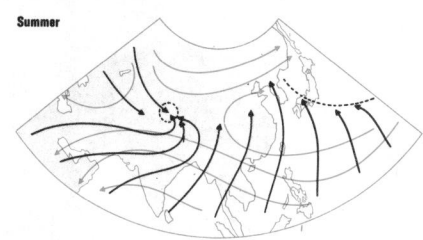

Summer

Winds near sea level ▬▶   Winds at about 20,000 ft (6000 m) ▬▶

Winter

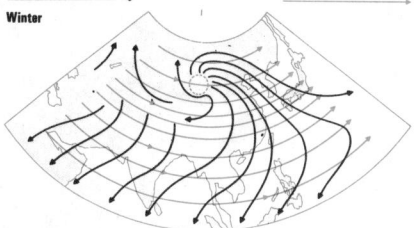

After the hurricane *left*
Whereas a tornado can cause buildings to explode, as a result of the sudden violent difference in pressure between inside and outside, a hurricane just blows. But the wind can demolish sound houses, such as this residence in Biloxi, Mississippi.

Blown snow *above*
When the wind blows in polar regions it soon begins to lift dry powdery snow and ice granules from the surface. As the wind increases in strength this drifting snow forms a thicker layer, as at this British base in Antarctica. When the entrained material reaches eye level it is known as blown snow. Any further rise in wind velocity swiftly increases the concentration of particulate matter, causing the visibility rapidly to fall to zero. When this is the case the term blizzard is appropriate, as it also is when high winds are combined with a heavy snowfall.

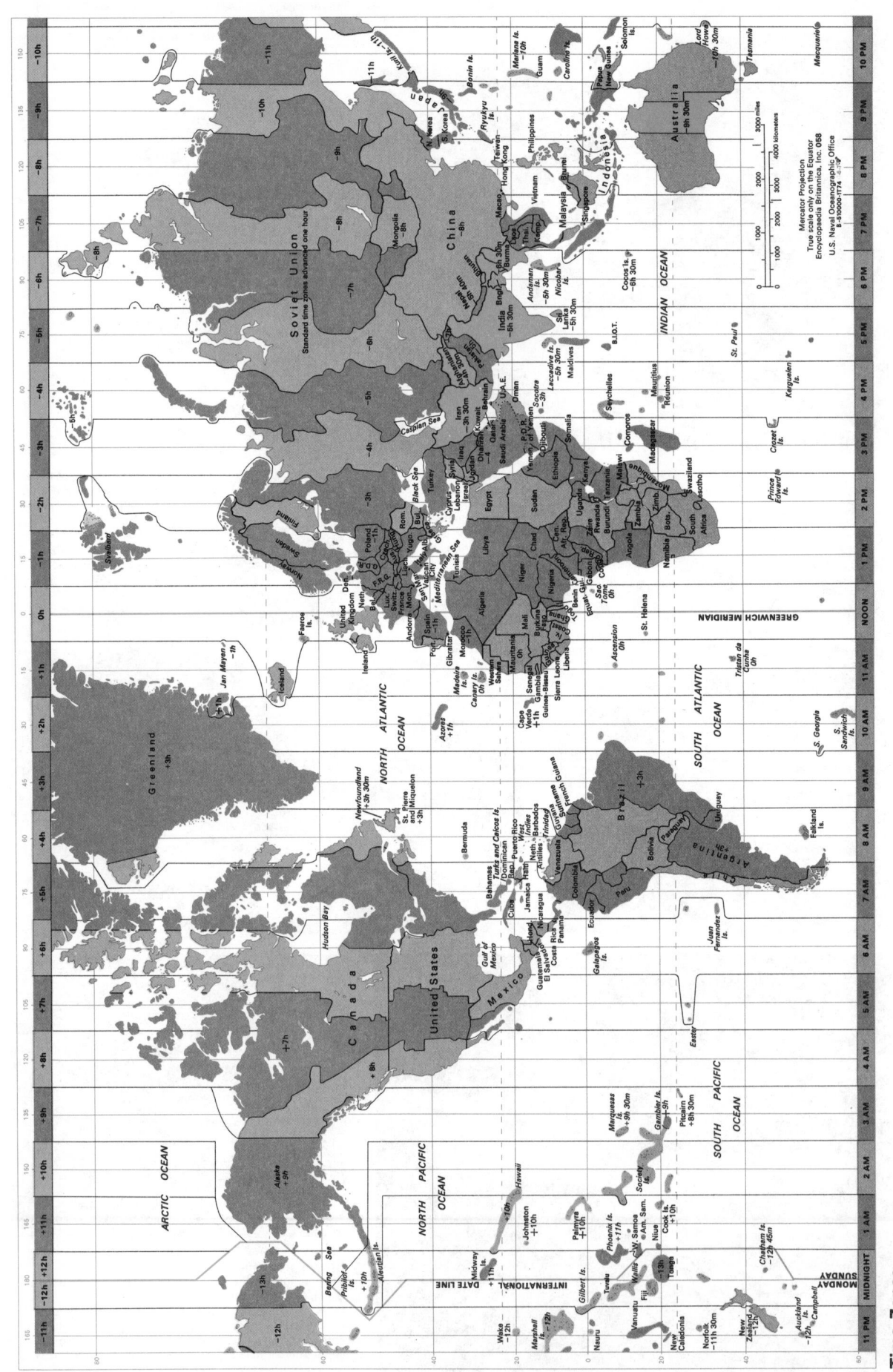

The standard time zone system, fixed by international agreement and by law in each country, is based on a theoretical division of the globe into 24 zones of 15° longitude each. The mid-meridian of each zone fixes the hour for the entire zone. The zero time zone extends 7½° east and 7½° west of the Greenwich meridian, 0° longitude. Since the earth rotates toward the east, time zones to the west of Greenwich are earlier, to the east, later.
Plus and minus hours at the top of the map are added to or subtracted from local time to find Greenwich time. Local standard time can be determined for any area in the world by adding one hour for each time zone counted in an easterly direction from

one's own, or by subtracting one hour for each zone counted in a westerly direction. To separate one day from the next, the 180th meridian has been designated as the international date line. On both sides of the line the time of day is the same, but west of the line it is one day later than it is to the east. Countries that adhere to the international zone system adopt the zone applicable to their location. Some countries, however, establish standard zones based on political boundaries, or adopt the time zone of a neighboring unit. For all or part of the year some countries also advance their time by one hour, thereby utilizing more daylight hours each day.

Mercator Projection
True scale only on the Equator
Encyclopaedia Britannica, Inc. 058
U.S. Naval Oceanographic Office
B-40000-1T74

Time Zones

☐	Standard time zone of even-numbered hours from Greenwich time
☐	Standard time zone of odd-numbered hours from Greenwich time
☐	Time varies from the standard time zone by half an hour
☐	Time varies from the standard time zone by other than half an hour

h m   hours, minutes

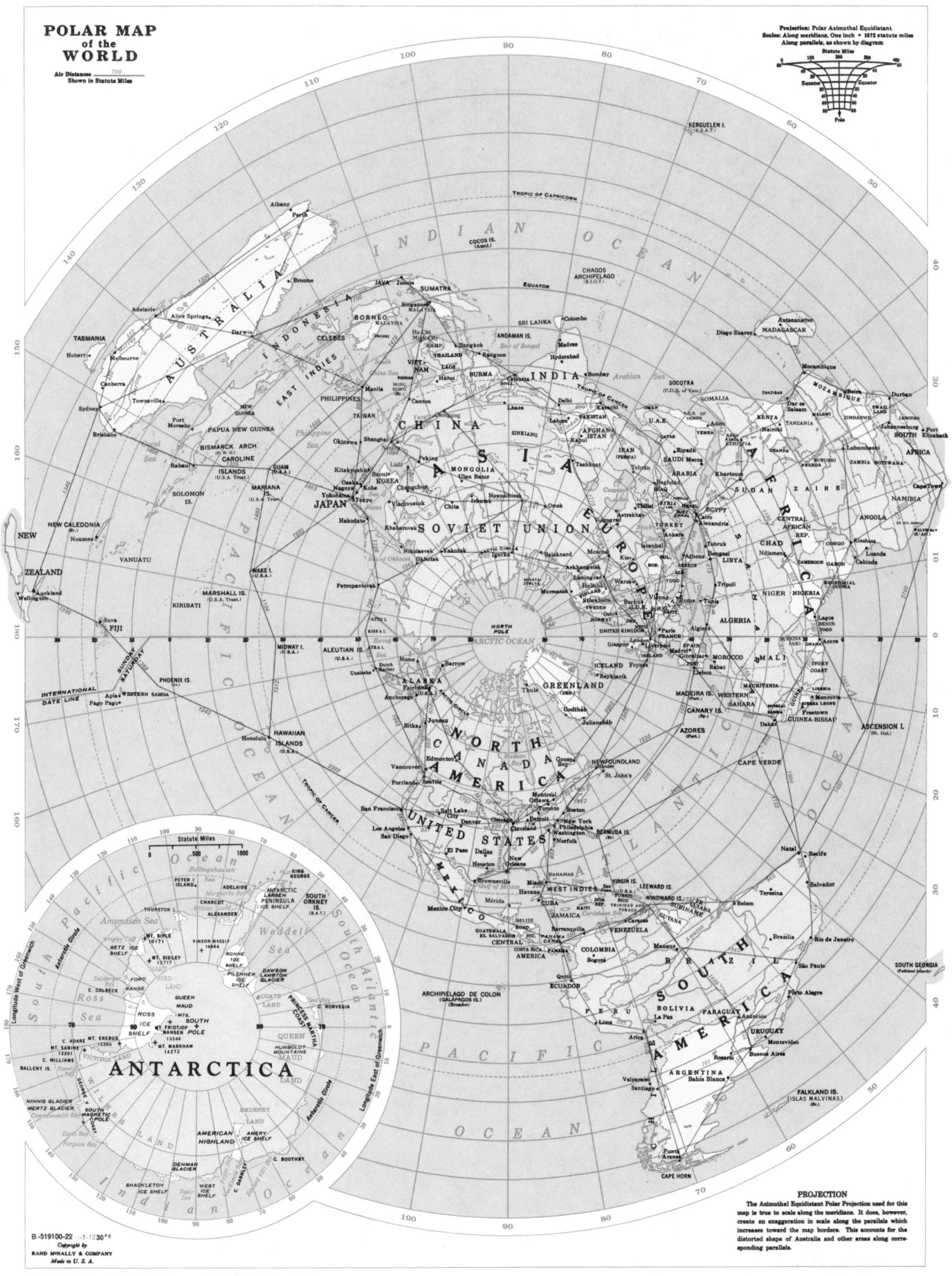

POLAR MAP
of the
WORLD

Air Distances ——700——
Shown in Statute Miles

Projection: Polar Azimuthal Equidistant
Scales: Along meridians, One inch = 1872 statute miles
Along parallels, as shown by diagram

PROJECTION

The Azimuthal Equidistant Polar Projection used for this map is true to scale along the meridians. It does, however, create an exaggeration in scale along the parallels which increases toward the map borders. This accounts for the distorted shape of Australia and other areas along corresponding parallels.

B-519100-22 -7-1230 P8
Copyright by
RAND McNALLY & COMPANY
Made in U.S.A.

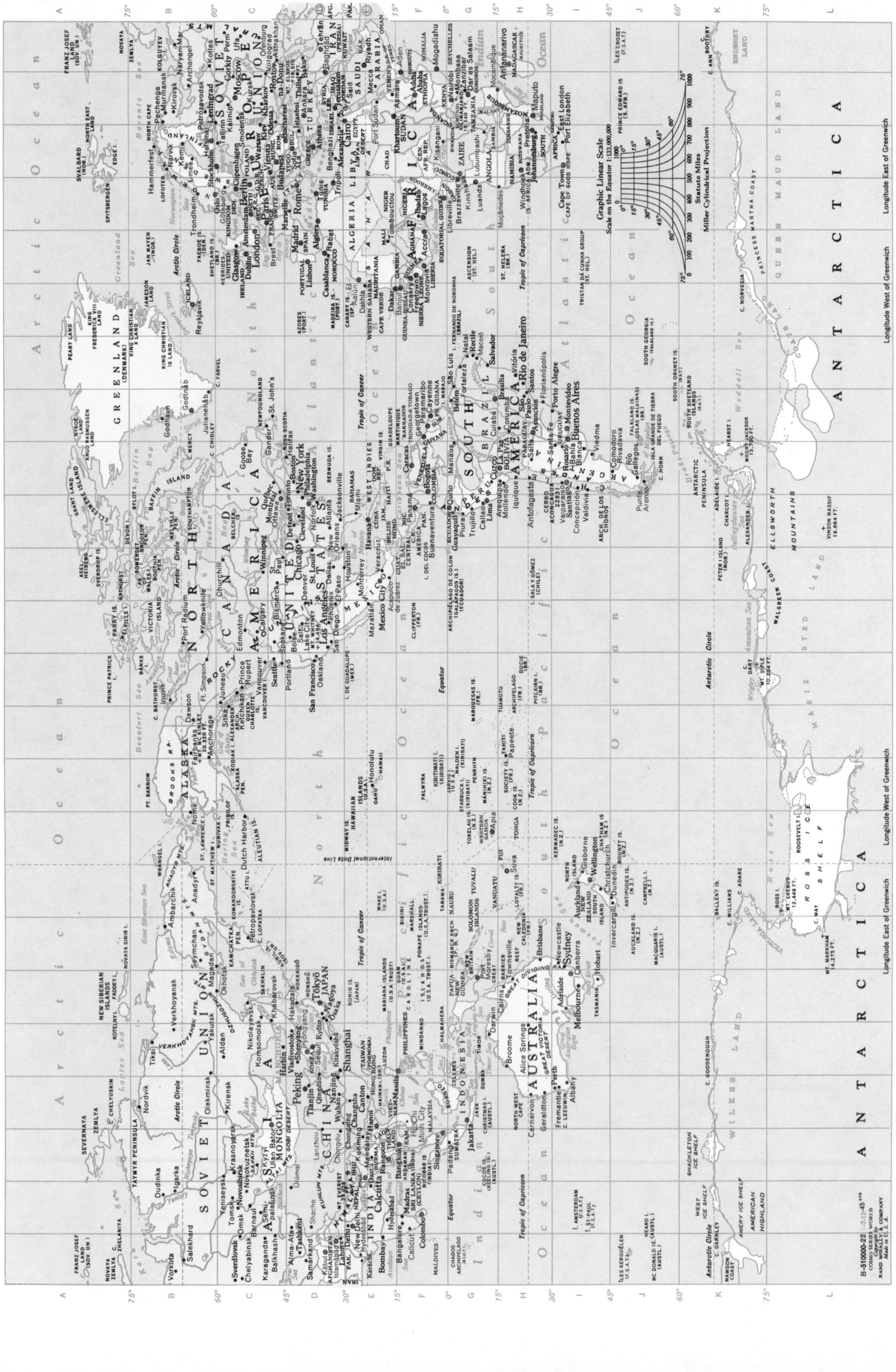

GRAPHIC LINEAR SCALE

Graphic Linear Scale
Scale on the Equator 1:133,000,000
Statute Miles
Miller Cylindrical Projection

Longitude East of Greenwich
Longitude West of Greenwich

Arctic Ocean

GREENLAND (DENMARK)

NORTH AMERICA

CANADA

UNITED STATES

SOUTH AMERICA

BRAZIL

EUROPE

AFRICA

SOVIET UNION

ASIA

CHINA

MONGOLIA

INDIA

AUSTRALIA

ANTARCTICA

QUEEN MAUD LAND

Atlantic Ocean

Pacific Ocean

Indian Ocean

North Pacific Ocean

South Pacific Ocean

Equator

Tropic of Cancer

Tropic of Capricorn

Arctic Circle

Antarctic Circle

International Date Line

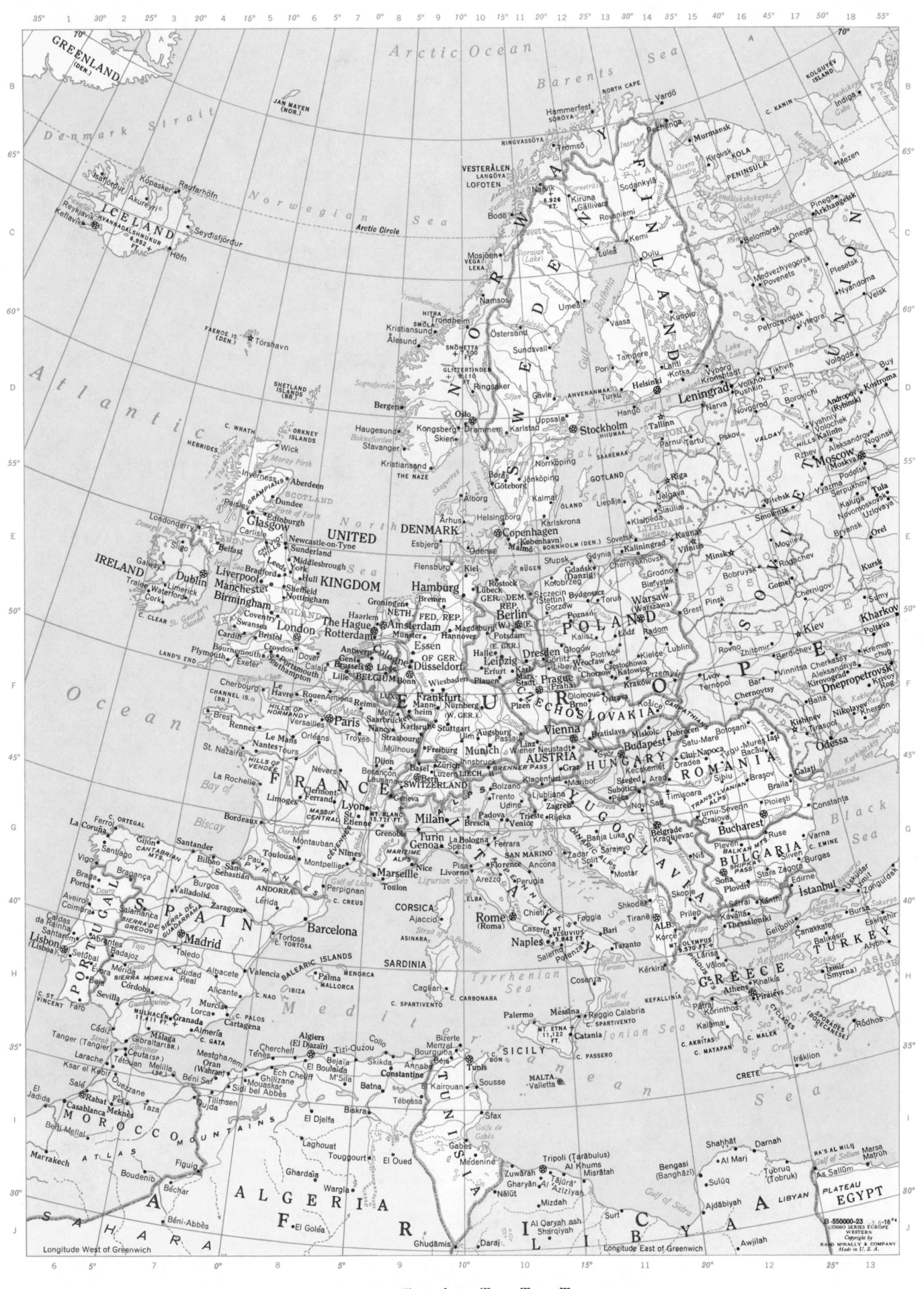

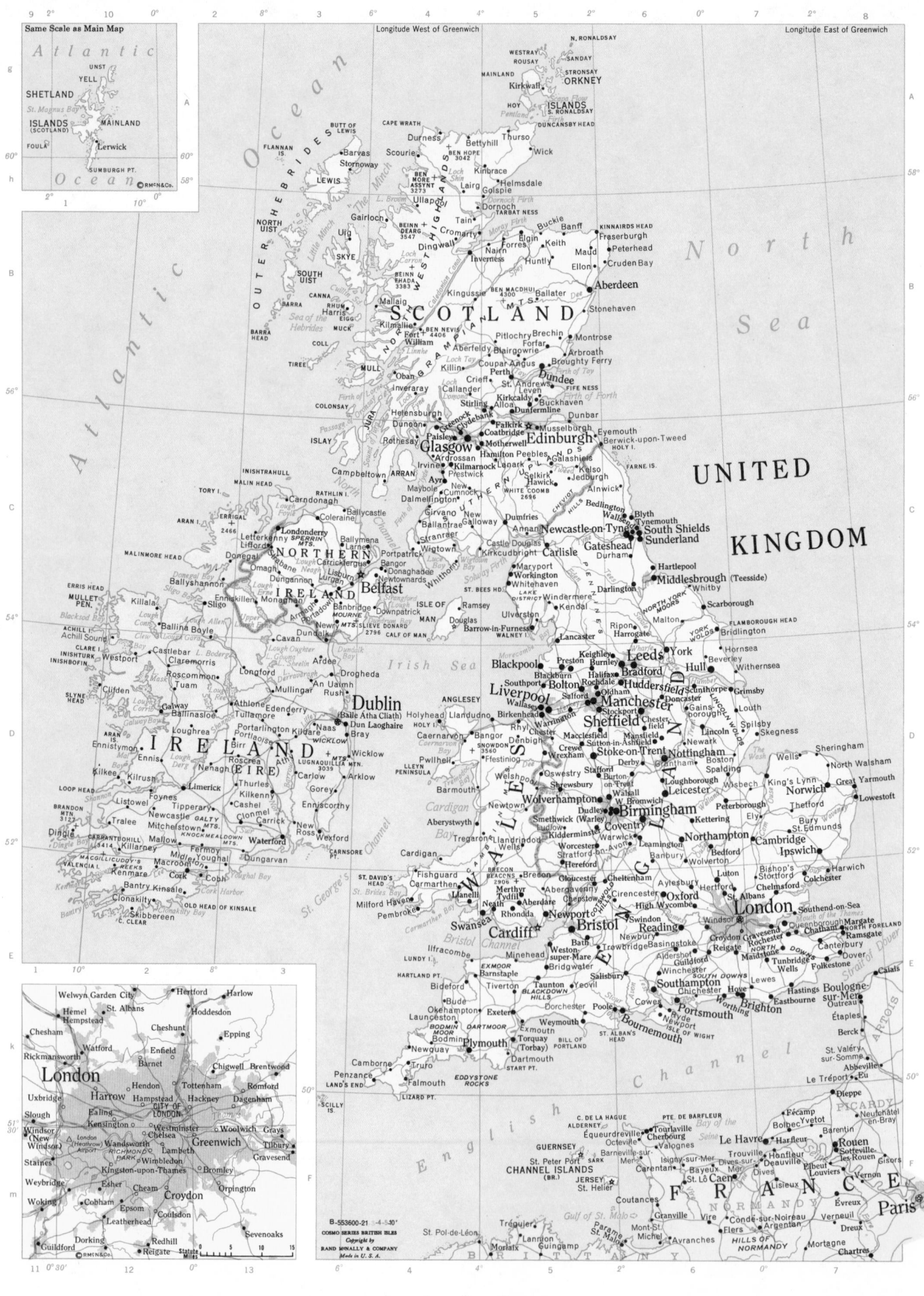

Same Scale as Main Map

Longitude West of Greenwich

Longitude East of Greenwich

SCOTLAND

UNITED

KINGDOM

NORTHERN
IRELAND

IRELAND
(EIRE)

WALES

ENGLAND

London

FRANCE

Atlantic Ocean

North Sea

Irish Sea

English Channel

BRITANNY

NORMANDY

PICARDY

Conic Projection

B-553600-21 -4-5-30'

COSMO SERIES BRITISH ISLES
Copyright by
RAND McNALLY & COMPANY
Made in U.S.A.

Statute Miles 25 0 25 50 75

Kilometers 25 0 25 50 100

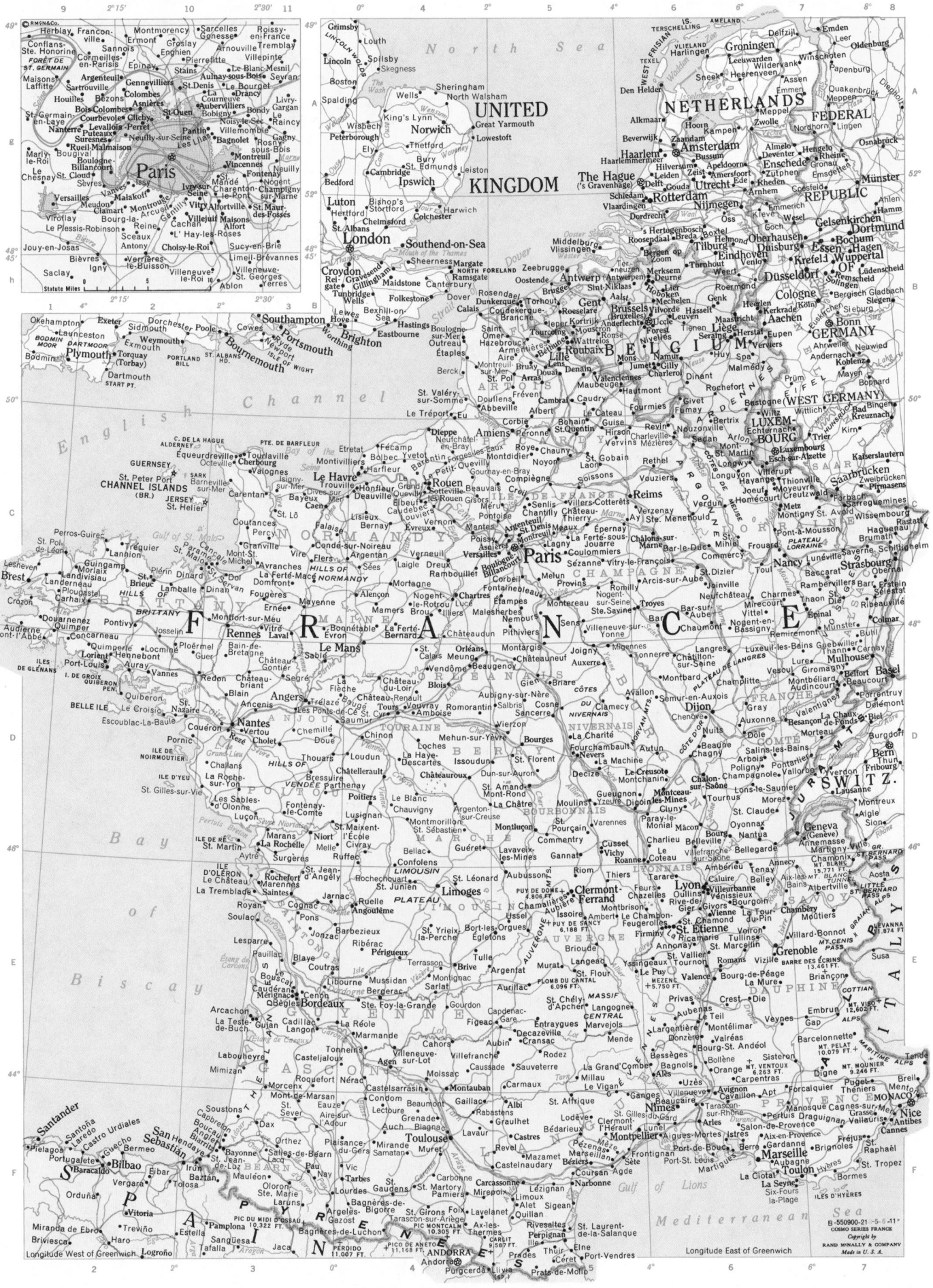

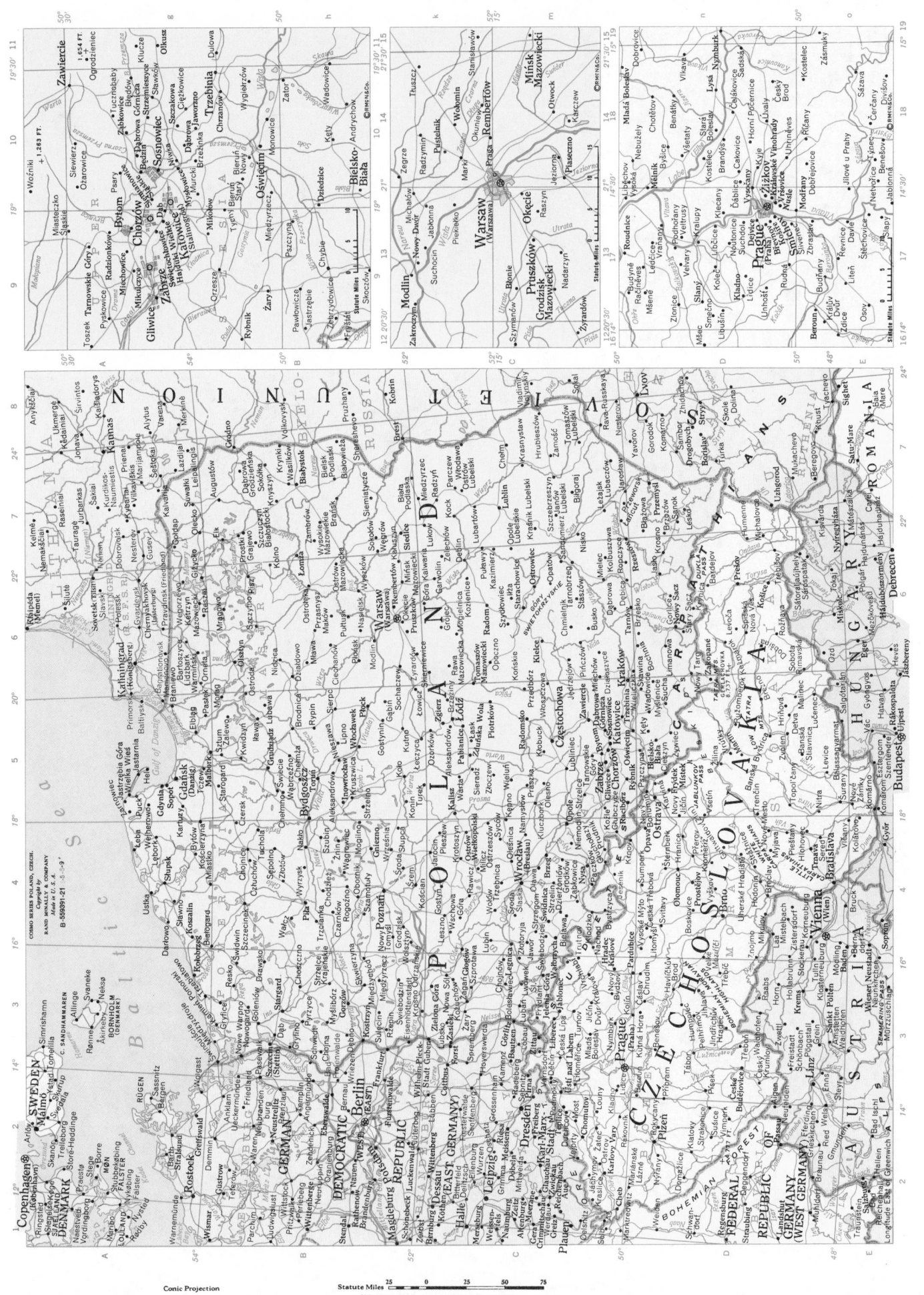

Conic Projection

Statute Miles

Kilometers

Statute Miles 25 0 25 50 75

Kilometers 25 0 25 50 100

Conic Projection

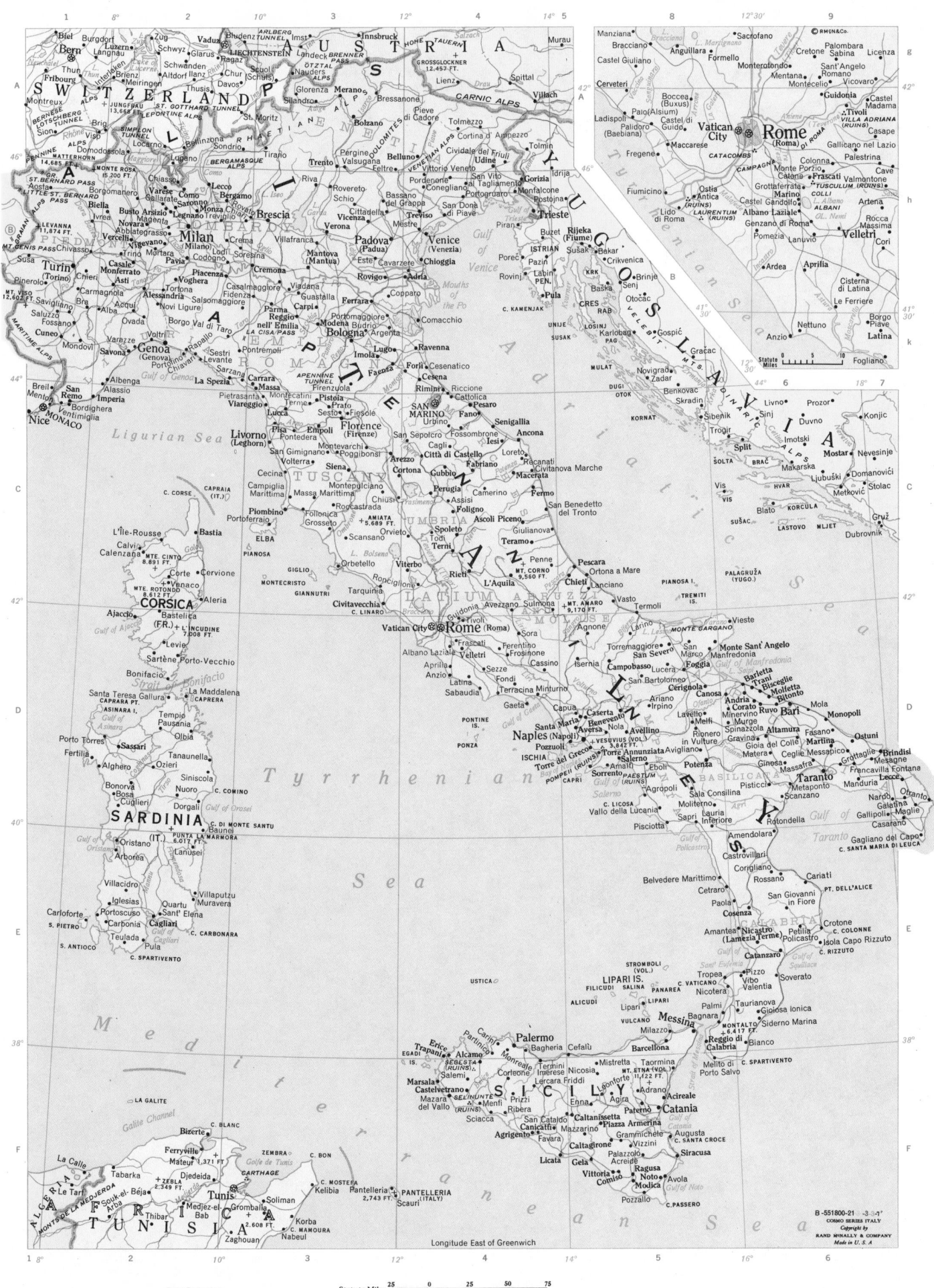

Statute Miles 25   0   25   50   75

Kilometers   25   0   25   50   100

Conic Projection

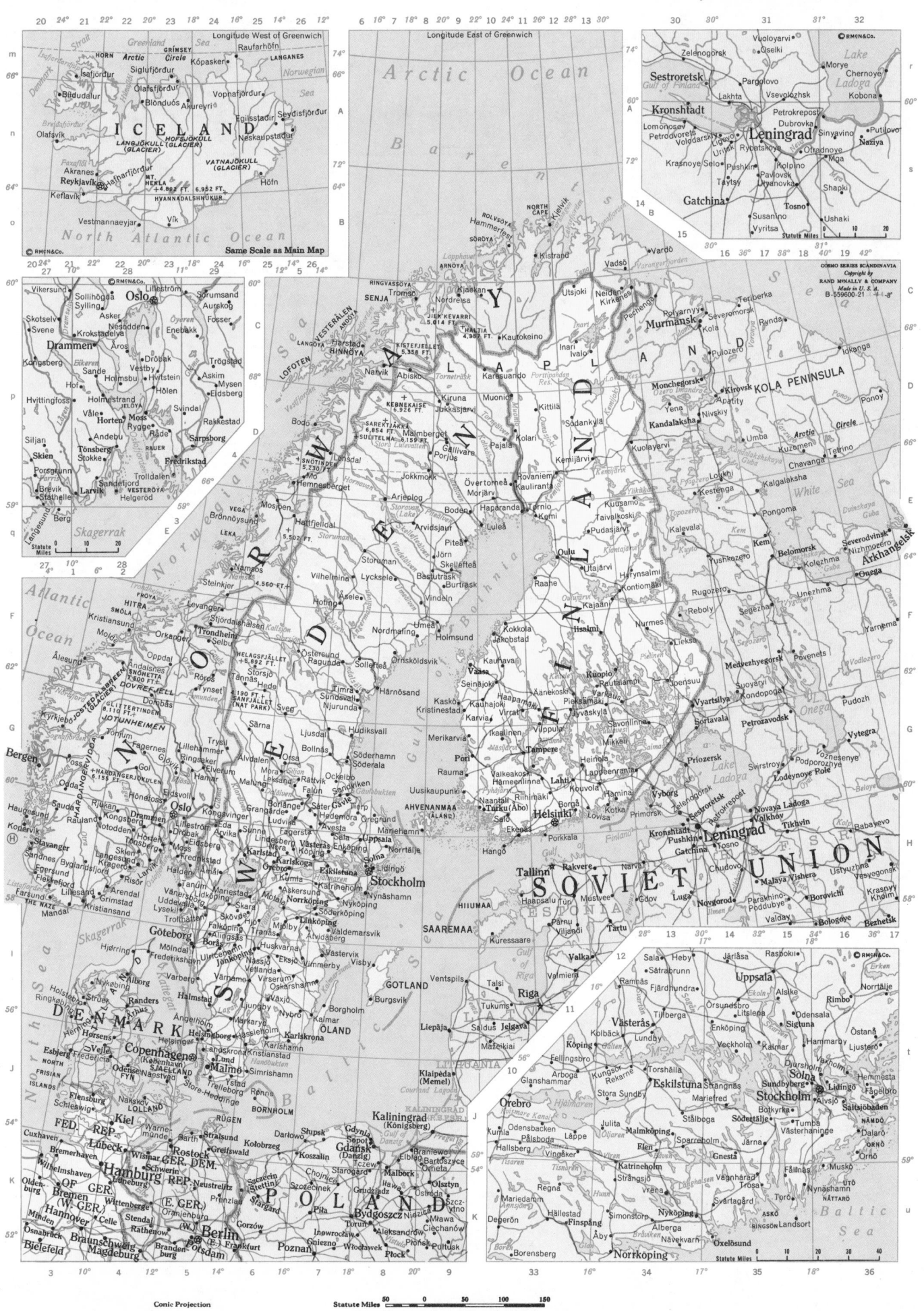

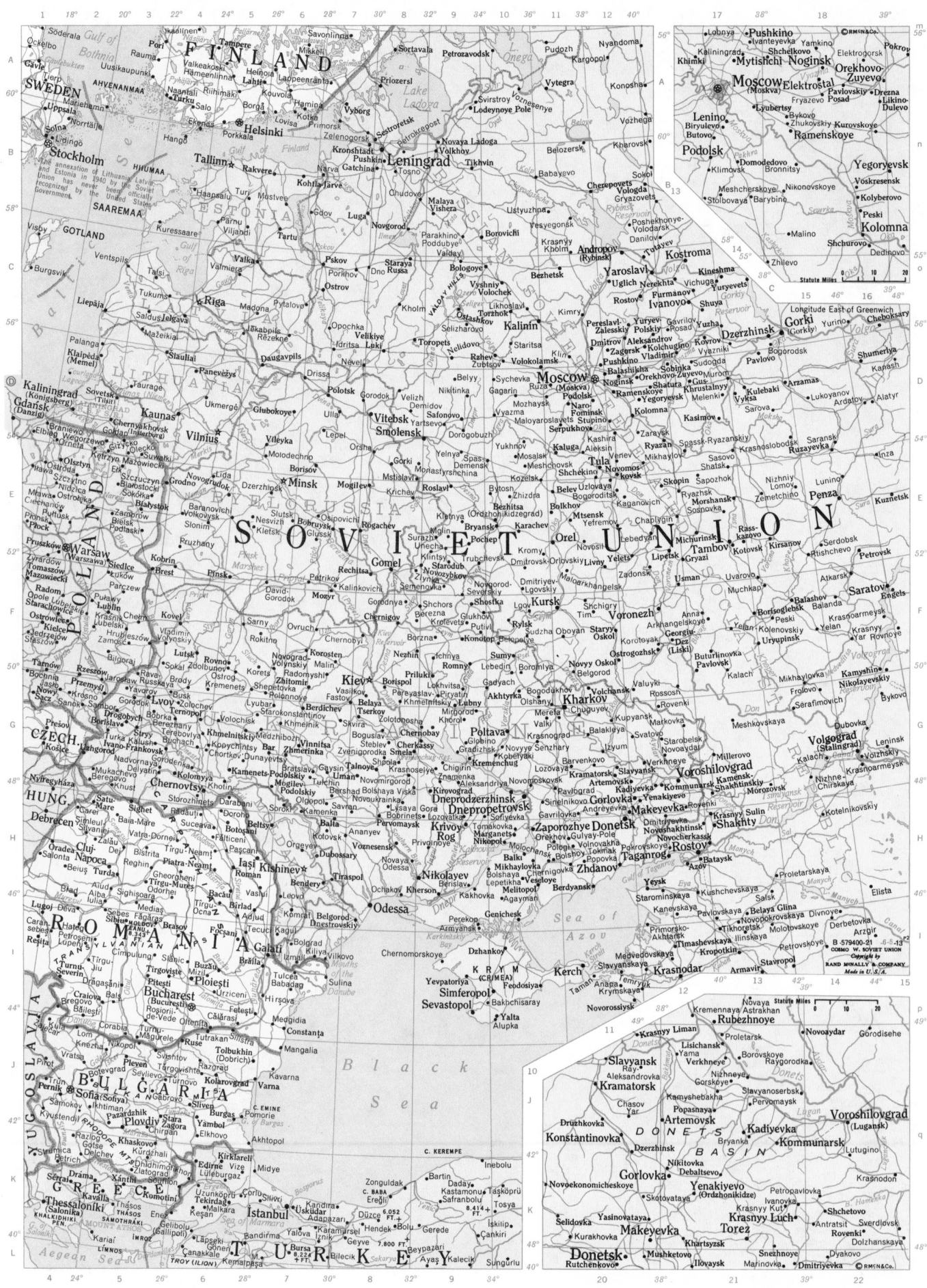

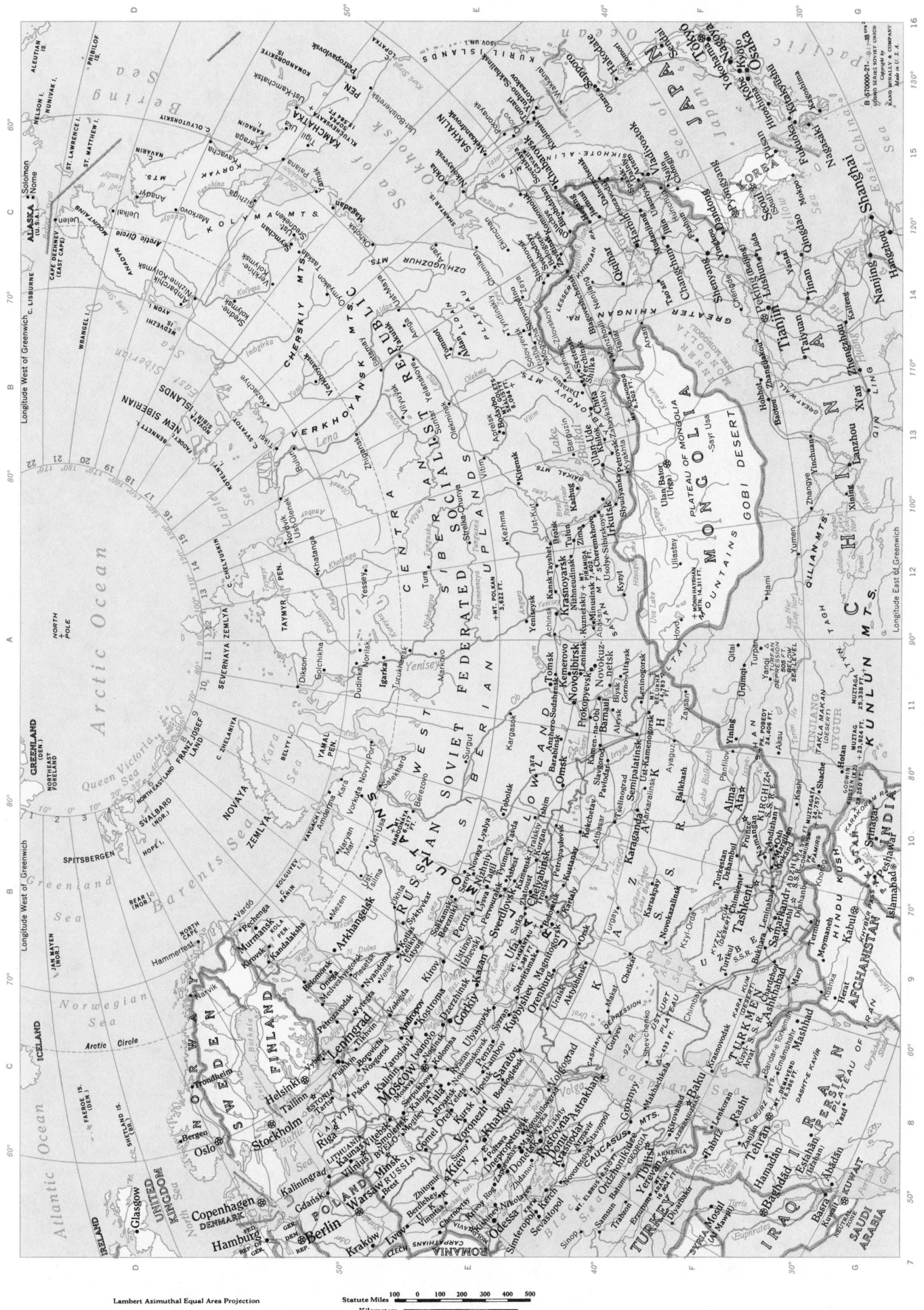

Lambert Azimuthal Equal Area Projection

Statute Miles
Kilometers

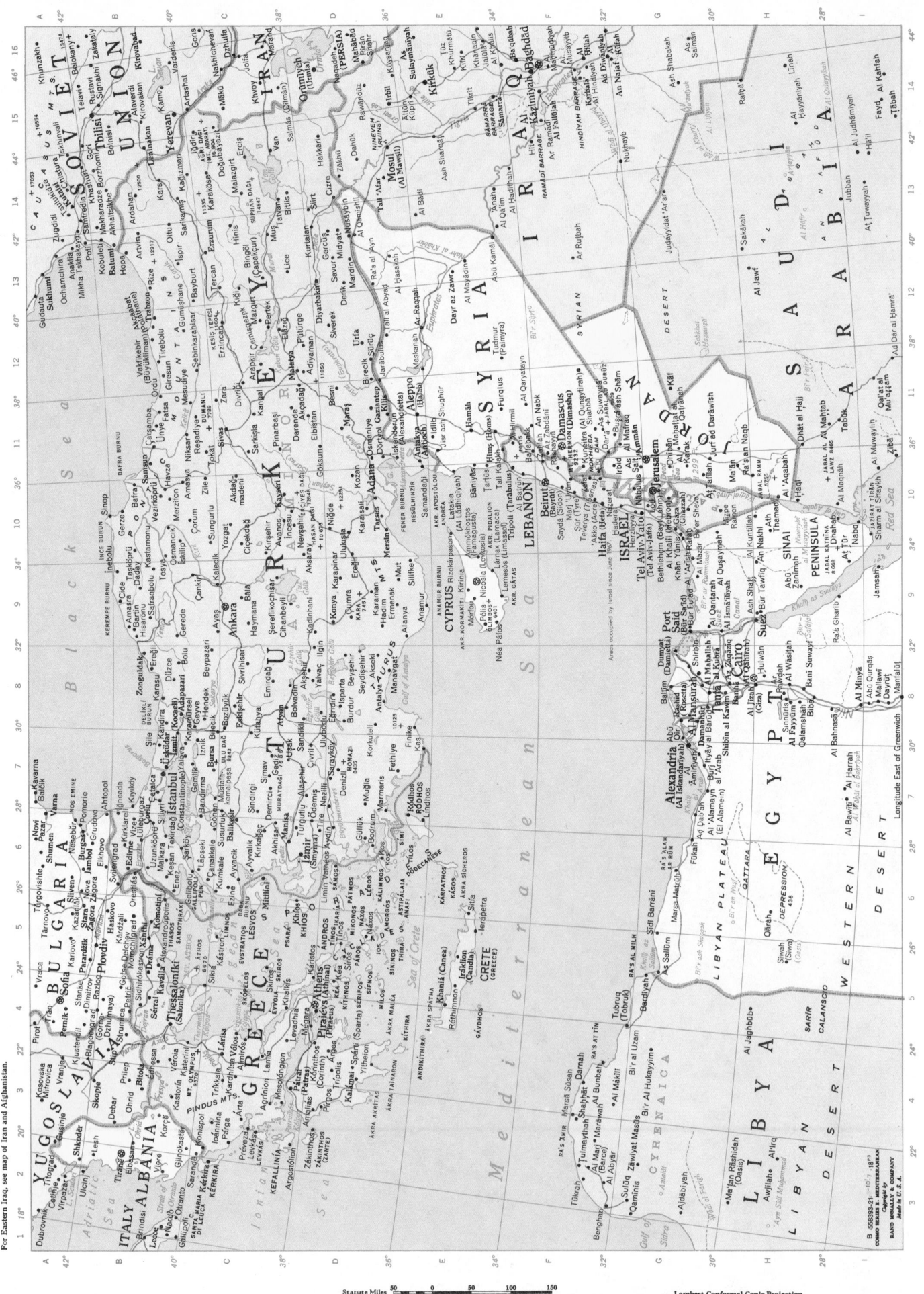

For Eastern Iraq, see map of Iran and Afghanistan.

Statute Miles   50   0   50   100   150

Kilometers   50   0   50   100   200

Lambert Conformal Conic Projection

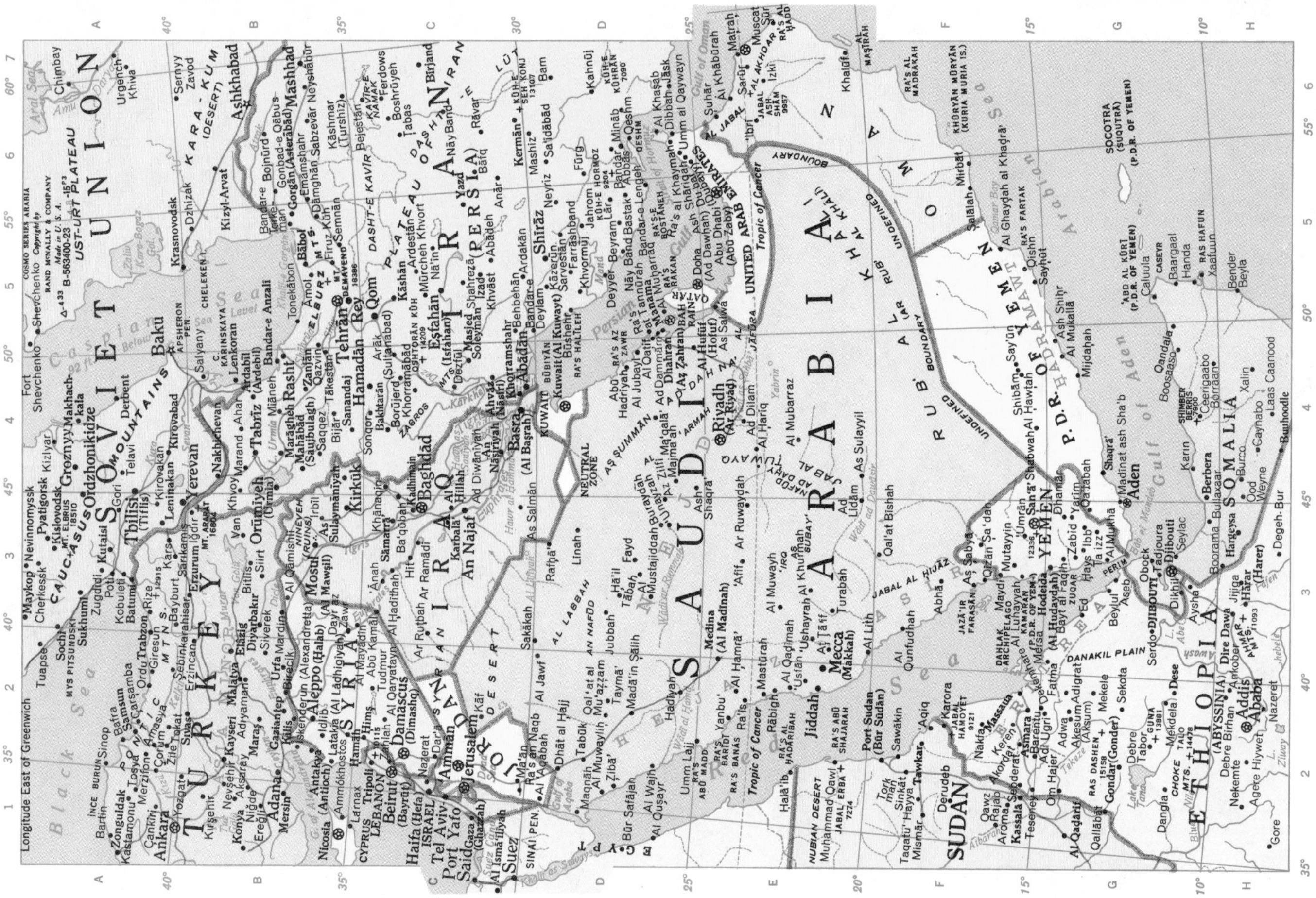

Israel and Arabia

SOVIET UNION

TURKEY

S Y R I A

I R A N

I R A Q

S A U D I   A R A B I A

JORDAN

ISRAEL

LEBANON

EGYPT

SUDAN

ETHIOPIA

SOMALIA

YEMEN

P.D.R. OF YEMEN

UNITED ARAB EMIRATES

OMAN

QATAR

KUWAIT

NEUTRAL ZONE

RUB' AL KHALI

SINAI PENINSULA

GAZA STRIP

Black Sea

Caspian Sea

Mediterranean Sea

Red Sea

Persian Gulf

Gulf of Oman

Gulf of Aden

Arabian Sea

Gulf of Aqaba

Dead Sea

Aral Sea

KARA-KUM (DESERT)

UST-URT PLATEAU

Tropic of Cancer

SOCOTRA (SUQUTRA) (P.D.R. OF YEMEN)

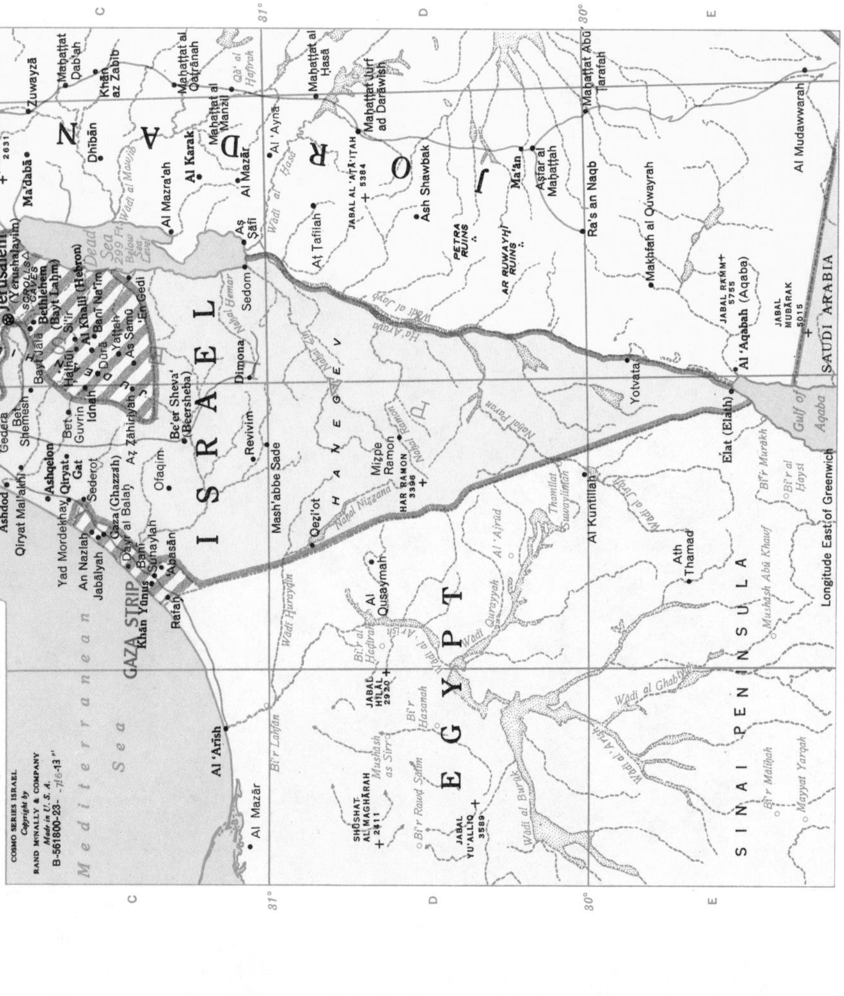

'ABD AL KURI (P.D.R. OF YEMEN)

KHORYAN MORYAN (KURIA MURIA ISJ.)

DANAKIL PLAIN

NUBIAN DESERT

Longitude East of Greenwich

Lambert Conformal Conic Projection

Statute Miles

Kilometers

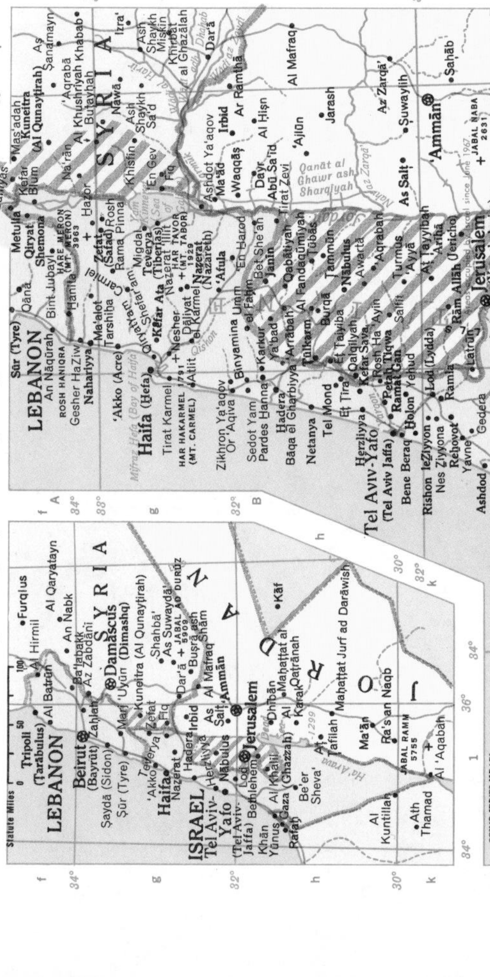

Lambert Conformal Conic Projection

COSMO SERIES ISRAEL
RAND M°NALLY & COMPANY
Made in U.S.A.
B-561800-23 —76-43™

ABBYSSINIA (Etheopia)

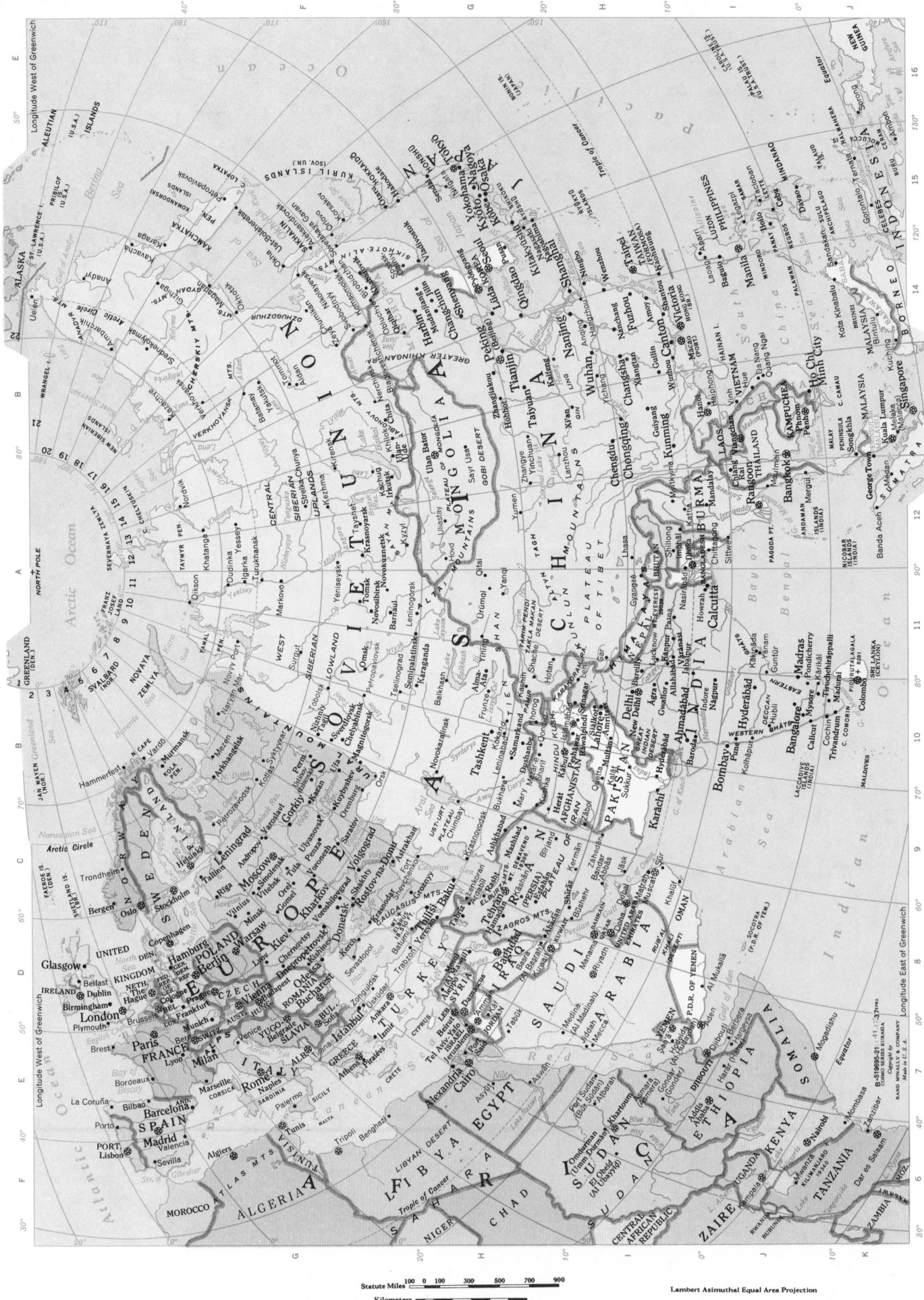

Statute Miles 100 0 100 300 500 700 900

Kilometers 100 0 100 300 700 1100

Lambert Azimuthal Equal Area Projection

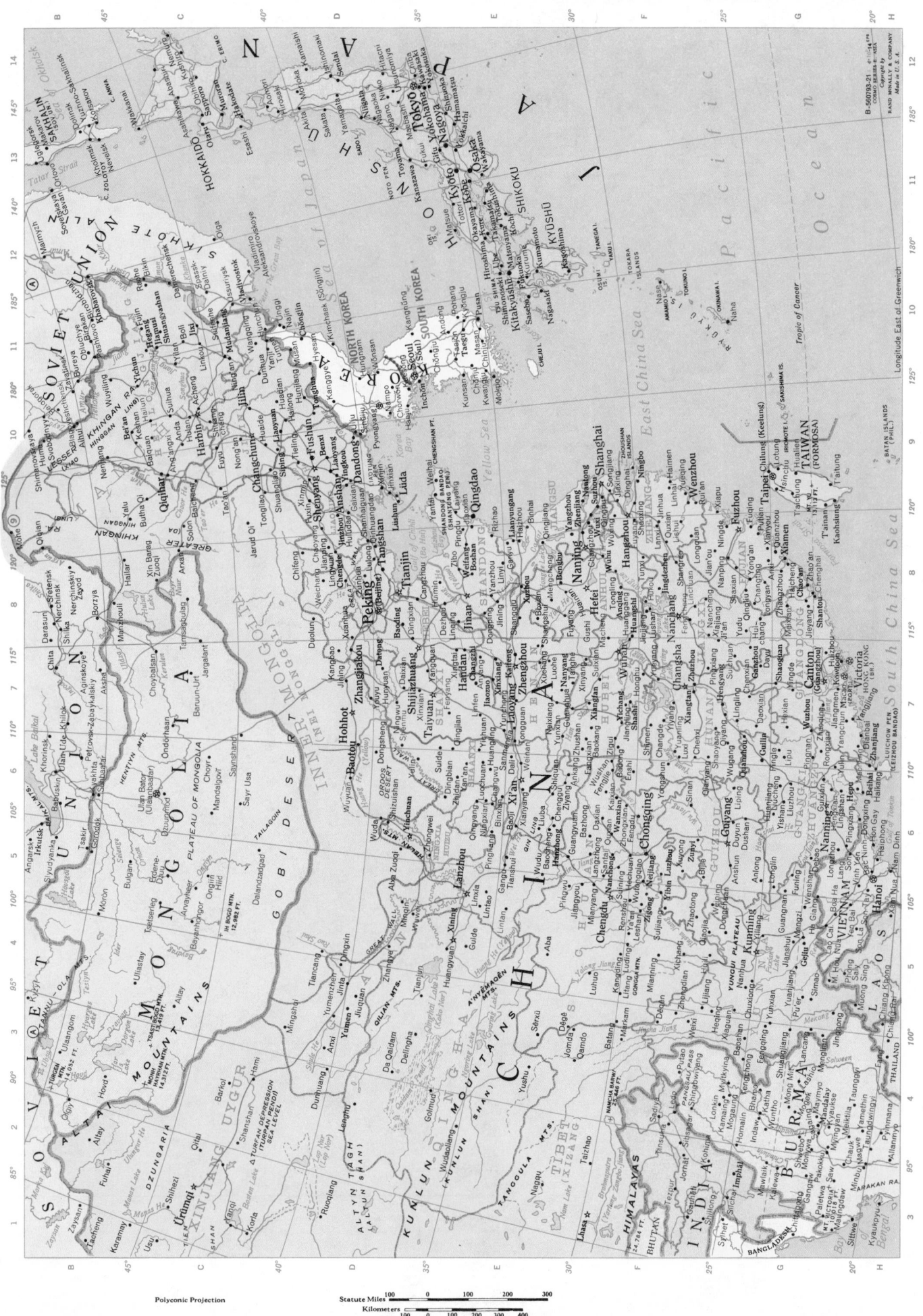

Polyconic Projection

Statute Miles   100   0   100   200   300

Kilometers   100   0   100   200   300   400

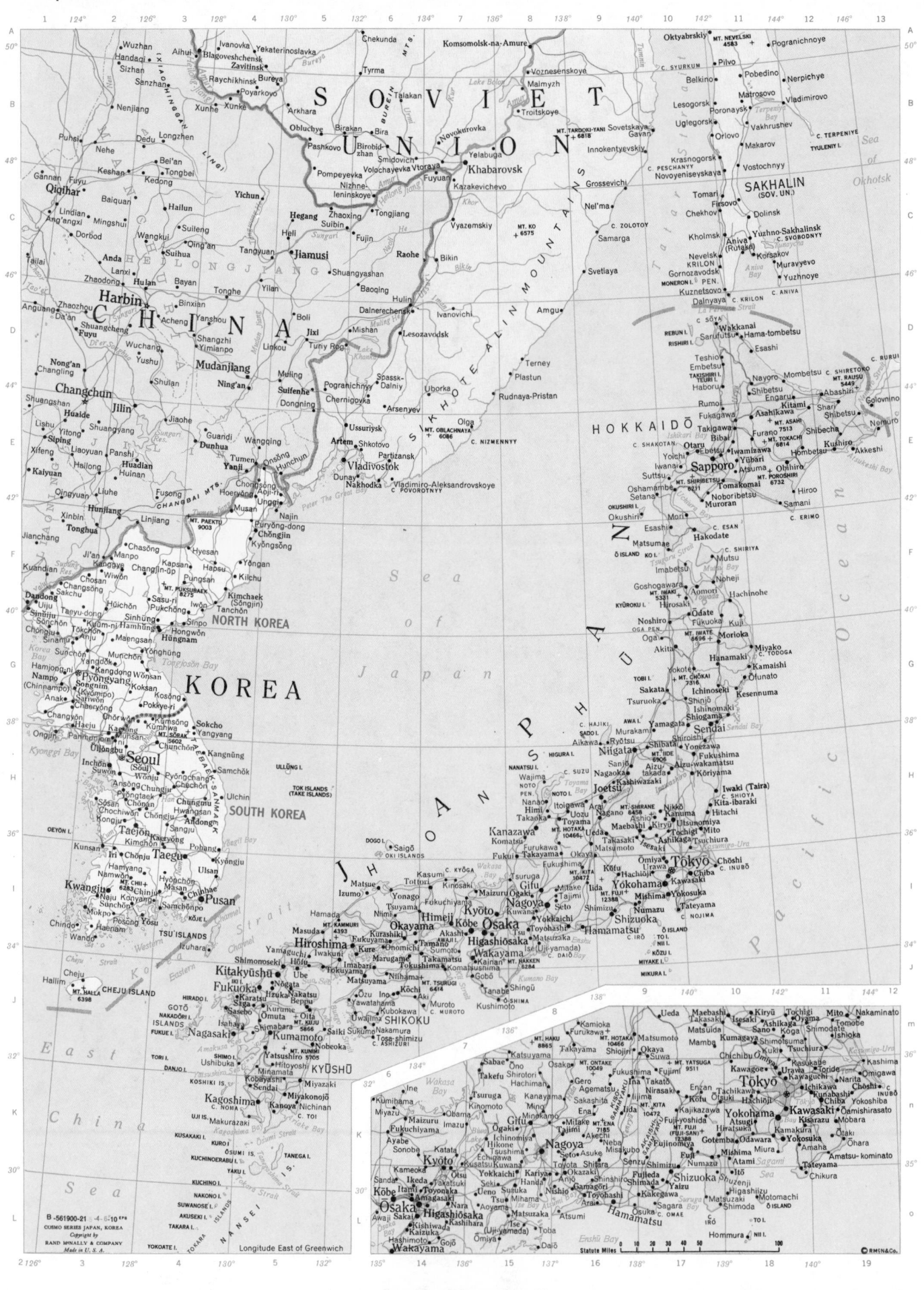

Longitude East of Greenwich

Statute Miles
Kilometers

Lambert Conformal Conic Projection

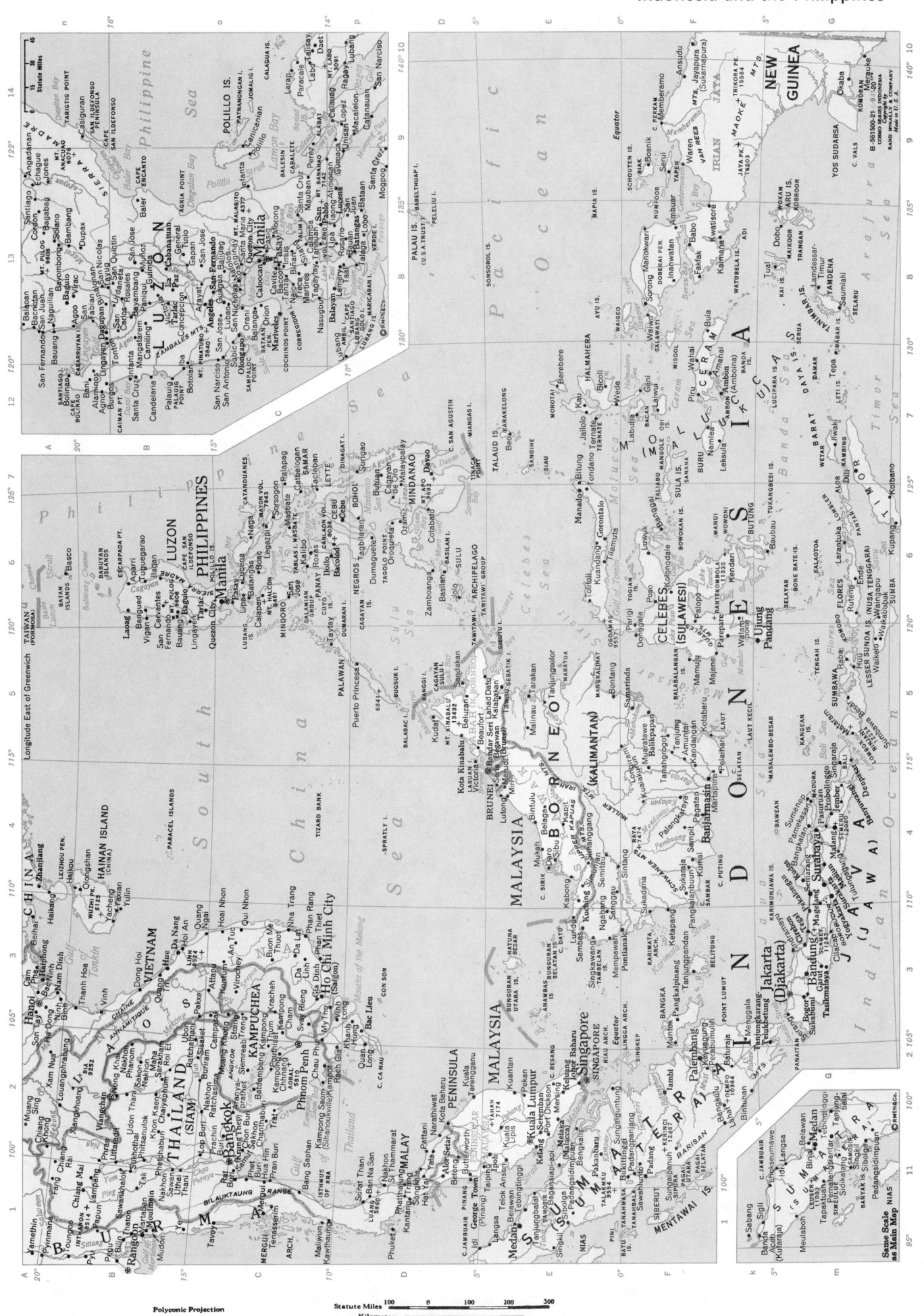

Polyconic Projection

Statute Miles 100 0 100 200 300

Kilometers 100 0 100 200 300 400

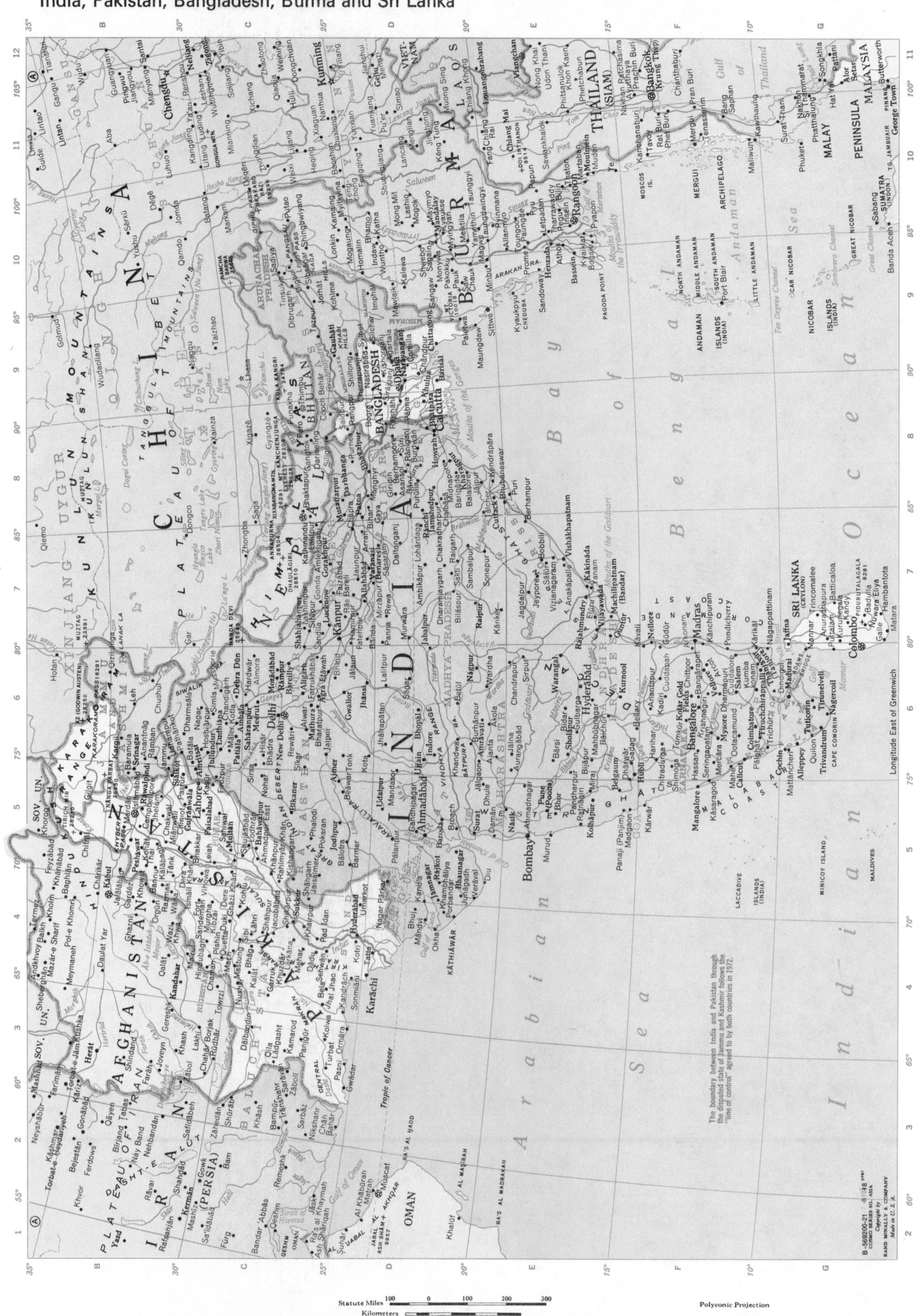

The boundary between India and Pakistan through
the disputed state of Jammu and Kashmir follows the
"line of control" agreed to by both countries in 1972.

Statute Miles 100 0 100 200 300
Kilometers 100 0 100 200 300 400

Polyconic Projection

B-569200-21
COSMO SERIES SO. ASIA
Copyright by
RAND M°NALLY & COMPANY
Made in U.S.A.

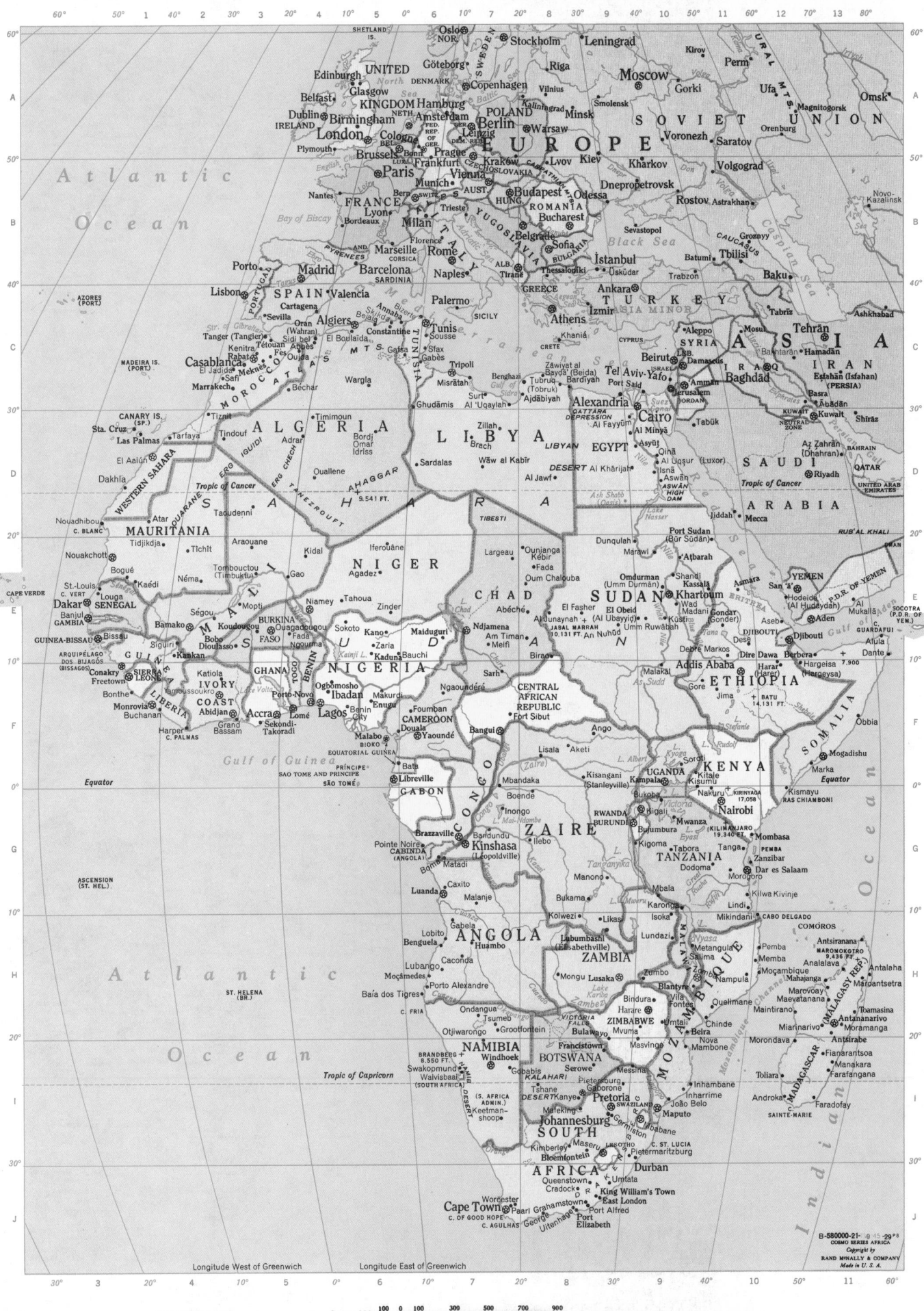

B-580000-21- -9-15 -29P8
COSMO SERIES AFRICA
Copyright by
RAND MCNALLY & COMPANY
Made in U.S.A.

Sinusoidal Projection

Statute Miles   100 0 100   300   500   700   900

Kilometers   100 0 100 300 500 700 900 1100 1300

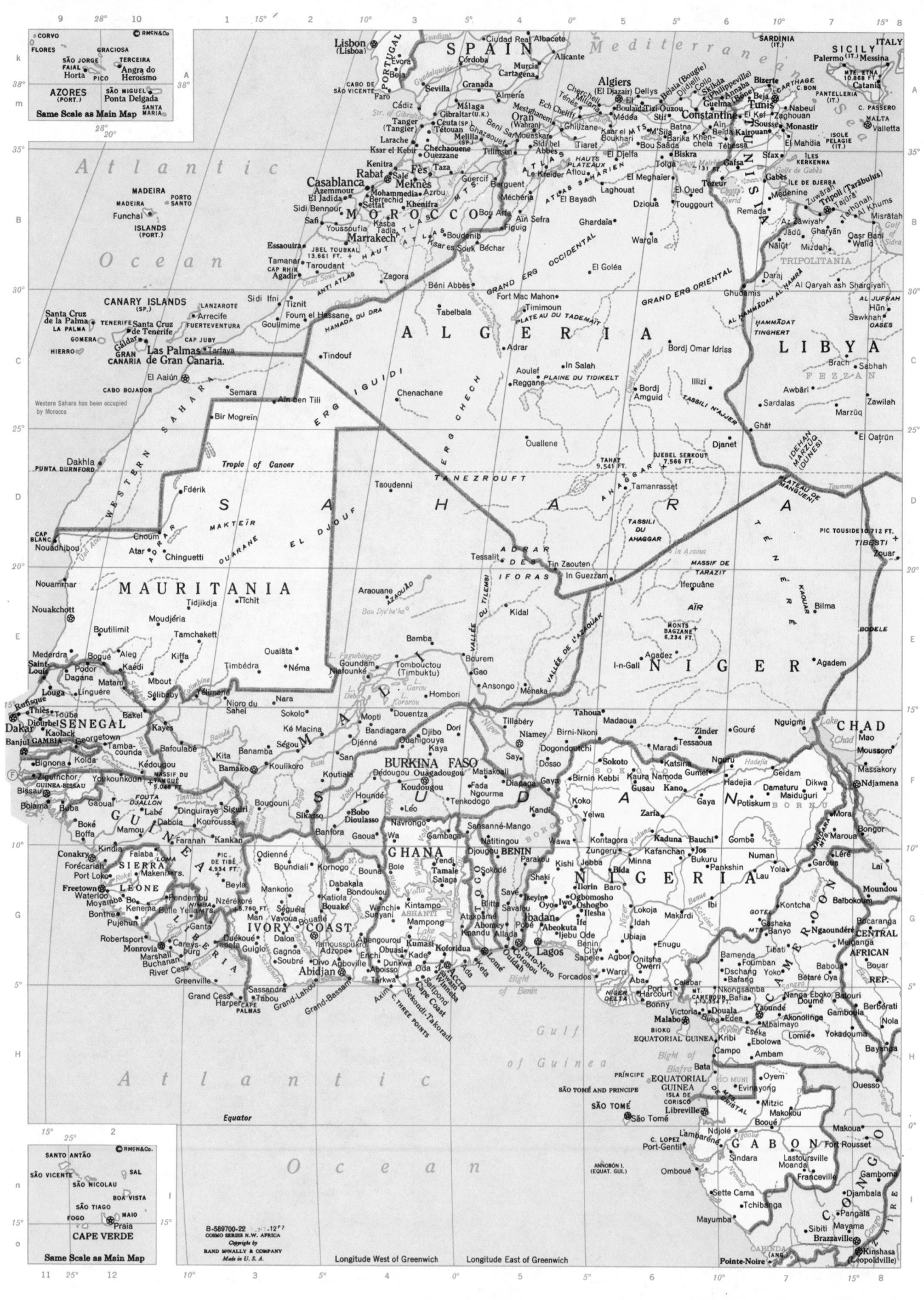

Statute Miles 100   0   100   200   300

Kilometers 100 0 100 200 400

Sinusoidal Projection

B-589700-22 ...-12″²
COSMO SERIES N.W. AFRICA
Copyright by
RAND McNALLY & COMPANY
Made in U.S.A.

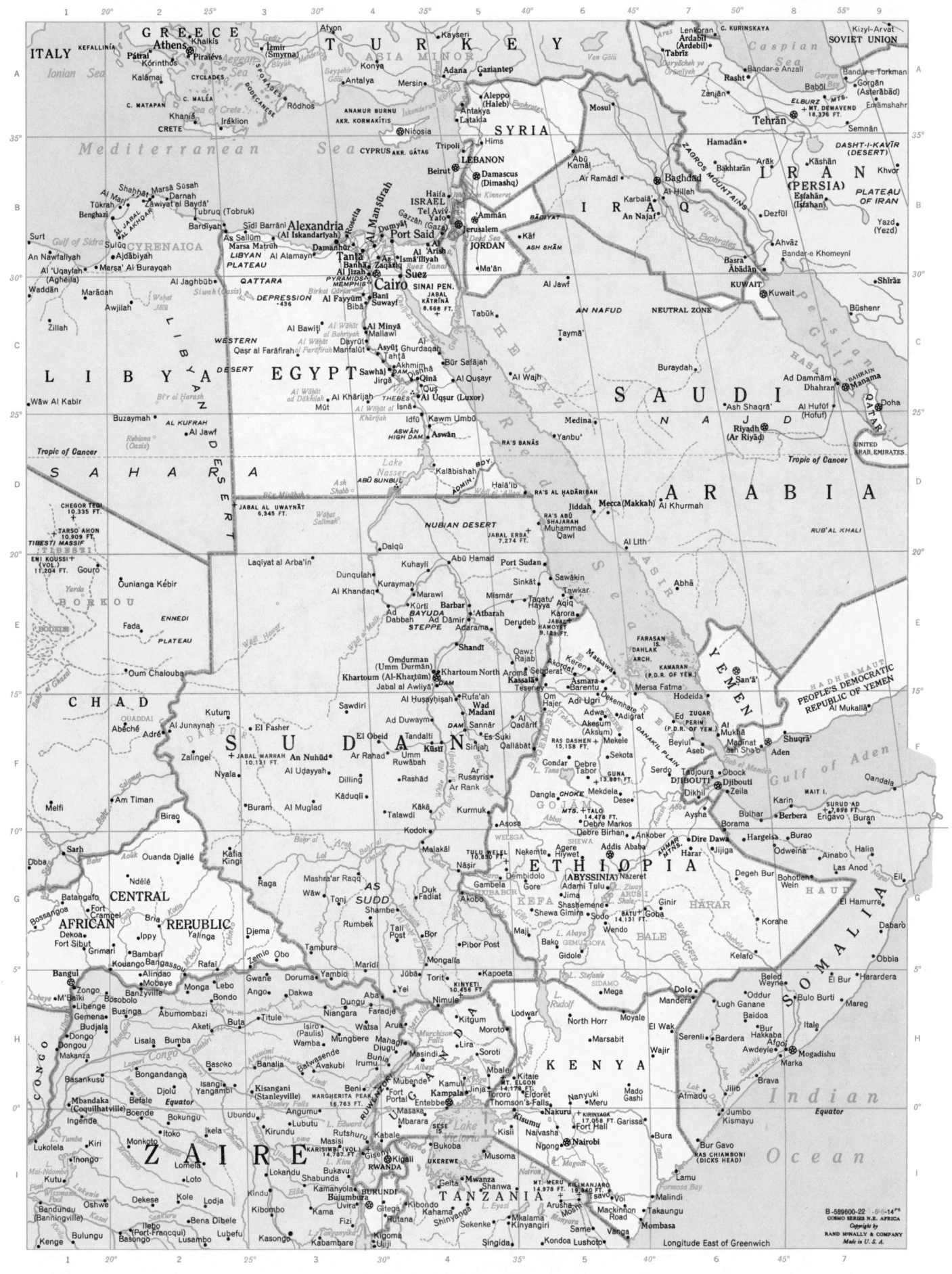

Statute Miles 100 0 100 200 300

Kilometers 100 0 100 200 300 400

B-589600-22
COSMO SERIES N.E. AFRICA
Copyright by
RAND M9NALLY & COMPANY
Made in U.S.A.

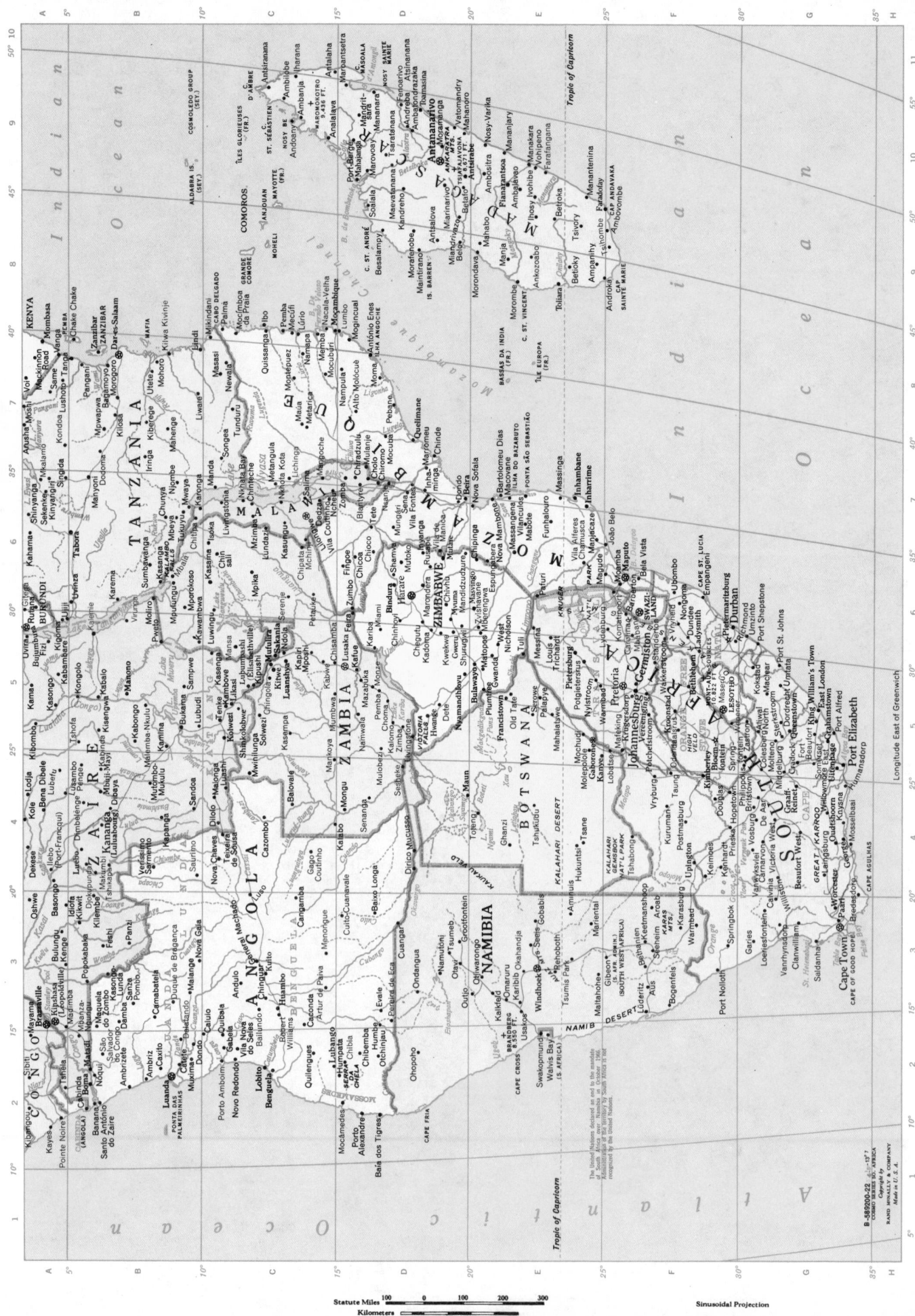

Statute Miles   100   0   100   200   300

Kilometers   100   0   100   200   300   400

Sinusoidal Projection

B-589200-22
COSMO SERIES SO. AFRICA
Copyright by
RAND McNALLY & COMPANY
Made in U.S.A.

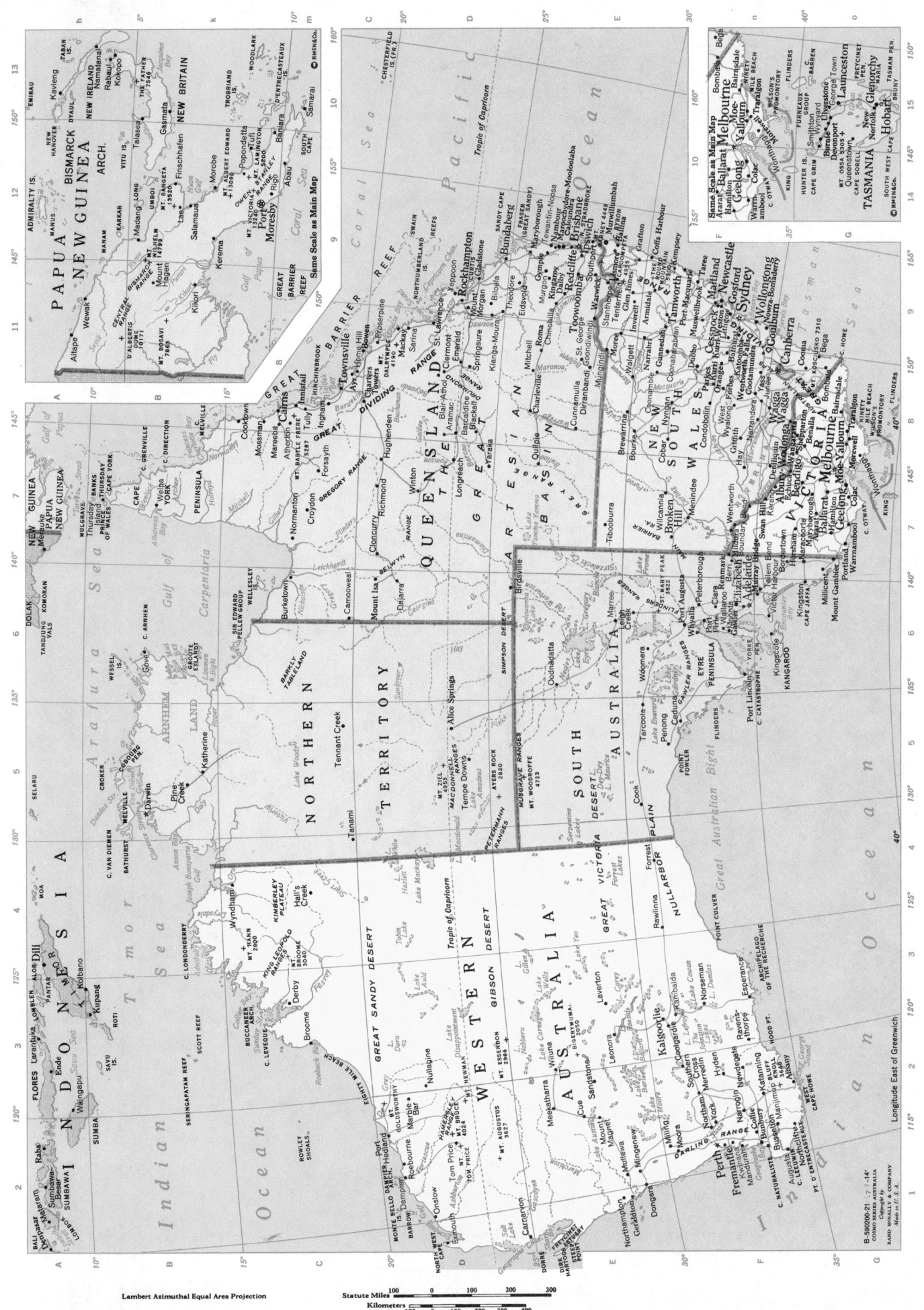

Lambert Azimuthal Equal Area Projection

Statute Miles
100   0   100   200   300

Kilometers
100   0   100   200   300   400

B-590200-21 -7-1-14'
COSMO SERIES Australia
Copyright by
RAND M^cNALLY & COMPANY
Made in U.S.A.

Statute Miles

Kilometers

Lambert Conformal Conic Projection

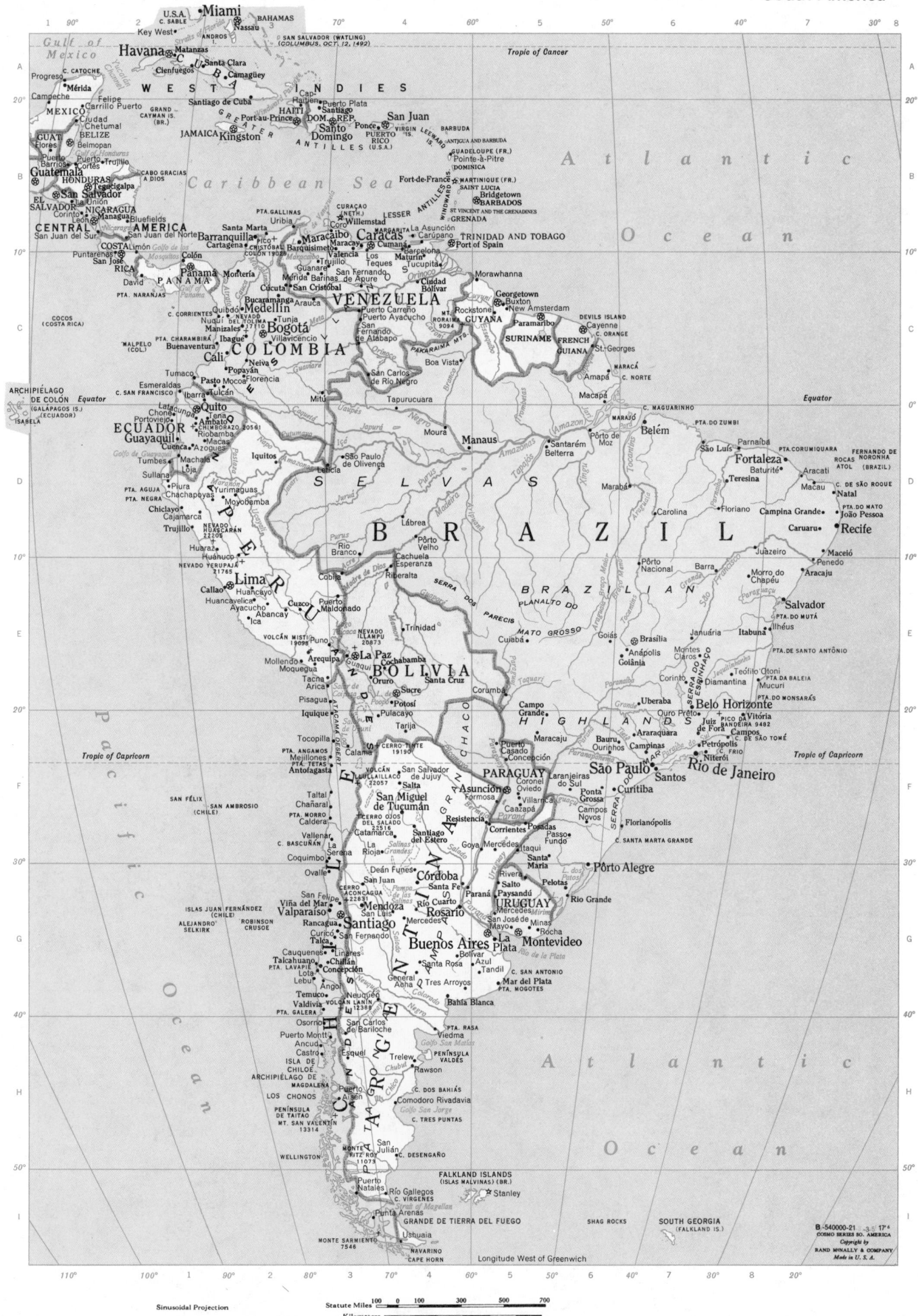

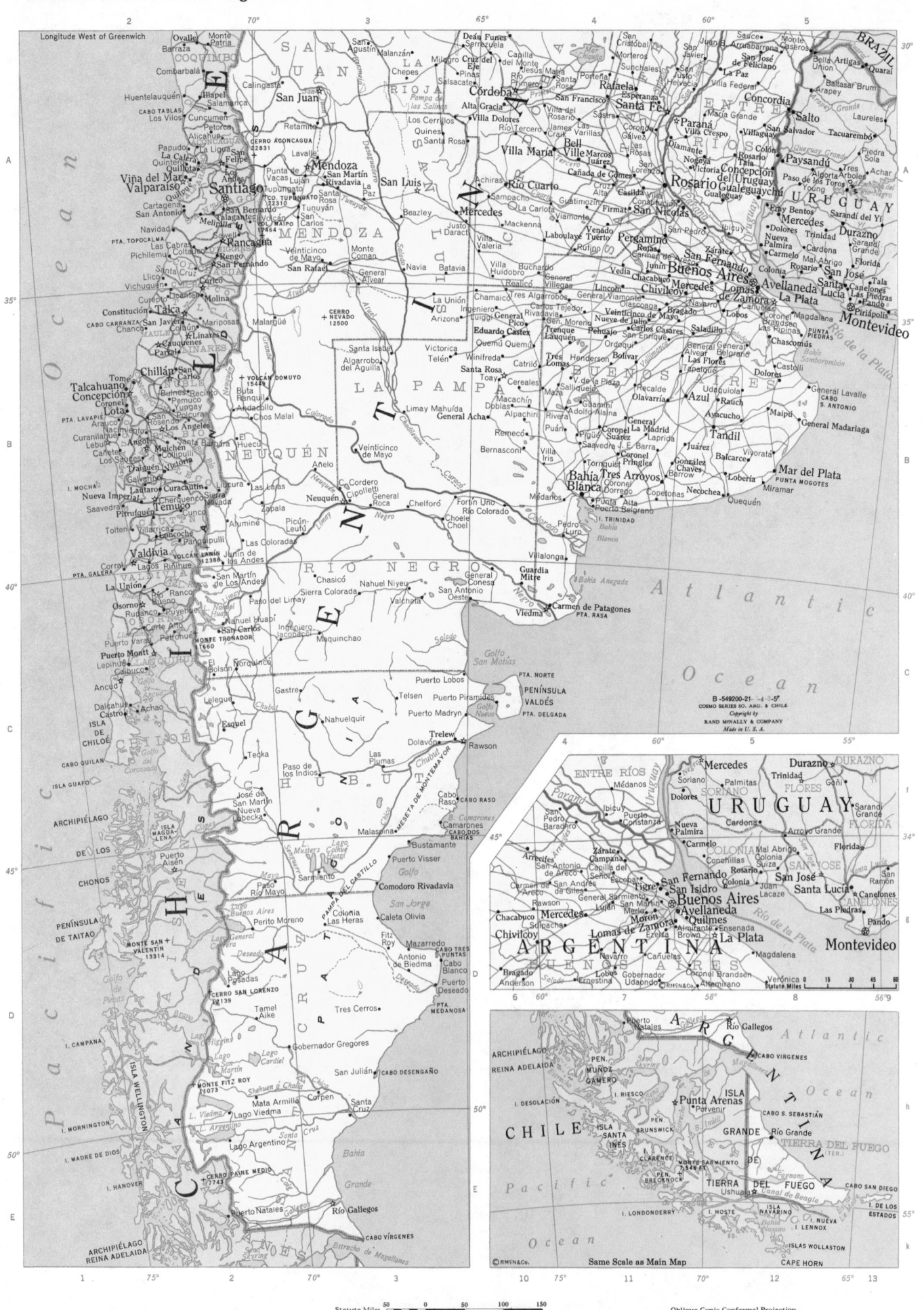

Statute Miles

Kilometers

Oblique Conic Conformal Projection

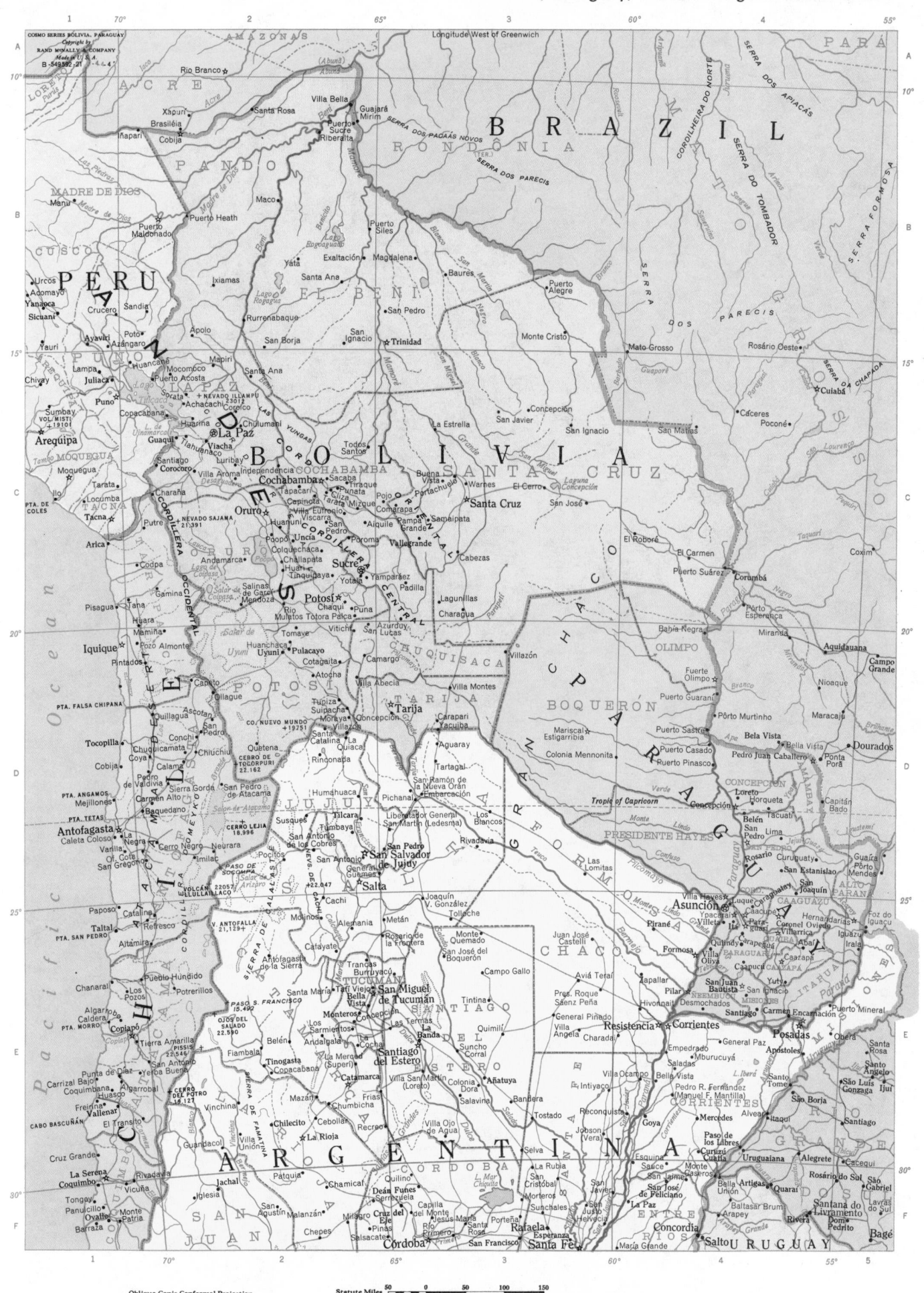

Oblique Conic Conformal Projection

Statute Miles
50   0   50   100   150

Kilometers
50   0   50   100   150   200

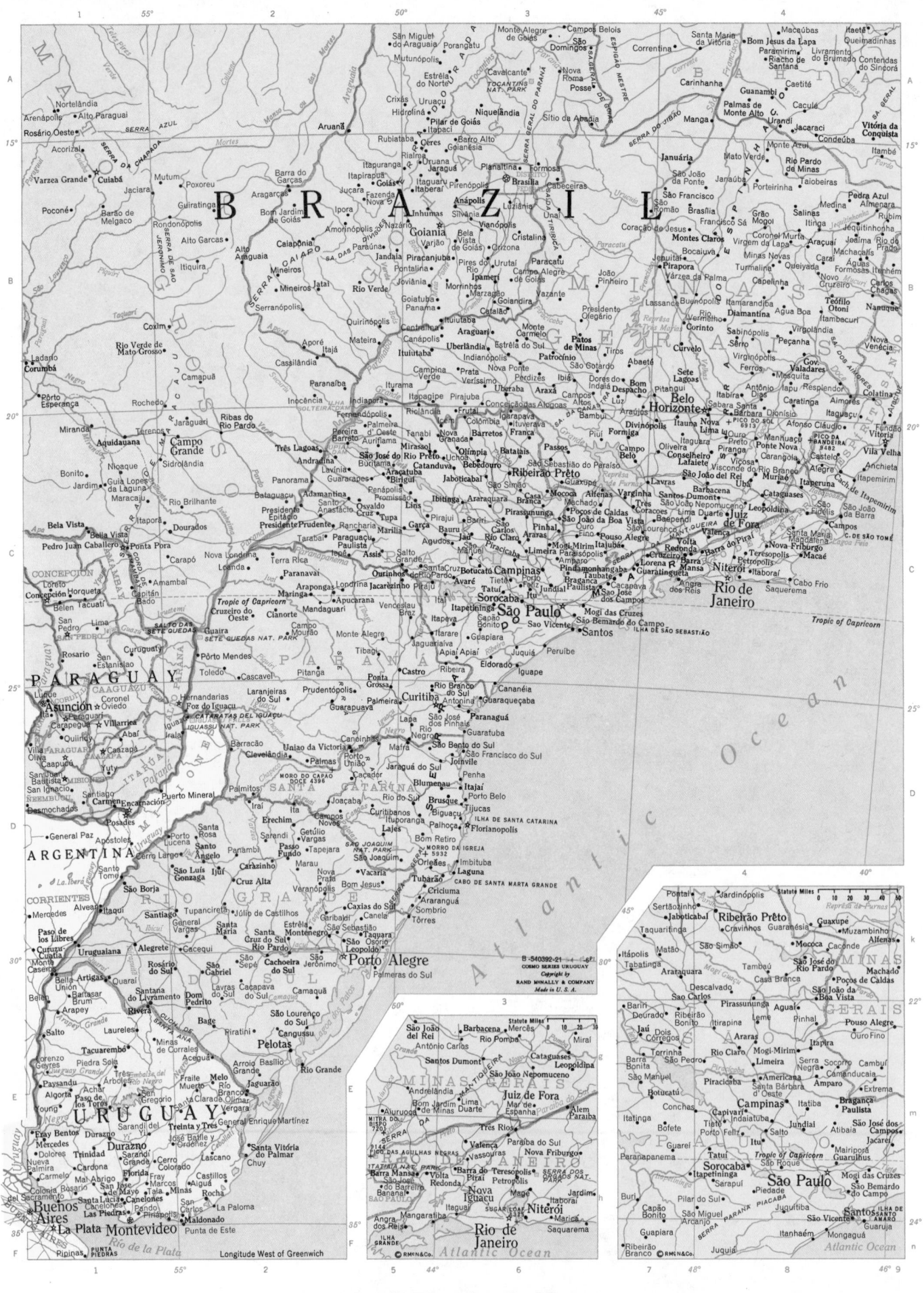

Statute Miles 50 0 50 100 150

Kilometers 50 0 50 100 150 200

Oblique Conic Conformal Projection

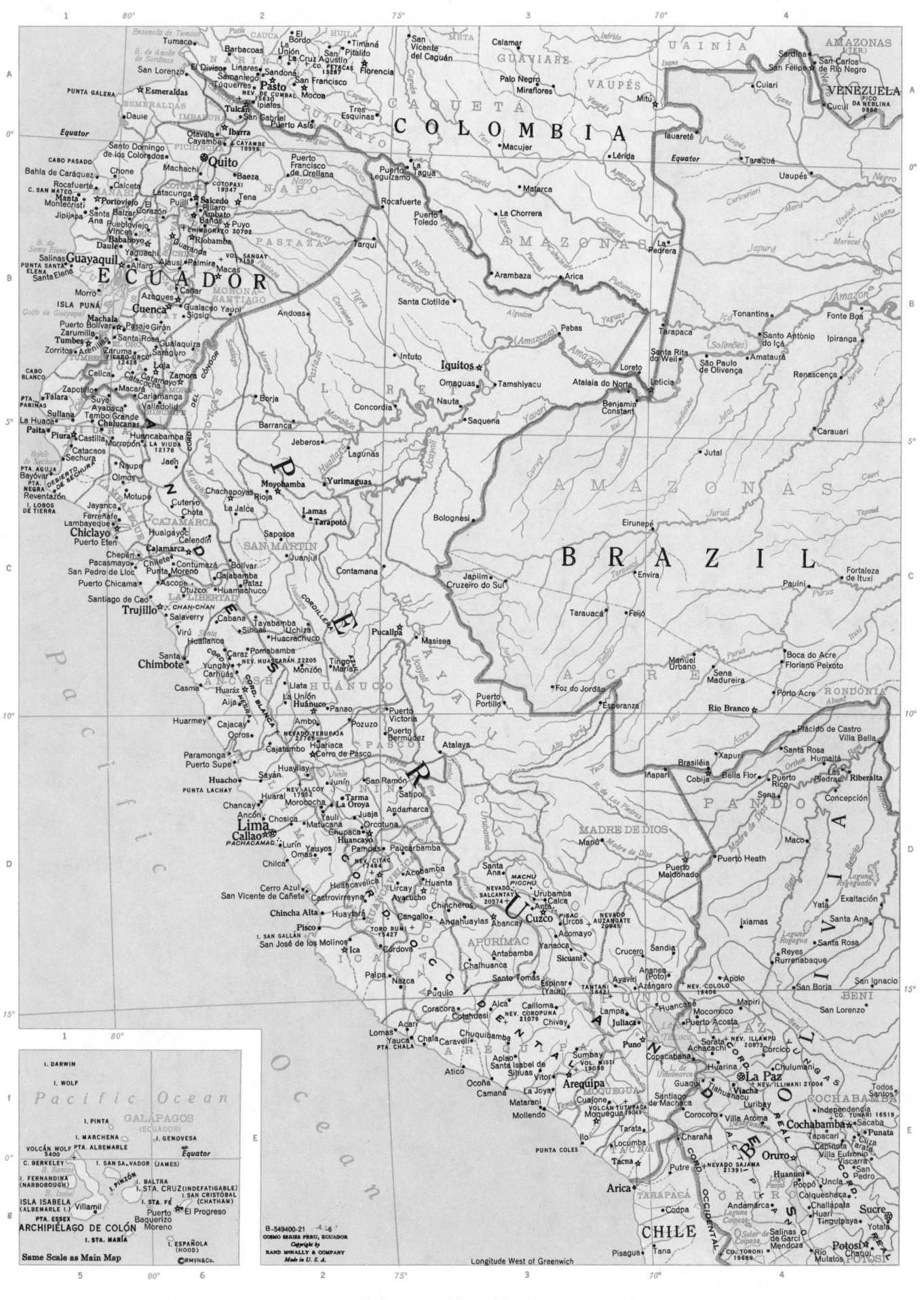

B-549400-21
COSMO SERIES PERU, ECUADOR
Copyright by
RAND McNALLY & COMPANY
Made in U.S.A.

Obliqu Conic Conformal Projection

Longitude West of Greenwich

Statute Miles
50   0   50   100   150

Kilometers
50   0   50   100   150   200

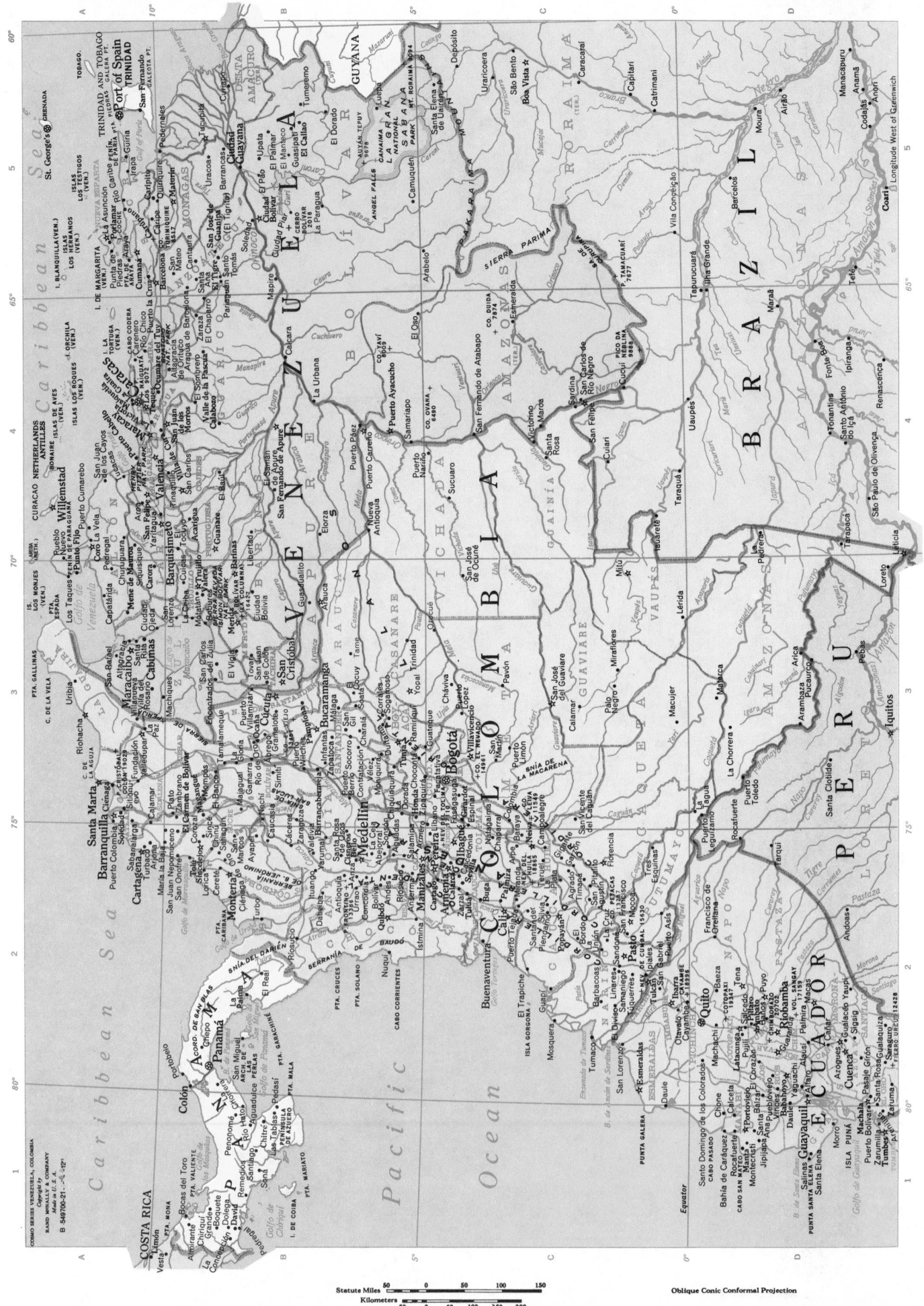

Statute Miles

Kilometers

Oblique Conic Conformal Projection

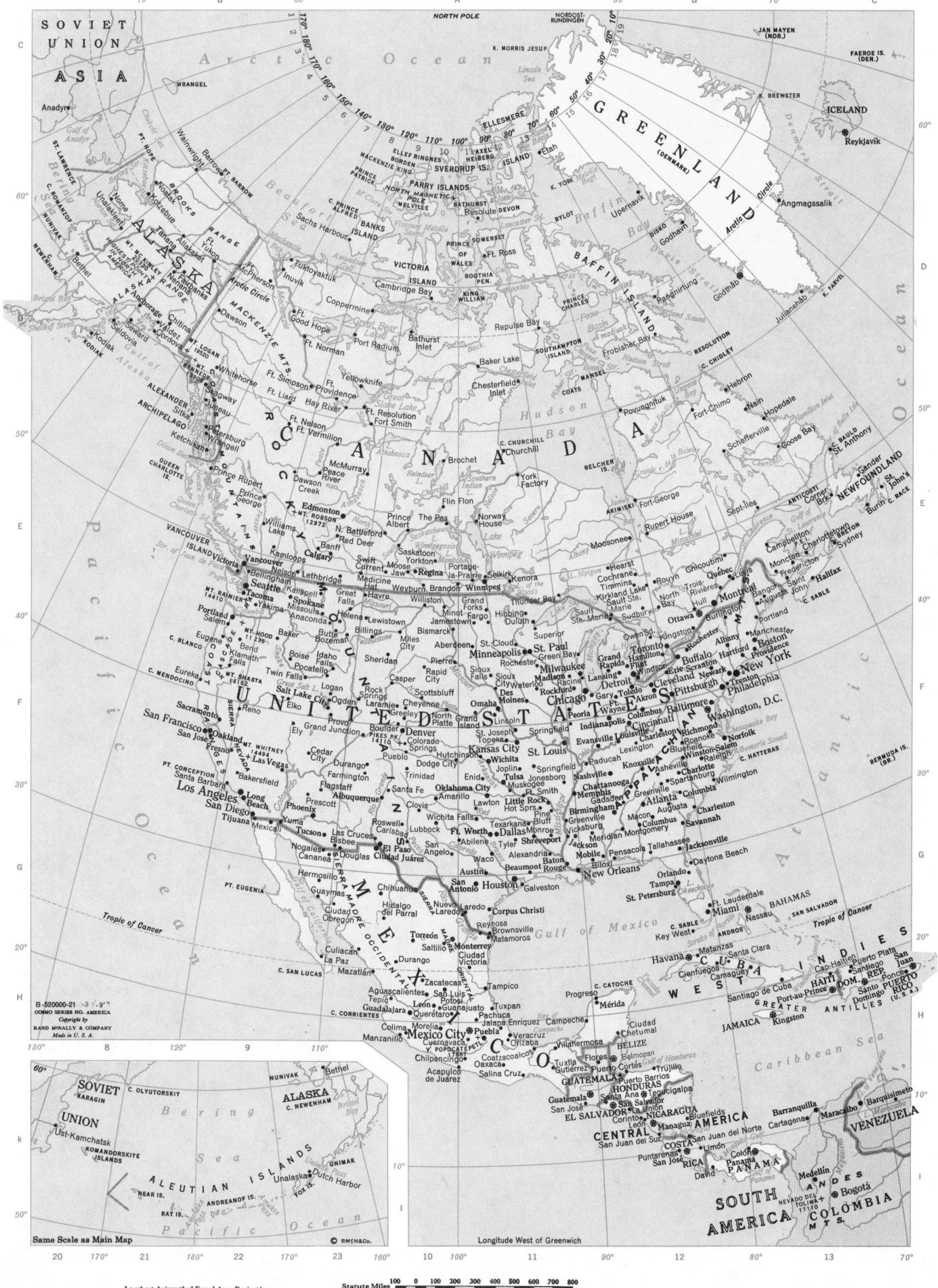

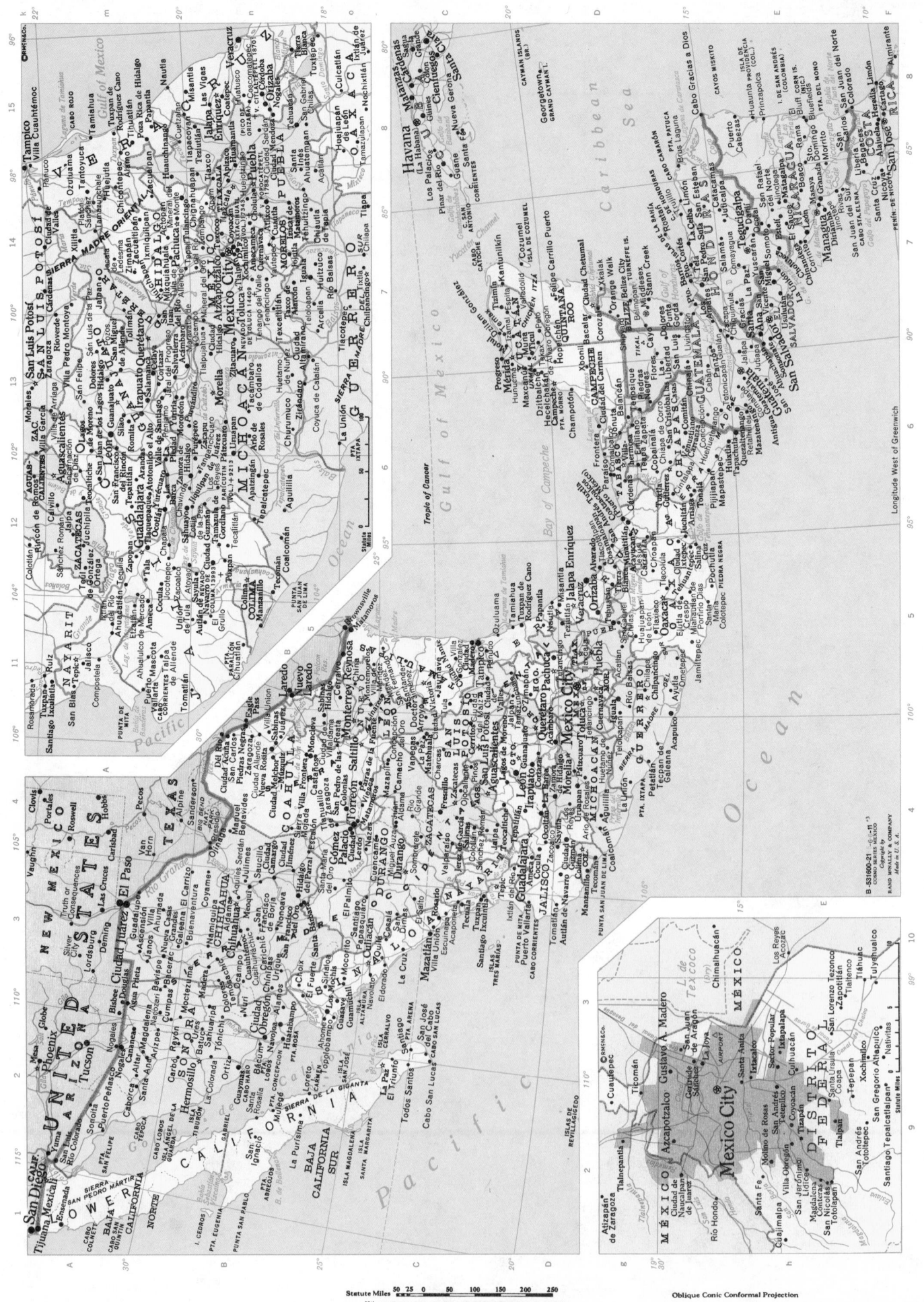

Statute Miles 50 25 0   50   100   150   200   250
Kilometers   50 0   100   200   300

Oblique Conic Conformal Projection

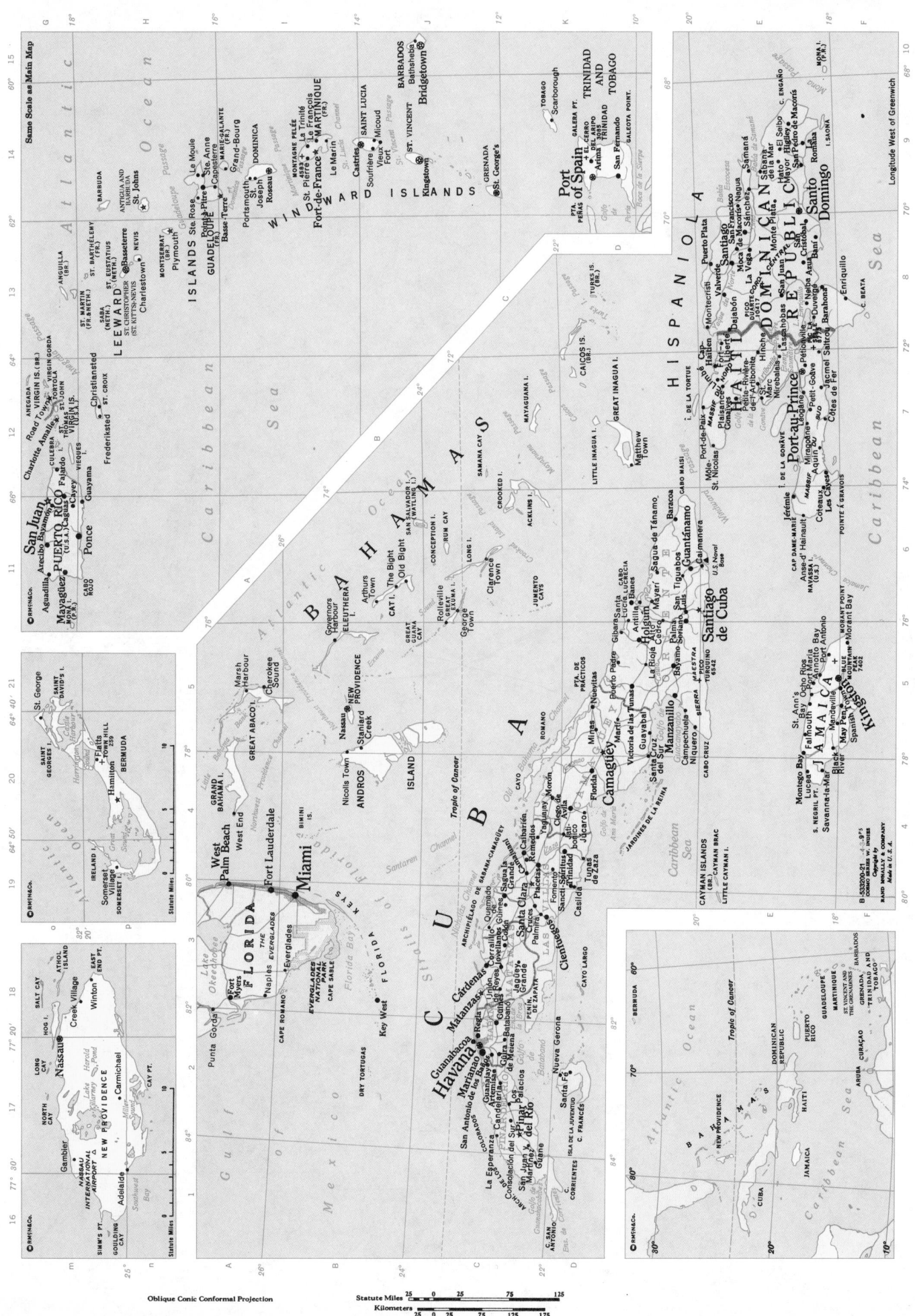

Oblique Conic Conformal Projection

Statute Miles 25 0 25 75 125

Kilometers 25 0 25 75 125 175

Longitude West of Greenwich

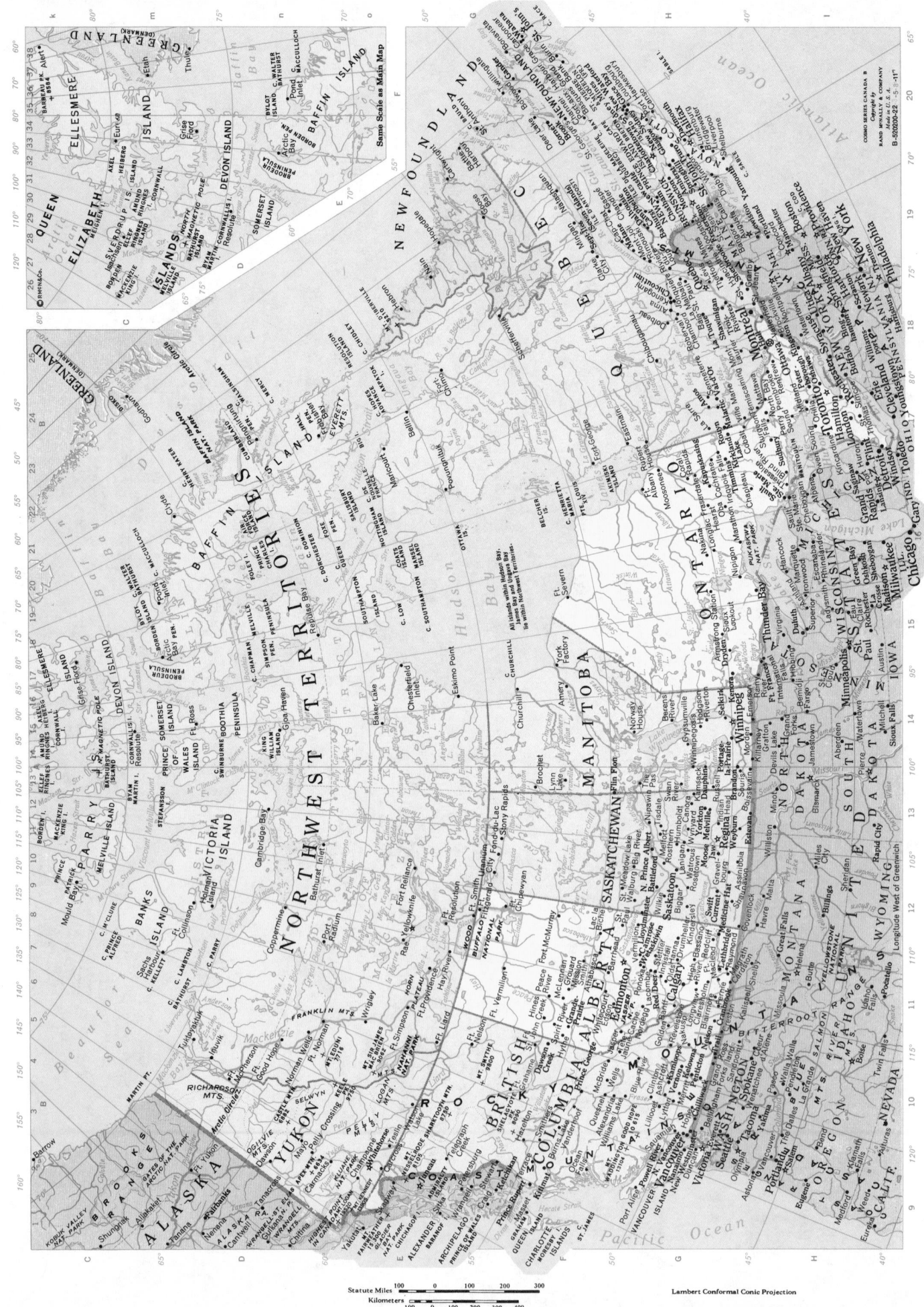

Statute Miles
100   0   100   200   300

Kilometers
100   0   100   200   300   400

Lambert Conformal Conic Projection

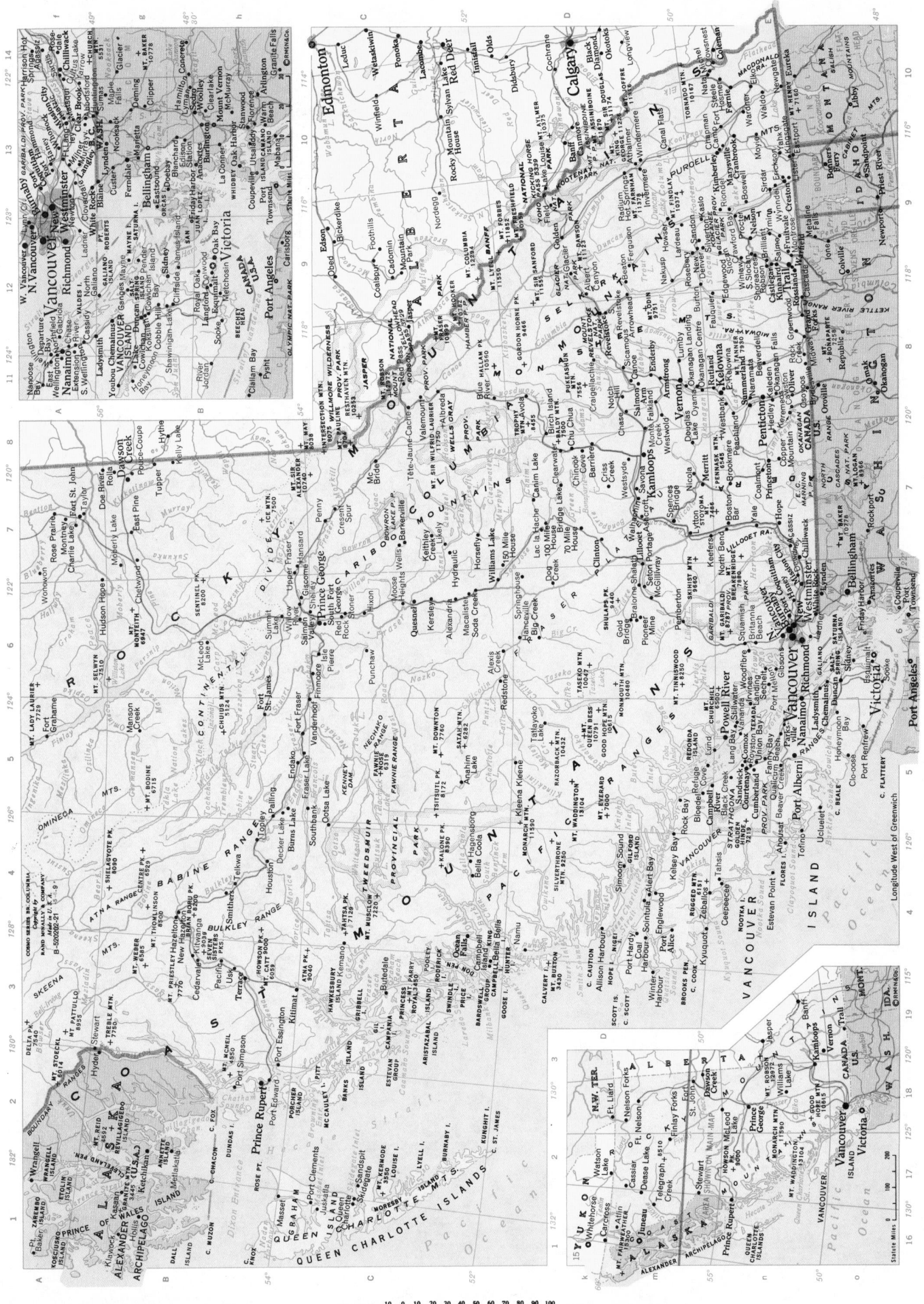

Oblique Cylindrical Projection

Statute Miles 10 0 10 20 30 40 50 60 70 80 90 100

Kilometers 10 0 10 20 40 60 80 100 120 140

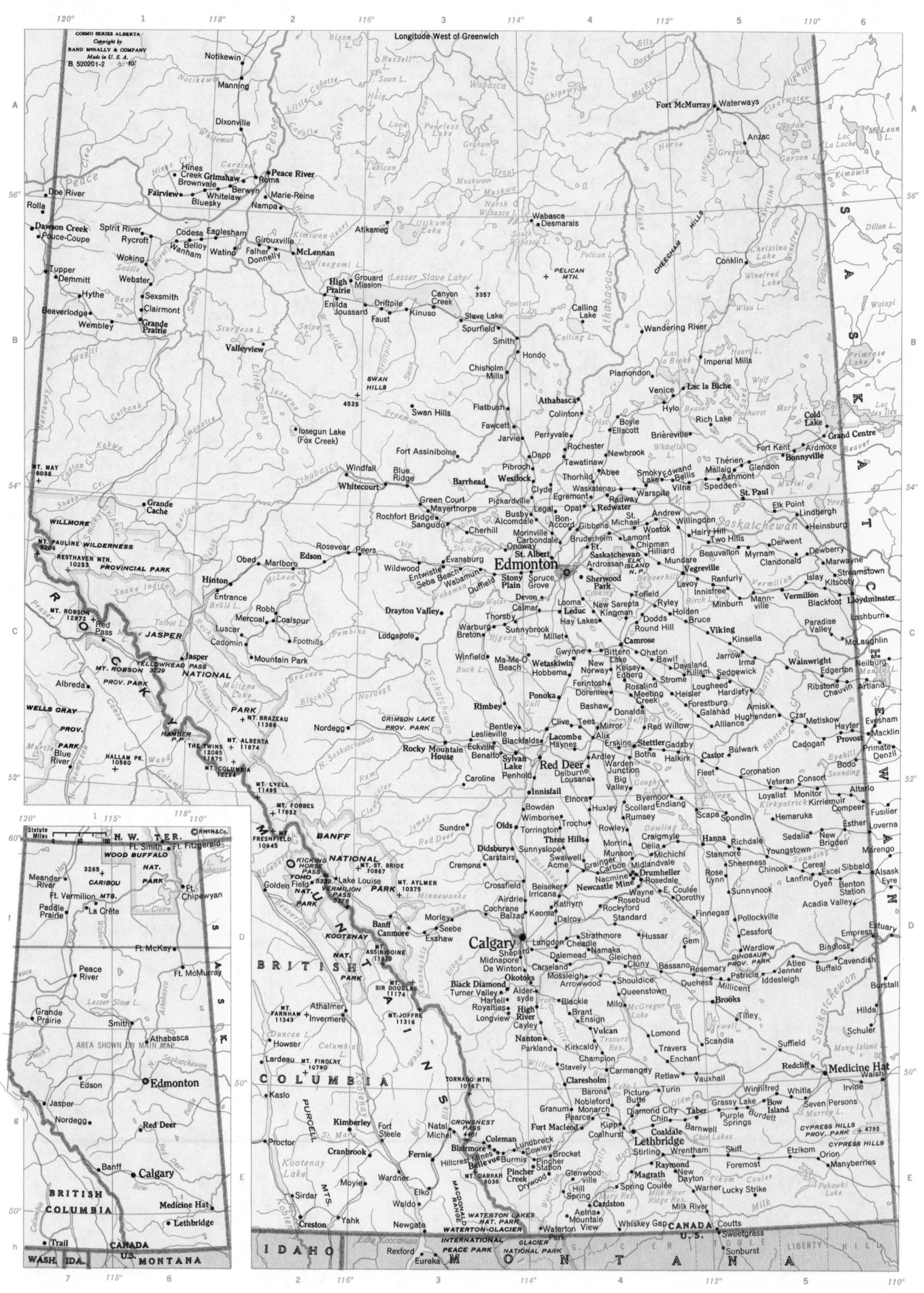

Oblique Cylindrical Projection

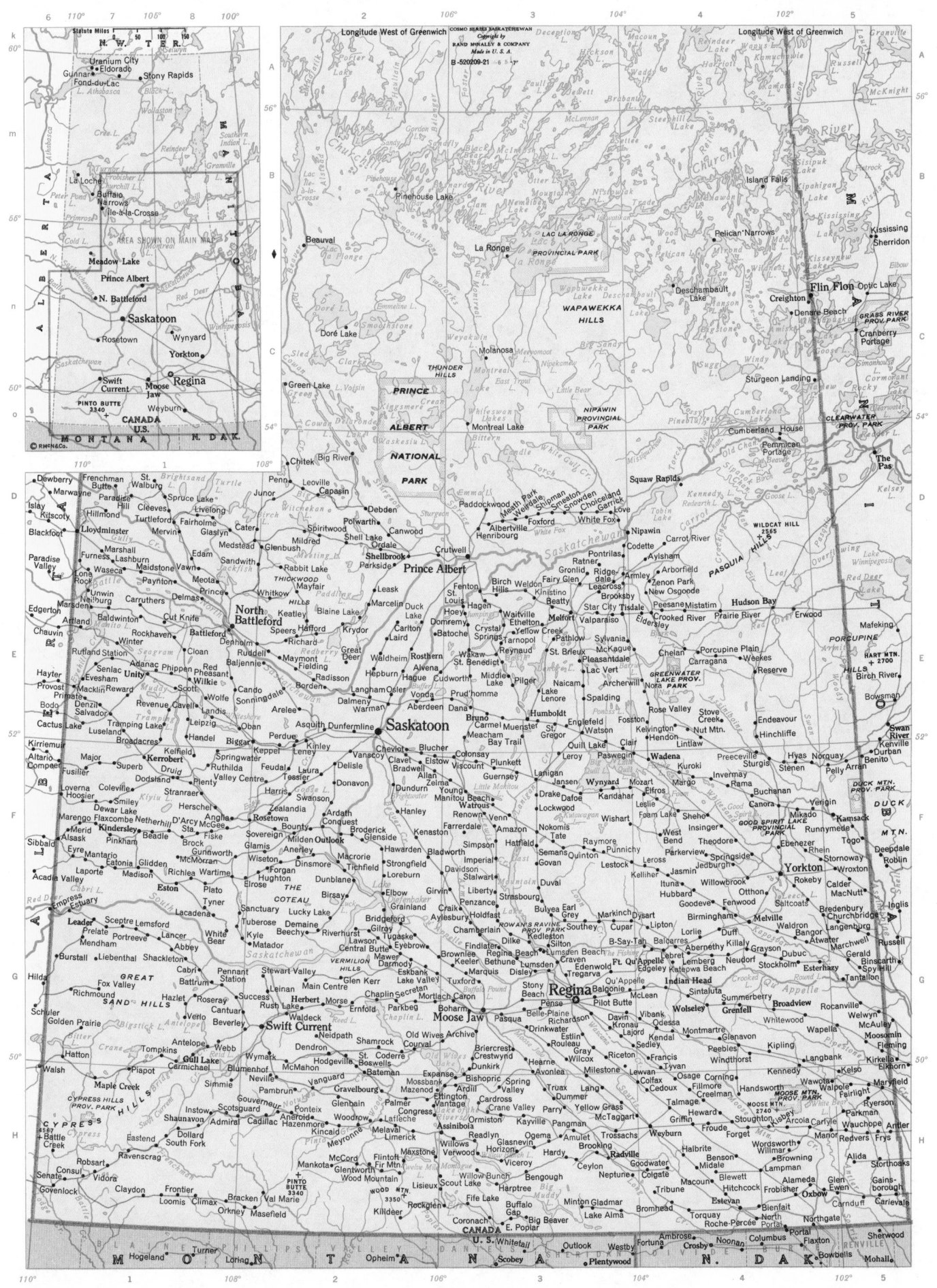

Oblique Cylindrical Projection

Statute Miles

Kilometers

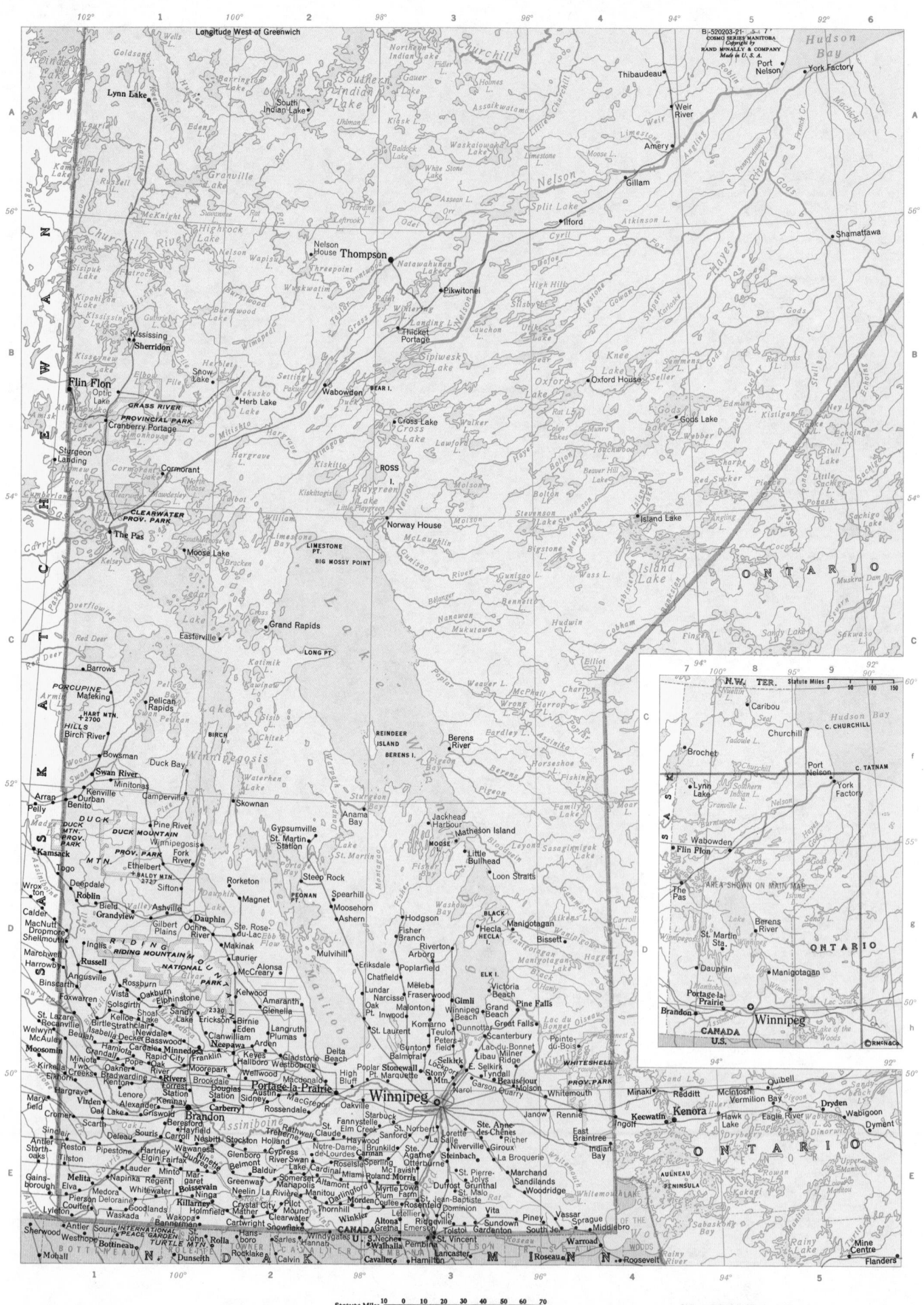

Statute Miles 10 0 10 20 30 40 50 60 70
Kilometers 10 0 10 20 30 40 60 80 100

Oblique Cylindrical Projection

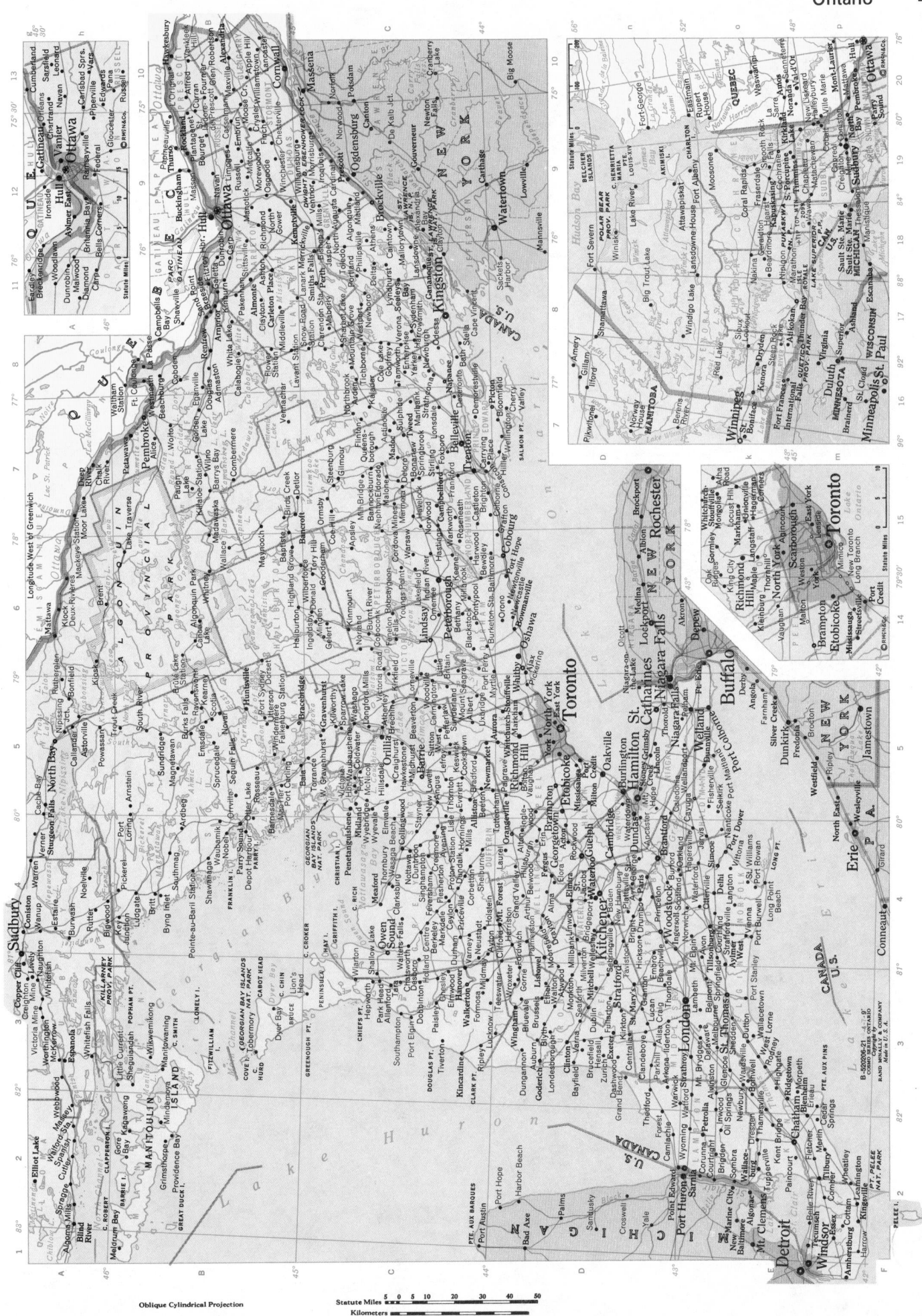

Oblique Cylindrical Projection

Statute Miles

Kilometers

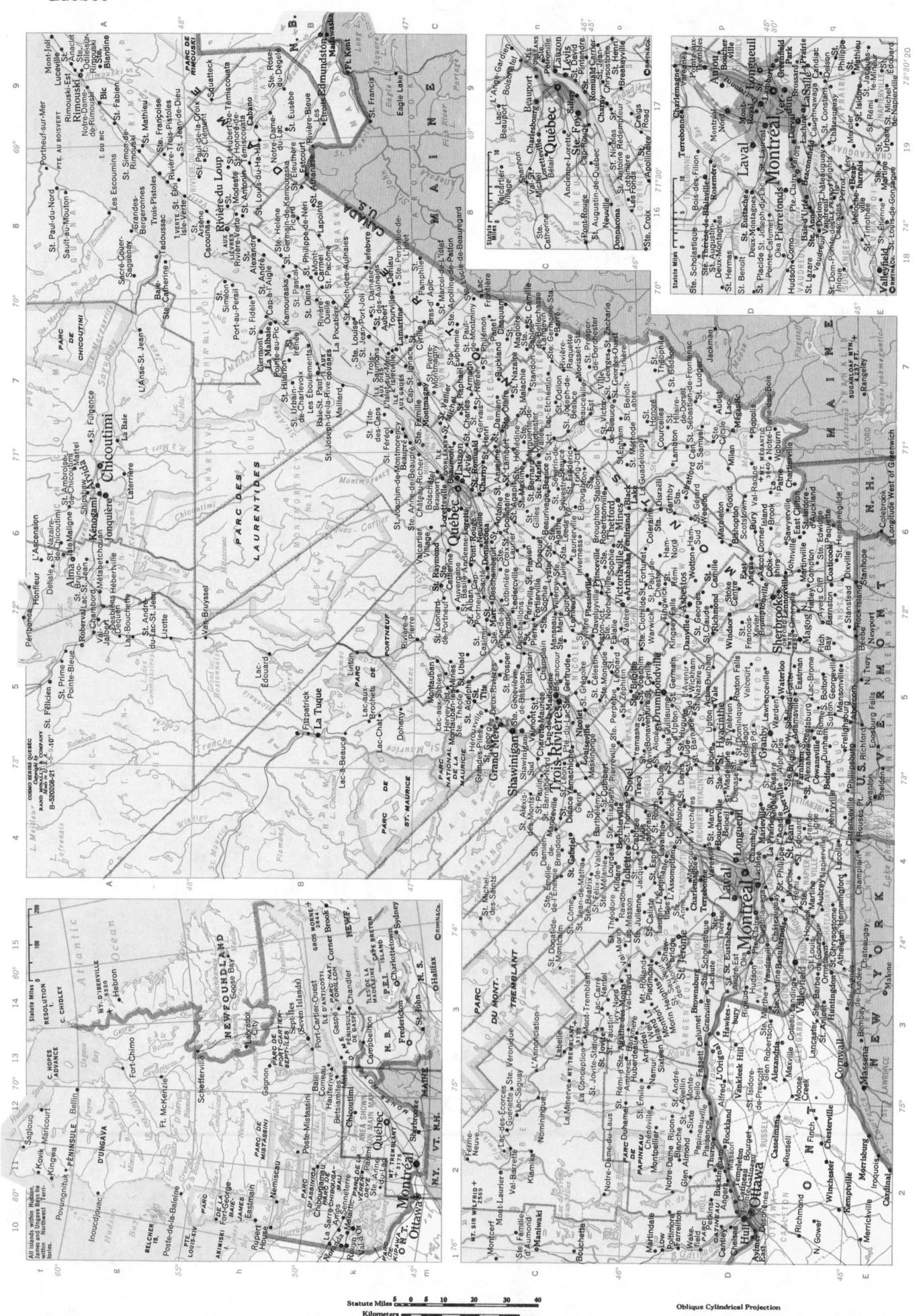

Statute Miles 5 0 5 10 20 30 40
Kilometers 5 0 5 15 25 35 45 55

Oblique Cylindrical Projection

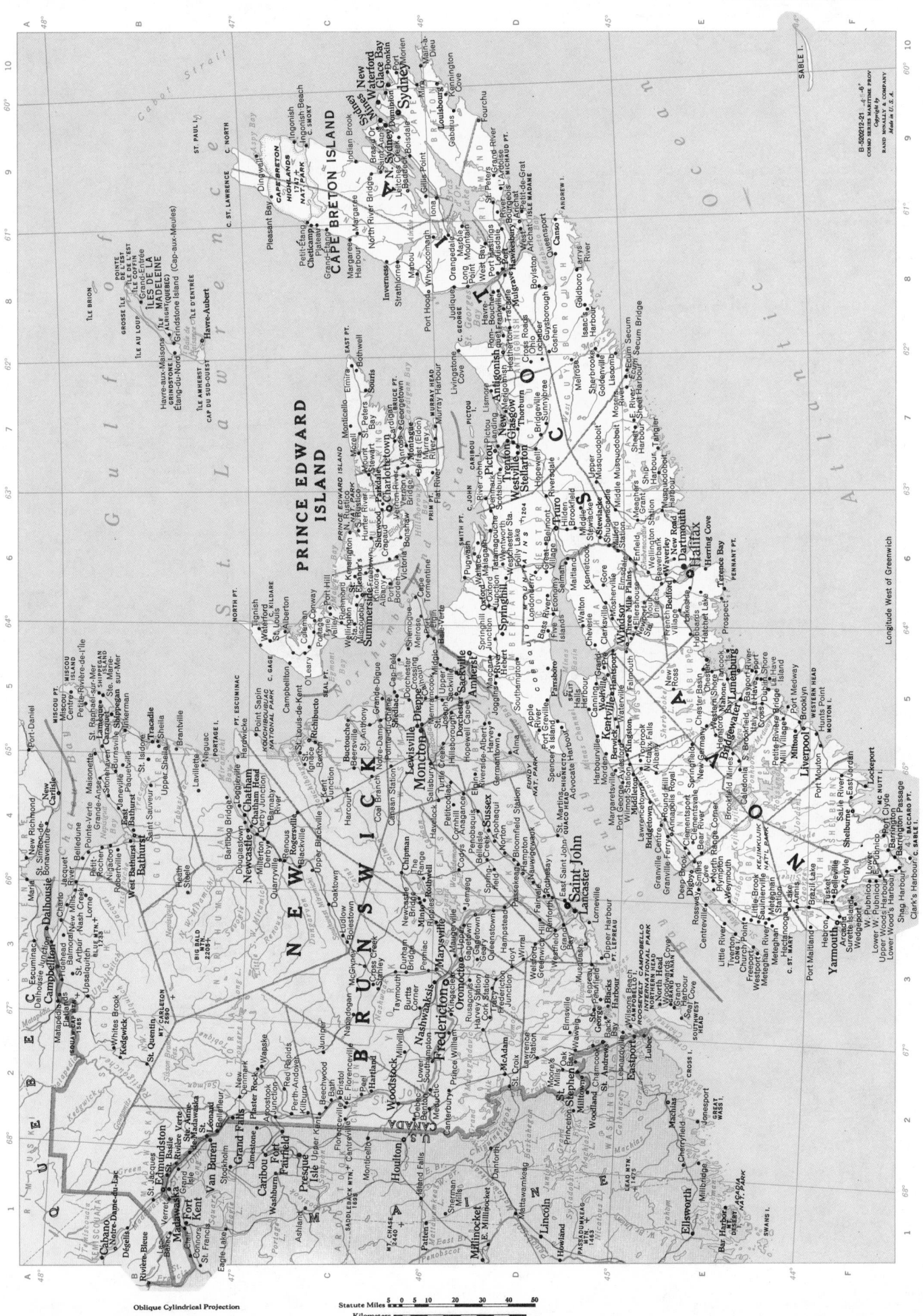

Oblique Cylindrical Projection

Statute Miles

Kilometers

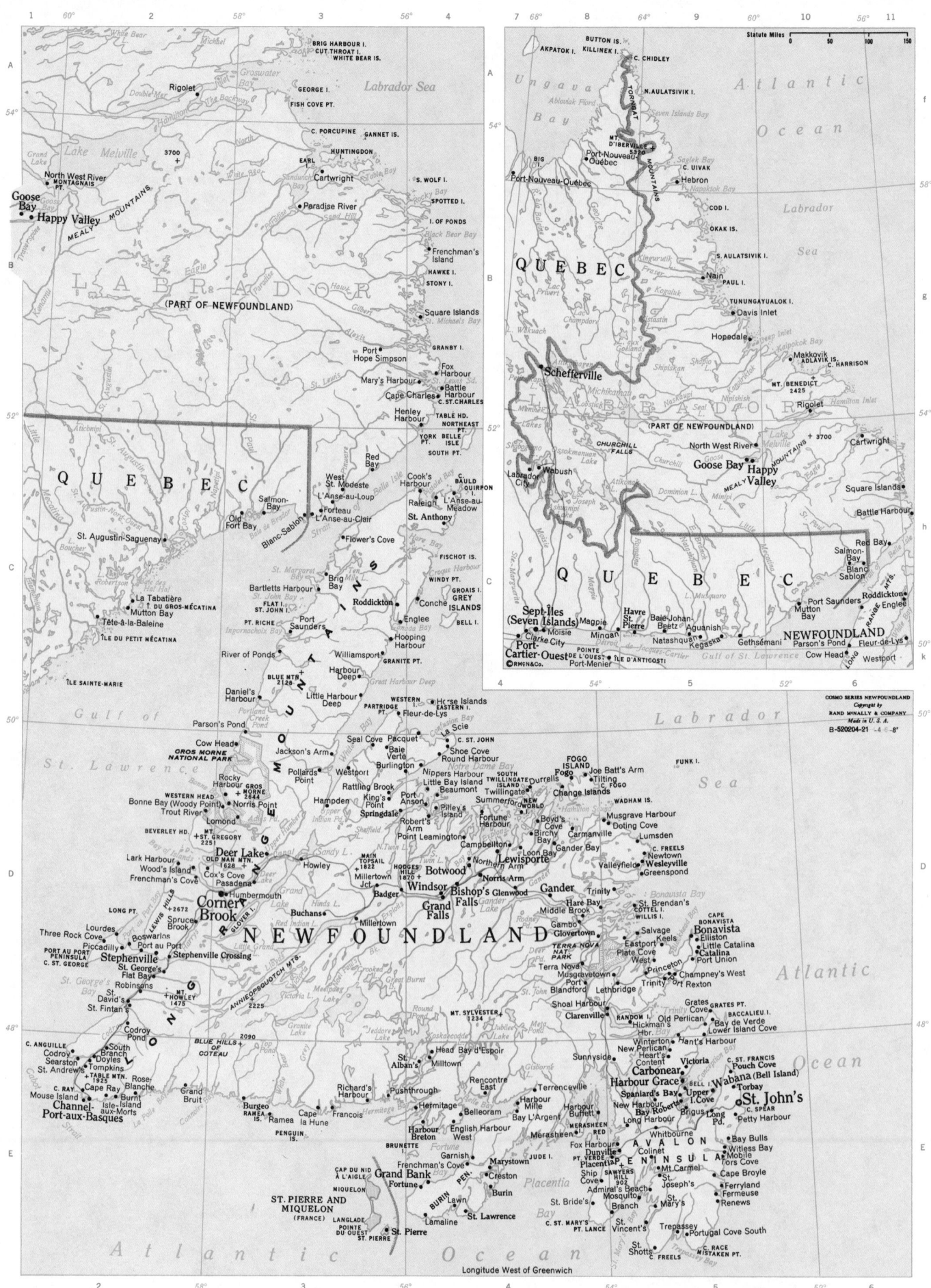

Lambert Conformal Conic Projection

Statute Miles
Kilometers

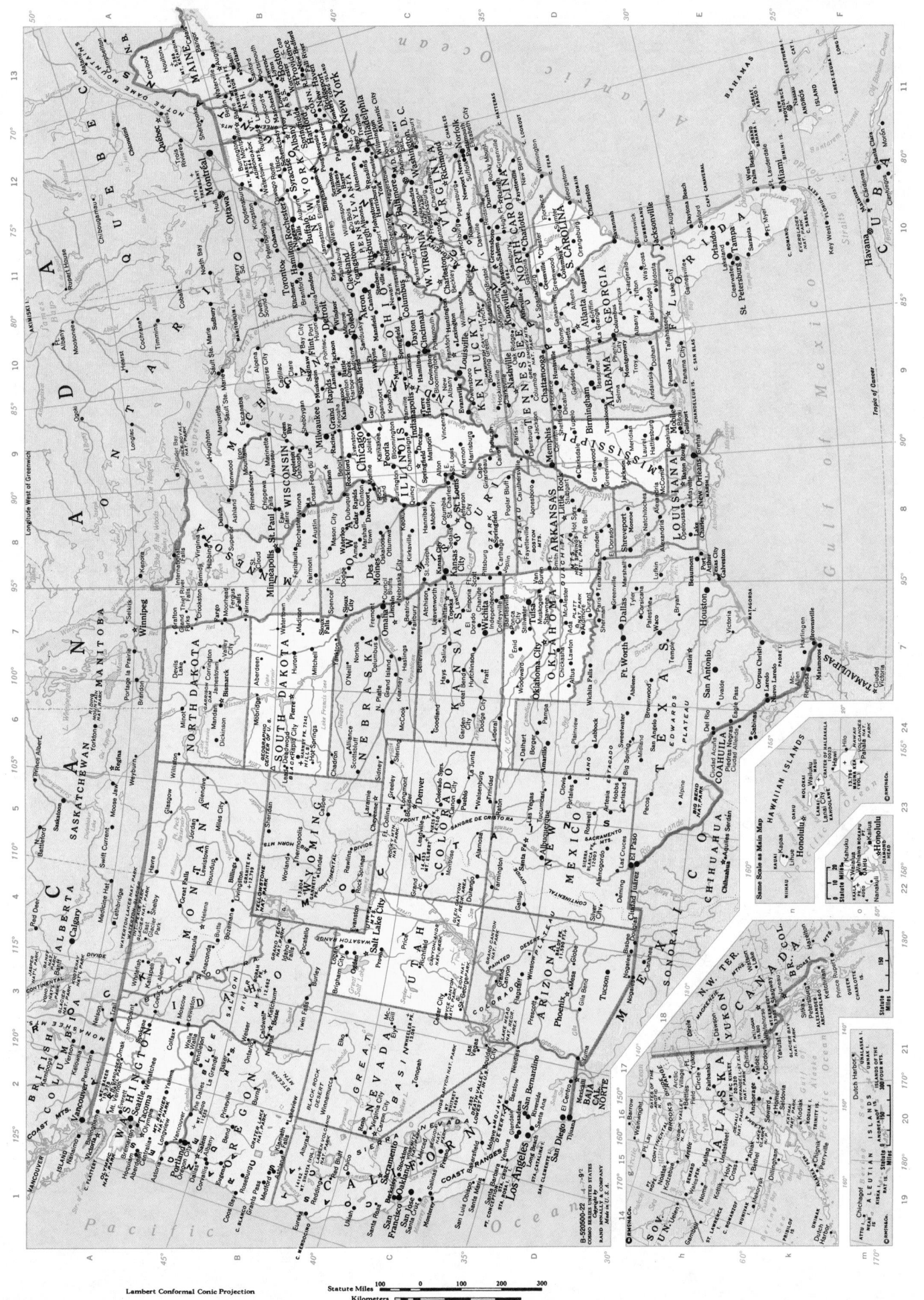

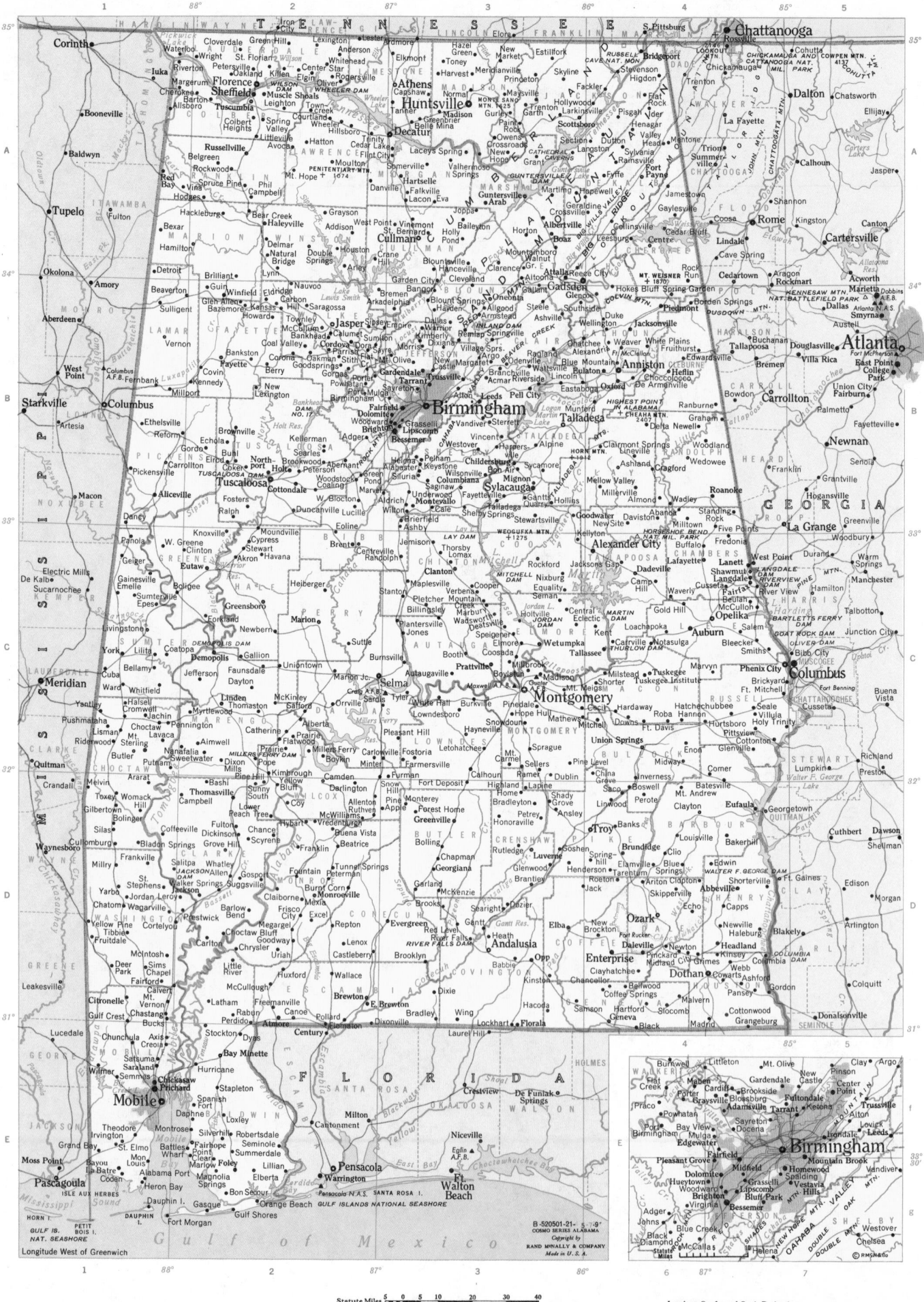

Statute Miles

Kilometers

Lambert Conformal Conic Projection

B-520501-21-
COSMO SERIES ALABAMA
Copyright by
RAND McNALLY & COMPANY
Made in U.S.A.

Longitude West of Greenwich

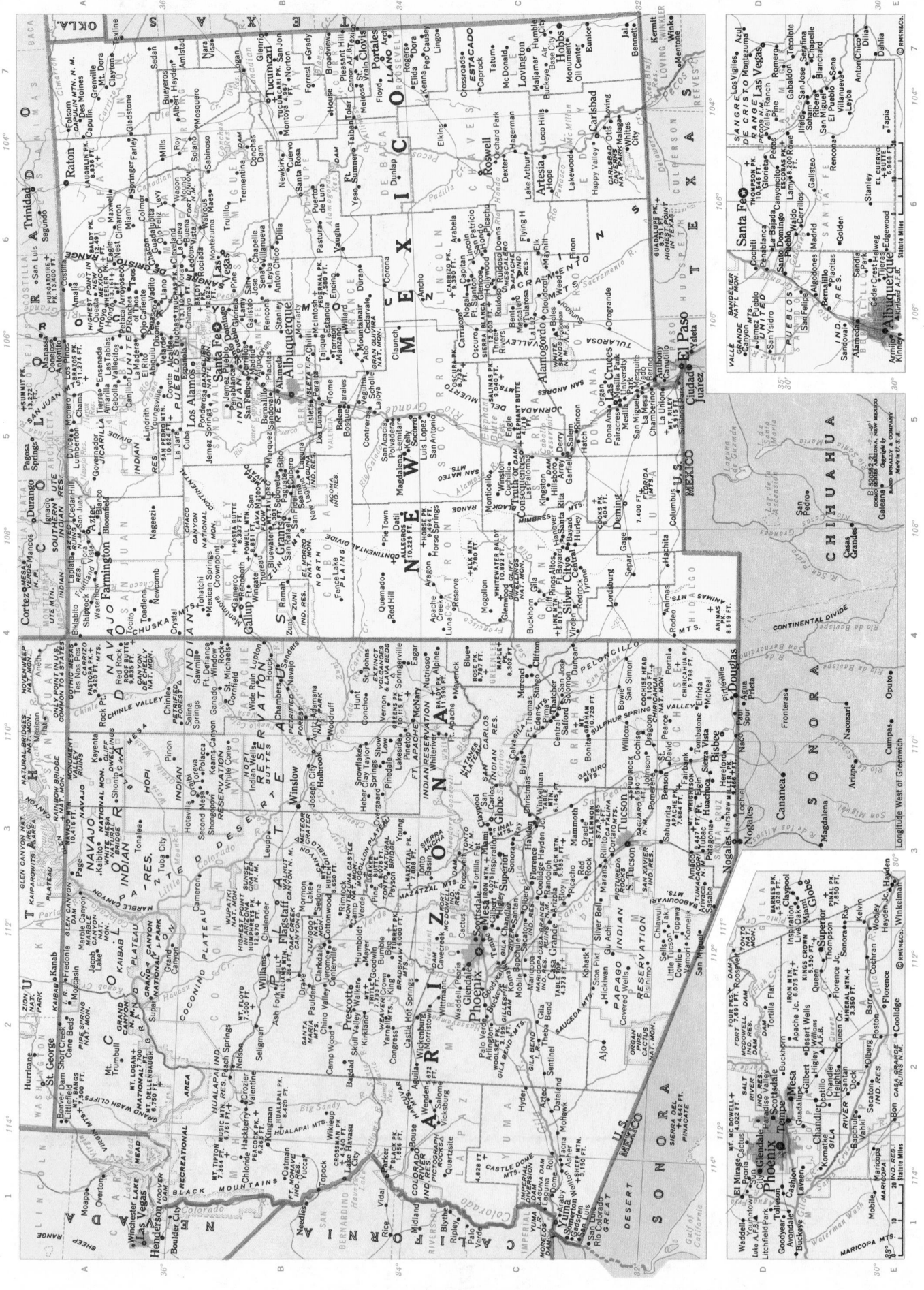

Statute Miles 10 0 10 20 30 40 50 60 70 80 90

Kilometers 10 0 10 20 40 60 80 100 120

Lambert Conformal Conic Projection

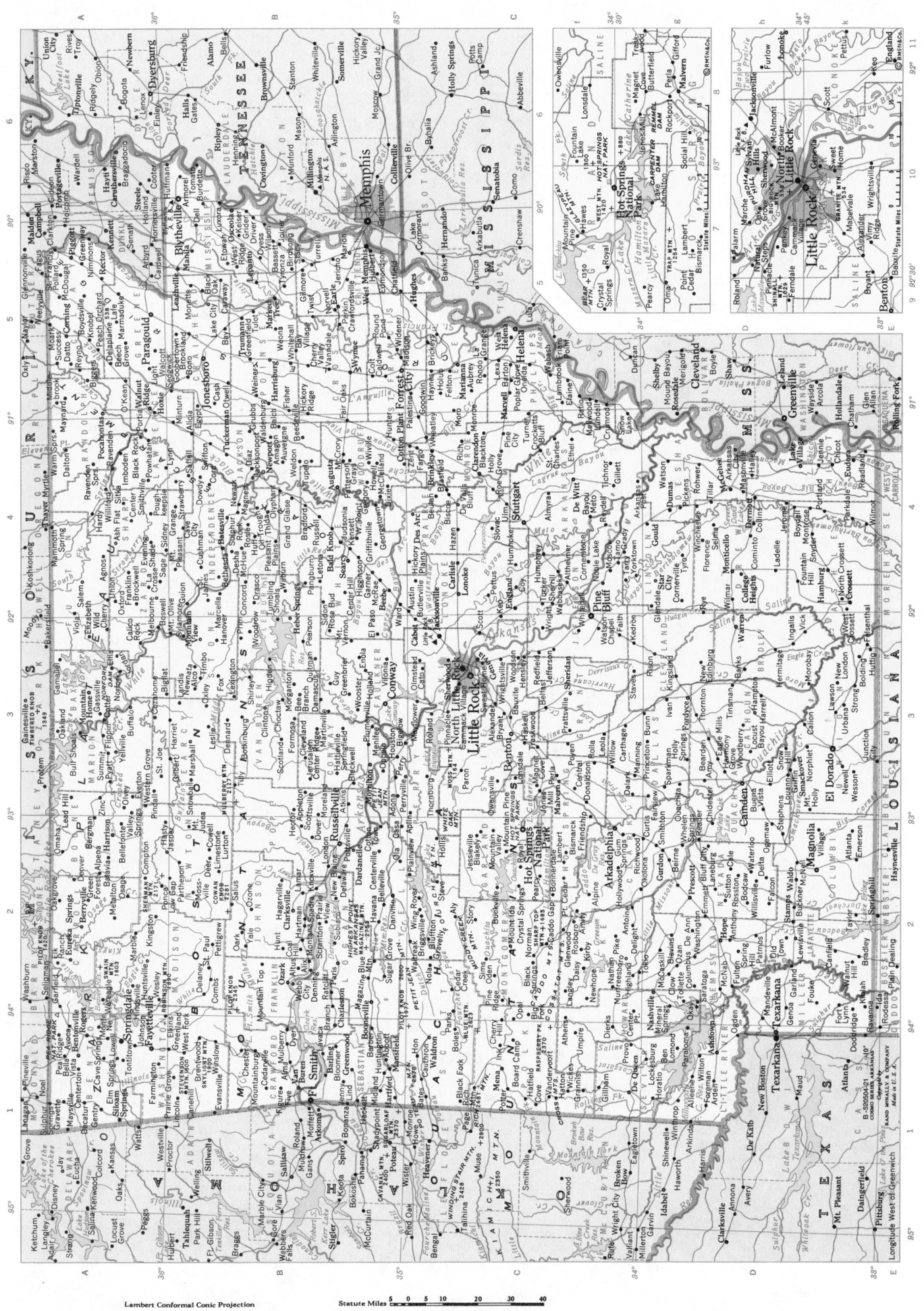

Statute Miles

Kilometers

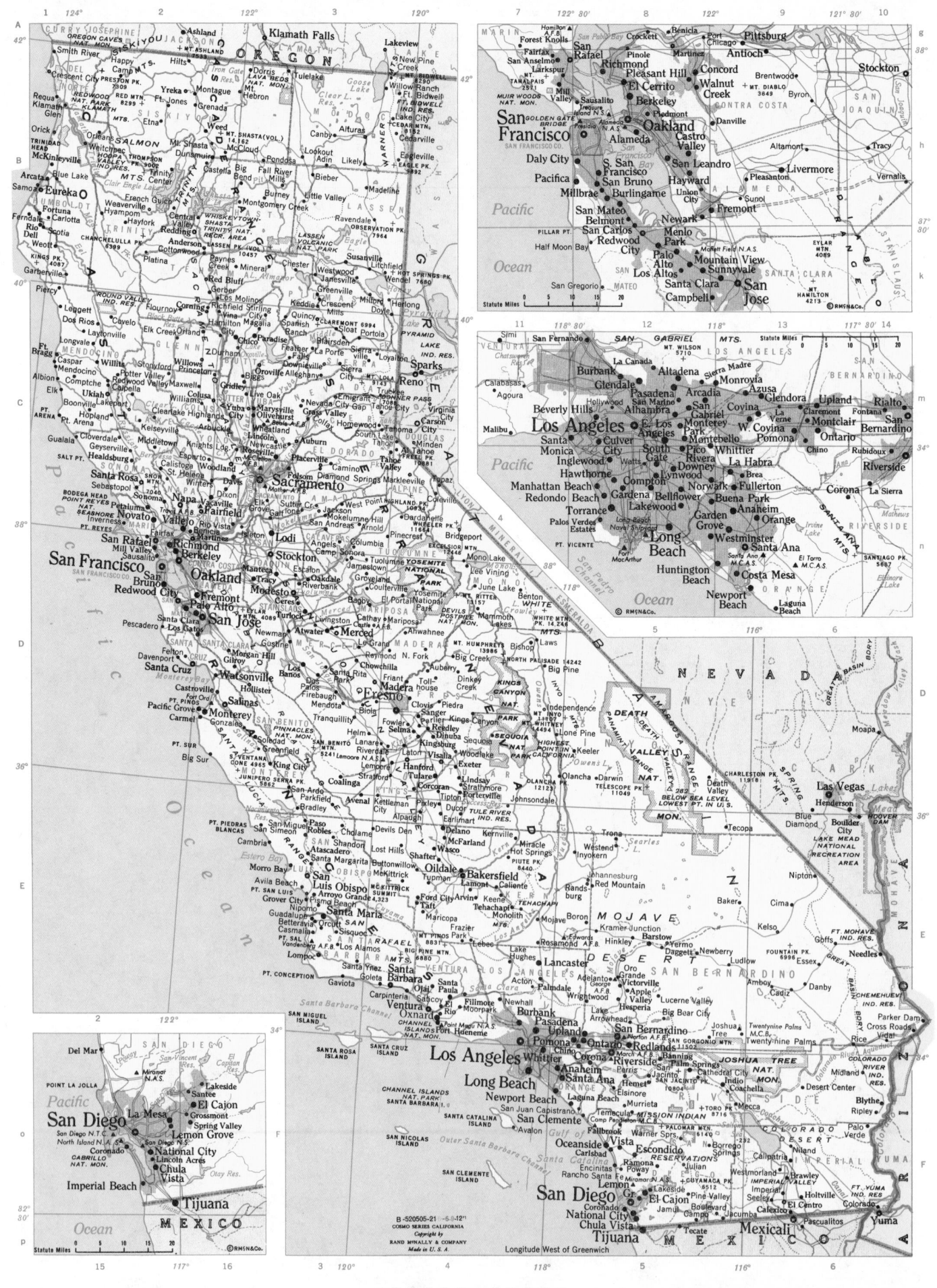

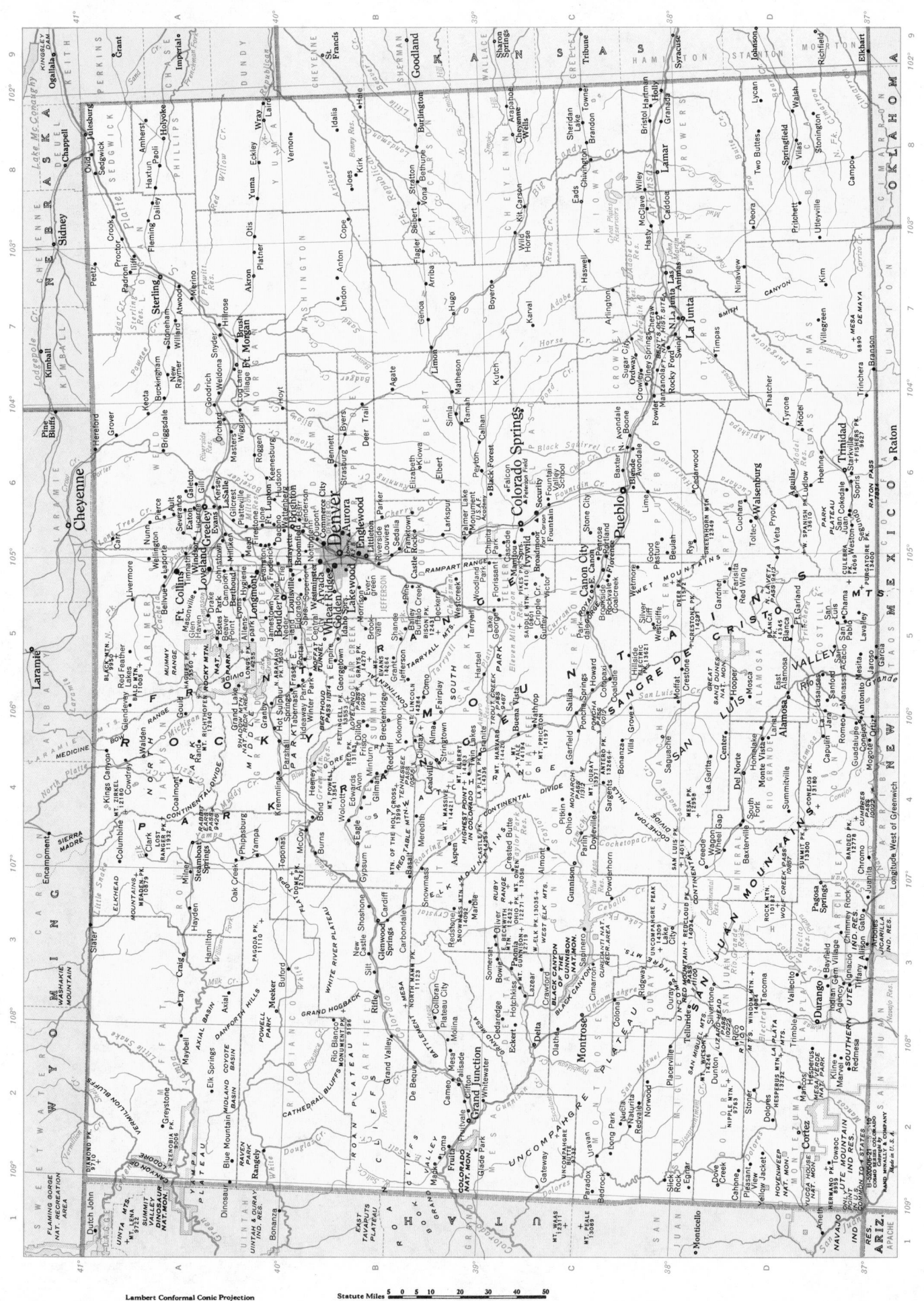

Lambert Conformal Conic Projection

Statute Miles 5 0 5 10 20 30 40 50

Kilometers 5 0 5 15 25 35 45 55 65 75

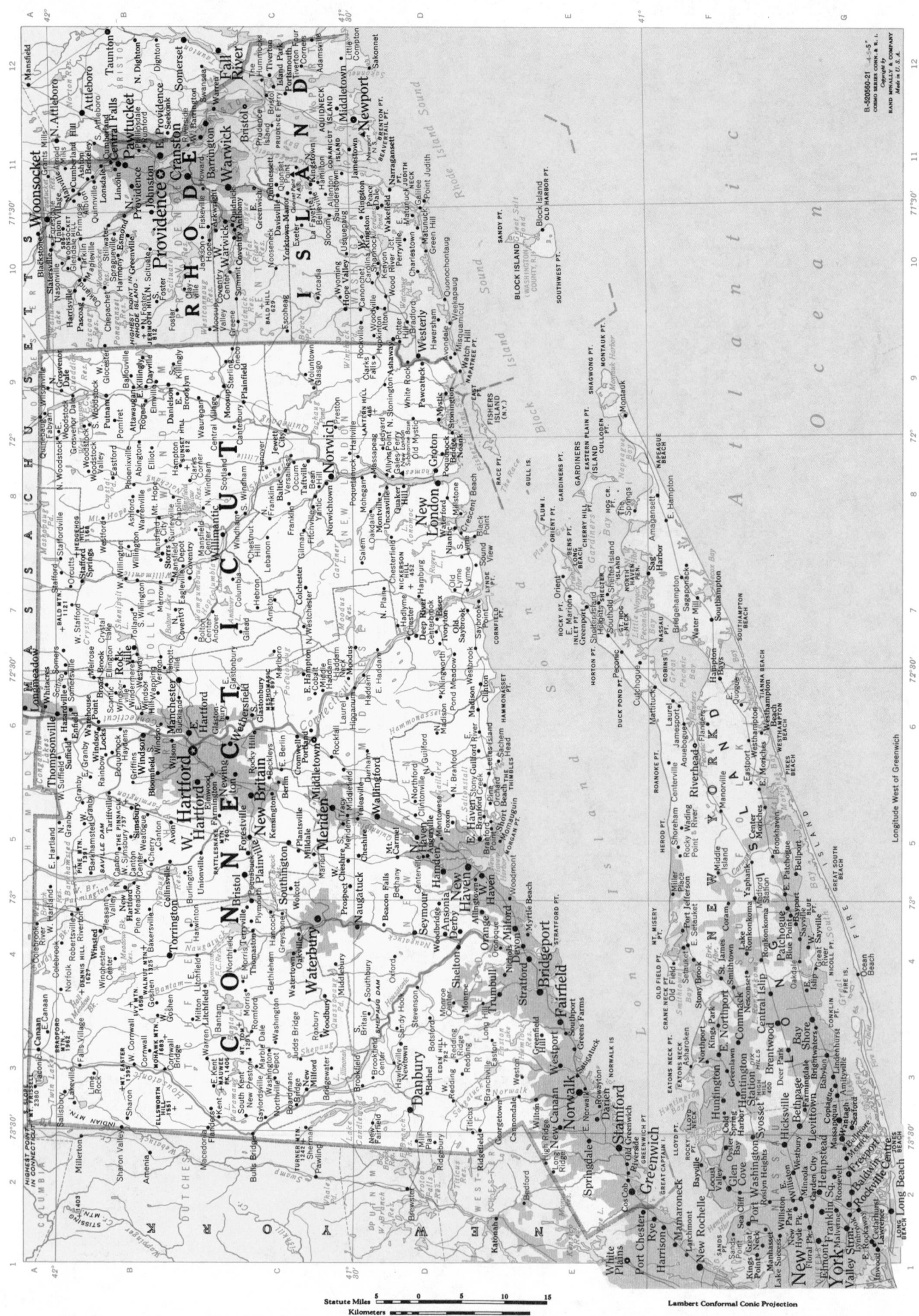

Statute Miles 5   0   5   10   15

Kilometers 5   0   5   10   15   20

Lambert Conformal Conic Projection

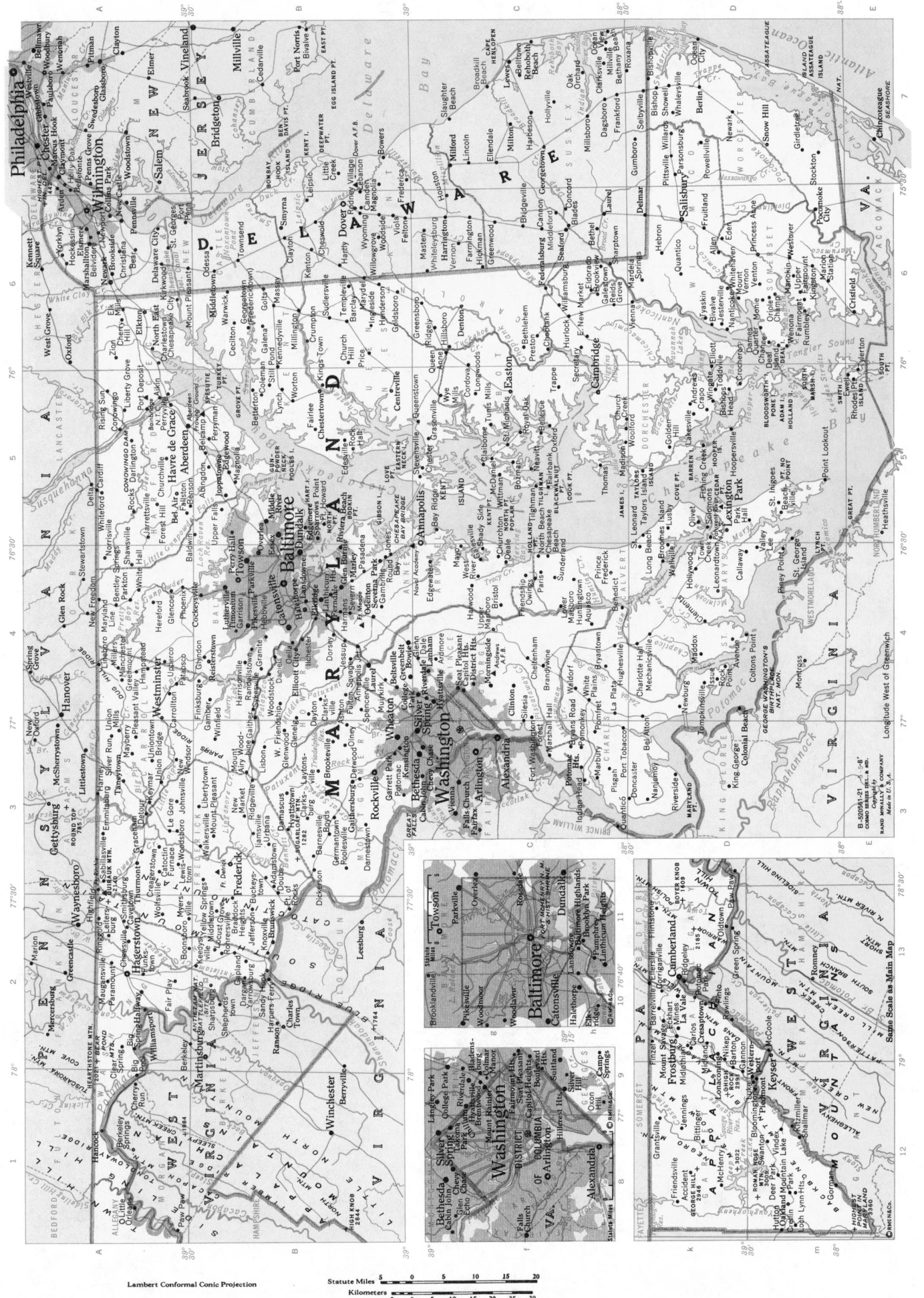

Lambert Conformal Conic Projection

Statute Miles 5 0 5 10 15 20

Kilometers 5 0 5 10 15 20 25 30

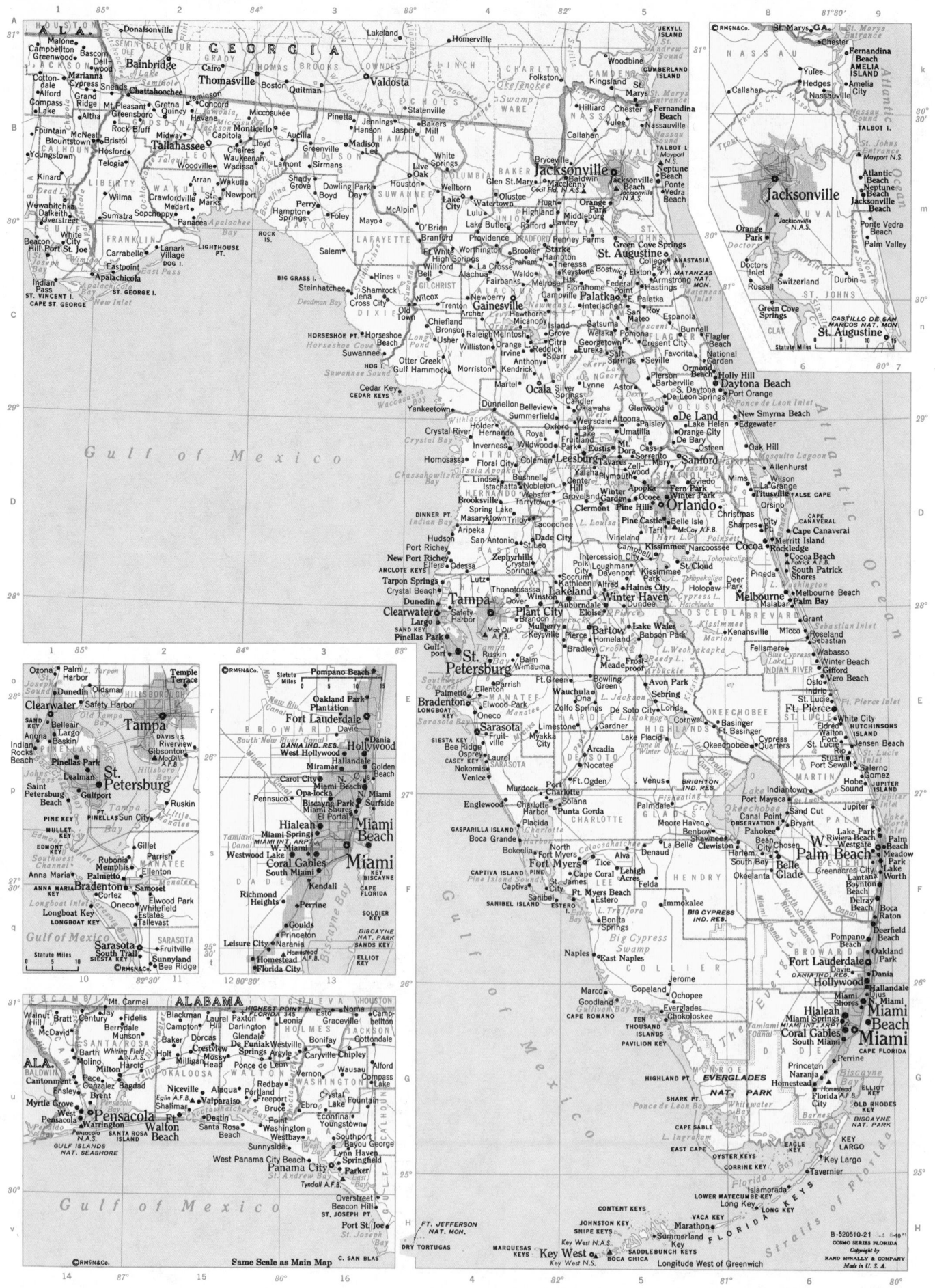

Statute Miles 5 0 5 10 20 30 40 50
Kilometers 5 0 5 15 25 35 45 55 65

Lambert Conformal Conic Projection

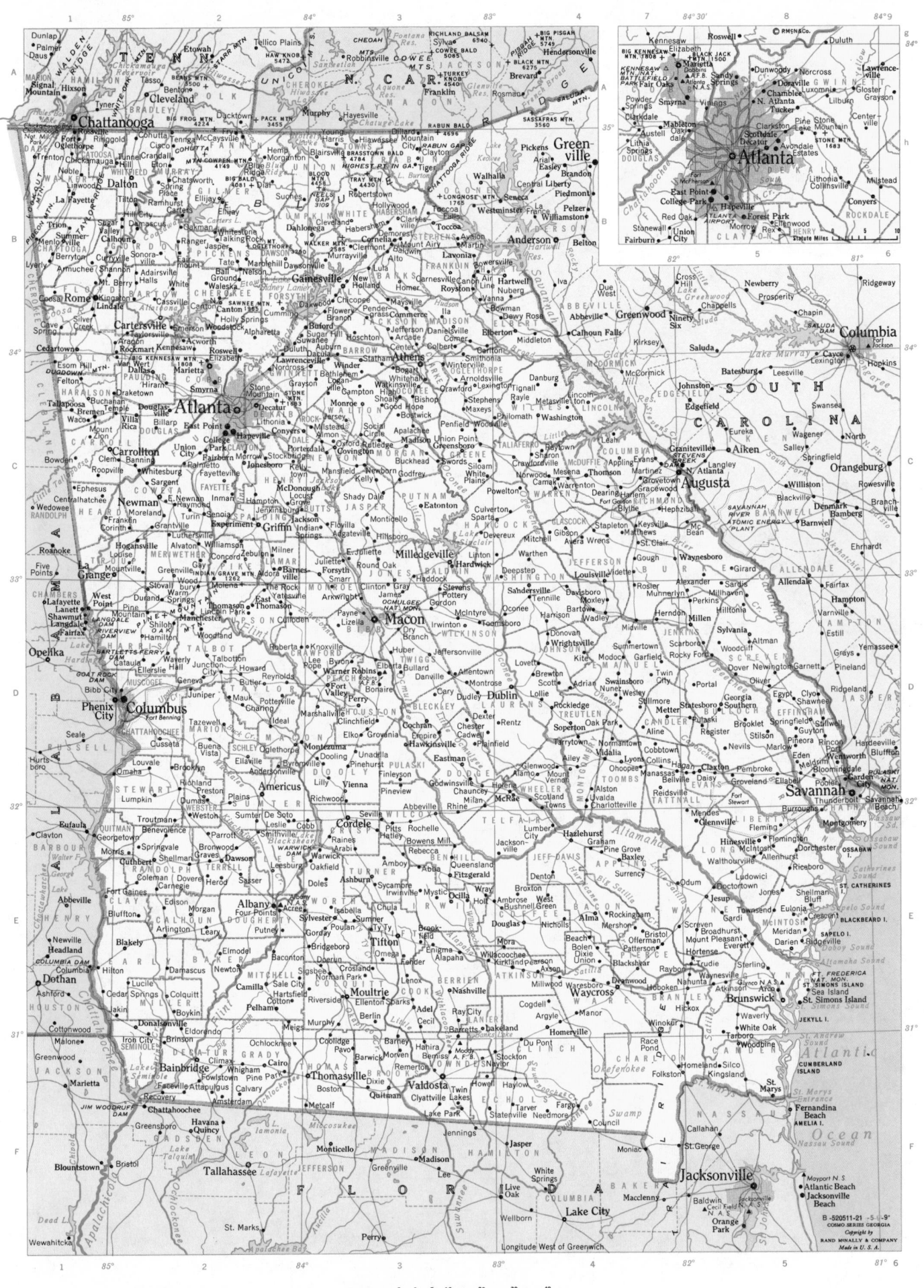

Statute Miles
5 0 5 10 20 30 40

Kilometers
5 0 5 15 25 35 45 55

B-520511-21 -5 -9°

COSMO SERIES GEORGIA

Copyright by
RAND M℡NALLY & COMPANY
Made in U.S.A.

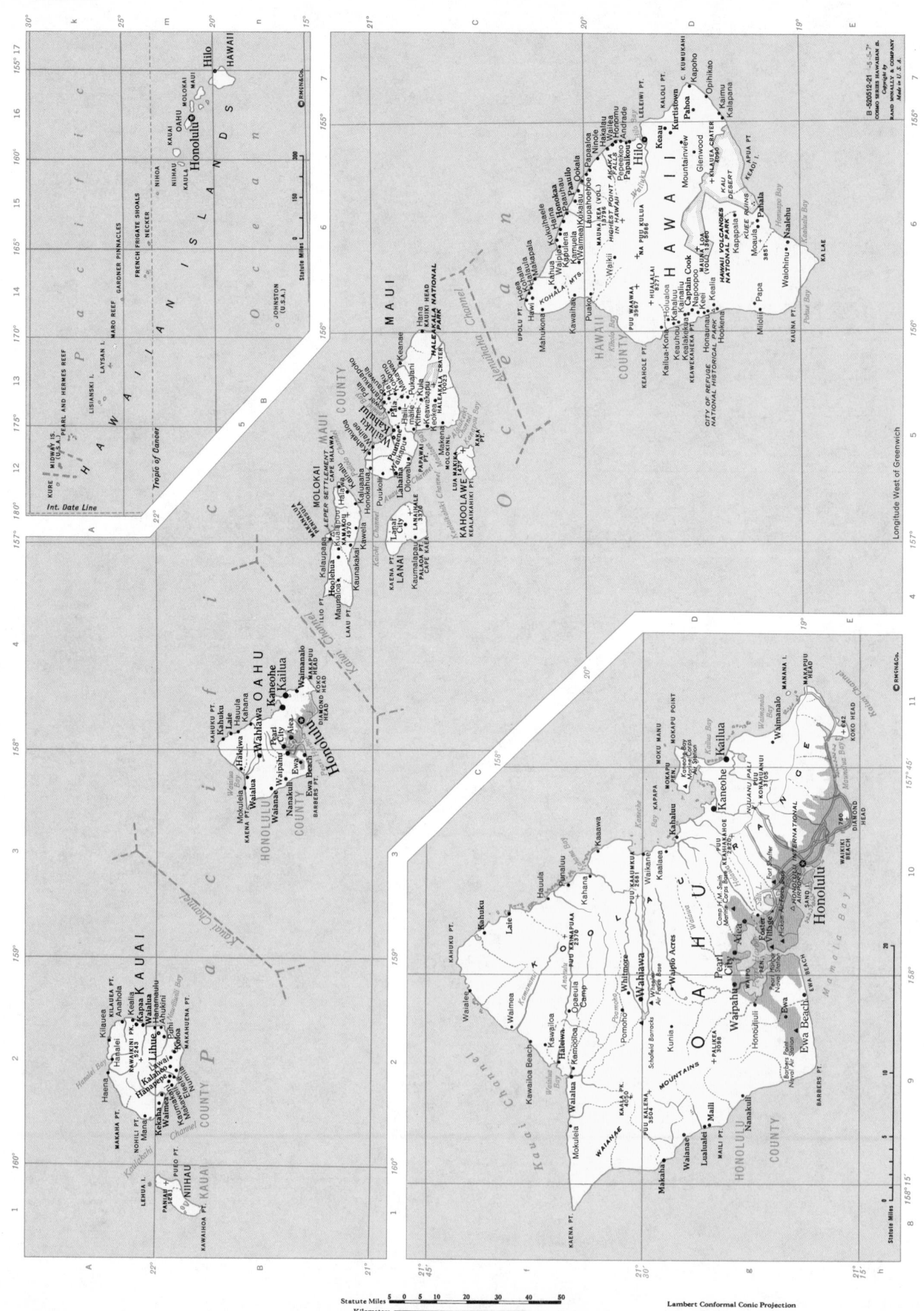

Statute Miles 5 0 5 10   20   30   40   50

Kilometers 5 0 5 10   20   30   40   50   60

Lambert Conformal Conic Projection

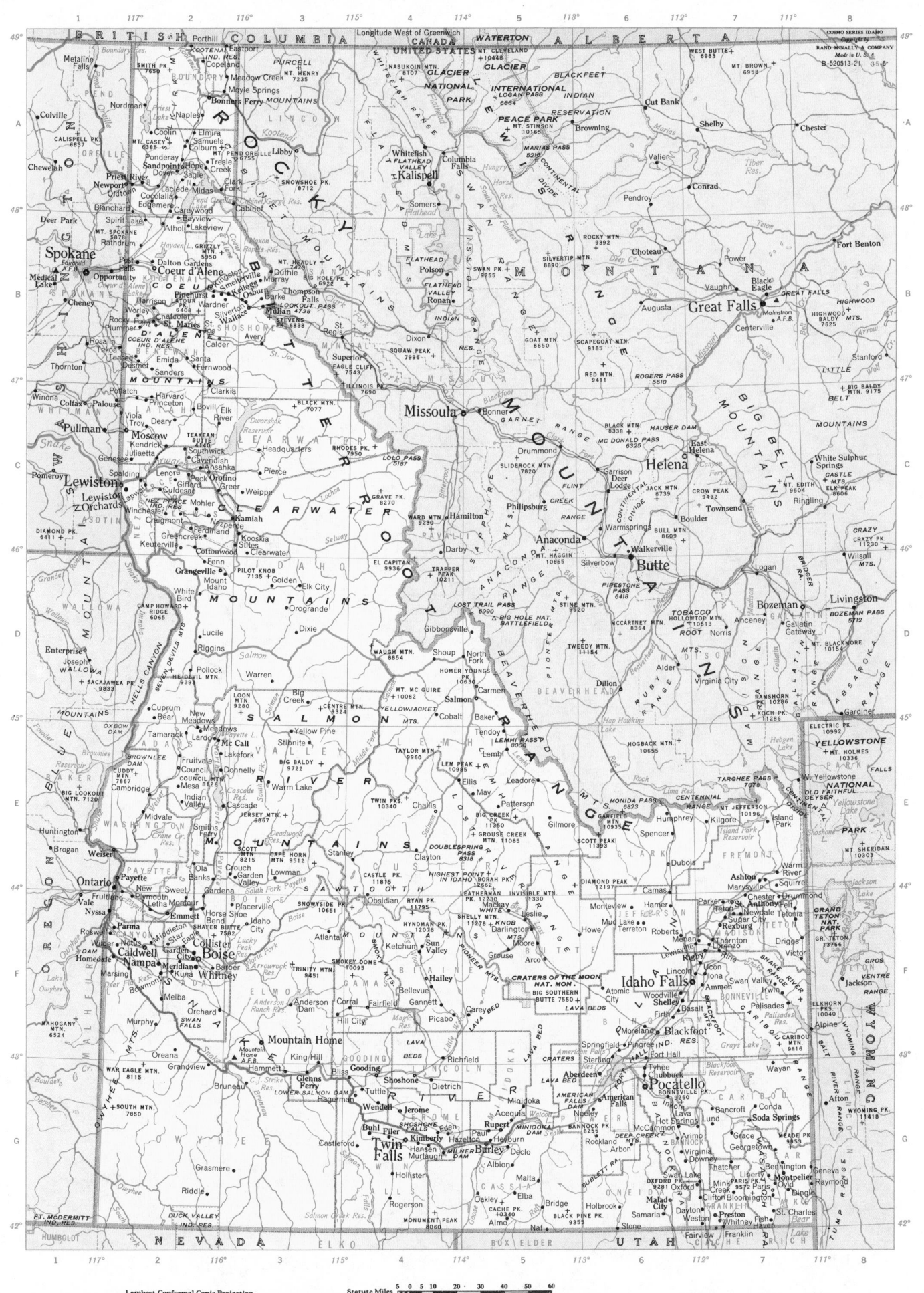

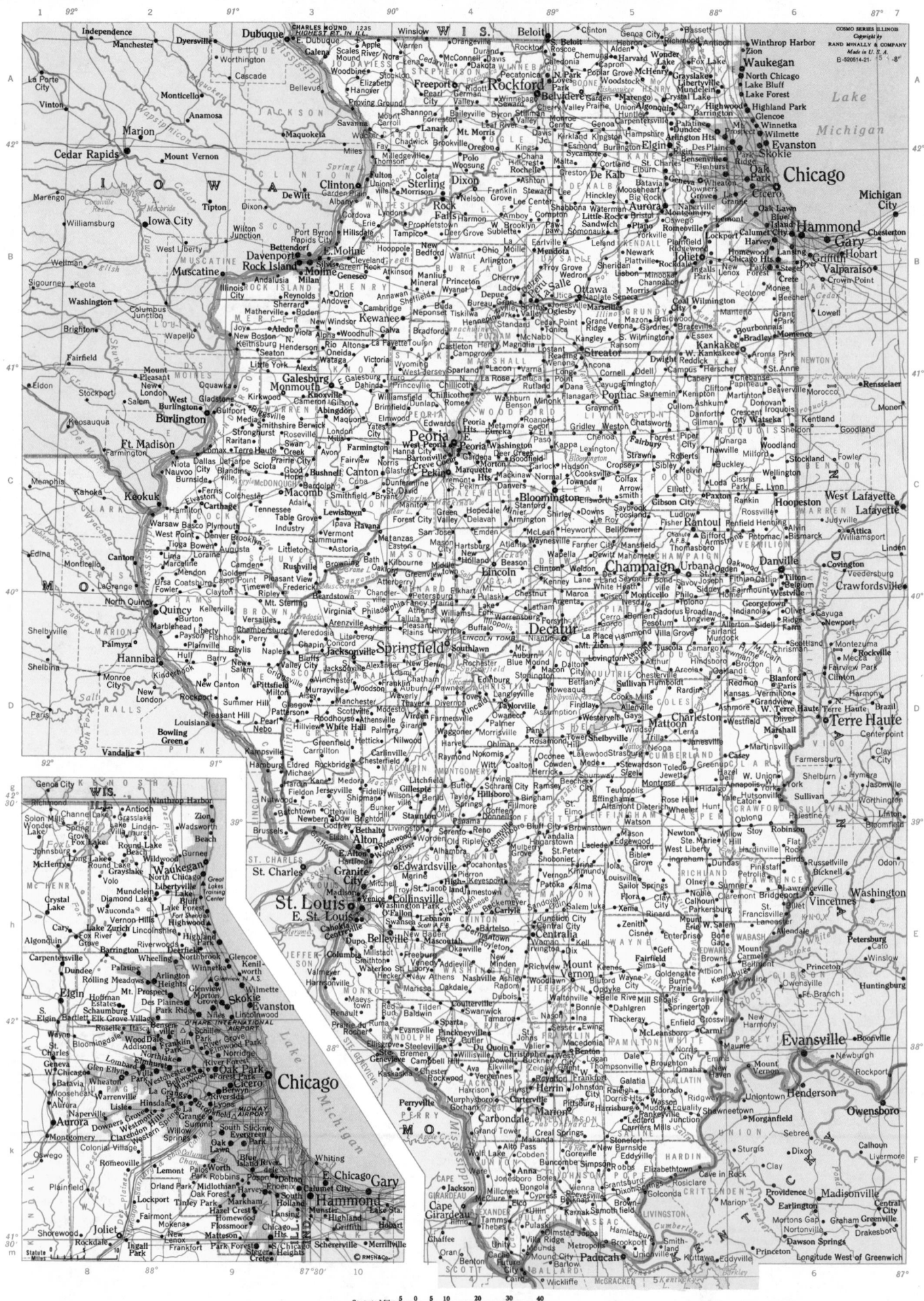

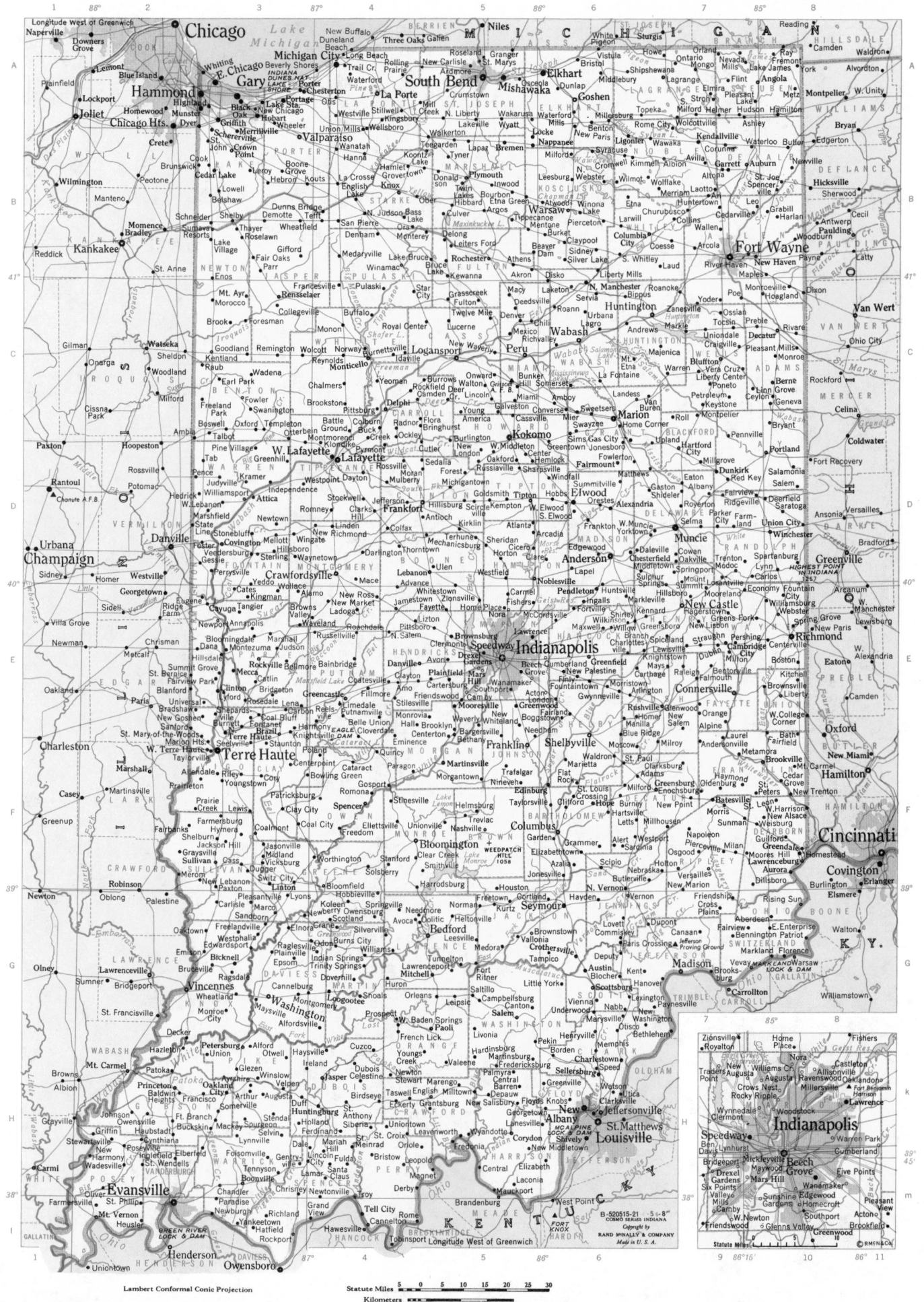

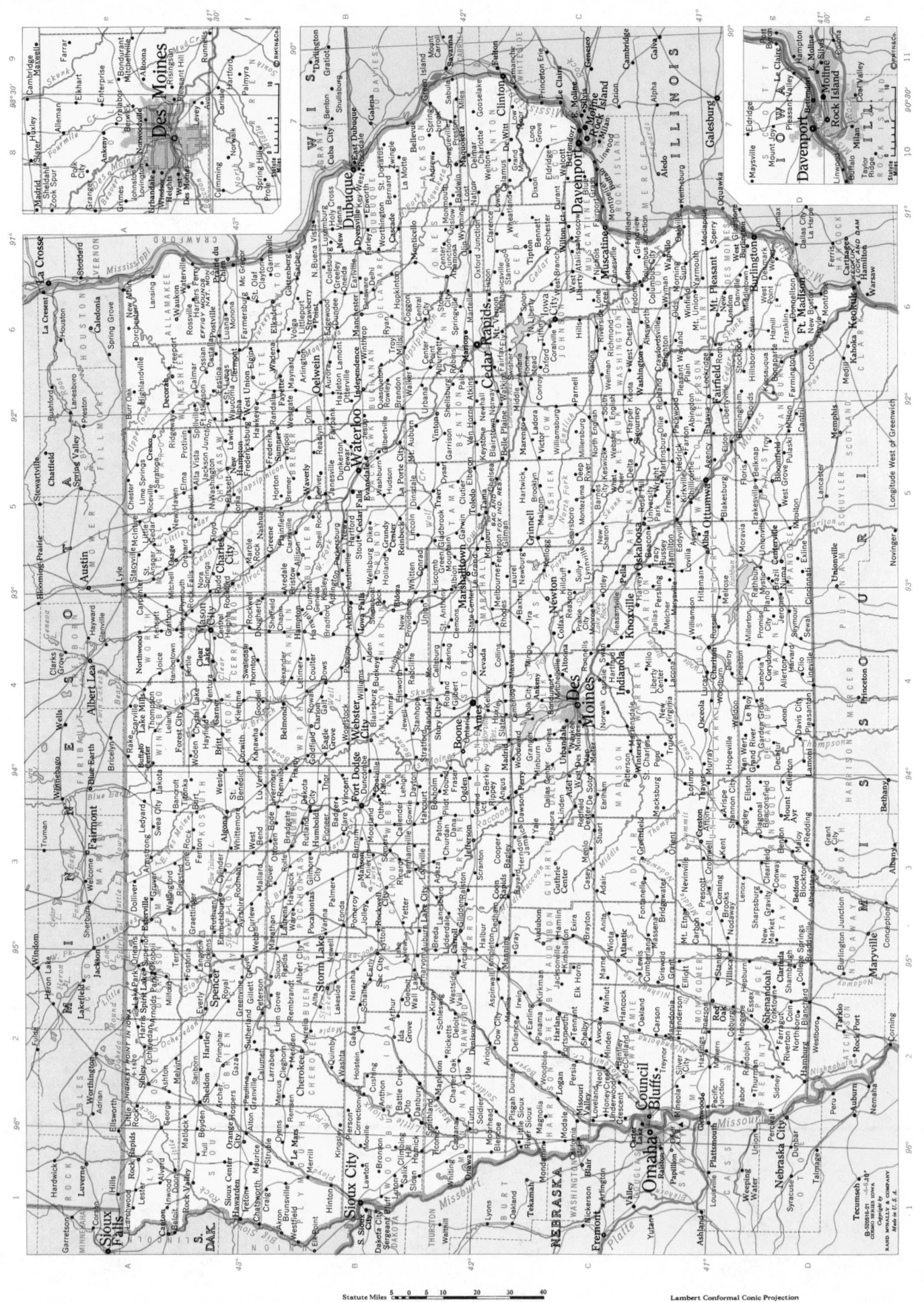

Statute Miles 5 0 5 10   20   30   40

Kilometers 5 0 5 15 25 35 45 55

Lambert Conformal Conic Projection

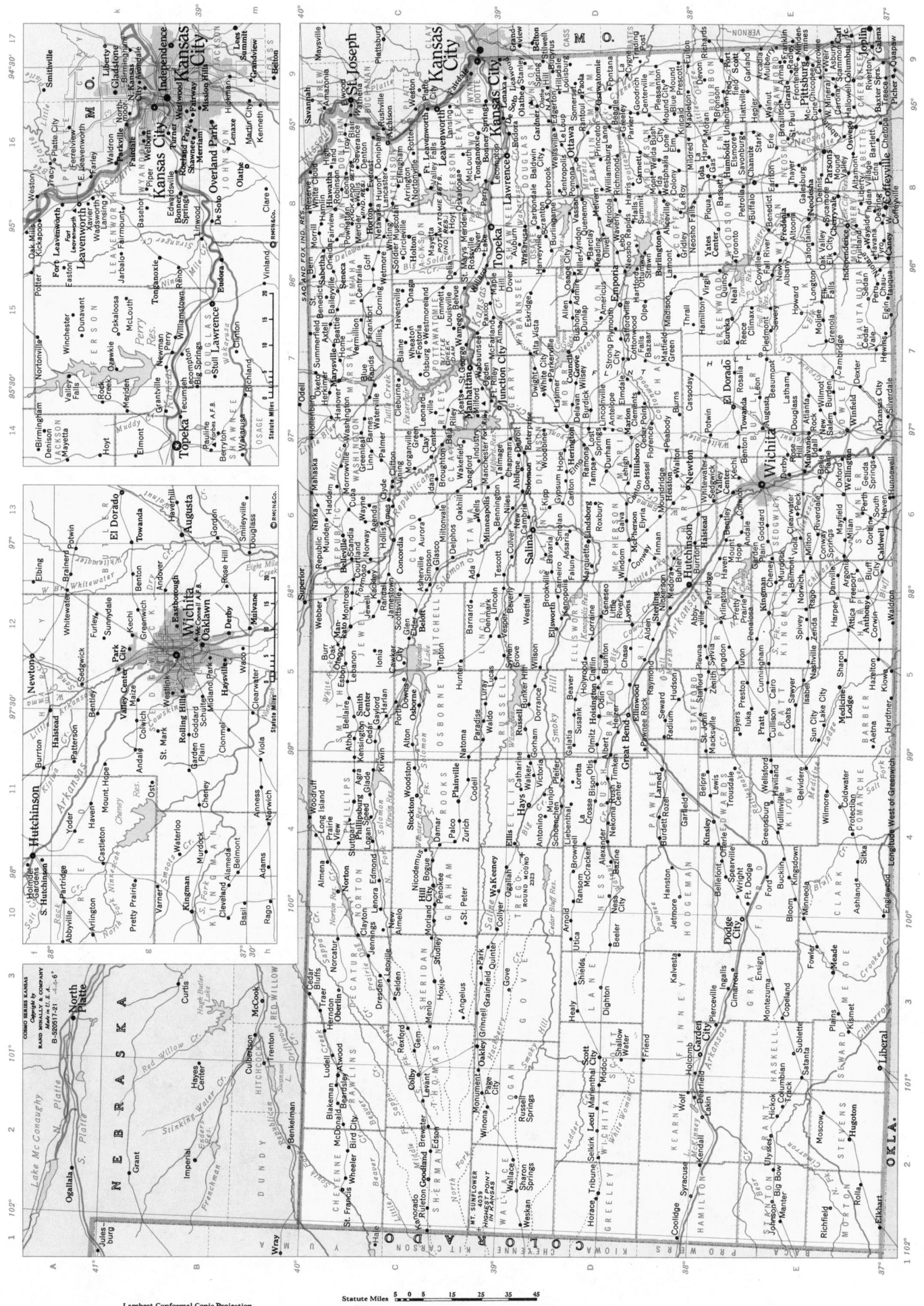

Lambert Conformal Conic Projection

Statute Miles 5 0 5 15 25 35 45
Kilometers 5 0 5 15 25 35 45 55 65

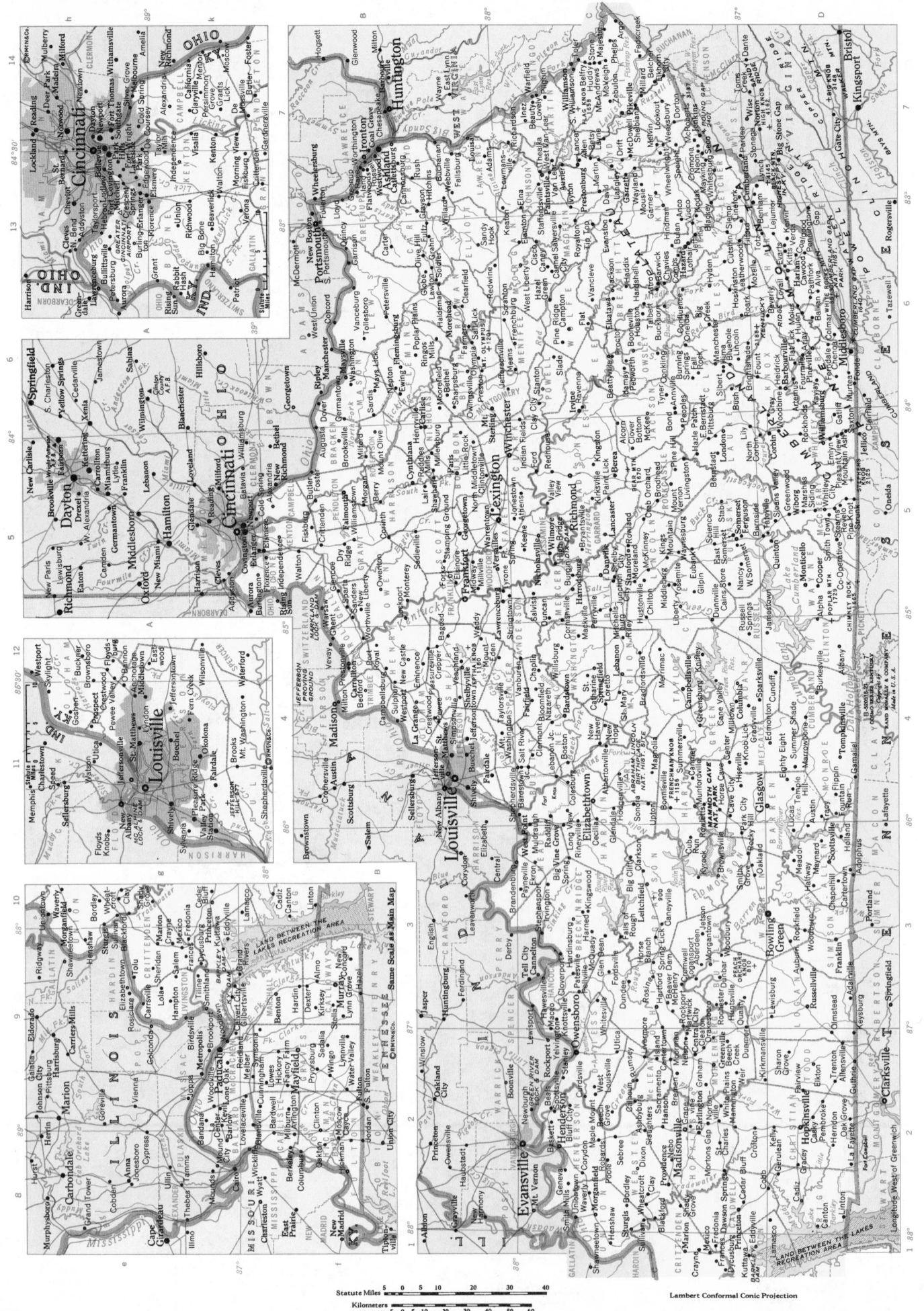

Statute Miles
Kilometers

Lambert Conformal Conic Projection

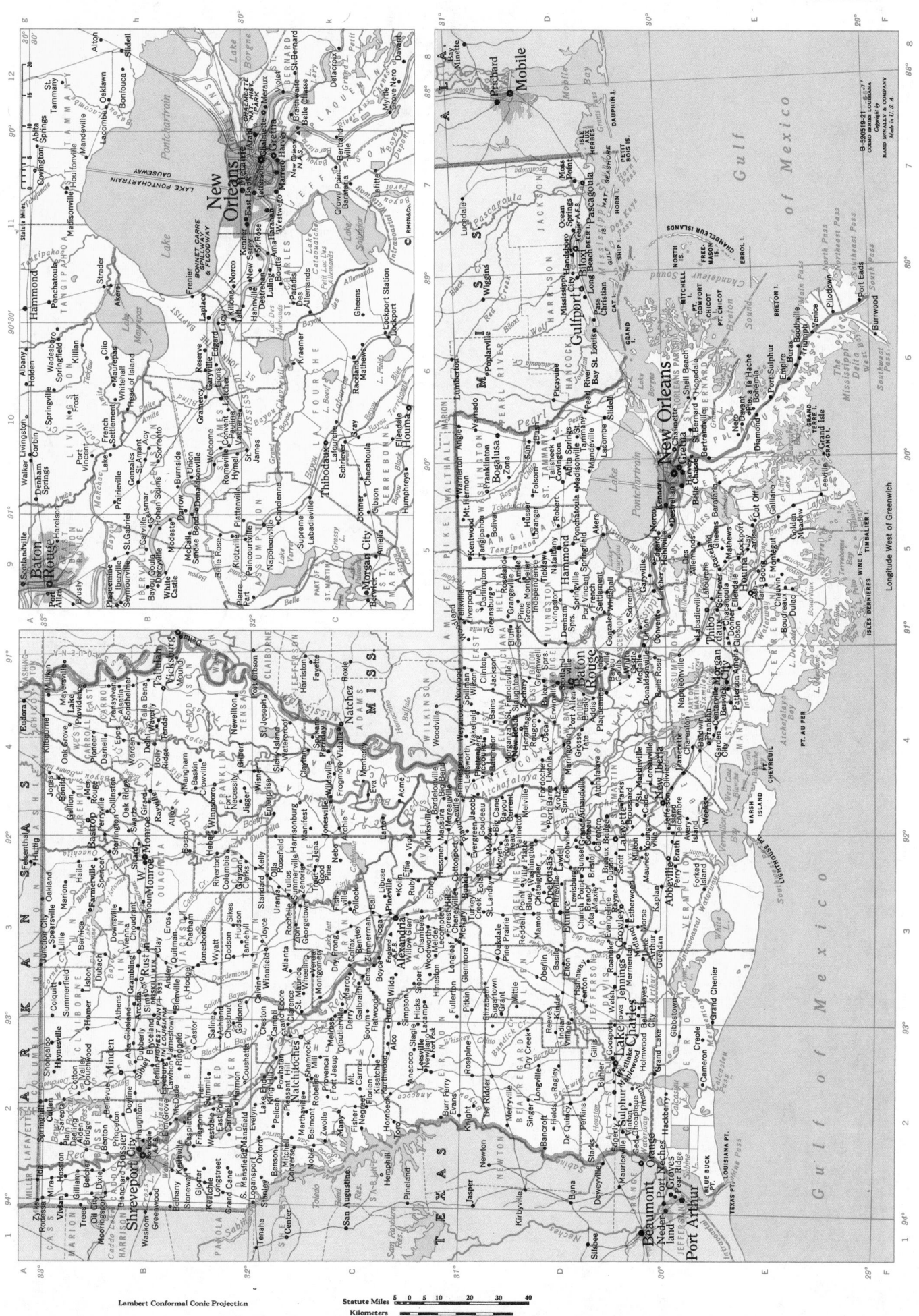

Lambert Conformal Conic Projection

Statute Miles

Kilometers

B-500519-21
COSMO SERIES LOUISIANA
Copyright by
RAND MCNALLY & COMPANY
Made in U.S.A.

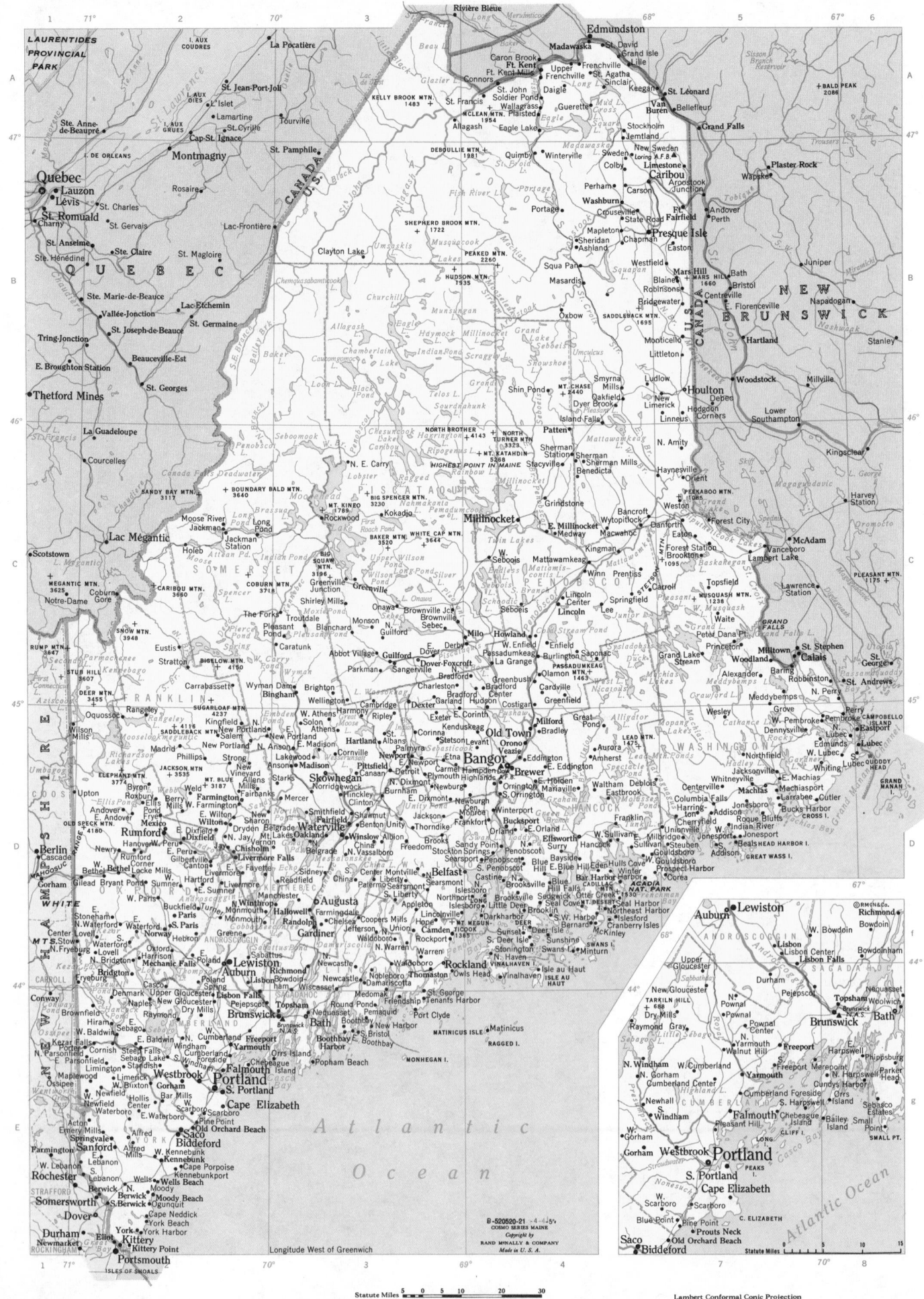

Statute Miles 5 0 5 10 20 30
Kilometers 5 0 5 10 20 30 40

Longitude West of Greenwich

B-520520-21 · 4-4-45-
COSMO SERIES MAINE
Copyright by
RAND McNALLY & COMPANY
Made in U.S.A.

Lambert Conformal Conic Projection

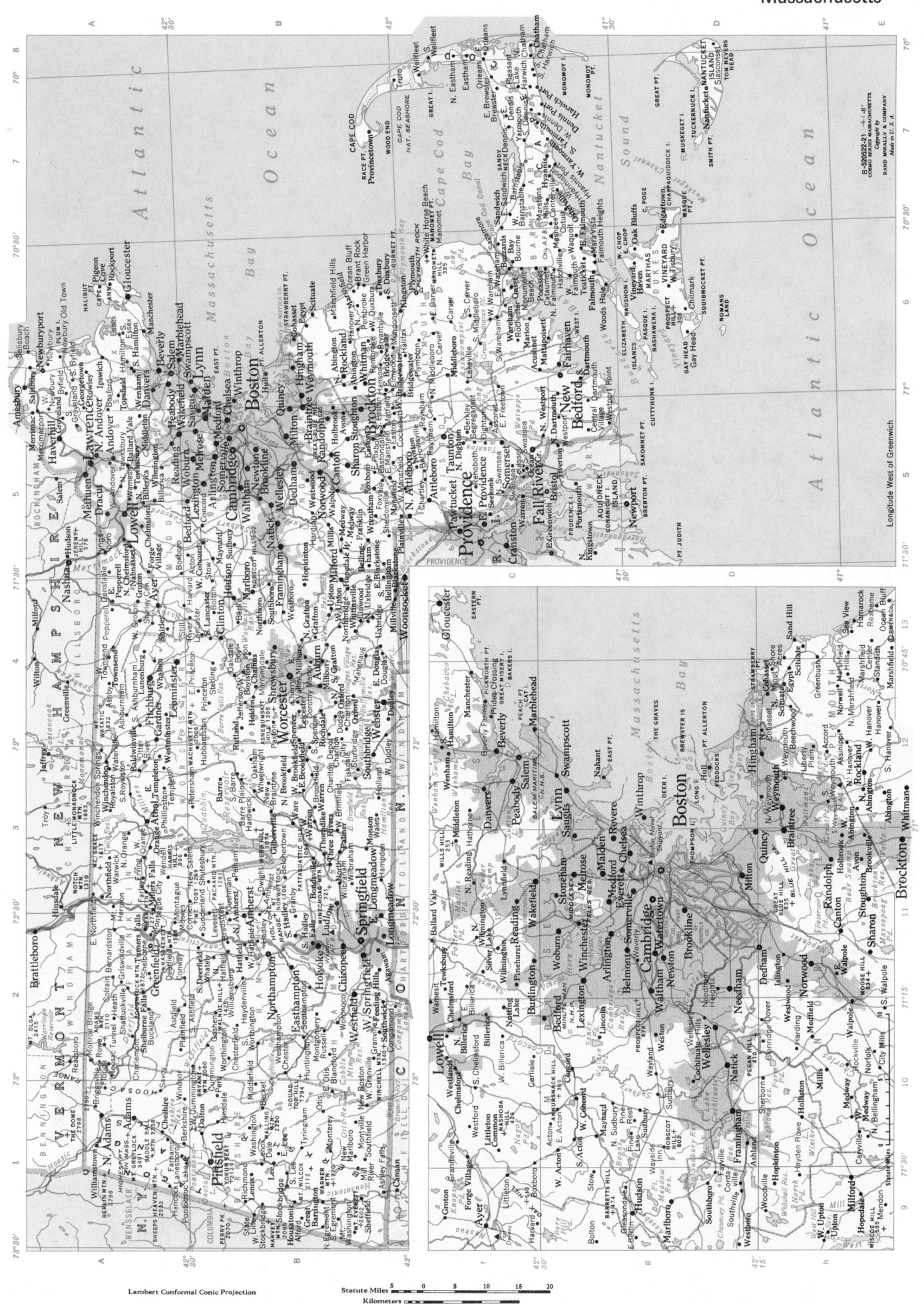

Lambert Conformal Conic Projection

Statute Miles
Kilometers

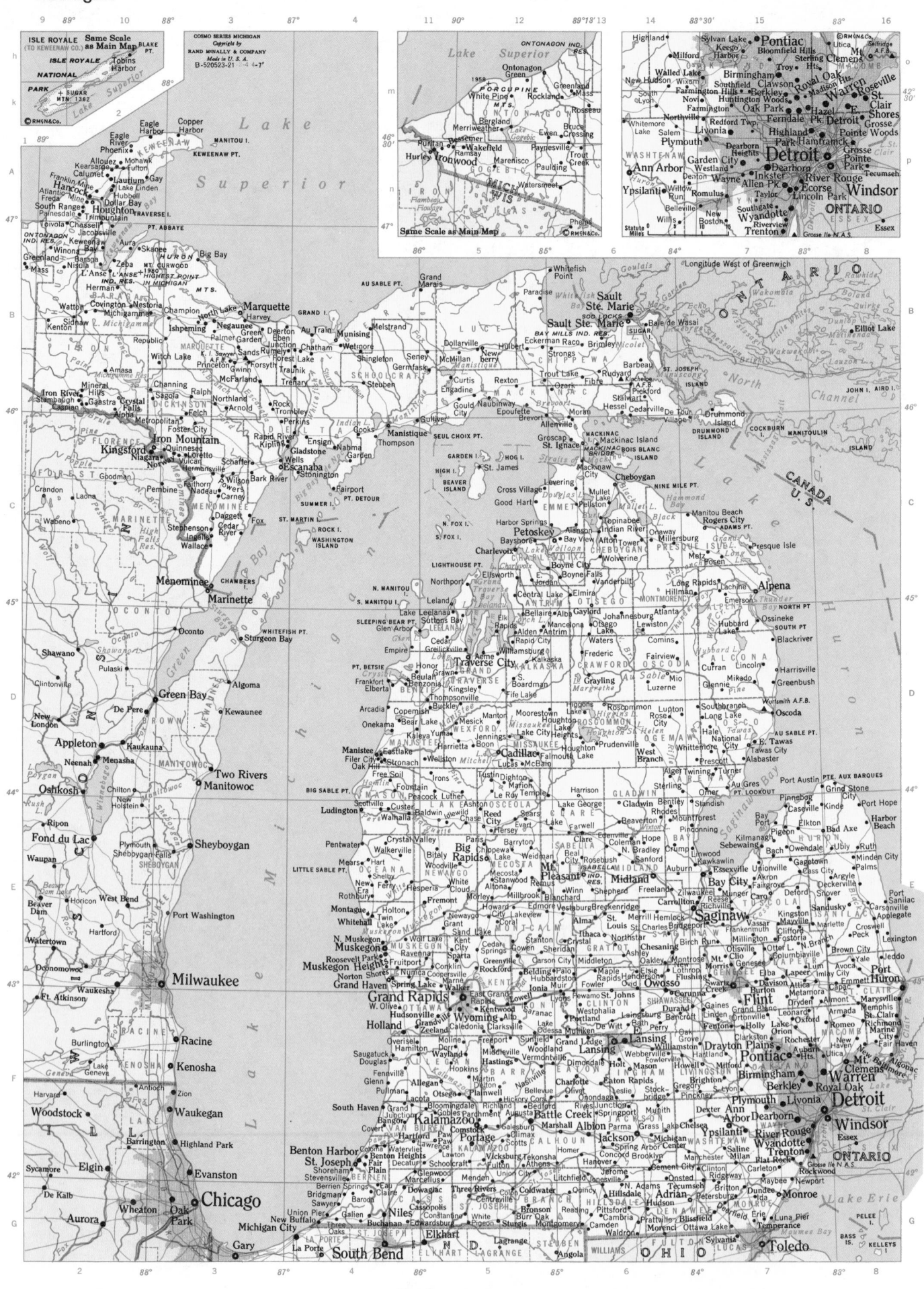

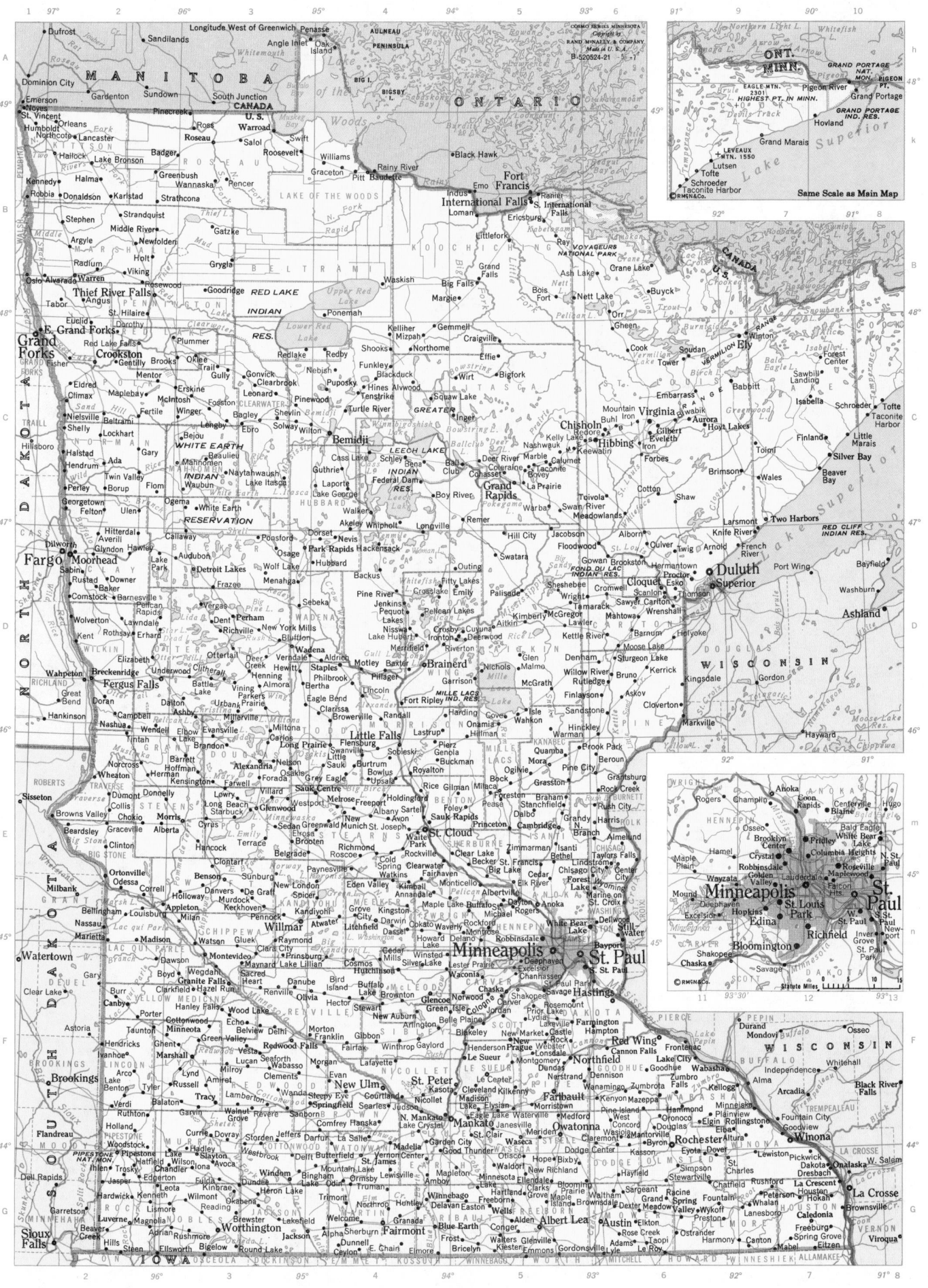

Statute Miles 5 0 5 10 20 30 40 50

Kilometers 5 0 5 15 25 35 45 55 65

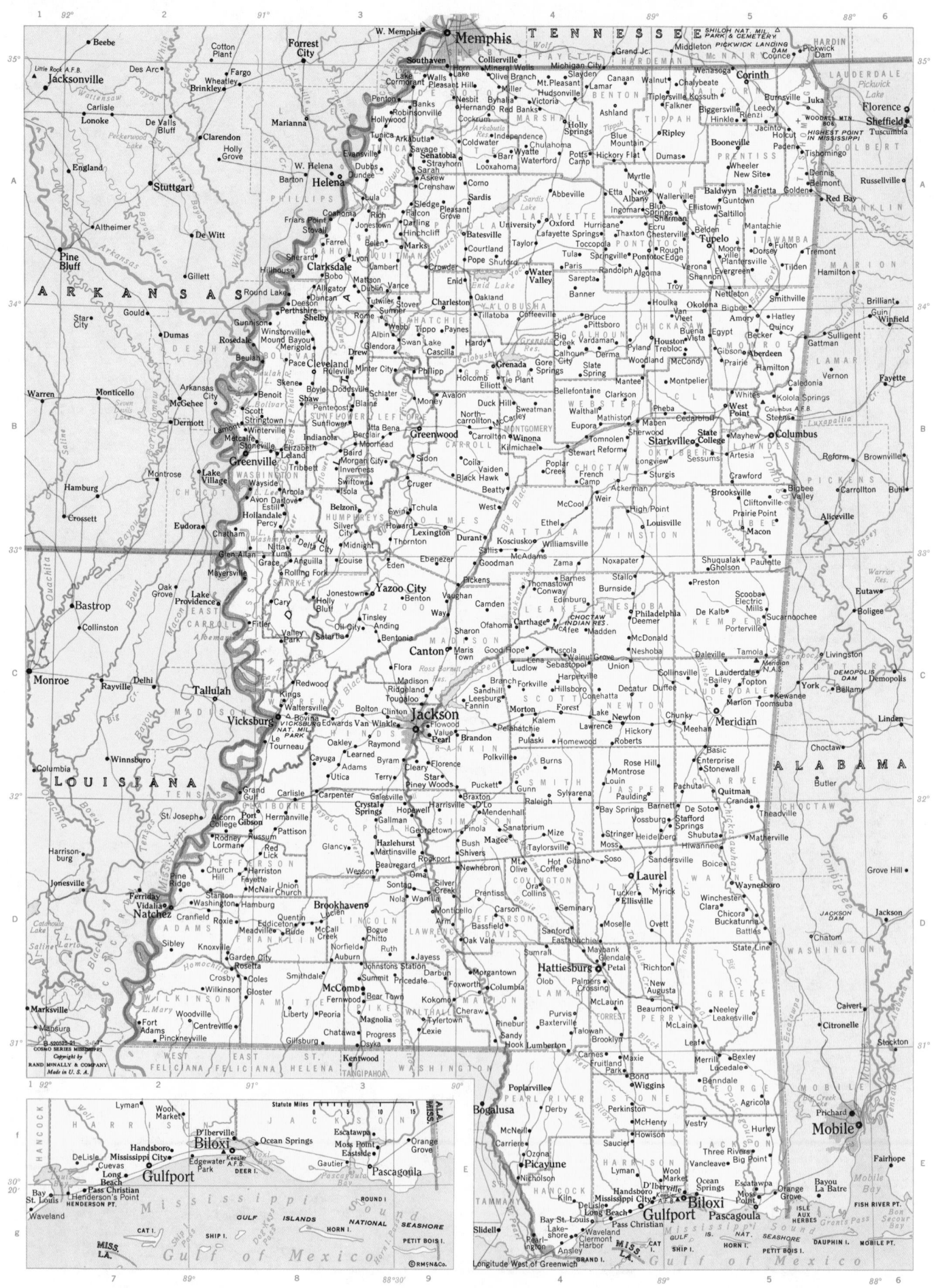

Statute Miles

Kilometers

Lambert Conformal Conic Projection

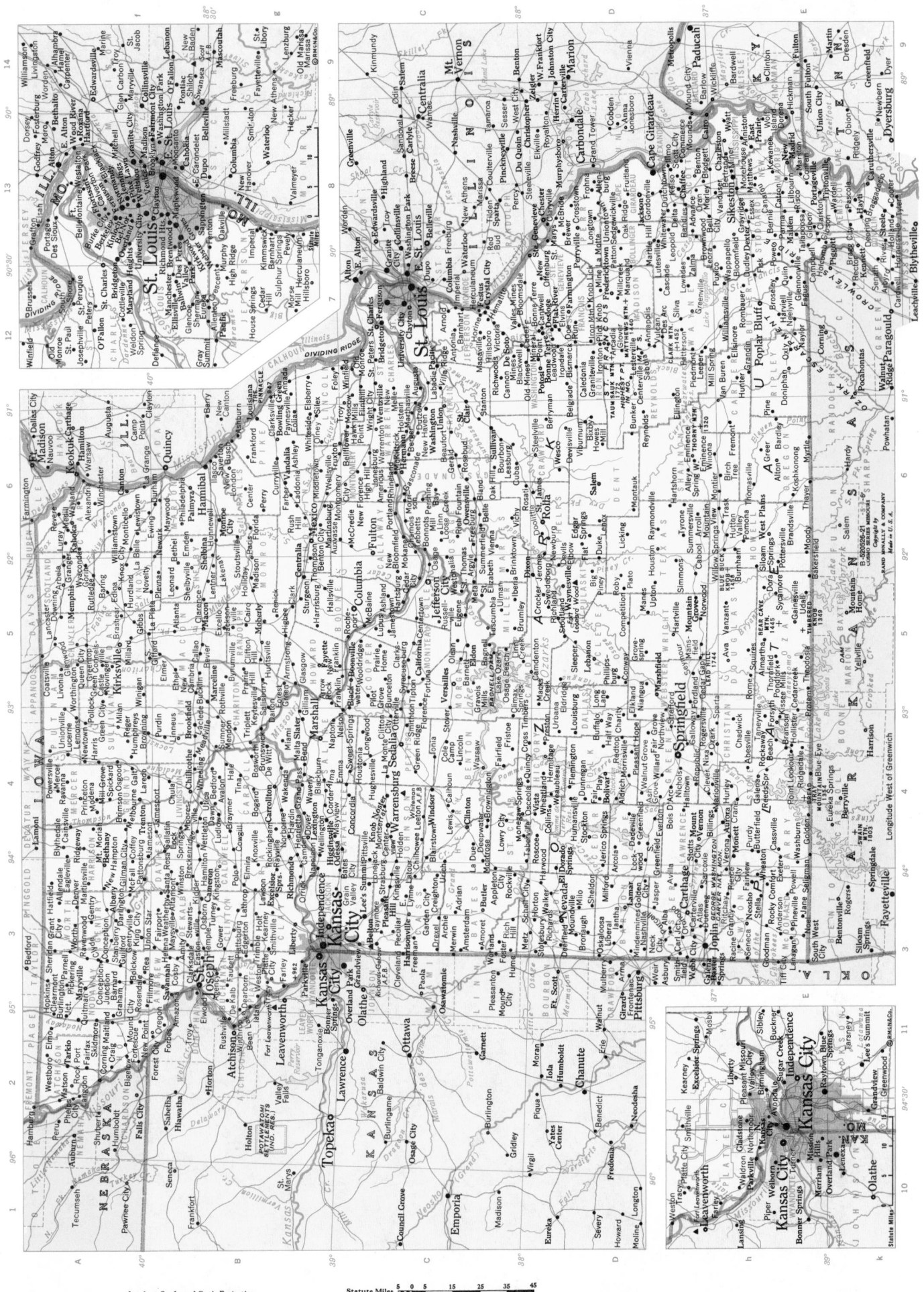

Statute Miles 5 0 5 15 25 35 45

Kilometers 5 0 5 15 25 35 45 55 65

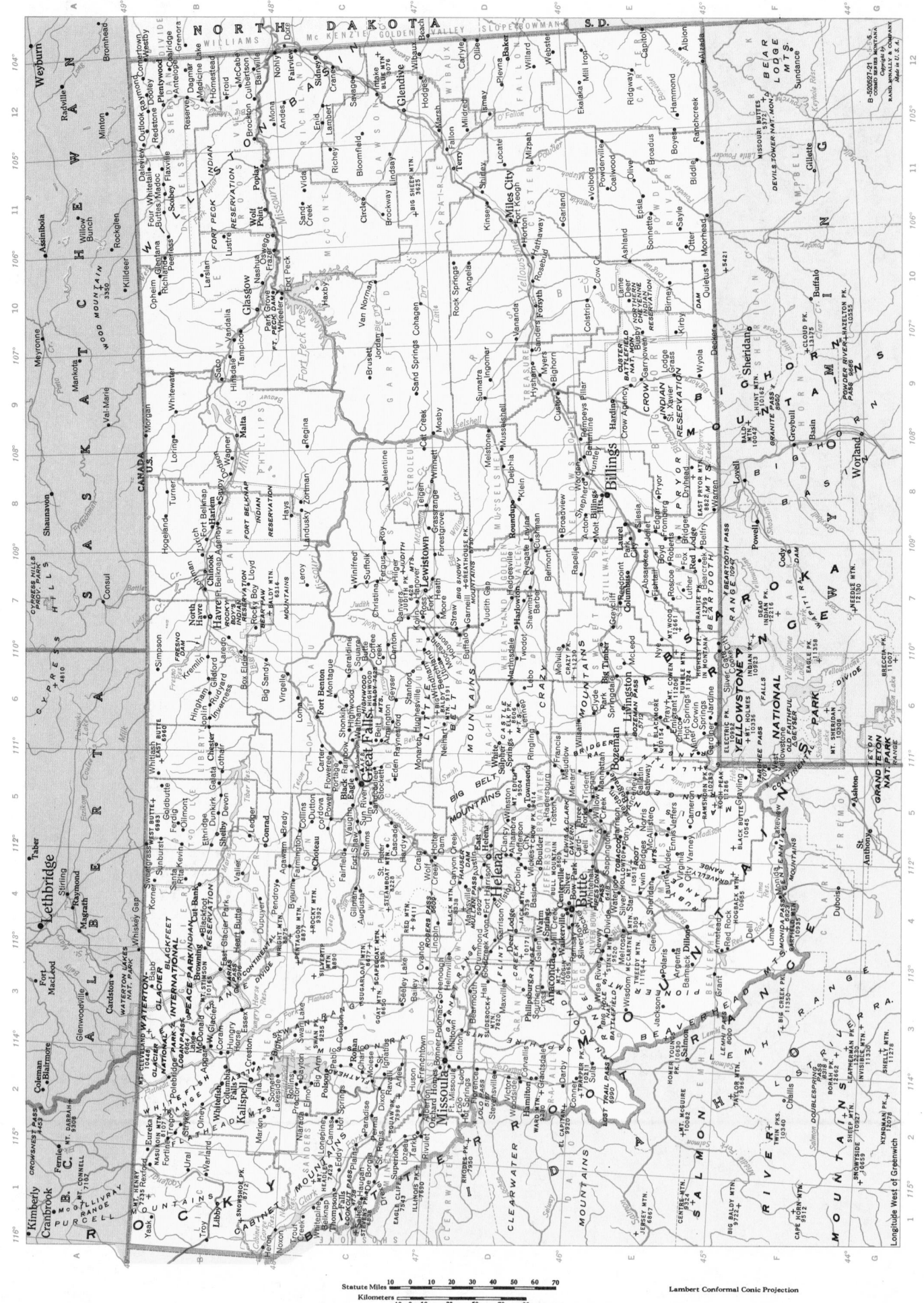

Statute Miles 10 0 10 20 30 40 50 60 70
Kilometers 10 0 10 30 50 70 90

Lambert Conformal Conic Projection

Longitude West of Greenwich

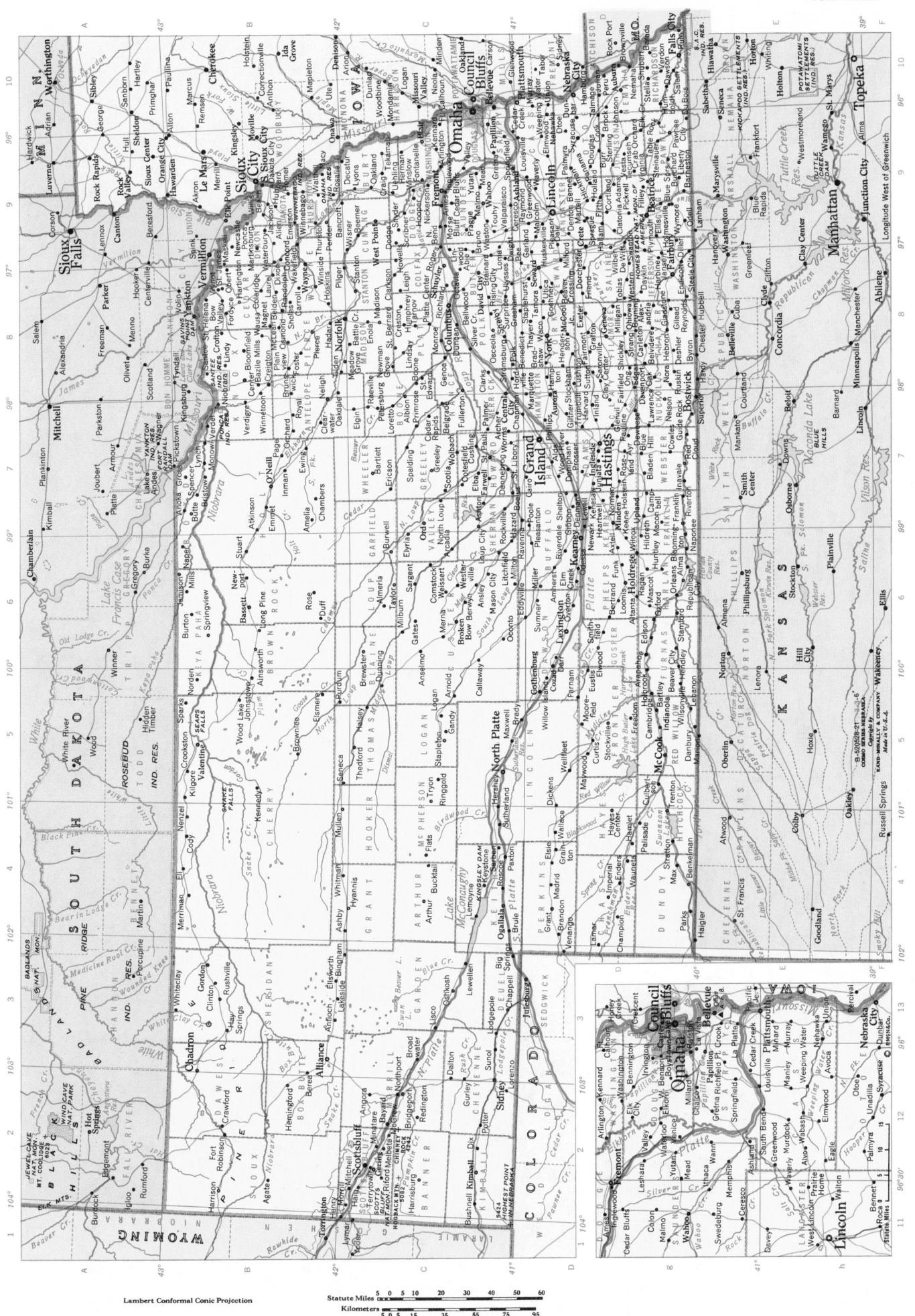

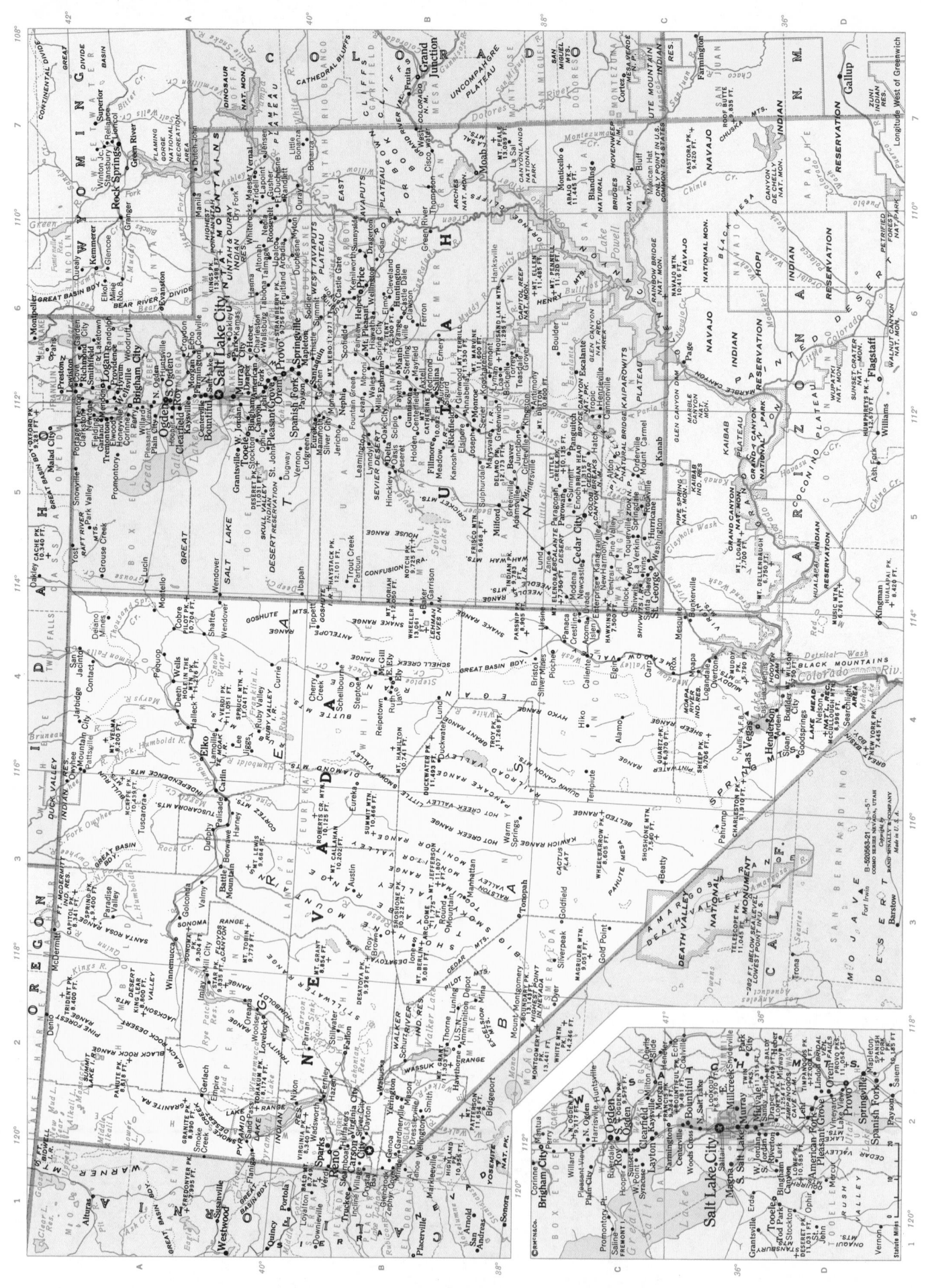

Statute Miles 5 0 5 10 20 30 40 50 60 70 80
Kilometers 5 0 10 20 40 60 80 100 120

Lambert Conformal Conic Projection

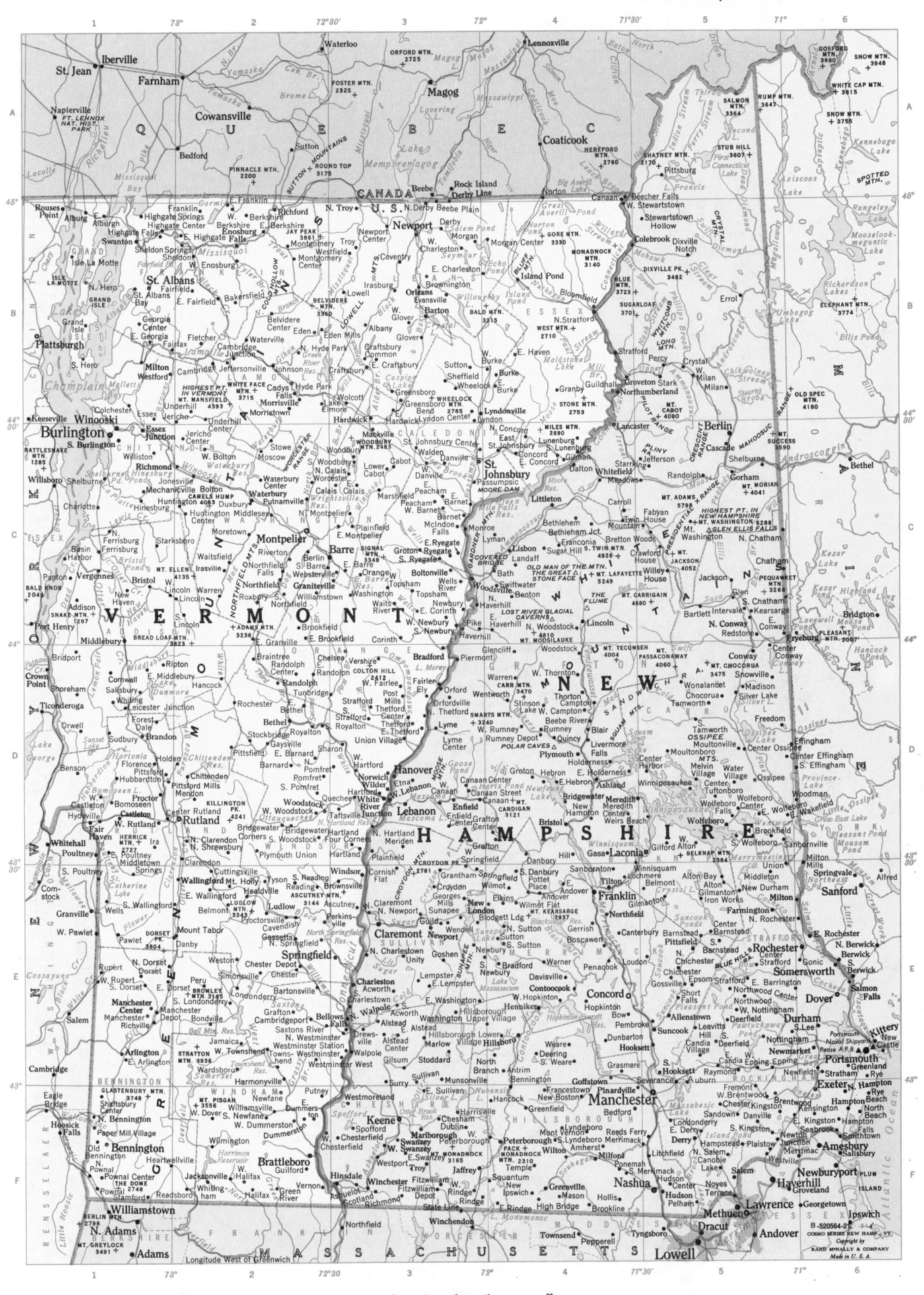

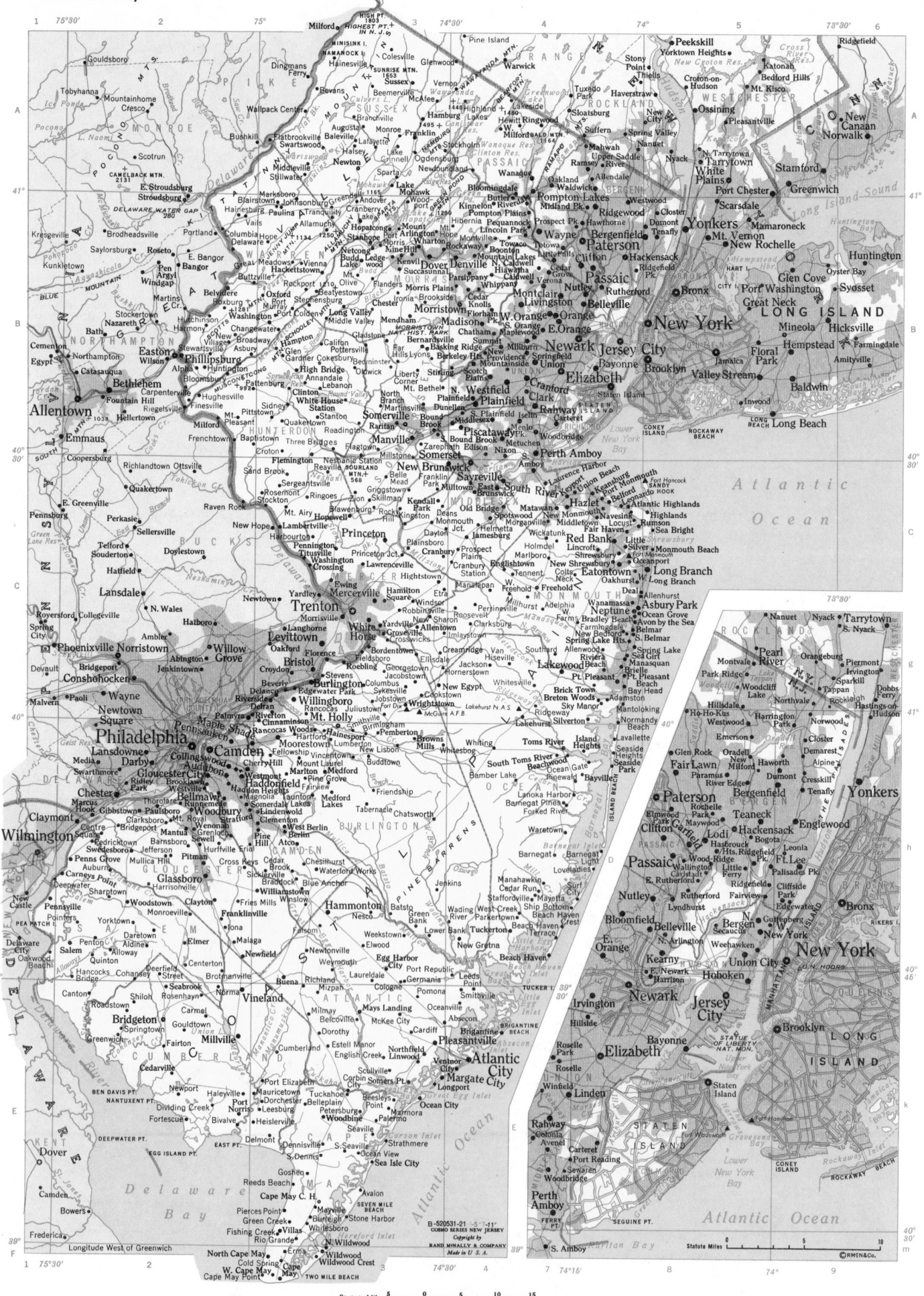

Lambert Conformal Conic Projection

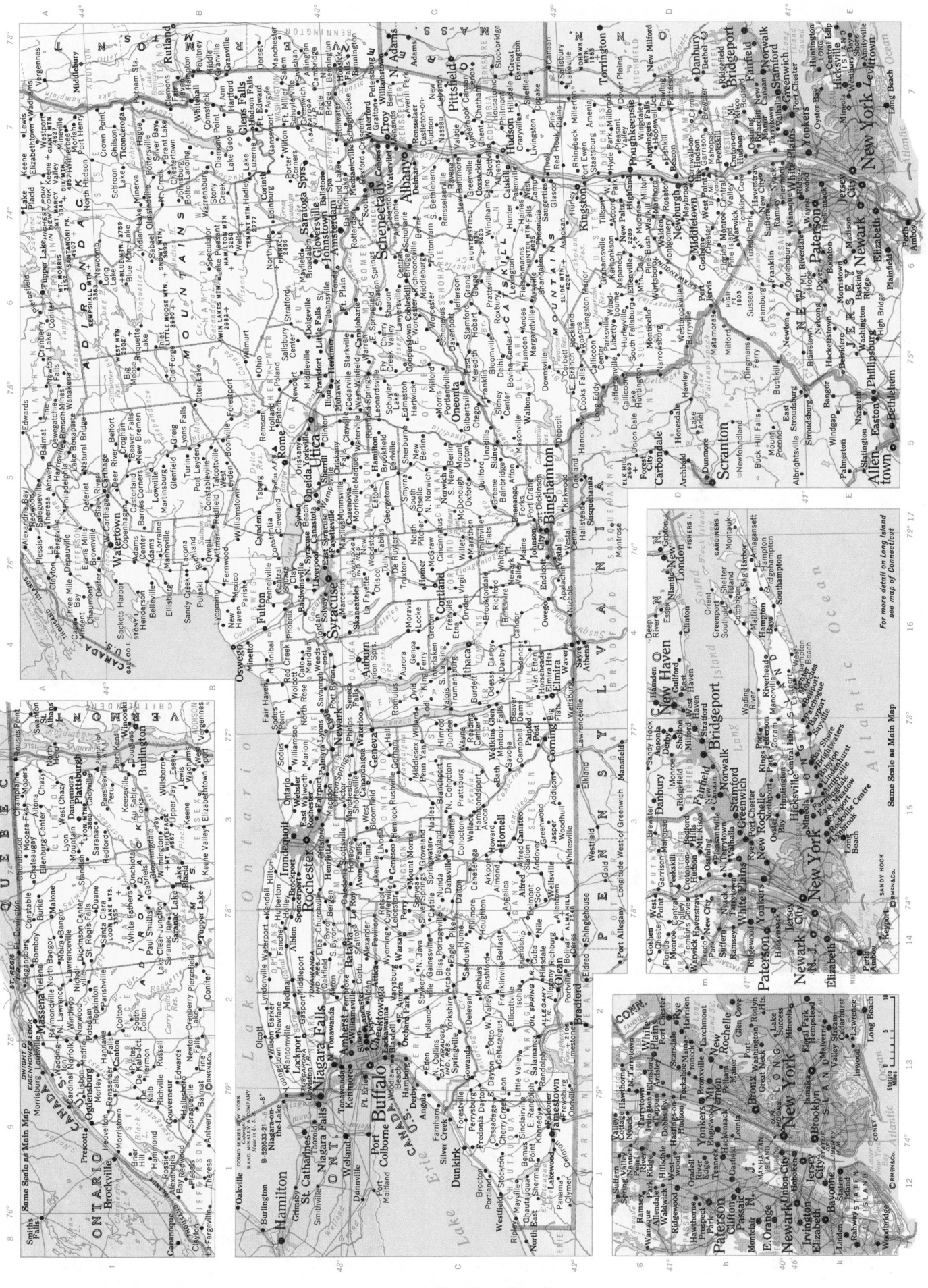

Lambert Conformal Conic Projection

Statute Miles
Kilometers

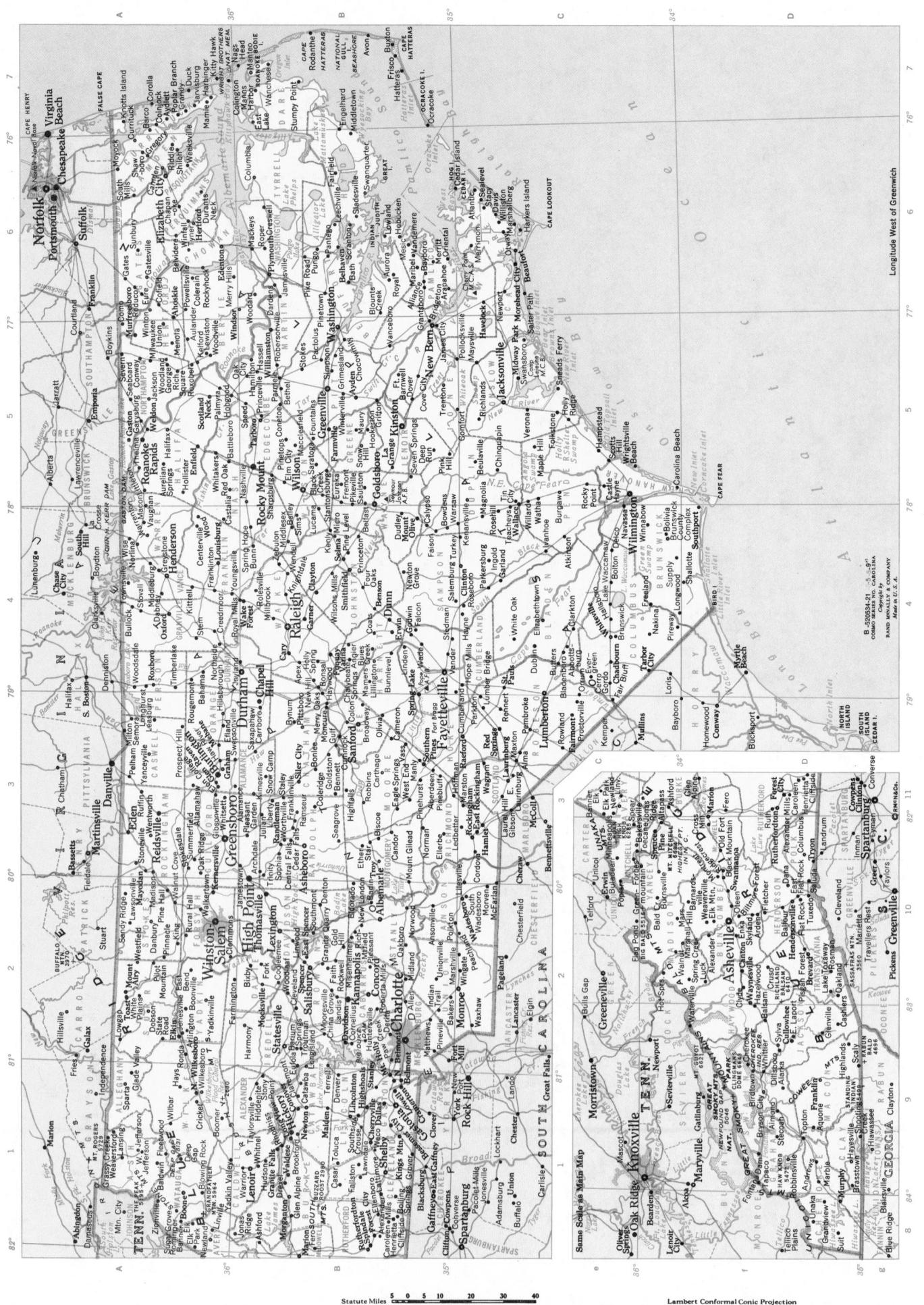

Statute Miles 5 0 5 10 20 30 40
Kilometers 5 0 5 15 25 35 45 55

Lambert Conformal Conic Projection

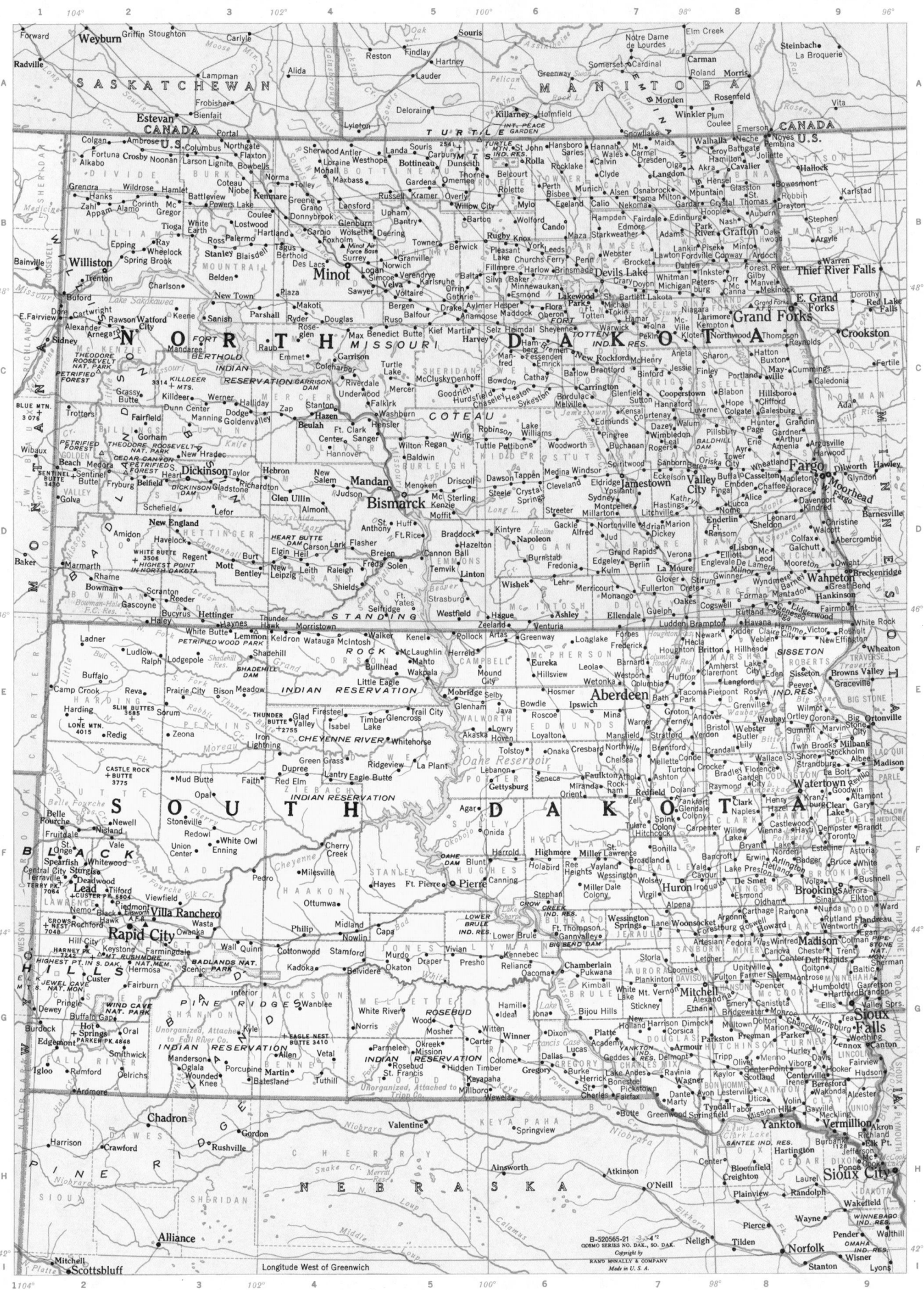

Lambert Conformal Conic Projection

Statute Miles
5 0 5 10 20 30 40 50 60

Kilometers
5 0 5 15 25 35 45 55 65 75

Longitude West of Greenwich

B-520565-21
COSMO SERIES NO. DAK., SO. DAK.
Copyright by
RAND McNALLY & COMPANY
Made in U.S.A.

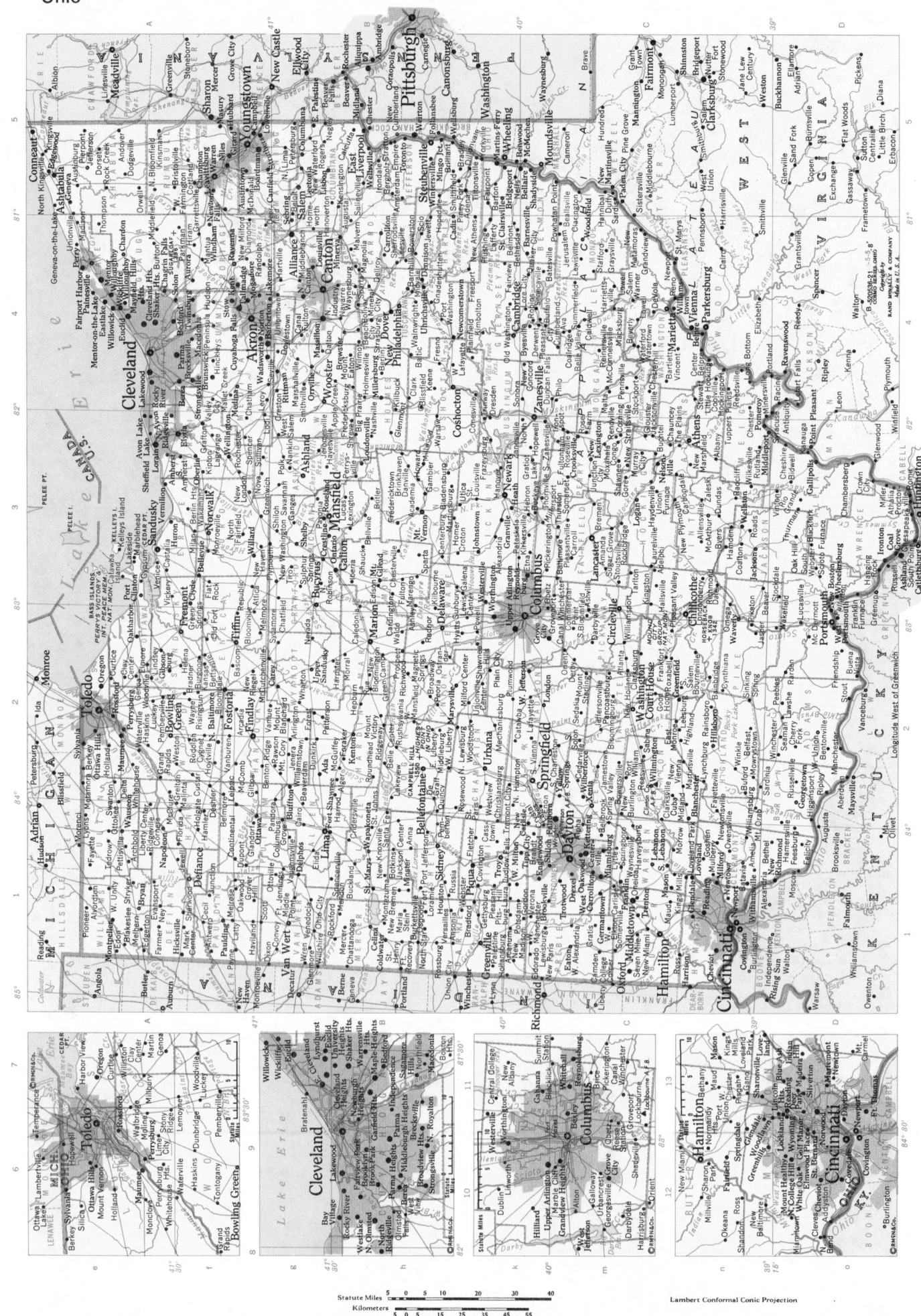

Lambert Conformal Conic Projection

Statute Miles 5 0 5 10   20   30   40

Kilometers 5 0 5 10 15 20 25 35 45 55

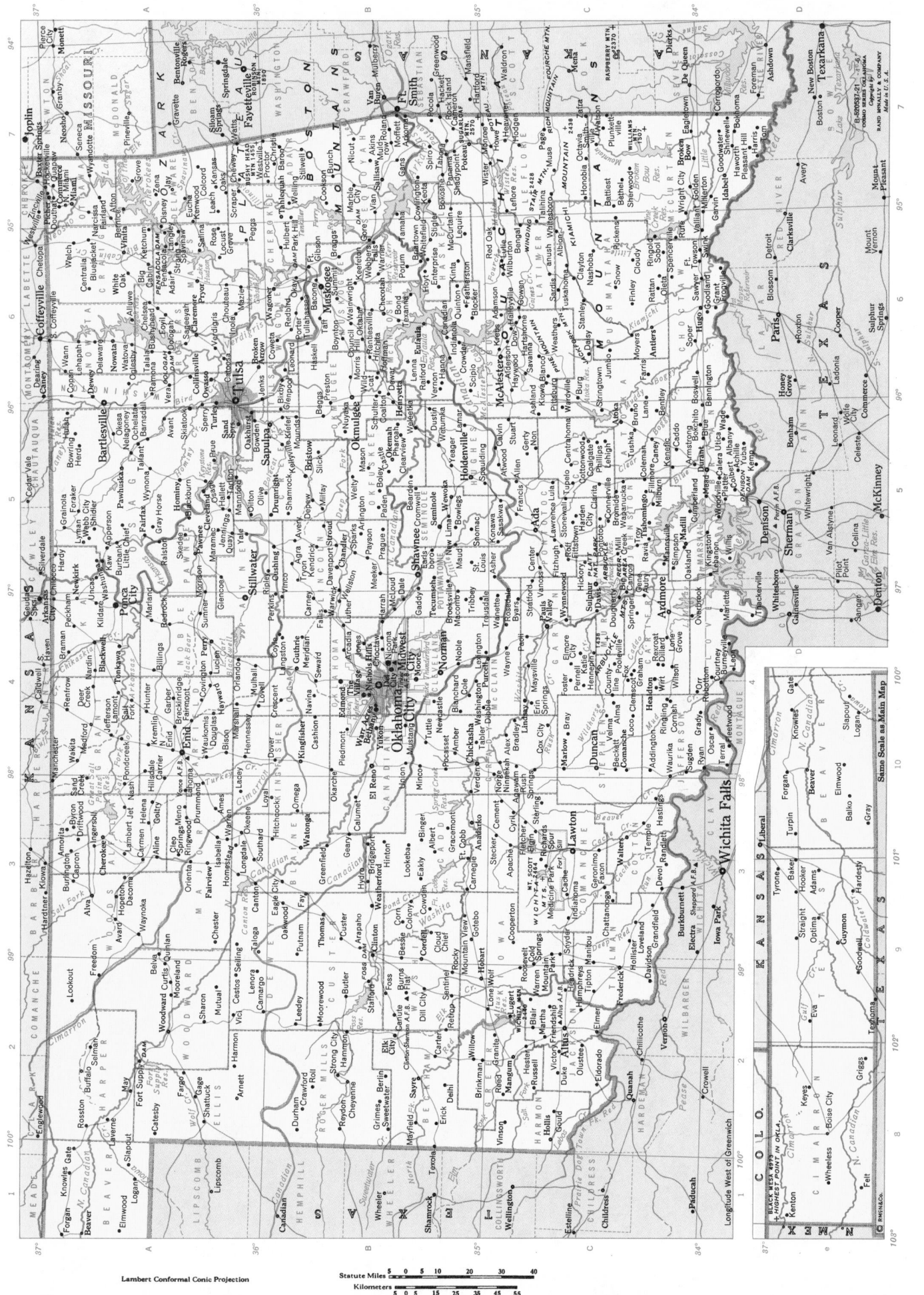

Lambert Conformal Conic Projection

Statute Miles

Kilometers

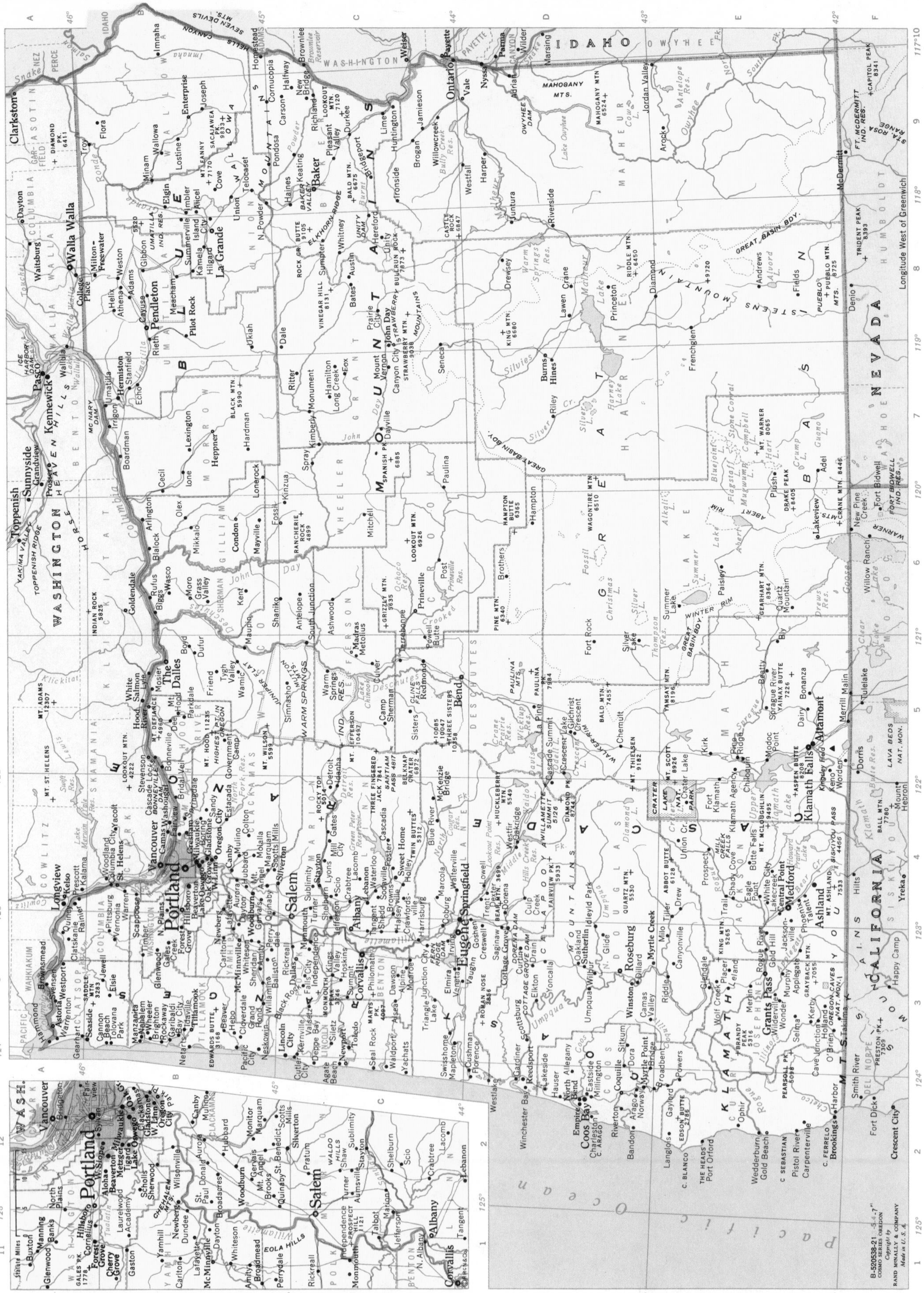

Statute Miles 5 0 5 10 20 30 40 50
Kilometers 5 0 5 15 35 55 65 75

Lambert Conformal Conic Projection

B-520538-21—S-47
COSMO SERIES OREGON
Copyright by
RAND MCNALLY & COMPANY
Made in U.S.A.

Lambert Conformal Conic Projection

Statute Miles

Kilometers

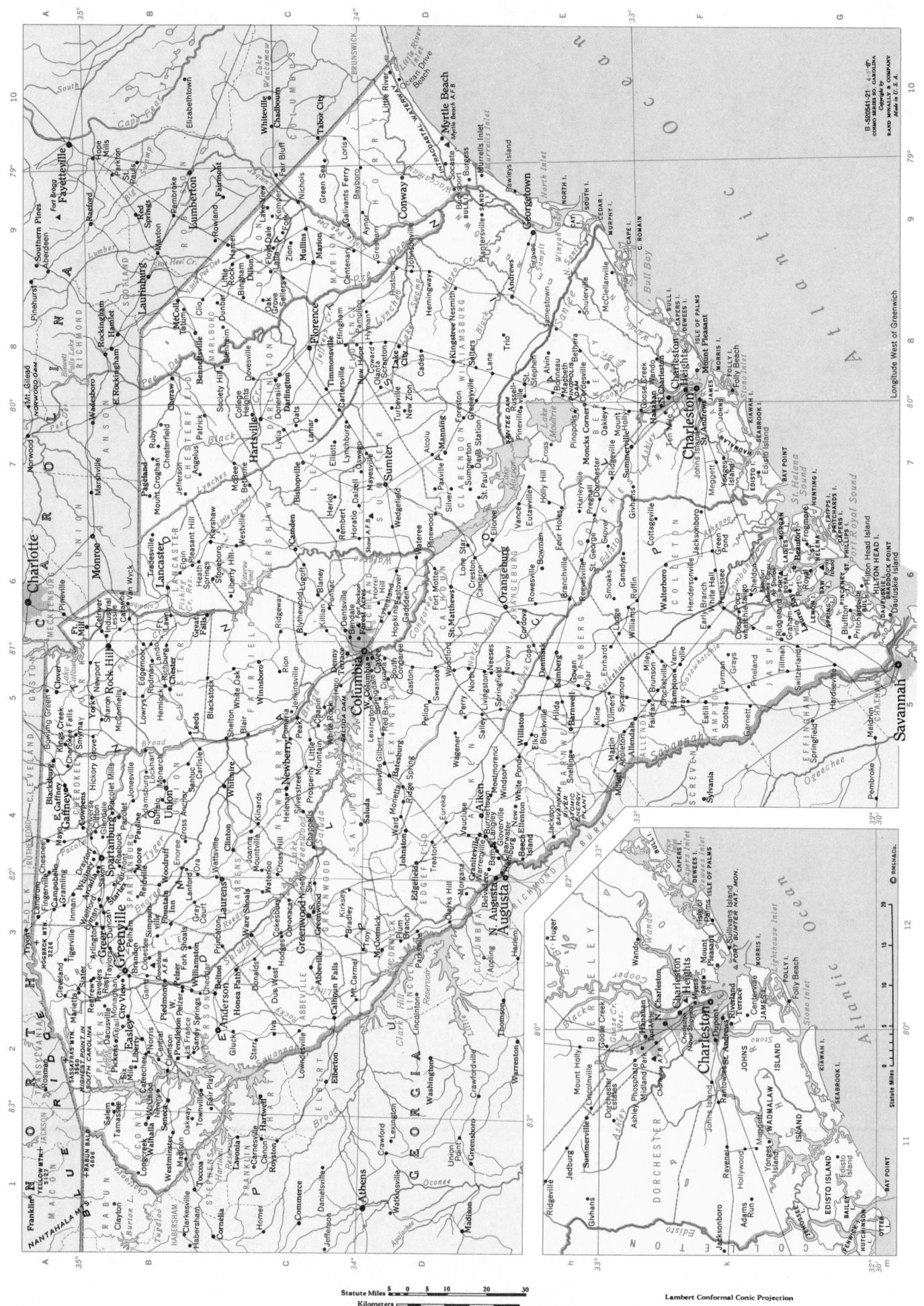

Statute Miles
Kilometers

Lambert Conformal Conic Projection

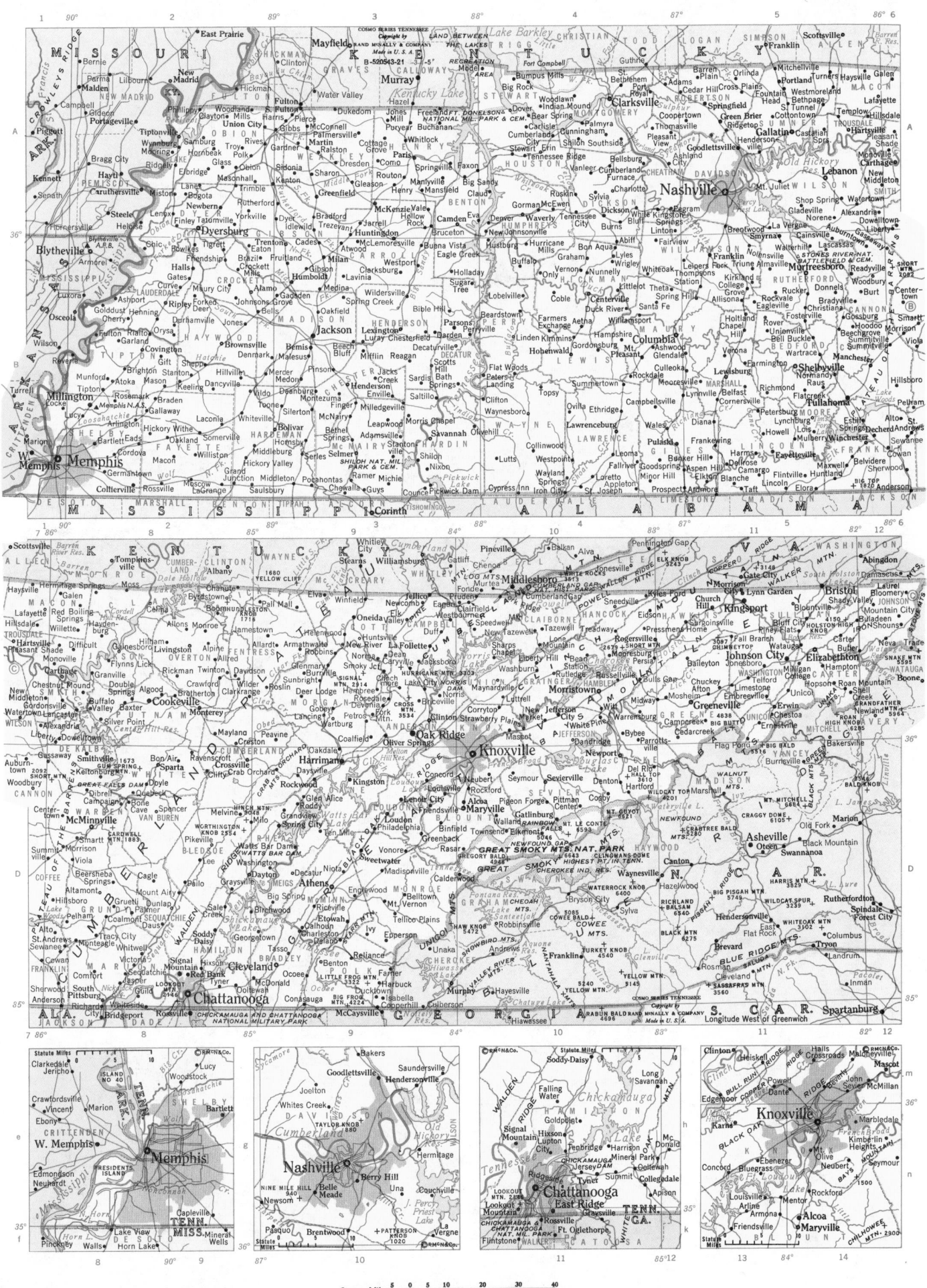

Lambert Conformal Conic Projection

Statute Miles   5 0 5   10   20   30   40

Kilometers   5 0 5   15   25   35   45   55

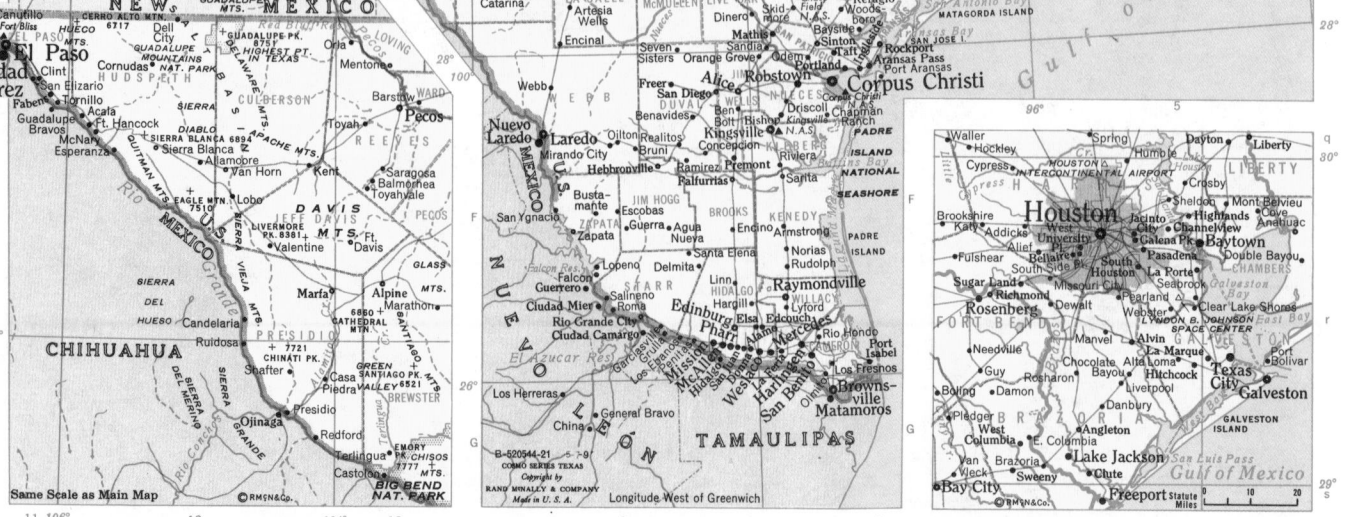

Statute Miles 10 0 10 20 30 40 50 60 70 80 90 100

Kilometers 10 0 10 20 40 60 80 100 120 140

Lambert Conformal Conic Projection

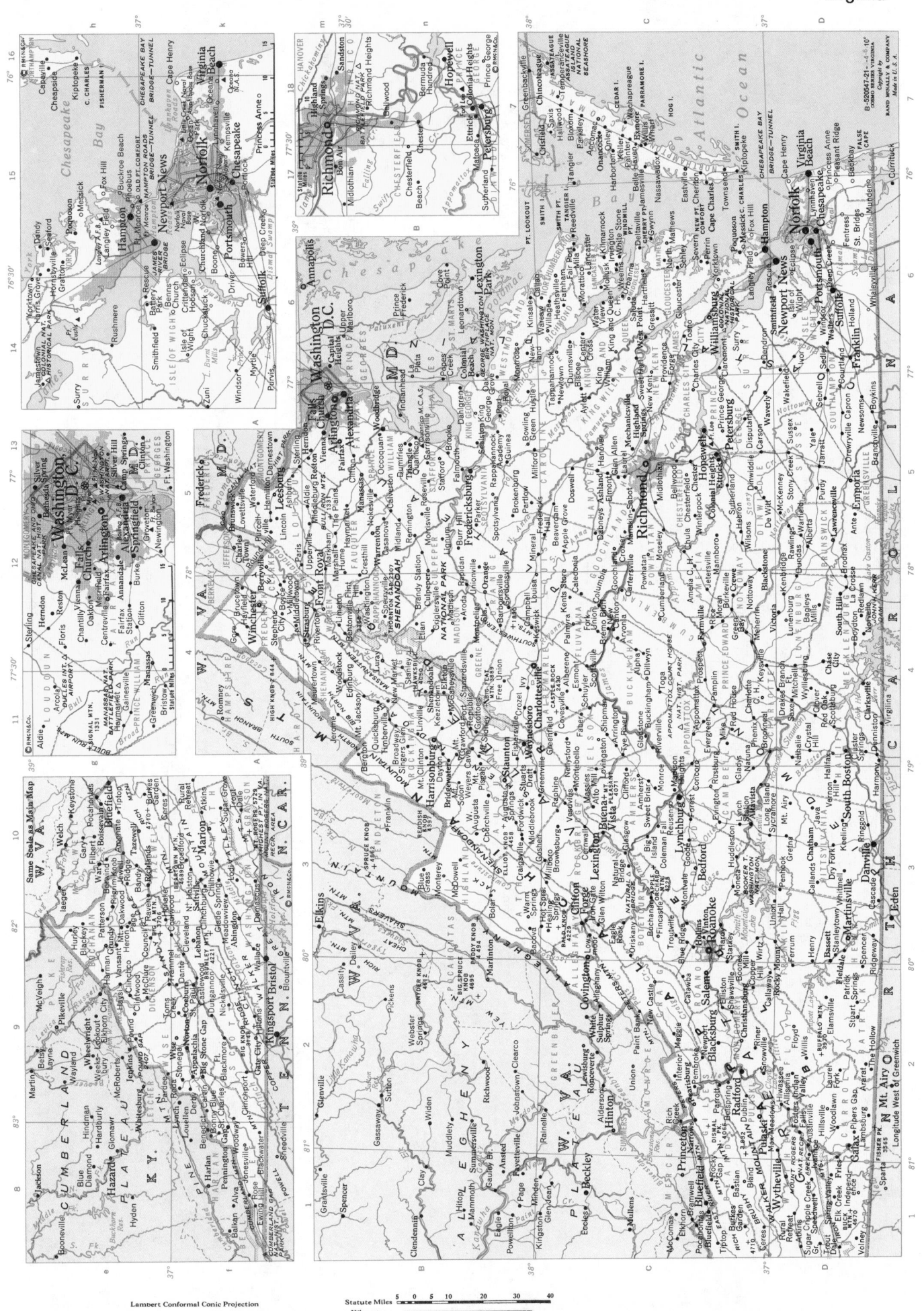

Lambert Conformal Conic Projection

Statute Miles

Kilometers

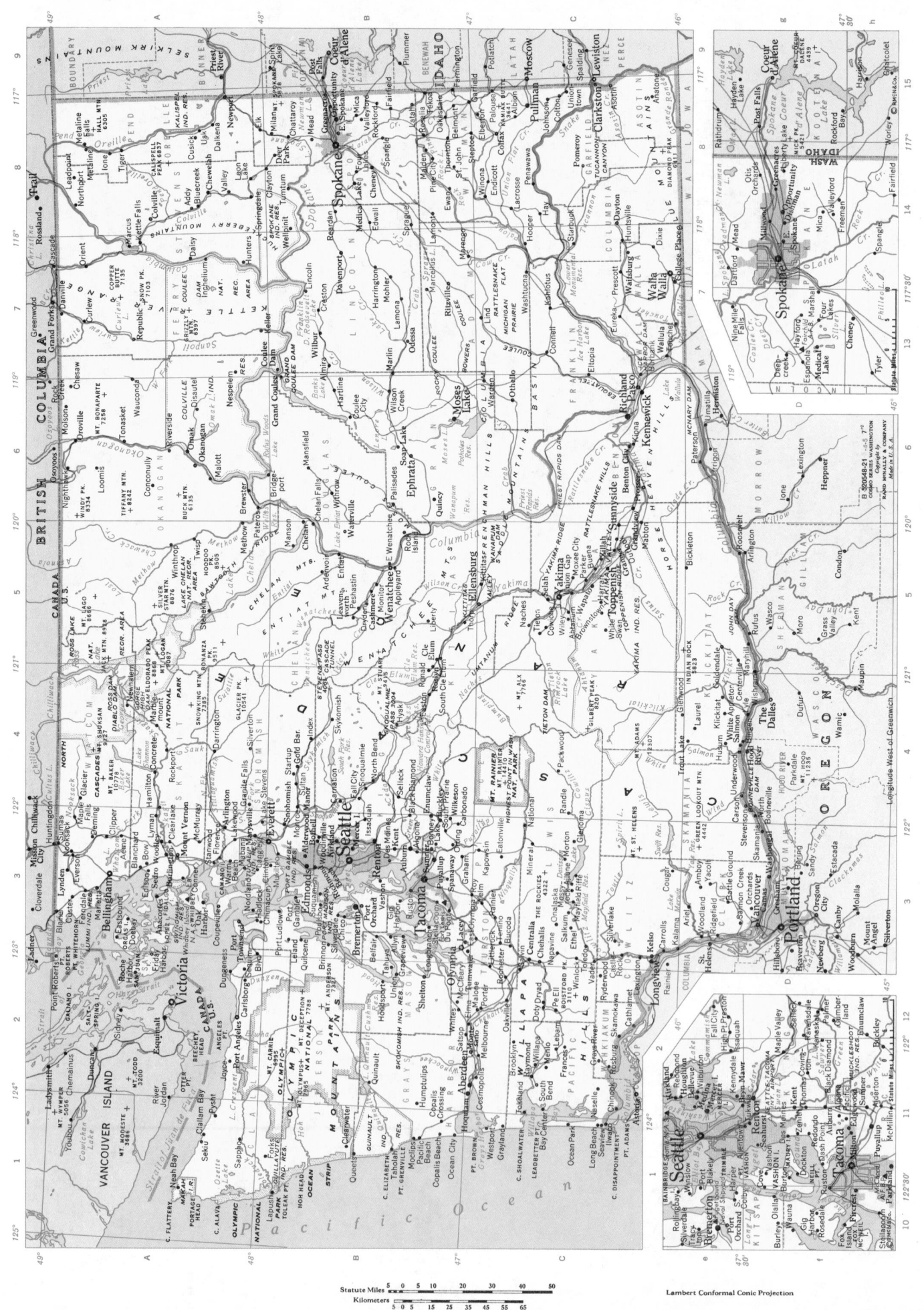

Statute Miles

Kilometers

Lambert Conformal Conic Projection

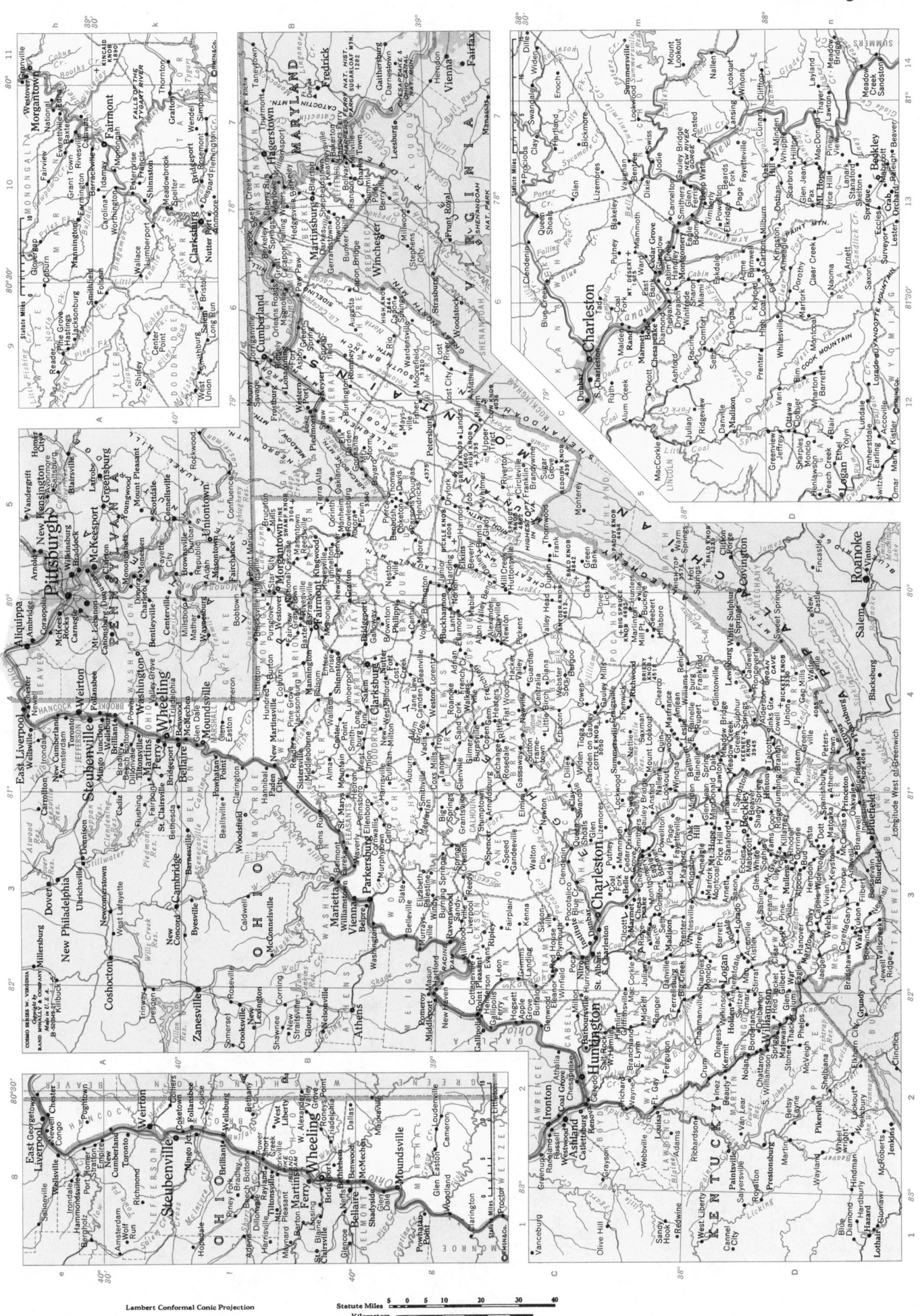

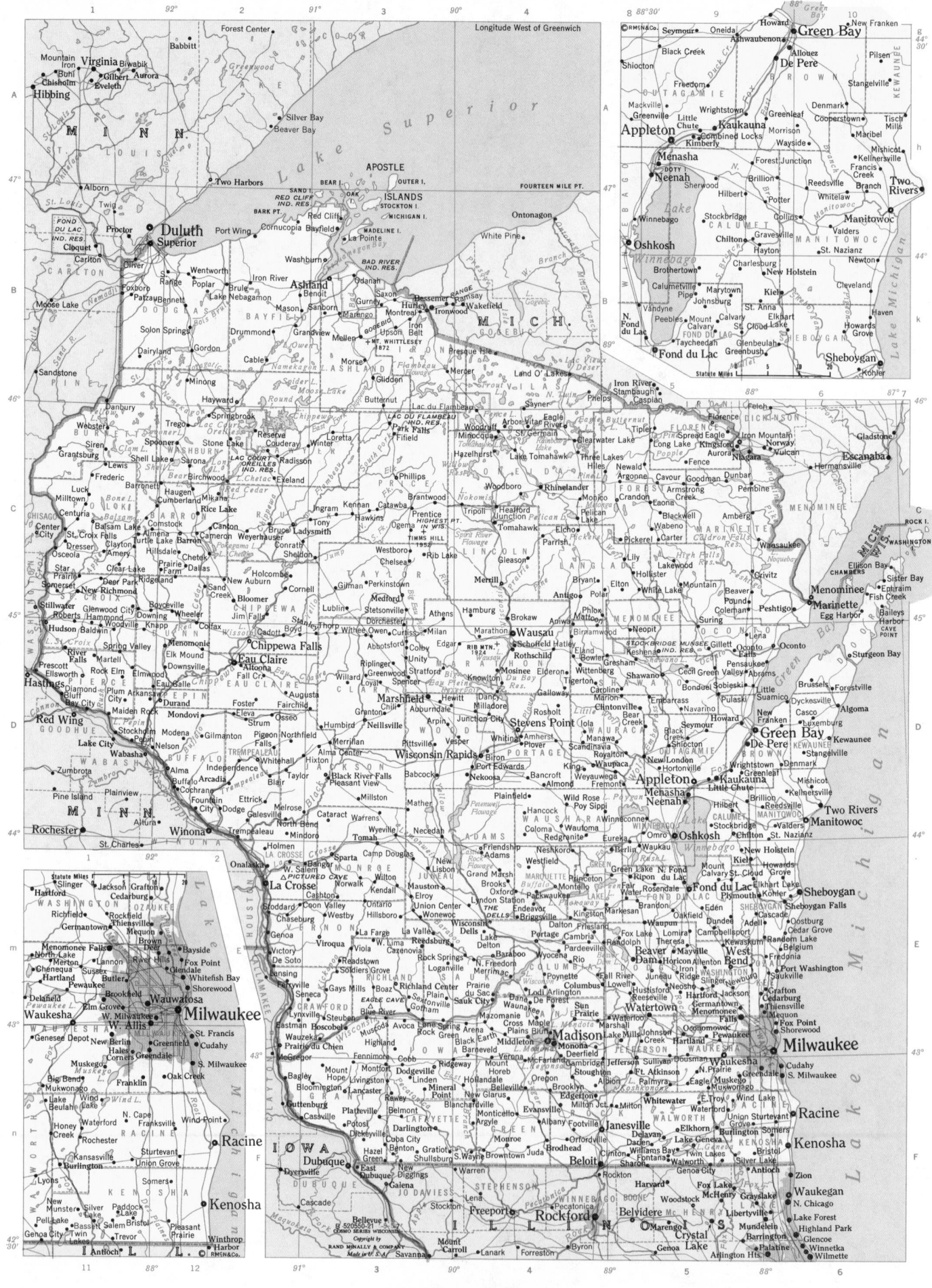

Longitude West of Greenwich

Lambert Conformal Conic Projection

Statute Miles

Kilometers

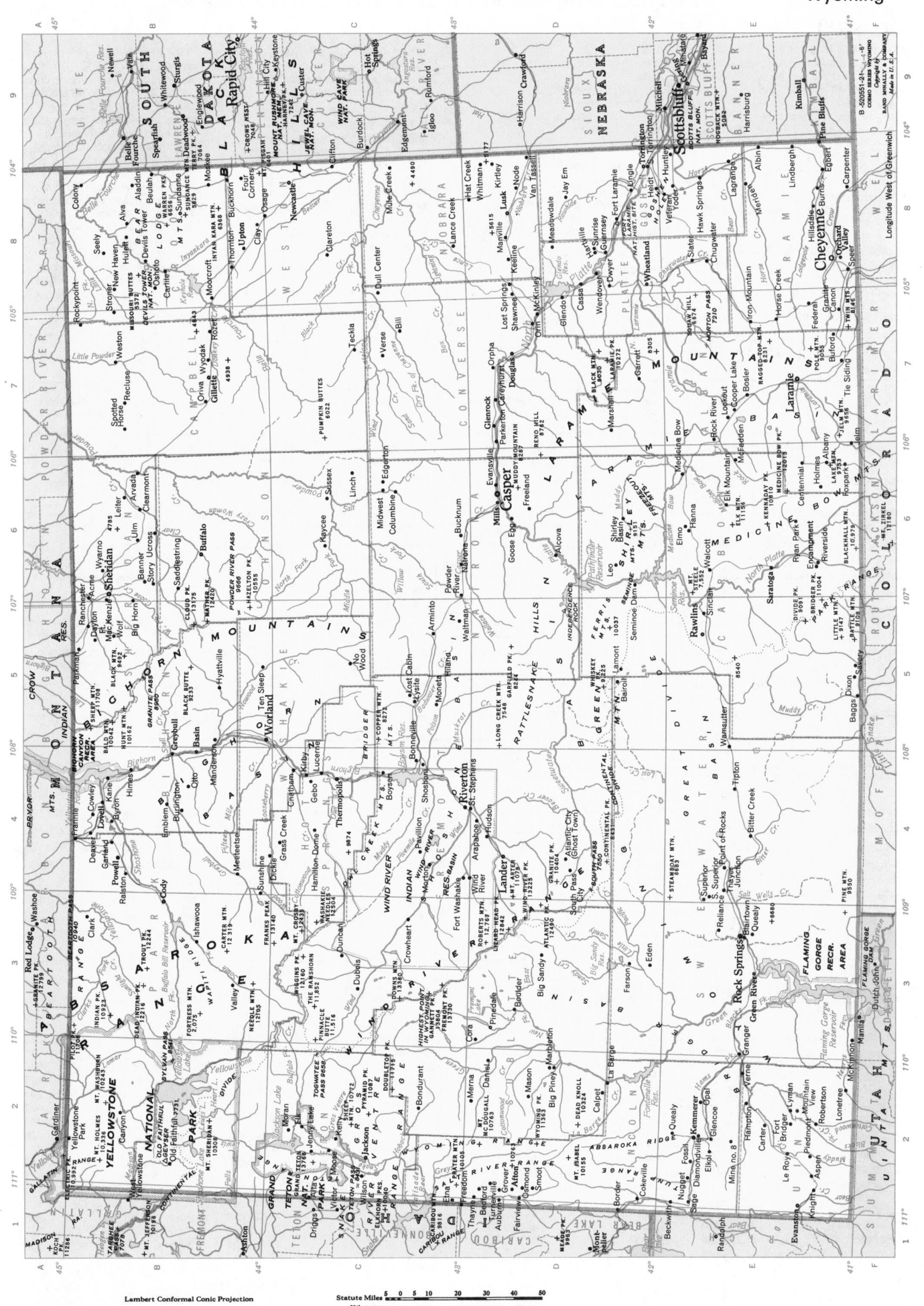

Statute Miles 5 0 5 10 20 30 40 50

Kilometers 5 0 5 15 25 35 45 55 65 75

WORLD GEOGRAPHICAL INFORMATION

GENERAL

MOVEMENTS OF THE EARTH

The earth makes one complete revolution around the sun every 365 days, 5 hours, 48 minutes, and 46 seconds.

The earth makes one complete rotation on its axis in 23 hours, 56 minutes and 4 seconds.

The earth revolves in its orbit around the sun at a speed of 66,700 miles per hour.

The earth rotates on its axis at an equatorial speed of more than 1,000 miles per hour.

MEASUREMENTS OF THE EARTH

Estimated age of the earth, at least 4.6 billion years.
Equatorial diameter of the earth, 7,926.38 miles.
Polar diameter of the earth, 7,899.80 miles.
Mean diameter of the earth, 7,917.52 miles.
Equatorial circumference of the earth, 24,901.45 miles.
Polar circumference of the earth, 24,855.33 miles.

Difference between equatorial and polar circumference of the earth, 46.12 miles.
Weight of the earth, 6,600,000,000,000,000,000,000 tons, or 6,600 billion billion tons.
Total area of the earth, 197,000,000 square miles.
Total land area of the earth (including inland water and Antarctica), 57,800,000 square miles.

THE EARTH'S INHABITANTS

Total population of the earth is estimated to be 4,975,000,000 (January 1, 1987).
Estimated population density of the earth, 86 per square mile.

THE EARTH'S SURFACE

Highest point on the earth's surface, Mount Everest, China (Tibet)-Nepal, 29,028 feet.
Lowest point on the earth's land surface, shores of the Dead Sea, Israel-Jordan, 1,312 feet below sea level.
Greatest ocean depth, the Mariana Trench, southwest of Guam, Pacific Ocean, 35,810 feet.

EXTREMES OF TEMPERATURE AND RAINFALL OF THE EARTH

Highest temperature ever recorded, 136° F. at Al 'Azīzīyah, Libya, Africa, on September 13, 1922.
Lowest temperature ever recorded, –129° F. at Vostok, Antarctica, on July 21, 1983.
Highest mean annual temperature, 94° F. at Dallol, Ethiopia.
Lowest mean annual temperature, –70° F. at Plateau Station, Antarctica.
The greatest local average annual rainfall is at Mt. Waialeale, Kauai, Hawaii, 460 inches.
The greatest 24-hour rainfall, 74 inches is at Cilaos, Reunion Island, March 15–16, 1952.
The lowest local average annual rainfall is at Arica, Chile, .03 inches.
The longest dry period, over 14 years, is at Arica, Chile, October 1903 to January 1918.

THE CONTINENTS

CONTINENT	Area (sq. mi.)	Estimated Population Jan. 1, 1987	Population per sq. mi.	Mean Elevation (feet)	Highest Elevation (Feet)	Lowest Elevation (Feet)	Highest Recorded Temperature	Lowest Recorded Temperature
North America	9,400,000	407,200,000	43	2,000	Mt. McKinley, United States (Alaska), 20,320	Death Valley, California, 282 below sea level	Death Valley, California, 134° F.	Snag, Yukon, Canada, –81° F.
South America	6,900,000	276,700,000	40	1,800	Cerro Aconcagua, Argentina, 22,831	Salinas Chicas, Argentina, 138 below sea level	Rivadavia, Argentina, 120° F.	Sarmiento, Argentina, –27° F.
Europe	3,800,000	680,100,000	179	980	Mt. Elbrus, Soviet Union, 18,510	Caspian Sea, Soviet Union-Iran, 92 below sea level	Sevilla (Seville), Spain, 122° F.	Ust-Shchugor, Soviet Union, –67° F.
Asia	17,300,000	2,985,300,000	173	3,000	Mt. Everest, China (Tibet)-Nepal, 29,028	Dead Sea, Israel-Jordan, 1,312 below sea level	Tirat Zevi, Israel, 129° F.	Oymyakon, Soviet Union, –90° F.
Africa	11,700,000	600,600,000	51	1,900	Mt. Kilimanjaro, Tanzania, 19,340	Lac Assal, Djibouti, 509 below sea level	Al 'Azīzīyah, Libya, 136° F.	Ifrane, Morocco, –11° F.
Oceania, incl. Australia	3,300,000	25,100,000	7	....	Mt. Wilhelm, Papua New Guinea, 14,793	Lake Eyre, South Australia, 52 below sea level	Cloncurry, Queensland, Australia, 128° F.	Charlotte Pass, New South Wales, Australia, –8° F
Australia	2,966,153	16,065,000	5	1,000	Mt. Kosciusko, New South Wales, 7,310	Lake Eyre, South Australia, 52 below sea level	Cloncurry, Queensland, 128° F.	Charlotte Pass, New South Wales, –8° F.
Antarctica	5,400,000	Uninhabited	....	6,000	Vinson Massif, 16,864	Unknown	Esperanza (Antarctic Peninsula), 59° F.	Vostok, –129° F.
World	57,800,000	4,975,000,000	86	....	Mt. Everest, China (Tibet)-Nepal, 29,028	Dead Sea, Israel-Jordan, 1,312 below sea level	Al 'Azīzīyah, Libya, 136° F.	Vostok, Antarctica, –129° F.

HISTORICAL POPULATIONS *

AREA	1650	1750	1800	1850	1900	1914	1920	1939	1950	1987
North America	5,000,000	5,000,000	13,000,000	39,000,000	106,000,000	141,000,000	147,000,000	186,000,000	219,000,000	407,200,000
South America	8,000,000	7,000,000	12,000,000	20,000,000	38,000,000	55,000,000	61,000,000	90,000,000	111,000,000	276,700,000
Europe	100,000,000	140,000,000	190,000,000	265,000,000	400,000,000	470,000,000	453,000,000	526,000,000	530,000,000	680,100,000
Asia	335,000,000	476,000,000	593,000,000	754,000,000	932,000,000	1,006,000,000	1,000,000,000	1,247,000,000	1,418,000,000	2,985,300,000
Africa	100,000,000	95,000,000	90,000,000	95,000,000	118,000,000	130,000,000	140,000,000	170,000,000	199,000,000	600,600,000
Oceania, incl. Australia	2,000,000	2,000,000	2,000,000	2,000,000	6,000,000	8,000,000	9,000,000	11,000,000	13,000,000	25,100,000
Australia					4,000,000	5,000,000	6,000,000	7,000,000	8,000,000	16,065,000
World	550,000,000	725,000,000	900,000,000	1,175,000,000	1,600,000,000	1,810,000,000	1,810,000,000	2,230,000,000	2,490,000,000	4,975,000,000

* Figures prior to 1987 are rounded to the nearest million. Figures in italics represent very rough estimates.

LARGEST COUNTRIES : POPULATION

		Population 1/1/87
1	China (excl. Taiwan)	1,069,410,000
2	India (incl. part of Jammu and Kashmir)	773,430,000
3	Soviet Union	280,830,000
4	United States	241,960,000
5	Indonesia	168,460,000
6	Brazil	140,440,000
7	Japan	121,770,000
8	Nigeria	107,250,000
9	Pakistan (incl. part of Jammu and Kashmir)	103,510,000
10	Bangladesh	102,510,000
11	Mexico	81,230,000

		Population 1/1/87
12	Vietnam	62,670,000
13	Federal Republic of Germany (West Germany)	60,925,000
14	Italy	57,300,000
15	United Kingdom	56,510,000
16	Philippines	55,930,000
17	France	55,500,000
18	Turkey	53,450,000
19	Thailand	52,690,000
20	Egypt	50,540,000
21	Iran	46,130,000
22	Ethiopia	45,170,000
23	South Korea	42,200,000
24	Spain	39,680,000
25	Burma	37,970,000

LARGEST COUNTRIES : AREA

		Area (sq. mi.)
1	Soviet Union	8,600,387
2	Canada	3,849,674
3	China (excl. Taiwan)	3,718,783
4	United States	3,679,245
5	Brazil	3,286,488
6	Australia	2,966,153
7	India (incl. part of Jammu and Kashmir)	1,237,062
8	Argentina	1,073,400
9	Sudan	967,500
10	Algeria	919,595
11	Zaire	905,568
12	Greenland	840,004
13	Saudi Arabia	830,000
14	Mexico	761,605
15	Indonesia	741,101

		Area (sq. mi.)
16	Libya	679,362
17	Iran	636,296
18	Mongolia	604,250
19	Peru	496,225
20	Chad	495,755
21	Niger	489,191
22	Angola	481,354
23	Mali	478,767
24	Ethiopia	472,435
25	Colombia	440,831
26	South Africa	433,680
27	Bolivia	424,165
28	Mauritania	397,956
29	Egypt	386,662
30	Tanzania	364,900
31	Nigeria	356,669

PRINCIPAL MOUNTAINS

NORTH AMERICA

Height (feet)

McKinley, Mt., Δ Alaska (Δ United States; Δ North America) 20,320
Logan, Mt., Δ Canada (Δ St. Elias Mts.; Δ Yukon) 19,524
Citlaltépetl, Volcán, Δ Mexico 18,701
St. Elias, Mt., Alaska—Canada 18,008
Popocatépetl, Volcán, Mexico 17,887
Foraker, Mt., Alaska 17,400
Ixtacihuatl, Mexico 17,343
Lucania, Mt., Canada 17,147
Fairweather, Mt., Alaska—Canada (Δ British Columbia) 15,300
Whitney, Mt., Δ California 14,494
Elbert, Mt., Δ Colorado (Δ Rocky Mts.) 14,433
Massive, Mt., Colorado 14,421
Harvard, Mt., Colorado 14,420
Rainier, Mt., Δ Washington (Δ Cascade Range) 14,410
Williamson, Mt., California 14,375
Blanca Pk., Colorado (Δ Sangre de Cristo Mts.) 14,345
La Plata Pk., Colorado 14,336
Uncompahgre Pk., Colorado (Δ San Juan Mts.) 14,309
Grays Pk., Colorado (Δ Front Range) 14,270
Evans, Mt., Colorado 14,264
Longs Pk., Colorado 14,255
Wrangell, Mt., Alaska 14,163
Shasta, Mt., California 14,162
Pikes Pk., Colorado 14,110
Colima, Nevado de, Mexico 13,993
Tajumulco, Volcán, Δ Guatemala (Δ Central America) 13,846
Gannett Pk., Δ Wyoming 13,804
Mauna Kea, Δ Hawaii 13,796
Grand Teton, Wyoming 13,770
Mauna Loa, Hawaii 13,679
Kings Pk., Δ Utah 13,528
Cloud Pk., Wyoming (Δ Bighorn Mts.) 13,167
Wheeler Pk., Δ New Mexico 13,161
Boundary Pk., Δ Nevada 13,140
Waddington, Mt., Canada (Δ Coast Mts.) 13,104
Robson, Mt., Canada (Δ Canadian Rockies) 12,972
Granite Pk., Δ Montana 12,799
Borah Pk., Δ Idaho 12,662
Humphreys Pk., Δ Arizona 12,633
Chirripó, Cerro, Δ Costa Rica 12,533
Columbia, Mt., Canada (Δ Alberta) 12,294
Adams, Mt., Washington 12,276
Gunnbjørn Fjeld, Δ Greenland 12,139
San Gorgonio Mtn., California 11,499
Barú, Volcán, Δ Panama 11,411
Hood, Mt., Δ Oregon 11,235
Lassen Pk., California 10,457
Duarte, Pico, Δ Dominican Rep. (Δ West Indies) 10,417
Haleakala Crater, Hawaii (Δ Maui) 10,023
Paricutín, Mexico 9,213
Pital, Cerro el, Δ El Salvador—Honduras 8,957
La Salle, Pic, Δ Haiti 8,773
Guadalupe Pk., Δ Texas 8,749
Olympus, Mt., Washington (Δ Olympic Mts.) 7,965
Blue Mountain Pk., Δ Jamaica 7,402
Harney Pk., Δ South Dakota (Δ Black Hills) 7,242
Mitchell, Mt., Δ North Carolina (Δ Appalachian Mts.) 6,684
Clingmans Dome, North Carolina—Δ Tennessee (Δ Great Smoky Mts.) 6,643
Turquino, Pico, Δ Cuba 6,542
Washington, Mt., Δ New Hampshire (Δ White Mts.) 6,288
Rogers, Mt., Δ Virginia 5,729
Marcy, Mt., Δ New York (Δ Adirondack Mts.) 5,344
Katahdin, Δ Maine 5,268
Kawaikini, Hawaii (Δ Kauai) 5,243
Spruce Knob, Δ West Virginia 4,862
Pelée, Montagne, Δ Martinique 4,583
Mansfield, Mt., Δ Vermont (Δ Green Mts.) 4,393
Punta, Cerro de, Δ Puerto Rico 4,389
Black Mtn., Δ Kentucky—Virginia 4,145
Kaala, Hawaii (Δ Oahu) 4,040

SOUTH AMERICA

Aconcagua, Cerro, Δ Argentina (Δ Andes Mts.; Δ South America) 22,831
Ojos del Salado, Nevado, Argentina—Δ Chile 22,572
Bonete, Cerro, Argentina 22,546
Pissis, Monte, Argentina 22,241
Huascarán, Nevado, Δ Peru 22,123
Llullaillaco, Volcán, Argentina—Chile 22,110
Yerupaja, Nevado, Peru 21,765
Tupungato, Cerro, Argentina—Chile 21,490
Sajama, Nevado, Δ Bolivia 21,463
Illampu, Nevado, Bolivia 20,873
Chimborazo, Δ Ecuador 20,702
Antofalla, Volcán, Argentina 20,013
Cotopaxi, Ecuador 19,347
Misti, Nevado, Peru 19,101
Cristóbal Colón, Pico, Δ Colombia 19,029
Huila, Nevado del, Colombia (Δ Cordillera Central) 18,865
Bolívar, Pico, Δ Venezuela 16,427
Fitzroy, Monte (Cerro Chaltel), Argentina—Chile 11,073
Neblina, Pico da, Δ Brazil—Venezuela 9,888

EUROPE

Elbrus, Mt., Soviet Union (Δ Caucasus Mts.; Δ Europe) 18,510
Dykh-Tau, Mt., Soviet Union 17,073
Shkhara, Mt., Soviet Union 16,627
Blanc, Mont (Monte Bianco), Δ France—Δ Italy (Δ Alps) 15,771
Rosa, Monte (Dufourspitze), Italy—Δ Switzerland 15,203
Weisshorn, Switzerland 14,780
Matterhorn, Italy—Switzerland 14,692
Finsteraarhorn, Switzerland 14,022
Jungfrau, Switzerland 13,642
Barre des Écrins, France 13,458
Viso, Mt., Italy (Δ Cottian Alps) 12,602
Grossglockner, Δ Austria 12,457
Teide, Pico de, Δ Spain (Δ Canary Is.) 12,198
Mulhacén, Δ Spain (continental) 11,411
Aneto, Pico de, Spain (Δ Pyrenees) 11,168
Perdido (Perdu), Spain 11,007
Etna, Mt., Italy (Δ Sicily) 10,902
Zugspitze, Austria—Δ Germany, Fed. Rep. of 9,716
Musala, Δ Bulgaria 9,596
Corno Grande, Italy (Δ Apennines) 9,554
Olympus, Mount, Δ Greece 9,570
Triglav, Δ Yugoslavia 9,393
Korab, Δ Albania—Yugoslavia 9,026
Cinto, Monte, France (Δ Corsica) 8,878
Gerlachovka, Δ Czechoslovakia (Δ Carpathian Mts.) 8,711
Moldoveanu, Δ Romania 8,343
Rysy, Czechoslovakia—Δ Poland 8,199
Glittertinden, Δ Norway (Δ Scandinavia) 8,110
Parnassós, Greece 8,061
Ida, Mount, Greece (Δ Crete) 8,058
Pico, Ponta do, Δ Portugal (Δ Azores Is.) 7,713
Hvannadalshnúkur, Δ Iceland 6,952
Kebnekaise, Δ Sweden 6,926
Estrela, Δ Portugal (continental) 6,539
Narodnaya, Mt., Soviet Union (Δ Ural Mts.) 6,217
Sancy, Puy de, France (Δ Massif Central) 6,184
La Marmora, Punta, Italy (Δ Sardinia) 6,017
Hekla, Mt., Iceland 4,892
Nevis, Ben, Δ United Kingdom (Δ Scotland) 4,406
Haltia, Δ Finland—Norway 4,357
Vesuvius, Italy 4,190
Snowdon, Δ Wales 3,560
Carrantuohill, Δ Ireland 3,414
Kékes, Δ Hungary 3,330
Scafell Pikes, Δ England 3,210

ASIA

Everest, Mt., Δ China—Δ Nepal (Δ Tibet; Δ Himalayas; Δ Asia; Δ World) 29,028
K2 (Godwin Austen), China—Δ Pakistan (Δ Kashmir; Δ Karakoram Range) 28,250
Kānchenjunga, Nepal—Δ India 28,208
Makālu, China—Nepal 27,825
Dhaulāgiri, Nepal 26,810
Nānga Parbat, Pakistan 26,660
Annapurna, Nepal 26,504
Gasherbrum, China—Pakistan 26,470
Xixabangma Mtn. (Gosainthan), China 26,291
Nanda Devi, India 25,645
Kāmet, China—India 25,447
Namcha Barwa, China 25,446
Muztag, China (Δ Kunlun Mts.) 25,338
Tirich Mīr, Pakistan (Δ Hindu Kush) 25,230
Gongga Mtn. (Minya Konka), China 24,790
Muztagata, China 24,757
Kula Kangri, Δ Bhutan 24,784
Communism Pk., Δ Soviet Union (Δ Pamir Mts.) 24,590
Nowshāk, Δ Afghanistan—Pakistan 24,557
Pobedy, Pk., China—Soviet Union (Δ Tien Shan) 24,406
Chomo Lhāri, Bhutan—China 23,997
Lenin Pk., Soviet Union 23,406
Api, Nepal 23,399
Kangrinboqê Mtn., China 22,028
Hkakabo Razi, Δ Burma 19,296
Demavend, Mt., Δ Iran 18,386
Ararat, Mt., Δ Turkey 16,804
Jaya Pk., Δ Indonesia (Δ New Guinea) 16,503
Fūlādī, Kūh-e, Afghanistan 16,243
Klyuchevskaya Sopka, Soviet Union (Δ Kamchatka Peninsula) 15,584
Trikora Pk., Indonesia 15,584
Belukha, Mt., Soviet Union 14,783
Süphan Dağı, Turkey 14,547
Kinabalu, Mt., Δ Malaysia (Δ Borneo) 13,432
Yü, Mt., Δ Taiwan 13,114
Türgen Mtn., Mongolia 13,051
Erciyeş Dağı, Turkey 12,848
Kerinci, Indonesia (Δ Sumatra) 12,467
Fuji, Mt., Δ Japan (Δ Honshu) 12,388
Nabi Shuayb, Mt., Δ Yemen (Δ Arabian Peninsula) 12,336
Rinjani, Indonesia (Δ Lombok) 12,224
Semeru, Indonesia (Δ Java) 12,060
Rantekombola, Indonesia (Δ Celebes) 11,335
Slamet, Indonesia 11,247
Fan-si-pan, Δ Vietnam 10,312
Shām, Jabal ash, Δ Oman 9,957
Apo, Mt., Δ Philippines (Δ Mindanao) 9,692
Pulog, Mt., Philippines (Δ Luzon) 9,606
Bia, Δ Laos 9,252
Hermon, Mt., Lebanon—Δ Syria 9,232
Paektu, Mt., Δ North Korea—China 9,003
Inthanon, Δ Thailand 8,514
Pidurutalagala, Δ Sri Lanka 8,281
Mayon Volcano, Philippines 7,943
Asahi, Mt., Japan (Δ Hokkaido) 7,513
Tahan, Malaysia (Δ Malaya) 7,174
Ólimbos, Δ Cyprus 6,401
Halla, Mt., Δ South Korea 6,398
Kujū, Mt., Japan (Δ Kyushu) 5,866
Aoral, Δ Kampuchea 5,810
Ramm, Jabal, Δ Jordan 5,755
Meron, Mt., Δ Israel 3,963
Carmel, Mt., Israel 1,791

AFRICA

Kilimanjaro, Δ Tanzania (Δ Africa) 19,340
Kirinyaga (Mt. Kenya), Δ Kenya 17,058
Margherita Pk., Δ Zaire—Δ Uganda 16,763
Ras Dashen Terara, Δ Ethiopia 15,158
Meru, Mt., Tanzania 14,978
Karisimbi, Volcan, Δ Rwanda—Zaire 14,787
Elgon, Mt., Kenya—Uganda 14,178
Toubkal, Jbel, Δ Morocco (Δ Atlas Mts.) 13,665
Cameroun, Mont, Δ Cameroon 13,353
Thabana Ntlenyana, Δ Lesotho 11,425
Koussi, Emi, Δ Chad (Δ Tibesti Mts.) 11,204
Injasuti, Δ South Africa 11,182
Kinyeti, Δ Sudan 10,456
Santa Isabel, Pico de, Δ Equatorial Guinea (Δ Bioko) 9,868
Tahat, Δ Algeria (Δ Ahaggar Mts.) 9,541
Maromokotro, Δ Madagascar 9,436
Kātrīnā, Jabal, Δ Egypt 8,668
São Tomé, Pico de, Δ Sao Tome 6,640

OCEANIA

Wilhelm, Mt., Δ Papua New Guinea 14,793
Giluwe, Mt., Papua New Guinea 14,330
Bangeta, Mt., Papua New Guinea 13,520
Victoria, Mt., Papua New Guinea (Δ Owen Stanley Range) 13,240
Cook, Mt., Δ New Zealand (Δ South Island) 12,349
Ruapehu, Mt., New Zealand (Δ North Island) 9,177
Balbi, Papua New Guinea (Δ Solomon Is.) 9,000
Egmont, Mt., New Zealand 8,260
Sinewit, Mt., Papua New Guinea (Δ Bismarck Archipelago) 8,000
Orohena, Δ French Polynesia (Δ Tahiti) 7,352
Kosciusko, Mt., Δ Australia (Δ New South Wales) 7,310
Silisili, Mt., Δ Western Samoa 6,096
Panié, Mont, Δ New Caledonia 5,341
Ossa, Mt., Australia (Δ Tasmania) 5,305
Bartle Frere, Mt., Australia (Δ Queensland) 5,285
Woodroffe, Mt., Australia (Δ South Australia) 4,721
Tomanivi (Victoria), Δ Fiji (Δ Viti Levu) 4,341
Bruce, Mt., Australia (Δ Western Australia) 4,052
Ayers Rock, Australia 2,844

ANTARCTICA

Vinson Massif, (Δ Antarctica) 16,864
Kirkpatrick, Mt. 14,856
Markham, Mt. 14,275
Jackson, Mt. 13,750
Sidley, Mt. 13,717
Wade, Mt. 13,399

Δ Highest mountain in state, country, range, or region named.

OCEANS, SEAS AND GULFS

	Area (sq. mi.)	Greatest Depth (ft.)		Area (sq. mi.)	Greatest Depth (ft.)		Area (sq. mi.)	Greatest Depth (ft.)
Pacific Ocean	63,800,000	35,810	South China Sea	1,331,000	18,241	Okhotsk, Sea of	619,000	11,063
Atlantic Ocean	31,800,000	28,232	Caribbean Sea	1,063,000	25,197	Norwegian Sea	597,000	13,189
Indian Ocean	28,900,000	23,376	Mediterranean Sea	967,000	16,470	Mexico, Gulf of	596,000	14,370
Arctic Ocean	5,400,000	17,881	Bering Sea	876,000	25,194	Hudson Bay	475,000	850
Arabian Sea	1,492,000	19,029	Bengal, Bay of	839,000	17,251	Greenland Sea	465,000	15,899

PRINCIPAL LAKES

	Area (sq. mi.)		Area (sq. mi.)		Area (sq. mi.)
Caspian Sea, Iran—Soviet Union (salt)	143,240	Ladoga, L., Soviet Union	6,835	Nettilling Lake, Canada	2,140
Superior, L., Canada—United States	31,700	Chad, L., Cameroon—Chad—Nigeria	6,300	Winnipegosis, L., Canada	2,075
Victoria, L., Kenya—Tanzania—Uganda	26,820	Onega, L., Soviet Union	3,750	Bangweulu, L., Zambia	1,930
Aral Sea, Soviet Union (salt)	24,750	Eyre, L., Australia (salt)	Δ 3,668	Nipigon, L., Canada	1,872
Huron, L., Canada—United States	23,000	Titicaca, Lago, Bolivia—Peru	3,200	Urmia, L., Iran (salt)	Δ 1,815
Michigan, L., United States	22,300	Nicaragua, Lago de, Nicaragua	3,150	Manitoba, L., Canada	1,799
Tanganyika. L., Burundi—Tanzania—Zaire—Zambia	12,350	Mai-Ndombe, Lac, Zaire	Δ 3,100	Kyoga, L., Uganda	1,710
Baikal, L., Soviet Union	12,160	Athabasca, L., Canada	3,064	Woods, Lake of the, Canada—United States	1,695
Great Bear Lake, Canada	12,028	Reindeer Lake, Canada	2,568	Great Salt Lake, United States (salt)	1,680
Nyasa, L., Malawi—Mozambique—Tanzania	11,150	Tonle Sap, Kampuchea	Δ 2,500	Mweru, L., Zaire—Zambia	1,680
Great Slave Lake, Canada	11,031	Rudolf, L., Ethiopia—Kenya (salt)	2,473	Gairdner, L., Australia (salt)	Δ 1,660
Erie, L., Canada—United States	9,910	Issyk-Kul, L., Soviet Union (salt)	2,425	Peipus, L., Soviet Union	1,660
Winnipeg, L., Canada	9,417	Torrens, L., Australia (salt)	2,278	Qinghai Lake (Koko Nor), China (salt)	1,650
Ontario, L., Canada—United States	7,540	Albert, L., Uganda—Zaire	2,160	Khanka, L., China—Soviet Union	1,620
Balkhash, L., Soviet Union	Δ 7,065	Vänern, Sweden	2,156	Van Gölü, Turkey (salt)	1,420

Δ *Due to seasonal fluctuations in water level, areas of these lakes vary considerably.*

PRINCIPAL RIVERS

	Length (miles)		Length (miles)		Length (miles)
Nile—Kagera, Africa	4,145	Pilcomayo, South America	1,550	Xiang Jiang, Asia	930
Amazon—Ucayali, South America	4,000	Euphrates (Firat), Asia	1,510	Canadian, North America	906
Yangtze (Chang Jiang), Asia	3,915	Ural, Asia	1,509	Brazos, North America	870
Mississippi—Missouri, North America	3,740	Arkansas, North America	1,459	Salado, South America	870
Huang He (Yellow), Asia	3,395	Colorado, North America (U.S.—Mexico)	1,450	Darling, Australia	864
Ob—Irtysh, Asia	3,362	Aldan, Asia	1,412	Fraser, North America	850
Rio de la Plata—Paraná, South America	3,030	Dnepr, Europe	1,368	Parnaíba, South America	850
Congo (Zaïre), Africa	2,900	Araguaia, South America	1,367	Colorado, North America (Texas)	840
Paraná, South America	2,796	Kasai (Cassai), Africa	1,338	Dnestr, Europe	840
Amur—Argun, Asia	2,761	Tarim He, Asia	1,328	Rhine, Europe	820
Lena, Asia	2,734	Kolyma, Asia	1,323	Narmada, Asia	800
Mackenzie, North America	2,635	Negro, South America	1,305	Saint Lawrence, North America	800
Mekong, Asia	2,600	Orange, Africa	1,300	Ottawa, North America	790
Niger, Africa	2,600	Red, North America	1,270	Athabasca, North America	765
Yenisey, Asia	2,543	Juruá, South America	1,250	Northern Donets, Europe	735
Mississippi, North America	2,348	Columbia, North America	1,243	Pecos, North America	735
Murray—Darling, Australia	2,330	Irrawaddy, Asia	1,238	Green, North America	730
Missouri, North America	2,315	Xingu, South America	1,230	Cumberland, North America	720
Ob, Asia	2,287	Ucayali, South America	1,220	Elbe (Labe), Europe	720
Volga, Europe	2,194	Saskatchewan—Bow, North America	1,205	White (Arkansas—Missouri), North America	720
Madeira—Mamoré, South America	1,988	Peace, North America	1,195	James, North America (N./S. Dakota)	710
São Francisco, South America	1,988	Tigris (Dicle), Asia	1,180	Gambia, Africa	680
Yukon, North America	1,979	Don, Europe	1,162	Yellowstone, North America	671
Grande, Rio, North America	1,885	Songhua Jiang, Asia	1,140	Tennessee, North America	652
Syr Darya, Asia	1,876	Pechora, Europe	1,124	Gila, North America	630
Purús, South America	1,860	Kama, Europe	1,122	Wisła (Vistula), Europe	630
Indus, Asia	1,800	Angara, Asia	1,105	Loire, Europe	625
Danube, Europe	1,776	Limpopo, Africa	1,100	Tagus (Tejo) (Tajo), Europe	625
Brahmaputra, Asia	1,770	Snake, North America	1,038	North Platte, North America	618
Salween (Nu Jiang), Asia	1,750	Uruguay (Uruguai), South America	1,025	Albany, North America	610
Zambezi, Africa	1,700	Churchill, North America	1,000	Tisza (Tisa), Europe	607
Vilyuy, Asia	1,647	Marañón, South America	1,000	Back, North America	605
Tocantins, South America	1,640	Tobol, Asia	989	Ouachita, North America	605
Paraguay (Paraguai), South America	1,610	Ohio, North America	981	Cimarron, North America	600
Orinoco, South America	1,600	Magdalena, South America	950	Sava, Europe	585
Amu Darya, Asia	1,578	Roosevelt, South America	950	Nemunas (Neman), Europe	582
Murray, Australia	1,566	Oka, Europe	932	Branco, South America	580
Ganges, Asia	1,560	Godāvari, Asia	930	Oder (Odra), Europe	565

PRINCIPAL ISLANDS

	Area (sq. mi.)		Area (sq. mi.)		Area (sq. mi.)
Greenland, North America	840,004	Banks I., Canada	27,038	Ceram, Indonesia	6,046
New Guinea, Indonesia—Papua New Guinea	303,090	Tasmania, Australia	26,383	New Caledonia, Oceania	5,671
Borneo (Kalimantan), Asia	258,855	Sri Lanka, Asia	24,962	Flores, Indonesia	5,513
Madagascar, Africa	226,658	Devon I., Canada	21,331	Samar, Philippines	5,050
Baffin I., Canada	195,928	Novaya Zemlya (N. part), Soviet Union	18,882	Negros, Philippines	4,907
Sumatra (Sumatera), Indonesia	182,860	Tierra del Fuego, Isla Grande de, South America	18,600	Palawan, Philippines	4,550
Great Britain, United Kingdom	88,795	Melville I., Canada	16,274	Panay, Philippines	4,446
Honshū, Japan	87,804	Southampton I., Canada	15,913	Jamaica, North America	4,244
Ellesmere I., Canada	83,896	Spitsbergen, Norway	15,260	Hawaii, United States	4,021
Victoria I., Canada	75,767	New Britain, Papua New Guinea	14,592	Cape Breton I., Canada	3,981
Celebes (Sulawesi), Indonesia	73,057	Kyūshū, Japan	14,154	Bougainville, Papua New Guinea	3,880
South I., New Zealand	58,093	Taiwan, China	13,885	Mindoro, Philippines	3,759
Java (Jawa), Indonesia	51,038	Hainan I., China	13,127	Kodiak I., United States	3,670
North I., New Zealand	44,297	Timor, Indonesia	13,094	Cyprus, Asia	3,572
Newfoundland, Canada	43,359	Prince of Wales I., Canada	12,872	Puerto Rico, North America	3,515
Cuba, North America	40,519	Vancouver I., Canada	12,079	Corsica, France	3,352
Luzon, Philippines	40,420	Sicily, Italy	9,926	New Ireland, Papua New Guinea	3,205
Iceland, Europe	39,769	Somerset I., Canada	9,570	Crete, Greece	3,189
Mindanao, Philippines	36,537	Sardinia, Italy	9,301	Wrangel I., Soviet Union	2,819
Ireland, Europe	32,588	Shikoku, Japan	7,053	Leyte, Philippines	2,785
Hokkaidō, Japan	30,088	North East Land, Norway	6,350	Guadalcanal, Solomon Islands	2,500
Sakhalin, Soviet Union	29,498			Long I., United States	1,401
Hispaniola, North America	29,418				

This table lists the area, population, population density, form of government, political status, capital and predominant languages for every country in the world.

The populations are estimates for January 1, 1987 made by Rand McNally & Company on the basis of official data, United Nations estimates, and other available information. Area figures include inland water.

The political units listed in the table are categorized by political status, as follows:

A–independent countries; B–internally independent political entities which are under the protection of other countries in matters of defense and foreign affairs; C–colonies and other dependent political units; D–the major administrative subdivisions of Australia, Canada, China, the Soviet Union, the United Kingdom, and the United States. For comparison, the table also includes the continents and the world.

All footnotes to this table appear on page 228.

Country, Division or Region English (Conventional)	Area in sq. mi.	Estimated Population 1/1/87	Pop. per sq. mi.	Form of Government and Political Status		Capital	Predominant Languages
Afars and Issas see Djibouti	—	—	—				
†Afghanistan	245,664	18,950,000	77	Socialist Republic	A	Kabul	Dari, Pushtu
Africa	11,700,000	600,600,000	51				
Alabama	51,704	4,065,000	79	State (U.S.)	D	Montgomery	English
Alaska	591,004	530,000	0.9	State (U.S.)	D	Juneau	English, indigenous languages
†Albania	11,100	3,045,000	274	Socialist Republic	A	Tirana	Albanian
Alberta	255,287	2,395,000	9.4	Province (Canada)	D	Edmonton	English
†Algeria	919,595	23,135,000	25	Socialist Republic	A	Algiers (El Djazaïr)	Arabic, Berber dialects
American Samoa	77	37,000	481	Unincorporated Territory (U.S.)	C	Pago Pago	English, Samoan
Andorra	175	50,000	286	Coprincipality (Spanish and French protection)	B	Andorra	Spanish, French
†Angola	481,354	9,150,000	19	Socialist Republic	A	Luanda	Portuguese, indigenous languages
Anguilla	35	7,000	200	Associated State (U.K. protection)	B	The Valley	English
Anhui	54,054	52,720,000	975	Province (China)	D	Hefei	Chinese (Mandarin)
Antarctica	5,400,000	—(1)	—				
†Antigua and Barbuda	171	83,000	485	Parliamentary State	A	St. John's	English, local dialects
†Argentina	1,073,400	31,300,000	29	Republic	A	Buenos Aires	Spanish
Arizona	114,002	3,220,000	28	State (U.S.)	D	Phoenix	English
Arkansas	53,191	2,395,000	45	State (U.S.)	D	Little Rock	English
Armenia	11,506	3,370,000	293	Soviet Socialist Republic (Soviet Union)	D	Yerevan	Armenian, Russian
Aruba	75	77,000	1,027	Self-governing Territory (Netherlands protection)	B	Oranjestad	Dutch, English, Papiamento, Spanish
Ascension	34	1,700	50	Dependency (St. Helena)	C	Georgetown	English
Asia	17,300,000	2,985,300,000	173				
†Australia	2,966,153	16,065,000	5.4	Federal Parliamentary State	A	Canberra	English
Australian Capital Territory	927	260,000	280	Territory (Australia)	D	Canberra	English
†Austria	32,377	7,550,000	233	Federal Republic	A	Vienna (Wien)	German
Azerbaijan	33,436	6,710,000	201	Soviet Socialist Republic (Soviet Union)	D	Baku	Turkish, Russian, Armenian
†Bahamas	5,382	235,000	44	Parliamentary State	A	Nassau	English
†Bahrain	256	435,000	1,699	Constitutional Monarchy	A	Manama	Arabic, English
†Bangladesh	55,598	102,510,000	1,844	Republic	A	Dacca (Dhaka)	Bangla, English
†Barbados	166	255,000	1,536	Parliamentary State	A	Bridgetown	English
†Belgium	11,783	9,855,000	836	Constitutional Monarchy	A	Brussels (Bruxelles)	Dutch (Flemish), French, German
†Belize	8,866	170,000	19	Parliamentary State	A	Belmopan	English, Spanish, indigenous languages
†Benin	43,484	4,095,000	94	Socialist Republic	A	Porto-Novo	French, Adja, Fon, indigenous languages
Bermuda	21	59,000	2,810	Dependency (U.K.)	C	Hamilton	English
†Bhutan	18,147	1,445,000	80	Monarchy (Indian protection)	B	Thimbu	Dzongkha, English, Nepalese dialects
†Bolivia	424,165	6,700,000	16	Republic	A	Sucre and La Paz	Aymara, Quechua, Spanish
Bophuthatswana(2)	15,444	1,730,000	112	Black National State (South African protection)	B	Mmabatho	Setswana, English
†Botswana	224,711	1,155,000	5.1	Republic	A	Gaborone	English, Setswana
†Brazil	3,286,488	140,440,000	43	Federal Republic	A	Brasília	Portuguese
British Columbia	365,948	2,925,000	8.0	Province (Canada)	D	Victoria	English
British Indian Ocean Territory	23	300	13	Dependency (U.K.)	C		English
†Brunei	2,226	235,000	106	Constitutional Monarchy	A	Bandar Seri Begawan	English, Malay, Chinese
†Bulgaria	42,823	8,985,000	210	Socialist Republic	A	Sofia (Sofiya)	Bulgarian
†Burkina Faso	105,792	7,195,000	68	Provisional Military Government	A	Ouagadougou	French, indigenous languages
†Burma	261,228	37,970,000	145	Socialist Republic	A	Rangoon	Burmese, indigenous languages
†Burundi	10,745	5,000,000	465	Republic	A	Bujumbura	French, Kirundi, Swahili
†Byelorussia	80,155	10,110,000	126	Soviet Socialist Republic (Soviet Union)	D	Minsk	Byelorussian, Polish, Russian
California	158,704	26,715,000	168	State (U.S.)	D	Sacramento	English
Cambodia see Kampuchea	—	—	—				
†Cameroon	183,569	10,145,000	55	Republic	A	Yaoundé	English, French, indigenous languages
†Canada	3,849,674	25,740,000	6.7	Federal Parliamentary State	A	Ottawa	English, French
†Cape Verde	1,557	320,000	206	Republic	A	Praia	Portuguese, Crioulo
Cayman Islands	100	22,000	220	Dependency (U.K.)	C	Georgetown	English
†Central African Republic	240,535	2,785,000	12	Republic	A	Bangui	French, Sango
Ceylon see Sri Lanka	—	—	—				
†Chad	495,755	5,265,000	11	Republic	A	N'Djamena	Arabic, French, indigenous languages
Channel Islands	75	134,000	1,787	Dependency (U.K.)	C		English, French
†Chile	292,135	12,330,000	42	Republic	A	Santiago	Spanish
†China (excl. Taiwan)	3,718,783	1,069,410,000	288	Socialist Republic	A	Peking (Beijing)	Chinese dialects
Christmas Island	52	3,900	75	External Territory (Australia)	C		English
Ciskei(2)	2,080	770,000	370	Black National State (South African protection)	B	Bisho	Xhosa, Afrikaans
Cocos (Keeling) Islands	5.4	700	130	Part of Australia			English, Malay
†Colombia	440,831	29,340,000	67	Republic	A	Bogotá	Spanish
Colorado	104,094	3,265,000	31	State (U.S.)	D	Denver	English
†Comoros (excl. Mayotte)	838	435,000	519	Republic	A	Moroni	Arabic, French, Swahili, Malagasy
†Congo	132,047	2,000,000	15	Socialist Republic	A	Brazzaville	French, indigenous languages
Connecticut	5,019	3,195,000	637	State (U.S)	D	Hartford	English
Cook Islands	91	18,000	198	Self-governing Territory (New Zealand protection)	B	Avarua	English, Malay-Polynesian languages
†Costa Rica	19,730	2,690,000	136	Republic	A	San José	Spanish
†Cuba	42,804	10,225,000	239	Socialist Republic	A	Havana (La Habana)	Spanish
†Cyprus	3,572	675,000	189	Republic	A	Nicosia (Levkosía)	Greek, Turkish
†Czechoslovakia	49,384	15,525,000	314	Federal Socialist Republic	A	Prague (Praha)	Czech, Slovak, Hungarian
Delaware	2,045	630,000	308	State (U.S.)	D	Dover	English
†Denmark	16,633	5,120,000	308	Constitutional Monarchy	A	Copenhagen (København)	Danish
District of Columbia	69	630,000	9,130	Federal District (U.S.)	D	Washington	English
†Djibouti	8,880	310,000	35	Republic	A	Djibouti	French, Afar, Somali
†Dominica	290	75,000	259	Republic	A	Roseau	English, French
†Dominican Republic	18,704	6,460,000	345	Republic	A	Santo Domingo	Spanish
†Ecuador	109,484	9,770,000	89	Republic	A	Quito	Spanish, Quechua
†Egypt	386,662	50,540,000	131	Socialist Republic	A	Cairo (Al Qāhirah)	Arabic
Ellis Islands see Tuvalu	—	—	—				
†El Salvador	8,124	5,000,000	615	Republic	A	San Salvador	Spanish
England	50,363	46,975,000	933	Administrative Division (U.K.)	D	London	English
†Equatorial Guinea	10,831	325,000	30	Republic	A	Malabo	Spanish, English, indigenous languages
Estonia	17,413	1,545,000	89	Soviet Socialist Republic (Soviet Union)	D	Tallinn	Estonian, Russian
†Ethiopia	472,435	45,170,000	96	Provisional Military Government	A	Addis Ababa	Amharic, indigenous languages
Europe	3,800,000	680,100,000	179				
Faeroe Islands	540	46,000	85	Part of Danish Realm	B	Tórshavn	Faroese, Danish
Falkland Islands (excl. Dependencies)(3)	4,700	2,000	0.4	Dependency (U.K.)	C	Stanley	English
†Fiji	7,078	720,000	102	Parliamentary State	A	Suva	English, Fijian, Hindustani
†Finland	130,559	4,950,000	38	Republic	A	Helsinki (Helsingfors)	Finnish, Swedish
Florida	58,668	11,520,000	196	State (U.S.)	D	Tallahassee	English
†France (excl. Overseas Departments)	211,208	55,500,000	263	Republic	A	Paris	French
French Guiana	35,135	85,000	2.4	Overseas Department (France)	D	Cayenne	French
French Polynesia	1,544	185,000	120	Overseas Territory (France)	C	Papeete	French, Tahitian
Fujian	47,491	27,700,000	583	Province (China)	D	Fuzhou	Chinese dialects
†Gabon	103,347	1,030,000	10	Republic	A	Libreville	French, indigenous languages
†Gambia	4,361	780,000	179	Republic	A	Banjul	English, indigenous languages
Gansu	150,580	20,855,000	138	Province (China)	D	Lanzhou	Chinese (Mandarin), Mongolian, Tibetan dialects
Georgia	58,914	6,050,000	103	State (U.S.)	D	Atlanta	English

Country, Division or Region English (Conventional)	Area in sq. mi.	Estimated Population 1/1/87	Pop. per sq. mi.	Form of Government and Political Status		Capital	Predominant Languages
Georgia	26,911	5,280,000	196	Soviet Socialist Republic (Soviet Union)	D	Tbilisi	Georgic, Armenian, Russian
† German Democratic Republic (East Germany)	41,828	16,595,000	397	Socialist Republic	A	Berlin (East)	German
† Germany, Federal Republic of (West Germany)	96,032	60,925,000	634	Federal Republic	A	Bonn	German
† Ghana	92,098	13,630,000	148	Provisional Military Government	A	Accra	English, Akan, indigenous languages
Gibraltar	2.3	31,000	13,478	Dependency (U.K.)	C	Gibraltar	English, Spanish
Gilbert Islands see Kiribati	—	—	—	....			
Great Britain see United Kingdom							
† Greece	50,944	9,995,000	196	Republic	A	Athens (Athínai)	Greek
Greenland	840,004	54,000	0.1	Part of Danish Realm	B	Godthåb	Danish, indigenous languages
† Grenada	133	86,000	647	Parliamentary State	A	St. George's	English
Guadeloupe (incl. Dependencies)	687	335,000	488	Overseas Department (France)	D	Basse-Terre	French, Creole
Guam	209	125,000	598	Unincorporated Territory (U.S.)	C	Agana	English, Chamorro
Guangdong	89,190	63,950,000	717	Province (China)	D	Canton (Guangzhou)	Chinese dialects, Miao-Yao
Guangxi Zhuangzu	91,506	39,570,000	432	Autonomous Region (China)	D	Nanning	Chinese dialects, Thai, Miao-Yao
† Guatemala	42,042	8,310,000	198	Republic	A	Guatemala	Spanish, indigenous languages
Guernsey (incl. Dependencies)	30	79,000	2,633	Bailiwick (Channel Islands)	C	St. Peter Port	English, French
† Guinea	94,926	6,330,000	67	Republic	A	Conakry	French, indigenous languages
† Guinea-Bissau	13,948	880,000	63	Republic	A	Bissau	Portuguese, indigenous languages
Guizhou	67,182	30,370,000	452	Province (China)	D	Guiyang	Chinese (Mandarin), Thai, Miao-Yao
† Guyana	83,000	795,000	9.6	Republic	A	Georgetown	English, indigenous languages
† Haiti	10,714	5,925,000	553	Republic	A	Port-au-Prince	French, Creole
Hawaii	6,473	1,065,000	165	State (U.S.)	D	Honolulu	English, Hawaiian, Japanese
Hebei	78,379	56,680,000	723	Province (China)	D	Shijiazhuang	Chinese (Mandarin)
Heilongjiang	177,607	33,795,000	190	Province (China)	D	Harbin	Chinese dialects, Mongolian, Tungus
Henan	64,479	78,820,000	1,222	Province (China)	D	Zhengzhou	Chinese (Mandarin)
Holland see Netherlands				....			
† Honduras	43,277	4,710,000	109	Republic	A	Tegucigalpa	Spanish
Hong Kong	412	5,535,000	13,434	Dependency (U.K.)	C	Victoria (Hong Kong)	Chinese (Cantonese), English
Hubei	72,587	50,370,000	694	Province (China)	D	Wuhan	Chinese dialects
Hunan	81,468	57,430,000	705	Province (China)	D	Changsha	Chinese dialects, Miao-Yao
† Hungary	35,921	10,655,000	297	Socialist Republic	A	Budapest	Hungarian
† Iceland	39,769	245,000	6.2	Republic	A	Reykjavik	Icelandic
Idaho	83,566	1,015,000	12	State (U.S.)	D	Boise	English
Illinois	57,872	11,690,000	202	State (U.S.)	D	Springfield	English
† India (incl. part of Jammu and Kashmir)	1,237,062	773,430,000	625	Federal Republic	A	New Delhi	English, Hindi, indigenous languages
Indiana	36,417	5,565,000	153	State (U.S.)	D	Indianapolis	English
† Indonesia	741,101	168,460,000	227	Republic	A	Jakarta	Indonesian, Malay-Polynesian languages
Inner Mongolia (Nei Monggol)	463,323	20,535,000	44	Autonomous Region (China)	D	Hohhot	Mongolian
Iowa	56,275	2,930,000	52	State (U.S.)	D	Des Moines	English
† Iran	636,296	46,130,000	72	Islamic Republic	A	Tehrān	Farsi, Turkish, Kurdish, Arabic
† Iraq	169,235	16,250,000	96	Republic	A	Baghdād	Arabic, Kurdish
† Ireland	27,136	3,590,000	132	Republic	A	Dublin (Baile Átha Cliath)	English, Irish Gaelic
Isle of Man	227	65,000	286	Self-governing Territory (U.K. protection)	B	Douglas	English
† Israel (excl. Occupied Areas)	7,848	4,220,000	508	Republic	A	Jerusalem (Yerushalayim)	Hebrew, Arabic
Israeli Occupied Areas[4]	2,703	1,730,000	640	....			Hebrew, Arabic
† Italy	116,319	57,300,000	493	Republic	A	Rome (Roma)	Italian
† Ivory Coast	123,847	10,680,000	86	Republic	A	Abidjan and Yamoussoukro[5]	French, indigenous languages
† Jamaica	4,244	2,305,000	543	Parliamentary State	A	Kingston	English
† Japan	145,834	121,770,000	835	Constitutional Monarchy	A	Tōkyō	Japanese
Jersey	45	55,000	1,222	Bailiwick (Channel Islands)	C	St. Helier	English, French
Jiangsu	39,382	63,520,000	1,613	Province (China)	D	Nanjing (Nanking)	Chinese dialects
Jiangxi	63,707	35,395,000	556	Province (China)	D	Nanchang	Chinese dialects
Jilin	72,201	23,525,000	326	Province (China)	D	Changchun	Chinese (Mandarin), Mongolian, Korean
† Jordan (excl. West Bank)	35,135	2,795,000	80	Constitutional Monarchy	A	'Ammān	Arabic
† Kampuchea (Cambodia)	69,898	6,465,000	92	Socialist Republic	A	Phnom Penh (Phnum Pénh)	Khmer
Kansas	82,282	2,495,000	30	State (U.S.)	D	Topeka	English
Kazakh S.S.R.	1,049,156	16,090,000	15	Soviet Socialist Republic (Soviet Union)	D	Alma-Ata	Turkish, Russian
Kentucky	40,414	3,775,000	93	State (U.S.)	D	Frankfort	English
† Kenya	224,961	24,555,000	109	Republic	A	Nairobi	English, Swahili, indigenous languages
Kirghiz S.S.R.	76,641	4,045,000	53	Soviet Socialist Republic (Soviet Union)	D	Frunze	Turkish, Farsi, Russian
Kiribati	275	65,000	236	Republic	A	Bairiki	English, Gilbertese
Korea, North	46,540	20,745,000	446	Socialist Republic	A	Pyŏngyang	Korean
Korea, South	38,025	42,200,000	1,110	Republic	A	Seoul (Sŏul)	Korean
† Kuwait	6,880	1,800,000	262	Constitutional Monarchy	A	Kuwait	Arabic, English
† Laos	91,429	3,720,000	41	Socialist Republic	A	Viangchan (Vientiane)	Lao, French
Latvia	24,595	2,640,000	107	Soviet Socialist Republic (Soviet Union)	D	Rīga	Latvian, Russian
† Lebanon	4,015	2,700,000	672	Republic	A	Beirut (Bayrūt)	Arabic, English, French
† Lesotho	11,720	1,575,000	134	Monarchy	A	Maseru	Sesotho, English
Liaoning	58,301	37,645,000	646	Province (China)	D	Shenyang (Mukden)	Chinese (Mandarin), Mongolian
† Liberia	43,000	2,290,000	53	Republic	A	Monrovia	English, indigenous languages
† Libya	679,362	3,930,000	5.8	Socialist Republic	A	Tripoli (Ṭarābulus)	Arabic
† Liechtenstein	62	28,000	452	Constitutional Monarchy	A	Vaduz	German
Lithuania	25,174	3,625,000	144	Soviet Socialist Republic (Soviet Union)	D	Vilnius	Lithuanian, Polish, Russian
Louisiana	47,750	4,550,000	95	State (U.S.)	D	Baton Rouge	English
† Luxembourg	998	365,000	366	Constitutional Monarchy	A	Luxembourg	French, Luxembourgish, German, English
Macao	6.2	405,000	65,323	Overseas Province (Portugal)	C	Macao	Portuguese, Chinese (Cantonese)
† Madagascar	226,658	10,375,000	46	Socialist Republic	A	Antananarivo	French, Malagasy
Maine	33,265	1,185,000	36	State (U.S.)	D	Augusta	English
† Malawi	45,747	7,405,000	162	Republic	A	Lilongwe	Chichewa, English
† Malaysia	127,502	15,975,000	125	Federal Constitutional Monarchy	A	Kuala Lumpur	Malay, Chinese dialects, Tamil, English
† Maldives	115	190,000	1,652	Republic	A	Male	Divehi
† Mali	478,767	7,985,000	17	Republic	A	Bamako	French, Bambara, indigenous languages
† Malta	121	355,000	2,934	Republic	A	Valletta	English, Maltese
Manitoba	250,947	1,085,000	4.3	Province (Canada)	D	Winnipeg	English
Marshall Islands	70	37,000	529	Part of Trust Territory of the Pacific Islands	B	Majuro (island)	Malay-Polynesian languages, English
Martinique	425	330,000	776	Overseas Department (France)	D	Fort-de-France	French, Creole
Maryland	10,461	4,455,000	426	State (U.S.)	D	Annapolis	English
Massachusetts	8,286	5,905,000	713	State (U.S.)	D	Boston	English
† Mauritania	397,956	1,710,000	4.3	Islamic Republic	A	Nouakchott	Arabic, French
† Mauritius (incl. Dependencies)	788	1,025,000	1,301	Parliamentary State	A	Port Louis	Creole, English, French
Mayotte[6]	144	60,000	417	Overseas Department (France)	D	Dzaoudzi and Mamoudzou[5]	French, Swahili
† Mexico	761,605	81,230,000	107	Federal Republic	A	Mexico City (Ciudad de México)	Spanish, indigenous languages
Michigan	97,107	9,220,000	95	State (U.S.)	D	Lansing	English
Micronesia, Federated States of	271	99,000	365	Part of Trust Territory of the Pacific Islands	B	Kolonia	Malay-Polynesian languages, English
Midway Islands	2.0	500	250	Unincorporated Territory (U.S.)	C		English
Minnesota	86,614	4,260,000	49	State (U.S.)	D	St. Paul	English
Mississippi	47,691	2,640,000	55	State (U.S.)	D	Jackson	English
Missouri	69,697	5,105,000	73	State (U.S.)	D	Jefferson City	English
Moldavia	13,012	4,185,000	322	Soviet Socialist Republic (Soviet Union)	D	Kishinev	Moldavian, Russian, Ukrainian
Monaco	0.6	28,000	46,667	Constitutional Monarchy	A	Monaco	French, English, Italian, Monegasque
† Mongolia	604,250	1,965,000	3.3	Socialist Republic	A	Ulan Bator (Ulaanbaatar)	Khalkha Mongol
Montana	147,045	845,000	5.7	State (U.S.)	D	Helena	English
Montserrat	40	12,000	300	Dependency (U.K.)	C	Plymouth	English
† Morocco (excl. Western Sahara)	172,414	23,915,000	139	Constitutional Monarchy	A	Rabat	Arabic, French, Berber dialects
† Mozambique	308,642	14,210,000	46	Socialist Republic	A	Maputo	Portuguese, indigenous languages
Namibia (excl. Walvis Bay)[7]	318,261	1,180,000	3.7	Under South African administration	C	Windhoek	Afrikaans, indigenous languages
Nauru	8.1	9,000	1,111	Republic	A	Yaren District	Nauruan, English

Country, Division or Region English (Conventional)	Area in sq. mi.	Estimated Population 1/1/87	Pop. per sq. mi.	Form of Government and Political Status		Capital	Predominant Languages
Nebraska	77,350	1,620,000	21	State (U.S.)	D	Lincoln	English
† Nepal	56,827	17,310,000	305	Constitutional Monarchy	A	Kathmandu	Nepali, indigenous languages
† Netherlands	16,042	14,570,000	908	Constitutional Monarchy	A	Amsterdam and The Hague ('s-Gravenhage)	Dutch
Netherlands Antilles	309	235,000	761	Self-governing Territory (Netherlands protection)	B	Willemstad	Dutch, English, Papiamento, Spanish
Nevada	110,562	945,000	8.5	State (U.S.)	D	Carson City	English
New Brunswick	28,355	725,000	26	Province (Canada)	D	Fredericton	English, French
New Caledonia	7,366	155,000	21	Overseas Territory (France)	C	Nouméa	French, Malay-Polynesian languages
Newfoundland	156,649	585,000	3.7	Province (Canada)	D	St. John's	English
New Hampshire	9,278	1,015,000	109	State (U.S.)	D	Concord	English
New Hebrides see Vanuatu	—	—	—				
New Jersey	7,787	7,670,000	985	State (U.S.)	D	Trenton	English
New Mexico	121,594	1,475,000	12	State (U.S.)	D	Santa Fe	English, Spanish
New South Wales	309,500	5,585,000	18	State (Australia)	D	Sydney	English
New York	52,737	18,025,000	342	State (U.S.)	D	Albany	English
† New Zealand	103,515	3,315,000	32	Parliamentary State	A	Wellington	English, Maori
† Nicaragua	50,193	3,390,000	68	Republic	A	Managua	Spanish, English
† Niger	489,191	6,820,000	14	Provisional Military Government	A	Niamey	French, Hausa, indigenous languages
† Nigeria	356,669	107,250,000	301	Provisional Military Government	A	Lagos and Abuja(5)	English, Hausa, Ibo, Yoruba, indigenous languages
Ningxia Huizu	25,483	4,280,000	168	Autonomous Region (China)	D	Yinchuan	Chinese (Mandarin)
Niue	102	3,000	29	Self-governing Territory (New Zealand protection)	B	Alofi	English, Malay-Polynesian languages
Norfolk Island	14	2,000	143	Part of Australia	C	Kingston	English, Tahitian
North America	9,400,000	407,200,000	43				
North Carolina	52,669	6,340,000	120	State (U.S.)	D	Raleigh	English
North Dakota	70,702	700,000	9.9	State (U.S.)	D	Bismarck	English
Northern Ireland	5,453	1,575,000	289	Administrative Division (U.K.)	D	Belfast	English
Northern Mariana Islands	184	21,000	114	Part of Trust Territory of the Pacific Islands	B	Saipan (island)	English, Carolinian, Chamorro
Northern Territory	519,771	145,000	0.3	Territory (Australia)	D	Darwin	English, indigenous languages
Northwest Territories	1,322,910	52,000		Territory (Canada)	D	Yellowknife	English, indigenous languages
† Norway (incl. Svalbard and Jan Mayen)	149,158	4,170,000	28	Constitutional Monarchy	A	Oslo	Norwegian
Nova Scotia	21,425	890,000	42	Province (Canada)	D	Halifax	English
Oceania (incl. Australia)	3,300,000	25,100,000	7.6				
Ohio	44,786	10,890,000	243	State (U.S.)	D	Columbus	English
Oklahoma	69,957	3,340,000	48	State (U.S.)	D	Oklahoma City	English
† Oman	82,030	1,285,000	16	Monarchy	A	Muscat	Arabic
Ontario	412,581	9,225,000	22	Province (Canada)	D	Toronto	English
Oregon	97,076	2,735,000	28	State (U.S.)	D	Salem	English
Pacific Islands, Trust Territory of the	717	170,000	237	United Nations Trusteeship (U.S. administration)	B	Saipan (island)	English, Malay-Polynesian languages
† Pakistan (incl. part of Jammu and Kashmir)	339,732	103,510,000	305	Federal Republic	A	Islāmābād	Urdu, Punjabi, Sindhi, English
Palau (Belau)	192	13,000	68	Part of Trust Territory of the Pacific Islands	B	Koror	English, Malay-Polynesian languages
† Panama	29,762	2,250,000	76	Republic	A	Panamá	Spanish, English
† Papua New Guinea	178,704	3,440,000	19	Parliamentary State	A	Port Moresby	English, Papuan and Negrito languages
† Paraguay	157,048	4,070,000	26	Republic	A	Asunción	Spanish, Guarani
Peking (Beijing)	6,487	9,840,000	1,517	Autonomous City (China)	D	Peking (Beijing)	Chinese (Mandarin)
Pennsylvania	46,047	12,000,000	261	State (U.S.)	D	Harrisburg	English
† Peru	496,225	20,435,000	41	Republic	A	Lima	Spanish, Quechua, Aymara
† Philippines	115,831	55,930,000	483	Republic	A	Manila	Pilipino, English, Tagalog, Cebuano
Pitcairn (incl. Dependencies)	19	55	2.9	Dependency (U.K.)	C	Adamstown	English, Tahitian
† Poland	120,728	37,635,000	312	Socialist Republic	A	Warsaw (Warszawa)	Polish
† Portugal	35,516	10,320,000	291	Republic	A	Lisbon (Lisboa)	Portuguese
Prince Edward Island	2,185	130,000	59	Province (Canada)	D	Charlottetown	English
Puerto Rico	3,515	3,310,000	942	Commonwealth (U.S. protection)	B	San Juan	English, Spanish
† Qatar	4,247	310,000	73	Monarchy	A	Doha	Arabic, English
Qinghai	278,380	4,170,000	15	Province (China)	D	Xining	Tibetan dialects, Mongolian, Turkish dialects, Chinese (Mandarin)
Quebec	594,860	6,675,000	11	Province (Canada)	D	Québec	French, English
Queensland	666,876	2,600,000	3.9	State (Australia)	D	Brisbane	English
Reunion	967	540,000	558	Overseas Department (France)	D	Saint-Denis	French
Rhode Island	1,212	990,000	817	State (U.S.)	D	Providence	English
Rhodesia see Zimbabwe	—	—	—				
† Romania	91,699	22,905,000	250	Socialist Republic	A	Bucharest (Bucureşti)	Romanian
Russian Soviet Federative Socialist Republic	6,592,849	145,470,000	22	Soviet Socialist Republic (Soviet Union)	D	Moscow (Moskva)	Russian, Finno-Ugric languages, Farsi, Turkish, Mongolian
† Rwanda	10,169	6,505,000	640	Republic	A	Kigali	French, Kinyarwanda
† St. Christopher-Nevis	104	40,000	385	Parliamentary State	A	Basseterre	English
St. Helena (incl. Dependencies)	162	8,100	50	Dependency (U.K.)	C	Jamestown	English
† St. Lucia	238	139,000	584	Parliamentary State	A	Castries	English, French
St. Pierre and Miquelon	93	6,100	66	Overseas Department (France)	D	Saint-Pierre	French
† St. Vincent and the Grenadines	150	104,000	693	Parliamentary State	A	Kingstown	English
San Marino	24	23,000	958	Republic	A	San Marino	Italian
† Sao Tome and Principe	372	110,000	296	Republic	A	São Tomé	Portuguese, indigenous languages
Saskatchewan	251,866	1,030,000	4.1	Province (Canada)	D	Regina	English
† Saudi Arabia	830,000	11,685,000	14	Monarchy	A	Riyadh (Ar Riyāḍ)	Arabic
Scotland	29,794	5,150,000	173	Administrative Division (U.K.)	D	Edinburgh	English, Scots Gaelic
† Senegal	75,955	6,515,000	86	Republic	A	Dakar	French, Wolof, indigenous languages
† Seychelles	175	65,000	371	Republic	A	Victoria	English, French, Creole
Shaanxi	75,676	30,690,000	406	Province (China)	D	Xi'an (Sian)	Chinese (Mandarin)
Shandong	59,074	78,600,000	1,331	Province (China)	D	Jinan	Chinese (Mandarin)
Shanghai	2,239	12,405,000	5,540	Autonomous City (China)	D	Shanghai	Chinese (Wu)
Shanxi	60,618	26,840,000	443	Province (China)	D	Taiyuan	Chinese (Mandarin)
Sichuan	219,692	104,160,000	474	Province (China)	D	Chengdu	Chinese (Mandarin), Tibetan dialects, Miao-Yao
† Sierra Leone	27,925	3,795,000	136	Republic	A	Freetown	English, Krio, indigenous languages
† Singapore	239	2,620,000	10,962	Republic	A	Singapore	Chinese (Mandarin), English, Malay, Tamil
† Solomon Islands	11,506	285,000	25	Parliamentary State	A	Honiara	English, Malay-Polynesian languages
† Somalia	246,201	7,935,000	32	Socialist Republic	A	Mogadishu (Muqdisho)	Arabic, Somali
† South Africa (incl. Walvis Bay)	433,680	33,585,000	77	Republic	A	Pretoria, Cape Town, and Bloemfontein	English, Afrikaans, indigenous languages
South America	6,900,000	276,700,000	40				
South Australia	379,925	1,390,000	3.7	State (Australia)	D	Adelaide	English
South Carolina	31,116	3,390,000	109	State (U.S.)	D	Columbia	English
South Dakota	77,120	725,000	9.4	State (U.S.)	D	Pierre	English
Southern Yemen see Yemen, P.D.R. of	—	—	—				
South Georgia (incl. Dependencies)	1,450	20		Dependency (Falkland Islands)	C		English
South West Africa see Namibia							
† Soviet Union	8,600,387	280,830,000	33	Federal Socialist Republic	A	Moscow (Moskva)	Russian and other Slavic languages, various ethnic languages
† Spain	194,885	39,680,000	204	Constitutional Monarchy	A	Madrid	Spanish
Spanish North Africa(8)	12	150,000	12,500	Five possessions (Spain)	C		Spanish, Arabic, Berber dialects
Spanish Sahara see Western Sahara							
† Sri Lanka	24,962	16,195,000	649	Socialist Republic	A	Colombo and Jayawardenapura(5)	Sinhala, Tamil, English
† Sudan	967,500	23,730,000	25	Republic	A	Khartoum (Al Kharţūm)	Arabic, English, indigenous languages
† Suriname	63,037	405,000	6.4	Republic	A	Paramaribo	Dutch, English, Sranan Tongo, Hindi, Javanese

Country, Division or Region English (Conventional)	Area in sq. mi.	Estimated Population 1/1/87	Pop. per sq. mi.	Form of Government and Political Status	Capital	Predominant Languages
† Swaziland	6;704	700,000	104	Monarchy ... A	Mbabane	English, siSwati
† Sweden	158,661	8,350,000	53	Constitutional Monarchy ... A	Stockholm	Swedish
Switzerland	15,943	6,465,000	406	Federal Republic ... A	Bern (Berne)	German, French, Italian, Romansch
† Syria	71,498	10,790,000	151	Socialist Republic ... A	Damascus (Dimashq)	Arabic
Taiwan	13,900	19,685,000	1,416	Republic ... A	T'aipei	Chinese dialects
Tajik S.S.R.	55,251	4,575,000	83	Soviet Socialist Republic (Soviet Union) ... D	Dushanbe	Tajik, Turkish, Russian
† Tanzania	364,900	22,810,000	63	Republic ... A	Dar es Salaam and Dodoma[5]	English, Swahili, indigenous languages
Tasmania	26,178	450,000	17	State (Australia) ... D	Hobart	English
Tennessee	42,143	4,815,000	114	State (U.S.) ... D	Nashville	English
Texas	266,805	16,600,000	62	State (U.S.) ... D	Austin	English, Spanish
† Thailand	198,115	52,690,000	266	Constitutional Monarchy ... A	Bangkok (Krung Thep)	Thai
Tianjin (Tientsin)	4,247	8,235,000	1,939	Autonomous City (China) ... D	Tianjin (Tientsin)	Chinese (Mandarin)
Tibet (Xizang)	471,817	2,030,000	4.3	Autonomous Region (China) ... D	Lhasa	Tibetan dialects
† Togo	21,925	3,165,000	144	Republic ... A	Lomé	French, indigenous languages
Tokelau	4.6	1,500	326	Island Territory (New Zealand) ... C		English, Tokelauan
Tonga	270	99,000	367	Constitutional Monarchy ... A	Nuku'alofa	Tongan, English
Transkei[2]	16,816	2,765,000	164	Black National State (South African protection) ... B	Umtata	Xhosa, Afrikaans
† Trinidad and Tobago	1,980	1,215,000	614	Republic ... A	Port of Spain	English
Tristan da Cunha	40	300	7.5	Dependency (St. Helena) ... C	Edinburgh	English
† Tunisia	63,170	7,500,000	119	Republic ... A	Tunis	Arabic, French
† Turkey	300,948	53,450,000	178	Republic ... A	Ankara	Turkish, Kurdish
Turkmen S.S.R.	188,456	3,230,000	17	Soviet Socialist Republic (Soviet Union) ... D	Ashkhabad	Turkish, Russian
Turks and Caicos Islands	166	8,900	54	Dependency (U.K.) ... C	Grand Turk	English
Tuvalu	10	8,400	840	Parliamentary State ... A	Funafuti	Tuvaluan, English
† Uganda	93,104	15,505,000	167	Republic ... A	Kampala	English, Swahili, indigenous languages
† Ukraine	233,090	51,675,000	222	Soviet Socialist Republic (Soviet Union) ... D	Kiev	Ukrainian, Russian
† United Arab Emirates	32,278	1,345,000	42	Federation of Monarchs ... A	Abu Dhabi (Abū Ẕaby)	Arabic, English, Farsi, Hindi, Urdu
† United Kingdom	93,629	56,510,000	604	Constitutional Monarchy ... A	London	English
† United States	3,679,245	241,960,000	66	Federal Republic ... A	Washington	English
Upper Volta *see* Burkina Faso	—	—		...		
† Uruguay	68,037	2,965,000	44	Republic ... A	Montevideo	Spanish
Utah	84,902	1,670,000	20	State (U.S.) ... D	Salt Lake City	English
Uzbek S.S.R.	172,742	18,280,000	106	Soviet Socialist Republic (Soviet Union) ... D	Tashkent	Turkish, Sart, Russian
† Vanuatu	4,706	138,000	29	Republic ... A	Port-Vila	Bislama, English, French
Vatican City	0.2	700	3,500	Ecclesiastical State ... A	Vatican City	Italian, Latin
Venda[2]	2,393	410,000	171	Black National State (South African protection) ... B	Thohoyandou	Venda, Afrikaans
† Venezuela	352,145	17,990,000	51	Federal Republic ... A	Caracas	Spanish
Vermont	9,614	530,000	55	State (U.S.) ... D	Montpelier	English
Victoria	87,877	4,200,000	48	State (Australia) ... D	Melbourne	English
† Vietnam	127,242	62,670,000	493	Socialist Republic ... A	Hanoi	Vietnamese
Virginia	40,763	5,785,000	142	State (U.S.) ... D	Richmond	English
Virgin Islands (U.S.)	133	116,000	872	Unincorporated Territory (U.S.) ... C	Charlotte Amalie	English, Spanish
Virgin Islands, British	59	12,000	203	Dependency (U.K.) ... C	Road Town	English
Wake Island	3.0	300	100	Unincorporated Territory (U.S.) ... C		English
Wales	8,019	2,810,000	350	Administrative Division (U.K.) ... D	Cardiff	English, Welsh Gaelic
Wallis and Futuna	98	14,000	143	Overseas Territory (France) ... C	Mata-Utu	French, Uvean, Futunan
Washington	68,139	4,475,000	66	State (U.S.) ... D	Olympia	English
Western Australia	975,101	1,435,000	1.5	State (Australia) ... D	Perth	English
Western Sahara	102,703	95,000	0.9	Occupied by Morocco ... C	El Aaiún	Arabic
† Western Samoa	1,097	165,000	150	Constitutional Monarchy ... A	Apia	English, Samoan
West Virginia	24,236	1,960,000	81	State (U.S.) ... D	Charleston	English
Wisconsin	66,213	4,840,000	73	State (U.S.) ... D	Madison	English
Wyoming	97,808	510,000	5.2	State (U.S.) ... D	Cheyenne	English
Xinjiang Uygur	635,910	13,900,000	22	Autonomous Region (China) ... D	Ürümqi	Turkish dialects, Mongolian, Tungus
† Yemen	75,290	9,495,000	126	Republic ... A	San'ā'	Arabic
† Yemen, People's Democratic Republic of	128,560	2,400,000	19	Socialist Republic ... A	Aden ('Adan)	Arabic
† Yugoslavia	98,766	23,365,000	237	Federal Socialist Republic ... A	Belgrade (Beograd)	Serbo-Croatian, Slovene, Macedonian
Yukon Territory	186,661	23,000	0.1	Territory (Canada) ... D	Whitehorse	English, Inuktitut, indigenous languages
Yunnan	168,341	34,865,000	207	Province (China) ... D	Kunming	Chinese (Mandarin), Tibetan dialects, Khmer, Miao-Yao
† Zaire	905,568	31,740,000	35	Republic ... A	Kinshasa	French, Kikongo, Lingala, Swahili, Tshiluba
† Zambia	290,586	6,965,000	24	Republic ... A	Lusaka	English, indigenous languages
Zhejiang	39,382	41,170,000	1,045	Province (China) ... D	Hangzhou	Chinese dialects
† Zimbabwe	150,873	8,800,000	58	Republic ... A	Harare (Salisbury)	English, indigenous languages
World	57,800,000	4,975,000,000	86	...		

† Member of the United Nations (1986).
— None, or not applicable.
(1) No permanent population.
(2) Bophuthatswana, Ciskei, Transkei, and Venda are not recognized by the United Nations.
(3) Claimed by Argentina.
(4) Includes West Bank, Golan Heights, and Gaza Strip.
(5) Future capital.
(6) Claimed by Comoros.
(7) In October 1966 the United Nations terminated the South African mandate over Namibia, a decision which South Africa did not accept.
(8) Comprises Ceuta, Melilla, and several small islands.

Abbreviations

admin	administered	Grc	Greece	Om	Oman
Afg	Afghanistan	Grnld	Greenland	Ont	Ontario
Afr	Africa	Guad	Guadeloupe	Oreg	Oregon
Ala	Alabama	Guat	Guatemala	Pa	Pennsylvania
Alb	Albania	Guy	Guyana	Pac. O.	Pacific Ocean
Alg	Algeria	Hai	Haiti	Pak	Pakistan
Alsk	Alaska	Haw	Hawaii	Pan	Panama
Alta	Alberta	Hond	Honduras	Pap. N. Gui	Papua New Guinea
Am	American	Hung	Hungary	Par	Paraguay
Am. Sam.	American Samoa	I	Island	par	parish
And	Andorra	I.C.	Ivory Coast	P.D.R. of Yem	Yemen, People's
Ang	Angola	Ice	Iceland		Democratic Republic of
Ant	Antarctica	Ill	Illinois	P.E.I	Prince Edward Island
Arc	Arctic	incl	includes, including	pen	peninsula
arch	archipelago	Ind	Indiana	Phil	Philippines
Arg	Argentina	Indian res	Indian reservation	Pol	Poland
Ariz	Arizona	Indon	Indonesia	pol. dist	political district
Ark	Arkansas	I. of Man	Isle of Man	pop	population
Atl. O.	Atlantic Ocean	Ire	Ireland	Port	Portugal, Portuguese
Aus	Austria	is	islands	poss	possession
Austl	Australia, Australian	isl	island	P.R.	Puerto Rico
auton	autonomous	Isr	Israel	pref	prefecture
Az. Is	Azores Islands	It	Italy	prot	protectorate
Ba	Bahamas	Jam	Jamaica	prov	province, provincial
Barb	Barbados	Jap	Japan	pt	point
B. C.	British Columbia	Kam	Kampuchea	Que	Quebec
Bel	Belgium, Belgian	Kans	Kansas	reg	region
Bhu	Bhutan	Ken	Kenya	rep	republic
Bis. Arch	Bismarck Archipelago	Kor	Korea	res	reservation, reservoir
Bngl	Bangladesh	Kuw	Kuwait	R.I	Rhode Island
Bol	Bolivia	Ky	Kentucky	riv	river
Bots	Botswana	La	Louisiana	Rom	Romania
Br	British	Leb	Lebanon	S. A	South America
Braz	Brazil	Le. Is	Leeward Islands	S. Afr	South Africa
Bru	Brunei	Leso	Lesotho	Sal	El Salvador
Bul	Bulgaria	Lib	Liberia	Sask	Saskatchewan
Bur	Burma	Liech	Liechtenstein	Sau. Ar	Saudi Arabia
Calif	California	Lux	Luxembourg	S.C.	South Carolina
Cam	Cameroon	Mad	Madagascar	Scot	Scotland
Can	Canada	Mad. Is	Madeira Islands	S. Dak	South Dakota
Can. Is	Canary Islands	Mala	Malaysia	Sen	Senegal
Cen. Afr. Rep.	Central African Republic	Man	Manitoba	S.L.	Sierra Leone
Cen. Am	Central America	Mart	Martinique	Sol. Is	Solomon Islands
co	county	Mass	Massachusetts	Som	Somalia
Col	Colombia	Maur	Mauritania	Sov. Un	Soviet Union
Colo	Colorado	Md	Maryland	Sp	Spain, Spanish
Con	Congo	Medit	Mediterranean	St., Ste	Saint, Sainte
Conn	Connecticut	Mex	Mexico	Sud	Sudan
cont	continent	Mich	Michigan	Sur	Suriname
C. R.	Costa Rica	Minn	Minnesota	Swaz	Swaziland
C. V.	Cape Verde	Miss	Mississippi	Swe	Sweden
Cyp	Cyprus	Mo	Missouri	Switz	Switzerland
Czech	Czechoslovakia	Mong	Mongolia	Syr	Syria
D.C.	District of Columbia	Mont	Montana	Tan	Tanzania
Del	Delaware	Mor	Morocco	Tenn	Tennessee
Den	Denmark	Moz	Mozambique	ter	territories, territory
dep	dependency, dependencies	mtn	mount, mountain	Tex	Texas
dept	department	mts	mountains	Thai	Thailand
dist	district	mun	municipality	Trin	Trinidad & Tobago
div	division	N.A.	North America	trust	trusteeship
Dji	Djibouti	nat. mon	national monument	Tun	Tunisia
Dom. Rep	Dominican Republic	nat. park	national park	Tur	Turkey
Ec	Ecuador	N.B.	New Brunswick	U.A.E	United Arab Emirates
Eg	Egypt	N.C.	North Carolina	Ug	Uganda
Eng	England	N. Cal	New Caledonia	U.K.	United Kingdom
Equat. Gui	Equatorial Guinea	N. Dak	North Dakota	Ur	Uruguay
Eth	Ethiopia	Nebr	Nebraska	U.S.	United States
Eur	Europe	Nep	Nepal	Va	Virginia
Falk. Is	Falkland Islands	Neth	Netherlands	Ven	Venezuela
Fed	Federation	Nev	Nevada	Viet	Vietnam
Fin	Finland	Newf	Newfoundland	Vir. Is	Virgin Islands
Fla	Florida	N.H.	New Hampshire	vol	volcano
Fr	France, French	Nic	Nicaragua	Vt	Vermont
Fr. Gu	French Guiana	Nig	Nigeria	Wash	Washington
Ga	Georgia	N. Ire	Northern Ireland	W.I.	West Indies
Gam	Gambia	N.J.	New Jersey	Win. Is	Windward Islands
Ger., Fed. Rep. of	Federal Republic of Germany	N. Mex	New Mexico	Wis	Wisconsin
		Nor	Norway, Norwegian	W. Sah.	Western Sahara
		N.S.	Nova Scotia	W. Sam	Western Samoa
Ger. Dem. Rep	German Democratic Republic	N.W. Ter	Northwest Territories	W. Va	West Virginia
		N.Y.	New York	Wyo	Wyoming
		N.Z.	New Zealand	Yugo	Yugoslavia
Gib	Gibraltar	occ	occupied area	Zimb	Zimbabwe
		Okla	Oklahoma		

Index

This universal index includes in a single alphabetical list all important names that appear on the reference maps. Each place name is followed by its location, the map index key, and the page number of the map.

State locations are given for all places in the United States. Province and country locations are given for all places in Canada. All other place name entries show only country locations.

The index reference key, always a letter and figure combination, and the map page number are the last items in each entry. Because some places are shown on both a main map and an inset map, more than one index key may be given for a single map page number. Reference also may be made to more than a single map. In each case, however, the index key *letter and figure* precede the map page number to which reference is made. A lowercase key letter indicates reference to an inset map which has been keyed separately.

Each major and minor political division is followed both by a descriptive term (co., dist., region, prov.; dept.; state, etc.) indicating political status, and by the name of the country in which it is located. United States counties are listed with state locations; all other divisions are given with country references.

The more important physical names that are shown on the maps are listed in the index. Each entry is followed by a descriptive term (bay, hill, range, riv., mtn., isl., etc.), to indicate its nature.

Country locations are given for all names except features entirely within a state of the United States or a province of Canada, in which case this division is given.

Some names included in the index were omitted from the maps because of scale size or lack of space. These entries are identified by an asterisk (*), and reference is given to the approximate location on the map.

A long name may appear on the map in a shortened form, with the full name given in the index. The part of the name not on the map then appears in italics, thus: St. Gabriel-*de-Brandon.*

The system of alphabetizing used in the index is standard. When more than one name with the same spelling is shown, place names are listed *first* and political divisions *second.*

A

Aachen, Ger., Fed. Rep. of	C3	6
Aalen, Ger., Fed. Rep. of	D5	6
Aalst, Bel.	B6	5
Äänekoski, Fin.	F11	11
Aarau, Switz.	E4	6
Aargau, canton, Switz.	*E3	6
Aba, China	E5	17
Aba, Nig.	G6	22
Ābādān, Iran	B7	23
Abaetetuba, Braz.	*D6	27
Abakan, Sov. Un.	D12	13
Abancay, Peru	D3	31
Abashiri, Jap.	D12	18
Abbeville, Ala.	D4	46
Abbeville, Fr.	B4	5
Abbeville, La.	E3	63
Abbeville, S.C.	C3	82
Abbeville, co., S.C.	C2	82
Abbiategrasso, It.	C2	82
Abbotsford, B.C., Can.	f13	37
Abbotsford, Wis.	D3	88
Åbenrå, co., Den.	*J3	11
Abeokuta, Nig.	G5	22
Aberdare, Wales	E5	4
Aberdeen, Idaho	G6	57
Aberdeen, Md.	A5	53
Aberdeen, Miss.	B5	68
Aberdeen, N.C.	B3	76
Aberdeen, Scot.	B5	4
Aberdeen, S. Dak.	E7	77
Aberdeen, Wash.	C2	86
Aberdeen, co., Scot.	*B5	4
Abergavenny, Wales	E5	4
Abernathy, Tex.	C2	84
Aberystwyth, Wales	D4	4
Abidjan, I.C.	G4	22
Abilene, Kans.	D6	61
Abilene, Tex.	C3	84
Abingdon, Ill.	C3	58
Abingdon, Va.	f10	85
Abington, Mass.	B6, h12	65
Abington, Pa.	o12	81
Abitibi, co., Que., Can.	*h12	42
Åbo, see Turku, Fin.		
Abomey, Benin	G5	22
Abony, Hung.	B5	10
Abra, prov., Phil.	*B6	19
Abruzzi, reg., It.	C4	9
Abruzzi e Molise, pol. dist., It.	C4	9
Absecon, N.J.	E3	74
Abu Dhabi (Abū Zaby)	E5	15
Abū Kamāl, Syr.	E13	14
Aby, Swe.	u34	11
Acadia, par., La.	D3	63
Acámbaro, Mex.	C4, m13	34
Acaponeta, Mex.	C4	34
Acapulco *de Juárez,* Mex.	D5	34
Acarigua, Ven.	B4	32
Acatlán *de Osorio,* Mex.	D5, m14	34
Acayucan, Mex.	D6	34
Accomack, co., Va.	C7	85
Accoville, W. Va.	D3, n12	87
Accra, Ghana	G4	22
Achinsk, Sov. Un.	D12	13
Acireale, It.	F5	9
Ackerman, Miss.	B4	68
Ackley, Iowa	B4	60
Acmetonia, Pa.	*E1	81
Aconcagua, prov., Chile	A2	28

Aconcagua, peak, Arg.	A3	28
Acqui, It.	*B2	9
Acre, state, Braz.	C3	31
Acre, riv., Braz.	D4	31
Acton, Ont., Can.	D4	41
Acton Vale, Que., Can.	D5	42
Açu, Braz.	*D7	27
Acushent, Mass.	*C6	65
Acworth, Ga.	B2	55
Ada, Minn.	C2	67
Ada, Ohio	B2	78
Ada, Okla.	C5	79
Ada, Yugo.	C5	10
Ada, co., Idaho	F2	57
Adair, co., Iowa	C3	60
Adair, co., Ky.	C4	62
Adair, co., Mo.	A5	69
Adair, co., Okla.	B7	79
Adairsville, Ga.	B2	55
Adam, mtn., Wash.	C4	86
Adamantina, Braz.	C2	30
Adams, Mass.	A1	65
Adams, Minn.	G6	67
Adams, N.Y.	B4	75
Adams, Wis.	E4	88
Adams, co., Colo.	B6	51
Adams, co., Idaho	E2	57
Adams, co., Ill.	D2	58
Adams, co., Ind.	C8	59
Adams, co., Iowa	C3	60
Adams, co., Miss.	D2	68
Adams, co., Nebr.	D7	71
Adams, co., N. Dak.	D3	77
Adams, co., Ohio	D2	78
Adams, co., Pa.	G7	81
Adams, co., Wash.	B7	86
Adams, co., Wis.	D4	88
Adams, mtn., Mass.	A2	65
Adams, mtn, Wash.	C4	86
Adams Center, N.Y.	B5	75
Adamston, N.J.	C4	74
Adamstown, Pa.	F9	81
Adamsville, Ala.	f7	46
Adamsville, Tenn.	B3	83
Adana, Tur.	D10	14
Adapazari, Tur.	B8	14
Ad Dāmir, Sud.	E4	23
Addis Ababa, Eth.	G5	23
Addison, Ill.	k9	58
Addison, co., Vt.	C1	73
Ad Dīwānīyah, Iraq	C3	15
Ad Duwaym, Sud.	F4	23
Addyston, Ohio	o12	78
Adel, Ga.	E3	55
Adel, Iowa	C3	60
Adelaide, Austl.	F6	25
Adelphi, Md.	*C4	53
Aden, P.D.R. of Yem.	G4	15
Adena, Ohio	B5	78
Adigrat, Eth.	F5	23
Adirondack, mts., N.Y.	A6, f10	75
Adi Ugri, Eth.	F5	23
Adiyaman, Tur.	C12	14
Adjuntas, P.R.	*G11	35
Admiralty, is., Pap. N. Gui.	h12	25
Ado-Ekiti, Nig.	*E6	22
Adrano, It.	F5	9
Adria, It.	B4	9
Adrian, Mich.	G6	66

Adrian, Minn.	G3	67
Adrian, Mo.	C3	69
Adrianople, see Edirne, Tur.		
Adwā, Eth.	F5	23
Afars & Issas, see Djibouti, country, Fr.		
Affton, Mo.	C7	69
Afghanistan, country, Asia	B4	20
Africa, cont.		21
Afton, Iowa	C3	60
Afton, N.Y.	C5	75
Afton, Okla.	A7	79
Afton, Wyo.	D2	89
'Afula, Isr.	B3	15
Afyon, Tur.	C8	14
Agadèz, Niger.	E6	22
Agadir, Mor.	B3	22
Agana, Guam	*F6	2
Agartala, India	D9	20
Agate Beach, Oreg.	C2	80
Agawam, Mass.	B2	65
Agboville, I.C.	G4	22
Agde, Fr.	F5	5
Agematsu, Jap.	n16	18
Agen, Fr.	E4	5
Agira, It.	F5	9
Agnone, It.	D5	9
Āgra, India	C6	20
Agrícola Oriental, Mex.	*D5	34
Agrigento, It.	F4	9
Agrínion, Grc.	C3	14
Aguada, P.R.	*G11	35
Aguadas, Col.	B2	32
Aguadilla, P.R.	G11	35
Aguascalientes, Mex.	C4, m12	34
Aguascalientes, state, Mex.	C4, k12	34
Aguilar, Colo.	D6	51
Aguita, Mex.	*B4	34
Agusan prov., Phil.	*D7	19
Ahlen, Ger., Fed. Rep. of	C3	6
Ahmadabad, India	D5	20
Ahmadnagar, India	E5	20
Ahmadpur East, Pak.	C5	20
Ahoskie, N.C.	A6	76
Ahrweiler, Ger., Fed. Rep. of	C3	6
Ahuachapan, Sal.	E7	34
Ahualulco de Mercado, Mex.	m12	34
Ahvāz, Iran	B7	23
Ahvenanmaa (Åland), prov. Fin.	G8	11
Aibonito, P.R.	*G11	35
Aichi, pref., Jap.	*I8	18
Aiea, Haw.	B4, g10	56
Aihui, China	A10	17
Aikawa, Jap.	G9	18
Aiken, S.C.	D4	82
Aiken, co., S.C.	D4	82
Aiken West, S.C.	*D4	82
Aimorés, Braz.	B4	30
Aïn, dept.	*D6	5
Aïn Sefna, Alg.	B4	22
Ainsworth, Nebr.	B6	71
Aire-sur-la-Lys, Fr.	B5	5
Aisén; prov., Chile	D2	28
Aitkin, Minn.	D5	67
Aitkin, co., Minn.	D5	67
Aitolía kai Akarnanía	*C3	14
Aitolikón, Grc.	C3	24
Aiud, Rom.	B6	10
Aix-en-Provence, Fr.	F6	5

Aix-la-Chapelle, see Aachen, Ger., Fed. Rep. of		
Aix-les-Bains, Fr.	E6	5
Aíyina, Grc.	D4	14
Aíyion, Grc.	C4	14
Aizu-wakamatsu, Jap.	H9	18
Ajaccio, Fr.	D2	9
Ajax, Ont. Can.	D6	41
Ajmer, India	C5	20
Ajo, Ariz.	C2	48
Akashi, Jap.	I7	18
Akcaabat, Tur.	B12	14
Akershus, co., Nor.	*H4	11
Aketi, Zaire	H2	23
Akhaía (Achaea), prov., Grc.	*C3	14
Akharnaí, Grc.	g11	14
Akhisar, Tur.	C6	14
Akhtyrka, Sov. Un.	F10	13
Aki, Jap.	J6	18
Akita, Jap.	G10	18
Akita, pref., Jap.	*G1	18
Akkeshi, Jap.	E12	18
'Akko (Acre), Isr.	B3, g5	15
Akola, India	D6	20
Akron, Colo.	A7	51
Akron, Ind.	B5	59
Akron, Iowa	B1	60
Akron, N.Y.	B2	75
Akron, Ohio	A4	78
Akron, Pa.	F9	81
Aksaray, Tur.	C10	14
Akşehir, Tur.	C8	14
Aksenovo-Zilovskove, Sov. Un.	D14	13
Aktyubinsk, Sov. Un.	D8	13
Akureyri, Ice.	n23	11
Alabama, state, U.S.		46
Alabaster, Ala.	B3	46
Alachua, Fla.	C4	54
Alachua, co., Fla.	C4	54
Alagôa Grande, Braz.	*D7	27
Alagôas, state, Braz.	*D7	27
Alagoinhas, Braz.	*E7	27
Alajuela, C.R.	E8	34
Al 'Alamayn (El Alamein), Eg.	G7	14
Alamance, co. N.C.	B3	76
Alameda, Calif.	h8	50
Alameda, N. Mex.	B5, D5	48
Alameda, co. Calif.	D3	50
Alamo, Calif.	*D3	50
Alamo, Tenn.	B2	83
Alamo, Tex.	F3	84
Alamogordo, N. Mex.	C6	48
Alamo Heights, Tex.	E3, k7	84
Alamosa, Colo.	D5	51
Alamosa, co., Colo.	D5	51
Alanya, Tur.	D9	14
Alaşehir, Tur.	C7	14
Alaska, State, U.S.		47
Alassio, It.	C2	9
Alatyr, Sov. Un.	D16	12
Alava prov., Sp.	*A4	8
Alba, It.	B2	9
Albacete, Sp.	C5	8
Alba Iulia, Rom.	B6	10
Albania, country, Eur.	B2	10
Albano Laziale, It.	D4, h9	9
Albany, Ga.	E2	55
Albany, Ind.	D7	59
Albany, Ky.	D4	62

Albany, Minn. E4 67
Albany, Mo. A3 69
Albany, N.Y. C7 75
Albany, Oreg. C3, k11 80
Albany, Tex. C3 84
Albany, Wis. F4 88
Albany, co., N.Y. C6 75
Albany, co., Wyo. E6 89
Albany, riv., Ont. o18 41
Al Batrūn, Leb. f5 15
Albay, prov., Phil. *C6 19
Albemarle, N.C. B2 76
Albemarle, co., Va. C4 85
Albenga, It. B2 9
Albert, Fr. B5 5
Albert, co., N.B., Can. D5 43
Albert, Lake, Ug., Zaire H4 23
Alberta, prov., Can. 38
Alberta, mtn., Alta., Can. C2 38
Albert Edward, mtn., Pap. N. Gui. . k12 25
Albert Lea, Minn. G5 67
Albertson, N.Y. *G2 52
Albertville, Ala. A3 46
Albertville, Fr. E7 5
Albi, Fr. F5 5
Albia, Iowa C5 60
Albion, Ill. E5 58
Albion, Ind. B7 59
Albion, Mich. F6 66
Albion, Nebr. C7 71
Albion, N.Y. B2 75
Albion, R.I. B11 52
Ålborg, Den. I3 11
Albuñol, Sp. D4 8
Albuquerque, N. Mex. B5, D5 48
Alburquerque, Sp. C2 8
Alburtis, Pa. F10 81
Albury-Wodonga, Austl. G8 25
Alcalá de Guadaira, Sp. D3 8
Alcala de Henares, Sp. B4, p18 8
Alcamo, It. F4 9
Alcanar, Sp. B6 8
Alcañiz, Sp. B5 8
Alcalá de Henares, Sp. B4, p18 8
Alcalá de los Gazules, Sp. D3 8
Alcamo, It. F4 9
Alcanar, Sp. B6 8
Alcañiz, Sp. B5 8
Alcaraz, Sp. C4 8
Alcaudete, Sp. D3 8
Alcázar de San Juan, Sp. C4 8
Alcazarquivir, see Ksar el Kebir, Mor.
Alcoy, Sp. C5 8
Alcoy, Nevado, mtn., Peru D2 31
Aldan, Pa. *G11 81
Aldan, Sov. Un. D15 13
Aldan, riv., Sov. Un. C16 13
Alden, Iowa B4 60
Alden, N.Y. C2 75
Alden, Pa. D9 81
Aldershot, Eng. E6 4
Alderson, W. Va. D4 87
Alderwood Manor, Wash. B3 86
Aledo, Ill. B3 58
Alegre, Braz. C4 30
Alegrete, Braz. D1 31
Aleksandriya, Sov. Un. G9 12
Aleksandrov, Sov. Un. C12 12
Aleksandrovsk -Sakhalinskiy,
  Sov. Un. D17 13
Aleksandrów, Pol. B5 7
Aleksinac, Yugo. D5 10
Alençon, Fr. C4 5
Aleppo (Halab), Syr. D11 14
Alert Bay, B.C., Can. D4 37
Alès, Fr. E6 5
Alessandria, It. B2 9
Alesund, Nor. F2 11
Alexander, co., Ill. F4 58
Alexander, co., N.C. B1 76
Alexander City, Ala. C4 46
Alexander Mills, N.C. B1, f11 76
Alexandria, Ont., Can. B10 41
Alexandria (Al Iskandariyah), Eg. . G7 14
Alexandria, Ind. D6 59
Alexandria, Ky. B5, k14 62
Alexandria, La. C3 63
Alexandria, Minn. E3 67
Alexandria, Rom. D7 10
Alexandria
  (Independent City), Va. B5, g12 85
Alexandria Bay, N.Y. A5, f9 75
Alexandria Southwest, La. *C3 63
Alexandroúpolis, Grc. B5 14
Alexis, Ill. B3 58
Aleysk, Sov. Un. D11 13
Alfalfa, co., Okla. A3 79
Al Fallūjah, Iraq F14 14
Alfaro, Sp. A5 8
Al Fayyūm, Eg. H8 14
Alfenas, Braz. C3, k9 30
Alfortville, Fr. g10 5

Alfred, Ont., Can., ... B10 41
Alfred, N.Y. C3 75
Algarve, prov., Port. D1 8
Algarve, reg., Port. *D2 8
Algeciras, Sp. D3 8
Algemesí, Sp. C5 8
Alger, Ohio B2 78
Alger, co., Mich. B4 66
Algeria, country, Afr. C3 22
Alghero, It. D2 9
Al Ghurdaqah, Eg. C4 23
Algiers (El Djazair), Alg. A5 22
Algoma, dist., Ont., Can. A2 41
Algoma, Wis. D6 88
Algona, Iowa A3 60
Algona, Wash. B3, f11 86
Algonac, Mich. F8 66
Algonquin, Ill. A5, h8 58
Al Hadīthah, Iraq E14 14
Alhama, Sp. D5 8
Alhambra, Calif. m12 50
Alhaurín el Grande, Sp. D3 8
Al Ḥillah, Iraq F15 14
Al Hufhūf (Hofhof), Sau. Ar. D4 15
Al Ḥusayhisah, Sud. F4 23
Alicante, Sp. C5 8
Alice, Tex. F3 84
Alice, Southwest, Tex. *F3 84
Aliceville, Kans. D8 61
Alīgarh, India C6 20
Alingsås, Swe. I5 11
Aliquippa, Pa. E1, h13 81
Al Iskandariyah, see Alexandria, Eg.
Al Isma 'īliyah, Eg. G9 14
Alistrái, Grc. B4 14
Aliwal North, S. Afr. G5 24
Al Jawf (Jauf), Sau. Ar. D2 15
Al Jīzah (Giza), Eg. H8 14
Al Junaynah, Sud. F2 23
Aljustrel, Port. D1 8
Al Karak, Jordan C3, h5 15
Al Kāzimiyah, Iraq F14 14
Al Khābūkrah, Om. D2 20
Al Khalil (Hebron), Jordan ... C3, h5 15
Al Kharijah, Eg. C4 23
Alkmaar, Neth. A6 5
Al Kūfah, Iraq F15 14
Al Lādhiqiyah, see Latakia, Syr.
Allahābād, India C7 20
Allmakee, co., Iowa A6 60
Allanmyo, Bur. E10 20
Allariz, Sp. A2 8
Allaykha, Sov. Un. B17 13
Allegan, Mich. F5 66
Allegan, co., Mich. F4 66
Allegany, N.Y. C2 75
Allegany, co., Md. A1 53
Allegany, co., N.Y. C2 75
Allegany, co., N.C. A1 76
Allegany, co., Va. C3 85
Allegheny, co., Pa. E1 81
Allegheny, mts., U.S. C10 45
Allegheny, riv., Pa. E2 81
Allen, Okla. C5 79
Allen, co., Ind. B7 59
Allen, co., Kans. E8 61
Allen, co., Ky. D3 62
Allen, co., Ohio B1 78
Allen, par., La. D3 63
Allendale, N.J. A4 74
Allendale, S.C. E5 82
Allendale, co., S.C. F5 82
Allen Park, Mich. p15 66
Allenport, Pa. F1 81
Allenstein, see Olsztyn, Pol.
Allentown, N.J. C3 74
Allentown, Pa. E11 81
Alleppey, India G6 20
Aller (Cabañaquinta), Sp. A3 8
Alliance, Nebr. B3 71
Alliance, Ohio B4 78
Allier, dept., Fr. D5 5
Allinge, Den. A3 7
Allison, Iowa B5 60
Allison, Pa. G2 81
Allison Park, Pa. h14 81
Allison, Ont., Can. C5 41
Al Līth, Sau. Ar. D6 23
Alloa, Scot. B5 4
Allouez, Wis. h9 88
Al Luhayyah, Yemen F3 15
Alma, Ark. B1 49
Alma, Ga. E4 55
Alma, Kans. C7 61
Alma, Mich. E6 66
Alma, Nebr. D6 71
Alma, Wis. D2 88
Alma-Ata, Sov. Un. E10 13
Almada, Por. f9 8
Almadén, Sp. C3 8
Al Madīnah, see Medina, Sau. Ar.
Almagro, Sp. C4 8
Al Maḥallah al Kubrā, Eg. *G8 14

Almansa, Sp. C5 8
Al Manşūra, Eg. G8 14
Al Marj, Libya B2 23
Al Mawşil, see Mosul, Iraq
Almeirim, Port. C1 8
Almelo, Neth. A7 5
Almendralejo, Sp. C2 8
Almería, Sp. D4 8
Al Minyā, Eg. C4 23
Almiros, Grc. C4 14
Almodóvar, Sp. C3 8
Almogía, Sp. D3 8
Almon, Ga. C3 55
Almonesson, N.J. D2 74
Almont, Mich. F7 66
Almonte, Ont., Can. B8 41
Almora, Minn. *D3 67
Almoradí, Sp. C5 8
Al Mukallā, P.D.R. of Yem. G4 15
Al Mukhā, Yemen G3 15
Almuñécar, Sp. D4 8
Alnwick, Eng. C6 4
Aloha, Oreg. h12 80
Alor Setar, Mala. D2 19
Alorton (Fireworks), Ill. *E3 58
Alosno, Sp. D2 8
Alpaugh, Calif. E4 50
Alpena, Mich. C7 66
Alpena, co., Mich. C7 66
Alpes-Maritimes, dept., Fr. *F7 5
Alpha, N.J. B2 74
Alpharetta, Ga. B2 55
Alpiarça, Port. C1 8
Alpine, Calif. *F5 50
Alpine, N.J. *h9 74
Alpine, Tex. o13 84
Alpine, co., Calif. C4 50
Alpoca, W. Va. D3 87
Al Qadarif, Sud. F5 23
Al Qāhirah, see Cairo, Eg.
Al Qantarah, Eg. G9 14
Al Qaṭīf, Sau. Ar. D4 15
Al Qunayṭirah, see Kuneitra, Syr.
Alsfeld, Ger., Fed. Rep of C4 6
Alsip, Ill. B6 58
Alta, Iowa B2 6
Alta Gracia, Arg. A4 28
Alta Loma, Tex. r14 84
Altamont, Ill. D5 58
Altamont, N.Y. C6 75
Altamont, Oreg. E5 80
Altamonte Springs, Fla. *D5 54
Altamura, It. D6 9
Altavista, Va. C3 85
Altay, China B2 17
Altdorf, Switz. E4 6
Altenburg, Mo. D8 69
Altheimer, Ark. C4 49
Alto, Tex. D5 84
Alto Alentejo, prov., Port. *C2 8
Alton, Ill. E3 58
Alton, Iowa B1 60
Altona, Man., Can. E3 40
Altoona, Ala. A3 46
Altoona, Iowa C4 6
Altoona, Pa. F5 81
Altoona, Wis. D2 88
Alto Paraná, dept., Par. D4 29
Alturas, Calif. B3 50
Altus, Okla. C2 79
Alula, Som. F8 23
Al Uqşur (Luxor), Eg. C4 23
Alva, Ky. D6 62
Alva, Okla. A3 79
Alvarado, Tex. C4, n9 84
Alvin, Tex. E5, r4 84
Älvsborg, so., Swe. *H5 11
Alwar, India C6 20
Alx, mtn., Wash. C4 86
Alytus, Sov. Un. A8 7
Amador, co., Calif. C3 50
Amagansett, N.Y. n16 75
Amagasaki, Jap. o14 18
Amål, Swe. H5 11
Amalias, Grc. D3 14
Amambay, dept., Par. D4 29
Amamtea, It. E6 9
Amapá, Braz. C5 27
Amarillo, Tex. B2 84
Amaroúsion, Gr. g11 14
Amasya (Amasia), Tur. *B10 14
Amazonas, comisaría, Col. D3 32
Amazonas, dept., Peru B2 31
Amazonas, state, Braz. C3 31
Amazonas, (Amazon) riv.,
  Braz., Peru D5 27
Amazon, see Amazonas, riv., Braz., Peru
Ambāla, India B6 20
Ambarchik, Sov. Un. C19 13
Ambato, Ec. B2 31
Amberg, Ger. Fed. Rep. of D5 6

Ambérieu -en Bugey, Fr. E5 6
Amberley, Ohio *C1 78
Ambikapur, India D7 20
Ambler, Pa. F11, o21 81
Amboise, Fr. D4 5
Ambon (Amboina), Indon. F7 19
Amboy, Ill. B4 58
Ambridge, Pa. E1, h13 81
Ambridge Heights, Pa. *E1 81
Amderma, Sov. Un. C9 13
Ameca, Mex. C4, m11 34
Amecameca de Juárez, Mex. n14 34
Amelia, La. E4, k9 63
Amelia, Ohio C1 78
Amelia, co., Va. C4 85
Amelia Court House, Va. C5 85
Amenia, N. Dak. D8 77
Amenia, N.Y. D7 75
American Falls, Idaho G6 57
American Fork, Utah A6, D2 72
American Samoa,
  U.S. dep., Oceania *G9 2
Americus, Ga. D2 55
Amersfoort, Neth. A6 5
Amery, Wis. C1 88
Ames, Iowa B4 60
Amesbury, Mass. A6 65
Amfissa, Grc. C4 14
Amga, Sov. Un. C16 13
Amherst, N.S., Can. D5 43
Amherst, Mass. B2 65
Amherst, (Eggertsville), N.Y. *C2 75
Amherst, Ohio A3 78
Amherst, Tex. B1 84
Amherst, Va. C3 85
Amherst, co., Va. C3 85
Amherstburg, Ont., Can. E1 41
Amherstdale, W. Va. D3, n12 87
Amiens, Fr. C5 5
Amite, La. D5 63
Amite, co., Miss. D3 68
Amityville, N.Y. E7, n15 75
'Ammān, Jordan C3, h5 15
Ammon, Idaho F7 57
Amory, Miss. B5 68
Amos, Que., Can. o20 41
Amoy, see Xiamen, China
Amparo, Braz. C3, m8 30
Amqui, Que., Can. *k13 42
Amravati, India D6 20
Amritsar, India B5 20
Amsterdam, Neth. A6 5
Amsterdam, N.Y. C6 75
Amsterdam, Ohio B5 78
Amstetten, Aus. D7 6
Amu Darya, riv., Sov. Un. FI9 13
Amur, riv., China, Sov. Un. E16 13
'Ānah, Iraq C3 15
Anaconda, Mont. D4 70
Anacortes, Wash. A3 86
Anadarko, Okla. B3 79
Anadyr, Sov. Un. C20 13
Anaheim, Calif. F5, n13 50
Anahuac, Tex. E5, r15 84
Anakapallei, India E7 20
Analalava, Mad. C9 24
Anamosa, Iowa B6 60
Anandale, Lal. *C3 63
Anantapur, India F6 20
Anantnag, India B6 20
Ananyev, Sov. Un. H7 12
Anápolis, Braz. B3 30
Añatuya, Arg. E3 29
Anawalt, W. Va. D3 87
Ancash, dept., Peru C2 31
Anchorage, Alsk. C10, g17 47
Anchorage, Ky. g11 62
Ancienne Lorette, Que., Can. .. C6, n17 42
Ancon, C.Z. B2 32
Ancona, It. C4 9
Anda, China C2 18
Andalusia, Ala. D3 46
Andalusia reg., Sp. D3 8
Andaman and Nicobar Islands,
  ter., India F9, G9 20
Anderlecht, Bel. B6 5
Andernach, Ger., Fed. Rep of C3 6
Anderson, Calif. B2 50
Anderson, Ind. D6 59
Anderson Mo. E3 69
Anderson, S.C. B2 82
Anderson, co., Kans. D8 61
Anderson, co., Ky. C4 62
Anderson, co., S.C. B2 82
Anderson, co., Tenn. C9 83
Anderson, co., Tex. D5 84
Anderson, mtn., Wash. B2 86
Andes, Col. B2 32
Andhra Pradesh, state, India E6 20
Andizhan, Sov. Un. E10 13
Andkhui, Afg. A4 20
Andoany, Mad. *C9 24
Andong, Kor. H4 18

Andorra, And. A6 8
Andorra, country, Eur. A6 8
Andover, Mass. A5 65
Andover, N.B., Can. C2 43
Andover, N.Y. C3 75
Andover, Ohio A5 78
Andraitx, Sp. C7 8
Andrew, co., Mo. B3 69
Andrew Jackson, mtn., Ant. K16 2
Andrews, Ind. C6 59
Andrews, N.C. f9 76
Andrews, S.C. El8 82
Andrews, Tex. C1 84
Andrews, co., Tex. C1 84
Andreyevka, Sov. Un. G11 12
Andria, It. D6 9
Androscoggin, co., Maine D2 64
Andropov (Rybinsk), Sov. Un. B12 12
Andros, isl., Ba. B4 35
Andrychów, Pol. h10 7
Andújar, Sp. C3 8
Aneto, mtn., Sp. A6 8
Angara, riv., Sov. Un. D13 13
Angarsk, Sov. Un. *D13 13
Angelholm, Swe. I5 11
Angelica, N.Y. C2 75
Angelina, co., Tex. D5 84
Angels Camp, Calif. C3 50
Angermunde, Ger. Dem. Rep. B7 6
Angers, Fr. D3 5
Angier, N.C. B4 76
Anglesey, is., Wales D4 4
Anglet, Fr. F3 5
Angleton, Tex. E5, r14 84
Ango, Zaire H3 23
Angol, Chile B2 28
Angola, Ind. A8 59
Angola, N.Y. C1 75
Angola, country, Afr. C3 24
Angoulême, Fr. E4 5
Angra do Heroismo, Port. k10 22
Angra dos Reis, Braz. C4, h5 30
Anguang, China D1 18
Angus, co., Scot. *B5 4
Anhui, prov., China E8 17
Anina, Rom. C5 10
Anita, Iowa C3 60
Anita, Pa. D4 81
Aniva (Rutaka), Sov. Un. *C11 18
Anjo, Jap. o16 18
Anjou, Que., Can. p19 42
Anjou, former prov. Fr. D3 5
Anju, Kor. G2 18
Ankang, China E6 17
Ankara, Tur. C9 14
Ankeny, Iowa C4, e8 60
Anklam, Ger. Dem. Rep. B6 6
Annaba (Bône), Alg. A6 22
An Najaf, Iraq C3 15
Annalee Heights, Va. *B5 85
Annam, reg., Viet. *B3 19
Annandale, Minn. E4 67
Annandale, Va. g12 85
Annapolis, Md. C5 53
Annapolis Royal, N.S. E4 43
Annapurna 1, peak, Nep. C7 20
Ann Arbor, Mich. F7, p14 66
An Nasiriya, Iraq C4 15
Anne Arundel co., Md. B4 53
Annecy, Fr. E7 5
Annemasse, Fr. D7 5
Anniston, Ala. B4 46
Annonay, Fr. E6 5
An Nuhūd, Sud. F3 23
Annville, Pa. F8 81
Anoka, Minn. E5, m12 67
Anoka, co., Minn. E5 67
Ansbach, Ger., Fed. Rep. of D5 6
Anserma, Col. B2 32
Anshan, China C9 17
Anshun, China F6 17
Anson, Maine D3 64
Anson, Tex. C3 84
Anson, co., N.C. B2 76
Ansong, Kor. H3 18
Ansonia, Conn. D4 52
Ansonia, Ohio B1 78
Ansted, W.Va. C3, m13 87
Anta, Peru D3 31
Antakay (Antioch), Tur. D11 14
Antalaha, Mad. C10 24
Antalya (Adalia), Tur. D8 14
Antananarive, Mad. D9 24
Antarctic, pen., Ant. K16 2
Antelope, co., Nebr. B7 71
Anthon, Iowa B2 60
Anthony, Kans. E5 61
Anthony, N. Mex. D5 48
Anthony, R.I. C10 52
Antibes, Fr. F7 5
Antigo, Wis. C4 88
Antigonish, N.S., Can. D8 43

Antigonish, co., N.S., Can. D8 43
Antigua and Barbuda, country, N.A. H14 35
Antigua, Guatemala, Guat. E6 34
Antilla, Cuba D6 35
Antioch, Calif. h9 50
Antioch, Ill. A5, h8 58
Antioquia, Col. B2 32
Antioquia, dept. Col. B2 32
Antique, prov., Phil. *C6 19
Antlers, Okla. C6 79
Antofagasta, Chile D1 29
Antofagasta, prov., Chile D1 29
Anton, Tex. C1 84
Antonina, Braz. D3 30
António Enes, Moz. D7 24
Antonito, Colo. D5 51
Antony, Fr. g10 5
Antratsit, Sov. Un. g22 12
Antrim, co., Mich. C5 66
Antrim, co. N. Ire. *C3 4
Antsirabe, Mad. D9 24
Antsiranana, Mad. C9 24
Antwerp, N.Y. A5, f9 75
Antwerp, Ohio A1 78
Antwerp (Antwerpen), Bel. B6 5
Antwerpen, prov., Bel. *B6 5
Anuadhapura, Sri Lanka G7 20
Anyang, China D7 17
Anzhero-Sudzhensk, Sov. Un. D11 13
Anzio, It. D4, k7 9
Anzoátequi, state, Ven. B5 32
Aomori, Jap. F10 18
Aomori, pref., Jap. *F10 18
Aosta, It. B1 9
Apache, Okla. C3 79
Apache co., Ariz. B4 48
Apache mts., Tex. o12 84
Apache Junction, Ariz. D2 48
Apalachicola, Fla. C2 54
Apalachin, N.Y. C4 75
Apam, Mex. n14 34
Aparri, Phil. B6 19
Apatin, Yugo. C4 10
Apeldoorn, Neth. A6 5
Apex, N.C. B4 76
Apia, W. Sam. G9 2
Apizaco, Mex. n14 34
Aplao, Peru E3 31
Apington, Iowa B5 60
Apo, vol., Phil. D7 19
Apolda, Ger. Dem. Rep. C5 6
Apollo, Pa. E2 8
Apopka, Fla. D5 54
Appalachia, Va. f9 85
Appalachian, mts., U.S. F12 33
Appanoose, co., Iowa D5 60
Appenzell, canton, Switz. *B7 6
Apple Orchard, mtn., Va. C3 85
Appleton, Minn. E2 67
Appleton, Wis. D5, h9 88
Appleton City, Mo. C3 69
Appleyard, Wash. B5 86
Appling, co., Ga. E4 55
Appomattox, Va. C4 85
Appomattox, co., Va. C4 85
Aprelsk, Sov. Un. D14 13
Apt, Fr. F6 5
Apulia, reg., It. D6 9
Apure, riv., Ven. B4 32
Apurímac, riv., Peru D3 31
Aquidauana, Braz. C1 30
Arab, Ala. A3 46
Arabi, La. k11 62
Arabia, see Saudi Arabia, Asia
Aracaju, Braz. E7 27
Aracati, Braz. D7 27
Arçatuba, Braz. C2 30
Arad, Rom. B5 10
Aragon, Ga. B1 55
Aragua, state, Ven. A4 32
Araguaia, riv., Braz. D6 27
Araguari, Braz. *E5 27
Arai, Jap. o16 18
Arāk (Sultanabad), Iran B7 23
Aral, sea, Sov. Un. E8 13
Aranda de Duero, Sp. B4 8
Arandas, Mex. m12 34
Aranjuez, Sp. B4 8
Aranos, S.W. Afr. B2 24
Aranyaprathet, Thai. C2 19
Arapahoe, Nebr. D6 71
Arapkir, Tur. C12 14
Arapohoe, co., Colo. B6 51
Araraquara, Braz. C3, k7 30
Araras, Braz. m8 30
Ararat, Austl. G7, n14 25
Ararat, see Buyuk Agri Dagi, mtn., Tur.
Arauca, Col. B3 32
Arauca, intendencia, Col. B3 32
Arauco, prov., Chile *B2 28
Araxá, Braz. B3 30

Arboga, Swe. t33 11
Arborg, Man., Can. D3 40
Arbor Terrace, Mo. *C7 69
Arbroath, Scot. B5 4
Arbuckle, Calif. C2 50
Arcade, N.Y. C2 75
Arcadia, Calif. m12 50
Arcadia, Fla. E5 54
Arcadia, Ind. D5 59
Arcadia, La. B3 63
Arcadia, Wis. D2 88
Arcanum, Ohio C1 78
Arcata, Calif. B1 50
Archangel, see Arkhangelsk, Sov. Un.
Archbald, Pa. m18 81
Archbold, Ohio A1 78
Archdale, N.C. B3 76
Archer, co., Tex. C3 84
Archer City, Tex. C3 84
Archidona, Sp. D3 8
Archuleta, co., Colo. D3 51
Arcila, Mor. E2 8
Arco, Ga. E5 55
Arco, Idaho F5 57
Arcola, Ill. D5 58
Arcoverde, Braz. *D6 27
Arctic, Ocean A6 2
Arcueil, Fr. g10 5
Ardabil (Ardebil), Iran B4 15
Ardatov, Sov. Un. D16 12
Ardèche, dept., Fr. *E6 5
Arden (Ardentown), Del. A7 53
Arden Hills, Minn. *E7 67
Ardennes, dept., Fr. *C6 5
Ardmore, Okla. C4 79
Ardmore, Pa. g20 81
Ardrossan, Scot. C4 4
Ardsley, N.Y. g13 75
Arecibo, P.R. g11 35
Areia Branca, Braz. *D7 27
Arenac, co., Mich. D7 66
Arendal, Nor. H3 11
Arequipa, Peru E3 31
Arequipa, dept., Peru E3 31
Arezzo, It. C3 9
Argenta, Ill. D5 58
Argenta, It. B3 8
Argentan, Fr. C4 5
Argenteuil, Fr. C5, g10 5
Argenteuil, co. Que. D3 42
Argentina, country, S.A. G4 27
Argenton-sur-Creuse, Fr. D4 5
Argolis, prov., Grc. *D4 14
Argos, Grc. D4 14
Argos, Ind. B5 59
Argostólion, Grc. C3 14
Argyll, co., Scot. *B4 4
Århus, Den. I4 11
Århus, co., Den. *I4 11
Ariail, S.C. B2 82
Ariano Irpino, It. D5 9
Arica, Chile C1 29
Ariège, dept., Fr. *F4 5
Arīhā (Jericho), Jordan C3 15
Ario de Rosales, Mex. D4, n13 34
Aripo, El Cerro del, mtn., Trin. K14 34
Arizona, state, U.S. 48
Arjay, Ky. D6 62
Arjona, Col. A2 32
Arjona, Sp. D3 8
Arkadelphia, Ark. C2 49
Arkadhia (Arcadia), prov., Grc. *D4 14
Arkansas, state, U.S. 49
Arkansas, co., Ark. C4 49
Arkansas, riv., U.S. C8 45
Arkansas City, Ark. D4 49
Arkansas City, Kans. E6 61
Arkhangelsk, Sov. Un. C7 13
Arkoma, Okla. B7 79
Arkonam, India F6 20
Arkport, N.Y. C3 75
Arkwright, R.I. C10 52
Arkwright, S.C. *B4 82
Arles, Fr. F6 5
Arlington, Ga. E2 55
Arlington, Mass. B5, g11 65
Arlington, Minn. F4 67
Arlington, N.Y. *D7 75
Arlington, Ohio B2 78
Arlington, S.C. B3 82
Arlington, S. Dak. F8 77
Arlington, Tex. n9 84
Arlington, Vt. E1 73
Arlington, Wash. A3 86
Arlington, co., Va. B5, g12 85
Arlington Heights, Ill. A5, a9 58
Arlington Heights, Ohio *C1 78
Arlon, Bel. *C6 5

Arma, Kans. E9 61
Armada, Mich. F8 66
Armagh, N. Ire. C3 4
Armagh, Que., Can. C7 42
Armagh, co., N. Ire. *C3 4
Armavir, Sov. Un. I13 12
Armenia, Col. C2 32
Armenia (S.S.R.), rep. Sov. Un. A4 15
Armentières, Fr. B5 5
Armero, Col. C3 32
Armidale, Austl. F9 25
Armijo, N. Mex. E5 48
Armona, Calif. *D4 50
Armonk, N.Y. *D7 75
Armour, S. Dak. G7 77
Armstrong, B.C., Can. D8 37
Armstrong, Iowa A3 60
Armstrong, co., Pa. E3 81
Armstrong, co., Tex. B2 84
Arnaudville, La. D4 63
Arnedo, Sp. A4 8
Arnhem, Neth. B6 5
Arnissa, Grc. *I5 14
Arnold, Mo. C7 69
Arnold, Nebr. C5 71
Arnold, Pa. h14 81
Arnolds Park, Iowa A2 60
Arnouville -les-Gonesse, Fr. g10 5
Arnprior, Ont., Can. B8 41
Arnsberg, Ger., Fed. Rep. of. C4 6
Arnstadt, Ger. Dem. Rep. C5 6
Aroostook, co., Maine B4 64
Arp, Tex. C5 84
Arrah, India C7 20
Ar Ramādī, Iraq F14 14
Ar Raqqah, Syr. E12 14
Arras, Fr. B5 5
Arrecife, Sp. m15 8
Arrecifes, Arg. g6 28
Arroyo, P.R. *G11 35
Arroyo Grande, Calif. E3 50
Árta, Grc. C3 14
Arta, prov., Grc. *C3 14
Artem, Sov. Un. E16 13
Artemisa, Cuba C2 35
Artemovsk, Sov. Un. G12, o21 12
Arter, mtn., Wyo. D4 89
Artesia, Calif. *F4 50
Artesia, N. Mex. C6 48
Arthabaska, Que., Can. C6 42
Arthabaska, co., Que., Can C5 42
Arthur, Ill. D5 58
Arthur, co., Nebr. C4 71
Artigas, Ur. E1 30
Artois, former prov., Fr. B5 5
Aruba, Neth. dep A4 32
Arunachal Pradesh, ter., India C9 20
Arusha, Tan. I5 23
Arvada, Colo. B5 51
Arvida, Que., Can. A6 42
Arvidsjaur, Swe. E8 11
Arvika, Swe. H5 11
Arvin, Calif. E4 50
Arzamas, Sov. Un. D14 12
Arzúa, Sp. A1 8
As, Czech. C2 7
Asahi-Dake, mtn., Jap. E11 18
Asahikawa, Jap. E11 18
Asan, Guam *F6 2
Asansol, India D8 20
Asbest, Sov. Un. D9 13
Asbestos, Que., Can. D6 42
Asbury Park, N.J. C4 74
Ascension, par., La. D5 63
Ascension Isl. Br. dep., Atl. O. G20 2
Aschaffenburg, Ger., Fed. Rep. of D4 6
Aschersleben, Ger. Dem. Rep. C5 6
Ascoli Piceno, It. C4 9
Asenovgrad, Bul. E7 10
Ashaway, R.I. D9 52
Ashburn, Ga. E3 55
Ashburnham, Mass. A4 65
Ashburton, N.Z. O13 26
Ashby, Ala. B3 46
Ashcroft, B.C., Can. D7 37
Ashdown, Ark. D1 49
Ashe, co., N.C. A1 76
Asheboro, N.C. B3 76
Asheboro South, N.C. *B3 76
Asheboro West, N.C. *B3 76
Asherton, Tex. E3 84
Asheville, N.C. f10 76
Ashford, Ala. D4 46
Ash Grove, Mo. D4 69
Ashikaga, Jap. H9, m18 18
Ashio, Jap. H9 18
Ashkhabad, Sov. Un. F8 13
Ashland, Ala. B4 46
Ashland, Ill. D3 58
Ashland, Kans. E4 61
Ashland, Ky. B7 62

Ashland, Maine,	B4	64
Ashland, Mass.	g10	65
Ashland, Nebr.	C9, g12	71
Ashland, N.H.	D4	73
Ashland, Ohio	B3	78
Ashland, Oreg.	E4	80
Ashland, Pa.	E9	81
Ashland, Va.	C5	85
Ashland, Wis.	B3	88
Ashland, co., Ohio	B3	78
Ashland, co., Wis.	B3	88
Ashland, mtn. Oreg.	E4	80
Ashland City, Tenn.	A4	83
Ashley, N. Dak.	D6	77
Ashley, Ohio	B5	78
Ashley, Pa.	n17	81
Ashley, co., Ark.	D4	49
Ashmūn, Eg.	*G8	14
Ashqelon, Isr.	C2	15
Ash Shāmīyah, Iraq	*G15	14
Ash Shatt, Eg.	H9	14
Ash Shihr, P.D.R. of Yem.	C6	15
Ashtabula, Ohio	A5	78
Ashtabula, co., Ohio	A5	78
Ashton, Idaho	E7	57
Ashton, Ill.	B4	58
Ashton, R.I.	B11	52
Ashville, Ala.	B3	46
Ashville, Ohio	C3	78
Ashwaubenon, Wis.	g9	88
Asia, cont.	F9	16
Asir, reg., Sau. Ar.	E6	23
Asmara, Eth.	E5	23
Asnières -sur Seine, Fr.	g10	5
Asotin, co., Wash.	C8	86
Aspe, Sp.	C5	8
Aspen, Colo.	B4	51
Aspermont, Tex.	C2	84
Aspinwall, Pa.	k14	81
As Salt, Jordan	B3, g5	15
Assam, state, India	C9	20
Assateague, isl. Va.	C7	85
Assen, Neth.	A7	5
Assens, co. Den.	*J3	11
Assiniboia, Sask. Can.	H3	39
Assiniboine, mtn., Alta.	D3	38
Assini, I.C.	G4	22
Assis, Braz.	C2	30
Assisi, It.	C4	9
As Sulaymānīyah, Iraq	B3	15
Assumption, Ill.	D4	58
Assumption, par., La.	E4	63
As Suwaydā, Syr	F11	14
Asti, It.	B2	9
Aston, Pa.	*G11	81
Astorga, Sp.	A2	8
Astoria, Ill.	C3	58
Astoria, Oreg.	A3	80
Astrakhan, Sov. Un.	E7	13
Asturias, reg., Sp.	A2	8
Asunción, Par.	E4	29
Aswan, Eg.	D4	23
Asyut, Eg.	C4	23
Atacama, prov., Chile	E1	29
Atami, Jap.	n18	18
Atascadero, Calif.	E3	50
Atascosa, co., Tex.	E3	84
'Atbarah, Sud	E4	23
Atbasar, Sov. Un.	D9	13
Atchison, Kans.	C8	61
Atchison, co., Kans.	C8	61
Atchison, co., Mo.	A2	69
Atco, N.J.	D3	74
Athabasca, Alta., Can.	B4, g8	38
Athabasca, lake, Alta., Can.	m6	39
Athabasca, riv., Can.	E11	36
Athena, Oreg.	E8	80
Athens, Ala.	A3	46
Athens, Ont., Can.	C9	41
Athens, Ga.	C3	55
Athens (Athinai), Grc.	C4	14
Athens, Ill.	C4	58
Athens, Mich.	F5	66
Athens, N.Y.	C7	75
Athens, Ohio	C3	78
Athens, Pa.	C9	81
Athens, Tenn.	D9	83
Athens, Tex.	C5	84
Athens, W. Va.	D3	87
Athens, co., Ohio	C3	78
Atherton, Austl.	C8	25
Atherton, Calif.	*D2	60
Athis-Mons, Fr.	h10	5
Athleague, Ire.	D3	4
Athok, Bur.	E10	20
Athol, Mass.	A3	65
Atibaia, Braz.	m8	30
Atikokan, Ont., Can.	E8	41
Atkarsk, Sov. Un.	F15	12
Atkins, Ark.	B3	49
Atkinson, Ill.	B3	58
Atkinson, Nebr.	B7	71
Atkinson, co., Ga.	E4	55
Atlanta, Ga.	C2, h8	55
Atlanta, Ill.	C4	58
Atlanta, Tex.	C5	84
Atlantic, Iowa	C2	60
Atlantic, N.C.	C6	76
Atlantic, co., N.J.	E3	74
Atlantic, ocean	D17	2
Atlantic peak, Wyo.	D3	89
Atlantic Beach, N.Y.	n15	75
Atlantic City, N.J.	E4	74
Atlantic Highlands, N.J.	C4	74
Atlántico, dept., Col.	A2	32
Atlas, Pa.	*D8	81
Atlixco, Mex.	n14	34
Atmore, Ala.	D2	46
Atna, peak, B.C., Can.	C3	37
Atoka, Okla.	C5	79
Atoka, co., Okla.	C5	79
Atotonilco el Alto, Mex.	m12	34
Atrisco, N. Mex.	*B5	48
Atsugi, Jap.	n18	18
At Tafilah, Jordan	D3, h5	15
At Ta'if, Sau. Ar.	E3	15
Attala, co., Miss.	B4	68
Attalia, Ala.	A3	46
At Tayyibah, Jordan	C3	15
Attica, Ind.	D3	59
Attica, Kans.	E5	61
Attica, N.Y.	C2	75
Attica, Ohio	A3	78
Attika (Attica), prov., Grc.	*C4	14
Attleboro, Mass.	C5	65
Atvidaberg, Swe.	H6	11
Atwater, Calif.	D3	50
Atwater, Minn.	E4	67
Atwood, Ill.	D5	58
Atwood, Kans.	C2	61
Atzcapotzalco (Azcapotzalco), Mex.	h9, n14	34
Atzmon, mtn., Isr.	A3	15
Aubagne, Fr.	F3	5
Aube, dept., Fr.	*C6	5
Aubervilliers, Fr.	g10	5
Aubin, Fr.	E5	5
Auburn, Ala.	C4	46
Auburn, Ill.	D4	58
Auburn, Ind.	B7	59
Auburn, Kans.	D8	61
Auburn, Ky.	D3	62
Auburn, Maine	D2, f7	64
Auburn, Mass.	B4	65
Auburn, Mich.	E6	66
Auburn, Nebr.	D10	71
Auburn, N.Y.	C4	75
Auburn, Pa.	E9	81
Auburn, Wash.	B3, f11	86
Auburndale, Fla.	D5	54
Auburn Heights, Mich.	F7	66
Aubusson, Fr.	E5	5
Auch, Fr.	F4	5
Auckland, N.Z.	L15	26
Aude, dept. Fr.	*C6	5
Audincourt, Fr.	D7	5
Audrain, co., Mo.	B6	69
Audubon, Iowa	C3	60
Audubon, N.J.	D2	74
Audubon, co., Iowa	C3	60
Audubon Park, N.J.	*C3	74
Aue, Ger. Dem. Rep.	C6	6
Auglaize, co., Ohio	B1	78
Augsburg, Ger., Fed. Rep. of	D5	6
Augusta, Ark.	B4	49
Augusta, Ga.	C5	55
Augusta, Ill.	C3	58
Augusta, It.	F6	9
Augusta, Kans.	E6, g13	61
Augusta, Ky.	B5	62
Augusta, Maine	D3	64
Augusta, Mich.	F5	66
Augusta, Wis.	D2	88
Augusta co., Va.	B3	85
Augustów, Pol.	B7	7
Augustus, mtn., Austl.	D2	25
Aulander, N.C.	A5	76
Aulnay-sous-Bois, Fr.	g11	5
Auray, Fr.	D2	5
Aurelia, Iowa	B2	60
Aurich, Ger., Fed. Rep. of	B3	6
Aurillac, Fr.	E5	5
Aurora, Ont.,Can.	D5	42
Aurora, Colo.	B6	51
Aurora, Ill.	B5, k8	58
Aurora, Ind.	F8	59
Aurora, Minn.	C6	67
Aurora, Mo.	E4	69
Aurora, Nebr.	D7	71
Aurora, Ohio	A4	78
Aurora, S. Dak.	G7	77
Aurora, co., S. Dak.	D7	77
Au Sable Forks, N.Y.	f11	75
Aust-Agder, co., Nor	*H3	11
Austell, Ga.	h7	55
Austin, Ind.	G6	59
Austin, Minn.	C6	67
Austin, Tex.	D4	84
Austin, co., Tex.	E4	84
Austintown, Ohio	A5	78
Australia, country, Oceania		25
Australian Capital Territory, Aust.	*G8	25
Austria, country, Eur.	E6	6
Autauga, co., Ala.	C3	46
Autlán de Navarro	D4, n11	34
Autun, Fr.	D6	5
Auvergne, former prov., Fr.	E5	5
Auxerre, Fr.	D5	5
Auxier, Ky.	C7	62
Ava, Mo.	E5	69
Avalon, Calif.	F4	50
Avalon, Pa.	h13	81
Avanos, Tur	C10	14
Avaré, Braz.	C3	30
Aveiro, Port.	B1	8
Avella, Pa.	F1	81
Avellaneda, Arg.	A5, g7	28
Avellino, It	D5	9
Avenal, Calif.	E3	50
Avenel, N.J.	k7	74
Aversa, It.	D5	9
Avery, co., N.C.	e11	76
Avesta, Swe.	G7	11
Aveyron, dept., Fr.	*E5	5
Avezzano, It.	C4	9
Avigliano, It.	D5	9
Avignon, Fr.	F6	5
Ávila, Sp.	B3	8
Avilés, Sp.	A3	8
Avilla, Ind.	B7	59
Avis, Pa.	D7	81
Avoca, Ala.	A2	46
Avoca, Iowa	C2	60
Avoca, N.Y.	C3	75
Avoca, Pa.	m18	81
Avola, It.	F5	9
Avon, Conn	B5	52
Avon, Ill.	C3	58
Avon, Mass.	B5, a11	65
Avon, N.Y.	C3	75
Avon, Ohio	A3	78
Avon, Pa.	*F9	81
Avon by the Sea, N.J.	C4	74
Avondale, Ariz.	D1	48
Avondale, Pa.	G10	81
Avondale Estates, Ga.	h8	55
Avon Lake, Ohio	A3	78
Avonmore, Pa.	E3	81
Avon Park, Fla.	E5	54
Avoyelles, par., La.	C3	63
Avranches, Fr.	C3	5
Axim, Ghana	H4	22
Axis, Ala.	E1	46
Ay, Fr.	C5	5
Ayabe, Jap.,	n14	18
Ayacucho, Arg.	B5	28
Ayacucho, Peru	D3	31
Ayacucho, dept., Peru	D3	31
Ayaguz, Sov. Un.	E11	13
Ayamonte, Sp.	D2	8
Ayan, Sov. Un.	D16	13
Ayaviri, Peru	D3	31
Ayden, N.C.	B5	76
Aydin, Tur.	D6	14
Ayer, Mass.	A4, f9	65
Ayion Oros (Mount Athos) prov., Grc.	*B5	14
Áyios Dhimitrios, Grc.	*C4	14
Aylesbury, Eng.	E6	4
Aylesford, N.S., Can.	D5	43
Aylmer East, Que., Can.	D2	42
Aylmer West, Ont., Can.	E4	41
Ayora, Sp.	C5	8
Ayr, Scot	C4	4
Ayr, co., Scot.	*C4	4
Aytos, Bul.	D8	10
Ayutthaya, Thai.	C2	19
Ayvalik, Tur	C6	14
Azalea Park, Fla.	*D5	54
Azemmour, Mor.	B3	22
Azerbaidzhan (S.S.R.)	*E7	16
Azle, Tex.	n9	84
Azogues, Ec.	B2	31
Azores Islands, reg., Port.	C3	21
Azov, Sov. Un.	H12	12
Azrou, Mor.	B3	22
Aztec, N. Mex.	A4	48
Azua, Dom. Rep.	E8	35
Azuay, prov., Ec.	B2	31
Azul, Arg.	B5	28
Azuza, Calif.	m13	50
Az Zaqāziq, Eg.	B4	23
Az Zarqā', Jor.	B4	15

B

Babaeski, Tur.	E8	10
Babahoyo, Ec.	B2	31
Babayevo, Sov. Un.	B11	12
Babbitt, Minn.	*C7	67
Babbitt, Nev.	*B2	72
Bābol, Iran	A8	23
Babson Park, Fla.	E5	54
Babyak, Bul.	E6	10
Babylon, N.Y.	n15	75
Baca, co.,Colo.	D8	51
Bacalar, Mex.	D7	34
Bacău, Rom.	B8	10
Baccarat, Fr.	C7	5
Back, riv., Can.	C12	36
Bac Kan, Viet.	*G5	17
Backa Palanka, Yugo.	C4	10
Backa Topola, Yugo.	C4	10
Bac Lieu, Viet.	*D3	19
Bacliff, Tex.	*E5	84
Bac Ninh, Viet.	G6	17
Bacolod, Phil.	C6	19
Bacon, co., Ga.	E4	55
Bacsalmas, Hung.	B4	10
Bács-Kiskun, co., Hung.	*B4	10
Badajoz, Sp.	C2	8
Badalona, Sp.	B7	8
Bad Axe, Mich.	E8	66
Baddeck, N.S., Can.	C9	43
Bad Doberan, Ger. Dem Rep.	A5	6
Baden, Aus.	D8	6
Baden, Ont., Can.	D4	41
Baden, Pa.	E1	81
Baden, Switz.	E4	6
Baden, reg., Ger. Fed. Rep. of	D4	6
Baden-Baden, Ger., Fed. Rep. of	D4	6
Baden-Württemberg, state, Ger., Fed. Rep. of	*D4	6

Bad Freienwalde, Ger.
  Dem. Rep. B7   6
Badger, Newf., Can. D3 44
Bad Hersfeld, Ger., Fed.
  Rep. of...................... C4   6
Badin, N.C. B2 76
Bad Ischl, Aus. E6   6
Bad Kissingen, Ger., Fed.
  Rep. of...................... C5   6
Bad Kreuznach, Ger., Fed.
  Rep. of...................... D3   6
Bad Langensalza, Ger.
  Dem. Rep. C5   6
Bad Oldesloe, Ger., Fed.
  Rep. of...................... B5   6
Bad Reichenhall, Ger., Fed.
  Rep. of...................... E6   6
Bad Salzuflen, Ger., Fed.
  Rep. of...................... B4   6
Bad Tölz, Ger., Fed.
  Rep. of...................... E5   6
Badulla, Sri Lanka G7 20
Baffin, isl., Can. B19 36
Bafra, Tur. B10 14
Bagdad, Ariz. B2 48
Bagdad, Fla. u14 54
Bagé, Braz. E2 30
Baghdåd, Iraq C3 15
Bagheria, It. E4   9
Baghlan, Afg. A4 20
Bagley, Minn. C3 67
Bagnara Calabra, It. E5   9
Bagnères-de-Bigorre, Fr. F4   5
Bagnolet, Fr. g10 5
Bagnols sur-Cèze, Fr. E6   5
Bagot, co., Que., Can. D5 42
Bahamas, country, N.A. B11 35
Bahāwalpur, Pak. C5 20
Bahia, see Salvador, Braz.
Bahia, state, Braz A4 30
Bahía Blanca, Arg. B4 28
Bahia de Caráquiz, Ec. B1 31
Bahrain (Bahrein), country, Asia.....C8 23
Baia-Mare, Rom. B6 10
Baicheng, China B9 17
Baie-Comeau, Que.. Can. k13 42
Baie-St. Paul, Que., Can. B7 42
Baie Verte, Newf., Can. D3 44
Baikal, lake, Sov. Un. D13 13
Baile Atha Cliath, see
  Dublin, Ire.
Bailén, Sp. C4   8
Bailesti, Rom. C6 10
Bailey, co., Tex. B1 84
Bailundo, Ang. C3 24
Bainbridge, Ga. F2 55
Bainbridge, N.Y. C5 75
Bainbridge, Ohio C2 78
Baird, Tex. C3 84
Baixo Alentejo, prov., Port. *C2   8
Baja, Hung. B4 10
Baja, California, state, Mex. A1 34
Baja California Sur, ter., Mex. ...C2 34
Baker, La. *D4 63
Baker, Mont. D12 70
Baker, Oreg. C9 80
Baker, co., Fla. B4 54
Baker, co., Ga. E2 55
Baker, co., Oreg. C9 80
Bakersfield, Calif. E4 50
Bakerton, see Elmora, Pa.
Bakhtarān, Iran B7 23
Baku, Sov. Un. E7 13
Ba'labakk, Leb. g6 15
Bala-Cynwyd, Pa. *F11 81
Balaguer, Sp. B6   8
Balakleya, Sov. Un.,...........G11 12
Balanda, Sov. Un. F15 12
Balanga, Phil *C6 19
Balashov, Sov. Un. F14 12
Balasore, India D8 20
Balassagyarmat, Hung. A4 10
Balboa, Pan. *B2 32
Balcarce, Arg. B5 28
Balch, Ark. B4 49
Balcones Heights, Tex. *E3 84
Bald Eagle, Minn. E7 67
Bald Knob, Ark. B4 49
Baldwin, La. E4 63
Baldwin, Mich. E5 66
Baldwin, N.Y. G2 52
Baldwin, N.Y. *k14 81
Baldwin, Wis. D1 88
Baldwin co., Ala. E2 46
Baldwin co., Ga. C3 55
Baldwin City, Kans. D8 61
Baldwin Park, Calif. *F4 50
Baldwinsville, N.Y. B4 75
Baldwinville, Mass. A3 65
Baldwyn, Miss. A5 68
Balearic, is., Sp. C6   8
Baler, Phil. B6 19
Balfour, N.C. f10 76

Balikesir, Tur. C6 14
Balikpapan, Indon..............F5 19
Balkh, Afg. A4 20
Balkhash, Sov. Un. E10 13
Balkhash, lake, Sov. Un. E10 13
Balki, Sov. Un. H10 12
Ballarat, Austl.................G7, n14 25
Ballard, co., Ky. e8 62
Ballard Vale, Mass. A5, f11 65
Ballina, Austl. E9 25
Ballina, Ire. C2   4
Ballinasloe, Ire. D2   4
Ballinger, Tex. D3 84
Ballston Lake, N.Y. C7 75
Ballston Spa, N.Y. B7 75
Ballville, Ohio *A2 78
Ballwin, Mo. g12 69
Bally, Pa. F10 81
Ballymena, N. Ire. C3   4
Balm, Fla. E4 54
Balmazújváros, Hung. B5 10
Balmville, N.Y. *D6 75
Bals, Rom. C7 10
Baltã, Sov. Un. H7 12
Baltic, Conn. C8 52
Baltic, sea, Eur. I8 11
Baltimore, Ohio C3 78
Baltimore, co., Md. B4 53
Baltimore (Independent City),
  Md. B4, g11 53
Baluchistan, reg., Iran, Pak. C4 20
Bamako, Mali F3 22
Bamberg, Ger., Fed. Rep. of D5   6
Bamberg, S.C. E5 82
Bamberg, co., S.C. E5 82
Banat, reg. Rom. C5 10
Banbridge, N. Ire. C3   4
Banbury, Eng. D6   4
Bancroft, Ont., Can. B7 41
Bancroft, Iowa A3   6
Banda, India C7 20
Banda Aceh, Indon. k11 19
Bandar 'Abbās, Iran *D6 15
Bandar-e Anzalī, Iran B7 23
Bandar Seri Begawan,
  (Brunei), Bru. E4 19
Bande, Sp. A2   8
Bandeira, peak, Braz. C4 30
Bandera, Tex. E3 84
Bandera co., Tex. E3 84
Bandirma, Tur. B6 14
Bandon, Oreg. D2 80
Bandung, Indon. G3 19
Banes, Cuba D6 35
Banff, Alta., Can. D3, g7 38
Banff, co., Scot. *B5   4
Bangalore, India F6 20
Banggai, Indon. F6 19
Bangkok (Krung Thep), Thai. C2 19
Bangladesh, country, Asia D9 20
Bangor, Maine D4 64
Bangor, Mich. F4 66
Bangor, N. Ire. C4   4
Bangor, Pa. E11 81
Bangor, Wales D4   4
Bangor, Wis. E3 88
Bangs, Tex. D3 84
Bangued, Phil B6 19
Bangui, Cen. Afr. Rep. H1 23
Bangweulu, lake, Zambia C6 24
Banhã, Eg. G8 14
Baní, Dom. Rep. E8 35
Bani Suwayf, Eg. C4 23
Banja Luka, Yugo. C3 10
Banjarmasin, Indon. F4 19
Banjul, Gam. F1 22
Banks, co., Ga. B3 55
Banks isl., Can. B9 36
Bankura, India D8 20
Banner, co., Nebr. C2 71
Bannertown, N.C. *A2 76
Bannock, co., Idaho G6 57
Bannu, Pak. B5 20
Bañolas, Sp. A7   8
Banska Bystrica, Czech. D5   7
Banska Stiavnica, Czech. D5   7
Bansko, Bul. E6 10
Bantam, Conn. C4 52
Banyuwangi, Indon. G4 19
Baoding, China D8 17
Baoji, China E6 17
Baotou, China C7 17
Ba'qūbah, Iraq C3 15
Bar, Sov. Un. G6 12
Barabinsk, Sov. Un. D10 13
Baraboo, Wis. E4 88
Baracaldo, Sp. A4   8
Baracoa, Cuba D6 35
Baradero, Arg. F7 28
Baraga, Mich. B2 66
Baraga, co., Mich. B2 66
Barahona, Dom. Rep. E8 35
Baramula, India B5 20

Baranovichi, Sov. Un. E3 12
Baraanya, co., Hung. *B4 10
Barataria, La. E5, k11 63
Barbacena, Braz. C4, g6 30
Barbar, Sud. E4 23
Barbados, country, N.A. J15 35
Barbastro, Sp. A6   8
Barbate, Sp. D3   8
Barber, co., Kans E5 61
Barberton, Ohio A4 78
Barberton, S. Afr. F6 24
Barbour, co., Ala D4 46
Barbour, co., W. Va. B4 87
Barboursville, W. Va. C2 87
Barbourville, Ky. D6 62
Barbuda, isl., Antigua and Barbuda..H14 35
Barcarrota, Sp. C2   8
Barcellona Pozzo di Gotto, It. ...E5   9
Barcelona, Sp. B7   8
Barcelona, Ven................A5 32
Barcelos, Port. B1   8
Bardejov, Czech. D6   7
Bardstown, Ky. C4 62
Bardwell, Ky. f8 62
Bareilly, India C6   2
Baresville, Pa. *G8 81
Barguzin, Sov. Un. D13 13
Bar Harbor, Maine D4 64
Bari, It. D6   9
Barinas, state, Ven. B3 32
Baripāda, India D8 20
Barirí, Braz. C3, m7 30
Barisāl, Bngl. D9 20
Barking, Eng. k13   4
Barkol, China C3 17
Bar-le-Duc, Fr. C6   5
Barletta, It. D6   9
Barling, Ark. B1 49
Barmer, India C5 20
Barnaul, Sov. Un. D11 13
Barnegat, N.J. D4 74
Barnes, co., N. Dak. C7 77
Barnesboro, Pa. E4 81
Barnesville, Ga. C2 55
Barnesville, Minn. D2 67
Barnesville, Ohio C4 78
Barnhill, Ohio B4 78
Barnsboro, N.J. D2 74
Barnsdall, Okla. A5 79
Barnsley, Eng. *D6   4
Barnstable, Mass. C7 65
Barnstable, co., Mass. C7 65
Barnstaple, Eng. E4   4
Barnwell, S.C. E5 82
Barnwell co., S.C. E4 82
Baroda, India D5 20
Barquisimeto, Ven. A4 32
Barra, Braz. *E5 27
Barraba, Austl. E8 26
Barrackville, W. Va. B4, h10 87
Barra do Piraí, Braz. C4, h6 30
Barra Mansa, Braz. C4, h6 30
Barrancabermeja, Col. B3 32
Barranquilla, Col. A3 32
Barre, Mass. B3 65
Barre, Vt. C3 73
Barreiras, Braz. *E5 27
Barreiro, Port. C1, f9 8
Barreiros, Braz. *D7 27
Barren, co., Ky. D4 62
Barretos, Braz. C3 30
Barrett, Tex. *E5 84
Barrhead, Alta., Can. B3 38
Barrie, Ont., Can. C5 41
Barrigada, Guam *F6   2
Barrington, Ill. A5, h8 58
Barrington, N.J. *D2 74
Barrington, R.I. C11 52
Barrington Hills, Ill. *A5 58
Barron, Wis. C2 88
Barron, co., Wis. C2 88
Barrow, Alsk. A8 47
Barrow, co., Ga. B3 55
Barrow-in Furness, Eng. C5   4
Barruelo de Santullán, Sp. A3   8
Barry, Ill. D2 58
Barry, co., Mich. F5 66
Barry, co., Mo. E4 69
Barrys Bay, Ont., Can. B7 41
Bārsi, India E6 20
Barstow, Calif. E5 50
Barth, Fla. u14 54
Barth, Ger. Dem. Rep. A6   6
Bartholomew, co., Ind. F6 59
Bartin, Tur. B9 14
Bartle Frere, mtn., Austl. C8 25
Bartlesville, Okla. A6 79
Bartlett, Ill. h8 58
Bartlett, Tex. D4 84
Barton, Ala. A2 46
Barton, Ohio B5 78
Barton, Vt. *B3 73
Barton, co., Kans. D5 61

Barton, co. Mo. D3 69
Bartonville, Ill. C4 58
Bartow, Fla. E5 54
Bartow, co., Ga. B2 55
Barvas, Scot. A3   4
Barvenkovo, Sov. Un. G11 12
Basel, Switz. E3   6
Basel-Land, sub canton, Switz. ...*E3   6
Basel-Stadt, sub canton, Switz. ...*E3   6
Basildon, Eng. *E7   4
Basile, La. D3 63
Basilicata, pol. dist., It. *D5   9
Basin, Wyo B4 89
Basingstoke, Eng. E6   4
Baskin, Fla. P10 54
Basking Ridge, N.J. *B3 74
Basque Provinces, reg., Sp. A4   8
Basra, Iraq B7 23
Bas-Rhin, dept. Fr. *C7   5
Bassac, Laos C3 19
Bassano, Alta., Can. D4 38
Bassano del Grappa, It. B3   9
Bassein, Bur. E9 20
Basses-Alpes, dept. Fr. *E7   5
Basses-Pyrénées, dept. Fr. *F3   5
Basse-Terre, Guad. I14 35
Basseterre, St. Christopher-
  Nevis-Anguilla H13 35
Bassett, Nebr. B6 71
Bassett, Va. D3 85
Bastia, Fr. C2   9
Bastogne, Bel. B6   5
Bastrop. La. B4 63
Bastrop, co., Tex. D4 84
Basutoland, see Lesotho,
  county, Afr.
Bata, Equat., Gui. H6 22
Bataan, prov., Phil. *C6 19
Batāla, India B6 20
Batanes, prov., Phil. *A6 19
Batangas, Phil. p13 19
Batangas, prov., Phil. *C6 19
Bátaszék, Hung. B4 10
Batatais, Braz. C3 30
Batavia,·Ill. B5, k8 58
Batavia, N.Y. C2 75
Batavia, Ohio C1 78
Batavia, see Jakarta, Indon.
Bataysk, Sov. Un. H12 12
Bates, co., Mo. *C3 69
Batesburg, S.C. D4 82
Batesville, Ark. B4 49
Batesville, Ind. F7 57
Batesville, Miss. A4 68
Bath, Eng. E5   4
Bath, Maine E3, g8 64
Bath, N.Y. C3 75
Bath, Pa. E11 81
Bath, S.C. D4 82
Bath, co., Ky. B6 62
Bath, co., Va. B3 85
Bathurst, Austl. F8 25
Bathurst, N.B., Can. B4 43
Bathurst, see Banjul, Gam.
Batna, Alg. H6 22
Baton Rouge, La. D4, h9 63
Batouri, Cam. H7 22
Battambang, Kam. C2 19
Batticaloa, Sri Lanka G7 20
Battle Creek, Mich. F5 66
Battleford, Sask., Can. E1 39
Battle Ground, Ind. C4 59
Battle Ground, Wash. D3 86
Battonya, Hung. B5 10
Batumi, Sov. Un. E7 13
Batu Pahat (Bandar
  Penggaram), Mala. *E2 19
Baturité, Braz. D7 27
Bat Yam, Isr. *B2 15
Bauchi, Nig. F6 22
Baudette, Minn. B4 67
Bauru, Braz. C3 30
Bautzen, Ger. Dem. Rep. C7   6
Bauxite, Ark. C3, k9 49
Bavaria, reg., Ger.,
  Fed. Rep. of D5   6
Bavispe, Mex. A3 34
Bawcomville, La. *B3 63
Baxley, Ga. E4 55
Baxter, Minn. D4 67
Baxter, co., Ark. A3 49
Baxter Estates, N.Y. *E7 75
Baxter Springs, Kans. E9 61
Bay, co., Fla. B1, u16 54
Bay, co., Mich. E6 66
Bayamo, Cuba D5 35
Bayamón, P.R. G1 35
Bayan, China C3 18
Bayanovka, Sov. Un. C8 13
Bayard, Nebr. C2 71
Bayard, N. Mex. C4 48
Baybay, Phil. *C6 19

Bayburt, Tur. — B13 14
Bay City, Mich. — E7 66
Bay City, Oreg. — B3 80
Bay City, Tex. — E5, s14 84
Bay de Verde, Newf. — D5 44
Bayern, state, Ger. Fed. Rep. of — *D5 6
Bayeux, Fr. — C3 5
Bayfield. Wis. — B3 88
Bayfield, co., Wis. — B2 88
Bay Harbor Island, Fla. — *F3 54
Bay Head, N.J. — C4 74
Bayindir, Tur. — *C6 14
Baylor, co., Tex. — C3 84
Bay Minette, Ala. — E2 46
Bayombong, Phil. — *B6 19
Bayonne, Fr. — F3 5
Bayonne, N.J. — B4, k8 74
Bayou Cane, La. — *E5 63
Bayou LaBatre, Ala. — E1 46
Bay Park, N.Y. — *E7 75
Bayport, N.Y. — n15 75
Bayport, Min. — E6 67
Bayreuth, Ger.
    Fed. Rep. of — D5 6
Bay Roberts, Newf., Can. — E5 44
Bay St. Louis, Miss. — E4, g7 68
Bay Shore, N.Y. — E7, n15 75
Bayshore Gardens, Fla. — *E4 54
Bayside, Wis. — m12 88
Bay Springs, Miss. — D4 68
Bayt Lahm, see Bethlehem, Jordan
Baytown, Tex. — E5, r15 84
Bay View, Ala. — f7 46
Bayview, Calif. — *B1 50
Bayview, Mass. — A6 65
Bay Village, Ohio — h9 78
Bayville, N.Y. — F2 52
Baztán, Sp. — A5 8
Beach. N. Dak. — D2 77
Beach City, Ohio — B4 78
Beach Haven, New Jersey — D4 74
Beachville, Ont., Can — D4 41
Beachwood, N.J. — *D4 74
Beachwood, Ohio — A4 78
Beacon, N.Y. — D7 75
Beacon Falls, Conn. — D4 52
Beacon Hill, Wash. — *C3 86
Beaconsfield, Que., Can. — D8 42
Beadle, co., S.Dak. — F7 77
Bearden, Ark. — D3 49
Beardstown, Ill. — C3 58
Bear Lake, co.,Idaho — G7 57
Bear River,N.S., Can. — E4 43
Bear Town, Miss. — D3 68
Beas de Segura, Sp. — C4 8
Beatrice, Nebr. — D9 71
Beattyville, Ky. — C6 62
Beaucaire, Fr. — F6 5
Beauce, co., Que., Can. — C7 42
Beauceville Est., Que., Can. — *C7 42
Beauceville Quest, Que., Can. — *C7 42
Beaufort, N.C. — C6 76
Beaufort, S.C. — G6 82
Beaufort, co., N.C. — B5 76
Beaufort, co., S.C. — G6 82
Beaufort West, S. Afr. — G4 24
Beauharnois, que., Can. — D4, q19 42
Beauharnois, co., Que. Can. — D3 42
Beaumont, Calif. — *F5 50
Beaumont, Tex. — D5 84
Beaumont Place, Tex. — *E5 84
Beaune, Fr. — D6 5
Beauport, Que., Can. — C6, n17 42
Beaupré, Que., Can. — B7 42
Beauregard, par., La. — D2 63
Beaurepaire, Que., Can. — D8 42
Beauséjour, Man., Can. — D3 40
Beauvais, Fr. — C5 5
Beaver, Okla. — A1, e10 79
Beaver, Pa. — E1 81
Beaver, Utah — B5 72
Beaver, co., Okla. — A1 79
Beaver, co., Pa. — E1 81
Beaver, co., Utah — B5 72
Beaver Bank, N.S., Can. — E6 43
Beaver City, Nebr. — D6 71
Beaverdale, Pa. — F4 81
Beaver Dam, Ky. — C3 62
Beaver Dam, Wis. — E5 88
Beaver Falls, Pa. — E1 81
Beaver (Glen Hedrick),
    W. Va. — D3, n13 87
Beaverhead, co., Mont. — E3 70
Beaverlodge, Alta., Can. — B1 38
Beaver Meadows, Pa. — *E10 81
Beaverton, Ont., Can. — C5 42
Beaverton, Mich. — E6 66
Beaverton, Oreg. — B4, h12 80
Beãwar, India — C5 20
Bebedouro, Braz. — C3 30
Bečej, Yugo. — C5 10
Béchar, Alg. — B4 22
Bechuanaland, see Botswana,
    country, Afr.

Becker, co., Minn. — D3 67
Beckham, co., Okla. — B2 79
Beckley, W. Va. — D3, n13 87
Bédarieux, Fr. — F5 5
Bedford, N.S., Can. — E6 43
Bedford, Eng. — D6 4
Bedford, Ind. — G5 59
Bedford, Iowa — D3 60
Bedford, Mass. — B5, g10 65
Bedford, Ohio — A4, h9 78
Bedford, Pa. — F4 81
Bedford, Tex. — *C4 84
Bedford, Va. — C3 85
Bedford, co., Eng. — *D6 4
Bedford, co., Pa. — G4 81
Bedford, co. Tenn. — B5 83
Bedford, co., Va. — C3 85
Bedford Heights, Ohio, — *A4 78
Bedford Hills, N.Y. — m15 75
Bedlington, Eng. — C6 4
Bedminster, N.J. — B3 74
Bedzin, Pol. — g10 7
Bee, co., Tex — E4 84
Beebe, Ark. — B4 49
Beebe, Que., Can. — D5 42
Beecher, Ill. — B6 58
Beech Grove, Ind. — E5, m10 59
Beenleigh, Austl. — C9 26
Bee Ridge, Fla. — E4, q11 54
Be'er Sheva' (Beersheba),
    Isr. — C2, h5 15
Beeskow, Ger. Dem. Rep. — B7 6
Beeton, Ont., Can. — C5 41
Beeville, Tex. — E4 84
Bègles, Fr. — E3 5
Beida, Libya — B2 23
Bei'an, China — B10 17
Beihai, China — G6 17
Beijing, see Peking, China
Beira, Moz. — D6 24
Beira, reg. Port. — B2 8
Beira Alta, prov., Port. — *B2 8
Beira Baixa, prov., Port. — *C2 8
Beira Litoral, prov., Port. — *B1 8
Beirut (Bayrūt), Leb. — g5 15
Beja, Port. — C2 8
Béja, Tun. — A6 22
Bejaïa (Bougie), Alg. — A5 22
Bejeda (Ras Dashan), mtn., Eth. — F5 23
Békés, Hung. — B5 10
Békés, co., Hung. — *B5 10
Békéscaba, Hung. — B5 10
Bela, India — C7 20
Bela Crkva, Yugo. — C5 10
Bel Air, Md. — A5 53
Belalcázar, Sp. — C3 8
Bela Vista, Braz. — C1 30
Belaya Tserkov, Sov. Un. — G8 12
Belchertown, Mass. — B3 65
Belding, Mich. — E5 66
Belém, Braz. — D6 27
Belen,N. Mex. — B5 48
Belén, Par. — D4 29
Belev, Sov. Un. — E11 12
Belfair, Wash. — B3 86
Belfast, Maine — D3 64
Belfast, N.Y. — C2 75
Belfast, N.C. — B4 76
Belfast, N. Ire. — C4 4
Belfield, N. Dak. — D3 77
Belfort, N.J. — C4 74
Belfort, Fr. — D7 5
Belfort, dept., Fr. — *D7 5
Belfry, Ky. — C7 62
Belgaum, India — E5 20
Belgium, country, Eur. — B6 5
Belgorod, Sov. Un. — F11 12
Belgorod-Dnestrovskiy, Sov. Un. — H8 12
Belgrade, Mont. — E5 70
Belgrade (Beograd), Yugo. — C5 10
Belhaven, N.C. — B6 76
Belington, W. Va. — B5 87
Belize, country, N.A. — D7 34
Belize City, Belize — D7 34
Belknap, co., N.H. — D5 73
Bell, Calif. — *F4 50
Bell, co., Ky. — D6 62
Bell, co., Tex. — D4 84
Bell Acres, Pa. — *E1 81
Bellaire, Ohio — C5 78
Bellaire, Tex. — r14 84
Bellary, India — E6 20
Bella Unión, Ur. — E1 30
Bella Vista, Arg. — E2 29
Bella Vista, Arg. — E4 29
Bella Vista, Par. — D4 29
Bellbrook, Ohio — C1 78
Belle, Mo. — C6 69
Belle, W. Va. — C6 87
Belleair, Fla. — p10 54
Belle Center, Ohio — B2 78
Bellechasse, co., Que., Can. — C7 42
Bellefontaine, Ohio — B2 78

Bellefontaine Neighbors, Mo. — *C7 69
Bellefonte, Del. — A7 53
Bellefonte, Pa. — E6 81
Belle Fourche, S. Dak. — F2 77
Bellegarde -sur-Valserine, Fr. — D6 5
Belle Glade, Fla. — F6 54
Belle Isle, Fla. — D5 54
Bellemead, Md. — *C4 53
Belle Plaine, Iowa — C5 60
Belle Plaine, Kans. — E6 61
Belle Plaine, Minn. — F5 67
Belle River, Ont., Can. — *E2 41
Bellerose, N.Y. — *E7 75
Belleterre, Que., Can. — *o20 41
Belle Vernon, Pa. — F2 81
Belleview, Fla. — C4 54
Belleville, Ont., Can. — C7 41
Belleville, Ill. — E4 58
Belleville, Kans. — C6 61
Belleville, Mich. — p15 66
Belleville, N.J. — B4, h8 74
Belleville, Pa. — E6 81
Belleville, Wis. — F4 88
Bellevue, Ill. — *C4 58
Bellevue, Iowa — B7 60
Bellevue, Ky. — h13 62
Bellevue, Mich. — F5 66
Bellevue, Nebr. — C10, g3 71
Bellevue, Ohio — A3 78
Bellevue, Wash. — e11 86
Belley, Fr. — E6 5
Bellflower, Calif. — n12 50
Bell Gardens, Calif. — *F4 50
Bellingham, Mass. — B5, h10 65
Bellingham, Wash — A3 86
Bellinzona, Switz. — E4 6
Bellmawr, N.J. — D2 74
Bellmead, Tex. — *D4 84
Bellmore, N.Y. — G2 52
Bello, Col. — B2 32
Bellows Falls, Vt. — E3 73
Bellport, N.Y. — G5 52
Bells, Tenn. — B2 83
Belluno, It. — A4 9
Bell Ville, Arg. — A4 28
Bellville, Ohio — B3 78
Bellville, Tex. — E4 84
Bellwood, Ill. — k9 58
Bellwood, Pa. — E5 81
Belmar, N.J. — C4 74
Bélmez, Sp. — C3 8
Belmond, Iowa — B4 60
Belmont, Calif. — h8 50
Belmont, Mass. — g11 65
Belmont, Miss. — A5 68
Belmont, N.Y. — C2 75
Belmont, N.C. — B1 76
Belmont, co., Ohio — C4 78
Belmonte, Braz. — *E7 27
Belmopan, Belize — D7 34
Bel-Nor, Mo. — f13 69
Beloeil, Que., Can. — D4 42
Belo Horizonte, Braz. — B4 30
Beloit, Kans. — C5 61
Beloit, Ohio — B5 78
Beloit, Wis. — F4 88
Beloit West, Wis. — *F4 88
Belomorsk, Sov. Un. — C6 13
Belopolye, Sov. Un. — F10 12
Beloretsk, Sov. Un. — D8 13
Belovo, Sov. Un. — *D11 13
Belpre, Ohio — C4 78
Bel-Ridge, Mo. — *C7 69
Belton, Mo. — C3 69
Belton, S.C. — B3 82
Belton, Tex. — D4 84
Beltrami, co., Minn. — B3 67
Beltsville, Md. — B4 53
Beltsy, Sov. Un. — H6 12
Belukha, mtn., Sov. Un. — E11 13
Belvedere, Calif. — *C2 50
Belvedere, Va. — *B5 85
Belvedere Marittimo, It. — E5 9
Belvidere, Del. — A6 53
Belvidere, Ill. — A5 58
Belvidere, N.J. — B2 74
Belzoni, Miss. — B3 68
Bement, Ill. — D5 58
Bemidji, Minn. — C4 67
Bemis, Tenn. — B3 83
Benalla, Austl. — G8 25
Benares, see Varanasi, India
Benavente, Sp. — A3 8
Ben Avon, Pa. — *E1 81
Benbrook, Tex. — *C4 84
Bend, Oreg. — C5 80
Bendale, S.C. — C6 82
Bendery, Sov. Un. — H7 12
Bendigo, Austl. — G7 25
Bene Beraq, Isr. — B2 15
Beneŝov, Czech. — D3, o18 7
Benevento, It. — D5 9

Benewah, Idaho — B2 57
Benewah, co., Idaho — B2 57
Bengal, reg., Bngl., India — D8 20
Bengasi (Banghāzī), Libya — B2 23
Bengbu, China — E8 17
Bengkulu, Indon. — F2 19
Benguela, Ang. — C2 24
Benguela, dist., Ang. — C3 24
Benham, Ky. — D7 62
Ben Hill, co., Ga. — D3 55
Benicarló, Sp. — B6 8
Benicia, Calif. — C2, g8 50
Benin, country, Afr. — G5 22
Benin City, Nig. — G6 22
Benisa, Sp. — C6 8
Benkelman, Nebr. — D4 71
Benld, Ill. — D4 58
Ben Lomond, Calif. — *D2 50
Bennett, co., S. Dak. — G4 77
Bennettsville, S.C. — *B8 82
Bennettsville Southwest, S.C. — *B8 82
Ben Nevis, mtn., Scot. — B4 4
Bennington, Vt. — F1 73
Bennington, co., Vt. — E1 73
Bensenville, Ill. — B6, k9 58
Bensheim, Ger., Fed. Rep of — D4 6
Benson, Ariz. — D3 48
Benson, Minn. — E3 67
Benson, N.C. — B4 76
Benson, co., N. Dak. — B6 77
Bent, co., Colo. — D7 51
Bentleyville, Pa. — F1 81
Benton, Ark. — C3, k9 49
Benton, Ill. — E5 58
Benton, Ky. — f9 62
Benton, La. — B2 63
Benton, Pa. — D9 81
Benton, Tenn. — D9 83
Benton, Wis. — F3 88
Benton, co., Ark. — A1 29
Benton, co., Ind. — C3 59
Benton, co., Iowa — B5 60
Benton, co.,Minn. — E4 67
Benton, co., Miss. — A4 68
Benton, co., Mo. — C4 69
Benton, co., Oreg. — C3 80
Benton, co., Tenn. — A3 83
Benton, co.,Wash. — C6 86
Benton City, Wash. — C6 86
Benton Harbor, Mich. — F4 66
Benton Heights, Mich. — F4 66
Bentonville, Ark. — A1 49
Benwood, W. Va. — A4, f8 87
Benzie, co., Mich. — D4 66
Benxi, China — C9 17
Beograd, see Belgrade, Yugo.
Beppu, Jap. — J5 18
Berat, Alb. — *B2 14
Berat, pref., Alb. — *B2 14
Berbera, Som. — F7 23
Berchtesgaden, Ger., Fed. Rep. of — E6 6
Berck, Fr. — B4 5
Berdichev, Sov. Un. — G7 12
Berdyansk, Sov. Un. — H11 12
Berea, Ky. — C5 62
Berea, Ohio — A4, h9 78
Beregovo, Sov. Un. — G4 12
Beresford, S. Dak. — G9 77
Berettyóújfalu, Hung. — B5 12
Berezhany, Sov. Un. — G5 12
Berezna, Sov. Un. — F8 12
Berezniki, Sov. Un. — D8 13
Berg, Nor. — q27 11
Berga, Sp. — A6 8
Bergama, Tur. — *C6 14
Bergamo, It. — B2 9
Bergen, Ger. Dem. Rep. — A6 6
Bergen, N.Y. — B3 75
Bergen, Nor. — G1 11
Bergen, see Mons, Bel.
Bergen, co., N.J. — A4 74
Bergen, co., Nor. — *G1 11
Bergenfield, N.J. — B5, h8 74
Bergen op Zoom, Neth. — B6 5
Bergerac, Fr. — E4 5
Bergholz, Ohio — B5 78
Bergisch Gladback, Ger.
    Fed. Rep. of — C3 6
Berhampore, India — D8 20
Berhampur, India — E7 20
Bering, sea, Alsk., Sov. Un. — D21 16
Berislav, Sov. Un. — H9 12
Berja, Sp. — D4 8
Berkeley, Calif. — D2 50
Berkeley, Ill. — *B6 58
Berkeley, Mo. — f13 69
Berkeley, R.I. — B11 52
Berkeley, co., S.C. — E7 82
Berkeley, co., W. Va. — B6 87
Berkeley Heights, N.J. — B4 74
Berkeley Springs (Bath), W. Va. — B6 87
Berkley, Mich. — F7, o15 66
Berkovitsa, Bul. — D6 10

Berks, co., Pa. ... F9 81
Berkshire, Md. ... *C4 53
Berkshire, co., Eng. ... *E6 4
Berksire, co., Mass. ... B1 65
Berlin, Md. ... D7 53
Berlin, N.H. ... C5 73
Berlin, N.J. ... D3 74
Berlin, N.Y. ... C7 75
Berlin, Pa. ... E5 81
Berlin, Wis. ... E5 88
Berlin, East, Ger., Dem. Rep. ... B6 6
Berlin, West, Ger., Fed. Rep. of ... B6 6
Berlin, West, state, Ger.,
  Fed. Rep. of ... *B6 6
Bermeo, Sp. ... A4 8
Bermuda, Br. dep.,N.A. ... p20 35
Bern, Switz. ... E3 6
Bern, canton, Switz. ... *E3 6
Bernalillo, N. Mex. ... B5, D6 48
Bernalillo, co., N. Mex. ... B5 48
Bernardsville, N.J. ... B3 74
Bernau, Ger. Dem. Rep. ... B6 6
Bernay, Fr. ... C4 5
Bernberg, Ger. Dem. Rep. ... C5 6
Berndorf, Aus. ... E8 6
Berne, Ind. ... C8 59
Bernice, La. ... B3 63
Bernie, Mo. ... E8 69
Bernville, Pa. ... F9 81
Beroun, Czech ... D3, o17 7
Berri, Austl. ... F7 25
Berrien, co., Ga. ... E3 55
Berrien, co., Mich. ... F4 66
Berrien Springs, Mich. ... G4 66
Berry, former prov., Fr. ... D4 5
Berry Hill, Tenn. ... g10 83
Berryville, Ark. ... A2 49
Berryville, Va. ... A5 85
Bershad, Sov. Un. ... G7 12
Berthier, co., Que., Can. ... *C3 42
Bethierville, Que., Can. ... C4 42
Berthoud, Colo. ... A5 51
Bertie, co., N.C. ... A5 76
Bertram, Tex. ... D4 84
Bertrand, Mich. ... *G4 66
Berwick, N.S., Can. ... D5 43
Berwick, La. ... E4 63
Berwick, Maine ... E2 64
Berwick, Pa. ... D9 81
Berwick, co., Scot ... *C5 4
Berwick-upon-Tweed, Eng. ... C6 4
Berwind, W. Va. ... D3 87
Berwyn, Ill. ... k9 58
Berwyn, Pa. ... o20 81
Berwyn Heights, Md. ... *B4 53
Besa, Indon. ... E7 19
Besancon, Fr. ... D7 5
Besni, Tur. ... D11 14
Bessèges, Fr. ... E6 5
Bessemer, Ala. ... B3, g7 46
Bessemer, Mich. ... n11 66
Bessemer, Pa. ... E1 81
Bessemer City, N.C. ... B1 76
Bethalto, Ill. ... E3 58
Bethany, Conn. ... D5 52
Bethany, Ill. ... D5 58
Bethany, Mo. ... A3 69
Bethany, Okla. ... B4 79
Bethany, W. Va. ... f8 87
Bethayres-Huntingdon
  Valley, Pa. ... *F11 81
Bethel, Alsk. ... C7 47
Bethel, Conn. ... D3 52
Bethel, Maine ... D2 64
Bethel, N.C. ... B6 76
Bethel, Ohio ... D1 78
Bethel (Bethel, Park) Pa. ... k13 81
Bethesda, Md. ... C3, f8 53
Bethesda, Ohio ... B4 78
Bethlehem (Bayt Lahm),
  Jordon ... C3, h5 15
Bethlehem, Pa. ... E11 81
Bethlehem, S. Afr. ... F5 24
Bethlehem, W. Va. ... f8 87
Bethpage, N.Y. ... G3 52
Béthune, Fr. ... B5 5
Bettendorf, Iowa ... C7, g11 60
Betül, India ... D6 20
Beulah, N. Dak. ... C4 77
Beulaville, N.C. ... C5 76
Beverley, Eng ... D6 4
Beverly, Mass. ... A6, f12 65
Beverly, N.J. ... C3 74
Beverly, Ohio ... C4 78
Beverly Gardens, Ohio ... *C1 78
Beverly Hills, Calif. ... m12 50
Beverly Hills, Mich. ... *F7 66
Beverwijk, Neth. ... A6 5
Bexar, co., Tex. ... E3 84
Bexhill-on-Sea, Eng. ... E7 4
Bexley, Ohio ... m11 78
Beypazari, Tur. ... *B8 14
Bezerros, Braz. ... *D7 27

Bezhetsk, Sov. Un. ... C11 12
Bezhitsa, Sov. Un. ... E10 12
Béziers, Fr. ... F5 5
Bezons, Fr. ... g9 5
Bhadgaon, Nep. ... C8 20
Bhagalpur, India ... C8 20
Bhakkar, Pak. ... B5 20
Bhamo, Bur. ... D10 20
Bharatpur, India ... C6 20
Bhatpara, India ... D8 20
Bhaunagar, India ... D5 20
Bhind, India ... C6 20
Bhopal, India ... D6 20
Bhor, India ... E5 20
Bhuj, India ... D4 20
Bhutan, country, Asia ... C9 20
Biała Podlaska, Pol. ... B7 7
Białogard, Pol. ... A4 7
Białystok, Pol. ... B7 7
Bianco, It. ... E6 9
Biarritz, Fr. ... F3 5
Bibai, Jap. ... E10 18
Bibb, co., Ala. ... C2 46
Bibb, co., Ga. ... D3 55
Bibb City, Ga. ... D2 55
Biberach, Ger., Fed. Rep. of ... D4 6
Bic, Que., Can. ... A9 42
Bicknell, Ind. ... G3 59
Bicske, Hung. ... B4 10
Bida, Nig. ... G6 22
Bidar, India ... E6 20
Biddeford, Maine ... E2, g7 64
Bideford, Eng. ... E4 4
Biel, Switz. ... E3 6
Bielawa, Pol. ... C4 7
Bielefeld, Ger., Fed. Rep. of ... B4 6
Biella, It. ... B2 9
Bielsko-Biala, Pol. ... D5, h10 7
Bielsk Podlaski, Pol. ... B7 7
Bienfait, Sask.,Can. ... H4 39
Beinville, par., La. ... B2 63
Biga, Tur. ... *B7 14
Big Bear City, Calif. ... E5 50
Big Bear Lake, Calif. ... *E5 50
Big Beaver, Pa. ... *E1 81
Big Flats, N.Y. ... C4 75
Biggar, Sask., Can. ... E1 39
Biggs, Calif. ... C3 50
Big Horn, co., Mont. ... E9 70
Big Horn, co., Wyo. ... B4 89
Big Lake, Tex. ... D2 84
Biglerville, Pa. ... G7 81
Big Pine, Calif. ... D4 50
Big Rapids, Mich. ... E5 66
Big River, Sask., Can. ... D2 39
Big Run, Pa. ... E4 81
Big Sandy, Mont. ... B6 70
Big Spring, Tex. ... C2 84
Big Stone, co., Minn. ... E2 67
Big Stone Gap, Va. ... f9 85
Big Timber, Mont. ... E7 70
Big Wells, Tex. ... E3 84
Bihac, Yugo. ... C2 10
Bihar, India ... C8 20
Bihar, state, India ... D8 20
Bijapur, India ... E6 20
Bijeljina, Yugo. ... C4 10
Bikaner, India ... C5 20
Bikin, Sov. Un. ... C7 18
Bilaspur, India ... D7 20
Bilbao, Sp. ... A4 8
Bileca, Yugo ... D4 10
Bilin, Bur. ... E10 20
Billerica, Mass. ... A5, f10 65
Billings, Mont. ... E8 70
Billings, co., N. Dak. ... C2 77
Billings Heights, Mont. ... E8 70
Biloela, Austl. ... B8 26
Biloxi, Miss. ... E5, f8 68
Bilqas Qism Awwal ... *G8 14
Biltmore Forest, N.C. ... f10 76
Binalbagan, Phil. ... *C6 19
Bindura, Zimb. ... D6 24
Bingen, Ger., Fed. Rep. of ... D3 6
Bingham, Maine ... C3 64
Bingham, co., Idaho ... F6 57
Bingham Canyon, Utah ... A5, D2 72
Binghamton, N.Y. ... C5 75
Binjai, Indon. ... m11 19
Bintulu, Mala. ... E4 19
Binxian, China ... D3 18
Bío-Bío, prov., Chile ... B2 28
Bioko, isl., Equat. Gui. ... H6 22
Birakan, Sov. Un. ... B54 18
Bi'r Ar Rummanah, Eg. ... G9 14
Birch Run, Mich. ... E7 66
Bird Island, Minn. ... F4 67
Birdsboro, Pa. ... F10 81
Birecik, Tur. ... D11 14
Bir Hasnnah, well, Eg. ... *G8 14
Birkenhead, Eng. ... D5 4
Birlad, Rom. ... B8 10
Birmingham, Ala. ... B3, f7 46

Birmingham, Eng. ... D6 4
Birmingham, Mich. ... F7, o15 66
Birobidzhan, Sov. Un. ... E16 12
Birtle, Man., Can. ... D1 40
Bisbee, Ariz. ... D4 48
Biscayne Park, Fla. ... s13 54
Bisceglie, It. ... D6 9
Biscoe, N.C. ... B3 76
Bishop, Calif. ... D4 50
Bishop, Tex. ... F4 84
Bishop's Falls, Newf., Can. ... D4 44
Bishop's Stortford, Eng. ... E7 4
Bishopville, S.C. ... C7 82
Biskra, Alg. ... B6 22
Bismarck, Mo. ... D7 69
Bismarck, N. Dak. ... D5 77
Bissau, Guinea-Bissau, ... F1 22
Bissett, Man., Can. ... D4 40
Bistrita, Rom. ... B7 10
Bitlis, Tur. ... C14 14
Bitola, Yugo. ... E5 10
Bitonto, It. ... D6 9
Bitterfeld, Ger. Dem. Rep. ... *C6 6
Biwabik, Minn. ... C6 67
Bixby, Okla. ... B6 79
Biysk, Sov. Un. ... D11 12
Bizerte, Tun. ... A6 22
Bjelovar, Yugo. ... C3 10
Black, mtn., Ky. ... D7 62
Black, sea, Eur ... G14 3
Blackburn, Eng. ... D5 4
Black Diamond, Alta. ... D3 38
Black Diamond, Wash. ... B4, f11 86
Black Eagle, Mont. ... C5 70
Blackford, co., Ind. ... D7 59
Black Forest, Colo. ... C6 51
Black Hawk, co., Iowa ... B5 60
Black Lake, Que., Can. ... C6 42
Black Mountain, N.C. ... f10 76
Black Oak, Ind. ... *A3 59
Black Point, Calif. ... *C2 50
Blackpool, Eng. ... D5 4
Black River, N.Y. ... A5 75
Black River Falls, Wis. ... D3 88
Blacksburg, S.C. ... A4 82
Blacksburg, Va. ... C2 85
Blackshear, Ga. ... E4 55
Blackstone, Mass. ... B4 65
Blackstone, Va. ... C5 85
Blackville, S.C. ... E5 82
Blackwell, Okla. ... A4 79
Blackwood, N.J. ... *D2 74
Bladen, co., N.C. ... C4 76
Bladenboro, N.C. ... C4 76
Bladensburg, Md. ... f9 53
Blagoevgrad (Gorna-
  Dzhumaya), Braz. ... D6 10
Blagoveshchensk, Sov. Un. ... D15 13
Blain, Fr. ... D3 5
Blaine, Minn. ... m12 67
Blaine, Wash. ... A3 86
Blaine, co., Idaho ... F4 57
Blaine, co., Mont. ... B7 70
Blaine, co., Nebr. ... C5 71
Blaine, Okla. ... B3 79
Blair, Nebr. ... C9 71
Blair, Okla. ... C2 79
Blair, Wis. ... D2 88
Blair, co., Pa. ... E5 81
Blairgowrie & Rattray,
  Scot. ... B5 4
Blairmore, Alta., Can. ... E3 38
Blairsville, Pa. ... F3 81
Blaj, Rom. ... B7 10
Blakely, Ga. ... E2 55
Blanc, mtn., Fr. ... E7 5
Blanca, pk., Colo. ... D5 51
Blanchard, Okla. ... B4 79
Blanchester, Ohio ... C2 78
Blanco, co., Tex. ... D3 84
Bland, co., Va. ... C1 85
Blanding, Utah ... C7 72
Blandinsville, Ill. ... C3 58
Blankenburg, Ger. Dem. Rep. ... C5 6
Blantyre, Malawi ... D6 24
Blasdell, N.Y. ... C2 75
Blato, Yugo ... D3 10
Blauvelt, N.Y. ... *D6 75
Blawnox, Pa. ... k14 81
Bleckley, co., Ga. ... D3 55
Bled-Grad, Yugo. ... B10 10
Bledsoe, co., Tenn. ... D8 83
Blekinge, co., Swe. ... *I6 11
Blenheim, Ont., Can. ... E2 41
Blenheim, N.Z. ... N14 26
Blind River, Ont., Can. ... A2 41
Blissfield, Mich. ... G7 66
Blitar, Indon. ... *G4 19
Bloemfontein, S. Afr. ... F5 24
Blois, Fr. ... D4 5
Blonie, Pol. ... m13 7
Bloomer, Wis. ... C2 88

Bloomfield, Ont., Can. ... D7 41
Bloomfield, Conn. ... B6 52
Bloomfield, Ind. ... F4 59
Bloomfield, Iowa ... D5 60
Bloomfield, Ky. ... C4 62
Bloomfield, Mo. ... E8 69
Bloomfield, Nebr. ... B2 71
Bloomfield, N.J. ... h8 74
Bloomfield, N. Mex. ... A3 48
Bloomfield Hills, Mich. ... o15 66
Bloomfield Village, Mich. ... *F7 66
Bloomingdale, Ga. ... D5 55
Bloomingdale, Ill. ... *B5 58
Bloomingdale, N.J. ... A4 74
Blooming Prairie, Minn. ... G5 67
Bloomington, Calif. ... *F5 50
Bloomington, Ill. ... C4 58
Bloomington, Ind. ... F4 59
Bloomington, Minn. ... n12 67
Bloomington, Tex. ... E4 84
Bloomsburg, Pa. ... E9 81
Bloomsbury, N.J. ... B2 74
Bloomville, Ohio ... A2 78
Blossburg, Pa. ... C7 81
Blossom Hill, Pa. ... *G9 81
Blount, co., Ala. ... B3 46
Blount, co., Tenn. ... D10 83
Blountstown, Fla. ... B1 54
Bludenz, Aus. ... E4 6
Blue Ash, Ohio ... o13 78
Blue Bell, Pa. ... *F11 81
Blue Earth, Minn. ... G4 67
Blue Earth, co., Minn. ... F4 67
Bluefield, Va. ... e10 85
Bluefield, W. Va. ... D3 87
Bluefields, Nic. ... E8 34
Blue Hills, Conn. ... *B6 52
Blue Island, Ill. ... B6, k9 58
Blue Lake, Calif. ... B2 50
Blue Mound, Ill. ... D4 58
Blue Mountain, pk., Jam. ... F5 35
Blue Point, N.Y. ... G4 52
Blue Rapids, Kans. ... C7 61
Blue Ridge, Ga. ... B2 55
Blue Ridge, Va. ... C3 85
Blue Ridge, mts., U.S. ... C10 45
Blue Springs, Mo. ... h11 69
Bluff City, Tenn ... C11 69
Bluff Park, Ala. ... g7 46
Bluffton, Ind. ... C7 59
Bluffton, Ohio ... B2 78
Blumenau, Braz. ... D3 30
Blyth, Eng. ... C6 4
Blyth, Calif. ... F6 50
Blytheville, Ark. ... B6 49
Boac, Phil. ... C6 19
Boalsburg, Pa. ... E6 81
Boardman, Ohio ... A5 78
Boaz, Ala. ... A3 46
Bobbili, India ... E7 20
Bobcaygeon, Ont., Can. ... C6 41
Bobigny, Fr. ... g10 5
Bobo Dioulasso, Burkina Faso. ... F4 22
Bobtinets, Sov. Un. ... G9 12
Bobrka, Sov. Un. ... G5 12
Bobruysk, Sov. Un. ... E7 12
Bobtown, Pa. ... G2 81
Bobures, Ven. ... B3 32
Boca Raton, Fla. ... F6 54
Bochnia, Pol. ... D6 7
Bochum, Ger., Fed. Rep. of ... C3 6
Bodaybo, Sov. Un. ... D14 13
Boden, Swe ... E9 11
Bodmin, Eng. ... E4 4
Bodö, Nor. ... D6 11
Boerne, Tex. ... E3, h7 84
Bogalusa, La. ... D6 63
Bogata, Tex. ... C5 84
Boger City,N.C. ... B1 76
Bogo, Phil. ... C6 19
Bogodukhov, Sov. Un. ... F10 12
Bogor (Buitenzorg). Indon. ... G3 19
Bogoroditsk, Sov. Un. ... E12 12
Bogorodsk, Sov. Un. ... C14 12
Bogotá, Col. ... C3 32
Bogota, N.J. ... h8 74
Bogra, Bngl. ... D8 20
Boguslav, Sov. Un. ... G8 12
Bohain -en-Vermandois, Fr. ... C5 5
Bohemia, N.Y. ... n15 75
Bohemia (Cechy), reg., Czech. ... D3 7
Bohol, prov., Phil. ... D6 19
Boiling Springs, N.C. ... B1 76
Boiling Springs, Pa. ... F7 81
Boischâtel, Que., Can. ... C6, n17 42
Bois-Colombes, Fr. ... G10 5
Bois-des-Filion, Que., Can. ... p19 42
Boise, Idaho ... F2 57
Boise, co., Idaho ... F3 57
Boise City, Okla. ... e8 79
Boissevain, Man., Can. ... E1 40
Boissevain, Va. ... e10 85
Bolbec, Fr. ... C4 5

Bolgrad, Sov. Un. I7 12
Boling, Tex. E5, r14 84
Boli, China B11 17
Bolívar, Arg. B4 28
Bolivar, Mo. D4 69
Bolivar, N.Y. C2 75
Bolivar, Ohio B4 78
Bolivar, Tenn. B3 83
Bolivar, co., Miss. B3 68
Bolívar, dept., Col. B2 32
Bolívar, prov., Ec. B2 31
Bolívar, state, Ven. B4 32
Bolívar, (La Columna), pk., Ven. B3 32
Bolivia, country, S.A. C2 29
Bolkhov, Sov. Un. E11 12
Bollinger, co., Mo. D7 69
Bollnäs, Swe. G7 11
Bollullos, Sp. D2 8
Bologna, It. B3 9
Bologoye, Sov. Un. C10 12
Bolshaya Lepetikha, Sov. Un. H9 12
Bolshaya Viska, Sov. Un. G8 12
Bolshoy Tokmak, Sov. Un. H10 12
Bolton, Ont., Can. D5 41
Bolton, Eng. D5 4
Bolton Landing, N.Y. B7 75
Bolu, Tur. B8 14
Bolvadin, Tur. C8 14
Bolzano, It. A3 9
Boma, Zaire B2 24
Bombay, India E5 20
Bom Conselho, Braz. *D7 27
Bom Despacho, Braz. B3 30
Bon Air, Pa. *G11 81
Bon Air, Va. m17 85
Bonaventure, Que., Can. *k13 42
Bonaventure, co., Que., Can. A3 43
Bonavista, Newf., Can. D5 44
Bond, co., Ill E4 58
Bondy, Fr. G10 5
Bone, see Annaba, Alg.
Bonham, Tex. C4 84
Bon Homme, co., S. Dak. G8 77
Bonifay, Fla. G3 54
Bonin, is., Jap. E6 2
Bonita, Calif. *E5 50
Bonita Springs, Fla. F5 54
Bonn, Ger., Fed. Rep. of C3 6
Bonner, co., Idaho A2 57
Bonners Ferry, Idaho A2 57
Bonner Springs, Kans. C9, k16 61
Bonne Terre, Mo. D7 69
Bonneville, co., Idaho F7 57
Bonnyville, Alta., Can. B5 38
Bonorva, It. D2 9
Bonoua, I.C. *E4 22
Bonthain, Indon. G5 19
Bontoc, Phil. *B6 19
Boomer, W. Va. C3, m13 87
Boone, Iowa B4 60
Boone, N.C. A1 76
Boone, co., Ark. A2 49
Boone, co., Ill. A5 58
Boone, co., Ind. D4 59
Boone, co., Iowa B4 60
Boone, co., Ky. B5 62
Boone, co., Mo. B5 69
Boone, co., Nebr. C7 71
Boone, co., W. Va. C3 87
Booneville, Ark B2 49
Booneville, Miss. A5 68
Boonsboro, Md. A2 53
Boon Terrace, Pa. *F1 81
Boonton, N.J. B4 74
Boonville, Calif. C2 50
Boonville, Ind. H3 59
Boonville, Mo. C5 69
Boonville, N.Y. B5 75
Boothbay Harbor, Maine E3 64
Boothwyn, Pa. *G11 81
Boppard, Ger., Fed. Rep. of C3 6
Boquerón, dept., Par. D3 29
Borah, pk., Idaho E3 57
Borås, Swe. I5 11
Bordeaux, Fr. E3 5
Borden, co., Tex. C2 84
Borden Springs, Ala. B4 46
Bordentown, N.J. C3 74
Bordighera, It. . . . . C1` 9
Borgå, Fin. G11 11
Borger, Tex. B2 84
Borgomanero, It. B2 9
Borgo Val di Taro, It. B2 9
Borislav, Sov. Un. G7 12
Borisoglebsk, Sov. Un. F13 12
Borisov, Sov. Un. D7 12
Borispol, Sov. Un. F8 12
Borja, Sp. B5 8
Borkou, reg., Chad. E1 23
Borlänge, Swe. G6 11
Borneo (Kalimantan), isl., Asia E4 19
Bornholm, co., Den. *A3 7
Bornos, Sp. D3 8

Boromlya, Sov. Un. F10 12
Borovan, Bul. D6 10
Borovichi, Sov. Un. B9 12
Borovskoye, Sov. Un. q21 12
Borsod-Abauj-Zemplen, co., Hung. . . *A5 10
Bort-les-Orgues, Fr. E5 5
Borüjerd, Iran C4 15
Borzna, Sov. Un. F9 12
Bosa, It. D2 9
Bosanska Gradiska, Yugo. C3 10
Bosanska Kostajnica, Yugo. C3 10
Bosanski Novi, Yugo. C3 10
Boscobel, Wis. E3 88
Boshan, China D8 17
Boskovice, Czech. D4 7
Bosnia, reg., Yugo C3 10
Bosnia-Hercegovian, rep., Yugo *C3 10
Bosque, co., Tex. D4 84
Bossier, par. La. B2 63
Bossier City, La. B2 63
Boston, Eng. D6 4
Boston,Ga. F3 55
Boston, Mass. B5, g11 65
Boston, Pa. *E1 65
Boswell, Ind. C3 59
Botetourt, co., Va. C3 85
Botevgrad, Bul. D6 10
Botkins, Ohio B1 78
Botosani, Rom. E8 10
Botswana, country, Afr. E4 24
Bottineau, N. Dak. A5 77
Bottineau, co.,N. Dak. B5 77
Botucatu, Braz. C3, m7 30
Botwood, Newf., Can. D4 44
Bouaké, I.C. G3 22
Boucherville, Que., Can. D4, p20 42
Bouches-du-Rhône, dept., Fr. *F6 5
Bougie, see Bejaïa, Alg.
Boulder, Colo. A5 51
Boulder, Mont. D4 70
Boulder, co., Colo. A5 51
Boulder City, Nev. D4 72
Boulder Creek, Calif. *D2 50
Boulogne-Billancourt, Fr. C5 5
Boulogne-sur-Mer, Fr. B4 5
Boundary, co., Idaho A2 57
Boundary, pk., Nev. C2 72
Bound Brook, N.J. B3 74
Bountiful, Utah A6, C2 72
Bourbon, Ind. B5 59
Bourbon, co., Kans. E9 61
Bourbon, co., Ky. B5 62
Bourbonnais, Ill. B6 58
Bourbonnais, former prov., Fr. D5 5
Bourg, Fr. D6 5
Bourg-de-Péage, Fr. E6 5
Bourg -de-Bresse, Fr. D6 5
Bourges, Fr. D5 5
Bourg-la-Reine, Fr. g10 5
Bourgoin -Jallieu, Fr. E6 5
Bournemouth, Eng. E6 4
Bovey, Minn. C5 67
Bovina, Tex. B1 84
Bowdon, Ga. C1 55
Bowie, Md. B4 53
Bowie, Tex. C4 84
Bowie, co., Tex. C5 84
Bow Island, Alta., Can. E5 38
Bowling Green, Fla. E5 54
Bowling Green, Ky. D3 62
Bowling Green, Mo. B6 69
Bowling Green, Ohio A2, f6 78
Bowling Green, S.C. A5 82
Bowman, N. Dak. D2 77
Bowman, S.C. E6 82
Bowman, co., N. Dak. D2 77
Bowmanstown, Pa. E10 81
Bowmanville, Ont. Can. D6 41
Bowral, Austl. G8 26
Box Butte, co., Nebr. B2 71
Box Elder, co., Utah A5 72
Boxian, China E8 17
Boxtel, Neth. B6 5
Boyacá, dept., Col. B3 32
Boyce, La. C3 63
Boyd, co., Ky. B7 62
Boyd, co., Nebr. B7 71
Boyertown, Pa. F10 81
Boyes Hot Springs, Calif. *C2 50
Boyle, co., Ky. C5 62
Boylston, Ala. C3 46
Boyne City, Mich. C5 66
Boynton Beach, Fla. F6 54
Boys Town, Nebr. g12 71
Bozeman, Mont. E5 70
Bozüyük, Tur. C8 14
Bra., It. B1 9
Brabant, prov., Bel. *B6 5
Bracciano, It. g8 9
Bracebridge, Ont., Can. B5 41
Bracken, co., Ky. B5 62
Brackenridge, Pa. h15 81

Brackettville, Tex. E2 84
Brad, Sov. Un. B6 10
Bradbury Heights, Md. *C3 53
Braddock, Pa. k14 81
Braddock Heights, Md. B2 53
Braddock Hills, Pa. *E1 81
Bradenton, Fla. E4, q10 54
Bradenton Beach, Fla. *E4 54
Bradenville, Pa. F3 81
Bradford, Ont., Can. C5 41
Bradford, Eng. D6 4
Bradford, Ill. B4 58
Bradford, Ohio B1 78
Bradford, Pa. C4 81
Bradford, R. I. D10 52
Bradford, co., Fla. C4 54
Bradford, co., Pa. C8 81
Bradfordwoods, Pa. h13 81
Bradley, Fla. E5 54
Bradley, Ill. B6 58
Bradley, co., Ark. D3 49
Bradley, co., Tenn. D9 83
Bradley Beach, N.J. C4 74
Bradley Gardens, N.J. *B3 74
Bradner, Ohio A2 78
Bradshaw, W. Va. D3 87
Brady, Tex. D3 84
Braga, Port. B1 8
Bragado, Arg. B4, g6 28
Bragança, Braz. *D6 27
Bragança, Port. B2 8
Bragança, Paulista, Braz. C3, m8 30
Brahmaputra, riv., Asia C9 10
Braidwood, Ill. B5 58
Brăila, Rom. C8 10
Brainerd, Minn. D4 67
Braintree, Mass. B5, h11 65
Brampton, Ont., Can. D5, m14 41
Bramwell, W. Va. D3 87
Branch, co., Mich. G5 66
Branchville, N.J. A3 74
Branchville, S.C. E6 82
Branco, riv., Braz. C5 32
Brandenburg, Ger. Dem. Rep. B6 6
Brandenburg, Ky. B3 62
Brandenburg, former state,
   Ger. Dem. Rep. B6 6
Brandenburg, reg.,
   Ger. Dem. Rep. B6 6
Brandon, Man., Can. E2, h7 40
Brandon, Fla. E4 54
Brandon, Miss. C4 68
Brandon, S.C. B3 82
Brandon, Vt. D1 73
Brandys nad Ladem, Czech. n18 7
Branford, Conn. D5 2
Branson, Mo. E4 69
Brant, co., Ont., Can. D4 41
Brantford, Ont., Can. D4 41
Brant Lake, N.Y. B7 75
Brantley, Ala. D3 46
Brantley, co., Ga. E4 55
Bras-d'or, N.S., Can. C9 43
Brasília, Braz. B3 30
Brasília (Federal District), Braz. B3 30
Brasov, Rom. C7 10
Bratenahl, Ohio g9 78
Bratislava, Czech. D4 7
Bratsk, Sov. Un. *D13 13
Bratslav, Sov. Un. G7 12
Brattleboro, Vt. F2 73
Braunau am Inn, Aus. D6 6
Braunschweig, Ger. Fed.
   Rep. of B5 6
Brawley, Calif. F6 50
Braxton, co., W. Va. C4 87
Bray, Ire. D3 4
Braymer, Mo. B4 69
Brazil, Ind. E3 59
Brazil, country, S.A. C3 30
Brazoria, Tex. r14 84
Brazoria, co., Tex. E5 84
Brazos, co., Tex. D4 84
Brazzaville, Con. C4 10
Brčko, Yugo. C3 10
Brea. Calif. n13 50
Breathitt, co., Ky. C6 62
Breaux Bridge, La. D4 63
Brechin, Scot. B5 4
Breckenridge, Mich. E6 66
Breckenridge, Minn. D2 67
Breckenridge, Tex. C3 84
Breckenridge Hills, Mo. *C7 69
Breckinridge, co.,Ky. C3 62
Brecknock, co., Wales *E5 4
Brecksville, Ohio A4, h9 78
Břeclav, Czech. D4 7
Brecon, Wales. E5 4
Breda, Neth. kB6 5
Breese, Ill. E4 58
Bregenz, Aus. E4 6
Bregovo, Bul. C6 10
Bremen, Ga. C1 55

Bremen, Ger., Fed. Rep. of B4 6
Bremen, Ind., ... B5 59
Bremen, Ohio C3 78
Bremen, state, Ger., Fed. Rep of, ... *B4 6
Bremer, co., Iowa B5 60
Bremerhaven, Ger., Fed. Rep. of B4 6
Bremerton, Wash. B3, e10 86
Bremerton East (Enetai), Wash. *B3 86
Bremond, Tex. D4 84
Breham, Tex. D4 84
Brent, Ala. C2 46
Brent, Fla. u14 54
Brenton, W. Va. D3 87
Brentwood, Calif. h9 50
Brentwood, Md. F9 53
Brentwood, Mo. f13 69
Brentwood, N.Y. F4 52
Brentwood, Pa. k14 81
Brescia, It. B3 9
Breslau, see Wroclaw, Pol.
Bressanone, It. A3 9
Bressler, Pa. *F8 81
Bressuire, Fr. D3 5
Brest, Fr. C1 4
Brest, Sov. Un. E4 12
Brenton Woods, N.J. C4 74
Brevard, co., Fla. E6 54
Brevard, N.C. f10 76
Brewer, Maine D4 64
Brestwer, N.Y. D7, m15 75
Brewster, Ohio B4 78
Brewster, Wash. A6 86
Brewster, co.,Tex. p13 84
Brewton, Ala. D2 46
Brezno nad Hronom, Czech. D5 7
Briançon, Fr. E7 5
Briarcliff, Pa. *G11 81
Briarcliff Manor, N.Y. D7 75
Briceville, Tenn. C9 83
Bridge City, Tex. *D6 84
Bridgehampton, N.Y. n16 75
Bridgeport, Ala. A4 46
Bridgeport, Ont., Can. *D4 41
Bridgeport, Conn. E4 52
Bridgeport, Ill. E6 58
Bridgeport, Mich. E7 66
Bridgeport, Nebr. C2 71
Bridgeport, Ohio B5 78
Bridgeport, Pa. F11, o20 81
Bridgeport, Tex. C4 84
Bridgeport, Wash. B6 86
Bridgeport, W. Va. B4, k10 87
Bridgeton, Mo. C7, f13 69
Bridgeton, N.J. E2 74
Bridgetown, Barb. J15 35
Bridgetown, N.S., Can. E4 43
Bridgetown, Ohio *C1 78
Bridgeview, Ill *B6 58
Bridgeville, Del. C6 53
Bridgeville, Pa. k13 81
Bridgewater, N.S., Can. E5 43
Bridgewater, Mass. C6 65
Bridgewater, Va. B4 85
Bridgman, Mich. G4 66
Bridgton, Maine D2 64
Bridgwater, Eng. E5 4
Bridlington, Eng. C6 4
Brielle, N.J. C4 74
Brigantine, N.J. E4 74
Bringham City, Utah A4, C2 72
Brighton, Ala. B3, g7 46
Brighton, Colo. B6 51
Brighton, Eng. E6 4
Brighton, Ill. D3 58
Brighton, Mich. F7 66
Brighton, N.Y. *B3 75
Brightwaters, N.Y. n15 75
Brignoles, Fr. F7 5
Brilliant, Ohio B5 78
Brillion, Wis. D5, h9 88
Brindisi, It. D6 9
Brinkley, Ark. C4 49
Brioude, Fr. E5 5
Brisbane, Austl. E9 25
Brisbane, Calif. *D2 50
Bricoe, co., Tex. B2 84
Bristol, Conn. C5 52
Bristol, Eng. A6 4
Bristol, Ind. a6 59
Bristol, N.H. D4 73
Bristol, Pa. F12 81
Bristol, R.I. C11 52
Bristol, Tenn. C11 83
Bristol, Vt. C1 73
Bristol (Independent City), Va. f9 85
Bristol, co., Mass. C5 65
Bristol, co., R.I. C11 52
Bristow, Okla. B5 79
Brittania Beach, B.C., Can. E6 37
British Columbia, prov., Can. 37
British Guiana, see Guyana,
   country, S.A.

British Honduras, see
  Belize, Br. dep., N.A.
British Indian Ocean
  Territory, ter., Ind. O. *B9 24
British North Borneo, see
  Sabah, reg., Mala.
Britt, Iowa........................ A4 60
Brittany (Bretagne),
  former Prov., Fr. C2 5
Britton, S. Dak. E8 77
Brive -la-Gaillarde, Fr. E4 5
Brno, Czech. D4 7
Broach, India..................... D5 20
Broadalbin, N.Y. B6 75
Broad Brook, Conn. B6 52
Broadmoor, Colo.................. C6 51
Broadview, Sask., Can............. G4 39
Broadview, Ill. *B6 58
Broadview, Ind. *F4 59
Broadview Heights, Ohio.......... B2 78
Broadwater, co., Mont. D5 70
Brockport, N.Y. B3 75
Brockton, Mass. B5, h11 65
Brockville, Ont., Can. C9 41
Brockway, Pa. D4 81
Brocton, Ill D6 58
Brod, Yugo. C4 10
Broderick, Calif. *C3 50
Brodhead, Wis. F4 88
Brodnica, Pol. B5 7
Brody, Sov. Un. F5 12
Broken Arrow, Okla. A6 79
Broken Bow, Nebr. C6 71
Broken Bow, Okla................. C7 79
Broken Hill, Austl. F7 25
Broken Hill, Zambia............... C5 24
Brome, co., Que., Can............. D5 42
Bromptonville, Que., Can. D6 42
Bronson, Mich. G5 66
Bronte, Tex. D2 84
Bronx, bourough and co., N.Y. F7 75
Bronxville, N.Y. h13 75
Brook, Ind. C3 59
Brooke, co., W. Va. A4 87
Brookfield, Ill. k9 58
Brookfield, Mass. B3 65
Brookfield, Mo. B4 69
Brookfield, Wis. m11 88
Brookhaven, Miss. *D3 68
Brookhaven, Pa. *G11 81
Brookings, Oreg. E2 80
Brookings. S. Dak., ... F9 77
Brookings, co., S. Dak. F9 77
Brrooklands, Man., Can............ *E3 40
Brooklands, Mich. *F7 66
Brooklawn, N.J. D2 74
Brookline, Mass. B5, g11 65
Brooklyn, Conn. B9 52
Brooklyn, Ind. E5 59
Brooklyn, Iowa C5 60
Brooklyn, Mich. F6 66
Brooklyn, Ohio h9 78
Brooklyn (Lovejoy), Ill. g13 69
Brooklyn, borough, N.Y. k13 75
Brooklyn Center, Minn. E6 67
Brooklyn Park, Minn. *E6 67
Brookneal, Va. C4 85
Brook Park, Ohio h9 78
Brookport, Ill. F5 58
Brooks, Alta, Can. D5 38
Brooks, co., Ga. F3 55
Brooks, co., Tex. F3 84
Brookshire, Tex. E5, r14 84
Brookside, Ala. f7 46
Brookside, Del. A6 53
Brookside, N.J. B3 74
Brookston, Ind. C4 59
Brooksville, Fla. D4 54
Brookville, Ind. F7 59
Brookville, Mass. h11 65
Brookville, N.Y. *G2 52
Brookville, Ohio C1 78
Brookville, Pa. D3 81
Brookmall, Pa. *G11 81
Broome, co., N.Y. C5 75
Broomfield, Colo. B5 51
Broughton, Pa. *E1 81
Broussard, La. D4 63
Broward, co., Fla. F6 54
Brown, co., Ill. D3 58
Brown, co., Ind. F5 59
Brown co., Kans. C8 61
Brown, co. , Minn. F4 67
Brown, co., Nebr. B6 71
Brown, co., Ohio D2 78

Brown, co., S. Dak. E7 77
Brown, co., Tex. D3 84
Brown, co., Wis. D6 88
Brown City, Mich. E8 66
Brown Deer, Wis. m12 88
Brownfield, Tex. C1 84
Browning, Mont. B3 70
Brownlee Park, Mich. *F5 66
Brownsburg, Que., Can............ D3 42
Brownsburg, Ind. E5 59
Browns Mills, N.J. D3 74
Brownstown, Ind. G5 59
Brownstown, Pa. *E4 81
Browns Valley, Minn. E2 67
Brownsville, La. *B3 63
Brownsville, Oreg. C4 80
Brownsville, Pa. F2 81
Brownsville, Tenn. B2 83
Brownsville, Tex. G4 84
Brownville, Ala. B2 46
Brownville, N.Y. A5 75
Brownville Junction, Maine. C3 64
Brownwood, Tex. D3 84
Broxton, Ga. E4 55
Brozas, Sp. C2 8
Bruay en-Artios, Fr. B5 5
Bruce, mtn., Austl. D2 25
Bruce, Miss. B4 68
Bruceton, Tenn. A3 83
Bruchsal, Ger., Fed. Rep. of D4 6
Bruck ander Leitha, Aus. D8 6
Bruck an der Mur, Aus. E7 6
Brugge (Bruges), Bel. B5 5
Brule, co., S. Dak. G6 77
Brumath, Fr. C7 5
Brundidge, Ala. D4 46
Brunei, see Bandar Seri
  Begawan, Bru.
Brunei, country, Asia E4 19
Brunswick, Ga. E5 55
Brunswick, Maine...............E3, g8 64
Brunswick, Md. B23 53
Brunswick, Mo. B4 69
Brunswick, Ohio A4 78
Brunswick, co., N.C. C4 76
Brunswick, co., Va. D5 85
Brush, Colo....................... A7 51
Brusly, La. D4, h9 63
Brusque, Braz. D3 30
Brussels (Bruxelles), Bel. B6 5
Brussels, Ont., Can. D3 41
Bruxelles, see Brussels, Bel.
Bryan, Ohio A1 78
Bryan, Tex. D4 84
Bryan, co., Ga. D5 55
Bryan, co., Okla. D5 79
Bryansk, Sov. Un. E10 12
Bryant, Fla. F6 54
Bryantville, Mass. B6 65
Bryn Athyn, Pa. o21 81
Bryn Mawr, Pa. o20 81
Bryn Mawr, Wash. D2 86
Bryson City, N.C. f9 76
Bryte, Calif. *C3 50
Brzeg, Pol. C4 7
Brzeziny, Pol..................... C5 7
Bsa, It. B1 9
Bucaramanga, Col. B3 32
Buchanan, Mich. G4 66
Buchanan, N.Y. *D7 75
Buchanan, Va. C3 85
Buchanan, co., Iowa B6 60
Buchanan, co., Mo. B3 69
Buchanan, co., Va. e9 85
Buchans, Newf., Can. D3 44
Bucharest (Bucuresti), Rom. C8 10
Buchloe, Ger., Fed. Rep. of D5 6
Buckeye, Ariz. C2, D1 48
Buckeye Lake, Ohio C3 78
Buckhannon, W. Va. C4 87
Buckhaven & Methil, Scot. B5 4
Buckhorn, Ariz. D2 48
Buckie, Scot. B5 4
Buckingham, Que.,Can. D2 42
Buckingham, co., Eng. *E6 4
Buckingham, co., Va. C4 85
Buckley, Wash. B3, f11 86
Bucknell Manor, Va. *B5 85
Buckner, Mo. *B3 69
Bucks, co., Pa. F11 81
Bucksport, Maine D4 64
Bucksport, S.C. D9 82
Bucovina, reg., Rom. B7 10
Bucovina, reg., Sov. Un. B7 10
Bucuresti, see Bucharest, Rom.

Bucyrus, Ohio B3 78
Budapest, Hung. B4 10
Budd Lake, N.J. B3 74
Bude, Eng. E4 4
Bude, Miss. D3 68
Budrio, It. B3 9
Buechel, Ky. B4, g11 62
Buena, N.J. D3 74
Buena Park, Calif. n13 50
Buenaventura, Col. C2 32
Buena Vista, Colo. C4 51
Buena Vista, Ga. D2 55
Buena Vista (Independent City),
  Va. C3 85
Buena Vista, co., Iowa B2 60
Buenos Aires, Arg. A5, g7 28
Buenos Aires, prov. B4, g7 28
Buffalo, Iowa C7, h10 60
Buffalo, Minn. E5 67
Buffalo, Mo. D4 69
Buffalo, N.Y. C2 75
Buffalo, Ohio C4 78
Buffalo, Okla. A2 79
Buffalo, S.C. B4 82
Buffalo, Tex. D4 84
Buffalo, Wyo. B6 89
Buffalo, co., Nebr. D6 71
Buffalo, co., S. Dak. F6 77
Buffalo, co., Wis. D2 88
Buffalo Center, Iowa A4 60
Buffalo Grove, Ill. *A6 58
Bufford, Ga. B3 55
Buga, Col. C2 32
Bugojno, Yugo. C3 10
Buhl, Idaho G4 57
Buhl, Minn. C6 67
Buhler, Kans. D6 61
Buhuşi, Rom. B8 10
Bujalance, Sp. D3 8
Bujumbura, Burundi I3 23
Bukama, Zaire B5 24
Bukavu, Zaire I3 23
Bukhara, Sov. Un. F9 13
Bukidnon, prov., Phil. *D6 19
Bukittinggi, Indon. F2 19
Bukoba, Tan. I4 23
Bulacan, prov., Phil. *C6 19
Bulan, Ky. C6 62
Bulan, Phil. *C6 19
Bulawayo, Zimb. E5 24
Bulgaria, country, Eur. D7 10
Bullas, Sp. C5 8
Bullitt, co., Ky. C4 62
Bulloch, co., Ga. D5 55
Bullock, co., Ala. C4 46
Bulun, Sov. Un. B15 13
Bunbury, Austl. F2 25
Buncombe, co., N.C. f10 76
Bundaberg, Austl. D9 25
Bunia, Zaire H4 23
Bunker Hill, Ill. D4 58
Bunker Hill, Ind. C5 59
Bunker Hill, Oreg. *D2 80
Bunker Hill, Tex. *E5 84
Bunkie, La. D3 63
Bunnell, Fla. C5 54
Bunny Run, Mich. *F7 66
Burao, Som. G7 23
Buras, La. E6 63
Buraydah, Sau. Ar. D3 15
Burbank, Calif. E4, m12 50
Burdur, Tur. D8 14
Burdwān, India D8 20
Bureau, co., Ill. B4 58
Bureya, Sov.Un. B4 18
Burgas, Bul. D8 10
Burgas, pol. div., Bul. *D8 10
Burgaw, N.C. C5 76
Burgdorf, Switz. E3 6
Burgeo, Newf., Can. E3 44
Burgettstown, Pa. F1 81
Burgos, Sp. A4 8
Burgos, prov., Sp. *A4 8
Burgundy (Burgogne)
  former prov., Fr. D6 5
Burhānpur, India D6 20
Burin, Newf., Can. E4 44
Buriram, Thai. *C2 19
Burkburnett, Tex. B3 84
Burke, co., Ga. C4 55
Burke, co., N.C. B2 76
Burke, co., N. Dak. B3 77
Burke City, Mo. f13 69
Burkina Faso, country, Afr. F4 22

Burks Falls, Ont., Can. B5 41
Burleigh, co., N. Dak. D5 77
Burleson, Tex. n9 84
Burleson, co., Tex. D4 84
Burlingame, Calif. h8 50
Burlingame, Kans. D8 61
Burlington, Ont., Can. D5 41
Burlington, Colo. B8 51
Burlington, Iowa D6 60
Burlington, Kans. D8 61
Burlington, Mass. f11 65
Burlington, N.J. C3 74
Burlington, N.C. A3 76
Burlington, Vt. C1 73
Burlington, Wash. A3 86
Burlington, Wis. F5, n11 88
Burlington, co., N.J. D3 74
Burma, country, Asia D10 20
Burnet, Tex. D3 84
Burnet, co., Tex. D3 84
Burnett, co., Wis. C1 88
Burney, Calif. B3 50
Burnham, Ill. *B6 58
Burnham, Pa. E6 81
Burnie, Austl. o15 25
Burnley, Eng. D5 4
Burns, Oreg. D7 80
Burns Flat, Okla. B2 79
Burns Lake, B.C., Can. B5 37
Burnsville, N.C. f10 76
Burnwell, Ala. f6 46
Burr Oak, Mich. G5 66
Bursa, Tur. B7 14
Burt, co., Nebr. C9 71
Burton, Mich. F7 66
Burton, Ohio A4 78
Burton-on-Trent, Eng. D6 4
Burundi, country, Afr. I3 23
Büshehr, Iran G8 16
Buskerud, co., Nor. *H4 11
Busko, Pol. C6 7
Bussum, Neth. A6 5
Busto Arsizio, It. B2 9
Buta, Zaire H2 23
Bute, co., Scot. *C4 4
Butha Qi, China B9 17
Butler, Ala. C1 46
Butler, Ga. D2 55
Butler, Ind. B8 59
Butler, Mo. C3 69
Butler, N.J. B4 74
Butler, Ohio B3 78
Butler, Pa. E2 81
Butler, Wis. m11 88
Butler, co., Ala. D3 46
Butler, co., Iowa B5 60
Butler, co., Kans. E7 61
Butler, co., Ky. C3 62
Butler, co., Mo. F7 69
Butler, co., Nebr. C8 71
Butler, co., Ohio C1 78
Butler, co., Pa. E2 81
Butner, N.C. *A4 76
Butte, Mont. D4 70
Butte, co., Calif. C3 50
Butte, co., Idaho F5 57
Butte, co., S. Dak. F2 77
Butterworth, Mala. D2 19
Buttonwillow, Calif. E4 50
Butts, co., Ga. C3 55
Butuan, Phil. D7 19
Buturlinovka, Sov. Un. F13 12
Bützow, Ger. Dem. Rep. B5 6
Buxtehude, Ger. Fed. Rep. of B4 6
Buxton, Guy. C5 27
Büyük Ağri Daği (Mt. Ararat),
  mtn., Tur. C15 14
Buzău, Rom. C8 10
Buzet, Yugo. C1 10
Buzzards Bay, Mass. C6 65
Byala Slatina, Bul. D6 10
Bydgoszcz, Pol. B5 7
Byelorussia (S.S.R.), rep.,
  Sov. Un. E5 12
Byesville, Ohio C4 78
Byfield, Mass. A6 65
Bykovo, Sov. Un. G15 12
Byron, Ga. D3 55
Byron, Ill. A4 58
Bystrzyca, Pol. C4 7
Bytom, Pol. C5, g9 7
Bytosh, Sov. Un. E10 12

C

Caacupé Par. ... E4 29
Caaguazú dept., Par. ... D4 29
Caapucú, Par. ... E4 29
Caazapá, Par. ... E4 29
Caazapá, dept., Par. ... E4 29
Cabaceiras, Braz. ... *D4 27
Cabana, Peru ... C2 31
Cabanatuan, Phil. ... o13 19
Cabano, Que., Can. ... B9 42
Cabarrus, co., N.C. ... B2 76
Cabedelo, Braz. ... *D7 27
Cabell, co., W. Va. ... C2 87
Cabeza, del Buey, Sp. ... C3 8
Cabimas, Ven. ... A3 32
Cabinda, Ang. ... B2 24
Cabinda, dist., Ang. ... B2 24
Cabin John, Md. ... C3, f8 53
Cabo, Braz. ... *D7 27
Cabool, Mo. ... D5 69
Caboolture, Austl. ... *E9 25
Caborca, Mex. ... A2 34
Cabo Frio, Braz. ... C4 30
Cabo Rojo, P.R. ... *G11 35
Cabo San Lucas, Mex. ... C3 34
Cabot, Ark. ... C3 49
Cacak, Yugo. ... D5 10
Caçapava, Braz. ... C3 30
Cacequi, Braz. ... D2 30
Cáceres, Sp. ... C2 8
Cáceres, prov., Sp. ... C2 8
Cachan, Fr. ... G10 5
Cache, Okla. ... C3 79
Cache, co., Utah ... A6 72
Cache, peak, Idaho ... G5 57
Cache Bay, Ont., Can. ... A5 41
Cachi, Arg. ... E2 29
Cachoeira, Braz. ... *E7 27
Cachoeira do Sul, Braz. ... E2 30
Cachoeiro do Itapemirim, Braz. ... C4 30
Cacouna, Que., Can. ... B8 42
Caddo, Okla. ... C5 79
Caddo, co., Okla. ... B3 79
Caddo, par., La. ... B2 63
Cadillac, Mich. ... D5 66
Cadillac, mtn., Maine ... D4 64
Cadiz, Ky. ... D2 62
Cadiz, Ohio ... B4 78
Cádiz, Sp. ... D2 8
Cádiz, prov., Sp. ... *D2 8
Cadott, Wis. ... D2 88
Cadyville, N.Y. ... f11 75
Caen, Fr. ... C3 5
Caernarvon, Wales ... D4 4
Caernarvon, co., Wales ... *D4 4
Cagayan, de Oro, Phil. ... D6 19
Cagayan, prov., Phil. ... *B6 19
Cagli, It. ... C4 9
Cagliari, It. ... E2 9
Cagnes-sur-Mer, Fr. ... F7 5
Caguas, P.R. ... G12 35
Cahaba Heights, Ala. ... *B3 46
Cahokia, Ill. ... E3 58
Cahors, Fr. ... E4 5
Caibarién, Cuba ... C4 35
Caicedonia, Col. ... C2 32
Caicó, Braz. ... *D7 27
Cailloma, Peru ... E3 31
Cairnbrook, Pa. ... F4 81
Cairns, Austl. ... C8 25
Cairo, Ga. ... F2 55
Cairo, Ill. ... F4 58
Cairo, Eg. ... B4 23
Caithness, co., Scot. ... *A5 4
Cajabamba, Peru ... C2 31
Cajacay, Peru ... D2 41
Cajamarca, Peru ... C2 31
Cajamarca, dept., Peru ... C2 31
Cajatambo, Peru ... D2 31
Cajázeiras, Braz. ... *D7 27
Cakovec, Yugo. ... B3 10
Calabar, Nig. ... H6 22
Calabria, pol. dist., It. ... *E5 9
Calabria, reg., It. ... E6 9
Calafat, Rom. ... D6 10
Calahorra, Sp. ... A5 8
Calais, Fr. ... B4 5
Calais, Maine ... C5 64
Calamar, Col. ... A3 32
Calamba, Phil. ... C6 19
Calañas, Sp. ... D2 8
Calapan, Phil. ... C6 19
Cãlárási, Rom. ... C8 10
Calarcá, Col. ... C2 32
Calasparra, Sp. ... C5 8
Calauag, Phil. ... P14 19
Calaveras, co., Calif. ... C3 50
Calca, Peru ... D3 31

Calcasieu, par., La. ... D2 63
Calceta, Ec. ... B1 31
Calcutta, India ... D8 10
Calcutta, Ohio ... B5 78
Caldas, dept. Col. ... B2 32
Caldas da Rainha, Port. ... C1 8
Caldwell, Idaho ... F2 57
Caldwell, Kans. ... E6 61
Caldwell, N.J. ... B4 74
Caldwell, Ohio ... C4 78
Caldwell, Tex. ... D4 84
Caldwell, co., Ky. ... C2 62
Caldwell, co., Mo. ... B3 69
Caldwell, co., N.C. ... B1 76
Caldwell, co., Tex. ... E4 84
Caldwell, par., La. ... B3 63
Caledonia, Ont., Can. ... D5 41
Caledonia, Minn. ... G7 67
Caledonia, N.Y. ... C3 75
Caledonia, Ohio ... B3 78
Caledonia, co., Vt. ... C3 73
Calella, Sp. ... B7 8
Calera, Ala. ... B3 46
Calera, Chile ... A2 28
Calexico, Calif. ... F6 50
Calgary, Alta., Can. ... D3, g8 38
Calhoun, Ga. ... B2 55
Calhoun, co., Ala. ... B4 46
Calhoun, co., Ark. ... D3 49
Calhoun, co., Fla. ... B1 54
Calhoun, co., Ga. ... E2 55
Calhoun, co., Ill. ... D3 58
Calhoun, co., Iowa ... B4 60
Calhoun, co., Mich. ... F5 66
Calhoun, co., Miss. ... B4 68
Calhoun, co., S.C. ... D6 82
Calhoun, co., Tex. ... E4 84
Calhoun, co., W. Va. ... C3 87
Calhoun City, Miss. ... B4 68
Calhoun Falls, S.C. ... C2 82
Cali, Col. ... C2 32
Calico Rock, Ark. ... A3 49
Calicut, India ... F6 20
Caliente, Nev. ... C4 72
California, Mo. ... C5 69
California, Pa. ... F2 81
California, state, U.S. ... C2 50
Calipatria, Calif. ... F6 50
Calispell, peak, Wash. ... A8 86
Calistoga, Calif. ... C2 50
Callahan, co., Tex. ... C3 84
Callander, Ont., Can. ... A5 41
Callander, Scot. ... B4 4
Callao, Peru ... D2 31
Callao, prov., Peru ... D2 31
Callaway, co., Mo. ... C6 69
Callicoon, N.Y. ... D5 75
Calloway, co., Ky. ... f9 62
Calmar, Alta., Can. ... C4 38
Calmar, Iowa ... A6 60
Caloundra, Austl. ... C9 26
Caltagirone, It. ... F5 9
Caltanissetta, It. ... F5 9
Caluire -et-Cuire, Fr. ... E6 5
Calumet, Que., Can. ... D3 42
Calumet, Mich. ... A2 66
Calumet, Pa. ... *F2 81
Calumet, co., Wis. ... D5 88
Calumet City, Ill. ... B6, k9 58
Calumet Park, Ill. ... *B6 58
Calvados, dept., Fr. ... *C3 5
Calvert, Tex. ... D4 84
Calvert, co., Md. ... C4 53
Calvert City, Ky. ... e9 62
Calverton Park, Mo., ... A8 69
Calvillo, Mex. ... m12 34
Calwa, Calif. ... *D4 50
Camacho, Mex. ... C4 34
Camagüey, Cuba ... D5 35
Camagüey, prov., Cuba ... D5 35
Camaná, Peru ... E2 31
Camanche, Iowa ... C7 60
Camargo, see Ciudad
   Camargo, Mex.
Camarillo, Calif. ... *E4 50
Camarines Norte, prov., Phil. ... *C6 19
Camarines Sur, prov., Phil. ... *C6 19
Camas, Wash. ... D3 86
Camas, co., Idaho ... F4 57
Cambay, India ... *D5 20
Cambodia, see Kampuchea,
   country, Asia
Camborne -Redruth, Eng. ... E4 4
Cambrai, Fr. ... B5 5
Cambria, Calif. ... E3 50
Cambria, co., Pa. ... E4 81
Cambrian Park, Calif. ... *D3 50

Cambridge, Eng. ... D7 4
Cambridge, Ill. ... B3 58
Cambridge, Md. ... C5 53
Cambridge, Mass ... B5, g11 65
Cambridge, Minn. ... E5 67
Cambridge, Nebr. ... D5 71
Cambridge, N.J. ... *C3 74
Cambridge, N.Y. ... B7 75
Cambridge, Ohio ... B4 78
Cambridge & Isle of Ely,
   co., Eng. ... *D7 4
Cambridge City, Ind. ... E7 59
Cambridge Springs, Pa. ... C1 81
Camden, Ala. ... D2 46
Camden, Ark. ... D3 49
Camden, Del. ... B6 53
Camden, Maine ... D3 64
Camden, N.J. ... D2 74
Camden, N.Y. ... B5 75
Camden, Ohio ... C1 78
Camden, S.C. ... C6 82
Camden, Tenn. ... A3 83
Camden, Tex. ... D5 84
Camden, co., Ga. ... F5 55
Camden, co., Mo. ... C5 69
Camden, co., N.J. ... D3 74
Camden, co., N.C. ... A6 76
Camdenton Mo. ... D5 69
Camerino, It. ... C4 9
Cameron, La. ... E2 63
Cameron, Mo. ... B3 69
Cameron, Tex. ... D4 84
Cameron, W. Va. ... B4, g8 87
Cameron, Wis. ... C2 88
Cameron, co., Pa. ... D5 81
Cameron, co., Tex. ... F4 84
Cameron, par., La. ... E2 63
Cameroon, country, Afr. ... G7 22
Cameroun, Mont, mtn., Cam. ... H6 22
Camiling, Phil. ... o13 19
Camilla, Ga. ... E2 55
Camillus, N.Y. ... *B4 75
Camino, Calif. ... C3 50
Cammack Village, Ark. ... C3, h10 49
Camocim, Braz. ... *D6 27
Camp, co., Tex. ... C5 84
Campagna di Roma, reg., It. ... h9 9
Campana, Arg. ... g7 28
Campanario, Sp. ... C3 8
Campania, pol. dist., It. ... *D5 9
Campania, reg., It. ... D5 9
Campbell, Calif. ... k8 50
Campbell, Mo. ... E7 69
Campbell, Ohio ... A5 78
Campbell, co., Ky. ... B5 62
Campbell, co., S. Dak. ... E5 77
Campbell, co, Tenn. ... C9 83
Campbell, co., Va. ... C3 85
Campbell, co., Wyo. ... B7 89
Campbell, hill, Ohio ... B2 78
Campbellford, Ont., Can. ... C7 41
Campbellpore, Pak. ... B5 20
Campbell River, B.C. ... D5 37
Campbells Bay, Que., Can. ... B8 41
Campbellsport, Wis. ... E5 88
Campbellsville, Ky. ... C4 62
Campbellton, N.B., Can. ... A3 43
Campbelltown, Pa. ... *F9 81
Campbeltown, Scot. ... C4 4
Campeche, Mex. ... D6 34
Camp Hill, Ala. ... C4 46
Camp Hill, Pa. ... F8 81
Campiglia Marittima, It. ... C3 9
Campina Grande, Braz. ... D7 27
Campinas, Braz. ... C3, m8 30
Campoalegre, Col. ... C2 32
Campobasso, It. ... D5 9
Campo Belo, Braz. ... C3 30
Campo de Criptana, Sp. ... C4 8
Campo Grande, Braz. ... C2 30
Campo Maior, Braz. ... *D6 27
Campo Maior, Port. ... C2 8
Campos, Braz. ... C4 30
Camp Point, Ill. ... C2 58
Camp Springs, Md. ... f9 53
Campti, La. ... C2 63
Camrose, Alta., Can. ... C4 38
Canaan, Conn. ... A3 52
Canada, country, N.A. ... D10 33
Cañada de Gómez, Arg. ... A4 28
Canadensis, Pa. ... D11 81
Canadian, Tex. ... B2 84
Canadian, co., Okla. ... B3 79
Canadian, riv., U.S. ... C6 45
Canajoharie, N.Y. ... C6 75
Çanakkale, Tur. ... B6 14

Canal Fulton, Ohio ... B4 78
Canal Point, Fla. ... F6 54
Canal Winchester, Ohio ... C3, m11 78
Canandaigua, N.Y. ... C3 75
Cananea, Mex. ... A2 34
Cañar, prov., Ec. ... B2 31
Canary Islands, reg., Sp. ... C1 22
Cañas, C.R. ... *E7 75
Canastota, N.Y. ... B5 34
Canavieiras, Braz. ... *E7 27
Canberra, Austl. ... G8 25
Canby, Minn. ... F2 67
Canby, Oreg. ... B4, h12 80
Candeleda, Sp. ... B3 8
Candia, see Iraklion, Grc.
Candiac, Que., Can. ... q19 42
Candler, co., Ga. ... D4 75
Cando, N. Dak. ... B6 77
Candor, N.Y. ... C4 75
Canelones, Ur. ... E1 30
Canelones, dept. Ur. ... *E1 30
Cañete, Peru ... D2 31
Caney, Kans. ... E8 61
Canfield, Ohio ... A5 78
Cangallo, Peru ... D3 31
Cangas, Sp. ... A1 8
Cangzhou, China ... D8 17
Canicatti, It. ... F4 9
Caniles, Sp. ... D4 8
Canisteo, N.Y. ... C3 75
Çankiri (Changra), Tur. ... B9 14
Canmore, Alta, Can. ... D3 38
Cannelton, Ind. ... I4 59
Cannes, Fr. ... F7 5
Canning, N.S., Can. ... D5 43
Cannington, Ont., Can. ... C5 41
Cannon, co., Tenn. ... B5 83
Cannon Falls, Minn. ... F6 67
Canoas, Braz. ... *D2 30
Canoinhas, Braz. ... D2 30
Canon City, Colo ... C5 51
Canonsburg, Pa. ... F1 81
Canora, Sask., Can. ... F4 39
Canosa de Puglia, It. ... D6 9
Canso, N.S., Can. ... D8 43
Cantal, dept., Fr. ... *E5 5
Canterbury, Eng. ... E7 4
Can Tho, Viet. ... *C3 19
Cantilan, Phil. ... *D7 19
Canton, China ... G7 17
Canton, Ga. ... B2 55
Canton, Ill. ... C3 58
Canton, Mass. ... B5, h11 65
Canton, Miss. ... C3 68
Canton, Mo. ... A6 69
Canton, N.Y. ... F9 75
Canton, N.C. ... D3 76
Canton, Ohio ... B4 78
Canton, Okla. ... A3 79
Canton, Pa. ... C8 81
Canton, S. Dak. ... G9 77
Canton, Tex. ... C5 84
Cantonment, Fla. ... u14 54
Cantwell, Mo. ... D7 69
Canutillo, Tex. ... o11 84
Canyon, Tex. ... B2 84
Canyon, co., Idaho ... F2 57
Canyonville, Oreg. ... E3 80
Cao Bang, Viet. ... G6 17
Capac, Mich. ... F8 66
Cap Chat, Que., Can. ... G20 36
Cap-de-la-Madeleine, Que., Can. ... C5 42
Cape, prov., S. Afr. ... G4 24
Cape Breton, N.S., Can. ... G21 36
Cape Breton, co., N.S., Can. ... D9 43
Cape Canaveral, Fla. ... D6 54
Cape Charles, Va. ... C6 85
Cape Coast, Ghana ... G4 22
Cape Coral, Fla. ... F5 54
Cape Elizabeth, Maine ... E2, g7 64
Cape Girardeau, Mo. ... D8 69
Cape Girardeau, co., Mo. ... D8 69
Cape Horn, mtn., Idaho ... E3 57
Capels, W. Va. ... D3 87
Cape May, N.J. ... F3 74
Cape May, co., N.J. ... E3 74
Cape May Court House, N.J. ... E3 74
Capesterre, Guad. ... H14 35
Cape Town (Kaapstad), S. Afr. ... G3 24
Cape Verde, country, Afr. ... O12 22
Cape Vincent, N.Y. ... A4 75
Cap-Haïtien, Hai. ... F7 35
Capiata, Par. ... *E4 29
Capistrano Beach, Calif. ... *F5 50
Capitan, N. Mex. ... C6 48
Capitola, Calif. ... *D2 50

Capitol Heights, Md. C4, f9 53
Capivarí, Braz. m8 30
Capiz, prov., Phil *C6 19
Capoompeta, mtn., Austl. E9 25
Cap-Pelé, N.B., Can. C5 43
Capreol, Ont., Can. p19 41
Cap-St. Ignace, Que., Can. B7 42
Captain Cook, Haw. D6 56
Capua, It. D5   9
Caquetá, intendencia, Col. C3 32
Carabobo, state, Ven. A4 32
Caracal, Rom. C7 10
Caracas, Ven. A4 32
Caraguatay, Par. E4 29
Carangola, Braz. C4 30
Caransebes, Rom. C6 10
Carapeguá, Par. E4 29
Caraquet, N.B., Can. B5 43
Caratinga, Braz. B4 20
Caravelí, Peru E3 31
Caraway, Ark. B5 49
Caraz, Peru C2 31
Carázinho, Braz. D2 30
Carballino, Sp. A1   8
Carballo, Sp. A1   8
Carberry, Man., Can. E2 40
Carbó, Mex. B2 34
Carbon, co., Mont. E7 70
Carbon, co. Pa. E10 81
Carbon, co., Utah B6 72
Carbon, co., Wyo. E5 89
Carbondale, Ill. F4 58
Carbondale, Pa. C10 81
Carbonear, Newf., Can. E5 44
Carbon Hill, Ala. B2 46
Carbonia, It. E2   9
Carcagente, Sp. C5   8
Carcar, Phil. *C6 19
Carcassonne, Fr. F5   5
Carchi, prov., Ec. A2 31
Cardale, Pa. *G2 81
Cárdenas, Cuba C3 35
Cárdenas, Mex. D6 34
Cárdenas, Mex. m14 34
Cardiff, Wales E5   4
Cardiff-by-the-Sea, Calif. *F5 50
Cardigan, Wales D4   4
Cardigan, co., Wales *D4   4
Cardinal, Ont., Can. C9 41
Cardington, Ohio B3 78
Cardston, Alta., Can. E4 38
Cardwell, Mo. E7 69
Carei, Rom. B6 10
Carencro, La. D3 63
Carenero, Ven. A4 32
Caretta, W. Va. D3 87
Carey, Ohio B2 78
Carhuaz, Peru C2 31
Cariati, It. E6   9
Caribbean, sea, N.A. H13 33
Cariboo mts., B.C. C7 37
Caribou, Maine B5 64
Caribou, co., Idaho F6 57
Caribou, mtn., Idaho F7 57
Caribou, mtn., Maine C2 64
Carichic, Mex. B3 34
Carini, It. E4   9
Carinthia, reg., Aus. E6   6
Caripito, Ven. A5 32
Carle Place, N.Y. *G2 52
Carleton, Mich. F7 66
Carleton, co., N.B., Can. C2 43
Carleton, mtn., N.B., Can. B3 43
Carleton Place, Ont., Can. B8 41
Carletonville, S. Afr. *F5 24
Carlin, Nev. A3 72
Carlinville, Ill. D4 58
Carlisle, Ark. C4 49
Carlisle, Eng. C5   4
Carlisle, Iowa C4 60
Carlisle, Ky. B5 62
Carlisle, Pa. F7 81
Carlisle, co., Ky. f8 62
Carl Junction, Mo. D3 69
Carloforte, It. E2   9
Carlos Casares, Arg. B4 28
Carlow, Ire. D3   4
Carlow, co., Ire. *D3   4
Carlsbad, Calif. F5 50
Carlsbad, N. Mex. C6 48
Carlstadt, N.J. h8 74
Carlton, Oreg. B3, h11 80
Carlton, co., Minn. D6 67
Carlyle, Sask., Can. H4 39
Carlyle, Ill. E4 58
Carmagnola, It. B1   9
Carman, Man., Can. E2 40
Carman, hill, Pa. C6 81
Carmanville, Newf., Can. D4 44
Carmarthen, Wales E4   4
Carmarthen, co.,Wales *E4   4
Carmaux, Fr. E5   5
Carmel, Calif. D3 50

Carmel, Ind. E5 59
Carmel, N.Y. D7 75
Carmel, mtn., Isr. B3 15
Carmelo, Ur. E1 30
Carmel Valley, Calif. *D3 50
Carmel Woods, Calif. *D3 50
Carmen, Par. E4 29
Carmen de Patagones, Arg. C4 28
Carmi, Ill. E5 58
Carmichael, Calif. *C3 50
Carmichaels, Pa. G2 81
Carmona, Sp. D3   8
Carnarvon, Austl. D1 25
Carnduff, Sask., Can. H5 39
Carnegie,Okla. B3 79
Carnegie, Pa. F1, k13 81
Carneys Point, N.J. D2 74
Caro, Mich. E7 66
Carol City, Fla. s13 54
Caroleen, N.C. B1, f11 76
Carolina, P.R. *G11 35
Carolina Beach, N.C. C5 76
Caroline, co., Md. C6 53
Caroline, co., Va. C5 85
Caroline, arch., Pac. O. F6   2
Carora, Ven. A3 32
Carouge, Switz. E3   6
Carpentersville, Ill. A5, h8 58
Carpentras, Fr. E6   5
Carpi, It. B3   9
Carpinteria, Calif. E4 50
Carrabelle, Fla. C2 54
Carrantuohill, mtn., Ire. D1   4
Carrara, It. B3   9
Carrboro, N.C. B3 76
Carrickfergus, N. Ire. C4   4
Carrie, mtn., Wash. B2 86
Carriers Mills, Ill. F5 58
Carrington, N. Dak. C6 77
Carrizo, see El Carrizo, Mex.
Carrizo Springs, Tex. E3 84
Carrizozo, N. Mex. C6 48
Carroll, Iowa B3 60
Carroll, co., Ark. A2 49
Carroll, co., Ga. C1 55
Carroll, co., Ill. A4 58
Carroll, co., Ind. C4 59
Carroll, co., Iowa B3 60
Carroll, co., Ky. B4 62
Carroll, co., Md. A3 53
Carroll, co., Miss. B4 68
Carroll, co., Mo. B4 69
Carroll, co., N.H. D5 73
Carroll, co., Ohio B4 78
Carroll, co., Tenn. B3 83
Carroll, co., Va. D2 85
Carrollton, Ga. C1 55
Carrollton, Ill. D3 58
Carrollton, Ky. B4 62
Carrollton, Md. A4 53
Carrollton, Mich. E7 66
Carrollton, Mo. B4 69
Carrollton, Ohio B4 78
Carrollton, Tex. *C4 84
Carrolltown, Pa. E4 81
Carrot River, Sask., Can. D4 39
Carrville, Ala. *C4 46
Çarşamba, Tur. B11 14
Carson, Calif. *n12 50
Carson, Iowa C10 71
Carson, co., Tex. B2 84
Carson City, Mich. E6 66
Carson City, Nev. B2 72
Carsonville, Mo. *C7 69
Cartagena, Col. A2 32
Cartagena, Sp. D5   8
Cartago, Col. C2 32
Cartago, C.R. F8 34
Cartago, prov., C.R. *I12 33
Cartaxo, Port. C1   8
Cartaya, Sp. D2   8
Carter, co., Ky. B6 62
Carter, co., Mo. E7 69
Carter, co., Mont. E12 70
Carter, co., Okla. C4 79
Carter, co., Tenn. C11 83
Carteret, N.J. B4, k8 74
Carteret, co., N.C. C6 76
Carter Lake, Iowa C2 60
Cartersville, Ga. B2 55
Carterville, Ill. F4 58
Carterville, Mo. D3 69
Carthage, Ill. C2 58
Carthage, Ind. E6 59
Carthage, Miss. C4 68
Carthage, Mo. D3 69
Carthage, N.Y. B5 75
Carthage, N.C. B3 76
Carthage, Tenn. C8 83
Carthage, Tex. C5 84
Caruaru, Braz. D7 27
Carúpano, Ven. A5 32
Caruthersville, Mo. E8 69

Carver, Minn. F5 67
Carver, co., Minn. F5 67
Carville, La. h9 63
Cary, Ill. A5, h8 58
Cary, N.C. B4 76
Caryville, Tenn. C9 83
Casablanca, Mor. B3 22
Casa Branca, Braz. C3, k8 30
Casa Grande, Ariz. C3 48
Casale Monferrato, It. B2   9
Casarano, It. D7   9
Casas Adobes, Ariz. *C3 48
Cascade, Idaho E2 57
Cascade, Iowa B6 60
Cascade, co., Mont. C5 70
Cascade, range, Can., U.S. B2 45
Cascais, Port. C1, f9   8
Caseros (Tres de Febrero), Arg. ... *A5 28
Caserta, It. D5   9
Casey, Ill. D6 58
Casey, co., Ky. C4 62
Casey, mtn., Idaho A2 57
Caseyville, Ill. *E3 58
Cashion, Ariz. D1 48
Cashmere, Wash. B5 86
Cashton, Wis. E3 88
Casilda, Arg. A4 28
Casino, Austl. D9 26
Casma, Peru C2 31
Caspe, Sp. B5   8
Casper, Wyo. D6 89
Caspian, Mich. B2 66
Caspian, sea, Asia E7 13
Cassadaga, N.Y. C1 75
Cass, co., Ill. D3 58
Cass, co., Ind. C5 59
Cass, co., Iowa C3 60
Cass, co., Mich. G4 66
Cass, co., Minn. D4 67
Cass, co., Mo. C3 69
Cass, co., Nebr. D9 71
Cass, co., N. Dak. C8 77
Cass, co., Tex. C5 84
Cass, co., Mich. E7 66
Casselberry, Fla. *D5 54
Casselman, Ont., Can. B9 41
Casselton, N. Dak. D8 77
Cassia, co., Idaho G5 57
Cassino, It. D4   9
Cass Lake Minn. C4 67
Cassopolis, Mich. G4 66
Cassville, Mo. E4 69
Cassville, Wis. F3 88
Castalia, Ohio A3 78
Castanea, Pa. D7 81
Castaños, Mex. B4 34
Castellammare di Stabia, It. *D5   9
Castellón (Castellón
  de la Plana), prov., Sp. *C5   8
Castellón de la Plana, Sp. C5   8
Castelnaudary, Fr. F4   5
Castelo Branco, Port. C2   8
Castelvetrano, It. F4   9
Castile, N.Y. C2 75
Castilla, Peru C1 31
Castle, peak, Idaho E4 57
Castle Douglas, Scot. C5   4
Castlegar, B.C., Can. E9 37
Castle Hills, Tex. *E3 84
Castlemaine, Austl. H5 26
Castle Park, Calif. *F5 50
Castle Rock, Colo. B6 51
Castle Rock, Wash. C3 86
Castle Rock, mtn., Oreg. C8 80
Castle Rock, mtn., Va. C4 85
Castle Shannon, Pa. k13 81
Castleton-on-Hudson, N.Y. C7 75
Castor, Alta, Can. C5 38
Castres, Fr. F5   5
Castries, St. Lucia J14 35
Castro, Braz. C3 30
Castro, co., Tex. B1 84
Castro Alves, Braz. *E7 27
Castropol, Sp. A2   8
Castro Valley, Calif. h8 50
Castrovillari, It. E6   9
Castroville, Calif. D3 50
Castroville, Tex. E3 84
Castrovirreyna, Peru D2 31
Castuera, Sp. C3   8
Caswell, co., N.C. A3 76
Catacaos, Peru C1 31
Catacocha, Ec. B2 31
Cataguases, Braz. C4, g6 30
Catahoula, par., La. C4 63
Cataingan, Phil. *C6 19
Catalao, Braz. B3 30
Çatalca, Tur. B7 14
Catalina, Newf., Can. D5 44
Catamarca, Arg. E2 29
Catamarca, prov., Arg. E2 29

Catanduva, Braz. C3 30
Catania, It. F5   9
Cataño, P.R. *G11 35
Catañzaro, It. E6   9
Catarman, Phil. C6 19
Catarroja, Sp. C5   8
Catasauqua, Pa. E11 81
Catawba, co., N.C. B1 76
Catawissa, Pa. E9 81
Catbalogan, Phil. C6 19
Cathedral, mtn., Tex. o13 84
Cathedral City, Calif. F5 50
Catlettsburg, Ky. B7 62
Catlin, Ill. C6 58
Catonsville, Md. B4, g10 53
Catoosa, co., Ga. B1 55
Catron, co., N. Mex. C4 48
Catskill, N.Y. C7 75
Catskill, mts., N.Y. C6 75
Catt, mtn., B.C., Can. B3 37
Cattaraugus, N.Y. C2 75
Cattaraugus, co.,N.Y. C2 75
Cattolica, It. C4   9
Cauca, dept., Col. C2 32
Caucasia, Col. B2 32
Caudebec -lès-Elbeuf, Fr. C4   5
Caudete, Sp. C5   8
Caudry, Fr. B5   5
Caughnawaga, Que., Can. D4, q19 42
Cauquenes, Chile B2 28
Causapscal, Que., Can. *h14 42
Cautín, prov., Chile B2 28
Cavadas, Mex. m12 34
Cavaillon, Fr. F6   5
Cavalier, N. Dak. B8 77
Cavalier, co., N. Dak. B7 77
Cavan, co., Ire. *D3   4
Cavarzere, It. B4   9
Cave, It. h9   9
Cave City, Ky. C4 62
Cave Junction, Oreg. E3 80
Cave Spring, Ga. B1 55
Cavite, Phil. o13 19
Cavite, prov., Phil. *C6 19
Cawnpore, see Kanpur, India
Cawood, Ky. D6 62
Caxias, Braz. *D6 27
Caxias do Sul., Braz. D2 30
Caxito, Ang. B2 24
Cayambe, Ec. A2 31
Cayce, S.C. D5 82
Cayenne, Fr. Gu. C5 27
Cayey, P.R. G11 35
Cayman Islands, Br. dep.,N.A. F3 35
Cayuga, Ont., Can. E5 41
Cayuga, Ind. E3 59
Cayuga, co., N.Y. C4 75
Cayuga Heights, N.Y. *C4 75
Cazalla de la Sierra, Sp. D3   8
Cazenovia, N.Y. C5 75
Cazorla, Sp. D4   8
Ceará, state, Braz. *D7 27
Ceará Mirim, Braz. *D7 27
Cebu, Phil. C6 19
Cebu, prov., Phil. *C6 19
Cecil, Pa. F1 81
Cecil, co., Md. A6 53
Cecina, It. C3   9
Cedar, co., Iowa C6 60
Cedar, co., Mo. D4 69
Cedar, co., Nebr. B8 71
Cedar, mtn., Cal. B3 50
Cedar Bluff, Va. e10 85
Cedarburg, Wis. E5, m12 88
Cedar City, Utah C5 72
Cedar Falls, Iowa B5 60
Cedar Grove, N.J. *B4 74
Cedar Grove, W. Va. C3, m13 87
Cedar Grove, Wis. E6 88
Cedar Hammock, Fla. *E4 54
Cedar Heights, Md. *C4 53
Cedar Hill, Tex. n10 84
Cedar Hills, Oreg. *B4 80
Cedarhurst, N.Y. k13 75
Cedar Key, Fla. C3 54
Cedar Knolls, N.J. B4 74
Cedar Lake, Ind. B3 59
Cedar Rapids, Iowa C6 60
Cedar Springs, Mich. E5 66
Cedar Terrace, S.C. *D5 82
Cedartown, Ga. B1 55
Cedar Vale, Kans. E7 61
Cedarville, Calif. B3 50
Cedarville, N.J. E2 74
Cedarville, Ohio C2 78
Cedarwood Park, N.J. *C4 74
Ceduna, Austl. F5 25
Cefalù, It. E5   9
Cegléd, Hung. B4 10
Ceglie Messapico, It. D6   9
Celákovice, Czech. n18   7
Celaya, Mex. m13 34
Celebes (Sulawesi), isl., Indon. ... F6 19

Celendín, Peru C2 31
Celina, Ohio B1 78
Celina, Tenn. C8 83
Celina, Tex. C4 84
Celje, Yugo. B2 10
Celle, Ger., Fed. Rep. of. B5 6
Celoron, N.Y. C1 75
Cement, Okla. C3 79
Cementon, Pa. E10 81
Cenon, Fr. E3 5
Centennial, mts., Mont. F4 70
Center, Colo. D4 51
Center, Tex. D5 84
Centerburg, Ohio B3 78
Centereach, N.Y. E3 75
Center Line, Mich. *F8 66
Center Moriches, N.Y. n16 75
Center Point, Ala. f7 46
Center Point, Iowa B6 60
Centerport, N.Y. *n15 75
Centerville, Ind. E8 59
Centerville, Iowa D5 60
Centerville, Mont. D4 70
Centerville, Ohio C1 78
Centerville, Pa. F2 81
Centerville, S. Dak. G9 77
Centerville, Tenn. B4 83
Centerville, Tex. D5 84
Centerville, Utah A6, C2 72
Central, N. Mex. C4 48
Central, S.C. B2 62
Central, mts., Dom. Rep. E8 35
Central African Republic,
  country, Afr. G2 23
Central America, reg., N.A. E6 34
Central Avenue Park, Ohio *A2 78
Central City, Ill. E4 58
Central City, Iowa B6 60
Central City, Ky. C2 62
Central City, Nebr. C7 71
Central City, Pa. F4 81
Central Falls, R.I. B11 52
Central Heights, Ariz. *C3 48
Central Heights, Iowa A4 60
Centralia, Ill. E4 58
Centralia, Mo. B5 69
Centralia, Pa. *D8 81
Centralia, Wash. C3 86
Central Islip, N.Y. E7, n15 75
Central Nyack, N.Y. *D7 75
Central Park, Ill. *C6 58
Central Park, Wash. *C2 86
Central Point, Oreg. E4 80
Central Square, N.Y. B4 75
Central Valley, Calif. B2 50
Central Valley, N.Y. D6, m14 75
Centre, Ala. A4 46
Centre, co., Pa. E6 81
Centre, mtn., Idaho D3 57
Centre, peak, B.C., Can. B4 37
Centre Hall, Pa. E6 81
Centreville, Ala. C2 46
Centreville, Ill. E3 58
Centreville, Md. B5 53
Centreville, Mich. G5 66
Centreville, Miss. D2 68
Century, Fla. u14 54
Ceram, isl., Indon. F7 19
Ceredo, W. Va. C2 87
Ceres, Calif. D3 50
Cereté, Col. B2 32
Cerignola, It. D5 9
Cernavoda, Rom. C9 10
Cerralvo, Mex. B5 34
Cerritos, Calif. *F4 50
Cerritos, Mex. C4 34
Cerro Alto, mtn., Tex. o12 84
Cerro Azul, Peru D2 31
Cerro de Pasco, Peru D2 31
Cerro Gordo, Ill. D5 58
Cerro Gordo, co., Iowa A4 60
Cerro Largo, dept., Ur. *E2 30
Cervantes, Sp. A2 8
Cerva del Rio Alhama, Sp. A2 8
Cesena, It. B4 9
Cesenatico, It. B4 9
Česká Lípa, Czech. C3 7
Česká Trebova, Czech. D4 7
České Budejovice, Czech. D3 7
Český Brod, Czech. n8 7
Český Krumlov, Czech. D3 7
Cessnock, Austl. F9 25
Cetinje, Yugo. D4 10
Cetraro, It. E5 9
Ceuta, Sp. dep., Afr. A3 2
Ceylon, see Sri Lanka,
  country, Asia.
Chacabuco, Arg. A4, m9 28
Chachapoyas, Peru C2 31
Chaco, prov., Arg. E3 29
Chad, country, Afr. F1 23
Chad, lake, Cam., Nig. E7 22
Chadbourn, N.C. C4 76

Chadron, Nebr. B3 71
Chadwicks, N.Y. *B5 75
Chaffee, Mo. D8 69
Chaffee, co., Colo. C4 51
Chaffins, Mass. *B4 65
Chagrin Falls, Ohio A4 78
Chahar Burjak, Afg. B3 20
Chaibāsā, India D8 20
Chakradharpur, India D8 20
Chakwāl, Pak. B5 20
Chalchuapa, Sal. *E7 34
Chalfant, Pa. *E1 81
Chalhuanca, Peru D3 31
Chalk River, Ont., Can. A7 41
Chalkville, Ala. *E4 46
Chalmette, La. E6, k11 63
Châlons-sur-Marne, Fr. C6 5
Chalon-sur-Saône, Fr. E6 5
Chama, N. Mex. A5 48
Chamalières, Fr. E5 5
Chaman, Pak. B4 20
Chamberlain, S. Dak. G6 77
Chamberlayne Heights, Va. *C5 85
Chambers, co., Ala. C4 46
Chambers, co., Tex. E5 84
Chambersburg, Pa. G6 81
Chambéry, Fr. E6 5
Chamblee, Ga. h8 55
Chambly, Que., Can. D4 42
Chambly, co., Que., Can. D4 42
Chambord, Que., Can. A5 42
Champaign, Ill. C5 58
Champaign, co., Ill. C5 58
Champaign, co., Ohio B2 78
Champigny-sur-Marne, Fr. g11 5
Champion, Ohio A5 78
Champlain, N.Y. f11 75
Champlain, co., Que., Can. B4 42
Champlin, Minn. m12 67
Champotán, Mex. D6 34
Chañaral, Chile F3 27
Chancay, Peru D2 31
Chanchelulla, peak, Calif. B2 50
Chanchiang (Tsamkkong), China . G7 17
Chandīgarh, India B6 20
Chandīgarh, ter., India *B6 20
Chandler, Ariz. C3, D2 48
Chandler, Que., Can. K14 42
Chandler, Ind. H3 59
Chandler, Okla. B5 79
Chāndpur, Bngl. D9 20
Chandrapur, India E6 20
Changchun (Hsinking), China C10 17
Changde, China F7 17
Changhua, Taiwan *G9 17
Changjin, Kor. F3 18
Changsha, China F7 17
Changting, China F8 17
Changyon, Kor. G2 18
Changahi, China D7 17
Changzhou, China E8 17
Channel Lake, Ill. H8 58
Channel-Port-aux-Basques,
  Newf., Can. E2 44
Channelview, Tex. r14 84
Chantada, Sp. A2 8
Chanthaburi, Thai. C2 19
Chantilly, Fr. C5 5
Chanute, Kans. E8 61
Chao'an, China G8 17
Chaoyang, China C9 17
Chapala, Mex. m12 34
Chaparral, Col. C2 32
Chapel Hill, N.C. B3 76
Chapleau, Ont., Can. p19 41
Chaplygin, Sov. Un. E12 12
Chapman, Ala. D3 46
Chapman, Kans. D7 61
Chapmanville, W. Va. D2 87
Chappaqua, N.Y. *D7 75
Chappell, Nebr. C3 71
Chapra, India C7 20
Charalá, Col. B2 32
Charcas, Mex. C4 34
Chardon, Ohio A4 78
Chardzhou, Sov. Un. F9 13
Charente, dept., Fr. *E4 5
Charente-Maritime, dept., Fr. *D3 5
Charenton-le-Pont, Fr. g10 5
Charikar, Afg. A4 20
Chariton, Iowa C4 60
Chariton, co., Mo. B4 69
Charlack, Mo. *C7 69
Charlemagne, Que., Can. D4, p19 42
Charleroi, Bel. B6 5
Charleroi, Pa. F2 81
Charleroix West, co., Que.,
  Can. B7 42
Charles, co., Md. C3 53
Charlesbourg, Que., Can. N17 42
Charles City, Iowa A5 60

Charles City, co., Va. C5 85
Charles Mix, co., S. Dak. G7 77
Charleston, Ark. B1 49
Charleston, Ill. D5 58
Charleston, Miss. A3 68
Charleston, Mo. E8 69
Charleston, S.C. F8, k12 82
Charleston, W. Va. C3, m12 87
Charleston, Utah C4 72
Charleston, co., S.C. F8 82
Charlestown, Ind. H6 59
Charlestown, N.H. E3 73
Charlestown, St. Kitts-
  Nevis-Anguilla H13 35
Charles Town, W. Va. B7 87
Charleville, Austl. E8 25
Charlevoix, Mich. C5 66
Charlevoix, co., Mich. C5 66
Charlieu, Fr. D6 5
Charlotte, Mich. F6 66
Charlotte, N.C. B2 76
Charlotte, Tex. E3 84
Charlotte, co., N.B., Can. D3 43
Charlotte, co., Fla. F5 54
Charlotte, co., Va. D4 85
Charlotte Amalie, Vir. Is.
  (U.S.) G12 35
Charlotte Harbor, Fla. F4 54
Charlottesville
  (Independent City), Va. B4 85
Charlottetown, P.E.I., Can. C6 43
Charlton, City, Mass. B4 65
Charlton, co., Ga. F4 55
Charmco, W. Va. *D4 87
Charny, Que., Can. C6, o17 42
Charter Oak, Calif. *E4 50
Charters Towers, Austl. D8 25
Chartres, Fr. C4 5
Chascomús, Arg. B5 28
Chase, B.C., Can. D8 37
Chase, Kans. D5 61
Chase, co., Kans. D7 61
Chase, co., Nebr. D4 71
Chase City, Va. D4 85
Chase, mtn., Maine B4 64
Chaska, Minn. F5, n11 67
Chasong, Kor. F3 18
Chasov Yar, Sov., Un. q20 12
Chataignier, La. D3 63
Châteaubriant, Fr. D3 5
Châteaudun, Fr. C4 5
Chateaugay, N.Y. f11 10
Châteauguay, Que., Can. D4, q19 42
Châteauguay, co., Que.,
  Can. D4 42
Châteauguay Heights,
  Que., Can. q19 42
Château-Richer, Que., Can. C6 42
Châteauroux, Fr. D4 5
Château-Theirry, Fr. C5 5
Châtellerault, Fr. D4 5
Chatfield, Minn. G6 67
Chatham, N.B., Can. B4 43
Chatham, Ont., Can. E2 41
Chatham, Eng. *E7 4
Chatham, Ill. D4 58
Chatham, Mass. C8 65
Chatham, N.J. B4 74
Chatham, N.Y. C7 75
Chatham, Va. D3 85
Chatham, co., Ga. E5 55
Chatham, co., N.C. B3 76
Chatom, Ala. D1 46
Chatsworth, Ga. B2 55
Chatsworth, Ill. C5 58
Chattahoochee, Fla. B2 54
Chattahoochee, co., Ga. D2 55
Chattanooga, Tenn. D8, h11 83
Chattaroy, W. Va. D2 87
Chattooga, co.,Ga. B1 55
Chatwood, Pa. *G10 81
Chau Doc, Viet. *C3 19
Chauk, Bur. D9 20
Chaumont, Fr. C6 5
Chauncey, Ohio C3 78
Chauny, Fr. C5 5
Chautauqua, co., Kans. E7 61
Chautauqua, co., N.Y. C1 75
Chauvin, La. E5 63
Chaves, Port. B2 8
Chaves, co., N. Mex. C6 48
Chavinda, Mex. m12 34
Chazelles sur-Lyon, Fr. E6 5
Chazy, N.Y. f11 75
Cheatham, co., Tenn. A4 83
Cheb, Czech. C2 7
Chebanse, Ill. C6 58
Cheboksary, Sov. Un. C16 12
Cheboygan, Mich. C6 66
Cheboygan, co., Mich. C6 66
Chechaouene, Mor. A3 22
Checotah, Okla. B6 79

Cheddar, S.C. B3 82
Cheektowaga, N.Y. C2 75
Chefoo, see Yantai, China
Chehalis, Wash. C3 86
Cheju, Kor. J3 18
Chekhov, Sov. Un. C10 18
Chelan, Wash. B5 86
Chelan, co., Wash. B4 86
Chelan, mts., Wash. A5 86
Chelkar, Sov. Un. E3 13
Chełm *Lubelski*, Pol. C7 7
Chelmno, Pol. B5 7
Chelmsford, Ont., Can. *A3 41
Chelmsford, Eng. E7 4
Chelmsford, Mass. A5, f10 65
Chełmza, Pol. B5 7
Chelsea, Mass. B5, g11 65
Chelsea, Miss. F6 66
Chelsea, Okla. A6 79
Cheltenham, Eng. E5 4
Cheltenham, Md. C4 53
Cheltenham, Pa. *F11 81
Chelyabinsk, Sov. Un. D9 13
Chemainus, B.C., Can. E6, g12 37
Chemnitz, see Karl-Marx-
  Stadt, Ger. Dem. Rep.
Chemung, co., N.Y. C4 75
Chenango, co., N.Y. *C5 75
Chenango Bridge, N.Y. *C5 75
Cheney, Kans. E6, g11 61
Cheney, Wash. B8, h13 86
Cheneyville, La. C3 63
Chengde, China C8 17
Chengdu, China E5 17
Chenghai, China G8 17
Chenoa, Ill. C5 58
Chenxian, China F7 17
Chepén, Peru C2 31
Chepstow, Wales E5 4
Cher, dept., Fr. *D5 5
Cheraw, S.C. B8 82
Cherbourg, Fr. C3 5
Cheremkhovo, Sov. Un. D13 13
Cherepovets, Sov. Un. B11 12
Cherkassy, Sov. Un. G9 12
Cherkassy, Sov. Un. G9 12
Chernigov, Sov. Un. F8 12
Chernobay, Sov. Un. G9 12
Chernobyl, Sov. Un. F8 12
Chernovtsy, Sov. Un. G5 12
Chernyakhovsk, (Insterburg),
  Sov. Un. D3 12
Cherokee, Ala. A2 46
Cherokee, Iowa B2 60
Cherokee, Kans. E9 61
Cherokee, Okla. A3 79
Cherokee, co. Ala. A4 46
Cherokee, co., Ga. B2 55
Cherokee, co., Iowa B2 60
Cherokee, co., Kans. E9 61
Cherokee, co., N.C. f8 76
Cherokee, co., Okla. B6 79
Cherokee, co., S.C. A4 82
Cherokee, co., Tex. D5 84
Cherokee Forest, S.C. *B3 82
Cherokee Ranch, Pa. *F9 81
Cherry, co., Nebr. B4 71
Cherry Grove, Ohio *C1 78
Cherry Hill, N.J. D2 74
Cherry Hills Village, Colo. *B6 51
Cherryvale, Kans. E8 61
Cherry Valley, Ill. A5 58
Cherry Valley, Mass. B4 65
Cherryville, N.C. B1 76
Chesaning, Mich. E6 66
Chesapeake, Ohio D3 78
Chesapeake (Independent
  City), Va. D6, k15 85
Chesapeake, W. Va. C3 87
Chesapeake City, Md. A6 53
Chesham, Eng. k11 4
Cheshire, Conn. D5 52
Cheshire, Mass. A1 65
Cheshire, co., Eng. *D5 4
Cheshire, co., N.H. E3 73
Cheshunt, Eng. k12 4
Chesley, Ont., Can. C3 41
Chesnee, S.C. A4 82
Chester, Calif. B3 50
Chester, N.S., Can. E5 43
Chester, Conn. D7 52
Chester, Eng. D5 4
Chester, Ill. F4 58
Chester, Md. C5 53
Chester, Mass. B2 65
Chester, Mont. B6 70
Chester, N.J. B3 74
Chester, N.S., Can. E5 43
Chester, N.Y. D6, m14 75
Chester, Pa. G11, p20 81
Chester, S.C. B5 82
Chester, Vt. E3 73
Chester, W. Va. C5, n18 85
Chester, W. Va. A4, e8 87

Chester, co., Pa. ...G10 81
Chester, co., S.C. ...B5 82
Chester, co., Tenn. ...B3 83
Chesterfield, Eng. ...D6 4
Chesterfield, Ind. ...D6 59
Chesterfield, S.C. ...B7 82
Chesterfield, co., S.C. ...B7 82
Chesterfield, co., Va. ...C5 85
Chesterhill, Ohio ...C4 78
Chesterton, Ind. ...A3 59
Chestertown, Md. ...B5 53
Chesterville, Ont., Can. ...B9 41
Cheswick, Pa. ...h14 81
Chetek, Wis. ...C2 88
Cheticamp, N.S., Can. ...C8 43
Chetopa, Kans. ...E8 61
Chetumal, see Ciudad
  Chetumal, Mex.
Chetwynd, B.C., Can. ...B7 37
Cheverly, Md. ...*C4 53
Cheviot, Ohio ...C1, o12 78
Chevy Chase, Md. ...C3, f8 53
Chevy Chase Heights, Pa. ...*E3 81
Chevy Chase Section
  Four, Md. ...*C3 53
Chevy Chase View, Md. ...*C3 53
Chewelah, Wash. ...A8 86
Chews (Chews Landing), N.J. ...*C4 74
Cheyenne, Okla. ...B2 79
Cheyenne, Wyo. ...E8 89
Cheyenne, co., Colo. ...C8 51
Cheyenne, co., Kans. ...C2 61
Cheyenne, co., Nebr. ...C2 71
Cheyenne Wells, Colo. ...C8 51
Chiai, Taiwan ...*G9 17
Chiang Khong, Thai. ...A2 19
Chiang Mai,Thai. ...B1 19
Chiang Rai, Thai ...B1 19
Chiapa de Corzo, Mex. ...D6 34
Chiapas, state, Mex. ...D6 34
Chiari, It. ...B2 9
Chiautla de Tapia, Mex. ...n14 34
Chiavari, It. ...B2 9
Chiba, Jap. ...I10, n19 18
Chiba, pref., Jap. ...*I10 18
Chicago, Ill. ...B6, k9 58
Chicago Heights, Ill. ...B6, k9 58
Chicago Ridge, Ill. ...*B6 58
Chichester, Eng. ...E6 4
Chichibu, Jap. ...m18 18
Chickamauga, Ga. ...B1 55
Chickasaw, Ala. ...E1 46
Chickasaw, co., Iowa ...A5 60
Chickasaw, co.,Miss. ...B5 68
Chickasha, Okla. ...B4 79
Chiclana, Sp. ...D2 8
Chiclayo, Peru ...C2 31
Chico, Calif. ...C3 50
Chico, Tex. ...C4 84
Chico, Wash. ...B3 86
Chicontepec, Mex. ...m14 34
Chicopee, Ga. ...B3 55
Chicopee, Mass. ...B2 65
Chicora, Pa. ...E2 81
Chicot, co., Ark. ...D4 49
Chicoutimi, Que., Can. ...A6, k12 42
Chicoutimi, co., Que., Can. ...A6 42
Chico Vecino, Calif. ...*C3 50
Chiefland, Fla. ...C4 54
Chieri, It. ...B1 9
Chieti, It. ...C5 9
Chifeng, China ...C8 17
Chigasaki, Jap. ...*I9 18
Chigirin, Sov. Un. ...G9 12
Chignahuapan, Mex. ...n14 34
Chigwell, Eng. ...k13 4
Chihuahua, Mex. ...B3 34
Chihuahua, state, Mex. ...B3 34
Chii-san, mtn., Korea ...I3 18
Chikura, Jap. ...o18 18
Chilapa de Alvarez, Mex. ...D5, o14 34
Childersburg, Ala. ...B3 46
Chilca, Peru ...D2 31
Childress, Tex. ...B2 84
Childress, co., Tex. ...*B2 84
Chile, country, S.A. ...E2 29
Chilecito, Arg. ...E2 29
Chilhowie, Va. ...f10 85
Chillán, Chile ...B2 28
Chillicothe, Ill. ...C4 58
Chillicothe, Mo. ...B4 69
Chillicothe, Ohio ...C3 78
Chillicothe, Tex. ...B3 84
Chilliwack, B.C., Can. ...E7, f14 37
Chillum, Md. ...*C3 53
Chiloé, prov., Chile ...C2 28
Chiloquin, Oreg. ...E5 80
Chilpancingo de los
  Bravos, Mex. ...D5, o14 34
Chilton, Tex. ...D4 84
Chilton, Wis. ...D5, h10 88
Chilton, co., Ala. ...C3 46
Chilung, Taiwan ...F9 17

Chimalhuacán, Mex. ...h10 34
Chimayo, N. Mex. ...B6 48
Chimbay, Sov. Un. ...E8 13
Chimborazo, prov., Ec. ...B2 31
Chimborazo, vol., Ec. ...B2 31
Chimbote, Peru ...C2 31
Chimkent, Sov. Un. ...E19 13
China, Mex. ...B5 34
China, country, Asia ...E4 17
China Grove, N.C. ...B2 76
Chinandega, Nic. ...E7 34
Chinati, peak, Tex. ...p12 84
Chincha Alta, Peru ...D2 31
Chincheros, Peru ...D3 31
Chinchilla, Austl. ...E9 25
Chinchilla, Pa. ...*D10 81
Chincoteague, Va. ...C7 85
Chindo,Kor. ...I3 18
Chingford, Eng. ...k13 4
Chingola, Zam. ...*C5 24
Chinhae, Kor. ...I4 18
Chiniot,Pak. ...B5 20
Chinju, Kor. ...I4 18
Chinnampo (Nampo), Kor. ...G2 18
Chino, Calif. ...F5, m13 50
Chinook, Mont. ...B7 70
Chinquapin, N.C. ...C5 76
Chiñú, Col. ...B3 32
Chioggia, It. ...B4 9
Chipley, Fla. ...u16 54
Chipman, N.B., Can. ...C4 43
Chippewa, co., Mich. ...B6 66
Chippewa, co. Minn. ...E3 67
Chippewa, co., Wis. ...C2 88
Chippewa Falls, Wis. ...D2 88
Chiquimula, Guat. ...E7 34
Chiquinquira, Col. ...B3 32
Chiriqui Grande, Pan. ...B1 32
Chirpan, Bul. ...D7 10
Chisago, co., Minn. ...E6 67
Chisholm, Maine ...D2 64
Chisholm, Minn. ...C6 67
Chişineu-Criş, Rom. ...B5 10
Chisos, mts., Tex. ...p13 84
Chita, Sov. Un. ...D14 13
Chitradurga, India ...F6 20
Chitré, Pan. ...B1 32
Chittagong, Bngl. ...D9 20
Chittenango, N.Y. ...*B5 75
Chittenden, co.,Vt. ...C1 73
Chittoor, India ...F6 20
Chiusi, It. ...C3 9
Chivasso, It. ...B1 9
Chivay, Peru ...E3 31
Chivilcoy,Arg. ...A4, g6 28
Chochiwŏn, Kor. ...H3 18
Chocó, dept., Col. ...C2 32
Chocontá, Col. ...B3 32
Choctaw, co., Ala. ...C1 46
Choctaw, co., Miss. ...B4 68
Choctaw, co., Okla. ...C6 79
Chodziez, Pol. ...B4 7
Choisy-le-Roi, Fr. ...g10 5
Choix, Mex. ...B3 34
Chojna, Pol. ...B3 7
Chojnice, Pol. ...B4 7
Chojnów, Pol. ...C3 7
Chokai-zan mtn., Jap. ...G10 18
Cholet, Fr. ...D3 5
Cholula de Rivadabia, Mex. ...n14 34
Choluteca, Hond. ...E7 34
Chomutov, Czech. ...C2 7
Chonan, Kor. ...H3 18
Chon Buri,Thai. ...C2 19
Chone, Ec. ...B1 31
Chongjin, Kor. ...F4 18
Chongju, Kor. ...H3 18
Chongqing, China ...F6 17
Chonju, Kor. ...I3 18
Chorrilos, Peru ...D2 31
Chŏrwŏn, Kor. ...G3 18
Chorzów, Pol. ...g9 7
Chosen, Fla. ...F6 54
Chosen, see Korea, Asia
Choshi, Jap. ...I10, n19 18
Chosica, Peru ...D2 31
Chota, Peru ...C2 31
Choteau, Mont. ...C4 70
Choum, Maur. ...D2 22
Chouteau, Okla. ...A6 79
Chouteau, co., Mont. ...C6 70
Chowan, co., N.C. ...A6 76
Chowchilla,Calif. ...D3 50
Chrisman, Ill. ...D6 58
Christchurch, N.Z. ...O14 26
Christian, co., Ill. ...D4 58
Christian, co., Ky. ...D2 62
Christian, co., Mo. ...E4 69
Christiana, Pa. ...G9 81
Christiansburg, Va. ...C2 85
Christiansted, Vir. Is. (U.S.) ...H12 35
Christmas Island, Austl.
  dep., Oceania ...G4 2

Christopher, Ill. ...F4 58
Chrudim, Czech. ...D3 7
Chrzanów, Pol. ...g10 7
Chubbuck, Idaho ...G6 57
Chubut, prov.,Arg. ...C3 28
Chugiak, Alsk. ...C10, g17 47
Chuguyev, Sov. Un. ...G11 12
Chuius, mtn., B.C., Can. ...B5 37
Chula Vista, Calif. ...F5, o15 50
Chuluchana, Peru ...B1 31
Chumikǎn, Sov. Un. ...D16 13
Chunchŏn, Kor. ...H3 18
Chungju, Kor ...H3 18
Chungking, see Chongqing, China
Chupaca, Peru ...D2 31
Chuquibamba, Peru ...E3 31
Chuquisaca, dept., Bol. ...D3 29
Chur, Switz. ...E4 6
Church, mtn., B.C., Can. ...f14 37
Church Hill, Tenn. ...C11 83
Churchhill, Man., Can. ...f9 40
Churchill, Pa. ...*E1 81
Churchill, co., Nev. ...B2 72
Churchhill, riv., Man.,
  Sask.,Can. ...B2 39
Church Point, La. ...D3 63
Churchs Ferry, N. Dak. ...B6 77
Churchville, Pa. ...*F11 81
Churubusco, Ind. ...B7 59
Churmuco, Mex. ...n13 34
Chusovoy, Sov. Un. ...*D8 13
Cibola, co, N. Mex. ...B4 48
Cicero, Ill. ...B6, k9 58
Cicero, Ind. ...D5 59
Ciechanów, Pol. ...B6 7
Ciego de Avila, Cuba ...D4 35
Ciénaga, Col. ...A3 32
Ciénaga de Oro, Col. ...B2 32
Cienfuegos, Cuba ...C3 35
Cieszyn, Pol. ...D5 7
Cihuatlán, Mex. ...n11 34
Cilacap, Indon. ...G3 19
Cimarron, Kans. ...E3 62
Cimarron, N. Mex. ...A6 48
Cimarron, co., Okla. ...e8 79
Cimarron, riv., U.S. ...C7 45
Cîmpina, Rom. ...C7 45
Cîmpulung, Rom. ...C7 10
Cîmpulung Moldovenesc, Rom. ...B7 10
Cincinnati, Ohio ...C1, o12 78
Cinnaminson, N.J. ...D3 74
Cinnaminson Township, N.J. ...*C2 74
Cintalapa de Figueroa, Mex. ...D6 34
Cinto, mtn., Fr. ...C7 45
Circle, Mont. ...C11 70
Circle Pines, Minn. ...*E5 67
Circleville, Ohio ...C3 78
Cirebon, Indon. ...G3 19
Cirencester, Eng. ...E6 4
Cisco, Tex. ...C3 84
Cisneros, Col. ...B2 32
Cissna Park, Ill. ...C6 58
Cisterna di Latina, It. ...h9 9
Citac, mtn., Peru ...D2 31
Citlaltépet (Pico de
  Orizaba), vol., Mex. ...n15 34
Citronelle, Ala. ...D1 46
Citrus, co., Fla. ...D4 54
Citrus Heights, Calif. ...*C3 50
Cittadella, It. ...B3 9
Città de Castello, It. ...C4 9
City View, S.C. ...B3 82
Ciudad Acuña, Mex. ...B4 34
Ciudad Allende, Mex. ...B4 34
Ciudad Altamirano, Mex. ...n13 34
Ciudad Bolívar, Ven. ...B5 32
Ciudad Camargo, Mex. ...B3 34
Ciudad Chetumal, Mex. ...D7 34
Ciudad del Carmen, Mex. ...D6 34
Ciudad del Maíz, Mex. ...C5 34
Ciudad de Naucalpan de
  Juárez, Mex. ...h9 34
Ciudad de Valles, Mex. ...C5, m14 34
Ciudad de Villaldama, Mex. ...B4 34
Ciudad Dr. Hernández
  Alvarez, Mex. ...*m13 34
Ciudad Guzmán, Mex. ...D4, n12 34
Ciudad Hidalgo, Mex. ...n13 34
Ciudad Ixtepec, Mex. ...D5 34
Ciudad Jiménez, Mex. ...B4 34
Ciudad Juárez, Mex. ...A3 34
Ciudad Lerdo, Mex. ...B4 34
Ciudad Madero, Mex. ...C5 34
Ciudad Mante, Mex. ...C5 34
Ciudad Melchor Múzquiz,
  Mex. ...B4 34
Ciudad Mendoza, Mex. ...n15 34
Ciudad Obregón, Mex. ...B3 34
Ciudad Ojeda, Ven. ...A3 32
Ciudad Real, Sp. ...*C4 8
Ciudad Real, prov., Sp. ...*C4 8
Ciudad Serdán, Mex. ...n14 34
Ciudad Victoria, Mex. ...C5 34

Cividale de Friuli, It. ...A4 9
Civitanova Marche, It. ...C4 9
Civitavecchia, It. ...C3 9
Cizre, Tur ...D14 14
Clackamas, Oreg. ...h12 80
Clackamas, co., Oreg. ...B4 80
Clackmannan, co., Scot ...*B5 4
Claflin, Kans. ...D5 61
Claiborne, co.,Miss. ...D3 68
Claiborne, co., Tenn. ...C10 83
Claiborne, par.,La. ...B2 63
Clairfield, Tenn. ...C10 83
Clairton, Pa. ...F2 81
Clallam, co.,Wash. ...A1 86
Clamart, Fr. ...g10 5
Clamecy, Fr. ...D5 5
Clanton, Ala. ...C3 46
Clara City, Minn. ...F3 67
Clare, Austl. ...F6 25
Clare, Mich. ...E6 66
Clare, co., Ire. ...D2 4
Clare, co., Mich. ...E6 66
Claremont, Calif. ...m13 50
Claremont, N.H. ...E3 73
Claremont, mtn., Cal. ...C3 50
Claremore, Okla. ...A6 79
Clarence, Iowa ...C6 60
Clarence, Mo. ...B5 69
Clarence, N.Y. ...*C2 75
Clarendon, Ark. ...C4 49
Clarendon, Tex. ...B2 84
Clarendon, co., S.C. ...D7 82
Clarendon Hills, Ill. ...k9 58
Clarenville, Newf., Can. ...D4 44
Claresholm, Alta., Can. ...D4 38
Claridge, Pa. ...F2 81
Clarinda, Iowa ...D2 60
Clarion, Iowa ...B4 60
Clarion, Pa. ...D3 81
Clarion, co.,Pa. ...D2 81
Clark, N.J. ...B4 74
Clark, S. Dak. ...F8 77
Clark, co., Ark. ...C2 49
Clark, co., Idaho ...E6 57
Clark, co., Ill. ...D6 58
Clark, co., Ind. ...H6 59
Clark, co., Kans. ...E4 61
Clark, co., Ky. ...C5 62
Clark, co., Mo. ...A6 69
Clark, co., Nev. ...C4 72
Clark, co., Ohio ...C2 78
Clark, co., S. Dak. ...F8 77
Clark, co., Wash. ...D3 86
Clark, co., Wis. ...D3 88
Clark, mtn.,Mo. ...D7 69
Clarkdale, Ariz. ...B2 48
Clarke, co., Ala. ...D2 46
Clarke, co., Ga. ...C3 55
Clarke, co., Iowa ...D4 60
Clarke, co., Miss. ...C5 68
Clark, co., Va. ...A4 85
Clarks Harbour, N.S., Can. ...F4 43
Clarkfield, Minn. ...F3 67
Clark Mills, N.Y. ...*B5 75
Clarks, La. ...B3 63
Clarksburg, W. Va. ...B4, k10 87
Clarksdale, Miss. ...A3 68
Clarks Green, Pa. ...*D10 81
Clarks Harbour, N.S., Can. ...F4 43
Clarks Summit, Pa. ...m18 81
Clarkston, Ga. ...h8 55
Clarkston, Wash. ...C8 86
Clarksville, Ark. ...B2 49
Clarksville, Ind. ...H6 59
Clarksville, Iowa ...B5 60
Clarksville, Tenn. ...A4 83
Clarksville, Tex. ...C5 84
Clarksville, Va. ...D4 85
Clarkton, Mo. ...E8 69
Clatskanie, Oreg. ...A3 80
Clatsop, co., Oreg. ...A3 80
Claude, Tex. ...B3 84
Clausthal-Zellerfeld, Ger.,
  Fed. Rep of ...C5 6
Clawson, Mich. ...o15 66
Claxton, Ga. ...D5 55
Clay, Ky. ...C2 62
Clay, co., Ala. ...B4 46
Clay, co., Ark. ...A5 49
Clay, co., Fla. ...B5 54
Clay, co., Ga. ...E2 55
Clay, co., Ill. ...E5 58
Clay, co., Ind. ...F3 59
Clay, co., Iowa ...A2 60
Clay, co., Kans. ...C6 61
Clay, co., Ky. ...C6 62
Clay, co., Minn. ...D2 67
Clay, co., Miss. ...B5 68
Clay, co., Mo. ...B3 69
Clay, co., Nebr. ...D7 71
Clay, co., N.C. ...f9 76
Clay, co., S. Dak. ...H9 77
Clay, co., Tenn. ...C8 83

Clay, co., Tex. C3 84
Clay, co., W. Va. C3 87
Clay Center, Kans. C6 61
Clay City, Ill. E5 58
Clay City, Ind. F3 59
Claycomo Mo. *B3 69
Claymont, Del. A7 53
Claypool, Ariz. C3, D3 48
Claysburg, Pa. F5 81
Clayville, Pa. F1 81
Clayton, Ala. D4 46
Clayton, Del. B6 53
Clayton, Ga. B3 55
Clayton, Ill. C3 58
Clayton, La. C4 63
Clayton, Mo. C7, f13 69
Clayton, N.J. D2 74
Clayton, N. Mex. A7 48
Clayton, N.Y. A4, f8 75
Clayton, N.C. B4 76
Clayton, Okla. C6 79
Clayton, co., Ga. C2 55
Clayton, co., Iowa B6 60
Clear Brook, B.C., Can. f13 37
Clear Creek, co., Colo. B5 51
Clearfield, Pa. D5 81
Clearfield, Utah A5 72
Clearfield, co., Pa. D4 81
Clear Lake, Iowa A4 60
Clear Lake, S. Dak. F9 77
Clearlake Highlands, Calif. C2 50
Clear Lake Shores, Tex. r14 84
Clearwater, Fla. E4, p10 54
Clearwater, Kans. E6 61
Clearwater, S. C. E4 82
Clearwater, co., Idaho C3 57
Clearwater co., Minn. C3 67
Clearwater, mts., Idaho C2 57
Cleburne, Tex. C4, n9 84
Cleburne, co., Ala. B4 46
Cleburne, co., Ark. B3 49
Cle Elum, Wash. B5 86
Clementon, N.J. D3 74
Clemmons, N.C. A2 76
Clemson, S.C. B2 82
Clemson College, S.C. *B2 82
Clendenin, W. Va. C3, m13 87
Cleona, Pa. F9 81
Clermont, Austl. D8 25
Clermont, Que., Can. B7 42
Clermont, Fla. D5 54
Clermont, co., Ohio C1 78
Clermont-Ferrand, Fr. E5 5
Clermont-l'Hérault, Fr. F5 5
Cleveland, Miss. B3 68
Cleveland, Ohio A4, h9 78
Cleveland, Okla. A5 79
Cleveland, Tenn. D9 83
Cleveland, Tex. D5 84
Cleveland, co.,Ark. D3 49
Cleveland, co., N.C. B1 76
Cleveland, co., Okla. B4 79
Cleveland, mtn., Mont. B3 70
Cleveland Heights, Ohio A4, g9 78
Cleves, Ohio o12 78
Clewiston, Fla. F6 54
Clichy -la-Garenne, Fr. C5, g10 5
Cliffside, N.C. B1, f11 76
Cliffside Park, N.J. h9 74
Cliffwood, N.J. *C4 74
Cliffwood Beach, N.J. *C4 74
Clifton, Ariz. C4 48
Clifton, Ill. C6 58
Clifton, N.J. B4, h8 74
Clifton, S.C. B4 82
Clifton, Tex. D4 84
Clifton Forge (Independent City),
  Va. D3 85
Clifton Heights, Pa. p20 81
Clifton Springs, N.Y. C3 75
Climax, Colo. B4 51
Clinch, co., Ga. F4 55
Clinch, mtn., Tenn. f8 83
Clinchco, co., Va. e9 85
Clinchfield, N.C. *F10 76
Clingmans Dome, mtn.,
  N. Car. f9 76
Clint, Tex. o11 84
Clinton, Ark. B3 49
Clinton, B.C., Can. D7 37
Clinton, Ont., Can. D3 41
Clinton, Conn. D6 52
Clinton, Ill. D5 58
Clinton, Ind. E3 59
Clinton, Iowa C7 60
Clinton, Ky. f9 62
Clinton, La. D4 63
Clinton, Maine D3 64
Clinton, Md. C4 53
Clinton, Mass. B4 65
Clinton, Mich. F7 66
Clinton, Miss. C3 68
Clinton, Mo. C4 69

Clinton, N.J. B3 74
Clinton, N.Y. B5 75
Clinton, N.C. C4 76
Clinton, Ohio *A4 78
Clinton, Okla. B3 79
Clinton, S.C. C4 82
Clinton, Tenn. C9, m13 83
Clinton, Utah B3 72
Clinton, Wash. B3 86
Clinton, Wis. F5 88
Clinton, co., Ill. E4 58
Clinton, co., Ind. D4 59
Clinton, co., Iowa C7 60
Clinton, co., Ky. D4 62
Clinton, co., Mich. F6 66
Clinton, co., Mo. B3 69
Clinton, co., N.Y. f11 75
Clinton, co., Ohio C2 78
Clinton, co., Pa. D6 81
Clintonville, Wis. D5 88
Clintwood, Va. e9 85
Clio, Ala. D4 46
Clio, Mich. E7 66
Clio, S.C. B8 82
Cloncurry, Austl. D7 25
Clonmel, Ire. D3 4
Cloquet, Minn. D6 67
Closter, N.J. B5, h9 74
Clothier, W. Va. n12 87
Cloud, co., Kans. C6 61
Cloud, peak, Wyo. A5 89
Clover, S.C. A5 82
Cloverdale, Calif. C2 50
Cloverdale, B.C., Can. f13 37
Cloverleaf, Tex. *E5 84
Cloverport, Ky. C3 62
Clovis, Calif. D4 50
Clovis, N. Mex. B7 48
Cluj-Napoca, Rom. B6 10
Clute, Tex. r14 84
Clyde, Kans. C6 61
Clyde, N.Y. B4 75
Clyde, Ohio A3 78
Clyde, Tex. C3 84
Clydebank, Scot. C4 4
Clyde Hill, Wash. *B3 86
Clymer, Pa. E3 81
Coachella, Calif. F5 50
Coahoma, Tex. C2 84
Coahoma, co., Miss. A3 68
Coahuila, state, Mex. B4 34
Coal, co., Okla. C5 79
Coal City, Ill. B5 58
Coalcomán de
  Matamoros, Mex. D4, n12 34
Coaldale, Alta., Can. E4 38
Coaldale, Pa. E10 81
Coal Fork, W. Va. C3, m12 87
Coalgate, Okla. C5 79
Coalgood, Ky. D6 62
Coal Grove, Ohio D3 78
Coal Hill, Ark. B2 49
Coalinga, Calif. D3 50
Coalport, Pa. E4 81
Coaltown, Pa. *E1 81
Coalville, Utah A6, C2 72
Coalwood, W. Va. *D3 87
Coast, mts., B.C. B3, m16 37
Coast, ranges, Cal. B2 50
Coamo, P.R. *G11 35
Coatbridge, Scot. C5 4
Coatepec, Mex. n15 34
Coatepeque, Guat. *E6 34
Cobalt, Ont. p19 41
Cobán, guat. d6 34
Cobden, Ont.,Can. B8 41
Cobden, Ill. F4 58
Cobequid, mts., N.S., Can. D5 43
Cobh, Ire. E2 4
Cobija, Bol. E4 27
Cobleskill, N.Y. C6 75
Cobourg, Ont., Can. D6 41
Coburg, Ger. Fed. Rep. of C5 6
Coburn, mtn., Maine C2 64
Cocentaina, Sp. C5 8
Cochabamba, Bol. C2 29
Cochabamba, dept., Bol. C2 29
Cochin, India G6 20
Cochin China, reg., Viet. *D3 19
Cochise, co., Ariz. D4 48
Cochituate, Mass. g10 65
Cochran, Ga. D3 55
Cochran, co., Tex. C1 84
Cochrane, Alta., Can. D3 38
Cochrane, Ont., Can. o19 41
Cochrane, dist., Ont. e9 41
Cochranton, Pa. C1 81
Cocke, co., Tenn. D10 83
Cockeysville, Md. B4 53
Cockrell Hill, Tex. n10 84
Cocoa, Fla. D6 54
Cocoa Beach, Fla. D6 54
Cocoa West, Fla. *D6 54

Coconino, co., Ariz. B2 48
Cocula, Mex. C4, m12 34
Codington, co.,S. Dak. F8 77
Codogno, It. B2 9
Cody,Wyo. B3 89
Coeburn, Va. f9 85
Coesfeld, Ger., Fed. Rep. of C3 6
Coeur d'Alene, Idaho B2 57
Coeur d'Alene, mts., Idaho B2 57
Coffee, co., Ala. D3 46
Coffee, co., Ga. E4 55
Coffee, co., Tenn. B5 83
Coffey, co., Kans. D8 61
Coffeyville, Kans. E8 61
Coffs Harbour, Austl. E9 26
Cognac, Fr. E3 5
Cohasset, Mass. B6, h12 65
Cohocton, N.Y. C3 75
Cohoes, N.Y. C7 75
Coimbatore, India F6 20
Coimbra, Port. B1 8
Coín, Sp. D3 8
Cojedes, state, Ven. B4 32
Cojutepeque, Sal. *E7 34
Cokato, Minn. E4 67
Coke, co., Tex. D2 84
Cokeburg, Pa. *F1 81
Colac, Austl. I4 26
Cobert, co., Ala. A2 46
Colborne, Ont., Can. C7 41
Colby, Kans. C2 61
Colby, Wis. D3 88
Colchagua, prov., Chile A2 28
Colchester, Conn. C7 52
Colchester, Eng. E7 4
Colchester, Ill. C3 58
Colchester, co., N.S., Can. D6 43
Cold Lake, Alta., Can. B5 38
Cold Spring, Ky. A5, h14 62
Cold Spring, Minn. E4 67
Cold Spring, N.Y. *D7 75
Cold Spring Harbor, N.Y. F3 52
Coldwater, Kans. E4 61
Coldwater, Mich. G5 66
Coldwater, Miss. A4 68
Coldwater, Ohio B1 78
Cole, co., Mo. C5 69
Colebrook, N.H. B5 73
Cole Camp, Mo. C4 69
Coleman, Alta., Can. F3 52
Coleman, Fla. D4 54
Coleman, Mich. E6 66
Coleman, Tex. D3 84
Coleman, co., Tex. D3 84
Coleraine, Minn. C5 67
Coleraine, N. Ire. C3 4
Coles, co, Ill. D5 58
Colfax, Calif. C3 50
Colfax, Ill. C5 58
Colfax, Iowa C4 60
Colfax, La. C3 63
Colfax, Wash. C8 86
Colfax, Wis. D1 88
Colfax, co., Nebr. C8 71
Colfax, co., N. Mex. A6 48
Colima, Mex. D4, n12 34
Colima, state, Mex. D4, n12 34
College, Alsk. C10 47
Collegedale, Tenn. h11 83
College Heights, S.C. C7 82
College Park, Ga. C2, h8 55
College Park, Md. f9 53
College Place, Wash. C7 86
College Station, Tex. D4 84
Collegeville, Ind. C3 59
Collegeville (P.O.), Minn. *E4 67
Collegeville, Pa. F11 81
Colleton, co, S.C. F6 82
Colleyville, Tex. *C4 84
Collie, Austl. F2 25
Collier, co., Fla. F5 54
Collierville, Tenn. B2 83
Collin, co., Tex. C4 84
Collingdale, Pa. p20 81
Collingswood, N.J. D2 74
Collingsworth, co., Tex. B2 84
Collingwood, Ont., Can. C4 41
Collins, Miss. D4 68
Collins Park, Del. *A6 53
Collinsville, Ala. A4 46
Collinsville, Conn. B5 52
Collinsville, Ill. E4 58
Collinsville, Okla. A6 79
Collinsville, Va. *D3 85
Collister, Idaho F2 57
Colmar, Fr. C7 5
Colmar Manor, Md. f9 53
Colmenar Viejo, Sp. B4, o17 8
Cologne (Köln), Ger.,
  Fed. Rep. of C3 6
Coloma, Fla. F4 66
Colomb-Bechar, see Bechar, Alg.
Colombes, Fr. g10 5

Colombia, Col. C3 32
Colombia, country, S.A. C3 32
Colombo, Sri Lanka G6 20
Colón, Arg. A5 28
Colón, Cuba C3 35
Colon, Mich. G5 66
Colón, Pan. B2 32
Colón, Archipiélago de,
  (Galapagos Islands), is., Ec ... g5 31
Colonia, N.J. *k7 74
Colonia, dept., Ur. *E1 30
Colonia del Sacramento, Ur. E1 30
Colonia Gustavo A. Madero,
  Mex. h9 34
Colonial Beach, Va. B6 85
Colonial Heights,
  (Independent City), Va. C5, n18 85
Colonial Manor, N.J. *D2 74
Colonial Park, Pa. *F8 81
Colonia Suiza, Ur. g8 28
Colonie, N.Y. *C7 75
Colorado, co., Tex. E4 84
Colorado, state, U.S. 51
Colorado, riv., Mex., U.S. C5 45
Colorado, riv., Tex. D3 84
Colorado City, Tex. C2 84
Colorado Springs, Colo. C6 51
Colored Hill, W. Va. *D3 87
Colotlan, Mex. C4, k12 34
Colquitt, Ga. E2 55
Colquitt, co., Ga. E3 55
Colton, Calif. *E5 50
Columbia, Ill. E3 58
Columbia, Ky. C4 62
Columbia, La. B3 63
Columbia, Miss. D4 68
Columbia, Mo. C5 69
Columbia, N.C. B6 76
Columbia, Pa. F9 81
Columbia, S.C. C5 82
Columbia, Tenn. B4 83
Columbia, co., Ark. D2 49
Columbia, co., Fla. B4 54
Columbia, co., Ga. C4 55
Columbia, co., N.Y. C7 75
Columbia, co., Oreg. B3 80
Columbia, co., Pa. D8 81
Columbia, co., Wash. C7 86
Columbia, co., Wis. E4 88
Columbia, mtn., Alta, Can. C2 38
Columbia, riv., Can.,U.S. G9 36
Columbia City, Ind. B7 59
Columbia Falls, Mont. B2 70
Columbia Heights, Minn. m12 67
Columbia Heights, Wash. *C3 86
Columbiana, Ala. B3 46
Columbiana, Ohio B5 78
Columbiana, co., Ohio B5 78
Columbia Station, Ohio *A3 78
Columbiaville, Mich. E7 66
Columbus, Ga. D2 55
Columbus, Ind. F6 59
Columbus, Kans. E9 61
Columbus, Miss. B5 68
Columbus, Mont. E7 70
Columbus, Nebr. C8 71
Columbus, Ohio C3, m11 78
Columbus, Tex. E4 84
Columbus, Wis. E4 88
Columbus, co., Ga. D2 55
Columbus, co., N.C. C4 76
Columbus Grove, Ohio B1 78
Columbus Junction, Iowa *C6 60
Colusa, Calif. C2 50
Colusa, co., Calif. C2 50
Colver, Pa. E4 81
Colville, Wash. A8 86
Colwood, B.C.,Can. h12 37
Colwyn, Pa. *G11 81
Comacchio, It. B4 9
Comal, co., Tex. E3 84
Comalapa, Guat. E6 34
Comalcalco, Mex. D6 34
Comanche, Okla. C4 79
Comanche, Tex. D3 84
Comanche, co., Kans. E4 61
Comanche, co., Okla. C3 79
Comanche, co., Tex. D3 84
Combined Locks, Wis. h9 88
Combs, Ky. C6 62
Comerío, P.R. *G11 35
Comfort, Tex. E3 84
Comilla, Pak. D9 20
Comiso, It. F5 9
Comitán de Dominguez,
  Mex. D6 34
Commack, N.Y. *n15 75
Commentry, Fr. D5 5
Commerce, Calif. *E4 50
Commerce, Ga. B3 55
Commerce, Mich. *F7 66
Commerce, Okla. A7 79
Commerce, Tex. C5 84

Commerce City, Colo. B6 51
Commercy, Fr. C6 5
Communism, peak, Sov. Un. F10 13
Como, Que., Can. q18 42
Como, Colo. e11 86
Como, It. B2 9
Comodoro Rivadavia, Arg. D3 28
Comoros, country, Afr............... C8 24
Comox, B.C., Can. E5 37
Compiègne, Fr. C5 5
Compostela, Mex. m11 34
Compton, Calif. n12 50
Compton, co., Que., Can. D6 42
Comstock, Mich. F5 66
Comstock Park, Mich............... *E5 66
Conakry, Guinea G2 22
Concarneau, Fr. D2 5
Concepción, Arg. E2 29
Concepción, Chile B2 28
Concepción, prov., Chile B2 28
Concepción, Par. D4 29
Concepción, dept., Par. D4 29
Concepción del Oro, Mex. C4 34
Concepción del Uruguay, Arg. A5 28
Concho, co., Tex. D3 84
Concord, Calif. D4 50
Concord, Mass. B5, g10 65
Concord, Mich. F6 66
Concord, N.H. E4 73
Concord, N.C. B2 76
Concordia, Arg. A5 28
Concordia, Col. B2 32
Concordia, Kans. C6 61
Concordia, Mo. C4 69
Concordia, par., La. C4 63
Concrete, Wash. A4 86
Condobolin, Austl. F8 25
Condon, Oreg. B6 80
Conecuh, co., Ala. D2 46
Conegliano, It. B4 9
Conejos, co., Colo. D4 51
Conemaugh, Pa. F4 81
Conflans-Ste. Honorine, Fr. g9 5
Confluence, Pa. G3 81
Congamond, Mass. B2 65
Congers, N.Y. *D7 75
Congo, country, Afr. I7 22
Congo, The (Republic of
the Congo), see Zaire, country, Afr.
Congo (Zaire), riv., Afr. H2 21
Conil, Sp. D2 8
Coniston, Ont., Can. A4, p19 41
Conjeeveram, see
Kanchipuram, India
Connacht, prov., Ire. *D2 4
Conneaut, Ohio A5 78
Conneautville, Pa. C1 81
Connecticut, state, U.S. 52
Connell, Wash. C7 86
Connellsville, Pa. F2 81
Connersville, Ind. E7 59
Conning Towers, Conn. *D8 52
Conover, N.C. B1 76
Conrad, Iowa B5 60
Conrad, Mont. B5 70
Conroe, Tex. D5 84
Conselheiro Lafaiete, Braz. C4 30
Conshohocken, Pa. F11, o20 81
Consolación del Sur, Cuba C2 35
Constanţa, Rom. C9 10
Constantia, N.Y. B5 75
Constantina, Sp. D3 8
Constantine, Alg. A6 22
Constantine, Mich................... G5 66
Constantinople, see Istanbul,
Tur.
Continental, peak, Wyo............. D4 89
Constitución, Chile B2 28
Consuegra, Sp. C4 8
Contamana, Peru C2 31
Continental, Ohio A1 78
Contra Costa, co., Calif. D2 50
Contratación, Col. B3 32
Contrecoeur, Que., Can. D4 42
Contreras, Mex. h9 34
Contumaza, Peru C2 31
Convent, La. D5, h10 63
Converse, Ind. C6 59
Converse, S.C. B4 82
Converse, co., Wyo. C7 89
Convoy, Ohio B1 78
Conway, Ark. B3 49
Conway, Fla. *D5 54
Conway, N.H. D5 73
Conway, Pa. E1 81
Conway, S.C. D9 82
Conway, co., Ark. B3 49
Conway Springs, Kans. E6 61
Conyers, Ga. C2, h8 55
Cooch Behar, India C8 20
Cook, co., Ga. E3 55
Cook, co., Ill. B6 58

Cook, co.,Minn..................... C8 67
Cooke, co., Tex. C4 84
Cookeville, Tenn. C8 83
Cookshire, Que., Can. D6 42
Cookstown, Ont., Can. C5 41
Cooleemee, N.C. B2 76
Coolidge, Ariz. C3, E2 48
Coolidge, Tex. D4 84
Cool Ridge, W. Va. D3 87
Cool Valley, Mo. *C7 69
Cooma, Austl. G8 25
Coonabarabran, Austl. F8 25
Coonamble, Austl. F8 25
Coon Rapids, Iowa C3 60
Coon Rapids, Minn. m12 67
Cooper, Tex. C5 84
Copper, co., Mo. C5 69
Coopersburg, Pa. E11 81
Cooperstown, N.Y. C6 75
Cooperstown, N. Dak. C7 77
Coopersville, Mich. E5 66
Coos, co., N.H. B5 73
Coos, co., Oreg. D2 80
Coosa, co., Ala. C3 46
Coos Bay, Oreg. D2 80
Cootamundra, Austl. G7 26
Copainalá, Mex. D6 34
Copenhagen (København), Den. J5 11
Copiague, N.Y. G3 52
Copiah, co., Miss. D3 68
Copiapó, Chile E1 29
Coplay, Pa. *E10 81
Copley, Ohio *A4 78
Copparo, It. B3 9
Copper, mtn., Wyo. C5 89
Copperas Cove, Tex. D4 84
Copper Cliff, Ont., Can. A3 41
Copperhill, Tenn. D9 83
Coquille, Oreg. D2 80
Coquimbo, Chile E1 29
Coquimbo, prov., Chile A2 28
Corabia, Rom. D7 10
Coracora, Peru E3 31
Coral Gables, Fla. G6, s13 54
Coralville, Iowa D6 60
Coram, N.Y. n15 75
Coraopolis, Pa. E1, h13 81
Corato, It. D6 9
Corbeil, Fr. C5 5
Corbin, Ky. D5 62
Corcoran, Calif. D4 50
Corcoran, Minn. *E5 67
Cordele, Ga. E3 55
Cordell, Okla. B3 79
Cordillera, dept., Par. D4 29
Córdoba, Arg. A4 28
Córdoba, Mex. n15 34
Córdoba, Sp. D3 8
Córdoba, prov.,Sp. *D3 8
Córdoba, prov., Arg. A4 28
Cordova, Ala. B2 46
Cordova, Alsk. C10, g19 47
Cordova, N.C. C3 76
Córdova, Peru D2 31
Cori, It. h9 9
Corigliano, It. E6 9
Corinna, Maine D3 64
Corinne, W. Va. D3 87
Corinth, Miss. A5 68
Corinth, N.Y. B7 75
Corinth, see Korinthos, Grc.
Corinto, Braz. B4 30
Corinto, Nic. H12 33
Cork, Ire. E2 4
Cork, co., Ire. E3 4
Corleone, It. F4 9
Çorlu, Tur. B6 14
Cormeilles-en-Parisis, Fr. g9 5
Cornelia, Ga. B3 55
Cornelius, N.C. B2 76
Cornelius, Oreg. g11 80
Cornell, Wis. C2 88
Corner Brook, Newf., Can. D3 44
Corning, Ark. A5 49
Corning, Calif. C2 50
Corning, Iowa D3 60
Corning, N.Y. C3 75
Corning, Ohio C3 78
Corno, mtn., It. C4 9
Cornwall, Ont., Can. B10 41
Cornwall, N.Y. D6 75
Cornwall, Pa. F9 81
Cornwall, see Cornwall-on-
the-Hudson, N.Y.
Cornwall, co. ,Eng. *E4 4
Cornwall-on-the-Hudson, N.Y........ D6 75
Cornwells Heights, Pa. o22 81
Coro, Ven. A4 31
Corona, Calif. F5, n13 50
Coronado, Calif. F5, o15 50
Coronation, Alta., Can. C5 38
Coronel, Chile B2 28
Coronel Dorrego, Arg. B4 28

Coronel Oviedo, Par. E4 29
Coronel Pringles, Arg. B4 28
Coronel Suárez, Arg. B4 28
Coropuna, mtn., Peru E3 31
Corozal, Col. B2 32
Corpus Christi, Tex. F4 84
Corral de Almaguer, Sp. C4 8
Corrales, Col. B3 32
Corralillo, Cuba C3 35
Correctionville, Iowa B2 60
Corréze, dept., Fr. *E4 5
Corrientes, Arg. E4 29
Corrigan, Tex. D5 84
Corry, Pa. C2 81
Corse, dept., Fr. *C2 9
Corisica, isl. , Eur. C2 9
Corsicana, Tex. C4 84
Corson, co., S. Dak. E4 77
Cortazar, Mex. C4, m13 34
Cortegana, Sp. D2 8
Corte Madera, Calif. *C2 50
Cortez, Colo. D1 51
Cortez, Fla. q10 54
Cortland, N.Y. C4 75
Cortland, Ohio A5 78
Cortland, co., N.Y. C4 75
Cortona, It. C3 9
Corumbá, Braz. B1 30
Çorum (Chorum), Tur. B10 14
Corunna, Ont., Can. E2 41
Corvallis, Oreg. C3, k11 80
Corunna, Mich. F6 66
Corydon, Ind. H5 59
Corydon, Iowa D4 60
Coryell, co., Tex. D4 84
Cosalá, Mex. C3 34
Cosamaloapan de Carpio, Mex. D5 34
Coscomatepec de Bravo, Mex. n15 34
Cosenza, It. E6 9
Coshocton, Ohio B4 78
Coshocton, co., Ohio B3 78
Cosmopolis, Wash. C2 86
Cosne -sur-Loire, Fr. C5 5
Costa Mesa, Calif. n13 50
Costa Rica, country, N.A. E8 34
Costilla, N. Mex. A6 48
Costilla, co., Colo. D5 51
Cotabato, Phil. D6 19
Cotabato, prov., Phil *D6 19
Cotahuasi, Peru D2 31
Cotati,Calif. *C2 50
Côte-d'or, dept., Fr. *D6 5
Côtes-du-Nord, dept., Fr. *C2 5
Côtes-St. Luc., Que., Can. *D4 42
Cotija de la Paz, Mex. n12 34
Cotonou, Benin G5 22
Cotopaxi, prov., Ec. B2 31
Cotopaxi, vol., Ec. A2 31
Cottage City, Md. *C4 53
Cottage Grove, Oreg. D3 80
Cottage Grove, Wis. *E4 88
Cottage Hills, Ill. *E3 58
Cottbus, Ger. Dem. Rep. C7 6
Cotter, Ark. A3 49
Cottle, co., Tex. B2 84
Cotton, co., Okla. C3 79
Cottondale, Fla. B1, u16 54
Cotton Plant, Ark. B4 49
Cottonport, La. D3 63
Cotton Valley, La. B2 63
Cottonwood, Ala. D4 46
Cottonwood, Ariz. B3 48
Cottonwood, Calif. B2 50
Cottonwood, Idaho C2 57
Cottonwood, co., Minn. F3 67
Cottonwood Falls, Kans. D6 61
Cottonwood Heights, Utah D2 72
Cotuit, Mass. C7 65
Cotulla, Tex. E3 84
Coudekerque-Branche, Fr. B5 5
Coudersport, Pa. C5 81
Coulee City, Wash. B6 86
Coulee Dam, Wash. B7 86
Coulommiers, Fr. C5 5
Coulterville, Ill. D4 58
Council, Idaho E2 57
Council,mtn., Idaho E2 57
Council Bluffs, Iowa C2 60
Council Grove, Kans. D7 61
Country Club Hills, Ill. *B6 58
Country Club Hills, Mo. *C7 69
Country Homes, Wash. *B8 86
Coupar Angus, Scot. B5 4
Courbevoie, Fr. g10 5
Courtdale, Pa. *D9 81
Courtenay, B.C., Can. E5 37
Courtland, Calif. *C3 50
Courtland, Va. D5 85
Courtrai, see Kortrijk, Bel.
Coushatta, La. B2 63
Coutances, Fr. C3 5
Coutras, Fr. E3 5

Covedale, Ohio o12 78
Covelo, Calif. C2 50
Coventry, Conn. B7 52
Coventry, Eng. D6 4
Coventry, R.I. C10 52
Covilhã, Port. B2 8
Covina, Calif. m13 50
Covington, Ga. C3 55
Covington, Ind. D3 59
Covington, Ky. A5, h13 62
Covington, La. D5, h11 63
Covington, Ohio B1 78
Covington, Tenn. B2 83
Covington, (Independent City)
Va. C3 85
Covington, co., Ala. D3 46
Covington, co., Miss. D4 68
Cowan, Tenn. B5 83
Cowansville, Que., Can. D5 42
Cowansville, Pa. E2 81
Cowen, mtn., Mont. E6 70
Cowes, Eng. E6 4
Coweta, Okla. B6 79
Coweta, co., Ga. C2 55
Cowley, co., Kans. E7 61
Cowlitz, co., Wash. C3 86
Cowpens, S.C. A4 82
Cowra, Austl. F7 26
Coxsackie, N.Y. C7 75
Coyame, Mex. B3 34
Coyoacán, Mex. H9, n14 34
Coyuca de Catalán, Mex. n13 34
Cozad, Nebr. D6 71
Cozumel, Mex. C7 34
Crab Orchard, W. Va. n13 87
Crabtree, Pa. F3 81
Crabtree Mills, Que., Can. D4 42
Cradock, S. Afr. G5 24
Crafton, Pa. k13 81
Craig, Colo. A3 51
Craig, co., Okla. A6 79
Craig, co., Va. C2 85
Craig Beach, Ohio *B5 78
Craighead, co., Ark. B5 49
Craigsville, Va. B3 85
Crailsheim, Ger., Fed. Rep of D5 6
Craiova, Rom. C6 10
Cramerton, N.C. B1 76
Cranberry Portage, Man., Can. B10 40
Cranbrook, B.C.,Can. E10 37
Cranbury, N.J. C3 74
Crandon, Wis. C5 88
Crane, Mo. E4 39
Crane, Tex. D1 84
Crane, co., Tex. D1 84
Crane, mtn., Oreg. E6 80
Cranford, N.J. B4 74
Cranston, R.I. B11 52
Crateús, Braz. *D6 27
Crato, Braz. *D7 27
Craven, co., N.C. B5 76
Crawford, Nebr. B2 71
Crawford, co., Ark. B1 49
Crawford, co., Ga. D2 55
Crawford, co., Ill. D6 58
Crawford, co., Ind. H4 59
Crawford, co., Iowa B2 60
Crawford, co., Kans. E9 61
Crawford, co., Mich. D6 66
Crawford, co., Mo. D6 69
Crawford, co., Ohio B2 78
Crawford, co., Pa. C1 81
Crawford, co., Wis. E3 88
Crawfordsville, Ind. D4 59
Crawfordville, Ga. C4 55
Crazy, peak, Mont. D6 70
Creedmoor, N.C. A4 76
Creek, co., Okla. B5 79
Creemore, Ont., Can. C4 41
Creighton, Sask., Can. C5 39
Creighton, Nebr. B8 71
Creighton, Pa. h14 81
Creighton Mine, Ont., Can. A3, p19 41
Creil, Fr. C5 5
Crema, It. B2 9
Cremona, It. B3 9
Crenshaw, Miss. A3 68
Crenshaw, co., Ala. D3 46
Cresaptown, Md. k13 53
Crescent, Okla. B4 79
Crescent City, Calif. B1 50
Crescent City, Fla. C5 54
Crescent City Northwest, Calif. ... *B1 50
Crescent Springs, Ky. h13 62
Cresco, Iowa A5 60
Cresskill, N.J. h9 74
Cresson, Pa. F4 81
Cressona, Pa. E9 81
Crest, Fr. E6 4
Crest Hill, Ill. *B5 58
Crestline, Calif. *E5 50
Crestline, Ohio B3 78
Crestmont, Pa. *F11 81

Creston, B.C., Can.	E9 37	Cross Plains, Tex.	C3 84
Creston, Newf., Can.	E4 44	Cross Plains, Wis.	E4 88
Creston, Iowa	C3 60	Crossville, Ill.	E5 58
Creston, Ohio	B4 78	Crossville, Tenn.	D8 83
Crestview, Fla.	u15 54	Croswell, Mich.	E8 66
Crestwood, Ill.	*B6 58	Crothersville, Ind.	G6 59
Crestwood, Mo.	*C7 69	Crotone, It.	E6 9
Crete, Ill.	B6, m9 58	Croton-on-Hudson, N.Y.	D7, m15 75
Crete, Nebr.	D9 71	Crouse, N.C.	B1 76
Crete, isl., Grc.	E5 14	Crow, peak, Mont.	D5 70
Crete, sea, Grc.	E5 14	Crow Agency, Mont.	E9 70
Creuse, dept., Fr.	*D4 5	Crowell, Tex.	C3 84
Creutzwald, Fr.	C7 5	Crowley, La.	D3 63
Creve Coeur, Ill.	C4 58	Crowley, co., Colo.	C7 51
Creve Coeur, Mo.	*C7 69	Crown Point, Ind.	B3 59
Crevillente, Sp.	C5 8	Crown Point, N.Y.	B7 75
Crewe, Eng.	D5 4	Crow Wing, co., Minn.	D4 67
Crewe, Va.	C4 85	Croydon, Pa.	F12 81
Cricket, N.C.	A1 76	Crozet, Va.	B4 85
Cridersville, Ohio	B1 78	Cruces, Cuba	C3 35
Crieff, Scot.	B5 4	Crucible, Pa.	G1 81
Crimmitschau, Ger. Dem. Rep.	C6 6	Cruden Bay, Scot.	B6 4
Crisana, reg., Rom.	B6 10	Crum Lynne, Pa.	*E1 81
Crisfield, Md.	E6 53	Cruz Alta, Braz.	D2 30
Crisp, co., Ga.	E3 55	Cruz del Eje, Arg.	A4 28
Cristóbal Colón, mtn., Col.	A3 32	Cruzeiro, Braz.	C4 30
Crittenden, co., Ark.	B5 49	Crystal, Minn.	m12 67
Crittenden, co., Ky.	e9 62	Crystal Beach, Fla.	D4 54
Croatia, reg. Yugo.	*C2 10	Crystal City, Mo.	C7, g13 69
Croatia, rep., Yugo.	C2 10	Crystal City, Tex.	E3 84
Crocker, Mo.	D5 69	Crystal Falls, Mich.	B2 66
Crockett, Calif.	g8 50	Crystal Lake, Fla.	u16 54
Crockett, Tex.	D5 84	Crystal Lake, Ill.	A5, h8 58
Crockett, co., Tenn.	B2 83	Crystal Lakes, Ohio	C1 78
Crockett, co., Tex.	B2 84	Crystal River, Fla.	D4 54
Croghan, N.Y.	B5 75	Crystal Springs, Miss.	D3 68
Cromona, Ky.	C7 62	Csongrád, Hung.	B5 10
Cromwell, Conn.	C6 52	Csongrád, co., Hung.	*B5 10
Crook, co., Oreg.	C6 80	Csorna, Hung.	B3 10
Crook, co., Wyo.	B8 89	Cuajimalpa, Mex.	h9 34
Crookston, Minn.	C2 67	Cuauhtémoc, Mex.	B3 34
Crooksville, Ohio	C3 78	Cuautepec, Mex.	g9 34
Crosby, Minn.	D5 67	Cuautla, Mex.	n14 34
Crosby, Miss.	D2 68	Cuba, Ill.	C3 58
Crosby, N. Dak.	A2 77	Cuba, Mo.	C6 69
Crosby, Tex.	r14 84	Cuba, N.Y.	C2 75
Crosby, co., Tex.	C2 84	Cuba, country, N.A.	C3 35
Crosby, mtn., Wyo.	C3 89	Cuba City, Wis.	F3 88
Crosbyton, Tex.	C2 84	Cucamonga, Calif.	*E5 50
Cross, co., Ark.	B5 49	Cúcuta, Col.	B3 32
Cross City, Fla.	C3 54	Cudahy, Calif.	*F4 50
Crossett, Ark.	D4 49	Cudahy, Wis.	F6, n12 88
Cross Mill, N.C.	f10 76	Cuddalore, India	F6 20

Cuddapah, India	F6 20	Cunnamulla, Austl.	E8 25
Cuddy, Pa.	*B5 81	Cupertino, Calif.	*D2 50
Cuenca, Ec.	B2 31	Curaçao, isl.,Neth.	
Cuenca, Sp.	B4 8	Antilles	A4 32
Cuenca, prov. Sp.	*B4 8	Curacautín, Chile	B2 28
Cuencamé de Ceniceros, Mex.	C4 34	Curicó, Chile	B2 28
Cuernavaca, Mex.	D5, n14 34	Curicó, prov., Chile	A2 28
Cuero, Tex	E4 84	Curitiba, Braz.	D3 30
Cuetzalan, Mex.	m15 34	Currais Novos, Braz.	*D7 27
Cuevas, Sp.	D5 8	Currituck, co.,N.C.	A6 76
Cuiabá, Braz.	B1 30	Curry, co., N. Mex.	B7 48
Cuicatlán, Mex.	o15 34	Curry, co., Oreg.	E2 80
Culberson, co., Tex.	o12 84	Curtea-de-Arges, Rom.	C7 10
Culbertson, Mont.	B12 70	Curtici, Rom.	B5 10
Culbertson, Nebr.	D5 71	Curtis, Nebr.	D5 71
Culhuacán, Mex.	h9 34	Curtisville, Pa.	E1, h14 81
Culiacán, Mex.	C3 34	Curug, Yugo.	C5 10
Cúllar de Baza, Sp.	D4 8	Curuzú Cuatia, Arg.	E4 29
Cullen, La.	B2 63	Curvelo, Braz.	B4 30
Cullera, Sp.	C5 8	Curwensville, Pa.	E4 81
Cullman, Ala.	A3 46	Cushing, Okla.	B5 79
Cullman, co., Ala.	A3 46	Cusset, Fr.	D5 5
Culloden, W. Va.	*C2 87	Custer, S. Dak.	G2 77
Cullowhee, N.C.	f9 76	Custer, co., Colo.	C5 51
Culmore, Va.	*B5 85	Custer, co., Idaho	E4 57
Culpeper, Va.	B4 85	Custer, co., Mont.	D11 70
Culpeper, co., Va.	B5 85	Custer, co., Nebr.	C6 79
Culver, Ind.	B5 59	Custer, co., Okla.	B2 71
Culver City, Calif.	m12 50	Custer, co., S. Dak.	G2 77
Cumaná, Ven.	A5 32	Cut Bank, Mont.	B4 70
Cumberland, B.C., Can.	E5 37	Cutchogue, N.Y.	m16 75
Cumberland, Ind.	E6, k11 59	Cutervo, Peru	C2 31
Cumberland, Ky.	D7 62	Cuthbert, Ga.	E2 55
Cumberland, Md.	k13 53	Cutler, Calif.	*D4 50
Cumberland, Wis.	C2 88	Cutler Ridge, Fla.	*G6 54
Cumberland, co., N.S., Can.	D5 43	Cutack, India	D8 20
Cumberland, co., Eng.	*C5 4	Cutten, Calif.	*B1 50
Cumberland, co.,Ill.	D5 58	Cuxhaven, Ger., Fed. Rep. of	B4 6
Cumberland, co., Ky.	D4 62	Cuyahoga, co., Ohio	A4 78
Cumberland, co., Maine	E2 64	Cuyahoga Falls, Ohio	A4 78
Cumberland, co., N.J.	E2 74	Cuzco, Peru	D3 31
Cumberland, co., N.C.	C4 76	Cuzco, dept., Peru	D3 31
Cumberland, co., Pa.	F7 81	Cynthiana, Ky.	B5 62
Cumberland, co., Tenn.	D8 83	Cypress, Calif.	*F4 50
Cumberland, co., Va.	C4 85	Cypress Quarters, Fla.	E6 54
Cumberland, mtn., Ky., Tenn.	*C9 83	Cyprus, country, Asia	E9 14
Cumberland, riv., U.S.	C10 45	Cyprus, isl., Asia	E9 14
Cuming, co., Nebr.	C9 71	Cyrenaica, prov., Libya	B2 23
Cumming, Ga.	B2 55	Cyril, Okla.	C3 79
Cumpas, Mex.	A3 34	Czechoslovakia, country, Eur.	D4 7
Çumra, Tur.	D9 14	Czersk, Pol.	B4 7
Cundinamarca, dept., Col.	C3 32	Częstochowa, Pol.	C5 7
Cuneo, It.	B1 9		

D

Da'an, China	D2 18	Dahlonega, Ga.	B3 55
Dab, Pol., (part of Katowice)	g9 7	Dailey, W. Va.	C5 87
Dab, Pol., (part of Szczecin)	B3 7	Daimiel, Sp.	C4 8
Dabeiba, Col.	B2 32	Daingerfield, Tex.	C5 84
Dablice, Czech.	n18 7	Daio, Jap.	o15 18
Dąbrowa, Pol.	C6 7	Dairen, see Lüda, China	
Dąbrowa Gornicza, Pol.	C5, g10 7	Dairy Valley, Calif.	*F4 50
Dacca, see Dhaka, Bngl.		Daisetta, Tex.	D5 84
Dachau, Ger., Fed. Rep. of	D5 6	Daisytown, Pa.	*F1 81
Dade,co., Fla	G6 54	Dajabon, Dom. Rep.	E8 35
Dade, co., Ga.	B1 55	Dakar, Sen.	F1 22
Dade, co., Mo.	D4 69	Dakota, co., Minn.	F5 67
Dade City, Fla.	D4 54	Dakota, co., Nebr.	B9 71
Dadeville, Ala.	C4 46	Dakota City, Nebr.	B9 71
Dadra and Nagar Haveli,		Da Lat, Viet.	C3 19
ter., India	*D5 20	D'Albertis Dome, mtn.,	
Dadu, Pak.	C4 20	Pap. N. Gui.	h11 25
Daet, Phil.	*C6 19	Dalby, Austl.	E9 25
Daggett, co., Utah	A7 72	Dale, Ind.	H4 59
Dagupan, Phil	n13 19	Dale, Pa.	*E4 81
Dahlgren, Va.	B5 85	Dale, co., Ala.	D4 46

Daleville, Ind.	D6 59	Dalnyaya, Sov. Un.	D11 18
Dalhart, Tex.	A1 84	Dalrymple, mtn., Austl.	D8 25
Dalhousie, N.B., Can.	A3 43	Dalton, Ga.	B2 55
Dall, mtn., Alsk.	f15 47	Dalton, Mass.	B1 65
Dallam, co., Tex.	A1 84	Dalton, Ohio	B4 78
Dallas, Ga.	C2 55	Dalton, Pa.	C10 81
Dallas, N.C.	B1 76	Daltonganj, India	D7 20
Dallas, Oreg.	C3 80	Dalton Gardens, Idaho	B2 57
Dallas, Pa.	D10, m17 81	Daly City, Calif.	h8 50
Dallas, Tex.	C4, n10 84	Damān, India	D5 20
Dallas, co., Ala.	C2 46	Damanhûr, Eg.	G8 14
Dallas, co., Ark.	D3 49	Damariscotta, Maine	D3 64
Dallas, co., Iowa	C3 60	Damascus, Md.	B3 53
Dallas, co., Mo.	D4 69	Damascus, Va.	f10 85
Dallas, co., Tex.	C4 84	Damascus (Dimashq), Syr.	F11 14
Dallas Center, Iowa	C4 60	Da Nang, Viet.	B3 19
Dallas City, Ill.	C2 58	Dana Point, Calif.	*F5 50
Dallastown, Pa.	G8 81	Danbury, Conn.	D3 52
Dalmatia, reg., Yugo	*D3 10	Dandong, China	C9 17
Dalmellington, Scot.	C4 4	Dane, co., Wis.	E4 88
Dalnerechensk, Sov. Un.	E16 13	Dania, Fla.	F6, r13 54

Daniels, co., Mont. B11 70
Danielson, Conn. B9 52
Dannemora, N.Y. f11 75
Dannevirke, N.Z. N16 26
Dans, mtn., Md. k13 53
Dansalan, Phil. *D6 19
Dansville, N.Y. C3 75
Dante, Som. F8 23
Dante, Va. f9 85
Danube, riv., Eur. F10 3
Danubyu, Bur. *E10 20
Danvers, Mass. A6, f12 65
Danville, Ark. B2 49
Danville, Calif. h9 50
Danville, Que., Can. D5 42
Danville, Ill. C6 58
Danville, Ind. E4 59
Danville, Ky. C5 62
Danville, Ohio B3 78
Danville, Pa. E8 81
Danville (Independent City), Va. D3 85
Danville East, Pa. *D8 81
Danzig see Gdánsk, Pol.
Daphne, Ala. E2 46
Dar'a, Syr. F11 14
Darabani, Rom. A8 10
Darasun, Sov. Un. D14 13
Darbhanga, India C8 20
Darby, Pa. G11, p20 81
Dardanelle, Ark. B2 49
Dare, co., N.C. B7 76
Darenbe, Tur. C11 14
Dar-es-Salaam, Tan. B7 24
Darien, Conn. E3 52
Darien, Wis. F5 88
Darjeeling, India C8 20
Dark Cove, Newf., Can. *D4 44
Darke, co., Ohio B1 78
Darling Rante, mts., Austl. F2 25
Darling, riv., Aust. E5 26
Darlington, Eng. C6 4
Darlington, S.C. C8 82
Darlington, Wis. F3 88
Darlington, co., S.C. C7 82
Darlowo, Pol. A4 7
Darmstadt, Ger., Fed.
    Rep. of D4 6
Darnah (Derna), Libya. B2 23
Darrah, mtn., Alta. E3 38
Darrington, Wash. A4 86
Darrow, La. h10 63
Dartmouth, N.S., Can. E6 43
Dartmouth, Eng. E5 4
Daruvar, Yugo. C3 10
Darwin, Austl. B5 25
Dassel, Minn. E4 67
Datong, China D7 17
Daugavpils, Sov. Un. D6 12
Dauphin, Man., Can. D1, g7 40
Dauphin, co., Pa. F8 81
Dauphiné, former prov., Fr. E6 5
Davao, Phil. D7 19
Davao, prov., Phil. *D7 19
Davenport, Fla. D5 54
Davenport, Iowa C7, g10 60
Davenport, Okla. B5 79
Davenport, Wash. B7 86
David, Pan. B1 32
David City, Nebr. C8 71
Davidson, Sask., Can. F3 39
Davidson, N.C. B2 76
Davidson, co., N.C. B2 76
Davidson, co., Tenn. A5 83
Davie, Fla. F6, r13 54
Davie, co., N.C. B2 76
Daviess, co., Ind. G3 59
Daviess, co., Ky. C2 72
Daviess, co., Mo. B3 69
Davis, Calif. C3 50
Davis, Okla. C4 79
Davis, W. Va. B5 87
Davis, co., Iowa D4 60
Davis, co., Utah A5 72
Davis, mtn. Pa. G3 81
Davison, Mich. E7 66
Davison, co., S. Dak. G7 77
Davisville, R.I. C11 52
Davos, Switz. E4 6
Davy, W. Va. D3 87
Dawes, co., Nebr. B2 71
Dawson, Ga. E2 55
Dawson, Minn. F2 67
Dawson, Tex. D4 84
Dawson, co., Ga. B2 55
Dawson, co., Mont. C11 70
Dawson, co., Nebr. D6 71
Dawson, co., Tex. C1 84
Dawson, mtn., B.C., Can. D9 37
Dawson Creek, B.C., Can. B7, m8 37
Dawson Springs, Ky. C2 62
Dax, Fr. F3 5
Daxian, China E6 17

Day, co., S. Dak. E8 77
Dayrūt, Eg. C4 23
Dayton, Ky. h14 62
Dayton, Ohio C1 78
Dayton, Tenn. D8 83
Dayton, Tex. D5, q15 84
Dayton, Va. B4 85
Dayton, Wash. C8 86
Daytona Beach, Fla. C5 54
Daytona Beach Shores, Fla. *C6 54
De Aar, S. Afr. G4 24
Dead Indian, peak, Wyo. B3 89
Dead Knoll, mtn., Wyo. D2 89
Deadwood, S. Dak. F2 77
Deaf Smith, co., Tex. B1 84
Deal N.J. C4 74
Deale, Md. C4 53
Déan Funes, Arg. A4 28
Dearborn, Mich. F7, p15 66
Dearborn, co., Ind. F8 59
Dearborn Heights, Mich. p15 66
Death, valley, Calif. D5 50
Deauville, Fr. C4 5
De Baca, co., N. Mex. B6 48
Debaltsevo, Sov. Un. q21 12
Debar, Yugo. E5 10
De Bary, Fla. D5 54
Dębica, Pol. C6 7
Dębno, Pol. B3 7
Deboullie, mtn., Maine B4 64
Debrecen, Hung. B5 10
Decatur, Ala. A3 46
Decatur, Ga. C2, h8 55
Decatur, Ill. D5 58
Decatur, Ind. C8 59
Decatur, Mich. F5 66
Decatur, Miss. C4 68
Decatur, Tex. C4 84
Decatur, co., Ga. F2 55
Decatur, co., Ind. F6 59
Decatur, co., Iowa D5 60
Decatur, co., Kans. C3 61
Decatur, co., Tenn. B3 83
Decazeville, Fr. E5 5
Deccan, reg., India E6 20
Deception, mtn.,Wash. B2 86
Decherd, Tenn. B5 83
Děčín, Czech. C3 7
Decorah, Iowa A6 60
Dededo, Guam *F6 2
Dedham, Mass. B5, h11 65
Dedinovo, Sov. Un. n19 12
Dedu, China B3 18
Deephaven, Minn. F5, n11 67
Deep River, Ont., Can. A7 41
Deep River, Conn. D7 52
Deepwater, N.J. D2 74
Deer, mtn., Maine C2 74
Deerfield, Ill. h9 58
Deerfield, Mich. G7 66
Deerfield Beach, Fla. F6 54
Deer Lake, Newf., Can. D3 44
Deer Lodge, Mont. D4 70
Deer Lodge, co., Mont. D3 70
Deer Park, N.Y. *F3 75
Deer Park, Wash. B8 86
Deer Park, Ohio o13 78
Deer Park, Tex. *E5 84
Deer River, Minn. C5 67
Defense Highway, Md. *C4 53
Defiance, Ohio A1 78
Defiance, co., Ohio A1 78
Defiance, mtn., Oreg. B5 80
De Forest, Wis. E4 88
De Funiak Springs, Fla. u15 54
Dégê, China E4 17
Deggendorf, Ger., Fed.
    Rep. of D6 6
De Graff, Ohio B2 78
Dehiwaia-Mount Lavinia,
    Sri Lanka. *G7 20
Dehra Dūn, India B6 20
Dej, Rom. B6 10
De Kalb, Ill. B5 58
De Kalb, Miss. C5 68
De Kalb, Tex. C5 84
De Kalb, co., Ala. A4 46
De Kalb, co., Ga. C2 55
De Kalb, co., Ill. B5 58
De Kalb, co., Ind. B7 59
De Kalb, co., Mo. B3 69
De Kalb, co., Tenn. D8 83
Delafield, Wis. *E5 88
Del Aire, Calif. *F4 50
Delanco, N.J. C3 74
De Land, Fla. C5 54
Delano, Calif. E4 50
Delano, Minn. E5 67
Delavan, Ill. C4 58
Delavan, Wis. F5 88
Delaware, Ohio B2 78
Delaware, co., Ind. D7 59

Delaware, co., Iowa B6 60
Delaware, co., N.Y. C5 75
Delaware, co., Ohio B2 78
Delaware, co., Okla. A7 79
Delaware, co., Pa. G11 81
Delaware, state, U.S. C11 45
Delaware, bay, Del. B7 53
Delaware City, Del. A6 53
Delbarton, W. Va. D2 87
Delcambre, La. E4 63
Del city, Okla. B4 79
Delemont, Switz. E3 6
De Leon, Tex. C3 84
De Leon Springs, Fla. C5 54
Delft, Neth. A6 5
Delfzijl, Neth. A7 5
Delhi, Calif. *D3 50
Delhi, Ont., Can. E4 41
Delhi, India C6 20
Delhi, ter., India *C6 20
Delhi, La. B4 63
Delhi, N.Y. C6 75
Delhi Hills, Ohio *C1 78
Delisle, Que., Can. A6 42
Delitzsch, Ger. Dem. Rep. C6 6
Dell Rapids, S. Dak. G9 77
Dellenbaugh, mtn., Ariz. A2 48
Dellwood, Mo. *C7 69
Del Mar, Calif. o15 50
Delmar, Del. D6 53
Delmar, Md. D6 53
Delmar, N.Y. C7 75
Delmenhorst, Ger., Fed.
    Rep. of B4 6
Delmont, Pa. *F2 81
Del Monte Park, Calif. *D3 50
Del Norte, Colo. D4 51
Del Norte, co., Calif. B2 50
Deloraine, Man., Can. E1 40
Delphi, Ind. C4 59
Delphos, Ohio B1 78
Delran, N.J. C3 74
Delray Beach, Fla. F6 54
Del Rey Oaks, Calif. *D3 50
Del Rio, Tex. E2 84
Delson, Que., Can. q19 42
Delta, Colo. C2 51
Delta, Ohio A2 78
Delta, Pa. G9 81
Delta, Utah B5 72
Delta, co., Colo. C3 51
Delta, co., Mich. G3 66
Delta, co., Tex. C5 84
Delta, peak, B.C., Can. A3 37
Delta Amacuro, ter., Ven. B5 32
Deltaville, Va. C6 85
Demarest, N.J. h9 74
Demavend, mtn.,Iran F8 16
Demidov, Sov.,Un. D8 12
Deming, N. Mex. C5 48
Demirci, Tur. C7 14
Demmin, Ger., Dem. Rep. B6 6
Demopolis, Ala. C2 46
Demorest, Ga. B3 55
Demotte, Ind. B3 59
Dempo, mtn., Indon. F2 19
Denain, Fr. B5 5
Denbigh, Wales D5 4
Denbigh, co., Wales. *D5 4
Denham Springs, La. D5, h10 63
Den Helder, Neth. A6 5
Denia, Sp. C6 8
Deniliquin, Austl. G7 25
Denison, Iowa B2 60
Denison, Tex. C4 84
Denizli, Tur. D7 14
Denmark, S.C. E5 82
Denmark, Wis. D6, h10 88
Denmark, country, Eur. I3 11
Dennison, Ohio B4 78
Dennis Port, Mass. C7 65
Denny Terrace, S.C. C5 82
Denpasar, Indon. G5 19
Dent, co., Mo. D6 69
Denton, Ga. E4 55
Denton, Md. C6 53
Denton, N.C. B2 76
Denton, Tex. C4 84
Denton, co., Tex. C4 84
Dentsville, S.C. C6 82
Denver, Colo. B6 51
Denver, Iowa B5 60
Denver, Pa. F9 81
Denver, co., Colo. B6 51
Denver City, Tex. C1 84
Denville, N.J. *B4 74
Departure Bay, B.C., Can. f12 37
De Pere, Wis. D5, h9 88
Depew, N.Y. C2 75
Deposit, N.Y. C5 75
Depue, Ill. B4 58
De Queen, Ark. C1 49
De Quincy, La. D2 63

Dera Ghazi Khan, Pak. B5 20
Dera Ismail Khan, Pak. B5 20
Derby, Austl. C3 25
Derby, Colo. *B6 51
Derby, Conn. D4 52
Derby, Eng. D6 4
Derby, Kans. E6 61
Derby, N.Y. C2 75
Derby, co., Eng. *D6 4
Derecske, Hung. B5 10
De Ridder, La. D2 63
Derita, N.C. B2 76
Dermott, Ark. D4 49
Derry, N.H. F5 73
Derry, Pa. F3 81
Derventa, Yugo. C3 10
Derzhavinskoye, Sov. Un. D9 16
Des Allemands, La. E5, k11 63
Des Arc, Ark. C4 49
Desbiens, Que., Can. A6 42
Deschaillons sur St. Laurent,
    Que., Can. *C5 42
Deschambault, Que.,Can. C6 42
Deschênes, Que., Can. D2 42
Deschutes, co., Oreg. D5 80
Dese, Eth. F5 23
Deseronto, Ont., Can. C7 41
Desert Hot Springs, Calif. *F5 50
Desha, co.,Ark. D4 49
Deshler, Nebr. D8 71
Deshler, Ohio A2 78
Desloge, Mo. D7 69
De Smet, S. Dak. F8 77
Des Moines, Iowa C4, e8 60
Des Moines, Wash. B3, f11 86
Des Moines, co., Iowa D6 60
De Soto, Kans. D9, m16 61
De Soto, Mo. C7 69
De Soto, Tex. *C4 84
De Soto, co., Fla. E5 54
De Soto, co., Miss. A3 68
De Soto, co., par.,La. B2 63
Des Peres, Mo. f13 69
Des Plaines, Ill. A6, h9 58
Dessau, Ger. Dem. Rep. C6 6
Destin, Fla. u15 54
Detmold, Ger., Fed. Rep of D4 6
Detroit, Mich. F7, p15 66
Detroit Beach, Mich. *G7 66
Detroit Lakes, Minn. D3 67
Detva, Czech. D5 71
Deuel, co.,Nebr. C3 71
Deuel, co., S. Dak. F9 77
Deurne, Bel. B6 5
Deux-Montagnes, Que.,Can. p19 42
Deuz-Sèvres, dept., Fr. *D3 5
Deva, Rom. C6 10
Dévaványa, Hung. B5 10
Deventer, Neth. A7 5
Devils Lake, N. Dak. B7 77
Devine, Tex. E3 84
De Vola, Ohio C4 84
Devon, Alta., Can. C4 38
Devon, Pa. *G10 81
Devon, co., Eng. *E5 4
Devon, isl.,Can. *A15 36
Devonport, Austl. o15 25
Devonport, N.Z. L15 26
Dewar, Okla. B6 79
Dewey, Okla. A6 79
Dewey, co., Okla. B2 79
Dewey, co., S.C. E5 77
De Witt, Ark. C4 49
De Witt, Iowa C7 60
De Witt, Mich. F6 66
De Witt, N.Y. *B4 75
De Witt, co., Ill. C5 58
De Witt, co., Tex. E4 84
Dewsbury, Eng. A6 4
Dexter, Maine C3 64
Dexter, Mich. F7 66
Dexter, Mo. E8 69
Dexter, N.Y. A4 75
Dezful, Iran C4 15
Dezhou, China D8 17
Dhahran (Az Zahran), Sau. Ar. D5 15
Dhaka (Dacca), Bngl. D9 20
Dhanbad, India *D8 20
Dharamjaygarth, India D7 20
Dharmapuri, India F6 20
Dharmsala, India B6 20
Dharwar, India E6 20
Dhaulagiri, peak, Nep. C7 20
Dhidhimótikhon, Grc. E8 10
Dhule, India D5 20
Diablo, Calif. *D2 50
Diablo,mtn.,Calif. h9 50
Diablo Heights, Pan. *B2 32
Diamante, Arg. A4 28
Diamantina, Braz. E6 27
Diamantina, Braz. B4 30
Diamond, peak, Oreg. D4 80
Diamond Springs, Calif. C3 50

Diber (Dibra), pref., Alb. *E5 10
D'Iberville, Miss. E5, f8 68
Diboll, Tex. D5 84
Dickens, co., Tex. C2 84
Dickenson, co., Va. e9 85
Dickey, co., N. Dak. D7 77
Dickinson, N. Dak. D3 77
Dickinson, Tex. *E5 84
Dickinson, co., Iowa A2 60
Dickinson, co., Kans. D6 61
Dickinson, co., Mich. B3 66
Dickson, Tenn. A4 83
Dickson, co., Tenn. A4 83
Dickson City, Pa. D10, m18 81
Didsbury, Alta., Can. D3 38
Dien Bien Phu, Viet. *A2 19
Diepholz, Ger., Fed. Rep. of B4 6
Dieppe, N.B., Can. C5 43
Dieppe, Fr. C4 5
Dierks, Ark. C1 49
Digboi, India C10 20
Digby, N.S., Can. E4 43
Digby, co., N.S., Can. E4 43
Dighton, Kans. D3 61
Digne, Fr. E7 5
Digoin, Fr. D5 5
Dijon, Fr. D6 5
Dikson, Sov. Un. B11 16
Dili, Indon. G7 19
Dilley, Tex. E3 84
Dilligen an der Donau,
 Ger., Fed. Rep. of D5 6
Dillon, Mont. E4 70
Dillon, S.C. C9 82
Dillon, co., S.C. C9 82
Dillonvale, Ohio B5 78
Dillsburg, Pa. F7 81
Dilworth, Minn. D2 67
Dimitrovgrad, Bul. D7 10
Dimmit, co., Tex. E3 84
Dimmitt, Tex. B2 84
Dimona, Isr. C3 15
Dimondale, Mich. F6 66
Dinan, Fr. C3 5
Dinant, Bel. B6 5
Dinard, Fr. C2 5
Dindigul, India F6 20
Dingwall, Scot. B4 4
Dinh Lap, Viet. *G6 17
Dinuba, Calif. D4 50
Dinwiddie, co., Va. C5 85
Diourbel, Sen. F1 22
Dipolog, Phil *D6 19
Dire Dawa, Eth. G6 23
Diriamba, Nic. E7 34
Dirranbandi, Austl. E8 25
Dishman, Wash. g14 86
Dismal, peak, Va. C2 85
Disraëli, Que., Can. D6 42
District Heights, Md. *C4 53
District of Columbia, U.S. C3, f8 53
Distrito Federal, fed. dist.,
 Mex. D5 34
Distrito Federal, fed. dist.,
 Ven. A4 32
Disūq, Eg. *G8 14
Diu, India D5 20
Divernon, Ill. D4 58
Dives-sur-Mer, Fr. C3 5
Divide, co., N. Dak. B2 77
Divide, peak, Wyo. E5 89
Divinópolis, Braz. C4 30
Divnoye, Sov. Un. I14 12
Dix, mtn., N.Y. A7 75
Dixfield, Maine D2 64
Dixiana, Ala. B3 46
Dixie, co., Fla. C3 54
Dixmoor, Ill. *B6 58
Dixon, Calif. C3 50
Dixon, Ill. B4 58
Dixon, Mo. D5 69
Dixon, co., Nebr. B9 71
Dixonville, Pa. E3 81
Diyarbakir, Tur. *D13 14
Djajapura, see Jayapura, Indon.
Djakarta, see Jakarta, Indon.
Djakovica, Yugo. D5 10
Djakovo, Yugo. D4 10
Djibouti, Dji. F6 23
Djibouti, country, Afr. F6 23
Djombang, Indon. *G4 19
Djurdjevac, Yugo. B3 10
Djursholm, Swe. t36 11
Dmitriyevka, Sov. Un. H12, r21 12
Dmitrov, Sov. Un. C11 12
Dmitrovsk-Orlovskiy, Sov. Un. E10 12
Dnepr, riv., Sov. Un. H9 12
Dneprodzerzhinsk, Sov. Un. G10 12
Dnepropetrovsk, Sov. Un. G10 12
Dnestr, riv., Sov. Un. H7 12
Dno, Sov. Un. C7 12
Dobbs Ferry, N.Y. g13 75
Döbeln, Ger. Dem. Rep. C6 6

Doboj, Yugo. C4 10
Dobrich, see Tolbukhin, Bul.
Dobrogea, reg., Rom. *C9 10
Dobruja, reg., Bul. C9 10
Dobruja, reg., Rom. D9 10
Docena, Ala. f7 46
Doddridge, co., W. Va. B4 87
Dodge, co., Ga. D3 55
Dodge, co., Minn. G6 67
Dodge, co., Nebr. C9 71
Dodge, co., Wis. E5 88
Dodge Center, Minn. F6 67
Dodge City, Kans. E3 61
Dodgeville, Wis. F3 88
Dodoma, Tan. B7 24
Doerun, Ga. E3 55
Doe Run, Mo. D7 69
Doha (Ad Dawḥah), Qatar D5 15
Doi Inthanon, mtn., Thai. E10 20
Dolbeau, Que., Can. G19 36
Dôle, Fr. D6 5
Dolgeville, N.Y. B6 75
Dolina, Sov. Un. D8 7
Dolinsk (Ochiai), Sov. Un. C11 18
Dolomite, Ala. B3, g7 46
Dolores, Arg. B5 28
Dolores, Ur. E1 30
Dolores, co., Colo. D2 51
Dolores Hidalgo, Mex. m13 34
Dolton, Ill. k9 58
Dolzhanskaya, Sov. Un. q22 12
Domažlice, Czech. D2 7
Dominguez, Calif. *F4 50
Dominica, country, N.A. I14 35
Dominican Republic,
 country, N.A. E8 35
Dominion, N.S., Can. C9 43
Domodossola, It. A2 9
Dom Pedrito, Braz. E2 30
Don, riv., Sov. Un. H13 12
Dona Ana, co., N. Mex. C5 48
Donaghadee, N. Ire. C4 4
Donaldsonville, La. D4, h10 63
Donalsonville, Ga. E2 55
Don Benito, Sp. C3 8
Doncaster, Eng. D6 4
Donegal, co., Ire. *C2 4
Doneraile, S.C. C8 82
Donets, riv., Sov. Un. G13 12
Donetsk, Sov. Un. H11, r20 12
Dongchuan, China F5 17
Donggala, Indon. F5 19
Dong Hoi, Viet. B3 19
Doniphan, Mo. E7 69
Doniphan, co., Kans. C8 61
Donkin, N.S., Can. C10 43
Donley, co., Tex. B2 84
Donna, Tex. F3 84
Donnacona, Que., Can. C6, o16 42
Donora, Pa. F2 81
Donzère, Fr. E6 5
Doolittle, Mo. D6 69
Dooly, co., Ga. D3 55
Door, co., Wis. D6 88
Dora, Ala. B2 46
Doraville, Ga. h8 55
Dorbod, China C2 18
Dorchester, N.B., Can. D5 43
Dorchester, Eng. E5 4
Dorchester, co., Que., Can. C7 42
Dorchester, co., Md. D5 53
Dorchester, co., S.C. E6 82
Dordogne, dept., Fr. *E4 5
Dordrecht, Neth. B6 5
Dores do Indaiá, Braz. B3 30
Dorgali, It. D2 9
Dorion-Vaudreuil, Que., Can. q18 42
Dorking, Eng. m12 4
Dormont, Pa. k13 81
Dornbirn, Aus. E4 6
Dornoch, Scot. B4 4
Dorohoi, Rom. B8 10
Dorris, Calif. B3 50
Dorset, co., Eng. *F5 4
Dortmund, Ger., Fed. Rep. of C3 6
Dorton, Ky. C7 62
Dörtyol, Tur. D11 14
Dorval, Que., Can. q19 42
Dos Hermanas, Sp. D3 8
Dos Palos, Calif. D3 50
Dothan, Ala. D4 46
Douai, Fr. B5 5
Douala, Cam. H6 22
Douarnenez, Fr. C1 5
Doubletop, peak, Wyo. C2 89
Doubs, dept., Fr. *D7 5
Dougherty, co., Ga. E2 55
Douglas, Alsk. D13, k22 47
Douglas, Ariz. D6 48
Douglas, Ga. E4 55
Douglas, I. of Man C4 4
Douglas, Wyo. D7 89
Douglas, co., Colo. B6 51

Douglas, co., Ga. C2 55
Douglas, co., Ill. D5 58
Douglas, co., Kans. D8 61
Douglas, co., Minn. E3 67
Douglas, co., Mo. E5 69
Douglas, co., Nebr. C9 71
Douglas, co., Nev. B2 72
Douglas, co., Oreg. D3 80
Douglas, co., S. Dak. G7 77
Douglas, co., Wash. B6 86
Douglas, co., Wis. B1 88
Douglass, Kans. E7 61
Douglasville, Ga. C2 55
Doullens, Fr. B5 5
Douro Litoral, prov., Port. *B1 8
Dove Creek, Colo. D2 51
Dover, Del. B6 53
Dover, Eng. E7 4
Dover, Fla. D4 54
Dover, Mass. h10 65
Dover, N.H. E6 73
Dover, N.J. B3 74
Dover, Ohio B4 78
Dover, Pa. F8 81
Dover, Tenn. A4 83
Dover-Foxcroft, Maine C3 64
Dover Plains, N.Y. D7 75
Dowagiac, Mich. G4 66
Down, co., N. Ire. *C4 4
Downers Grove, Ill. B5, k8 58
Downey, Calif. n12 50
Downington, Pa. F10 81
Downpatrick, N. Ire. C4 4
Downs, Kans. C5 61
Downs, mtn., Wyo. C3 89
Downton, mtn., B.C., Can. C5 37
Dows, Iowa B4 60
Doylestown, Ohio B4 78
Doylestown, Pa. F11 81
Doyline, La. B2 63
Dracut, Mass. A5 65
Draganovo, Bul. D7 10
Drăgăsani, Rom. C7 10
Dragerton, Utah *B6 72
Draguignan, Fr. F7 5
Drain, Oreg. D3 80
Drake, peak, Oreg. E6 80
Drakesboro, Ky. C2 62
Drama, Grc. B5 14
Drama, prov., Grc. *B5 14
Drammen, Nor. H4, p28 11
Drancy, Fr. g10 5
Draper, Utah A6, D2 72
Dravosburg, Pa. *E1 81
Drayton, N. Dak. A8 77
Drayton, S.C. B4 82
Drayton Plains, Mich. F7 66
Drayton Valley, Alta., Can. C3 38
Drenthe, prov., Neth. *A7 5
Dresden, Ont., Can. E2 41
Dresden, Ger. Dem. Rep. C6 6
Dresden, Ohio B3 78
Dresden, Tenn. A3 83
Dreux, Fr. C4 5
Drew, Miss. B3 68
Drew, co., Ark. D4 49
Drexel, N.C. B1 76
Drexel, Ohio C1 78
Drexel Hill, Pa. *G11 81
Drift, Ky. C7 62
Drifton, Pa. D10 81
Driggs, Idaho F7 57
Driskill, mtn., La. B3 63
Drissa, Sov. Un. D6 12
Drogheda, Ire. D3 4
Drogobych, Sov. Un. G4 12
Druid Hills, N.C. *f10 76
Drumheller, Alta., Can. D4 38
Drummond, co., Que., Can. D5 42
Drummond Range, mts., Austl. D8 25
Drummondville, Que., Can. D3 42
Drummondville Ouest, Que., Can. ... *D5 42
Drumright, Okla. B5 79
Druzhkovka, Sov. Un. q20 12
Dryden, Ont., Can. o16 41
Dryden, N.Y. C4 75
Duarte, Calif. *E5 50
Duarte, peak, Dom. Rep. E8 35
Dubach, La. B3 63
Dubai (Dubayy), U.A.E. D6 15
Dubawnt, lake, N.W. Ter., Can. D13 36
Dubbo, Austl. F8 25
Dublin, Ga. D4 55
Dublin, Ind. E7 59
Dublin (Baile Átha Cliath),
 Ire. D3 4
Dublin, Tex. C3 84
Dublin, Va. C2 85
Dublin, co. Ire. D3 4
Dubois, co., Ind. H4 59
Du Bois, Pa. D4 81
Duboistown, Pa. D7 81
Dubossary, Sov. Un. H7 12

Dubovka, Sov. Un. G15 12
Dubrovnik, Yugo. D4 10
Dubuque, Iowa B7 60
Dubuque, co., Iowa B7 60
Duchesne, co., Utah A6 72
Duchov, Czech. C2 7
Duck, mtn., Man., Can. D1 40
Ducktown, Tenn. D9 83
Dudinka, Sov. Un. C11 13
Dudley, Eng. D5 4
Dudley, Mass. B4 65
Due West, S.C. D3 82
Dufferin, co., Ont., Can. C4 41
Dugger, Ind. F3 59
Duisburg, Ger., Fed. Rep. of C3 6
Duitama, Col. B3 32
Dukes, co., Mass. B6 65
Dulawan, Phil. *D6 19
Duluth, Ga. B2, g8 55
Duluth, Minn. D6 67
Dumaguete, Phil. D6 19
Dumas, Ark. D4 49
Dumas, Tex. B2 84
Dumfries, Scot. C5 4
Dumfries, Va. B5 85
Dumfries, co., Scot. *C5 4
Dumont, N.J. B5, h9 74
Dumyât (Damietta), Eg. G8 14
Dunaföldvár, Hung. B4 10
Dunapataj, Hung. B4 10
Dunaujváros, Hung. B4 10
Dunayevsty, Sov. Un. G6 12
Dunbar, Pa. G2 81
Dunbar, Scot. B5 4
Dunbar, W. Va. C3, m12 87
Dunbarton, co., Scot. *B4 4
Duncan, Ariz. C4 48
Duncan, B.C., Can. E6, g12 37
Duncan, Okla. C4 79
Duncan, S.C. B3 82
Duncannon, Pa. F7 81
Duncansville, Pa. F5 81
Duncanville, Tex. n10 34
Dundalk, Ont., Can. C4 41
Dundalk, Ire. C3 4
Dundalk, Md. B4, g11 53
Dundas, Ont., Can. D5 41
Dundas, co., Ont., Can. B9 41
Dundee, Ill. A5, h6 58
Dundee, Fla. D5 54
Dundee, Mich. G7 66
Dundee, N.Y. C4 75
Dundee, Scot. B5 4
Dundee, S. Afr. F6 24
Dundy, co., Nebr. D4 71
Dunean, S.C. *B3 82
Dunedin, Fla. D4, o10 54
Dunedin, N.Z. P13 26
Dunellen, N.J. B4 74
Dunfermline, Scot. B5 4
Dungannon, N. Ire. C3 4
Dungarvan, Ire. D3 4
Dungulah, Sud. E4 23
Dunhua, China C10 17
Dunkerque, Fr. B5 5
Dunkirk, Ind. D7 59
Dunkirk, N.Y. C1 75
Dunkirk, Ohio B2 78
Dunkirk, see Dunkerque, Fr.
Dunklin, co., Mo. E7 69
Dun Laoghaire, Ire. D3 4
Dunlap, Ind. A6 59
Dunlap, Iowa C2 60
Dunlap, Tenn. D8 83
Dunlo, Pa. F4 81
Dunmore, Pa. D10, m18 81
Dunn, N.C. B4 76
Dunn, co., N. Dak. C3 77
Dunn, co., Wis. D2 88
Dunnellon, Fla. C4 54
Dunn Loring, Va. *B5 85
Dunnville, Ont., Can. E5 41
Dunoon, Scot. C4 4
Dunseith, N. Dak. A5 77
Dunsmuir, Calif. B2 50
Dunville, Newf., Can. E5 44
Du Page, co., Ill. A5 58
Duparquet, Que., Can. *D3 42
Duplin, co., N.C. C5 76
Dupnitsa, see Stanke Dimitrov, Bul.
Dupo, Ill. E3 58
Dupont, Pa. n18 81
Duque de Caxais, Braz. *C4 30
Duquesne, Pa. F2, k14 81
Du Quoin, Ill. E4 58
Dūra, Jordan C3 15
Durand, Mich. F6 66
Durand, Wis. D2 88
Durango, Colo. D3 51
Durango, Mex. C4 34
Durango, state, Mex. C4 34
Durant, Iowa C7 60
Durant, Miss. B4 68

Durant, Okla. ... D5 79
Durazno, Ur. ... E1 30
Durazno, dept., Ur. ... *E1 30
Durban, S. Afr. ... F6 24
Düren, Ger., Fed. Rep. of ... C3 6
Durg, India ... *D7 20
Durham, Calif. ... C3 50
Durham, Maine ... g7 64
Durham, Ont., Can. ... C4 41
Durham, Eng. ... C6 4
Durham, N.H. ... E6 73
Durham, N.C. ... B4 76

Durham, co., Ont., Can. ... C6 41
Durham, co., Eng. ... *C6 4
Durham, co., N.C. ... A4 76
Durres, Alb. ... *B2 14
Duryea, Pa. ... D10, m17 81
Dushanbe, Sov. Un. ... F9 13
Duson, La. ... D3 63
Düsseldorf, Ger., Fed. Rep. of ... C3 6
Dutchess, co., N.Y. ... D7 75
Dutton, Ont., Can. ... E3 41
Duval, co., Fla. ... B5 54
Duval, co., Tex. ... F3 84

Duvergé, Dom. Rep. ... *E8 35
Duxbury, Mass. ... B6 65
Duyun, China ... F6 17
Düzce, Tur. ... B8 14
Dvůr Králové nad Labem, Czech. ... C3 7
Dwight, Ill. ... B5 58
Dyer, Ind. ... A2 59
Dyer, Tenn. ... A3 83
Dyer, co., Tenn. ... A3 83
Dyersburg, Tenn. ... A2 83
Dyersville, Iowa ... B6 60
Dyrlow, see Darlowo, Pol.

Dysart, Iowa ... B5 60
Dzaudzhikau, see
  Ordzhonikidze,Sov. Un.
Dzerzhinsk, Sov. Un. ... q20 12
Dzerzhinsk, Sov. Un. ... C14, d7 12
Dzhambul, Sov. Un. ... E10 13
Dzhankoy, Sov. Un. ... I1 12
Dzialdowo, Pol. ... B6 7
Dzeirzlow, see Darlowo, Pol.
Dzierżoniów, Pol. ... C4 7
Dzilam Gonzáles, Mex. ... C7 34
Dzitbalché, Mex. ... C6 34

E

Eads, Colo. ... C8 51
Eagan, Tenn. ... C10 83
Eagle, W. Va. ... C3, m13 87
Eagle, co., Colo. ... B4 51
Eagle, mtn., Tex. ... o12 84
Eagle, peak, Calif. ... B3 50
Eagle Grove, Iowa ... B4 60
Eagle Lake, Fla. ... *E5 54
Eagle Lake, Maine ... A4 64
Eagle Lake, Tex. ... E4 84
Eagle Pass, Tex. ... E2 84
Eagle River, Wis. ... C4 88
Eagleton Village, Tenn. ... *D10 83
Eagleville, Pa. ... o20 81
Earle, Ark. ... B5 49
Earlimart, Calif. ... E4 50
Earlington, Ky. ... C2 62
Earlville, Ill. ... B5 58
Earlville, N.Y. ... C5 75
Early, Iowa ... B2 60
Early, co., Ga. ... E2 55
Earth, Tex. ... B1 84
Easley, S.C. ... B2 82
East, div., Ice. ... *n15 11
East Alamosa, Colo. ... D5 51
East Alliance, Ohio ... *B5 78
East Alton, Ill. ... E3 58
East Angus, Que., Can. ... D6 42
East Aurora, N.Y. ... C2 75
East Bangor, Pa. ... E11 81
East Bank, La. ... k7 63
Eastbank, W. Va. ... m13 87
East Bathurst, N.B., Can. ... B4 43
East Baton Rouge, par., La. ... D4 63
East Berlin, Pa. ... G8 81
East Bernstadt, Ky. ... C5 62
East Berwick, Pa. ... *D9 81
East Bethel, Minn. ... *E5 67
East Billerica, Mass. ... f11 65
Eastborough, Kans. ... g12 61
Eastbourne, Eng. ... E7 4
East Brady, Pa. ... E2 81
East Brewton, Ala. ... D2 46
East Bridgewater, Mass. ... B6 65
East Brookfield, Mass. ... B3 65
East Brooklyn, Conn. ... *B9 52
East Broughton Station,
  Que., Can. ... C6 42
East Brunswick, N.J. ... C4 74
East Butler, Pa. ... E2 81
East Canon, Colo. ... C5 51
East Canton, Ohio ... *B4 78
East Carroll, par., La. ... B4 63
East Chelmsford, Mass. ... f10 65
Eastchester, N.Y. ... *E7 75
East Chicago, Ind. ... A3 59
East Chicago Heights, Ill. ... *B6 58
East China, sea, China ... F9 17
East Cleveland, Ohio ... g9 78
East Conemaugh
  (Conemaugh), Pa. ... *E4 81
East Coulée, Alta., Can. ... D4 38
East Detroit, Mich. ... p16 66
East Douglas, Mass. ... B4 65
East Dubuque, Ill. ... A3 58
East Dundee, Ill. ... *A5 58
East Ely, Nev. ... D7 72
Eastern, reg., Nig. ... G6 22
Eastern Valley, Ala. ... *f6 46
East Falmouth, Mass. ... C6 65
East Farmington Heights, Conn. ... *B6 52
East Faxon, Pa. ... *D7 81
East Fayetteville, N.C. ... *B3 76
East Feliciana, par., La. ... *D4 63
East Flanders, prov., Bel. ... *B5 5
East Flat Rock, N.C. ... f10 76
East Gaffney, S.C. ... A4 82
Eastgate, Wash. ... *B3 86

East Glenville, N.Y. ... *C7 75
East Grand Forks, Minn. ... C2 67
East Grand Rapids, Mich. ... F5 66
East Greenbush, N.Y. ... *C7 75
East Greenville, Pa. ... F10 81
East Greenwich, R.I. ... C11 52
East Hampden, Maine ... *D4 64
East Hampton, Conn. ... C6 52
Easthampton, Mass. ... B2 65
East Hampton, N.Y. ... m16 75
East Hartford, Conn. ... B6 52
East Haven, Conn. ... D5 52
East Hazelcrest, Ill. ... *B6 58
East Helena, Mont. ... D5 70
East Herkimer, N.Y. ... *B6 75
East Hickory, N.C. ... *B1 76
East Hills, N.Y. ... *E7 75
East Islip, N.Y. ... G4 52
East Jordan, Mich. ... C5 66
East Keansburg, N.J. ... *C4 74
East Kingsford, Mich. ... *C2 66
Eastlake, Ohio ... A4 78
Eastland, Tex. ... C3 84
Eastland, co., Tex. ... C3 84
East Lansdowne, Pa. ... *G11 81
East Lansing, Mich. ... F6 66
East Liverpool, Ohio ... B5 78
East London, S. Afr. ... G5 24
East Longmeadow, Mass. ... B2 65
East Los Angeles, Calif. ... m12 50
East Lothian, co., Scot. ... *C5 4
East McKeesport, Pa. ... *F2 81
Eastman, Ga. ... D3 55
East Marietta, Ga. ... *A5 55
East Meadow, N.Y. ... n15 75
East Millbury, Mass. ... *B4 65
East Millinockot, Maine ... C4 64
East Moline, Ill. ... B3 58
East Moriches, N.Y. ... F5 52
East Naples, Fla. ... F5 54
East Newark, N.J. ... k8 74
East Newnan, Ga. ... C2 55
East Northport, N.Y. ... F3 52
East Norwich, N.Y. ... *F2 52
Easton, Calif. ... *D4 50
Easton, Maine ... B5 64
Easton, Md. ... C5 53
Easton, Pa. ... E11 81
East Orange, N.J. ... B4, h8 74
East Palatka, Fla. ... C5 54
East Palestine, Ohio ... B5 78
East Palo Alto, Calif. ... *D2 50
East Patchogue, N.Y. ... G5 52
East Peoria, Ill. ... C4 58
East Pepperell, Mass. ... A4 65
East Petersburg, Pa. ... F9 81
East Pines, Md. ... *C4 53
East Pittsburgh, Pa. ... *k14 81
East Point, Ga. ... C2, h8 55
Eastport, Newf., Can. ... D5 44
Eastport, Maine ... D6 64
Eastport, N.Y. ... n16 75
East Prairie, Mo. ... E8 69
East Pryor, mtn., Mont. ... E8 70
East Providence, R.I. ... B11 52
East Quincy, Calif. ... *C3 50
East Quogue, N.Y. ... *n16 75
East Richmond, Calif. ... *D2 50
East Ridge, Tenn. ... h11 83
East Rochester, N.Y. ... B3 75
East Rochester, Pa. ... *E1 81
East Rockaway, N.Y. ... G2 52
East Rockingham, N.C. ... C3 76
East Rockwood, Mich. ... *F7 66
East Rutherford, N.J. ... h8 74
East St. John, N.B., Can. ... D3 43
East St. Louis, Ill. ... E3 58
East Setauket, N.Y. ... F4 52

Eastside, Oreg. ... D2 80
East Sparta, Ohio ... B4 78
East Spencer, N.C. ... B2 76
East Stroudsburg, Pa. ... D11 81
East Sudbury, Mass. ... g10 65
East Syracuse, N.Y. ... B4 75
East Tawas, Mich. ... D7 66
East Templeton, Mass. ... A3 65
East Troy, Wis. ... F5 88
East Uniontown, Pa. ... *G2 81
East Vandergrift, Pa. ... *F2 81
East Walpole, Mass. ... D2 65
East Wareham, Mass. ... C6 65
East Washington, Pa. ... F1 81
East Wenatchee, Wash. ... B5 86
East Whittier, Calif. ... *F4 50
East Williston, N.Y. ... G2 52
Eastwood, Mich. ... *E5 66
East York, Ont., Can. ... *m15 41
East York, Pa. ... *G8 81
Eaton, Colo. ... A6 51
Eaton, Ind. ... D7 59
Eaton, Ohio ... C1 78
Eaton, co., Mich. ... F6 66
Eaton Rapids, Mich. ... F6 66
Eatonton, Ga. ... C3 55
Eatontown, N.J. ... C4 74
Eatonville, Wash. ... C3 86
Eau Claire, Wis. ... D2 88
Eau Claire, co., Wis. ... D2 88
Ebensburg, Pa. ... F4 81
Eberswalde,Ger. Dem. Rep. ... B6 6
Ebetsu, Jap. ... E10 18
Ebingen, Ger., Fed. Rep. of ... D4 6
Eboli, It. ... D5 9
Eccles, W. Va. ... D3, n13 87
Eceabat (Maydos), Tur. ... B6 14
Ech Cheliff, Alg. ... A5 22
Echigawa, Jap. ... n15 18
Echols, co., Ga. ... F3 55
Echuca, Austl. ... G7 25
Écija, Sp. ... D3 8
Eckernförde, Ger., Fed.
  Rep. of ... A4 6
Eckert, Colo. ... C3 51
Eckhart Mines, Md. ... k13 53
Eckman, W. Va. ... *D3 87
Eclectic, Ala. ... C3 46
Economy, Pa. ... *E1 81
Ecorse, Mich. ... p15 66
Ector, co., Tex. ... D1 84
Ecuador, country, S.A. ... 31
Edcouch, Tex. ... F4 84
Eddiceton, Miss. ... D3 68
Eddy, co., N. Mex. ... C6 48
Eddy, co., N. Dak. ... C7 77
Eddystone, Pa. ... p20 81
Eddyville, Iowa ... C5 60
Eddyville, Ky. ... e9 62
Ede, Neth. ... A6 5
Ede, Nig. ... *G5 22
Edea, Cam. ... H7 22
Eden, N.Y. ... C2 75
Eden, N.C. ... A3 76
Eden, Tex. ... D3 84
Edenborn, Pa. ... G2 81
Edenton, N.C. ... A6 76
Edgar, Wis. ... D4 88
Edgar, co., Ill. ... D6 58
Edgartown, Mass. ... D6 65
Edgecombe, co., N.C. ... B5 76
Edgefield, S.C. ... D4 82
Edgefield, co., S.C. ... D3 82
Edgeley, N. Dak. ... D7 77
Edgely, Pa. ... *F11 81
Edgemere, Md. ... *B5 53
Edgemont, Calif. ... *F5 50
Edgemont, S. Dak. ... G2 77

Edgerton, Minn. ... G2 67
Edgerton, Ohio ... A1 78
Edgerton, Wis. ... F4 88
Edgewater, Ala. ... f7 46
Edgewater, Colo. ... B5 51
Edgewater, Fla. ... D6 54
Edgewater, Md. ... C4 53
Edgewater, N.J. ... h9 74
Edgewater Park, N.J. ... C3 74
Edgewood, Ind. ... D6 59
Edgewood, Ky. ... A7 62
Edgewood, Md. ... B5 53
Edgewood, Ohio ... A5 78
Edgewood, Pa. ... k14 81
Edgeworth, Pa. ... h13 81
Edgewood, Pa. ... *D8 81
Edhessa, Grc. ... B4 14
Edina, Minn. ... n12 67
Edina, Mo. ... A5 69
Edinboro, Pa. ... C1 81
Edinburg, Ill. ... D4 58
Edinburg, Ind. ... F6 59
Edinburg, Miss. ... C4 68
Edinburg, Tex. ... F3 84
Edinburg, Scot. ... C5 4
Edirne, Tur. ... B6 14
Edison, Ga. ... E2 55
Edison, N.J. ... B4 74
Edisto Island, S.C. ... F7, k11 82
Edmeston, N.Y. ... C5 75
Edmond, Okla. ... B4 79
Edmonds, Wash. ... B3 86
Edmonson, co., Ky. ... C3 62
Edmonston, Md. ... *C4 53
Edmonton, Alta., Can. ... C4, g8 38
Edmonton, Eng. ... K12 4
Edmore, Mich. ... E5 66
Edmundson, Mo. ... *C7 69
Edmundston, N.B., Can. ... B1 43
Edna, Tex. ... E4 84
Edremit, Tur. ... *C6 14
Edson, Alta., Can. ... C7, g7 38
Edwards, Miss. ... C3 68
Edwards, co., Ill. ... E5 58
Edwards, co., Kans. ... E4 61
Edwards, co., Tex. ... E2 84
Edwardsburg, Mich. ... G4 66
Edwardsville, Ill. ... E4 58
Edwardsville, Pa. ... n17 81
Eferding, Aus. ... D7 6
Effingham, Ill. ... D5 58
Effingham, co., Ga. ... D5 55
Effingham, co., Ill. ... D5 58
Eganville, Ont., Can. ... B7 41
Eger, Hung. ... B5 7
Egg Harbor City, N.J. ... D3 74
Egmont, mtn. N.Z. ... M15 26
Eğridir, Tur. ... D8 14
Egypt, Mass. ... B6, h12 65
Egypt, Pa. ... E10 81
Egypt, country, Afr. ... C3 23
Ehime, pref., Jap. ... *J6 18
Ehrenfeld, Pa. ... F4 81
Éibar, Sp. ... A4 8
Eichstätt, Ger., Fed. Rep. of ... D5 6
Eidsberg, Nor. ... H4, p29 11
Eidsvoll, Nor. ... G4 11
Eilenburg, Ger. Dem. Rep. ... C6 6
Einbeck, Ger., Fed. Rep. of ... C4 6
Eindhoven, Neth. ... B6 5
Eire, see Ireland, country, Eur.
Eisenach, Ger. Dem. Rep. ... C5 6
Eisenhüttenstadt, Ger.
  Dem. Rep. ... B7 6
Eisenstadt, Aus. ... E8 6
Eisleben, Ger. Dem. Rep. ... C5 6

Ekalaka, Mont. ... E12 70
Eksjö, Swe. ... I6 11
El Aaiún, W. Sah. ... C2 22
El Arahal, Sp. ... D3 8
Elâziǧ, Tur. ... C12 14
Elba, Ala. ... D3 46
El Banco, Col. ... B3 32
El Barco, Sp. ... A2 8
El Barco, Sp. ... A2 8
Elbasan, Alb. ... B3 14
Elbasan, pref., Alb. ... *B3 14
Elbe, (Labe), riv., Eur. ... B5 6
Elbert, Colo. ... B4 51
Elbert, co., Colo. ... B6 51
Elbert, co., Ga. ... B4 55
Elberton, Ga. ... B4 55
Elbeuf, Fr. ... C4 5
Elbing, see Elblag, Pol.
Elbistan, Tur. ... C11 14
Elblag, Pol. ... A5 7
El Bonillo, Sp. ... C4 8
El Bordo, Col. ... C2 32
El Boulaïda, Alg. ... A5 22
Elbow Lake, Minn. ... E3 67
Elbrus, mtn., Sov. Un. ... E7 13
Elburn, Ill. ... B5 58
El Cajon, Calif. ... F5, o16 50
El Campo, Tex. ... E4 84
El Camp South, Tex. ... *E4 84
El Capitan, mtn., Mont. ... D2 70
El Carmen de Bolivar, Col. ... B2 32
El Carrizo, Mex. ... B3 34
El Centro, Calif. ... F6 50
El Cerrito, Calif. ... h8 50
Elche, Sp. ... C5 8
El Cocuy, Col. ... B3 32
Elda, Sp. ... C5 8
El Djelfa, Alg. ... B5 22
Eldon, Iowa ... D5 60
Eldon, Mo. ... C5 69
Eldora, Iowa ... B4 60
El Dorado, Ark. ... D3 49
Eldorado, Ill. ... F5 58
El Dorado, Kans. ... E7, g13 61
Eldorado, Mex. ... C3 34
Eldorado, Tex. ... D2 84
El Dorado, co., Calif. ... C3 50
Eldorado, peak, Wash. ... A4 86
El Dorado Springs, Mo. ... D3 69
Eldoret, Ken. ... H5 23
Eldred, Pa. ... C5 81
Eldridge, Iowa ... C7, g10 60
Eleanor, W. Va. ... C3 87
Electra, Tex. ... C3 84
Electric, peak, Mont. ... D6 70
Eleele, Haw. ... B2 56
Elektrostal, Sov. Un. ... n18 12
Elephant, mtn., Maine ... D2 64
Elevsís (Eleusis), Grc. ... g11 14
El Fasher, Sud. ... F3 23
El Ferrol *del Caudillo*, Sp. ... A1 8
El Fuerte, Mex. ... B3 34
Elgin, Ill. ... A5, h8 58
Elgin, Iowa ... B6 60
Elgin, N. Dak. ... D4 77
Elgin, Oreg. ... B9 80
Elgin, Scot. ... B5 4
Elgin, Tex. ... D4 84
Elgin, co., Ont., Can. ... E3 41
Elgon, mtn., Ken., Ug. ... H4 23
El Grullo, Mex. ... n11 34
Elida, Ohio ... B1 78
Elim, Pa. ... *E4 81
Eliot, Maine ... E2 64
Elizabeth, Austl. ... F6 25
Elizabeth, Ga. ... C2, h7 55
Elizabeth, La. ... D3 63
Elizabeth, N.J. ... B4, k8 74
Elizabeth, Pa. ... *E1 81
Elizabeth City, N.C. ... A6 76
Elizabeth Lake Estates, Mich. ... *F7 66
Elizabethton, Tenn. ... C11 83
Elizabethtown, Ky. ... C4 62
Elizabethtown, N.C. ... C4 76
Elizabethtown, Pa. ... F8 81
Elizabethville, Pa. ... E8 81
El Jadida, Mor. ... B3 22
Elk, Pol. ... B7 7
Elk, co., Kans. ... E7 61
Elk, co., Pa. ... D4 81
Elk, mtn., Wyo. ... E6 89
Elk, peak, Mont. ... D6 70
Elkader, Iowa ... B6 60
Elk City, Okla. ... B2 79
El Kef, Tun. ... A6 22
Elk Grove, Calif. ... C3 50
Elk Grove Village, Ill. ... h9 58
Elkhart, Ind. ... A6 59
Elkhart, Kans. ... E2 61
Elkhart, co., Ind. ... A6 59
Elkhorn, W. Va. ... *D3 87
Elkhorn, Wis. ... F5 88
Elkhorn City, Ky. ... C7 62
Elkhovo, Bul. ... D8 10

Elkin, N.C. ... A2 76
Elkins, W. Va. ... C5 87
Elkins Park, Pa. ... o21 81
Elkland, Pa. ... C7 81
Elk Mountain, N.C. ... f10 76
Elko, Nev. ... A4 72
Elko, co., Nev. ... A4 72
Elk Point, S. Dak. ... H9 77
Elk Rapids, Mich. ... D5 66
Elkridge, Md. ... B4, h10 53
Elkridge, W. Va. ... m13 87
Elk River, Idaho ... C2 57
Elk River, Minn. ... E5 67
Elk Run Heights, Iowa ... *B5 60
Elkton, Ky. ... D2 62
Elkton, Md. ... A6 53
Elkton, Mich. ... E7 66
Elkton, Va. ... B4 85
Elkville, Ill. ... F4 58
Ellaville, Ga. ... D2 55
Ellendale, N. Dak. ... E7 77
Ellensburg, Wash. ... C5 86
Ellenton, Fla. ... E4, p10 54
Ellenville, N.Y. ... D6 75
Ellerbe, N.C. ... B3 76
Ellesmere, isl., N.W. Ter., Can. ... k34 36
Ellettsville, Ind. ... F4 59
Ellicott City, Md. ... B4 53
Ellicottville, N.Y. ... C2 75
Ellijay, Ga. ... B2 55
Ellington, Mo. ... D7 69
Ellinwood, Kans. ... D5 61
Elliott, co., Ky. ... B6 62
Ellis, Kans. ... D4 61
Ellis, co., Kans. ... D4 61
Ellis, co., Okla. ... A2 79
Ellis, co., Tex. ... C4 84
Ellisville, Miss. ... D4 68
Ellisville, Mo. ... f12 69
Ellon, Scot. ... B5 4
Ellport, Pa. ... E1 81
Ellsworth, Kans. ... D5 61
Ellsworth, Maine ... D4 64
Ellsworth, Pa. ... F1 81
Ellsworth, Wis. ... D1 88
Ellsworth, co., Kans. ... D5 61
Ellwangen, Ger., Fed. Rep. of ... D5 6
Ellwood City, Pa. ... E1 81
Elma, N.Y. ... *C2 75
Elma, Wash. ... C2 86
El Mahdia, Tun. ... A7 22
Elmali, Tur. ... *D7 14
Elmer, N.J. ... D2 74
Elmer, Wis. ... *m11 88
Elm Grove, Wis. ... *m11 88
Elmhurst, Ill. ... B6, k9 58
Elmira, Ont., Can. ... D4 41
Elmira, N.Y. ... C4 75
El Mirage, Ariz. ... D1 48
Elmira Heights, N.Y. ... C4 75
Elmont, N.Y. ... *G2 52
El Monte, Calif. ... *E4 50
Elmora, Pa. ... E4 81
Elmore, Minn. ... G4 67
Elmore, Ohio ... A2 78
Elmore, co., Ala. ... C3 46
Elmore, co., Idaho ... F3 57
Elmore City, Okla. ... C4 79
Elmsford, N.Y. ... g13 75
Elmshorn, Ger., Fed. Rep. of ... B4 6
Elmwood, Ill. ... C4 58
Elmwood Park, Ill. ... k9 58
Elmwood Park, N.J. ... h8 74
Elmwood Place, Ohio ... o13 78
El Nevado, mtn., Col. ... C3 32
Elnora, Ind. ... G3 59
Elon College, N.C. ... A3 76
Elora, Ont., Can. ... D4 41
Eloise, Fla. ... E5 54
Elon College, N.C. ... A3 76
El Oro, prov., Ec. ... B2 31
Eloy, Ariz. ... C3 48
El Paso, Ill. ... C4 58
El Paso, Tex. ... o11 84
El Paso, co., Colo. ... C6 51
El Paso, co., Tex. ... o11 84
El Portal, Fla. ... s13 54
El Porto Beach, Calif. ... *F4 50
El Puerto de Santa María, Sp. ... D2 8
Elrama, Pa. ... F2 81
El Reno, Okla. ... B4 79
El Rio, Calif. ... E4 50
Elroy, Wis. ... E3 88
Elsa, Tex. ... F3 84
El Salto, Mex. ... C3 34
El Salvador, country, N.A. ... E7 34
Elsberry, Mo. ... B6 69
El Segundo, Calif. ... *F4 50
El Seibo, Dom. Rep. ... E9 35
Elsie, Mich. ... E6 66
Elsinore, Calif. ... F5 50
Elsmere, Del. ... A6 53
Elsmere, Ky. ... B5, h13 62
El Sobrante, Calif. ... *D2 50

Elsterwerda, Ger. Dem. Rep. ... C6 6
El Tigre, Ven. ... B5 32
El Tocuyo, Ven. ... B4 32
Elton, La. ... D3 63
Elūru, India ... E7 20
Elvas, Port. ... C2 8
El Verano, Calif. ... *C2 50
Elverum, Nor. ... G4 11
El Viejo, mtn., Col. ... B3 32
Elvins, Mo. ... D7 69
Elwood, Ind. ... D6 59
Elwood, Kans. ... C9 61
Elwood, N.Y. ... n15 75
Elwyn, Pa. ... *G11 81
Ely, Eng. ... D7 4
Ely, Minn. ... C7 67
Ely, Nev. ... B4 72
Elyria, Ohio ... A3 78
Elysburg, Pa. ... E8 81
Emãnshahr, Iran ... B6 15
Emanuel, co., Ga. ... D4 55
Embetsu, Jap. ... E10 18
Embrun, Ont., Can. ... B9 41
Emden, Ger., Fed. Rep. of ... B3 6
Emerson, Man., Can. ... E3 40
Emerson, Nebr. ... B9 71
Emerson, N.J. ... H8 74
Emery, co., Utah ... B6 72
Emeryville, Calif. ... *D3 50
Emi Koussi, vol., Chad ... E1 23
Emilia, reg., It. ... B3 9
Emilia-Romagna, pol. dist., It. ... B3 9
Emiliano Zapata, Mex. ... D6 34
Eminence, Ky. ... B4 62
Emirdaǧ, Tur. ... C8 14
Emlenton, Pa. ... D2 81
Emmaus, Pa. ... E11 81
Emmen, Neth. ... A7 5
Emmerald, Austl. ... D8 25
Emmerich, Ger., Fed. Rep. of ... C3 6
Emmet, co., Iowa ... A3 60
Emmet, co., Mich. ... C6 66
Emmetsburg, Iowa ... A3 60
Emmett, Idaho ... F2 57
Emmitsburg, Md. ... A3 53
Emmons, co., N. Dak. ... D5 77
Empire, Calif. ... *D3 50
Empire, La. ... E6 63
Empire, Nev. ... A2 72
Empoli, It. ... C3 9
Emporia, Kans. ... D7 61
Emporia, Va. ... D5 85
Emporium, Pa. ... D5 81
Emsdetten, Ger., Fed. Rep. of ... B3 6
Emsworth, Pa. ... h13 81
Ena, Jap. ... n16 18
Encarnación, Par. ... E4 29
Encarnación de Díaz, Mex. ... m12 34
Encinal, Tex. ... E3 84
Encinitas, Calif. ... F5 50
Encino, N. Mex. ... C4 48
Ende, Indon. ... G6 19
Enderby, B.C., Can. ... D8 37
Enderlin, N. Dak. ... D8 77
Endicott, N.Y. ... C4 75
Endwell, N.Y. ... *C4 75
Enfield, Conn. ... B6 52
Enfield, Ill. ... E5 58
Enfield, N.H. ... D3 73
Enfield, N.C. ... A5 76
Engaru, Jap. ... D11 18
Engels, Sov. Un. ... F16 12
Enghien, Fr. ... g10 5
England, Ark. ... C4, k11 49
England, reg., U.K. ... D6 4
Englee, Newf., Can. ... C3, h10 44
Englewood, Colo. ... B6 51
Englewood, Fla. ... *B5 54
Englewood, Fla. ... F4 54
Englewood, Ind. ... *G5 59
Englewood, N.J. ... h9 74
Englewood, Ohio ... C1 78
Englewood, Oreg. ... *D2 80
Englewood, Tenn. ... D9 83
Englewood Cliffs, N.J. ... B5 74
Englishtown, N.J. ... C4 74
Enguera, Sp. ... C5 8
Enhaut, Pa. ... *F8 81
Enid, Okla. ... A4 79
Enka, N.C. ... f10 76
Enköping, Swe. ... H7, t35 11
Enna, It. ... F5 9
Ennis, Ire. ... D2 4
Ennis, Tex. ... C4, n10 84
Enniscorthy, Ire. ... D3 4
Enniskillen, N.Ire. ... C3 4
Enns, Aus. ... D7 6
Enola, Pa. ... F8 81
Enon, Ohio ... C2 78
Enoree, S.C. ... B4 82
Enosburg Falls, Vt. ... B2 73
Enriquillo, Dom. Rep. ... F8 35
Enschede, Neth. ... A7 5
Ensenada, Arg. ... g8 28

Ensenada, Mex. ... A1 34
Ensenada, P.R. ... G11 35
Ensley, Fla. ... u14 54
Entebbe, Ug. ... H4 23
Enterprise, Ala. ... D4 46
Enterprise, Calif. ... *B2 50
Enterprise, Kans. ... D6 61
Enterprise, Oreg. ... B9 80
Entiat, mts., Wash. ... B5 86
Entre Minho e Douro, reg., Port. ... B1 8
Entre Ríos, prov., Arg. ... A5, f7 28
Enugu, Nig. ... G6 22
Enumclaw, Wash. ... B4, f12 86
Enzan, Jap. ... n17 18
Épernay, Fr. ... C5 5
Ephraim, Utah ... B6 72
Ephrata, Pa. ... F9 81
Ephrata, Wash. ... B6 86
Épila, Sp. ... B5 8
Épinal, Fr. ... C7 5
Épinay-sur-Seine, Fr. ... g10 5
Epirus, reg., Grc. ... *C3 14
Epping, Eng. ... k13 4
Epping, N.H. ... E5 73
Epsom (& Ewell) Eng. ... m12 4
Epworth, Iowa ... B7 60
Equatorial Guinea, country, Afr. ... H6 22
Erath, La. ... E3 63
Erath, co., Tex. ... C3 84
Ercis, Tur. ... C14 14
Erciyes Dagi, mtn., Tur. ... C10 14
Érd, Hung. ... B4 10
Erdek, Tur. ... *B6 14
Erdenheim, Pa. ... o21 81
Erding, Ger., Fed. Rep. of ... D5 6
Ereǧli, Tur. ... B8 14
Ereǧli, Tur. ... D10 14
Erfurt, Ger. Dem. Rep. ... C5 6
Erice, It. ... E4 9
Erick, Okla. ... B2 79
Erickson, B.C., Can. ... E9 37
Erie, Colo. ... A5 51
Erie, Ill. ... B3 58
Erie, Kans. ... E8 61
Erie, Pa. ... B1 81
Erie, co., N.Y. ... C2 75
Erie, co., Ohio ... A3 78
Erie, co., Pa. ... C1 81
Erie, lake, Can., U.S. ... B10 45
Erin, Tenn. ... A4 83
Eritrea, prov., Eth. ... E5 23
Erlangen, Ger., Fed. Rep. of ... D5 6
Erlanger, Ky. ... A5, h13 62
Ermenak, Tur. ... D9 14
Ermont, Fr. ... g10 5
Ernakulam, India ... *G6 20
Ernest, Pa. ... E3 81
Errigal, mtn., Ire. ... C2 4
Errol Heights, Oreg. ... *B4 80
Erstein, Fr. ... C7 5
Erwin, N.C. ... B4 76
Erwin, Tenn. ... C11 83
Erzincan, Tur. ... C12 14
Erzurum, Tur. ... C13 14
Esashi, Jap. ... D11 18
Esashi, Jap. ... F10 18
Esbjerg, Den. ... J3 11
Escada, Braz. ... *D7 27
Escalante, Utah ... C6 72
Escalon, Calif. ... D3 50
Escalón, Mex. ... B4 34
Escambia, co., Ala. ... D2 46
Escambia, co., Fla. ... u14 54
Escanaba, Mich. ... C3 66
Escatawpa, Miss. ... E5, f8 68
Esch-sur-Alzette, Lux. ... C7 5
Eschwege, Ger., Fed. Rep. of ... C5 6
Eschweiler, Ger., Fed. Rep. of ... C3 6
Escondido, Calif. ... F5 50
Escoublac-La-Baule, Fr. ... D2 5
Escuintla, Guat. ... E6 34
Escuinapa *de Hidalgo*, Mex. ... C3 34
Esfahãn (Isfajamn), Iran ... C5 15
Esher, Eng. ... m12 4
Eskdale, W. Va. ... C3, m13 87
Eskilstuna, Swe. ... H7, t34 11
Eskisehir, Tur. ... C8 14
Esmeralda, co., Nev. ... C3 72
Esmeraldas, Ec. ... A2 31
Esmeraldas, prov., Ec. ... A2 31
Esmond, R.I. ... B10 52
Espanola, Ont., Can. ... A3 41
Espanola, N. Mex. ... B5 48
Esperanza, Arg. ... A4 28
Espinal, Col. ... C3 32
Espírito Santo, state, Braz. ... C4 30
Espita, Mex. ... C7 34
Espy, Pa. ... D9 81
Esquel, Arg. ... C2 28
Esquimalt, B.C., Can. ... E6, h12 37
Essaouira, Mor. ... B3 22
Essen, Ger., Fed. Rep. of ... C3 6
Essendon, mtn., Austl. ... D3 25

Essex, Ont., Can. E2 41
Essex, Conn. D7 52
Essex, Md. B5 52
Essex, co., Ont., Can. E2 41
Essex, co., Eng. *E7 41
Essex, co., Mass. A5 65
Essex, co., N.J. B4 74
Essex, co., N.Y. B4 75
Essex, co., Vt. B4 73
Essex, co., Va. C6 85
Essex Fells, N.J. *B4 74
Essex Junction, Vt. C1 73
Essexville, Mich. E7 66
Essington, Pa. *G11 81
Esslingen, Ger., Fed. Rep. of D4 6
Estacada, Oreg. B4 80
Estancia, Braz. *E7 27
Estancia, N. Mex. B5 48
Este, It. B3 9
Esteli, Nic. E7 34
Estepa, Sp. D3 8
Esterhazy, Sask., Can. G4 39
Estes Park, Colo. A5 51
Estevan, Sask., Can. H4 39
Esther, Mo. *D7 69
Estherville, Iowa A3 60
Estill, S.C. F5 82
Estill, co., Ky. C5 62
Eston, Sask., Can. F1 39
Estonia (S.S.R.), rep., Sov. Un. B5 12
Estremadura, prov., Port. *C1 8
Estremadura, reg., Port. *C1 8

Estremoz, Port. C2 8
Esztergom, Hung. B4 10
Étampes, Fr. C5 5
Étaples, Fr. B4 5
Etawah, India C6 20
Ethel, W. Va. D5 87
Ethiopia (Abyssinia), country, Afr. G5 23
Etna, Pa. k14 41
Etna, Monte, vol., It. F5 9
Etobicoke, Ont., Can. D5, m14 41
Etowah, Tenn. D9 83
Etowah, co., Ala. A3 46
Ettrick, Va. C5, n18 85
Etzatlan, Mex. m11 34
Eu, Fr. B4 5
Euclid, Ohio A4, g9 78
Euclid Center, Mich. *F4 66
Eudora, Ark. D4 49
Eudora, Kans. D8, m15 61
Eufaula, Ala. D4 46
Eufaula, Okla. B6 79
Eugene, Oreg. C3 80
Euless, Tex. *C4 84
Eunice, La. D3 63
Eunice, N. Mex. C7 48
Eupen, Bel. B7 5
Euphrates, see Firat, riv., Asia
Eupora, Miss. B4 68
Eure, dept., Fr. *C4 5
Eure-et-Loir, dept., Fr. *C4 5
Eureka, Calif. B1 50
Eureka, Ill. C4 58

Eureka, Kans. E7 61
Eureka, Mo. f12 69
Eureka, Mont. B1 70
Eureka, S. Dak. E6 77
Eureka, Utah B5 72
Eureka, co., Nev. B3 72
Eureka Springs, Ark. A2 49
Europe, cont. 3
Euskirchen, Ger., Fed. Rep. of C3 6
Eustis, Fla. D5 54
Eutaw, Ala. C2 46
Evangeline, La. D3 63
Evangeline, par., La. D3 63
Evans, Colo. A6 51
Evans, co., Ga. D5 55
Evans, mtn., Colo. B5 51
Evans City (Evansburg), Pa. E1 81
Evansdale, Iowa B5 60
Evanston, Ill. A6, h9 58
Evanston, Wyo. E2 89
Evansville, Ill. E4 58
Evansville, Ind. I2 59
Evansville, Wis. F4 88
Evart, Mich. E5 66
Evarts, Ky. D6 62
Eveleth, Minn. C6 67
Even Yehuda, Isr. *B2 15
Everard, mtn., B.C., Can. D5 37
Everest, peak, China, Nep. C8 20
Everett, Mass. g11 65
Everett, Pa. F5 81
Everett, Wash. B3 86

Everett, mtn., Mass. B1 65
Everglades, Fla. G5 54
Evergreen, Ala. D3 46
Evergreen Park, Ill. k9 58
Everman, Tex. *C4 84
Everson, Pa. F2 81
Évora, Port. C2 8
Évreux, Fr. C4 5
Évros, prov., Grc. *B5 14
Evvoia (Euboea), prov., Grc. *C4 14
Ewa, Haw. B3, g9 56
Ewa Beach, Haw. g9 56
Ewing, N.J. C3 74
Ewing, Va. f8 85
Excelsior, Minn. F5, n11 67
Excelsior, mtn., Cal. C4 50
Excelsior Springs, Mo. B3, h11 69
Exeter, Calif. D4 50
Exeter, Ont., Can. D3 41
Exeter, Eng. E5 4
Exeter, N.H. F6 73
Exeter, Pa. D10, n17 81
Exira, Iowa C3 60
Exmore, Va. C7 85
Exmouth, Austl. D1 25
Exmouth, Eng. E5 4
Experiment, Ga. C2 55
Export, Pa. F2 81
Eyemouth, Scot. C5 4
Eylar, mtn., Calif. D3 50
Eyre, lake, Austl. E6 25
Ezine, Tur. C6 14

F

Fabens, Tex. o11 84
Fabriano, It. C4 9
Facatativá, Col. C3 32
Factoryville, Pa. C10 81
Fada Ngourma, Burkina Faso E6 21
Faenza, It. B3 9
Faeroe Islands, Dan. dep. Eur. C6 3
Fafe, Port. B1 8
Făgăraș, Rom. C7 10
Fagatogo, Am. Sam. *G9 2
Fagersta, Swe. G6 11
Faifo, Viet. *B3 19
Fairbank, Iowa B5 60
Fairbanks, Alsk. C10 47
Fair Bluff, N.C. C3 76
Fairborn, Ohio C1 78
Fairburn, Ga. C2, h7 55
Fairbury, Ill. C5 58
Fairbury, Nebr. D8 71
Fairchance, Pa. G2 81
Fairdale, Ky. g11 62
Fairfax, Ala. C4 46
Fairfax, Calif. C2, h7 50
Fairfax, Del. *A6 53
Fairfax, Iowa C6 60
Fairfax, Minn. F4 67
Fairfax, Mo. A2 69
Fairfax, Ohio C1 78
Fairfax, Okla. A5 79
Fairfax, S.C. F5 82
Fairfax (Independent City)
  Va. B5, g12 85
Fairfax, co., Va. B5 85
Fairfield, Ala. B3, f7 46
Fairfield, Calif. C2 50
Fairfield, Conn. E3 52
Fairfield, Ill. E5 58
Fairfield, Iowa D6 60
Fairfield, Maine D3 64
Fairfield, Mont. C5 70
Fairfield, N.J. *B4 74
Fairfield, Ohio n12 78
Fairfield, Tex. D4 84
Fairfield, co., Conn. D3 52
Fairfield, co., Ohio C3 78
Fairfield, co., S.C. C5 82
Fairgrove, Mich. E7 66
Fair Grove, N.C. *B2 76
Fairhaven, Mass. C6 65
Fair Haven, Mich. F8 66
Fair Haven, N.J. C4 74
Fair Haven, N.Y. B4 75
Fair Haven, Vt. D1 73
Fairhope, Ala. E2 46

Fairhope, Pa. *G2 81
Fairland, Ind. E6 59
Fairland, Okla. A7 79
Fair Lawn, N.J. h8 74
Fairlawn, Ohio *A4 78
Fairless Hills, Pa. *F11 81
Fairmont, Ill. k8 58
Fairmont, Minn. G4 67
Fairmont, N.C. C3 76
Fairmont, Wash. *B3 86
Fairmont, W. Va. B4, k10 87
Fairmont City, Ill. f13 69
Fairmount, Ill. C6 58
Fairmount, Ind. D6 59
Fairmount, N.Y. *B4 75
Fairmount Heights, Md. f9 53
Fair Oaks, Calif. C3 50
Fair Oaks, Calif. *E3 50
Fair Oaks, Ga. h7 55
Fairoaks, Pa. h13 81
Fair Plain, Mich. F4 66
Fairpoint, Ohio B5 78
Fairport, N.Y. B3 75
Fairport Harbor, Ohio A4 78
Fairton, N.J. E2 74
Fairvale, N.B., Can. D4 43
Fairview, Alta., Can. A1 38
Fairview, Ill. C3 58
Fairview, Mont. C12 70
Fairview, N.J. D3 74
Fairview, N.J. h8 74
Fairview, N.Y. *D7 75
Fairview, Ohio B4 78
Fairview, Okla. A3 79
Fairview, Pa. *D8 81
Fairview, Pa. *E11 81
Fairview, Pa. B1 81
Fairview, Tenn. B4 83
Fairview, Utah B6 72
Fairview, Wash. *C5 86
Fairview, peak, Oreg. D4 80
Fairview Park, Ind. E3 59
Fairview Park, Ohio h9 78
Fairview Shores, Fla. *D5 54
Fairvilla, Fla. *D5 54
Fairway, Kans. B9 61
Faisalabad, Pak. B5 20
Faizabad, Afg. A5 20
Faizābād, India C7 20
Fajardo, P.R. G12 35
Fakfak, Indon. F8 19
Fălciu, Rom. B9 10
Falxón, state, Ven. A3 32
Falconer, N.Y. C1 75

Falcon Heights, Minn. n12 67
Falconwood, N.Y. *C2 75
Faleshty, Sov. Un. B8 10
Falfurrias, Tex. F3 84
Falher, Alta., Can. B2 38
Falkirk, Scot. C5 4
Falkland Islands, Br. dep., S.A. I5 27
Falköping, Swe. H5 11
Fall Branch, Tenn. C11 83
Fallbrook, Calif. F5 50
Fallon, Nev. B2 72
Fallon, co., Mont. D12 70
Fall River, Mass. C5 65
Fall River, co., S.Dak. G2 77
Fall Rock, Ky. C6 62
Falls, co., Tex. D4 84
Falls Church (Independent
  City), Va. g12 85
Falls City, Nebr. D10 71
Falls City, Oreg. C3 80
Falls Creek, Pa. D4 81
Fallsington, Pa. *F11 81
Falmouth, Eng. E4 4
Falmouth, Jam. E5 35
Falmouth, Ky. B5 62
Falmouth, Maine E5 64
Falmouth, Mass. C6 65
Falmouth, N.S. E5 43
Falmouth, Va. B5 85
Falticeni, Rom. B8 10
Falun, Swe. G6 11
Fannin, co., Ga. B2 55
Fannin, co., Tex. C4 84
Fanny, mtn., Oreg. B9 80
Fano, It. C4 9
Fanwood, N.J. B4 74
Faradofay, Mad. E9 24
Farafangana, Mad. E9 24
Farah, Afg. B3 20
Faranah, Guinea F2 22
Fargo, N.Dak. D9 77
Faribault, Minn. F5 67
Faribault, co., Minn. G5 67
Farina, Ill. E5 58
Farley, Iowa B6 60
Farmer City, Ill. C5 58
Farmers Branch, Tex. n10 84
Farmersburg, Ind. F3 59
Farmersville, Tex. C4 84
Farmerville, La. B3 63
Farmingdale, Maine D3 64
Farmingdale, N.J. *C4 74
Farmingdale, N.Y. G3 52

Farmington, Conn. C5 52
Farmington, Ill. C3 58
Farmington, Iowa D6 60
Farmington, Maine D2 64
Farmington, Mich. p15 66
Farmington, Minn. F5 67
Farmington, Mo. D7 69
Farmington, N.H. E5 73
Farmington, N. Mex. A4 48
Farmington, Utah A6, C2 72
Farmington Hills, Mich. o15 66
Farmingville, N.Y. n16 75
Farmland, Ind. D7 59
Farmville, N.C. B5 76
Farmville, Va. C4 85
Farnham, Que., Can. D5 42
Farnham, mtn., B.C. D9 37
Faro, Port. D2 8
Farrell, Pa. D1 81
Farrukhābād, India C6 20
Farwell, Mich. E6 66
Farwell, Tex. B1 84
Fasano, It. D6 9
Fastov, Sov. Un. F7 12
Fatehpur, India C6 20
Fatsa, Tur. B11 14
Faulk, co., S.Dak. E6 77
Faulkner, co., Ark. B3 49
Faulkton, S.Dak. E6 77
Fauquier, co., Va. B5 85
Faust, Alta., Can. B3 38
Favara, It. F4 9
Fawnie Nose, mtn., B.C.,
  Can. C5 37
Faxon, Pa. *D7 81
Fayette, Ala. B2 46
Fayette, Iowa B6 60
Fayette, Miss. D2 68
Fayette, Mo. B5 69
Fayette, Ohio A1 78
Fayette, co., Ala. B2 46
Fayette, co., Ga. C2 55
Fayette, co., Ill. D4 58
Fayette, co., Ind. E7 59
Fayette, co., Iowa B6 60
Fayette, co., Ky. B5 62
Fayette, co., Ohio C2 78
Fayette, co., Pa. G2 81
Fayette, co., Tenn. B2 83
Fayette, co., Tex. E4 84
Fayette, co., W.Va. C3 87
Fayette City, Pa. *G2 81
Fayetteville, Ark. A1 49
Fayetteville, Ga. C2 55

Fayetteville, N.Y. B5 75
Fayetteville, N.C. B4 76
Fayetteville, Pa. G6 81
Fayetteville, Tenn. B5 83
Fayetteville, W.Va. C3,m13 87
Fayville, Mass. g9 65
Feasterville, Pa. o21 81
Feather Falls, Calif. C3 50
Fécamp, Fr. C4 5
Federalsburg, Md. C6 53
Federal Way, Wash. *B3 86
Fedscreek, Ky C7 62
Feeding Hills, Mass. B2 65
Feilding, N.Z. N15 26
Feira de Santana, Braz. *E7 27
Fejér, co., Hung. *B4 10
Felanitx, Sp. C7 8
Feldkirch, Aus. E4 6
Felicity, Ohio D1 78
Felipe Carrillo Puerto, Mex. D7 34
Fellsmere, Fla. E6 54
Felton, Calif. D2 50
Feltre, It. A3 9
Fenelon Falls, Ont., Can. D4 41
Fengshan, Taiwan *G9 17
Fennimore, Wis. F3 88
Fennville, Mich. F4 66
Fenton, Mich. F7 66
Fenton, Mo. f13 69
Fentress, co., Tenn. C9 83
Fenyang, China D7 17
Fedosiya, Sov. Un. I10 12
Ferdinand, Ind. H4 59
Ferentino, It. D4 9
Fergana, Sov. Un. *E10 13
Fergus, Ont., Can. D4 41
Fergus, co., Mont. C7 70
Fergus Falls, Minn. D2 67
Ferguson, Mo. C7, f13 69
Fermanagh, co., N.Ire. *C3 4
Ferme-Neuve, Que., Can. C2 42
Fermo, It. C4 9
Fernandina Beach, Fla. B5, k9 54
Fern Creek, Ky. g11 62
Ferndale, Calif. B1 50
Ferndale, Md. B4 53
Ferndale, Mich. *F7 66
Ferndale, Pa. F4 81
Ferndale, Wash. A3 86
Fernie, B.C., Can. E10 37
Fern Park, Fla. D5 54
Fernwood, N.Y. B4 75
Ferrara, It. B3 9
Ferreñafe, Peru C2 31
Ferriday, La. C4 63
Ferris, Ont., Can. *A5 41
Ferris, Tex. C4, n10 84
Ferris, mts., Wyo D5 89
Ferry, co., Wash. A7 86
Ferryland, Newf., Can. E5 44
Ferrysburg, Mich. *E4 66
Ferryville, Tun. F2 9
Fertile, Minn. C2 67
Fès, Mor. B3 22
Fessenden, N. Dak. C6 77
Festus, Mo. C7, g13 69
Fetesti, Rom. C8 10
Fetters Hot Springs, Calif. *C2 50
Ffestiniog, Wales D5 4
Fianarantsoa, Malag. E9 24
Fidenza, It. B3 9
Fieldale, Va. D3 85
Fier, Alb. *B2 14
Fierro Urco, vol., Peru B2 31
Fife, co., Sask., Can. *B5 4
Fife, Wash. *B3 86
Figeac, Fr. E4 5
Figueira da Foz, Port. B1 8
Figueras, Sp. A7 8
Fiji, country, Oceania H8 2
Filer, Idaho G4 57
Filiatra, Grc. D3 14
Fillmore, Calif. E4 50
Fillmore, Utah B5 72
Fillmore, co., Minn. G6 67
Fillmore, co., Nebr. D8 71
Finderne, N.J. *B3 74
Findlay, Ohio A2 78
Findlay, Ill. D5 58
Findlay, mtn., B.C., Can. D9 37
Finistère, dept., Fr. *C2 5
Finland, country, Eur. E12 11
Finney, co., Kans. D3 61
Finneytown, Ohio *C1 78
Finnmark, co., Nor. *B13 11
Finspång, Swe. u33 11
Finsterwalde, Ger. Dem. Rep. *C6 6
Firat (Euphrates), riv.,
  Asia D12 14
Fircrest, Wash. f10 86
Firebaugh, Calif. D3 50
Firenze, see Florence, It.

Firenzuola, It. B3 9
Firminy, Fr. E6 5
Firozabad, India *C6 20
Firozpur, India B5 20
Fisher, Ill. C5 58
Fisher, co., Tex. C2 84
Fisher, peak, Va. D2 85
Fishersville, Va. B4 85
Fishguard, Wales E4 4
Fishing Creek, Md. D5 53
Fishkill, N.Y. D7 75
Fiskdale, Mass. D3 65
Fitchburg, Mass. A4 65
Fitzgerald, Ga. E3 55
Fitz Roy, mtn., Arg. D2 28
Fiume, see Rijeka, Yugo.
Five Points, N.Mex. *B3 48
Flagler, co., Fla. C5 54
Flagler Beach, Fla. C5 54
Flagstaff, Ariz. B3 48
Flagtown, N.J. B3 74
Flanagan, Ill. C5 58
Flanders, N.Y. *n16 75
Flandreau, S.Dak. F9 77
Flat Creek, Ala. B2, f6 46
Flathead, co., Mont. B2 70
Flathead, mts., Mont. B2 70
Flatonia, Tex. E4 84
Flat River, Mo. D7 69
Flat Rock, Newf., Can. *E5 44
Flat Rock, Mich. F7 66
Flat Rock, N.C. f10 76
Flatwoods, Ky. B7 62
Fleetwing Estates, Pa. *F11 81
Fleetwood, Pa. F10 81
Fleming, co., Ky. B6 62
Flemingsburg, Ky. B6 62
Flemington, N.J. B3 74
Flemington, Pa. D7 81
Flensburg, Ger., Fed. Rep. of A4 6
Flers, Fr. C3 5
Fletcher, N.C. f10 76
Fletcher, Okla. C4 79
Flin Flon, Man., Can. B1, g7 40
Flint, Mich. F7 66
Flint, co., Wales *D5 4
Flintridge, Calif. *F4 50
Flomaton, Ala. D2 46
Floodwood, Minn. D6 67
Flora, Ill. E5 58
Flora, Ind. C4 59
Florala, Ala. D3 46
Floral City, Fla. D4 54
Floral Park, Mont. *D4 70
Floral Park, N.Y. k13 75
Flordell Hills, Mo. *C7 69
Florence, Ala. A2 46
Florence, Ariz. C3, D2 48
Florence, Calif. *E4 50
Florence, Colo. C5 51
Florence (Firenze), It. C3 9
Florence, Kans. D7 61
Florence, KY. B5, k13 62
Florence, N.J. C3 74
Florence, Oreg. D2 80
Florence, S.C. C8 82
Florence, Wis. C5 88
Florence, co., S.C. C8 82
Florence, co., Wis. C5 88
Florence (Firenze), It. C3 9
Florencia, Col. C2 32
Flores, Guat. H12 33
Flores, isl., Indon. G6 19
Flores, dept., Ur. *E1 30
Floresville, Tex. E3, k7 84
Florham Park, N.J. B4 74
Floriano, Braz. D6 27
Florianópolis, Braz. D3 30
Florida, Cuba D4 35
Florida, N.Y. D6, m14 75
Florida, Ur. E1 30
Florida, dept., Ur. *E1 30
Florida, state, U.S. E10 45
Florida, bay, Fla. E10 54
Florida City, Fla. G6, t13 54
Florida Keys, is., Fla. H6 54
Florina, Grc. E5 10
Flórina, prov., Grc. *B3 14
Florissant, Mo. f13 69
Flossmoor, Ill. k9 58
Flourtown, Pa. o21 81
Flower Hill, N.Y. *E7 75
Floyd, co., Ga. B1 55
Floyd, co., Ind. H6 59
Floyd, co., Iowa A5 60
Floyd, co., Ky. C7 62
Floyd, co., Tex. B2 84
Floyd, co., Va. D2 85
Floydada, Tex. C2 84
Flushing, Mich. E7 66
Flushing, Ohio B4 78
Fluvanna, co., Va. C4 85
Foam Lake, Sask., Can. F4 39

Foard, co., Tex. B3 84
Focşani, Rom. C8 10
Foggia, It. D5 9
Fogo, Newf., Can. D4 44
Fohnsdorf, Aus. E7 6
Foix, Fr. F4 5
Folcroft, Pa. *G11 81
Foley, Ala. E2 46
Foley, Minn. E5 67
Foligno, It. C4 9
Folkestone, Eng. E7 4
Folkston, Ga. F4 55
Follansbee, W. Va. A4, f8 87
Follonica, It. C3 9
Folly Beach, S.C. F8, k12 82
Folsom, Calif. C3 50
Folsom, Pa. *G11 81
Fomento, Cuba C4 35
Fonda, Iowa B3 60
Fonda, N.Y. C6 75
Fond du Lac, Wis. E5, k9 88
Fond du Lac, co., Wis. E5 88
Fondi, It. D4 9
Fonsagrada, Sp. A2 8
Fontainebleau, Fr. C5 5
Fontana, Calif. m14 50
Fontana, Wis. F5 88
Fontanelle, Iowa C3 60
Fontenay-le-Comte, Fr. D3 5
Fontenay -sous-Bois, Fr. g10 5
Foochow, see Fuzhou, China
Footville, Wis. F4 88
Forbach, Fr. C7 5
Forbes, Austl. F8 25
Forbes, mtn., Alta., Can. D2 38
Forchheim, Ger., Fed. Rep. of D5 6
Ford, co., Ill. C5 58
Ford, co., Kans. E4 61
Ford City, Calif. E4 50
Ford City, Pa. E2 81
Fords, N.J. *B4 74
Fords Prairie, Wash. *C3 86
Fordyce, Ark. D3 49
Foreman, Ark. D1 49
Forest, Bel. B6 5
Forest, Ont., Can. D2 41
Forest, Miss. C4 68
Forest, Ohio B2 78
Forest, co., Pa. C3 81
Forest, co., Wis. C5 88
Forest Acres, S.C. C6 82
Forestburg, Alta., Can. C4 38
Forest City, Iowa A4 60
Forest City, N.C. B1, f11 76
Forest City, Pa. C11 81
Forest Grove, Oreg. B3, g11 80
Forest Heights, Md. *C4 53
Forest Hill, Tex. *C4 84
Forest Hills, N.B., Can. *D4 43
Forest Hill, Tex. *C4 84
Forest Hills, Pa. k14 81
Forest Homes, Ill. *E3 58
Forest Knolls, Calif. g7 50
Forest Lake, Minn. E6 67
Forest Park, Ga. h8 55
Forest Park, Ill. k9 58
Forestview, Ill. *B6 58
Forestville, Md. *C4 53
Forestville, N.Y. C1 75
Forfar, Scot. *B5 4
Forge Village, Mass. A5, f10 65
Forked River, N.J. D4 74
Forks, Wash. B1 86
Forli, It. B4 9
Formiga, Braz. C3 30
Formosa, Arg. E4 29
Formosa, prov., Arg. E4 29
Formosa, see Taiwan, Asia
Forney, Tex. C4, n10 84
Forres, Scot. B5 4
Forrest, Ill. C5 58
Forrest, co., Miss. D4 68
Forreston, Ill. A4 58
Forrest City, Ark. B5 49
Forsayth, Austl. C8 25
Forst, Ger. Dem. Rep. C7 6
Forster-Tuncurry,
  Austl. F9 26
Forsyth, Ga. C3 55
Forsyth, Mont. D10 70
Forsyth, co., Ga. B2 55
Forsyth, co., N.C. A2 76
Fortaleza, Braz. D7 27
Fort Atkinson, Wis. F5 88
Fort Bend, co., Tex. E5 84
Fort Benton, Mont. C6 70
Fort Bragg, Calif. C2 50
Fort Branch, Ind. H2 59
Fort Chipewyan, Alta., Can. f8 38
Fort Cobb, Okla. B3 79
Fort Collins, Colo. A5 51
Fort Collins West, Colo. *A5 51
Fort Coulonge, Que., Can. B8 41
Fort Covington, N.Y. f10 75
Fort Davis, Tex. o13 84

Fort-de France, Mart. I14 35
Fort Deposit, Ala. D3 46
Fort Dodge, Iowa B3 60
Fort Edward, N.Y. B7 75
Fort Erie, Ont., Can. E6 41
Fort Fairfield, Maine B7 64
Fort Frances, Ont., Can. o16 41
Fort Gaines, Ga. E1 55
Fort-George, Que., Can. h11 42
Fort Gibson, Okla. B6 79
Fort Hall, Idaho F6 57
Fort Hancock, Tex. o12 84
Fort Howard, Md. B5 53
Fort Johnson, N.Y. *C6 75
Fort Kent, Maine A4 64
Fort-Lamy, see Ndjamena, Chad
Fort Langley, B.C., Can. f13 37
Fort Lauderdale, Fla. F6, r13 54
Fort Lee, N.J. h9 74
Fort Leavenworth, Kans. C8, k15 61
Fort-Liberté, Hai. E8 35
Fort Loramie, Ohio B1 78
Fort Lupton, Colo. A6 51
Fort Macleod, Alta.,Can. E4 38
Fort Madison, Iowa D6 60
Fort McKinley, Ohio *C1 78
Fort Meade, Fla. E5 54
Fort Mill, S.C. A6 82
Fort Morgan, Colo. A7 51
Fort Myers, Fla. F5 54
Fort Myers Beach, Fla. F5 54
Fort Nelson, B.C., Can. m18 37
Fort Oglethorpe, Ga. B1 55
Fort Payne, Ala. A4 46
Fort Peck, Mont. B10 70
Fort Pierce, Fla. E6 54
Fort Pierre, S. Dak. F5 77
Fort Plain, N.Y. C6 75
Fort Qu'Appelle, Sask., Can. G4 39
Fort Recovery, Ohio B1 78
Fort Riley, Kans. C7 61
Fort St. James, B.C., Can. B5 37
Fort St. John, B.C., Can. A7, m18 37
Fort Saskatchewan, Alta., Can. C4 38
Fort Scott, Kans. E9 61
Fort Shawnee, Ohio B1 78
Fort Smith, Ark. B1 49
Fort. St. John, B.C., Can. A7, m18 37
Fort Stockton, Tex. D1 84
Fort Sumner, N. Mex. B6 48
Fort Thomas, Ky. h14 62
Fortuna, Calif. B1 50
Fortune, Newf., Can. E4 44
Fort Valley, Ga. D3 55
Fort Vermilion, Alta., Can. f7 38
Fortville, Ind. E6 59
Fort Walton Beach, Fla. u15 54
Fort Washington, Pa. o21 81
Fort Washington Forest,
  Md. C4 53
Fort Wayne, Ind. B7 59
Fort William, Scot. B4 4
Fort Worth, Tex. C4, n9 84
Fort Wright, Ky. h13 62
Fort Yates, N. Dak. D5 77
Forty Fort, Pa. D10, n17 81
Fossano, It. B1 9
Fosses, Scot. C3 67
Fossombrone, It. C4 9
Fossil, Oreg. B6 80
Fosston, Minn. C3 67
Foster, co., N. Dak. C7 77
Foster Brook, Pa. C4 81
Foster Village, Haw. g10 56
Fostoria, Ohio A2 78
Fougères, Fr. C3 5
Foumban, Cam. G7 22
Fountain, Colo. C6 51
Fountain, co., Ind. D3 59
Fountain, peak, Calif. E6 50
Fountain City, Ind. E8 59
Fountain City, Wis. D2 88
Fountain Green, Utah B7 72
Fountain Hill, Pa. E11 81
Fountain Inn, S.C. B3 82
Fountain Place, La. *D4 63
Fountain Valley, Calif. *F5 50
Four Corners, Oreg. *C4 80
Fourmies, Fr. B6 5
Four Oaks, N.C. B4 76
Fowler, Calif. D4 50
Fowler, Colo. C6 51
Fowler, Ind. C3 59
Fowler, Kans. E3 61
Fowler, Mich. E6 66
Fowlerville, Mich. F6 66
Foxboro, Mass. B5 65
Fox Chapel, Pa. *E1 81
Fox Farm, Wyo *E8 89
Fox Harbour, Newf., Can. A5 44
Fox Lake, Ill. A5, h8 58
Fox Lake, Wis. E5 88
Fox Point, Wis. E5, m12 88
Fox River Grove, Ill. h8 58

Foxworth, Miss. ... D4 68
Frackville, Pa. ... E9 81
Fraga, Sp. ... B6 8
Framingham, Mass. ... B5, g10 65
Franca, Braz. ... C3 30
Francavilla Fontana, It. ... D6 9
France, country, Eur. ... 5
Francesville, Ind. ... C4 9
Franche-Comté reg., Fr. ... D6 5
Francistown, Bots. ... E5 24
Franconville, Fr. ... g9 5
Frankenberg, Ger., Fed. Rep. of ... C4 6
Frankenmuth, Mich. ... E7 66
Frankenthal, Ger., Fed. Rep. of ... D4 6
Frankford, Ont., Can. ... C7 41
Frankfort, Ill. ... m9 58
Frankfort, Ind. ... D4 59
Frankfort, Kans. ... C7 61
Frankfort, Ky. ... B5 62
Frankfort, Mich. ... D4 66
Frankfort, N.Y. ... B5 75
Frankfurt am Main,
  Ger., Fed. Rep. of ... C4 6
Frankfurt an der Oder,
  Ger. Dem. Rep ... B7 6
Franklin, Idaho ... *F2 57
Franklin, Ind. ... F5 59
Franklin, Kans. ... E9 61
Franklin, Ky. ... D3 62
Franklin, La. ... E4 63
Franklin, Mass. ... B5 65
Franklin, Mich. ... *F7 66
Franklin, Nebr. ... D7 71
Franklin, N.H. ... E4 73
Franklin, N.J. ... A3 74
Franklin, N.C. ... f9 76
Franklin, Ohio ... C1 78
Franklin, Pa. ... *E4 81
Franklin, Pa. ... D2 81
Franklin, Tenn. ... B5 83
Franklin, Tex. ... D4 84
Franklin (Independent City)
  Va. ... D6 85
Franklin, Wis. ... n11 88
Franklin, co., Ala. ... A2 46
Franklin, co., Ark. ... B2 49
Franklin, co., Fla. ... C2 54
Franklin, co., Ga. ... B3 55
Franklin, co., Idaho ... G7 57
Franklin, co., Ill. ... E5 58
Franklin, co., Ind. ... F7 59
Franklin, co. Iowa ... B4 60
Franklin, co., Kans. ... D8 61
Franklin, co., Ky. ... B5 62
Franklin, co., Maine ... C2 64
Franklin, co., Mass. ... A2 65
Franklin, co., Miss. ... D3 68
Franklin, co., Mo. ... C6 69
Franklin, co., Nebr. ... D7 71
Franklin, co., N.Y. ... A6 75
Franklin, co., N.C. ... A4 76
Franklin, co., Ohio ... B2 78
Franklin, co., Pa. ... G6 81
Franklin, co., Tenn. ... B5 83
Franklin, co., Tex. ... C5 84
Franklin, co., Vt. ... B2 73
Franklin, co., Va. ... D3 85
Franklin, co., Wash. ... C6 86
Franklin, dist., N. W. Ter., Can. ... B13 36
Franklin, par.,La. ... B4 63
Franklin Furnace, Ohio ... D3 78
Franklin Grove, Ill. ... B4 58
Franklin Lakes, N.J. ... *B4 74

Franklin Park, Ill. ... k9 58
Franklin Park, N.J. ... C3 74
Franklin Park, Va. ... *B5 85
Franklin Square, N.Y. ... G2 52
Franklinton La. ... D5 63
Franklinton, N.C. ... A4 76
Franklinville, N.J. ... D2 74
Franklinville, N.Y. ... C2 75
Franklinville, N.C. ... B3 76
Frankston, Tex. ... C5 84
Frankton, Ind. ... D6 59
Frascati, It. ... D4, h9 9
Fraser, Mich. ... *F8 66
Fraser, riv., B.C., Can. ... C6 37
Fraser, mtn., B.C., Can. ... C8 37
Fraserburgh, Scot. ... B6 4
Frauenfeld, Switz. ... E4 6
Fray Bentos, Ur. ... E1 30
Frazee, Minn. ... D3 67
Frazeyburg, Ohio ... B3 78
Frazier Park, Calif. ... E4 50
Frederic, Wis. ... C1 88
Fredericia, Den. ... J3 11
Frederick, Md. ... B3 53
Frederick, Okla. ... C2 79
Frederick, co., Md. ... B3 53
Frederick, co., Va. ... A4 85
Fredericksburg, Iowa ... B5 60
Fredericksburg, Pa. ... *F9 81
Fredericksburg, Tex. ... D3 84
Fredericksburg (Independent City),
  Va. ... B5 85
Fredericktown, Mo. ... D7 69
Fredericktown, Ohio ... B3 78
Fredericktown, Pa. ... F1 81
Fredericton, N.B., Can. ... D3 43
Frederiksborg, co., Den. ... *J5 11
Frederikshavn, Den. ... I4 11
Frederiksted, Vir. Is., (U.S.) ... H12 35
Fredonia, Kans. ... E8 61
Fredonia, N.Y. ... C1 75
Fredonia, Pa. ... D1 81
Fredonia, Wis. ... E6 88
Fredrikstad, Nor. ... H4, p28 11
Freeborn, co., Minn. ... G5 67
Freeburg, Ill. ... E4 58
Freedom, Calif. ... *D3 50
Freedom, Pa. ... E1 81
Freehold, N.J. ... C4 74
Freel, peak, Calif. ... C4 50
Freeland, Mich. ... E6 66
Freeland, Pa. ... D10 81
Freelandville, Ind. ... G3 59
Freeman, S. Dak. ... G8 77
Freemansburg, Pa. ... E11 81
Freeport, Fla. ... u15 54
Freeport, Ill. ... A4 58
Freeport, Maine ... E2, g7 64
Freeport ,Minn. ... E4 67
Freeport, N.Y. ... G2 52
Freeport, Pa. ... E2 81
Freeport, Tex. ... E5, s14 84
Freer, Tex. ... F3 84
Freestone, co., Tex. ... *D4 84
Freetown, N.Y. ... *m16 75
Freetown, S.L. ... G2 22
Fregenal de la Sierra, Sp. ... C2 8
Freiberg, Ger. Dem. Rep ... C6 6
Freiburg im Breisgau,
  Ger., Fed. Rep. of ... D3 6
Freising, Ger., Fed. Rep. of ... D5 6
Freistadt, Aus. ... D7 6
Fréjus, Fr. ... F3 5

Fremantle, Austl. ... F2 25
Fremont, Calif. ... D2, h9 50
Fremont, Ind. ... A8 59
Fremont, Mich. ... E5 66
Fremont, Nebr. ... C9, g11 71
Fremont, N.C. ... B5 76
Fremont, Ohio ... A2 78
Fremont, co., Colo. ... C5 51
Fremont, co., Idaho ... E7 57
Fremont, co., Iowa ... D2 60
Fremont, co., Wyo. ... C4 89
French Camp, Calif. ... *D3 50
French Guiana, dep., S.A. ... C5 27
French Lick, Ind. ... G4 59
French Polynesia,
  Fr. dep., Oceania ... *H11 2
Frenchtown, N.J. ... B2 74
Frenchville, Maine ... A4 64
Freshfield, mtn., Alta., Can. ... D9 37
Freshwater, Newf., Can. ... *f9 44
Fresnillo de González
  Echeverría, Mex. ... C4 34
Fresno, Calif. ... D4 50
Fresno, co., Calif. ... D4 50
Freudenstadt, Ger., Fed.
  Rep. of ... D4 6
Frewsburg, N.Y. ... C1 75
Friant, Calif. ... D4 50
Friars Point, Miss. ... A3 68
Frias, Arg. ... E2 29
Fribourg, Switz. ... E8 6
Fribourg, canton, Switz. ... *E3 6
Friday Harbor, Wash. ... A2 86
Fridley, Minn. ... m12 67
Friedberg, Ger., Fed. Rep. of ... B6 6
Friedens, Pa. ... F4 81
Friedland, Ger. Dem. Rep. ... B6 6
Friedrichshafen, Ger.,
  Fed. Rep. of ... E4 6
Friend, Nebr. ... D8 71
Friendship, N.Y. ... C2 75
Friern Barnet, Eng. ... k12 4
Fries, Va. ... D2 85
Friesland, prov., Neth. ... *A6 5
Frio, co., Tex. ... E3 84
Friona, Tex. ... B1 84
Frisco, Pa. ... *E1 81
Frisco, Tex. ... *C4 84
Frisco City, Ala. ... D2 46
Fritch, Tex. ... B2 84
Fritzlar, Ger., Fed. Rep. of ... C4 6
Friuli-Venezia Giulia, reg., It. ... *B4 9
Frontenac, Kans. ... E9 61
Frontenac, Mo. ... *C7 69
Frontenac, co., Ont., Can. ... C8 41
Frontenac, co., Que., Can. ... D7 42
Frontera, Mex. ... D6 34
Frontier, co., Nebr. ... D5 71
Frontignan, Fr. ... F5 5
Frontino, peak, Col. ... B2 32
Front Royal, Va. ... B4 85
Frosinone, It. ... D4 9
Frostburg, Md. ... k13 53
Frostproof, Fla. ... E5 54
Frouard, Fr. ... C7 4
Fruita, Colo. ... B2 51
Fruitdale, Oreg. ... *E3 80
Fruitland, Idaho ... F2 57
Fruitland, Ill. ... *B3 58
Fruitland, Md. ... D6 53
Fruitland Park, Fla. ... D5 54
Fruitport, Mich. ... E4 66
Fruitvale, Wash. ... *C5 86

Fruitville, Fla. ... E4, q11 54
Frunze, Sov. Un. ... E10 13
Frýdek-Místek,Czech. ... D5 7
Fryeburg, Maine ... D2 64
Fthiotis (Phthiotis), prov., Grc. ... *C4 14
Fuchou see Fuzhou, China
Fuchu, Jap. ... *I9 18
Fuente Alamo, Sp. ... D5 8
Fuente de Cantos, Sp. ... C2 8
Fuenteovejuna, Sp. ... C3 8
Fuhai, China ... B2 17
Fuji, Jap. ... n17 18
Fuji, vol., Jap. ... I9, n17 18
Fujian, prov., China ... F8 17
Fujieda, Jap. ... o17 18
Fujimi, Jap. ... n17 18
Fujin, China ... B11 17
Fujinomiya, Jap. ... n17 18
Fujisawa, Jap. ... *I9 18
Fuji-yoshida, Jap. ... n17 18
Fukagawka, Jap. ... E10 18
Fukuchiyama, Jap. ... I7, n14 18
Fukui, Jap. ... H8 18
Fukui, pref., Jap. ... *H8 18
Fukuoka, Jap. ... F10 18
Fukuoka, Jap. ... J5 18
Fukuoka, pref., Jap. ... *J5 18
Fukushima, Jap. ... I8, n16 18
Fukushima, Jap. ... H10 18
Fukushima, pref., Jap. ... *H10 18
Fukuyama, Jap. ... I6 18
Fulda, Ger., Fed. Rep. of ... C4 6
Fulda, Minn. ... G3 67
Fullerton, Calif. ... n13 50
Fullerton, Ky. ... B7 62
Fullerton, Nebr. ... C8 71
Fulton, Ill. ... B3 58
Fulton, Ky. ... f9 62
Fulton, Miss. ... A5 68
Fulton, Mo. ... C6 69
Fulton, N.Y. ... B4 75
Fulton, co., Ark. ... A4 49
Fulton, co., Ga. ... C2 55
Fulton, co., Ill. ... C3 58
Fulton, co., Ind. ... B5 59
Fulton, co., Ky. ... B2 62
Fulton, co., N.Y. ... B6 75
Fulton, co., Ohio ... A1 78
Fulton, co., Pa. ... G5 81
Fultondale, Ala. ... f7 46
Fumay, Fr. ... C6 5
Funabashi, Jap. ... n19 18
Funchal, Port. ... h12 8
Fundación, Col. ... A3 32
Funkstown, Md. ... A2 53
Fuquay-Varina, N.C. ... *B4 76
Furano, Jap. ... E11 18
Furman University,S.C. ... *B3 82
Furnas, co., Nebr. ... D6 71
Fürstenfeld, Aus. ... E8 6
Fürstenwalde, Ger. Dem. Rep. ... B7 6
Fürth, Ger., Fed. Rep. of ... D5 6
Furukawa, Jap. ... H8, m16 18
Fusagasugá, Col. ... C3 32
Fushun, China ... C9 17
Fusong, China ... E3 18
Füssen, Ger., Fed. Rep. of ... E5 6
Fuxin, China ... C9 17
Fuyang, China ... E8 17
Fuyu, China ... B9 17
Fuyuan, China ... B7 18
Fuzhou, China ... F8 17

G

Gabès, Tun. ... B7 22
Gabin, Pol. ... B5 7
Gabon (Gabun),country, Afr. ... I7 22
Gaborone, Bots. ... E5 24
Gabrovo, Bul. ... D7 10
Gadag, India ... E6 20
Gadsden, Ala. ... A3 46
Gadsden, co., Fla. ... B2 54
Gadyach, Sov.Un. ... F9 12
Gãesti, Rom. ... C7 10
Gaeta, It. ... D4 9
Gaffney, S.C. ... A4 82
Gafsa, Tun. ... B6 22
Gage, co., Nebr. ... D9 71
Gages Lake, Ill. ... *A5 58

Gagnon, Que., Can. ... h13 42
Gagny, Fr. ... g11 5
Gahanna, Ohio ... k11 78
Gaillac, Fr. ... F4 5
Gaines, co., Tex. ... C1 84
Gainesboro, Tenn. ... C8 83
Gainesville, Fla. ... C4 54
Gainesville, Ga. ... B3 55
Gainesville, Tex. ... C4 84
Gainsborough, Eng. ... D6 4
Gairdner, lake, Austl. ... F6 25
Gairloch, Scot. ... B4 4
Gaithersburg, Md. ... B3 53
Gaixian, China ... C9 17
Galacz, see Galati, Rom.

Galápagos, prov., Ec. ... g5 31
Galashiels, Scot. ... C5 4
Galati, Rom. ... C8 10
Galatia, Ill. ... F5 58
Galatina, It. ... D7 9
Galax (Independent City), Va. ... D2 85
Gáldar, Sp. ... m14 8
Galeana, Mex. ... A3 34
Galena, Ill. ... A3 58
Galena, Kans. ... E9 61
Galena Park, Tex. ... r14 84
Gales, peak, Oreg. ... g11 80
Galesburg, Ill. ... C3 58
Galesburg, Mich. ... F5 66
Galesville, Md. ... C4 53

Galesville, Wis. ... D2 88
Galeton, Pa. ... C6 81
Galeville, N.Y. ... *B4 75
Galicia, reg., Pol., Sov. Un. ... D6 7
Galicia, reg., Sp. ... A1 8
Galien, Mich. ... G4 66
Galion, Ohio ... B3 78
Gallarate, It. ... B1 9
Gallatin, Mo. ... B4 69
Gallatin, Tenn. ... A5 83
Gallatin, co., Ill. ... F5 58
Gallatin, co., Ky. ... B5 62
Gallatin, co., Mont. ... E5 70
Galle, Sri Lanka ... G7 20
Gallia, co., Ohio ... D3 78

Gallipoli, It. ... D6 9
Gallipoli, see Gelibolu, Tur.
Gallipolis, Ohio ... D3 78
Gallitzin, Pa. ... F4 81
Gällivare, Swe. ... D9 11
Galloway, W. Va. ... B4 87
Gallup, N. Mex. ... B4 48
Galt, Calif. ... C3 50
Galt, Ont., Can. ... D4 41
Galty, mts., Ire. ... D2 4
Galva, Ill. ... B3 58
Galveston, Ind. ... C5 59
Galveston, Tex. ... E5, r15 84
Galveston, co., Tex. ... E5 84
Galway, Ire. ... D2 4
Galway, co., Ire. ... *D2 4
Gamagori, Jap. ... o16 18
Gamarra, Col. ... B3 22
Gambia, country, Afr. ... F1 32
Gambia, riv., Afr. ... F2 32
Gambier, Ohio ... B3 78
Gamboa, Pan. ... *B2 32
Gambrills, Md. ... B4 53
Ganado, Tex. ... E4 84
Gananoque, Ont.,Can. ... C8 41
Gand, see Gent, Bel.
Gander, Newf., Can. ... D4 44
Gandhinagar, India ... D5 20
Gandía, Sp. ... C5 8
Gangaw, Bur. ... D9 20
Ganges, riv., Asia ... D8 20
Gangtok, India ... C8 20
Gannat, Fr. ... D5 5
Gannett, peak, Wyo. ... C3 89
Gansu, prov., China ... D5 17
Gantt, S.C. ... B3 82
Ganzhou, China ... F7 17
Gao, Mali ... E5 22
Gap, Fr. ... E7 5
Gap, Pa. ... G9 81
Gar, China ... B7 20
Garanhuns, Braz. ... *D7 27
Garber, Okla. ... A4 79
Garberville, Calif. ... B2 50
Garça, Braz. ... C3 30
Garciasville, Tex. ... F3 84
Gard, dept., Fr. ... *F6 5
Gardelegen, Ger. Dem. Rep. ... B5 6
Garden, co., Nebr. ... C3 71
Gardena, Calif. ... n12 50
Garden City, Ga. ... D5 55
Garden City, Idaho ... *F2 57
Garden City, Kans. ... E3 61
Garden City, Mich. ... p15 66
Garden City, Mo. ... C3 69
Garden City, N.Y. ... G2 52
Garden City, Pa. ... *G11 81
Garden City Park, N.Y. ... *G2 52
Gardendale, Ala. ... B3, f7 46
Garden Grove, Calif. ... n13 50
Garden Home, Oreg. ... *B4 80
Garden Lakes, Ga. ... *B1 55
Garden View, Pa. ... *D7 81
Gardiner, Maine ... D3 64
Gardiner, Mont. ... E6 70
Gardner, Ill. ... B5 58
Gardner, Kans. ... D9 61
Gardner, Mass. ... A4 65
Garfield, N.J. ... h8 74
Garfield, Wash. ... B8 86
Garfield, co., Colo. ... B2 51
Garfield, co., Mont. ... C9 70
Garfield, co., Nebr. ... C6 71
Garfield, co., Okla. ... A4 79
Garfield, co., Utah ... C6 72
Garfield, co., Wash. ... C8 86
Garfield Heights, Ohio ... h9 78
Garfield peak, Wyo. ... D5 89
Gargaliánoi, Grc. ... D3 14
Garibaldi, Oreg. ... B3 80
Garibaldi, mtn., B.C., Can. ... E6 37
Garland, Md. ... *B4 53
Garland, N.C. ... C4 76
Garland, Tex. ... n10 84
Garland, Utah ... A5 72
Garland, co., Ark. ... C2 49
Garmisch-Partenkirchen, Ger., Fed. Rep. of ... E5 6
Garnavillo, Iowa ... B6 60
Garner, Iowa ... A4 60
Garner, N.C. ... B4 76
Garnett, Kans. ... D8 61
Garoua, Cam. ... G7 22
Garrard, co., Ky. ... C5 62
Garrett, Ind. ... B7 59
Garrett, Ky. ... C7 62
Garrett, co., Md. ... k12 53
Garrett Park, Md. ... B3 53
Garrett Park Estates, Md. ... *B3 53
Garrettsville, Ohio ... A4 78
Garrison, Md. ... *B4 53
Garrison, N.Dak. ... C4 77

Garrison, Tex. ... D5 84
Garrovillas, Sp. ... C2 8
Garson, Ont., Can. ... *p19 41
Garut, Indon. ... G3 19
Garvin, co., Okla. ... C4 79
Garwolin, Pol. ... C6 7
Garwood, N.J. ... *B4 74
Gary, Ind. ... A3 59
Gary, W. Va. ... D3 87
Garyville, La. ... D5, h10 63
Garza, co., Tex. ... C2 84
Garzón, Col. ... C2 32
Gas City, Ind. ... D6 59
Gasconade, co., Mo. ... C6 69
Gascony (Gascogne), former prov., Fr. ... E3 5
Gaspé, Que., Can. ... k14 42
Gaspe East, co., Que., Can. ... *k14 42
Gaspe West, co., Que., Can. ... *k13 42
Gasport, N.Y. ... B2 75
Gassaway, W. Va. ... C4 87
Gaston, Ind. ... D7 59
Gaston, N.C. ... A5 76
Gastonia, co., N.C. ... B1 76
Gastonia, N.C. ... B1 76
Gatchina, Sov. Un. ... H14, s31 11
Gate City, Va. ... f9 85
Gates, N.Y. ... *B3 75
Gates, co., N.C. ... A6 76
Gateshead, Eng. ... C6 4
Gates Mills, Ohio ... *A4 78
Gatesville, Tex. ... D4 84
Gatineau, Que., Can. ... D2 42
Gatineau, co., Que., Can. ... C2 42
Gatlinburg, Tenn. ... D10 83
Gatton, Austl. ... C9 26
Gatun, Pan. ... *B2 32
Gauhāti, India ... C9 20
Gauley Bridge, W. Va. ... C3, m13 87
Gävle, Swe. ... G7 11
Gävleborg, co., Swe. ... *G7 11
Gavrilovka, Sov. Un. ... G11 12
Gawler, Austl. ... G2 26
Gaya, India ... D7 20
Gaylord, Mich. ... C6 66
Gaylord, Minn. ... F4 67
Gays Mills, Wis. ... E3 88
Gaza (Ghazzah), Gaza Strip ... C2 15
Gaza Strip, Israeli occ., Asia ... C2 15
Gaziantep, Tur. ... D11 14
Gdańsk (Danzig), Pol. ... A5 7
Gdynia, Pol. ... A5 7
Gearhart, mtn., Oreg. ... E6 80
Geary, N.B., Can. ... D3 43
Geary, Okla. ... B3 79
Geary, co., Kans. ... D7 61
Geauga, co., Ohio ... A4 78
Gediz, Tur. ... C7 14
Geelong, Austl. ... G7, n14 25
Geislingen, Ger., Fed. Rep of ... D4 6
Geistown, Pa. ... F4 81
Gela, It. ... F5 9
Gelderland, prov., Neth. ... *A6 5
Gelibolu, Tur. ... B6 14
Gelsenkirchen, Ger. Fed. Rep of ... C3 6
Gem, co., Idaho ... E2 57
Gemlik, Tur. ... B7 14
General Belgrano, Arg. ... B5 28
General Madariaga, Arg. ... B5 28
General Pico, Arg. ... B4 28
General Roca, Arg. ... B3 28
Genessee, Idaho ... C2 57
Genesee, Mich. ... E7 66
Genesee, co., Mich. ... E7 66
Genesee, co., N.Y. ... B2 75
Geneseo, Ill. ... B3 58
Geneseo, N.Y. ... C3 75
Geneva, Ala. ... D4 46
Geneva, Ill. ... F1 58
Geneva, Ind. ... C8 59
Geneva, Nebr. ... D8 71
Geneva, N.Y. ... C4 75
Geneva, Ohio ... A5 78
Geneva-on-the-Lake, Ohio ... A5 78
Geneva, co., Ala. ... D4 46
Genève (Geneva), Switz. ... E3 6
Genève, canton, Switz. ... *E3 6
Genevia, Ark. ... C3, k10 49
Genichesk, Sov. Un. ... H10 12
Genk, Bel. ... B6 5
Gennevilliers, Fr. ... g10 5
Genoa, Ill. ... A5 58
Genoa (Genova), It. ... B2 9
Genoa, Nebr. ... C8 71
Genoa, Ohio ... A2, e7 78
Genoa City, Wis. ... F5, n11 88
Genova, see Genoa, It.
Gent (Ghent), Bel. ... B5 5
Genthin, Ger. Dem. Rep. ... B6 6
Gentilly, Fr. ... g10 5

Gentry, co., Mo. ... A3 69
Genzano di Roma, It. ... h9 9
George, Iowa ... A2 60
George, S. Afr. ... G4 24
George, co., Miss. ... E5 68
George, hill, Md. ... k12 53
George Town, Austl. ... o15 25
Georgetown, Ont., Can. ... D5 41
Georgetown, P.E.I., Can. ... C7 43
Georgetown, Conn. ... D3 52
Georgetown, Del. ... C7 53
Georgetown, Guy. ... C5 27
Georgetown, Idaho ... G7 57
Georgetown, Ill. ... D6 58
Georgetown, Ind. ... H6 59
Georgetown, Ky. ... B5 62
Georgetown, Mass. ... A6 65
Georgetown, Ohio ... D2 78
Georgetown, S.C. ... E9 82
George Town (Pinang), Mala. ... D2 19
Georgetown, co., S.C. ... E9 82
George West, Tex. ... E3 84
Georgia (Georgian S.S.R.), rep., Sov. Un. ... *A3 15
Georgia, state, U.S. ... 55
Georgiana, Ala. ... D3 46
Gera, Ger. Dem. Rep. ... C6 6
Geraldton, Austl. ... E1 25
Geraldton, Ont., Can. ... o18 41
Gerber, Calif. ... B2 50
Gering, Nebr. ... C2 71
Gerlachovka, mtn., Czech. ... D6 7
German Democratic Republic, country, Eur. ... E10 6
Germantown, Ill. ... E4 58
Germantown, Ohio ... C1 78
Germantown, Tenn. ... B2 83
Germantown, Wis. ... E5, m11 88
Germany, East, see German Democratic Republic, country, Eur.
Germany, Federal Republic of, country, Eur. ... E9 6
Germany, West, see Germany, Federal Republic of, country, Eur.
Germiston, S. Afr. ... F5 24
Gero, Jap. ... n16 18
Gerona, Sp. ... B7 8
Gerona, prov., Sp. ... *B7 8
Gers, dept., Fr. ... *F4 5
Getafe, Sp. ... B4, p17 8
Gertrudis Sánchez, Mex. ... h9 34
Gettysburg, Pa. ... G7 81
Gettysburg, S.Dak. ... E6 77
Geyserville, Calif. ... C2 50
Ghana, country, Afr. ... G4 22
Gharyān, Libya ... B7 22
Ghazni, Afg. ... B4 20
Ghazzah, see Gaza, Gaza Strip
Ghent, see Gent, Bel.
Gheorgheni, Rom. ... B7 10
Gherla, Rom. ... B6 10
Ghilizane, Alg. ... A5 22
Gia Dinh, Viet. S. ... C3 19
Giant, mtn., N.Y. ... A7 75
Gibara, Cuba ... D5 35
Gibbon, Minn. ... F4 67
Gibbon, Nebr. ... D7 71
Gibbstown, N.J. ... D2 74
Gibraleón, Sp. ... D2 8
Gibraltar, Gib. ... D3 8
Gibraltar, Mich. ... *F7 66
Gibraltar, Br. dep., Eur. ... *D3 8
Gibsland, La. ... B2 63
Gibson, co., Ind. ... H2 59
Gibson, co., Tenn. ... A3 83
Gibsonburg, Ohio ... A2, e7 78
Gibson City, Ill. ... C5 58
Gibsonia, Pa. ... h14 81
Gibsons, B.C., Can. ... E6 37
Gibsonton, Fla. ... p11 54
Gibsonville, N.C. ... A3 76
Giddings, Tex. ... D4 84
Gideon, Mo. ... E8 69
Gien, Fr. ... D5 5
Giessen, Ger., Fed. Rep. of ... C4 6
Gifford, Fla. ... E6 54
Gifu, Jap. ... I8, n15 18
Gifu, pref., Jap. ... *I8 18
Gigante, Col. ... C2 32
Gig Harbor, Wash. ... B3, f10 86
Gijon, Sp. ... A3 8
Gila, co., Ariz. ... C3 48
Gila, riv., Ariz., N.Mex. ... D4 45
Gila Bend, Ariz. ... C2 48
Gilbert, Ariz. ... C3, D2 48
Gilbert, Minn. ... C6 67
Gilbert, peak, Wash. ... C4 86
Gilberton, Pa. ... *E9 81
Gilbert Plains, Man., Can. ... D1 40
Gilbertsville, Pa. ... F10 81
Gilbertville, Iowa ... B5 60

Gilbertville, Mass. ... B3 65
Gilchrist, co., Fla. ... C4 54
Giles, co., Tenn. ... B4 83
Giles, co., Va. ... C2 85
Gilford Park, N.J. ... *D4 74
Gillespie, Ill. ... D4 58
Gillespie, co., Tex. ... D3 84
Gillett, Wis. ... D5 88
Gillette, Wyo. ... B7 89
Gilliam, co., Oreg. ... B6 80
Gillingham, Eng. ... E7 4
Gilly, Bel. ... B6 5
Gilman, Ill. ... C5 58
Gilmer, Tex. ... C5 84
Gilmer, co., Ga. ... B2 55
Gilmer, co., W.Va. ... C4 87
Gilmore City, Iowa ... B3 60
Gilpin, co., Colo. ... B5 51
Gilroy, Calif. ... D3 50
Gimli, Man., Can. ... D3 40
Ginosa, It. ... D6 9
Ginzo, Sp. ... A2 8
Gioia del Colle, It. ... D6 9
Gioiosa Ionica, It. ... E6 9
Girard, Ill. ... D4 58
Girard, Kans. ... E9 61
Girard, Ohio ... A5 78
Girard, Pa. ... B1 81
Girardot, Col. ... C3 32
Girardville, Pa. ... E9 81
Giresun, Tur. ... B12 14
Giridih, India ... D8 20
Girishk, Afg. ... B3 20
Gironde, dept., Fr. ... *E3 5
Girvan, Scot. ... C4 4
Gisborne, N.Z. ... M17 26
Giscome, B.C., Can. ... B6 37
Gisors, Fr. ... C4 5
Gitega, Burundi ... I4 23
Giulianova, It. ... C4 9
Giurgiu, Rom. ... D7 10
Giv'atayim, Isr. ... *B2 15
Givet, Fr. ... B6 5
Givors, Fr. ... E6 5
Gjinokaster, Alb. ... B3 14
Gjinokaster, pref., Alb. ... *B3 14
Gjøvik, Nor. ... G4 11
Glace Bay, N.S., Can. ... C10 43
Glacier, co., Mont. ... B3 70
Glacier, peak, Wash. ... A4 86
Gladbrook, Iowa ... B5 60
Glades, co., Fla. ... F5 54
Glade Spring, Va. ... f10 85
Gladewater, Tex. ... C5 84
Gladstone, Austl. ... D9 25
Gladstone, Man., Can. ... D2 40
Gladstone, Mich. ... C4 66
Gladstone, Mo. ... h10 69
Gladstone, N.J. ... B3 74
Gladstone, Oreg. ... B4, h12 80
Gladwin, Mich. ... E6 66
Gladwin, co., Mich. ... *D6 66
Gladwyne, Pa. ... *F11 81
Glamoč, Yugo. ... C3 10
Glamorgan, co., Wales ... *E5 4
Glandorf, Ohio ... A1 78
Glarus, Switz. ... E4 6
Glarus, canton, Switz. ... *E4 6
Glasco, Kans. ... C6 61
Glasco, N.Y. ... C7 75
Glascock, co., Ga. ... C4 55
Glasford, Ill. ... C4 58
Glasgow, Ky. ... C4 62
Glasgow, Mo. ... B5 69
Glasgow, Mont. ... B10 70
Glasgow, Scot. ... C4 4
Glasgow, Va. ... C3 85
Glasgow, W.Va. ... m13 87
Glassboro, N.J. ... D2 74
Glasscock, co., Tex. ... D2 84
Glassport, Pa. ... F2 81
Glastonbury, Conn. ... C6 52
Glauchau, Ger. Dem. Rep. ... C6 6
Gleason, Tenn. ... A3 83
Gleasondale, Mass. ... g9 65
Glenarden, Md. ... *C4 53
Glen Allen, Va. ... C5 85
Glen Alpine, N.C. ... B1, f11 76
Glen Avon Heights, Calif. ... *F5 50
Glenboro, Man., Can. ... E2 40
Glen Burnie, Md. ... B4 53
Glen Carbon, Ill. ... E4 58
Glencoe, Ala. ... B4 46
Glencoe, Ont., Can. ... E3 41
Glencoe, Ill. ... A6, h9 58
Glencoe, Minn. ... F4 67
Glen Cove, N.Y. ... h13 75
Glendale, Ariz. ... C2, D1 48
Glendale, Calif. ... m12 50
Glendale, Mo. ... *C7 69
Glendale, Ohio ... C1, m13 78
Glendale, S.C. ... B4 82
Glen Dale, W.Va. ... B4 87

Glendale, Wis. *E6 88
Glendive, Mont.................... C12 70
Glendora, Calif. m13 50
Glendora, N.J. *D2 74
Glen Ellyn, Ill. k8 58
Glen Gardner, N.J. B3 74
Glengarry, co., Ont., Can. B10 41
Glen Head, N.Y. *F2 52
Glen Innes, Austl. E9 25
Glen Jean, W.Va. D3, n13 87
Glen Lake, B.C., Can. E5 37
Glen Lyon, Pa. D9 81
Glen Moore, Pa. *G9 81
Glenmora, La. D3 63
Glenn, co., Calif. C2 50
Glenn Dale, Md. C4 53
Glenns Ferry, Idaho G3 57
Glennville, Ga. E5 55
Glenolden, Pa. p20 81
Glenorchy, Austl. o15 25
Glen Raven, N.C. A3 76
Glen Rock, Pa. G8 81
Glenrock, Wyo. D7 89
Glen Rose, Tex. C4 84
Glens Falls, N.Y. B7 75
Glenshaw, Pa. *E1 81
Glenside, Pa. o21 81
Glen Ullin, N. Dak. D4 77
Glenview, Ill. h9 58
Glenview Countryside, Ill. *E2 58
Glenville, Minn. G5 67
Glenville, W. Va. C4 87
Glenwillard, Pa. *E1 81
Glenwood, Newf., Can. D4 44
Glenwood, Iowa C2 60
Glenwood, Minn. E3 67
Glenwood, Pa. *D3 85
Glenwood Landing, N.Y. *F2 52
Glenwood Springs, Colo. B3 51
Glidden, Iowa B3 60
Glidden, Wis. B3 88
Gliwice, Pol. C5, g9 7
Globe, Ariz. C3, D3 48
Globino, Sov. Un. G9 12
Gloucester, Eng. E5 4
Gloucester, Mass. A6, f13 65
Gloucester, co., N.B., Can. B4 43
Gloucester, co.,Eng. *E5 4
Gloucester, co., N.J. D2 74
Gloucester, co., Va. C6 85
Gloucester City, N.J. D2 74
Glouster, Ohio C3 78
Gloversville, N.Y. B6 75
Glovertown, Newf., Can. D4 44
Glovertown South, Newf., Can. *D5 44
Gloverville, S.C. E4 82
Glubczyce, Pol. C4 7
Glubokoye, Sov. Un. D6 12
Głuchołazy, Pol. C4 7
Gluck, S.C. C2 82
Gluckhov, Sov. Un. F9 12
Glussk, Sov. Un. E7 12
Glyndon, Md. B4 53
Glynn, co., Ga. E5 55
Gmunden, Aus. E6 6
Gnadenhutten, Ohio B4 78
Gniezno, Pol. B4 7
Goa, Daman and Diu, ter.,
  India D5, E5 20
Goat, mtn., Mont. *C3 70
Gobles, Mich. F5 66
Gobo, Jap. J7 18
Goch, Ger., Fed. Rep. of C3 6
Godãvari, riv., India E6 20
Goderich, Ont., Can. D3 41
Godfrey, Ill. E3 58
Godwin Austen, peak, Pak.......... A6 20
Goffstown, N.H. E4 73
Gogebic, co., Mich. n12 66
Goiânia, Braz. B3 30
Goiás, state, Braz. B2 30
Gojo, Jap. o14 18
Golan Heights, hills, Syria *B3 15
Golchika, Sov. Un. B11 13
Golconda, Ill. F5 58
Gold Beach, Oreg. E2 80
Gold Coast, see Ghana, country, Afr.
Gold Coast, see Southport, Austl.
Golden, B.C., Can. D9 37
Golden, Colo. B5 51
Golden City, Mo. D3 69
Goldendale, Wash. D5 86
Golden Hill, Minn. *F6 67
Golden Hinde, mtn., B.C., Can. E5 37
Golden Meadow, La. E5 63
Golden Valley, Minn. n12 67
Golden Valley, co., Mont. D7 70
Golden Valley, co., N. Dak. D2 77
Gold Hill, Ore. E3 80
Goldsboro, N.C. B5 76
Goldsmith, Tex. D1 84
Goldthwaite, Tex. D3 84
Goleta, Calif. E4 50

Golf Manor, Ohio o13 78
Goliad, Tex. E4 84
Goliad, co., Tex. E4 84
Golspie, Scot. A5 4
Gomel, Sov. Un. E8 12
Gómez Palacio, Mex. B4 34
Gonaïves, Hai. E7 35
Gonda, India C7 20
Gondar, Eth. F5 23
Gönen, Tur. B6 14
Gonesse, Fr. g10 5
Gongga, mtn., China F5 17
Gonzales, Calif. D3 50
Gonzales, La. D5, h10 63
Gonzales, Tex. E4 84
Gonzales, co., Tex. E4 84
Goochland, co., Va. C5 85
Goodhue, co., Minn. F6 67
Gooding, Idaho G4 57
Gooding, co., Idaho F4 57
Goodland, Ind. C3 59
Goodland, Kans. C2 61
Goodman, Miss. C4 68
Good Pine, La. C3 63
Goodsprings, Ala. B2 46
Goodview, Minn. F7 67
Goodwater, Ala. B3 46
Goodwell, Okla. e9 79
Goodyear, Ariz. C3, D2 48
Goondiwindi, Austl. E9 25
Goose Bay, Newf., Can. B1, h9 44
Goose Creek, S.C. F7, k11 82
Goppingen, Ger., Fed. Rep. of D4 6
Gorakhpur, India C7 20
Gordo, Ala. B2 46
Gordon, Ga. D3 55
Gordon, Nebr. B3 71
Gordon, Pa. *E9 81
Gordon, co., Ga. B1 55
Gordonsville, Va. B4 85
Gore, Eth. G5 23
Gore, N.Z. Q10 26
Gore Bay, Ont., Can. B2 41
Gorgan, Iran B5 15
Gorgas, Ala. B2 46
Gorham, Maine E2, g7 64
Gorham, N.H. C5 73
Gorham, N.Y. C3 75
Gorizia, It. B4 9
Gorki (Gorkiy), Sov. Un. D7 13
Gorlice, Pol. D6 7
Görlitz, Ger. Dem. Rep. C7 6
Gorlovka, Sov. Un. G12, q21 12
Gorman, Tex. C3 84
Gorna-Dzhumaya,see
  Blagoevgrad, Bul.
Gorna Oryakhovitsa, Bul. D7 10
Gorno-Altaysk, Sov. Un. *D11 12
Gorodenka, Sov. Un. G5 12
Gorodishche, Sov. Un. q22 12
Gorodnya, Sov. Un. F8 12
Gorodok, Sov. Un. D7 12
Gorodok, Sov. Un. G4 12
Gorontalo, Indon. E6 19
Gorzów Wielkopolski, Pol. B3 7
Gosford, Austl. F8 26
Goshen, Calif. *D4 50
Goshen, Ind. A6 59
Goshen, N.Y. D6, m14 75
Goshen, Ohio C1 78
Goshen, co., Wyo. D8 89
Goshogawara, Jap. F10 18
Goslar, Ger., Fed. Rep. of C5 6
Gosper, co., Nebr. D6 71
Gosport, Ind. F4 59
Gospic, Yugo. C2 10
Gostivar, Yugo. E5 10
Gostyń, Pol. C4 7
Gostynin, Pol. B5 7
Goteborg, Swe. *I4 11
Göteborg, och Bohus, co., Swe. *I4 11
Gotemba, Jap. n18 18
Gotha, Ger. Dem. Rep. C5 6
Gothenburg, Nebr. D5 71
Gotland, co., Swe. *I8 11
Göttingen, Ger., Fed. Rep. of C4 6
Gottwaldov, (Zlín), Czech. D4 7
Gouda, Neth. A6 5
Goulburn, Austl. F8 25
Gould, Ark. D4 49
Goulding, Fla. *u14 54
Goulds, Fla. s13 54
Gournay-en-Bray, Fr. C4 5
Gouverneur, N.Y. f9 75
Gove, co., Kans. D3 61
Governador Valadares, Braz. B4 30
Gowanda, N.Y. C2 75
Gowrie, Iowa B3 60
Goya, Arg. B4 29
Graat-Reinet, S. Afr. G4 24
Gračanica, Yugo. C4 10
Grace, Idaho G7 57
Grace, mtn., Mass. A3 65

Grace Park, Pa. *G11 81
Graceville, Fla. u16 54
Graceville, Minn. E2 67
Gradacac, Yugo. C4 10
Gradizhsk, Sov. Un. G9 12
Grado, Sp. A2 8
Graehl, Alsk. *C10 47
Graettinger, Iowa A3 60
Grafton, Austl. E9 25
Grafton, Ill. E3 58
Grafton, Mass. B4 65
Grafton, N. Dak. B8 77
Grafton, Ohio A3 78
Grafton, Va. h15 85
Grafton, W.Va. B4, k10 87
Grafton, Wis. E5, m12 88
Grafton, co., N.H. D4 73
Graham, N.C. A3 76
Graham, Tex. C3 84
Graham, co., Ariz. C3 48
Graham, co., Kans. C4 61
Graham, co., N.C. f9 76
Grahamstown, S.Afr. G5 24
Grainger, co., Tenn. C10 83
Grajewo, Pol. B7 7
Gramalote, Col. B3 32
Grambling, La. B3 63
Gramercy, La. h10 63
Grammichele, It. F5 9
Granada, Nic. E7 34
Granada, Sp. D4 8
Granada, prov., Sp. *D4 8
Granbury, Tex. C4 84
Granby, Que., Can. D5 42
Granby, Mo. E3 69
Grand, co., Colo. A4 51
Grand, co., Utah B7 72
Grand, isl., La. E6 63
Grand Bank, Newf., Can. E4 44
Grand Bassam, I.C. G4 22
Grand Bay, N.B., Can. D3 43
Grand Bend, Ont., Can. D3 41
Grand Blanc, Mich. F7 66
Grand-Bourg, Guad. I14 35
Grand Centre, Alta., Can. B5 38
Grand Coteau, La. D3 63
Grand Coulee, Wash. B6 86
Grande-Entrée, Que., Can. B8 43
Grande Prairie, Alta., Can. B1, f7 38
Grande Rivière, Que., Can. *k14 42
Grandes-Bergeronnes,
  Que. A8 42
Grand Falls, N.B., Can. B2 43
Grand Falls, Newf., Can. D4 44
Grandfalls, Tex. D1 84
Grandfather, mtn., N.C. A1 76
Grandfield, Okla. C3 79
Grand Forks, B.C., Can. E8 37
Grand Forks, N. Dak. C8 77
Grand Forks, co., N.Dak. C8 77
Grand Gorge, N.Y. C6 75
Grand Haven, Mich. E4 66
Grand Island, Nebr. D7 71
Grand Island, N.Y. *B2 75
Grand Isle, La. E6 63
Grand Isle, co., Vt. B1 73
Grand Junction, Colo. B2 51
Grand Junction, Iowa B3 60
Grand Ledge, Mich. F6 66
Grand Marais, Minn. k9 67
Grand Meadow, Minn. G6 67
Grand' Mère, Que., Can. C5 42
Grand Prairie, Tex. n10 84
Grand Rapids, Man., Can. C2 40
Grand Rapids, Mich. F5 66
Grand Rapids, Minn. C5 67
Grand Rapids, Ohio A2, f6 78
Grand Saline, Tex. C5 84
Grand Terrace, Calif. *F5 50
Grand Teton, mtn., Wyo. C2 89
Grand Tower, Ill. F4 58
Grand Traverse, co., Mich. D5 66
Grand Valley, Ont., Can. D4 41
Grandview, Man., Can. D1 40
Grandview, Ill. D6 58
Grand View, Ind. I4 59
Grandview, Mo. C3, k10 69
Grandview, Tex. *C4 84
Grandview, Wash. C6 86
Grandview Heights, Ohio m10 78
Grandview Heights, Pa. *G9 81
Grandville, Mich. F5 66
Granger, Tex. C4 84
Granger, Utah *A5 72
Granger, Wash. C5 86
Grangeville, Idaho D2 57
Grangeville, Pa. *G8 81
Granite, Md. *B4 53
Granite, Okla. C2 79
Granite, co., Mont. D3 70
Granite, peak, Mont. E7 70

Granite, peak, Wyo. D4 89
Granite City, Ill. E3 58
Granite Falls, Minn. F3 67
Granite Falls, N.C. B1 76
Granite Falls, Wash. A4 86
Granite Quarry, N.C. B2 76
Graniteville, Mass. f10 65
Graniteville, S.C. *D4 82
Granja de Torrehermosa, Sp. C3 8
Granollers, Sp. B7 8
Grant, Mich. E5 66
Grant, Nebr. D4 71
Grant, co., Ark. C3 49
Grant, co., Ind. C6 59
Grant, co., Kans. E2 61
Grant, co., Ky. B5 62
Grant, co., Minn. E2 67
Grant, co., Nebr. C4 71
Grant, co., N. Mex. C4 48
Grant, co., N. Dak. D4 77
Grant, co., Okla. A4 79
Grant, co., Oreg. C7 80
Grant, co., S. Dak. E9 77
Grant, co., Wash. B6 86
Grant, co., W.Va. B5 87
Grant, co., Wis. F3 88
Grant, par., La. C3 63
Grant City, Mo. A3 69
Grantham, Eng. D6 4
Grant Park, Ill. B6 58
Grants, N. Mex. B5 48
Grantsboro, N.C. B6 76
Grantsburg, Wis. C1 88
Grants Pass, Oreg. E3 80
Grantsville, Utah A5, D1 72
Grantsville, W. Va. C3 87
Grant Town, W. Va. B4 h10 87
Grantville, Ga. C2 55
Granville, Fr. C3 5
Granville, Ill. B4 58
Granville, N.Y. B7 75
Granville, Ohio B3 78
Granville, W. Va. h11 87
Granville, co., N.C. A4 76
Grapeland, Tex. D5 84
Grapeville, Pa. *F2 81
Grapevine, Ky. C2 62
Grapevine, Tex. C4, n9 84
Grasonville, Md. C5 53
Grasse, Fr. F7 5
Grassflat, Pa. D5 81
Grass Lake, Mich. F6 66
Grass Valley, Calif. C3 50
Gratiot, co., Mich. E6 66
Graton, Calif. *C2 50
Graubünden, canton, Switz. *E4 6
Graulhet, Fr. F5 5
Gravatá, Braz. *D7 27
Grave, peak, Idaho C4 57
Gravelbourg, Sask., Can. H2 39
Gravenhurst, Ont., Can. C5 41
Graves, co., Ky. f9 62
Gravesend, Eng. E7, m13 4
Gravina in Puglia, It. D6 9
Gray, Ga. C3 55
Gray, Ky. D5 62
Gray, co., Kans. E3 61
Gray, co., Tex. B2 84
Grayling, Mich. D6 66
Grays, peak, Colo. B5 51
Grays Harbor, co., Wash. B2 86
Grayslake, Ill. A5, h8 58
Grayson, Ky. B7 62
Grayson, co., Ky. C3 62
Grayson, co., Tex. C4 84
Grayson, co., Va. D1 85
Graysville, Ala. f7 46
Grayville, Ill. E5 58
Graz, Aus. E7 6
Great Barrington, Mass. B1 65
Great Bear, lake, Can. C9 36
Great Bend, Kans. D5 61
Great Bend, Pa. C10 81
Great Blue, hill, Mass. B5 65
Great Divide, basin, Wyo. E4 89
Greater Antilles, is., W.I. B3 27
Great Falls, Mont. G5 70
Great Falls, S.C. B6 82
Greathouse, peak, Mont. D7 70
Great Neck, N.Y. h13 75
Great Neck Estates, N.Y. n15 75
Great Salt, lake, Utah A5 72
Great Slave, lake, Can. D11 36
Great Yarmouth, Eng. D7 4
Greece, Ill. *B3 75
Greece, country, Eur. C4 14
Greeley, Colo. A6 51
Greeley, Nebr. C7 71
Greeley, co., Kans. D2 61
Greeley, co., Nebr. C7 71
Green, co., Ky. C4 62
Green, co., Wis. F4 88
Green, riv., U.S. B6 72

Greenacres, Calif. *E4 50
Greenacres, Wash.............. B8, g14 86
Greenacres City, Fla. F6 54
Greenback, Tenn..................... D9 83
Green Bay, Wis. D6, g10 88
Greenbelt, Md. B4 53
Greenbrae, Calif. *D2 50
Greenbrier, co., W. Va. D4 87
Green Brook, N.J. *B4 74
Greenbush, Mass. h12 65
Gfeenbush, Minn. B2 67
Greencastle, Ind. E4 59
Greencastle, Pa. G6 81
Green City, Mo. A5 69
Green Cove Springs, Fla. C5, n8 54
Greendale, Ind. F8 59
Greendale, Wis. F6, n12 88
Greene, Iowa B5 60
Greene, N.Y. C5 75
Greene, co., Ala. C1 46
Greene, co., Ark. A5 49
Greene, co., Ga. C3 55
Greene, co., Ill. D3 58
Greene, co., Ind. F4 59
Greene, co., Iowa B3 60
Greene, co., Miss. D5 68
Greene, co., Mo. D4 69
Greene, co., N.Y. D6 75
Greene, co., N.C. B5 76
Greene, co., Ohio C2 78
Greene, co., Pa. G1 81
Greene, co., Tenn. C11 83
Greene, co., Va. B4 85
Greeneville, Tenn. C11 83
Greenfield, Calif. D3 50
Greenfield, Ill. D3 58
Greenfield, Ind. E6 59
Greenfield, Iowa C3 60
Greenfield, Mass. A2 65
Greenfield, Mo. D4 69
Greenfield, Ohio C2 78
Greenfield, Tenn. A3 83
Greenfield, Wis. n12 88
Greenfield Park, Que., Can. q20 42
Green Forest, Ark. A2 49
Green Harbor, Mass. B6 65
Greenhills, Ohio n12 78
Green Island, N.Y. *C7 75
Green Lake, Sask., Can............. C2 39
Green Lake, Wis. E5 88
Green Lake, co., Wis. E4 88
Greenland, Dan. dep., N.A. B16 33
Greenlawn, N.Y. F3 52
Greenlee, co., Ariz. C4 48
Green Lookout, mtn., Wash. D3 86
Green Manorville, Conn. *B6 52
Green Meadows, Md. *C4 53
Greenock, Pa. *E1 81
Greenock, Scot. C4 4
Greenport, N.Y. m16 75
Green Ridge, Pa. *G11 81
Green River, Utah B6 72
Green River, Wyo. E3 89
Greensboro, Ala. C2 46
Greensboro, Fla. B2 54
Greensboro, Ga. C3 55
Greensboro, Md. C6 53
Greensboro, N.C. A3 76
Greensburg, Ind. F7 59
Greensburg, Kans. E4 61
Greensburg, Ky. C4 62
Greensburg, Pa. F2 81
Green's Harbour, Newf., Can. E5 44
Greenspond, Newf., Can. D5 44
Green Springs, Ohio A2 78
Greensville, co., Va. D5 85
Greentown, Ind. D6 59
Green Tree, Pa. *E1 81
Greenup, Ill. D5 58
Greenup, Ky. B7 62
Greenup, co., Ky. B6 62
Greenvale, N.Y. *F2 52
Greenview, Ill. C4 58
Greenville, Ala. D3 46
Greenville, co., S.C. A3 82
Greenville, Calif. B3 50

Greenville, Fla. B3 54
Greenville, Ill. E4 58
Greenville, Ky...................... C2 62
Greenville, Maine C3 64
Greenville, Mich. E5 66
Greenville, Miss. B2 68
Greenville, N.H. F4 73
Greenville, N.Y. h13 75
Greenville, N.C..................... B5 76
Greenville, Ohio B1 78
Greenville, Pa. D1 81
Greenville, R.I. B10 52
Greenville, S.C. B3 82
Greenville, Tex. C4 84
Greenville Junction, Maine C3 64
Greenwich, Conn. E2 52
Greenwich, Eng., (part of London)... m13 4
Greenwich, N.Y. B7 75
Greenwich, Ohio A3 78
Greenwood, Ark. B1 49
Greenwood, B.C., Can. E8 37
Greenwood, Ind. E5, m10 59
Greenwood, Miss. B3 68
Greenwood, Pa. E5 81
Greenwood, S.C. D3 82
Greenwood, Wis. D3 88
Greenwood, co., Kans. E7 61
Greenwood, co., S.C. C3 82
Greenwood Lake, N.Y. *D6 75
Greer, S.C. B3 82
Greer, co., Okla. C2 79
Gregg, co., Tex. C5 84
Gregory, S. Dak. G6 77
Gregory, Tex. *F4 84
Gregory, co., S. Dak. G6 77
Greifswald, Ger. Dem. Rep. A6 6
Greilickville, Mich. D5 66
Greiz, Ger. Dem. Rep. C6 6
Grenada, Miss. B4 68
Grenada, co., Miss. B4 68
Grenada, country, N.A. J14 35
Grenfell, Sask., Can. G4 39
Grenloch, N.J. D2 74
Grenoble, Fr. E6 5
Grenville, Que., Can. D3 42
Grenville, co., Ont., Can. C9 41
Gresham, Oreg. B4 80
Gretna, Fla. B2 54
Gretna, La. E5, k11 63
Gretna, Nebr. C9, g12 71
Gretna, Va. D3 85
Grey, co., Ont., Can. C4 41
Greybull, Wyo. B4 89
Greylock, mtn., Mass. A1 65
Greymouth, N.Z. O13 26
Gridley, Calif. C3 50
Gridley, Ill. C5 58
Griffin, Ga. C2 55
Griffing Park, Tex. *E5 84
Griffith, Austl. F8 25
Griffith, Ind. A3 59
Grifton, N.C. B5 76
Griggs, co., N. Dak. C7 77
Griggsville, Ill. D3 58
Grimes, co., Tex. D4 84
Grimma, Ger. Dem. Rep. C6 6
Grimsby, Ont., Can. D5 41
Grimsby, Eng. D6 4
Grimshaw, Alta., Can. A2 38
Grindstone, Pa. *G2 81
Grinnell, Iowa C5 60
Griswold, Iowa C2 60
Grodno, Sov. Un. E4 12
Grodzisk, Pol. B4 7
Grodzisk Mazowiecki, Pol. m13 7
Groesbeck, Ohio *C1 78
Groesbeck, Tex. D4 84
Grójec, Pol. C6 7
Grombalia, Tun. F3 9
Gronau, Ger., Fed. Rep. of B3 6
Groningen, Neth. A7 5
Groningen, prov., Neth. *A7 5
Grosse Ile, Mich. *B7 66
Grosse Pointe, Mich............... p16 66
Grosse Pointe Farms, Mich. *p16 66
Grosse Pointe Park, Mich........... p16 66

Grosse Pointe Shores, Mich. F8 66
Grosse Pointe Woods, Mich. p16 66
Grosseto, It. C3 9
Grossglockner, mtn., Aus. E6 6
Grossmont, Calif. o16 50
Gros Ventre, range, Wyo. C2 89
Groton, Conn. D8 52
Groton, Mass. A4, f9 65
Groton, N.Y. C4 75
Groton, S. Dak. E7 77
Grottaferrata, It. h9 9
Grottaglie, It. D6 9
Grottoes, Va. B4 85
Grove City, Ohio C2, m10 78
Grove City, Pa. D1 81
Grove Hill, Ala. D2 46
Groveland, Fla. D5 54
Groveland, Mass. A5 65
Groveport, Ohio C2, m11 78
Grover City, Calif. E3 50
Groves, Tex. E6 84
Groveton, N.H. B4 73
Groveton, Tex. D5 84
Groveton, Va. g12 85
Grovetown, Ga. C4 55
Groveville, N.J. C3 74
Groznyy, Sov. Un. E7 13
Grudziądz, Pol. B5 7
Grulla, Tex. F3 84
Grundy, Va. e9 85
Grundy, co., Ill. B5 58
Grundy, co., Iowa B5 60
Grundy, co., Mo. A4 69
Grundy, co., Tenn. D8 83
Grundy Center, Iowa B5 60
Gruver, Tex. A2 84
Gruz, Yugo. D4 10
Gryazi, Sov. Un. E12 12
Guadalajara, Mex. C4, m12 34
Guadalajara, Sp. B4 8
Guadalajara, prov., Sp. *B4 8
Guadalcanal, Sp. C3 8
Guadalupe, Ariz. D2 48
Guadalupe, Calif. E3 50
Guadalupe, co., N. Mex. B6 48
Guadalupe, co., Tex. E4 84
Guadalupe, peak, Tex. o12 84
Guadeloupe, Fr. dep., N.A. H14 35
Guaira, dept., Par. E4 29
Gualeguay, Arg. A5 28
Gualeguaychú, Arg. A5 28
Guam, U.S., dep., Oceania *F6 2
Guanabacoa, Cuba C2 35
Guanacaste, prov., C.R. *E8 34
Guanajay, Cuba C2 35
Guanajuato, Mex. C4, m13 34
Guanajuato, state, Mex. C4 34
Guanare, Ven. B4 32
Guane, Cuba C1 35
Guangdong, prov., China G7 17
Guangxi Zhuangzu, auton reg.,
    China G6 17
Guánica, P.R. *G11 35
Guantánamo, Cuba D6 35
Guarabira, Braz. *D7 27
Guaranda, Ec. B2 31
Guarapuava, Braz. D2 30
Guaratinguetá, Braz. C3 30
Guarda, Port. B2 8
Guareña, Sp. C2 8
Guárico, state, Ven. B4 32
Guarujá, Braz. n8 30
Guatemala, Mex. E6 34
Guatemala, country, N.A. D6 34
Guavaire, comisaría, Col. C3 32
Guaxupé, Braz. C3, k8 30
Guayabal, Cuba D5 35
Guayama, P.R. n13 36
Guayaquil, Ec. B2 31
Guayas, prov., Ec. B1 31
Guaymas, Mex. B2 34
Gubakha, Sov. Un. *D8 13
Gubat, Phil. *C6 19
Gubbio, It. C4 9
Gūdūr, India F6 20
Guebwiller, Fr. D7 5

Guecho, Sp. A4 8
Guelma, Alg. A6 22
Guelph, Ont., Can. D4 41
Güemes, Arg. D2 29
Guéret, Fr. D4 5
Guerneville, Calif................... *C2 50
Guernsey, Wyo. D8 89
Guernsey, Br. dep., Eur. F5 4
Guernsey, co., Ohio B4 78
Guerrero, state, Mex. D5 34
Gueydan, La. D3 63
Guiana, French, see French
    Guiana, dep., S.A.
Guiana, Netherlands,
    see Surinam, Neth. dep., S.A.
Guidonia, It. D4, h9 9
Guildford, Eng. E6, m11 4
Guilford, Conn. D6 52
Guilford, Maine C3 64
Guilford, N.C. *A3 76
Guilford, co., N.C. A3 76
Guilin, China F7 17
Guimarães, Port. B1 8
Guin, Ala. B2 46
Guinea, country, Afr. F2 22
Guinea-Bissau, country, Afr. E4 21
Güines, Cuba C2 35
Guingamp, Fr. C2 5
Guipúzcoa, prov., Sp. *A4 8
Güira de Melena, Cuba C2 35
Güiria, Ven. A5 32
Guise, Fr. C5 5
Guiyang, China F6 17
Guizhou, prov., China F6 17
Gujarat, state, India D5 20
Gujrānwāla, Pak. B5 20
Gujrat, Pak. *B5 20
Gulbarga, India E6 20
Gulf, co., Fla. C1 54
Gulf Hammock, Fla. C4 54
Gulfport, Fla. E4, p10 54
Gulfport, Miss. E4, f7 68
Gull Lake, Sask., Can. G1 39
Gulyay-Pole, Sov. Un. H11 12
Gumma, pref., Jap. *H9 18
Gummersbach, Ger., Fed.
    Rep. of *C3 6
Gunnedah, Austl. E8 26
Gunnison, Colo. C4 51
Gunnison, Utah B6 72
Gunnison, co., Colo. C3 51
Guntersville, Ala. A3 46
Guntūr, India E7 20
Gurabo, P.R. *G11 35
Gurdon, Ark. D2 49
Gurnee, Ill. E2 58
Guryev, Sov. Un. E8 13
Gusav, Nig. F6 22
Gusev, Sov. Un. A7 7
Gusinje, Yugo. D4 10
Gus-Khrustalnyy, Sov. Un. D13 12
Gustavo A. Madero, Mex. h9 34
Gustine, Calif. D3 50
Güstrow, Ger. Dem. Rep. B6 6
Gütersloh, Ger., Fed. Rep of C4 6
Guthrie, Ky. D2 62
Guthrie, Okla. B4 79
Guthrie, co., Iowa C3 60
Guthrie Center, Iowa C3 60
Guttenberg, Iowa B6 60
Guttenberg, N.J. h8 74
Guyana, country, S.A. C5 27
Guyenne, former prov., Fr. E4 5
Guymon, Okla. e9 79
Guysborough, co., N.S., Can. D8 43
Gvardeysk, Sov. Un. A6 7
Gwādar, Pak. C3 20
Gwalior, India C6 20
Gweru, Zimb. D5 24
Gwinn, Mich. .... Be 66
Gwinnett, co., Ga. C2 55
Gyangzê, China *C8 20
Gympie, Austl. E9 25
Gyöngyös, Hung. B4 10
Győr, Hung. B3 10
Gyor-Sopron, co., Hung. *B3 10
Gyula, Hung. B5 10

H

Haakon, co., S. Dak. ... F4 77
Haapsalu, Sov. Un. ... B4 12
Haarlem, Neth. ... A6 5
Habersham, Ga. ... B3 55
Habersham, co., Ga. ... B3 55
Haboru, Jap. ... D10 18
Hachiman, Jap. ... n15 18
Hachinohe, Jap. ... F10 18
Hachioji, Jap. ... I9, n18 18
Hackberry, La. ... E2 63
Hackensack, N.J. ... B4, h8 74
Hackettstown, N.J. ... B3 74
Haddonfield, N.J. ... D2 74
Haddon Heights, N.J. ... D2 74
Hadera, Isr. ... B2, g5 15
Haderslev, co., Den. ... *J3 11
Hadramawt, reg., P.D.R. of Yem. ... G4 15
Hadley, Mass. ... B2 65
Haeju, Kor. ... G2 18
Hagaman, N.Y. ... *C6 75
Hagar Shores (Lake Michigan Beach), Mich. ... *F4 66
Hagen, Ger., Fed. Rep. of ... C3 6
Hagerman, N. Mex. ... C6 48
Hagerstown, Ind. ... E7 59
Hagerstown, Md. ... A2 53
Hagersville, Ont., Can. ... E4 41
Hagi, Jap. ... I5 18
Ha Giang, Viet. ... G6 17
Haguenau, Fr. ... C7 5
Hague, The ('s Gravenhage), see The Hague, Neth.
Hahira, Ga. ... F3 55
Hahnville, La. ... E5, k11 63
Hai Duong, Viet. ... *A3 19
Haifa (Hefa), Isr. ... B3, g5 15
Hā'il, Sau. Ar. ... D3 15
Hailar, China ... B8 17
Hailey, Idaho ... F4 57
Haileybury, Ont., Can. ... p20 41
Haileyville, Okla. ... C6 79
Hailong, China ... E2 18
Hailun, China ... C3 18
Hainan, isl., China ... B4 19
Hainaut, prov., Bel. ... *B5 5
Haines City, Fla. ... D5 54
Haines Falls, N.Y. ... C6 75
Hainesport, N.J. ... D3 74
Haiphong, Viet. ... A3 19
Haiti, country, N.A. ... E7 35
Hajdu-Bihar, co., Hung. ... *B5 10
Hajduhadház, Hung. ... B5 10
Hajdunánás, Hung. ... B5 10
Hajduszoboszló, Hung. ... B5 10
Hakalau, Haw. ... D6 56
Hakodate, Jap. ... F10 18
Halawa Heights, Haw. ... g10 56
Halberstadt, Ger. Dem. Rep. ... C5 6
Halden, Nor. ... H4 11
Haldensleben, Ger. Dem. Rep. ... B5 6
Haldimand, co., Ont., Can. ... E5 41
Hale, co., Ala. ... C2 46
Hale, co., Tex. ... B2 84
Haleakala, crater, Haw. ... C5 56
Hale Center, Tex. ... B2 84
Haledon, N.J. ... *B4 74
Haleiwa, Haw. ... B3, f9 56
Hales Corners, Wis. ... n11 88
Halesite, N.Y. ... *n15 75
Halethorpe, Md. ... B4, h10 53
Haleyville, Ala. ... A2 46
Half Moon Bay, Calif. ... k8 50
Halfway, Md. ... A2 53
Haliburton, Ont., Can. ... B6 41
Haliburton, co., Ont., Can. ... B6 41
Halifax, N.S., Can. ... E6 43
Halifax, Eng. ... D6 4
Halifax, N.C. ... A5 76
Halifax, Mass. ... C6 65
Halifax, Pa. ... F8 81
Halifax, Va. ... D4 85
Halifax, co., N.C. ... A5 76
Halifax, co., N.S., Can. ... E7 43
Halifax, co., Va. ... D4 85
Hall, Aus. ... E5 6
Hall, co., Ga. ... B3 55
Hall, co., Nebr. ... D7 71
Hall, co., Tex. ... B2 84
Halland, co., Swe. ... I15 11
Hallandale, Fla. ... G6, s13 54
Halle, Ger. Dem. Rep. ... C5 6
Hallein, Aus. ... E6 6
Hallettsville, Tex. ... E4 84
Hallock, Minn. ... B2 67
Hallowell, Maine ... D3 64
Halls, Tenn. ... B2 83
Hallstead, Pa. ... C10 81

Hallsville, Tex. ... C5 84
Halmstad, Swe. ... I5 11
Halstad, Minn. ... C2 67
Halstead, Kans. ... E6, g11 61
Haltom City, Tex. ... *C4 84
Halton, co., Ont., Can. ... D4 41
Hamada, Jap. ... I6 18
Hamadān, Iran ... F7 16
Hamāh, Syr. ... E11 14
Hamamatsu, Jap. ... I8, o16 18
Hamar, Nor. ... G4 11
Hama-tombetsu, Jap. ... D11 18
Hambantota, Sri Lanka ... G7 20
Hamblen, co., Tenn. ... C10 83
Hamburg, Ark. ... D4 49
Hamburg, Ger., Fed. Rep. of ... B5 6
Hamburg, Iowa ... D2 60
Hamburg, N.J. ... A3 74
Hamburg, N.Y. ... C2 75
Hamburg, Pa. ... E10 81
Hamburg, state, Ger. Fed. Rep. of ... *B5 6
Hamburg, mts., N.J. ... A3 74
Hamden, Conn. ... D6 52
Hamden, Ohio ... C3 78
Häme, prov., Fin. ... G11 11
Hämeenlinna, Fin. ... G11 11
Hamel, Minn. ... *E5 67
Hameln, Ger., Fed. Rep. of ... B4 6
Hamhung, Kor. ... G3 18
Hami, China ... C3 17
Hamilton, Ala. ... A2 46
Hamilton, Austl. ... G7 25
Hamilton, Bermuda ... p20 35
Hamilton, Ill. ... C2 58
Hamilton, Mass. ... A6, f12 65
Hamilton, Mich. ... F4 66
Hamilton, Mo. ... B3 69
Hamilton, Mont. ... D2 70
Hamilton, N.Y. ... C5 75
Hamilton, N.Z. ... L15 26
Hamilton, Ohio ... C1 78
Hamilton, Scot. ... C4 4
Hamilton, Tex. ... D3 84
Hamilton, co., Fla. ... B3 54
Hamilton, co., Ill. ... E5 58
Hamilton, co., Ind. ... D5 59
Hamilton, co., Iowa ... B4 60
Hamilton, co., Kans. ... E2 61
Hamilton, co., Nebr. ... D7 71
Hamilton, co., N.Y. ... C5 75
Hamilton, co., Ohio ... C1 78
Hamilton, co., Tenn. ... D8 83
Hamilton, co., Tex. ... D3 84
Hamilton, mtn., N.Y. ... B6 75
Hamilton Park, Pa. ... *G9 81
Hamilton Square, N.J. ... C3 74
Hamina, Fin. ... G12 11
Hamiota, Man., Can. ... D1 40
Hamīrpur, India ... C7 20
Hamlet, N.C. ... C3 76
Hamlin, Tex. ... C2 84
Hamlin, co., S. Dak. ... F8 77
Hamm in Westfalen, Ger., Fed. Rep. of ... C3 6
Hammon, Okla. ... B2 79
Hammond, Ind. ... A2 59
Hammond, La. ... D5, h11 63
Hammond, Wis. ... D1 88
Hammond East, La. ... *D5 63
Hammondsport, N.Y. ... C3 75
Hammonton, N.J. ... D3 74
Hampden, Newf., Can. ... D3 44
Hampden, Maine ... *D4 64
Hampden, co., Mass. ... B2 65
Hampden Highlands, Maine ... D4 64
Hampshire, Ill. ... A5 58
Hampshire, co., Eng. ... *E6 4
Hampshire, co., Mass. ... B2 65
Hampshire, co., W.Va. ... B6 87
Hampstead, Que., Can. ... *D4 42
Hampton, Ark. ... D3 49
Hampton, Ga. ... C2 55
Hampton, Iowa ... B4 60
Hampton, N.H. ... F6 73
Hampton, N.J. ... B3 74
Hampton, S.C. ... F5 82
Hampton, Tenn. ... C11 83
Hampton (Independent City), Va. ... C6, h15 85
Hampton, co., S.C. ... F5 82
Hampton Bays, N.Y. ... n16 75
Hamtramck, Mich. ... p15 66
Hana, Haw. ... C6 56
Hanahan, S.C. ... F7, k11 82
Hanamaki, Jap. ... G10 18

Hanamaulu, Haw. ... B2 56
Hanapepe, Haw. ... B2 56
Hanau, Ger., Fed. Rep. of ... C4 6
Hanceville, Ala. ... A3 46
Hancock, Md. ... A1 53
Hancock, Mich. ... A2 66
Hancock, Minn. ... E3 67
Hancock, N.Y. ... D5 75
Hancock, co., Ga. ... C3 55
Hancock, co., Ill. ... C2 58
Hancock, co., Ind. ... E6 59
Hancock, co., Iowa ... A4 60
Hancock, co., Ky. ... C3 62
Hancock, co., Maine ... D4 64
Hancock, co., Miss. ... E4 68
Hancock, co., Ohio ... A2 78
Hancock, co., Tenn. ... C10 83
Hancock, co., W. Va. ... A4 87
Hand, co., S. Dak. ... F6 77
Handa, Jap. ... o15 18
Handan, China ... D7 17
Handley, W. Va. ... m13 87
Haney, B.C., Can. ... E6, f13 37
Hanford, Calif. ... D4 50
Hanford Northwest, Calif. ... *D4 50
Hangchou, see Hangzhou, China
Hangö, Fin. ... H10 11
Hangzhou, China ... E8 17
Hankinson, N. Dak. ... D9 77
Hanley Hills, Mo. ... *C7 69
Hanna, Alta., Can. ... D5 38
Hanna, Wyo. ... E6 89
Hanna City, Ill. ... C4 58
Hannibal, Mo. ... B6 69
Hannibal, N.Y. ... B4 75
Hannover (Hanover), Ger., Fed. Rep. of ... B4 6
Hanoi, Viet. ... G6 17
Hanover, Ont., Can. ... C3 41
Hanover, Ill. ... A3 58
Hanover, Ind. ... G7 59
Hanover, Kan. ... C7 61
Hanover, Mass. ... B6, h12 65
Hanover, N.H. ... D3 73
Hanover, N.J. ... *B4 74
Hanover, Pa. ... G8 81
Hanover, co., Va. ... C5 85
Hanover, reg., Ger., Fed. Rep. of ... B4 6
Hanover Green, Pa. ... *D9 81
Hansford, co., Tex. ... A2 84
Hanson, Mass. ... B6 65
Hanson, co., S. Dak. ... G8 77
Hants, co., N.S., Can. ... D6 43
Hantsport, N.S., Can. ... D5 43
Hanzhong, China ... E6 17
Hapeville, Ga. ... C2, h8 55
Happy Valley, Newf., Can. ... B1, h9 44
Harahan, La. ... k11 63
Haralson, co., Ga. ... C1 55
Harar, Eth. ... G6 23
Harare, (Salisbury), Zimb. ... D6 24
Harbin, China ... B10 17
Harbor Beach, Mich. ... E8 66
Harborcreek, Pa. ... B2 81
Harbor Isle, N.Y. ... *E7 75
Harbor Springs, Mich. ... C6 66
Harbour Breton, Newf., Can. ... E4 44
Harbour Grace, Newf., Can. ... E5 44
Harbour Main, Newf., Can. ... E5 44
Hardee, co., Fla. ... E5 54
Hardeeville, S.C. ... G5 82
Hardeman, co., Tenn. ... B2 83
Hardeman, co., Tex. ... B3 84
Hardin, Ill. ... D3 58
Hardin, Mo. ... B4 69
Hardin, co., Ill. ... F5 58
Hardin, co., Iowa ... B4 60
Hardin, co., Ky. ... C3 62
Hardin, co., Mont. ... E9 70
Hardin, co., Ohio ... B2 78
Hardin, co., Tenn. ... B3 83
Hardin, co., Tex. ... D5 84
Harding, co., N. Mex. ... B7 48
Harding, co., S. Dak. ... E2 77
Hardinsburg, Ky. ... C3 62
Hardshell, Ky. ... C6 62
Hardwar, India ... C6 20
Hardwick, Vt. ... B3 73
Hardy, co., W. Va. ... B6 87
Hare Bay, Newf., Can. ... D4 44
Harfleur, Fr. ... C4 5
Harford, co., Md. ... A5 53
Hargeisa, Som. ... G6 23
Harihar, India ... F6 20
Harkers Island, N.C. ... C6 76

Harlan, Iowa ... C2 60
Harlan, Ky. ... D6 62
Harlan, co., Ky. ... D6 62
Harlan, co., Nebr. ... D6 71
Harlem, Fla. ... F6 54
Harlem, Ga. ... C4 55
Harlem, Mont. ... B8 70
Harlingen, Neth. ... A6 5
Harlingen, Tex. ... F4 84
Harlow, Eng. ... k13 4
Harlowton, Mont. ... D7 70
Harmarville, Pa. ... h14 81
Harmon, co., Okla. ... C2 79
Harmony, Ind. ... E3 59
Harmony, Minn. ... G6 67
Harmony, Pa. ... E1 81
Harnett, co., N.C. ... B4 76
Harney, co., Oreg. ... D7 80
Harney, peak, S. Dak. ... F2 77
Harnösand, Swe. ... F8 11
Haro, Sp. ... A4 8
Harper, Kans. ... E5 61
Harper, Lib. ... H3 22
Harper, co., Kans. ... E5 61
Harper, co., Okla. ... A2 79
Harper Woods, Mich. ... *F7 66
Harrah, Okla. ... B4 79
Harriman, Tenn. ... D1 83
Harrington, Del. ... C6 53
Harrington Park, N.J. ... h9 74
Harris, co., Ga. ... D1 55
Harris, co., Tex. ... E5 84
Harris, hill, Mass. ... A3 65
Harrisburg, Ark. ... B5 49
Harrisburg, Ill. ... F5 58
Harrisburg, Oreg. ... C3 80
Harrisburg, Pa. ... F8 81
Harris Hill, N.Y. ... *C2 75
Harrison, Ark. ... A2 49
Harrison, Mich. ... D6 66
Harrison, N.J. ... k8 74
Harrison, N.Y. ... D2, h13 75
Harrison, Ohio ... C3 78
Harrison, co., Ind. ... H5 59
Harrison, co., Iowa ... C2 60
Harrison, co., Ky. ... B5 62
Harrison, co., Miss. ... E4 68
Harrison, co., Mo. ... A3 69
Harrison, co., Ohio ... B4 78
Harrison, co., Tex. ... C5 84
Harrison, co., W. Va. ... B4 87
Harrisonburg, La. ... C4 63
Harrisonburg (Independent city), Va. ... B4 85
Harrisonville, Mo. ... C3 69
Harriston, Ont., Can. ... D4 41
Harrisville, Pa. ... D2 81
Harrisville, R.I. ... B10 52
Harrisville, W. Va. ... B3 87
Harrisville, N.Y. ... A5 75
Harrodsburg, Ky. ... C5 62
Harrogate, Eng. ... C6 4
Harrow, Ont., Can. ... E2 41
Hart, Mich. ... E4 66
Hart, co., Ga. ... B3 55
Hart, co., Ky. ... C4 62
Hart, mtn. Man., Can. ... C1 40
Hartford, Ala. ... D4 46
Hartford, Conn. ... B6 52
Hartford, Ill. ... E3 58
Hartford, Ky. ... C3 62
Hartford, Mich. ... F4 66
Hartford, Wis. ... E5, m11 88
Hartford, co., Conn. ... B5 52
Hartford City, Ind. ... D7 59
Hartington, Nebr. ... B8 71
Hartland, N.B., Can. ... C2 43
Hartland, Maine ... D3 64
Hartland, Wis. ... E5, m11 88
Hartlepool, Eng. ... C6 4
Hartley, Iowa ... A2 60
Hartley, co., Tex. ... B1 84
Hartsdale, N.Y. ... *D7 75
Hartselle, Ala. ... A3 46
Hartshorne, Okla. ... C6 79
Hartsville, S.C. ... C7 82
Hartsville, Tenn. ... A5 83
Hartville, Ohio ... B4 78
Hartwell, Ga. ... B4 55
Hartwick, N.Y. ... C5 75
Harvard, Ill. ... A5 58
Harvard, Nebr. ... D7 71
Harvard, mtn., Colo. ... C4 51
Harvey, Ill. ... B6, k9 58
Harvey, La. ... E5, k11 63
Harvey, Mich. ... B3 66
Harvey, N. Dak. ... C6 77
Harvey, co., Kans. ... D6 61

Harvey, mtn., Mass. B1 65
Harwich, Eng. E7 4
Harwich, Mass. C7 65
Harwich Port, Mass. C7 65
Harwick, Pa. *E1 81
Harwood Heights, Ill. *B6 58
Haryāna, state, India C5 20
Hasbrouck Heights, N.J. h8 74
Hashimoto, Jap. o14 18
Haskell, Okla. B6 79
Haskell, Tex. C3 84
Haskell, co., Kans. E3 61
Haskell, co., Okla. B6 79
Haskell, co., Tex. *C3 84
Haslett, Mich. *F6 66
Hassan, India F6 20
Hasselt, Bel. B6 5
Hässleholm, Swe. I5 11
Hastings, Ont., Can. C7 41
Hastings, Eng. E7 4
Hastings, Fla. C4 54
Hastings, Mich. F5 66
Hastings, Minn. F6 67
Hastings, Nebr. D7 71
Hastings, N.Z. M16 26
Hastings, Pa. E4 81
Hastings, co., Ont., Can. C7 41
Hastings-on-Hudson, N.Y. h13 75
Hatboro, Pa. F11 81
Hatch, N. Mex. C5 48
Hatfield, Mass. B2 65
Hatfield, Pa. F11 81
Hathras, India *C6 20
Ha Tien, Viet. C2 19
Hatteras, N.C. B7 76
Hattiesburg, Miss. D4 68
Hatton, N. Dak. C8 77
Hatton Fields, Calif. *D3 50
Hatvan, Hung. B4 10
Hatzic, B.C., Can. f13 37
Haubstadt, Ind. H2 59
Haugesund, Nor. H1 11
Hauppauge, N.Y. *D3 75
Haute-Garonne, dept., Fr. *F4 5
Haute-Loire, dept., Fr. *E5 5
Haute-Marne, dept., Fr. *C6 5
Hauterive, Que., Can. k13 42
Hautes-Alpes, dept., Fr. *E7 5
Hautes-Saône, dept., Fr. *D6 5
Haute-Savoie, dept., Fr. *D7 5
Hautes-Pyrénées, dept., Fr. *F4 5
Haute-Vienne, dept., Fr. *E4 5
Hautmont, Fr. B6 5
Haut-Rhin, dept., Fr. *C7 5
Hauula, Haw. B4, f10 56
Havana (La Habana), Cuba C2 35
Havana, Fla. B2 54
Havana, Ill. *C3 58
Havelock, Ont., Can. C7 41
Havelock, N.C. C6 76
Haven, Kans. E6, g11 61
Haverford, Pa. *F10 81
Haverhill, Mass. A5 65
Haverstraw, N.Y. D7, m15 75
Havertown, Pa. *G10 81
Haviland, Kans. E4 61
Havlíčkuv Brod, Czech. *D3 7
Havre, Mont. B7 70
Havre, see Le Havre, Fr.
Havre-Aubert, Que., Can. B8 43
Havre de Grace, Md. A5 53
Havza, Tur. B10 14
Hawaii, co., Haw. D5 56
Hawaii, state, U.S. D5 56
Hawaii, isl., Haw. D6 56
Hawaiian Gardens, Calif. *F4 50
Hawarden, Iowa A1 60
Hawera, N.Z. M15 26
Hawesville, Ky. C3 62
Hawi, Haw. C6 56
Hawick, Scot. C5 4
Hawkesbury, Ont., Can. B10 41
Hawkins, co., Tenn. C10 83
Hawkinsville, Ga. D3 55
Hawk Run, Pa. E5 81
Hawks Bill, mtn., Va. B4 85
Hawley, Minn. D2 67
Hawley, Pa. D11 81
Haworth, N.J. h9 74
Haw River, N.C. A3 76
Hawthorne, Calif. n12 50
Hawthorne, Fla. C4 54
Hawthorne, Nev. E2 72
Hawthorne, N.J. B4 74
Hawthorne, N.Y. g13 75
Haxtun, Colo. A8 51
Hayange, Fr. C7 5
Hayden, Ariz. C3, D3 48
Hayden, Idaho B2 57
Haydenville, Mass. B2 65
Haydenville, Ohio C3 78
Hayes, La. D3 63
Hayes, co., Nebr. D4 71

Hayesville, Oreg. *C4 80
Hayfield, Minn. G6 67
Haynau, see Chojnow, Pol.
Haynesville, La. B2 63
Hay River, N. W. Ter., Can. D10 36
Hays, Kans. D4 61
Hays, Mont. C8 70
Hays, co., Tex. D3 84
Hay Springs, Nebr. B3 71
Haysville, Kans. B5 61
Hayti, Mo. E8 69
Hayward, Calif. h8 50
Hayward, Wis. B2 88
Haywood, N.C. B3 76
Haywood, co., N.C. f9 76
Haywood, co., Tenn. B2 83
Hazard, Ky. C6 62
Hazardville, Conn. B6 52
Hazebrouck, Fr. B5 5
Hazel Crest, Ill. k9 58
Hazel Dell, Wash. *D3 86
Hazel Green, Wis. F3 88
Hazel Park, Mich. p15 66
Hazelwood, Mo. *C7 69
Hazelwood, N.C. f10 76
Hazen, Ark. C4 49
Hazen, N. Dak. C4 77
Hazlehurst, Ga. E4 55
Hazlehurst, Miss. D3 83
Hazlet, N.J. C4 74
Hazleton, Iowa B6 60
Hazleton, Pa. E10 81
Hazelton, peak, Wyo. C3 89
Headland, Ala. D4 46
Healdsburg, Calif. C2 50
Healdton, Okla. C4 79
Heard, co., Ga. C1 55
Hearne, Tex. D4 84
Hearst, Ont., Can. o19 41
Heart's Content, Newf., Can. E5 44
Heart's Delight, Newf., Can. *E5 44
Heath, Ohio B3 78
Heavener, Okla. C7 79
Hebbronville, Tex. F3 84
Hebei, prov., China D8 17
Heber, Utah A6, D2 72
Heber Springs, Ark. B3 49
Hébertville, Que., Can. A6 42
Hébertville Station,
    Que., Can. *A6 42
Hebrides, sea, Scot. B3 4
Hebron, Ill. A5 58
Hebron, Ind. B3 59
Hebron, Nebr. D8 71
Hebron, N. Dak. D3 77
Hebron, Ohio C3 78
Hecelchakán, Mex. C6 34
Hechingen, Ger., Fed. Rep. of D4 6
Hechuan, China E6 17
Hector, Minn. F4 67
Hedemora, Swe. G6 11
Hedmark, co., Nor. *G4 11
Hedwing, Iowa C5 60
Hedrick Village, Tex. *E5 84
Heerlen, Neth. B6 5
Hefei, China E8 17
Heflin, Ala. B4 46
Hegang, China B11 17
Hegeler, Ill. *C6 58
Hegins, Pa. E8 81
Heide, Ger., Fed. Rep. of A4 6
Heidelberg, Ger., Fed. Rep. of D4 6
Heidelberg, Miss. D5 68
Heidelberg, Pa. *E1 81
Heidenheim, Ger., Fed. Rep. of D5 6
Heidrick, Ky. D6 62
Heibronn, Ger., Fed. Rep. of D4 6
Heiligenstadt, Ger. Dem. Rep. C5 6
Heilongjiang, prov., China B10 17
Heislerville, N.J. E3 74
Hejaz, pol. div., Sau. Ar. D2 15
Hekla, peak, Ice. n23 11
Helena, Ark. C5 49
Helena, Ga. D4 55
Helena, Mont. D5 70
Helensburgh, Scot. B4 4
Heli, China C5 18
Hellam, Pa. G8 81
Hellertown, Pa. E11 81
Helmetta, N.J. C4 74
Helmond, Neth. B6 5
Helmstedt, Ger., Fed. Rep. of B5 6
Helper, Utah B6 72
Helsingborg, Swe. I5 11
Helsingfors, see Helsinki, Fin.
Helsingor, Den. I5 11
Helsinki, Fin. G11 11
Hemel Hempstead, Eng. k12 4
Hemet, Calif. F5 50
Hemingford, Nebr. B2 71
Hemingway, S.C. D9 82
Hemlock, Mich. E6 66
Hemlock (Eureka), S.C. B5 82

Hemmingford, Que.,Can. D4 42
Hemphill, Tex. D6 84
Hemphill, co., Tex. B2 84
Hempstead, N.Y. k13 75
Hempstead, Tex. D4 84
Hempstead, co., Ark. D2 49
Henan, prov., China E7 17
Hendaye, Fr. F3 5
Hendek, Tur. B8 14
Henderson, Ky. C2 62
Henderson, Minn. F5 67
Henderson, Nebr. D8 71
Henderson, Nev. C4 72
Henderson, N.C. A4 76
Henderson, Tenn. B3 83
Henderson, Tex. C5 84
Henderson, co., Ill. C3 58
Henderson, co., Ky. C2 62
Henderson, co., N.C. f10 76
Henderson, co., Tenn. B3 83
Henderson, co., Tex. C5 84
Hendersonville, N.C. f10 76
Hendersonville, Tenn. A5, g10 83
Hendricks, Minn. F2 67
Hendricks, co., Ind. E4 59
Hendry, co., Fla. F5 54
Hengelo, Neth. A7 5
Hengyang, China F7 17
Henlawson, W. Va. n12 87
Hennebont, Fr. D2 5
Hennepin, co., Minn. E5 67
Hennessey, Okla. A4 79
Henning, Minn. D3 67
Henrico, co., Va. C5 85
Henrietta, N.Y. B3 75
Henrietta, N.C. B2, f11 76
Henrietta, Tex. C3 84
Henry, Ill. B4 58
Henry, co., Ala. D4 46
Henry, co., Ga. C2 55
Henry, co., Ill. B3 58
Henry, co., Ind. E7 59
Henry, co., Iowa C6 60
Henry, co., Ky. B4 62
Henry, co., Mo. C4 69
Henry, co., Ohio A1 78
Henry, co., Tenn. A3 83
Henry, co., Va. D3 85
Henryetta, Okla. B6 79
Hensall, Ont., Can. D3 41
Henryville, Que., Can. D4 42
Henzada, Bur. E10 20
Heppner, Oreg. B7 80
Hepu, China G6 17
Heqing, China F5 17
Herat, Afg. B3 20
Hérault, dept., Fr. *F5 5
Herbert, Sask., Can. G2 39
Herblay, Fr. g9 5
Hercegovina, reg., Yugo. D3 10
Herculaneum, Mo. C7, g13 69
Heredia, C.R. E8 34
Heredia, prov., C.R. *E8 34
Hereford, Eng. D5 4
Hereford, Tex. B1 84
Hereford, co., Eng. *D5 4
Herencia, Sp. C4 8
Herford, Ger., Fed. Rep. of B4 6
Herington, Kans. D7 61
Herisau, Switz. E4 6
Herkimer, N.Y. B6 75
Herkimer, co., N.Y. B5 75
Herman, Minn. E2 67
Hermann, Mo. C6 69
Hermansville, Mich. C3 66
Hermantown, Minn. D6 67
Herminie, Pa. F2 81
Hermiston, Oreg. B7 80
Herman, Minn. f9 75
Hermosa Beach, Calif. *F4 50
Hermosillo, Mex. B2 34
Hernando, Miss. A4 68
Hernando, co., Fla. D4 54
Herndon, Va. B5, g12 85
Herning, Den. I3 11
Heron Lake, Minn. G3 67
Herrin, Ill. F4 58
Hershey, Pa. F8 81
Herstal, Bel. B6 5
Hertford, Eng. E6, k12 4
Hertford, N.C. A6 76
Hertford, co., Eng. *E6 4
Hertford, co., N.C. A5 76
Herzliyya, Isr. B2, g5 15
Hesperia, Mich. E4 66
Hesperia, Calif. F5 50
Hesse, reg., Ger., Fed. Rep. of ... C4 6
Hessen, state, Ger., Fed. Rep. of . *C4 6
Hesston, Kans. D6 61
Hettinger, N. Dak. D3 77
Hettinger, co., N. Dak. D3 77
Heuvelton, N.Y. f9 75
Heves, Hung. *B5 10
Heves, co., Hung. *B5 10

Hewitt, N.J. A4 74
Hewlett, N.Y. *G2 52
Hewlett Harbor, N.Y. *G2 52
Heyworth, Ill. C5 58
Hialeah, Fla. G6, s13 54
Hiawatha, Iowa *C6 60
Hiawatha, Kans. C8 61
Hiawatha, Utah B6 72
Hibbing, Minn. C6 67
Hibernia, N.J. B4 74
Hickman, Ky. f8 62
Hickman, co., Ky. f8 62
Hickman, co., Tenn. B4 83
Hickory, co., Mo. D4 69
Hickory Hills, Ill. *B6 58
Hicksville, N.Y. E7, n15 75
Hicksville, Ohio A1 78
Hico, Tex. D3 84
Hidalgo, Tex. F3 84
Hidalgo, co., N. Mex. D4 48
Hidalgo, co., Tex. F3 84
Hidalgo, state, Mex. C5, m14 34
Hidalgo del Parral, Mex. B3 34
Higashiizu, Jap. o18 18
Higashiosaka, Jap. I7, o14 18
Higbee, Mo. B5 69
Higgins, Tex. A2 84
Higginsville, Mo. B4 69
High Bridge, N.J. B3 74
Highgrove, Calif. *F5 50
High Knob, mtn., Va. A4 85
Highland, Calif. *E5 50
Highland, Ill. E4 58
Highland, Ind. A3 59
Highland, Kans. C8 61
Highland, Mich. o14 66
Highland, N.Y. D7 75
Highland, Wis. E3 88
Highland, co., Ohio C2 78
Highland, co., Va. *B3 85
Highland City, Fla. *E5 54
Highland Creek, Ont., Can. D5 41
Highland Crest, Kans. *B8 61
Highland Falls, N.Y. *D7 75
Highland Heights, Ky. *A5 62
Highland Heights, Ohio A4 78
Highland Park, Ill. A6, h9 58
Highland Park, Mich., ... p15 66
Highland Park, N.J. *C4 74
Highland Park, Pa. *F6 81
Highland Park, Tex. B5 84
Highlands, Fla. *B5 54
Highlands, N.J. C5 74
Highlands, Tex. r14 84
Highlands, co., Fla. E5 54
Highland Springs, Va. C5, m18 85
Highmore, S. Dak. F6 77
High Point, N.C. B3 76
High Point, mtn., N.J. A3 74
High Prairie, Alta., Can. B2 38
High River, Alta., Can. D4 38
Highshoals, N.C. B1 76
High Spire, Pa. F8 81
High Springs, Fla. C4 54
Hightstown, N.J. C3 74
Highway City, Calif. *D4 50
Highway Village, Tex. *F4 84
Highwood, Ill. A6, h9 58
High Wycombe, Eng. E6 4
Higüey, Dom. Rep. E9 35
Hikone, Jap. n15 18
Hilbert, Wis. E3 88
Hildburghausen, Ger. Dem. Rep. C5 6
Hildesheim, Ger., Fed. Rep. of B4 6
Hill, co., Mont. B6 70
Hill, co., Tex. D4 84
Hillburn, N.Y. *D6 75
Hill City, Kans. C4 61
Hillcrest, N.J. *B2 74
Hillcrest, N.Y. *D6 75
Hillcrest Center, Calif. *E4 50
Hillcrest Heights, Md. *C3 53
Hillcrest Mines, Alta., Can. E3 38
Hiller, Pa. *G2 81
Hilliard, Fla. B4 54
Hilliard, Ohio k10 78
Hillsboro, Ill. D4 58
Hillsboro, Kans. D6 61
Hillsboro, N.H. E4 73
Hillsboro, N. Dak. C8 77
Hillsboro, Ohio C2 78
Hillsboro, Oreg. B3, g12 80
Hillsboro, Tenn. B6 83
Hillsboro, Tex. C4 84
Hillsboro, Wis. E3 88
Hillsboro, co., N.H. F4 73
Hillsborough, Calif. *D2 50
Hillsborough, N.B., Can. D5 43
Hillsborough, N.C. A3 76
Hillsborough, co., Fla. E4 54
Hillsborough Lower Village, N.H. .. E3 73
Hillsborough Upper Village, N.H. .. E4 73
Hillsdale, Mich. G6 66

Hillsdale, Mo. *C7   69
Hillsdale, N.J. g8   74
Hillsdale, co., Mich. G6   66
Hillside, Ill. *B6   58
Hillside, N.J. k8   74
Hillside Manor, N.Y. *G2   52
Hillsville, Pa. D1   81
Hillsville, Va. D2   85
Hilltop, N.J. *D2   74
Hillwood, Va. *B5   85
Hilo, Haw. D6, n16   56
Hilton, N.Y. B3   75
Hilversum, Neth. A6   5
Himachal Pradesh, state, India *B6   20
Himalayas, mts., India. C7   20
Himeji, Jap. I7   18
Himi, Jap. H8   18
Ḥimṣ, (Homs), Syr. B5   23
Hinche, Hai E7   35
Hinckley, Ill. B5   58
Hinckley, Minn. D6   67
Hindenburg, see Zabrze, Pol.
Hinds, co., Miss. C3   68
Hines, Oreg. D7   80
Hinesville, Ga. D5   55
Hingham, Mass. B6, h12   65
Hinojosa del Duque, Sp. C3   8
Hinsdale, Ill. k9   58
Hinsdale, Mass. B1   65
Hinsdale, N.H. F3   73
Hinsdale, co., Colo. D3   51
Hinton, Alta., Can. C2   38
Hinton, Okla. B3   79
Hinton, W. Va. D4   87
Hirakata, Jap. *I7   18
Hiram, Ohio A4   78
Hiratsuka, Jap. n17   18
Hiroo, Jap. E11   18
Hirosaki, Jap. F10   18
Hiroshima, Jap I6   18
Hiroshima, pref., Jap. *I6   18
Hirson, Fr. C5   5
Hisār, India. C6   20
Hispaniola, isl., N.A. D8   35
Hita, Jap. *J5   18
Hitachi, Jap. H10   18
Hitchcock, Tex. r14   84
Hitchcock, co., Nebr. D4   71
Hitchins, Ky. B7   62
Hitoyoshi, Jap. J5   18
Hixon, Tenn. D8, h11   83
Hjørring, Den. I3   11
Hjørring, co., Den. I3   11
Hlohovec, Czech. D4   7
Hlomsak, Thai. *E11   20
Hoa Binh, Viet. *A3   19
Hobart, Austl. o15   25
Hobart, Ind. A3   59
Hobart, Okla. B2   79
Hobbs, N. Mex. C7   48
Hoboken, Bel. B6   5
Hoboken, N.J. k8   74
Ho Chi Minh City
   (Saigon), Viet. C3   19
Hocking, co., Ohio C3   78
Hockley, co., Tex. C1   84
Hoddesdon, Eng. k13   4
Hodeida, Yemen F6   23
Hodgeman, co., Kans. D4   61
Hodgenville, Ky. C4   62
Hodgkins, Il. *B6   58
Hódmezővásárhely, Hung. B5   10
Hodonín, Czech. D4   7
Hoeryong, Kor. E4   18
Hof, Ger., Fed.,Rep of C5   6
Hoffman, Minn. E3   67
Hoffman Estates, Ill. h8   58
Hofu, Jap. I5   18
Hogansville, Ga. C2   55
Hogback, mtn., S.C. A3   82
Hohenwald, Tenn. B4   83
Hohhot, China C7   17
Ho-Ho-Kus (Hohokus) N.J. h8   74
Hoisington, Kans. D5   61
Hokah, Minn. G7   67
Hoke, co.,N.C. B3   76
Hokendauqua, Pa. *E10   81
Hokes Bluff, Ala. B4   46
Hokkaido, pref., Jap. *E10   18
Hokkaido, isl., Jap. E10   18
Holbaek, co., Den. *J4   11
Holbrook, Ariz. B3   48
Holbrook, Mass. B5, h11   65
Holbrook N.Y. *n15   75
Holden, Mass. B4   65
Holden, Mo. C4   69
Holden, W. Va. D2   87
Holdrege, Nebr. D6   71
Holgate, Ohio A1   78
Holguín, Cuba D5   35
Hollabrunn, Aus. D8   6
Holladay, Utah *C3   72

Holland, Mich. F4   66
Holland, N.Y. C2   75
Holland, Ohio A2, e6   78
Hollandale, Miss. B3   68
Holley, N.Y. B2   75
Holliday, Tex. C3   84
Hollidaysburg, Pa. F5   81
Hollins, Va. C3   85
Hollis, Alsk. n23   47
Hollis, Okla. C2   79
Hollister, Calif. D3   50
Hollister, Mo. E4   69
Holliston, Mass. h10   65
Holloway Terrace, Del. *A6   53
Hollsopple, Pa. F4   81
Holly, Colo. C8   51
Holly, Mich. . . . . , . F7   66
Holly Hill, Fla. C5   54
Holly Hill, S.C. E7   82
Holly Oak, Del. A7   53
Holly Ridge, N.C. C5   76
Holly Springs, Miss. A4   68
Hollywood, Fla. f6, r13   54
Hollywood, La. *D2   63
Hollywood, Pa. *F11   81
Hollywood Heights, Ill. *E3   58
Holmdel Gardens, Kans. *D6   61
Holmen, Wis. E2   88
Holmes, Pa. *G11   81
Holmes, co., Fla. u16   54
Holmes, co., Miss. B3   68
Holmes, co., Ohio B4   78
Holmes, mtn., Wyo. B2   89
Holmes Beach, Fla. *E4   54
Holmes Run Acres, Va. *B5   85
Holmes Run Park, Va. *B5   85
Holon, Isr. B2   15
Holopaw, Fla. D5   54
Holstebro, Den. I3   11
Holstein, Iowa B2   60
Holt, Ala. B2   46
Holt, Mich. F6   66
Holt, co., Mo. A2   69
Holt, co., Nebr. B7   71
Holton, Kans. C8   61
Holtville, Calif. F6   50
Holyhead, Wales D4   4
Holyoke, Colo. A8   51
Holyoke, Mass. B2   65
Holyoke, range, Mass. B2   65
Holyrood, Kans. D5   61
Holzminden, Ger., Fed. Rep of C4   6
Homalin, Bur. D9   20
Homeacre, Pa. *E2   81
Home Corner, Ind. C6   59
Homécourt, Fr. C6   5
Homedale, Idaho F2   57
Homedale, Ohio *B2   78
Home Gardens, Calif. *F5   50
Home Hill, Austl. C8   25
Homer, Alsk. D6, h16   47
Homer, Ill. C6   58
Homer, La. B2   63
Homer, Mich. F6   66
Homer, N.Y. C4   75
Homer City, Pa. E3   81
Homerville, Ga. E4   55
Homestead, Fla. G6, t13   54
Homestead, Pa. k14   81
Homestead Valley, Calif. *C2   50
Hometown, Ill. *B6   58
Homewood, Ala. g7   46
Homewood, Calif. C3   50
Homewood, Ill. B6, k9   58
Homeworth, Ohio B4   78
Hominy, Okla. A5   79
Honaker, Va. e10   85
Honan, see Henan, China
Honda, Col. B3   32
Hondo, Tex. E3   84
Honduras, country, N.A. D7   34
Honea Path, S.C. C3   82
Honeoye Falls, N.Y. C3   75
Honesdale, Pa. C11   81
Honey Brook, Pa. F10   81
Honey Grove, Tex. *C5   84
Honfleur, Fr. C4   5
Hon Gai, Viet. *A3   19
Hongwon, Kor. G3   18
Hong Kong, Br. dep.,Asia G7   17
Honokaa, Haw. C6   56
Honolulu, Haw. B4, g10   56
Honolulu, co., Haw. B3   56
Honshū, isl., Jap. H8   18
Honto, see Nevelsk, Sov. Un.
Hood, co., Tex. C4   84
Hood, mtn., Oreg. B5   80
Hoodoo, peak, Wash. A5   86
Hood River, Oreg. B5   80
Hood River, co., Oreg. B5   80
Hoodsport, Wash. B2   86
Hooghly-Chinsura, India *D8   20
Hooker, Okla. e9   79
Hooker, co., Nebr. C4   71

Hooker, mtn., B.C., Can. C8   37
Hooks, Tex. *C5   84
Hooksett, N.H. E5   73
Hoolehua, Haw. B4   56
Hooper, Nebr. C9   71
Hooper, Utah A5, C2   72
Hooper Bay, Alsk. C6   47
Hoopeston, Ill. C6   58
Hoorn, Neth. A6   5
Hoosac, range, Mass. A1   65
Hoosick Falls, N.Y. C7   75
Hoosier, Pa. F4   81
Hope, Ark. D2   49
Hope, B.C., Can. E7   37
Hope, Ind. F6   59
Hopedale, Ill. C4   58
Hopedale, La. E6   63
Hopedale, Mass. B4, h9   65
Hopedale, Ohio B5   78
Hopelawn, N.J. *B4   74
Hope Mills, N.C. C4   76
Hope Ranch, Calif. *E4   50
Hope Valley, R.I. C10   52
Hopewell, N.J. C3   74
Hopewell
   (Independent City), Va. C5, n18   85
Hopewell Junction, N.Y. D7   75
Hopkins, Minn. n12   67
Hopkins, Mo. A3   69
Hopkins, co., Ky. C2   62
Hopkins, co., Tex. C5   84
Hopkinsville, Ky. D2   62
Hopkinton, Iowa B6   60
Hopkinton, Mass. B4, h9   65
Hopland, Calif. C2   50
Hopwood, Pa. G2   81
Hoquiam, Wash. C2   86
Hordaland, co., Nor. *G1   11
Horicon, Wis. E5   88
Hornell, N.Y. C3   75
Hornersville, Mo. E7   69
Horní Počernice, Czech. n18   7
Hornsea, Eng. D6   4
Hornsey, Eng. k12   4
Horqueta, Par. D4   29
Horry, co., S.C. D9   82
Horseback Knob, hill, Ohio C2   78
Horse Cave, Ky. C4   62
Horseheads, N.Y. C4   75
Horsens,Den. J3   11
Horsham, Austl. G7   25
Horsham, Pa. *F11   81
Horta, Port. (Azores) k9   22
Horten, Nor. H4, p28   11
Horton, Kans. C8   61
Hortonville, Wis. D5   88
Hoshiārpur, India B6   20
Hospers, Iowa A2   60
Hospitalet, Sp. B7   8
Hotan, China A6   20
Hot Springs, N.C. f10   76
Hot Springs, S. Dak. G2   77
Hot Springs, co., Ark. C2   49
Hot Springs, co., Wyo. C4   89
Hot Springs, see Truth or
   Consequences, N. Mex.
Hot Springs National Park, Ark. . . . C2, f7   49
Houghton, Mich. A2   66
Houghton, N.Y. C2   75
Houghton, Wash. e11   86
Houghton, co., Mich. B2   66
Houghton Lake, Mich. D6   66
Houghton Lake Heights, Mich. D6   66
Houilles, Fr. g9   5
Houlton, Maine B5   64
Houma, La. E5, k10   63
Housatonic, Mass. B1   65
Houston, B.C., Can. B4   37
Houston, Minn. G7   67
Houston, Miss. B4   68
Houston, Mo. D6   69
Houston, Pa. F1   81
Houston, Tex. E5, r14   84
Houston, co., Ala. D4   46
Houston, co., Ga. D3   55
Houston, co., Minn. G7   67
Houston, co., Tenn. A4   83
Houston, co., Tex. D5   84
Houtzdale,Pa. E5   81
Hove, Eng. E6   4
Howard, Kans. E7   61
Howard, S. Dak. F8   77
Howard, Wis. D5, g9   88
Howard, co., Ark. C2   49
Howard, co., Ind. C5   59
Howard, co., Iowa A5   60
Howard, co., Md. B4   53
Howard, co., Mo. B5   69
Howard, co., Nebr. C7   71
Howard, co., Tex. C2   84
Howard City, Mich. E5   66
Howard Lake, Minn. E4   67

Howe, Ind. A7   59
Howell, Mich. F7   66
Howell, co., Mo. E6   69
Howells, Nebr. C8   71
Howick, Que., Can. D4   42
Howland, Maine C4   64
Howley, mtn., Newf., Can. D2   44
Howrah, India D8   20
Howson, peak, B.C., Can. B4, n17   37
Hoxie, Ark. A5   49
Hoxie, Kans. C3   61
Hoya, Ger., Fed. Rep. of B4   6
Hoyerswerda, Ger. Dem Rep. C7   6
Hoyt Lakes, Minn. C6   67
Hradec Králové, Czech. C3   7
Hranice, Czech. D4   7
Hriňová, Czech. D5   7
Hrubieszów, Pol. C7   7
Hsinchu, Taiwan G9   17
Hsinkao, mtn., Taiwan G9   17
Hsipaw, Bur. *D10   20
Huacho, Peru D2   31
Huadian, China C10   17
Huaide, China E2   18
Huailley, Peru D2   31
Huainan, China E8   17
Hualgayoc, Peru C2   3
Hualien,Taiwan G9   17
Huamachuco, Peru C2   31
Huamantla, Mex. n15   34
Huambo, Ang. C3   24
Huancabamba, Peru C2   31
Huancané, Peru E4   31
Huancavelica, Peru D2   31
Huancavelica, dept., Peru D2   31
Huancayo, Peru D2   31
Huang He (Yellow), riv., China F13   16
Huangshi, China E8   17
Huanta, Peru D3   31
Huánuco, Peru C2   31
Huánuco, dept., Peru C2   31
Huaral, Peru D2   31
Huaráz, Peru C2   31
Huariaca, Peru D2   31
Huascaran, mtn., Peru C2   31
Huatabampo, Mex. B3   34
Huatusco de Chicuellar, Mex. n15   34
Huauchinango, Mex. m14   34
Huaytará, Peru D2   31
Hubbard, Iowa B4   60
Hubbard, Ohio A5   78
Hubbard, Tex. D4   84
Hubbard, co., Minn. C3   67
Hubbell, Mich. A2   66
Hubei, prov., China E7   17
Huberdeau, Que., Can. D3   42
Huber Heights, Ohio *C1   78
Hubli, India. E6   20
Huddersfield, Eng. D6   4
Hudiksvall, Swe. G7   11
Hudson, Que., Can. D3, q18   42
Hudson, Iowa B5   60
Hudson, Mass. B4, g9   65
Hudson, Mich. g6   66
Hudson, N.H. F5   73
Hudson, N.Y. C7   75
Hudson, N.C. B1   76
Hudson, Ohio A4   78
Hudson, Pa. *D9   81
Hudson, Wis. D1   88
Hudson, co., N.J. B4   74
Hudson, bay, Can. D16   36
Hudson, riv., Maine B3   64
Hudson Bay, Sask., Can. E4   39
Hudson Falls, N.Y. B7   75
Hudsonville, Mich. F5   66
Hudspeth, co.,Tex. o12   84
Hue, Viet. B3   19
Hueco, mts., Tex. o11   84
Huedin, Rom. B6   10
Huehuetenango, Guat. *D6   34
Huelma, Sp. D4   8
Huelva, Sp. D2   8
Huelva, prov., Sp. *D2   8
Huércal-Overa, Sp. D5   8
Huerfano, co., Colo. C6   51
Huesca, Sp. A5   8
Huesca, prov., Sp. *A5   8
Huéscar, Sp. D4   8
Hueytown, Ala. g6   46
Hughes, Ark. C5   49
Hughes, co., Okla. B5   79
Hughes, co., S. Dak. F6   77
Hughes Springs, Tex. *C5   84
Hughestown, Pa. *D9   81
Hughesville, Pa. D8   81
Hughson, Calif. *D3   50
Hugo, Colo. B7   51
Hugo, Okla. C6   79
Hugoton, Kans. E2   61
Huguley, Ala. *C4   6
Huichon, Kor. F3   18
Huila, dept., Col. C2   32

Huixtla, Mex.	D6	34
Huizhou, China	G7	17
Hukou, China	F8	17
Hulan, China	B10	17
Hulen, Ky.	D6	62
Hull, Que., Can.	D2	42
Hull, Eng.	D6	4
Hull, Iowa	A1	60
Hull, Mass.	B6, g12	65
Hull, co., Que., Can.	D2	42
Hulmeville, Pa.	*F11	81
Humacao, P.R.	*G12	35
Humansville, Mo.	D4	69
Humble, Tex.	E5, q14	84
Humboldt, Sask., Can.	E3	39
Humboldt, Iowa	B3	60
Humboldt, Kans.	E8	61
Humboldt, Nebr.	D10	71
Humboldt, Tenn.	B3	83
Humboldt, co., Calif.	B2	50
Humboldt, co., Iowa	B3	60
Humboldt, co., Nev.	A2	72
Humenné, Czech.	D6	7
Humeston, Iowa	D4	60
Hummelstown, Pa.	*F8	81
Humphrey, Nebr.	C8	71
Humphreys, co., Miss.	B3	68
Humphreys, co., Tenn.	A4	83
Humphreys, peak, Ariz.	B2	48
Humpolec, Czech.	D3	7
Hunan, prov., China	F7	17
Hunchun, China	C11	17
Hunedoara, Rom.	C6	10
Hungary, country, Eur.	B4	10
Hungnam, Kor.	G3	18
Hunjiang, China	C10	17
Hunt, mtn., Wyo	B5	89
Hunt, co., Tex.	C4	84
Hunterdon, N.J.	B3	74
Huntersville, N.C.	B2	76
Huntingburg, Ind.	H4	59
Huntingdon, Que., Can.	D3	42
Huntingdon, Pa.	F6	81
Huntingdon, Tenn.	A3	83
Huntingdon, co., Que., Can.	D3	42
Huntingdon, co., Pa.	F5	81
Huntingdon & Peterborough, co., Eng.	*D7	4
Huntington, Ind.	C7	59
Huntington, Mass.	B2	65
Huntington, N.J.	B2	74
Huntington, N.Y.	E7, n15	75
Huntington, Oreg.	C9	80
Huntington, Tex.	D5	84
Huntington, Utah	B6	72
Huntington, W. Va.	C2	87
Huntington, co., Ind.	C6	59
Huntington Bay, N.Y.	*G3	52
Huntington Beach, Calif.	n13	50
Huntington Beach, N.Y.	*D3	75
Huntington Park, Calif.	F4	50
Huntington Station, N.Y.	F3	52
Huntington Woods, Mich.	p15	66
Huntingtown, Md.	C4	53
Huntley, Ill.	A5	58
Huntly, Scot.	B5	4
Huntsville, Ala.	A3	46
Huntsville, Ark.	A2	49
Huntsville, Ont., Can.	B5	41
Huntsville, Mo.	B5	69
Huntsville, Tex.	D5	84
Hurley, N. Mex.	C4	48
Hurley, N.Y.	D6	75
Hurley, Wis.	B3	88
Hurleyville, N.Y.	D6	75
Hurlock, Md.	C3	53
Huron, Calif.	*D4	50
Huron, Ohio	A3	78
Huron, S. Dak.	F7	77
Huron, co., Ont., Can.	D3	41
Huron, co., Mich.	E7	66
Huron, co., Ohio	A3	78
Huron, lake, Can.	B10	45
Hurricane, Utah	C5	72
Hurricane, W. Va.	C2	87
Hurst, Ill.	F4	58
Hurst, Tex.	*C4	84
Hurtsboro, Ala.	C4	46
Huşi, Rom.	B9	10
Hustisford, Wis.	E5	88
Husum, Ger., Fed. Rep. of	A4	6
Hutchins, Tex.	n10	84
Hutchinson, Kans.	D6, f11	61
Hutchinson, Minn.	F4	67
Hutchinson, co., S. Dak.	G8	77
Hutchinson, co., Tex.	B2	84
Huttig, Ark.	D3	49
Huxley, Iowa	C4, e8	60
Huy, Bel.	B6	5
Hvannadalshnúkur, mtn., Ice.	o24	11
Hvittingfoss, Nor.	p28	11
Hwange, Zimb.	D5	24
Hyannis, Mass.	C7	65
Hyannis Port, Mass.	C7	65
Hyattsville, Md.	C4, f9	53
Hyde, Pa.	D5	81
Hyde, co., N.C.	B6	76
Hyde, co., S. Dak.	F6	77
Hyde Park, N.Y.	D7	75
Hyde Park, Pa.	*F9	81
Hyderābād, India	E6	20
Hyderābād, Pak.	C4	20
Hyde Villa, Pa.	*F9	81
Hydro, Okla.	B3	79
Hyères, Fr.	F7	5
Hymera, Ind.	F3	59
Hyndman, Pa.	G4	81
Hyogo, pref., Jap.	*I7	18
Hyopchon, Kor.	I4	18
Hyrum, Utah	A6	72
Hyrynsalmi, Fin.	E13	11
Hythe, Alta., Can.	B1	38
Hythe, Eng.	E7	4

I

Iaeger, W. Va.	D3	87
Iasi, Rom.	B8	10
Iba, Phil.	*B5	19
Ibadan, Nig.	G5	22
Ibagué, Col.	C2	32
Ibaraki, Jap.	*o14	18
Ibaraki, pref., Jap.	*H10	18
Ibarra, Ec.	A2	31
Ibb, Yemen	G3	15
Iberia, Mo.	C5	69
Iberia, par., La.	E4	63
Iberville, Que., Can.	D4	42
Iberville, co.,Que., Can.	D4	42
Iberville, par., La.	D4, h9	63
Iberville, mtn., Newf.	f9	44
Ibitinga, Braz.	C3	30
Ibiza, Sp.	C6	8
Ica, Peru	D2	31
Ica, dept., Peru	D2	31
Ice, mtn., B.C., Can.	B7	37
Iceland, country, Eur.	*n23	11
Ichihara, Jap.	*n19	18
Ichikawa, Jap.	n18	18
Ichinomiya, Jap.	n15	18
Ichinoseki, Jap.	G10	18
Ichnya, Sov. Un.	F9	12
Ida, Mich.	G7	66
Ida, co., Iowa	B2	60
Idabel, Okla.	D7	79
Ida Grove, Iowa	B2	60
Idaho, co., Idaho	D3	57
Idaho,state, U.S.		57
Idaho Falls, Idaho	F6	67
Idaho Springs, Colo.	B5	51
Idalou, Tex.	C2	84
Idamay, W. VA.	k10	87
Idanha-a-Nova, Port.	C2	8
Idaville, Ind.	C4	59
Idrija, Yugo.	B2	10
Ieper (Ypres), Bel.	B5	5
Ierápetra, Grc.	E5	14
Iesi, It.	C4	9
Ife, Nig.	G5	22
Igarapava, Braz.	C3	30
Igarka, Sov. Un.	C11	13
Iğdir, Tur.	*C15	14
Iglesias, It.	E2	9
Igloo, S. Dak.	G2	77
Igualada, Sp.	B6	8
Iguatu, Braz.	*D7	27
Iida, Jap.	I8, n16	18
Iide-san, mtn., Jap.	H9	18
Iijima, Jap.	n16	18
Iisalmi, Fin.	F12	11
Iizuka, Jap.	J5	18
Ijebu Ode, Nig.	G5	22
Ijuí, Braz.	D2	30
Ikeda, Jap.	D14	18
Ikerre, Nig.	*G6	22
Ikhtiman, Bul.	D6	10
Ila, Nig.	E5	22
Ilagan, Phil.	B6	19
Ilan, Taiwan	*G9	17
Ilawe, Nig.	*E6	22
Ile-a-la-Cross, Sask., Can.	m7	39
Ilebo (Port-Francqui), Zaire	I2	23
Ile-de-France, former prov., Fr.	C5	5
Ile-Perrot, Que., Can.	q19	42
Ilesha, Nig.	G5	22
Ilford, Eng.	k13	4
Ilfracombe, Eng.	E4	4
Ilgin, Tur.	C8	14
Ilhavo, Port.	B1	8
Ilhéus, Braz.	E7	27
Ilia (Elis), prov., Grc.	*D3	14
Ilinskaya, Sov. Un.	I13	12
Ilion, N.Y.	B5	75
Illampu, mtn., Bol.	C2	29
Illapel, Chile	A2	28
Ille-et-Vilaine, dept., Fr.	*C3	5
Illinois, state, U.S.		58
Illinois, peak, Idaho	B3	57
Illinois, peak, Mont.	C1	70
Illiopolis, Ill.	D4	58
Illmo, Mo.	D8	69
Illora, Sp.	D4	8
Ilmenau, Ger. Dem. Rep.	C5	6
Ilo, Peru	E3	31
Ilocos Norte, prov., Phil	*B6	19
Ilocos Sur, prov., Phil.	C6	19
Iloilo, Phil.	C6	19
Iloilo, prov., Phil.	*C6	19
Ilorin, Nig.	G5	22
Ilovaysk, Sov. Un.	r21	12
Imabari, Jap.	I6	18
Imabetsu, Jap.	F10	18
Imari, Jap.	*J4	18
Imazu, Jap.	n15	18
Imbābah, Eg.	*G8	14
Imbabura, prov., Ec.	A2	31
Imlay City, Mich.	E7	66
Immenstadt, Ger., Fed. Rep. of	E5	6
Immokalee, Fla.	F5	54
Imola, It.	B3	9
Imperia, It.	C2	9
Imperial, Calif.	F6	50
Imperial, Sask., Can.	F3	39
Imperial, Mo.	C7, g13	69
Imperial, Nebr.	D4	71
Imperial, Pa.	k13	81
Imperial, co., Calif.	F6	50
Imperial Beach, Calif.	o15	50
Imperoyal, N.S.,Can.	E6	43
Imphāl, India	D9	20
Ina, Jap.	n16	18
Inca, Sp.	C7	8
Inchon, Kor.	H3	18
Indaw, Bur.	D10	20
Independence, Calif.	D4	50
Independence, Iowa	B6	60
Independence, Kans.	E8	61
Independence, La.	D5	63
Independence, Minn.	*F5	67
Independence, Mo.	B3, h11	69
Independence, Ohio	h9	78
Independence, Oreg.	C3, k11	80
Independence, Wis.	D2	88
Independence, co., Ark.	B4	49
Independence Hill, Ind.	*B3	59
India, country, Asia	D6	20
Indialantic, Fla.	*D6	54
Indian, ocean	G2	2
Indiana, Pa.	E3	81
Indiana, co., Pa.	E3	81
Indiana, state, U.S.		59
Indianapolis, Ind.	E5, k10	59
Indian Head, Sask., Can.	G4	39
Indian Head, Md.	C3	53
Indian Hill, Ohio	o13	78
Indian Lake, N.Y.	B6	75
Indian Mound Beach, Mass.	*C6	65
Indianola, Iowa	C4	60
Indianola, Miss.	B3	68
Indianola, Nebr.	D5	71
Indianola, Pa.	*E1	81
Indian, peak, Wyo.	B3	89
Indian River, co., Fla.	E6	54
Indian Rocks, Beach, Fla.	p10	54
Indiantown, Fla.	E6	54
Indio, Calif.	F5	50
Indochina, reg., Asia	B3	19
Indonesia, country, Asia	F6	19
Indore, India	D6	20
Indramayu, Indon.	G3	19
Indre, dept., Fr.	*D4	5
Indre-et-Loire, dept., Fr.	*D4	5
Indus, riv., Asia	C4	20
Industrial, S.C.	B6	82
Industry, Pa.	*E1	81
Ine, Jap.	n14	18
Infantes, Sp.	C4	8
Infiesto, Sp.	A3	8
Ingalls, Ind.	E6	59
Ingalls Park, Ill.	B5	58
Ingersoll, Ont., Can.	D4	41
Ingham, Austl.	C8	25
Ingham, co., Mich.	F6	66
Ingleside, Nebr.	D7	71
Ingleside, Tex.	F4	84
Inglewood, Calif.	n12	50
Inglewood, Nebr.	C9, g11	71
Ingolstadt, Ger., Fed. Rep. of	D5	6
Ingomar, Pa.	h13	81
Ingonish Beach, N.S., Can.	C9	43
Ingram, Pa.	k13	81
Inhambane, Moz.	E7	24
Inharrime, Moz.	E7	24
Inishbofin, isl., U.K.	D1	4
Inishtrahull, isl., U.K.	C3	4
Inishturk, isl., U.K.	D1	4
Inkerman, Pa.	*D9	81
Inkom, Idaho	G6	57
Inkster, Mich.	p15	66
Inman, Kans.	D6	61
Inman, S.C.	A3	82
Inman Mills, S.C.	*A3	82
Inner Mongolia, prov., China	C8	17
Innisfail, Alta., Can.	C4	38
Innisfail, Austl.	C8	25
Innsbruck, Aus.	E5	6
Ino, Jap.	J6	18
Inowroclaw, Pol.	B5	7
Insein, Bur.	E10	20
Institute, W. Va.	C3	87
Intercesion City, Fla.	D5	54
Intercity, Wash.	*B3	86
Interlaken, N.J.	*C4	74
International Falls, Minn.	B5	67
Intersection, mtn., B.C. Can.	C7	37
Invercargill, N.Z.	Q12	26
Inverell, Austl.	E9	25
Invermere, B.C. Can.	D9	37
Inverness, Calif.	C2	50
Inverness, N.S., Can.	C8	43
Inverness, Fla.	D4	54
Inverness, Ill.	*B6	58

Inverness, Miss. B3 68
Inverness, Scot. B4 4
Inverness, co., N.S. Can. C8 43
Inverness, co., Scot. *B4 4
Invisible, mtn.,Idaho F5 57
Inwood, Iowa A1 60
Inwood, N.Y. k13 75
Inyan Kara, mtn., Wyo. B8 89
Inyo,co., Calif. D5 50
Inyokern, Calif. E5 50
Ioánnina, Grc. *C3 14
Ioannina, prov.,Grc. *C3 14
Iola, Kans. E8 61
Iola, Wis. D4 88
Iona, Idaho F7 57
Ione, Calif. D3 50
Ionia, Mich. F5 66
Ionia, co., Mich. F5 66
Iosco, co., Mich. D7 66
Iota, La. D3 63
Iowa, La. D2 63
Iowa, co.,Iowa C5 60
Iowa, co., Wis. E3 88
Iowa, state, U.S. 60
Iowa City, Iowa C6 60
Iowa Falls, Iowa B4 60
Iowa Park, Tex. C3 84
Ipameri, Braz. B3 30
Ipava, Ill. C3 58
Ipiales, Col. C2 32
Ipin, China F5 17
Ipoh, Mala. E2 19
Ipswich, Austl. E9 25
Ipswich, Eng. D7 4
Ipswich, Mass. A6 55
Ipswich, S. Dak. E6 77
Iquique, Chile D2 29
Iquitos, Peru B3 31
Iraan, Tex. D2 84
Iraklion (Candia), Grc. E5 14
Iraklion, prov., Grc. *E5 14
Iran, (Persia), country, Asia F8 16
Irapuato, Mex. C4, m13 34
Iraq, country, Asia F5 16
Irbid, Jordan B3, g5 15
Irbil, Iraq D15 14
Iredell, co., N.C. B2 76
Ireland (Eire), country, Eur. D3 4
Ireton, Iowa B1 60
Iri, Kor. I3 18
Iringa, Tan. B7 24
Irion, co.,Tex. D2 84
Irkutsk, Sov. Un. D13 13
Iron, co., Mich. B2 66
Iron, co., Mo. D7 69
Iron, co., Utah C5 72
Iron, co., Wis. B3 88
Iron, mts., Va. f10 85

Irondale, Ala. f7 46
Irondale, Ohio B5 78
Irondequoit, N.Y. B3 75
Ironia, N.J. B3 74
Iron Mountain, Mich. C2 66
Iron River, Mich. B2 66
Iron River, Wis. B2 88
Ironton, Minn. D5 67
Ironton, Mo. D7 69
Ironton, Ohio D3 78
Ironwood, Mich. .... nII 66
Iroquois, N.B., Can. *B1 43
Iroquois, Ont., Can. C9 41
Iroquois, co., Ill. C6 58
Iroquois Falls, Ont., Can. *o19 41
Irosin, Phil. *C6 19
Irrawaddy, riv., Bur. D10 20
Irtysh, riv., Sov. Un. D10 13
Irún, Sp. A5 8
Irvine, Ky. C6 62
Irvine, Scot. C4 4
Irving, Tex. n10 84
Irvington, Ky. C3 62
Irvington, N.J. k8 74
Irvington, N.Y. g13 75
Irvona, Pa. E4 81
Irwin, Pa. F2 81
Irwin, S.C. *B6 82
Irwin, co., Ga. E3 55
Irwindale, Calif. *E4 50
Isabell, mtn., Wyo. D2 89
Isabela, P.R. *G11 35
Isabela, prov.,Phil. *D6 19
Isabella, Pa. G2 81
Isabella, Tenn. D9 83
Isabella, co., Mich. E6 66
Isahaya, Jap. J5 18
Isanti, Minn. E5 67
Isanti,co., Minn. E5 67
Ise (Uji-yamada), Jap. I8. o15 18
Iselin, N.J. B4 74
Iselin, Pa. E3 81
Isère, dept., Fr. *E6 5
Iserlohn, Ger., Fed. Rep. of *C3 6
Isernia, It. D5 9
Isesaki, Jap. H9. m18 18
Iseyin, Nig. G5 22
Ishikawa, pref., Jap. *H8 18
Ishim, Sov. Un. D9 13
Ishimbay, Sov. Un. *D8 13
Ishinomaki, Jap. G10 18
Ishioka, Jap. m19 18
Ishpeming, Mich. B3 66
Isigny-sur-Mer, Fr. C3 5
Isiro (Paulis), Zaire H3 23
Iskenderun (Alexandretta), Tur. D11 14
Iskilip, Tur. B10 14
Isla Cristina, Sp. D2 8

Islâmâbâd, Pak. B5 20
Islamorado,Fla. H6 54
Island, co., Wash. A3 86
Island Falls, Maine B4 64
Island Heights, N.J. D4 74
Island Lake, Ill. *E2 58
Island Park, N.Y. *E7 75
Island Pond, Vt. B4 73
Islav, isl., U.K. C3 4
Isle, Minn. D5 67
Isle-aux-Morts, Newf., Can. E2 44
Isle of Ely, co., Eng. *D7 4
Isle of Man, Br. dep: Eur. *C4 4
Isle of Man, isl., U.K. C4 4
Isle of Palms, S.C. k12 82
Isle of Wight, co., Eng. *E6 4
Isle of Wight, co., Va. D6 85
Isle of Wight, isl., U.K. E6 4
Isle Royale, isl., Mich. h9 66
Isleton, Calif. C3 50
Isle-Verte, Que., Can. A8 42
Islington, Mass. h11 65
Islip, N.Y. n15 75
Islip Terrace, N.Y. *n15 75
Isola Capo Rizzuto, It. E6 9
Isparta, Tur. D8 14
Israel, country, Asia C2 15
Issaquah, Wash. e11 86
Issaquena, co., Miss. C2 68
Issoire, Fr. E5 5
Issoudun, Fr. D4 5
Issyk-kul, lake, Sov. Un. E10 13
Issy les-Moulineaux, Fr. g10 5
Istanbul (Constantinople).
   Tur. B7 14
Istmina, Col. B2 32
Itá, Par. E4 29
Itabaiana, Braz. *E7 27
Itabaiana, Braz. *D7 27
Itaberaba, Braz. *E6 27
Itabira, Braz. B4 30
Itabuna, Braz. E7 27
Itajai, Braz. D3 30
Itajubá, Braz. C3 30
Italy, Tex. C4 84
Italy, country, Eur. 9
Itami, Jap. o14 18
Itaperuna, Braz. C4 30
Itapetininga, Braz. C3. m7 30
Itapeva, Braz. C3 30
Itápolis, Braz. k7 30
Itapúa, dept., Par. E4 29
Itaqui, Braz. D1 30
Itararé, Braz. C3 30
Itasca, Ill. k8 58
Itasca, Tex. C4 84
Itasca, co., Minn. C5 67
Itatiba, Braz. m8 30

Itauna, Braz. C4 30
Itawamba, co., Miss. A5 68
Ithaca, Mich. E6 66
Ithaca, N.Y. C4 75
Itō, Jap. o18 18
Itoigawa, Jap. H8 18
Itta Bena, Miss. B3 68
Itu, Braz. C3. m8 30
Ituango, Col. B2 32
Ituiutaba, Braz. B3 30
Ituna, Sask., Can. F4 39
Itzehoe, Ger.,Fed. Rep. of B4 6
Iuka, Miss. A4 68
Iva, S.C. C2 82
Ivanhoe, Calif. *D4 50
Ivanhoe, Minn. F2 67
Ivanhoe, Va. D2 85
Ivano-Frankovsk, Sov. Un. G5 12
Ivanovka, Sov. Un. q21 12
Ivanovo, Sov. Un. C13 12
Ivanteyevka, Sov. Un. n17 12
Ivory Coast, country, Afr. G3 22
Ivoryton, Conn. D7 52
Ivrea, It. B1 9
Ivry-sur-Seine, Fr. g10 5
Ivywild, Colo. C6 51
Iwaki (Tairi), Jap. H10 18
Iwaki-yama, mtn., Jap. F10 18
Iwakuni, Jap. I6 18
Iwamizawa, Jap. E10 18
Iwanai, Jap. E10 18
Iwate, pref., Jap. *G10 18
Iwate-yama, mtn., Jap. G10 18
Iwo, Nig. G5 22
Ixmiquilpan, Mex. m14 34
Ixtacalco, Mex. h9 34
Ixtacihuatl, mtn., Mex. n14 34
Ixtapalapa, Mex. h9 34
Ixtlán de Juárez, Mex. o15 34
Ixtlán del Rio, Mex. C4. m11 34
Izamal, Mex. C7 34
Izard, co., Ark. A4 49
Izhevsk, see Ustinov, Sov. Un.
Izmail, Sov. Un. I7 12
Izmir (Smyrna), Tur. C6 14
Izmit (Kocaeli), Tur. B7 14
Izúcar de Matamoros, Mex. n14 34
Izuhara, Jap. I4 18
Izumo, Jap. I6 18
Izyum, Sov. Un. G11 12

J

Jabalpur (Jubbulpore), India D6 20
Jaboatão, Braz. *D7 27
Jaboticabal, Braz. C3, k7 30
Jaca, Sp. A5 8
Jacala de Ledesma, Mex. m14 34
Jacarei, Braz. m9 30
Jacarèzinho, Braz. C3 30
Jáchymov, Czech. C2 7
Jacinto City, Tex. r14 84
Jack, co., Tex. C3 84
Jack, mtn., Mont. D4 70
Jack, mtn., Va. B3 85
Jackfork, mtn., Okla. C6 79
Jacks, mtn., Pa. E6 81
Jacksboro, Tex. C3 84
Jackson, Ala. D2 46
Jackson, Calif. C3 50
Jackson, Ga. C3 55
Jackson, Ky. C6 62
Jackson, La. D4 63
Jackson, Mich. F6 66
Jackson, Minn. G3 67
Jackson, Miss. C3 68
Jackson, Mo. D8 69
Jackson, N.C. A5 76
Jackson, Ohio C3 78
Jackson, S.C. E4 82
Jackson, Tenn. B3 83
Jackson, Wyo. C2 89
Jackson, co., Ala. A3 46
Jackson, co., Ark. B4 49

Jackson, co., Colo. A4 51
Jackson, co., Fla. B1 54
Jackson, co., Ga. B3 55
Jackson, co., Ill. F4 58
Jackson, co., Ind. G5 59
Jackson, co., Iowa B7 60
Jackson, co., Kans. C8 61
Jackson, co., Ky. C5 62
Jackson, co., Mich. F6 66
Jackson, co., Minn. G3 67
Jackson, co., Miss. E5 68
Jackson, co., Mo. C3 69
Jackson, co., N.C. f9 76
Jackson, co., Ohio C3 78
Jackson, co., Okla. C2 79
Jackson, co., Oreg. E3 80
Jackson, co., S. Dak. G4 77
Jackson, co., Tenn. C8 83
Jackson, co., Tex. E4 84
Jackson, co., W. Va. C3 87
Jackson, co., Wis. D3 88
Jackson, par., La. B3 63
Jackson, mtn., Maine D2 64
Jackson Center, Ohio B1 78
Jacksonville, Ala. B4 46
Jacksonville, Ark. C3, h10 49
Jacksonville, Fla. B5, m8 54
Jacksonville, Ill. D3 58
Jacksonville, N.C. C5 76
Jacksonville, Oreg. E4 80
Jacksonville, Tex. D5 84

Jacksonville Beach, Fla. B5, m9 54
Jacmel, Hai. E7 35
Jacobâbâd, Pak. C4 20
Jacobina, Braz. *E6 27
Jacomino, Cuba *C2 35
Jacques Cartier, mtn.,
   Que., Can. k13 42
Jaén, Sp. D4 8
Jaén, prov., Sp. *D4 8
Jaffna, Sri Lanka G7 20
Jaffrey, N.H. F3 73
Jaguarão, Braz. E2 30
Jaguey Grande, Cuba C3 35
Jaipur, India C6 20
Jaisalmer, India C5 20
Jajce, Yugo. C3 10
Jájpur, India D8 20
Jakarta (Djakarta), Indon. G3 19
Jakobstad (Pietersaari), Fin. F10 11
Jal, N. Mex. C7 48
Jalalabad, Afg. B5 20
Jalapa, Guat. *F6 34
Jalapa Enriquez, Mex. D5, n15 34
Jalca Grande, Peru C2 31
Jálgaon, India D6 20
Jalisco,state, Mex. C4, m12 34
Jálna, India E6 20
Jalpa, Mex. C4, m12 34
Jalpan, Mex. C5, m14 34
Jamaica, country, N.A. E5 35
Jambi, Indon. *F2 19

James, riv., S. Dak. F7 77
Jamesburg, N.J. C4 74
James City, N.C. B5 76
James City, co., Va. C6 85
Jamesport, Mo. B4 69
Jamestown, Calif. D3 50
Jamestown, Ind. E4 59
Jamestown, Ky. D4 62
Jamestown, N.Y. C1 75
Jamestown, N.C. B3 76
Jamestown, N. Dak. D7 77
Jamestown, Ohio C2 78
Jamestown, Pa. D1 81
Jamestown, R.I. D11 52
Jamestown, Tenn. C9 83
Jamesville, N.Y. *C4 75
Jamiltepec, Mex. D5 34
Jammu, India B5 20
Jammu and Kashmir, Disputed reg.,
   India, Pak. B6 20
Jāmnagar, India D5 20
Jamshedpur, India D8 20
Jämtland, co., Swe. *F6 11
Janesland, Iowa B5 60
Janesville, Minn. F5 67
Janesville, Wis. F4 88
Janin, Jordan B3 15
Janos, Mex. A3 34
Jánoshalma, Hung. B4 10
Janów, Lubelski, Pol. C7 7
Januária, Braz. B4 30

Jaoho (Tuanshantzu), China B11 17
Japan, country, Asia I6 18
Japan, sea, Asia F6 18
Jaral del Progreso, Mex. m13 34
Jarales, N. Mex. B5 48
Jarocin, Pol. C4 7
Jaroslaw, Pol. C7 7
Jarvis, Ont., Can. E4 41
Jarvisburg, N.C. A7 76
Jasonville, Ind. F3 59
Jasper, Ala. B2 46
Jasper, Alta., Can. C1 38
Jasper, Fla. B4 54
Jasper, Ga. B2 55
Jasper, Ind. H4 59
Jasper, Minn. G2 67
Jasper, Mo. D3 69
Jasper, Tenn. D8 83
Jasper, Tex. D6 84
Jasper, co., Ga. C3 55
Jasper, co., Ill. D5 58
Jasper, co., Ind. B3 59
Jasper, co., Iowa C4 60
Jasper, co., Miss. C4 68
Jasper, co., Mo. D3 69
Jasper, co., S.C. G5 82
Jasper, co., Tex. D5 84
Jászapáti, Hung. B5 10
Jászbereny, Hung. B4 10
Jatibonico,Cuba D4 35
Játiva, Sp. C5 8
Jaú, Braz. C3, m7 30
Jauja, Peru D2 31
Jaumave, Mex. C5 34
Jaunpur, India C7 20
Java, isl., Indon. G3 19
Javellanos, Cuba *C3 35
Jawor, Pol. C4 7
Jaworzno, Pol. g10 7
Jay, Fla. u14 54
Jay, N.Y. f11 75
Jay, Okla. A7 79
Jay, co., Ind. D7 59
Jayanca, Peru C2 31
Jayapura (Sukarnapura), Indon. F10 19
Jeanerette, La. E4 63
Jeannette, Pa. F2 81
Jeberos, Peru C2 31
Jedburgh, Scot. C5 4
Jedrzejów, Pol. C6 7
Jeff, Ky. C6 62
Jeff Davis, co., Ga. E4 55
Jeff Davis, co., Tex. o12 84
Jefferson, Ga. B3 55
Jefferson, Iowa B3 60
Jefferson, La. k11 63
Jefferson, Mass. B4 65
Jefferson, N.C. A1 76
Jefferson, Ohio A5 78
Jefferson, Oreg. C3, k11 80
Jefferson, Pa. *E1 81
Jefferson, Tex. C5 84
Jefferson, Wis. E5 88
Jefferson, co., Ala. B3 46
Jefferson, co., Ark. C3 49
Jefferson, co., Colo. B5 51
Jefferson, co., Fla. B3 54
Jefferson, co., Ga. C4 55
Jefferson, co., Idaho F6 57
Jefferson, co., Ill. E5 58
Jefferson, co., Ind. G7 59
Jefferson, co., Iowa C6 60
Jefferson, co., Kans. C8 61
Jefferson, co., Ky. B4 62
Jefferson, co., Miss. D2 68
Jefferson, co., Mo. C7 69
Jefferson, co., Mont. D4 70
Jefferson, co., Nebr. D8 71
Jefferson, co., N.Y. A5 75
Jefferson, co., Ohio B5 78
Jefferson, co., Okla. C4 79
Jefferson, co., Oreg. C5 80
Jefferson, co., Pa. D3 81
Jefferson, co., Tenn. C10 83
Jefferson, co., Tex. E5 84
Jefferson, co., Wash. B2 86
Jefferson, co., W. Va. B7 87
Jefferson, co., Wis. E5 88
Jefferson, par., La. E5 63

Jefferson City, Mo. C5 69
Jefferson City, Tenn. C10 83
Jefferson Davis, co., Miss. D4 68
Jefferson Davis, par., La. D3 63
Jeffersontown, Ky. B4, g11 62
Jefferson Village, Va. *B5 85
Jeffersonville, Ga. D3 55
Jeffersonville, Ind. H6 59
Jeffersonville, Ky. C6 62
Jeffrey City, Wyo. *D4 89
Jehossee, isl., S.C. k11 81
Jekabpils, Sov. Un. C5 12
Jelenia Góra, Pol. C3 7
Jelgava, Sov. Un. C4 12
Jellico, Tenn. C9 83
Jelm, mtn., Wyo. E7 89
Jember, Indon. G4 19
Jemison, Ala. C3 46
Jena, Ger. Dem. Rep. C5 6
Jena, La. C3 63
Jenison, Mich. *F4 66
Jenkins, Ky. C7 62
Jenkins, co., Ga. D4 55
Jenkinsville, S.C. C5 82
Jenkintown, Pa. F11, o21 81
Jenks, Okla. A6 79
Jenners, Pa. F3 81
Jennings, Fla. B3 54
Jennings, La. D3 63
Jennings, Mo. f13 69
Jennings, co., Ind. G6 59
Jennings Lodge, Oreg. *B4 80
Jensen Beach, Florida E6 54
Jenny Jump, mtn., N.J. B3 74
Jequié, Braz. *E6 27
Jerauld, co., S. Dak. F7 77
Jérémie, Hai E6 35
Jerez de García Salinas, Mex. C4 34
Jerez, de la Frontera, Sp. D2 8
Jericho, N.Y. *E7 75
Jericho, Va. *D6 85
Jermyn, Pa. C10 81
Jerome, Idaho G4 57
Jerome, Ill. *D4 58
Jerome, Pa. F4 81
Jerome, co., Idaho G4 57
Jersey, Br. dep., Eur. F5 4
Jersey, co., Ill. D3 58
Jersey City, N.J. B4, k8 74
Jersey Shore, Pa. D7 81
Jerseyside, Newf., Can. *E5 44
Jerseyville, Ill. D3 58
Jerusalem (Yerushalayim), Isr. .. C3, h5 15
Jerusalem, Jordan C3, h5 15
Jesenik, Czech. C4 7
Jessamine, co., Ky. C5 62
Jessup, Md. B4 53
Jessup, Pa. m18 81
Jesup, Ga. E5 55
Jesup, Iowa B5 60
Jesús Carranza, Mex. D6 34
Jesús María, Arg. A4 28
Jetmore, Kans. D4 61
Jever, Ger., Fed. Rep. of B3 6
Jewell, Iowa B4 60
Jewell, Kans. C5 61
Jewell, co., Kan. C5 61
Jewett, Ohio B4 78
Jewett City, Conn. C9 52
Jeypore, India E7 20
Jhang Maghiana, Pak. *B5 20
Jhālrapātan, India D6 20
Jhānsi, India C6 20
Jhelum, Pak. B5 20
Jiamusi, China C5 18
Ji'an, China F3 18
Jiangling, China E7 17
Jiangmen, China G7 17
Jiangsu, prov., China E9 17
Jiangxi, prov., China F9 17
Jiaoxian, China D9 17
Jiaozuo, China D7 17
Jiaxing, China E9 17
Jicin, Czech. C3 7
Jiddah, Sau. Ar. E2 15
Jieyang, China G8 17
Jihlava, Czech. D3 7
Jilin, China C10 17
Jilin, prov., China C9 17

Jima, Eth. G5 23
Jimbolia, Rom. C5 10
Jimena, Sp. D3 8
Jim Hogg, co., Tex. F3 84
Jim Thorpe, Pa. E10 81
Jim Wells, co., Tex. F3 84
Jinan, China D8 17
Jindřichuv Hradec, Czech. D3 7
Jingdezhen, China F8 17
Jining, China D8 17
Jining, China C7 17
Jinja, Ug. H4 23
Jinotepe, Nic. E7 34
Jinxian, China D9 17
Jinzhou, China C9 17
Jipijapa, Ec. B1 31
Jiquilpan de Juárez, Mex. n12 34
Jiujiang, China F8 17
Jixi, China B11 17
Joanna, S.C. C4 82
João Pessoa, Braz. D7 27
Jocobus, Pa. *G8 81
Jocotepec, Mex. m12 34
Jo Daviess, co., Ill. A3 58
Jodhpur, India C5 20
Joe Batt's, Arm, Newf., Can. D4 44
Joensuu, Fin. F13 11
Joeuf, Fr. C6 5
Joffre, mtn., Alta., Can. D3 38
Joffre, mtn., B.C.,Can. D10 37
Joggins, N.S., Can. D5 43
Jogjakarta, see
  Yogyakarta, Indon.
Johannesburg, S. Afr. F5 24
John Day, Oreg. C8 80
Johns Island, S.C. F7, k11 82
Johnson, Kans. E2 61
Johnson, Vt. B2 73
Johnson, co., Ark. B2 49
Johnson, co., Ga. D4 55
Johnson, co., Ill. F5 58
Johnson, co., Ind. F5 59
Johnson, co., Iowa C6 60
Johnson, co., Kans. D9 61
Johnson, co., Ky. C7 62
Johnson, co., Mo. C4 69
Johnson, co., Nebr. D9 71
Johnson, co., Tenn. C12 83
Johnson, co., Tex. C4 84
Johnson, co., Wyo. B6 89
Johnsonburg, Pa. D4 81
Johnson City, N.Y. C5 75
Johnson City, Tenn. C11 83
Johnson City, Tex. D3 84
Johnson Creek, Wis. E5 88
Johnsonville, S.C. D9 82
Johnston, Iowa E8 60
Johnston, R.I. B10 52
Johnston, S.C. D4 82
Johnston, co., N.C. B4 76
Johnston, co., Okla. C5 79
Johnston City, Ill. F5 58
Johnstown, Colo. A6 51
Johnstown, N.Y. B6 75
Johnstown, Ohio B3 78
Johnstown, Pa. F4 81
Johor, state, Mala. *E2 19
Johor Baharu, Mala. E2 19
Joigny, Fr. D5 5
Joinville, Braz. D3 30
Jojutla, Mex. n14 34
Joliet, Ill. B5, k8 58
Joliette, Que., Can. C4 42
Joliette, co., Que.,Can. C3 42
Jolo, Phil. D6 19
Jonava, Sov. Un. A8 7
Jones, Okla. B4 79
Jones, co., Ga. C3 55
Jones, co., Iowa B6 60
Jones, co., Miss. D4 68
Jones, co., N.C. B5 76
Jones, co., S. Dak. G5 77
Jones, co., Tex. C3 84
Jonesboro, Ark. B5 49
Jonesboro, Ga. C2 55
Jonesboro, Ill. F4 58
Jonesboro, Ind. D6 59
Jonesboro, La. B3 63

Jonesboro, Tenn. C11 83
Jones Mill, Ark. C3, g8 49
Jonesport, Maine D5 64
Jonesville, La. C4 63
Jonesville, Mich. G6 66
Jonesville, N.C. A2 76
Jonesville, S.C. B4 82
Jonesville, Va. f8 85
Jönköping, Swe. I6 11
Jönköping, co., Swe. *I5 11
Jonquière, Que., Can. A6 42
Jonuta, Mex. D6 34
Joplin, Mo. D3 69
Joppa, Ill. F5 58
Jordan, Minn. F5 67
Jordan, N.Y. B4 75
Jordan, country, Asia C3 15
Jorhāt, India C9 20
Jos, Nig. G6 22
José Battle y Ordóñez, Ur. E1 30
Joseph, Oreg. B9 80
Josephine, Oreg. E3 80
Joshua Tree, Calif. E5 50
Jourdanton, Tex. E3 84
Jovellanos, Cuba C3 35
Juab, co., Utah B5 72
Juana Díaz, P.R. *G11 35
Juan Aldama, Mex. C4 34
Juanita, Wash. *B3 86
Juanjui, Peru C2 31
Juárez, Arg. B5 28
Juarez, Mex. B4 34
Juàzeiro, Braz. D6 27
Juazeiro do Norte, Braz. *D7 27
Jūbā, Sud. H4 23
Júcaro, Cuba D4 35
Juchipila, Mex. m12 34
Juchitán de Zaragoza, Mex. D6 34
Jude, isl.,Newf., Can. E4 44
Judenburg, Aus. E7 6
Judith Basin, co., Mont. C6 70
Judith, mtn., Mont. C7 70
Judith, peak, Mont. C7 70
Judson, S.C. *B3 82
Judsonia, Ark. B4 49
Juiz de Fora, Braz. C4, g6 30
Jujuy, Arg. D2 29
Jujuy, prov., Arg. D2 29
Julesburg, Colo. A8 51
Juliaca, Peru E3 31
Julian, Calif. F5 50
Julianehab, Grnld. C16 33
Jullundur, India B6 20
Julimes, Mex. B3 34
Jumet, Bel. B6 5
Jumilla, Sp. C5 8
Junāgadh, India D5 20
Juncos, P.R. *G12 35
Junction, Tex. D3 84
Junction City, Ark. D3 49
Junction City, Kans. C7 61
Junction City, Ky. C5 62
Junction City, Ohio C3 78
Junction City, Oreg. C3 80
Jundiaí, Braz. C3, m8 30
Juneau, Alsk. D13, k22 47
Juneau, Wis. E5 88
Juneau, co., Wis. E3 88
Junee, Austl. F8 25
Jungfrau, mtn., Switz. E3 6
Juniata, co., Pa. F6 81
Juniata Terrace, Pa. E6 81
Junín, Arg. A4 28
Junín, Peru D2 31
Junin, dept., Peru D2 31
Juniper, N.B., Can. C2 43
Junipero Serra, peak, Calif. D3 50
Jupiter, Fla. F6 54
Jura, dept., Fr. *D6 5
Jura, isl., Scot. C4 4
Jurbarkas, Sov. Un. A7 7
Juruá, riv. C4 31
Justice, Ill. *B6 58
Jüterbog, Ger. Dem. Rep. C6 6
Jutiapa, Guat. E7 34
Juwain, Afg. B3 20
Jyvaskylä, Fin. F11 11

K

Kaala, peak, Haw. f9 56
Kaalaea, Haw. g10 56
Kabaena, isl., Mala. G6 19
Kabong, Mala. E4 19
Kabul, Afg. B4 20
Kachuga, Sov. Un. D13 13
Kadinhani, Tur. C9 14
Kadiri, India F6 20
Kadiyevka, Sov. Un. G12, o21 12
Kaduna, Nig. F6 22
Kaédi, Maur. E2 22
Kaeryong, Kor. H4 18
Kaesong, Kor. G3 18
Kāf, Sau. Ar. C2 15
Kafr az Zayyat, Eg. D2 14
Kagawa, pref., Jap. *I7 18
Kağizman, Tur. B14 14
Kagoshima, Jap. K5 18
Kagoshima, pref., Jap. *K5 18
Kagul, Sov. Un. C9 10
Kahoolawe, isl., Haw. C5 56
Kahuka, Haw. B4, f10 56
Kahului, Haw. C5 56
Kaifeng, China E7 17
Kailua, Haw. g11 56
Kaimana, Indon. F8 19
Kainan, Jap. I7 18
Kairouan, Tun. A6 22
Kaiserslautern, Ger., Fed. Rep.
  of D3 6
Kaiyuan, China E2 18
Kaizuka, Jap. o14 18
Kajaani, Fin. E12 11
Kajikazawa, Jap. n17 18
Kakegawa, Jap. o17 18
Kākināda, India E7 20
Kakogawa, Jap. *I7 18
Kālābagh, Pak. B5 20
Kalach, Sov. Un. F13 12
Kalaheo, Haw. B2 56
Kalama, Wash. C3 86
Kalamai (Kalamata), Grc. D4 14
Kalamazoo, Mich. F5 66
Kalamazoo, co., Mich. F5 66
Kalaotoa, isl., Indon. G6 19
Kalapana, Haw. D7 56
Kalemie, Zaire B5 24
Kalgoorlie, Austl. F3 25
Kálimnos, Grc. *D6 14
Kalinin, Sov. Un. C10 12
Kaliningrad, Sov. Un. n17 12
Kalingrad (Königsbert), Sov. Un. . . . D3 12
Kalinkovichi, Sov. Un. E7 12
Kalispell, Mont. B2 70
Kalisz, Pol. C5 7
Kalkaska, Mich. D5 66
Kalkaska, co., Mich. D5 66
Kallithéa, Grc. *D4 14
Kalmar, Swe. I7 11
Kalmar, co., Swe. *I7 11
Kalocsa, Hung. B4 10
Kalona, Iowa C6 60
Kalone, peak, B.C., Can. C4 37
Kaluga, Sov. Un. D11 12
Kalush, Sov. Un. G5 12
Kama, riv., Sov. Un. D8 13
Kamaishi, Jap. G10 18
Kamakura, Jap. n18 18
Kamarhati, India *D8 20
Kamenets-Podolskiy, Sov. Un. G6 12
Kamen-na-Obi, Sov. Un. D11 13
Kamensk-Shakhtinskiy, Sov. Un. . . . G13 12
Kamensk-Uralskiy, Sov. Un. D9 13
Kamenz, Ger. Dem. Rep. C7 6
Kameoka, Jap. o14 18
Kamiah, Idaho C2 57
Kamioka, Jap. m16 18
Kamloops, B.C., Can. D7, n18 37
Kammuri-Yama, mtn., Jap. I6 18
Kamouraska, co., Que., Can. B8 42
Kampala, Ug. H4 23
Kampen, Neth. A6 5
Kampot, Kam. C2 19
Kampuchea, country, Asia C2 19
Kamsack, Sask., Can. F5 39
Kamuela, Haw. C6 56
Kamyshin, Sov. Un. F15 12
Kanab, Utah C5 72
Kanabec, co., Minn. E5 67
Kanagawa, pref., Jap. *I9 18
Kananga (Luluabourg), Zaire B4 24
Kanash, Sov. Un. D16 12
Kanawha, Iowa B4 60
Kanawha, co., W. Va. C3 87
Kanayama, Jap. n16 18
Kanazawa, Jap. H8 18
Kanchanaburi, Thai. C1 19

Kānchenjunga, peak, Nep.,
  India C8 20
Kānchipuram, India F7 20
Kandahar, Afg. B4 20
Kandalaksha, Sov. Un. C6 13
Kandangan, Indon. F5 19
Kandira, Tur. B8 14
Kandiyohi, co., Minn. E3 67
Kandy, Sri Lanka G7 20
Kane, Pa. C4 81
Kane, co., Ill. B5 58
Kane, co., Utah C5 72
Kaneohe, Haw. B4, g10 56
Kangding, China E5 17
Kanggye, Kor. F3 18
Kangnung, Kor. H4 18
Kanjiža, Yugo. B5 10
Kankakee, Ill. B6 58
Kankakee, co., Ill. B6 58
Kankan, Guinea F3 22
Kānker, India D7 20
Kannapolis, N.C. B2 76
Kano, Nig. F6 22
Kanopolis, Kans. D5 61
Kanoya, Jap. K5 18
Kansas, Ill. D6 58
Kansas, state, U.S. 61
Kansas, riv., Kans. C7 61
Kansas City, Kans. C9, k16 61
Kansas City, Mo. B3, h10 69
Kansk, Sov. Un. D12 13
Kansong, Kor. G4 18
Kantunilkin, Mex. C7 34
Kanye, Bots. E5 24
Kaohsiung, Taiwan G9 17
Kaolack, Sen. F1 22
Kapaa, Haw. A2 56
Kapanga, Zaire B4 24
Kapfenberg, Aus. E7 6
Kapit, Mala. E4 19
Kaplan, La. D3 63
Kaposvár, Hung. B3 10
Kapuskasing, Ont., Can. o19 41
Kapuvár, Hung. B3 10
Karachev, Sov. Un. E10 12
Karāchi, Pak. D4 20
Karaga, Sov. Un. D19 13
Karaganda, Sov. Un. E10 13
Karaköse, Tur. C14 14
Karaman, Tur. D9 14
Karamay, China B1 17
Karapinar, Tur. D9 14
Karatsu, Jap. J4 18
Karbalā, Iraq C3 15
Karcag, Hung. B5 10
Kardhitsa, Grc. C3 14
Karelia (Kerelo-Finnish S.S.R.),
  former rep., Sov. Un. *C6 16
Kargil, India B6 20
Kargopol, Sov. Un. A12 12
Kariba, Zimb. D5 24
Kārikal, India F6 20
Karkaralinsk, Sov. Un. E10 13
Karl-Marx-Stadt (Chemnitz),
  Ger. Dem. Rep. C6 6
Karlovac, Yugo. C2 10
Karlóvasi, Grc. D6 14
Karlovy Vary, Czech. C2 7
Karlshamn, Swe. I6 11
Karlskoga, Swe. H6 11
Karlskrona, Swe. I6 11
Karlsruhe, Ger., Fed. Rep. of D4 6
Karlstad, Minn. B2 67
Karlstad, Swe. H5 11
Karmutzen, mtn., B.C., Can. D4 37
Karnak, Ill. F5 58
Karnataka, state, India F6 20
Karnes, co., Tex. E4 84
Karnes City, Tex. E4 84
Kars, Tur. B14 14
Karsakpay, Sov. Un. E9 13
Karshi, Sov. Un. F9 13
Kartal, Tur. *B7 14
Kartaly, Sov. Un. D9 13
Kartuzy, Pol. A5 7
Karviná, Czech. D5 7
Kārwār, India F5 20
Kāsaragod, India F6 20
Kasba Tadla, Mor. B3 22
Kāshān, Iran B8 23
Kashi, China F10 16
Kashima, Jap. n19 18
Kashira, Sov. Un. D12 12
Kashiwa, Jap. *n18 18
Kashiwazaki, Jap. H9 18
Kasimov, Sov. Un. D13 12

Kaslo, B.C., Can. E9 37
Kasota, Minn. F5 67
Kassalā, Sud. E5 23
Kassel, Ger., Fed. Rep. of C4 6
Kasson, Minn. F6 67
Kastamonu, Tur. B9 14
Kastoria, Grc. B3 14
Kasugai, Jap. *n15 18
Kasukabe, Jap. n18 18
Kasumi, Jap. I7 18
Kasur, Pak. B5 20
Katahdin, mtn., Maine C4 64
Katanga, prov., Zaire C5 24
Katanning, Austl. F2 25
Katata, Jap. (part of Otsu) n14 18
Kateríni, Grc. B4 14
Katherine, Austl. B5 25
Kathleen, Fla. D4 54
Kathmandu, Nep. *C8 20
Kathwood, S.C. *D4 82
Katiola, I.C. G4 22
Katonah, N.Y. A5 75
Katoomba-Wentworth Falls, Austl. . . . F8 26
Katowice (Stalinogród), Pol. C5, g10 7
Kātrīnā, mtn., Eg. C4 23
Katrineholm, Swe. H7, u34 11
Katsina, Nig. F6 22
Katsuyama, Jap. m15 18
Katy, Tex. r14 84
Kauai, isl., Haw. A2 56
Kauai, co., Haw. B2 56
Kaufbeuren, Ger., Fed. Rep. of E5 6
Kaufman, Tex. C4 84
Kaufman, co., Tex. C4 84
Kaukauna, Wis. D5, h9 88
Kaukakai, Haw. B2 56
Kaunakakai, Haw. B4 56
Kaunas, Sov. Un. D4 12
Kavaje, Alb. *B2 14
Kaválla, Grc. B5 14
Kaválla, prov., Grc. *B5 14
Kavarna, Bul. D9 10
Kawagoe, Jap. n18 18
Kawaguchi, Jap. n18 18
Kawaikini, peak, Haw. A2 56
Kawasaki, Jap. I9, n18 18
Kawkareik, Bur. *B1 19
Kawkawlin, Mich. E7 66
Kawn Umbū, Eg. D4 23
Kay, co., Okla. A4 79
Kayes, Mali F2 22
Kayford, W. Va. C3, m13 87
Kayseri, Tur. C10 14
Kaysville, Utah A6, C2 72
Kazachye, Sov. Un. B16 13
Kazakh S.S.R., rep., Sov. Un. *E9 16
Kazan, Sov. Un D7 13
Kazanluk, Bul. D7 10
Keaau, Haw. D6 56
Keansburg, N.J. C4 74
Kearney, Nebr. D6 71
Kearney, Mo. B3, h11 69
Kearney, co., Nebr. D7 71
Kearns, Utah *A5 72
Kearny, N.J. h8 74
Kearny, co., Kans. D2 61
Kearsarge, Mich. A2 66
Keasbey, N.J. *B4 74
Kebnekaise, mtn., Swe. D8 11
Kecskemét, Hung. B4 10
Kedah, state, Mala. *D2 19
Kedainiai, Sov. Un. A7 7
Kedgwick, N.B., Can. B2 43
Kediri, Indon. *G4 19
Kedong, China C3 18
Keegan, Maine A5 64
Keego Harbor, Mich. o15 66
Keeling, Tex. F3 73
Keene, N.H. n9 84
Keene, Tex. f11 75
Keeseville, N.Y. E4 40
Keewatin, Ont., Can. C4 67
Keewatin, Minn. D15 36
Keewatin, dist., N.W. Ter., Can. *C3 14
Kefallinia, prov., Grc. B3 15
Kefar Ata, Isr. B2 15
Kefar Sava, Isr. D6 4
Keighley, Eng. B5 4
Keith, Scot. C4 71
Keith, co., Nebr. B3 58
Keithsburg, Ill. *C4 80
Keizer, Oreg. B2 56
Kekaha, Haw. K4 19
Kelang, Mala. D2 19
Kelantan, state, Mala. n9 84
Keller, Tex. B2 46
Kellerman, Ala. B2 57
Kellogg, Idaho . . . .

Kellogg, Iowa C5 60
Kelly Brook, mtn., Maine A3 64
Kelly Lake, Minn. C5 67
Kelowna, B.C., Can. E8 37
Kelseyville, Calif. C2 50
Kelso, Mo. D8 69
Kelso, Scot. C5 4
Kelso, Wash. C3 86
Keltys, Tex. *D5 84
Keluang, Mala. E2 19
Kelvington, Sask., Can. E4 39
Kem, Sov. Un. E16 11
Kemah, Tex. *E5 84
Kemerovo, Sov. Un. D11 13
Kemi, Fin. E11 11
Kemmerer, Wyo. E2 89
Kemp, Tex. C4 84
Kemper, co., Miss. C5 68
Kempsey, Austl. F9 25
Kempshall, mtn., N.Y. A6 75
Kempten, Ger., Fed. Rep. of E5 6
Kemptville, Ont., Can. B9 41
Kenansville, N.C. C4 76
Kenbridge, Va. D4 85
Kendal, Eng. C5 4
Kendall, Fla. s13 54
Kendall, co., Ill. B5 58
Kendall, co., Tex. E3 84
Kendall Park, N.J. C3 74
Kendallville, Ind. B7 59
Kendari, Indon. F6 19
Kendrāpāra, India D8 20
Kendrick, Fla. C4 54
Kenedy, Tex. E4 84
Kenedy, co., Tex. F4 84
Kenhorst, Pa. *F9 81
Kenilworth, Ill. H9 58
Kenilworth, N.J. *B4 74
Kenitra, Mor. B3 22
Kenly, N.C. B4 76
Kenmare, N. Dak. B3 77
Kenmawr, Pa. *E1 81
Kenmore, N.Y. C2 75
Kenmore, Wash. *B3 86
Kennaday, peak, Wyo. E6 89
Kennebec, co., Maine D3 64
Kennebunk, Maine E2 64
Kennebunkport, Maine E2 64
Kennedale, Tex. n9 84
Kennedy, N.Y. C1 75
Kennesaw, Ga. B2, g7 55
Kenneth City, Fla. *E4 54
Kennett, Mo. E7 69
Kennett Square, Pa. G10 81
Kennewick, Wash. C6 86
Kennydale, Wash. e11 86
Kénogami, Que., Can. A6 42
Kenora, Ont., Can. o16 41
Kenora, dist., Ont., Can. o16 41
Kenosha, Wis. F6, n12 88
Kenosha, co., Wis. F5 88
Kenova, W. Va. C2 87
Kensington, Calif. *D3 50
Kensington, Conn. C5 52
Kensington, Kans. C4 61
Kensington, Md. B3 53
Kensington, N.Y. *G2 52
Kensington Estates, Md. *B3 53
Kensington Park, Fla. *E4 54
Kent, Conn. C2 52
Kent, Ohio A4 78
Kent, Wash. B3, f11 86
Kent, co., N.B., Can. C4 43
Kent, co., Ont., Can. E2 41
Kent, co., Del. B6 53
Kent, co., Eng. *E7 4
Kent, co., Md. B5 53
Kent, co., Mich. E5 66
Kent, co., R.I. C10 52
Kent, co., Tex. C2 84
Kent City, Mich. E5 66
Kentfield, Calif. *C2 50
Kentland, Ind. C3 59
Kentland, Md. *C4 53
Kenton, Ohio B2 78
Kenton, Tenn. A2 83
Kenton, co., Ky. B5 62
Kentucky, state, U.S. 62
Kent Village, Md. *C4 53
Kentville, N.S., Can. D5 43
Kentwood, La. D5 63
Kentwood, Mich. F5 66
Kenvil, N.J. B3 74
Kenvir, Ky. D6 62
Kenwood, Ohio *C1 78
Kenya, country, Afr. H5 23

Kenyon, Minn. F6 67
Keokuk, Iowa D6 60
Keokuk, co., Iowa C5 60
Keosauqua, Iowa D6 60
Keota, Iowa C6 60
Keota, Okla. B7 79
Kepno, Pol. C5 7
Kerala, state, India F6 20
Kerang, Austl. G7 25
Kerby, Oreg. E3 80
Kerch, Sov. Un. I11 12
Keremeos, B.C., Can. E8 37
Kerens, Tex. C4 84
Kerhonkson, N.Y. D6 75
Kerinci, mtn., Indon. F2 19
Kerkhoven, Minn. E3 67
Kérkira, Grc. C2 14
Kérkira, prov., Grc. *C2 14
Kerkrade, Neth. B7 5
Kerman, Calif. *D4 50
Kermān, Iran C6 15
Kermānshāh, see Bakhtarān, Iran
Kermit, Tex. D1 84
Kermit, W. Va. D2 87
Kermode, mtn., B.C., Can. C2 37
Kern, co., Calif. E4 50
Kernersville, N.C. A2 76
Kernville, Calif. E4 50
Kerr, co., Tex. D3 84
Kerrobert, Sask., Can. F1 39
Kerrville, Tex. D3 84
Kerry, co., Ire. *D2 4
Kershaw, S.C. B6 82
Kershaw, co., S.C. C6 82
Keşan, Tur. B6 14
Kesennuma, Jap. G10 18
Keshan, China B10 17
Keski-Suomi, prov., Fin. *K5 11
Keswick, Ont., Can. C5 41
Keszthely, Hung. B3 10
Keta, Ghana G5 22
Ketapang, Indon. F3 19
Ketchikan, Alsk. D13, n24 47
Ketchum, Idaho F4 57
Ketona, Ala. f7 46
Ketrzyn Mazowiecki, Pol. A6 7
Kettering, Eng. D6 4
Kettering, Ohio C1 78
Kettle Falls, Wash. A7 86
Kety, Pol. D5, h10 7
Kewanee, Ill. B4 58
Kewaskum, Wis. E5 88
Kewaunee, Wis. D6 88
Kewanna, Ind. B5 59
Kewaunee, co., Wis. D6 88
Keweenaw, co., Mich. A2 66
Keya Paha, co., Nebr. B6 71
Key Biscayne, Fla. *G6 54
Keyes, Calif. *D4 50
Keyes, Okla. e8 79
Keyport, N.J. C4 74
Keyser, W. Va. B6 87
Keystone, Iowa C5 60
Keystone, W. Va. D3 87
Keysville, Fla. E2 54
Keysville, Va. C4 85
Keytesville, Mo. B5 69
Key West, Fla. H5 54
Kezar Falls, Maine E2 64
Kezhma, Sov. Un. D13 13
Kežmarok, Czech. D6 7
Khabarovsk, Sov. Un. E16 13
Khairpur, Pak. C4 20
Khalkidhikí (Chalcidice),
    prov., Grc. *B4 14
Khalkis, Grc. C4 14
Khalūf, Om. E6 15
Khambhāliya, India D4 20
Khanabad, Afg. A4 20
Khānaqīn, Iraq E15 15
Khandwa, India D6 20
Khaniá (Canea), Grc. E5 14
Khaniá, prov., Grc. *E4 14
Khānpur, Pak. C5 20
Khān Yūnus, Gaza Strip C2, h5 15
Kharagpur, India D8 20
Kharkov, Sov. Un. G11 12
Kharmanli, Bul. E7 10
Kharovsk, Sov. Un. B13 12
Khartoum (Al-Kharṭūm), Sud. E4 23
Khartoum North, Sud. E4 23
Khartsyzsk, Sov. Un. q21 12
Khash, Afg. B3 20
Khaskovo, Bul. E7 10
Khatanga, Sov. Un. B13 16
Khenifra, Mor. B3 22
Kherson, Sov. Un. H9 12
Khilok, Sov. Un. D14 13
Khimki, Sov. Un. n17 12
Khíos, Grc. C6 14
Khíos, (Chios), prov., Grc. *C6 14
Khmelnik, Sov. Un. G6 12
Khmelnitskiy, Sov. Un. G6 12

Kholm, Sov. Un. C8 12
Khong, Laos C3 19
Khong Sedone, Laos *B3 19
Khorog, Sov. Un. F10 13
Khorol, Sov. Un. G9 12
Khorramābād, Iran C4 15
Khorramshahr, Iran C4 15
Khotin, Sov. Un. G6 12
Khulna, Bngl. D8 20
Khust, Sov. Un. G4 12
Kiamichi, mtn., Okla. C6 79
Kiangsu, prov., China E8 17
Kičevo, Yugo. E5 10
Kidder, co., N. Dak. C6 77
Kidderminster, Eng. D5 4
Kiel, Ger., Fed. Rep. of A5 6
Kiel, Wis. E5, k9 88
Kielce, Pol. C6 7
Kiester, Minn. G5 67
Kiev (Kiyev), Sov. Un. F8 12
Kifisiá, Grc. g11 14
Kigali, Rwanda I4 23
Kikinda, Yugo. C5 10
Kikládhes (Cyclades), prov., Grc. *D5 14
Kikwit, Zaire B3 24
Kilauea, crater, Haw. D6 56
Kilbride, Newf., Can. *E5 44
Kilchu, Kor. F4 18
Kildare, co., Ire. *D3 4
Kilgore, Tex. C5 84
Kilimanjaro, mtn., Tan. I5 23
Kilis, Tur. D11 14
Kiliya, Sov. Un. I7 12
Kilkenny, Ire. D3 4
Kilkenny, co., Ire. *D3 4
Kilkís, Grc. E6 10
Kilkís, prov., Grc. *B4 14
Killaloe Station, Ont., Can. B7 41
Killarney, Man., Can. E2 40
Killarney, Ire. D2 4
Killbuck, Ohio B4 78
Killeen, Tex. D4 84
Killian, S.C. C6 82
Killona, La. h11 63
Kilmallie, Scot. B4 4
Kilmarnock, Scot. C4 4
Kilmarnock, Va. C6 85
Kimchaek, (Songjin), Kor. F4 18
Kimball, Minn. E4 67
Kimball, Nebr. C2 71
Kimball, S. Dak. G7 77
Kimball, co., Nebr. C2 71
Kimberly, B.C., Can. E9 37
Kimberly, S. Afr. F4 24
Kimberly, Ala. B3 46
Kimberly, Idaho G4 57
Kimberly, W. Va. D6 87
Kimberly, Wis. h9 88
Kimble, co., Tex. D3 84
Kimry, Sov. Un. C11 12
Kinabalu, mtn., Mala. D5 19
Kincaid, Ill. D4 58
Kincardine, Ont., Can. C3 41
Kincardine, co., Scot. *B5 4
Kinde, Mich. E8 66
Kinder, La. D3 63
Kinderhook, N.Y. C7 75
Kindersley, Sask., Can. F1 39
Kindia, Guinea F2 22
Kindu, Zaire I3 23
Kineo, mtn., Maine C3 64
Kineshma, Sov. Un. C14 12
King, N.C. A2 76
King, co., Tex. C2 84
King, co., Wash. B4 86
King, mtn., Oreg. D8 80
King, mtn., Oreg. E3 80
King and Queen, co., Va. C6 85
Kingaroy, Austl. E9 25
King City, Calif. D3 50
King City, Ont., Can. k14 41
King City, Mo. A3 69
Kingfield, Maine D2 64
Kingfisher, Okla. B4 79
Kingfisher, co., Okla. B3 79
King George, co., Va. B5 85
King George, mtn., B.C., Can. D10 37
Kingman, Ariz. B1 48
Kingman, Kans. E5, g10 61
Kingman, co., Kans. E5 61
King of Prussia, Pa. *F11 81
Kings, co., Calif. D3 50
Kings, co., N.B., Can. D4 43
Kings, co., N.S., Can. E5 43
Kings, co., P.E.I., Can. C7 43
Kings (Brooklyn Borough), co.,
    N.Y. E7 75
Kings, peak, Calif. B1 50
Kings, peak, Utah A6 72
Kingsburg, Calif. D4 50
Kingsbury, co., S. Dak. F7 77
Kingscote, Austl. G6 25
Kingsford, Mich. C2 66

Kingsford Heights, Ind. *A4 59
Kings Gardens, Kans. A4 61
Kingsley, Iowa B2 60
Kingsley, Mich. D5 66
King's Lynn, Eng. D7 4
Kings Mills, Ohio C1, n13 78
Kings Mountain, N.C. B1 76
Kings Park, N.Y. n15 75
King's Point, Newf., Can. D3 44
Kings Point, N.Y. F1 52
Kingsport, Tenn. C11 83
Kingston, Austl. G6 25
Kingston, Ont., Can. C8 41
Kingston, Idaho B2 57
Kingston, Jam. F5 35
Kingston, Mass. C6 65
Kingston, N.H. F6 73
Kingston, N.J. C3 74
Kingston, N.Y. D6 75
Kingston, Ohio C3 78
Kingston, Okla. D5 79
Kingston, Pa. D10, n17 81
Kingston, R.I. D10 52
Kingston, Tenn. D9 83
Kingston, W. Va. D3, n13 87
Kingstree, S.C. D8 82
Kingsville, Ont., Can. E2 41
Kingsville, Ohio A5 78
Kingsville, Tex. F4 84
King William, co., Va. C5 85
King William's Town, S. Afr. G5 24
Kingwood, W. Va. B5 87
Kinistino, Sask., Can. E3 39
Kinloch, Mo. f13 69
Kinmundy, Ill. E5 58
Kinnaird, B.C., Can. E9 37
Kinnelon, N.J. B4 74
Kinney, co., Tex. E2 84
Kinross, co., Scot. *B5 4
Kinshasa (Leopoldville), Zaire A3 24
Kinsley, Kans. E4 61
Kinsman, Ohio A5 78
Kinston, N.C. B5 76
Kinwood, Tex. *E5 84
Kiowa, Kans. E5 61
Kiowa, Okla. C6 79
Kiowa, co., Colo. C8 51
Kiowa, co., Kans. E4 61
Kiowa, co., Okla. C2 79
Kiparissia, Grc. D3 14
Kipling, Sask., Can. G4 39
Kipushi, Zaire C5 24
Kirbyville, Tex. D6 84
Kirensk, Sov. Un. D13 13
Kirghiz, S.S.R., rep., Sov. Un. E10 16
Kiribati, country, Oceania F8 2
Kirikkale, Tur. *C9 14
Kirin, prov., China C9 17
Kirinyaga, mts., Ken. I5 23
Kirkcaldy, Scot. B5 4
Kirkcudbright, co., Scot. *C4 4
Kirkland, Ill. A5 58
Kirkland, Wash. B3, e11 86
Kirkland Lake, Ont., Can. o19 41
Kirklareli, Tur. B6 14
Kirklin, Ind. D5 59
Kirksville, Mo. A5 69
Kirkūk, Iraq E15 14
Kirkwood, Md. *C3 53
Kirkwood, Mo. f13 69
Kirn, Ger., Fed. Rep. of D3 6
Kirov, Sov. Un. D7 13
Kirovabad, Sov. Un. E7 13
Kirovograd, Sov. Un. G9 12
Kirovsk, Sov. Un. C6 13
Kirsanov, Sov. Un. E14 12
Kirşehir, Tur. C10 14
Kirtland, Ohio *A4 78
Kiruna, Swe. D9 11
Kiryū, Jap. H9, m18 18
Kisarazu, Jap. n18 18
Kiselevsk, Sov. Un. *D11 13
Kishangarh, India C5 20
Kishinev, Sov. Un. H7 12
Kishiwada, Jap. o14 18
Kishorganj, Bngl. D9 20
Kiskoros, Hung. B4 10
Kiskundorozsma, Hung. B5 10
Kiskunfelegyháza, Hung. B4 10
Kiskunhalas, Hung. B4 10
Kiskunmajsa, Hung. B4 10
Kislovodsk, Sov. Un. *E7 13
Kiso-sammyaku, mts., Jap. n16 18
Kissimmee, Fla. D5 54
Kistler, W. Va. D3, D5 87
Kisújszállás, Hung. B5 10
Kisumu, Ken. I4 23
Kisvárda, Hung. A6 10
Kita-dake, mtn., Jap. I9 18
Kitakyūshū, Jap. J5 18
Kitale, Ken. H4 23
Kitami, Jap. E11 18

Kit Carson, co., Colo. B8 51
Kitchener, Ont., Can. D4 41
Kitimat, B.C., Can. B3 37
Kitsap, co., Wash. B3 86
Kittanning, Pa. E2 81
Kittery, Maine E2 64
Kittery Point, Maine E2 64
Kittitas, co., Wash. B5 86
Kitts, Ky. D6 62
Kittson, co., Minn. B2 67
Kitwe, Zam. *C5 24
Kitzbühel, Aus. E6 6
Kitzingen, Ger., Fed. Rep. of D5 6
Kitzmiller, Md. m12 53
Kizel, Sov. Un. *D8 13
Kizyl-Arvat, Sov. Un. F8 13
Kladno, Czech. C3, n17 7
Klagenfurt, Aus. E7 6
Klaipeda (Memel), Sov. Un. D3 12
Klamath, co., Oreg. E4 80
Klamath, mts., Calif. B2 50
Klamath Falls, Oreg. E5 80
Klamath Glen, Calif. B2 50
Klatovy, Czech. D2 7
Kleberg, Tex. *C4 84
Kleberg, co., Tex. F4 84
Klemme, Iowa A4 60
Kletnya, Sov. Un. E9 12
Kletsk, Sov. Un. E6 12
Kleve, Ger., Fed. Rep. of C3 6
Klickitat, Wash. D4 86
Klickitat, co., Wash. D5 86
Klintsy, Sov. Un. E9 12
Ključ, Yugo. C3 10
Kobuck, Pol. C5 7
Kłodzko, Pol. C4 7
Klosterneuburg, Aus. D8 6
Kluczbork, Pol. C5 7
Klyuchevskaya, vol., Sov. Un. D19 13
Knezha, Bul. D7 10
Knightdale, N.C. B4 76
Knights Landing, Calif. C3 50
Knightstown, Ind. E6 59
Knightsville, Ind. E3 59
Knittlefeld, Aus. E7 6
Knob Noster, Mo. C4 69
Knockmealdown, mts., Ire. D2 4
Knollwood, Ohio *C2 78
Knoolwood Park, Mich. *F6 66
Knot, co., Ky. C6 62
Knox, Ind. B4 59
Knox, Pa. *E1 81
Knox, co., Ill. B3 58
Knox, co., Ind. G3 59
Knox, co., Ky. D6 62
Knox, co., Maine D4 64
Knox, co., Mo. A5 69
Knox, co., Nebr. B8 71
Knox, co., Ohio B3 78
Knox, co., Tenn. C10 83
Knox, co., Tex. C3 84
Knox City, Tex. C3 84
Knoxville, Ill. C3 58
Knoxville, Iowa C5 60
Knoxville, Tenn. D10, n14 83
Knysna, S. Afr. G4 24
Kōbe, Jap. o14 18
København, see Copenhagen, Den.
Koblenz, Ger., Fed. Rep. of
    . . . . C3 6
Kobrin, Sov. Un. E5 12
Kočani, Yugo. E6 10
Koch, mtn., Mont. E5 70
Kochi, Jap. J6 18
Kochi, pref., Jap. *J6 18
Kodaira, Jap. *n18 18
Kodak, Ky. C6 62
Kodiak, Alsk. D9 47
Kodiak, isl., Alsk. D9 47
Koforidua, Ghana G4 22
Kofu, Jap. I9, n17 18
Koga, Jap. m18 18
Kohala, Haw. C6 56
Kohat, Pak. B5 20
Kohler, Wis. E5, k10 88
Kokand, Sov. Un. E10 13
Kokchetav, Sov. Un. D9 13
Kokkola, Fin. F10 11
Kokomo, Ind. D5 59
Kokstad, S.Afr. G5 24
Kolar Gold Fields, India F6 20
Kolarovo, Bul. D8 10
Kolárovo, Czech. E4 7
Kolhapur, India E5 20
Kolín, Czech. C3 7
Köln, see Cologne, Ger.
Koło, Pol. B5 7
Koloa, Haw. B2 56
Kolomna, Sov. Un. D12, n18 12
Kolomyya, Sov. Un. G5 12
Kolonodale, Indon. F6 19
Kolpino, Sov. Un. s31 1

Kolpino, Sov. Un. ... s31 11
Kolwezi, Zaire ... C5 24
Kolyberovo, Sov. Un. ... n18 12
Kolyma, riv., Sov. Un. ... C18 16
Komádi, Hung. ... B5 10
Komandorski Village, Calif. ... *D2 50
Komárno, Czech. ... E5 7
Komarno, Sov. Un. ... D7 7
Komárom, Hung. ... B4 10
Komárom, co., Hung. ... *B4 10
Komatsu, Jap. ... H8 18
Komatsushima, Jap. ... I7 18
Kommunarsk, Sov. Un. ... G12, q21 12
Komotiní, Grc. ... B5 14
Kompong Cham, Kam. ... C3 19
Kompong Chhnang, Kam. ... C2 19
Kompong Kleang, Kam. ... *C2 19
Kompong Speu, Kam. ... *C2 19
Kompong Thom, Kam. ... C2 19
Komrat, Sov. Un. ... H7 12
Komsomolsk -na Amure,
  Sov. Un. ... D16 13
Konawa, Okla. ... C5 79
Kondoa, Tan. ... A7 24
Kondopoga, Sov. Un. ... F16 11
Kong, reg., I.C. ... G4 22
Kongju, Kor. ... H3 18
Kongsberg, Nor. ... H3 11
Konin, Pol. ... B5 7
Konosha, Sov. Un. ... A13 12
Konotop, Sov. Un. ... F9 12
Końskie, Pol. ... C6 7
Konstantinovka, Sov. Un. ... q20 12
Konstanz, Ger., Fed. Rep. of ... E4 6
Kontum, Viet. ... C3 19
Konya, Tur. ... D9 14
Konyang, Kor. ... I3 18
Koochiching, co., Minn. ... B4 67
Koontz Lake, Ind. ... B5 59
Kooskia, Idaho ... C3 57
Kootenai, co., Idaho ... B2 57
Kopeysk, Sov. Un. ... *D9 13
Köping, Swe. ... H6, t33 11
Kopparberg, co., Swe. ... *G6 11
Koppel, Pa. ... E1 81
Koprivnica, Yugo. ... B3 10
Kopychintsy, Sov. Un. ... G5 12
Korçë, Alb. ... B3 14
Korçë, pref., Alb. ... *B3 14
Korea, North, country, Asia ... F4 18
Korea, South, country, Asia ... H4 18
Korets, Sov. Un. ... F6 12
Korhogo, I.C. ... G3 22
Kórinthos (Corinth), Grc. ... D4 14
Kóriyama, Jap. ... H10 18
Korkino, Sov. Un. ... *D9 13
Korla, China ... C2 17
Körmend, Hung. ... B3 10
Korneuburg, Aus. ... D8 6
Koropí, Grc. ... h11 14
Korosten, Sov. Un. ... F7 12
Korsakov, Sov. Un. ... E17 13
Kortrijk, Bel. ... B5 5
Kos, Grc. ... D6 14
Kościan, Pol. ... B4 7
Kościerzyna, Pol. ... A4 7

Kosciusko, Miss. ... B4 68
Kosciusko, co., Ind. ... B6 59
Kosciusko, mtn., Austl. ... G8 25
Košice, Czech. ... D6 7
Kosong, Kor. ... G4 18
Kosove (Kosovo), pref., Alb. ... *A3 14
Kosovska Mitrovica, Yugo. ... D5 10
Kossuth, co., Iowa ... A3 60
Kostroma, Sov. Un. ... C13 12
Kostrzyn, Pol. ... B3 7
Koszalin, Pol. ... A4 7
Koszeg, Hung. ... B3 10
Kota, India ... C6 20
Kota Baharu, Mala. ... D2 19
Kotabaru, Indon. ... F5 19
Kota Kinabalu, Mala. ... I14 19
Kotelnikovskiy, Sov. Un. ... H14 12
Köthen, Ger. Dem. Rep. ... C5 6
Kotka, Fin. ... G12 11
Kotlas, Sov. Un. ... C7 13
Kotor, Yugo. ... D4 10
Kotovsk, Sov. Un. ... H7 12
Koudougou, Burkina Faso ... F4 22
Kountze, Tex. ... D5 84
Kouts, Ind. ... B3 59
Kouvola, Fin. ... G12 11
Kovel, Sov. Un. ... F5 12
Kovrov, Sov. Un. ... C13 12
Kowa, Jap. ... o15 18
Kowloon, Hong Kong ... G7 17
Kowon, Kor. ... G3 18
Kozan, Tur. ... D10 14
Kozáni, Grc. ... B3 14
Kozáni, prov., Grc. ... *B3 14
Kozienice, Pol. ... C6 7
Koźle, Pol. ... C5 7
Kozloduy, Bul. ... D6 10
Kozuchów, Pol. ... C3 7
Kragujevac, Yugo. ... D5 10
Kraków, Pol. ... C5 7
Kraljevo, Yugo. ... D5 10
Kralupy nad Vltavou, Czech. ... n17 7
Kramatorsk, Sov. Un. ... G11, q20 12
Kranj, Yugo. ... B2 10
Kraslice, Czech. ... C2 7
Kraśnik Lubelski, Pol. ... C7 7
Krasnoarmeysk, Sov. Un. ... F15 12
Krasnodar, Sov. Un. ... I12 12
Krasnograd, Sov. Un. ... G10 12
Krasnoselye, Sov. Un. ... G9 12
Krasnoslobodsk, Sov. Un. ... D14 12
Krasnovodsk, Sov. Un. ... E8 13
Krasnoyarsk, Sov. Un. ... D12 13
Krasnystaw, Pol. ... C7 7
Krasnyy Liman, Sov. Un. ... q20 12
Krasnyy Luch, Sov. Un. ... q21 12
Krasnyy Sulin, Sov. Un. ... H13 12
Krasnyy Yar, Sov. Un. ... F15 12
Kratie, Kam. ... C3 19
Krebs, Okla. ... C6 79
Krefeld, Ger., Fed. Rep. of ... C3 6
Kremenchug, Sov. Un. ... G9 12
Kremenets, Sov. Un. ... F5 12
Kremennaya, Sov. Un. ... p21 12
Krems, Aus. ... D7 6

Krichev, Sov. Un. ... E8 12
Krishnagiri, India ... F6 20
Kristiansand, Nor. ... H2 11
Kristianstad, Swe. ... I6 11
Kristianstad, co., Swe. ... *I5 11
Kristiansund, Nor. ... F2 11
Krivoy Rog, Sov. Un. ... H9 12
Križevci, Yugo. ... B3 10
Krnov, Czech. ... C4 7
Kroměříž, Czech. ... D4 7
Kromy, Sov. Un. ... E10 12
Kronoberg, co., Swe. ... *I6 11
Kronshtadt, Sov. Un. ... B7 12
Kroonstad, S. Afr. ... F5 24
Kropotkin, Sov. Un. ... I13 12
Krosno, Pol. ... D6 7
Krosno Odrzańskie, Pol. ... B3 7
Krotoszyn, Pol. ... C4 7
Krotz Springs, La. ... D4 63
Krsko, Yugo. ... C2 10
Krugersdorp, S. Afr. ... *F5 24
Krumroy, Ohio ... *A4 78
Kruševac, Yugo. ... D5 10
Krusevo, Yugo. ... E6 10
Krymskaya, Sov. Un. ... I11 12
Krynki, Pol. ... B7 7
Ksar el Kebir, Mor. ... B3 22
Ksar es Souk, Mor. ... B4 22
Kuala Lipis, Mala. ... E2 19
Kuala Lumpur, Mala. ... E2 19
Kuala Terengganu, Mala. ... D2 19
Kuantan, Mala. ... E2 19
Kubokawa, Jap. ... J6 18
Kuching, Mala. ... E4 19
Kudat, Mala. ... D5 19
Kudus, Indon. ... G4 19
Kufstein, Aus. ... E6 6
Kuji, Jap. ... F10 18
Kuju-San, mtn., Jap. ... J5 18
Kuki, Jap. ... m18 18
Kula, Bul. ... D6 10
Kula, Tur. ... *C7 14
Kula, Yugo. ... C4 10
Kula Kangri, peak, Bhutan,
  China ... C9 20
Kulebaki, Sov. Un. ... D14 12
Kulmbach, Ger., Fed. Rep. of ... C5 6
Kulpmont, Pa. ... E9 81
Kumagaya, Jap. ... m18 18
Kumamoto, Jap. ... J5 18
Kumamoto, pref., Jap. ... *J5 18
Kumanovo, Yugo. ... D5 10
Kumasi, Ghana ... G4 22
Kumbakonam, India ... F6 20
Kumchon, Kor. ... H4 18
Kumha, Kor. ... G3 18
Kumihama, Jap. ... n14 19
Kumla, Swe. ... H6, t33 11
Kumo, Nig. ... D7 22
Kuna, Idaho ... F2 57
Kuneitra (Al Qunaytirah), Syr. ... F10 14
Kunming (Yunnanfu), China ... F5 17
Kunsan, Kor. ... I3 18
Kunszentmárton, Hung. ... B5 10
Kuolayarvi, Sov. Un. ... D13 11
Kuopio, Fin. ... F12 11

Kuopio, prov., Fin. ... *F12 11
Kupang, Indon. ... H6 19
Kupyansk, Sov. Un. ... G11 12
Kurashiki, Jap. ... I6 18
Kuraymah, Sud. ... E4 23
Kurdzhali, Bul. ... E7 10
Kure, Jap. ... I6 18
Kuressaare, Sov. Un. ... B4 12
Kurgan, Sov. Un. ... D9 13
Kurnool, India ... E6 20
Kurri Kurri-Weston, Austl. ... F8 26
Kursk, Sov. Un. ... F11 12
Kurthwood, La. ... C2 63
Kurtistown, Haw. ... D6 56
Kurume, Jap. ... J5 18
Kurunegala, Sri Lanka ... G7 20
Kusatsu, Jap. ... n14 18
Kushchevskaya, Sov. Un. ... H12 12
Kushevat, Sov. Un. ... C9 13
Kushimoto, Jap. ... J7 18
Kushiro, Jap. ... E12 18
Kushka, Sov. Un. ... F9 13
Kustanay, Sov. Un. ... D9 13
Küsti, Sud. ... F4 23
Küstrin, see Kostrzyn, Pol.
Kütahya (Kutaiah), Tur. ... C7 14
Kutaisi, Sov. Un. ... A14 14
Kutná Hora, Czech. ... D3 7
Kutno, Pol. ... B5 7
Kutztown, Pa. ... E10 81
Kuwait, Kuw. ... D4 15
Kuwait, country, Asia ... D4 15
Kuwana, Jap. ... I8, n18 18
Kuybyshev, Sov. Un. ... D8 13
Kuybyshev, Sov. Un. ... D10 13
Kuznetsk, Sov. Un. ... E16 12
Kwangju, Kor. ... I3 18
Kwidzyń, Pol. ... B5 7
Kyabram, Austl. ... H5 26
Kyaiklat, Bur. ... E10 20
Kyaikto, Bur. ... *B1 19
Kyakhta, Sov. Un. ... D13 13
Kyaukse, Bur. ... D10 20
Kybartai, Sov. Un. ... A7 7
Kyje, Czech. ... n18 7
Kyle, Sask., Can. ... G1 39
Kyle, Tex. ... E4 84
Kylestrome, Scot. ... *A4 4
Kyllburg, Ger., Fed. Rep. of ... *C3 6
Kymi, prov., Fin. ... *G12 11
Kynlyn, Del. ... *A6 53
Kyomipo, see Songnim, Kor.
Kyongju, Kor. ... I4 18
Kyongsong, Kor. ... F4 18
Kyōto, Jap. ... I7, n14 18
Kyoto, pref., Jap. ... *I7 18
Kyritz, Ger. Dem. Rep. ... B6 6
Kyshtym, Sov. Un. ... *D9 13
Kyūshū, isl., Jap. ... J5 18
Kyustendil, Bul. ... D6 10
Kyzyl, Sov. Un. ... D12 13
Kzyl-Orda, Sov. Un. ... *E9 13

L

Labadieville, La. ... E5, k10 63
La Barca, Mex. ... C4, m12 34
La Barge, Wyo. ... D2 89
Labe, Guinea ... F2 22
Labelle, Que., Can. ... C3 42
La Belle, Fla. ... F5 54
La Belle, Mo. ... A6 69
Labelle, co., Que., Can. ... C2 42
Labette, co., Kans. ... E8 61
Labin, Yugo. ... C2 10
La Boca, Pan. ... *B2 32
Laboulaye, Arg. ... A4 28
Labrador, reg., Newf., Can. ... g9 44
Laburnum Manor, Va. ... *C5 85
La Canada, Calif. ... m12 50
La Carlota, Phil. ... *C6 19
La Carolina, Sp. ... C4 8
Lac au Saumon, Que., Can. ... *k13 42

Lac-aux-Sables, Que., Can. ... *C5 42
Lac-Beauport, Que., Can. ... C9 42
Lac-Bouchette, Que., Can. ... A5 42
Lac-Brome, Que., Can. ... D5 42
Laccadive, is., India ... F5 20
Lac-Carre, Que., Can. ... C3 42
Lac-du-Bonnet, Man., Can. ... D3 40
Lac du Flambeau, Wis. ... B4 88
La Ceiba, Hond. ... D7 34
La Ceja, Col. ... B2 32
Lac-Etchemin, Que., Can. ... C7 42
Lacey, Wash. ... B3 86
Lacey Park, Pa. ... *F11 81
La Chaux-de-Fonds, Switz. ... E3 6
Lachine, Que., Can. ... D4, q19 42
La Chorrera, Pan. ... B2 32
Lachute, Que., Can. ... D3 42
La Ciotat, Fr. ... F6 5

Lackawanna, N.Y. ... C2 75
Lackawanna, co., Pa. ... D10 81
Lac la Biche, Alta., Can. ... B5 38
Lac la Hache, B.C., Can. ... D7 37
Laclede, co., Mo. ... D5 69
Lac-Mégantic, Que., Can. ... D7 42
Lacolle, Que., Can. ... D4 42
Lacombe, Alta., Can. ... C4 38
Lacombe, La. ... D6, h12 63
Lacon, Ill. ... B4 58
Laconia, N.H. ... D5 73
La Conner, Wash. ... A3 86
Lacoochee, Fla. ... D4 54
La Coruña, Sp. ... A1 8
La Coruña, prov., Sp. ... *A1 8
La Courneuve, Fr. ... g10 5
Lac Qui Parle, co., Minn. ... F2 67
La Crescent, Minn. ... G7 67

La Crescenta, Calif. ... *F4 50
La Cresta Village, Calif. ... *E4 50
La Crosse, Ind. ... B4 59
La Crosse, Kans. ... D4 61
La Crosse, Va. ... D5 85
La Crosse, Wis. ... E2 88
La Crosse, co., Wis. ... *E2 88
La Cruz, Col. ... C2 32
La Cruz, Mex. ... C3 34
Lac-St.-Jean-Est, co., Que., Can. ... A6 42
Lac-St.-Jean-Ouest, co.,
  Que., Can. ... A5 42
La Cygne, Kans. ... D9 61
Lacy-Lakeview, Tex. ... *D4 84
Ladd, Ill. ... B4 58
Ladera Heights, Calif. ... *F4 50
Ladner, B.C., Can. ... E6, f12 37
Ladoga, Ind. ... E4 59

Ladoga, lake, Sov. Un. A8 12
Ladonia, Tex. C5 84
La Dorado, Col. B3 32
Ladue, Mo. *C7 69
Lady Laurier, mtn., B.C., Can. A6 37
Ladysmith, B.C., Can. E6, g12 37
Ladysmith, S. Afr. F5 24
Ladysmith, Wis. C2 88
Lae, Pap. N. Gui. k12 25
La Esperanza, Cuba C2 35
La Estrada, Sp. A1 8
La Farge, Wis. E3 88
Lafayette, Ala. C4 46
Lafayette, Calif. *D2 50
Lafayette, Colo. B5 51
La Fayette, Ga. B1 55
Lafayette, Ind. D4 59
Lafayette, La. D3 63
Lafayette, N.J. A3 74
Lafayette, Oreg. B3, h11 80
Lafayette, Tenn. C7 83
Lafayette, co., Ark. D2 49
Lafayette, co., Fla. C3 54
Lafayette, co., Miss. A4 68
Lafayette, co., Mo. C4 69
Lafayette, co., Wis. F3 88
Lafayette, par., La. D3 63
Lafayette Hill, Pa. *F11 81
La Feria, Tex. F4 84
La Ferté-Bernard, Fr. C4 5
Lafferty, Ohio B4 78
Lafitte, La. k11 63
Laflèche, (Mackayville),
Que., Can. *D4 42
Laflèche, Sask., Can. H2 39
La Flèche, Fr. D3 5
La Follette, Tenn. C9 83
La Fontaine, Ind. C6 59
Lafourche, par., La. E5 63
La France, S.C. B2 82
Laghouat, Alg. B5 22
La Gloria, Col. B3 52
Lagny, Fr. C5 5
Lagos, Nig. G5 22
Lagos, Port. D1 8
Lagos, de Moreno, Mex. C4, m13 34
La Grand' Combe, Fr. E5 5
La Grande, Oreg. B8 80
La Grange, Ga. C1 55
La Grange, Ill. B6, k9 58
Lagrange, Ind. A7 59
La Grange, Ky. B4 62
La Grange, Mo. A6 69
La Grange, N.C. B5 76
Lagrange, Ohio A3 78
La Grange, Tex. E4 84
Lagrange, co., Ind. A7 59
La Grange Highlands, Ill. *B6 58
La Grange Park, Ill. k9 58
Lagro, Ind. C6 59
La Guadeloupe, Que., Can. D7 42
La Guaira, Ven. A4 32
La Guajira, intendencia, Col. A3 32
La Guardia, Sp. B1 8
Laguna, Braz. D3 30
Laguna, prov., Phil. *C6 19
Laguna Beach, Calif. F5, n13 50
Lagunas, Peru C2 31
Laguna Shores, Tex. *F4 84
La Habra, Calif. n13 50
La Habra Heights, Calif. *F4 50
Lahad Datu, Mala. D5 19
La Harpe, Ill. C3 58
Lahij, P.D.R. of Yem. G3 15
Lahore, Pak. B5 20
Lahr, Ger., Fed. Rep. of D3 6
Lahti, Fin. G11 11
La Huaca, Peru B1 31
Laie, Haw. B4, f10 56
Laigle, Fr. C4 5
Laingsburg, Mich. F6 66
Lairg, Scot. A4 4
La Jara, Colo. D5 51
Lajes, Braz. D2 30
Lajosmizse, Hung. B4 10
La Joya, Mex. h9 34
La Junta, Colo. D7 51
Lake, co., Calif. C2 50
Lake, co., Colo. b4 51
Lake, co., Fla. D5 54
Lake, co., Ill. a6 58
Lake, co., Ind. B3 59
Lake, co., Mich. E3 66
Lake, co., Minn. C7 67
Lake, co., Mont. C2 70
Lake, co., Ohio A4 78
Lake, co., Oreg. E6 80
Lake, co., S. Dak. F8 77
Lake, co., Tenn. A2 83
Lake, mtn., Wyo. E6 89
Lake Alfred, Fla. D5 54
Lake Andes, S. Dak. G7 77

Lake Arrowhead, Calif. E5 50
Lake Arthur, La. D3 63
Lake Barcroft, Va. *B5 85
Lake Benton, Minn. F2 67
Lake Bluff, Ill. A6, h9 58
Lake Butler, Fla. B4 54
Lake Charles, La. D2 63
Lake City, Fla. B4 54
Lake City, Iowa B3 60
Lake City, Mich. D5 66
Lake City, Minn. F6 67
Lake City, Pa. B1 81
Lake City, S.C. D8 82
Lake City, Tenn. C9 83
Lake Cowichan, B.C., Can. g11 37
Lake Crystal, Minn. F4 67
Lake Delton, Wis. E4 88
Lake Erie Beach, N.Y. *C1 75
Lake Fenton, Mich. *F7 66
Lakefield, Ont., Can. C6 41
Lakefield, Minn. G3 67
Lake Forest, Ill. A6, h9 58
Lake Forest, S.C. *B3 82
Lake Forest Park, Wash. *B3 86
Lake Geneva, Wis. F5 88
Lake George, N.Y. B7 75
Lake Hamilton, Fla. *D5 54
Lake Harbor, Fla. *F6 54
Lake Helen, Fla. D5 54
Lake Hiawatha, N.J. B4 74
Lake Hills, Wash. *B3 86
Lake Hopatcong, N.J. *B3 74
Lakehurst, N.J. C4 74
Lake in the Hills, Ill. *A5 58
Lake Jackson, Tex. E5, r14 84
Lake James, Ind. A7 59
Lakeland, Fla. D5 54
Lakeland, Ga. E3 55
Lakeland Village, Calif. *F5 50
Lake Linden, Mich. A2 66
Lake Lotawana, Mo. *C3 69
Lake Luzerne, N.Y. B7 75
Lake Mary, Fla. D5 54
Lake Mills, Iowa A4 60
Lake Mills, Wis. E5 88
Lake Mohawk, N.J. A3 74
Lakemont, Pa. F5 81
Lakemore, Ohio A4 78
Lake Odessa, Mich. F5 66
Lake of the Woods, lake,
Can., U.S. A4 67
Lake of the Woods, co., Minn. B3 67
Lake Orion, Mich. *F7 66
Lake Orion Heights, Mich. *F7 66
Lake Oswego, Oreg. B4, h12 80
Lake Ozark, Mo. C5 69
Lake Park, Fla. F6 54
Lake Park, Iowa A2 60
Lake Park, Minn. D2 67
Lake Placid, Fla. E5 54
Lake Placid, N.Y. A7, f10 75
Lakeport, Calif. C2 50
Lake Preston, S. Dak. F8 77
Lake Providence, La. B4 63
Lake Ronkonkoma, N.Y. F4 52
Lakeside, Calif. F5, o16 50
Lakeside, N.S., Can. E6 43
Lakeside, La. *C3 63
Lakeside, Ohio A3 78
Lakeside, Oreg. D2 80
Lakeside, Va. *C5 85
Lakeside Park, Ky. h13 62
Lake Station, Ind. A3 59
Lake Stevens, Wash. A3 86
Lake Success, N.Y. h13 75
Lake Telemark, N.J. *B3 74
Lake Toxaway, N.C. f10 76
Lake View, Iowa B2 60
Lakeview, Mich. *F5 66
Lakeview, Mich. E5 66
Lake View, N.Y. *C2 75
Lakeview, Ohio B2 78
Lakeview, Oreg. E6 80
Lake View, S.C. C9 82
Lakeview, Tex. *E6 84
Lake Villa, Ill. h8 58
Lake Village, Ark. D4 49
Lakeville, Conn. B3 52
Lakeville, Ind. A5 59
Lakeville, Minn. F5 67
Lakeville, N.Y. C3 75
Lakeville, Ohio A5 78
Lake Waccamaw, N.C. C4 76
Lake Wales, Fla. E5 54
Lakewood Calif. n12 50
Lakewood, N.B., Can. *C2 43
Lakewood, Colo. B5 51
Lakewood, N.J. C4 74
Lakewood, N.Y. C1 75
Lakewood, Ohio A4, h9 78
Lakewood, Tex. *E5 84
Lakewood Center, Wash. *B3 86
Lake Worth, Fla. F6 54

Lake Zurich, Ill. h8 58
Lakhīmpur, India C7 20
Lakin, Kans. E2 61
Lakonia (Laconia), prov., Grc. *D4 14
Lakota, N. Dak. B7 77
Lakshadweep, ter., India *F5 20
La Laguna, Sp. m13 8
La Libertad, dept., Peru C2 31
Lalín, Sp. A1 8
La Linea, Sp. D3 8
Lalitpur, India D6 20
La Loche, Sask., Can. m7 39
La Maddalena, It. D2 9
La Malbaie, Que., Can. B7 42
Lamar, Colo. C8 51
Lamar, Mo. D3 69
Lamar, S.C. C7 82
Lamar, co., Ala. B1 46
Lamar, co., Ga. C2 55
Lamar, co., Tex. C5 84
Lamar, co., Miss. D4 68
La Marque, Tex. r15 84
Lamartine, Que., Can. B7 42
Lamas, Peru C2 31
Lamb, co., Tex. B1 84
Lamballe, Fr. C2 5
Lambayeque, Peru C2 31
Lambayeque, dept., Peru C2 31
Lambert, Miss. A3 68
Lamberton, Minn. F3 67
Lambertville, Mich. *G7 66
Lambertville, N.J. C3 74
Lambeth, Ont., Can. E3 41
Lambton, Que., Can. D6 42
Lambton, co., Ont., Can. E2 41
Lamego, Port. B2 8
Lamèque, N.B., Can. B5 43
La Mesa, Calif. o15 50
Lamesa, Tex. C2 84
Lamia, Grc. C4 14
La Mirada, Calif. *F4 50
La Moille, Ill. B4 58
Lamoille, co., Vt. B2 73
Lamoni, Iowa D4 60
Lamont, Calif. E4 50
Lamont, Alta., Can. C4 38
Lamont, Okla. A4 79
La Monte, Mo. C4 69
La Moure, N. Dak. D7 77
La Moure, co., N. Dak. D7 77
Lampa, Peru E3 31
Lampang, Thai. *B1 19
Lampasas, Tex. D3 84
Lampasas, co., Tex. D3 84
Lamphun, Thai. *B1 19
Lampman, Sask., Can. H4 39
Lanai City, Haw. C5 56
Lanao del Norte, prov., Phil. *D6 19
Lanark, Ont., Can. C8 41
Lanark, Ill. A4 58
Lanark, Scot. C5 4
Lanark, co., Ont., Can. C8 41
Lanark, co., Scot. *C5 4
Lanark Village, Fla. C2 54
Lancashire, co., Eng. *C5 4
Lancaster, Calif. E4 50
Lancaster, N.B., Can. D3 43
Lancaster, Ont., Can. B10 41
Lancaster, Eng. C5 4
Lancaster, Ky. C5 62
Lancaster, Mass. B4 65
Lancaster, Mo. A5 69
Lancaster, N.H. C4 73
Lancaster, N.Y. C2 75
Lancaster, Ohio G3 78
Lancaster, Pa. F9 81
Lancaster, S.C. B6 82
Lancaster, Tex. n10 84
Lancaster, Wis. F3 88
Lancaster, co., Nebr. D9 71
Lancaster, co., Pa. G9 81
Lancaster, co., S.C. B6 82
Lancaster, co., Va. C6 85
Lancaster Mills, S.C. *B6 82
Lancer, Ky. C7 62
Lanciano, It. C5 9
Lancut, Pol. C7 7
Landau an der Isar, Ger
Fed., Rep. of D6 6
Landau in der Pfalz, Ger.,
Fed. Rep. of D4 6
Landeck, Aus. E5 6
Lander, Wyo. D4 89
Lander, co., Nev. A3 72
Landerneau, Fr. C1 5
Landes, dept., Fr. *F3 5
Landing, N.J. *B3 74
Landis, N.C. B2 76
Landisville, Pa. *F11 81
Landivisiau, Fr. C1 5
Lando, S.C. B5 82
Landover Hills, Md. *C4 53
Landrum, S.C. A3 82

Landsberg, Ger., Fed. Rep. of D5 6
Landshut, Ger., Fed. Rep of D6 6
Landskrona, Swe. J5 11
Lane, co., Kans. D3 61
Lane, co., Oreg. D4 80
Lanesboro, Mass. A1 65
Lanesboro, Minn. G7 67
Lanett, Ala. C4 46
Langadhas, Grc. *B4 14
Langdale, Ala. C4 46
Langdon, N. Dak. B7 77
L'Ange-Gardien, Que., Can. n17 42
Langeloth, Pa. F1 81
Langenburg, Sask., Can. G5 39
Langenthal, Switz. E3 6
Langesund, Nor. H3, p27 11
Langford, B.C., Can. h12 37
Langhorne, Pa. F12 81
Langlade, co., Wis. C4 88
Langley, B.C., Can. f13 37
Langley, Ky. C7 62
Langley, S.C. D4 82
Langley Park, Md. *C3 53
Langnau in Emmental, Switz. E3 6
Langon, Fr. E3 5
Langreo, Sp. A3 8
Langres, Fr. D6 5
Langsa, Indon. E1, m11 19
Lang Son, Viet. *G13 16
Langstaff, Ont., Can. k15 41
Languedoc, former prov., Fr. F5 5
Lanham, Md. C4 53
Lanier, co., Ga. E3 55
Lannion, Fr. C2 5
Lannon, Wis. m11 88
L'Annonciation, Que., Can. C3 42
Lanoraie, Que., Can. D4 42
Lansdale, Pa. F11 81
Lansdowne, Md. B4 53
Lansdowne, Pa. G11, p20 81
Lansdowne House, Ont., Can. n18 41
L'Anse, Mich. B2 66
Lansford, Pa. E10 81
Lansing, Ill. B6, k9 58
Lansing, Iowa A6 60
Lansing, Kans. B8 61
Lansing, Mich. F6 66
Lansing, Ohio *C4 78
Lantana, Fla. F6 54
Lanús, Arg. *A5 28
Lanxi, China C3 18
Lanzhou, China D5 17
Laoag, Phil. B6 19
Laoighis, co., Ire. *D3 4
Lao Kay, Viet. *G13 16
Laon, Fr. C5 5
Laona, Wis. C5 88
La Oroya, Peru D2 31
Laos, country, Asia B2 19
Lapa, Braz. D3 30
La Palma, Sp. D2 8
La Pampa, prov., Arg. B3 28
La Paz, Arg. A4 28
La Paz, Bol. C2 29
La Paz, Col. A3 32
La Paz, Mex. C2 34
La Paz, co., Ariz. C1 48
La Paz, dept., Bol. C2 29
Lapeer, Mich. E7 66
Lapeer, co., Mich. E7 56
Lapel, Ind. D6 59
La Piedad Cavadas, Mex. m12 34
Laplace, La. h11 63
Lapland, reg., Eur. C12 11
La Plata, Arg. A5, g8 28
La Plata, Col. C2 32
La Plata, Md. C4 53
La Plata, Mo. A5 69
La Plata, co., Colo. D3 51
La Pocatière, Que., Can. B7 42
La Pocatiêwe, Que. Can. B7 42
La Pola, Sp. A3 8
La Porte, Ind. A4 59
La Porte, Tex. r14 84
La Porte, co., Ind. A4 59
La Porte City, Iowa B5 60
Lappeenranta, Fin. *G13 11
Lappi, prov., Fin. *D11 11
La Prairie, Que., Can. D4, q20 42
Laprairie, co., Que., Can. D4, q20 42
La Presa, Calif. *F5 50
La Providence, Que., Can. *D5 42
La Pryor, Tex. E3 84
La Puebla, Sp. C7 8
La Puebla de Montalbán, Sp. C3 8
La Puente, Calif. *F4 50
La Purisima, Mex. B2 34
La Quiaca, Arg. D2 29
L'Aquila, It. C4 9
Lara, state, Ven. A3 32
Larache, Mor. A3 22
Laramie, Wyo. E7 89
Laramie, co., Wyo. E8 89

Laramie, peak, Wyo.	D7	89
Larchmont, N.Y.	h13	75
Laredo, Sp.	A4	8
Laredo, Tex.	F3	84
Largo, Fla.	E4, p10	54
Lariat, Colo.	D4	51
La Ricamarie, Fr.	E6	5
Larimer, Pa.	*F2	81
Larimer, co., Colo.	A5	51
Larimore, N. Dak.	C8	77
Larino, It.	D5	9
La Rioja, Arg.	E2	29
La Rioja, prov., Arg.	E2	29
La Rioja, Cuba	D5	35
Lárisa (Larissa), Grc.	C4	14
Lárisa (Larissa), prov., Grc.	*C4	14
Lārkāna, Pak.	C4	20
Larkspur, Calif.	h7	50
Larksville, Pa.	n17	81
Larne, N. Ire.	C4	4
Larned, Kans.	D4	61
La Rochelle, Fr.	D3	5
La Roche-sur-Yon, Fr.	D3	5
La Roda, Sp.	C4	8
La Romana, Dom. Rep.	E9	35
La Ronge, Sask., Can.	B3	39
Larose, La.	E5	63
La Rue, Ohio	B2	78
La Rue, co., Ky.	C4	62
Larvik, Nor.	H4, p28	11
Larwill, Ind.	B6	59
La Salle, Que., Can.	q19	42
La Salle, Colo.	A6	51
La Salle, Ill.	B4	58
La Salle, co., Ill.	B5	58
La Salle, co. Tex.	E3	84
La Salle, par.,La.	C3	63
Las Animas, Colo.	C7	51
Las Animas, co., Colo.	D6	51
La Sarre, Que., Can.	o20	41
Lascahobas, Hai.	E8	35
L'Ascension, Que., Can.	A6	42
La Scie, Newf., Can.	D4	44
Las Conchas, Arg.	g7	28
Las Cruces, N. Mex.	C5	48
La Selle, peak, Hai.	E8	37
La Serena, Chile	E1	29
La Seyne -sur-Mer, Fr.	F6	5
Las Flores, Arg.	B5	28
La Sierra, Calif.	n14	50
Lasithi (Lasithion), prov., Grc.	*E5	14
Las Matas de Farfan, Dom. Rep.	*E8	35
La Solana, Sp.	C4	8
Las Palmas de Gran Canaria, Sp.	m14	8
Las Palmas, prov., Sp.	m14	8
La Spezia, It.	B2	9
Las Piedras, Ur.	E1	30
Lassen, co., Calif.	B3	50
Lassen, peak, Calif.	B3	50
L'Assomption, Que., Can.	D4	42
L'Assomption, co., Que., Can.	D4	42
Las Varillas, Arg.	A4	28
Las Vegas, Nev.	C4	72
Las Vegas, N. Mex.	B6, D7	48
Las Villas, prov., Cuba	C3	35
Lataunga, Ec.	B2	31
Latah, co., Idaho	C2	57
Latakia (Al Lādhiqīyah), Syr.	E10	14
Laterrière, Que., Can.	A6	42
La Teste-de-Bunch, Fr.	D3	5
Latham, N.Y.	*C7	75
Lathrop, Calif.	*D3	50
Lathrop, Mo.	B3	69
Lathrup Village, Mich.	*F7	66
Latimer, co.,Okla.	C6	79
Latina, It.	D4, k9	9
Latium, reg., It.	C4	9
Laton, Calif.	D4	50
Latour, peak, Idaho	B2	57
La Trinité, Mart.	I14	35
Latrobe, Pa.	F3	81
Latta, S.C.	C9	82
Lattimer Mines, Pa.	E10	81
Lattingtown, N.Y.	*E7	75
La Tuque, Que., Can.	B5	42
Latvia (S.S.R.), rep., Sov. Un.	C4	12
Lauderdale, Minn.	n12	67
Lauderdale, co., Ala.	A2	46
Lauderdale, co., Miss.	C5	68
Lauderdale, co., Tenn.	B2	83
Lauderdale-by-the-Sea, Fla.	*F6	54
Launceston, Austl.	o15	25
Launceston, Eng.	E4	4
La Unión, Chile	C5	28
La Unión, Col.	C2	32
La Unión, Mex.	D4, o13	34
La Unión, Peru	C2	31
La Unión, Sal.	E7	34
La Unión, Sp.	D5	8
La Union prov., Phil.	*B6	19
Laupheim, Ger., Fed. Rep. of	D4	6
Laurel, Del.	C6	53
Laurel, Fla.	E4	54
Laurel, Ind.	F7	59
Laurel, Md.	B4	53
Laurel, Miss.	D4	68
Laurel, Mont.	E8	70
Laurel, Nebr.	B8	71
Laurel, Va.	C5	85
Laurel, co., Ky.	C5	62
Laurel Bay, S.C.	G6	82
Laureldale, Pa.	F10	81
Laurel Gardens, Pa.	*E1	81
Laurel Heights, Wash.	*B3	86
Laurel Hill, N.C.	C3	76
Laurel Run, Pa.	n17	81
Laurel Springs, N.J.	*D3	74
Laurence Harbor, N.J.	C4	74
Laurens, Iowa	B3	60
Laurens, S.C.	B3	82
Laurens, co., Ga.	D3	55
Laurens, co., S.C.	C3	82
Laurentides, Que., Can.	D4	42
Laurier, Que., Can.	C6	42
Laurierville, Que., Can.	C6	42
Laurinburg, N.C.	C3	76
Laurium, Mich.	A2	66
Lausanne, Switz.	E3	6
Lautaro, Chile	B2	28
Lauzon, Que., Can.	C6, n17	42
Lavaca, co., Tex.	E4	84
Lava Hot Springs, Idaho	G6	57
Laval, Fr.	C3	5
Laval, Que., Can.	D4	42
Laval-des-Rapides, Que., Can.	*D4	42
La Vale, Md.	k13	53
Lavalleja, dept., Ur.	*E1	30
Lavallette, N.J.	D4	74
Laval-Ouest, Que., Can.	*p19	42
Lavaltrie, Que., Can.	D4	42
Lavaur, Fr.	F4	5
La Vega, Dom. Rep.	E8	35
Lavello, It.	D5	9
La Verne, Calif.	m13	50
Laverne, Okla.	A2	79
Laviania, Sp.	A3	8
La Victoria, Ven.	A4	32
La Villa, Tex.	*F4	84
La Vista, Ga.	C2	55
La Vista, Nebr.	g13	71
La Viuda, mtn., Peru	C2	31
Lavonia, Ga.	B3	55
Lavras da Mangabeira, Braz.	*D7	27
Lawn, Newf., Can.	E4	44
Lawndale, Calif.	*F4	50
Lawndale, N.C.	B1	76
Lawnside, N.J.	*D2	74
Lawton, Pa.	*F8	81
Lawrence, Ind.	E5, k10	59
Lawrence, Kans.	D9, m15	61
Lawrence, Mass.	A5	65
Lawrence, Mich.	F4	66
Lawrence, N.Y.	G2	52
Lawrence, Pa.	F1	81
Lawrence, co., Ala.	A2	46
Lawrence, co., Ark.	A4	49
Lawrence, co., Ill.	E6	58
Lawrence, co., Ind.	G4	59
Lawrence, co., Ky.	B7	62
Lawrence, co., Miss.	D3	68
Lawrence, co., Mo.	D4	69
Lawrence, co., Ohio	D3	78
Lawrence, co., Pa.	E1	81
Lawrence, co., S. Dak.	F2	77
Lawrence, co., Tenn.	B4	83
Lawrenceburg, Ind.	F8	59
Lawrenceburg, Ky.	B5	62
Lawrenceburg, Tenn.	B4	83
Lawrence Park, Pa.	B1	81
Lawrenceville, Ga.	C3, h9	55
Lawrenceville, Ill.	E6	58
Lawrenceville, N.J.	C3	74
Lawrenceville, Va.	D5	85
Lawson, Mo.	B3	69
Lawtey, Fla.	B4	54
Lawton, Mich.	F5	66
Lawton, Okla.	C3	79
Layland, W. Va.	n14	87
Layton, Utah	C2	72
Laytonville, Calif.	C2	50
Lazio, reg., It.	*D4	9
Lea, co., N. Mex.	C7	48
Leachville, Ark.	B5	49
Lead, S. Dak.	F2	77
Lead, mtn., Maine	D4	64
Leader, Sask., Can.	G1	39
Leadville, Colo.	B4	51
Leadwood, Mo.	D7	69
League City, Tex.	*E5	84
Leake, co., Miss.	C4	68
Leakey, Tex.	E3	84
Leakesville, Miss.	D5	68
Lealman, Fla.	p10	54
Leamington, Ont., Can.	E2	41
Leamington, Eng.	D6	4
Leaside, Ont., Can.	m15	41
Leatherhead, Eng.	m12	4
Leatherwood, Ky.	C6	62
Leavenworth, Kans.	C9, k16	61
Leavenworth, Wash.	B5	86
Leavenworth, co., Kans.	C8	61
Leavittsburg, Ohio	A5	78
Leawood, Kans.	D9	61
Lebanon, Ill.	E4	58
Lebanon, Ind.	D5	59
Lebanon, Ky.	C4	62
Lebanon, Mo.	D5	69
Lebanon, N.H.	D3	73
Lebanon, N.J.	B3	74
Lebanon, Ohio	G1	78
Lebanon, Oreg.	C4, k12	80
Lebanon, Pa.	F9	81
Lebanon, Tenn.	A5	83
Lebanon, Va.	f9	85
Lebanon, co., Pa.	F9	81
Lebanon, country, Asia	F10	14
Lebanon Junction, Ky.	C4	62
Lebedyan, Sov. Un.	E12	12
Le Blanc, Fr.	D4	5
Le Blanc-Mesnil, Fr.	g10	5
Lębork, Pol.	A4	7
Le Bourget, Fr.	g10	5
Le Bouscat, Fr.	E3	5
Lebrija, Sp.	D2	8
Le Cateau, Fr.	B5	5
Lecce, It.	D7	9
Lecco, It.	B2	9
Le Center, Minn.	F5	67
Le Chambon-Feugerolles, Fr.	E6	5
Le Chesnay, Fr.	g9	5
Le Claire, Iowa	C7, g11	60
Lecompte, La.	C3	63
Le Coteau, Fr.	D6	5
Le Creusot, Fr.	D6	5
Łęczyca, Pol.	B5	7
Ledgewood, N.J.	B3	74
Ledo, India	C10	20
Leduc, Alta, Can.	C4	38
Lee, Mass.	B1	65
Lee, co., Ala.	C4	46
Lee, co., Ark.	C5	49
Lee, co., Fla.	F5	54
Lee, co., Ga.	E2	55
Lee, co., Ill.	B4	58
Lee, co., Iowa	D6	60
Lee, co., Ky.	C6	62
Lee, co., Miss.	A5	68
Lee, co., N.C.	B3	76
Lee, co., S.C.	C7	82
Lee, co., Tex.	D4	84
Lee, co., Va.	f8	85
Leechburg, Pa.	E2	81
Leedon, Estates, Pa.	*G11	81
Leeds, Ala.	B3, f7	46
Leeds, Eng.	D6	4
Leeds, co., Ont., Can.	C8	41
Leelanau, co., Mich.	D5	66
Lee Park, Pa.	n17	81
Leer, Ger., Fed. Rep. of	B3	6
Leesburg, Fla.	D5	54
Leesburg, N.J.	E3	74
Leesburg, Ohio	C2	78
Leesburg, Va.	A5	85
Lee's Summit, Mo.	C3, k11	69
Leesville, La.	C2	63
Leeville, S.C.	D4	82
Leetes Island, Conn.	D6	52
Leeton, Austl.	G6	26
Leetonia, Ohio	B5	78
Leetsdale, Pa.	h13	81
Leeuwarden, Neth.	A6	5
Leeward, is., see Antigua, Montserrat, St. Kitts-Nevis-Anguilla, and Virgin Islands, (Br.), Br. dep., N.A.		
Leflore, co., Miss.	B3	68
Le Flore, co., Okla.	C7	79
Lefors, Tex.	B2	84
Le François, Mart.	I14	37
Leganés, Sp.	p17	8
Legaspi, Phil.	C6	19
Legion, Tex.	*E3	84
Legnano, It.	B2	9
Legnica, Pol.	C4	7
Lago, mtn., Wash.	A5	86
Le Grand, Calif.	D3	50
Le Harve, Fr.	C3	5
Lehi, Utah	A6, D2	72
Lehigh, Iowa	B3	60
Lehigh, co.,Pa.	E10	81
Lehigh Acres, Fla.	F5	54
Lehighton, Pa.	E10	81
Lehrte, Ger., Fed. Rep of	B4	6
Leiah, Pak.	B5	20
Leicester, Eng.	D6	4
Leicester, Mass.	B4	65
Leicester, co.,Eng.	*D6	4
Leiden, Neth.	A6	5
Leigh Creek, Austl.	F6	25
Leighton, Ala.	A2	46
Leinster, prov., Ire.	*D3	4
Leipsic, Ohio	A2	78
Leipzig, Ger. Dem. Rep	C6	6
Leira, Port.	C1	8
Leisure City, Fla.	s13	54
Leitchfield, Ky.	C3	62
Leith, Pa.	*G2	81
Leitrim, co., Ire.	*D3	4
Leiva, mtn., Col.	C3	32
Lejunior, Ky.	D6	62
Leksand, Swe.	G6	11
Leland, Miss.	B3	68
Leland Grove, Ill.	*D4	58
Le Locle, Switz.	E3	6
Le Mans, Fr.	D4	5
Le Marin, Mart.	I14	35
Le Mars, Iowa	B1	60
Lemay (Luxemburg), Mo.	*C7	69
Leme, Braz.	m8	30
Lemeta, Alsk.	*C10	47
Lemgo, Ger., Fed. Rep. of	B4	6
Lemhi, co., Idaho	E4	57
Lemmon, S. Dak.	E3	77
Lemon Grove, Calif.	F5, o15	50
Lemont, Ill.	B6, k9	58
Lemont, Pa.	E6	81
Lemoore, Calif.	D4	50
Le Moule, Guad.	H14	35
Le Moyen, Fr.	D3	63
Lemoyne, Pa.	*F8	81
Le Moyne, Que, Can.	*D4	42
Lena, Ill.	A4	58
Lena, Sp.	A3	8
Lena, riv.,Sov. Un.	C15	13
Lenawee, co., Mich.	G6	66
Lenexa, Kans.	D9	61
Leninabad, Sov. Un.	E9	13
Leninakan, Sov. Un.	B14	14
Leningrad, Sov. Un.	H14, s31	11
Leninogorsk, Sov. Un.	D11	3
Leninsk, Sov. Un.	G15	12
Leninsk-Kuznetskiy, Sov. Un.	D11	13
Lenkoran, Sov. Un.	F7	13
Lennox, Calif.	*E4	50
Lennox, S. Dak.	G9	77
Lennox & Addington, co., Ont., Can.	C7	41
Lennoxville, Que., Can.	D6	42
Lenoir, N.C.	B1	76
Lenoir, co., N.C.	B5	76
Lenoir City, Tenn.	D9	83
Lenox, Iowa	D3	60
Lenox, Mass.	B1	65
Lenox Avenue, N.Y.	*C4	75
Lenwood, Calif.	*E5	50
Leo, Ind.	B7	59
Leoben, Aus.	E7	6
Léogâne, Hai.	E7	35
Leominster, Mass.	A4	65
Leon, Iowa	D4	60
León (de los Aldamas), Mex.	C4, m13	34
León, Nic.	E7	34
León, Sp.	A3	8
Leon, co., Fla.	B2	54
Leon, co., Tex.	D5	84
León, prov., Sp.	*A3	8
León, reg., Sp.	B3	8
Leonard, Tex.	C4	84
Leonardo, N.J.	C4	74
Leonardtown, Md.	D4	53
Leonforte, It.	F5	9
Leonia, N.J.	h9	74
Leonora, Austl.	E3	25
Leopoldina, Braz.	C4, g6	30
Leoti, Kans.	D2	61
Leovo,Sov. Un.	H7	12
Lepanto, Ark.	B5	49
Lepe, Sp.	D2	8
Lepel, Sov. Un.	D7	12
Le Petit-Quevilly, Fr.	C4	5
L'Epiphanie, Que., Can.	D4	42
Le Puy -en-Velay, Fr.	E5	5
Le Raincy, Fr.	g11	5
Lercara Friddi, It.	F4	9
Lérida, Sp.	B6	8
Lérida, prov., Sp.	*B6	8
Le Roy, Ill.	C5	58
Le Roy, Kans.	D8	61
Le Roy, Minn.	G6	67
Le Roy, N.Y.	C3	75
Lerwick, Scot.	g10	4
Léry, Que., Can.	q19	42
Les Cayes, Hai.	E7	35
Les Eboulements, Que.,Can.	B7	42
Lesh, Alb.	B2	14
Leshan, China	F5	17
Leskovac, Yugo.	D5	10
Leslie, Mich.	F6	66
Leslie, co., Ky.	C6	62

Les Lilas, Fr. g10 5
Lesotho, country, Afr. F5 24
Les Sables-d'Olonne, Fr. D3 5
Lesser Antilles, is., W.I. B4 27
Lester, Pa. *G11 81
Lester, W. Va. n13 87
Lester Prairie, Minn. F4 67
Le Sueur, Minn. F5 67
Le Sueur, co., Minn. F5 67
Lesvos (Lesbos), prov., Grc. *C6 14
Leszno, Pol. C4 7
Letcher, co., Ky. C7 62
Le Teil, Fr. E6 5
Lethbridge, Alta., Can. E4, h8 38
Leticia, Col. D4 32
Letpadan, Bur. *H12 16
Le Tréport, Fr. B4 5
Leucadia, Calif. *F5 50
Leuser mtn., Indon. m11 19
Leuven, Bel. B6 5
Levack, Ont., Can. *A3 41
Levadhia, Grc. C4 14
Levallois-Perret, Fr. C4, g10 5
Level Green, Pa. *F2 81
Levelland, Tex. C1 84
Level Park, Mich. *F5 66
Leven, Scot. B5 4
Leverkusen, Ger., Fed. Rep. of ... *C3 6
Levice, Czech. D5 7
Levin, N.Z. N15 26
Lévis, Que., Can. C6, n17 42
Lévis, co., Que., Can. C6 42
Levittown, N.Y. *G2 52
Levittown, Pa. *F12 81
Levkas, Grc. C3 14
Levoća, Czech. D6 7
Levy, co., Fla. C4 54
Lewes, Del. C7 53
Lewes, Eng. E7 4
Lewis, co., Idaho C2 57
Lewis, co., Ky. B6 62
Lewis, co., Mo. A6 69
Lewis, co., N.Y. B5 75
Lewis, co., Tenn. B4 83
Lewis, co., Wash. C3 86
Lewis, co., W. Va. C4 87
Lewis and Clark, co., Mont. C4 70
Lewisburg, Ohio C1 78
Lewisburg, Pa. E8 81
Lewisburg, Tenn. B5 83
Lewisburg, W. Va. D4 87
Lewisdale, Md. *C3 53
Lewis Gardens, Va. *C5 85
Lewisporte, Newf., Can. D4 44
Lewis Run, Pa. C4 81
Lewiston, Idaho C1 57
Lewiston, Maine D2, f7 64
Lewiston, Mich. D6 66
Lewiston, Minn. G7 67
Lewiston, N.Y. B1 75
Lewiston, Utah A6 72
Lewiston Orchards, Idaho C1 57
Lewistown, Ill. C3 58
Lewistown, Mont. C7 70
Lewistown, Pa. E6 81
Lewisville, Ark. D2 49
Lewisville, Ind. F7 59
Lewisville, N.B., Can. C5 43
Lewisville, Tex. C4, m10 84
Lexington, Ill. C5 58
Lexington, Ky. B5 62
Lexington, Mass. B5, g11 65
Lexington, Mich. E8 66
Lexington, Minn. *E5 67
Lexington, Miss. B3 83
Lexington, Mo. B4 69
Lexington, Nebr. D6 71
Lexington, N.C. B2 76
Lexington, Ohio B3 78
Lexington, Okla. B4 79
Lexington, S.C. D5 82
Lexington, Tenn. B3 83
Lexington (Independent city), Va. .. C3 85
Lexington, co., S.C. D5 82
Lexington Park, Md. *D5 53
Leyte, prov., Phil. *C6 19
Leyte, isl., Phil. C6 19
Leyton, Eng. k12 4
Lézignan, Fr. F5 5
Lezirias, reg., Port. f10 8
Lgov, Sov. Un. F10 12
Lhasa, China F3 17
L'Hay-les-Roses, Fr. g10 5
Lianyungang, China E8 17
Liaoning, prov., China C9 17
Liaoyang, China C9 17
Liaoyuan, China C10 17
Líbano,Col. C3 32
Libby, Mont. B1 70
Liberal, Mo. D3 69
Liberec, Czech. C3 7
Liberia, country, Afr. *G3 22
Liberty, Ind. *E8 59

Liberty, Ky. C5 62
Liberty, Mo. B3, h11 69
Liberty, N.Y. D6 75
Liberty, N.C. B3 76
Liberty, Pa. *E1 81
Liberty, S.C. B2 82
Liberty, Tex. D5, q15 84
Liberty, co., Fla. B2 54
Liberty, co., Ga. E5 55
Liberty, co., Mont. B5 70
Liberty, co., Tex. D5 84
Liberty Acres, Calif. *E4 50
Liberty Center, Ohio A1 78
Liberty Corner, N.J. B3 74
Liberty Lake, Wash. g14 86
Liberty Plain, Mass. h12 65
Libertyville, Ill. A6, h9 58
Libourne, Fr. E3 5
Library, Pa. *E1 81
Libreville, Gabon H6 22
Libya, country, Afr. C2 32
Licata, It. F4 9
Lice, Tur. C13 14
Licking, Mo. D6 69
Licking, co., Ohio B3 78
Lida, Sov. Un. E5 12
Lidgerwood, N. Dak. D8 77
Lidice, Czech. C3, n17 7
Lidingö, Swe. H8, t36 11
Lidköping, Swe. H5 11
Liechtenstein, country, Eur. E4 6
Liège, Bel. B6 5
Liège, prov., Bel. B6 5
Lienz, Aus. E6 6
Liepāja, Sov. Un. C3 12
Lier, Bel. B6 5
Liestal, Switz. E3 6
Lighthouse Point, Fla. *F6 54
Lighthouse, point, Fla. C2 80
Lighthouse, point, Mich. C5 66
Ligonier, Ind. B6 59
Ligonier, Pa. F3 81
Liguria, pol. dist., It. *B2 9
Liguria, reg., It. B2 9
Lihue, Haw. B2 56
Likasi, Zaire C5 24
Likhoslavl, Sov. Un. C10 12
Likino-Dulevo, Sov. Un. n18 12
Lilbourn, Mo. E8 69
Lilesville, N.C. C2 76
Lille, Fr. B5 5
Lillehammer, Nor. G4 11
Lillestrom, Nor. H4, p29 11
Lillington, N.C. B4 76
Lillooet, B.C., Can. D7 37
Lillooet, range, B.C., Can. E7 37
Lilongwe, Malawi C6 24
Lima, N.Y. C3 75
Lima, Ohio B1 78
Lima, Peru D2 31
Lima, dept., Peru D2 31
Limbé, Hai. E7 35
Limburg, Ger., Fed. Rep. of C4 6
Limburg, prov., Bel. *B6 5
Limburg, prov., Neth. *B6 5
Limeil-Brévannes, Fr. h10 5
Limeira, Braz. m8 30
Limerick, Ire. D2 4
Limerick, co., Ire. *D2 4
Limestone, Maine B5 64
Limestone, co., Ala. A2 46
Limestone, co., Tex. D4 84
Limoeiro do Norte, Braz. *D7 27
Limoges, Fr. E4 5
Limon, Colo. B7 51
Limón, C.R. F8 34
Limón, prov., C.R. *I12 33
Limousin, former prov., Fr. E4 5
Limoux, Fr. F5 5
Linares, Chile B2 28
Linares, Col. C2 32
Linares, Mex. C5 34
Linares, Sp. C4 8
Linares, prov. Chile B2 28
Linch, Wyo. *C6 89
Linchuan, China F8 17
Lincoln, Arg. A4 28
Lincoln, Calif. *C3 50
Lincoln, Ont., Can. D5 41
Lincoln, Eng. D6 4
Lincoln, Ill. C4 58
Lincoln, Kans. C5 61
Lincoln, Maine C4 64
Lincoln, Mass. g10 65
Lincoln, Nebr. D9, h11 71
Lincoln, N.H. *C4 73
Lincoln, Pa. *E1 81
Lincoln, R.I. B11 52
Lisboa, see Lisbon, Port. C6 60
Lincoln, co., Ark. D4 49
Lincoln, co., Colo. C7 51
Lincoln, co., Eng. *D6 4
Lincoln, co., Ga. C4 55
Lincoln, co., Idaho G4 57

Lincoln, co., Kans. C5 61
Lincoln, co., Ky. C5 62
Lincoln, co., Maine D3 64
Lincoln, co., Minn. F2 67
Lincoln, co., Miss. D3 68
Lincoln, co., Mo. B6 69
Lincoln, co., Mont. B1 70
Lincoln, co., Nebr. D5 71
Lincoln, co., Nev. C4 72
Lincoln, co., N. Mex. C6 48
Lincoln, co., N.C. B1 76
Lincoln, co., Okla. B5 79
Lincoln, co., Oreg. C3 80
Lincoln, co., S. Dak. G9 77
Lincoln, co., Tenn. B5 83
Lincoln, co., Wash. B7 86
Lincoln, co., W. Va. C2 87
Lincoln, co., Wis. C4 88
Lincoln, co., Wyo. D2 89
Lincoln, par., La. B3 63
Lincoln Acres, Calif. o15 50
Lincoln City, Oreg. C3 80
Lincoln Heights, Ohio o13 78
Lincoln Highway, Nebr. *C5 71
Lincoln Park, Colo. *C5 51
Lincoln Park, Ga. D2 55
Lincoln Park, Mich. p15 66
Lincoln Park, N.J. B4 74
Lincoln Park, N.Y. *D6 75
Lincoln Park, Pa. *F9 81
Lincolnton, Ga. C4 55
Lincolnton, N.C. B1 76
Lincoln Village, Calif. *D3 50
Lincoln Village, Ohio *C3 78
Lincolnwood, Ill. h9 58
Lincroft, N.J. C4 74
Lind, Wash. D7 86
Linda, Calif. *C3 50
Lindale, Ga. B1 55
Lindale, Tex. C5 84
Lindau, Ger., Fed. Rep. of E4 6
Linden, Ala. C2 46
Linden, Ind. D4 59
Linden, Mich. F7 66
Linden, N.J. k8 74
Linden, Tenn. B4 83
Linden, Tex. C5 84
Lindenhurst, Ill. h8 58
Lindenhurst, N.Y. *G3 52
Lindenwold, N.J. D3 74
Lindesberg, Swe. H6 11
Lindi, Tan. B7 24
Lindon, Utah *A6 72
Lindsay, Calif. D4 50
Lindsay, Ont., Can. C6 41
Lindsay, Okla. C4 79
Lindsborg, Kans. D6 61
Lindstrom, Minn. E6 67
Linesville, Pa. C1 81
Lineville, Ala. B4 46
Linfen, China D7 17
Lingayen, Phil. B6 19
Lingen, Ger., Fed. Rep. of B3 6
Linglestown, Pa. F8 81
Lingyuan, China C8 17
Linhai, China F9 17
Linière, Que., Can. C7 42
Linköping, Swe. H6 11
Linn, Mo. C6 69
Linn, co., Iowa B6 60
Linn, co., Kans. D9 61
Linn, co., Mo. B4 69
Linn, co., Oreg. C4 80
Linntown, Pa. *E7 81
Lino Lakes, Minn. *E5 67
Linqing, China D8 17
Lins, Braz. C3 30
Linthicum Heights, Md. B4, h11 53
Linton, Ind. F3 59
Linton, N. Dak. D5 77
Linwood, Mass. B4 65
Linwood, Mich. E7 66
Linwood, N.J. E3 74
Linwood, Pa. *G11 81
Linworth, Ohio k10 78
Linxia, China D5 17
Linyi, China D8 17
Linz, Aus. D7 6
Lipa, Phil. C6, p13 19
Lipari, It. E5 9
Lipetsk, Sov. Un. E12 12
Lipkany, Sov. Un. A8 10
Lipno, Pol. B5 7
Lipova, Rom. B5 10
Lippstadt, Ger., Fed. Rep. of B3, g7 6
Lipscomb, Ala. B3, g7 46
Lipscomb, co., Tex. A2 84
Liria, Sp. C5 8
Lisboa, see Lisbon, Port. C6 60
Lisbon, Iowa C6 60
Lisbon, Maine D2, f7 64
Lisbon, N.H. C4 73
Lisbon, N. Dak. D8 77
Lisbon, Ohio B5 78

Lisbon (Lisboa), Port. C1, f9 8
Lisbon Falls, Maine D5, f7 64
Lisburn, N. Ire. C3 4
Lishu, China E2 18
Lisichansk, Sov. Un. q21 12
Lisieux, Fr. C4 5
Lisle, Ill. k8 58
L'Islet, co., Que., Can. B7 42
L'Islet-sur-Mer, Que.,Can. B7 42
L'isletville, Que., Can. B7 42
Lisman, Ala. C1 46
Lismore, Austl. E9 25
Listowel, Ont., Can. D4 41
Litchfield, Conn. B4 52
Litchfield, Ill. D4 58
Litchfield, Mich. F6 66
Litchfield, Minn. E4 67
Litchfield, co., Conn. B3 52
Litchfield Park, Ariz. D1 48
Lithgow, Austl. F9 25
Lithonia, Ga. C2, h8 55
Lithuania (S.S.R) rep., Sov. Un. ... D4 12
Lititz, Pa. F9 81
Litókhoron, Grc. *B4 14
Litoměřice, Czech. C3 7
Litomyšl, Czech. D7 7
Little, mtn., Wyo. E5 89
Little Belt, mtn., Mont. D6 70
Little Canada, Minn. *E5 67
Little Catalina, Newf. D4 44
Little Chute, Wis. D5, h9 88
Little Current, Ont., Can. B3 41
Little Falls, Minn. E4 67
Little Falls, N.J. B4 74
Little Falls, N.Y. B6 75
Little Ferry, N.J. h8 74
Littlefield, Tex. C1 84
Littlefork, Minn. B5 67
Little River, co., Ark. D1 49
Little Rock, Ark. C3, k10 49
Little Rock, river, Iowa A1 70
Little Silver, N.J. C4 74
Littletown, Pa. G7 81
Littleton, Colo. B6 51
Littleton, Mass. f9 65
Littleton, N.H. C4 73
Littleton, N.C. A5 76
Littleton Common, Mass. f10 65
Little Valley, N.Y. C2 75
Liuhe, China E2 18
Liuzhou, China G6 17
Lively, Ont., Can. A3 41
Live Oak, Calif. C3 50
Live Oak, Fla. B4 54
Live Oak, Co., Tex. E3 84
Livermore, Calif. h9 50
Livermore, Ky. C2 62
Livermore, peak, Tex. o12 84
Livermore Falls, Maine D2 64
Liverpool, N.S., Can. E5 43
Liverpool, Eng. D5 4
Liverpool, N.Y. B4 75
Liverpool, Pa. E7 81
Livingston, Ala. C1 46
Livingston, Calif. D3 50
Livingston, Guat. D7 34
Livingston, Ill. D5, g10 63
Livingston, La. D5, g10 63
Livingston, Mont. E6 70
Livingston, N.J. B4 74
Livingston, Tenn. C8 83
Livingston, Tex. D5 84
Livingston, Zambia D5 24
Livingston, co.,Ill. C5 58
Livingston, co., Ky. e9 62
Livingston, co., Mich. F6 66
Livingston, co., Mo. B4 69
Livingston, co., N.Y. C3 75
Livingston, par., La. D5 63
Livingston Manor, N.Y. D6 75
Livno, Yugo. D3 10
Livny, Sov. Un. E11 12
Livonia, Mich. F7 66
Livonia, N.Y. C3 75
Livorno (Leghorn), It. C3 9
Livry-Gargan, Fr. g11 5
Lizard Head, peak, Wyo. D3 89
Ljubljana, Yugo. B2 10
Ljungby, Swe. I5 11
Llandrindod Wells, Wales D5 4
Llandudno, Wales D5 4
Llanelli, Wales E4 4
Llanes, Sp. A3 8
Llano, Tex. D3 84
Llano, co.,Tex. D3 84
Llanquihue, prov.,Chile C2 28
Lloyd, N.Y. B7 62
Lloyd Harbor, N.Y. *G3 52
Lloydminster, Alta., Sask., Can. ... D1 39
Lloyd Palce, Va. *D6 85
Lluchmayor, Sp. C7 8
Llullaillaco, vol., Chile D2 29
Löbau, Ger. Dem. Rep. C7 6

Lobería, Arg. B5 28
Lobito, Arg. C2 24
Lobos, Arg. B5, g7 28
Locarno, Switz. E4 6
Lochdale, B.C., Can. f12 37
Lochearn, Md. *B4 53
Loches, Fr. D4 5
Loch Raven, Md. *B4 53
Lockeport, N.S.,Can. F4 43
Lockhart, Tex. E4, h8 84
Lock Haven, Pa. D7 81
Lockland, Ohio o13 78
Lockney, Tex. B2 84
Lockport, Ill. B5, k8 58
Lockport, La. F5, k10 62
Lockport, N.Y. B2 75
Lockwood, Mo. D4 69
Locumba, Peru E3 31
Locust, N.J. C4 74
Locust Grove, Okla. A6 79
Locust Valley, N.Y. F2 52
Lod (Lydda), Isr. C2, h5 15
Lodève, Fr. F5 5
Lodeynoye Pole, Sov. Un. A9 12
Lodge Grass, Mont. E9 70
Lodhrān, Pak. C5 20
Lodi, Calif. C3 50
Lodi, N.J. h8 74
Lodi, Ohio A3 78
Lodi, Wis. E4 88
Łódź, Pol. *C5 7
Loei,Thai. *B2 19
Logan, Iowa C2 60
Logan, Kans. C4 61
Logan, Ohio C3 78
Logan, Utah A6 72
Logan, W. Va. D3, n12 87
Logan, co.,Ark. B2 49
Logan, co., Colo. A7 51
Logan, co., Ill. C4 58
Logan, co., Kans. D2 61
Logan, co., Ky. D3 62
Logan, co., Nebr. C5 71
Logan, co., N. Dak. D6 77
Logan, co., Ohio B2 78
Logan, co., Okla. B4 79
Logan, co., W. Va. D3 87
Logan, mtn, Yukon, Can. D6 36
Logansport, Ind. C5 59
Logansport, La. C2 63
Loganville, Ga. C3 55
Loggieville, N.C., Can. B4 43
Logroño, Sp. A4 8
Logroño, prov., Sp. *A4 8
Logrosán, Sp. C3 8
Lohārdaga, India D7 20
Lohrville, Iowa B3 60
Loire, dept., Fr. *E6 5
Loire, riv., Fr. D3 5
Loire-atlantique, dept., Fr. *D3 5
Loiret, dept., Fr. *D4 5
Loir-et-Cher, dept., Fr. *D4 5
Loja, Ec. B2 31
Loja, Sp. D3 8
Loja, prov.,Ec. B2 31
Lokhvitsa, Sov. Un. F9 12
Lom, Bul. D6 10
Loma Linda, Calif. *E5 50
Lombard, Ill. k8 58
Lombardia, reg., It. *B2 9
Lombardy, reg.,It. B2 9
Lomé, Togo G5 22
Lometa, Tex. D3 84
Lomira, Wis. E5 88
Lomita, Calif. *E4 50
Lomas de Zamora, Arg. A5, g7 28
Lomonosov, Sov. Un. s30 11
Lompoc, Calif. E3 50
Łomza, Pol. B7 7
Lonaconing, Md. k13 53
London, Ont., Can. E3 41
London, Eng. E6, k12 4
London, Ky. C5 62
London, Ohio C2 78
London, Greater, co., Eng. *E6 4
Londonderry, N. Ire. C3 4
Londonderry, co., N. Ire. *C3 4
London Mills, Ill. C3 58
Londrina, Braz. C2 30
Lone Oak, Ky. e9 62
Lone Pine, Calif. D4 50
Lone Star, Tex. *C5 84
Lone Wolf, Okla. C2 79
Lone Tree, Iowa C6 60
Long, co., Ga. E5 55
Long Beach, Calif. F4, n12 50
Long Beach, Ind. A4 59
Long Beach, Miss. E4, f7 68
Long Beach,*N.Y. E7, n15 75
Long Beach, Wash. C1 86
Longboat Key, Fla. q10 54
Long Branch, Ont., Can. m14 41
Long Branch, N.J. C5 74

Long Creek, mtn., Wyo D4 89
Longford, co., Ire. *D3 4
Longhurst, N.C. A4 76
Long Island, isl, N.Y. n15 75
Long Lake, Ill. h8 58
Long Lake, Minn. *F5 67
Long Lake, N.Y. B6 75
Longleaf, La. C3 63
Long Leaf Park, N.C. *C5 76
Longmeadow, Mass. B2 65
Longmont, Colo. A5 51
Long Pond, Newf., Can. E5 44
Longport, N.J. E13 74
Long Prairie, Minn. E4 67
Longreach, Austl. D7 25
Lourdes, Newf., Can. D2 44
Long Range, mts., Newf., Can. ..E2, k10 44
Longueuil, Que.,Can. D4 42
Long Valley, N.J. B3 74
Longview, Alta, Can. D3 38
Long View, Ky. C4 62
Long View, N.C. B1 76
Longview, Tex. C5 84
Longview, Wash. C3 86
Longwood, Fla. *D4 54
Longwood Park, N.C. *B3 76
Longwy, Fr. C6 5
Long Xuyen, Viet. *C3 19
Lonoke, Ark. C4, h11 49
Lonoke, co., Ark. C4 49
Lons-le-Saunier, Fr. D6 5
Loogootee, Ind. G4 59
Lookout, Ky. C7 62
Lookout Mountain, Tenn. h11 83
Loon Lake, mtn. N.Y. f10 75
Lora, Sp. D3 8
Lorado, W. Va. D3, n12 87
Lorain, Ohio A3 78
Lorain, Pa. *E4 81
Lorain, co., Ohio A3 78
Loraine, Tex. C2 84
Lorca, Sp. D5 8
Lordsburg, N. Mex. C4 84
Loreauville, La. D4 63
Lorena, Braz. G3 30
Lorenzo, Tex. C2 84
Loreto, Mex. B2 34
Loreto, Par. D4 29
Loreto, dept., Peru C3 31
Loretteville, Que., Can. C6, n17 42
Loretto, Pa. F4 81
Loretto, Tenn. B4 83
Lorica, Col. B2 32
Lorient, Fr. D2 5
L'Orignal, Ont., Can. B10 41
Loris, S.C. C10 82
Lorne, N.B., Can. D3 43
Lorneville, N.B., Can. B3 43
Lörrach, Ger., Fed. Rep. of E3 6
Lorraine, former prov., Fr. C6 5
Los Alamitos, Calif. *F5 50
Los Alamos, N. Mex. B5 48
Los Alamos, co., N. Mex. B5 48
Los Altos, Calif. k8 50
Los Altos Hills, Calif. *D2 50
Los Andes, Chile A2 28
Los Angeles, Calif. E4, m12 50
Los Angeles, Chile B2 28
Los Angeles, co., Calif. E4 50
Los Banos, Calif. D3 50
Los Barrios, Sp. D3 8
Los Fresnos, Tex. F4 84
Los Gatos, Calif. D2 50
Los Mochis, Mex. B3 34
Los Nietos, Calif. *E4 50
Los Palacios, Cuba C2 35
Los Reyes de Salgado, Mex. ...D4, n12 34
Los Rios, prov., Ec. B2 31
Los Tequés, Ven. A4 32
Lost Nation, Iowa C7 60
Lot, dept., Fr. *E4 5
Lota, Chile B2 28
Lotbinière, co., Que. Can. C6 42
Lot-et-Garonne, dept., Fr. *E4 5
Lothair, Ky. C6 62
Lott, Tex. D4 84
Loudon, Tenn. D9 83
Loudon, co., Tenn. D9 30
Loudonville, N.Y. *D6 75
Loudonville, Ohio B3 78
Loudoun, co., Va. B5 85
Loudun, Fr. D4 5
Loughborough, Eng. D6 4
Louisa, Ky. B7 62
Louisa, co., Iowa C6 60
Louisa, co., Va. C5 85
Louisbourg, N.S., Can. D10 43
Louisburg, Kans. D9 61
Louisburg, N.C. A4 76
Louise, N.S. D8 43
Louisiana, Mo. B6 69
Louisiana, state, U.S.   63
Louis Trichardt, S. Afr. E5 24

Louisville, Que., Can. C5 42
Louisville, Colo. B5 51
Louisville, Ga. C4 55
Louisville, Ill. E5 58
Louisville, Ky. B4, g11 62
Louisville, Miss. B4 68
Louisville, Nebr. D9, h12 71
Louisville, Ohio B4 78
Loulé, Port. D1 8
Louny, Czech. C2 7
Loup, co., Nebr. C6 71
Loup, riv., Nebr. C8 71
Loup City, Nebr. C7 71
Lourdes, Fr. F4 5
Lourenço Marques, see
   Maputo, Moz.
Loures, Port. f9 8
Louth, Eng. D7 4
Louth, co., Ire. *C3 4
Loutrá Aidhipsoú Grc. C4 14
Louvain, see Leuven, Bel.
Louviers, Fr. C4 5
Love, co., Okla. D4 79
Lovech, Bul. D7 10
Lovejoy,Ill. *E3 58
Loveland, Colo. A5 51
Loveland, Ohio C1, n12 78
Loveland Park, Ohio C1, n13 78
Lovell, Wyo. B4 89
Lovelock, Nev. A2 72
Lovely, Ky. C7 62
Loves Park, Ill. A4 58
Lovilia, Iowa C5 60
Loving, N. Mex. C6 48
Loving, co., Tex. o13 84
Lovington, Ill. D5 58
Lovington, N. Mex. C7 48
Lowden, Iowa C7 60
Lowell, Ind. B3 59
Lowell, Mass. A5, f10 65
Lowell, Mich. F5 66
Lowell, N.C. B1 76
Lowell, Ohio C4 78
Lowell, Wash. *B3 86
Lowellville, Ohio A5 78
Lower Burrell, Pa. *F2 81
Lower Caraquet, N.B., Can. *B5 43
Lower Hutt, N.Z. *N15 26
Lower Paia, Haw C5 56
Lower West Pubnico, N.S., Can. ...F4 43
Lowestoft, Eng. D7 4
Łowicz, Pol. B5 7
Lowmoore, Va. C3 85
Lowndes, co., Ala. C3 46
Lowndes, co., Ga. F3 55
Lowndes, co., Miss. B5 68
Lowville, N.Y. B5 75
Loxton, Austl. G3 26
Loyal, Wis. D3 88
Loyalhanna, Pa. *F2 81
Loyall, Ky. D6 62
Loyalton, Calif. C3 50
Loyalty is., Pac. O. H8 2
Lozère, dept., Fr. *E5 5
Loznica, Yugo. C4 10
Lozovatka, Sov. Un. G9 12
Luanda, Ang. B2 24
Luang Prabang, Laos B2 19
Luanshya, Zambia C5 24
Lubań, Pol. C3 7
Lubango, Ang. C2 24
Lubartów, Pol. C7 7
Lübben, Ger. C6 6
Lubbock, Tex. C2 84
Lubbock, co., Tex. C2 84
Lubec, Maine D6 64
Lübeck, Ger., Fed. Rep. of B5 6
Lublin, Pol. C7 7
Lubliniec, Pol. C5 7
Lubny, Sov. Un. F9 12
Lubrin, Sp. D4 8
Lubumbashi (Elisabethville)
   Zaire C5 24
Lubutu, Zaire I3 23
Lucan, Ont., Can. D3 41
Lucas, Ohio B3 78
Lucas, co., Iowa C4 60
Lucas, co., Ohio A2 78
Lucasville, Ohio D3 78
Lucca, It. C3 9
Luce, co., Mich. B5 66
Lucedale, Miss. E5 68
Lucena, Phil. C6, p13 19
Lucenec, Czech. D5 7
Lucera, It. D5 9
Lucerne, see Luzern, Switz.
Lucernemines, Pa. E3 81
Luceville, Que. Can. A9 42
Luck, Wis. C1 88
Luckau, Ger. C6 6
Luckenwalde, Ger. Dem. Rep. B6 6

Luckey, Ohio A2, f7 78
Lucknow, Ont., Can. D3 41
Lucknow, India C7 20
Lucknow, Pa. *F8 81
Loçon, Fr. D3 5
Lucy, La. h10 63
Lüda, China D9 17
Lüdenscheid, Ger., Fed. Rep. of ..C3 6
Ludhiana, India B6 20
Ludington, Mich. E4 66
Ludlam, Fla. *G6 54
Ludlow, Eng. D5 4
Ludlow, Ky. h13 62
Ludlow, Mass. B3 65
Ludlow, Pa. C4 81
Ludlow, Vt. E2 73
Ludowici, Ga. E5 55
Ludvika, Swe. G6 11
Ludwigsburg, Ger., Fed. Rep. of ..D4 6
Ludwigshafen, Ger., Fed. Rep. of .D4 6
Ludwigslust, Ger. Dem. Rep. B5 6
Lueders, Tex. C3 84
Lufkin, Tex. D5 84
Luga, Sov. Un. B7 12
Lugano, Switz. E4 6
Lugansk, see Voroshilovgrad
   Sov. Un.
Lugo, It. B3 9
Lugo, Sp. A2 8
Lugo, prov., Sp. *A2 8
Lugoff, S.C. C6 82
Lugoj, Rom. C5 10
Luján, Arg. g7 28
Lukovit, Bul. D7 10
Luków, Pol. C7 7
Lukoyanov, Sov. Un. D15 12
Luleå, Swe. E10 11
Luling, La. k11 63
Luling, Tex. E4, h8 84
Luluabourg, see Kananga, Zaire
Lumber City, Ga. E4 55
Lumberport, W.Va. B4, k10 87
Lumberton, Miss. D4 68
Lumberton, N.J. D3 74
Lumberton, N.C. C4 76
Lumby, B.C., Can. D8 37
Lumpkin, B.C., Can. D8 37
Lumpkin, Ga. D2 55
Lumpkin, co., Ga. B2 55
Lumsden, Sask., Can. G3 39
Luna, co., N. Mex. C5 48
Luna Pier (Lakewood), Mich. G7 66
Lund, Swe. J5 11
Lundale, W. Va. D3, n12 87
Lundar, Man., Can. D2 40
Lüneburg, Ger., Fed. Rep. of B5 6
Lunel, Fr. F6 5
Lunenburg, N.S., Can. E5 43
Lunenburg, Mass. A4 65
Lunenburg, co., N.S., Can. E5 43
Lunenburg, co., Va. D4 85
Lunéville, Fr. C7 5
Lunino, Sov. Un. E15 12
Luohe, China E7 17
Luoyang, China E7 17
Lupeni, Rom. C6 10
Luque, Par. E4 29
Luray, Va. B4 85
Lure, Fr. D7 5
Luragn, N. Ire. C3 4
Lusaka, Zambia D5 24
Lusambo, Zaire I2 23
Luseland, Sask.,Can. E1 39
Lushan, China F8 17
Lüshun (Port Arthur), China D9 17
Lusk, Wyo. D8 89
Lutcher, La. D5, h10 63
Lutesville, Mo. D8 69
Lutherville-Timonium, Md. B4 53
Luton, Eng. E6 4
Lutsk, Sov. Un. F5 12
Lutugino, Sov. Un. q22 12
Lutz, Fla. D4 54
Luverne, Ala. D3 46
Luverne, Minn. G2 67
Luwuk, Indon. F6 19
Luxembourg, Lux. C7 5
Luxembourg, country, Eur. C7 5
Luxembourg, prov., Bel. *C6 5
Luxembourg, Wis. D6 88
Luxeuil-les-Bains, Fr. D7 5
Luxor, see Al Uqsur, Eg.
Luxora, Ark. B6 49
Luzern, Switz. *E4 6
Luzern, canton, Switz. *E4 6
Luzerne, Pa. n17 81
Luzerne, co., Pa. D9 81
Luzhou, China F6 17
Luzon, isl., Phil. B6 19
Lvov, Sov. Un. G5 12
Lyaskovets, Bul. D7 10
Lycoming, co., Pa. D7 81
Lydia Mills, S.C. *C4 82

Lydick, Ind. *A5 59
Lyell, mtn., B.C., Can............... D9 37
Lyford, Tex.......................... F4 84
Lykens, Pa. E8 81
Lyle, Minn. G6 67
Lyman, Nebr. C1 71
Lyman, S.C. B3 82
Lyman, co., S. Dak. G6 77
Lyman, N.Y. G2 52
Lynbrook, N.Y. G2 52
Lynch, Ky. D7 62
Lynchburg, Ohio C2 78
Lynchburgh (Independent
  City), Va. C3 85
Lynden, Wash. A3 86

Lyndhurst, N.J. h8 74
Lyndhurst, Ohio g9 78
Lyndon, Kans. D8 61
Lyndon, Ky. g11 62
Lyndonville, N.Y. B2 75
Lyndonville, Vt. B3 73
Lyndora, Pa. E2 81
Lynn, Ind. D8 59
Lynn, Mass. B6, g12 65
Lynn, co., Tex. C2 84
Lynnfield, Mass. f11 65
Lynn Garden, Tenn. C11 83
Lynn Haven, Fla. u16 54
Lynn Lake, Man............... A1, f7 40

Lynville, Ky. f9 62
Lynnwood, Pa. *D9 81
Lynnwood, Wash. *B3 36
Lynwood, Calif. n12 50
Lyon, Fr. E6 4
Lyon, co., Iowa A1 60
Lyon, co., Kans. D7 61
Lyon, co., Ky. C1 62
Lyon, co., Minn. F3 67
Lyon, co., Nev. B2 72
Lyon Mountain, N.Y. f11 75
Lyonnais, former prov.,Fr. E6 5
Lyons, Ga. D4 55
Lyons, Ill. k9 58

Lyons, Ind. G3 59
Lyons, Kans. D5 61
Lyons, Mich. F6 66
Lyons, Nebr. C9 71
Lyons, N.Y. B4 75
Lyons Falls, N.Y. B5 75
Lysá, Czech. n18 7
Lysaya Gora, Sov. Un. G8 12
Lysekil, Swe. H4 11
Lyster Station, Que, Can. C6 42
Lysva, Sov. Un. D8 13
Lytle, Tex. E3 84
Lyubar, Sov. Un. G6 12
Lyubertsy, Sov. Un. N17 12

M

Ma'alot Tarshiha, Isr. A3 15
Maastricht, Neth. B6 5
Mabank, Tex......................... C4 84
Mabel, Minn. G7 67
Mableton, Ga. h7 55
Mabscott, W. Va. D3, n13 87
Mabton, Wash. C5 86
McAdam, N.B., Can. D2 43
McAdenville, N.C.................... *B1 76
McAdoo, Pa. E9 81
Macaé, Braz. C4 30
McAlester, Okla. C6 79
McAllen, Tex. F3 84
Macamic, Que. *o20 41
Macao, Port. dep., Asia G7 17
Macapá, Braz. C5 27
McArthur, Ohio C3 78
Macas, Ec. D3 27
Macau, Braz. D7 27
McBee, S.C. C7 82
McBride, B.C., Can. C7 37
McCall, Idaho E2 57
McCamey, Tex. D1 84
McCarthy, mtn., Mont. E4 70
McCaysville, Ga. B2 55
McChesneytown, Pa. *F2 81
McClain, co., Okla. C4 79
McCleary, Wash. B2 86
MacClenny, Fla. B4 54
Macclesfield, Eng. D5 4
McCloud, Calif...................... B2 50
McClure, Ohio A2 78
McClure, Pa. E7 81
McColl, S.C. B8 82
McComas, W. Va. D3 87
McComb, Miss. D3 68
McComb, Ohio A2 78
McCone, co., Mont. C11 70
McConnellsburg, Pa. G6 81
McConnelsville, Ohio C4 78
McCook, Nebr. D5 71
McCook, co., S. Dak. G8 77
McCormick, S.C. D3 82
McCormick, co., S.C. D3 82
McCracken, co., Ky. e9 62
McCreary, Man., Can. D2 40
McCreary, co., Ky. D5 62
McCrory, Ark. B4 49
McCulloch, co., Tex. D3 84
McCurtain, Okla. B7 79
McCurtain, co., Okla. C7 79
McDermott, Ohio D2 78
McDonald, Ohio A5 78
McDonald, Pa....................... k13 81
MacDonald, W. Va. D3, D7 87
McDonald, co., Mo. E3 69
McDonough, Ga. C2 55
McDonough, co., Ill. C3 58
McDowell, co., N.C. f10 76
McDowell, co., W. Va. D3 87
McDuffie, co., Ga. C4 55
Macedon, N.Y. B3 75
Macedonia, reg., Eur. *B4 14
Macedonia, rep., Yugo. *D5 10
Maceió, Braz. D7 27
Macerata, It. C4 9
McEwen, Tenn. A4 83
McFarland, Calif. E4 50
McFarland, Wis. E4 88
McGehee, Ark. *D4 49

McGill, Nev. B4 72
MacGillicuddy's Reeks, mts., Ire. .. E2 4
McGrann, Pa. *E2 81
McGraw, N.Y. C4 75
MacGregor, Man., Can. E2 40
McGregor, Iowa A6 60
McGregor, Tex...................... D4 84
McGuffey, Ohio B2 78
McGuire, mtn., Idaho D4 57
Machado, Braz. C3, k9 30
Machala, Ec. B2 31
McHenry, Ill. A5, h8 58
McHenry, co., Ill. A5 58
McHenry, co., N. Dak. B5 77
Machias, Maine D5 64
Machida, Jap. *n18 18
Machilipatnam (Bandar),
  India E7 20
Măcin, Rom. C9 10
McIntosh, Minn. C3 67
McIntosh, co., Ga. E5 55
McIntosh, co., N. Dak. D6 77
McIntosh, co., Okla. B6 79
Mack, Ohio *D2 78
Mackay, Austl. D8 25
Mackay, Idaho F5 57
McKean, co., Pa. C4 81
McKeesport, Pa. F4, r14 81
McKees Rocks, Pa. F1, k13 81
McKenney, Va. D5 85
McKenzie, Tenn. A3 83
McKenzie, co., N. Dak. C2 77
Mackenzie, dist., N.W.
  Ter., Can. D11 36
McKenzie, mts., Can. C7 33
McKenzie, riv., N.W. Ter., Can. C8 36
Mackinac, co., Mich. B5 66
Mackinac Island, Mich. C6 66
Mackinaw, Ill. C4 58
Mackinaw City, Mich. C6 66
McKinley, Minn. C6 67
McKinley, co., N. Mex. B4 48
McKinley, mtn., Alsk. C9 47
McKinley Heights, Ohio *A5 78
McKinleyville, Calif. B1 50
McKinney, Tex. C4 84
McKittrick Summit, mtn., Calif. E4 50
Macklin, Sask., Can. E1 39
McKnight, Pa. *E1 81
McKnownville, N.Y. *C7 75
McLaughlin, S. Dak. E5 77
McLean, Tex. B2 84
McLean, Va. g12 85
McLean, co., Ill. C5 58
McLean, co., Ky. C2 62
McLean, co., N. Dak. C4 77
McLean, mtn., Maine A4 64
McLeansboro, Ill. E5 58
McLennan, Alta., Can. B2 38
McLennan, co., Tex. D4 84
McLeod, co., Minn. F4 67
McLeod Lake, B.C., Can. B6, n18 37
McLoud, Okla. B4 79
McLoughlin, mtn., Oreg. E4 80
McLouth, Kans. C8, k15 61
McMasterville, Que., Can. *D4 42
McMechen, W. Va. B4, g8 87
McMillan Manor, Calif. *E4 50
McMinn, co., Tenn. D9 83
McMinnville, Oreg............... B3, h11 80

McMinnville, Tenn. D8 83
McMullen, co., Tex. E3 84
McMurray, Alta., Can. A5, f8 38
McNair, Tex. E5 84
McNairy, co., Tenn. B3 83
McNary, Ariz. B4 48
McNeill, mtn., B.C., Can. B2 37
Macomb, Ill. C3 58
Macomb, co., Mich. F8 66
Macon, Fr. D6 5
Macon, Ga. D3 55
Macon, Ill. D5 58
Macon, Miss. B5 68
Macon, Mo. B5 69
Macon, co., Ala. C4 46
Macon, co., Ga. D2 55
Macon, co., Ill. D5 58
Macon, co., Mo. B5 69
Macon, co., N.C. f9 76
Macon, co., Tenn. C7 83
Macoupin, co., Ill. D4 58
McPherson, Kans. D6 61
McPherson, co., Kans. D6 61
McPherson, co., Nebr. C4 71
McPherson, co., S. Dak. E6 77
McRae, Ga. D4 55
McRoberts, Ky. C7 62
McSherrystown, Pa. G7 81
Macksville, Kans. E5 61
MacTier, Ont., Can. B5 41
Macungie, Pa. E10 81
McVeigh, Ky. C7 62
Ma'dabā, Jordan C3 15
Madagascar, country, Afr. E9 24
Madawaska, Maine A4 64
Madawaska, co., N.B., Can. B1 43
Madeira, Ohio o13 78
Madeira Beach, Fla. *E4 54
Madeira Is., reg., Port. B1 22
Madelia, Minn. F4 67
Madera, Calif. D3 50
Madera, Mex. B3 34
Madera, co., Calif. D4 50
Madgaon, India E5 20
Madhya Pradesh, state, India D6 20
Madill, Okla. C5 79
Madīnat ash Sha'b, P.D.R. of
  Yem............................... G4 15
Madison, Ala. A3 46
Madison, Ala. C3 46
Madison, Conn. D6 52
Madison, Fla. B3 54
Madison, Ga. C3 55
Madison, Ill. E3 58
Madison, Ind. G7 59
Madison, Kans. D7 61
Madison, Maine D3 64
Madison, Minn. E2 67
Madison, Mo. B5 69
Madison, Nebr. C8 71
Madison, N.J. B4 74
Madison, N.C. A3 76
Madison, Ohio A4 78
Madison, S. Dak. G9 77
Madison, W. Va. C3, m12 87
Madison, Wis. E4 88
Madison, co., Ala. A3 46
Madison, co., Ark. B2 49
Madison, co., Fla. B3 54

Madison, co., Ga. B3 55
Madison, co., Idaho F7 57
Madison, co., Ill. E4 58
Madison, co., Ind. D6 59
Madison, co., Iowa C3 60
Madison, co., Ky. C5 62
Madison, co., Miss. C4 68
Madison, co., Mo. D7 69
Madison, co., Mont. E4 70
Madison, co., Nebr. C8 71
Madison, co., N.Y. C5 75
Madison, co., N.C. f10 76
Madison, co., Ohio C2 78
Madison, co., Tenn. B3 83
Madison, co., Tex. D5 84
Madison, co., Va. B4 85
Madison, par., La. B4 63
Madison Heights, Mich. o15 66
Madison Heights, Va. C3 85
Madisonville, Ky. C2 62
Madisonville, La. D5, h11 63
Madisonville, Tenn. D9 83
Madisonville, Tex. D5 84
Madium, Indon. *G4 19
Madoc, Ont., Can. C7 41
Madras, India F7 20
Madras, Oreg. C5 80
Madre de Dios, dept., Peru D3 31
Madrid, Iowa C4, e8 60
Madrid, N.Y. f9 75
Madrid, Sp. B4, p17 8
Madrid, prov., Sp. *B4 8
Madridejos, Phil. *C6 19
Madridejos, Sp. C4 8
Madurai, India G6 20
Maebashi, Jap. H9, m18 18
Maeser, Utah A7 72
Mafeking, S. Afr. F5 24
Mafra, Braz. D3 30
Magadan, Sov. Un. D18 13
Magallanes, prov., Chile E2, h11 28
Magangué, Col. B3 32
Magdalena, Mex. A2 34
Magdalena, N. Mex. B5 48
Magdalena, dept., Col. A3 32
Magdalena, riv., Col. C3 27
Magdalena Contreras, Mex. h9 34
Magdalen Islands, co.,
  Que., Can. B8 43
Magdeburg, Ger. Dem. Rep. B5 6
Magé, Braz. h6 30
Magee, Miss. D4 68
Magelang, Indon. G4 19
Magenta, It. B2 9
Maglie, It. D7 9
Magna, Utah A5, C2 72
Magnitogorsk, Sov. Un. D8 13
Magnolia, Ark. D2 49
Magnolia, Miss. D3 68
Magnolia, N.J. D2 74
Magnolia, N.C. C4 76
Magnolia, Ohio B4 78
Magoffin, co., Ky. C6 62
Magog, Que., Can. D5 42
Magrath, Alta., Can. E4 38
Magwe, Bur. D9 20
Mahameru, mtn., Indon. G4 19
Mahanoy City, Pa. E9 81
Maharashtra, state, India D5 20
Mahaska, co., Iowa C5 60

Mahbūbnagar, India E6 20
Mahe, India F6 20
Mahnomen, Minn. C3 67
Mahnomen, co., Minn. C2 67
Mahogany, mtn., Oreg. D9 80
Mahomet, Ill. C5 58
Mahón, Sp. C8 8
Mahone Bay, N.S., Can. E5 43
Mahoning, co., Ohio B5 78
Mahopac, N.Y. D7, m15 75
Mahtomedi, Minn. E7 67
Mahwah, N.J. A4 74
Maiden, N.C. B1 76
Maidstone, Sask., Can. D1 39
Maidstone, Eng. E7 4
Maiduguri, Nig. F7 22
Maimana, Afg. A3 20
Maine, former prov., Fr. C3 5
Maine, state, U.S. 64
Maine-et-Loire, dept., Fr. *D3 5
Maintirano, Mad. D8 24
Main Topsail, mtn., Newf., Can. ... D3 44
Mainz, Ger., Fed. Rep. of C4 6
Maipú, Arg. B5 28
Maiquetía, Ven. A4 32
Maisonette, N.B., Can. B4 43
Maisons-Alfort, Fr. g10 5
Maisons-Laffitte, Fr. g9 5
Maitland, Austl. F9 25
Maitland (Lake Maitland), Fla. *D5 54
Maize, Kans. g12 61
Maizuru, Jap. I7, n14 18
Majagual, Col. B3 32
Majestic, Ky. C7 62
Major, co., Okla. A3 79
Makaha, Haw. g9 56
Makajanga, Mad. D9 24
Makarov Shirutoru, Sov. Un. B11 18
Makarska, Yugo. D3 10
Makasar, see Ujung Pandang, Indon.
Makati, Phil. *o3 19
Makawao, Haw. C5 56
Makaweli, Haw. B2 56
Makeyevka, Sov. Un. G11, q20 12
Makhachkala, Sov. Un. E7 13
Makhlata, Bul. D7 10
Makurazaki, Jap. K5 18
Makurdi, Nig. G6 22
Malabar, Fla. D6 54
Malabo, Equat. Gui. H6 22
Malacca, state, Mala. E2 19
Malad City, Idaho G6 57
Málaga, Col. B3 32
Malaga, N.J. D2 74
Málaga, Sp. D3 8
Málaga, prov., Sp. *D3 8
Malagasy Republic, see
  Madagascar, country, Afr.
Malakāl, Sud. G4 23
Malakoff, Fr. g10 5
Malakoff, Tex. C4 84
Malang, Indon. G4 19
Malanje, Ang. B3 24
Malartic, Que., Can. k11 42
Malatya, Tur. C12 14
Malawi, country, Afr. C6 24
Malaya Vishera, Sov. Un. B9 12
Malaybalay, Phil. *D7 19
Malaysia, country, Asia E4 19
Malbork, Pol. A5 7
Malchin, Ger. Dem. Rep. B6 6
Malden, Mass. B5, g11 65
Malden, Mo. E8 69
Malden, W. Va. m12 87
Maldives, country, Asia G5 20
Maldonado, Ur. E2 30
Maldonado, dept., Ur. *E2 30
Malegaon, India *D5 20
Māler Kotla, India B6 20
Malheur, co., Oreg. D9 80
Mali, country, Afr. F3 22
Malibu, Calif. m11 50
Malin, Oreg. E5 80
Malinec, Czech. D5 7
Malita, Phil. *D7 19
Malkara, Tur. B6 14
Mallacoota, prov., Chile B2 28
Mallory, W. Va. *D3 87
Mallow, Ire. D2 4
Malmédy, Bel. B7 5
Malmö, Swe. J5 11
Malmöhus, co., Swe. *J5 11
Maloarkhangelsk, Sov. Un. E11 12
Malolos, Phil. o13 19
Malone, Fla. B1 54
Malone, N.Y. f10 75
Maloyaroslavets, Sov. Un. D11 12
Malta, Mont. B9 70
Malta, Ohio C4 78
Malta, country, Eur. A7 22
Malton, Eng. C6 4
Malvern, Ark. C3, g8 49

Malvern, Iowa D2 60
Malvern, Ohio B4 78
Malvern, Pa. F10, o19 81
Malverne, N.Y. *G2 52
Mamanguape, Braz. *D7 27
Mamaroneck, N.Y. h13 75
Mamba, Jap. m17 18
Mamers, Fr. C4 5
Mammoth, Ariz. C3 48
Mammoth, W. Va. C3, m13 87
Mamou, Guinea F2 22
Mamou, La. D3 63
Man, W. Va. D3, n12 87
Man, Isle of, see Isle of
  Man, Br. dep., Eur.
Manabi, prov., Ec. B1 31
Manacor, Sp. C7 8
Manado, Indon. E6 19
Managua, Nic. E7 34
Manahawkin, N.J. D4 74
Manakara, Mad. E9 24
Manama, Bahrain D5 15
Mananjary, Mad. E9 24
Manasquan, N.J. C4 74
Manassas, Va. B5, g12 85
Manassas Park, Va. *B5 85
Manatee, co., Fla. E4 54
Manatí, P.R. *G11 35
Manaus, Braz. D4 27
Manawa, Wis. D5 88
Mancelona, Mich. D5 66
Mancha, reg., Sp. C4 8
Mancha Real, Sp. D4 8
Manchaug, Mass. B4 65
Manche, dept., Fr. *C3 5
Manchester, Conn. B6 52
Manchester, Eng. D5 4
Manchester, Ga. D2 55
Manchester, Iowa B6 60
Manchester, Ky. C6 62
Manchester, Md. A4 53
Manchester, Mass. A6, f12 65
Manchester, Mich. F6 66
Manchester, Mo. f12 69
Manchester, N.H. F5 73
Manchester, N.Y. C3 75
Manchester, Ohio D2 78
Manchester, Pa. F8 81
Manchester, Tenn. B5 83
Manchester Depot, Vt. E1 73
Manchuria, reg., China B10 17
Mandalay, Bur. D10 20
Mandan, N. Dak. D5 77
Mandasor, India D6 20
Manderson, Wyo. B5 89
Mandeville, Jam. E5 35
Mandeville, La. D5, h11 63
Mandurah, Austl. F2 25
Manduria, It. D6 9
Māndvi, India D4 20
Manfalūt, Eg. C4 23
Manfredonia, It. D5 9
Mangalore, India F5 20
Mangham, La. B4 63
Mangum, Okla. C2 79
Manhasset, N.Y. F2 52
Manhattan, Ill. *B6 58
Manhattan, Kans. C7 61
Manhattan, N.Y. *B5 75
Manhattan Beach, Calif. n12 50
Manheim, Pa. F9 81
Manhuaçu, Braz. C4 30
Manila, Ark. B5 49
Manila, Phil. o13 19
Manilla, Iowa C2 60
Manipur, state, India D9 20
Manisa, Tur. C6 14
Manistee, Mich. D4 66
Manistee, co., Mich. D4 66
Manistique, Mich. C4 66
Manito, Ill. C4 58
Manitoba, prov., Can. 40
Manitoba, lake, Man., Can. D2 40
Manitou, Man., Can. E2 40
Manitou Beach, Mich. *G6 66
Manitoulin, dist., Ont., Can. B2 41
Manitou Springs, Colo. C6 51
Manitowoc, Wis. D6, h10 88
Manitowoc, co., Wis. D6 88
Maniwaki, Que., Can. C2 42
Manizales, col. B2 32
Manjimup, Austl. F2 25
Mankato, Kans. C5 61
Mankato, Minn. F5 67
Manlius, N.Y. C5 75
Manlléu, Sp. A7 8
Manly, Iowa A4 60
Mannar, Sri Lanka G6 20
Mannheim, Ger., Fed. Rep. of D4 6
Manning, Alta., Can. A2 38
Manning, Iowa C2 60
Manning, S.C. D7 82
Mannington, W. Va. B4, h10 87

Mannum, Austl. G2 26
Mannville, Alta., Can. C5 38
Manomet, Mass. C6 65
Manomet, hill, Mass. C6 65
Manono, Zaire B5 24
Manor, Pa. *F2 81
Manorhaven, N.Y. *E7 75
Manosque, Fr. F6 5
Manresa, Sp. B6 8
Manseau, Que., Can. C5 42
Mansfield, Eng. D6 4
Mansfield Ill. C5 58
Mansfield, La. B2 63
Mansfield, Mass. B5 65
Mansfield, Ohio B3 78
Mansfield, Pa. C7 81
Mansfield, Tex. n9 84
Mansfield, mtn., Vt. B2 73
Mansfield Southeast, Ohio *B3 78
Manson, Iowa B3 60
Mansura, La. C3 63
Manta, Ec. B1 31
Manteca, Calif. D3 50
Manteno, Ill. B6 58
Manti, Utah B6 72
Manton, Mich. D5 66
Mantova, It. D3 9
Mantua, N.J. D2 74
Mantua, Ohio A4 78
Manuel Benavides, Mex. B4 34
Manuels, Newf., Can. *E5 44
Manukau, N.Z. *L15 26
Manville, N.J. B3 74
Manville, R.I. B11 52
Many, La. C2 63
Manzanares, Sp. C4 8
Manzanillo, Cuba D5 35
Manzanillo, Mex. D4, n11 34
Manzhouli, China B8 17
Maoming, China G7 17
Mapastepec, Mex. D6 34
Maple, Ont., Can. k14 41
Maple Bluff, Wis. E4 88
Maple Creek, Sask., Can. H1 39
Maple Heights, Ohio h9 78
Maple Lake, Minn. E4 67
Maple Lane, Ind. *A5 59
Maple Mount, Ky. C2 62
Maple Plain, Minn. m11 67
Maple Rapids, Mich. E6 66
Maple Shade, N.J. D2 74
Mapleton, Iowa B2 60
Mapleton, Maine B4 64
Mapleton, Minn. G5 67
Mapleton, Oreg. C3 80
Mapleton, Utah D2 72
Maplewood, La. D2 63
Maplewood, Minn. m12 67
Maplewood, Mo. f13 69
Maplewood, N.J. B4 74
Maplewood, N.Y. *C7 75
Maplewood Park, Pa. *G11 81
Maputo, Moz. F6 24
Maquoketa, Iowa B7 60
Marabá, Braz. D6 27
Maracaibo, Ven. A3 32
Maracaju, Braz. *F5 27
Maracay, Ven. A4 32
Maradi, Niger F6 22
Marāgheh, Iran B4 15
Maragogipe, Braz. *E7 27
Marana, Ariz. C3 48
Maranguape, Braz. *D7 27
Maranhão, state, Braz. *D6 27
Marañón, riv., Peru B2 31
Maraş, Tur. D11 14
Marathon, Fla. H5 54
Marathon, Iowa B3 60
Marathon, N.Y. C4 75
Marathon, Tex. D1, o13 84
Marathon, Wis. D4 88
Marathon, co., Wis. D4 88
Maravatío de Ocampo, Mex. n13 34
Mara Vista, Mass. C6 65
Marawi, Sud. E4 23
Marbella, Sp. D3 8
Marble, Minn. C5 67
Marble Cliff, Ohio m10 78
Marble Falls, Tex. D3 84
Marblehead, Mass. B6, f12 65
Marblehead, Ohio A3 78
Marbleton, Que., Can. D6 42
Marburg, Ger., Fed. Rep. of C4 6
Marbury, Md. C3 53
Marceline, Mo. B5 69
Marcellus, Mich. F5 66
Marcellus, N.Y. C4 75
Marche, former prov., Fr. D4 5
Marche, pol. dist., It. *C4 9
Marchena, Sp. D3 8
Marches, reg., It. C4 9

Marcola, Oreg. C4 80
Marcos Juarez, Arg. A4 28
Marcus, Iowa B2 60
Marcus Hook, Pa. G11 81
Marcy, mtn., N.Y. A7 75
Mardān, Pak. B5 20
Mar Del Plata, Arg. B5 28
Mardin, Tur. D13 14
Marechal Deodoro, Braz. *D7 27
Marengo, Ill. A5 58
Marengo, Ind. H5 59
Marengo, Iowa C5 60
Marengo, co., Ala. C2 46
Marenisco, Mich. n12 66
Marfa, Tex. o12 84
Margaret, Ala. B3 46
Margaretville, N.Y. C6 75
Margate, Eng. E7 4
Margate, Fla. *F6 54
Margate City, N.J. E3 74
Margelan, Sov. Un. E10 13
Margherita, mtn., Ug. H3 23
Maria la Baja, col. A2 32
Mariana, is., Pac. O. E6 2
Marianna, Ark. C5 49
Marianna, Fla. B1 54
Marianna, Pa. *F1 81
Mariánské Lázně, Czech. D2 7
Maribo, Den. *J4 11
Maribor, Yugo. B2 10
Maricopa, Calif. E4 50
Maricopa, co., Ariz. C2 48
Mariemont, Ohio o13 78
Marienville, Pa. D3 81
Maries, co., Mo. C6 69
Mariestad, Swe. H5 11
Marietta, Ga. C2, h7 55
Marietta, Ohio C4 78
Marietta, Okla. D4 79
Marietta, Pa. F8 81
Marietta, S.C. A2 82
Marieville, Que., Can. D4 42
Marília, Braz. C3 30
Marin, Sp. A1 8
Marin, co., Calif. C2 50
Marin City, Calif. *C2 50
Marinduque, prov., Phil. *C6 19
Marine, Ill. E4 58
Marine City, Mich. F8 66
Marinette, Wis. C6 88
Marinette, co., Wis. C5 88
Maringouin, La. D4 63
Marinha Grande, Port. C1 8
Marino, It. H9 9
Marion, Ala. C2 46
Marion, Ill. F5 58
Marion, Ind. C6 59
Marion, Iowa B6 60
Marion, Kans. D6 61
Marion, Ky. e9 62
Marion, La. B3 63
Marion, Mass. C6 65
Marion, Mich. D5 66
Marion, N.Y. B3 75
Marion, N.C. B1, f10 76
Marion, Ohio B2 78
Marion, S.C. C9 82
Marion, Va. f10 85
Marion, Wis. D5 88
Marion, co., Ala. A2 46
Marion, co., Ark. A3 49
Marion, co., Fla. C4 54
Marion, co., Ga. D2 55
Marion, co., Ill. E5 58
Marion, co., Ind. E5 59
Marion, co., Iowa C4 60
Marion, co., Kans. D6 61
Marion, co., Ky. C4 62
Marion, co., Miss. D4 68
Marion, co., Mo. B6 69
Marion, co., Ohio B2 78
Marion, co., Oreg. C4 80
Marion, co., S.C. C9 82
Marion, co., Tenn. D8 83
Marion, co., Tex. C5 84
Marion, co., W. Va. B4 87
Marion Heights, Pa. *D8 81
Marionville, Mo. D4 69
Mariposa, Calif. D4 50
Mariposa, co., Calif. D3 50
Marissa, Ill. E4 58
Maris Town, Miss. C3 68
Mariupol, see Zhdanov, Sov. Un.
Marka, Som. H6 23
Markdale, Ont., Can. C4 41
Marked Tree, Ark. B5 49
Markesan, Wis. E5 88
Markham, Ont., Can. D5, k15 41
Markham, Ill. k9 58
Markham, mtn., Ant. L7 2
Markle, Ind. C7 59
Markovka, Sov. Un. G12 12
Marks, Miss. A3 68

Marksville, La. C3 63
Marktredwitz, Ger., Fed.
Rep. of C6 6
Marlbank, Ont., Can. C7 41
Marlboro, Mass. B4, g9 65
Marlboro, N.J. C4 74
Marlboro, N.Y. D6 75
Marlboro, co., S.C. B8 82
Marlborough, N.H. F3 73
Marlette, Mich. E7 66
Marley, Md. B4 53
Marlin, Tex. D4 84
Marlinton, W. Va. C4 87
Marlow, Okla. C4 79
Marlowe, W.Va. B7 87
Marlton, N.J. D3 74
Marmande, Fr. E4 5
Marmet, W. Va. C3, m12 87
Marmora, Ont., Can. C7 41
Marmora, N.J. E3 74
Marmora, peak, It. D2 9
Marne, Mich. E5 66
Marne, dept., Fr. *C6 5
Maroa, Ill. C5 58
Maroantsetra, Mad. D9 24
Maromokotro, mtn., Mad. C9 24
Maroochydore-Mooloolaba,
Austl. C9 26
Maroua, Cam. F7 22
Marovoay, Mad. D9 24
Marquesas, is., Fr. Polynesia G11 2
Marquette, Kans. D6 61
Marquette, Mich. B3 66
Marquette, co., Mich. B3 66
Marquette, co., Wis. E4 88
Marquette Heights, Ill. C4 58
Marrakech, Mor. B3 22
Marrero, La. k11 63
Marromeu, Moz. D7 24
Mars, Pa. E1 81
Mars, hill, Maine g7 64
Marsala, It. F4 9
Marsa Matruh, Eg. B3 23
Marseille, Fr. F6 5
Marseilles, Ill. B5 58
Marshall, Ark. B3 49
Marshall, Ill. D6 58
Marshall, Mich. F6 66
Marshall, Minn. F3 67
Marshall, Mo. B4 69
Marshall, N.C. F10 76
Marshall, Tex. C5 84
Marshall, Va. B5 85
Marshall, Wis. E4 88
Marshall, co., Ala. A3 46
Marshall, co., Ill. B4 58
Marshall, co., Ind. B5 59
Marshall, co., Iowa C4 60
Marshall, co., Kans. C7 61
Marshall, co., Ky. f9 62
Marshall, co., Minn. B2 67
Marshall, co., Miss. A4 68
Marshall, co., Okla. C5 79
Marshall, co., S. Dak. E8 77
Marshall, co., Tenn. B5 83
Marshall, co., W. Va. B4 87
Marshallberg, N.C. C6 76
Marshall Northeast, Tex. *C5 84
Marshallton, Del. A6 35
Marshallton, Pa. *D8 81
Marshalltown, Iowa B5 60
Marshallville, Ga. D3 55
Marshallville, Ohio B4 78
Marshfield, Mass. B6, h13 65
Marshfield, Mo. D5 69
Marshfield, Wis. D3 88
Marshfield Hills, Mass. B6, h13 65
Mars Hill, Ind. E5, m10 59
Mars Hill, Maine B5 64
Mars Hill, N.C. f10 76
Marshville, N.C. C2 76
Marsing, Idaho F2 57
Marston, Mo. E8 69
Mart, Tex. D4 84
Martel, Que., Can. A6 42
Martí, Cuba D5 35
Martigues, Fr. F6 5
Martin, Ky. C7 62
Martin, Mich. F5 66
Martin, S. Dak. G4 77
Martin, Tenn. A3 83
Martin, co., Fla. E6 54
Martin, co., Ind. G4 59
Martin, co., Ky. C7 62
Martin, co., Minn. G4 67
Martin, co., N.C. B5 76
Martin, co., Tex. C2 84
Martina Franca, It. D6 9
Martinez, Calif. C2, h8 50
Martinez, Ga. C4 55
Martinique, Fr. dep., N.A. I14 35
Martinsburg, Pa. F5 81
Martinsburg, W. Va. B7 87

Martins Creek, Pa. B2 81
Martins Ferry, Ohio B5 78
Martinsville, Ill. D6 58
Martinsville, Ind. F5 59
Martinsville, N.J. B3 74
Martinsville (Independent City),
Va. D3 85
Martos, Sp. D4 8
Marudi, Mala. E5 19
Maruf, Afg. B4 20
Marugame, Jap. I6 18
Marvell, Ark. C5 49
Mary, Sov. Un. F9 13
Maryborough, Austl. E9 25
Maryborough, Austl. G7 25
Maryfield, Sask., Can. H5 39
Maryland, state, U.S. 53
Maryland Heights, Mo. f13 69
Maryport, Eng. C5 4
Marys, peak, Oreg. C3 80
Mary's Harbour, Newf., Can. B4 44
Marystown, Newf., Can. E4 44
Marysville, Calif. C3 50
Marysville, B.C., Can. E10 37
Marysville, Kans. C7 61
Marysville, Mich. F8 66
Marysville, Ohio B2 78
Marysville, Pa. F8 81
Marysville, Wash. A3 86
Maryvale, Ariz. *C2 48
Maryville, Mo. A3 69
Maryville, Tenn. D10, n14 83
Masan, Kor. I4 18
Masaya, Nic. E7 34
Masbate, Phil. C6 19
Masbate, prov., Phil. *H7 19
Mascot, Tenn. C10, m14 83
Mascota, Mex. m11 34
Mascouche, Que., Can. D4 42
Mascoutah, Ill. E4 58
Mashhad (Meshed), Iran B6 15
Masindi, Ug. H4 23
Masisea, Peru C3 31
Masjed, Soleyman, Iran C4 15
Maskinongé, Que., Can. C4 42
Maskinongé, co., Que., Can. C4 42
Mason, Mich. F6 66
Mason, Ohio C1, n13 78
Mason, Tex. D3 84
Mason, W. Va. B2 87
Mason, co., Ill. C4 58
Mason, co., Ky. B6 62
Mason, co., Mich. D4 66
Mason, co., Tex. D3 84
Mason, co., Wash. B2 86
Mason, co., W. Va. C3 87
Mason City, Ill. C4 58
Mason City, Iowa A4 60
Masontown, Pa. G2 81
Masontown, W. Va. B5 87
Mass, Mich. B1, m12 66
Massa, It. B3 9
Massac, co., Ill. F5 58
Massachusetts, state, U.S. 65
Massaemett, mtn., Mass. A2 65
Massafra, It. D6 9
Massa Marittima, It. C3 9
Massanutten, mtn., Va. B4 85
Massapequa, N.Y. G3 52
Massapequa Park, N.Y. *E7 75
Massawa, Eth. E5 23
Massena, N.Y. f10 75
Masset, B.C., Can. C1 37
Massey, Ont., Can. A2 41
Massillon, Ohio B4 78
Massive, mtn., Colo. B4 51
Masson, Que., Can. D2 42
Masterton, N.Z. N15 26
Mastic, N.Y. *n15 75
Mastic Beach, N.Y. *F4 52
Mastung, Pak. C4 20
Masuda, Jap. I5 18
Masuria, reg., Pol. B6 7
Masury, Ohio A5 78
Masvingo, Zimb. E6 24
Matachewan, Ont. Can. p19 41
Matadi, Zaire B2 24
Matador, Tex. C2 84
Matagalpa, Nic. E7 34
Matagorda, co., Tex. E5 84
Matamoras, Pa. D12 81
Matamoros, Mex. *B5 34
Matamoros de la Laguna, Mex. B4 34
Matane, Que., Can. G20 36
Matane, co., Que., Can. *G20 36
Matanzas, Cuba C3 35
Matanzas, prov., Cuba C3 35
Matapedia, co., Que., Can. *G20 36
Matara, Sri Lanka G7 20
Mataram, Indon. G5 19
Mataró, Sp. B7 8
Matawan, N.J. C4 74
Matehuala, Mex. C4 34

Matera, It. D6 9
Mátészalka, Hung. B6 10
Mateur, Tun. F2 9
Matewan, W. Va. D2 87
Matfield, Mass. B6 65
Mather, Pa. G1 81
Mather, peak, Wyo. B5 89
Mathews, co., Va. C6 85
Mathis, Tex. E4 84
Mathura, India C6 20
Matoaca, Va. n18 85
Matoaka, W. Va. D3 87
Mato Grosso, state, Braz. B1 30
Matozinhos, Port. B1 8
Matrāh, Om. E6 15
Matsudo, Jap. *I9 18
Matsue, Jap. I6 18
Matsuida, Jap. m17 18
Matsumae, Jap. F10 18
Matsumoto, Jap. H9, m16 18
Matsuyama, Jap. J6 18
Matsuzaka, Jap. I8, o15 18
Matsuzaki, Jap. o17 18
Mattapoisett, Mass. C6 65
Mattawa, Ont., Can. A6, p20 41
Mattawamkeag, Maine C4 64
Matterhorn, mtn., Switz. E3 6
Matteson, Ill. k9 58
Matthews, Ind. D7 59
Matthews, N.C. B2 76
Matthews, mtn. Mo. D7 69
Matthew Town, Ba. D7 35
Mattituck, N.Y. n16 75
Mattoon, Ill. D5 58
Mattydale, N.Y. *B4 75
Matucana, Peru D2 31
Matun, Afg. B4 20
Maturín, Ven. B5 32
Maubeuge, Fr. B5 5
Maubin, Bur. *E10 20
Mauch Chunk, see Jim Thorpe, Pa.
Maud, Ohio C1, n13 78
Maud, Okla. B5 79
Maud, Tex. C5 84
Maugansville, Md. A2 52
Maugerville, N.B., Can. D3 43
Maui (incl. Kalawao), co., Haw. B6 56
Maui, isl., Haw. C6 56
Mauldin, S.C. *B3 82
Maule, prov., Chile B2 28
Maumee, Ohio A2, e6 78
Mauna Kea, vol., Haw. D6 56
Maunaloa, Haw. B4 56
Mauna Loa, vol., Haw. D6 56
Mauritania, country, Afr. E2 22
Mauritius, country, Afr. *H24 2
Maury, co., Tenn. B4 83
Mauston, Wis. E3 88
Maverick, co., Tex. E2 84
Maxcanú, Mex. C7 34
Max Meadows, Va. D2 85
Maxton, N.C. C3 76
Maxwell, Iowa C4, e9 60
May, mtn., Alta., Can. B1 38
Mayagüez, P.R. G11 35
Mayari, Cuba D6 35
Maybee, Mich. F7 66
Maybeury, W.Va. *D3 87
Maybole, Scot. C4 4
Maybrook, N.Y. D6 75
Mayen, Ger., Fed. Rep of C3 6
Mayenne, Fr. C3 5
Mayenne, dept., Fr. *C3 5
Mayer, Ariz. B2 48
Mayerthorpe, Alta., Can. C3 38
Mayes, co., Okla. A6 79
Mayesville, S.C. D7 82
Mayfield, Ky. f9 62
Mayfield, N.Y. B6 75
Mayfield, Ohio *A4 78
Mayfield, Pa. C11 81
Mayfield Heights, Ohio A4 78
Mayking, Ky. C7 62
Maynard, Iowa B6 60
Maynard, Mass. B5, g10 65
Mayo, Yukon, Can. D6 36
Mayo, Fla. B3 54
Mayo, Md. C4 53
Mayo, S.C. A4 82
Mayo, co., Ire. *D2 4
Mayodan, N.C. A3 76
Mayon, vol., Phil. C6 19
Mayotte, Fr. ter., Afr. C9 24
May Pen, Jam. F5 35
Mays Landing, N.J. E3 74
Maysville, Ky. B6 62
Maysville, Mo. B3 69
Maysville, N.C. C5 76
Maysville, Okla. C4 79
Mayville, Mich. E7 66
Mayville, N.J. E3 74

Mayville, N.Y. C1 75
Mayville, N. Dak. C8 77
Mayville, Wis. E5 88
Maywood, Calif. *F4 50
Maywood, Ill. k9 58
Maywood, N.J. h8 74
Maywood, N.Y. *C7 75
Mazamet, Fr. F5 5
Mazapil, Mex. C4 34
Mazara Del Vallo, It. F4 9
Mazar-I-Sharif, Afg. A4 20
Mazarrón, Sp. D5 8
Mazatenango, Guat. E6 34
Mazatlán, Mex. C3 34
Mazomanie, Wis. E4 88
Mazon, Ill. B5 58
Mazzarino, It. F5 9
Mbabane, Swaz. F6 24
Mbala, Zambia B6 24
Mbalmayo, Cam. H7 22
Mbandaka, Zaire H1 23
Mbanza-Ngungu, Zaire B2 24
Mbeya, Tan. B6 24
Mead, Wash. B8, g14 86
Meade, Kans. E3 61
Meade, co., Kans. E3 61
Meade, co., Ky. C3 62
Meade, co., S. Dak. F3 77
Meade, peak, Idaho G7 57
Meaderville, Mont. *D4 70
Meadowbrook, Ind. *B7 59
Meadowbrook, W. Va. k10 87
Meadow Lake, Sask., Can. n7 39
Meadow Lands, Pa. F1 81
Meadow Park, Fla. F6 54
Meadowview, Va. f10 85
Meadville, Pa. C1 81
Meaford, Ont., Can. C4 41
Meagher, co., Mont. D6 70
Meath, co., Ire. *D3 4
Meaux, Fr. C5 5
Mebane, N.C. A3 76
Mecca, Ind. E3 59
Mecca (Makkah), Sau. Ar. E2 15
Mechanic Falls, Maine D2 64
Mechanicsburg, Ohio B2 78
Mechanicsburg, Pa. F7 81
Mechanicsville, Iowa C6 60
Mechanicsville, Va. C5 85
Mechanicville, N.Y. C7 75
Mechelen, Bel. B6 5
Mecklenburg, co., N.C. B2 76
Mecklenburg, co., Va. D4 85
Mecklenburg, state, Ger.
Dem. Rep. *B6 6
Mecosta, co., Mich. E5 66
Medan, Indon. E1, m11 19
Medaryville, Ind. B4 59
Medéa, Alg. A5 22
Medellín, Col. B2 32
Medfield, Mass. h10 65
Medford, Mass. B5, g11 65
Medford, N.J. D3 74
Medford, Okla. A4 79
Medford, Oreg. E4 80
Medford, Wis. C3 88
Medford Lakes, N.J. D3 74
Medgidia, Rom. C9 10
Media, Pa. G11, p20 81
Mediapolis, Iowa C6 60
Medias, Rom. B7 10
Medical Lake, Wash. B8, g13 86
Medicine Bow, peak, Wyo. E6 89
Medicine Hat, Alta., Can. D5, g8 38
Medicine Lodge, Kans. E5 61
Medicine Park, Okla. C3 79
Medina, N.Y. B2 75
Medina, Ohio A4 78
Medina (Al Madīnah), Sau. Ar. E2 15
Medina, Wash. e11 86
Medina, co., Ohio A4 78
Medina, co., Tex. E3 84
Medina del Campo, Sp. B3 8
Medina Sidonia, Sp. D3 8
Mediterranean, sea D21 2
Medora, Ind. G5 59
Medvezhegorsk, Sov. Un. F16 11
Medway, Mass. B5, h10 65
Medzhibozh, Sov. Un. G6 12
Meekatharra, Austl. E2 25
Meeker, Colo. A3 51
Meeker, Okla. B5 79
Meeker, co., Minn. E4 67
Meerane, Ger. Dem. Rep. C6 6
Meerut, India C6 20
Mégantic, co., Que., Can. C6 42
Mégantic, mtn., Que., Can. D6 42
Megara, Grc. C4 14
Meggett, S.C. F7, k11 82
Meghalaya, state, India C9 20
Megunticook, mtn., Maine D3 64
Mehun-sur-Yèvre, Fr. D5 5
Meigs, Ga. E2 55

Meigs, co., Ohio C3 78
Meigs, co., Tenn. D9 83
Meiktila, Bur. D10 20
Meiners Oaks, Calif. *E4 50
Meiningen, Ger. Dem. C5 6
Meissen, Ger. Dem. Rep. C6 6
Meixian, China G8 17
Mejillones, Chile F3 27
Meknès, Mor. B3 22
Mekong, riv., Asia B2 19
Melaka (Malacca), Mala. E2 19
Melbourne, Austl. G8, n15 25
Melbourne, Fla. D6 54
Melbourne, Iowa C4 60
Melbourne Beach, Fla. D6 54
Melcher, Iowa C4 60
Melfi, It. D5 9
Melfort, Sask., Can. E3 39
Melilla, Sp. dep., Afr. A4 22
Melipilla, Chile A2 28
Melito di Porto Salvo, It. F5 9
Melitopol, Sov. Un. H10 12
Mellen, Wis. B3 88
Mellette, co., S. Dak. G5 77
Mělník, Czech. n18 7
Melo, Ur. E2 30
Melocheville, Que., Can. q19 42
Melouprey, Camb. *C3 19
Melrose, Fla. C4 54
Melrose, Mass. B5, g11 65
Melrose, Minn. E4 67
Melrose, N. Mex. B7 48
Melrose, Wis. D3 88
Melrose Park, Fla. *F6 54
Melrose Park, Ill. F2 58
Melrose Park, N.Y. *C4 75
Melrose Park, Pa. *F11 81
Melun, Fr. C5 5
Melville, Sask., Can. G4 39
Melville, La. D4 63
Melville, isl., N.W. Ter., Can. A11 36
Melvin, Ky. C7 62
Melvindale, Mich. *F7 66
Memel, see Klaipeda, Sov. Un.
Memmingen, Ger., Fed. Rep. of ... E5 6
Memphis, Fla. p10 54
Memphis, Mich. F8 66
Memphis, Mo. A5 69
Memphis, Tenn. B1, e9 83
Memphis, Tex. B2 84
Memramcook, N.B., Can. C5 43
Memramcook East, N.B., Can. *C5 43
Mena, Ark. C1 49
Menahga, Minn. D3 67
Menands, N.Y. *C7 75
Menard, Tex. D3 84
Menard, co., Ill. C4 58
Menard, co., Tex. D3 84
Menasha, Wis. D5, h9 88
Mende, Fr. E5 5
Mendenhall, Miss. D4 68
Mendham, N.J. B3 74
Mendocino, Calif. C2 50
Mendocino, co., Calif. C2 50
Mendon, Ill. C2 58
Mendon, Mass. h9 65
Mendon, Mich. F5 66
Mendon, Ohio B1 78
Mendota, Calif. D3 50
Mendota, Ill. B4 58
Mendota Heights, Minn. *F5 67
Mendoza, Arg. A3 28
Mendoza, prov., Arg. A3 28
Menemen, Tur. *C6 14
Menfi, It. F4 9
Mengzi, China G5 17
Menifee, co., Ky. C6 62
Menindee, Austl. F7 25
Menlo Park, Calif. k8 50
Menlo Park, N.J. B4 74
Menlo Park Terrace, N.J. *B4 74
Menominee, Mich. C3 66
Menominee, co., Mich. C3 66
Menominee, co., Wis. C5 88
Menominee, riv., Mich. C3 66
Menomonee Falls, Wis. E5, m11 88
Menomonie, Wis. D2 88
Mentana, It. g9 9
Menton, Fr. F7 5
Mentone, Calif. *E5 50
Mentone, Ind. B5 59
Mentor, Ohio A4 78
Mentor Headlands, Ohio *A4 78
Mentor-on-the-Lake, Ohio A4 78
Meoqui, Mex. B3 34
Meppel, Neth. A7 5
Meppen, Ger., Fed. Rep. of B3 6
Mequon, Wis. E6, m12 88
Merano, It. A3 9
Merauke, Indon. G10 19
Mercãra, India F6 20
Merced, Calif. D3 50

Merced, co., Calif. D3 50
Mercedes, Arg. E4 29
Mercedes, Arg. A5, g7 28
Mercedes, Arg. A3 28
Mercedes, Tex. F4 84
Mercedes, Ur. E1 30
Mercer, Pa. D1 81
Mercer, Wis. B3 88
Mercer, co., Ill. B3 58
Mercer, co., Ky. C5 62
Mercer, co., Mo. A4 69
Mercer, co., N.J. C3 74
Mercer, co., N. Dak. C4 77
Mercer, co., Ohio B1 78
Mercer, co., Pa. D1 81
Mercer, co., W. Va. D3 87
Mercer Island, Wash. B3, e11 86
Mercersburg, Pa. G6 81
Mercerville, N.J. C3 74
Merchantville, N.J. *D2 74
Meredith, N.H. D4 73
Meredosia, Ill. D3 58
Merefa, Sov. Un. G11 12
Mergui, Bur. F10 20
Mérida, Mex. C7 34
Mérida, Sp. C2 8
Mérida, Ven. B3 32
Mérida, state, Ven. B3 32
Meriden, Conn. C5 52
Meridian, Idaho F2 57
Meridian, Miss. C5 68
Meridian, Pa. *E2 81
Meridian, Tex. D4 84
Merioneth, co., Wales *D5 4
Merion Park, Pa. *F11 81
Merion Station, Pa. *F11 81
Meriwether, co., Ga. C2 55
Merkel, Tex. C3 84
Merksem, Bel. B6 5
Merlin, Ont., Can. E2 41
Merlo, Arg. g7 28
Mermentau, La. D3 63
Mermentau, riv., La. E2 63
Merredin, Austl. F2 25
Merriam, Kans. B8 61
Merrick, N.Y. G2 52
Merrick, co., Nebr. C7 71
Merrickville, Ont., Can. C9 41
Merrifield, Va. g12 85
Merrill, Iowa B1 60
Merrill, Mich. E6 66
Merrill, Oreg. E5 80
Merrill, Wis. C4 88
Merrillan, Wis. D3 88
Merrillville, Ind. B3 59
Merrimac, Mass. A5 65
Merrimack, N.H. F5 73
Merrimack, co., N.H. E4 73
Merritt, B.C., Can. D7 37
Merritt Island, Fla. D6 54
Mer Rouge, La. B4 63
Merryville, La. D2 63
Mersey, riv., Eng. D5 4
Merseburg, Ger. Dem. Rep. C4 6
Mersey, riv., Eng. D5 4
Mersin, Tur. D10 14
Mersing, Mala. E2 19
Merthyr Tydfil, Wales E5 4
Meru, mtn., Tan. I5 23
Merzifon, Tur. B10 14
Mesa, Ariz. C3, D2 48
Mesa, co., Colo. C2 51
Mesa de Tijuana, Mex. *A1 34
Meshkovskaya, Sov. Un. G13 12
Mesilla, N. Mex. E3 48
Mesilla Park, N. Mex. E3 48
Mesolongion, Grc. C3 14
Mesquite, Tex. n10 84
Messina, It. E5 9
Messina, S. Afr. E6 24
Messini, Grc. D3 14
Messinia (Messenia), prov.,
  Grc. *D4 14
Mestghanem, Alg. A5 22
Mestre, It. B4 9
Meta, dept., Col. C3 32
Meta, riv., Col. B4 32
Métabetchouan, Que., Can. A6 42
Metairie, La. k11 63
Metamora, Ill. C4 58
Metamora, Ohio A2 78
Metán, Arg. E3 29
Metcalfe, co., Ky. C4 62
Meteghan, N.S., Can. E3 43
Methuen, Mass. A5 65
Metkovic, Yugo. D3 10
Metropolis, Ill. F5 58
Metter, Ga. D5 55
Metuchen, N.J. B4 74
Metz, Fr. C7 5
Metzger, Oreg. h12 80
Meudon, Fr. g9 5
Meulaboh, Indon. m11 19

Meurthe-et-Moselle, dept., Fr. *C7 5
Meuse, dept., Fr. *C6 5
Mexia, Tex. D4 84
Mexicali, Mex. A1 34
Mexico, Ind. C5 59
Mexico, Maine D2 64
Mexico, Mo. B6 69
Mexico, N.Y. B4 75
Mexico, country, N.A. G10 33
México, state, Mex. D5, n14 34
México, gulf, N.A. G11 33
Mexico City, Mex. n14 34
Meyersdale, Pa. G3 81
Mezen, Sov. Un. C7 13
Mezőkövesd, Hung. B5 10
Mezőtúr, Hung. B5 10
Mglin, Sov. Un. E9 12
Miajadas, Sp. C3 8
Miami, Ariz. C3, D3 48
Miami, Fla. G6, s13 54
Miami, Okla. A7 79
Miami, W. Va. m13 87
Miami, co., Ind. C5 59
Miami, co., Kans. D9 61
Miami, co., Ohio B1 78
Miami Beach, Fla. G6, s13 54
Miamisburg, Ohio C1 78
Miami Shores, Fla. G6, s13 54
Miami Shores, Ohio *C1 78
Miami Springs, Fla. G6, s13 54
Miamitown, Ohio o12 78
Miānwāli, Pak. B5 20
Mianyang, China E5 17
Miaoli, Taiwan *G9 17
Miass, Sov. Un. *D9 13
Micanopy, Fla. C4 54
Michalovce, Czech. D6 7
Michigan, lake, U.S. E12 33
Michigan, state, U.S. 66
Michigan Center, Mich. F6 66
Michigan City, Ind. A4 59
Michoacán, state, Mex. D4, n13 34
Michurinsk, Sov. Un. E13 12
Mickleyville, Ind. m10 59
Micoud, St. Lucia J14 35
Middelburg, Neth. B5 5
Middelburg, S. Afr. G5 24
Middleboro, Mass. C6 65
Middlebranch, Ohio B4 78
Middle Brook, Newf., Can. D4 44
Middleburg, Fla. B5 54
Middleburg, N.Y. C6 75
Middleburg, Pa. E7 81
Middleburg, Va. B5 85
Middleburgh Heights, Ohio h9 78
Middlebury, Conn. C4 52
Middlebury, Ind. A6 59
Middlebury, Vt. C1 73
Middle Caraquet, N.B., Can. *B5 43
Middlefield, Conn. C5 52
Middlefield, Ohio A4 78
Middle Granville, N.Y. B7 75
Middle Haddam, Conn. C5 52
Middle Musquodoboit, N.S., Can. . D6 43
Middleport, N.Y. B2 75
Middleport, Ohio C3 78
Middleport, Pa. *E9 81
Middle River, Md. *B5 53
Middlesboro, Ky. D6 62
Middlesbrough (Teesside), Eng. ... C6 4
Middlesex, N.J. B4 74
Middlesex, N.C. B4 76
Middlesex, co., Ont., Can. D3 41
Middlesex, co., Conn. D6 52
Middlesex, co., Eng. *E6 4
Middlesex, co., Mass. A5 65
Middlesex, co., N.J. C4 74
Middlesex, co., Va. C6 85
Middleton, Conn. C6 52
Middleton, N.S., Can. E4 43
Middleton, Idaho F2 57
Middleton, Mass. A5, f11 65
Middleton, Wis. E4 88
Middletown, Calif. C2 50
Middletown, Del. B6 53
Middletown, Ind. D6 59
Middletown, Ky. g11 62
Middletown, Md. B2 53
Middletown, N.J. C4 74
Middletown, N.Y. D6 75
Middletown, Ohio C1 78
Middletown, Pa. F8 81
Middletown, R.I. C11 52
Middletown Heights, Pa. *G11 81
Middleville, Mich. F5 66
Middleville, N.Y. B6 75
Midfield, Ala. g7 46
Midland, Calif. F6 50
Midland, Ont.,Can. C5 41
Midland, La. D3 63
Midland, Md. K13 53
Midland, Mich. E6 66
Midland, N.C. B2 76

Midland, Pa. E1 81
Midland, Tex. D1 84
Midland, Wash. *D3 86
Midland, co., Mich. E6 66
Midland, co., Tex. D1 84
Midland Park, Kans. B5 61
Midland Park, N.J. B4 74
Midland Park, S.C. K11 82
Midleton, Ire. E2 4
Midlothian, Ill. k9 58
Midlothian, Tex. C4, n10 84
Midlothian, co., Scot. *C5 4
Midnapore, India D8 20
Midvale, Ohio B4 78
Midvale, Utah D2 72
Midway, Ky. B5 62
Midway, Oreg. *B4 80
Midway, Pa. G7 81
Midway City, Calif. *F5 50
Midway Park, N.C. C5 76
Midway Is., U.S. dep., Oceania ... E9 2
Midwest, Wyo. C6 89
Midwest City, Okla. B4 79
Mid-Western, reg., Nig. G6 22
Midyat, Tur. D13 14
Mie, pref., Jap. *I8 18
Miechów, Pol. C6 7
Miechowice, Pol. g9 7
Miedzyrzec, Pol. C7 7
Mielec, Pol. C6 7
Mieres, Sp. A3 8
Mifflin, co., Pa. F6 81
Mifflinburg, Pa. E7 81
Mifflintown, Pa. E7 81
Mifflinville, Pa. E9 81
Migennes, Fr. D5 5
Mignon, Ala. B3 46
Mihama, Jap. o15 18
Mihara, Jap. *I6 18
Mikhaylovgrad, Bul. D6 10
Mikhaylovka, Sov. Un. H10 12
Mikhaylovka, Sov. Un. F14 12
Mikindani, Tan. C8 24
Mikkeli, Fin. G12 11
Mikkeli, prov., Fin. *G12 11
Mikołów, Pol. g9 7
Mikulczyce, Pol. g8 7
Mikulov, Czech. D4 7
Milaca, Minn. E5 67
Milam, co., Tex. D4 84
Milan, Ill. B3 58
Milan, Ind. F7 59
Milan (Milano), It. B2 9
Milan, Mich. F7 66
Milan, Mo. A4 69
Milan, N. Mex. *B2 48
Milan, Ohio A3 78
Milan, Tenn. B3 83
Milano, see Milan, It.
Milas, Tur. *D6 14
Milazzo, It. E5 9
Milbank, S. Dak. E9 77
Milbridge, Maine D5 64
Mildmay, Ont., Can. C3 41
Mildred, Pa. D9 81
Mildura, Austl. F7 25
Miles, Austl. *E9 25
Miles, Tex. D2 84
Miles City, Mont. D11 70
Milford, Conn. E4 52
Milford, Del. C7 53
Milford, Ill. C6 58
Milford, Ind. B6 59
Milford, Iowa A2 60
Milford, Maine D4 64
Milford, Mass. B4, h9 65
Milford, Mich. F7, o14 66
Milford, Nebr. D8 71
Milford, N.H. F4 73
Milford, N.J. B2 74
Milford, N.Y. C6 75
Milford, Ohio C1 78
Milford, Pa. D12 81
Milford, Utah E2 72
Milford Center, Ohio B2 78
Milford Haven, Wales E4 4
Milford Station, N.S., Can. D6 43
Miliana, Alg. A5 22
Milk, riv., Alta., Can. E5 38
Milk River, Alta., Can. E4 38
Mill, riv., Mass. h9 65
Millard, Nebr. g12 71
Millard, co., Utah B5 72
Millau, Fr. E5 5
Millbourne, Pa. G11 81
Millbrae, Calif. h8 50
Millbrook, Ala. C3 46
Millbrook, Ont., Can. C6 41
Millbrook, N.J. *B3 74
Millbrook, N.Y. D7 75
Millburn, N.J. B4 74
Millbury, Mass. B4 65
Millbury, Ohio e7 78

Mill City, Oreg. C4 80
Milldale, Conn. C4 52
Milledgeville, Ga. C3 55
Milledgeville, Ill. B4 58
Mille Lacs, co., Minn. E5 67
Mille Lacs, lake, Minn. D5 67
Millen, Ga. D5 55
Miller, S. Dak. F7 77
Miller, co., Ark. D2 49
Miller, co., Ga. E2 55
Miller, co., Mo. C5 69
Millerovo, Sov. Un. G13 12
Millersburg, Ky. B5 62
Millersburg, Ohio B4 78
Millersburg, Pa. E8 81
Millers Falls, Mass. A3 65
Millersport, Ohio C3 78
Millersville, Pa. F9 81
Millerton, N.Y. D7 75
Mill Hall, Pa. D7 81
Millicent, Austl. G7 25
Milligan, Fla. u15 54
Millington, Mich. E7 66
Millington, N.J. *B3 74
Millington, Tenn. B2 83
Millinocket, Maine C4 64
Millis, Mass. B5, h10 65
Millport, Ala. B1 46
Mills, Wyo. D6 89
Mills, co., Iowa C2 60
Mills, co., Tex. D3 84
Millsboro, Del. C2 53
Millsboro, Pa. G1 81
Millside, Del. *A6 53
Millstadt, Ill. E3 58
Milltown, N.B., Can. D2 43
Milltown, Ind. H5 59
Milltown, Mont. D3 70
Milltown, N.J. C4 74
Milltown, Wis. C1 88
Millvale, Pa. k14 81
Mill Valley, Calif. D2, h7 50
Millville, Mass. B4 65
Millville, N.J. E2 74
Millville, Ohio n12 78
Millville, Pa. D9 81
Millwood, Wash. g14 86
Milmont Park, Pa. *G11 81
Milo, Maine C4 64
Milpitas, Calif. *D3 50
Milroy, Ind. F7 59
Milroy, Pa. E6 81
Milstead, Ga. C3, h8 55
Milton, N.S., Can. E5 43
Milton, Ont., Can. D5 41
Milton, Del. C7 53
Milton, Fla. u14 54
Milton, Ind. E7 59
Milton, Iowa D5 60
Milton, Mass. B5, g11 65
Milton, N.H. D5 73
Milton, N.J. A3 74
Milton, N.Y. D7 75
Milton, Pa. D8 81
Milton, Wash. f11 86
Milton, W. Va. C2 87
Milton, Wis. F5 88
Milton-Freewater, Oreg. B8 80
Milton-Freewater, Oreg. B8 80
Milton Junction, Wis. F5 88
Miltonvale, Kans. C6 61
Milverton, Ont., Can. D4 41
Milwaukee, Wis. E6, m12 88
Milwaukee, co., Wis. E6 88
Milwaukie, Oreg. B4, h12 80
Mims, Fla. D6 54
Minamata, Jap. J5 18
Minas, Ur. E1 30
Minas de Riotinto, Sp. D2 8
Minas Gerais, state, Braz. B4 30
Minatare, Nebr. C2 71
Minatitlán, Mex. D6 34
Minato, Jap. m19 18
Minbu, Bur. D9 20
Minco, Okla. B4 79
Mindanao, isl., Phil. D6 19
Minden, Ont., Can. C6 41
Minden, Ger., Fed. Rep. of B4 6
Minden, La. B2 63
Minden, Nebr. D7 71
Minden, W. Va. D3, n13 87
Mindoro, isl., Phil. C6 19
Minechoag, mtn.,Mass. B3 65
Minehead, Eng. E5 4
Mine Hill, N.J. *B3 74
Mineola, N.Y. E7, n15 75
Mineola, Tex. C5 84
Miner, Mo. E8 69
Miner, co., S. Dak. G8 77
Mineral, co., Colo. D4 51
Mineral, co., Mont. C1 70
Mineral, co., Nev. B2 72
Mineral, co., W. Va. B6 87
Mineral City, Ohio B4 78

Mineral del Oro, Mex. n13 34
Mineral Point, Wis. F3 88
Mineral Ridge, Ohio *A5 78
Mineral Wells, Tex. C3 84
Minersville, Pa. E9 81
Minerva, Ohio B4 78
Minerva Park, Ohio *C3 78
Minervino Murge, It. D6 9
Minetto, N.Y. B4 75
Mineville, N.Y. A7 75
Mingenew, Austl. E2 25
Mingo, co., W. Va. D2 87
Mingo Junction, Ohio B5 78
Mingshui, China C2 18
Minho, prov., Port. *B1 8
Minidoka, co., Idaho G5 57
Minier, Ill. C4 58
Minitonas, Man., Can. C1 40
Minna, Nig. G6 22
Minneapolis, Kans. C6 61
Minneapolis, Minn. F5, n12 67
Minnedosa, Man., Can. D2 40
Minnehaha, Wash. *D3 86
Minnehaha, co., S. Dak. G9 77
Minneola, Kans. E3 61
Minneota, Minn. F3 67
Minnesota, state, U.S. 67
Minnesota, riv., Minn. F3 67
Minnesota Lake, Minn. G5 67
Minnetonka, Minn. *F5 67
Minnetrista, Minn. *E5 67
Mino, Jap. n15 18
Minoa, N.Y. *B4 75
Minocqua, Wis. C4 88
Minokamo, Jap. n15 18
Minonk, Ill. C4 58
Minot, N. Dak. B4 77
Minquadale, Del. *A6 53
Minsk, Sov. Un. E6 12
Minster, Ohio B1 78
Minturno, It. D4 9
Minūf, Eg. *G8 14
Minusinsk, Sov. Un. D12 13
Miraflores, Col. C3 32
Miraflores, Peru A3 31
Miraj, Indai E5 20
Mira Loma, Calif. *E5 50
Miramar, Fla. s13 54
Miranda, state, Ven. A4 32
Miranda de Ebro, Sp. A4 8
Mirassol, Braz. C3 30
Mirebalais, Hai. E7 35
Mirecourt, Fr. C7 5
Mirgorod, Sov. Un. G9 12
Miri, Mala. E4 19
Mirpur-Khas, Pak. *C4 20
Mirror, Alta., Can. C4 38
Mirzāpur, India C7 20
Misakubo, Jap. n16 18
Misamis Occidental, prov., Phil. ... *D6 19
Misamis Oriental, prov., Phil. *D7 19
Misantla, Mex. D5, h15 34
Misenheimer, N.C. B2 76
Mishan, China D6 18
Mishawaka, Ind. A5 59
Mishicot, Wis. D6, h10 88
Mishima, Jap. I9, h17 18
Misiones, dept., Par. E4 19
Misiones, prov., Arg. E4 29
Miskolc, Hung. A5 10
Misrātah, Libya B8 22
Missaukee, co., Mich. D5 66
Mission, Kans. *B9 61
Mission, Tex. F3 84
Mission City, B.C., Can. E6, f13 37
Mission Hills, Kans. B9 61
Missisquoi, co., Que., Can. D4 42
Mississauga, Ont., Can. D5, m14 41
Mississippi, co., Ark. B5 49
Mississippi, co., Mo. E8 69
Mississippi, state, U.S. 68
Mississippi, riv., U.S. D8 45
Mississippi City, Miss. E4, f7 68
Missoula, Mont. D2 70
Missoula, co., Mont. D2 70
Missoula Southwest, Mont. *D2 70
Missouri, state, U.S. 69
Missouri, riv., U.S. B7 45
Missouri Valley, Iowa C2 60
Mistelbach an der Zaya, Aus. D8 6
Misti, vol., Peru E3 31
Mistretta, It. F5 9
Mitaka, Jap. *I9 18
Mitake, Jap. I8, n16 18
Mitchell, Austl. E8 25
Mitchell, Ont., Can. D3 41
Mitchell, Ind. G5 59
Mitchell, Nebr. C2 71
Mitchell, S. Dak. G7 77
Mitchell, co., Ga. E2 55
Mitchell, co., Iowa A5 60
Mitchell, co., Kans. C5 61
Mitchell, co., N.C. e10 76

Mitchell, co., Tex. C2 84
Mitchell, mtn., N.C. f10 76
Mitchellsberg, Ky. C5 62
Mitchellville, Iowa C4 60
Mitilini (Mytilene), Grc. C6 14
Mito, Jap. H10, m19 18
Mittagong, Austl. *F9 25
Mitterteich, Ger., Fed. Rep. of C6 6
Mittweida, Ger. Dem. Rep. C6 6
Mitú, Col. C3 32
Miura, Jap. n18 18
Mixquiahuala, Mex. m13 34
Miyagi, pref., Jap. *G10 18
Miyako, Jap. G10 18
Miyakonojo, Jap. K5 18
Miyazaki, Jap. K5 18
Miyazaki, pref., Jap. *K5 18
Miyazu, Jap. n14 18
Mizil, Rom. C8 10
Mizoram, ter., India *D9 20
Mjölby, Swe. H6 11
Mlada Boleslav, Czech. C3, n18 7
Mława, Pol. B6 7
Moab, Utah B7 72
Mobara, Jap. n19 18
Moberly, Mo. B5 69
Mobile, Ala. E1 46
Mobile, co., Ala. E1 46
Mobridge, S. Dak. E5 77
Moca, mun., P.R. E8 35
Moçambique, Moz. D8 24
Moçâmedes, Ang. D2 24
Mocanaqua, Pa. D9 81
Mochudi, Bots. E5 24
Mocksville, N.C. B2 76
Moclips, Wash. B1 86
Mocoa, Col. C2 32
Mococa, Braz. C3, k8 30
Mocorito, Mex. B3 34
Moctezuma, Mex. B3 34
Modena, It. B3 9
Modesto, Calif. D3 50
Modica, It. F5 9
Modjokerto, Indon. *G4 19
Modlin, Pol. B6, k13 7
Mödling, Aus. D8 6
Modoc, co.,Calif. B3 50
Modřany, Czech. o17 7
Moeo-Yallourn, Austl. I6 26
Moffat, co., Colo. A2 51
Mogadishu, Som. H7 23
Mogadore, Ohio A4 78
Mogaung, Bur. C10 20
Mogi das Cruzes, Braz. C3, m8 30
Mogilev, Sov. Un. E8 12
Mogilev-Podolskiy, Sov. Un. G6 12
Mogilno, Pol. B4 7
Mogi Mirim, Braz. C3, m8 30
Mogocha, Sov. Un. D14 13
Mogok, Bur. D10 20
Moguer, Sp. D2 8
Mohács, Hung. C4 10
Mohall, N. Dak. B4 77
Mohammedia, Mor. B3 22
Mohave, co., Ariz. B1 48
Mohawk, Mich. A2 66
Mohawk, N.Y. C5 75
Mohnton, Pa. F10 81
Moinesti, Rom. B8 10
Moissac, Fr. E4 5
Mojave, Calif. E4 50
Mokleumne Hill, Calif. C3 50
Mokena, Ill. k9 58
Mokpo, Kor. I3 18
Mol, Yugo. C5 10
Mola de Bari, It. D6 9
Molalla, Oreg. B4 80
Mold, Wales *D5 4
Moldavia, reg., Rom. B8 10
Moldavia (S.S.R.), rep., Sov. Un. ... H7 12
Molepolole, Bots. E5 24
Molfetta, It. D6 9
Molina, Chile B2 28
Molina de Segura, Sp. C5 8
Moline, Ill. B3 58
Moline, Kans. E7 61
Moline, Mich. F5 66
Moline Acres, Mo. *C7 69
Molino, Fla. u14 54
Molino de Rosas, Mex. h9 34
Moliterno, It. D5 9
Mollendo, Peru E3 31
Mölndal, Swe. I5 11
Molodechno, Sov. Un. E6 12
Molotovsk, Sov. Un. E18 11
Molotovskoye, Sov. Un. I13 12
Molus, Ky. D6 62
Mombasa, Ken. I5 23
Mombetsu, Jap. D11 18
Momence, Ill. B6 58
Momostenango, Guat. *D6 34
Mompós, Col. B3 32
Monaca, Pa. E1 81

Monaco, country, Eur. F7 5
Monagas, state, Ven. B5 32
Monaghan, S.C. B5 82
Monaghan, co., Ire. *C3 4
Monahans, Tex. D1 84
Monarch, S.C. B4 82
Monarch, mtn., B.C., Can. D5, n17 37
Monashee, mts., B.C., Can. D8 37
Monastir, Tur. A7 22
Monchegorsk, Sov. Un. D15 11
Mönchengladbach,
    Ger., Fed. Rep. of C3 6
Moncks Corner, S.C. E7 82
Monclova, Mex. B4 34
Moncton, N.B., Can. C5 43
Mondoñedo, Sp. A2 8
Mondovi, It. B1 9
Mondovi, Wis. D2 88
Monessen, Pa. F2 81
Monett, Mo. E4 69
Monette, Ark. B4 49
Monfalcone, It. B4 9
Monforte de Lemos, Sp. A2 8
Monfort Heights, Ohio *C1 78
Monghyr, India C8 20
Mong Mit, Bur. D10 20
Mongolia, country, Asia B4 17
Moniquirá, Col. B3 32
Moniteau, co., Mo. C5 69
Monmouth, Ill. C3 58
Monmouth, Oreg. C3, k11 80
Monmouth, co., N.J. C4 74
Monmouth, co., Wales *E5 4
Monmouth, mtn., B.C., Can. D6 37
Monmouth Beach, N.J. *C5 74
Monmouth Junction, N.J. *C3 74
Mono, co., Calif. D4 50
Monon, Ind. C4 59
Monona, Iowa A6 60
Monona, Wis. E4 88
Monona, co., Iowa B1 60
Monongah, W. Va. B4, k10 87
Monongahela, Pa. F2 81
Monongahela, riv., Pa. G2 81
Monongalia, co., W. Va. B4 87
Monopoli, It. D6 9
Monor, Hung. B4 10
Monóvar, Sp. C5 8
Monponsett, Mass. B9 65
Monreale, It. E4 9
Monroe, Conn. D3 52
Monroe, Ga. C3 55
Monroe, Iowa C4 60
Monroe, La. B3 63
Monroe, Mich. G7 66
Monroe, N.Y. D6, m14 75
Monroe, N.C. C2 76
Monroe, Ohio *C1 78
Monroe, Utah B5 72
Monroe, Va. C3 85
Monroe, Wash. B4 86
Monroe, Wis. F4 88
Monroe, co., Ala. D2 46
Monroe, co., Ark. C4 49
Monroe, co., Fla. G5 54
Monroe, co., Ga. D3 55
Monroe, co., Ill. E3 58
Monroe, co., Ind. F4 59
Monroe, co., Iowa D5 60
Monroe, co., Ky. D4 62
Monroe, co., Mich. G7 66
Monroe, co., Miss. B5 68
Monroe, co., Mo. B5 69
Monroe, co., N.Y. B3 75
Monroe, co., Ohio C4 78
Monroe, co., Pa. D11 81
Monroe, co., Tenn. D9 83
Monroe, co., W. Va. D4 87
Monroe, co., Wis. E3 88
Monroe City, Mo. B6 69
Monroeville, Ala. D2 46
Monroeville, Ind. *C8 59
Monroeville, Ohio A3 78
Monroeville, Pa. *E1 81
Monrovia, Calif. m13 50
Monrovia, Lib. G2 22
Mons, Bel. B5 5
Monson, Maine C3 64
Monson, Mass. B2 65
Montague, Calif. B2 50
Montague, P.E.I., Can. C7 43
Montague, Mass. A2 65
Montague, Mich. E4 66
Montague, co., Tex. C4 84
Montague City, Mass. A2 65
Mont Alto, Pa. G6 81
Montalvo, Calif. *E4 50
Montana, state, U.S. 70
Montánchez, Sp. C2 8
Montargis, Fr. D5 5
Montauban, Que., Can. C5 42
Montauban, Fr. E4 5
Montauk, N.Y. m17 75

Monta Vista, Calif. *B3 50
Monta Vista, Wash. *B33 86
Montbeliard, Fr. D7 5
Mont Belvieu, Tex. E5, r15 84
Montbrison, Fr. E6 5
Montcalm, co., Que., Can. C3 42
Montcalm, co., Mich. E5 66
Mont-Carmel, Que., Can. B8 42
Montceau-les-Mines, Fr. D6 5
Montchanin -les-Mines, Fr. D6 5
Montclair (Monte Vista), Calif. m13 50
Montclair, N.J. B4 74
Mont Clare, Pa. o19 81
Montcoal, W. Va. D3, n12 87
Mont-De-Marsan, Fr. F3 5
Montebello, Calif. m12 50
Montebello, Que., Can. D3 42
Monte Caseros, Arg. A5 28
Montecelio, It. g9 9
Montecristi, Dom. Rep. E8 35
Montefrio, Sp. D3 8
Montego Bay, Jam. E5 35
Montegut, La. E5 63
Monteith, mtn., B.C., Can. B6 38
Montélimar, Fr. E6 5
Montellano, Sp. D3 8
Montello, Wis. E4 88
Montemorelos, Mex. B5 34
Montemor-o-Novo, Port. C1 8
Montenegro, Braz. D2 30
Montenegro (Crna Gora),
  rep., Yugo. *D4 10
Monte Plata, Dom. Rep. E9 35
Montepulciano, It. C3 9
Montereau, Fr. C5 5
Monterey, Calif. D3 50
Monterey, Ohio *C1 78
Monterey, Tenn. C8 83
Monterey, co., Calif. D3 50
Monterey Park, Calif. m12 50
Montería, Col. B2 32
Monteros, Arg. E2 29
Monterotondo, It. g9 9
Monterrey, Mex. B4 34
Montesano, Wash. C2 86
Monte Sant' Angelo, It. D5 9
Montes Claros, Braz. B4 30
Monte Sereno, Calif. *D3 50
Montevallo, Ala. B3 46
Montevarchi, It. C3 9
Montevideo, Minn. F3 67
Montevideo, Ur. E1 30
Montevideo, dept., Ur. *E1 30
Monte Vista, Colo. D4 51
Montezuma, Ga. D2 55
Montezuma, Ind. E3 59
Montezuma, Iowa C5 60
Montezuma, co., Colo. D2 51
Montfort, Wis. F3 88
Montgomery, Ala. C3 46
Montgomery, Ill. B5, k8 58
Montgomery, La. C3 63
Montgomery, Minn. F5 67
Montgomery, N.Y. D6 75
Montgomery, Ohio *C1 78
Montgomery, Pa. D8 81
Montgomery, W. Va. C3, m13 87
Montgomery, co., Ala. C3 46
Montgomery, co., Ark. C2 49
Montgomery, co., Ga. D4 55
Montgomery, co., Ill. D4 58
Montgomery, co., Ind. D4 59
Montgomery, co., Iowa *C2 60
Montgomery, co., Kans. E8 61
Montgomery, co., Ky. B6 62
Montgomery, co., Md. B3 53
Montgomery, co., Miss. B4 68
Montgomery, co., Mo. C6 69
Montgomery, co., N.Y. C6 75
Montgomery, co., N.C. B3 76
Montgomery, co., Ohio C1 78
Montgomery, co., Pa. F11 81
Montgomery, co., Tenn. A4 83
Montgomery, co., Tex. D5 84
Montgomery, co., Va. *C2 85
Montgomery, co., Wales *D5 4
Montgomery City, Mo. C6 69
Monticello, Ark. D4 49
Monticello, Fla. B3 54
Monticello, Ga. C3 55
Monticello, Ill. C5 58
Monticello, Ind. C4 59
Monticello, Iowa B6 60
Monticello, Ky. D5 62
Monticello, Maine B5 64
Monticello, Minn. E5 67
Monticello, Miss. D3 68
Monticello, N.Y. D6 75
Monticello, Utah C7 72
Monticello, Wis. F4 88
Montigny -lès-Metz, Fr. *C7 5
Montijo, Port. C1, f10 8
Montijo, Sp. C2 8

Montilla, Sp. D3 8
Montivilliers, Fr. C4 5
Mont-Joli, Que., Can. G20 36
Mont-Laurier, Que., Can. C2 42
Montluçon, Fr. D5 5
Montmagny, Que., Can. C7 42
Montmagny, co., Que., Can. C7 42
Montmartre, Sask., Can. G4 39
Montmorenci, S.C. D4 82
Montmorency, Fr. g10 5
Montmorency, co., Mich. C6 66
Montmorency No. 1, co.,
  Que., Can. B6 42
Montmorency No. 2, co.,
  Que., Can. C7 42
Montmorillon, Fr. D4 5
Montoro, Sp. C3 8
Montour, co., Pa. D8 81
Montour Falls, N.Y. C4 75
Montoursville, Pa. D8 81
Montpelier, Idaho G7 57
Montpelier, Ind. C7 59
Montpelier, Ohio A1 78
Montpelier, Vt. C2 73
Montpellier, Fr. F5 5
Montréal, Que., Can. D4, q19 42
Montreal, Wis. B3 88
Montréal West, Que., Can. *D4 42
Montreuil-sous-Bois, Fr. C5 5
Montreux, Switz. E3 6
Mont-Rolland, Que., Can. D3 42
Montrose, Ala. E2 46
Montrose, Calif. *E4 50
Montrose, B.C., Can. E9 37
Montrose, Colo. C3 51
Montrose, Iowa D6 60
Montrose, Mich. E7 66
Montrose, Pa. *F10 81
Montrose, Pa. C10 81
Montrose, Scot. B5 4
Montrose, co., Colo. C2 51
Montrose Hill, Pa. *E1 81
Montrouge, Fr. g10 5
Mont-Royal, Que., Can. p19 42
Montserrat, Br. dep., N.A. H13 35
Montvale, N.J. g8 74
Montville, Conn. D8 52
Montville, N.J. B4 74
Monument, peak, Idaho G4 57
Monument Beach, Mass. C6 65
Monywa, Bur. D10 20
Monza, It. B2 9
Monzón, Peru C2 31
Moodus, Conn. D7 52
Moody, Tex. D4 84
Moody, co., S. Dak. F9 77
Mooers, N.Y. f11 75
Moonachie, N.J. *B4 74
Moon Crest, Pa. *E1 81
Moon Run, Pa. k13 81
Moonta, Austl. F6 25
Moora, Austl. F2 25
Moorcraft, Wyo. B8 89
Moore, Okla. B4 79
Moore, co., N.C. B3 76
Moore, co., Tenn. B5 83
Moore, co., Tex. B2 84
Moorefield, W. Va. B6 87
Moore Haven, Fla. F5 54
Mooreland, Okla. A2 79
Moorestown, N.J. D3 74
Mooresville, Ind. E5 59
Mooresville, N.C. B2 76
Moorhead, Minn. D2 67
Moorhead, Miss. B3 83
Mooringsport, La. B2 63
Moorpark, Calif. E4 50
Moose, mtn., Sask., Can. H4 39
Mooseheart, Ill. B5, k8 58
Moose Jaw, Sask., Can. G3, n7 39
Moose Lake, Minn. D6 67
Moosic, Pa. m18 81
Moosic, mts., Pa. m18 81
Moosomin, Sask., Can. G5 39
Moosonee, Ont., Can. o19 41
Moosup, Conn. C9 52
Mopti, Mali F4 22
Moquegua, Peru E3 31
Moquegua, dept., Peru E3 31
Mor, Hung. B4 10
Mora, Minn. E5 67
Mora, N. Mex. B6 48
Mora, Sp. C4 8
Mora, Swe. G6 11
Mora, co., N. Mex. A6 48
Morada, Calif. *D3 50
Morādābād, India C6 20
Moraine, Ohio *C1 78
Moramanga, Mad. D9 24
Moran, Kans. E8 61
Morant Bay, Jam. F5 35
Moratalla, Sp. C5 8
Moratuwa, Sri Lanka *G6 20

Moravia, Iowa D5 60
Moravia, N.Y. C4 75
Moravia (Morava), reg., Czech. D4 7
Moray, co., Scot. *B5 4
Morbihan, dept., Fr. *D2 5
Morden, Man., Can. E2 40
Moreauville, La. C4 63
Moree, Austl. E8 25
Morehead, Ky. B6 62
Morehead City, N.C. C6 76
Morehouse, par., La. B4 63
Morehouse, Mo. E8 69
Moreland Hills, Ohio *A4 78
Morelia, Mex. D4, n13 34
Morelos, state, Mex. D5, n14 34
Morenci, Ariz. C4 48
Morenci, Mich. G6 66
Möre og Romsdal, co., Nor. *F2 11
Morez, Fr. D7 5
Morgan, Minn. F4 67
Morgan, Utah A6 72
Morgan, co., Ala. A3 46
Morgan, co., Colo. A7 51
Morgan, co., Ga. C3 55
Morgan, co., Ill. D3 58
Morgan, co., Ind. F5 59
Morgan, co., Ky. C6 62
Morgan, co., Mo. C5 69
Morgan, co., Ohio C4 78
Morgan, co., Tenn. C9 83
Morgan, co., Utah A6 72
Morgan, co., W. Va. B6 87
Morgan City, La. E4, k9 63
Morganfield, Ky. C2 62
Morgan Hill, Calif. D3 50
Morganton, N.C. B1 76
Morgantown, Ind. F5 59
Morgantown, Ky. C3 62
Morgantown, W. Va. B5, h11 87
Morganza, La. D4 63
Mori, Jap. E10 18
Moriguchi, Jap. *I7 18
Morinville, Alta., Can. C4 38
Morioka, Jap. G10 18
Morlaix, Fr. C2 5
Morningdale, Mass. B4 65
Morningside, Md. *C4 53
Morningside, Minn. *F5 67
Morning Sun, Iowa C6 60
Morocco, Ind. C3 59
Morocco, country, Afr. B4 22
Morococha, Peru D2 31
Morogoro, Tan. B7 24
Moroléon, Mex. m13 34
Morón, Arg. g7 28
Morón, Cuba C4 35
Morona-Santiago, prov., Ec. B3 31
Morondava, Mad. E8 24
Moroni, Utah B6 72
Morozovsk, Sov. Un. G13 12
Morrill, Nebr. C2 71
Morrill, co., Nebr. C2 71
Morrilton, Ark. B3 49
Morris, Ala. B3 46
Morris, Man., Can. E3 40
Morris, Ill. B5 58
Morris, Minn. E3 67
Morris, N.Y. C5 75
Morris, Okla. B6 79
Morris, co., Kans. D7 61
Morris, co., N.J. B3 74
Morris, co., Tex. C5 84
Morris, mtn., N.Y. A6 75
Morrisburg, Ont., Can. C9 41
Morrisdale, Pa. E5 81
Morrison, Ill. B4 58
Morrison, Tenn. D8 83
Morrison, co., Minn. D4 67
Morrisonville, Ill. D4 58
Morris Plains, N.J. B4 74
Morristown, Ind. E6 59
Morristown, Minn. F5 67
Morristown, N.J. B3 74
Morristown, N.Y. f9 75
Morristown, Tenn. C10 83
Morrisville, N.Y. C5 75
Morrisville, Vt. B2 73
Morro Bay, Calif. E3 50
Morro do Chapéu, Braz. E6 27
Morropón, Peru C2 31
Morrow, Ohio C1 78
Morrow, co., Ohio B3 78
Morrow, co., Oreg. B7 80
Morse, La. D3 63
Morshansk, Sov. Un. E13 12
Mortara, It. B2 9
Morteros, Arg. A4 28
Morton, Ill. C4 58
Morton, Minn. F4 67
Morton, Miss. C4 68
Morton, Pa. *G11 81
Morton, Tex. C1 84
Morton, Wash. *C3 86

Morton, co., Kans. E2 61
Morton, co., N. Dak. D4 77
Morton Grove, Ill. h9 58
Mortons Gap, Ky. C2 62
Moruya, Austl. G8 26
Morven, N.C. C2 76
Morwell, Austl. G8, n15 25
Moscow, Idaho C2 57
Moscow, Pa. m18 81
Moscow (Moskva), Sov. Un. ... D11, n17 12
Moselle, dept., Fr. *C7 5
Moses Lake, Wash. B6 86
Moshi, Tan. I5 23
Mosinee, Wis. D4 88
Mosjoen, Nor. E5 11
Moskva, see Moscow, Sov. Un.
Mosonmagyaróvár, Hung. B3 10
Mosquera, Col. C2 32
Moss, Nor. H4, p28 11
Mossbank, Sask., Can. H3 39
Mosselbaai, S. Afr. G4 24
Mossman, Austl. C8 25
Mossoro, Braz. *D7 27
Moss Point, Miss. E5, f8 68
Moss Vale, Austl. *F9 25
Most, Czech. C2 7
Mostar, Yugo. D3 10
Mosul (Al Mawsil), Iraq D14 14
Motala, Swe. *H6 11
Motherwell & Wishaw, Scot. C5 4
Motley, co., Tex. B2 84
Motomachi, Jap. o18 18
Motril, Sp. D4 8
Mott, N. Dak. D3 77
Motul de Felipe Carrillo
  Puerto, Mex. C7 34
Motupe, Peru C2 31
Mouaskar, Alg. A5 22
Moulins, Fr. D5 5
Moulmein, Bur. E10 20
Moulton, Ala. A2 46
Moulton, Iowa D5 60
Moultrie, Ga. E3 55
Moultrie, co., Ill. D5 58
Mound, Minn. n11 67
Mound Bayou, Miss. B3 68
Mound City, Ill. F4 58
Mound City, Kans. D9 61
Mound City, Mo. A2 69
Moundridge, Kans. D6 61
Mounds, Ill. F4 58
Mounds, Okla. B5 79
Mounds View, Minn. *F5 67
Moundsville, W. Va. B4, g8 87
Moundville, Ala. C2 46
Mountain, prov., Phil. *B6 19
Mountainair, N. Mex. B5 48
Mountain Brook, Ala. g7 46
Mountain City, Tenn. C12 83
Mountain Dale, N.Y. D6 75
Mountain Grove, Mo. D5 69
Mountain Home, Ark. A3 49
Mountain Home, Idaho F3 57
Mountain Iron, Minn. C6 67
Mountain Lake, Minn. G4 67
Mountain Lake Park, Mo. m12 53
Mountain Lakes, N.J. B4 74
Mountain Pine, Ark. C2, f7 49
Mountainside, N.J. B4 74
Mountain View, Ark. B3 49
Mountain View, Calif. k8 50
Mountainview, Haw. D6 56
Mountain View, Idaho *F2 57
Mountain View, Mo. D6 69
Mountain View, Okla. B3 79
Mountain View, Wyo. E3 89
Mount Airy, Md. B3 53
Mount Airy, N.C. A2 76
Mount Angel, Oreg. B4, h12 80
Mount Arlington, N.J. B3 74
Mount Ayr, Iowa D3 60
Mount Berry, Ga. B1 55
Mount Bethel, N.J. B3 74
Mount Brydges, Ont., Can. E3 41
Mount Carmel, Ill. E6 58
Mount Carmel, Newf., Can. E5 44
Mount Carmel, Ohio o13 78
Mount Carmel, Pa. E9 81
Mount Carroll, Ill. A4 58
Mount Clare, W. Va. B4 87
Mount Clemens, Mich. F8, o16 66
Mount Dora, Fla. D5 54
Mount Edgecumbe, Alsk. m22 47
Mount Ephraim, N.J. *D2 74
Mount Forest, Ont., Can. D4 41
Mount Gambier, Austl. G7 25
Mount Gilead, N.C. B3 76
Mount Gilead, Ohio B3 78
Mount Healthy, Ohio o12 78
Mount Hermon, Mass. A3 65
Mount Holly, N.J. C3 74
Mount Holly, N.C. B1 76
Mount Holly Springs, Pa. F7 81

Mount Hope, Ont., Can. D5   42
Mount Hope, Kans. E6, g11 61
Mount Hope, N.J. B3 74
Mount Hope, W. Va. D3, n13 87
Mount Horeb, Wis. E4 88
Mount Houston, Tex. *E5 84
Mount Isa, Austl. D6 25
Mount Jackson, Va. B4 85
Mount Jewett, Pa. C4 81
Mount Joy, Pa. F9 81
Mount Kisco, N.Y. D7, m15 75
Mountlake Terrace, Wash. *B3 86
Mount Lebanon, Pa. F1 81
Mount Magnet, Austl. E2 25
Mount Morgan, Austl. D9 25
Mount Moriah, Newf., Can. *D2 44
Mount Morris, Ill. A4 58
Mount Morris, Mich. E7 66
Mount Morris, N.Y. C3 75
Mount Olive, Ala. B3, f7 46
Mount Olive, Ill. D4 58
Mount Olive, N.C. B4 76
Mount Oliver, Pa. k14 81
Mount Orab, Ohio C2 78
Mount Pearl Park, Newf., Can. f9 44
Mount Penn, Pa. *F10 81
Mount Pleasant, Iowa D6 60
Mount Pleasant, Mich. E6 66
Mount Pleasant, N.C. B2 76
Mount Pleasant, Pa. F2 81
Mount Pleasant, S.C. F8, k12 82
Mount Pleasant, Tenn. B4 83
Mount Pleasant, Tex. C5 84
Mount Pleasant, Utah B6 72
Mount Pocono, Pa. D11 81
Mount Prospect, Ill. A6, h9 58
Mount Pulaski, Ill. C4 58
Mountrail, co., N. Dak. B3 77
Mount Rainier, Md. f9 53
Mount Royal, N.J. D2 74
Mount Savage, Md. k13 53
Mount Shasta, Calif. B2 50
Mount Sterling, Ill. D3 58
Mount Sterling, Ky. B6 62
Mount Sterling, Ohio C2 78
Mount Union, Pa. F6 81
Mount Vernon, Ala. D1 46
Mount Vernon, Ga. D4 55
Mount Vernon, Ill. E5 58
Mount Vernon, Ind. I2 59
Mount Vernon, Iowa C6 60
Mount Vernon, Ky. C5 62
Mount Vernon, Md. D6 53
Mount Vernon, Mo. D4 69
Mount Vernon, N.Y. *C2 75
Mount Vernon, N.Y. h13 75
Mount Vernon, Ohio B3 78
Mount Vernon, Tex. C5 84
Mount Vernon, Wash. A3 86
Mount Victory, Ohio B2 78

Mountville, Pa. *G9 81
Mount Washington, Ky. B4, g11 62
Mount Wolf, Pa. F8 81
Mount Zion, Ill. D5 58
Moura, Port. C2   8
Mourne, mts., N. Ire. C3   4
Mouscron, Bel. B5   5
Mousie, Ky. C7 62
Moville, Iowa B1 60
Moweaqua, Ill. D4 58
Mower, co., Minn. G6 67
Moyeuvre -Grande, Fr. C7   5
Moyobamba, Peru C2 31
Mozambique, country, Afr. D7 24
Mozhaysk, Sov. Un. D11 12
Mozyr, Sov. Un. E7 12
Mtsensk, Sov. Un. E11 12
Muang Hot, Thai. *B1 19
Muang Nan, Thai. *B2 19
Muar (Bandar Maharani), Mala. *E2 19
Muchkap, Sov. Un. F14 12
Mucuri, Braz. E7 27
Mudanjiang, China C10 17
Mudanya, Tur. *B7 14
Mudgee, Austl. F7 26
Muenster, Tex. C4 84
Mufulira, Zambia C5 24
Mugía, Sp. A1   8
Muğla, Tur. D7 14
Mühldorf, Ger., Fed. Rep. of D6   6
Muhlenberg, co., Ky. C2 62
Muhlenberg Park, Pa. *F9 81
Mühlhausen, Ger. Dem. Rep. C5   6
Muir, Mich. E6 66
Mukachevo, Sov. Un. G4 12
Mukden, see Shenyang, China
Mukilteo, Wash. B3 86
Mukwonago, Wis. F5, n11 88
Mula, Sp. C5   8
Mulberry, Ark. B1 49
Mulberry, Fla. E5 54
Mulberry, Ind. D4 59
Mulberry, Kans. E9 61
Mulchén, Chile B2 28
Muldraugh, Ky. C4 26
Muldrow, Okla. B7 79
Mulege, Mex. B2 34
Muleshoe, Tex. B1 84
Mulga, Ala. B3, f7 46
Mulgrave, N.S., Can. D8 43
Mulhacén, mtn., Sp. D4   8
Mülheim an der Ruhr, Ger.
    Fed. Rep. of C3   6
Mulhouse, Fr. D7   5
Muling, China D5 18
Mullan, Idaho B3 57
Mullens, W. Va. D3 87
Mullewa, Austl. E2 25
Mullica Hill, N.J. D2 74
Mullingar, Ire. D3   4
Mullins, S.C. C9 82

Mūltan, Pak. B5 20
Multnomah, co., Oreg. B4 80
Mulvane, Kans. E6 61
Muna, Mex. C7 34
München, see Munich, Ger.,
    Fed. Rep. of
Munchon, Kor. G3 18
Muncie, Ind. D7 59
Muncy, Pa. D8 81
Mundare, Alta., Can. C4 38
Munday, Tex. C3 84
Mundelein, Ill. A5, h9 58
Münden, Ger., Fed. Rep. of C4   6
Munford, Tenn. B2 83
Munfordville, Ky. C4 62
Mungindi, Austl. E8 25
Munhall, Pa. k14 81
Munich (München), Ger.,
    Fed. Rep. of C5   6
Munising, Mich. B4 66
Munroe Falls, Ohio *A4 78
Munsan, Kor. H3 18
Munsey Park, N.Y. *E7 75
Munster, Fr. C7   5
Munster, Ind. A2 59
Münster in Westfalen, Ger.
    Fed. Rep. of C3   6
Munster, prov., Ire. *D2   4
Muntenia, prov., Rom. *C8 10
Muntenia, reg., Rom. C7 10
Muntok, Indon. F3 19
Muong Hou Nua, Laos, ... *D11 20
Muong Sing, Laos D11 20
Murakami, Jap. G9 18
Murcia, Sp. C5   8
Murcia, reg., Sp. C5   8
Murfreesboro, Ark. C2 49
Murfreesboro, N.C. A5 76
Murfreesboro, Tenn. B5 83
Murgon, Austl. E9 25
Muriae, Braz. C4 30
Murmansk, Sov. Un. C15 11
Murom, Sov. Un. D13 11
Muroran, Jap. E10 18
Muroto, Jap. J7 18
Murphy, Mo. g13 69
Murphy, N.C. f8 76
Murphysboro, Ill. F4 58
Murray, Iowa C4 60
Murray, Ky. f9 62
Murray, Utah A6, C2 72
Murray, co., Ga. B2 55
Murray, co., Minn. F3 67
Murray, co., Okla. C4 79
Murray, riv., Austl. G7 25
Murray Bridge, Austl. G6 25
Murray City, Ohio C3 78
Murrells Inlet, S.C. D9 82
Murrysville, Pa. k15 81
Murud, India E5 20
Murwāra, India D7 20

Murwillumbah, Austl. D9 26
Mürzzuschlag, Aus. E7   6
Mus, Tur. C13 14
Musala, peak, Bul. D6 10
Musan, Kor. E4 18
Musashino, Jap. *I9 18
Muscat, Om. D2 20
Muscat & Oman, see Oman,
    country, Asia.
Muscatine, Iowa C6 60
Muscatine, co., Iowa C6 60
Muscle Shoals, Ala. A2 46
Musclow, mtn., B.C., Can. C4 37
Muscoda, Wis. E3 88
Musconetcong, mtn., N.J. B2 74
Muse, Pa. F1 81
Musgravetown, Newf., Can. D5 44
Mushketovo, Sov. Un. r20 12
Muskego, Wis. F5, n11 88
Muskegon, Mich. E4 66
Muskegon, co., Mich. E4 66
Muskegon Heights, Mich. E4 66
Muskigum, co., Ohio B3 78
Muskö, Swe. u36 11
Muskogee, Okla. B6 79
Muskogee, co., Okla. B6 79
Muskoka, dist., Ont., Can. B5 41
Musquash, mtn., Maine C5 64
Musquodoboit Harbour, N.S., Can. . . . E6 43
Musselburgh, Scot. C5   4
Musselshell, co., Mont. D8 70
Mustafakemalpasa, Tur. B7 14
Muswellbrook, Austl. F9 25
Mutare, Zimb. D6 24
Mutsu, Jap. F10 18
Mutton, mts., Oreg. C5 80
Muttontown, N.Y. *E7 75
Muzaffarnagar, India *C6 20
Muzaffarpur, India C8 20
Muzambinho, Braz. k8 30
Muztag, mtn., Braz. A7 20
Muztag, mtn., China. A8 20
Mvuma, Zimb. D6 24
Mwanza, Tan. I4 23
Myers, S.C. k12 82
Myerstown, Pa. F9 81
Myingyan, Bur. D10 20
Myitkyina, Bur. C10 20
Myjava, Czech. D4   7
Myrtle Beach, S.C. D10 82
Myrtle Creek, Oreg. D3 80
Myrtle Grove, Fla. u14 54
Myrtle Point, Oreg. D2 80
Mysen, Nor. p29 11
Myślenice, Pol. D5   7
Mysłowice, Pol. g10   7
Mysore, India F6 20
Mysore, see Karnataka, state, India
Mystic, Conn. D9 52
Mystic, Iowa D5 60
My Tho, Viet. C3 19
Mytishchi, Sov. Un. n17 12

N

Naalehu, Haw. D6 56
Nabadwip, India *D8 20
Nabeul, Tun. A7 22
Nabnasset, Mass. A5 65
Nābulus, Jordan B3, g5 15
Naches, Wash. C5 86
Náchod, Czech. C4   7
Nacogdoches, Tex. D5 84
Nacogdoches, co., Tex. D5 84
Nacozari de García, Mex. A3 34
Nadiad, India *D5 20
Nădlac, Rom. B5 10
Nadvornaya, Sov. Un. G5 12
Naesong, Kor. H4 18
Naestved, Den. J4 11
Naga, Phil. C6 19
Nagaland, state, India *C9 20
Nagano, Jap. H9 18
Nagano, pref., Jap. *H9 18
Nagaoka, Jap. H9 18
Nagappattinam, India F6 20
Nagasaki, Jap. J4 18

Nagasaki, pref., Jap. *J4 18
Nāgercoil, India *G6 20
Nagoya, Jap. J8, n15 18
Nāgpur, India D6 20
Nags Head, N.C. B7 76
Nagua, Dom. Rep. E9 35
Nagykanizsa, Hung. B3 10
Nagykőrös, Hung. B4 10
Naha, Jap. F10 17
Nahant, Mass. g10 65
Nahariyya, Isr. A3 15
Nahunta, Ga. E5 55
Naicam, Sask., Can. E3 39
Nairn, Scot. *B5   4
Nairn, co., Scot. *B5   4
Nairobi, Ken. I5 23
Najin, Kor. E5 18
Nakaminato, Jap. m19 18
Nakamura, Jap. J6 18
Nakatsu, Jap. J5 18
Nakhichevan na Arakse,
    Sov. Un. F7 16

Nakhon Ratchasima, Thai. C2 19
Nakina, Ont., Can. o18 41
Nakło, Pol. B4   7
Nakskov, Den. J4 11
Nakuru, Ken. I5 23
Nakusp, B.C., Can. D9 37
Nalchik, Sov. Un. *E7 13
Namangan, Sov. Un. E10 12
Nambour, Austl. E9 25
Namcha Barwa, mtn., China F4 17
Nam Dinh, Viet. A3 19
Namibia (South West Africa),
    country, Afr. E3 24
Namiquipa, Mex. B3 34
Nampa, Idaho F2 57
Nampo (Chinnampo), Kor. G2 18
Namur, Bel. B6   5
Namur, prov., Bel. *B6   5
Namwŏn, Kor. I3 18
Nanaimo, B.C., Can. E5, f12 37
Nanakuli, Haw. B3, g9 56
Nanam, Kor. F4 18

Nanao, Jap. H8 18
Nance, co., Nebr. C7 71
Nanchang, China F8 17
Nanchong, China E6 17
Nancy, Fr. C7   5
Nanda Devi, peak, India B7 20
Nanded, India *E6 20
Nānga Parbat, peak, Pak. A5 20
Nanjing, China E8 17
Nanju, Kor. I3 18
Nanking, see Nanjing, China
Nanning, China G6 17
Nanping, China F8 17
Nanterre, Fr. g9   5
Nantes, Fr. D3   5
Nanticoke, Md. D6 53
Nanticoke, Pa. D10, n16 81
Nanton, Alta., Can. D4 38
Nantong, China E9 17
Nantucket, Mass. D7 65
Nantucket, co., Mass. D7 65
Nanty Glo, Pa. F4 81

Nanuet, N.Y. g12 75
Nanyang, China E7 17
Naoma, W. Va. n13 87
Naousa, Grc. B4 14
Napa, Calif. C2 50
Napa, co., Calif. C2 50
Napanee, Ont., Can. C8 41
Napanoch, N.Y. D6 75
Naperville, Ill. B5, k8 58
Napier, N.Z. M16 26
Napierville, Que., Can. D4 42
Napierville, co., Que., Can. D4 42
Naples, Fla. F5 54
Naples (Napoli), It. D5 9
Naples, N.Y. C3 75
Naples, Tex. C5 84
Napo, riv., Ec., Peru B2 31
Napoleon, N. Dak. D6 77
Napoleon, Ohio A1 78
Napoleonville, La. E4, k9 63
Napoli, see Naples, It.
Nappanee, Ind. B5 59
Naqadeh, Iran D15 14
Nara, Jap. o14 19
Naracoorte, Austl. G7 25
Naranja, Fla. G6, s13 54
Nārāyanganj, Bngl. D9 20
Narberth, Pa. o20 81
Narbonne, Fr. F5 5
Nardó, It. D7 9
Nariño, dept., Col. C2 32
Narita, Jap. n19 18
Narmada, riv., India D6 20
Narodnaya, mtn., Sov. Un. C9 13
Naro-Fominsk, Sov. Un. D11 12
Narol, Man., Can. D3 40
Narrabri, Austl. F8 25
Narragansett, R.I. D11 52
Narrandera, Austl. F8 25
Narrogin, Austl. F2 25
Narrows, Va. C2 85
Narrowsburg, N.Y. D5 75
Narva, Sov. Un. B7 12
Narvik, Nor. C7 11
Naryan-Mar, Sov. Un. C8 13
Nash, Tex. C5 84
Nash, co., N.C. A4 76
Nashua, Iowa B5 60
Nashua, Mont. B10 70
Nashua, N.H. F5 73
Nashville, Ark. D2 49
Nashville, Ga. E3 55
Nashville, Ill. E4 58
Nashville, Mich. F5 66
Nashville, N.C. B5 76
Nashville, Tenn. A5, g10 83
Nashwauk, Minn. C5 67
Našice, Yugo. C4 10
Nāsik, India E5 20
Nasirābād, Bngl. D9 20
Nassau, Ba. B5, m17 35
Nassau, N.Y. C7 75
Nassau, co., Fla. B5 54
Nassau, co., N.Y. E7 75
Nassawadox, Va. C7 85
Nässjö, Swe. I6 11
Nasukoin, mtn., Mont. B2 70
Natagaima, Col. C2 32
Natal, Braz. D7 27
Natal, B.C., Can. E10 37
Natal, prov., S. Afr. F6 24
Natalia, Tex. E3 84
Natchez, Miss. D2 68
Natchitoches, La. C2 63
Natchitoches, par., La. C2 63
Nathanya, Isr. B2 15
Natick, Mass. B5, g10 65
National City, Calif. F5, o15 50
National Park, N.J. *D2 74
Natívitas, Mex. h9 34
Natoma, Kans. C4 61
Natrona, co., Wyo. D6 89
Natrona Heights, Pa. E2, h15 81
Natural Bridge, N.Y. A5 75
Naturita, Colo. C2 51
Nauen, Ger. Dem. Rep. B6 6
Naugatuck, Conn. D4 52
Naughton, Ont., Can. A3 41
Naumburg an der Saale,
  Ger. Dem. Rep. C5 6
Nauru, country, Oceania G8 2
Nauta, Peru B3 31
Nautla, Mex. C5, m15 34
Nauvoo, Ill. C2 58
Navajo, co., Ariz. B3 48
Navalmoral de la Mata, Sp. C3 8
Navarre, Ohio B4 78
Navarre, reg., Sp. A5 8
Navarro, co., Tex. C4 84
Navasota, Tex. D4 84
Navassa, N.C. C4 76
Navesink, N.J. C4 74
Navojoa, Mex. B3 34

Navolato, Mex. C3 34
Navplion, Grc. D4 14
Navy Yard City, Wash. *B3 86
Nayarit, state, Mex. C4, m11 34
Nayoro, Jap. D11 18
Nazaré, Braz. *E7 27
Nazaré, Port. C1 8
Nazareth, Ky. C4 62
Nazareth, Pa. E11 81
Nazas, Mex. B4 34
Nazca, Peru D3 31
Nazerat (Nazareth), Isr. B3, g5 15
Nazilli, Tur. D7 14
Ndjemena, Chad. F8 22
Ndola, Zambia C5 24
Neah Bay, Wash. A1 86
Neath, Wales E5 4
Nebraska, state, U.S. 71
Nebraska City, Nebr. D10, h13 71
Necedah, Wis. D3 88
Nechako, mts., B.C., Can. C5 37
Necochea, Arg. B5 28
Nederland, Tex. E6 84
Nedrow, N.Y. *C4 75
Needham, Mass. g11 65
Needle, mtn., Wyo. B3 89
Needles, Calif. E6 50
Needville, Tex. r14 84
Neembucu, dept., Par. A4 29
Neenah, Wis. D5, h9 88
Neepawa, Man., Can. D2 40
Neffs, Ohio B5 78
Neffsville, Pa. F9 81
Negaunee, Mich. B3 66
Negley, Ohio B5 78
Negotin, Yugo. C6 10
Negra, mts., Peru C2 31
Negreira, Sp. A1 8
Negro, riv., S.A. D4 27
Negros Occidental, prov., Phil. *C6 19
Negros Oriental, prov., Phil. *D6 19
Neguac, N.B., Can. B4 43
Neiba, Dom. Rep. E8 35
Neijiang, China F6 17
Neillsville, Wis. D3 88
Neiva, Col. C2 32
Nejd, pol. div., Sau. Ar. D3 15
Nekoosa, Wis. D4 88
Neligh, Nebr. B7 71
Nellore, India F6 20
Nelson, B.C., Can. E9 37
Nelson, Nebr. D7 71
Nelson, N.Z. N14 26
Nelson, co., Ky. C4 62
Nelson, co., N. Dak. C7 77
Nelson, co., Va. C4 85
Nelsonville, Ohio C3 78
Nemacolin, Pa. G2 81
Nemaha, co., Kans. C7 61
Nemaha, co., Nebr. D10 71
Nemunas (Niemen), riv., Sov. Un. D3 12
Nemuro, Jap. E12 18
Nenjiang, China B10 17
Neodesha, Kans. E8 61
Neoga, Ill. D5 58
Neola, Iowa C2 60
Neon, Ky. C7 62
Neopit, Wis. D5 88
Nepal, country, Asia C7 20
Nephi, Utah B6 72
Neptune, N.J. C4 74
Neptune Beach, Fla. B5, m9 54
Neptune City, N.J. *C4 74
Nerchinsk, Sov. Un. D14 13
Nerekhta, Sov. Un. C13 12
Nerja, Sp. D4 8
Nerva, Sp. D2 8
Nesconset, N.Y. F4 52
Nescopeck, Pa. D9 81
Neshoba, co., Miss. C4 68
Nesquehoning, Pa. E10 81
Ness, co., Kans. D3 61
Ness City, Kans. D4 61
Nes Ziyyona, Isr. C2 15
Netarts, Oreg. B3 80
Netcong, N.J. B3 74
Netherlands, country, Eur. A6 5
Netherlands Antilles, dep., N.A. *A4 32
Nettleton, Miss. A5 68
Nettuno, It. k9 9
Neubrandenburg, Ger. Dem. Rep. B6 6
Neuburg, Ger., Fed. Rep. of D5 6
Neuchâtel, Switz. E3 6
Neuchâtel, canton, Switz. E3 6
Neufchâtel-en-Bray, Fr. C4 5
Neuilly sur-Marne, Fr. g11 5
Neuilly -sur-Seine, Fr. g10 5
Neumarkt, Ger., Fed. Rep. of D5 6
Neumünster, Ger., Fed. Rep. of A4 6
Neunkirchen, Aus. E8 6

Neunkirchen, Ger., Fed. Rep. of *D3 6
Neuquén, Arg. B3 28
Neuquén, prov., Arg. B3 28
Neuruppin, Ger. Dem. Rep. B6 6
Neuss, Ger., Fed. Rep. of *C3 6
Neustadt, Ont., Can. C4 41
Neustadt an der Aisch,
  Ger., Fed. Rep. of C5 6
Neustadt an der Weinstrasse,
  Ger., Fed. Rep. of D4 6
Neustadt bei Coburg,
  Ger., Fed. Rep. of D4 6
Neustadt im Schwarzwald,
  Ger., Fed. Rep. of A5 6
Neustadt in Holstein,
  Ger., Fed. Rep. of C5 6
Neustrelitz, Ger. Dem. Rep. B6 6
Neu-Ulm, Ger., Fed. Rep. of D5 6
Neuville, Que., Can. C6, o16 42
Neuwied, Ger., Fed. Rep. of C3 6
Nevada, Iowa B4 60
Nevada, Mo. D3 69
Nevada, Ohio B2 78
Nevada, co., Ark. D2 49
Nevada, co., Calif. C3 50
Nevada, state, U.S. 72
Nevada City, Calif. C3 50
Nevada de Colima, mtn., Mex. m12 34
Nevada de Toluca, mtn., Mex. n14 34
Nevado del Huilo, peak, Col. C2 32
Nevelsk, Sov. Un. C10 18
Nevers, Fr. D5 5
Nevesinje, Yugo. D4 10
Neville Island, Pa. *E1 81
Nevşehir, Tur. C10 14
New Albany, Ind. H6 59
New Albany, Miss. A4 68
New Albin, Iowa A6 60
New Alexandria, Va. *B5 85
New Amsterdam, Guy. C5 27
Newark, Ark. B4 49
Newark, Calif. h8 50
Newark, Del. A6 53
Newark, Eng. D6 4
Newark, N.J. B4, k8 74
Newark, N.Y. B3 75
Newark, Ohio B3 78
Newark Valley, N.Y. C4 75
New Athens, Ill. E4 58
Newaygo, Mich. E5 66
Newaygo, co., Mich. E5 66
New Baden, Ill. E4 58
New Baltimore, Mich. F8 66
New Baltimore, N.Y. C7 75
New Beaver, Pa. *E1 81
New Bedford, Mass. C6 65
Newberg, Oreg. B4, h12 80
New Berlin, Ill. D4 58
New Berlin, N.Y. C5 75
New Berlin, Wis. n11 88
New Berlinville, Pa. *F9 81
New Bern, N.C. B5 76
Newbern, Tenn. A2 83
Newberry, Fla. C4 54
Newberry, Mich. B5 66
Newberry, S.C. C4 82
Newberry, co., S.C. C4 82
New Bethlehem, Pa. D3 81
New Bloomfield (Bloomfield),
  Pa. F7 81
New Boston, Ill. B3 58
New Boston, Mich. p15 66
New Boston, Ohio D3 78
New Boston, Tex. C5 84
New Braunfels, Tex. E3, h7 84
New Bremen, Ohio B1 78
New Brighton, Minn. *E5 67
New Brighton, Pa. E1 81
New Britain, Conn. C5 52
New Britain, Isl., Pap. N. Gui. G7 2
New Brockton, Ala. D4 46
New Brunswick, N.J. C4 74
New Brunswick, prov., Can. C3 43
New Brunswick Heights, N.J. *C4 74
New Buffalo, Mich. G4 66
Newburg, Mo. D6 69
Newburgh, Ont., Can. C8 41
Newburgh, Ind. I3 59
Newburgh, N.Y. D6 75
Newburgh Heights, Ohio h12 78
Newbury, Eng. E6 4
Newbury, Mass. A6 65
Newburyport, Mass. A6 65
New Caledonia, Fr., dep., Oceania H7 2
New Canaan, Conn. E3 52
New Carlisle, Que., Can. A4 43
New Carlisle, Ind. A4 59
New Carlisle, Ohio C1 78
New Cassel, N.Y. *E7 75
New Castle, reg., Sp. C4 8
New Castle, Ala. B3, f7 46
Newcastle, Austl. F9 25
Newcastle, Calif. C3 50

Newcastle, N.B., Can. B4 43
Newcastle, Ont., Can. D6 41
New Castle, Del. A6 53
New Castle, Ind. E7 59
New Castle, Pa. D1 81
Newcastle, Tex. C3 84
Newcastle, Wyo. C8 89
New Castle, co., Del. A6 53
Newcastle Bridge, N.B., Can. C3 43
Newcastle Mine, Alta., Can. D4 38
New Castle Northwest, Pa. *E1 81
Newcastle-on-Tyne, Eng. C6 4
New Chicago, Ind. A3 59
New City, N.Y. D7, m15 75
Newcomb, N.Y. B6 75
Newcomerstown, Ohio B4 78
New Concord, Ohio C4 78
New Cumberland, Pa. F8 81
New Cumberland, W. Va. A4, f8 87
New Cumnock, Scot. C4 4
New Delhi, India C6 20
New Denver, B.C., Can. D9 37
New Eagle, Pa. *F1 81
New Egypt, N.J. C3 74
Newell, Iowa B2 60
Newell, W. Va. A4, e8 87
New Ellenton, S.C. E4 82
Newellton, La. B4 63
New England, N. Dak. D3 77
Newfane, N.Y. B2 75
Newfield, N.J. D2 74
New Florence, Mo. C6 69
New Florence, Pa. F3 81
Newfoundland, prov., Can. 44
Newfoundland, N.J. A4 74
New Franklin, Mo. B5 69
New Freedom, Pa. G8 81
New Germany, N.S., Can. E5 43
New Glarus, Wis. F4 88
New Glasgow, N.S., Can. D7 43
New Gretna, N.J. D4 74
New Guinea, isl., Oceania G6 2
New Guinea, Territory of, see
  Papua New Guinea, country, Oceania
Newgulf, Tex. *E5 84
Newhall, Calif. E4 50
Newhall, Iowa C6 60
New Hamburg, Ont., Can. D4 41
New Hampshire, state, U.S. 73
New Hampton, Iowa A5 60
New Hanover, co., N.C. C5 76
New Harbour, Newf., Can. E5 44
New Harmony, Ind. H2 59
New Hartford, Conn. B5 52
New Hartford, Iowa B5 60
New Hartford, N.Y. *B5 75
New Haven, Conn. D5 52
New Haven, Ill. F5 58
New Haven, Ind. B7 59
New Haven, Ky. C4 62
New Haven, Mich. F8 66
New Haven, Mo. C6 69
New Haven, W. Va. C3 87
New Haven, co., Conn. D4 52
New Hebrides, see Vanuatu,
  country, Oceania
New Holland, Ga. B3 55
New Holland, Ohio C2 78
New Holland, Pa. F9 81
New Holstein, Wis. E5, k9 88
New Hope, Ala. A3 46
New Hope, Minn. *E5 67
New Hope, Pa. F12 81
New Hudson, Mich. o14 66
New Hyde Park, N.Y. G2 52
New Iberia, La. D4 63
Newington, Conn. C6 52
New Jersey, state, U.S. 74
New Kensington, Pa. E2, h14 81
New Kent, co., Va. C6 85
Newkirk, Okla. A4 79
New Knoxville, Ohio B1 78
New Kowloon, Hong Kong *G7 17
Newland, N.C. A1, e11 76
New Lebanon, Ohio *C1 78
New Lenox, Ill. B6, k9 58
New Lexington, Ohio C3 78
New Lisbon, Wis. E3 88
New Liskeard, Ont. Can. p20 41
New London, Conn. C8 52
New London, Iowa D6 60
New London, Minn. E4 67
New London, Mo. B6 69
New London, N.H. E4 73
New London, Ohio A3 78
New London, Wis. D5 88
New London, co., Conn. D8 52
New Madison, Ohio C1 78
New Madrid, Mo. E8 69
New Madrid, co., Mo. E8 69
New Malden, Eng. m11 4
Newman, Calif. D3 50
Newman, Ill. D6 58

Newman Grove, Nebr.	C8	71
Newmanstown, Pa.	F9	81
Newmarket, Ont., Can.	C5	41
New Market, Ind.	E4	59
Newmarket, N.H.	E6	73
New Market, N.J.	*B4	74
New Market, Va.	B4	85
New Martinsville, W. Va.	B4	87
New Matamoras, Ohio	C4	78
New Meadows, Idaho	E2	57
New Mexico, state, U.S.		48
New Miami, Ohio	C1, n12	78
New Milford, Conn.	C3	52
New Milford, N.J.	h8	74
New Milford, Ohio	A4	78
New Milford, Pa.	C10	81
New Monmouth, N.J.	C4	74
Newnan, Ga.	C2	55
New Norfolk, Austl.	o15	25
New Orleans, La.	E5, h11	63
New Oxford, Pa.	G7	81
New Palestine, Ind.	E6	59
New Paltz, N.Y.	D6	75
New Paris, Ind.	B6	59
New Paris,Ohio	C1	78
New Philadelphia, Ohio	B4	78
New Philadelphia, Pa.	E9	81
New Plymouth, Idaho	F2	57
New Plymouth, N.Z.	M15	26
Newport, Ark.	B4	49
Newport, Del.	A6	53
Newport, Eng.	E6	4
New Port, Ind.	E3	59
Newport, Ky.	A5, h14	62
Newport, Maine	D3	64
Newport, Mich.	G7	66
Newport, Minn.	n13	67
Newport, N.H.	E3	73
Newport, N.J.	E2	74
New Port, N.Y.	B5	75
New Port, N.C.	C6	76
Newport, Ohio	C4	78
Newport, Oreg.	C2	80
Newport, Pa.	F7	81
Newport, R.I.	D11	52
Newport, Tenn.	D10	83
Newport, Vt.	B3	73
Newport, Wales	E5	4
Newport, Wash.	A8	86
Newport, co., R.I.	C11	52
Newport Beach, Calif.	F5, n13	50
Newport News (Independent City), Va.	D6, k15	85
New Port Richey, Fla.	D4	54
Newportville, Pa.	*F11	81
New Prague, Minn.	F5	67
New Providence, N.J.	B4	74
New Providence, isl., Ba.	B5, m17	35
Newquay, Eng.	E4	4
New Richland, Minn.	G5	67
New Richmond, Que., Can.	A4	43
New Richmond, Ohio	D1	78
New Richmond, Wis.	C1	88
New Road, N.S., Can.	E6	43
New Roads, La.	D4	63
New Rochelle, N.Y.	h13, n15	75
New Rockford, N. Dak.	C6	77
Newry, N. Ire.	C3	4
Newry, S.C.	B2	82
New Salem, N. Dak.	D4	77
New Salem, Pa.	*G2	81
New Sarpy, La.	k11	63
New Sharon, Iowa	C5	60
New Shrewsbury, N.J.	C4	74
New Smyrna Beach, Fla.	C6	54
New South Wales, state, Austl.	F8	25
New Straitsville, Ohio	C3	78
New Tazewell, Tenn.	C10	83
Newton, Ala.	D4	46
Newton, Ill.	E5	58
Newton, Iowa	C4	60
Newton, Kans.	D6, f12	61
Newton, Mass.	B5, g11	65
Newton, Miss.	C4	68
Newton, N.J.	A3	74
Newton, N.C.	B1	76
Newton, Tex.	D6	84
Newton, co., Ark.	B2	49
Newton, co., Ga.	C3	55
Newton, co., Ind.	B3	59
Newton, co., Miss.	C4	68
Newton, co., Mo.	E3	69
Newton, co., Tex.	D6	84
Newton Falls, N.Y.	A6, f9	75
Newton Falls, Ohio	A5	78
Newtonville, N.Y.	*C7	75
Newtown, Conn.	D3	52
Newtown, Ohio	C1, o13	78
Newtown, Pa.	F12	81
Newtown & *Llanllwchaiarn*, Wales	D5	4
Newtownards, N. Ire.	C4	4
Newtown Square, Pa.	p20	81
New Ulm, Minn.	F4	67
New Vienna, Ohio	C2	78
Newville, Pa.	F7	81
New Washington, Ohio	B3	78
New Waterford, N.S., Can.	C9	43
New Waterford, Ohio	B5	78
New Westminster, B.C., Can.	E6, f13	37
New Whiteland, Ind.	E5	59
New Wilmington, Pa.	D1	81
New Windsor, Ill.	B3	58
New Windsor, Md.	A3	53
New Windsor, N.Y.	*D6	75
New York, N.Y.	E7, h13	75
New York, co., N.Y.	k13	75
New York, state, U.S.		75
New York Mills, Minn.	D3	67
New York Mills, N.Y.	*B5	75
New Zealand, country, Oceania	N15	26
Nezhin, Sov. Un.	F8	12
Nez Perce, Idaho	C2	57
Nez Perce, co., Idaho	C2	57
Ngaoundéré, Cam	G7	22
Nha Trang, Viet.	C3	19
Niagara, Wis.	C6	88
Niagara, co., Ont., Can.	D5	41
Niagara, N.Y.	B2	75
Niagara Falls, Ont., Can.	D5	41
Niagara Falls, N.Y.	B1	75
Niagara-on-the-Lake, Ont., Can.	D5	41
Niagara University, N.Y.	*B1	75
Niamey, Niger	F5	22
Niantic, Conn.	D8	52
Niantic, Ill.	D4	58
Nicaragua, country, N.A.	E7	34
Nicaragua, lake, Nic.	E7	34
Nicastro (Lamezia Terme), It.	E6	9
Nice, Fr.	F7	5
Niceville, Fla.	u15	54
Nichinan, Jap.	K5	18
Nicholas, co., Ky.	B5	62
Nicholas, co., W. Va.	C4	87
Nicholasville, Ky.	C5	62
Nicholls, Ga.	E4	55
Nichols, N.Y.	C4	75
Nichols, S.C.	C9	82
Nichols Hills, Okla.	B4	79
Nicholson, Pa.	C10	81
Nickerson, Kans.	D5	61
Nicolet, Que., Can.	C5	42
Nicolet, co., Que., Can.	C5	42
Nicollet, Minn.	F4	67
Nicollet, co., Minn.	F4	67
Nicoma Park, Okla.	B4	79
Nicosia (Levkosia), Cyp.	A4	23
Nicosia, It.	F5	9
Nicotera, It.	E5	9
Nicoya, C.R.	E7	34
Niedersachsen (Lower Saxony), state, Ger., Fed. Rep. of	*B4	6
Nienburg, Ger., Fed. Rep. of	B4	6
Nievre, dept., Fr.	*D5	5
Niğde, Tur.	D10	14
Niger, country, Afr.	F6	22
Niger, riv., Afr.	F5	22
Nigeria, country, Afr.	G6	22
Nigrita, Grc.	B4	14
Niigata, Jap.	H9	18
Niigata, pref., Jap	*H9	18
Niihama, Jap.	J6	18
Niihau, isl., Haw.	B1	56
Niimi, Jap.	I6	18
Nijar, Sp.	D4	8
Nijmegen, Neth.	B6	5
Nikitovka, Sov. Un.	q21	12
Nikko, Jap.	H9	18
Nikolayev, Sov. Un.	H9	12
Nikopol, Sov. Un.	H10	12
Niland, Calif.	F6	50
Nile, riv., Afr.	C4	23
Niles, Ill.	h9	58
Niles, Mich.	G4	66
Niles, Ohio	A5	78
Nimes, Fr.	F6	5
Ninette, Man., Can.	E2	40
Ninety Six, S.C.	C3	82
Ning'an, China	D4	18
Ningbo, China	F9	17
Ningde, China	F8	17
Ningxia, Huizu, auton. reg., China	D6	17
Ningxian, China	D6	17
Ninh Binh, Viet.	A3	19
Niobrara, Nebr.	B7	71
Niobrara, co., Wyo.	C8	89
Niort, Fr.	D3	5
Niota, Tenn.	D9	83
Nipawin, Sask., Can.	D3	39
Nipigon, lake, Ont., Can.	o17	41
Nipissing, dist., Ont., Can.	A5	41
Nipomo, Calif.	E3	50
Niquero, Cuba	D5	35
Nirasaki, Jap.	n17	18
Nis, Yugo.	D5	10
Nisa, Port.	C2	8
Nishinomiya, Jap.	*I7	18
Nishio, Jap.	o16	18
Nisko, Pol.	C7	7
Nisswa, Minn.	D4	67
Niterói, Braz.	C4, h6	30
Nitra, Czech.	D5	7
Nitro, W. Va.	C3	87
Niue, N.Z., dep., Oceania	*H9	2
Nivelles, Bel.	B6	5
Nivernais, former prov., Fr.	D5	5
Niverville, Man., Can.	E3	40
Nixa, Mo.	D4	69
Nixon, N.J.	B4	74
Nixon, Tex.	E4, k8	84
Nizāmābād, India	*E6	20
Nizhneudinsk, Sov. Un.	D12	13
Nizhneye, Sov. Un.	q21	12
Nizhniy Tagil, Sov. Un.	D9	13
Nkangsamba, Cam	H6	22
Noank, Conn.	D9	52
Nobel, Ont., Can.	B4	41
Nobeoka, Jap.	J5	18
Noble, Ill.	E5	58
Noble, Okla.	B4	79
Noble, co., Ind.	B7	59
Noble, co., Ohio	C4	78
Noble, co., Okla.	A4	79
Nobles, co., Minn.	G3	67
Noblesville, Ind.	D6	59
Noboribetsu, Jap.	E10	18
Nocatee, Fla.	E5	54
Nochixtán, Mex.	o15	34
Nocona, Tex.	C4	84
Nodaway, co., Mo.	A3	69
Noel, Mo.	E3	69
Nogales, Ariz.	D3	48
Nogales, Mex.	A2	34
Nogales, Mex.	n15	34
Nogata, Jap.	J5	18
Nogent-le-Rotrou, Fr.	C4	18
Nogent *sur-Marne*, Fr.	g10	5
Noginsk, Sov. Un.	D12, n18	12
Nogoyá, Arg.	A5	28
Nógrád, co., Hung.	*A4	10
Nohar, India	C5	20
Noheji, Jap.	F10	18
Noisy-le-Sec, Fr.	g10	5
Nokomis, Sask., Can.	F3	39
Nokomis, Fla.	E4	54
Nokomis, Ill.	D4	58
Nola, It.	D5	9
Nolan, co., Tex.	C2	84
Nome, Alsk.	C6	47
Nominingue, Que., Can.	C2	42
Nomme, Sov. Un.	*B5	11
Nong'an, China	C10	17
Nonoava, Mex.	B3	34
Noranda, Que., Can.	*o20	41
Nora Springs, Iowa	A5	60
Norborne, Mo.	B4	69
Norco, Calif.	*F5	50
Norco, La.	D5, h11	63
Norcross, Ga.	C2, h8	55
Nord, dept., Fr.	*B5	5
Nordegg, Alta., Can.	C2, g7	38
Norden, Ger., Fed. Rep. of	B3	6
Nordenham, Ger., Fed. Rep. of	B4	6
Nordhausen, Ger. Dem. Rep.	C5	6
Nordhorn, Ger., Fed. Rep. of	B3	6
Nordland, co., Nor.	*D6	11
Nördlingen, Ger., Fed. Rep. of	D5	6
Nordrhein-Westfalen, state, Ger., Fed. Rep. of	*C3	6
Nord-Trøndelag, co., Nor.	*E4	11
Nordvik, Sov. Un.	B14	13
Norfolk, Nebr.	B8	71
Norfolk, N.Y.	f9	75
Norfolk (Independent City), Va.	D6, k15	85
Norfolk, co., Ont., Can.	E4	41
Norfolk, co., Eng.	*D7	4
Norfolk, co., Mass.	B5	65
Norilsk, Sov. Un.	C11	13
Norlina, N.C.	A4	76
Norma, N.J.	E2	74
Normal, Ala.	*A3	46
Normal, Ill.	C5	58
Norman, co., Minn.	C2	67
Norman, Okla.	B4	79
Normandin, Que., Can.	*G19	36
Normandy, Fla.	*B5	54
Normandy, Mo.	f13	69
Normandy, former prov., Fr.	C4	5
Normandy Heights, Ohio	n12	78
Normandy Park, Wash.	*B4	86
Norman's Cove, Newf.	*D5	44
Norquay, Sask., Can.	F4	39
Norridge, Ill.	k9	58
Norridgewock, Maine	D3	64
Norris, S.C.	B2	82
Norris, Tenn.	C9	83
Norris Arm, Newf., Can.	D4	44
Norris City, Ill.	F5	58
Norris Point, Newf., Can.	D3	44
Norristown, Pa.	F11, o20	81
Norrköping, Swe.	H7, u34	11
Norrtälje, Swe.	H8, t36	11
Norseman, Austl.	F3	25
Norte de Santander, dept., Col.	B3	32
North, S.C.	D5	82
North, isl., N.Z.	L14	26
North, sea, Eur.	D8	3
North Abington, Mass.	B6, h12	65
North Adams, Mass.	A1	65
North Adams, Mich.	G6	66
North Albany, Oreg.	k11	80
Northam, Austl.	F2	25
North America, cont.		33
North Amherst, Mass.	B2	65
North Amityville, N.Y.	*E7	75
Northampton, Austl.	E1	25
Northampton, Eng.	D6	4
Northampton, Mass.	B2	65
Northampton, Pa.	E11	81
Northampton, co., Eng.	*D6	4
Northampton, co., N.C.	A5	76
Northampton, co., Pa.	E11	81
Northampton, co., Va.	C7	85
North Andover, Mass.	A5	65
North Anson, Maine	D3	64
North Apollo, Pa.	E2	81
North Arlington, N.J.	h8	74
North Asheboro, N.C.	*B3	76
North Atlanta, Ga.	h8	55
North Attleboro, Mass.	C5	65
North Augusta, S.C.	E3	82
North Aurora, Ill.	k8	58
North Babylon, N.Y.	*n15	75
North Baltimore, Ohio	A2	78
North Bangor, N.Y.	f10	75
North Battleford, Sask., Can.	E1, n7	39
North Bay, Ont., Can.	A5, p20	41
North Bay, Fla.	*G6	54
North Belle Vernon, Pa.	*F2	81
North Bellmore, N.Y.	*E7	75
North Bellport, N.Y.	n15	75
North Belmont, N.C.	B1	76
North Bend, Nebr.	C9	71
North Bend, Ohio	o12	78
North Bend, Oreg.	D2	80
North Bend, Pa.	D6	81
North Bend, Wash.	B4	86
North Bennington, Vt.	F1	73
North Bergen, N.J.	h8	74
North Berwick, Maine	E2	64
North Billerica, Mass.	A5, f10	65
North Bonneville, Wash.	D4	86
Northboro, Mass.	B4	65
North Brabant, prov., Neth.	*B6	5
North Braddock, Pa.	k14	81
North Branch, Mich.	E7	66
North Branch, Minn.	E6	67
North Branch, N.J.	B3	74
Northbridge, Mass.	B4	65
Northbrook, Ill.	h9	58
North Brookfield, Mass.	B3	65
North Brother, mtn., Maine	C4	64
North Brunswick, N.J.	*C4	74
North Caldwell, N.J.	B4	74
North Canton, Ga.	B2	55
North Canton, Ohio	B4	78
North Carolina, state, U.S.		76
North Catasauqua, Pa.	*E11	81
North Cedar, Iowa	*B5	60
North Charleroi, Pa.	*F1	81
North Charleston, S.C.	F8, k12	82
North Chelmsford, Mass.	A5	65
North Chicago, Ill.	A6, h9	58
North Chili, N.Y.	*B3	75
North Chillicothe, Ill.	B4	58
North City, Wash.	*B3	86
Northcliffe, Austl.	F2	25
North Cohasset, Mass.	h12	65
North College Hill, Ohio	o12	78
North Collins, N.Y.	C2	75
North Conway, N.H.	B4	73
North Corbin, Ky.	D5	62
North Creek, N.Y.	B7	75
Northcrest, Calif.	*B1	50
North Dakota, state, U.S.		77
North Dartmouth, Mass.	C6	65
North Decatur, Ga.	*C2	55
North Dighton, Mass.	C5	65
North East, Md.	A6	53
North East, Nor.	E5	13
North East, Pa.	B2	81
Northeastern Polder, prov., Neth.	*A6	5
Northeast Harbor, Maine	D4	64
North Easton, Mass.	B5	65
Northeim, Ger., Fed. Rep. of	C4	6
North English, Iowa	C5	60
Northern Arm, Newf., Can.	D4	44

Northern, reg., Nig. ... F6 22
Northern Ireland, reg., U.K. ... C3 4
Northern Territory, ter., Austl. ... C5 25
North Fairfield, Ohio ... A3 78
North Falmouth, Mass. ... C6 65
Northfield, B.C., Can. ... f2 37
Northfield, Ill. ... *B6 58
Northfield, Mass. ... A3 65
Northfield, Minn. ... F5 67
Northfield, N.H. ... E4 73
Northfield, N.J. ... E3 74
Northfield, Ohio ... h9 78
Northfield, Vt. ... C2 73
North Fond du Lac, Wis. ... E5, k9 88
North Fork, Calif. ... D4 50
North Freedom, Wis. ... E4 88
North Glen Ellyn, Ill. ... *B5 58
Northglenn, Colo. ... B6 51
North Grafton, Mass. ... B4 65
North Great River, N.Y. ... n15 75
North Grosvenor Dale, Conn. ... B9 52
North Haledon, N.J. ... *B4 74
North Hampton, Ohio ... C2 78
North Hartsville, S.C. ... *C7 82
North Hatley, Que., Can. ... D6 42
North Haven, Conn. ... D5 52
North Head, N.S., Can. ... E3 43
North Henderson, N.C. ... *A4 76
North Highlands, Calif. ... *C3 50
North Holland (Noordholland), prov., Neth. ... *A6 5
North Hornell, N.Y. ... *C3 75
North Hudson, Wis. ... *D1 88
North Industry, Ohio ... B4 78
North Irwin, Pa. ... *F2 81
North Judson, Ind. ... B4 59
North Kamloops, B.C., Can. ... D7 37
North Kansas City, Mo. ... h10 69
North Kingstown, R.I. ... C11 52
North Kingsville, Ohio ... A5 78
North La Junta, Colo. ... C7 51
Northlake, Ill. ... K9 58
North Larchmont, N.Y. ... *D2 75
North Las Vegas, Nev. ... C4 72
North Lewisburg, Ohio ... B2 78
North Liberty, Ind. ... A5 59
North Lima, Ohio ... B5 78
North Lindenhurst, N.Y. ... n15 75
North Little Rock, Ark. ... C3, h10 49
North Manchester, Ind. ... C6 59
North Mankato, Minn. ... F4 67
North Massapequa, N.Y. ... *E7 75
North Merrick, N.Y. ... *E7 75
North Miami, Fla. ... G6, s13 54
North Miami Beach, Fla. ... s13 54
Northmoor, Mo. ... h10 69
North Muskegon, Mich. ... E4 66
North New Hyde Park, N.Y. ... *E7 75
North Norwich, N.Y. ... C5 75
North Ogden, Utah ... A6, C2 72
North Olmsted, Ohio ... h9 78
North Oxford, Mass. ... B4 65
North Palisade, mtn., Calif. ... D4 50
North Palm Beach, Fla. ... *F6 54
North Park, Ill. ... A4 58
North Patchogue, N.Y. ... n14 75
North Pembroke, Mass. ... B6 65
North Perkin, Ill. ... *C4 58
North Pelham, N.Y. ... h13 75
North Plainfield, N.J. ... B4 74
North Plains, Oreg. ... B4, g12 80
North Platte, Nebr. ... C5 71
North Platte, riv., U.S. ... B6 45
North Pleasanton, Tex. ... *E3 84

Northport, Ala. ... B2 46
Northport, Mich. ... C5 66
Northport, N.Y. ... n15 75
Northport, Wash. ... A8 86
North Prairie, Wis. ... F5 88
North Providence, R.I. ... B11 52
North Quincy, Ill. ... D2 58
North Reading, Mass. ... f11 65
North Richland Hills, Tex. ... C4 84
Northridge, Ohio ... *C1 78
North Riverside, Ill. ... *B6 58
North Rockville Centre, N.Y. ... *E7 75
North Rose, N.Y. ... B4 75
North Royalton, Ohio ... h9 78
North Sacramento, Calif. ... *C3 50
North Salem, Ind. ... E4 59
North Salt Lake, Utah ... *A6 72
North Scituate, Mass. ... h12 65
North Seaford, N.Y. ... *E7 75
North Shreveport, La. ... *B2 63
North Springfield, Va. ... *B5 85
North St. Paul, Minn. ... m13 67
North Sudbury, Mass. ... g10 65
North Swansea, Mass. ... C5 65
North Sydney, N.S., Can. ... C9 43
North Syracuse, N.Y. ... B4 75
North Tarrytown, N.Y. ... g13, m15 75
North Terre Haute, Ind. ... E3 59
North Tewksbury, Mass. ... A5 65
North Tonawanda, N.Y. ... B2 75
North Troy, Vt. ... B3 73
North Turlock, Calif. ... *D3 50
North Turner, mtn., Mass. ... C4 65
Northumberland, Pa. ... E8 81
Northumberland, co., N.B., Can. ... B3 43
Northumberland, co., Ont., Can. ... C6 41
Northumberland, co., Eng. ... *C6 4
Northumberland, co., Pa. ... D8 81
Northumberland, co., Va. ... C6 85
North Uxbridge, Mass. ... B4 65
Northvale, N.J. ... g9 74
North Valley Stream, N.Y. ... *E7 75
North Vancouver, B.C., Can. ... E6, f12 37
North Vandergrift, Pa. ... *E2 81
North Vassalboro, Maine ... D3 64
North Vernon, Ind. ... F6 59
Northville, Mich. ... p15 66
Northville, N.Y. ... B6 75
North Wales, Pa. ... F11 81
North Walsham, Eng. ... D7 4
North Warren, Pa. ... C3 81
Northwest Park, Md. ... *B3 53
North Westport, Mass. ... C5 65
North West River, Newf., Can. ... B1, h9 44
Northwest Territories, ter., Can. ... C10 36
North Wilbraham, Mass. ... B3 65
North Wildwood, N.J. ... E3 74
North Wilkesboro, N.C. ... A1 76
Northwood, Iowa ... A4 60
Northwood, Mich. ... *E5 66
Northwood, N.H. ... E5 73
Northwood, N. Dak. ... C8 77
Northwoods, Mo. ... *C7 69
North York, Pa. ... G8 81
North York, Ont., Can. ... D5, k15 41
Norton, N.S., Can. ... D4 43
Norton, Kans. ... C4 61
Norton, Mass. ... C5 65
Norton, Ohio ... A4 78
Norton (Independent City), Va. ... f9 85
Norton, co., Kans. ... C4 61
Norton Shores, Mich. ... E4 66
Nortonville, Kans. ... C8, k15 61

Nortonville, Ky. ... C2 62
Norvelt, Pa. ... *F2 81
Norwalk, Calif. ... n12 50
Norwalk, Conn. ... E3 52
Norwalk, Iowa ... C4, f8 60
Norwalk, Ohio ... A3 78
Norwalk, Wis. ... E3 88
Norway, Iowa ... C6 60
Norway, Maine ... D2 64
Norway, Mich. ... C3 66
Norway, S.C. ... E5 82
Norway, country, Eur. ... E5 11
Norway House, Man., Can. ... C3 40
Norwayne, Mich. ... *F7 66
Norwell, Mass. ... h12 65
Norwich, Ont., Can. ... E4 41
Norwich, Conn. ... C8 52
Norwich, Eng. ... D7 4
Norwich, N.Y. ... C5 75
Norwood, Ont., Can. ... C7 41
Norwood, Mass. ... B5, h11 65
Norwood, Minn. ... F5 67
Norwood, N.J. ... h9 74
Norwood, N.Y. ... f10 75
Norwood, N.C. ... B2 76
Norwood, Ohio ... o13 78
Norwood, Pa. ... p20 81
Norwood, Tenn. ... *D10 83
Norwottock, mtn., Mass. ... B2 65
Noshiro, Jap. ... F10 18
Nossa Senhora das Dores, Braz. ... *E7 27
Notch, mtn., Mass. ... A3 65
Noto, It. ... F5 9
Notodden, Nor. ... H3 11
Notre Dame, Ind. ... *A5 59
Notre-Dame-de-Lourdes, Man., Can. ... E2 40
Notre Dame du Lac, Que., Can. ... B9 42
Notre-Dame-du-Laus, Que., Can. ... C2 42
Nottingham, Eng. ... D6 4
Nottingham, Pa. ... *F11 81
Nottingham, co., Eng. ... *D6 4
Nottoway, co., Va. ... C4 85
Nouadhibou, Maur. ... D4 21
Nouakchott, Maur. ... E1 22
Nouméa, N. Cal. ... *H8 2
Nova Cruz, Braz. ... *D7 27
Nova Friburgo, Braz. ... C4, h6 30
Nova Iguaçu, Braz. ... h6 30
Nova Lima, Braz. ... C4 30
Nova Lisboa, see Huambo, Ang.
Novara, It. ... B2 9
Nova Scotia, prov., Can. ... D6 43
Novato, Calif. ... C2 50
Nova Varos, Yugo. ... D4 10
Novaya Ladoga, Sov. Un. ... A9 12
Novaya Zemlya, isl., Sov. Un. ... B8 16
Nova Zagora, Bul. ... D8 10
Nové Zámky, Czech. ... E5 7
Novgorod, Sov. Un. ... B8 12
Novgorod-Severskiy, Sov. Un. ... E9 12
Novi, Mich. ... p15 66
Novigrad, Yugo. ... C2 10
Novi Ligure, It. ... B2 9
Novi Pazar, Bul. ... D8 10
Novi Pazar, Yugo. ... D5 10
Novi Sad, Yugo. ... C4 10
Novoaydar, Sov. Un. ... G12, q21 12
Novocherkassk, Sov. Un. ... H13 12
Novoekonomicheskoye, Sov. Un. ... q20 12
Novogrudok, Sov. Un. ... E5 12
Novo-Kazalinsk, Sov. Un. ... E9 16
Novokuznetsk, Sov. Un. ... D11 13

Novomoskovsk, Sov. Un. ... G10 12
Novomoskovsk, Sov. Un. ... D12 12
Novorossiysk, Sov. Un. ... I11 12
Novoshakhtinsk, Sov. Un. ... H12 12
Novosibirsk, Sov. Un. ... D11 13
Novosil, Sov. Un. ... E11 12
Novoukrainka, Sov. Un. ... G8 12
Nový Bohumín, Czech. ... D5 7
Nový Bydžov, Czech. ... C3 7
Nový Jičín, Czech. ... D5 7
Novyye Senzhary, Sov. Un. ... G10 12
Novyy Oskol, Sov. Un. ... F11 12
Nowa Sól, Pol. ... C3 7
Nowata, Okla. ... A6 79
Nowata, co., Okla. ... A6 79
Nowra-Bomaderry, Austl. ... G8 26
Nowshera, Pak. ... B5 20
Nowy Dwór, Pol. ... k13 7
Nowy Sacz, Pol. ... D6 7
Nowy Targ, Pol. ... D6 7
Noxen, Pa. ... D9, n16 81
Noxubee, co., Miss. ... B5 68
Noya, Sp. ... A1 8
Noyon, Fr. ... C5 5
Nsawam, Ghana ... G4 22
Nuble, prov., Chile ... B2 28
Nuckolls, co., Nebr. ... D7 71
Nucla, Colo. ... C2 51
Nueces, co., Tex. ... F4 84
Nueva Atzacoálco, Mex. ... *D5 34
Nueva Casas Grandes, Mex. ... A3 34
Nueva Ecija, prov., Phil. ... *C6 19
Nueva Esparta, state, Ven. ... A5 32
Nueva Gerona, Cuba ... D2 35
Nueva Imperial, Chile ... B2 28
Nueva Rosita, Mex. ... B4 34
Neuva San Salvador, Sal. ... *E7 34
Neuva Vizcaya, prov., Phil. ... *B6 19
Nueve de Julio, Arg. ... B4 28
Nuevitas, Cuba ... D5 35
Nuevo Laredo, Mex. ... B5 34
Nuevo León, state, Mex. ... B5 34
Nukualofa, Tonga ... *H9 2
Nules, Sp. ... C5 8
Numazu, Jap. ... I9, n17 18
Nu Mine, Pa. ... E3 81
Nunda, N.Y. ... C3 75
Nuoro, It. ... D2 9
Nuquí, Col. ... C3 27
Nuremberg, Pa. ... E9 81
Nuri, Mex. ... B3 34
Nürnberg (Nuremberg), Ger., Fed. Rep. of ... D5 6
Nushki, Pak. ... C4 20
Nutley, N.J. ... B4, h8 74
Nutter Fort, W. Va. ... B4, k10 87
Nutting Lake, Mass. ... f10 65
Nuwara Eliya, Sri Lanka ... G7 20
Nyack, N.Y. ... D7, m15 75
Nyamandhlovu, Zimb. ... D5 24
Nyandoma, Sov. Un. ... A13 12
Nyasa, lake, Afr. ... C6 24
Nybro, Swe. ... I6 11
Nye, co., Nev. ... B3 72
Nyíregyháza, Hung. ... B5 10
Nykøbing Falster, Den. ... A1 7
Nykøbing Mors, Den. ... I3 11
Nyköping, Swe. ... H7, u34 11
Nyland Acres, Calif. ... *E4 50
Nymburk, Czech. ... C3, n19 7
Nynäshamn, Swe. ... H7, u35 11
Nyngan, Austl. ... F8 25
Nysa, Pol. ... C4 7
Nyssa, Oreg. ... D10 80

O

Oahu, isl., Haw. ... B4, g9 56
Oak Bay, B.C., Can. ... h12 37
Oak Bluffs, Mass. ... D6 65
Oakbrook Terrace, Ill. ... *F2 58
Oak Creek, Colo. ... A4 51
Oak Creek, Wis. ... n12 88
Oakdale, Calif. ... D3 50
Oakdale, La. ... D3 63
Oakdale, Mass. ... B4 65
Oakdale, N.Y. ... *n16 75
Oakdale, Pa. ... k13 81
Oakes, N. Dak. ... D7 77

Oakfield, Maine ... B4 64
Oakfield, N.Y. ... B2 75
Oakford, Pa. ... F12, o22 81
Oak Forest, Ill. ... k9 58
Oak Grove, Ga. ... *C2 55
Oak Grove, La. ... B4 63
Oak Grove, Oreg. ... B4, h12 80
Oakharbor, Ohio ... A2 78
Oak Harbor, Wash. ... A3 86
Oak Hill, Fla. ... D6 54
Oak Hill, Mich ... D4 66
Oak Hill, Ohio ... D3 78

Oak Hill, Tenn. ... *A5 83
Oak Hill, W. Va. ... D3, n13 87
Oakhurst, N.J. ... C4 74
Oakhurst, Okla. ... A5 79
Oakland, Calif. ... D2, h8 50
Oakland, Ill. ... D5 58
Oakland, Iowa ... C2 60
Oakland, Maine ... D3 64
Oakland, Md. ... m12 53
Oakland, Mo. ... *C7 69
Oakland, Nebr. ... C9 71
Oakland, N.J. ... A4 74

Oakland, Oreg. ... D3 80
Oakland, Pa. ... *D1 81
Oakland, co., Mich. ... F7 66
Oakland City, Ind. ... H3 59
Oaklandon, Ind. ... k11 59
Oakland Park, Fla. ... F6, r13 54
Oak Lawn, Ill. ... B6, k9 58
Oaklawn, Kans. ... B5 61
Oakley, Idaho ... G5 57
Oakley, Kans. ... C3 61
Oakley Park, Mich. ... *F7 66
Oaklyn, N.J. ... *D2 74

Oakman, Ala. B2 46
Oakmont, Pa. E2, h14 81
Oak Park, Ill. B6, k9 58
Oak Park, Mich. p15 66
Oak Ridge, N.C. A3 76
Oakridge, Oreg. D4 80
Oak Ridge, Tenn. C9 83
Oak Ridges, Ont., Can. k15 41
Oaks, Pa. o20 81
Oaktown, Ind. G3 59
Oak View, Calif. *E4 50
Oak View, Md. *C3 53
Oakville, Ont., Can. D5 41
Oakville, Conn. C4 52
Oakville, Mo. g13 69
Oakwood, Ill. C6 58
Oakwood, Ohio A1 78
Oakwood (Oakwood Village),
  Ohio *A4 78
Oakwood (Far Hills), Ohio C1 78
Oakwood, Pa. *E1 81
Oakwood, Tex. D5 84
Oakwood Beach, N.J. D1 74
Oakwood Villa, Fla. *B5 54
Oamaru, N.Z. P13 26
Oamishirasato, Jap. n19 18
Oaxaca de Juarez, Mex. D5 34
Oaxaca, state, Mex. D5 34
Ob, riv., Sov. Un. C9 13
Obama, Jap. n14 18
Oban, Scot. B4 4
Oberhausen, Ger., Fed. Rep. of C3 6
Oberlin, Kans. C3 61
Oberlin, La. D3 63
Oberlin, Ohio A3 78
Oberlin, Pa. *F8 81
Oberstdorf, Ger., Fed. Rep. of E5 6
Obetz, Ohio C3, m11 78
Obihiro, Jap. E11 18
Obion, Tenn. A2 83
Obion, co., Tenn. A2 83
Oblong, Ill. D6 58
Obluchye, Sov. Un. E16 13
O'Brien, co., Iowa A2 60
Observation, peak, Calif. B3 50
Obuasi, Ghana G4 22
Ocala, Fla. C4 54
Ocaña, Col. B3 32
Ocaña, Sp. C4 8
Occidental, mts., Peru D2 31
Ocean, co., N.J. D4 74
Oceana, W. Va. D3 87
Oceana, co., Mich. E4 66
Ocean Bluff, Mass. B6, h13 65
Ocean City, Md. D7 53
Ocean City, N.J. E3 74
Ocean Falls, B.C., Can. C4 37
Ocean Gate, N.J. D4 74
Ocean Grove, Mass. C5 65
Ocean Grove, N.J. C4 74
Oceanlake, Oreg. *C3 80
Oceano, Calif. *E3 50
Ocean Park, Wash. C1 86
Oceanport, N.J. C4 74
Oceanside, Calif. F5 50
Oceanside, N.Y. *G2 52
Ocean Springs, Miss. E5, f8 68
Oceanville, N.J. E4 74
Ocheyedan, Iowa A2 60
Ochiltree, co., Tex. A2 84
Ocilla, Ga. E3 55
Ockelbo, Swe. G7 11
Ocenle Mari, Rom. C7 10
Ocho Rios, Jam. E5 35
Ocoee, Fla. D5 54
Ocoña, Peru E3 31
Oconee, co., Ga. C3 55
Oconee, co., S.C. B1 82
Oconomowoc, Wis. E5 88
Oconto, Wis. D6 88
Oconto Falls, Wis. D5 88
Oconto, co., Wis. D6 88
Ocotlán, Mex. C4, m12 34
Ocracoke, N.C. B7 76
Ocros, Peru D2 31
Oda, Ghana G4 22
Ōdate, Jap. F10 18
Odawara, Jap. I9, n18 18
Odda, Nor. G2 11
Odebolt, Iowa B2 60
Odell, Ill. B5 58
Odem, Tex. F4 84
Ödemiş, Tur. C7 14
Odendaalsrus, S. Afr. F5 24
Odense, Den. J4 11
Odense, co., Den. *J4 11
Odenton, Md. B4 53
Oder (Odra), riv., Eur. B7 6
Odessa, Ont., Can. C8 41
Odessa, Mo. B4 69
Odessa, Sov. Un. H8 12
Odessa, Tex. D1 84

Odessa, Wash. B7 86
Odin, Ill. E4 58
Odin, mtn., B.C., Can. D8 37
Odon, Ind. G4 59
O'Donnell, Tex. C2 84
Odorhei, Rom. B7 10
Oella, Md. B4 53
Oelsnitz, Ger. Dem. Rep. C6 6
Oelwein, Iowa B6 60
O'Fallon, Ill. E4 58
O'Fallon, Mo. f12 69
Offaly, co., Ire. *D3 4
Offenbach, Ger., Fed. Rep. of C4 6
Offenburg, Ger., Fed. Rep. of D3 6
Ōfunato, Jap. G10 18
Oga, Jap. G9 18
Ōgaki, Jap. I8, n15 18
Ogallala, Nebr. C4 71
Ogbomosho, Nig. G5 22
Ogden, Iowa B3 60
Ogden, Kans. C7 61
Ogden, Utah A6, C2 72
Ogden, Utah *G11 81
Ogden Dunes, Ind. *A3 59
Ogdensburg, N.J. A3 74
Ogdensburg, N.Y. f9 75
Ogemaw, co., Mich. D6 66
Ogle, co., Ill. A4 58
Ogles, Ill. *E4 58
Oglesby, Ill. B4 58
Oglethorpe, Ga. D2 55
Oglethorpe, co., Ga. C3 55
Ogletown, Del. *A6 53
Ogoamas, mtn., Indon. E6 19
Ogulin, Yugo. C2 10
Ogunquit, Maine E2 64
Ōhara, Jap. n19 18
O'Higgins, prov., Chile A2 28
Ohio, co., Ind. G7 59
Ohio, co., Ky. C2 62
Ohio, co., W. Va. A4 87
Ohio, state, U.S. 78
Ohio, river, U.S. C10 45
Ohio City, Ohio B1 78
Ohioville, Pa. *E1 81
Ohrid, Yugo. E5 10
Oil City, La. B2 63
Oil City, Pa. D2 81
Oildale, Calif. E4 50
Oilton, Okla. A5 79
Oise, dept., Fr. *C5 5
Ōita, Jap. J5 18
Oita, pref., Jap. *J5 18
Ojai, Calif. E4 50
Ojinaga, Mex. B4 34
Ojocaliente, Mex. D4 34
Ojos del Salado, mtn.,
  Arg., Chile F4 27
Ojus, Fla. G6, s13 54
Oka, Que., Can. D3, q18 42
Oka, Nig. E6 22
Oka, river, Sov. Un. D11, o18 12
Okaloosa, co., Fla. u15 54
Okanagan Landing, B.C., Can. D8 37
Okanogan, Wash. A6 86
Okanogan, co., Wash. A6 86
Okara, Pak. *B5 20
Okarche, Okla. B4 79
Okauchee, Wis. *E5 88
Okawville, Ill. E4 58
Okaya, Jap. H9, m17 18
Okayama, Jap. I6 18
Okayama, pref., Jap. *I6 18
Okazaki, Jap. o16 18
Okecie, Pol., (part of
  Warsaw) B6, m13 7
Okeechobee, Fla. E6 54
Okeechobee, co., Fla. E5 54
Okeene, Okla. A3 79
Okehampton, Eng. E4 4
Okemah, Okla. B5 79
Okfuskee, co., Okla. B5 79
Okha, Sov. Un. D17 13
Okhotsk, Sov. Un. D17 13
Okhotsk, sea, Sov. Un. D17 13
Oklahoma, Pa. *F2 81
Oklahoma, co., Okla. B4 79
Oklahoma, state, U.S. 79
Oklahoma City, Okla. B4 79
Oklawaha, Fla. C5 54
Oklee, Minn. C3 67
Okmulgee, Okla. B6 79
Okmulgee, co., Okla. B5 79
Okolona, Ky. g11 62
Okolona, Miss. B5 68
Okotoks, Alta., Can. D4 38
Oktibbeha, co., Miss. B5 68
Okushiri, Jap. E9 18
Olancha, peak, Calif. D4 50
Olanta, S.C. D8 82
Olathe, Kans. D9 61
Olavarría, Arg. B4 28
Oława, Pol. C4 7

Olbia, It. D2 9
Olcott, N.Y. B2 75
Old Bethpage, N.Y. *E7 75
Old Bridge, N.J. C4 74
Old Brookville, N.Y. *E7 75
Old Castile, reg., Sp. B4 8
Oldenburg in Holstein, Ger.,
  Fed. Rep. of A5 6
Oldenburg, Ger., Fed. Rep. of B4 6
Oldenburg, Ind. F7 59
Old Forge, N.Y. B6 75
Old Forge, Pa. D10, m17 81
Old Fort, N.C. F10 76
Old Man, mtn., Newf., Can. D3 44
Old Orchard Beach, Maine E2, g7 64
Old Perlican, Newf., Can. D5 44
Olds, Alta., Can. D3 38
Oldsmar, Fla. o10 54
Old Speck, mtn., Maine D2 64
Old Tappan, N.J. *B4 74
Old Town, Maine D4 64
Oldtown, N.C. *A2 76
Old Westbury, N.Y. *E7 75
Orlean, N.Y. C2 75
O'Leary Station, P.E.I., Can. C5 43
Oleiros, Sp. A1 8
Olekminsk, Sov. Un. C15 13
Olesno, Pol. C5 7
Olhão, Port. D2 8
Olimpia, Braz. C3 30
Olimpo, dept., Par. D4 29
Olin, Iowa B6 60
Olinda, Braz. *D7 27
Oliva, Sp. C5 8
Oliva de la Frontera, Sp. C2 8
Olive Hill, Ky. B6 62
Olivehurst, Calif. C3 50
Oliveira, Braz. C4 30
Olivenza, Sp. C2 8
Oliver, B.C., Can. E8 37
Oliver, Pa. G2 81
Oliver, co., N. Dak. C4 77
Oliver Springs, Tenn. C9 83
Olivet, Mich. F6 66
Olivette, Mo. *C7 69
Olivia, Minn. F4 67
Olkusz, Pol. g11 7
Olla, La. C3 63
Olmos, Peru C2 31
Olmos Park, Tex. k7 84
Olmsted, Ohio *A4 78
Olmsted, co., Minn. G6 67
Olmsted Falls, Ohio h9 78
Olney, Md. B3 53
Olney, Tex. C3 84
Olomouc, Czech. D4 7
Oloron-Ste. Marie, Fr. F3 5
Olot, Sp. A7 8
Olpe, Kans. D7 61
Olshany, Sov. Un. F10 12
Olsztyn, Pol. B6 7
Olten, Switz. E3 6
Oltenia, prov., Rom. *C6 10
Oltenia, reg., Rom. C6 10
Oltenița, Rom. C8 10
Olton, Tex. B1 84
Olvera, Sp. D3 8
Olympia, Wash. B3 86
Olympia Fields, Ill. *B6 58
Olympus, mtn., Grc. B4 14
Olympus, mtn., Wash. B2 86
Olyphant, Pa. D10, m18 81
Omagh, N. Ire. C3 4
Omaha, Nebr. C10, g13 71
Omak, Wash. A6 86
Oman, country, Asia F6 15
Oman, Wash. D3, n12 87
Omdurman (Umm Durmān), Sud. E4 23
Omega, Ga. E3 55
Omemee, Ont., Can. C6 41
Omerville, Que., Can. D5 42
Ometepec, Mex. D5 34
Omigawa, Jap. n19 18
Omiya, Jap. I9, n18 18
Omro, Wis. D5 88
Omsk, Sov. Un. D10 13
Ōmuta, Jap. J5 18
Onalaska, Wis. E2 88
Onamia, Minn. D5 67
Onancock, Va. C7 85
Onarga, Ill. C5 58
Onawa, Iowa B1 60
Onaway, Mich. C6 66
Ondör Haan, Mong. B7 17
Oneco, Fla. E4, q10 54
Onega, Sov. Un. C6 13
Onega, lake, Sov. Un. G16 11

Oneida, Ill. B3 58
Oneida, N.Y. B5 75
Oneida, Ohio C1 78
Oneida, Tenn. C9 83
Oneida, co., Idaho G6 57
Oneida, co., N.Y. B5 75
Oneida, co., Wis. C4 88
O'Neill, Nebr. B7 71
Oneonta, Ala. B3 46
Oneonta, N.Y. C5 75
Ongjin, Kor. H2 18
Onitsha, Nig. G6 22
Ono, Jap. n15 18
Onoda, Jap. *J15 18
Onomichi, Jap. I6 18
Onondaga, N.Y. *C4 75
Onondaga, co., N.Y. C4 75
Onset, Mass. C6 65
Onslow, co., N.C. C5 76
Onsong, Kor. E4 18
Onsted, Mich. F6 66
Ontake-san, mtn., Jap. n16 18
Ontario, Calif. E5, m13 50
Ontario, N.Y. B3 75
Ontario, Ohio B3 78
Ontario, Oreg. C10 80
Ontario, co., Ont., Can. C5 41
Ontario, co., N.Y. C3 75
Ontario, prov., Can. 41
Onteniente, Sp. C5 8
Ontonagon, Mich. B1, m12 66
Ontonagon, co., Mich. m12 66
Oolitic, Ind. G4 59
Oostburg, Wis. E6 88
Oostende, Bel. B5 5
Ootacamund, India F6 20
Oot Park, N.Y. *B4 75
Opal Cliffs, Calif. *D2 50
Opa-Locka, Fla. s13 54
Opatów, Pol. C6 7
Opava, Czech. D4 7
Opelika, Ala. C4 46
Opelousas, La. D3 63
Opochka, Sov. Un. C7 12
Opoczno, Pol. C6 7
Opole, Pol. C4 7
Opole Lubelskie, Pol. C6 7
Opp, Ala. D3 46
Oppdal, Nor. F3 11
Oppeln see Opole, Pol.
Oppland, co., Nor. *G4 11
Opportunity, Wash. B8, g14 86
Oquawka, Ill. C3 58
Oradea, Rom. B5 10
Oradell, N.J. h8 74
Oran (Wahran), Alg. A4 22
Oran, Mo. D8 69
Oran, dept., Alg. *B5 22
Orange, Austl. F8 25
Orange, Calif. n13 50
Orange, Conn. D4 52
Orange, Fr. E6 5
Orange, Mass. A3 65
Orange, N.J. *B4 74
Orange, Ohio *A4 78
Orange, Tex. D6 84
Orange, Va. B4 85
Orange, co., Calif. F5 50
Orange, co., Fla. D5 54
Orange, co., Ind. G4 59
Orange, co., N.Y. D6 75
Orange, co., N.C. A3 76
Orange, co., Tex. D6 84
Orange, co., Vt. D3 73
Orange, co., Va. B4 85
Orange, riv., Afr. F3 24
Orangeburg, N.Y. *D6 75
Orangeburg, S.C. E6 82
Orangeburg, co., S.C. E6 82
Orange City, Fla. D5 54
Orange City, Iowa A1 60
Orange Cove, Calif. *D4 50
Orange Free State, prov., S. Afr. F5 24
Orange Grove, Tex. F4 84
Orange Park, Fla. B5, m8 54
Orangevale, Calif. *C3 50
Orangeville, Ont., Can. D4 41
Oranienburg, Ger. Dem. Rep. B6 6
Oras, Phil. *C7 19
Orăstie, Rom. C6 10
Oravița, Rom. C5 10
Orchard Avenue, Wash. *B8 86
Orchard Beach, Md. *B4 53
Orchard Homes, Mont. D2 70
Orchard Lake, Mich. *F7 66
Orchard Park, N.Y. C2 75
Orchard Valley, Wyo. E8 89
Orchards, Wash. D3 86
Orcotuna, Peru D2 31
Orcutt, Calif. E3 50
Ord, Nebr. C7 71
Órdenes, Sp. A1 8
Ordu, Tur. B11 14

Orduña, Sp. A4 8
Ordville, Nebr. *C2 71
Ordway, Colo. C7 51
Ordzhonikidze, Sov. Un. E7 13
Örebro, Swe. H6, t33 11
Örebro, co., Swe. *H6 11
Oregon, Ill. A4 58
Oregon, Mo. B2 69
Oregon, Ohio A2, e7 78
Oregon, Wis. F4 88
Oregon, co., Mo. E6 69
Oregon, state, U.S. 80
Oregon City, Oreg. B4, h12 80
Orehov, Sov. Un. H10 12
Orekhovo-Zuyevo,
   Sov. Un. D12, n18 12
Orel, Sov. Un. E11 12
Oreland, Pa. *F11 81
Orem, Utah A6 72
Orenburg, Sov. Un. D8 13
Orense, prov., Sp. *A2 8
Orestes, Ind. D6 59
Orestiás, Grc. B6 14
Orford, mtn., Que., Can. D5 42
Orfordville, Wis. F4 88
Orgeyev, Sov. Un. H7 12
Orick, Calif. B1 50
Orient, Ill. F5 58
Orient, N.Y. m16 75
Oriental, N.C. B6 76
Oriente, prov., Cuba D6 35
Orihuela, Sp. C5 8
Orillia, Ont., Can. C5 41
Orinda, Calif. *D2 50
Orinoco, river, Ven. B5 32
Orion, Ill. B3 58
Oriskany, N.Y. B5 75
Oriskany Falls, N.Y. C5 75
Orissa, state, India E7 20
Oristano, It. E2 9
Orizaba, Mex. D5, n15 34
Orkney, co., Scot. *A5 4
Orkney, isl., Scot. *A5 4
Orland, Calif. C2 50
Orlando, Fla. D5 54
Orland Park, Ill. k9 58
Orleanais, former prov., Fr. D4 5
Orleans, Calif. B2 50
Orléans, Ont., Can. h12 41
Orléans, Fr. D4 5
Orleans, Ind. G5 59
Orleans, Mass. C7 65
Orleans, Nebr. D6 71
Orleans, Vt. B3 73
Orleans, co., N.Y. B2 75
Orleans, co., Vt. B3 73
Orleans, par., La. E6 63
Orlovista, Fla. *D5 54
Ormoc, prov., Phil. *C6 19
Ormond Beach, Fla. C5 54
Ormstown, dept., Que., Can. D3 42
Orne, dept., Fr. *C3 5
Örnsköldsvik, Swe. F8 11
Orocué, Col. C3 32
Orofino, Idaho C2 57
Oro Grande, Calif. E5 50
Oromocto, N.B., Can. D3 43
Orono, Ont., Can. D6 41
Orono, Maine D4 64
Orono, Minn. *E5 67
Oronogo, Mo. D3 69
Oroquieta, Phil. *D6 19
Orosháza, Hung. B5 10
Oroville, Calif. C3 50
Oroville, Wash. A6 86
Orpington, Eng. m13 4
Orrick, Mo. B3 69
Orrville, Ohio B4 78
Orsha, Sov. Un. D8 12
Orsk, Sov. Un. D8 13
Orsova, Rom. C6 10

Orthez, Fr. F3 5
Ortigueria, Sp. A2 8
Orting, Wash. B3 86
Ortiz, Mex. B2 34
Ortona a Mare, It. C5 9
Ortonville, Mich. F7 66
Ortonville, Minn. E2 67
Orumiyeh (Urmia), Iran B4 15
Oruro, Bol. C2 29
Oruro, dept., Bol. C2 29
Orvieto, It. C4 9
Orwell, Ohio A5 78
Orwigsburg, Pa. E9 81
Oryakhovo, Bul. D6 10
Osage, Iowa A5 60
Osage, co., Kans. D8 61
Osage, co., Mo. C6 69
Osage Beach, Mo. C5 69
Osage City, Kans. D8 61
Ōsaka, Jap. I7, o14 18
Osaka, Jap. n16 18
Ōsaka, pref., Jap. *I7 18
Osakis, Minn. E3 67
Osawatomie, Kans. D9 61
Osborne, Kans. C5 61
Osborne, co., Kans. C5 61
Osbornsville, N.J. *C4 74
Osburn, Idaho B3 57
Osceola, Ark. B6 49
Osceola, Ind. A5 59
Osceola, Iowa C4 60
Osceola, Mo. C4 69
Osceola, Nebr. C8 71
Osceola, Wis. C1 88
Osceola, co., Fla. E5 54
Osceola, co., Iowa A2 60
Osceola, co., Mich. E5 66
Osceola Mills, Pa. E5 81
Oschatz, Ger. Dem. Rep. C6 6
Oschersleben, Ger. Dem. Rep. B5 6
Oscoda, Mich. D7 66
Oscoda, co., Mich. D6 66
Osgoode, Ont., Can. B9 41
Osgood, Ind. F7 59
Osh, Sov. Un. E10 13
Oshamambe, Jap. E10 18
Oshawa, Ont., Can. D6 41
Oshkosh, Nebr. C3 71
Oshkosh, Wis. D5, h8 88
Oshogbo, Nig. G5 22
Osijek, Yugo. C4 10
Osinniki, Sov. Un. *D11 13
Oskaloosa, Iowa C5 60
Oskaloosa, Kans. C8, k15 61
Oskarshamn, Swe. I7 11
Oslo, Nor. G4, p28 11
Oslo, co., Nor. *H4 11
Osmaniye, Tur. D11 14
Osmond, Nebr. B8 71
Osnabrück, Ger. Fed. Rep. of B4 6
Osorno, Chile C2 28
Osorno, prov., Chile C2 28
Osoyoos, B.C., Can. E8 37
Osprey, Fla. E4 54
Oss, Neth. B6 5
Ossa, mtn., Austl. o15 25
Osseo, Minn. m12 67
Osseo, Wis. D2 88
Ossian, Ind. C7 59
Ossian, Iowa A6 60
Ossining, N.Y. D7, m15 75
Ostashkov, Sov. Un. C9 12
Osteen, Fla. D5 54
Östergöland, co., Swe. *H6 11
Östersund, Swe. F6 11
Osterville, Mass. C7 65
Ostfold, co., Nor. *H4 11
Ostrava, Czech. D5 7
Ostróda, Pol. B5 7
Ostrogozhsk, Sov. Un. F12 12
Ostrołeka, Pol. B6 7

Ostrov, Czech. C2 7
Ostrov, Sov. Un. C7 12
Ostrowiec Swietokrzyski, Pol. C6 7
Ostrów Mazowiecka, Pol. B6 7
Ostrów Wielkopolski, Pol. C4 7
Ostrzeszów, Pol. C4 7
Ostuni, It. D6 9
Ōsuka, Jap. o16 18
Osuna, Sp. D3 8
Oswego, Ill. B5, k8 58
Oswego, Kans. E8 61
Oswego, N.Y. B4 75
Oswego, co., N.Y. B4 75
Oswestry, Eng. D5 4
Oświecim, Pol. C5, g10 7
Ota, Jap. *m18 18
Otaki, Jap. n19 18
Otaré, mtn., Col. C3 32
Otaru, Jap. E10 18
Otavalo, Ec. A2 31
Otay, Calif. *F5 50
Oteen, N.C. f10 76
Otego, N.Y. C5 75
Otero, co., Colo. D7 51
Otero, co., N. Mex. C6 48
Othello, Wash. C6 86
Otho, Iowa B3 60
Otis Orchards, Wash. g14 86
Otisville, Mich. E7 66
Otisville, N.Y. *D6 75
Otoe, co., Nebr. D9 71
Otsego, Mich. F5 66
Otsego, co., Mich. C6 66
Otsego, co., N.Y. C5 75
Ōtsu, Jap. o14 18
Otsuki, Jap. n17 18
Ottawa, Ont., Can. B9, h12 41
Ottawa, Ill. B5 58
Ottawa, Kans. D8 61
Ottawa, Ohio A1 78
Ottawa, co., Kans. C6 61
Ottawa, co., Mich. F4 66
Ottawa, co., Ohio A2 78
Ottawa, co., Okla. A7 79
Ottawa, river, Ont., Que., Can. E18 36
Ottawa-Carleton, co.,
   Ont., Can. B9 41
Ottawa Hills, Ohio A2, e6 78
Otterbien, Ind. D3 59
Otter Lake, Mich. E7 66
Otter River, Mass. A3 65
Otter Tail, co., Minn. D3 67
Otterville, Ont., Can. E4 41
Ottoville, Ohio B1 78
Ottumwa, Iowa C5 60
Otuzco, Peru C2 31
Otwell, Ind. H3 59
Otwock, Pol. m14 7
Ouachita, co., Ark. D3 49
Ouachita, par., La. B3 63
Ouachita, river, U.S. D8 45
Ouagadougou, Burkina Faso. F4 22
Ouahigouya, Burkina Faso. F4 22
Oudtshoorn, S. Afr. G4 24
Ouezzane, Mor. B3 22
Ouidah, Benin G5 22
Oujda, Mor. C5 21
Oulins, Fr. E6 5
Oulu, Fin. E11 11
Oulu, prov., Fin. *E11 11
Ouray, Colo. C3 51
Ouray, co., Colo. C3 51
Ourinhos, Braz. C3 30
Ouro Fino, Braz. C3, m8 30
Ouro Prêto, Braz. C4 30
Outagamie, co., Wis. D5 88
Outes, Sp. A1 8
Outlook, Sask., Can. F2 39
Outreau, Fr. B4 5
Outremont, Que., Can. p19 42
Ovada, It. B2 9

Ovalle, Chile A2 28
Ovar, Port. B1 8
Overbrook, Kans. D8 61
Overijssel, prov., Neth. *A7 5
Overland, Mo. f13 69
Overland Park, Kans. m16 61
Overlea, Md. B4, g11 53
Overton, Nebr. D6 71
Overton, Nev. C4 72
Overton, Tex. C5 84
Overton, co., Tenn. C8 83
Ovid, Mich. E6 66
Ovid, N.Y. C4 75
Oviedo, Fla. D5 54
Oviedo, Sp. A3 8
Oviedo, prov., Sp. *A3 8
Ovruch, Sov. Un. F7 12
Owasso, Okla. A6 79
Owatonna, Minn. F5 67
Owego, N.Y. C4 75
Owen, Wis. D3 88
Owen, co., Ind. F4 59
Owen, co., Ky. B5 62
Owens, N.C. *C4 76
Owensboro, Ky. C2 62
Owen Sound, Ont., Can. C4 41
Owensville, Ind. H2 59
Owensville, Mo. C6 69
Owensville, Ohio C1 78
Owenton, Ky. B5 62
Owings Mills, Md. *B4 53
Owingsville, Ky. B6 62
Owl Creek, mts., Wyo. C4 89
Owosso, Mich. E6 66
Owsley, co., Ky. C6 62
Owyhee, co., Idaho G2 57
Oxbow, Sask., Can. H4 39
Oxbow, Mich. *F6 66
Oxelösund, Swe. o35 11
Oxford, Ala. B4 46
Oxford, N.S., Can. D6 43
Oxford, Eng. E6 4
Oxford, Ga. C3 55
Oxford, Ind. C3 59
Oxford, Iowa C6 60
Oxford, Kans. E6 61
Oxford, Maine D2 64
Oxford, Md. C5 53
Oxford, Mass. B4 65
Oxford, Mich. F7 66
Oxford, Miss. A4 68
Oxford, Nebr. D6 71
Oxford, N.J. B3 74
Oxford, N.Y. C5 75
Oxford, N.C. A4 76
Oxford, Ohio C1 78
Oxford, Pa. G10 81
Oxford, co., Ont., Can. D4 41
Oxford, co., Eng. *E6 4
Oxford, co., Maine D2 64
Oxnard, Calif. E4 50
Oxnard Beach, Calif. *E4 50
Oyama, Jap. m18 18
Oyo, Nig. G5 22
Oyonnax, Fr. D6 5
Oyster Bay, N.Y. E7, n15 75
Oyster Bay Cove, N.Y. *E7 75
Ozamiz, Phil. D6 19
Ozark, Ala. D4 46
Ozark, Ark. B2 49
Ozark, Mo. D4 69
Ozark, co., Mo. E5 69
Ozaukee, co., Wis. E6 88
Ozd, Hung. A5 10
Ozieri, It. D2 9
Ozona, Fla. o10 54
Ozona, Tex. D2 84
Ozorków, Pol. C5 7
Ozu, Jap. J6 18

P

Paarl, S. Afr. G3 24
Paauilo, Haw. C6 56
Pabianice, Pol. C5 7
Pâbna, Bngl. D8 20
Pacasmayo, Peru C2 31
Pace, Fla. u14 54
Pacheco, Calif. *C2 50

Pachuca de Soto, Mex. C5, m14 34
Pacific, Mo. C7, g12 69
Pacific, Wash. f11 86
Pacific, co., Wash. C2 86
Pacific, ocean F6 2
Pacifica, Calif. h8 50
Pacific Grove, Calif. D3 50

Packard, mtn., Mass. B3 65
Pacolet, S.C. B4 82
Pacolet Mills, S.C. B4 82
Paczkow, Pol. C4 7
Padang, Indon. F2 19
Padangpanjang, Indon. F2 19
Padangsidempuan, Indon. E1, m11 19

Paddock Lake, Wis. n11 88
Paden City, W. Va. B4 87
Paderborn, Ger. Fed. Rep. of C4 6
Padova (Padua), It. B3 9
Paducah, Ky. A2 62
Paducah, Tex. B2 84
Paektu-san, mtn., Kor. F4 18

Pagadian, Phil. *D6 19
Page, Ariz. A4 48
Page, W. Va. C3, m13 87
Page, co., Iowa D2 60
Page, co., Va. B4 85
Pagedale, Mo. *C7 69
Pageland, S.C. B7 82
Page Manor, Ohio *C1 78
Pago Pago, Am. Sam. *G9 2
Pagosa Springs, Colo. D3 51
Pahala, Haw. D6 56
Pahang, state, Mala. E2 19
Pahoa, Haw. D7 56
Pahokee, Fla. F6 54
Paia, Haw. C5 65
Painesdale, Mich. A2 66
Painesville, Ohio A4 78
Paint, Pa. *F4 81
Painted Post, N.Y. C3 75
Paintsville, Ky. C7 62
Paisley, Ont., Can. C3 41
Paisley, Scot. C4 4
Paita, Peru C1 31
Pajaro, Calif. *D3 50
Pakanbaru, Indon. E2 19
Pakistan, country, Asia C4 20
Pakistan, East, see
  Bangladesh, country, Asia
Pakokku, Bur. D10 20
Paks, Hung. B4 10
Pakse, Laos B3 19
Palacios, Tex. E4 84
Palafrugell, Sp. B7 8
Palaiseau, Fr. h9 5
Palamós, Sp. B7 8
Palana, Sov. Un. D18 13
Pālanpur, India D5 20
Palas de Rey, Sp. A2 8
Palatine, Ill. A5, h8 58
Palatka, Fla. C5 54
Palawan, prov., Phil. C5 19
Palawan, isl., Phil. C5 19
Palayankottai, India *G6 20
Palazzolo Acreide, It. F5 9
Palembang, Indon. F2 19
Palencia, Sp. A3 8
Palencia, prov., Sp. *A3 8
Palermo, It. E4 9
Palestine, Ill. D6 58
Palestine, Tex. D5 84
Palestine, reg., Asia D2 15
Palestrina, It. h9 9
Pālghāt, India *F6 20
Palisades, Idaho *F7 57
Palisades Park, N.J. h8 74
Palma de Mallorca, Sp. C7 8
Palmares, Braz. *D7 27
Palma Soriano, Cuba D5 35
Palm Bay, Fla. D6 54
Palm Beach, Fla. F6 54
Palm Beach, co., Fla. F6 54
Palmdale, Calif. E4 50
Palm Desert, Calif. *F5 50
Palmeira dos Indios, Braz. *D7 27
Palmer, Alsk. C10, g17 47
Palmer, Mass. B3 65
Palmer, Mich. B3 66
Palmer, Tenn. D8 83
Palmer Heights, Pa. *E11 81
Palmer Park, Md. *C4 53
Palmerston, Ont., Can. D4 41
Palmerston North, N.Z. N15 26
Palmerton, Pa. E10 81
Palmetto, Fla. E4, p10 54
Palmetto, Ga. C2 55
Palm Harbor, Fla. o10 54
Palmi, It. E5 9
Palmira, Col. C2 32
Palmira, Cuba C3 35
Palm Springs, Calif. F5 50
Palm Springs, Fla. *F6 54
Palmyra, Ill. D4 58
Palmyra, Mo. B6 69
Palmyra, N.J. C2 74
Palmyra, N.Y. B3 75
Palmyra, Pa. F8 81
Palmyra, Wis. F5 88
Palo Alto, Calif. D2, k8 50
Palo Alto, Pa. *E9 81
Palo Alto, co., Iowa A3 60
Pálomar, mtn., Calif. F5 50
Palombara Sabina, It. g9 9
Palo Pinto, co., Tex. C3 84
Palopo, Indon. F6 19
Palos Heights, Ill. *B6 58
Palos Hills, Ill. *B6 58
Palos Park, Ill. k9 58
Palos Verdes Estates, Calif. n12 50
Palouse, Wash. C8 86
Palpa, Peru D3 31
Pamekasan, Indon. G4 19
Pamiers, Fr. F4 5
Pamlico, co., N.C. B6 76

Pampa, Tex. B2 84
Pampanga, prov., Phil. *B6 19
Pampas, Peru D3 31
Pampas, reg., Arg. *G4 27
Pamplico, S.C. C8 82
Pamplona, Col. B3 32
Pamplona, Sp. A5 8
Pana, Ill. D4 58
Panagyurishte, Bul. D7 10
Panaji (Panjim), India E5 20
Panama, Okla. B7 79
Panamá, Pan. B2 32
Panama, country, N.A. B2 32
Panama City, Fla. u16 54
Panao, Peru C2 31
Panay, isl., Phil. C6 19
Pancevo, Yugo. C5 10
Pandharpur, India E6 20
Pando, Ur. E1 30
Pando, dept., Bol. B2 29
Pandora, Ohio B2 78
Panevežys, Sov. Un. D5 12
Panfilov, Sov. Un. E10 13
Pangasinan, prov., Phil. *B6 19
Pangkalpinang, Indon. F3 19
Panguitch, Utah C5 72
Panhandle, Tex. B2 84
Pānīpat, India *C6 20
Panna, India D7 20
Panola, co., Miss. A3 68
Panola, co., Tex. C5 84
Panora, Iowa C3 60
Pantelleria, It. F3 9
Pantin, Fr. g10 5
Pánuco, Mex. C5, k14 34
Paola, It. E6 9
Paoli, Ind. G5 59
Paoli, Pa. o20 81
Paonia, Colo. C3 51
Pápa, Hung. B3 10
Papaikou, Haw. D6 56
Papantla de Olarte, Mex. C5, m15 34
Papeete, Fr. Polynesia H11 2
Papenburg, Ger., Fed. Rep. of ... B3 6
Papillion, Nebr. C9, g12 71
Papineau, co., Que., Can. D2 42
Papineauville, Que., Can. D2 42
Papua New Guinea,
  country, Oceania h11 25
Para, state, Braz. A4 29
Paracatu, Braz. B3 30
Paracin, Yugo. D5 10
Paradis, La. k11 63
Paradise, Calif. C3 50
Paradise Valley, Ariz. D2 48
Paragould, Ark. A5 49
Paraguaçu Paulista, Braz. C2 30
Paraguarí, Par. E4 29
Paraguarí, dept., Par. E4 29
Paraguay, country, S.A. D4 29
Paraguay, riv., Braz., Par. F5 27
Paraíba do Sul, Braz. h6 30
Paraíba do Sul, riv., Braz. F6 27
Paraíso, Pan. *B2 32
Paraíso, Mex. D6 34
Paraisópolis, Braz. C3 30
Parakhino-Paddubye, Sov. Un. B9 12
Paramaribo, Sur. C5 27
Paramount, Calif. *F4 50
Paramus, N.J. h8 74
Paraná, Arg. A4 28
Paraná, state, Braz. C2 30
Paraná, riv., S.A. E4 29
Paranaguá, Braz. D3 30
Paray-Le-Monial, Fr. D6 5
Parchim, Ger. Dem. Rep. B5 6
Parchment, Mich. F5 66
Pardeeville, Wis. E4 88
Pardes Hanna, Isr. B2 15
Pardubice, Czech. C3 7
Parecis, mts., Braz. E5 27
Parent, Que., Can. k12 42
Parepare, Indon. F5 19
Parintins, Braz. *D5 27
Paris, Ark. B2 49
Paris, Ont., Can. D4 41
Paris, Fr. C5, g10 5
Paris, Idaho G7 57
Paris, Ill. D6 58
Paris, Ky. B5 62
Paris, Mo. B6 69
Paris, S.C. *B3 82
Paris, Tenn. A3 83
Paris, Tex. C5 84
Paris, peak, Idaho G7 57
Park, co., Colo. B5 51
Park, co., Mont. E6 70
Park, co., Wyo. B3 89
Park City, Ill. *A6 58
Park City, Kans. B5 61
Park City, Utah A6, D2 72
Parkdale, P.E.I., Can. C6 43

Parke, co., Ind. E3 59
Parker, Ariz. B1 48
Parker, Fla. u16 54
Parker, Pa. D2 81
Parker, S. Dak. G8 77
Parker, co., Tex. C4 84
Parker City, Ind. D7 59
Parkersburg, Iowa B5 60
Parkersburg, W. Va. B3 87
Parkers Prairie, Minn. D3 67
Parkes, Austl. F7 26
Park Falls, Wis. C3 88
Park Forest, Ill. B6, m9 58
Parkhill, Ont., Can. D3 41
Park Hills, Ky. A7 62
Parkin, Ark. B5 49
Parkland, Pa. *F11 81
Parkland, Wash. f11 86
Parklawn, Va. *B5 85
Park Place, Pa. *B3 81
Park Rapids, Minn. D3 67
Park Ridge, Ill. B6, h9 58
Park Ridge, N.J. g8 74
Park Ridge Manor, Ill. *B6 58
Parkrose, Oreg. *B4 80
Parkside, Pa. *G11 81
Parksley, Va. C7 85
Parkston, S. Dak. G8 77
Parksville, B.C., Can. E5 37
Parksville, N.Y. D6 75
Parkton, N.C. C3 76
Parkview, Ohio *A4 78
Parkview, Pa. *E2 81
Parkville, Md. C3 53
Parkville, Mo. B3, h10 69
Parkville, Pa. *G8 81
Parkwood, Md. *B3 53
Parlier, Calif. D4 50
Parma, Idaho F2 57
Parma, It. B3 9
Parma, Mich. F6 66
Parma, Mo. E8 69
Parma, Ohio A4, h9 78
Parma Heights, Ohio h9 78
Parmer, co., Tex. B1 84
Parnaíba, Braz. D6 27
Parnaíba, riv., Braz. D6 27
Pärnu, Sov. Un. B5 12
Parowan, Utah C5 72
Parral, Chile B2 28
Parramatta, Austl. *F8 26
Parras de la Fuente, Mex. B4 34
Parrish, Ala. B2 46
Parrish, Fla. E4, p11 54
Parrsboro, N.S., Can. D5 43
Parry, isl., N.W. Ter., Can. m28 36
Parry, mtn., B.C., Can. C3 37
Parry Sound, Ont., Can. B4, p20 41
Parry Sound, dist., Ont., Can. .. B4 41
Parshall, N. Dak. C3 77
Parsippany, N.J. B4 74
Parsons, Kans. E8 61
Parsons, Tenn. B3 83
Parsons, W. Va. B5 87
Parthenay, Fr. D3 5
Partinico, It. E4 9
Partizansk, Sov. Un. E16 13
Pasadena, Calif. E4, m12 50
Pasadena, Md. B4 53
Pasadena, Tex. r14 84
Pasadena Hills, Mo. *C7 69
Pasadena Park, Wash. *B8 86
Pasay, Phil. C6, o13 19
Pascagoula, Miss. E5, f8 68
Pascani -Gara, Rom. B8 10
Pasco, Wash. C6 86
Pasco, co., Fla. D4 54
Pasco, dept., Peru D2 31
Pascoag, R.I. B2 52
Pas-de-Calais, dept., Fr. B5 5
Pasewalk, Ger. Dem. Rep. B7 6
Pasig, Phil. o13 19
Paso de los Libres, Arg. E4 29
Paso Robles, Calif. E3 50
Pasquotank, co., N.C. A6 76
Pasrur, Pak. B5 20
Passadumkeag, mtn., Maine C4 64
Passaic, N.J. B4, h8 74
Passaic, co., N.J. A4 74
Passau, Ger., Fed. Rep. of D6 6
Pass Christian, Miss. E4, g7 68
Passo Fundo, Braz. D2 30
Passos, Braz. C3 30
Pastaza, prov., Ec. B2 31
Pasto, Col. C2 32
Pasuruan, Indon. G4 19
Pataskala, Ohio C3 78
Patchogue, N.Y. n15 75
Paternò, It. F5 9
Paterson, N.J. B4, h8 74
Pathānkot, India u16 20

Pathfork, Ky. D6 62
Patiāla, India B6 20
Patna, India C8 20
Patos, Braz. *D7 27
Patos de Minas, Braz. B3 30
Patrai, Grc. C3 14
Patrick, co., Va. D2 85
Patrocinio, Braz. B3 30
Pattani, Thai. D2 19
Patten, Maine C4 64
Patterson, Calif. *D3 50
Patterson, La. E4 63
Patterson, N.Y. D7 75
Patterson Gardens, Mich. *G7 66
Patton, Pa. E4 81
Pattonsburg, Mo. A3 69
Pattullo, mtn., B.C., Can. A3 37
Pátzcuaro, Mex. D4, n13 34
Patzicia, Guat. *E6 34
Patzún, Guat. *E6 34
Pau, Fr. F3 5
Paucarbamba, Peru D3 31
Paudalho, Braz. *D7 27
Pauk, Bur. D9 20
Paulding, Ohio A1 78
Paulding, co., Ga. C2 55
Paulding, co., Ohio A1 78
Paulina (Remy), La. D5, h10 63
Paulina, mts., Oreg. D5 80
Paulina, peak, Oreg. D5 80
Pauline, mtn., B.C., Can. C8 37
Paullina, Iowa B2 60
Paulsboro, N.J. D2 74
Pauls Valley, Okla. C4 79
Paungde, Bur. E10 20
Pavia, It. B2 9
Pavlodar, Sov. Un. D10 13
Pavlograd, Sov. Un. G10 12
Pavlovo, Sov. Un. D14 12
Pavlovsk, Sov. Un. F13 12
Pavlovskiy Posad, Sov. Un. n18 12
Pawcatuck, Conn. D9 52
Paw Creek, N.C. B2 76
Pawhuska, Okla. A5 79
Pawling, N.Y. D7 75
Pawnee, Ill. D4 58
Pawnee, Okla. A5 79
Pawnee, co., Kans. D4 61
Pawnee, co., Nebr. D9 71
Pawnee, co., Okla. A5 79
Pawnee City, Nebr. D9 71
Paw Paw, Mich. F5 66
Paw Paw, W. Va. B6 87
Paw Paw Lake, Mich. *F4 66
Pawtucket, R.I. B11 52
Paxtang, Pa. *F8 81
Paxton, Ill. C5 58
Payette, Idaho E2 57
Payette, co., Idaho E2 57
Payne, Ohio A1 78
Payne, co., Okla. A4 79
Paynesville, Minn. E4 67
Paysandú, Ur. E1 30
Paysandú, dept., Ur. *E1 30
Payson, Utah A6, D2 72
Pazardzhik, Bul. D7 10
Pazin, Yugo. C1 10
Peabody, Kans. D6 61
Peabody, Mass. A6, f12 65
Peace, riv., Alta., B.C., Can. .. E10 36
Peace Dale, R.I. D11 52
Peace River, Alta., Can. A2, f7 38
Peach, co., Ga. D3 55
Peach Creek, W. Va. n12 87
Peaked, mtn., Maine B4 64
Pearisburg, Va. C2 85
Pearl, Miss. C3 68
Pearland, Tex. r14 84
Pearl Beach, Mich. *F8 66
Pearl City, Haw. B4, g10 56
Pearl River, La. D6 63
Pearl River, N.J. *g12 75
Pearl River, co., Miss. D6 63
Pear Ridge, Tex. E2 63
Pearsall, Tex. E3 84
Pearsall, peak, Oreg. E3 80
Pearson, Ga. E4 55
Pebane, Moz. D7 24
Peć, Yugo. D5 10
Peçanha, Braz. B4 30
Pecatonica, Ill. A4 58
Pechenga, Sov. Un. C6 13
Pechora, riv., Sov. Un. C8 13
Peckville (Blakely), Pa. A9 81
Pecos, N. Mex. *B6 48
Pecos, Tex. D1, o13 84
Pecos, co., Tex. D1 84
Pecos, riv., N. Mex., Tex. D6 45
Pécs, Hung. B4 10
Pedley, Calif. *F5 50
Pedreiras, Braz. *D6 27
Pedricktown, N.J. D2 74
Pedro Juan Caballero, Par. D4 29

Pedro Velho, Braz. *D7 27
Peebles, Ohio D2 78
Peebles, Scot. C5 4
Peebles, co., Scot. *C5 4
Peekaboo, mtn., Maine C5 64
Peekskill, N.Y. D7, m15 75
Peel, co., Ont., Can. D5 41
Pego, Sp. C5 8
Pegu, Bur. E10 20
Pehuajó, Arg. B4 28
Peine, Ger., Fed. Rep. of B5 6
Pekalongan, Indon. G3 19
Pekan, Mala. E2 19
Pekin, Ill. C4 58
Peking (Beijing), China D8 17
Pelahatchie, Miss. C4 68
Pelée, mtn., Mart. I14 35
Pelham, Ont., Can. D5 41
Pelham, Ga. E2 55
Pelham, N.Y. *D7 75
Pelham Manor, N.Y. h13 75
Pelhrimov, Czech. D3 7
Pelican Rapids, Minn. D2 67
Pelican, mtn., Alta., Can. B4 38
Pell Lake, Wis. n11 88
Pella, Iowa C5 60
Pella, prov., Grc. *B4 14
Pell City, Ala. B3 46
Peloponnesos (Peloponnesus),
  reg., Grc. D4 14
Pelotas, Braz. E2 30
Pelzer North, S.C. *B2 82
Pematangsiantar, Indon. m11 19
Pemba, Moz. C8 24
Pemberton, N.J. D3 74
Pemberville, Ohio A4 78
Pembina, co., N. Dak. B8 77
Pembroke, Ont., Can. B7, p20 41
Pembroke, Ga. D5 55
Pembroke, Mass. B6 65
Pembroke, N.C. C3 76
Pembroke, Va. C2 85
Pembroke, Wales E4 4
Pembroke, co., Wales *E4 4
Pembroke Pines, Fla. *F6 54
Pemiscot, co., Mo. E8 69
Penápolis, Braz. C2 30
Pen Argyl, Pa. E11 81
Peñarroya-Pueblonuevo, Sp. C3 8
Penbrook, Pa. F8 81
Pender, Nebr. B9 71
Pender, co., N.C. C4 76
Pendleton, Ind. E6 59
Pendleton, Oreg. B8 80
Pendleton, S.C. B2 82
Pendleton, co., Ky. B5 62
Pendleton, co., W. Va. C5 87
Pend Oreille, co., Wash. A8 86
Penedo, Braz. E7 27
Penetanguishene, Ont., Can. C5 41
Penfield, N.Y. *B3 75
Penfield Junction, Ohio *A3 78
Peniche, Port. C1 8
Peninsula, Ohio A4 78
Penn, Pa. *F3 81
Pennask, mtn., B.C., Can. E7 37
Penndel, Pa. *F12 81
Penne, It. C4 9
Penn Hills, Pa. F2 81
Pennines, mts., Eng. C5 4
Pennington, Ala. C1 46
Pennington, N.J. C3 74
Pennington, co., Minn. B2 67
Pennington, co., S. Dak. G3 77
Pennington Gap, Va. f8 85
Pennsauken, N.J. D2 74
Pennsboro, W. Va. B4 87
Pennsburg, Pa. F11 81
Penns Grove, N.J. D2 74
Pennside, Pa. *F10 81
Pennsville, N.J. D1 74
Pennsylvania, state, U.S. 81
Penn Valley, Pa. *F11 81
Penn Wynne, Pa. *C11 81
Penn Yan, N.Y. C3 75
Penny Hill, Del. *A6 53
Penobscot, co., Maine C4 64
Pensacola, Fla. u14 54
Pentecost, Miss. B3 68
Penticton, B.C., Can. E8 37
Penton, Miss. A3 68
Pentwater, Mich. E4 66
Penza, Sov. Un. D7 13
Penzance, Eng. E4 4
Penzberg, Ger., Fed. Rep. of E5 6
Penzhino, Sov. Un. C19 13
Peoria, Ariz. C2, D1 48
Peoria, Ill. C4 58
Peoria, co., Ill. C4 58
Peoria Heights, Ill. C4 58
Peotone, Ill. B6 58
Pepin, Wis. D1 88
Pepin, co., Wis. D2 88
Pepper Pike, Ohio *A4 78

Pequannock, N.J. B4 74
Perak, state, Mala. *E2 19
Percy, Ill. E4 58
Perdido, mtn., Sp. A6 8
Pereira Barreto, Braz. C2 30
Pereira, Col. C2 32
Perekop, Sov. Un. H9 12
Pereslavl-Zalesskiy, Sov. Un. C12 12
Pereyaslav-Khmelnitskiy,
  Sov. Un. F8 12
Pergamino, Arg. A4 28
Perham, Minn. D3 67
Périgueux, Fr. E4 5
Perija, mts.,Col. B3 32
Perkasie, Pa. F11 81
Perkins, co., Nebr. D4 71
Perkins, co., S. Dak. E3 77
Perleberg, Ger. Dem. Rep. B5 6
Perlis, state, Mala. *D2 19
Perl-Mack, Colo. *B6 51
Perm, Sov. Un. D8 13
Përmet, Alb. B3 14
Pernambuco, state, Braz. *D7 27
Pernik, Bul. D6 10
Perpignan, Fr. F5 5
Perquimans, co., N.C. A6 76
Perrine, Fla. G6, s13 54
Perris, Calif. F5 50
Perry, Fla. B3 54
Perry, Ga. D3 55
Perry, Iowa C3 60
Perry, Mich. F6 66
Perry, Mo. B6 69
Perry, N.Y. C3 75
Perry, Ohio A4 78
Perry, Okla. A4 79
Perry, co., Ala. C2 46
Perry, co., Ark. C3 49
Perry, co., Ill. E4 58
Perry, co., Ind. H4 59
Perry, co., Ky. C6 62
Perry, co., Miss. D4 68
Perry, co., Mo. D8 69
Perry, co., Ohio C3 78
Perry, co., Pa. F7 81
Perry, co., Tenn. B4 83
Perry, peak, Mass. B1 65
Perry Hall (Fullerton), Md. B5 53
Perry Heights, Ohio *B4 78
Perryman, Md. B5 53
Perryopolis, Pa. *F2 81
Perrysburg, Ohio A2, e6 78
Perryton, Tex. A2 84
Perryville, Mo. D8 69
Pershing, co., Nev. A2 72
Persia, see Iran, country, Asia
Persimmon Grove, Ky. k14 62
Person, co., N.C. A3 76
Perth, Austl. F2 25
Perth, N.S., Can. C2 43
Perth, Ont., Can. C8 41
Perth, Scot. B5 4
Perth, co., Ont., Can. D3 41
Perth, co., Scot. *B5 4
Perth Amboy, N.J. B4, k7 74
Pertuis, Fr. F6 5
Peru, Ill. B4 58
Peru, Ind. C5 59
Peru, Nebr. D10 71
Peru, country, S.A. D3 31
Perugia, It. C4 9
Pervomaysk, Sov. Un. G8 12
Pervomaysk, Sov. Un. q21 12
Pervouralsk, Sov. Un. D8 13
Pesaro, It. C4 9
Pescara, It. C5 9
Peshāwar, Pak. B5 20
Peshtera, Bul. D7 10
Peshtigo, Wis. C6 88
Peski, Sov. Un. F14 12
Peso da Régua, Port. B2 8
Pesqueira, Braz. *D7 27
Pest, co., Hung. *B4 10
Petacas, mtn., Col. C2 32
Petah Tiqwa, Isr. B2 15
Petal, Miss. D4 68
Petaling Jaya, Mala. *E2 19
Petaluma, Calif. C2 50
Petatlán, Mex. D4 34
Peterborough, Ont., Can. C6 41
Peterborough, Eng. D6 4
Peterborough (Peterboro), N.H. F4 73
Peterborough, co., Ont., Can. C6 41
Peterhead, Scot. B6 4
Petermann, ranges, Austl. D4 25
Peters, mtn., Va. C2 85
Petersburg, Alsk. D13, m23 47
Petersburg, Ill. C4 58
Petersburg, Ind. H3 59
Petersburg, Mich. G7 66
Petersburg, Tex. C2 84
Petersburg (Independent City),
  Va. C5, n18 85

Petersburg, W. Va. B5 87
Pétionville, Hai. E7 35
Petite-de Grat, N.S., Can. D9 43
Petite-Rivière-de-l'Artibonite,
  Hai. E7 35
Petit-Goâve, Hai. E7 35
Peto, Mex. C7 34
Petoskey, Mich. C6 66
Petrich, Bul. E6 10
Petrikov, Sov. Un. E7 12
Petrinja, Yugo. C3 10
Petrodvorets, Sov. Un. s30 11
Petrokrepost, Sov. Un. s32 11
Petroleum, co., Mont. C8 70
Petrolia, Ont., Can. E2 41
Petrolina, Braz. *D6 27
Petropavlovsk, Sov. Un. D9 13
Petropavlovsk
  -Kamchatskiy, Sov. Un. D18 13
Petrópolis, Braz. C4, h6 30
Petros, Tenn. C9 83
Petroseni, Rom. C6 10
Petrovgrad, see Zrenjanin, Yugo.
Petrovsk, Sov. Un. E15 12
Petrovskoye, Sov. Un. I14 12
Petrovsk-Zabaykalskiy,
  Sov. Un. D13 13
Petrozavodsk, Sov. Un. A10 12
Pettis, co., Mo. C4 49
Petty Harbour, Newf., Can. E5 44
Pewaukee, Wis. E5, m11 88
Pézenas, Fr. F5 5
Pforzheim, Ger., Fed. Rep. of D4 6
Phalodi, India C5 20
Phan Rang, Viet. C3 19
Phan Thiet, Viet. C3 19
Pharr, Tex. F3 84
Phelps, Ky. C7 62
Phelps, N.Y. C3 75
Phelps, co., Mo. D6 69
Phelps, co., Nebr. D6 71
Phenix City, Ala. C4 46
Phet Buri, Thai. C1 19
Phetchabun, Thai. B2 19
Phichit, Thai. *B2 19
Philadelphia, Miss. C4 68
Philadelphia, N.Y. A5 75
Philadelphia, Pa. G11, p21 81
Philadelphia, co., Pa. G11 81
Phil Campbell, Ala. A2 46
Philip, S. Dak. C4 77
Philippeville, Bel. *B6 5
Philippi, W. Va. B4 87
Philippines, country, Asia B6 19
Philippolis, S. Afr. G5 24
Philipsburg, Mont. D3 70
Philipsburg, Pa. E5 81
Phillips, Tex. B2 84
Phillips, Wis. C3 88
Phillips, co., Ark. C5 49
Phillips, co., Colo. A8 51
Phillips, co., Kans. C4 61
Phillips, co., Mont. B8 70
Phillipsburg, Kans. C4 61
Phillipsburg, N.J. B2 74
Phillipsville, N.C. *f9 76
Philmont, N.Y. C7 75
Philo, Ohio C4 78
Philomath, Ga. C4 55
Philomath, Oreg. C3 80
Phitsanulok, Thai. B2 19
Phnom Penh, Kam. C2 19
Phoenix, Ariz. C2, D2 48
Phoenix, Ariz. k9 58
Phoenix, N.Y. B4 75
Phoenixville, Pa. F10, o19 81
Phong Saly, Laos G5 17
Phrae, Thai. *B2 19
Phucket, Thai. D1 19
Piacenza, It. B2 9
Pialba, Austl. B9 26
Piaseczno, Pol. m14 7
Piatra-Neamt, Rom. B8 10
Piatt, co., Ill. D5 58
Piauí, state, Braz. *D6 27
Piazza Armerina, It. F5 9
Picardy (Picardie),
  former prov., Fr. C5 5
Picayune, Miss. E4 68
Picher, Okla. A7 79
Pichincha, prov., Ec. B2 31
Pickaway, co., Ohio C2 78
Pickens, S.C. B2 82
Pickens, co., Ala. B1 46
Pickens, co., Ga. B2 55
Pickens, co., S.C. B2 82
Pickering, Ont., Can. D5 41
Pickett, co., Tenn. C8 83
Pickstown, S. Dak. H7 77
Pico Duarte, peak, Dom. Rep. E8 35
Pico Rivera, Calif. N12 50
Picton, Ont., Can. D7 41
Pictou, N.S., Can. D7 43

Pidurutalagala, peak, Sri Lanka G7 20
Piedmont, Ala. B4 46
Piedmont, Calif. h8 50
Piedmont, Mo. D7 69
Piedmont, S.C. B3 82
Piedmont, W. Va. B5 87
Piedmont, reg., It. B1 9
Piedrabuena, Sp. C3 8
Piedras Negras, Mex. B4 34
Pieksämäki, Fin. F12 11
Piélagos, Sp. A4 8
Piemonte, pol. dist., It. *B1 9
Piendamó, Col. C2 32
Pierce, Fla. E5 54
Pierce, Nebr. B8 71
Pierce, co., Ga. E4 55
Pierce, co., Nebr. B8 71
Pierce, co., N. Dak. B5 77
Pierce, co., Wash. C3 86
Pierce, co., Wis. D1 88
Pierce City, Mo. E3 69
Pierceton, Ind. B6 59
Piermont, N.Y. D7 75
Pierre, S. Dak. F5 77
Pierrefitte sur-Seine, Fr. g10 5
Pierrefonds, Que.,Can. q19 42
Pierreville, Que., Can. C5 42
Pierz, Minn. E4 67
Pieš'any, Czech. D4 7
Pietermaritzburg, S. Afr. F6 24
Pietersburg, S. Afr. E5 24
Pigeon, Mich. E7 66
Pigeon Cove, Mass. A6 65
Piggott, Ark. A5 49
Pigüé, Arg. B4 28
Pike, co., Ala. D4 46
Pike, co., Ark. C2 49
Pike, co., Ga. C2 55
Pike, co., Ill. D3 58
Pike, co., Ind. H3 59
Pike, co., Ky. C7 62
Pike, co., Miss. D3 68
Pike, co., Mo. B6 69
Pike, co., Ohio C2 78
Pike, co., Pa. D11 81
Pikes, peak, Colo. C5 51
Piketon, Ohio C2 78
Pikeville, Ky. C7 62
Pikesville, Md. B4, g10 53
Pikeville, Tenn. D8 83
Piła, Pol. B6 7
Pilar, Braz. *D7 27
Pilar, Par. E4 29
Pilcomayo, riv., S.A. D3 29
Pilgrim Gardens, Pa. *B11 81
Pilot Mound, Man., Can. E2 40
Pilot Mountain, N.C. A2 76
Pilot, peak, Wyo. B3 89
Pilot Point, Tex. C4 84
Pilot Rock, Oreg. B8 80
Pima, co., Ariz. C2 48
Pimmit Hills, Va. *B5 85
Pinal co., Ariz. C3 48
Pinang, see George Town, Mala.
Pinang, state, Mal. D2 19
Pinar del Rio, Cuba C2 35
Pinar del Rio, prov., Cuba C2 35
Pinardville, N.H. *E4 73
Pincher Creek, Alta., Can. E4 38
Pinckneyville, Ill. E4 58
Pinconning, Mich. E7 66
Pindamonhangaba, Braz. C3 30
Pine, co., Minn. D6 67
Pine, riv., Mich. D5 66
Pine Beach, N.J. *D4 74
Pine Bluff, Ark. C3 49
Pine Bluffs, Wyo. E8 89
Pine Bush, N.Y. D6 75
Pine Castle, Fla. D5 54
Pine City, Minn. E6 67
Pineda, Fla. D6 54
Pinedale, Ariz. B3 48
Pinedale, Wyo. D3 89
Pine Falls, Man., Can. D3 40
Pine Grove, Pa. E9 81
Pine Hill, N.J. D3 74
Pine Hills, Fla. *D5 54
Pinehurst, Idaho B2 57
Pinehurst, Mass. f11 65
Pinehurst, N.C. B3 76
Pinehurst, Wash. *B3 86
Pine Island, Minn. F6 67
Pine Island, N.Y. D6 75
Pine Knot, Ky. D5 62
Pine Lake, Ind. *A4 59
Pine Lake, Mass. g10 65
Pineland, Tex. D6 84
Pine Lawn, Mo. f13 69
Pinellas, co., Fla. D4 54
Pinellas Park, Fla. E4, p10 54
Pine Ridge, S. Dak. G3 77
Pinerolo, It. B1 9
Pinetops, N.C. B5 76

Pineville., Ky. ... D6 62
Pineville, La. ... C3 63
Pineville, N.C. ... B2 76
Pineville, W. Va. ... D3 87
Piney Point, Tex. ... *E5 84
Piney View, W. Va. ... D7 87
Pingliang, China ... D6 17
Pingtung, Taiwan ... *G9 17
Pingxiang, China ... F7 17
Pinhal, Braz. ... C3, m8 30
Pinkney (South Gastonia), N.C. ... *B1 76
Pinole, Calif. ... h8 50
Pinon, Ariz. ... A3 48
Pinos, Mex. ... C4 34
Pinoso, Sp. ... C5 8
Pinos-Puente, Sp. ... D4 8
Pinsk, Sov. Un. ... E6 12
Pinson, Ala. ... f7 46
Pioche, Nev. ... C4 72
Piombino, It. ... C3 9
Piotrków *Trybunalski*, Pol. ... C5 7
Piper City, Ill. ... C5 58
Pipestone, Minn. ... G2 67
Pipestone, co., Minn. ... F2 67
Piqua, Ohio ... B1 78
Piracicaba, Braz. ... C3, m8 30
Piraçununga, Braz. ... C3, k8 30
Piraeus, see Piraiévs, Grc.
Piraiévs (Piraeus), Grc. ... D4 14
Pirajú, Braz. ... C3 30
Pirajuí, Braz. ... C3 30
Piran, Yugo. ... B4 9
Pirapóra, Braz. ... B4 30
Pirgos, Grc. ... D3 14
Piriápolis, Ur. ... E1 30
Pirmasens, Ger., Fed. Rep. of ... D3 6
Pirna, Ger. Dem. Rep. ... C6 6
Pirot, Yugo. ... D6 10
Piryatin, Sov. Un. ... F9 12
Pisa, It. ... C3 9
Piscataquis, co., Maine ... C3 64
Piscataway, N.J. ... B4 74
Pisco, Peru ... D2 31
Pisek, Czech. ... D3 7
Pisinimo, Ariz. ... C2 48
Pismo Beach, Calif. ... E3 50
Pissis, mtn., Arg. ... E2 29
Pisticci, It. ... D6 9
Pistoia, It. ... C3 9
Pitalito, Col. ... C2 32
Pitangui, Braz. ... B4 30
Pitcairn, Pa. ... k14 81
Piteå, Swe. ... E9 11
Piteşti, Rom. ... C7 10
Pith'iviers, Fr. ... C5 5
Pitkin, co., Colo. ... B4 51
Pitlochry, Scot. ... B5 4
Pitman, N.J. ... D2 74
Pitrufquén, Chile ... B2 28
Pitt, co., N.C. ... B5 76
Pittsboro, N.C. ... B3 76
Pittsboro, Ind. ... E5 59
Pittsburg, Calif. ... g9 50
Pittsburg, Kans. ... E9 61
Pittsburg, Tex. ... C5 84
Pittsburg, co., Okla. ... C6 79
Pittsburgh, Pa. ... F1, k13 81
Pittsfield, Ill. ... D3 58
Pittsfield, Maine ... D3 64
Pittsfield, Mass. ... B1 65
Pittsfield, Mich. ... *F7 66
Pittsfield, N.H. ... E5 73
Pittsford, N.Y. ... B3 75
Pittston, Pa. ... D10, n17 81
Pittsylvania, co., Va. ... D3 85
Piura, Peru ... C1 31
Piura, dept., Peru ... C1 31
Piute, co., Utah ... B5 72
Pixley, Calif. ... E4 50
Pizzo, It. ... E6 9
Placentia, Calif. ... *F5 50
Placentia, Newf., Can. ... E5 44
Placer, co., Calif. ... C3 50
Placerville, Calif. ... C3 50
Placetas, Cuba ... C4 35
Placida, Fla. ... F4 54
Plain City, Ohio ... B2 78
Plain Dealing, La. ... B2 63
Plainfield, Conn. ... C9 52
Plainfield, Ill. ... B5, k8 58
Plainfield, Ind. ... E5 59
Plainfield, N.J. ... B4 74
Plainfield, Tenn. ... *D10 83
Plainfield Heights, Mich. ... *F5 66
Plainsboro, N.J. ... *C3 74
Plainsville, Pa. ... *D10 81
Plainview, Minn. ... F6 67
Plainview, Nebr. ... B8 71
Plainview, N.Y. ... *G3 52
Plainview, Tex. ... *B2 84
Plainville, Conn. ... C5 52
Plainville, Kans. ... C4 61
Plainwell, Mich. ... F5 66

Plaisance, Hai. ... E7 35
Plaistow, N.H. ... F5 73
Planada, Calif. ... *D3 50
Plandome, N.Y. ... *E7 75
Plandome Heights, N.Y. ... *E7 75
Plano, Calif. ... *D4 50
Plano, Ill. ... B5 58
Plano, Tex. ... C4, m10 84
Plantagenet, Ont., Can. ... B9 41
Plantation, Fla. ... r13 54
Plant City, Fla. ... D4 54
Plantsite, Ariz. ... *D6 48
Plantsville, Conn. ... C5 52
Plaquemine, La. ... D4, h9 63
Plaquemines, par., La. ... *D4 63
Plasencia, Sp. ... B2 8
Plaster Rock, N.B., Can. ... C2 43
Plato, Col. ... B3 32
Platón, Sánchez, Mex. ... m14 34
Platte, S. Dak. ... G7 77
Platte, co., Mo. ... B3 69
Platte, co., Nebr. ... C8 71
Platte, co., Wyo. ... D7 89
Platte City, Mo. ... B3, h10 69
Platteville, Wis. ... F3 88
Plattsburg, Mo. ... B3 69
Plattsburgh, N.Y. ... f11 75
Plattsmouth, Nebr. ... D10, h13 71
Plauen, Ger. Dem. Rep. ... C6 6
Pleasant Dale, Nebr. ... D9 71
Pleasant Gap, Pa. ... E6 81
Pleasant Grove, Ala. ... g7 46
Pleasant Grove, Utah ... A6, D2 72
Pleasant Hill, Calif. ... h8 50
Pleasant Hill, Ill. ... D3 58
Pleasant Hill, Iowa ... e8 60
Pleasant Hill, La. ... C2 63
Pleasant Hill, Mo. ... C3 69
Pleasant Hill, Ohio ... B1 78
Pleasant Hill, Pa. ... *F9 81
Pleasant Hill, Va. ... *D6 85
Pleasant Hills, Pa. ... *F2 81
Pleasanton, Calif. ... h9 50
Pleasanton, Kans. ... D9 61
Pleasanton, Tex. ... E3 84
Pleasant Ridge, Mich. ... *F7 66
Pleasants, co., W. Va. ... B3 87
Pleasant Valley, Mo. ... h11 69
Pleasant Valley, N.Y. ... D7 75
Pleasant View, Colo. ... *B5 51
Pleasant View, Utah ... A5 72
Pleasantville, Iowa ... C4 60
Pleasantville, N.J. ... E3 74
Pleasantville, N.Y. ... m15 75
Pleasantville, Pa. ... C2 81
Pleasure Beach, Conn. ... *E4 52
Pleasure Ridge Park, Ky. ... g11 62
Pleasureville, Pa. ... *G8 81
Pleiku, Viet. ... *C3 19
Plenita, Rom. ... C6 10
Plentywood, Mont. ... B12 70
Plesetsk, Sov. Un. ... C7 13
Plessisville, Que., Can. ... C6 42
Pleszew, Pol. ... C4 7
Pleven, Bul. ... D7 10
Pleven, co., Bul. ... *D7 10
Pljevlja, Yugo. ... D4 10
Płock, Pol. ... B5 7
Ploërmel, Fr. ... D2 5
Ploiesti, Rom. ... C8 10
Plomarion, Grc. ... C6 14
Płońsk, Pol. ... B6 7
Plovdiv, Bul. ... D7 10
Plovdiv, co., Bul. ... *D7 10
Plum, Pa. ... *E1 81
Plumas, co., Calif. ... B3 50
Plymouth, Conn. ... C4 52
Plymouth, Eng. ... E4 4
Plymouth, Ind. ... B5 59
Plymouth, Mass. ... C6 65
Plymouth, Mich. ... F7, p15 66
Plymouth, Minn. ... *F5 67
Plymouth, Mont. ... H13 35
Plymouth, N.H. ... D4 73
Plymouth, N.C. ... B6 76
Plymouth, Ohio ... B3 78
Plymouth, Pa. ... D10, n17 81
Plymouth, Wis. ... E6, k10 88
Plymouth, co., Iowa ... B1 60
Plymouth, co., Mass. ... C6 65
Plymouth Meeting, Pa. ... *F11 81
Plymouth Valley, Pa. ... *F11 81
Plymptonville, Pa. ... D5 81
Plzeň, Czech. ... D2 7
Pobedy, peak, Asia ... E11 13
Pocahontas, Ark. ... A5 49
Pocahontas, Iowa ... B3 60
Pocahontas, Va. ... e10 85
Pocahontas, co., Iowa ... B3 60
Pocahontas, co., W. Va. ... C4 87
Pocatello, Idaho ... G6 57
Pochep, Sov. Un. ... E9 12
Pochutla, Mex. ... D5 34

Pocomoke City, Md. ... D6 53
Poços de Caldas, Braz. ... C3, k8 30
Podgorica, see Titograd, Yugo.
Podolsk, Sov. Un. ... D11, n17 12
Podor, Sen. ... E2 22
Poe, S.C. ... *B3 82
Poggibonsi, It. ... C3 9
Pohang, Kor. ... H4 18
Pohjois-Karjala, prov., Fin. ... *F13 11
Poinsett, co., Ark. ... B5 49
Point Comfort, Tex. ... *E4 84
Pointe-à-Pitre, Guad. ... H14 35
Pointe-au-Pic, Que., Can. ... B7 42
Pointe-aux-Trembles, Que., Can. ... p20 42
Pointe-Claire, Que., Can. ... D4, q19 42
Pointe Coupee, par., La. ... D4 63
Pointe-du-Lac, Que., Can. ... C5 42
Point Edward, Ont., Can. ... D2 41
Pointe-Gatineau, Que., Can. ... D2 42
Pointe-Noire, Con. ... I7 22
Point Leamington, Newf., Can. ... D4 44
Point Lookout, Mo. ... E4 69
Point Marion, Pa. ... F2 81
Point Pleasant, N.J. ... C4 74
Point Pleasant Beach, N.J. ... C4 74
Poissy, Fr. ... C4 5
Poitiers, Fr. ... D4 5
Poitou, former prov., Fr. ... D3 5
Pokaran, India ... C5 20
Pokrovskoye, Sov. Un. ... H12 12
Poland, Ohio ... *A5 78
Poland, country, Eur. ... C5 7
Polgár, Hung. ... B5 10
Políkhnitos, Grc. ... C6 14
Polk, co., Ark. ... C1 49
Polk, co., Fla. ... E5 54
Polk, co., Ga. ... C1 55
Polk, co., Iowa ... C4 60
Polk, co., Minn. ... C2 67
Polk, co., Mo. ... D4 69
Polk, co., Nebr. ... C8 71
Polk, co., N.C. ... f10 76
Polk, co., Oreg. ... C3 80
Polk, co., Tenn. ... D9 83
Polk, co., Tex. ... D5 84
Polk, co., Wis. ... C1 88
Pollensa, Sp. ... C7 8
Pollocksville, N.C. ... C5 76
Polo, Ill. ... B4 58
Polotsk, Sov. Un. ... D7 12
Polson, Mont. ... C2 70
Poltava, Sov. Un. ... G10 12
Pomabamba, Peru ... C2 31
Pombal, Braz. ... *D7 27
Pomerania, reg., Pol. ... B4 7
Pomeroy, Iowa ... B3 60
Pomeroy, Ohio ... C4 78
Pomeroy, Pa. ... *G10 81
Pomeroy, Wash. ... C8 86
Pomoho, Haw. ... f9 56
Pomona, Calif. ... E5, m13 50
Pompano Beach, Fla. ... F6, r13 54
Pompton Lakes, N.J. ... A4 74
Pompton Plains, N.J. ... B4 74
Ponca, Nebr. ... B9 71
Ponca City, Okla. ... A4 79
Ponce, P.R. ... *G11 35
Ponchatoula, La. ... D5, h11 63
Pondera, co., Mont. ... B4 70
Pondicherry, India ... F6 20
Pondicherry, ter., India ... *F6 20
Ponferrada, Sp. ... A2 8
Ponoka, Alta., Can. ... C4 38
Ponorogo, Indon. ... *G4 19
Ponta Delgada (Azores Is.), Port. ... m10 22
Ponta Grossa, Braz. ... D2 30
Pont-A-Mousson, Fr. ... C7 5
Ponta Porã, Braz. ... C1 30
Pontarlier, Fr. ... D7 5
Pontedera, It. ... C3 9
Ponteix, Sask., Can. ... H2 39
Ponte Nova, Braz. ... C4 30
Pontevedra, Sp. ... A1 8
Pontevedra, prov., Sp. ... *A1 8
Pontiac, Ill. ... C5 58
Pontiac, Mich. ... F7, o15 66
Pontiac, co., Que., Can. ... A7 41
Pontianak, Indon. ... F3 19
Pontivy, Fr. ... C2 5
Pont-l'-Abbé, Fr. ... D1 5
Pontoise, Fr. ... C5 5
Pontotoc, Miss. ... A4 68
Pontotoc, co., Miss. ... A4 68
Pontotoc, co., Okla. ... C5 79
Pontremoli, It. ... B2 9
Pont-Rouge, Que., Can. ... C6, n16 42
Pont-Vieu, Que., Can. ... *D4 42
Poole, Eng. ... E5 4
Pooler, Ga. ... D5 55
Popasnaya, Sov. Un. ... q21 12
Popayán, Col. ... C2 32

Pope, co., Ark. ... B2 49
Pope, co., Ill. ... F5 58
Pope, co., Minn. ... D3 67
Poplar, Calif. ... *D4 50
Poplar, Mont. ... B11 70
Poplar Bluff, Mo. ... E7 69
Poplar Heights, Va. ... *B5 85
Poplarville, Miss. ... E4 68
Popocatepetl, vol., Mex. ... n14 34
Popovka, Sov. Un. ... H11 12
Popovo, Bul. ... D8 10
Poquonock, Conn. ... B6 52
Poquonock Bridge, Conn. ... D8 52
Poquoson, Va. ... h15 85
Porbandar, India ... D4 20
Porcuna, Sp. ... D3 8
Pordenone, It. ... B4 9
Porec, Yugo. ... C1 10
Pori, Fin. ... G9 11
Porlamar, Ven. ... A5 32
Poronaysk Shikuka, Sov. Un. ... E17 13
Porrentruy, Switz. ... E3 6
Porsgrunn, Nor. ... p27 11
Portadown, N. Ire. ... C3 4
Portage, Ind. ... A3 59
Portage, Mich. ... F5 66
Portage, Pa. ... F4 81
Portage, Wis. ... E4 88
Portage, co., Ohio ... A4 78
Portage, co., Wis. ... D4 88
Portage Lakes, Ohio ... *A4 78
Portage-la-Prairie, Man., Can. ... E2, h8 40
Portageville, Mo. ... E8 69
Port Alberni, B.C., Can. ... E5 37
Portalegre, Port. ... C2 8
Portales, N. Mex. ... B7 48
Port Alfred, S. Afr. ... G5 24
Port Alice, B.C., Can. ... D4 37
Port Allegany, Pa. ... C5 81
Port Allen, La. ... D4, h9 63
Port Angeles, Wash. ... A2 86
Port Angeles East, Wash. ... *A2 86
Port Antonio, Jam. ... E5 35
Port Arthur, see Lushun, China
Port Arthur, Tex. ... E6 84
Port Augusta, Austl. ... F6 25
Port-au-Prince, Hai. ... E7 35
Port Barre, La. ... D4 63
Port Blair, India ... F9 20
Port Byron, Ill. ... B3 58
Port Byron, N.Y. ... B4 75
Port Carbon, Pa. ... E9 81
Port-Cartier-Ouest, Que., Can. ... k13 42
Port Charlotte, Fla. ... F4 54
Port Chester, N.Y. ... E7, n15 75
Port Chicago, Calif. ... G8 50
Port Clinton, Ohio ... A3 78
Port Colborne, Ont., Can. ... E5 41
Port Coquitlam, B.C., Can. ... E6, f13 37
Port Crane, N.Y. ... C5 75
Port Credit, Ont., Can. ... D5, m14 41
Port-de-Bouc, Fr. ... F6 5
Port-de-Paix, Hai. ... E7 35
Port Deposit, Md. ... A5 53
Port Dickinson, N.Y. ... C5 75
Port Dickson, Mala. ... E2 19
Port Dover, Ont., Can. ... E4 41
Port Edward, B.C., Can. ... B2 37
Port Edwards, Wis. ... D4 88
Port Elgin, N.B., Can. ... C5 43
Port Elgin, Ont., Can. ... C3 41
Port Elizabeth, S. Afr. ... G5 24
Porter, Ind. ... A3 59
Porter, co., Ind. ... B3 59
Porterdale, Ga. ... C3 55
Porterville, Calif. ... D4 50
Port Ewen, N.Y. ... D7 75
Port-Francqui, see Ilebo, Zaire
Port-Gentil, Gabon ... I6 22
Port Gibson, Miss. ... D3 68
Port Hammond, B.C., Can. ... f13 37
Port Harcourt, Nig. ... H6 22
Port Hawkesbury, N.S., Can. ... D8 43
Port Hedland, Austl. ... D2 25
Port Henry, N.Y. ... A7 75
Port Hope, Ont., Can. ... D6 41
Port Hueneme, Calif. ... E4 50
Port Huron, Mich. ... F8 66
Portimão, Port. ... D1 8
Port Isabel, Tex. ... F4 84
Port Jefferson, N.Y. ... F4 52
Port Jefferson Station, N.Y. ... n15 75
Port Jervis, N.Y. ... D6 75
Portland, Austl. ... G7 25
Portland, Conn. ... C6 52
Portland, Ind. ... D8 59
Portland, Maine ... E2, g7 64
Portland, Mich. ... F6 66
Portland, Oreg. ... B4, g12 80
Portland, Tenn. ... A5 83
Port Lavaca, Tex. ... E4 84
Port Leyden, N.Y. ... B5 75

Port Lincoln, Austl.	F6	25
Port Louis, Mau.	*H24	2
Port McNicoll, Ont., Can.	C5	41
Port Macquarie, Austl.	F9	25
Port Monmouth, N.J.	C4	74
Port Moody, B.C., Can.	E6, f13	37
Port Moresby, Pap.	k12	25
Port Neches, Tex.	E6	84
Portneuf, Que., Can.	C5	42
Portneuf, co., Que., Can.	C5	42
Port Norris, N.J.	E2	74
Pôrto (Oporto), Port.	B1	8
Pôrto Alegre, Braz.	E2	30
Porto Alexandre, Ang.	D2	24
Porto de Moz, Braz.	D5	27
Pôrto Feliz, Braz.	C3, m8	30
Portoferraio, It.	C3	9
Port of Spain, Trin.	K14	35
Portogruaro, It.	B4	9
Portomaggiore, It.	B3	9
Porto Nacional, Braz.	E6	27
Port-Novo, Benin	G5	22
Port Orange, Fla.	C6	54
Port Orchard, Wash.	B3, e10	86
Port Orford, Oreg.	E2	80
Portolo, Calif.	C3	50
Porto Torres, It.	D2	9
Pôrto União, Braz.	D2	30
Porto Velho, Braz.	D4	27
Portoviejo, Ec.	B1	31
Portpatrick, Scot.	C4	4
Port Perry, Ont., Can.	C6	41
Port Pirie, Austl.	F6	25
Port Reading, N.J.	k8	74
Port Richey, Fla.	D4	54
Port Said (Būr Sa'īd), Eg.	G9	14
Port Saint Joe, Fla.	C1, v16	54
Port St. Lucie, Fla.	E6	54
Port Sewall, Fla.	E6	54
Portsmouth, Eng.	E6	4
Portsmouth, N.H.	D5	73
Portsmouth, Ohio	D3	78
Portsmouth, R.I.	C12	52
Portsmouth, (Independent City), Va.	D6, k15	85
Port Stanley, Ont., Can.	E3	41
Port Sudan, Sud.	E5	23
Port Sulphur, La.	E6	63
Port Talbot, Wales	*E5	4
Port Townsend, Wash.	A3	86
Portugal, country, Eur.	C1	8
Portugal Cove, Newf., Can.	*E5	44
Portugalete, Sp.	A4	8
Portuguesa, state, Ven.	B4	32
Portuguese Guinea, see Guinea-Bissau, country, Afr.		
Port Vue, Pa.	*F2	81
Port Wakefield, Austl.	*F6	25
Port Washington, N.Y.	h13	75
Port Washington, Wis.	E6	88
Port Wentworth, Ga.	D5	55
Posadas, Arg.	E4	29
Posadas, Sp.	D3	8
Posen, Ill.	k9	58
Posen, see Poznan, Pol.		
Posey, co., Ind.	H2	59
Poseyville, Ind.	H2	59
Poso, Indon.	F6	19
Post, Tex.	C2	84
Poste-de-la-Baleine, Que., Can.	g11	42
Poste-Mistassini, Que., Can.	h12	42
Post Falls, Idaho	B2	57
Postojna, Yugo.	C2	10
Poston, S.C.	D9	82
Postville, Iowa	A6	60
Potchefstroom, S. Afr.	F5	24
Poteau, Okla.	B7	79
Poteet, Tex.	E3	84
Potenza, It.	D5	9
Potgietersrus, S. Afr.	E5	24
Poth, Tex.	E3	84
Potlatch, Idaho	C2	57
Potomac, Md.	B3	53
Potomac Heights, Md.	C3	53
Potomac Park, Md.	k13	53
Potosi, Bol.	C2	29
Potosi, Mo.	D7	69
Potosí, dept., Bol.	C2	29
Pototan, Phil.	*C6	19
Potsdam, Ger. Dem. Rep.	B6	6
Potsdam, N.Y.	f10	75
Pottawatomie, co., Kans.	C7	61
Pottawatomie, co., Okla.	B5	79
Pottawattamie, co., Iowa	C2	60
Potter, co., Pa.	C6	81
Potter, co., S. Dak.	F5	77
Potter, co., Tex.	*B2	84
Potterville, Mich.	*F6	66
Pottstown, Pa.	F10	81
Pottsville, Pa.	E9	81
Pouch Cove, Newf., Can.	E5	44
Poughkeepsie, N.Y.	D7	75
Poulsbo, Wash.	B3	86
Poultney, Vt.	D1	73
Pound, Va.	e9	85
Pouso Alegre, Braz.	C3	30
Póvoa, de Varzim, Port.	B1	8
Powassan, Ont., Can.	A5	41
Poway, Calif.	F5	50
Powder River, co., Mont.	E11	70
Powell, Mo.	E3	69
Powell, Wyo.	B4	89
Powell, co., Ky.	C6	62
Powell, co., Mont.	D4	70
Powell River, B.C., Can.	E5	37
Powellton, W. Va.	C3	87
Power, co., Idaho	G6	57
Powers, Oreg.	E2	80
Poweshiek, co., Iowa	C5	60
Powhatan, co., Va.	C5	85
Powhatan Point, Ohio	C5	78
Poynette, Wis.	E4	88
Požarevac, Yugo.	C5	10
Poza Rica de Hidalgo, Mex.	m15	34
Poznań, Pol.	B4	7
Pozoblanco, Sp.	C3	8
Pozzallo, It.	F5	9
Pozzuoli, It.	D5	9
Prachin Buri, Thai.	C2	19
Prachuap Khiri Khan, Thai.	*C1	19
Praco, Ala.	f6	46
Prades, Fr.	F5	5
Praestö, co., Den.	*J5	11
Prague (Praha), Czech.	C3, n17	7
Prague, Okla.	B5	79
Praha, see Prague, Czech.		
Praia, C.V.	n12	22
Prairie, co., Ark.	C4	49
Prairie, co., Mont.	D11	70
Prairie City, Iowa	C4	60
Prairie du Chien, Wis.	E2	88
Prairie du Sac, Wis.	E4	88
Prairie Grove, Ark.	B1	49
Prairie Village, Kans.	*B9	61
Pran Buri, Thai.	C1	19
Prato, It.	C3	9
Pratt, Kans.	E5	61
Pratt, Minn.	*C6	87
Pratt, co., Kans.	E5	61
Prattville, Ala.	C3	46
Prattville, Okla.	*A5	79
Pravdinsk (Friedland), Sov. Un.	A6	7
Pravia, Sp.	A2	8
Preble, co., Ohio	C1	78
Premont, Tex.	F3	84
Prentiss, Miss.	D4	68
Prentiss, co., Miss.	A5	68
Prenzlau, Ger.	F6	6
Přerov, Czech.	D4	7
Prescott, Ariz.	B2	48
Prescott, Ark.	D2	49
Prescott, Ont., Can.	C9	41
Prescott, Wis.	D1	88
Prescott, co., Ont., Can.	B10	41
Presidencia Roque Sáenz Peña, Arg.	E3	29
Presidente Hayes, dept., Par.	D4	29
Presidente Prudente, Braz.	C2	30
Presidio, Tex.	p12	84
Presidio, co., Tex.	o12	84
Prešov, Czech.	D6	7
Presque Isle, Maine	B4	64
Presque Isle, co., Mich.	C6	66
Preston, Eng.	D5	4
Preston, Idaho	G7	57
Preston, Ky.	B6	62
Preston, Minn.	G6	67
Preston, co., W. Va.	B5	87
Preston, peak, Calif.	B2	50
Prestonburg, Ky.	C7	62
Prestonville, Ky.	B4	62
Prestwick, Scot.	C4	4
Pretoria, S. Afr.	F5	24
Préveza, Grc.	C3	14
Préveza, prov., Grc.	*C3	14
Prey Veng, Camb.	*C3	19
Pribram, Czech.	D3	7
Price, Que., Can.	*G20	36
Price, Utah	B6	72
Price, co., Wis.	C3	88
Pricedale, Pa.	*F2	81
Prichard, Ala.	E1	46
Priestly, mtn., B.C., Can.	B3	37
Priest River, Idaho	A2	57
Prilep, Yugo.	E5	10
Priluki, Sov. Un.	F9	12
Primera, Tex.	*F4	84
Primghar, Iowa	A2	60
Primorsk, Sov. Un.	A6	7
Primorsko-Akhtarsk, Sov. Un.	H12	12
Primos, Pa.	*G11	81
Primrose, Pa.	*E9	81
Prince, co., P.E.I., Can.	C5	43
Prince Albert, Sask., Can.	D3, n7	39
Prince Edward, co., Ont., Can.	C7	41
Prince Edward, co., Va.	C4	85
Prince Edward Island, prov., Can.	C6	43
Prince George, B.C., Can.	C6, n18	37
Prince George, co., Va.	C5	85
Prince Georges, co., Md.	C4	53
Prince of Wales, isl., N.W. Ter., Can.	B14	36
Prince Rupert, B.C., Can.	B2, n16	37
Princess Anne, Md.	D6	53
Princeton, Ala.	A3	46
Princeton, B.C., Can.	E7	37
Princeton, Fla.	G6, s13	54
Princeton, Ill.	B4	58
Princeton, Ind.	H2	59
Princeton, Ky.	C2	62
Princeton, Minn.	E5	67
Princeton, Mo.	A4	69
Princeton, N.J.	C3	74
Princeton, N.C.	B4	76
Princeton, W. Va.	D3	87
Princeton, Wis.	E4	88
Princeville, Que., Can.	C6	42
Princeville, Ill.	C4	58
Princeville, N.C.	B5	76
Prince William, co., Va.	B5	85
Prineville, Oreg.	C6	80
Prineville Southeast, Oreg.	*C6	80
Pringle, Pa.	*D10	81
Prinsburg, Minn.	F3	67
Priozersk, Sov. Un.	G14	11
Pristina, Yugo.	D5	10
Pritzwalk, Ger. Dem. Rep.	B6	6
Privas, Fr.	E6	5
Privolnoye, Sov. Un.	H9	12
Prizren, Yugo.	D5	10
Prizzi, It.	F4	9
Probolinggo, Indon.	G4	19
Proctor, Minn.	D6	67
Proctor, Vt.	D1	73
Proctorville, Ohio	D3	78
Progreso, Hond.	*D7	34
Progreso, Mex.	C7	34
Progress, Pa.	*F8	81
Prokopyevsk, Sov. Un.	D11	13
Prokuplje, Yugo.	D5	10
Proletarskaya, Sov. Un.	H13	12
Prome, Bur.	E10	20
Prophetstown, Ill.	B4	58
Propriá, Braz.	*D7	27
Proserpine, Austl.	D8	25
Prosotsáni, Grc.	*B4	14
Prospect, Conn.	C5	52
Prospect, Ohio	B2	78
Prospect, Pa.	E1	81
Prospect Heights, Ill.	*B6	58
Prospect Park, N.J.	B4	74
Prospect Park, Pa.	p20	81
Prosser, Wash.	C6	86
Prostějov, Czech.	D4	7
Provadiya, Bul.	D8	10
Providence, Ky.	C2	62
Providence, R.I.	B11	52
Providence, Tenn.	*A5	83
Providence, Utah	*A6	72
Providence, co., R.I.	B10	52
Provincetown, Mass.	B7	65
Provins, Fr.	C5	5
Provo, Utah	A6, D2	72
Provost, Alta., Can.	C5	38
Prowers, co., Colo.	D8	51
Prozor, Yugo.	D3	10
Prudnik, Pol.	C4	7
Pruszków, Pol.	B6, m13	7
Pruzhany, Sov. Un.	E5	12
Pryor, Okla.	A6	79
Pryor, mts., Mont.	E8	70
Przasnysz, Pol.	B6	7
Przemyśl, Pol.	D7	7
Przeworsk, Pol.	C7	7
Pskov, Sov. Un.	C7	12
Pszczyna, Pol.	D5, h9	7
Ptolemaïs, Grc.	*B3	14
Ptuj, Yugo.	B2	10
Puebla, state, Mex.	D5, n14	34
Puebla de Don Fadrique, Sp.	D4	8
Puebla del Caramiñal, Sp.	A1	8
Puebla de Zaragoza, Mex.	D5, n14	34
Pueblo, Colo.	C6	51
Pueblo, co., Colo.	C6	51
Puente Alvaro Obregón, Mex.	*D6	34
Puerto Armuelles, Pan.	*B1	32
Puerto Barrios, Guat.	D7	34
Puerto Berrio, Col.	B3	32
Puerto Cabello, Ven.	A4	32
Puerto Casado, Par.	D4	29
Puerto Cortés, Hond.	D7	34
Puerto de la Cruz, Sp.	m13	8
Puerto Eten, Peru	C2	31
Puerto La Cruz, Ven.	A5	32
Puertollano, Sp.	C3	8
Puerto Maldonado, Peru	D4	31
Puerto Montt, Chile	C2	28
Puerto Padre, Cuba	D5	35
Puerto Peñasco, Mex.	A2	34
Puerto Pinasco, Par.	D4	29
Puerto Plata, Dom. Rep.	E8	35
Puerto Rico, U.S., dep., N.A.	G11	35
Puerto Sastre, Par.	D4	29
Puerto Supe, Peru	D2	31
Puerto Tejada, Col.	C2	32
Puerto Vallarto, Mex.	C3, m11	34
Puerto Wilches, Col.	B3	32
Puglia, pol. dist., It.	*D6	9
Pugwash, N.S., Can.	D6	43
Puhi, Haw.	B2	56
Puhsi, China	B2	18
Pukchong, Kor.	F4	18
Puksubaek-san, mtn., Kor.	F3	18
Pula, Yugo.	C1	10
Pulaski, Miss.	C4	68
Pulaski, N.Y.	B4	75
Pulaski, Tenn.	B4	83
Pulaski, Va.	C2	85
Pulaski, Wis.	D5	88
Pulaski, co., Ark.	C3	49
Pulaski, co., Ga.	D3	55
Pulaski, co., Ill.	F4	58
Pulaski, co., Ind.	B4	59
Pulaski, co., Ky.	C5	62
Pulaski, co., Mo.	D5	69
Pulaski, co., Va.	C2	85
Pulawy, Pol.	C6	7
Pul-I-Khumri, Afg.	A4	20
Pullman, Wash.	C8	86
Pulog, mtn., Phil.	n13	19
Pułtusk, Pol.	B6	7
Pune (Poona), India	E5	20
Pungsan, Kor.	F4	18
Punjab, state, India	B5	20
Puno, Peru	E3	31
Puno, dept., Peru	E3	31
Punta Alta, Arg.	B4	28
Punta Arenas, Chile	h11	28
Punta Gorda, Fla.	F4	54
Puntarenas, C.R.	*F8	34
Puntarenas, prov., C.R.	*F8	34
Punxsutawney, Pa.	E4	81
Puquio, Peru	D3	31
Purcell, Mo.	D3	69
Purcell, Okla.	B4	79
Purcellville, Va.	A5	85
Purèpero, Mex.	n12	34
Puri, India	E8	20
Purnea, India	C8	20
Pursat, Kam.	C2	19
Pursglove, W. Va.	B4	87
Purūlia, India	D8	20
Purús, riv., Peru	D3	31
Purvis, Miss.	D4	68
Purwokerto, Indon.	*G3	19
Pusan, Kor.	I4	18
Pushkin, Sov. Un.	B8	12
Pushkino, Sov. Un.	C11, m17	12
Pushmataha, Ala.	C1	46
Pushmataha, co., Okla.	C6	79
Püspökladány, Hung.	B5	10
Pustelnik, Pol.	k14	7
Putao, Bur.	C10	20
Puteaux, Fr.	g9	5
Putivl, Sov. Un.	F9	12
Putnam, Conn.	B9	52
Putnam, co., Fla.	C5	54
Putnam, co., Ga.	C3	55
Putnam, co., Ill.	B4	58
Putnam, co., Ind.	E4	59
Putnam, co., Mo.	A4	69
Putnam, co., N.Y.	D7	75
Putnam, co., Ohio	B1	78
Putnam, co., Tenn.	C8	83
Putnam, co., W. Va.	C3	87
Puttalam, Sri Lanka	G6	20
Putumayo, comisaría, Col.	C2	32
Puukolii, Haw.	C5	56
Puunene, Haw.	C5	56
Puxico, Mo.	E7	69
Puyallup, Wash.	B3, f11	86
Puy-de-Dôme, dept., Fr.	*E5	5
Puyo, Ec.	B2	31
Pwllheli, Wales	D4	4
Pyapon, Bur.	E10	20
Pyatigorsk, Sov. Un.	*E7	13
Pyinmana, Bur.	E10	20
Pyŏngchang, Kor.	H4	18
Pyongtaek, Kor.	H3	18
Pyongyang, Kor.	G2	18
Pyrénées-Orientales, dept., Fr.	*F5	5
Pyskowice, Pol.	g9	7
Pyu, Bur.	E10	20

Q

Qamdo, China E4 17
Qāna, Leb. A3 15
Qaṣr al Farāfirah, Eg. C3 23
Qatar, country, Asia D5 15
Qazvin, Iran B5 15
Qiemo, China A8 20
Qina, Eg. C4 23
Qingdao, China. D9 17
Qinghai, prov., China D4 17
Qinghai, lake, China D4 17
Qingjiang, China E8 20
Qinhuangdao, China. D8 17
Qiqihar, China B9 17
Qitai, China C2 17
Qiryat Shemona, Isr. A3 15
Qiryat Yam, Isr. B3 15
Qom, Iran C5 15
Quakenbruck, Ger. Fed. Rep. of . . B3 6
Quaker Hill, Conn. D8 52
Quakertown, Pa. F11 81
Quanah, Tex. B3 84
Quang Ngai, Viet. B3 19
Quang Tri, Viet. B3 19

Quantico, Va. B5 85
Quanzhou, China G8 17
Quapaw, Okla. A7 79
Quarai, Braz. E1 30
Quarryville, Pa. G9 81
Quartu Sant' Elena, It. E2 9
Quartz Hill, Calif. *E4 50
Quay, co., N. Mex. B7 48
Québec., Que., Can. C6, n17 42
Québec, co., Que., Can. B5 42
Québec, prov., Can. 42
Québec-Quest, Que., Can. *C6 42
Quedlinburg, Ger. Dem. Rep. C5 6
Queen Annes, co., Md. B5 53
Queen Bess, mtn., B.C., Can. D5 37
Queen City, Tex. *C5 84
Queen Elizabeth, is., N.W. Ter.,
   Can. m31 36
Queens, borough and co., N.Y. E7 75
Queens, co., N.B., Can. D4 43
Queens, co., N.S., Can. E4 43
Queens, co., P.E.I., Can. C6 43
Queensland, state, Austl. D7 25

Queenstown, S. Afr. G5 24
Quelimane, Moz. D7 24
Querétaro, Mex. C4, m13 34
Querétaro, state, Mex. C4, m13 34
Quesada, Sp. D4 8
Quesnel, B.C., Can. C6 37
Questa, N. Mex. A6 48
Quetta, Pak. B4 20
Quezaltenango, Guat. E6 34
Quezaltepeque, Sal. *E7 34
Quezon, prov., Phil. *C6 19
Quezon City, Phil. C6 19
Quibdó, Col. B2 32
Quidnessett, R.I. C11 52
Quidnick, R.I. C10 52
Quiindy, Par. E4 29
Quilá, Mex. C3 34
Quillota, Chile A2 28
Quilmes, Arg. g7 28
Quilon, India G6 20
Quilpie, Austl. E7 25
Quilpué, Chile A2 28
Quimper, Fr. C2 5

Quimperlé, Fr. D2 5
Quincy, Calif. C3 50
Quincy, Fla. B2 54
Quincy, Ill. D2 58
Quincy, Mass. h11 65
Quincy, Mich. G6 66
Quincy, Wash. B6 86
Qui Nhon, Viet. C3 19
Quinnville, R.I. B11 52
Quintana de la Serena, Sp. C3 8
Quintanar, Sp. C4 8
Quintana Roo, state, Mex. D7 34
Quinter, Kans. C3 61
Quinton, Okla. B6 79
Quiroga, Sp. A2 8
Quitman, Ga. F3 55
Quitman, Miss. C5 68
Quitman, Tex. C5 84
Quitman, co., Ga. E1 55
Quitman, co., Miss. A3 68
Quito, Ec. B2 31
Quixadá, Braz. *D7 27
Quxian, China F8 17

R

Raba, Indon. G5 19
Rabat, Mor. B3 22
Rabaul, Pap. N. Gui. h13 25
Rabun, Ala. D2 46
Rabun, co., Ga. B3 55
Raceland, Ky. B7 62
Raceland, La. E5, k10 63
Rach Gia., Viet. *C2 19
Raciborz, Pol. C5 7
Racine, Wis. F6, n12 88
Racine, co., Wis. F5 88
Radauti, Rom. B7 10
Radcliff, Ky. C4 62
Radeberg, Ger. Dem. Rep. C6 6
Radford (Independent City), Va. C2 85
Radiant Valley, Md. C4 53
Radnor, Pa. *G11 81
Radnor, co., Wales *D5 4
Radom, Pol. C6 7
Radomir, Bul. D6 10
Radomsko, Pol. C5 7
Radville, Sask., Can. H3 39
Radzionków, Pol. g9 7
Rāe Bareli, India C7 20
Raeford, N.C. C3 76
Rafaela, Arg. A4 28
Rafaḥ, Gaza Strip C2 15
Ragland, Ala. B3 46
Ragusa, It. F5 9
Rahīmyār-Khān, Pak. C5 20
Rahway, N.J. B4, k7 74
Rāichūr, India E6 20
Raigarh, India D7 20
Rainbow City, Ala. *A3 46
Rainbow City, Pan. *B2 32
Rainier, Oreg. A4 80
Rainier, mtn., Wash. C4 86
Rains, co., Tex. C5 84
Rainsville, Ala. A4 46
Rainy River, Ont., Can. *o16 41
Rainy River, dist., Ont., Can. *o16 41
Raipur, India D7 20
Rājahmundry, India *E7 20
Rajapalaiyam, India *G6 20
Rājasthān, state, India C5 20
Rājkot, India D5 20
Rājshāhi, Bngl. D8 20

Rakovník, Czech. . . . . C2 · 7
Rakvere, Sov. Un. B6 12
Raleigh, N.C. B4 76
Raleigh, W. Va. n13 87
Raleigh, co., W. Va. D3 87
Ralls, Tex. C2 84
Ralls, co., Mo. B6 69
Ralston, Nebr. g12 71
Rām Allāh, Jordan C3 15
Ramat Gan, Isr. B2 15
Ramat HaSharon, Isr. *B2 15
Rambervillers, Fr. C7 5
Ramea, Newf. Can. E3 44
Ramenskoye, Sov. Un. D12, n18 12
Ramla, Isr. C2 15
Ramleh, Eg. *G8 14
Ramona, Calif. F5 50
Rāmpur, India C6 20
Ramsay, Mich. n12 66
Ramseur, N.C. B3 76
Ramsey, N.J. A4 74
Ramsey, co. Minn. E5 67
Ramsey, co., N. Dak. B7 77
Ramsgate, Eng. E7 4
Rancagua, Chile A2 28
Ranches of Taos, N. Mex. A6 48
Rānchī, India D8 20
Rancho Cordova, Calif. *C3 50
Rand, W. Va. m12 87
Randall, co., Tex. B2 84
Randallstown, Md. B4 53
Randers, Den. I4 11
Randers, co., Den. *I4 11
Randleman, N.C. B3 76
Randolph, Maine D3 64
Randolph, Mass. B5, h11 65
Randolph, Nebr. B8 71
Randolph, Vt. D2 73
Randolph, Wis. E4 88
Randolph, co., Ala. B4 46
Randolph, co., Ark. A4 49
Randolph, co., Ga. E2 55
Randolph, co., Ill. E4 58
Randolph, co., Ind. D7 59
Randolph, co., Mo. B5 69
Randolph, co., N.C. B3 76
Randolph, co., W. Va. C5 87

Randolph Hills, Md. *B3 53
Rangely, Colo. A2 51
Ranger, Tex. C3 84
Rangoon, Bur. E10 20
Rangpur, Bngl. C8 20
Rānīganj, India D8 20
Rankin, Pa. k14 81
Rankin, Tex. D2 84
Rankin, co., Miss. C4 68
Ranlo, N.C. *B1 76
Ranshaw, Pa. *E9 81
Ransom, co., N. Dak. D8 77
Ranson, W. Va. B7 87
Rantoul, Ill. C5 58
Rapallo, It. B2 9
Rapid City, S. Dak. F2 77
Rapides, par., La. C3 63
Rappahannock, co., Va. B4 85
Raritan, N.J. B3 74
Raseiniai, Sov. Un. A7 77
Rashīd (Rosetta), Eg. G8 14
Rasht, Iran A7 23
Rasskazovo, Sov. Un. E13 12
Rastatt, Ger. Dem. Rep. of D4 6
Rat Buri, Thai. C1 19
Rathenow, Ger. Dem. Rep. B6 6
Ratibor, see Raciborz, Pol.
Ratlām, India *D6 20
Ratnāgiri, India E5 20
Raton, N. Mex. A6 48
Rauch, Arg. B5 28
Rauma, Fin. G9 11
Raurkela, India *D7 20
Rava-Russkaya, Sov. Un. F4 12
Ravalli, co., Mont. D2 70
Rava-Russkaya, Sov. Un. e10 85
Raven, Va. e10 85
Ravena, N.Y. C7 75
Ravenna, It. B4 9
Ravenna, Ky. C6 62
Ravenna, Nebr. C7 71
Ravenna, Ohio A4 78
Ravensburg, Ger., Fed. Rep. of E4 6
Ravenswood, W. Va. C3 87
Rāwalpindi, Pak. B5 20
Rawa Mazowiecka, Pol. C6 7
Rawdon, Que., Can. C4 42
Rawicz, Pol. C4 7

Rawlins, Wyo. E5 89
Rawlins, co.,Kans. C2 61
Rawlins, co., Kan. C2 61
Ray, Ariz. C3, D3 48
Ray, N. Dak. B2 77
Ray, co., Mo. B3 69
Raybon, Ga. E5 55
Raychikhinsk, Sov. Un. B4 18
Raymond, Alta, Can. E4 38
Raymond, Miss. C3 68
Raymond, Wash. C2 86
Raymond Terrace, Austl. F8 26
Raymondville, Tex. F4 84
Rayne, La. D3 63
Raynham Center, Mass. C5 65
Rayong, Thai. *C2 19
Raytown, Ga. C4 55
Raytown, Mo. h11 69
Rayville, La. B4 63
Razgrad, Bul. D8 10
Razlog, Bul. E6 10
Reading, Eng. E6 4
Reading, Mass. A5, f11 65
Reading, Mich. G6 66
Reading, Ohio C1, o13 78
Reading, Pa. F10 81
Reagan, co., Tex. D2 84
Real, co., Tex. E3 84
Ream, Camb. *C2 19
Ream, W. Va. *D3 87
Reamstown, Pa. F9 81
Recanati, It. C4 9
Rechitsa, Sov. Un. E8 12
Recife (Pernambuco), Braz. D7 27
Recklinghausen, Ger., Fed.
   Rep. of C3 6
Reconquista, Arg. E4 29
Rector, Ark. A5 49
Red, riv., U.S. D8 45
Red, sea, Afr. D9 21
Red, sea, Asia D9 21
Red Bank, N.J. C4 74
Red Bank, Tenn. D8 83
Red Bay, Ala. A1 46
Red Bluff, Calif. B2 50
Red Boiling Springs, Tenn. C8 83
Red Bud, Ill. E4 58

Redcliff, Alta, Can................ D5 38
Red Cloud, Nebr.................. D7 71
Red Deer, Alta, Can.......... C4, g8 38
Reddell, La...................... D3 63
Redding, Calif................... B2 50
Redfield, Iowa................... C3 60
Redfield, S. Dak................. F7 77
Redford Township, Mich......... p15 66
Red Hill, N.C................... *F11 81
Red Hook, N.Y.................. D7 75
Redington, Beach, Fla.......... *E4 54
Redington Shores, Fla.......... *E4 54
Red Jacket, W. Va.............. D2 87
Red Key, Ind................... D7 59
Red Lake, Ont., Can............ o16 41
Red Lake, co., Minn............. C2 67
Red Lake Falls, Minn............ C2 67
Redlands, Calif................. E5 50
Red Lion, Pa.................... G8 81
Red Lodge, Mont................ E7 70
Redmond, Oreg.................. C5 80
Redmond, Wash................. e11 86
Red Oak, Ga..................... h7 55
Redon, Fr...................... D3 5
Redondela, Sp.................. A1 8
Redondo Beach, Calif........... n12 50
Redore, Minn................... C6 67
Red River, co., Tex............. C5 84
Red River, par., La............. B2 63
Red Springs, N.C............... C3 76
Redstown, Colo................. B3 51
Red Tank, C.Z.................. *B2 32
Redtop, Mo..................... D4 69
Redwater, Alta, Can............ C4 38
Red Willow, co., Nebr.......... D5 71
Red Wing, Minn................. F6 67
Redwood, co., Minn............. F3 67
Redwood City, Calif........... D2 k8 50
Redwood Estates, Calif......... *D3 50
Redwood Falls, Minn............ F3 67
Reed City, Mich................ E5 66
Reedley, Calif.................. D4 50
Reedsburg, Wis................. E3 88
Reeds Lake, Mich............... *F5 66
Reedsport, Oreg................ D2 80
Reedsville, Pa................. E6 81
Reese Village, Tex............. *C2 84
Reeves, co., Tex............... o13 84
Reform, Ala.................... B1 46
Refuge, Tex.................... D5 84
Refugio, co., Tex.............. E4 84
Regensburg, Ger., Fed. Rep. of...... D6 6
Reggio di Calabria, It.......... E5 9
Reggio nell 'Emilia, It......... B3 9
Reghin, Rom.................... B7 10
Regina, Sask., Can........... G3, n8 39
Region Occidental
  (Chaco), dept., Par........... *D3 29
Regla, Cuba, (part of Havanna)...... C2 35
Rehoboth Beach, Del............ C7 53
Reḥovot, Isr................... C2 15
Reichenback, Ger. Dem. Rep...... C6 6
Reidsville, Ga................. D4 55
Reidsville, N.C................ A3 76
Reigate, Eng............... E6, m12 4
Reims, Fr...................... C6 5
Reinbeck, Iowa................. B5 60
Reindeer, lake, Can............ E13 36
Reinosa, Sp.................... A3 8
Reisterstown, Md............... B4 53
Rembertów, Pol., (part of
  Warsaw)................... B6, k14 7
Remedios, Cuba................. C4 35
Remerton, Ga................... F3 55
Remington, Ind................. C3 59
Remiremont, Fr................. C7 5
Remscheid, Ger., Fed. Rep. of...... C3 6
Remsen, Iowa................... B2 60
Rendsburg, Ger., Fed. Rep. of...... A4 6
Renfrew, Ont., Can............. B8 41
Renfrew, co., Ont., Can........ B7 41
Renfrew, co., Scot............. *C4 4
Rengo, Chile................... A2 28
Rennes, Fr..................... C3 5
Reno, Nev...................... B2 72
Reno, co., Kans................ E5 61
Renovo, Pa..................... D6 81
Rensselaer, Ind................ C3 59
Rensselaer, N.Y................ C6 75
Rensselaer, co., N.Y........... C7 75
Renton, Wash............... B3, f11 86
Renville, Minn................. F3 67
Renville, co., Minn............ F3 67
Renville, co., N. Dak.......... B4 77
Republic, Mich................. B3 66
Republic, Mo................... D4 69
Republic, Pa................... G2 81
Republic, Wash................. A7 86
Republic, co., Kans............ C7 61
Requena, Sp.................... C5 8
Reserve, La.................... h10 63
Resistencia, Arg............... E4 29
Resita, Rom.................... C5 10

Restigouche. co., N.B., Can......... B2 43
Reston, Va..................... B5 85
Reszel, Pol.................... A6 7
Retalhuleu, Guat............... E6 34
Rethimni (Rhethymnon), prov.,
  Grc........................ *E5 14
Réthimnon, Grc................. E5 14
Reus, Sp....................... B6 8
Reutlingen, Ger., Fed. Rep. of...... D4 6
Revel, Fr...................... F5 5
Revelo, Ky..................... D5 62
Revelstoke, B.C., Can.......... D8 37
Revere, Mass................... g11 65
Revere, Minn................... F3 67
Revin, Fr...................... C6 5
Revloc, Pa..................... F4 81
Rewa, India.................... D7 20
Rewāri, India.................. C6 20
Rexburg, Idaho................. F7 57
Rey, Iran...................... C5 15
Reykjavik, Ice................. n22 11
Reynolds, Ga................... D2 55
Reynolds, co., Mo.............. D6 69
Reynoldsburg, Ohio........... C3, m11 78
Reynoldsville, Pa.............. D4 81
Reynosa (Reinosa), Mex......... B5 34
Rezé, Fr....................... D3 5
Rezekne, Sov. Un............... C6 12
Rhea, co., Tenn................ D9 83
Rheden, Neth................... A7 6
Rhein (Rhine), riv., Eur....... C3 6
Rheine, Ger., Fed. Rep. of..... B3 6
Rheinland-Pfalz, state, Ger.,
  Fed. Rep. of................ C3 6
Rheydt, Ger., Fed. Rep. of..... *C3 6
Rhineland, reg., Ger., Fed.
  Rep. of.................... C3 6
Rhinelander, Wis............... C4 88
Rhode Island, state, U.S....... 52
Rhodesia, see Zimbabwe, Afr.
Rhodhiss, N.C.................. B1 76
Rhondda, Wales................. E5 4
Rhône, dept., Fr............... *E6 5
Rhyl, Wales.................... D5 4
Rialto, Calif.................. m14 50
Rianjo, Sp..................... A1 8
Ribadavia, Sp.................. A1 8
Ribadeo, Sp.................... A2 8
Ribadesella, Sp................ A3 8
Ribatejo, prov., Port.......... *C1 8
Ribe, co., Den................. *J3 11
Ribeirão Prêto, Braz......... C3, k8 30
Ribera, It..................... F4 9
Ričany, Czech.................. o18 7
Rice, co., Kans................ D5 61
Rice, co., Minn................ F5 67
Rice Lake, Wis................. C2 88
Riceville, Iowa................ A5 60
Rich, Miss..................... A3 68
Rich, co., Utah................ A6 72
Richardson, Tex................ n10 84
Richardson, co., Nebr.......... D10 71
Richelieu, co., Que., Can...... C4 42
Richfield, Calif............... C2 50
Richfield, Minn................ n12 67
Richfield, Utah................ B5 72
Richfield Springs, N.Y......... C6 75
Richford, Vt................... B3 73
Rich Hill, Mo.................. C3 69
Richibucto, N.B., Can.......... C5 43
Richland, Ga................... D2 55
Richland, Mo................... D5 69
Richland, Pa................... *F9 81
Richland, Wash................. C6 86
Richland, co., Ill............. E5 58
Richland, co., Mont............ C12 70
Richland, co., N. Dak.......... D9 77
Richland, co., Ohio............ B3 78
Richland, co., S.C............. D6 82
Richland, co., Wis............. E3 88
Richland, par., La............. B4 63
Richland Center, Wis........... E3 88
Richland Hills, Tex............ *C4 84
Richlands, N.C................. C5 76
Richlands, Va.................. e10 85
Richmond, Calif............. D2, h8 50
Richmond, Que., Can............ D5 42
Richmond, Ind.................. E8 59
Richmond, Ky................... C6 62
Richmond, Maine............. D3, f8 64
Richmond, Mich................. F8 66
Richmond, Mo................... B4 69
Richmond, Tex............... E5, r14 84
Richmond, Utah................. A6 72
Richmond (Independent City),
  Va........................ C5, m18 85
Richmond (Staten Island), borough
  and co., N.Y................ E6 75
Richmond, co., N.S., Can....... D9 43
Richmond, co., Que., Can....... D5 42
Richmond, co., Ga.............. C4 55
Richmond, co., N.C............. B3 76

Richmond. co., Va.............. C6 85
Richmond Beach, Wash........... B3 86
Richmond Heights, Fla.......... s13 54
Richmond Heights, Mo........... f13 69
Richmond Highlands, Wash....... *B3 86
Richmond Hill, Ont., Can..... D5, k15 41
Richmond Hill., N.C............ *B3 76
Richmond-Windsor, Austl........ F8 26
Rich Square, N.C............... A5 76
Richton, Miss.................. D5 68
Richwood, Ohio................. B2 78
Richwood, W. Va................ C4 87
Riddle, Oreg................... E3 80
Ridge, Va...................... *C5 85
Ridgecrest, Calif.............. *E5 50
Ridgecrest, Wash............... *B3 86
Ridgedale, Mo.................. E4 69
Ridgedale, Tenn................ C10 83
Ridge Farm, Ill................ D6 58
Ridgefield, Conn............... D3 52
Ridgefield, N.J................ h8 74
Ridgefield Park, N.J........ B4, h8 74
Ridgeland, S.C................. G6 82
Ridgeley, W.Va................. B6 87
Ridgely, Tenn.................. A2 83
Ridgetown, Ont., Can........... E3 41
Ridgeville, Ind................ E5 55
Ridgeville, Ind................ D7 59
Ridgewood, Ill................. B5 58
Ridgewood, N.J................. B4 74
Ridgewood Heights, Ohio........ *C1 78
Ridgway, Ill................... F5 58
Ridgway, Pa.................... D4 81
Ridley Farms, Pa............... *G11 81
Ridley Park, Pa................ p20 81
Ried, Aus...................... D6 6
Riegelsville, Pa............... B2 81
Riesa, Ger. Dem. Rep........... C6 6
Rieti, It...................... C4 9
Rifle, Colo.................... B3 51
Rīga, Sov. Un.................. C5 12
Rigaud, Que., Can.............. D3 42
Rigby, Idaho................... F7 57
Riihimäki, Fin................. G11 11
Rijeka (Fiume), Yugo........... C2 10
Riley, co., Kans............... C7 61
Rimbey, Alta., Can............. C3 38
Rimersburg, Pa................. D2 81
Rimini, It..................... B4 9
Rîmnicu-Sărat, Rom............. C8 10
Rîmnicu-Vîlcea, Rom............ C7 10
Rimouski, Que., Can............ A9 42
Rimouski, co., Que., Can....... A9 42
Rincon, Ga..................... D5 55
Ringgold, Ga................... B1 55
Ringgold, La................... B2 63
Ringgold, co., Iowa............ D3 60
Ringkobing, co., Den........... *I3 11
Ringling, Okla................. C4 79
Ringsaker, Nor................. G4 11
Ringsted, Den.................. A1 7
Ringwood, N.J.................. A4 74
Rinjani, peak, Indon........... G5 19
Rio Arriba, co., N.Mex......... A5 48
Riobamba, Ec................... B2 31
Rio Blanco, co., Colo.......... B2 51
Rio Branco, Braz............... C4 31
Rio Caribe, Ven................ A5 32
Rio Claro, Braz............. C3, m8 30
Rio Cuarto, Arg................ A4 28
Rio de Janeiro, Braz........ C4, h6 30
Rio de Janeiro, state, Braz.. C4, h6 30
Rio Dell, Calif................ B1 50
Rio Gallegos, Arg.......... E3, h12 28
Rio Grande, Braz............... E2 30
Rio Grande, Mex................ C4 34
Rio Grande, N.J................ E3 74
Rio Grande, co., Colo.......... D4 51
Rio Grande (Rio Bravo del Norte),
  river, Mex., U.S............ E6 45
Rio Grande do Norte, state, Braz..... *D7 27
Rio Grande do Sul, state, Braz....... E2 30
Ríohacha, Col.................. A3 32
Rio Hondo, Tex................. F4 84
Rio Linda, Calif............... *C3 50
Riom, Fr....................... E5 5
Rio Muni, reg., Equat. Gui..... H7 22
Rio Negro, Braz................ D3 30
Rio Negro, dept. Ur............ *E1 30
Rio Negro, prov., Arg.......... C3 28
Rionero in Vulture, It......... D5 9
Rio Pardo, Braz................ *D2 30
Rio Piedras, P.R............... *G11 35
Rio Tercero, Arg............... A4 28
Rio Verde, Braz................ B2 30
Rio Verde (Rioverde), Mex...... m13 34
Rio Vista, Calif............... C3 50
Ripley, Miss................... A5 68
Ripley, N.Y.................... C1 75
Ripley, Ohio................... D2 78
Ripley, Tenn................... B2 83
Ripley, W. Va.................. C3 87
Ripley, co., Ind............... F7 59

Ripley, co., Mo................ E7 69
Ripoll, Sp..................... A7 8
Ripon, Calif................... *D3 50
Ripon, Eng..................... C6 4
Ripon, Wis..................... E5 88
Rishon leZiyyon, Isr........... C2 15
Rising Star, Tex............... C3 84
Rising Sun, Ind................ G8 59
Rison, Ark..................... D3 49
Ritchey, Mo.................... E3 69
Ritchie, co., W. Va............ B3 87
Rittman, Ohio.................. B4 78
Ritzville, Wash................ B7 86
Riva, It....................... B3 9
Rivadavia, Arg................. A3 28
Rive-de-Gier, Fr............... E6 5
Rivera, Ur..................... E1 30
Rivera, dept., Ur.............. *E1 30
Riverbank, Calif............... D3 50
Riverdale, Calif............... D4 50
Riverdale, Ill................. k9 58
Riverdale, Md............... C4, f9 53
Riverdale, N.J................. B4 74
Riverdale, N. Dak.............. C4 77
Riverdale, Oreg................ *B4 80
Riverdale, Utah................ *A6 72
Riverdale Heights, Md.......... *C4 53
River Edge, N.J................ h8 74
River Falls, Wis............... D1 88
River Forest, Ill.............. k9 58
River Grove, Ill............... k9 58
Riverhead, N.Y................. n15 75
River Hebert, N.S., Can........ D5 43
River Hills, Wis............... m12 88
Riverina, reg., Austl.......... F7 25
Riverland Terrace, S.C......... k12 82
River Pines, Mass.............. *A5 65
River Plaza, N.J............... *C4 74
River Rouge, Mich.......... F7, p15 66
Rivers, Man., Can.............. D1 40
Riverside, Calif........... F5, n14 50
Riverside, Ont., Can........... E2 41
Riverside, Colo................ B5 51
Riverside, Ill................. k9 58
Riverside, Mich................ *F6 66
Riverside, Mo.................. *B3 69
Riverside, N.J................. C3 74
Riverside, N.Y................. *C3 75
Riverside, Pa.................. E8 81
Riverside, S.C................. *B3 82
Riverside, co., Calif.......... F5 50
Riverton, Ill.................. D4 58
Riverton, N.J.................. C3 74
Riverton, Utah................. D2 72
Riverton, Wyo.................. C4 89
Riverton Heights, Wash......... *B3 86
River Vale, N.J................ *A5 74
River View, Ala................ C4 46
Riverview, Fla................. p11 54
Riverview, Mich................ p15 66
Riverview, Mo.................. *C7 69
Riverview (Pasco West), Wash... *C6 86
Rives, Mo...................... E7 69
Rivesville, W. Va.......... B4, h10 87
Riviera Beach, Fla............. F6 54
Riviera Beach, Md.............. *B4 53
Rivière-Bleue, Que., Can....... B8 42
Rivière-du-Loup, Que., Can..... B8 42
Rivière-du-Loup, co., Que., Can.. B9 42
Riyadh (Ar Riyād), Sau. Ar..... E4 15
Rizal, Prov., Phil............. *B6 19
Rize, Tur...................... B13 14
Rjukan, Nor.................... H3 11
Roachdale, Ind................. E4 59
Roane, co., Tenn............... D9 83
Roane, co., W. Va.............. C3 87
Roan Mountain, Tenn............ C11 83
Roanne, Fr..................... D5 5
Roanoke, Ala................... B4 46
Roanoke, Ill................... C4 58
Roanoke, Ind................... C7 59
Roanoke (Independent City), Va.. C3 85
Roanoke, co., Va............... C2 85
Roanoke Rapids, N.C............ A5 76
Roanoke Rapids West, N.C....... *A5 76
Roaring Springs, Pa............ F5 81
Robbins, Ill................... k9 58
Robbins, N.C................... B3 76
Robbinsdale, Minn........... E5, m12 67
Robersonville, N.C............. B5 76
Robert Lee, Tex................ D2 84
Roberts, co., S. Dak........... E9 77
Roberts, co., Tex.............. B2 84
Robertsdale, Pa................ F5 81
Robertsdale, Ala............... E2 46
Robertson, co., Ky............. B5 62
Robertson, co., Tenn........... A5 83
Robertson, co., Tex............ D4 84
Robertsonville, Que., Can...... C6 42
Roberval, Que., Can............ A5 42
Robeson, co., N.C.............. C3 76
Robesonia, Pa.................. *F9 81
Robinson, Ill.................. D6 58

Robinson, Pa. F3 81
Robinson, Tex. *D4 84
Robinsonville, Miss.............. A3 68
Roblin, Man., Can. D1 40
Robson, mtn., Can. C1 38
Robstown, Tex. F4 84
Roby, Mo. D5 69
Roby, Tex. C2 84
Roccastrada, It.................. C3 9
Rocha, Ur. E2 30
Rocha, dept., Ur. *E2 30
Rochdale, Eng. D5 4
Rochdale, Mass. B4 65
Rochefort, Fr.................... E3 5
Rochelle, Ga. E3 55
Rochelle, Ill.................... B4 58
Rochelle Park, N.J. h8 74
Rochester, Ind. B5 59
Rochester, Mich. F7 66
Rochester, Minn. F6 67
Rochester, N.H. E6 73
Rochester, N.Y. B3 75
Rochester, Pa. E1 81
Rock, co., Minn. G2 67
Rock, co., Nebr. B6 71
Rock, co., Wis. F4 88
Rockaway, N.J. B3 74
Rockaway, Oreg. B3 80
Rockbridge, co., Va. C3 85
Rockcastle, co., Ky. C5 62
Rockcliffe Park, Ont., Can. *B9 41
Rock Creek Hills, Md. *B3 53
Rockdale, Ill. B5, m8 58
Rockdale, Md. *B4 53
Rockdale, Tex. D4 84
Rockdale, co., Ga. C2 55
Rock Falls, Ill. B4 58
Rockford, Ill. A4 58
Rockford, Iowa A5 60
Rockford, Mich. E5 66
Rockford, Ohio B1 78
Rockford, Tenn. D10, n14 83
Rock Hall, Md. B5 53
Rockhampton, Austl. D9 25
Rock Hill, Mo. *C7 69
Rock Hill, S.C. B5 82
Rockingham, N.C. C3 76
Rockingham, co., N.H. E5 73
Rockingham, co., N.C. A3 76
Rockingham, co., Va. B4 85
Rock Island, Que., Can. D5 42
Rock Island, Ill. B3 58
Rock Island, co., Ill. B3 58
Rockland, Ont., Can. B9 41
Rockland, Maine B3 64
Rockland, Mass. B6, h12 65
Rockland, co., N.Y. D6 75
Rockledge, Fla. D6 54
Rockledge, Pa. o21 81
Rocklin, Calif. *C3 50
Rockmart, Ga. B1 55
Rockport, Ind. I3 59
Rockport, Maine D3 64
Rockport, Mass. A6 65
Rock Port, Mo. A2 69
Rockport, Tex. F4 84
Rock Rapids, Iowa A1 60
Rocksprings, Tex. D2 84
Rock Springs, Wyo. E3 89
Rockton, Ill. A4 58
Rock Valley, Iowa A1 60
Rockville, Conn. B7 52
Rockville, Ind. E3 59
Rockville, Md. B3 53
Rockville Center, N.Y. n15 75
Rockwall, Tex. C4, n10 84
Rockwall, co., Tex. C4 84
Rockwell City, Iowa B3 60
Rockwood, Mich. F7 66
Rockwood, Pa. F3 81
Rockwood, Tenn. D9 83
Rocky Ford, Colo. C7 51
Rocky Grove, Pa. D2 81
Rocky Hill, Conn. C6 52
Rocky Mount, N.C. B5 76
Rocky Mount, Va. C3 85
Rocky Mountain House,
  Alta., Can. C3 38
Rocky Point, N.Y. *n15 75
Rocky Point, Wash. *B3 86
Rocky Ripple, Ind. k10 59
Rocky River, Ohio A4, h9 78
Roddickton, Newf, Can. C3, h10 44
Rodeo, Calif. *D3 50
Roderfield, W. Va. D3 87
Rodessa, La. B1 63
Rodez, Fr. E5 5
Rodgers Forge, Md. *B4 53
Rodhópi (Rhodope), prov., Grc. .. *B5 14
Ródhos, Grc. D7 14
Rodney, Ont. Can. E3 41
Rodney Village, Del. *B6 53
Roebling, N.J. C3 74

Roeland Park, Kans. B9 61
Roermond, Neth. B6 5
Roeselare, Bel. B5 5
Roessleville, N.Y. *C7 75
Rogachev, Sov. Un. E8 12
Rogaland, co., Nor. *H1 11
Rogatica, Yugo D4 10
Roger Mills, co., Okla. B2 79
Rogers, Ark. A1 49
Rogers, Tex. D4 84
Rogers, Va. f10 85
Rogers, co.,Okla. A6 79
Rogers City, Mich. C7 66
Rogers Heights, Md. *C4 53
Rogersville, Tenn. C10 83
Rogoźno, Pol. B4 7
Rohnerville, Calif. *B1 50
Rohtak, India *C6 20
Roi Et, Thai. B2 19
Rojas, Arg. A4 28
Rokitno, Sov. Un. F6 12
Rokycany, Czech. D2 7
Roland Terrace, Md. *B4 53
Rolette, co., N. Dak. B6 77
Rolfe, Iowa B3 60
Rolla, Mo. D6 69
Rolla, N. Dak. A6 77
Rolling Fork, Miss. C3 68
Rolling Hills, Kans. B5 61
Rolling Hills Estates, Calif. ... *F4 50
Rolling Meadows, Ill. h8 58
Rollingwood, Calif. *D2 50
Roma, Austl. E8 25
Roma, Tex. F3 84
Roma, see Rome, It.
Roman, Rom. B8 10
Romania, country, Eur. B7 10
Romans -sur-Isère, Fr. E6 5
Romblon, Phil. *C6 19
Romblon, prov., Phil. *C6 19
Rome, Ga. B1 55
Rome, Ill. C4 58
Rome (Roma), It. D4, h8 9
Rome, N.Y. B5 75
Rome, Ohio *A5 78
Romeo, Ill. *B5 58
Romeo, Mich. F7 66
Romilly -sur-Seine, Fr. C5 5
Romita, Mex. m11 34
Romney, W.Va. B6 87
Romny, Sov. Un. F9 12
Romorantin, Fr. D4 5
Romulus, Mich. p15 66
Ronan, Mont. C2 70
Roncerverte, W. Va. D4 87
Ronciglione, It. C4 9
Ronda, Sp. D3 8
Rondônia, ter., Braz. B3 29
Ronkonkoma, N.Y. F4 52
Rønne, Den. A3 7
Ronse, Bel. B5 5
Roodhouse, Ill. D3 58
Rooks, co., Kans. C4 61
Roosendaal, Neth. B6 5
Roosevelt, N.Y. G2 52
Roosevelt, Utah A6 72
Roosevelt, co., Mont. B11 70
Roosevelt, co., N. Mex. B7 48
Roosevelt, riv., Braz. B3 29
Roosevelt Park, Mich. E4 66
Roquetas, Sp. B6 8
Rorschach, Switz. E4 6
Rosa, mtn., It., Switz. B2 9
Roraima, ter., Braz. C5 32
Rosario, Arg. A4 28
Rosário, Braz. *D6 27
Rosario, Mex. C3 34
Rosario, Par. D4 29
Rosario, Ur. E1 30
Rosário do Sul, Braz. E2 30
Rosario Tala, Arg. A5 28
Rosburg, Wash. B5 89
Roscoe, N.Y. D6 75
Roscoe, Pa. F2 81
Roscoe, Tex. C2 84
Roscommon, co., Ire. *D2 4
Roscommon, co., Mich. D6 66
Roseau, Dominica I14 35
Roseau, Minn. B3 67
Roseau, co., Minn. B3 67
Roseboro, N.C. C4 76
Rosebud, Tex. D4 84
Rosebud, co., Mont. D10 70
Roseburg, Oreg. D3 80
Rosedale, Fla. *E4 54
Rosedale, Miss. B2 68
Rosedale Station, Alta, Can. D4 38
Rose Hill, Kans. E6 61
Rose Hill, N.C. C4 76
Roseland, Fla. E4 54
Roseland, Ind. A5 59
Roseland, La. D5 63
Roseland, N.J. *B4 74

Roseland, Ohio B3 78
Roselle, Ill. k8 58
Roselle, N.J. k7 74
Roselle Park, N.J. k7 74
Rosemead, Calif. *F4 50
Rosemère, Que., Can. p19 42
Rosemont, Ill. *E3 58
Rosemont, Pa. *F11 81
Rosemount, Minn. F5 67
Rosenberg, Tex. E5, r14 84
Rosendael, Fr. B5 5
Rosendale, N.Y. *C6 75
Rosenheim, Ger., Fed. Rep of E6 6
Roseto, Pa. E11 81
Rosetown, Sask., Can. F1, n7 39
Roseville, Calif. C3 50
Roseville, Ill. C3 58
Roseville, Mich. o16 66
Roseville, Minn. m12 67
Roseville, Ohio C3 78
Rosewood, Calif. *B1 50
Rosewood Heights, Ill. *E3 58
Rosiclare, Ill. F5 58
Rosiorii-de-Vede, Rom. C7 10
Roskilde, co., Den. *J5 11
Roslavl, Sov. Un. E9 12
Roslyn, N.Y. *E7 75
Roslyn, Pa. *F11 81
Roslyn, Wash. B4 86
Roslyn Estates, N.Y. *G2 52
Roslyn Harbor, N.Y. *E7 75
Roslyn Heights, N.Y. D2, h13 75
Rosny-sous-Bois, Fr. g10 5
Ross, Calif. *C2 50
Ross, co., Ohio C2 78
Ross and Cromarty, co., Scot. ... *B4 4
Rossano, It. E6 9
Rossford, Ohio A2, e6 78
Rossiter, Pa. E4 81
Rossland, B.C., Can. E9 37
Rossmoor, Calif. *F5 50
Rossmoyne, Ohio *C1 78
Rossosh, Sov. Un. F12 12
Rossville, Ga. B1 55
Rossville, Ill. C6 58
Rosthern, Sask., Can. E2 39
Rostock, Ger. Dem. Rep. A6 6
Rostov, Sov. Un. C12 12
Rostov -na-Donu, Sov. Un. H12 12
Roswell, Ga. B2 55
Roswell, N. Mex. C6 48
Rotan, Tex. C2 84
Rotenburg an der Fulda,
  Ger., Fed. Rep of B4 6
Rothenburg ob der Tauber
  Ger., Fed. Rep of D5 6
Rothesay, Scot. C4 4
Rothschild, Wis. D4 88
Rothsville, Pa. F9 81
Rotondella, It. D6 9
Rotorua, N.Z. M16 26
Rotterdam, Neth. B6 5
Rotterdam, N.Y. *C6 75
Rottweil, Ger., Fed. Rep of D4 6
Roubaix, Fr. B5 5
Roudnice ned Labem, Czech. n7 17
Rouen, Fr. C4 5
Roulette, Pa. C5 81
Round Lake, Ill. h8 58
Roundlake, Miss. A3 68
Round Lake Beach, Ill. h8 58
Round Lake Heights, Ill. *h8 58
Round Lake Park, Ill. *h8 58
Round Pond, Ark. B5 49
Round Rock, Tex. D4 84
Roundup, Mont. D8 70
Rouses Point, N.Y. f11 75
Rouseville, Pa. D2 81
Routt, co., Colo. A3 51
Rouville, co., Que., Can. D4 42
Rouzerville, Pa. G7 81
Rovaniemi, Fin. D11 11
Rovato, It. B2 9
Rovenki, Sov. Un. G12, q22 12
Rovereto, It. B3 9
Rovigo, It. B3 9
Rovinj, Yugo. C1 10
Rovno, Sov. Un. F6 12
Rovnoye, Sov. Un. F16 12
Rowan, co., Ky. B6 62
Rowan, co., N.C. B2 76
Rowan Mill, N.C. B2 76
Rowes Run, Pa. *F2 81
Rowland, N.C. C3 76
Rowland, Pa. D11 81
Rowlesburg, W. Va. B5 87
Rowlett, Tex. *C4 84
Rowley, Mass. A6 65
Roxana, Ill. f13 69
Roxas (Capiz), Phil. C6 19
Roxboro, N.C. A4 76
Roxburgh, co., Scot. *C5 4
Roxton Falls, Que., Can. D5 42

Roy, N. Mex. B6 48
Roy, Utah A5, C2 72
Royal, Fla. D4 54
Royal Center, Ind. C4 59
Royal Mills, N.C. A4 76
Royal Oak, Mich. F7, o15 66
Royal Oak, Township,
  Mich. *F7 66
Royalton, Ill. F4 58
Royalton, Pa. *F8 81
Royan, Fr. E3 5
Royersford, Pa. F10 81
Royse City, Tex. C4 84
Royston, Ga. B3 55
Rožňava, Czech. D6 7
Rtishchevo, Sov. Un. E14 12
Ruapehu, mtn., N.Z. M15 26
Rubezhnoye, Sov. Un. p21 12
Rubidoux, Calif. n14 50
Ruda Slaska, Pol. *C5 7
Rudbar, Afg. B3 20
Rudolf, lake, Afr. F9 21
Rudolstadt, Ger. Dem. Rep. C5 6
Rueil-Malmaison, Fr. g9 5
Rufino, Arg. A4 28
Rufisque, Sen. F1 22
Rugby, Eng. D6 4
Rugby, N. Dak. B6 77
Ruidoso, N. Mex. C6 48
Rule, Tex. C3 84
Ruleville, Miss. B3 68
Ruma, Yugo C4 10
Rumford, Maine D2 64
Rumoi, Jap. E10 18
Rumson, N.J. C4 74
Runge, Tex. E4 84
Runnels, co., Tex. D3 84
Runnemede, N.J. D2 74
Rupert, Idaho G5 57
Rupert, W. Va. D4 87
Rural Hall, N.C. A2 76
Ruse (Ruschuk), Bul. *D7 10
Ruse (Ruschuk), co., Bul. *D8 10
Rush, co., Ind. E7 59
Rush City, Minn. E6 67
Rush, co., Kan. D4 61
Rushford, Minn. G7 67
Rush Springs, Okla. C4 79
Rushville, Ill. C3 58
Rushville, Ind. E7 59
Rushville, Nebr. B3 71
Rusk, Tex. D5 84
Rusk, co., Tex. C5 84
Rusk, co., Wis. C2 88
Ruskin, Fla. E4, p11 54
Russas, Braz. *D7 27
Russell (Russell City), Calif. .. *D3 50
Russell, Man., Can. D1 40
Russell, Kans. D5 61
Russell, Ky. B7 62
Russell, co., Ala. C4 46
Russell, co., Ont. Can. B9 41
Russell, co., Kans. D5 61
Russell, co., Ky. C4 62
Russell, co., Va. f9 85
Russell Gardens, N.Y. *E7 75
Russells Point, Ohio *B2 78
Russell Springs, Ky. C4 62
Russellton, Pa. E2 81
Russellville, Ala. A2 46
Russellville, Ark. B2 49
Russellville, Ky. D3 62
Russian Soviet Federated Socialist
  Republic, rep., Sov. Un. C8 12
Russiaville, Ind. D5 59
Rustavi, Sov. Un. B15 14
Ruston, La. B3 63
Rutchenkovo, Sov. Un. r20 12
Rute, Sp. D3 8
Ruteng, Indon. G6 19
Ruth, Miss. D3 68
Ruth, Nev. B4 72
Ruthenia, reg., Sov. Un. D7 7
Rutherford, N.J. B4, h8 74
Rutherford, Tenn. A3 83
Rutherford, co., N.C. B1 76
Rutherford, co., Tenn. B5 83
Rutherford Heights, Pa. *F8 81
Rutherfordton, N.C. B1, f11 76
Rutland, Mass. B4 65
Rutland, Vt. D2 73
Rutland, co., Eng. *D6 4
Rutland, co., Vt. D1 73
Rutledge, Pa. *G11 81
Ruvo di Puglia, It. *D6 9
Ruxton, Md. *B4 53
Ruzayevka, Sov. Un. D15 12
Ružomberok, Czech. D5 7
Rwanda, country, Afr. I3 23
Ryazan, Sov. Un. D12 12
Rybink, Pol. C5, g9 7
Rydal, Pa. *F11 81
Ryde, Eng. E6 4

Rye, N.Y. h13, n15 75
Rylsk, Sov. Un. F10 12

Ryotsu, Jap. G9 18
Rypin, Pol. B5 7

Ryukyu Islands, Jap. F10 7
Rzeszów, Po. C6 7

Rzhev, Sov. Un. C10 12

S

Saalfeld, Ger. Dem Rep. C5 6
Saar, state, Ger. Fed. Rep. of D3 6
Saarbrüken, Ger. Fed. Rep. of D3 6
Saarlouis, Ger., Fed. Rep. of D3 6
Sabac, Yugo. C4 10
Sabadell, Sp. B7 8
Sabae, Jap. n15 18
Sabah (North Borneo), reg., Mala. ... D5 19
Sabana de la Mar, Dom. Rep. E9 35
Sabana Grande, P.R. *G11 35
Sabanalarga, Col. A3 32
Sabang, Indon. k11 19
Sabará, Braz. B4 30
Sabaudia, It. D4 9
Sabetha, Kans. C8 61
Sabina, Ohio C2 78
Sabinal, Tex. E3 84
Sabinas, Mex. B4 34
Sabinas Hidalgo, Mex. B4 34
Sabine, co., Tex. D6 84
Sabine, par., La. C2 63
Sablé -sur-Sarthe, Fr. D3 5
Sabzawar, Afg. B3 20
Sac, co., Iowa B2 60
Sac City, Iowa B2 60
Sache, China F10 16
Sachsen, former state, Ger.
  Dem. Rep. *C6 6
Sachsen-Anhalt (Saxony-Anhalt), former
  state, Ger. Dem. Rep. *C5 6
Sackets Harbor, N.Y. B4 75
Sackets Harbor, N.Y. B4 75
Sackville, N.B., Can. D5 43
Saco, Maine E2, g7 64
Sacramento, Calif. A6 50
Sacramento, co., Calif. C3 50
Sacré-Coeur Saguenay, Que., Can. ... A8 42
Sa'dah, Yemen *F3 15
Saddle Brook, N.J. *A4 74
Saddle River, N.J. *A4 74
Saddle Rock, N.Y. *G2 52
Saegertown, Pa. C1 81
Saeki, Jap. J5 18
Safety Harbor, Fla. D4, p10 54
Safford, Ariz. C4 48
Safi, Mor. B3 22
Safranbolu, Tur. B9 14
Saga, China C8 20
Saga, Jap. J5 18
Saga, pref., Jap. *J5 18
Sagadahoc, co., Maine E3 64
Sagaing, Bur. D10 20
Sagamihara, Jap. *I9 18
Sagamore, Pa. E3 81
Sagamore Hills, Ohio h9 78
Sãgar, India D6 20
Sagara, Jap. o17 18
Sag Harbor, N.Y. n16 75
Saginaw, Mich. E7 66
Saginaw, Tex. n9 84
Saginaw, co., Mich. E6 66
Sagle, Idaho A2 57
Saguache, Colo. C4 51
Saguache, co., Colo. C4 51
Sagua de Tánamo, Cuba D6 35
Sagua la Grande, Cuba C3 35
Saguenay, co., Que., Can. A8 42
Sagunto, Sp. C5 8
Sahagún, Col. B2 32
Sahāranpur, India C6 20
Sahiwal, Pak. B5 20
Sahuaripa, Mex. B3 34
Sahuayo de Díaz, Mex. m12 34
Saida (Sidon), Leb. F10 14
Saidpur, Bngl. C8 20
Saigo, Jap. H6 18
Saigon, see Ho Chi Minh City, Viet.
Saijo, Jap. *I6 18
Saiki, Jap. J5 18
St. Affrique, Fr. F5 5
St. Agapit, Que., Can. C6 42
Ste. Agathe-des-Monts, Que., Can. .. C3 42
St. Alban, Que., Can. C5 42
St. Alban's, Newf., Can. E4 44
St. Albans, Eng. E6, k12 4
St. Albans, W. Va. C3 87
St. Albans, Vt. B1 73
St. Albans Bay, Vt. B1 73
St. Albert, Alta., Can. C4 38

St. Alexandre -de-Kamouraska,
  Que., Can. B8 42
St. Alexis-des-Monts, Que., Can. ... C3 42
St. Armand-Mont-Rond, Pr. D5 5
St. Ambroise-de-Chicoutimi,
  Que., Can. A6 42
St. André-Avellin, Que., Can. D2 42
St. Andrews, N.B., Can. D2 43
St. Andrews, Scot. B5 4
St. Andrews, S.C. F7, k11 82
St. Andrews East, Que., Can. D3 42
Ste. Anne, Que., Can. D4 42
Ste. Anne, Guad. H14 35
St. Anne, Ill. B6 58
Ste. Anne-de-Beaupré, Que., Can. ... B7 42
Ste. Anne -de-Bellevue,
  Que., Can. q10 42
Ste. Anne-de-la-Pérade, Que., Can. . C5 42
St. Anselme, Que., Can. C7 42
St. Ansgar, Iowa A5 60
St. Anthony, Newf., Can. C4 44
St. Anthony, Minn. *F5 67
St. Antoine des Laurentides,
  Que. Can. *D3 42
St. Apollinaire, Que., Can. C6, o16 42
St. Aubert, Que., Can. B7 42
St. Augustine, Fla. C5, n9 54
St. Avold, Fr. C7 5
St. Barthélémy, Que., Can. C4 42
St. Basile -de-Portneuf,
  Que., Can. C6 42
St. Bernard, Ohio o12 78
St. Bernard, par., La. E6 63
St. Bernice, Ind. E2 59
St. Bonaventure, N.Y. *C2 75
St. Bride, mtn., Alta., Can. D3 88
St. Brieuc, Fr. C2 5
St. Bruno-Lac-St. Jean, Que., Can. . A6 42
St. Camille -de-Belle-chasse,
  Que., Can. C7 42
St. Casimir, Que., Can. C5 42
St. Catharines, Ont., Can. D5 41
Ste. Catherine, Que., Can. C6, n16 42
St. Césaire, Que., Can. D4 42
St. Chamond, Fr. E6 5
St. Charles, Ill. B5 58
St. Charles, Mich. E6 66
St. Charles, Minn. G6 67
St. Charles, Mo. C7, f12 69
St. Charles, co., Mo. C7 69
St. Charles, par., La. E5 63
St. Charles -de-Bellechasse,
  Que., Can. C7 42
St. Christopher-Nevis, country,
  N.A. H13 35
St. Chrysostome, Que., Can. D4 42
St. Clair, Mich. F8 66
St. Clair, Mo. C6 69
St. Clair, Pa. E9 81
St. Clair, co., Ala. B3 46
St. Clair, co., Ill. E3 58
St. Clair, co., Mich. F8 66
St. Clair, co., Mo. C4 69
Ste. Clair, Que., Can. C7 42
St. Clair Haven, Mich. *F8 66
St. Clair Shores, Mich. *F8 66
St. Clairsville, Ohio B5 78
St. Claude, Man., Can. E2 40
St. Claude -sur-Bienne, Fr. D6 5
St. Cloud, Fla. D5 54
St. Cloud, Fr. g9 5
St. Cloud, Minn. E4 67
St. Constant, Que., Can. q19 42
St. Croix, Que., Can. C6, o16 42
St. Croix, co., Wis. C1 88
St. Croix Falls, Wis. C1 88
St. Cyrille -de-L'Islet,
  Que., Can. B7 42
St. Cyrille -de-Wendover,
  Que., Can. D5 42
St. Damase, Que., Can. D4 42
St. Davids, Pa. *G11 81
St. Denis, Fr. C5, g10 5
St. Denis, Reunion *H24 2
St. Denis -de-la-Bouteillerie,
  Que., Can. B8 42
St. Denis, River Richelieu,
  Que., Can. D4 42

St. Dié, Fr. C7 5
St. Dizier, Fr. C6 5
St. Donat-de-Mont-calm, Que., Can. . C3 42
St. Edward, Nebr. C8 71
St. Eleuthère, Que., Can. B8 42
St. Elias, mts., N.A. C11 47
St. Elmo, Ill. D5 58
Ste. Emélie-de-l'Energie,
  Que., Can. C4 42
St. Ephrem, Que., Can. C7 42
St. Esprit, Que., Can. D4 42
St. Etienne, Fr. E6 5
St. Eustache, Que., Can. D4, p19 42
St. Fabien, Que., Can. A9 42
St. Felicien, Que., Can. A5 42
St. Félix-de-Valois, Que., Can. C4 42
St. Ferdinand, Que., Can. C6 42
St. Flavien, Que., Can. C6 42
St. Flour, Fr. E5 5
Ste. Foy, Que., Can. c6 42
St. Francis, Kans. C2 61
St. Francis, Wis. E2 88
St. Francis, co., Ark. B4 49
St. François -de-Lac, Que., Can. ... C5 42
St. Francisville, Ill. E6 58
St. Francisville, La. D4 63
St. Francois, co., Mo. D7 69
St. Fulgence, Que., Can. A7 42
St. Gabriel -de-Brandon,
  Que., Can. C4 42
St. Gallen, see Sankt Gallen, Switz.
St. Gaudens, Fr. F4 5
Ste. Genevieve, Mo. D7 69
Ste. Genevieve, co., Mo. D7 69
Ste. Geneviève-de-Pierrefonds,
  Que., Can. *D4 42
St. George, Austl. E8 25
St. George, N.B., Can. D3 43
St. George, Ont., Can. D4 41
St. George, Mo. *C7 69
St. George, S.C. E6 82
St. Georges, Que., Can. C5 42
St. George's, Grenada J14 35
St. Georges -de-Windsor
  Que., Can. D6 42
St. Georges-Ouest, Que., Can. *C7 42
St. Gérard, Que., Can. D6 42
St. Germain -de-Grantham,
  Que., Can. D5 42
St. Germain-en-Laye, Fr. g9 5
St. Gervais, Que., Can. C7 42
St. Gilles, Que., Can. C6 42
St. Gilles-du-Gard, Fr. F6 5
St. Girons, Fr. F4 5
St. Helena, Calif. A5 50
St. Helena, Br. dep., Afr. H20 2
St. Helena, par., La. D5 63
St. Helens, Eng. *D5 4
St. Helens, Oreg. B4 80
St. Helier, Jersey F5 4
St. Henry, Ohio B1 78
St. Hilaire Est, Que., Can. D4 42
St. Hyacinthe, Que., Can. D5 42
St. Hyacinthe, co., Que., Can. D4 42
St. Ignace, Mich. C6 66
St. Jacobs, Ont., Can. D4 41
St. Jacques, Que., Can. D4 42
St. James, Man., Can. E3 40
St. James, Minn. G4 67
St. James, Mo. D6 69
St. James, N.Y. F4 75
St. James, par., La. D5 63
St. Jean, Que., Can. D4 42
St. Jean, co., Que., Can. D4 42
St. Jean-Baptiste, Man., Can. E3 40
St. Jean-D'Angély, Fr. E3 5
St. Jean-de-Dieu, Que., Can. A9 42
St. Jean-de-Luz, Fr. F3 5
St. Jean-de-Matha, Que., Can. C4 42
St. Jean-Eudes, Que., Can. *A7 42
St. Jéôme, Que., Can. D3 42
St. John, N.B., Can. D3 43
St. John, Ind. B3 59
St. John, Kans. E5 61
St. John, co., N.B., Can. D4 43
St. John's, Antigua and Barbuda H14 35
St. Johns, Ariz. B4 48
St. John's, Newf., Can. E5 44

St. Johns, Mich. F6 66
St. Johns, Mo. *C7 69
St. Johns, co., Fla. B5 54
St. Johnsbury, Vt. C3 73
St. Johnsville, N.Y. *B6 75
St. John the Baptist, par., La. D5 63
St. Joseph, Ill. C5 58
St. Joseph, La. C4 63
St. Joseph, Mich. F4 66
St. Joseph, Minn. E4 67
St. Joseph, Mo. B3 69
St. Joseph, co., Ind. A5 59
St. Joseph, co., Mich. G5 66
St. Joseph-de-Beauce, Que., Can. ... C7 42
St. Joseph-de-Sorel, Que., Can. *D4 42
St. Joseph-de-St. Hyacinthe
  Que., Can. *D5 42
St. Jovite, Que., Can. C3 42
St. Junien, Fr. E4 5
St. Kitts-Nevis,see St.
  Christopher-Nevis, N.A.
St. Lambert, Que., Can. p19 42
St. Landry, par., La. D3 63
St. Laurent, Man., Can. D3 40
St. Laurent, Que., Can. p19 42
St. Lawrence, Newf., Can. E4 44
St. Lawrence, Pa. *F10 81
St.Lawrence, co., N.Y. A6 75
St. Lawrence, riv., N.A. G20 36
St. Léonard, N.B., Can. B2 43
St. Léonard -de-Noblat, Fr. E4 5
St. Lô, Fr. C3 5
St. Louis, Mich. E6 66
St.-Louis, Sen. E1 22
St. Louis (Independent City), Mo. .. C37 69
St. Louis, co., Minn. C6 67
St. Louis, co., Mo. C7 69
St. Louis Park, Minn. n12 67
St. Lucia, country, N.A. J14 35
St. Lucie, co., Fla. E6 54
St. Maixent-l' Ecole, Fr D3 5
St. Malo, Fr. C2 5
St. Mandé, Fr. g10 5
St. Marc, Hai. E7 35
St. Marc -des-Carrières,
  Que., Can. C5 42
Ste. Maire-Beauce, Que., Can. C6 42
St. Maries, Idaho B2 57
St. Martin, par., La. D4 63
St. Martinville, La. D4 63
St. Mary, par., La. E4 63
St. Mary, peak, Austl. *F6 25
St. Mary-of-the-woods, Ind. E3 59
St. Mary's, Ont., Can. D3 41
St. Marys, Ga. F5 55
St. Marys, Ind. A5 59
St. Marys, Kans. C7 61
St. Marys, Ohio B3 78
St. Marys, Pa. D4 81
St. Marys, W. Va. B3 87
St. Marys, co., Md. D4 53
St. Matthews, Ky. B4, g11 62
St. Matthews, S.C. D6 82
St. Maur-des-Fossés, Fr. g10 5
St. Maurice, co., Que., Can. C4 42
St. Michael, Minn. E5 67
St. Michael, Pa. *E4 81
St. Michaels, Md. C5 53
St. Nazaire, Fr. D2 5
St. Noël, Que., Can. *G20 36
St. Norbert, Man., Can. E3 40
St. Omer, Fr. B5 5
St. Ouen, Fr. g10 5
St. Pacôme, Que., Can. B8 42
St. Pamphile, Que., Can. C8 42
St. Paris, Ohio B2 78
St. Pascal, Que., Can. B8 42
St. Paul, Alta., Can. B5 38
St. Paul, Minn. E5, n12 67
St. Paul, Nebr. C7 71
St. Paul, Va. f9 85
St. Paulin, Que., Can. C4 42
St. Paul Park, Minn. F5, n12 67
St. Pauls, N.C. C4 76
St. Peter, Minn. F5 67
St. Peter Port, Guernsey F5 4
St. Petersburg, Fla. E4, p10 54

St. Petersburg Beach, Fla............ p10 54
St. Pie, Que., Can............. D5 42
St. Pierre, Mart................ I14 35
St. Pierre-Jolys, Man., Can. E3 40
St. Pierre & Miquelon,
   Fr. Dep., N.A.............. E3 44
St. Pol-de-Léon, Fr............... C2 5
St. Pourçain, -sur-Sioule, Fr. D5 5
St. Prosper, Que., Can............. C7 42
St. Quentin, N.B., Can............. B2 43
St. Quentin, Fr.................. C5 5
St. Raphaël, Que., Can............ C7 42
St. Raphaël, Fr................. F7 5
St. Raymond, Que., Can........... C6 42
St. Rémi, Que., Can........ D4, q19 42
St. Romuald, Que., Can........ C6, n17 42
Ste. Rose, Que., Can............. D4 42
Ste. Rose, Guad............... H14 35
St. Rose, La.................. k11 63
Ste. Rose-du-Dégelé, Que., Can. B9 42
St. Rose-du-Lac, Man., Can. D2 40
Saintes, Fr................... E3 5
St. Sauveur -des-Monts,
   Que., Can................ D3 42
Ste. Savine, Fr................ C5 5
St. Siméon, Que., Can............ B8 42
St. Simons Island, Ga. E5 55
St. Stephen, N.B., Can............ D2 43
St. Stephen, S.C. E8 82
St. Tammany, par., La. D5 63
Ste. Thérèse-de-Blainville,
   Que., Can.............. D4, p19 42
St. Thomas, Ont., Can............ E3 41
St. Tite, Que., Can.............. C5 42
St. Ulric, Que., Can............. *K13 52
St. Vincent and the Grenadines,
   country, N.A............... J9 35
St. Vincent-de-Paul, Que., Can. *D4 42
St. Walburg, Sask., Can........... D1 39
St. Yrieix-la-Perche, Fr. E4 5
Saintonge, former prov., Fr. E3 5
Saitama, pref., Jap.............. *I9 18
Sajama, mtn., Bol............... C2 29
Sakai, Jap.................. o14 18
Sakākah, Sau. Ar............... D3 15
Sakania, Zaire................ C5 24
Sakashita, Jap................ n16 18
Sakata, Jap.................. G9 18
Sakchu, Kor.................. F2 18
Sakhalin, isl., Sov. Un........... D17 16
Sakon Nakhon, Thai. B2 19
Sakti, India.................. D7 20
Sala, Swe................. H7, t34 11
Sala Consilina, It............... D5 9
Saladillo, Arg................. B5 28
Salado, riv., Arg............... A3 28
Salamá, Guat................. *D7 34
Salamanca, Mex............... m13 34
Salamanca, N.Y................ C2 75
Salamanca, Sp................ B3 8
Salamanca, prov., Sp. *B3 8
Salamina, Col................. B2 32
Salamis, Grc................. D4 14
Salas, Sp................... A2 8
Salatiga, Indon............... *G4 19
Salaverry, Peru................ C2 31
Salcedo, Ec.................. B2 31
Saldanha, S. Afr............... G3 24
Saldus, Sov. Un............... C4 12
Sale, Austl.................. I6 26
Salé, Mor................... B3 22
Salekhard, Sov. Un.............. C9 13
Salem, Ill................... E5 58
Salem, India................. *F6 20
Salem, Ind.................. G5 59
Salem, Mass.............. A6, f12 65
Salem, Mo.................. D6 69
Salem, N.H.................. F5 73
Salem, N.J.................. D2 74
Salem, N.Y.................. B7 75
Salem, Ohio................. B5 78
Salem, Oreg.............. C4, k12 80
Salem, S. Dak................ G8 77
Salem, Utah................. D2 72
Salem, Va. (Independent City) C2 85
Salem, W. Va............... B4, k9 87
Salem, co., N.J................ D2 74
Salem Depot, N.H.............. F5 73
Salemi, It................... F4 9
Salerno, It.................. D5 9
Salford, Eng................. D5 4
Salgótarján, Hung.............. A4 10
Salida, Calif................. *D3 50
Salida, Colo................. C5 51
Salies-de-Béarn, Fr. F3 5
Salihli, Tur.................. *C7 4
Salin, Bur.................. *D9 20
Salina, Kans................. D6 61
Salina, Okla................. A6 79
Salina, Utah................. B6 72
Salinas, Calif................. *D3 50
Salinas, P.R................. *G11 35

Salina Springs, Ariz............. A4 48
Saline, Mich................. F7 66
Saline, co., Ark............... C3 49
Saline, co., Ill................ F5 58
Saline, co., Kans.............. D6 61
Saline, co., Mo............... B4 69
Saline, co., Nebr.............. D8 71
Salineville, Ohio............... B5 78
Salisbury, Eng................ E6 4
Salisbury, Md................ D6 53
Salisbury, Mass............... A6 65
Salisbury, Mo................ B5 69
Salisbury, N.C................ B2 76
Salisbury, see Harare, Zimb.
Salisbury West, N.C............. *B2 76
Sallisaw, Okla................ B7 79
Salmon, Idaho................ D5 57
Salmon Arm, B.C., Can........... D8 37
Salmon Falls, N.H.............. E6 73
Salo, Fin................... G10 11
Salon-de-Provence, Fr. F6 5
Salonta, Rom................ B5 10
Salsk, Sov. Un................ H13 12
Salsomaggiore, It.............. B2 9
Salta, Arg.................. D2 29
Salta, prov., Arg............... D2 29
Saltillo, Mex................. B4 34
Salt Lake, co., Utah............. A5 72
Salt Lake City, Utah A6, C2 72
Salto, Braz................. m8 30
Salto, Ur................... E1 30
Salto, dept., Ur............... *E1 30
Saltpond, Ghana.............. G4 22
Salt River, Ky................ C4 62
Saltsburg, Pa................ F3 81
Salt Springs, Fla............... C5 54
Saltville, Va................. f10 85
Saluda, S.C................. D4 82
Saluda, co., S.C............... C4 82
Saluda Gardens, S.C............ *D5 82
Sālūr, India................. E7 20
Saluzzo, It.................. B1 9
Salvador, Braz................ E7 27
Salvatierra, Mex.............. m13 34
Salween, riv., Asia............. D10 20
Salyersville, Ky............... C6 62
Salzburg, Aus................ E6 6
Salzburg, state, Aus............ E6 6
Salzgitter, Ger., Fed. Rep. of B5 6
Salzwedel, Ger. Dem Rep. B5 6
Samani, Jap................. E11 18
Samaniego, Col............... C2 32
Samar, prov., Phil.............. C7 19
Samar, isl.,Phil............... C7 19
Samarinda, Indon.............. F5 19
Samarkand, Sov. Un............ F9 13
Sāmarrā', Iraq................ E14 14
Sambalpur, India.............. D7 20
Sambas, Indon................ E3 19
Sambhal, India............... *C6 20
Sambor, Sov. Un............... G4 12
Samchŏk, Kor................ H4 18
Samchonpo, Kor............... I4 18
Samokov, Bul................ D6 10
Samos, prov., Grc.............. *D6 14
Samoset, Fla................. q10 54
Sampson, co., N.C.............. B4 76
Samson, Ala................. D3 46
Samsun, Tur................. B11 14
Samtown, La................. *C3 63
San'ā', Yemen................ F3 15
San Agustín, Col............... C2 32
San Andreas, Calif............. C3 50
San Andrés de Giles, Arg. g7 28
San Andre's Tuxtla, Mex. *D5 34
San Angelo, Tex............... D2 84
San Anselmo, Calif............. h7 50
San Antonio, Chile.............. A2 28
San Antonio, Tex............ E3, k7 84
San Antonio de Areco, Arg. g7 28
San Antonio de los Baños, Cuba C2 35
San Antonio Heights, Calif. *E5 50
San Augustine, Tex............. D5 84
San Augustine, co., Tex. D5 84
San Bartolomeo in Galdo, It. D5 9
San Benedetto del Tronto, It. C4 9
San Benito, Tex............... F4 84
San Benito, co., Calif. D3 50
San Bernardino, Calif. E5, m14 50
San Bernardino, co., Calif. E5 50
San Bernardo, Chile............. A2 28
Sanborn, Iowa................ A2 60
Sanborn, co., S. Dak. G7 77
San Bruno, Calif............. D2, h8 50
San Carlos, Arg............... C2 28
San Carlos, Calif.............. k8 51
San Carlos, Chile.............. A2 28
San Carlos, Phil.............. o13 19
San Carlos, Ur................ E2 30
San Carlos de Bariloche, Arg. C2 28
San Cataldo, It................ F4 9
Sanch'ung, Tai................ *G9 17

San Clemente, Calif. F5 50
San Clemente, Sp.............. C4 8
San Cristóbal, Dom Rep. E8 35
San Cristóbal, Ven.............. B3 22
San Cristóbal Las Casas, Mex. D6 34
Sancti-Spíritus, Cuba D4 35
Sanda, Jap................. o14 18
Sandakan, Mala............... D5 19
Sandefjord, Nor............... p28 11
Sanders, co., Mont. C1 70
Sanderville, Ga............... D4 55
Sandia, Peru................. D4 31
San Diego, Calif............F5, o15 50
San Diego, Tex................ F3 84
San Diego, co., Calif. F5 50
Sandıklı, Tur................. C8 14
Sandila, India................ C7 20
San Dimas, Calif............... *F4 50
Sandoa, Zaire................ B4 24
Sandomierz, Pol............... C6 7
Sandoná, Col................ C2 32
San Donà di Piave, It............ B4 9
Sandoval, Ill................. E4 58
Sandoval, co., N. Mex. B5 48
Sandpoint, Idaho.............. A2 57
Sandpit, B.C., Can.............. C2 37
Sands Point, N.Y.............. *G2 52
Sand Springs, Okla............. A5 79
Sandstone, Minn............... D6 67
Sandusky, Mich............... E8 66
Sandusky, Ohio............... A3 78
Sandusky, co., Ohio............ A2 78
Sandusky South, Ohio........... *A3 78
Sandviken, Swe............... G7 11
Sandwich, Ill................. B5 58
Sandwich, Mass............... C7 65
Sandy, Oreg................. B4 80
Sandy, Pa.................. *D4 81
Sandy, Utah................. D2 72
Sandy Beach, N.Y.............. *C2 75
Sandy Hook, Conn.............. D3 52
Sandy Springs, Ga.............. h8 55
San Elizario, Tex.............. o11 84
San Estanislao, Par............. D4 29
San Felipe, Chile.............. A2 28
San Felipe, N. Mex........... B5, D6 48
San Felipe, Ven............... A4 32
San Felipe de Jesus, Mex. *D5 34
San Feliu de Guixols, Sp. B7 8
San Fernando, Arg........... A5, g7 28
San Fernando, Calif............. m12 50
San Fernando, Chile............. A2 28
San Fernando, Phil........... B6, n13 19
San Fernando, Phil............. o13 19
San Fernando, Sp.............. D2 8
San Fernando, Trin............. A5 32
San Fernando de Apure, Ven. B4 32
San Fernando de Atabapo, Ven. C4 32
Sanford, Fla................. D5 54
Sanford, Maine............... E4 64
Sanford, N.C................ B3 76
San Francisco, Arg............. A4 28
San Francisco, Calif. D2, h8 50
San Francisco, Col............. C2 32
San Fransico del Oro, Mex. B3 34
San Fransico del Rincón, Mex. m13 34
San Fransico de Macorís, Dom. Rep... E8 35
San Gabriel, Calif.............. m12 50
San Gabriel, Ec............... A2 31
San Gabriel Chilac, Mex. D5, n15 34
Sangamon, co., Ill.............. D4 58
Sanger, Calif................ D4 50
Sanger, Tex................. C4 84
Sangerhausen, Ger. Dem Rep C5 6
San Germán, P.R............... *G11 35
San Gil, Col................. B3 32
San Giovanni in Fiore, It. E6 9
Sangju, Kor................. H4 18
Sāngli, India................. *E5 20
San Gorgonio, mtn., Calif. E5 50
San Ignacio, Pr............... E4 29
San Jacinto, Calif.............. F5 50
San Jacinto, co., Tex. D5 84
San Javier, Chile.............. B2 28
Sanjo, Jap................. H9 18
San Joaquin, co., Calif. C3 50
San Jose, Ariz............... C4 48
San Jose, Calif............. D3, k9 50
San José, C.R................ F8 34
San Jose, Ill................. C4 58
San José, Ur................. E1 30
San José, dept. Ur............. *E1 30
San José, prov., C.R. *F8 34
San José de Feliciano, Arg. A5 28
San José de los Molinos, Peru....... D2 31
San Juan, Arg................ A3 28
San Juan, Colo............... D6 51
San Juan, Dom. Rep. E8 25
San Juan, P.R............... *G11 35
San Juan, Tex................ G2 84
San Juan, co., Colo............. D3 51

San Juan, co., N. Mex. A4 28
San Juan, co., Utah............. C6 72
San Juan, co., Wash............. A2 86
San Juan, prov., Arg............. A3 28
San Juan Bautista, Calif. *D3 50
San Juan Bautista, Par. E4 29
San Juan Capistrano, Calif. F5 50
San Juan de los Lagos, Mex. m12 34
San Juan de los Morros, Ven. B4 32
San Juan del Río, Mex. m13 34
San Julián, Arg............... D3 28
San Justo, Arg............... *B5 28
Sankt Gallen, Switz............. E4 6
Sankt Gallen, canton, Switz. *E4 6
Sankt Pölten, Aus.............. D7 6
Sankt Veit an der Glan, Aus. E7 6
San Leandro, Calif.............. h8 50
San Lorenzo, Art............... A4 28
San Lorenzo, Calif.............. *D2 50
San Lorenzo, P.R.............. *G12 35
San Lorenzo del Escorial, Sp. ... B3, 016 8
Sanlúcar, Sp................. D2 8
San Luis, Arg................ A3 28
San Luis, Colo............... D5 51
San Luis, Cuba............... D6 35
San Luis, prov., Arg............. A3 28
San Luis de la Paz., Mex. m13 34
San Luis Obispo, Calif. E3 50
San Luis Obispo, co., Calif. E3 50
San Luis Potosí, Mex. C4, k13 34
San Luis Potosí, state, Mex. C4, k13 34
San Manuel, Ariz.............. *C3 48
San Marco in Lamis, It. C5 9
San Marcos, Tex........... E4, h8 84
San Marino, Calif.............. m12 50
San Marino, country, Eur. C4 9
San Martín, Arg............... A3 28
San Martín (General San Martín)
   Arg.................... g7 28
San Martin, Calif.............. *D3 50
San Martín, dept., Peru C2 31
San Mateo, Calif.............. h8 50
San Mateo, Ven............... B5 32
San Mateo, co., Calif. D2 50
Sanmenxia, China.............. E7 17
San Miguel, Sal............... E7 34
San Miguel, co., Colo. D2 51
San Miguel, co., N. Mex. B6 48
San Miguel de Allende, Mex. m13 34
San Miguel del Padrón, Cuba *C2 35
San Miguel de Tucumán, Arg. F4 27
San Nicolás, Arg.............. A4 28
San Nicolás Totolapan, Mex. h9 34
Sannois, Fr................. g10 5
Sano, Jap................. m18 18
Sanok, Pol................. D7 7
San Onofre, Col............... B2 32
San Pablo, Calif.............. *D2 50
San Patricio, co., Tex. E4 84
San Pedro, Arg............... D3 29
San Pedro, Arg............. A5, f7 28
San Pedro, Par............... D4 29
San Pedro, Tex............... *F4 84
San Pedro, dept., Par. D4 29
San Pedro de las Colonias, Mex. B4 34
San Pedro de Lloc, Peru C2 31
San Pedro de Macorís, Dom. Rep. E9 35
San Pedro Mártir, mts., Mex. A1 34
San Pedro Sula, Hond. D7 34
Sanpete, co., Utah............. B6 72
San Rafael, Arg............... A3 28
San Rafael, Calif............. D2, h7 50
San Rafael, mts., Calif. E4 50
San Ramon, Peru.............. D2 31
San Ramon, Ur................ g9 28
San Remo, It................ C1 9
San Roque, Sp............... D3 8
San Saba, Tex................ D3 84
San Saba, co., Tex. D3 84
San Salvador, Sal.............. E7 34
San Salvador de Jujuy, Arg. F4 27
San Sebastián, P.R............. *G11 35
San Sebastián, Sp.............. A4 8
San Sepolcro, It............... C4 9
San Severo, It................ D5 9
Sansom Park Village, Tex. *C4 84
Sans Souci, S.C............... *B3 82
Santa, Peru................. C2 31
Santa Ana, Calif........... F5, n13 50
Santa Ana, Mex............... A2 34
Santa Ana, Sal............... E7 34
Santa Ana, mts., Calif. n13 50
Santa Antia, Mex.............. h9 34
Santa Anna, Tex............... D3 84
Santa Bárbara d'Oeste, Braz. m8 30
Santa Barbara, Calif............ E4 50
Santa Bárbara, Mex............ B3 34
Santa Barbara, co., Calif. E3 50
Santa Catalina, isl., Calif. F4 50
Santa Catarina, state, Braz. D2, k9 50
Santa Clara, Calif............ D2, k9 50
Santa Clara, Cuba.............. C4 35
Santa Clara, Ur................ E2 30

Santa Clara, co., Calif. ... D3 50
Santa Cruz, Bol. ... C3 29
Santa Cruz, Calif. ... D2 50
Santa Cruz, C.R. ... E7 34
Santa Cruz, co., Ariz. ... D3 48
Santa Cruz, co., Calif. ... D2 50
Santa Cruz, prov., Arg. ... D3 28
Santa Cruz de la Palma, Sp. ... m13 8
Santa Cruz de la Zarza, Sp. ... C4 8
Santa Cruz del Sur. ... D5 35
Santa Cruz de Tenerife, Sp. ... m13 8
Santa Cruz de Tenerife, prov., Sp. ... *m13 8
Santa Cruz do Rio Pardo, Braz. ... *C3 30
Santa Cruz do Sul., Braz. ... D2 30
Santa Elena, Tex. ... F3 84
Santa Eugenia de Ribeira, Sp. ... A1 8
Santa Eulalia del Rio, Sp. ... C6 8
Santa Fe, Arg. ... A4 28
Santa Fé, Cuba, (part of Havanna) ... D2 35
Santa Fe, Mex. ... h9 34
Santa Fe, N. Mex. ... B6, D6 48
Santafé, Sp. ... D4 8
Santa Fe, co., N. Mex. ... B5 48
Santa Fe, prov., Arg. ... A4 28
Santa Fe Springs, Calif. ... F4 50
Santai, China ... E6 17
Santa Inés, Ahuatempan, Mex. ... n14 34
Santa Isabel, P.R. ... *G11 35
Santa Lucía, Cuba ... D6 35
Santa Lucia, Ur. ... E1 30
Santa Margarita, Calif. ... E3 50
Santa Maria, Braz. ... D2 30
Santa Maria, Calfi. ... E3 50
Santa Maria Capua Vetere, It. ... D5 9
Santa Maria Colotepec, Mex. ... D5 34
Santa María del Oro, Mex. ... B3 34
Santa Marta, Col. ... A3 32
Santa Marta, Sp. ... C2 8
Santa Monica, Calif. ... m12 50
Santana, Port. ... h12 4
Santana do Livramento, Braz. ... E1 30
Santander, Col. ... C2 32
Santander, Sp. ... A4 8
Santander, dept., Col. ... B3 32
Santander, prov., Sp. ... *A4 8
Santanyí, Sp. ... C7 8
Santa Paula, Calif. ... E4 50
Santaquin, Utah ... B6 72
Santarém, Braz. ... D5 27
Santarém, Port. ... C1 8
Santa Rita, Braz. ... *D7 27
Santa Rita, Guam ... *F6 2
Santa Rita, N. Mex. ... C4 48
Santa Rosa, Arg. ... B4 28
Santa Rosa, Calif. ... C2 50
Santa Rosa, N. Mex. ... B6 48
Santa Rosa, co., Fla. ... G2 54
Santa Rosa de Copán, Hond. ... *E7 34
Santa Rosa, de Osos, Col. ... B2 32
Santa Rosalia, Mex. ... B2 34
Santa Susana, Calif. ... *E4 50
Santa Tomé de Guayana, Ven. ... B5 32
Santa Ursula Coapa, Mex. ... h9 34
Santa Venetia, Calif. ... *D2 50
Santa Vitória do Palmar, Braz. ... E2 30
Santee, Calif. ... o16 50
Santiago, Braz. ... D2 30
Santiago, Chile ... A2 28
Santiago, Dom. Rep. ... E8 35
Santiago, Mex. ... C3 34
Santiago, Pan. ... B1 32
Santiago, Par. ... E4 29
Santiago, Sp. ... A1 8
Santiago, prov., Chile ... A2 28
Santiago, mts., Tex. ... D1 84
Santiago, peak, Calif. ... n14 50
Santiago, peak, Tex. ... p13 84
Santiago de Cao, Peru ... C2 31
Santiago de Cuba, Cuba ... D6 35
Santiago del Estero, Arg. ... E3 29
Santiago del Estero, prov., Arg. ... E3 29
Santiago Ixcuintla, Mex. ... C3, m11 34
Santiago Tepalcatlalpan, Mex. ... h9 34
Santisteban, del Puerto, Sp. ... C4 8
Santo Amaro, Braz. ... *E7 27
Santo Andre, Braz. ... *m8 30
Santo Ângelo, Braz. ... D2 30
Santo Antônio, Braz. ... *E7 27
Santo Domingo, Dom. Rep. ... E9 35
Santo Domingo Pueblo, N. Mex. ... B5 48
San Tomas, Calif. ... *D3 50
Santoña, Sp. ... A4 8
Santos, Braz. ... C3, m8 30
Santos Dumont, Braz. ... C4, g6 30
Santo Tomás, Peru ... D3 31
Santo Tomas, Ven. ... B5 32
Santo Tomé de Guayana, Ven. ... B5 32
San Valentin, mtn., Chile ... H3 27
San Vicente, Sal. ... E7 34
San Vicente de Alcántara, Sp. ... C2 8
San Vicente del Caguán, Col. ... C3 32
San Vito al Tagliamento, It. ... B4 9

San Ygnacio, Tex. ... F3 84
São Bernardo do Campo, Braz. ... C3, m8 30
São Borja, Braz. ... D1 30
São Carlos, Braz. ... C3, m8 30
São Caetano do sul, Braz. ... *m8 30
São Cristovão, Braz. ... *E7 27
São Francisco, riv., Braz. ... A4 30
São Francisco do Sul, Braz. ... D3 30
São Gabriel, Braz. ... E2 30
São João da Boa Vista, Braz. ... C3, k8 30
São João del Rei, Braz. ... C4, g5 30
São Joao de Meriti, Braz. ... C4, *h6 30
São José do Rio Pardo, Braz. ... k8 30
São José do Rio Prêto, Braz. ... C3 30
São José dos Campos, Braz. ... C3, m9 30
São Leopoldo, Braz. ... D2 30
São Lourenço, Braz. ... C3 30
São Luis, Braz. ... D6 27
São Luis Gonzaga, Braz. ... D2 30
São Manuel, Braz. ... C3, m7 30
Saône-et-Loire, dept., Fr. ... *D6 5
São Paulo, Braz. ... C3, m8 30
São Paulo, state, Braz. ... C3, m8 30
São Roque, Braz. ... m8 30
São Sebastião do Paraiso, Braz. ... C3 30
São Tomé, São Tomé & Principe ... H6 22
Sao Tome & Principe, country, Afr. ... H5 22
São Vicente, Port. ... h11 8
São Vincinte, Braz. ... C3 30
Sapai, Grc. ... B5 14
Sapele, Nig. ... G6 22
Saposoa, Peru ... C2 31
Sapozhok, Sov. Un. ... E13 12
Sapphire, mts., Mont. ... D3 70
Sappington, Mo. ... f13 69
Sapporo, Jap. ... E10 18
Sapri, It. ... D5 9
Sapulpa, Okla. ... B5 79
Sara Buri, Thai. ... *C2 19
Sarah, Miss. ... A3 68
Sarajevo, Yugo. ... D4 10
Sara Kaeo, Thai. ... *C2 19
Saraland, Ala. ... E1 46
Saranac, Mich. ... F5 66
Saranac, N.Y. ... f11 75
Saranac Lake, N.Y. ... B3 75
Saranap, Calif. ... *D2 50
Sarandí del Yí, Ur. ... E1 30
Sarandi Grande, Ur. ... E1 30
Saransk, Sov. Un. ... D15 12
Sarapul, Sov. Un. ... D8 12
Sarasota, Fla. ... E4, q10 54
Sarasota, co., Fla. ... E4 54
Saratoga, Calif. ... *D3 50
Saratoga, Tex. ... D5 84
Saratoga, Wyo. ... E6 89
Saratoga, co., N.Y. ... B7 75
Saratoga Place, Va. ... *D6 85
Saratoga Springs, N.Y. ... B7 75
Saratov, Sov. Un. ... F15 12
Saravane, Laos ... *B3 19
Sarawak, reg., Mala. ... E4 19
Saraykoy, Tur. ... D7 14
Sarcelles, Fr. ... g10 5
Sarcoxie, Mo. ... D3 69
Sardegna, pol. dist., It. ... *E2 9
Sardinia, Ohio ... C2 78
Sardinia, isl., It. ... D2 9
Sardis, Ala. ... C3 46
Sardis, B.C., Can. ... f14 37
Sardis, Miss. ... A4 68
Sardis, Ohio ... C5 78
Sarepta, La. ... B2 63
Sargent, Nebr. ... C6 71
Sargent, co., N. Dak. ... D8 77
Sargodha, Pak. ... *B5 20
Sarh, Chad ... G1 23
Sarikamiş, Tur. ... B14 14
Sarina, Austl. ... D8 25
Sariwon, Kor. ... G2 18
Sarlat, Fr. ... E4 5
Sarmiento, mtn., Chile ... I3 27
Sarnia, Ont., Can. ... E2 41
Sarny, Sov. Un. ... F6 12
Saronno, It. ... B2 9
Sárospatak, Hung. ... A5 10
Sarpsborg, Nor. ... p29 11
Sarpy, co., Nebr. ... C9 71
Sarreguemines, Fr. ... C7 5
Sartell, Minn. ... E4 67
Sartène, Fr. ... D2 9
Sarthe, dept., Fr. ... *D4 5
Sartrouville, Fr. ... g9 5
Sarufutsu, Jap. ... D11 18
Sárvár, Hung. ... B3 10
Sarzana, It. ... B2 9
Sāsarām, India ... D7 20
Sasebo, Jap. ... J4 18
Saskatchewan, prov., Can. ... 39
Saskatchewan, riv., Can. ... F13 36
Saskatoon, Sask., Can. ... E2, n7 39

Sasovo, Sov. Un. ... D13 12
Sassafras, mtn., S.C. ... A2 82
Sassari, It. ... D2 9
Satah, mtn., B.C., Can. ... C5 37
Satanta, Kans. ... E3 61
Saticoy, Calif. ... E4 50
Satka, Sov. Un. ... D8 13
Sátoraljaújhely, Hung. ... A5 10
Satsuma, Fla. ... E1 46
Sattahip, Thai. ... *C2 19
Satu-Mare, Rom. ... B6 10
Saucillo, Mex. ... B3 34
Sauda, Nor. ... H2 11
Saudi Arabia, country, Asia ... D3 15
Saugatuck, Mich. ... F4 66
Saugerties, N.Y. ... C7 75
Saugus, Mass. ... B5, g11 65
Sauk, co., Wis. ... E4 88
Sauk Centre, Minn. ... E4 67
Sauk City, Wis. ... E4 88
Sauk Rapids, Minn. ... E4 67
Sauk Village, Ill. ... *B6 58
Saukville, Wis. ... E6 88
Sault-au-Mouton, Que., Can. ... A8 42
Sault Ste. Marie, Mich. ... B6 66
Sault Ste. Marie, Ont., Can. ... p18 41
Saumur, Fr. ... D4 5
Saunders, co., Nebr. ... C9 71
Sauquoit, N.Y. ... *B5 75
Sausalito, Calif. ... D2, h8 50
Sava, Yugo. ... C4 10
Savage, Md. ... B4 53
Savage, Minn. ... F5, n11 67
Savanna, Ill. ... A3 58
Savanna, Okla. ... C6 79
Savanna-la-Mar, Jam. ... E4 35
Savannah, Ga. ... D5 55
Savannah, Mo. ... B3 69
Savannah, N.Y. ... B4 75
Savannah, Tenn. ... B3 83
Savannah Beach, Ga. ... D6 55
Saveni, Rom. ... B8 10
Saverne, Fr. ... C7 5
Savigliano, It. ... B1 9
Savoie, dept., Fr. ... *F3 5
Savona, B.C., Can. ... D7 37
Savona, It. ... B2 9
Savona, N.Y. ... C3 75
Savonlinna, Fin. ... G13 11
Savoy (Savoie), former prov., Fr. ... E7 5
Savran, Sov. Un. ... G8 12
Sawahlunto, Indon. ... F2 19
Sawakin, Sud. ... E5 23
Sawan Khalok, Thai. ... B1 19
Sawbill Landing, Minn. ... C7 67
Sawhāj, Eg. ... C4 23
Sawtooth, mts., Idaho ... E3 57
Sawyer, Mich. ... G4 66
Sawyer, co., Wis. ... C2 88
Sawyerville, Que., Can. ... D6 42
Sawyerwood, Ohio ... *A4 78
Saxapahaw, N.C. ... B3 78
Saxis, Va. ... C7 85
Saxon, S.C. ... B4 82
Saxony, reg., Ger. Dem. Rep. ... C6 6
Saxonburg, Pa. ... E2 81
Saxton, Pa. ... F5 81
Sayabec, Que., Can. ... *G19 36
Sayán, Peru ... D2 31
Saybrook, Ill. ... C5 58
Sahyūt, P.D.R. of Yem ... F5 15
Sayre, Ala. ... B3 46
Sayre, Okla. ... B2 79
Sayre, Pa. ... C9 81
Sayreton, Ala. ... B3, f7 46
Sayreville, N.J. ... C4 74
Sayula, Mex. ... D4, n12 34
Sayville, N.Y. ... G4 52
Scafell Pikes, mtn., Eng. ... C4 4
Scalp Level, Pa. ... F4 81
Scandia, Kans. ... C6 61
Scanlon, Minn. ... D6 67
Scansano, It. ... C3 9
Scapegoat, mtn., Mont. ... C4 70
Scappoose, Oreg. ... B4 80
Scarboro, Maine ... E2, g7 64
Scarborough, Ont., Can. ... m15 41
Scarborough, Eng. ... C6 4
Scarborough, Trin. ... K14 35
Scarbro, W. Va. ... n13 87
Scarsdale, N.Y. ... h13 75
Sceaux, Fr. ... g10 5
Schaefferstown, Pa. ... F9 81
Schaerbeek, Bel. ... *B6 5
Schaffhausen, Switz. ... E4 6
Schaffhausen, canton, Switz. ... *E4 6
Schaghticoke, N.Y. ... C7 75
Schaller, Iowa ... B2 60
Schaumburg, Ill. ... h8 58
Schefferville, Que., Can. ... h13 42
Schenectady, N.Y. ... C7 75
Schenectady, co., N.Y. ... C6 75
Schererville, Ind. ... B3 59

Schertz., Tex. ... h7 84
Schiedam, Neth. ... B6 5
Schiller Park, Ill. ... k9 58
Schiltigheim, Fr. ... C7 5
Schio, It. ... B3 9
Schivelbein, see Swidwin, Pol.
Schleicher, co., Tex. ... D2 84
Schleswig, Ger., Fed. Rep. of ... A4 6
Schleswig, Iowa ... B2 60
Schleswig-Holstein, reg., Ger., Fed. Rep. of ... A4 6
Schleswig-Holstein, state, Ger., Fed. Rep. of ... *A4 6
Schley, co., Ga. ... D2 55
Schlüchtern, Ger., Fed. Rep. of ... C4 6
Schmalkalden, Ger. Dem. Rep. ... C5 6
Schneidemuhl, see Pila, Pol.
Schofield, Wis. ... *D4 88
Schoharie, N.Y. ... C6 75
Schoharie, co., N.Y. ... C6 75
Schönebeck, Ger. Dem. Rep. ... B5 6
Schongau, Ger., Fed. Rep. of ... E5 6
Schoolcraft, Mich. ... F5 66
Schoolcraft, co., Mich. ... B4 66
Schooley, mtn., N.J. ... B3 74
Schramberg, Ger., Fed. Rep. of ... D4 6
Schram City, Ill. ... D4 58
Schriever, La. ... E5, k10 63
Schrobenhausen, Ger., Fed. Rep. of ... D5 6
Schroon Lake, N.Y. ... B7 75
Schulenburg, Tex. ... E4 84
Schuyler, Nebr. ... C8 71
Schuyler, co., Ill. ... C3 58
Schuyler, co., Mo. ... A5 69
Schuyler, co., N.Y. ... C4 75
Schuylerville, N.Y. ... B7 75
Schuylkill, co., Pa. ... E9 81
Schuylkill Haven, Pa. ... E9 81
Schwabach, Ger., Fed. Rep. of ... D5 6
Schwäbisch Gmünd, Ger., Fed. Rep. of ... D4 6
Schwäbisch Hall, Ger., Fed. Rep. of ... D4 6
Schwandorf, Ger., Fed. Rep. of ... D6 6
Schwaner, mts., Indon. ... F4 19
Schwaz, Aus. ... E5 6
Schwedt, Ger. Dem. Rep. ... B7 6
Schweinfurt, Ger., Fed. Rep. of ... C5 6
Schwerin, Ger. Dem. Rep. ... B5 6
Schwyz, Switz. ... E4 6
Schwyz, canton, switz. ... *E4 6
Sciacca, It. ... F4 9
Scio, Ohio ... B4 78
Scioto, co., Ohio ... D2 78
Sciotodale, Ohio ... *D2 78
Scituate, Mass. ... B6, h13 65
Scobey, Mont. ... B11 70
Scone, Austl. ... F8 26
Scotch Plains, N.J. ... B4 74
Scotia, Calif. ... B1 50
Scotia, N.Y. ... C7 75
Scotland, Ont., Can. ... D4 41
Scotland, S. Dak. ... C8 77
Scotland, co., Mo. ... A5 69
Scotland, co., N.C. ... C3 76
Scotland, reg., U.K. ... B4 4
Scotland Neck, N.C. ... A5 76
Scotlandville, La. ... D4, g9 63
Scotstown, Que., Can. ... D6 42
Scott, La. ... D3 63
Scott, co., Ark. ... C1 49
Scott, co., Ill. ... D3 58
Scott, co., Ind. ... G6 59
Scott, co., Iowa ... C7 60
Scott, co., Kans. ... D3 61
Scott, co., Ky. ... B5 62
Scott, co., Minn. ... F5 67
Scott, co., Miss. ... C4 68
Scott, co., Mo. ... D8 69
Scott, co., Tenn. ... C9 83
Scott, co., Va. ... f9 85
Scott, mtn., Idaho ... E3 57
Scott, mtn., Okla. ... C3 79
Scott, mtn., Oreg. ... E4 80
Scott, peak, Idaho ... E6 57
Scott City, Kans. ... D3 61
Scott City, Mo. ... D8 69
Scottdale, Ga. ... h8 55
Scottdale, Pa. ... F2 81
Scotts, mtn., N.J. ... B2 74
Scottsbluff, Nebr. ... C2 71
Scotts Bluff, co., Nebr. ... C2 71
Scottsboro, Ala. ... A3 46
Scottsburg, Ind. ... G6 59
Scottsdale, Ariz. ... C3, D2 48
Scottsville, Ky. ... D3 62
Scottsville, N.Y. ... B3 75
Scottville, Mich. ... E4 66
Scranton, Iowa ... B3 60
Scranton, Kans. ... D8 61
Scranton, Pa. ... D10, m18 81
Scranton, S.C. ... D8 82

Screven, Ga. E4 55
Screven, co., Ga. D5 55
Scribner, Nebr. C9 71
Scunthorpe, Eng. D6 4
Scurry, co., Tex. C2 84
Seaboard, N.C. A5 76
Sea Bright, N.J. C5 74
Seabrook, Md. *C4 53
Seabrook, N.J. E2 74
Seabrook, Tex. r14 84
Sea Cliff, N.Y. F2 52
Seadrift, Tex. E4 84
Seaford, Del. C6 53
Seaford, N.Y. G3 52
Seaford, Va. h15 85
Seaforth, Ont., Can. D3 41
Sea Girt, N.J. C4 74
Seagoville, Tex. n10 84
Seagraves, Tex. C1 84
Sea Isle City, N.J. E3 74
Seal Beach, Calif. *F5 50
Seal Cove, N.B., Can. E3 43
Sealevel, N.C. C6 76
Sealy, Tex. E4 84
Seaman, Ohio D2 78
Searcy, Ark. B4 49
Searsport, Maine D4 64
Seaside, Calif. *D3 50
Seaside, Oreg. B3 80
Seaside Heights, N.J. D4 74
Seaside Park, N.J. D4 74
Seat Pleasant, Md. C4, f9 53
Seattle, Wash. B3, e11 86
Seaview, Wash. C1 86
Sebastian, Fla. E6 54
Sebastian, co., Ark. B1 49
Sebastopol, Calif. C2 50
Sebeka, Minn. D3 67
Sebeş, Rom. C6 10
Sebewaing, Mich. E7 66
Şebinkarahisar, Tur. B12 14
Sebnitz, Ger. Dem. Rep. C7 6
Sebree, Ky. C2 62
Sebring, Fla. E5 54
Sebring, Ohio B4 78
Sebringville, Ont., Can. D3 41
Secane, Pa. *B11 81
Secaucus, N.J. h8 74
Sechura, Peru C1 31
Sector Popular, Mex. h9 34
Security, Colo. C6 51
Sedalia, Mo. C4 69
Sedan, Fr. C6 5
Sedan, Kans. E7 61
Sedgefield, N.C. *A3 76
Sedgewick, Alta., Can. C5 38
Sedgwick, Kans. E6, g12 61
Sedgwick, co., Colo. A8 51
Sedgwick, co., Kans. E6 61
Sedro Woolley, Wash. A3 86
Seekonk, Mass. C5 65
Seeley, Calif. F6 50
Seeley Lake, Mont. C3 70
Seelyville, Ind. F3 59
Segorbe, Sp. C5 8
Ségou, Mali F3 22
Segovia, Sp. B3 8
Segovia, prov., Sp. *B3 8
Segré, Fr. D3 5
Seguin, Tex. E4, h8 84
Sehwān, Pak. C4 20
Seiling, Okla. A3 79
Seinäjoki, Fin. *F10 11
Seine, dept., Fr. C5, g1 5
Seine-et-Marne, dept., Fr. *C5 5
Seine-et-Oise, dept., Fr. *C5 5
Seine-Maritime, dept., Fr. C4 5
Seixal, Port. f9 8
Seki, Jap. o15 18
Sekondi-Takoradi, Ghana H4 22
Selah, Wash. C5 86
Selanovtsi, Bul. D7 10
Selb, Ger., Fed. Rep. of C6 6
Selby, S. Dak. E5 77
Selbyville, Del. D7 53
Selden, N.Y. *E3 75
Sélestat, Fr. C7 5
Selidovka, Sov. Un. q20 12
Selkirk, Man., Can. D3 40
Selkirk, Scot. C5 4
Selkirk, co., Scot. *C5 4
Selle, Pic la, peak, Hai. E8 35
Sellersburg, Ind. H6 59
Sellersville, Pa. F11 81
Selma, Ala. C2 46
Selma, Calif. D4 50
Selma, Ind. D7 59
Selma, N.C. B4 76
Selmer, Tenn. B3 83
Selvas, reg., Braz. *D4 27

Selwyn, mtn., B.C., Can. B6 37
Semarang, Indon. G4 19
Sembilan, state, Mala. *E2 19
Semenovka, Sov. Un. E9 12
Semeru, mtn., Indon. G4 19
Seminoe, mts., Wyo. D6 89
Seminole, Ala. E2 46
Seminole, Fla. *E4 54
Seminole, Okla. B5 79
Seminole, Tex. C1 84
Seminole, co., Fla. D5 54
Seminole, co., Ga. F2 55
Seminole, co., Okla. B5 79
Semipalatinsk, Sov. Un. D11 13
Semnān, Iran A8 23
Senador Pompeu, Braz. *D7 27
Senath, Mo. E7 69
Senatobia, Miss. A4 68
Sendai, Jap. G10 18
Sendai (Kagoshima, Perf.), Jap. K5 18
Seneca, Ill. B5 58
Sececa, Kans. C7 61
Seneca, Mo. E3 69
Seneca, Pa. D2 81
Seneca, S.C. B2 82
Seneca, co., N.Y. C4 75
Seneca, co., Ohio A2 78
Seneca Falls, N.Y. C4 75
Senegal, country, Afr. F2 22
Senftenberg, Ger. Dem. Rep. C6 6
Senhor do Bonfim, Braz. *E7 27
Senigallia, It. C4 9
Senlis, Fr. C5 5
Senneterre, Que., Can. B2 42
Sens, Fr. C5 42
Senta, Yugo. C5 10
Sentinel, Okla. B2 79
Sentinel, peak, B.C., Can. B6 37
Seoul (Soul), Kor. H3 18
Sept Iles (Seven Islands),
  Que., Can. h13 42
Sequatchie, co., Tenn. D8 83
Sequim, Wash. A2 86
Sequoia, Calif. D4 50
Sequoyah, co., Okla. B7 79
Serafimovich, Sov. Un. G14 12
Seraing, Bel. B6 5
Serampore, India *D8 20
Serang, Indon. G3 19
Serbia, reg., Yugo. D5 10
Serbia, rep., Yugo. *D5 10
Serdobsk, Sov. Un. E15 12
Seremban, Mala. E2 19
Sergeant Bluff, Iowa B1 60
Sergipe, state, Braz. *E7 27
Seria, Bru. E4 19
Seringapatam, India F6 20
Serón, Sp. D4 8
Serov, Sov. Un. D9 13
Serowe, Bots. E5 24
Serpa, Port. D2 8
Serpukhov, Sov. Un. D11 12
Sérrai, Grc. B4 14
Sérrai, prov., Grc. *B4 14
Serra Talhada, Braz. *D7 27
Serrinha, Braz. *E7 27
Sêrxü, China E4 17
Sesser, Ill. E4 58
Sesto Fiorentino, It. *C3 9
Sestri Levante, It. B2 9
Sestroretck, Sov. Un. A8 12
Setana, Jap. E9 18
Setauket, N.Y. F4 52
Sète, Fr. F5 5
Sete Lagoas, Braz. B4 30
Seth, W. Va. C3, m12 87
Seth Ward, Tex. *B2 84
Seto, Jap. I8, n16 18
Settat, Mor. B3 22
Setúbal, Port. C1 8
Sevastopol, Sov. Un. I9 12
Seven Devils, mts., Idaho D2 57
Seven Harbors, Mich. *F7 66
Seven Hills, Ohio *A4 78
Seven Mile, Ohio C1 78
Sevenoaks, Eng. m13 4
Severn, Md. B4 53
Severna Park, Md. B4 53
Sevier, co., Ark. D1 49
Sevier, co., Tenn. D10 83
Sevier, co., Utah B6 72
Sevierville, Tenn. D10 83
Sevilla, Col. C2 32
Sevilla (Seville), Sp. D3 8
Sevilla (Seville), prov., Sp. *D3 8
Seville, Fla. C5 54
Seville, Ohio A4 78
Sevlievo, Bul. D7 10
Sevran, Fr. g11 5
Sèvres, Fr. g9 5
Sewanee, Tenn. *B6 83

Seward, Alsk. C10, g17 47
Seward, Nebr. D8 71
Seward, co., Kans. E3 61
Seward, co., Nebr. D8 71
Sewaren, N.J. k7 74
Sewell, N.J. D2 74
Sewickley, Pa. E1, h13 81
Sewickley Heights, Pa. *E1 81
Sexsmith, Alta., Can. B1 38
Seychelles, Br. dep., Afr. G24 2
Seymour, Conn. D4 52
Seymour, Ind. G6 59
Seymour, Iowa D4 60
Seymour, Mo. D5 69
Seymour, Tex. C3 84
Seymour, Wis. D5, g9 88
Seymourville, La. h9 63
Sezimbra, Port. C1 8
Sezze, It. D4 9
Sfax, Tun. B7 22
Sfintul-Gheorghe, Rom. C7 10
's Gravenhage, see The Hague, Neth.
Shaanxi, prov., China D6 17
Shabbona, Ill. B5 58
Shache, China F10 16
Shackelford, co., Tex. C3 84
Shady Cove, Oreg. E4 80
Shady Side, Md. C4 53
Shadyside, Ohio C5 78
Shaft (William Penn), Pa. *E9 81
Shafter, Calif. E4 50
Shāhjahanpur, India C7 20
Shaker Heights, Ohio A4, h9 78
Shakhty, Sov. Un. H13 12
Shaki, Nig. G5 22
Shakopee, Minn. F5, n11 67
Shalimar, Fla. u15 54
Shallowater, Tex. C2 84
Sham, Jabal ash, mtn., Om D2 20
Shamokin, Pa. E8 81
Shamokin Dam, Pa. E8 81
Shamrock, Fla. C3 54
Shamrock, Tex. B2 84
Shandaken, N.Y. C6 75
Shandi, Sud. E4 23
Shandong, prov., China D8 17
Shanghai, China E9 17
Shangqui, China D8 17
Shangshui, China E7 17
Shangzhi, China D3 18
Shanhaiguan, China C8 17
Shannon, Ga. B1 55
Shannon, Ill. A4 58
Shannon, co., Mo. D6 69
Shannon, co., S. Dak. G3 77
Shannontown, S.C. *D7 82
Shantou, China G8 17
Shanxi, prov., China D7 17
Shaoguan, China G7 17
Shaoxing, China E9 17
Shaoyang, China F7 17
Shari, Jap. E12 18
Sharkey, co., Miss. C3 68
Sharon, Mass. B5, h11 65
Sharon, Pa. D1 81
Sharon, Tenn. A3 83
Sharon, Wis. F5 88
Sharon Hill, Pa. p20 81
Sharon Park, Ohio n12 78
Sharon Springs, Kans. D2 61
Sharonville, Ohio n13 78
Sharp, co., Ark. A4 49
Sharpes, Fla. D6 54
Sharpsburg, Md. B2 53
Sharpsburg, Pa. k14 81
Sharpsville, Ind. D5 59
Sharpsville, Pa. D1 81
Sharptown, Md. C6 53
Shashi, China E7 17
Shasta, co., Calif. B3 50
Shasta, mtn., Calif. B2 50
Shastsk, Sov. Un. D13 12
Shattuck, Okla. A2 79
Shaunavon, Sask., Can. H1 39
Shavertown, Pa. *B8 81
Shaw, Miss. B3 68
Shawano, Wis. D5 88
Shawano, co., Wis. D5 88
Shawbridge, Que., Can. D3 43
Shawinigan, Que., Can. C5 42
Shawinigan-Sud, Que., Can. C5 43
Shawmut, Ala. C4 46
Shawnee, Kans. k16 61
Shawnee, Ohio C3 78
Shawnee, Okla. B5 79
Shawnee, co., Kans. D8 61
Shawneetown, Ill. F5 58
Shawville, Que., Can. B8 41
Shchelkovo, Sov. Un. n18 12
Shchetovo, Sov. Un. q22 12
Shchigry, Sov. Un. F11 12

Shchors, Sov. Un. F8 12
Sheartown, Newf., Can. *E5 44
Sheboygan, Wis. E5, k10 88
Sheboygan, co., Wis. E6 88
Sheboygan Falls, Wis. E5, k10 88
Shediac, N.B., Can. C5 43
Sheep, mtn., Wyo. B5 89
Sheep, mtn., Wyo. C2 89
Sheeps Heaven, mtn., Mass. A1 65
Sheet Harbour, N.S., Can. E7 43
Sheffield, Ala. A2 46
Sheffield, Eng. D6 4
Sheffield, Ill. B4 58
Sheffield, Iowa B4 60
Sheffield, Ohio A3 78
Sheffield, Pa. C3 81
Sheffield Lake, Ohio *A3 78
Shefford, co., Que., Can. D5 42
Sheila, N.B., Can. B5 43
Shelagyote, Ky. C7 62
Shelagyote, peak, B.C., Can. B4 37
Shelbiana, Ky. C7 62
Shelbina, Mo. B5 69
Shelburn, Ind. F3 59
Shelburne, N.S., Can. F4 43
Shelburne, Ont., Can. C4 41
Shelburne, co., N.S., Can. F4 43
Shelburne Falls, Mass. A2 65
Shelby, Ind. B3 59
Shelby, Iowa C2 60
Shelby, Mich. E4 66
Shelby, Miss. B3 68
Shelby, Mont. B5 70
Shelby, Nebr. C8 71
Shelby, N.C. B1 76
Shelby, Ohio B3 78
Shelby, co., Ala. B3 46
Shelby, co., Ill. D5 58
Shelby, co., Ind. E6 59
Shelby, co., Iowa C2 60
Shelby, co., Ky. B4 62
Shelby, co., Mo. B5 69
Shelby, co., Ohio B1 78
Shelby, co., Tenn. B2 83
Shelby, co., Tex. D5 84
Shelby City, Ky. C5 62
Shelby Village, Mich. *F7 66
Shelbyville, Ill. D5 58
Shelbyville, Ind. F6 59
Shelbyville, Ky. B4 62
Shelbyville, Mo. B5 69
Shelbyville, Tenn. B5 83
Sheldon, Ill. C6 58
Sheldon, Iowa A2 60
Shell Beach, Calif. *E3 50
Shellbrook, Sask., Can. D2 39
Shell Camp, Tex. *C5 84
Shelley, Idaho F6 57
Shell Lake, Wis. C2 88
Shellman, Ga. E2 55
Shellman Bluff, Ga. E5 55
Shell Rock, Iowa B5 60
Shellsburg, Iowa B6 60
Shelter Island, N.Y. m16 75
Shelton, Conn. D4 52
Shelton, Nebr. D7 71
Shelton, Wash. B2 86
Shenandoah, Iowa D2 60
Shenandoah, Pa. E9 81
Shenandoah, Va. B4 85
Shenandoah, co., Va. B4 85
Shenandoah, mtn., Va. B3 85
Shenandoah Heights, Pa. *E9 81
Shenorock, N.Y. *D7 75
Shensi, see Shaanxi, China
Shenyang, China C9 17
Shepetovka, Sov. Un. F6 12
Shepherd, Mich. E6 66
Shepherd Brook, mtn., Maine B3 64
Shepherdstown, W.Va. B7 87
Shepherdsville, Ky. C4, g11 62
Shepparton, Austl. H5 26
Sheppton, Pa. E9 81
Sherborn, Mass. h10 65
Sherbrooke, Que., Can. D6, k12 42
Sherbrooke, co., Que., Can. D5 42
Sherburn, Minn. G4 67
Sherburne, N.Y. C5 75
Sherburne, co., Minn. E5 67
Shereshevo, Sov. Un. B8 7
Sheridan, Ark. C3 49
Sheridan, Colo. B6 51
Sheridan, Ind. D5 59
Sheridan, Mich. E5 66
Sheridan, Mont. E4 70
Sheridan, Oreg. B3 80
Sheridan, Wyo. B8 89
Sheridan, co., Kans. C3 61
Sheridan, co., Mont. B12 70
Sheridan, co., Nebr. B3 71
Sheridan, co., N.Dak. C5 77
Sheridan, co., Wyo. B5 89

Sheridan, mtn., Wyo. B2 89
Sheridan Beach, Wash. *B3 86
Sheringham, Eng. D7 4
Sherman, N.Y. C1 75
Sherman, Tex. C4 84
Sherman, co., Kans. C2 61
Sherman, co., Nebr. C6 71
Sherman, co., Oreg. B6 80
Sherman, co., Tex. A2 84
Sherridon, Man., Can. B1 40
Sherrill, N.Y. B5 75
's Hertogenbosch, Neth. B6 5
Sherwood, Ark. C3, h10 49
Sherwood, Ohio A1 78
Sherwood, Oreg. h12 80
Sherwood, Tenn. B6 83
Sherwood Park, Alta., Can. C4 38
Sheshebee, Minn. D5 67
Shetland, co., Scot. *g10 4
Shetland, is., Scot. g1 4
Shiawassee, co., Mich. F6 66
Shibām, P.D.R. of Yem. F4 15
Shibarghan (Shibargan), Afg. A4 20
Shibata, Jap. H9 18
Shibecha, Jap. E12 18
Shibetsu, Jap. D11 18
Shibetsu, Jap. E12 18
Shibīn al Kawm, Eg. G8 14
Shickshinny, Pa. D9 81
Shidler, Okla. A5 79
Shiga, pref., Jap. *I8 18
Shijiazhuang, China D7 17
Shikārpur, Pak. .C4 20
Shikoku, isl., Jap. J6 18
Shilka, Sov. Un. D14 13
Shillington, Pa. F10 81
Shillong, India .C9 20
Shiloh, Ohio B3 78
Shiloh, Ohio C1 78
Shimabara, Jap. J5 18
Shimada, Jap. o17 18
Shimane, pref., Jap. *I16 18
Shimanovsk, Sov. Un. D15 13
Shimizu, Jap. I9, n17 18
Shimoda, Jap. o17 18
Shimodate, Jap. m18 18
Shimoga, India .F6 20
Shimonoseki, Jap. I5 18
Shimotsuma, Jap. m18 18
Shiner, Tex. *E4 84
Shinglehouse, Pa. C5 81
Shingu, Jap. J7 18
Shinjo, Jap. G10 18
Shinkolobwe, Zaire C5 24
Shinnston, W. Va. B4, k10 87
Shinshiro, Jap. o16 18
Shiocton, Wis. D5, h8 88
Shiogama, Jap. G10 18
Shiojiri, Jap. .m16 18
Ship Bottom, N.J. D4 74
Shipman, Va. C4 85
Shippegan, N.B., Can. B5 43
Shippegan Gully, N.B., Can. *B5 43
Shippensburg, Pa. F7 81
Shirane-san, mtn., Jap. H9 18
Shīrāz, Iran G8 16
Shīrbin, Eg. G8 14
Shiremanstown, Pa. *F8 81
Shiribeshi-yama, mtn., Jap. E10 18
Shirley, Ind. E6 59
Shirley, Mass. .A4 65
Shirley, Mont. .D11 70
Shirley, N.Y. *n15 75
Shirley, mtn., Wyo. D6 89
Shirntoru, see Makarov, Sov. Un.
Shiroishi, Jap. G10 18
Shirotori, Jap. n15 18
Shitara, Jap. .n16 18
Shively, Ky. B4, g11 62
Shizuoka, Jap. I9, o17 18
Shizuoka, pref., Jap. *I9 18
Shkodër (Scutari), Alb. A2 14
Shkodër (Scutari), pref., Alb. *A2 14
Shoal Lake, Man., Can. D1 40
Shoals, Ind. G4 59
Shoemakersville, Pa. E10 81
Sholāpur, India .E6 20
Shore Acres, Calif. *D2 50
Shore Acres, Mass. h13 65
Shoreview, Minn. *F5 67
Shorewood, Minn. *F5 67
Shorewood, Wis. E6, m12 88
Shorewood Hills, Wis. *E4 88
Short Beach, Conn. D5 52
Shortsville, N.Y. C3 75
Shoshone, Idaho G4 57
Shoshone, co., Idaho B3 57
Shoshoni, Wyo. C4 89
Show Low, Ariz. B3 48
Shpola, Sov. Un. G8 12
Shreve, Ohio B3 78
Shreveport, La. B2 63

Shrewsbury, Eng. D5 4
Shrewsbury, Mass. B4 65
Shrewsbury, Mo. *C7 69
Shrewsbury, N.J. C4 74
Shrewsbury, Pa. G8 81
Shropshire, co., Eng. *D5 4
Shrub Oak, N.Y. *D7 75
Shuangcheng, China D3 18
Shuangliao, China C9 17
Shuangshan, China E1 18
Shuangyang, China E2 18
Shuangyashan, China C5 18
Shubenacadie, N.S., Can. D6 43
Shubrā al Khaymah, Eg. *G8 14
Shuksan, mtn., Wash. A4 86
Shulan, China D3 18
Shulaps, peak, B.C., Can. D6 37
Shullsburg, Wis. F3 88
Shumen, Bul. D8 10
Shumen, co., Bul. *D8 10
Shumerlya, Sov. Un. D16 12
Shuya, Sov. Un. C13 12
Shuzenji, Jap. o17 18
Shwebo, Bur. .D10 20
Shwegyin, Bur. *B1 19
Siālkot, Pak. B5 20
Siam, see Thailand, Asia
Sian see Xi'an, China
Siauliai, Sov. Un. D4 12
Sibenik, Yugo. .D2 10
Sibert, Ky. C6 62
Sibi, Pak. C4 20
Sibiu, Rom. C7 10
Sibley, Iowa A2 60
Sibley, La. B2 63
Sibley, co., Minn. F4 67
Sibolga, Indon. E1 19
Sibsagar, India C9 20
Sibu, Mala. E4 19
Sicard, La. B3 63
Sichuan, prov., China E5 17
Sicilia, pol. dist., It. *F4 9
Sicily, isl., It. F4 9
Sicily Island, La. C4 63
Sicklerville, N.J. D3 74
Sicuaní, Peru D3 31
Siderno Marina, It. E6 9
Sidhirokastron, Grc. B4 14
Sidi bel Abbès, Alg. A4 22
Sidi Ifni, Mor. C2 22
Sidmouth, Eng. E5 4
Sidney, B.C., Can. E6, g12 37
Sidney, Iowa D2 60
Sidney, Mont. C12 70
Sidney, Nebr. C3 71
Sidney, N.Y. C5 75
Sidney, Ohio B1 78
Sidney Center, N.Y. C5 75
Siedlce, Pol. B7 7
Siegburg, Ger., Fed. Rep. of C3 6
Siegen, Ger., Fed. Rep. of C4 6
Siemianowice Slaskie, Pol. g10 7
Siem Reap, Kam. C2 19
Siena, It. C3 9
Sieradz, Pol. C5 7
Siero, Sp. A3 8
Sierpc, Pol. B5 7
Sierra, co., Calif. C3 50
Sierra, co., N.Mex. C5 48
Sierra Blanca, Tex. o12 84
Sierra Leone, country, Afr. G2 22
Sierra Madre, Calif. m12 50
Sierra Nevada, mts., Calif. C3 50
Sierraville, Calif. C3 50
Sierra Vieja, mts., Tex. o12 84
Sierra Vista, Ariz. *D3 48
Sifton, Man., Can. D1 40
Sighet, Rom. B6 10
Sighişoara, Rom. B7 10
Sigli, Indon. k11 19
Signal, mtn., Va. g11 85
Signal Hill, Calif. *F4 50
Signal Hill, Ill. *E3 58
Signal Mountain, Tenn. D8, h11 83
Sigourney, Iowa C5 60
Siguiri, Guinea .F3 22
Sihaus, Peru C2 31
Siirt, Tur. D13 14
Sīkar, India C6 20
Sikasso, Mali F3 22
Sikeston, Mo. E8 69
Sikionia, Grc. C4 14
Silao, Mex. m13 34
Silchar, India D9 20
Siler City, N.C. B3 76
Silesia, reg., Pol. C4 7
Siletz, Oreg. C3 80
Silifke, Tur. D9 14
Silīguri, India C8 20
Silistra, Bul. C8 10
Sillery, Que., Can. n17 42
Siloam Springs, Ark. A1 49

Silsbee, Tex. D5 84
Siluria, Ala. B3 46
Silva, Mo. D7 69
Silva Jardim, Braz. h6 30
Silver Bay, Minn. C7 67
Silver Bow, co., Mont. E4 70
Silver Bow Park, Mont. D4 70
Silver City, N. Mex. C4 48
Silver Creek, N.Y. C1 75
Silverdale, Wash. B3, e10 86
Silver Grove, Ky. h14 62
Silver Hill, Md. .f9 53
Silver Lake, Ind. B6 59
Silver Lake, Mass. f11 65
Silver Lake, Minn. F4 67
Silver Lake, Ohio *A4 78
Silver Lake, Wis. F5, n11 88
Silver Spring, Md. C3, f8 53
Silver Springs, N.Y. C2 75
Silverthrone, mtn., B.C., Can. D4 37
Silvertip, mtn., Mont. C3 70
Silverton, Colo. D3 51
Silverton, Idaho B3 57
Silverton, Ohio o13 78
Silverton, Oreg. B4, h12 80
Silverton, Tex. .B2 84
Silvia, Col. C2 32
Silvis, Ill. B3 58
Silvis Heights, Ill. *B3 58
Silwān, Jordan *C3 15
Simav, Tur. C7 14
Simcoe, Ont., Can. E4 41
Simcoe, co., Ont., Can. C4 41
Simferopol, Sov. Un. I10 12
Simi, Calif. m11 50
Simití, Col. B3 32
Simla, India B6 20
Simleul-Silvaniei, Rom. B6 10
Simmesport, La. D4 63
Simpson, N.C. .B5 76
Simpson, Pa. .C11 81
Simpson, co., Ky. D3 62
Simpson, co., Miss. D4 68
Simpsonville, S.C. B3 82
Simsbury, Conn. B5 52
Sinaia, Rom. C7 10
Sinajana, Guam *F6 2
Sinaloa de Leyva, Mex. B3 34
Sinaloa, state, Mex. C3 34
Sinanju, Kor. G2 18
Sincé, Col. B2 32
Sincelejo, Col. .B2 32
Sinclair, Wyo. E5 89
Sinclairville, N.Y. C1 75
Sind, reg., Pak. C4 20
Sinelnikovo, Sov. Un. G10 12
Sines, Port. D1 8
Singapore, Singapore E2 19
Singapore, country, Asia E2 19
Singaraja, Indon. G5 19
Singkawang, Indon. E3 19
Singleton, Austl. *F9 25
Sinhung, Kor. F3 18
Siniscola, It. D2 9
Sinj, Yugo. D3 10
Sinjah, Sud. F4 23
Sinking Spring, Pa. *F9 81
Sînnicolau-Mare, Rom. B5 10
Sinnūris, Eg. H8 14
Sinpo, Tur. A10 14
Sinpo, Kor. F4 18
Sintang, Indon. E4 19
Sint-Niklaas, Bel. B6 5
Sinton, Tex. E4 84
Sintra, Port. f9 8
Sinuiju, Kor. F2 18
Sion, Switz. E3 6
Sioux, co., Iowa A1 60
Sioux, co., Nebr. B2 71
Sioux, co., N. Dak. D5 77
Sioux Center, Iowa A1 60
Sioux City, Iowa B1 60
Sioux Falls, S. Dak. G9 77
Sioux Lookout, Ont., Can. o17 41
Sioux Rapids, Iowa B2 60
Sipes (Midway), Fla. *D5 54
Siping, China C9 17
Sipsey, Ala. B2 46
Siracusa, It. F5 9
Sirājganj, Bngl. D8 20
Sir Douglas, mtn., Alta., Can. D3 38
Siren, Wis. C1 88
Siret, Rom. B8 10
Siros, Grc. D5 14
Sirpur, India E6 20
Sirsa, India C6 20
Sir Wilfrid, mtn., Que., Can. C2 42
Sisak, Yugo. C3 10
Siskiyou, co., Calif. B2 50
Sisseton, S.Dak. E9 77
Sister Bay, Wis. C6 88
Sisters, Oreg. C5 80
Sistersville, W. Va. B4 87

Sītāpur, India C7 20
Sitionuevo, Col. A3 32
Sitka, Alsk. D12 47
Sittwe, Burma .D9 20
Sivas, Tur. C11 14
Siverek, Tur. .D12 14
Sivrihisar, Tur. .C8 14
Skagit, co., Wash. A4 86
Skamania, co., Wash. D3 86
Skanderborg, co., Den. *I3 11
Skaneateles, N.Y. C4 75
Skara, Swe. H5 11
Skegness, Eng. D7 4
Skellefteå, Swe. E9 11
Skidmore, Tex. E4 84
Skien, Nor. H3, p27 11
Skierniewice, Pol. C6 7
Skihist, mtn., B.C., Can. D7 37
Skikda (Phillippeville), Alg. A6 22
Skokie, Ill. A6, h9 58
Skole, Sov. Un. D7 7
Skopin, Sov. Un. E13 12
Skopje (Skoplje), Yugo. D5 10
Skövde, Swe. H5 11
Skovorodino, Sov. Un. D15 13
Skowhegan, Maine D3 64
Skradin, Yugo. D2 10
Skvira, Sov. Un. G7 12
Skyland, N.C. .f10 76
Sky Manor, N.J. C4 74
Slagelse, Den. .A1 7
Slamet, mtn., Indon. G3 19
Slănic, Rom. C7 10
Slany, Czech. .n17 7
Slater, Iowa C4, e8 60
Slater, Mo. B4 69
Slater, S.C. A3 82
Slatersville, R.I. B10 52
Slatina, Rom. C7 10
Slatington, Pa. E10 81
Slaton, Tex. C2 48
Slavgorod, Sov. Un. D10 13
Slavonia, reg., Yugo. C3 10
Slavonska Pozega, Yugo. C3 10
Slavyanoserbsk, Sov. Un. q21 12
Slavyansk, Sov. Un. G11, q20 12
Slavyanskaya, Sov. Un. I12 12
Slayton, Minn. .G3 67
Sleepy Eye, Minn. F4 67
Sleepy Hollow, Calif. *D2 50
Sleepy Hollow, Va. *B5 85
Slickville, Pa. F2 81
Slidell, La. D6, h12 63
Slide, mtn. C6 75
Sliderock, mtn., Mont. D3 70
Slieve Donard, mtn., N. Ire. C3 4
Sligo, Ire. C2 4
Sligo, Pa. D3 81
Sligo, co., Ire. *C2 4
Slinger, Wis. E5 88
Slingerlands, N.Y. *C7 75
Slippery Rock, Pa. D1 81
Sliven, Bul. D8 10
Sloan, Iowa B1 60
Sloan, N.Y. C2 75
Sloatsburg, N.Y. A4 75
Slobozia, Rom. C8 10
Slocomb, Ala. .D4 46
Slonim, Sov. Un. E5 12
Slope, co., N. Dak. D2 77
Slough, Eng. k11 4
Slovakia (Slovensko),
  reg., Czech. D5 7
Slovan, Pa. F1 81
Slovenia, reg., Yugo. C2 10
Slovenia, rep., Yugo. *C2 10
Słupca, Pol. B4 7
Słupsk, Pol. A4 7
Slutsk, Sov. Un. s31 12
Slyudyanka, Sov. Un. D13 13
Smackover, Ark. D3 49
Smederevo, Yugo. C5 10
Smela, Sov. Un. G8 12
Smelterville, Idaho B2 57
Smethport, Pa. C5 81
Smidovich, Sov. Un. B6 18
Smith, co., Kans. C5 61
Smith, co., Miss. C4 68
Smith, co., Tenn. C8 83
Smith, co., Tex. C5 84
Smith, peak, Idaho A2 57
Smith Center, Kans. C5 61
Smithers, B.C., Can. B4 37
Smithers, W. Va. C3, m13 87
Smithfield, N.C. B4 76
Smithfield, Ohio B5 78
Smithfield, Pa. *E5 81
Smithfield, Pa. .G2 81
Smithfield, Utah A6 72
Smithfield, Va. k14 85
Smithmill, Pa. E5 81
Smith River, Calif. B1 50

Smithsburg, Md. A2 53
Smiths Falls, Ont., Can. C8 41
Smithton, Austl. o15 25
Smithtown, N.Y. F4 52
Smithville, Mo. B3, h10 69
Smithville, Ohio B4 78
Smithville, Tenn. D8 83
Smithville, Tex. D4 84
Smock, Pa. *G2 81
Smokey Dome, mtn., Idaho F4 57
Smoky, mts., Idaho F4 57
Smoky Lake, Alta., Can. B4 38
Smolensk, Sov. Un. D8 12
Smooth Rock Falls, Ont., Can. o19 41
Smyre, N.C. *B1 76
Smyrna, Del. B6 53
Smyrna, Ga. C2, h7 55
Smyrna, Tenn. B5 83
Smyrna, see Izmir, Tur.
Smyth, co., Va. f10 85
Snake, riv., U.S. B3 45
Sneads, Fla. B2 54
Sneads Ferry, N.C. C5 76
Sneek, Neth. A6 5
Snezhnoye, Sov. Un. q21 12
Snohomish, Wash. B3 86
Snohomish, co., Wash. A4 86
Snoqualmie, Wash. B4 86
Snow, mtn., Calif. C2 50
Snow, mtn., Maine C2 64
Snow, peak, Wash. A7 86
Snowdon, mtn., Wales D4 4
Snowflake, Ariz. B3 48
Snow Hill, Md. D7 53
Snow Hill, N.C. B5 76
Snow Lake, Man., Can. B1 40
Snowshoe, peak, Mont. B1 70
Snowyside, peak, Idaho F4 57
Snyatyn, Sov. Un. A7 10
Snyder, Okla. C3 79
Snyder, Tex. C2 84
Snyder, co., Pa. E7 81
Soap Lake, Wash. B6 86
Soatá, Col. B3 32
Sobinka, Sov. Un. D13 12
Sobota Rimavská, Czech. D6 7
Sobral, Braz. *D6 27
Socaste, S.C. D9 82
Sochaczew, Pol. B6 7
Sochi, Sov. Un. *E6 13
Society, is., Fr. Polynesia H10 2
Society Hill, S.C. B8 82
Socorro, Col. B3 32
Socorro, N. Mex. B5 48
Socorro, co., N. Mex. C5 48
Soc Trang, Viet. D3 19
Socuéllamos, Sp. C4 8
Soda Springs, Idaho G7 57
Soddy-Daisy, Tenn. D8, h11 83
Söderhamn, Swe. G7 11
Södertälje, Swe. t35 11
Sodus, N.Y. B3 75
Soest, Ger., Fed. Rep. of C4 6
Sofia (Sofiya), Bul. D6 10
Sofiya, see Sofia, Bul.
Sofiya, co., Bul. *D6 10
Sofiyevka, Sov. Un. G9 12
Sogamoso, Col. B3 32
Sogn og Fjordane, co., Nor. *G1 11
Sointula, B.C., Can. D4 37
Soissons, Fr. C5 5
Sokal, Sov. Un. F5 12
Sokcho, Kor. G4 18
Söke, Tur. *D6 14
Soke of Peterborough, co., Eng. .. *D6 4
Sokol, Sov. Un. B13 12
Sokołow, Pol. B7 7
Sokoto, Nig. F6 22
Solana, Fla. F5 54
Solana Beach, Calif. *F5 50
Solano, Phil. *B6 19
Solano, co., Calif. C2 50
Soldiers Grove, Wis. E3 88
Soledad, Calif. D3 50
Soledad, Col. A3 32
Solihull, Eng. *D6 4
Soliman, Tun. F3 9
Solikamsk, Sov. Un. D8 13
Solingen, Ger., Fed. Rep. of C3 6
Solleftea, Swe. F7 11
Sóller, Sp. C7 8
Solna, Swe. H7 11
Solomon, Kans. D6 61
Solomon Is., country, Oceania G7 2
Solon, Iowa C6 60
Solon, Maine D3 64
Solon, Ohio A4 78
Solonika, see Thessaloniki, Grc.
Solon Springs, Wis. B2 88
Solothurn, Switz. E3 6
Solothurn, canton, Switz. E3 6
Solovyevsk, Sov. Un. D15 13
Soltau, Ger., Fed. Rep. of B4 6

Solvang, Calif. *E3 50
Solvay, N.Y. B4 75
Soma, Tur. *C6 14
Somalia, country, Afr. H6 23
Sombor, Yugo. C4 10
Sombra, Ont., Can. E2 41
Sombrerete, Mex. C4 34
Somerdale, N.J. D2 74
Somers, Conn. B7 52
Somers, Mont. B2 70
Somers, Man., Can. E2 40
Somerset, Ky. C5 62
Somerset, Md. *C3 53
Somerset, Mass. C5 65
Somerset, Ohio C3 78
Somerset, Pa. F3 81
Somerset, Wis. C1 88
Somerset, co., Eng. *E5 4
Somerset, co., Maine C2 64
Somerset, co., Md. D6 53
Somerset, co., N.J. C3 74
Somerset, co., Pa. G3 81
Somerset, isl., N.W. Ter., Can. ... B15 36
Somerset East, S.Afr. G5 24
Somers Point, N.J. E3 74
Somersworth, N.H. E6 73
Somerton, Ariz. C1 48
Somervell, co., Tex. C4 84
Somerville, Mass. B5, g11 65
Somerville, N.J. B3 74
Somerville, Tenn. B2 83
Somerville, Tex. D4 84
Somme, dept., Fr. C5 5
Somogy, co., Hung. *B3 10
Somonauk, Ill. B5 58
Sonchon, Kor. G2 18
Sønderborg, Den. A4 6
Sønderborg, co., Den. *A4 6
Sondershausen, Ger. Dem. Rep. .. C5 6
Sondrio, It. A2 9
Sonepur, India D7 20
Songjiang, China E9 17
Songjin, see Kimchaek, Kor.
Songkhla, Thai. D2 19
Songnim (Kyomipo), Kor. G2 18
Son La, Viet. G5 17
Sonneberg, Ger. Dem. Rep. C5 6
Sonobe, Jap. n14 18
Sonoma, Calif. C2 50
Sonoma, co., Calif. C2 50
Sonora, Ariz. C3, D3 48
Sonora, Calif. D3 50
Sonora, Tex. D2 84
Sonora, state, Mex. B2 34
Sonsón, Col. B2 32
Sonsonate, Sal. E7 34
Son Tay, Viet. G6 17
Soperton, Ga. D4 55
Sophia, W.Va. D3 87
Sopot, Pol. A5 7
Sopron, Hung. B3 10
Sora, It. D4 9
Sorbas, Sp. D4 8
Sorel, Que., Can. C4 42
Sorento, Ill. E4 58
Soresina, It. B2 9
Soria, Sp. B4 8
Soria, prov., Sp. *B4 8
Soriano, dept., Ur. *E1 30
Søro, Den. *J4 6
Sorocaba, Braz. C3, m8 30
Soroki, Sov. Un. G7 12
Sorong, Indon. F8 19
Soroti, Ug. H4 23
Sorrento, It. D5 9
Sorrento, La. D5, h10 63
Sorrento, Maine *D5 64
Sorsogon, Phil. C6 19
Sorsogon, prov., Phil. *C6 19
Sortavala, Sov. Un. G14 11
Sor Trondelag, co., Nor. *F4 11
Sosnovka, Sov. Un. E13 12
Sosnowiec, Pol. C5, g10 7
Sotteville-lès-Rouen, Fr. C4 5
Soudan, Minn. C6 67
Souderton, Pa. F11 81
Souflion, Grc. B6 14
Soufriere, St. Lucia J14 35
Souk-el Arba, Tun. F2 9
Soul, see Seoul, Kor.
Soulanges, co., Que., Can. D3 42
Sound Beach, N.Y. *n15 75
Soure, Braz. *D6 27
Souris, Man., Can. E1 40
Souris East, P.E.I., Can. C7 43
Sourlake, Tex. D5 84
Sousse, Tun. A7 22
South, div., Ice. *n21 11
South, isl., N.Z. O12 26
South Acton, Mass. g10 65
South Africa, country, Afr. F5 24
South Amboy, N.J. C4, m7 74
South America, cont. 27

South Amherst, Mass. B2 65
South Amherst, Ohio A3 78
Southampton, Ont., Can. C3 42
Southampton, Eng. E6 4
Southampton, N.Y. n16 75
Southampton, Pa. *F11 81
Southampton, co., Va. D5 85
Southampton Island, Can. D16 36
South Apopka, Fla. *D5 54
South Arabia, see Yemen, People's
  Democratic Republic of, country, Asia
South Ashburnham, Mass. A4 65
South Australia, state, Austl. E5 25
South Barre, Mass. B3 65
South Bathurst, N.S., Can. *B4 43
South Bay, Fla. F6 54
South Bellingham, Mass. B5 65
South Belmar, N.J. C4 74
South Belmont, N.C. *B1 76
South Beloit, Ill. A4 58
South Bend, Ind. A5 59
South Bend, Wash. C2 86
South Bennettsville, S.C. *B8 82
South Berwick, Maine E2 64
South Boise, Idaho *F2 57
Southboro, Mass. B4, g9 65
South Boston (Independent City),
  Va. D4 85
South Bound Brook, N.J. *B3 74
Southbridge, Mass. B3 65
South Broadway, Wash. *C5 86
South Brook, Newf., Can. *D3 44
South Burlington, Vt. *C1 73
South Carolina, state, U.S. 82
South Charleston, Ohio C2 78
South Charleston, W.Va. m12 87
South Chelmsford, Mass. C1 65
South Chicago Heights, Ill. m9 58
South China, sea, Asia H14 16
South Cleveland, Tenn. *D9 83
South Clinton, Tenn. *C9 83
South Coatesville, Pa. *G10 81
South Coffeyville, Okla. A6 79
South Congaree, S.C. D5 82
South Connellsville, Pa. G2 81
South Corning, N.Y. *C3 75
South Dakota, state, U.S. 77
South Dartmouth, Mass. C6 65
South Dayton, N.Y. C1 75
South Daytona, Fla. C5 54
South Decatur, Ga. *C2 55
South Deerfield, Mass. B2 65
South Dennis, Mass. C7 65
South Dum-Dum, India *D8 20
South Duxbury, Mass. B6 65
South Easton, Mass. B5 65
South Elgin, Ill. B5, h8 58
South El Monte, Calif. *E5 50
Southend-on-Sea, Eng. E7 4
Southern Cross, Austl. F2 25
Southern Pines, N.C. B3 76
Southern Shops, S.C. *B4 82
Southern View, Ill. *D4 58
Southern Yemen, see Yemen, Peoples
  Democratic Republic of, country, Asia
South Essex, Mass. A6 65
South Euclid, Ohio g9 78
South Fallsburg, N.Y. D6 75
South Farmingdale, N.Y. *E7 75
South Fayetteville, N.C. *B3 76
Southfield, Mass. B1 65
Southfield, Mich. o15 66
South Floral Park, N.Y. *E7 75
South Fork, Pa. F4 81
South Fort George, B.C., Can. C6 37
South Fulton, Tenn. A3 83
South Fulton, Tenn. A3 83
South Gate, Calif. n12 50
Southgate, Ky. h14 62
Southgate, Mich. p15 66
South Glastonbury, Conn. C6 52
South Glens Falls, N.Y. *B7 75
South Grafton, Mass. B4 65
South Greensburg, Pa. *F2 81
South Greenwood, S.C. C3 82
South Hackensack, N.J. *B4 74
South Hadley, Mass. B2 65
South Hadley Falls, Mass. B2 65
South Hamilton, Mass. A6, f12 65
South Hanover, Mass. h12 65
South Harriman, Tenn. *D9 83
South Harwich, Mass. C7 65
South Haven, Mich. F4 66
South Hempstead, N.Y. *E7 75
South Henderson, N.C. *A4 76
South Hill, Va. D4 85
South Holland, Ill. k9 58
South Holland (Zuid-Holland),
  prov., Neth. *A6 5
South Hooksett, N.H. D4 73
South Houston, Tex. r14 84
South Huntington, N.Y. *D3 75
South Hutchinson, Kans. f11 61

Southington, Conn. C5 52
South International Falls, Minn. ... B5 67
South Jacksonville, Ill. D3 58
South Jordan, Utah *A6 72
Southkent, Mich. *F5 66
South Laguna, Calif. *F5 50
Southlake, Tex. *C4 84
South Lake Tahoe, Calif. C4 50
South Lancaster, Mass. B4 65
Southland, Mich. *F6 66
Southlawn, Ill. *D4 58
South Lebanon, Ohio C1 78
South Lyon, Mich. F7, p14 66
South Mansfield, La. B2 63
South Miami, Fla. G6, s13 54
South Milwaukee, Wis. F6, n12 88
South Modesto, Calif. *D3 50
South Monroe, Mich. *G7 66
South Montrose, Pa. C10 81
South Mt. Vernon, Ohio *B3 78
South Nelson, N.S., Can. *C4 43
South Nelson Village, B.C., Can. .. *E9 37
South New Castle, Pa. *D1 81
South Nyack, N.Y. g9 75
South Ogden, Utah A6, C2 72
Southold, N.Y. m16 75
South Orange, N.J. B4 74
South Oroville, Calif. *C3 50
South Paris, Maine D2 64
South Park, Ill. *B5 58
South Pasadena, Calif. *E4 50
South Patrick Shores, Fla. D6 54
South Pekin, Ill. C4 58
South Pittsburg, Tenn. D8 83
South Plainfield, N.J. B4 74
South Point, Ohio D3 78
South Porcupine, Ont., Can. o19 41
Southport, Austl. E9 25
Southport, Eng. D5 4
Southport, Fla. u16 54
Southport, Ind. E5, m10 59
Southport, N.Y. *C4 75
Southport, N.C. D4 76
South Portland, Maine E2, g7 64
South Pottstown, Pa. *F10 81
South Range, Mich. A2 66
South Renovo, Pa. D6 81
South Revelstoke, B.C., Can. D8 37
South River, Ont., Can. B5 42
South River, N.J. C4 74
South Rockwood, Mich. *F7 66
South Roxana, Ill. *E4 58
South Russell, Ohio *A4 78
South St. Paul, Minn. F5, n12 67
South Salisbury, N.C. *B2 76
South Salt Lake, Utah C2 72
South San Francisco, Calif. h8 50
South San Gabriel, Calif. *F4 50
South Shields, Eng. C6 4
South Shore, Mo. f12 69
Southside Estates, Fla. *B5 54
South Side Place, Tex. r14 84
South Sioux City, Nebr. B9 71
South Stickney, Ill. k9 58
South Streator, Ill. *B5 58
South Swansea, Mass. C5 65
South Taft, Calif. *E4 50
South Temple, Pa. *F10 81
South Toms River, N.J. D4 74
South Torrington, Wyo. D8 89
South Trail, Fla. q10 54
South Tucson, Ariz. C3 48
South Uniontown, Pa. *G2 81
South Walpole, Mass. h10 65
South Waverly, Pa. C8 81
South Webster, Ohio D3 78
Southwest, Pa. F2 81
South West, div., Ice. n22 11
South West Africa, see Namibia,
  country, Afr.
South Westbury, N.Y. *E7 75
Southwest Dillon, S.C. *C9 82
Southwestern, mts., Va. B4 85
South West Fargo, N.Dak. D9 77
Southwest Greensburg, Pa. *F2 81
Southwest Harbor, Maine D4 64
South Whitley, Ind. B6 59
Southwick, Mass. B2 65
South Williamson, Ky. C7 62
South Williamsport, Pa. D7 81
South Wilmington, Ill. B5 58
South Windermere, S.C. *F8 82
South Windham, Maine E2, g7 64
South Windsor, Conn. B6 52
Southwood Acres, Conn. *B6 52
South Yarmouth, Mass. C7 65
South Zanesville, Ohio C3 78
Sovetsk (Tilsit), Sov. Un. A6 7
Sovetskaya Gavan, Sov. Un. E17 13
Soviet Union (U.S.S.R.), country,
  Eur. Asia 13

Spa, Bel. B6   5
Spain, country, Eur. 8
Spalding, Eng. D6   4
Spalding, Nebr. C7   71
Spalding, co., Ga. C2   55
Spanaway, Wash. B3   86
Spangler, Pa. E4   81
Spaniard's Bay, Newf., Can. E5   44
Spanish, Ont., Can. A2   41
Spanish Fork, Utah A6, D2   72
Spanish Sahara, see Western Sahara, Afr.
Spanish Town, Jam. F5   35
Sparkill, N.Y. *D6   75
Sparkman, Ark. D3   49
Sparks, Ga. E3   55
Sparks, Nev. B2   72
Sparlingville, Mich. *F8   66
Sparrows Point, Md. B5   53
Sparta, Ga. C4   55
Sparta, Ill. E4   58
Sparta, Mich. E5   66
Sparta, N.J. A3   74
Sparta, N.C. A1   76
Sparta, Tenn. D8   83
Sparta, Wis. E3   88
Sparta, mtn., N.J. B3   74
Spartanburg, S.C. B4   82
Spartanburg, co., S.C. B3   82
Sparti (Sparta), Grc. D4   14
Spassk-Dalniy, Sov. Un. E16   13
Spearfish, S.Dak. F2   77
Spearman, Tex. A2   84
Spearville, Kans. E4   61
Speed, Ind. H6   59
Speedway, Ind. E5, k10   59
Speers, Pa. *F2   81
Speight, Ky. C7   62
Spenard, Alsk. *C10   47
Spencer, Ind. F4   59
Spencer, Iowa A2   60
Spencer, Mass. B4   65
Spencer, Nebr. B7   71
Spencer, N.Y. C4   75
Spencer, N.C. B2   76
Spencer, Ohio A3   78
Spencer, Okla. *B4   79
Spencer, W.Va. C3   87
Spencer, Wis. D3   88
Spencer, co., Ind. H4   59
Spencer, co., Ky. B4   62
Spencerport, Ky. B3   75
Spencerville, Ohio B1   78
Sperry, Okla. A6   79
Speyer, Ger., Fed. Rep. of D4   6
Spiceland, Ind. E7   59
Spinazzola, It. D6   9
Spindale, N.C. B1   76
Spink, co., S. Dak. F7   77
Spirit Lake, Idaho B3   57
Spirit Lake, Iowa A2   60
Spirit River, Alta., Can. B1   38
Spiro, Okla. B7   79
Spišská Nová Ves, Czech. D6   7
Spittal an der Drau, Aus. E6   6
Split, Yugo. D3   10
Spokane, Wash. B8, g14   86
Spokane, co., Wash. B8   86
Spoleto, It. C4   9
Spooner, Wis. C2   88
Spotswood, N.J. C4   74
Spotsylvania, co., Va. B5   85
Sprague, W.Va. n13   87
Spray, N.C. A3   76
Spreckels, Calif. *D3   50
Spreckelsville, Haw. *C5   56
Spremberg, Ger. Dem. Rep. C7   6
Spring, Tex. q14   84
Spring Arbor, Mich. F6   66
Springboro, Ohio C1   78
Spring City, Pa. F10   81
Spring City, Tenn. D9   83
Springdale, Ark. A1   49
Springdale, Newf., Can. D3   44
Springdale, Ohio n13   78
Springdale, Pa. E2, h14   81
Springdale, S.C. *D5   82
Springer, N. Mex. A6   48
Springfield, Colo. D8   51
Springfield, Fla. v16   54
Springfield, Ill. D4   58
Springfield, Ky. C4   62
Springfield, Mass. B2   65
Springfield, Minn. F4   67
Springfield, Mo. D4   69
Springfield, Nebr. C9, g12   71
Springfield, N.J. B4   74
Springfield, Ohio C2   78
Springfield, Oreg. *C4   80
Springfield, Pa. *B11   81
Springfield, S.C. E5   82
Springfield, S.Dak. H8   77
Springfield, Tenn. A5   83
Springfield, Vt. E3   73

Springfield, Va. g12   85
Springfield Place, Mich. *F5   66
Spring Glen, Fla. *B5   54
Spring Green, Wis. E3   88
Spring Grove, Minn. G7   67
Spring Grove, Pa. G8   81
Springhill, N.S., Can. D6   43
Spring Hill, Kans. D9   61
Springhill, La. A2   63
Spring Hill Pa. *F4   81
Spring Hope, N.C. B4   76
Spring Lake, Mich. E4   66
Spring Lake, N.J. C4   74
Spring Lake, N.C. B3   76
Spring Lake Heights, N.J. C4   74
Spring Lake Park, Minn. *E5   67
Springlee, Ky. *H6   62
Spring Mills, S.C. *B6   82
Springmont, Pa. *F10   81
Springport, Mich. F6   66
Springs, S. Afr. *F5   24
Springsure, Aust. B8   25
Springvale, Maine E2   64
Spring Valley, Calif. o16   50
Spring Valley, Ill. B4   58
Spring Valley, Minn. G6   67
Spring Valley, N.Y. g12   75
Spring Valley, Ohio C1   78
Spring Valley, Tex. *E5   84
Springville, Iowa B6   60
Springville, N.Y. C2   75
Springville, Utah A6, D2   72
Spruce Knob, mtn., W.Va. C5   87
Spruce Pine, N.C. f10   76
Spur, Tex. C2   84
Squamish, B.C., Can. E6   37
Squatteck, Que., Can. B9   42
Squaw Lake, Minn. C4   67
Squaw Rapids, Sask., Can. D4   39
Srbobran, Yugo. C4   10
Sredne-Kolymsk, Sov. Un. C18   13
Sremska Mitrovica, Yugo. C4   10
Sretensk, Sov. Un. D14   13
Sri Lanka, country, Asia G7   20
Srīnagar, India B6   20
Staatsburg, N.Y. D7   75
Stade, Ger., Fed. Rep. of B4   6
Stafford, Eng. D5   4
Stafford, Kans. E5   61
Stafford, Tex. *E5   84
Stafford; co., Eng. *D5   4
Stafford, co., Kans. D5   61
Stafford, co., Va. B5   85
Stafford Springs, Conn. B7   52
Staffordsville, Ky. C7   62
Staines, Eng. m11   4
Stains, Fr. g10   5
Stambaugh, Mich. B2   66
Stamford, Conn. E2   52
Stamford, N.Y. C6   75
Stamford, Tex. C3   84
Stamps, Ark. D2   49
Stanaford, W.Va. D3, n13   87
Stanberry, Mo. A3   69
Standale, Mich. *F5   66
Standerton, S. Afr. F5   24
Standish, Mich. E7   66
Stanfield, Oreg. B7   80
Stanford, Calif. *D2   50
Stanford, Ky. C5   62
Stanford, Mont. C6   70
Stanhope, N.J. B3   74
Stanislaus, co., Calif. D3   50
Stanke Dimitrov, Bul. D6   10
Stanley, Falk. Is. I5   27
Stanley, N.C. B1   76
Stanley, N.Dak. B3   77
Stanley, Va. B4   85
Stanley, Wis. D3   88
Stanley, co., S.Dak. F5   77
Stanleytown, Va. D3   85
Stanleyville, N.C. *A2   76
Stanly, co., N.C. B2   76
Stanstead, Que., Can. D5   42
Stanstead, co., Que., Can. D5   42
Stanthorpe, Austl. E9   25
Stanton, Calif. *F5   50
Stanton, Del. *A6   53
Stanton, Mich. E5   66
Stanton, Nebr. C8   71
Stanton, Tex. C2   84
Stanton, co., Kans. E2   61
Stanton, co., Nebr. C8   71
Stantonsburg, N.C. B5   76
Stanwood, Wash. A3   86
Staples, Minn. D4   67
Star, N.C. B3   76
Starachowice, Pol. C6   7
Staraya Russa, Sov. Un. C8   12
Stara Zagora, Bul. D7   10
Stara-Zagora, co., Bul. *D7   10
Starbuck, Minn. *E3   67
Star City, Ark. D4   49

Star City, W.Va. B5   87
Stargard, Pol. B3   7
Stargo, Ariz. C4   48
Starjunction, Pa. *F2   81
Stark, co., Ill. B4   58
Stark, co., N.Dak. D3   77
Stark, co., Ohio B4   78
Starke, Fla. C4   54
Starke, co., Ind. B4   59
Starkey, Va. C3   85
Starkville, Miss. B5   68
Starobelsk, Sov. Un. G12   12
Starodub, Sov. Un. E9   12
Starogard, Pol. B5   7
Starr, co., Tex. F3   84
Startex, S.C. B3   82
Staryy Oskol, Sov. Un. F11   12
Stassfurt, Ger. Dem. Rep. C5   6
State Center, Iowa B4   60
State College, Miss. B5   68
State College, Pa. E6   81
State Road, N.C. A2   76
Statesboro, Ga. D5   55
Statesville, N.C. A2   76
Staunton, Ill. D4   58
Staunton (Independent City), Va. B3   85
Stavanger, Nor. H1   11
Stavropol, Sov. Un. I13   12
Stawell, Austl. H4   26
Stayner, Ont., Can. C4   41
Stayton, Oreg. C4, k12   80
Steamboat Springs, Colo. A4   51
Stearns, Ky. D5   62
Stearns, co., Minn. E4   67
Steblev, Sov. Un. G8   12
Steele, Mo. E8   69
Steele, co., Minn. F5   67
Steele, co., N.Dak. C8   77
Steeleville, Ill. E4   58
Steelton, Pa. F8   81
Steelville, Mo. D6   69
Steep Rock Lake, Ont., Can. o17   41
Stefanesti, Rom. B8   10
Steger, Ill. B6, m9   58
Steiermark (Styria), state, Aus. *E7   6
Steilacoom, Wash. B3, f10   86
Steinbach, Man., Can. E3   40
Stellarton, N.S., Can. D7   43
Stendal, Ger. Dem. Rep. B5   6
Stephen, Minn. B2   67
Stephens, Ark. D2   49
Stephens, co., Ga. B3   55
Stephens, co., Okla. C4   79
Stephens, co., Tex. C3   84
Stephens City, Va. A4   85
Stephenson, Mich. C3   66
Stephenson, co., Ill. A4   58
Stephenville, Newf., Can. D2   44
Stephenville, Tex. C3   84
Stephenville Crossing, Newf., Can. . . . D2   44
Sterling, Colo. A7   51
Sterling, Ill. B4   58
Sterling, Kans. D5   61
Sterling, Mass. B4   65
Sterling, co., Tex. D2   84
Sterling City, Tex. D2   84
Sterling Heights, Mich. o15   66
Sterlington, La. B3   63
Sterlitamak, Sov. Un. D8   13
Šternberk, Czech. D4   7
Stettin, see Szczecin, Pol.
Stettler, Alta., Can. C4   38
Stetson, mtn., Maine C4   64
Steuben, co., Ind. A7   59
Steuben, co., N.Y. C3   75
Steubenville, Ohio B5   78
Stevenage, Eng. *E6   4
Stevens, co., Kans. E3   61
Stevens, co., Minn. E2   67
Stevens, co., Wash. A7   86
Stevenson, Ala. A4   46
Stevenson, Wash. D4   86
Stevensville, Mich. F4   66
Stevensville, Mont. D2   70
Steveston, B.C., Can. F12   37
Stewardson, Ill. D5   58
Stewart, Minn. F4   67
Stewart, co., Ga. D2   55
Stewart, co., Tenn. A4   83
Stewart Manor, N.Y. *E7   75
Stewartstown, Pa. G8   81
Stewartsville, N.J. B2   74
Stewartville, Minn. G6   67
Stewiacke, N.S., Can. D6   43
Steyr, Aus. D7   6
Stickney, Ill. *B6   58
Stif, Alg. A6   22
Stigler, Okla. B6   79
Stillwater, Minn. E3   67
Stillwater, N.Y. C7   75
Stillwater, Okla. A4   79
Stillwater, co., Mont. E7   70
Stilwell, Okla. B7   79

Stinnett, Tex. B2   84
Štip, Yugo. E6   10
Stirling, Ont., Can. C7   41
Stirling, N.J. B4   74
Stirling, Scot. B5   4
Stirling, co., Scot. *B5   4
Stittsville, Ont., Can. B9   41
Stockbridge, Ga. C2   55
Stockbridge, Mass. B1   65
Stockbridge, Mich. F6   66
Stockdale, Tex. E4, k8   84
Stockerau, Aus. D8   6
Stockholm, Swe. H8, t36   11
Stockholm, co., Swe. *H8   11
Stockport, Eng. D5   4
Stockton, Ala. E2   46
Stockton, Calif. D3, h10   50
Stockton, Ill. A3   58
Stockton, Kans. C4   61
Stockton, Mo. D4   69
Stoddard, co., Mo. E8   69
Stoke-on-Trent, Eng. D5   4
Stokes, co., N.C. A2   76
Stokesdale, N.C. A3   76
Stokke, Nor. p28   11
Stolberg, Ger., Fed. Rep. of C3   6
Stone, Ky. C7   62
Stone, co., Ark. B3   49
Stone, co., Miss. E4   68
Stone, co., Mo. E4   69
Stoneboro, Pa. D1   81
Stonega, Va. f9   85
Stoneham, Mass. g11   65
Stone Harbor, N.J. E3   74
Stonehaven, Scot. B5   4
Stoneleigh, Md. *B4   53
Stone Mountain, Ga. C2, h8   55
Stone Park, Ill. *B6   58
Stones River Homes, Tenn. *B5   83
Stoneville, N.C. A3   76
Stonewall, Man., Can. D3   40
Stonewall, Miss. C5   68
Stonewall, co., Tex. C2   84
Stoney Creek, Ont., Can. D5   41
Stonington, Conn. D9   52
Stonington, Ill. D4   58
Stonington, Maine D4   64
Stony Brook, N.Y. *n15   75
Stony Creek Mills, Pa. *F10   81
Stony Mountain, Man., Can. D3   40
Stony Plain, Alta., Can. C3   38
Stony Point, N.Y. A5   75
Stony Point, N.C. B1   76
Stony Prairie, Ohio *A2   78
Storey, co., Nev. B2   72
Storm Lake, Iowa B2   60
Stormont, co., Ont., Can. B9   41
Stornoway, Scot. A3   4
Storozhinets, Sov. Un. G5   12
Storrs, Conn. B7   52
Story, co., Iowa B4   60
Story City, Iowa B4   60
Stottville, N.Y. C7   75
Stoughton, Sask., Can. H4   39
Stoughton, Mass. B5, h11   65
Stoughton, Wis. F4   88
Stovall, Miss. A3   68
Stover, Mo. C4   69
Stow, Ohio A4   78
Stowe, Pa. F10   81
Stowe Township, Pa. *E2   81
Stoyoma, mtn., B.C., Can. E7   37
Strabane, N. Ire. C3   4
Strabane, Pa. F1   81
Strafford, Mo. D4   69
Strafford, Pa. *G10   81
Strafford, co., N.H. E5   73
Strakonice, Czech. D2   7
Straldzha, Bul. D8   10
Stralsund, Ger. Dem. Rep. A6   6
Strängnäs, Swe. t35   11
Stranraer, Scot. C4   4
Strasbourg, Sask., Can. F3   39
Strasbourg, Fr. D3   6
Strasburg, N.Dak. D5   77
Strasburg, Ohio B4   78
Strasburg, Pa. G9   81
Strasburg, Va. B4   85
Stratford, Calif. D4   50
Stratford, Ont., Can. D3   41
Stratford, Conn. E4   52
Stratford, Iowa B4   60
Stratford, N.J. D2   74
Stratford, Okla. C5   79
Stratford, Tex. A1   84
Stratford, Wis. D3   88
Stratford Hills, Va. *C5   85
Stratford-on-Avon, Eng. D6   4
Strathmore, Calif. D4   50
Strathmore, Alta., Can. D4   38
Strathroy, Ont., Can. *E3   41
Straubing, Ger., Fed. Rep. of D6   6
Strawberry, mts., Oreg. C8   80

Strawberry Point, Calif. *C2 50
Strawberry Point, Iowa B6 60
Strawn, Tex. C3 84
Strážnice, Czech. D4 7
Streamwood, Ill. *A5 58
Streator, Ill. B5 58
Streetsboro, Ohio *A4 78
Streetsville, Ont., Can. m14 41
Strehaia, Rom. C6 10
Stringtown, Ky. B5 62
Stromsburg, Nebr. C8 71
Strong City, Kans. D7 61
Stronghurst, Ill. C3 58
Strongsville, Ohio A4 78
Stroud, Okla. B5 79
Stroudsburg, Pa. E11 81
Stroudsburg West, Pa. *E11 81
Struer, Den. I3 11
Strum, Wis. D2 88
Strumica, Yugo. E6 10
Struthers, Ohio A5 78
Stryker, Ohio A1 78
Stryy, Sov. Un. G4 12
Strzegom, Pol. C4 7
Strzelce, Pol. C5 7
Strzelin, Pol. C4 7
Strzelno, Pol. B5 7
Strzemieszyce, Pol. g10 7
Stuart, Fla. E6 54
Stuart, Iowa C3 60
Stuart, Nebr. B6 71
Stuart, Va. D2 85
Stuarts Draft, Va. B3 85
Stung Treng, Kam. C3 19
Sturbridge, Mass. B3 65
Sturgeon, Mo. B5 69
Sturgeon, Pa. *F1 81
Sturgeon Bay, Wis. D6 88
Sturgeon Falls, Ont., Can. A5 41
Sturgis, Sask., Can. F4 39
Sturgis, Ky. C2 62
Sturgis, Mich. G5 66
Sturgis, S.Dak. F2 77
Sturtevant, Wis. F6, n12 88
Stutsman, co., N. Dak. C7 77
Stuttgart, Ark. C4 49
Stuttgart, Ger., Fed. Rep. of D4 6
Styria, reg., Aus. E7 6
Suao, Taiwan *G9 17
Sublette, Kans. E3 61
Sublette, co., Wyo. D2 89
Subotica, Yugo. B4 10
Succasunna, N.J. B3 74
Suceava, Rom. B8 10
Sucha, Pol. D5 7
Suchitoto, Sal. *E7 34
Suchow see Xuzhou China
Sucre, Bol. *C2 29
Sucre, state, Ven. A5 32
Sucy-en-Brie, Fr. g11 5
Sudan, Tex. *B1 84
Sudan, country, Afr. E8 21
Sudan, reg., Afr. E7 21
Sudbury, Ont., Can. A4, p19 41
Sudbury, Mass. B5, g10 65
Sudbury, dist., Ont., Can. A3 41
Sudbury Center, Mass. *B5 65
Sudirman, mts., Indon. F9 19
Sudzha, Sov. Un. F10 12
Sueca, Sp. C5 8
Suez, Eg. H9 14
Suffern, N.Y. D6, m14 75
Suffield, Conn. B6 52
Suffolk (Independent City), Va. .. D6, k14 85
Suffolk, co., Eng. *D7 4
Suffolk, co., Mass. B5 65
Suffolk, co., N.Y. n15 75
Sugar, mtn., Mich. k9 66
Sugar Creek, Mo. h11 69
Sugarcreek, Ohio *B4 78
Sugar Grove, Va. D1, f10 85
Sugar Hill, Ga. B2 55
Sugar Land, Tex. E5, r14 84
Sugarloaf, mtn., Maine C2 64
Sugar Notch, Pa. n17 81
Şuḥār, Om. E6 15
Suhl, Ger. Dem. Rep. C5 6
Suibin, China C5 18
Suihua, China B10 17
Suileng, China C3 18
Suining, China E6 17
Suita, Jap. *I7 18
Suitland, Md. f9 53
Suixian, China E7 17
Sukabumi, Indon. G3 19
Sukaraja, Indon. F4 19

Sukarnapura, see Jayapura, Indon.
Sukhumi, Sov. Un. A13 14
Sukumo, Jap. J6 18
Sukkur, Pak. C4 20
Sulawesi, see Celebes, isl., Indon.
Sullana, Peru B1 31
Sulligent, Ala. B1 46
Sullivan, Ill. D5 58
Sullivan, Ind. F3 59
Sullivan, Mo. C6 69
Sullivan, co., Ind. F3 59
Sullivan, co., Mo. A4 69
Sullivan, co., N.H. E3 73
Sullivan, co., N.Y. D6 75
Sullivan, co., Pa. D8 81
Sullivan, co., Tenn. C11 83
Sullivans Island, S.C. k12 82
Sully, Iowa C5 60
Sully, co., S. Dak. F5 77
Sulmona, It. C4 9
Sulphur, La. D2 63
Sulphur, Okla. C5 79
Sulphur South, La. *D2 63
Sulphur Springs, Tex. C5 84
Sultan, Wash. B4 86
Sulu, prov., Phil. *D6 19
Sumach, Wash. *C5 86
Sumas, Wash. A3 86
Sumatra, isl., Indon. F2 19
Sumenep, Indon. G4 19
Sumiton, Ala. B2 46
Summerdale, Pa. *F8 81
Summerfield, N.C. A3 76
Summerland, B.C., Can. E8 37
Summers, co., W. Va. D4 87
Summerside, P.E.I., Can. C6 43
Summersville, W. Va. C4, m14 87
Summerton, S.C. D7 82
Summerville, Ga. B1 55
Summerville, Pa. D3 81
Summerville, S.C. E7, h11 82
Summit, Ill. k9 58
Summit, Miss. D3 68
Summit, N.J. B4 74
Summit, co., Colo. B4 51
Summit, co., Ohio A4 78
Summit, co., Utah A6 72
Summit Hill, Pa. E10 81
Summitville, Ind. D6 59
Sumner, Ill. E6 58
Sumner, Iowa B5 60
Sumner, Wash. B3 86
Sumner, co., Kans. E6 61
Sumner, co., Tenn. A5 83
Sumoto, Jap. I7 18
Šumperk, Czech. D4 7
Sumter, S.C. D7 82
Sumter, co., Ala. C1 46
Sumter, co., Fla. D4 54
Sumter, co., Ga. D2 55
Sumter, co., S.C. D7 82
Sumy, Sov. Un. F10 12
Sun, La. D6 63
Sunburst, Mont. B5 70
Sunbury, Ohio B3 78
Sunbury, Pa. E8 81
Sunbury, co., N.B., Can. D3 43
Sunchŏn, Kor. I3 18
Sunchŏn, Kor. G2 18
Sun City, Ariz. D1 48
Suncook, N.H. E5 73
Sun Crest, Calif. *F5 50
Sundance, Wyo. B8 89
Sundance, mtn., Wyo. B8 89
Sundbyberg, Swe. t35 11
Sunderland, Ont., Can. C5 41
Sunderland, Eng. C6 4
Sundown, Tex. C1 84
Sundre, Alta., Can. D3 38
Sundsvall, Swe. F7 11
Sunfield, Mich. F5 66
Sunflower, co., Miss. B3 68
Sungari, riv., China C5 18
Sungchiang, China E7 17
Sungurlu, Tur. B10 14
Suniland, Fla. *G6 54
Sunman, Ind. F7 59
Sunnyland, Fla. q11 54
Sunnyland, Ill. *C4 58
Sunnymead, Calif. *F5 50
Sunnyside, Utah B6 72
Sunnyside, Wash. C5 86
Sunnyvale, Calif. k8 50
Sunol, Calif. h9 50
Sun Prairie, Wis. E4 88
Sunray, Tex. B2 84

Sunridge, Ont., Can. B5 41
Sunrise Heights, Mich. *F5 66
Sunset, La. D3 63
Sunset, Utah *A5 72
Sunset Beach, Calif. *F5 50
Sunset Hills, Mo. *C7 69
Sunset Park, Kans. *B5 61
Superior, Ariz. C3, D3 48
Superior, Mont. C2 70
Superior, Nebr. E7 71
Superior, W.Va. *D3 87
Superior, Wis. B1 88
Superior, Wyo. E4 89
Superior, lake, Can., U.S. A9 45
Suquamish, Wash. B3 86
Şūr (Tyre), Leb. F10 14
Şūr, Om. E6 15
Surabaja, see Surabaya, Indon.
Surabaya, Indon. G4 19
Surakarta, Indon. G4 19
Šurany, Czech. D5 7
Surat, India D5 20
Suresnes, Fr. g9 5
Surfside, Fla. s13 54
Surgoinsville, Tenn. C11 83
Surgut, Sov. Un. C10 13
Surī, India D8 20
Surigao, Phil. D7 19
Surigao del Norte, prov., Phil. *D7 19
Surigao del sur, prov., Phil. *D7 19
Suriname, dep., S.A. C5 27
Suriname, riv., Sur. C5 27
Surrey, co., Eng. *E6 4
Surry, N.H. E3 73
Surry, co., N.C. A2 76
Surry, co., Va. C6 85
Susa, It. B1 9
Susana Knolls, Calif. *E4 50
Susanville, Calif. B3 50
Sušice, Czech. D2 7
Susquehanna, Pa. C10 81
Susquehanna, co., Pa. C10 81
Sussex, N.B., Can. D4 43
Sussex, N.J. A3 74
Sussex, Wis. m11 88
Sussex, co., Del. C6 53
Sussex, co., Eng. *E7 4
Sussex, co., N.J. A3 74
Sussex, co., Va. D5 85
Susurluk, Tur. C7 14
Sutersville, Pa. *F2 81
Sutherland, Iowa B2 60
Sutherland, Nebr. C4 71
Sutherland, co., Scot. *B4 4
Sutherlin, Oreg. D3 80
Sutter, Calif. *C3 50
Sutter, co., Calif. C3 50
Sutter Creek, Calif. C3 50
Sutton, Que., Can. D5 42
Sutton, Nebr. D8 71
Sutton, W. Va. C4 87
Sutton, co., Tex. D2 84
Sutton-in-Ashfield, Eng. D6 4
Sutton West, Ont., Can. C5 41
Suttsu, Jap. E10 18
Suva, Fiji H8 2
Suwa, Jap. m17 18
Suwalki, Pol. A7 7
Suwannee, Fla. C3 54
Suwannee, co., Fla. B3 54
Suwŏn, S. Kor. H3 18
Suyo, Peru B1 31
Suzhou, China E9 17
Suzuka, Jap. o15 18
Svalbard (Spitzbergen).
  Nor., dep. B5 13
Svedala, Swe. A2 7
Svendborg, co., Den. *J4 11
Sverdlovsk, Sov. Un. D9 13
Sverdrup, is., Can. m30 36
Svetlaya, Sov. Un. C9 18
Svilajnac, Yugo. C5 10
Svilengrad, Bul. E8 10
Svirstroy, Sov. Un. A9 12
Svishtov, Bul. D7 10
Svitavy, Czech. D4 7
Svobodnyy, Sov. Un. D15 13
Swain, co., N.C. f9 76
Swainsboro, Ga. D4 55
Swampscott, Mass. B6, g12 65
Swan Hill, Aust. G7 25
Swan Hills, Alta., Can. B3 38
Swanlake, Idaho G6 57
Swan Lake, Miss. B3 68
Swannanoa, N.C. f10 76
Swan River, Man., Can. C1 40

Swansboro, N.C. C5 76
Swansea, Ill. f14 69
Swansea, Mass. C5 65
Swansea, S.C. D5 82
Swansea, Wales E5 4
Swansea Center, Mass. *C5 65
Swanton, Ohio A2 78
Swanton, Vt. B1 73
Swarthmore, Pa. q20 81
Swartz Creek, Mich. F7 66
Swayzee, Ind. C6 59
Swaziland, country, Afr. F6 24
Swea City, Iowa A3 60
Swedeborg, Mo. D5 59
Swedeland, Pa. o20 81
Sweden, country, Eur. F7 11
Swedesboro, N.J. D2 74
Sweeny, Tex. r14 84
Sweet, Idaho F2 57
Sweet Briar, Va. C3 85
Sweet Grass, co., Mont. E7 70
Sweet Home, Oreg. C4 80
Sweetsburg, Que., Can. D5 42
Sweetsers, Ind. C6 59
Sweet Springs, Mo. C4 69
Sweetwater, Tenn. D8 83
Sweetwater, Tex. C2 84
Sweetwater, co., Wyo. E3 89
Swepsonville, N.C. A3 76
Swidnica, Pol. C4 7
Swidwin, Pol. B3 7
Swiebodzice, Pol. C4 7
Swiebodzin, Pol. B3 7
Swiecie, Pol. B5 7
Świętochłowice, Pol. g9 7
Swift, co., Minn. E3 67
Swift Current, Sask., Can. G2, n7 39
Swindon, Eng. E6 4
Swinemünde, see
  Swinoujscie, Pol.
Świnoujście, Pol. B3 7
Swisher, co., Tex. B2 84
Swissvale, Pa. k14 81
Switzer, W. Va. D3 87
Switzerland, co., Ind. G7 59
Switzerland, country, Eur. E4 6
Swoyerville, Pa. D10, n17 81
Sycamore, Ill. B5 58
Sycamore, Ohio B2 78
Sycamore Hills, Mo. *C7 69
Sydenham, Ont., Can. C8 41
Sydney, Austl. F9 25
Sydney, N.S., Can. C9 43
Sydney Mines, N.S., Can. C9 43
Sykesville, Md. B4 53
Sykesville, Pa. D4 81
Syktyvkar, Sov. Un. C8 13
Sylacauga, Ala. B3 46
Sylhet, Bngl. D9 20
Sylva, N.C. f9 76
Sylvan, Oreg. f12 80
Sylvan Beach, N.Y. B5 75
Sylvania, Ala. A4 46
Sylvania, Ga. D5 55
Sylvania, Ky. g11 62
Sylvania, Ohio A2, e6 78
Sylvan Lake, Alta., Can. C3 38
Sylvester, Ga. E3 55
Syosset, N.Y. F2 52
Syracuse, Ind. B6 59
Syracuse, Kans. E2 61
Syracuse, Nebr. D9, h12 71
Syracuse, N.Y. B4 75
Syracuse, Ohio D4 78
Syracuse, Utah C2 72
Syr Darya, riv., Sov. Un. E9 13
Syria, country, Asia F6 16
Syriam, Bur. *B1 19
Syzran, Sov. Un. D7 13
Szabadszállás, Hung. B4 10
Szabolcs-Szatmár, co., Hung. *B5 10
Szamotuly, Pol. B4 7
Szarvas, Hung. B5 10
Szczebrzeszyn, Pol. C7 7
Szczecin (Stettin), Pol. B3 7
Szczecinek, Pol. B4 7
Szechwan, see Sichuan, China
Szeged, Hung. B5 10
Székesfehérvár, Hung. B4 10
Szekszárd, Hung. B4 10
Szentendre, Hung. B4 10
Szentes, Hung. B5 10
Szolnok, Hung. B5 10
Szolnok, co., Hung. *B5 10
Szombathely, Hung. B3 10

T

Tabaco, Phil. *C6 19
Tabasco, state, Mex. D6 34
Taber, Alta., Can. E4 38
Taboada, Sp. A2 8
Tábor, Czech. D3 7
Tabor, Iowa D2 60
Tabor, N.J. *B4 74
Tabora, Tan. B6 24
Tabor City, N.C. C4 76
Tabrīz, Iran B4 15
Tabūk, Sau. Ar. D2 15
Tachikawa, Jap. n18 18
Táchira, state, Ven. B3 32
Tacloban, Phil. C6 19
Tacna, Peru E5 31
Tacna, dept., Peru E3 31
Tacoma, Wash. B3, f11 86
Tacuarembó, Ur. E1 30
Tacuarembó, dept., Ur. *E1 30
Tadoussac, Que., Can. A8 42
Tadzhik, rep., Sov. Un. F9 16
Taegu, Kor. I4 18
Taejon, Kor. H3 18
Tafalla, Sp. A5 8
Taff Viejo, Arg. E2 29
Tafí Viejo, Arg. E2 29
Taft, Calif. E4 50
Taft, Fla. D5 54
Taft, Tex. F4 84
Taft Heights, Calif. *E4 50
Taft Southwest, Tex. *F4 84
Taganrog, Sov. Un. H12 12
Tahät, mtn., Alg. D6 22
Tahlequah, Okla. B7 79
Tahoka, Tex. C2 84
Tahoua, Niger F6 22
T'aichung, Taiwan G9 17
Tailai, China C1 18
T'ainan, Taiwan G9 17
Taipei, Taiwan G9 17
Taiping, Mala. E2 19
T'aitung, Taiwan G9 17
Taiwan (Formosa), country
   (Nationalist China), Asia G9 17
Taiyuan, China D7 17
Taizz, Yemen G3 15
Tajimi, Jap. I8, n16 18
Tajrīsh, Iran *B5 15
Tājūrā, Libya B7 22
Tak, Thai. *B1 19
Takada, Jap. H9 18
Takamatsu, Jap. I7 18
Takaoka, Jap. H9 18
Takasaki, Jap. H9, m17 18
Takatsuki, Jap. o14 18
Takawa, Jap. *J5 18
Takayama, Jap. H8, m16 18
Takefu, Jap. n15 18
Takeo, Kam. *C2 19
Takingeun, Indon. *m11 19
Takoma Park, Md. f8 53
Takut, Bur. *D10 20
Talā, Eg. *G8 14
Tala, Mex. m12 34
Tala, Ur. E1 30
Talagante, Chile A2 28
Talara, Peru B1 31
Talavera de la Reina, Sp. C3 8
Talbert, Ky. C6 62
Talbot, co., Ga. D2 5
Talbot, co., Md. C5 53
Talbotton, Ga. D2 55
Talca, Chile B2 28
Talca, prov., Chile B2 28
Talcahuano, Chile B2 28
Tālcher, India D8 20
Talco, Tex. C5 84
Taliaferro, co., Ga. C4 55
Talihina, Okla. C6 79
Talisayan, Phil. *D6 19
Talladega, Ala. B3 46
Talladega, co., Ala. B3 46
Tallahassee, Fla. B2 54
Tallahatchie, co., Miss. B3 68
Tallapoosa, Ga. C1 55
Tallapoosa, co., Ala. C4 46
Tallassee, Ala. C4 46
Talleyville, Del. *A6 53
Tallinn, Sov. Un. B5 12
Tallmadge, Ohio A4 78
Tallulah, La. B4 63
Talnoye, Sov. Un. G8 12
Talsi, Sov. Un. C4 12
Taltal, Chile E1 29
Tama, Iowa C5 60
Tama, co., Iowa B5 60
Tamale, Ghana G4 22

Taman, Sov. Un. I11 12
Tamano, Jap. I6 18
Tamanrasset, Alg. D6 22
Tamaqua, Pa. E10 81
Tamaulipas, state, Mex. C5 34
Tamazula de Gordiano, Mex. n12 34
Tambov, Sov. Un. E13 12
Tamil Nadu, state, India F6 20
Tampa, Fla. E4, p11 54
Tampere, Fin. G10 11
Tampico, Mex. C5, k15 34
Tams, W.Va. D3 87
Tamworth, Austl. F9 25
Tanabe, Jap. J7 18
Tananarive, see Antananarive, Mad.
Tanchon, Kor. F4 18
Tandag, Phil. *D7 19
Tāndārei, Rom. C8 10
Taney, co., Mo. E4 69
Taneytown, Md. A3 53
Tanga, Tan. B7 24
Tanganyika, lake, Afr. C6 24
Tanger (Tangier), Mor. A3 22
Tangermünde, Ger. Dem. Rep. B5 6
Tangier, Va. C7 85
Tangipahoa, par., La. D5 63
Tangshan, China D8 17
Tangyuan, China C4 18
Tanjay, Phil. *D6 19
Tanjore, see Thanjavūr, India
Tanjungkarang-Telukbetung,
   Indon. G3 19
Tanjungpandan, Indon. F3 19
Tānk, Pak. B5 20
Tanque Verde, Ariz. *C4 48
Tanshui, Taiwan *F9 17
Tanță, Eg. G8 14
Tanzania, country, Afr. B6 24
Tao'an, China B9 17
Taormina, It. F5 9
Taos, N.Mex. A6 48
Taos, co., N.Mex. A6 48
Tapachula, Mex. E6 34
Tappahannock, Va. C6 85
Tappan, N.Y. g13 75
Taquara, Braz. D2 30
Taquaritinga, Braz. k7 30
Tara, Mo. *C7 69
Tara, Sov. Un. D10 13
Tarābulus, see Tripoli, Leb.
Tarakan, Laos *B2 19
Tarancon, Sp. B4 8
Taranto, It. D6 9
Tarapacá, prov., Chile D1 29
Tarapoto, Peru C2 31
Tarare, Fr. E6 5
Tarascon-sur-Ariège, Fr. F6 5
Tarazona, Sp. B5 8
Tarbes, Fr. F4 5
Tarboro, N.C. B5 76
Taree, Austl. E9 26
Tarentum, Pa. E2, h14 81
Tarfaya, Mor. C2 22
Tarifa, Sp. D3 8
Tarija, Bol. D3 29
Tarija, dept., Bol. D3 29
Tarkio, Mo. A2 69
Tarkwa, Ghana G4 22
Tarlac, Phil. B6, o13 19
Tarlac, prov., Phil. *B6 19
Tarma, Peru D2 31
Tarn, dept., Fr. *F5 5
Tarn-et-Garonne, dept., Fr. *E4 5
Tarnobrzeg, Pol. C6 7
Tarnów, Pol. C6 7
Tarnowskie Góry, Pol. g9 7
Taroudant, Mor. B3 22
Tarpon Springs, Fla. D4 54
Tarquinia, It. C3 9
Tarragona, Sp. B6 8
Tarragona, prov., Sp. *B6 8
Tarrant, Ala. B3, f7 46
Tarrant, co., Tex. C4 84
Tarrasa, Sp. B7 8
Tarrytown, N.Y. D7, m15 75
Tarsney, Mo. k11 69
Tarsus, Tur. D10 14
Tartu, Sov. Un. B6 12
Tashkent, Sov. Un. E9 1
Tashkurghan, Afg. A4 20
Taskmalaya, Indon. *G3 19
Tasmania, state, Austl. o14 25
Tatabánya, Hun. B4 10
Tatamagouche, N.S., Can. D6 43
Tate, Ga. B2 55
Tate, co., Miss. A4 68

Tateville, Ky. D5 62
Tateyama, Jap. I9, n18 18
Tatta, Pak. D4 20
Tattnall, co., Ga. D4 55
Tatui, Braz. C3, m8 30
Tatum, N.Mex. C7 48
Taubaté, Braz. C3 30
Taung, S.Afr. F4 24
Taungdwingyi, Bur. D10 20
Taunggyi, Bur. D10 20
Taunton, Eng. E5 4
Taunton, Mass. C5 65
Taurage, sov. Un. D4 12
Tauranga, N.Z. L16 26
Taurianova, It. E6 9
Tauste, Sp. B5 8
Tavares, Fla. D5 54
Tavas, Tur. *D7 14
Tavda, Sov. Un. D9 13
Tavira, Port. D2 8
Tavistock, Ont., Can. D4 41
Tavoy, Bur. F10 20
Tavsanli, Tur. *C7 14
Tawas City, Mich. D7 66
Taylor, Mich. p15 66
Taylor, Pa. D10, m18 81
Taylor, Tex. D4 84
Taylor, co., Fla. B3 54
Taylor, co., Ga. D2 55
Taylor, co., Iowa D3 60
Taylor, co., Ky. C4 62
Taylor, co., Tex. C3 84
Taylor, co., W.Va. B4 87
Taylor, co., Wis. C3 88
Taylor Mill, Ky. k14 62
Taylors, S.C. B3 82
Taylorsport, Ky. h13 62
Taylorsville, Ky. B4 62
Taylorsville, Miss. D4 68
Taylorsville, N.C. B1 76
Taylorville, Ill. D4 58
Tayshet, Sov. Un. D12 13
Taza, Mor. B4 22
Tazewell, Tenn. C10 83
Tazewell, Va. e10 85
Tazewell, co., Ill. C4 58
Tazewell, co., Va. e10 85
Tbilisi, Sov. Un. E7 13
Tchula, Miss. B3 68
Tczew, Pol. A5 7
Teague, Tex. D4 84
Teaneck, N.J. h8 74
Tecuala, Mex. C3 34
Tecuci, Rom. C8 10
Tecumseh, Ont., Can. E2 41
Tecumseh, Mich. F7 66
Tecumseh, Nebr. D9 71
Tecumseh, Okla. B5 79
Tegal, Indon. *G3 19
Tegucigalpa, Hond. E7 34
Teguise, sp. m15 8
Tehachapi, Calif. E4 50
Tehama, co., Calif. B2 50
Tehrān, Iran B5 15
Tehuacan, Mex. D5, n15 34
Tehuantepec, Mex. D5 34
Tekamah, Nebr. C9 71
Tekax de Alvaro Obregón, Mex. C7 34
Tekirdag, Tur. B6 14
Tekoa, Wash. B8 86
Tela, Hond. *D7 34
Tel Aviv-Yafo (Tel Aviv Jaffa),
   Isr. B2, g5 15
Telde, Sp. m14 8
Telemark, co., Nor. *H3 11
Telfair, co., Ga. E3 55
Telford, Pa. F11 81
Tell, Wis. I4 59
Tell City, Ind. I4 59
Teller, co., Colo. C5 51
Telluride, Colo. D3 51
Telok Anson, Mala. E2 19
Teloloapan, Mex. D5, n14 34
Temirtau, Sov. Un. *D10 13
Témiscouata, co., Que., Can. B9 42
Temora, Austl. *F8 25
Tempe, Ariz. C3, D2 48
Temperance, Mich. G7 66
Tempio Pausania, It. D2 9
Temple, Okla. C3 79
Temple, Pa. F10 81
Temple, Tex. D4 84
Temple City, Calif. *F5 50
Temple Hill, Ky. D4 62
Temple Terrace, Fla. o11 54

Templeton, Que., Can. D2 42
Templeton, Mass. A3 65
Templin, Ger. Dem. Rep. B6 6
Temryuk, Sov. Un. I11 12
Temuco, Chile B2 28
Tenafly, N.J. B5, h9 74
Tenaha, Tex. D5 84
Tenāli, India *E7 20
Tenancingo, de Degollado, Mex. . . D5, n14 34
Tenango del Valle, Mex. n14 34
Tenasserim, Bur. F10 20
Tenchong, China F4 17
Tenino, Wash. C3 86
Tennessee, state, U.S. 83
Tennessee, riv., U.S. D9 45
Tensas, par., La. B4 63
Teocaltiche, Mex. C4 34
Teófilo Otoni, Braz. B4 30
Tepatitlán de Morelos, Mex. C4, m12 34
Tepic, Mex. C4, m11 34
Teplice, Czech. C2 7
Teramo, It. C4 9
Teresina, Braz. D6 27
Teresópolis, Braz. C4, h6 30
Termez, Sov. Un. F9 13
Termini Imerese, It. F4 9
Termoli, It. C5 9
Ternate, Indon. E7 19
Terneuzen, Neth. B5 5
Terney, Sov. Un. D8 18
Terni, It. C4 9
Ternopol, Sov. Un. G5 12
Terra Alta, W.Va. B5 87
Terrace, B.C., Can. B3 37
Terrace Park, Ohio *C1 78
Terracina, It. D4 9
Terra Linda, Calif. *D2 50
Terrebonne, Que., Can. D4, p19 42
Terrebonne, co., Que., Can. D3 42
Terrebonne, par., La. E5 63
Terre Haute, Ind. F3 59
Terre Hill, Pa. F9 81
Terrell, Tex. C4 84
Terrell, co., Ga. E2 55
Terrell, co., Tex. D1 84
Terrell Hills, Tex. k7 84
Terry, Mont. D11 70
Terry, co., Tex. C1 84
Terrytown, La. *k11 63
Terrytown, Nebr. C2 71
Terryville, Conn. C4 52
Teruel, Sp. *B5 8
Teruel, prov., Sp. *B5 8
Tesanj, Yugo. C3 10
Teterow, Ger. Dem. Rep. B6 6
Teton, co., Idaho F7 57
Teton, co., Mont. C4 70
Teton, co., Wyo. C2 89
Tétouan, Mor. A3 22
Tetovo, Yugo. D5 10
Teutopolis, Ill. D5 58
Teverya (Tiberias), Isr. B3, g5 15
Tewantin-Noosa, Austl. C9 26
Tewksbury, Mass. A5, f11 65
Texarkana, Ark. D1 49
Texarkana, Tex. C5 84
Texas, Md. B4 53
Texas, co., Mo. D5 69
Texas, co., Okla. e9 79
Texas, state, U.S. 84
Texas City, Tex. E5, r15 84
Texhoma, Okla. e9 79
Teziutlán, Mex. D5, n15 34
Thailand (Siam), country, Asia B2 19
Thames, N.Z. L15 26
Thamesville, Ont., Can. E3 41
Thāna, India *E5 20
Thanh Hoa, Viet. B3 19
Thanjāvūr (Tanjore), India F6 20
Thann, Fr. D7 5
Thaon -les-Vosges, Fr. C7 5
Tharptown, Pa. *E8 81
Tharrawaddy, Bur. E10 20
Thatcher, Ariz. C4 48
Thatcher, Idaho G7 57
Thaton, Bur. E10 20
Thayer, Mo. E6 69
Thayer, co., Nebr. D8 71
Thayetmyo, Bur. *E10 20
The Dalles, Oreg. B5 80
The Entrance, Austl. *F8 26
The Father, mtn., N.Gui. k13 25
The Hague ('s Gravenhage), Neth. A6 5
The Pas, Man., Can. C1, g7 40
The Plains, Ohio C3 78
Theresa, N.Y. A5, f9 75
Thermalito, Calif. *C3 50

Thermopolis, Wyo. C4 89
Thesprotia, prov., Grc. *C3 14
Thessalon, Ont., Can. p19 41
Thessaloniki (Salonika), Grc. B4 14
Thessaloniki (Salonika),
  prov., Grc. *B4 14
Thessaly, reg., Grc. C4 14
Thetford Mines, Que., Can. C6 42
The Village, Okla. *B4 79
Thibodaux, La. E5, k10 63
Thief River Falls, Minn. B2 67
Thiensville, Wis. E6, m12 88
Thiers, Fr. E5 5
Thiès, Sen. F1 22
Thimbu, Bhu. C8 20
Thionville, Fr. C7 5
Thisted, co., Den. *I3 11
Thivai (Thebes), Grc. C4 14
Thomas, Okla. B3 79
Thomas, W.Va. B5 87
Thomas, co., Ga. F3 55
Thomas, co., Kans. C2 61
Thomas, co., Nebr. C5 71
Thomason, Ga. D2 55
Thomaston, Ala. C2 46
Thomaston, Conn. C4 52
Thomaston, Maine D3 64
Thomaston, N.Y. *E7 75
Thomasville, Ala. D2 46
Thomasville, Ga. F3 55
Thomasville, N.C. B2 76
Thompson, Conn. B9 52
Thompson Falls, Mont. C1 70
Thompsonville, Conn. A6 52
Thomson, Ga. C4 55
Thon Buri, Thai. *C2 19
Thorburn, N.S., Can. D7 43
Thornbury, Ont., Can. C4 41
Thorndale, Tex. D4 84
Thornton, Colo. *B6 51
Thornton, Idaho *F7 57
Thornton, Ill. *B6 58
Thornton, Miss. B3 68
Thorntown, Ind. D4 59
Thornwood, N.Y. *D7 75
Thorofare, N.J. D2 74
Thorold, Ont., Can. D5 41
Thorp, Wis. D3 88
Thorpe, W.Va. D3 87
Thorsby, Ala. C3 46
Thorshavn, Faer. Is. C6 3
Thouars, Fr. D3 5
Thousand Oaks, Calif. *E4 50
Three Forks, Mont. E5 70
Three Hills, Alta., Can. D4 38
Three Oaks, Mich. G4 66
Three Rivers, Mass. B3 65
Three Rivers, Mich. G5 66
Three Rivers, Miss. E5 68
Three Rivers, Tex. E3 84
Throckmorton, Tex. C3 84
Throckmorton, co., Tex. C3 84
Throop, Pa. m18 81
Thule, Grnld. *B14 33
Thun, Switz. E3 6
Thunder Bay, Ont., Can. o17 41
Thunder Bay, dist., Ont., Can. o17 41
Thunderbolt, Ga. D5 55
Thurgau, canton, Switz. *E4 6
Thüringia, former state, Ger. Dem.
  Rep. *C5 6
Thüringia, reg., Ger. Dem. Rep. *C5 6
Thurles, Ire. D3 4
Thurmont, Md. A3 53
Thurrock, Eng. *E7 4
Thursday Island, Austl. B7 25
Thurso, Que., Can. D2 42
Thurso, Scot. A5 4
Thurston, co., Nebr. B9 71
Thurston, co., Wash. C3 86
Tianjin, China D8 17
Tianshui, China E6 17
Tibet, auton., reg., China B8 20
Tiburon, Calif. *C2 50
Tice, Fla. F5 54
Tickfaw, La. D5 63
Ticonderoga, N.Y. B7 75
Ticul, Mex. C7 34
Tidioute, Pa. C3 81
Tieling, China C9 17
Tienen, Bel. B6 5
Tientsin, see Tianjin, China
Tie Plant, Miss. B4 68
Tierra Blanca, Mex. D5, n15 34
Tierra del Fuego, isl., Chile h12 28
Tietê, Braz. C3, m8 30
Tiff City, Mo. E3 69
Tiffin, Ohio A2 78
Tiflis, see Tbilisi, Sov. Un.
Tift, co., Ga. E3 55
Tifton, Ga. E3 55
Tiftona, Tenn. *D8 83

Tigard, Oreg. h12 80
Tigil, Sov. Un. D18 13
Tignish, P.E.I., Can. C6 43
Tigre, Arg. g7 28
Tigris, riv., Asia F7 13
Tijuana, Mex. A1 34
Tikhvin, Sov. Un. B9 12
Tiksi, Sov. Un. B15 13
Tilburg, Neth. B6 5
Tilbury, Ont., Can. E2 41
Tilden, Ill. E4 58
Tilden, Nebr. B8 71
Tilghman, Md. C5 53
Tilimsen, Alg. B4 22
Tiline, Ky. e9 62
Tillamook, Oreg. B3 80
Tillamook, co., Oreg. B3 80
Tillicum, Wash. *B2 86
Tillman, co., Okla. C2 79
Tillsonburg, Ont., Can. E4 41
Tilton, Ill. C6 58
Tilton, N.H. E4 73
Tiltonsville, Ohio B5 78
Timaru, N.Z. P13 26
Timbaúba, Braz. *D7 27
Times Beach, Mo. *C7 69
Timiskaming, dist., Ont., Can. O19 41
Timisoara, Rom. C5 10
Timmins, Ont., Can. o19 41
Timmonsville, S.C. C8 82
Timoneng, Guam *F6 2
Timor, isl., Indon. G6 19
Timpson, Tex. D5 84
Tinley Park, Ill. k9 58
Tinsley, Miss. C3 68
Tioga, N. Dak. B2 77
Tioga, co., N.Y. C4 75
Tioga, co., Pa. C7 81
Tippah, co., Miss. A5 68
Tipp City, Ohio C1 78
Tippecanoe, co., Ind. D4 59
Tipperary, Ire. D2 4
Tipperary, co., Ire. *D3 4
Tipton, Calif. D4 50
Tipton, Ind. D5 59
Tipton, Iowa C6 60
Tipton, Mo. C5 69
Tipton, Okla. C2 79
Tipton, co., Ind. D5 59
Tipton, co., Tenn. B2 83
Tiptonville, Tenn. A2 83
Tiranë (Tirana), Alb. B2 14
Tiranë (Tirana), pref., Alb. *B2 14
Tirano, It. A3 9
Tiraspol, Sov. Un. H7 12
Tire, Tur. C6 14
Tîrgoviste, Rom. C7 10
Tîrgu-jiu, Rom. C6 10
Tîrgu-Neamt, Rom. B8 10
Tîrgul-Ocna, Rom. B8 10
Tîrgu-Mures, Rom. B7 10
Tîrgu-Sacuesc, Rom. B8 10
Tîrnaveni, Rom. B7 10
Tîrnavos, Grc. *C4 14
Tirol, state, Aus. E5 6
Tirol, reg., Aus. E5 6
Tiruchchirappalli, India F6 20
Tirunelveli, India G6 20
Tiruppur, India *F6 20
Tisdale, Sask., Can. E3 39
Tishomingo, Okla. C5 79
Tishomingo, co., Miss. A5 68
Tiskilwa, Ill. B4 58
Tisza, riv., Hung., Yugo. B5 10
Tiszafüred, Hung. B5 10
Tiszakécske, Hung. B5 10
Titicaca, lake, Bol., Peru C2 29
Titograd, Yugo. D4 10
Titovo Užice, Yugo. D4 10
Titov Veles, Yugo. E5 10
Titus, co., Tex. C5 84
Titusville, Fla. D6 54
Titusville, N.J. C3 74
Titusville, Pa. C2 81
Tiverton, Eng. E5 4
Tiverton, R.I. C12 52
Tivoli, It. D4, h9 9
Tivoli, Tex. E4 84
Tixtla, Mex. p14 34
Tizapán, Mex. h9 34
Tizimín, Mex. C7 34
Tizi-Ouzou, Alg. A5 22
Tiznit, Mor. C3 22
Tjiandjur, Indon. *G3 19
Tjimahi, Indon. *G3 19
Tlalpan, Mex. h9 34
Tlaxcala, state, Mex. D5 34
Tlaxiaco, Mex. D5 34
Toamasina, Mad. D9 24
Toast, N.C. A2 76
Toba, Jap. o15 18

Tobarra, Sp. C5 8
Tobol, riv., Sov. Un. D9 13
Tobolsk, Sov. Un. D9 13
Tobyhanna, Pa. D11 81
Tocantins, riv., Braz. D6 27
Toccoa, Ga. B3 55
Toccoa Falls, Ga. B3 55
Tochigi, Jap. H9, m18 18
Tochigi, pref., Jap. *H9 18
Tocopilla, Chile D1 29
Todd, co., Ky. D2 62
Todd, co., Minn. D4 67
Todd, co., S. Dak. G5 77
Togo, country, Afr. G5 22
Tokat, Tur. B11 14
Tokenon, Kor. G2 18
Toki, Jap. *n16 18
Tokorozawa, Jap. n18 18
Tokushima, Jap. I7 18
Tokushima, pref., Jap. *I7 18
Tokuyama, Jap. I5 18
Tōkyō, Jap. I9, n18 18
Tokyo, pref., Jap. *I9 18
Tolbukhin (Dobrich), Bul. D8 10
Toledo, Ill. D5 58
Toledo, Iowa B5 60
Toledo, Ohio A2, e6 78
Toledo, Oreg. C3 80
Toledo, Sp. C3 8
Toledo, prov., sp. *C3 8
Toler, Ky. C7 62
Toliara, Mad. E8 24
Tolima, Dept., Col. C2 32
Tolland, co., Conn. B7 52
Tolleson, Ariz. D1 48
Tolmin, Yugo. B1 10
Tolna, Hung. B4 10
Tolna, co., Hung. *B4 10
Tolono, Ill. D5 58
Tolosa, Sp. A4 8
Toluca, Ill. B4 58
Toluca de Lerdo, Mex. D5, n14 34
Tolyatti, Sov. Un. *D7 13
Tomah, Wis. E3 88
Tomahawk, Wis. C4 88
Tomakomai, Jap. E10 18
Tomakovka, Sov. Un. H10 12
Tomar, Port. C1 8
Tomari, Sov. Un. E17 13
Tomaszow Lubelski, Pol. C7 7
Tomaszow Mazowiecki, Pol. C6 7
Tomball, Tex. D5 84
Tombouctou (Timbuktu), Mali E4 22
Tombstone, Ariz. D4 48
Tomé, Chile B2 28
Tomelloso, Sp. C4 8
Tom Green, co., Tex. D2 84
Tomkins Cove, N.Y. D7, m14 75
Tommot, Sov. Un. D15 13
Tompkins, co., N.Y. C4 75
Tompkinsville, Ky. D4 62
Tom Price, Austl. D2 25
Tomsk, Sov. Un. D11 13
Toms River, N.J. D4 74
Tonalá, Mex. D6 34
Tonasket, Wash. A6 86
Tonawanda, N.Y. B2 75
Tondano, Indon. E6 19
Tønder, Den. A4 6
Tønder, co., Den. *J3 11
Tonga, Br. dep., Oceania H9 2
Tonganoxie, Kans. C8, k15 61
Tongua, China F2 18
Tongliao, China C9 17
Tongling, China E8 17
Tonk, India C6 20
Tonka Bay, Minn. *F5 67
Tonkawa, Okla. A4 79
Tonkin, reg., Viet. A3 19
Tonopah, Nev. E4 72
Tönsberg, Nor. H4, p28 11
Tooele, Utah A5, D2 72
Tooele, co., Utah A5 72
Toole, co., Mont. B5 70
Toombs, co., Ga. D4 55
Toowoomba, Austl. E9 25
Topanga, Calif. *F4 50
Topeka, Kans. C8, k13 61
Topol'čany, Czech. D5 7
Topolovgrad, Bul. D8 10
Toppenish, Wash. C5 86
Topsfield, Mass. A6 65
Topsham, Maine E3, g8 64
Topton, Pa. F10 81
Torbay, Newf., Can. E5 44
Torez, Sov. Un. q21 12
Torhout, Bel. B5 5
Toride, Jap. n19 18
Torino, see Turin, It.
Toro, Sp. B3 8
Törökszentmiklós, Hung. B5 10
Toronto, Ont., Can. D5, m15 41

Toronto, Ohio B5 78
Toropets, Sov. Un. *C8 12
Topquay (Torbay), Eng. E5 4
Torrance, Calif. n12 50
Torrance, co., N. Mex. B5 48
Torre Annunziata, It. D5 9
Torre del Greco, It. D5 9
Torredonjimeno, Sp. D4 8
Torrelavega, Sp. A3 8
Torremaggiore, It. D5 9
Torrens, lake, Austl. F6 25
Torrente, Sp. C5 8
Torreón, Mex. B4 34
Torre Pacheco, Sp. D5 8
Torres Novas, Port. C1 8
Torrevieja, Sp. D5 8
Torrington, Conn. B4 52
Torrington, Wyo. D8 89
Torrox, Sp. D4 8
Tortilla Flat, Ariz. C3 48
Tortona, It. B2 9
Tortosa, Sp. B6 8
Toruń, Pol. B5 7
Torzhok, Sov. Un. C10 12
Toscana, pol. dist., It. *C3 9
Tosno, Sov. Un. C10 12
Tosya, Tur. B10 14
Totana, Sp. D5 8
Totkomlós, Hung. B5 10
Totonicapán, Guat. D6 34
Totowa, N.J. B4 74
Tottori, Jap. *I7 18
Tottori, pref., Jap. *I7 18
Totz, Ky. D6 62
Toubkal, Jbel, mtn., Mor. B3 22
Tougaloo, Miss. C3 68
Touggourt, Alg. B6 22
Toul, Fr. C3 68
Toulon, Fr. F6 5
Toulon, Ill. B4 58
Toulouse, Fr. F4 5
Toungoo, Bur. E10 20
Touraine, former prov., Fr. D4 5
Tourcoing, Fr. B5 5
Tourlaville, Fr. C3 5
Tours, Fr. D4 5
Towaco, N.J. B4 74
Towanda, Kans. E7, k12 61
Towanda, Pa. C9 81
Tower City, Pa. E8 81
Town and Country, Mo. *C7 69
Towner, N. Dak. B5 77
Towner, co., N. Dak. B6 77
Townley, Ala. B2 46
Town of Pines, Ind. *A4 59
Town of Tonawanda, N.Y. *B2 75
Towns, co., Ga. B3 55
Townsend, Mass. A4 65
Townsend, Mont. D5 70
Townsville, Austl. C8 25
Towson, Md. B4, g11 53
Toyama, Jap. H8 18
Toyama, pref., Jap. *H8 18
Toyohashi, Jap. I8, o16 18
Toyokawa, Jap. *I8 18
Toyonaka, Jap. o14 18
Toyota, Jap. n16 18
Tozeur, Tun. B6 22
Trabzon, Tur. B12 14
Tracadie, N.B., Can. B5 43
Tracy, Calif. D3, h10 50
Tracy, Minn. F3 67
Tracy City, Tenn. D7 83
Traer, Iowa B5 60
Trafford, Pa. k14 81
Traiguén, Chile B2 28
Trail, B.C., Can. E9, o19 37
Trail Creek, Ind. A4 59
Trailer Estates, Fla. *E4 54
Traill, co., N. Dak. C8 77
Trainer, Pa. *G11 81
Tralee, Ire. D2 4
Tranås, Swe. H6 11
Trani, It. D6 9
Transilvania, prov., Rom. *B6 10
Transvaal, prov., S. Afr. E5 24
Transylvania, co., N.C. f10 76
Transylvania, reg., Rom. B6 10
Trapani, It. E4 9
Trappe, Pa. *F11 81
Traralgon, Austl. I6 26
Trás-os-Montes, reg., Port. B2 8
Trás-os-Montes e Alto Douro,
  prov., Port. *B2 8
Traunstein, Ger. Fed. Rep. of E6 6
Travelers Rest, S.C. B3 82
Traverse, co., Minn. E2 67
Traverse City, Mich. D5 66
Travis, co., Tex. D4 84
Travnik, Yugo. C3 10
Treasure, co., Mont. D9 70
Treasure Island, Fla. *E4 54

Trebič, Czech. D3   7
Trebinje, Yugo. D4 10
Trebisŏv, Czech. D6   7
Trego, co., Kans. D4 61
Treinta y Tres, Ur. E2 30
Treinta y Tres, dept., Ur. *E2 30
Trélazé, Fr. D3   5
Trelew, Arg. C3 28
Trelleborg, Swe. J5 11
Tremont, Ill. C4 58
Tremont, Pa. E9 81
Tremonton, Utah A5 72
Trempealeau, co., Wis. D2 88
Trenčín, Czech. D5   7
Trenggauu, state, Mala. *D2 19
Trenque Lauquén, Arg. B4 28
Trentino-Alto-Adige, pol. dist.,
  It. *A3   9
Trento, It. A3   9
Trenton, N.S., Can. D7 43
Trenton, Ont., Can. C7 41
Trenton, Fla. C4 54
Trenton, Ga. B1 55
Trenton, Ill. E4 58
Trenton, Mich. F7, p15 66
Trenton, Mo. A4 69
Trenton, Nebr. D4 71
Trenton, N.J. C3 74
Trenton, Ohio C1 78
Trenton, Tenn. B3 83
Trentwood, Wash. *B8 86
Tres Arroyos, Arg. B4 28
Tresckow, Pa. E10 81
Três Coraçoes, Braz. C3 30
Três Lagoas, Braz. C2 30
Treutlen, co., Ga. D4 55
Treviglio, It. B2   9
Treviso, It. B4   9
Trevorton, Pa. E8 81
Trevose, Pa. *F12 81
Trevose Heights, Pa. *F12 81
Treynor, Iowa C2 60
Trezevant, Tenn. A3 83
Triangle, Va. B5 85
Tribbett, Miss. B3 68
Tribune, Kans. D2 61
Trichinopoly, see
  Tiruchchirãppalli, India
Trichūr, India F6 20
Trier, Ger., Fed. Rep. of D3   6
Trieste, It. B4   9
Trigg, co., Ky. D2 62
Triglav, mtn., Yugo. B1 10
Trigueros, Sp. D2   8
Trikkala, Grc. C3 14
Trikkala, prov., Grc. *C3 14
Tri Lakes, Ind. *B7 59
Trimble, co., Ky. B4 62
Trimont, Minn. G4 67
Trincomalee, Sri Lanka G7 20
Tring-Jonction, Que., Can. C6 42
Trinidad, Braz. B3 29
Trinidad, Colo. D6 51
Trinidad, Cuba D4 35
Trinidad, Tex. C4 84
Trinidad, Ur. E1 30
Trinidad & Tobago, country, N.A. . . . A5 32
Trinité, Mart. I14 35
Trinity, Tex. D5 84
Trinity, co., Calif. B2 50
Trinity, co., Tex. D5 84
Trinity, mts., Calif. B2 50

Trino, It. B2   9
Trion, Ga. B1 55
Tripoli, Iowa B5 60
Tripolis, Grc. D4 14
Tripoli (Tarābulus), Leb. f5 15
Tripoli (Tarābulus), Libya B7 22
Tripp, S. Dak. G8 77
Tripp, co., S. Dak. G6 77
Tripura, state, India D9 20
Tristate Village, Ill. *B5 58
Triumph, La. E6 63
Trivandrum, India G6 20
Trnava, Czech. D4   7
Trois-Pistoles, Que., Can. A8 42
Trois-Rivières, Que., Can. C5 42
Troitsk, Sov. Un. D9 13
Trollhättan, Swe. H5 11
Troms, co., Nor. C8 11
Tromsö, Nor. *C8 11
Trona, Calif. E5 50
Trondheim, Nor. F4 11
Troodos, mtn., Cyp. E9 14
Tropea, It. E5   9
Trotwood, Ohio C1 78
Troup, Tex. C5 84
Troup, co., Ga. C1 55
Trousdale, co., Tenn. A5 83
Trouville, Fr. C3   5
Trowbridge, Eng. E5   4
Troy, Ala. D4 46
Troy, Ill. E4 58
Troy, Kans. C8 61
Troy, Mich. o15 66
Troy, Mo. C7 69
Troy, N.Y. C7 75
Troy, N.C. B3 76
Troy, Ohio B1 78
Troy, Pa. C8 81
Troyes, Fr. C6   5
Trubchevsk, Sov. Un. E9 12
Trucial States, see United Arab
  Emirates, country, Asia
Trucksville, Pa. *D10 81
Trujillo, Peru C2 31
Trujillo, Sp. C3   8
Trujillo, Ven. B3 32
Trujillo, state, Ven. B3 32
Truman, Minn. G4 67
Trumann, Ark. B5 49
Trumansburg, N.Y. C4 75
Trumbull, Conn. E4 52
Trumbull, co., Ohio A5 78
Truro, N.S., Can. D6 43
Truro, Eng. E4   4
Trussville, Ala. B3, f7 46
Truth or Consequences, N. Mex. C5 48
Trutnov, Czech. C3   7
Tryon, N.C. f10 76
Trysil, Nor. G5 11
Tselinograd, Sov. Un. D10 13
Tsitsihar, see Qiqhar, China
Tskhinvali, Sov. Un. A14 14
Tsu, Jap. I8, o15 18
Tsuchiura, Jap. H10, m19 18
Tsun Wan, Hong Kong *G7 17
Tsuruga, Jap. I8, n15 18
Tsuruoka, Jap. G9 18
Tsushima, Jap. n15 18
Tsuyama, Jap. I7 18
Tubarão, Braz. D3 30
Tübingen, Ger., Fed. Rep. of D4   6
Tubruq, (Tobruk), Libya B2 23

Tuchola, Pol. B4   7
Tuckahoe, N.Y. h13 75
Tucker, Ga. h8 55
Tucker, co., W. Va. B5 87
Tuckerman, Ark. B4 49
Tuckerton, N.J. D4 74
Tucson, Ariz. C3 48
Tucumán, Arg. E2 29
Tucumán, prov., Arg. E2 29
Tucumcari, N. Mex. B7 48
Tudela, Sp. A5   8
Tuguegarao, Phil. B6 19
Tukoyaktuk, N.W. Ter., Can. C7 36
Tukwila, Wash. f11 86
Tula, Sov. Un. D11 12
Tulancingo, Mex. C5, m14 34
Tulare, Calif. D4 50
Tulare, co., Calif. D4 50
Tularosa, N. Mex. C5 48
Tulcán, Ec. A2 31
Tulcea, Rom. C9 10
Tulelake, Calif. B3 50
Tulia, Tex. B2 84
Tūlkarm, Jordan B3 15
Tullahoma, Tenn. B5 83
Tullamore, Ire. D3   4
Tulle, Fr. E4   5
Tullytown, Pa. *F12 81
Tulsa, Okla. A6 79
Tulsa, co., Okla. B6 79
Tuluá, Col. C2 32
Tulun, Sov. Un. D13 13
Tulungagung, Indon. G4 19
Tumaco, Col. C2 32
Tumbarumba, Austl. G7 26
Tumbes, Peru B1 31
Tumen, China C10 17
Tumkūr, India F6 20
Tumuti, Austl. *G8 26
Tumwater, Wash. B3 86
Tunbridge Wells, Eng. E7   4
Tungurahua, prov., Ec. B2 31
Tunica, Miss. A3 68
Tunica, co., Miss. A3 68
Tunis, Tun. A7 22
Tunisia, country, Afr. A6 22
Tunja, Col. B3 32
Tunkhannock, Pa. C10 81
Tuntutuliak, Alsk. C7 47
Tunxi, China F8 17
Tuolumne, Calif. D3 50
Tuolumne, co., Calif. C4 50
Tupelo, Miss. A5 68
Tupper Lake, N.Y. A6, f10 75
Tupungato, mtn., Arg. A3 28
Tura, Sov. Un. C13 13
Turbaco, Col. A2 32
Turčiansky Svaty Martin, Czech. D5   7
Turda, Rom. B6 10
Tuerk, Pol. B5   7
Turgay, Sov. Un. E9 13
Turgovishte, Bul. D8 10
Turgutlu, Tur. C6 14
Turin (Torino), It. B1   9
Turka, Sov. Un. G4 12
Turkestan, Sov. Un. E9 13
Túrkeve, Hung. B5 10
Turkey, Tex. B2 84
Turkey, country, Asia, Eur. C9 14
Turkmen, S.S.R., rep., Sov. Un. *F8 16
Turks & Caicos Islands, Br. dep.,
  N.A. D8 35

Turku (Abo), Fin. G10 11
Turku-Pori, prov., Fin. *G10 11
Turley, Okla. A6 79
Turlock, Calif. D3 50
Turner, Kans. B8 61
Turner, co., Ga. E3 55
Turner, co., S. Dak. G8 77
Turners Falls, Mass. A2 65
Turner Valley, Alta., Can. D3 38
Turnhout, Bel. B6   5
Turnov, Czech. C3   7
Turnovo, Bul. D7 10
Turnu Măgurele, Rom. D7 10
Turnu Severin, Rom. C6 10
Turquino, peak, Cuba D5 35
Turtkul, Sov. Un. E9 13
Turtle Creek, Pa. k14 81
Tuscaloosa, Ala. B2 46
Tuscaloosa, co., Ala. B2 46
Tŏscany, reg., It. C3   9
Tuscarawas, co., Ohio B4 78
Tuscola, Ill. D5 58
Tuscola, co., Mich. E7 66
Tusculum College, Tenn. *C5 83
Tuscumbia, Ala. A2 46
Tuskegee, Ala. C4 46
Tuskegee Institute, Ala. C4 46
Tustin, Calif. *F5 50
Tuticorin, India G6 20
Tutrakan, Bul. C8 10
Tuttlingen, Ger., Fed. Rep. of E4   6
Tutwiler, Miss. A3 68
Tuvalu, country, Oceania G8   2
Tuxedo, Md. C4 53
Tuxedo Park, N.Y. D6, m14 75
Tuxpan, Mex. C3, m11 34
Tuxpan, Mex. n12 34
Tuxpan de Rodriguez Cano, Mex. C5, m15 34
Tuxtla Gutiérrez, Mex. D6 34
Tuy, Sp. A1   8
Tuzla, Yugo. C4 10
Tweed, Ont., Can. C7 41
Twenty-Nine Palms, Calif. E5 50
Twig, Minn. D6 67
Twiggs, co., Ga. D3 55
Twillingate, Newf., Can. D4 44
Twin City, Ga. D4 55
Twin Falls, Idaho G4 57
Twin Falls, co., Idaho G4 57
Twin Lakes, Calif. *D2 50
Twin Lakes, Ohio *A4 78
Twin Lakes, Wis. F5, n11 88
Twin Oaks, Pa. *G11 81
Twin Orchards, N.Y. *C5 75
Twin Rocks, Pa. F4 81
Twinsburg, Ohio A4 78
Two Harbors, Minn. D7 67
Two Rivers, Wis. D6, h10 88
Tyler, Minn. F2 67
Tyler, Tex. C5 84
Tyler, co., Tex. D5 84
Tyler, co., W. Va. B4 87
Tyler Park, Va. *B5 85
Tylertown, Miss. D3 68
Tyndall, S. Dak. H8 77
Tynemouth, Eng. C6   4
Tyre, see Sūr, Leb.
Tyrrell, co., N.C. B6 76
Tyrone, Pa. E5 81
Tyrone, co., N. Ire. *C3   4
Tyumen, Sov. Un. D9 13

U

Ubá, Braz. C4, g6 30
Ube, Jap. J5 18
Ubeda, Sp. C4   8
Uberaba, Braz. B3 30
Uberlândia, Braz. B3 30
Ubon Ratchathani, Thai. B2 19
Uccle, Bel. B6   5
Udaipur, India D5 20
Uddevalla, Swe. H4 11
Udine, It. A4   9

Udon Thani, Thai. B2 19
Ueda, Jap. H9, m17 18
Uelen, Sov. Un. C21 13
Uelkal, Sov. Un. C21 13
Uelzen, Ger., Fed. Rep. of B5   6
Ueno, Jap. o15 18
Ufa, Sov. Un. D8 13
Uganda, country, Afr. H4 23
Uglegorsk (Esutoru), Sov. Un. B11 18
Uglich, Sov. Un. C12 12

Uherské Hradistě, Czech. D4   7
Uhrichsville, Ohio B4 78
Uijongbu, Kor. H3 18
Uinta, co., Wyo. E2 89
Uintah, co., Utah B7 72
Uitenhage, S. Afr. *G5 24
Uji, Jap. *o14 18
Ujjain, India D6 20
Ujung Pandang, Indon. G5 19
Ukhta, Sov. Un. C8 13

Ukiah, Calif. C2 50
Ukraine (S.S.R.), rep., Sov. Un. *E6 16
Ulan Bator, Mong. B6 17
Ulan-Ude, Sov. Un. D13 13
Ulhasnagar, India *E5 20
Uliastay, Mong. B4 17
Ulla, Sov. Un. D7 12
Ulm, Ger., Fed. Rep. of D4   6
Ulman, Mo. C5 69
Ulsan, Kor. I4 18

Ulster, co., N.Y. D6 75
Ulster, prov., Ire. *C3 4
Ulverston, Eng. C5 4
Ulyanovsk, Sov. Un. D7 13
Ulysses, Kans. E2 61
Uman, Sov. Un. G8 12
Umatilla, Fla. D5 54
Umatilla, co., Oreg. B7 80
Umbria, pol. dist., It. *C4 9
Umbria, reg., It. C4 9
Umeå, Swe. F9 11
Umm Durmãn, see Omdurman,
  Sud.
Umm Ruwābah, Sud. F4 23
'Umrãn, Yemen F3 15
Una, S.C. *B4 82
Unadilla, Ga. D3 55
Unadilla, N.Y. C5 75
'Unayzah, Sua., Ar. D3 15
Uncasville, Conn. D8 52
Uncompahgre, mts., Colo. C3 51
Underwood, N. Dak. C4 77
Unecha, Sov. Un. E9 12
Unggi, Kor. .... E5 18'
Unicoi, co., Tenn. C11 83
Unidad de San Juan de Aragón,
  Mex. *D5 34
Union, Miss. C4 68
Union, Mo. C6 69
Union, N.J. B4 74
Union, Ohio C1 78
Union, Oreg. B9 80
Union, S.C. B4 82
Union, co., Ark. D3 49
Union, co., Fla. B4 54
Union, co., Ga. B2 55
Union, co., Ill. F4 58
Union, co., Ind. E8 59
Union, co., Iowa C3 60
Union, co., Ky. C1 62
Union, co., Miss. A4 68
Union, co., N.J. B4 74
Union, co., N.Mex. A7 48
Union, co., N.C. B2 76
Union, co., Ohio B2 78
Union, co., Oreg. B8 80

Union, co., Pa. E7 81
Union, co., S.C. B4 82
Union, co., S. Dak. H9 77
Union, co., S. Dak. C10 83
Union, co., Tenn. .... :... C10 83
Union, par., La. B3 63
Union Beach, N.J. C4 74
Union City, Calif. h8 50
Union City, Ga. C2 55
Union City, Ind. D8 59
Union City, Mich. F5 66
Union City, N.J. h8 74
Union City, Ohio B1 78
Union City, Pa. C2 81
Union City, Tenn. A2 83
Uniondale, N.Y. *G2 52
Unión de Reyes, Cuba C3 35
Union Gap, Wash. C5 86
Union Grove, Wis. F5, n11 88
Union Lake, Mich. *F7 66
Union of Soviet Socialist Republics,
  country, Europe, Asia 13
Union Park Fla. *D5 54
Union Point, Ga. C3 55
Union Springs, Ala. C4 46
Union Springs, N.Y. C4 75
Uniontown, Ala. C2 46
Uniontown, Ky. C2 62
Uniontown, Ohio B4 78
Uniontown, Pa. G2 81
Union Village, R.I. B10 52
Unionville, Conn. B5 52
Unionville, Mo. A4 69
United, Pa. F3 81
United Arab Emirates, country, Asia . E5 15
United Arab Republic, see
  Egypt, country, Afr.
United Kingdom of Great Britain
  and Northern Ireland, country, Eur. 4
United States, country, N.A. 45
United States Air Force Acad., Colo. . . C6 51
Unity, Sask., Can. E1 39
University, Miss. A4 68
University City, Mo. C7, f13 69
University Gardens, Md. *C4 53
University Heights, Ohio h9 78
University Hills, Md. *C4 53

University Park, Md. *C4 53
University Park, N. Mex. *C5 48
University Park, Tex. n10 84
University View, Ohio *C3 78
Unterwalden, canton, Switz. *E4 6
Ünye, Tur. B11 14
Upington, S. Afr. F4 24
Upland, Calif. E5, m13 50
Upland, Ind. D7 59
Upland, Pa. *G10 81
Upper Arlington, Ohio B3, k10 78
Upper Brookville, N.Y. *E7 75
Upper Darby, Pa. G11, p20 81
Upper Nyack, N.Y. *D7 75
Upper Saddle River, N.J. A4 74
Upper Sandusky, Ohio B2 78
Upper Silesia, reg., Pol. g9 7
Uppsala, Swe. H7, t35 11
Uppsala, co., Swe. *H7 11
Upshur, co., Tex. C5 84
Upshur, co., W. Va. C4 87
Upson, co., Ga. D2 55
Upton, Mass. B4, h9 65
Upton, Wyo. B8 89
Upton, co., Tex. D2 84
Ural, riv., Sov. Un. E8 13
Uralsk, Sov. Un. D8 13
Urania, La. C3 63
Uranium City, Sask., Can. E12 36
Uravan, Colo. C2 51
Urawa, Jap. I9, n18 18
Urbana, Ill. C5 58
Urbana, Ohio B2 78
Urbancrest, Ohio m10 78
Urbandale, Iowa C4, e8 60
Urbino, It. C4 9
Urfa, Tur. D12 14
Uri, canton, Switz. E4 6
Urla, Tur. *C6 14
Urmia, salt lake, Iran D15 14
Urupan del Progresso,
  Mex. D4, n13 34
Urugualana, Braz. D1 30
Uruguay, country, S.A. E1 30
Uruguay, riv., Arg., Ur. E1 30
Urumqi, China C2 17

Urusha, Sov. Un. D15 13
Uryupinsk, Sov. Un. F14 12
Uşak, Tur. C7 14
Üsküdar, Tur. B7 14
Usman, Sov. Un. E12 12
Usolye-Sibirskoye, Sov. Un. D13 13
Ussuriysk, Sov. Un. E16 13
Ustí nad Labem, Czech. C3 7
Ustinov, Sov. Un. D8 13
Ust-Kamenogórsk, Sov. Un. E11 13
Ust-Kut, Sov. Un. D13 13
Ust-Maya, Sov. Un. C16 13
Ust-Srednikan, Sov. Un. C18 13
Ust-Tsilma, Sov. Un. C8 13
Ust-Usa, Sov. Un. C8 13
Ustyuzhna, Sov. Un. B11 12
Usu, China C1 17
Usumbura, see Bujumbura, Burundi
Utah, co., Utah A6 72
Utah, state, U.S. 72
Utica, Ill. B4 58
Utica, Mich. F7, o15 66
Utica, N.Y. B5 75
Utica, Ohio B3 78
Utica, S.C. *B1 82
Utica Heights, Mich. *F8 66
Utiel, Sp. C5 8
Utrecht, Neth. A6 5
Utrecht, prov., Neth. *A6 5
Utrera, Sp. D3 8
Utsunomiya, Jap. H9 18
Uttaradit, Thai. *B2 19
Uttar Pradesh, state, India C6 20
Utuado, P.R. *G11 35
Uusimaa, prov., Fin. *G11 11
Uvalde, Tex. E3 84
Uvalde, co., Tex. E3 84
Uvaly, Czech. n18 7
Uwajima, Jap. J6 18
Uxbridge, Ont., Can. C5 41
Uxbridge, Mass. B4 65
Uzbek S.S.R., rep., Sov. Un. *E9 16
Uzhgorod, Sov. Un. G4 12
Uzunköprü, Tur. B6 14

V

Vaasa, Fin. F9 11
Vaasa, prov., Fin. *F9 11
Vác, Hung. B4 10
Vacaville, Calif. C3 50
Vacherie, La. h10 63
Vadnais Heights, Minn. *F5 67
Vaduz, Liech. E4 6
Vail Homes, N.J. *C4 74
Valais, canton, Switz. E3 6
Valatie, N.Y. C7 75
Val-Barrette, Que., Can. *G20 36
Val-David, Que., Can. C3 42
Valdepeñas, Sp. C4 8
Valdese, N.C. B1 76
Valdivia, Chile B2 28
Valdivia, prov., Chile B2 28
Val-d' Or, Que., Can. o20 41
Valdosta, Ga. F3 55
Vale, Oreg. D9 80
Valença, Braz. E7 27
Valence, Fr. E6 5
Valencia, Sp. C2 8
Valencia, Sp. C5 8
Valencia, Ven. A4 32
Valencia, co., N. Mex. B4 48
Valencia, prov., Sp. *C2 8
Valenciennes, Fr. B5 5
Valentine, Nebr. B5 71
Valera, Ven. B3 32
Valhalla, N.Y. D7, m15 75
Valjevo, Yugo. C4 10
Valka, Sov. Un. C6 12
Valki, Sov. Un. G10 12
Valladolid, Sp. B3 8
Valladolid, prov., Sp. *B3 8
Valle d' Aosta, pol. dist., It. *B1 9
Valle de la Pascua, Ven. B4 32
Valle del Cauca, dept., Col. C2 32
Valle de Santiago, Mex. m13 34
Valledupar, Col. A3 32
Vallée-Jonction, Que., Can. C7 42
Vallejo, Calif. C2 50
Valletta, Malta A7 22
Valley, Nebr. C9, g12 71

Valley, co., Idaho E3 57
Valley, co., Mont. B10 70
Valley, co., Nebr. C6 71
Valley Brook, Okla. *B4 79
Valley Center, Kans. E6, g12 61
Valley City, N. Dak. D7 77
Valley Cottage, N.Y. g13 75
Valleydale, Calif. *F4 50
Valley Falls, Kans. C8, k15 61
Valleyfield, Que., Can. D3, q18 42
Valley Mills, Tex. D4 84
Valley Park, Miss. C3 68
Valley Park, Mo. f12 69
Valley Station, Ky. g11 62
Valley Stream, N.Y. k13 75
Valley View, Ill. *B5 58
Valley View, Ohio *A4 78
Valley View, Tex. E9 81
Valmiera, Sov. Un. C5 12
Valparai, India *F6 20
Valparaíso, Chile A2 28
Valparaiso, Fla. u15 54
Valparaiso, Ind. B3 59
Valparaíso, prov., Chile A2 28
Valverde, Dom. Rep. E8 35
Val Verde, co., Tex. E2 84
Van, Tex. C5 84
Van, Tur. C14 14
Van, prov., Tur. *C14 14
Van Alstyne, Tex. C4 84
Van Buren, Ark. B1 49
Van Buren, Ind. C6 59
Van Buren, Maine A5 64
Van Buren, co., Ark. B3 49
Van Buren, co., Iowa D5 60
Van Buren, co., Mich. F4 66
Van Buren, co., Tenn. D8 83
Vance, co., N.C. A4 76
Vanceburg, Ky. B6 62
Vancouver, B.C., Can. E6, f12 37
Vancouver, Wash. D3 86
Vancouver, isl., B.C., Can. G8 36
Vandalia, Ill. E4 58
Vandalia, Mo. B6 69

Vandalia, Ohio *C1 78
Vanderbilt, Pa. F2 81
Vanderburgh, co., Ind. H2 59
Vandercook Lake, Mich. *F6 66
Vandergrift, Pa. E2 81
Vanderhoof, B.C., Can. C5 37
Vandling, Pa. C11 81
Vänern (Väner), lake, Swe. H5 11
Vänersborg, Swe. H5 11
Van Horn, Tex. o12 84
Vankleek Hill, Ont., Can. B10 41
Van Lear, Ky. C7 62
Vannes, Fr. D2 5
Vanuatu, country, Oceania H8 2
Vanves, Fr. g10 5
Van Wert, Ohio B1 78
Van Wert, co., Ohio B1 78
Van Winkle, Miss. C3 68
Van Yen, Viet. *G5 17
Van Zandt, co., Tex. C5 84
Var, dept., Fr. *F7 5
Vārānasi (Benares), India C7 20
Varaždin, Yugo. B3 10
Varazze, It. B2 9
Varberg, Swe. I5 11
Varel, Ger., Fed. Rep. of B4 6
Varese, It. B2 9
Varginha, Braz. C3 30
Varkaus, Fin. F12 11
Varmland, co., Swe. *H5 11
Värnamo, Swe. I6 11
Varnsdorf, Czech. C3 7
Varnville, S.C. F5 82
Vas, co., Hung. *B3 10
Vasilkov, Sov. Un. F8 12
Vaslui, Rom. B8 10
Vassar, Mich. E7 66
Västerås, Swe. H7, t34 11
Västerbotten, co., Swe. *F9 11
Västernörrland, co., Swe. *F8 11
Västervik, Swe. I7 11
Västmanland, co., Swe. *H7 11
Vasto, It. C5 9

Vatican City, country, Eur. D4, h8 9
Vaucluse, dept., Fr. *F6 5
Vaud, canton, Switz. *E2 6
Vaudreuil, Que., Can. D3, a18 42
Vaudreuil, co., Que., Can. D3 42
Vaughan, Ont., Can. D5, k14 41
Vaughn, N. Mex. B6 48
Vaupés, comisaría, Col. C3 32
Växjö, Swe. I6 11
Veachland, Ky. B4 62
Veazie, Maine *D4 64
Vecsés, Hung. B4 10
Veedersburg, Ind. D3 59
Vegas Heights, Nev. *G6 72
Vegreville, Alta., Can. C4 38
Vejle, Den. J3 11
Vejle, co., Den. *J3 11
Velbert, Ger., Fed. Rep. of *C3 6
Velda Village Hills, Mo. *C7 69
Vélez-Rubio, Sp. D4 8
Velikiye Luki, Sov. Un. C8 12
Velikiy Ustyug, Sov. Un. C7 13
Velizh, Sov. Un. D8 12
Velletri, It. D4, h9 9
Vellore, India F6 20
Velma, Okla. C4 79
Velsen, Neth. B2 6
Velsk, Sov. Un. C7 13
Velva, N. Dak. B5 77
Venado Tuerto, Arg. A4 28
Venango, co., Pa. D2 81
Vendée, hills, Fr. *D3 5
Venetian Village, Ill. *A6 58
Veneto, pol. dist., It. *B4 9
Veneto, reg., It. A3 9
Venezia, see Venice, It B4 9
Venezuela, country, S.A. C4 27
Venice, Fla. E4 54
Venice, Ill. E3 58
Venice (Venezia), It. B4 9
Vénissieux, Fr. E6 5
Venlo, Neth. B7 5
Ventimiglia, It. C1 9
Ventnor City, N.J. E4 74

Ventspils, Sov. Un. C3   12
Ventura, Calif. E4   50
Ventura, co., Calif. E4   50
Ventura North (Chrisman), Calif. *E4   50
Veracruz Llave, Mex. D5, n15   34
Veracruz, state, Mex. D5, n15   34
Veradale, Wash. *B8   86
Verãval, India D5   20
Vercelli, It. B2   9
Verchères, Que., Can. D4   42
Verchères, Que., Can. D9   42
Verden, Ger., Fed. Rep. of B4   6
Verdun, Que., Can. g19   42
Verdun -Sur-Meuse, Fr. C6   5
Verdunville, W.Va. D2   87
Vereeniging, S.Afr. F5   24
Verga, N.J. *D2   74
Vergennes, Vt. C1   73
Verkhneye, Sov. Un. G12, q21   12
Verkhoyansk, Sov. Un. C16   13
Vermilion, Alta., Can. C5   38
Vermilion, Ohio A3   78
Vermilion, co., Ill. C6   58
Vermilion, par.,La. E3   63
Vermilion Heights, Ill. *C6   58
Vermillion, S. Dak. H9   77
Vermillion, co., Ind. E3   59
Vermilion Heights, Ill. *C6   58
Vermont, state, U.S.   73
Vernal, Utah A7   72
Vernon, Ala. B1   46
Vernon, B.C., Can. D8, n19   37
Vernon, Fr. C4   5
Vernon, N.Y. *B5   75
Vernon, Tex. B3   84
Vernon, co., Mo. D3   69
Vernon, co., Wis. E3   88
Vernon, par.,La. C2   63
Vernonia, Oreg. B3   80
Vernon Valley, N.Y. n15   75
Vernona, N.J. B4   74
Vernona, Pa. k14   81
Vernona, Wis. E4   88
Vero Beach, Fla. E6   54
Verona, It. B3   9
Verona Park, Mich. *F5   66
Verplanck, N.Y. *D7   75
Versailles, Fr. C4, g9   5
Versailles, Ind. F7   59
Versailles, Ky. B5   62
Versailles, Mo. C5   69
Versailles, Ohio B1   78
Versailles, Pa. *F2   81
Verviers, Bel. B6   5
Veseloye, Sov. Un. H10   12
Vesoul, Fr. D7   5
Vest-Agder, co., Nor. *H2   11
Vestal, N.Y. C4   75
Vestavia Hills, Ala. g7   46
Vestfold, co., Nor. *H4   11
Vestry, Miss. E5   68
Vesuvius, vol., It. D5   9
Veszprém, Hung. B3   10
Veszprem, co., Hung. *B3   10
Veszto, Hung. B5   10
Vevay, Ind. G7   59
Vevey, Switz. C3   6
Vezirköprü, Tur. B10   14
Viadana, It. B3   9
Vian, Okla. B7   79
Viangchan, Laos B2   19
Viareggio, It. C3   9

Viborg, co., Den. *I3   11
Vibo Valentia, It. E6   9
Vicco, Ky. C6   62
Vicente López, Arg. *g7   28
Vicenza, It. B3   9
Vichada, comisaría, Col. C3   32
Vichy, Fr. D5   5
Vicksburg, Mich. F5   66
Vicksburg,Miss. C3   68
Victor, N.Y. C3   75
Victor Harbour, Austl. G2   26
Victoria, Arg. A4   28
Victoria, B.C., Can. E6, f12   37
Victoria, Newf., Can. E5   44
Victoria, Chile B2   28
Victoria, Hong Kong G7   17
Victoria, Kans. D4   61
Victoria, Tex. E4   84
Victoria, Va. D4   85
Victoria, co., N.B., Can. B2   43
Victoria, co., N.S., Can. C9   43
Victoria, co., Ont., Can. C6   43
Victoria, co., Tex. E4   84
Victoria, state, Austl. G7   25
Victoria, isl., Can. B11   36
Victoria, lake, Afr. I4   23
Victoria, mtn., Pap. k12   25
Victoria de las Tunas, Cuba D5   35
Victoria Harbour, Ont., Can. C5   41
Victoriaville, Que., Can. C6   42
Victor Mills, S.C. *B3   82
Victorville, Calif. E5   50
Victory Gardens, N.J. *B3   74
Victory Heights, N.Y. *C4   75
Vidalia, Ga. D4   55
Vidalia, La. C4   63
Vidin, Bul. D6   10
Vidor, Tex. D6   84
Vienna (Wien), Aus. D8   6
Vienna, Ga. D3   55
Vienna, Ill. F5   58
Vienna, Va. B5, g12   85
Vienna, W. Va. B3   87
Vienne, Fr. E6   5
Vienne, dept., Fr. *D4   5
Vierzon, Fr. D5   5
Vieste, It. D6   9
Vietnam, country, Asia B3   19
View Park, Calif. *E4   50
Vigan, Phil. B6   19
Vigevano, It. B2   9
Vigo, Sp. A1   8
Vigo, co., Ind. F3   59
Vijayawãda, India E7   20
Vila Nova de Gaia, Port. B1   8
Vila Velha, Braz. C4   30
Vieleyka, Sov. Un. D6   12
Viljandi, Sov. Un. B5   12
Vilkovo, Sov. Un. I7   12
Villacarrillo, Sp. C4   8
Villach, Aus. E6   6
Villa Dolores, Arg. A3   28
Villafranca, It. B3   9
Villafranca de los Barros, Sp. C2   8
Villafranca del Panadés, Sp. B6   8
Villafranca di Verona, It. B3   9
Villagarcía de Arosa, Sp. A1   8
Village-Richelieu, Que., Can. *D4   42
Villa Grove, Ill. D5   58
Villaguay, Arg. A5   28
Villa Heights, Md. *C4   53
Villahermosa, Mex. D6   34

Villa María, Arg. A4   28
Villanova, Pa. *G11   81
Villanueva de Córdoba, Sp. C3   8
Villanueva del Arzobispo, Sp. C4   8
Villanueva de La Serena, Sp. C3   8
Villanueva y Geltrú, Sp. B6   8
Villa Obregón, Mex. h9   34
Villa Park, Ill. k8   58
Villa Rica, Ga. C2   55
Villarreal, Sp. C5   8
Villarrica, Par. E4   29
Villarrobledo, Sp. C4   8
Villas, N.J. E3   74
Villavicencio, Col. C3   32
Villefranche-sur-Saône, Fr. E6   5
Villejuif, Fr. g10   5
Ville Marie, Que., Can. p20   41
Villemomble, Fr. g10   5
Villeneuve-le-Roi, Fr. h10   5
Villeneuve-St. Georges, Fr. h10   5
Villeneuve-sur-Lot, Fr. E4   5
Ville Platte, La. D3   63
Ville St. Georges, Que., Can. *C7   42
Villeta, Par. E4   29
Villeurbanne, Fr. E6   5
Villigen-Schwenningen, Ger.,
    Fed. Rep. of *D4   6
Villisca, Iowa D3   60
Vilnius, Sov. Un. D5   12
Vilvoorde, Bel. B6   5
Vilyuy, riv., Sov. Un. C15   13
Vilyuysk, Sov. Un. C15   13
Vimianzo, Sp. A1   8
Viña del Mar, Chile A2   28
Vinalhaven, Maine D4   64
Vincennes, Fr. g10   5
Vincennes, Ind. G3   59
Vincent, Ala. B3   46
Vincent, Ohio *A3   78
Vindeln, Swe. E8   11
Vine Grove, Ky. C4   62
Vine Hill (Martinez East), Calif. *C2   50
Vineland, N.J. E2   74
Vineyard Haven (Tisbury), Mass. D6   65
Vinh Yen, Viet. G6   17
Vinita, Okla. A6   79
Vinita Park, Mo. *C7   69
Vinkovci, Yugo. C4   10
Vinnitsa, Sov. Un. G7   12
Vinson Massif, mtn., Ant. L15   2
Vinton, Iowa B5   60
Vinton, La. D2   63
Vinton, Va. C3   85
Vinton, co., Ohio C3   78
Vintondale, Pa. F4   81
Virden, Man., Can. E1   40
Virden, Ill. D4   58
Virginia, Ill. D3   58
Virginia, Minn. C6   67
Virginia, state, U.S.   85
Virginia Beach
    (Independent City), Va. D7, k16   85
Virginia City, Nev. B2   72
Virginia Gardens, Fla. *G6   54
Virgin Islands, Br. dep., N.A. G12   35
Virgin Islands of the U.S.,
    dep., N.S. G12   35
Viroflay, Fr. g9   5
Viroqua, Wis. E3   88
Virovitica, Yugo. C3   10
Visalia, Calif. D4   50
Visby, Swe. I8   11
Vishãkhapatnam, India E7   20

Vista, Calif. F5   50
Vista Park, Calif. *E4   50
Vitanovak, Yugo. D5   10
Vitebsk, Sov. Un. D8   12
Viterbo, It. C4   9
Vitim, Sov. Un. D14   13
Vitória, Braz. C4   30
Vitoria, Sp. A4   8
Vitória da Conquista, Braz. A4   30
Vitry -sur-Seine, Fr. g10   5
Vittoria, It. F5   9
Vittorio Veneto, It. B4   9
Vivian, La. B2   63
Vizcaya, prov., Sp. *A4   8
Vizianagaram, India E7   20
Vizzini, It. F5   9
Vlaardingen, Neth. B6   5
Vladimir, Sov. Un. C13   12
Vladimiro Aleksandrovskoye,
    Sov. Un. E6   18
Vladimir Volynskiy, Sov. Un. F5   12
Vladivostok, Sov. Un. E5   18
Vlasotince, Yugo. D6   10
Vlissingen, Neth. B5   5
Vlonë, pref., Alb. *B2   14
Vlorë, Alb. B2   14
Vodnany, Czech. *D3   7
Voeune Sai, Camb. F7   22
Voghera, It. B2   9
Voiron, Fr. E6   5
Volga, riv., Sov. Un. E7   12
Volgograd, Sov. Un. G14   12
Volkhov, Sov. Un. B9   12
Volkovysk, Sov. Un. E5   12
Vologda, Sov. Un. B12   12
Volokolamsk, Sov. Un. C10   12
Volos, Grc. C4   14
Volsk, Sov. Un. *D7   13
Volta Redonda, Braz. C4, h5   30
Volterra, It. C3   9
Volusia, co., Fla. C5   54
Volzhskiy, Sov. Un. G15   12
Voorheesville, N.Y. *C7   75
Vorarlberg, state, Aus. E4   6
Vordingborg, Den. A1   7
Vorkuta, Sov. Un. C9   13
Voronezh, Sov Un F12   12
Voroshilovgrad (Lugansk),
    Sov. Un. G12, q22   12
Vosges, dept., Fr. *C7   5
Votkinsk, Sov. Un. *D8   13
Voznesensk, Sov. Un. H8   12
Vranje, Yugo. D5   10
Vratsa, Bul. D6   10
Vratsa, co., Bul. D6   10
Vršac, Yugo. C5   10
Vsetín, Czech. D5   7
Vukovar, Yugo. C4   10
Vulcan, Alta., Can. D4   38
Vulcan, Mo. D7   69
Vung Tau, Viet. *C3   17
Vyazma, Sov. Un. D10   12
Vyazniki, Sov. Un. C14   12
Vyborg, Sov. Un. A7   12
Vyksa, Sov. Un. D14   12
Vyshniy Volochek, Sov. Un. C10   12
Vysoké Tatry, Czech. D6   7
Vytegra, Sov. Un. A11   12

W

Wabana (Bell Island), Newf., Can. E5   44
Wabash, Ind. C6   59
Wabash, co., Ill. E6   58
Wabash, co., Ind. C6   59
Wabasha, Minn. F6   67
Wabasha, co., Minn. F6   67
Wabasso, Fla. E6   54
Wabaunsee, co., Kans. D7   61
Wacissa, Fla. B3   54
Waco, Tex. D4   84
Waconia, Minn. F5   67
Waddington, B.C., Can. F8   36
Waddington, N.Y. f9   75
Wadena, Sask., Can. F4   39
Wadena, Minn. D3   67
Wadena, co., Minn. D4   67

Wadesboro, N.C. C2   76
Wadley, Ga. D4   55
Wad Madanî, Sud. F4   23
Wadsworth, Ohio A4   78
Waelder, Tex. E4   84
Wagga Wagga, Austl. *G8   25
Wagner, S.Dak. G7   77
Wagoner, Okla. B6   79
Wagoner, co., Okla. B6   79
Wagon Mound, N.Mex. B6   48
Wagrowiec, Pol. B4   7
Wah Cantonment, Pak. *B5   20
Wahiawa, Haw. B3, f9   56
Wahkiakum, co., Wash. C2   86
Wahneta, Fla. *E5   54
Wahoo, Nebr. C9, g11   71

Wahpeton, N.Dak. D9   77
Waialua, Haw. B3, f9   56
Waianae, Haw. B3, g9   56
Waikabubak, Indon. G5   19
Wailua, Haw. A2   56
Wailuku, Haw. C5   56
Waimanalo, Haw. B4, g11   56
Waimea, Haw. B2   56
Waimea, Haw. f9   56
Wainwright, Alta., Can. C5   38
Waipahu, Haw. B3, g9   56
Waipio Acres, Haw. g9   56
Waite Park, Minn. E4   67
Waitsburg, Wash. C7   86
Wajima, Jap. H8   18
Wakarusa, Ind. A5   59

Wakaw, Sask., Can. E3   39
Wakayama, Jap. I7, o14   18
Wakayama, pref., Jap. *I7   18
Wake, co., N.C. B4   76
WaKeeney, Kans. C4   61
Wakefield, Mass. B5, f11   65
Wakefield, Mich. n12   66
Wakefield, Nebr. B9   71
Wakefield, R.I. D11   52
Wakefield, Va. D6   85
Wake Forest, N.C. B4   76
Wakkanai, Jap. D10   18
Wakulla, co., Fla. B2   54
Walbridge, Ohio e6   78
Walbrzych, Pol. C4   7
Walden, N.Y. D6   75

Waldo, Ark. ... D2 49
Waldo, co., Maine ... D3 64
Waldorf, Md. ... C4 53
Waldron, Ark. ... C1 49
Waldwick, N.J. ... A4 74
Wales, reg., U.K. ... D5 4
Walhalla, N.Dak. ... A8 77
Walhalla, S.C. ... B1 82
Walker, La. ... g10 63
Walker, Mich. ... E5 66
Walker, Minn. ... C4 67
Walker, co., Ala. ... B2 46
Walker, co., Ga. ... B1 55
Walker, co., Tex. ... D5 84
Walkersville, Md. ... B3 53
Walkerton, Ont., Can. ... C3 41
Walkerton, Ind. ... B5 59
Walkertown, N.C. ... A2 76
Walkerville, Mont. ... D4 70
Wall, Pa. ... *F2 81
Wallace, Idaho ... B3 57
Wallace, N.C. ... C4 76
Wallace, co., Kans. ... D2 61
Wallaceburg, Ont., Can. ... E2 41
Wallasey, Eng. ... D5 4
Walla Walla, Wash. ... C7 86
Walla Walla, co., Wash. ... C7 86
Walled Lake, Mich. ... o15 66
Waller, Tex. ... D5 84
Waller, co., Tex. ... E4 84
Wallingford, Conn. ... D5 52
Wallingford, Vt. ... E2 73
Wallington, Eng. ... m12 4
Wallington, N.J. ... h8 74
Wallis, Tex. ... E4 84
Wallkill, N.Y. ... D6 75
Wallowa, Oreg. ... B9 80
Wallowa, co., Oreg. ... B9 80
Wallsend, Eng. ... C6 4
Walnut, Calif. ... *F4 50
Walnut, Ill. ... B4 58
Walnut Cove, N.C. ... A2 76
Walnut Creek, Calif. ... h8 50
Walnut Heights, Calif. ... *D2 50
Walnut Park, Calif. ... *F4 50
Walnutport, Pa. ... E10 81
Walnut Ridge, Ark. ... A5 49
Walpole, Mass. ... B5, h10 65
Walsall, Eng. ... D6 4
Walsenburg, Colo. ... D6 51
Walsh, co., N.Dak. ... B8 77
Walterboro, S.C. ... F6 82
Walters, Okla. ... C3 79
Walthall, co., Miss. ... D3 68
Waltham, Mass. ... B5, g11 65
Walthill, Nebr. ... B9 71
Walton, Ind. ... C5 59
Walton, Ky. ... B5, k13 62
Walton, N.Y. ... C5 75
Walton, co., Fla. ... u15 54
Walton, co., Ga. ... C3 55
Walton Hills, Ohio ... *A4 78
Walvisbaai, S.Afr. ... E2 24
Walworth, Wis. ... F5 88
Walworth, co., S.Dak. ... E5 77
Walworth, co., Wis. ... F5 88
Wamac, Ill. ... E4 58
Wamego, Kans. ... C7 61
Wampum, Pa. ... E1 81
Wanamassa, N.J. ... C4 74
Wanaque, N.J. ... A4 74
Wanganui, N.Z. ... M15 26
Wangaratta, Austl. ... H6 26
Wangqing, China ... C10 17
Wantagh, N.Y. ... G2 52
Wanxian, China ... E6 17
Wapakoneta, Ohio ... B1 78
Wapato, Wash. ... C5 86
Wapello, Iowa ... C6 60
Wapello, co., Iowa ... C5 60
Wappingers Falls, N.Y. ... D7 75
War, W.Va. ... D3 87
Warangal, India ... E6 20
Ward, W. Va. ... m13 87
Ward, co., N. Dak. ... B4 77
Ward, co., Tex. ... D1 84
Warden, Wash. ... C6 86
Ward Ridge, Fla. ... *C1 54
Wardville, La. ... *C3 63
Ware, Mass. ... B3 65
Ware, co., Ga. ... E4 55
Wareham, Mass. ... C6 65
Warehouse Point, Conn. ... B6 52
Waren, Ger. Dem. Rep. ... B6 6
Ware Shoals, S.C. ... C3 82
Warfield, B.C., Can. ... E9 37
Wargla, Alg. ... B6 22
Warner Robins, Ga. ... D3 55
Warr Acres, Okla. ... B4 79
Warragul, Austl. ... *G8 25
Warren, Ark. ... D3 49
Warren, Ill. ... A4 58
Warren, Ind. ... C7 59

Warren, Mass. ... B3 65
Warren, Mich. ... F7, p16 66
Warren, Minn. ... B2 67
Warren, Ohio ... A5 78
Warren, Pa. ... C3 81
Warren, R.I. ... C11 52
Warren, co., Ga. ... C4 55
Warren, co., Ill. ... C3 58
Warren, co., Ind. ... D3 59
Warren, co., Iowa ... C4 60
Warren, co., Ky. ... C3 62
Warren, co., Miss. ... C3 68
Warren, co., Mo. ... C6 69
Warren, co., N.J. ... B3 74
Warren, co., N.Y. ... B7 75
Warren, co., N.C. ... A4 76
Warren, co., Ohio ... C1 78
Warren, co., Pa. ... C3 81
Warren, co., Tenn. ... D8 83
Warren, co., Va. ... B4 85
Warrensburg, Mo. ... C4 69
Warrensburg, N.Y. ... B7 75
Warrensville Heights, Ohio ... h9 78
Warrenton, Ga. ... C4 55
Warrenton, Mo. ... C6 69
Warrenton, N.C. ... A4 76
Warrenton, Oreg. ... A3 80
Warrenton, Va. ... B5 85
Warrenville, Ill. ... k8 58
Warrenville, S.C. ... D4 82
Warri, Nig. ... G6 22
Warrick, co., Ind. ... H3 59
Warrington, Eng. ... D5 4
Warrington, Fla. ... u14 54
Warrior, Ala. ... B3 46
Warrnambool, Austl. ... G7, n14 25
Warroad, Minn. ... B3 67
Warsaw, Ill. ... C2 58
Warsaw, Ind. ... B6 59
Warsaw, Mo. ... C4 69
Warsaw, N.Y. ... C2 75
Warsaw, N.C. ... B4 76
Warsaw (Warszawa), Pol. ... B6, m14 7
Warson Woods, Mo. ... *C7 69
Warwick, Que., Can. ... D6 42
Warwick, Eng. ... D6 4
Warwick, N.Y. ... D6, m14 75
Warwick, R.I. ... C10 52
Warwick, co., Eng. ... *D6 4
Wasatch, co., Utah ... A6 72
Wasco, Calif. ... E4 50
Wasco, co., Oreg. ... B5 80
Waseca, Minn. ... F5 67
Waseca, co., Minn. ... F5 67
Washakie, co., Wyo. ... C5 89
Washburn, Ill. ... C4 58
Washburn, Maine ... B4 64
Washburn, Wis. ... B3 88
Washburn, co., Wis. ... C2 88
Washington, D.C. ... C3, f8 53
Washington, Ga. ... C4 55
Washington, Ill. ... C4 58
Washington, Ind. ... G3 59
Washington, Iowa ... C6 60
Washington, Kans. ... C6 61
Washington, La. ... D3 63
Washington, Mo. ... C6 69
Washington, N.J. ... B3 74
Washington, N.C. ... B5 76
Washington, Pa. ... F1 81
Washington, co., Ala. ... D1 46
Washington, co., Ark. ... A1 49
Washington, co., Colo. ... B7 51
Washington, co., Fla. ... u16 54
Washington, co., Ga. ... C3 55
Washington, co., Idaho ... E2 57
Washington, co., Ill. ... E4 58
Washington, co., Ind. ... G5 59
Washington, co., Iowa ... C6 60
Washington, co., Kans. ... C6 61
Washington, co., Ky. ... C4 62
Washington, co., Maine ... D5 64
Washington, co., Md. ... A2 53
Washington, co., Minn. ... E6 67
Washington, co., Miss. ... B3 66
Washington, co., Mo. ... D7 69
Washington, co., Nebr. ... C9 71
Washington, co., N.Y. ... B7 75
Washington, co., N.C. ... B6 76
Washington, co., Ohio ... C4 78
Washington, co., Okla. ... A6 79
Washington, co., Oreg. ... B3 80
Washington, co., Pa. ... F1 81
Washington, co., R.I. ... D10 52
Washington, co., Tenn. ... C10 83
Washington, co., Tex. ... D4 84
Washington, co., Utah ... C5 72
Washington, co., Vt. ... C2 73
Washington, co., Va. ... f9 85
Washington, co., Wis. ... E5 88
Washington, par., La. ... D5 63
Washington, state, U.S. ... 86
Washington, mtn., N.H. ... C5 73

Washington Court House, Ohio ... C2 78
Washington Heights, N.Y. ... *D6 75
Washington North, Pa. ... *F1 81
Washington Park, Ill. ... E3 58
Washington Terrace, Utah ... *A5 72
Washingtonville, N.Y. ... *D6 75
Washington West, Pa. ... *F1 81
Washita, co., Okla. ... B2 79
Washoe, co., Nev. ... A2 72
Washougal, Wash. ... D3 86
Washtenaw, co., Mich. ... F7 66
Waskom, Tex. ... C5 84
Watauga, co., N.C. ... A1 76
Watchung, N.J. ... *B4 74
Waterbury, Conn. ... C4 52
Waterbury, Vt. ... C2 73
Waterford, Calif. ... *D3 50
Waterford, Ont., Can. ... E4 41
Waterford, Conn. ... D8 52
Waterford, Ire. ... D3 4
Waterford, N.Y. ... C7 75
Waterford, Pa. ... C1 81
Waterford, Wis. ... F5, n11 88
Waterford, co., Ire. ... *D3 4
Waterloo, Ont., Can. ... D4 41
Waterloo, Que., Can. ... D5 42
Waterloo, Ill. ... E3 58
Waterloo, Ind. ... B7 59
Waterloo, Iowa ... B5 60
Waterloo, N.Y. ... C4 75
Waterloo, Wis. ... E5 88
Waterloo, co., Ont., Can. ... D4 41
Waterman, Ill. ... B5 58
Waterproof, La. ... C4 63
Watertown, Conn. ... C4 52
Watertown, Fla. ... B4 54
Watertown, Mass. ... g11 65
Watertown, Minn. ... *F5 67
Watertown, N.Y. ... B5 75
Watertown, S. Dak. ... F8 77
Watertown, Tenn. ... A5 83
Watertown, Wis. ... E5 88
Water Valley, Miss. ... A4 68
Waterville, Que., Can. ... D6 42
Waterville, Maine ... D3 64
Waterville, Minn. ... F5 67
Waterville, N.Y. ... C5 75
Waterville, Ohio ... A2, f6 78
Waterville, Wash. ... B5 86
Watervliet, Mich. ... F4 66
Watervliet, N.Y. ... C7 75
Watford, Ont., Can. ... E3 41
Watford City, N. Dak. ... C2 77
Watkins Glen, N.Y. ... C4 75
Watonga, Okla. ... B3 79
Watonwan, co., Minn. ... F4 67
Watrous, Sask., Can. ... F3 39
Watseka, Ill. ... C6 58
Watsontown, Pa. ... D8 81
Watsonville, Calif. ... D3 50
Wattrelos, Fr. ... B5 5
Wattsville, S.C. ... B4 82
Wauchope, Austl. ... *E9 26
Wauchula, Fla. ... E5 54
Wauconda, Ill. ... h8 58
Waukegan, Ill. ... A6, h9 58
Waukesha, Wis. ... E5 88
Waukesha, co., Wis. ... E5 88
Waukon, Iowa ... A6 60
Waunakee, Wis. ... E4 88
Waupaca, Wis. ... D4 88
Waupaca, co., Wis. ... D5 88
Waupun, Wis. ... E5 88
Waurika, Okla. ... C4 79
Wausau, Wis. ... D4 88
Wauseon, Ohio ... A1 78
Waushara, co., Wis. ... D4 88
Wautoma, Wis. ... D4 88
Wauwatosa, Wis. ... m11 88
Waverly, Ill. ... D4 58
Waverly, Iowa ... B5 60
Waverly, N.Y. ... C4 75
Waverly, Ohio ... C3 78
Waverly, Tenn. ... A4 83
Waverly, Va. ... C5 85
Waxahachie, Tex. ... C4, n10 84
Waycross, Ga. ... E4 55
Wayland, Ky. ... C7 62
Wayland, Mass. ... g10 65
Wayland, Mich. ... F5 66
Wayland, N.Y. ... C3 75
Waymart, Pa. ... C11 81
Wayne, Mich. ... p15 66
Wayne, Nebr. ... B8 71
Wayne, N.J. ... B4 74
Wayne, Pa. ... F11, o20 81
Wayne, W. Va. ... C2 87
Wayne, co., Ga. ... E4 55
Wayne, co., Ill. ... E5 58
Wayne, co., Ind. ... E5 59
Wayne, co., Iowa ... *D4 60
Wayne, co., Ky. ... *D5 62

Wayne, co., Mich. ... F7 66
Wayne, co., Miss. ... D5 68
Wayne, co., Mo. ... D7 69
Wayne, co., Nebr. ... B8 71
Wayne, co., N.Y. ... B3 75
Wayne, co., N.C. ... B4 76
Wayne, co., Ohio ... B4 78
Wayne, co., Pa. ... C11 81
Wayne, co., Tenn. ... B4 83
Wayne, co., Utah ... B6 72
Wayne, co., W. Va. ... C2 87
Waynesboro, Ga. ... C4 55
Waynesboro, Miss. ... D5 68
Waynesboro, Pa. ... G6 81
Waynesboro, Tenn. ... B4 83
Waynesboro (Independent City),
   Va. ... B4 85
Waynesburg, Ohio ... B4 78
Waynesburg, Pa. ... G1 81
Waynesville, Mo. ... D5 69
Waynesville, N.C. ... f10 76
Waynesville, Ohio ... C1 78
Waynoka, Okla. ... A3 79
Wayzata, Minn. ... *F5 67
Weakley, co., Tenn. ... A3 83
Weatherford, Okla. ... B3 79
Weatherford, Tex. ... C4 84
Weatherly, Pa. ... E10 81
Weaver, Ala. ... B4 46
Weaverville, Calif. ... B2 50
Weaverville, N.C. ... f10 76
Webb, co., Tex. ... F3 84
Webb City, Mo. ... D3 69
Weber, co., Utah ... A6 72
Weber City, Va. ... *f9 85
Webster, Mass. ... B4 65
Webster, N.Y. ... B3 75
Webster, S. Dak. ... E8 77
Webster, co., Ga. ... D2 55
Webster, co., Iowa ... B3 60
Webster, co., Ky. ... C2 62
Webster, co., Miss. ... B4 68
Webster, co., Mo. ... D5 69
Webster, co., Nebr. ... D7 71
Webster, co., W. Va. ... C4 87
Webster, par., La. ... B2 63
Webster City, Iowa ... B4 60
Webster Groves, Mo. ... f13 69
Webster Springs (Addison), W. Va. ... C4 87
Wedgeport, N.S., Can. ... F4 43
Wedowee, Ala. ... B4 46
Weed, Calif. ... B2 50
Weed Heights, Nev. ... *B2 72
Weedon, Que., Can. ... D6 42
Weedsport, N.Y. ... B4 75
Weehawken, N.J. ... h8 79
Weeks, La. ... E4 63
Weeping Water, Nebr. ... D9, h12 71
Weert, Neth. ... B6 5
Weiden, Ger., Fed. Rep. of ... D6 6
Weifang, China ... D8 17
Weihai, China ... D9 17
Weilheim, Ger., Fed. Rep. ... E5 6
Weimar, Ger. Dem. Rep. ... C5 6
Weimar, Tex. ... E4 84
Weinan, China ... E6 17
Weinheim, Ger., Fed. Rep. of ... D4 6
Weippe, Idaho ... C3 57
Weirton, W. Va. ... A4, f8 87
Weiser, Idaho ... E2 57
Weissenburg in Bayern,
   Ger., Fed. Rep. of ... D5 6
Weissenfels, Ger. Dem. Rep. ... *C5 6
Wejherowo, Pol. ... A5 7
Welborn, Kans. ... B8 61
Welch, W. Va. ... D3 87
Welcome, S.C. ... *B3 82
Weld, co., Colo. ... A6 51
Weldon, N.C. ... A5 76
Weleetka, Okla. ... B5 79
Welkom, S. Afr. ... *F5 24
Welland, Ont., Can. ... E5 41
Wellesley, Mass. ... B5, g10 65
Wellford, S.C. ... B3 82
Wellington, Austl. ... F7 26
Wellington, Ont., Can. ... D7 41
Wellington, Kans. ... E6 61
Wellington, N.Z. ... N15 26
Wellington, Ohio ... A3 78
Wellington, Tex. ... B2 84
Wellington, Utah ... B6 72
Wellington, co., Ont., Can. ... D4 41
Wellman, Iowa ... C6 60
Wells, B.C., Can. ... C7 37
Wells, Minn. ... G5 67
Wells, Nev. ... A4 72
Wells, co., Ind. ... C7 59
Wells, co., N.Dak. ... C6 77
Wells, co., Pa. ... C7 81
Wellsboro, Pa. ... C7 81
Wellsburg, W. Va. ... A4, f8 87
Wellston, Mo. ... f13 69
Wellston, Ohio ... C3 78
Wellsville, Kans. ... D8 61

Wellsville, Mo. B6 69
Wellsville, N.Y. C3 75
Wellsville, Ohio B5 78
Wellsville, Utah A6 72
Wels, Aus. D7 6
Welsh, La. D3 63
Wembley, Eng. k11 4
Wenatche, Wash. B5 86
Wenatche, Wash. B5 86
Wenzhou, China F9 17
Wendell, Idaho G4 57
Wendell, N.C. B4 76
Wenham, Mass. A6, f12 65
Wenona, Ill. *B4 58
Wenonah, N.J. D2 74
Wentworth, co., Ont., Can. D4 41
Wentzville, Mo. C7 67
Werdau, Ger. Dem. Rep. C6 6
Wernersville, Pa. *F9 81
Wernigerode, Ger. Dem. Rep. C5 6
Wesel, Ger., Fed. Rep. of C3 6
Weslaco, Tex. F3 84
Weslaco North, Tex. *F3 84
Wesleyville, Newf., Can. D5 44
Wesleyville, Pa. B2 81
Wessington Springs, S. Dak. F7 77
Wesson, Miss. D3 68
West, Tex. D4 84
West Alexandria, Ohio C1 78
West Allis, Wis. m12 88
West Amityville, N.Y. *E7 75
West Babylon, N.Y. *n15 75
West Baden Springs, Ind. G4 59
West Barrington, R.I. B11 52
West Baton Rouge, par., La. D4 63
West Belmar, N.J. *C4 74
West Bend, Iowa B3 60
West Bend, Wis. E5 88
West Bengal, state, India *D8 20
West Berlin, N.J. D3 74
West Blocton, Ala. B2 46
West Bountiful, Utah *A6 72
West Boylston, Mass. B4 65
West Branch, Iowa C6 60
West Branch, Mich. D6 66
West Bridgewater, Mass. B5 65
West Bridgewater, Pa. *E1 81
West Bromwich, Eng. D6 4
Westbrook, Maine E2, g7 64
Westbrook, Minn. F3 67
West Brookfield, Mass. B3 65
Westbrook Park, Pa. *B11 81
West Brownsville, Pa. *F2 81
West Brunswick, N.J. *C4 74
West Burlington, Iowa D6 60
Westbury, N.Y. E7 75
Westby, Wis. E3 88
West Caldwell, N.J. *B4 74
West Cape May, N.J. F3 74
West Carroll, par., La. B4 63
West Carrollton, Ohio C1 78
West Carthage, N.Y. B5 75
Westchester, Ill. k9 58
West Chester, Pa. G10 81
Westchester, co., N.Y. D7 75
West Chicago, Ill. k8 58
West City, Ill. F8 58
West Clarkston, Wash. *C8 86
West Collingswood, N.J. *D2 74
West Collingswood Heights, N.J. .. *D2 74
West Columbia, S.C. B5 82
West Columbia, Tex. E5, r14 84
West Concord, Mass. B5, g10 65
West Concord, N.C. *B2 76
West Conshohocken, Pa. o20 81
West Corners, N.Y. *C5 75
West Covina, Calif. m13 50
Westdale, Ill. *B6 58
West Decatur, Pa. E5 81
West Derry, Pa. *F3 81
West Des Moines, Iowa C4, e8 60
West Easton, Pa. *E11 81
West Elizabeth, Pa. *F2 81
West Elkton, Ohio *C1 75
West Elmira, N.Y. *C4 75
West End, Fla. *C4 54
West End, N.Y. *C5 75
West End Anniston, Ala. *B4 46
West Endicott, N.Y. *C5 75
Westerly, R.I. D9 52
Western, reg., Nig. G5 22
Western Australia, state, Austl. . D3 25
Western Hills, Colo. *B6 51
Western Peninsula, div., Ice. ... *m21 11
Westernport, Md. m12 53
Western Sahara, country, Afr. ... D2 22
Western Samoa, country, Oceania . G9 2
Western Springs, Ill. k9 58
Westerville, Ohio B3, k11 78
West Fairview, Pa. F8 81
West Farmington, Maine D2 64
West Feliciana, par., La. D4 63
Westfield, Ind. D5 59
Westfield, Mass. B2 65

Westfield, N.J. B4 74
Westfield, N.Y. C1 75
Westfield, Pa. C6 81
Westfield, Wis. E4 88
West Flanders, prov., Bel. *B5 5
West Frankford, Ill. F5 58
Westgate, Fla. F6 54
West Glens Falls, N.Y. *B7 75
West Grove, Pa. G10 81
Westhampton Beach, N.Y. n16 75
West Hartford, Conn. B6 52
West Hartsville, S.C. *C7 82
West Haven, Conn. D5 52
West Haverstraw, N.Y. *D7 75
West Hazleton, Pa. E9 81
West Helena, Ark. C5 49
West Hempstead, N.Y. *G2 52
West Hillsboro, N.C. *A3 76
West Hollywood, Calif. *E4 50
West Hollywood, Fla. r13 54
West Homestead, Pa. *F2 81
West Indies,
  reg., Atl. O. 35
West Islip, N.Y. *n15 75
West Jefferson, N.C. A1 76
West Jefferson, Ohio C2, m10 78
West Jordan, Utah A5, D2 78
West Kingston, R.I. D10 52
West Kittanning, Pa. *E3 81
West Lafayette, Ind. D4 59
West Lafayette, Ohio B4 78
Westlake, La. D2 63
Westlake, Ohio h9 78
Westland, Mich. p15 66
Westlands, Mass. f10 65
West Lanham Hills, Md. *C4 53
West Lawn, Pa. F10 81
West Lebanon, Pa. *F9 81
West Leechburg, Pa. *E2 81
West Leisenring, Pa. G2 81
West Liberty, Iowa C6 60
West Liberty, Ky. C6 62
West Liberty, Ohio B2 78
West Liberty, W. Va. f8 87
West Linn, Oreg. B4, h12 80
Westlock, Alta., Can. B4 38
West Long Branch, N.J. *C4 74
West Lorne, Ont., Can. E3 41
West Lothian, Scot. *C5 4
West Manayunk, Pa. *F11 81
West Marion, N.C. *f10 76
West Mayfield, Pa. *E1 81
Westmeath, co., Ire. *D3 4
West Medway, Mass. B5, h10 65
West Melbourne, Fla. *D6 54
West Memphis, Ark. B5 49
West Miami, Fla. s13 54
West Middlesex, Pa. D1 81
West Mifflin, Pa. F2 81
West Milton, Ohio C1 78
West Milwaukee, Wis. m12 88
Westminster, Calif. n12 50
Westminster, Colo. A6 51
Westminster, Md. A4 53
Westminster, Mass. A4 65
Westminster, S.C. B1 82
West Monroe, La. B3 63
Westmont, Ill. k9 58
Westmont, N.J. D2 74
Westmont, Pa. F4 81
Westmoreland, co., Pa. F2 81
Westmoreland, co., Va. B6 85
Westmoreland City, Pa. *F2 81
Westmorland, Calif. F6 50
Westmorland, co., N.B., Can. ... C5 43
Westmorland, co., Eng. *C5 4
Westmount, Que., Can. *D4 42
West Mystic, Conn. D9 52
West Newton, Pa. F2 81
West New York, N.J. h8 74
West Nyack, N.Y. *D7 75
Weston, Ont., Can. m14 41
Weston, Conn. E3 52
Weston, Mass. g10 65
Weston, Mo. B3, h10 69
Weston, Ohio A2 78
Weston, W. Va. B4 87
Weston, co., Wyo. C8 89
Weston-Super-Mare, Eng. E5 4
West Orange, N.J. B4 74
West Orange, Tex. *D6 84
Westover, W.Va. B5, h11 87
West Palm Beach, Fla. F6 54
West Paterson, N.J. *B4 74
West Pensacola, Fla. v14 54
West Pittston, Pa. m17 81
West Plains, Mo. E6 69
West Point, Ga. D1 55
West Point, Ky. C4 62
West Point, Miss. B5 68
West Point, Nebr. C9 71
West Point, N.Y. D7, m15 75
West Point, Va. C6 85
Westport, Conn. E3 52

West Portland, Oreg. *B4 80
West Portland Park, Oreg. *B4 80
West Portsmouth, Ohio D2 78
West Pueblo, Colo. *C6 51
West Rockingham, N.C. *B3 76
West Rutland, Vt. D1 73
West Sacramento, Calif. *C3 50
West Salem, Ill. E5 58
West Salem, Ohio B3 78
West Salem, Wis. E2 88
West Sayville, N.Y. G4 52
West Seneca, N.Y. *C2 75
West Slope, Oreg. g12 80
West Spitsbergen, isl., Nor. A21 2
West Springfield, Mass. B2 65
West St. Paul, Minn. n12 67
West Terre Haute, Ind. F3 59
West Union, Iowa B6 60
West Union, Ohio D2 78
West Union, W.Va. B4, k9 87
West Unity, Ohio A1 78
West University Place, Tex. ... r14 84
West View, Ohio h9 78
West View, Pa. h13 81
West Van Lear, Ky. C7 62
West Virginia, state, U.S. 87
West Warren, Mass. B3 65
West Warwick, R.I. C10 52
Westwego, La. k11 63
West Wenatchee, Wash. *B5 86
West Winfield, N.Y. C5 75
West Winter Haven, Fla. *D5 54
Westwood, Calif. B3 50
Westwood, Kans. k16 61
Westwood, Ky. B7 62
Westwood, Mass. B5, h11 65
Westwood, Mich. *F5 66
Westwood, N.J. D5, h8 74
Westwood Lakes, Fla. s13 54
Westworth Village, Tex. *C4 84
West Wyalong, Austl. F6 26
West Wyoming, Pa. n17 81
West Wyomissing, Pa. *F9 81
West Yarmouth, Mass. C7 65
West York, Pa. G8 81
West Yuma, Ariz. *C1 48
Wetaskiwin, Alta., Can. C4 38
Wethersfield, Conn. C6 52
Wetumka, Okla. B5 79
Wetumpka, Ala. C3 46
Wetzel, co., W. Va. B4 87
Wetzlar, Ger., Fed. Rep. of C4 6
Wewahitchka, Fla. B1 54
Wewoka, Okla. B5 79
Wexford, Ire. D3 4
Wexford, co., Ire. *D3 4
Wexford, co., Mich. D5 66
Weyauwega, Wis. D5 88
Weyburn, Sask., Can. H4, o8 39
Weymouth, N.S., Can. E4 43
Weymouth, Mass. B6, h12 65
Weymouth & Melcombe Regis, Eng. .. E5 4
Whangarei, N.Z. K15 26
Wharton, N.J. B3 74
Wharton, Tex. E4 84
Wharton, W. Va. D6 87
Wharton, co., Tex. E4 84
Wharton West, Tex. *E4 84
What Cheer, Iowa C5 60
Whatcom, co., Wash. A4 86
Wheatland, Wyo. D8 89
Wheatland, co., Mont. D7 70
Wheatley, Ont., Can. E2 41
Wheaton, Ill. B5, k8 58
Wheaton, Md. *B3 53
Wheaton, Minn. E2 67
Wheat Ridge, Colo. *B5 51
Wheeler, Tex. B2 84
Wheeler, co., Ga. D4 55
Wheeler, co., Nebr. C7 71
Wheeler, co., Oreg. C6 80
Wheeler, co., Tex. B2 84
Wheeler, peak, N. Mex. A6 48
Wheelersburg, Ohio D3 78
Wheeling, Ill. h9 58
Wheeling, W.Va. A4, f8 87
Wheelwright, Ky. C7 62
Whippany, N.J. B4 74
Whitaker, Pa. *F2 81
Whitakers, N.C. A5 76
Whitby, Ont., Can. D6 41
Whitby, Eng. C6 4
Whitchurch-Stouffville,
  Ont., Can. D5, k15 41
White, co., Ark. B4 49
White, co., Ga. B3 55
White, co., Ill. E5 58
White, co., Ind. C4 59
White, co., Tenn. D8 83
White Bear Lake, Minn. E5, m12 67
White Castle, La. D4, h9 63

White City, Fla. C1 54
White Cloud, Mich. E5 66
White Deer, Tex. B2 84
Whitefield, N.H. C4 73
Whitefish, Mont. B2 70
Whitefish Bay, Wis. *E6 88
White Hall, Ill. D3 58
Whitehall, Mich. E4 66
Whitehall, Mont. E4 70
Whitehall, N.Y. B7 75
Whitehall, Ohio m11 78
Whitehall, Pa. *F1 81
Whitehall, Wis. D2 88
Whitehaven, Eng. C5 4
White Haven, Pa. D10 81
Whitehorse, Yukon, Can. *n12 67
Whitehouse, Ohio A2, e6 78
White Lake, Mich. *F7 66
Whiteland, Ind. *E5 59
White Oak, N.C. C4 76
White Oak, Ohio o12 78
White Oak, Pa. *F2 81
White Oak, Tex. *C5 84
White Pigeon, Mich. G5 66
White Pine, co., Nev. B4 72
White Pine, Tenn. C10 83
White Plains, N.Y. D7, m15 75
White River Junction, Vt. D3 73
White Rock, B.C., Can. E6, f13 37
White Salmon, Wash. D4 86
Whitesboro, N.Y. *B5 75
Whitesboro, Tex. C4 84
Whitesburg, Ky. C7 62
Whites Creek, Tenn. g10 83
White Settlement, Tex. *B5 84
Whiteside, co., Ill. B3 58
White Stone, Va. C6 85
White Sulphur Springs, Mont. ... D6 70
White Sulphur Springs, W.Va. .. D4 87
Whitesville, W.Va. n12 87
Whiteville, N.C. C4 76
Whitewright, Tex. C4 84
Whitfield, co., Ga. B1 55
Whiting, Ind. A3 59
Whiting, Wis. D4 88
Whitinsville, Mass. B4 65
Whitley, co., Ind. B6 59
Whitley, co., Ky. D5 62
Whitley City, Ky. D5 62
Whitman, Mass. B6, h12 65
Whitman, co., Wash. B8 86
Whitmire, S.C. N4 82
Whitmore City, Haw. f9 56
Whitnel, N.C. B1 76
Whitney, Idaho F2 57
Whitney, S.C. B4 82
Whitney, Tex. D4 84
Whitney, mtn., Calif. D4 50
Whitney Point, N.Y. C5 75
Whittier, Calif. F4, n12 50
Whitwell, Tenn. D8 83
Wiarton, Ont., Can. C3 41
Wibaux, co., Mont. D12 70
Wichita, Kans. E6, g12 61
Wichita, Oreg. *B4 80
Wichita, co., Kans. D2 61
Wichita, co., Tex. B3 84
Wichita Falls, Tex. C3 84
Wickenburg, Ariz. C2 48
Wickett, Tex. D1 84
Wickliffe, Ky. A2 62
Wickliffe, Ohio A4, g9 78
Wickliffe, Ohio *A5 78
Wicklow, co., Ire. *D3 4
Wicomico, co., Md. D6 53
Wiconisco, Pa. E8 81
Widnes, Eng. *D5 4
Wieluń, Pol. C6 7
Wiener Neustadt, Aus. E8 6
Wiesbaden, Ger., Fed. Rep. of ... C4 6
Wiggins, Miss. E4 68
Wigtown, co., Scot. *C4 4
Wilbarger, co., Tex. B3 84
Wilber, Nebr. D9 71
Wilberforce, Ohio C2 78
Wilbur, Wash. B7 86
Wilburton, Okla. C6 79
Wilcox, co., Ala. D2 46
Wilcox, co., Ga. E3 55
Wilder, Vt. D3 73
Wildwood, Fla. D4 54
Wildwood, N.J. F3 74
Wildwood, Pa. *E2 81
Wildwood Crest, N.J. F3 74
Wilhelm, mtn., N.Gui. k12 25
Wilhelmina, mtn., Indon. F9 19
Wilhelm-Pieck-Stadt Guben,
  Ger. Dem. Rep. C7 6
Wilhelmshaven, Ger., Fed. Rep. of ... B4 6
Wilkes, co., Ga. C4 55
Wilkes, co., N.C. A1 76
Wilkes-Barre, Pa. D10, n17 81
Wilkesboro, N.C. A1 76
Wilkie, Sask., Can. E1 39

Wilkin, co., Minn. ... D2 67
Wilkinsburg, Pa. ... F2, k14 81
Wilkinson, co., Ga. ... D3 55
Wilkinson, co., Miss. ... D2 68
Will, co., Ill. ... B6 58
Willacoochee, Ga. ... E3 55
Willacy, co., Tex. ... F4 84
Willamina, Oreg. ... B3 80
Willard, Ohio ... A3 78
Willcox, Ariz. ... C4 48
Willemstad, Neth. Antilles ... A4 32
Williams, Ariz. ... B2 48
Williams, Calif. ... C2 50
Williams, co., N.Dak. ... B2 77
Williams, co., Ohio ... A1 78
Williams Bay, Wis. ... F5 88
Williamsburg, Iowa ... C5 60
Williamsburg, Ky. ... D5 62
Williamsburg, Ohio ... C1 78
Williamsburg, Pa. ... F5 81
Williamsburg (Independence City),
Va. ... C6 85
Williamsburg, co., S.C. ... D8 82
Williams Lake, B.C., Can. ... C6, n18 37
Williamson, N.Y. ... B3 75
Williamson, W.Va. ... D2 87
Williamson, co., Ill. ... F4 58
Williamson, co., Tenn. ... A5 83
Williamson, co., Tex. ... D4 84
Williamsport, Ind. ... D3 59
Williamsport, Md. ... A2 53
Williamsport, Pa. ... D7 81
Williamston, Mich. ... F6 66
Williamston, N.C. ... B5 76
Williamston, S.C. ... B3 82
Williamstown, Ky. ... B5 62
Williamstown, Mass. ... A1 65
Williamstown, N.J. ... D3 74
Williamstown, Pa. ... E8 81
Williamstown, W. Va. ... B3 87
Williamsville, N.Y. ... C2 75
Willimantic, Conn. ... C8 52
Willingboro (Levittown), N.J. ... *C3 74
Willis Beach, Nebr. ... B9 71
Williston, Fla. ... C4 54
Williston, N.Dak. ... B2 77
Williston, S.C. ... E5 82
Williston Park, N.Y. ... G2 52
Willits, Calif. ... C2 50
Willmar, Minn. ... E3 67
Willoughby, Ohio ... A4 78
Willow Brook, Calif. ... *F4 50
Willow Grove, Pa. ... F11 021 81
Willowick, Ohio ... A4, g9 78
Willow Run, Mich. ... p14 66
Willows, Calif. ... C2 50
Willow Springs, Ill. ... k9 58
Willow Springs, Mo. ... E6 69
Wills Point, Tex. ... *C5 84
Wilmer, Tex. ... n10 84
Wilmerding, Pa. ... B6 81
Wilmette, Ill. ... A6, h9 58
Wilmington, Del. ... A6 53
Wilmington, Ill. ... B5 58
Wilmington, Mass. ... A5, f11 65
Wilmington, N.C. ... C5 76
Wilmington, Ohio ... C2 78
Wilmington Manor, Del. ... *A6 53
Wilmore, Ky. ... C5 62
Wilson, Ark. ... B5 49
Wilson, Conn. ... B6 52
Wilson, Kans. ... D5 61
Wilson, N.Y. ... B2 75
Wilson, N.C. ... B5 76
Wilson, Okla. ... C4 79
Wilson, Pa. ... E11 81
Wilson, co., Kans. ... E8 61
Wilson, co., N.C. ... B5 76
Wilson, co., Tenn. ... A5 83
Wilson, co., Tex. ... E3 84
Wilton, Conn. ... E3 52
Wilton, Maine ... D2 64
Wilton, N.H. ... F4 73
Wilton Junction (Wilton), Iowa ... C6 60
Wilton Manors, Fla. ... *F6 54
Wiltshire, co., Eng. ... *F6 4
Winamac, Ind. ... B4 59
Winchendon, Mass. ... A3 65
Winchester, Ont., Can. ... B9 41
Winchester, Eng. ... E6 4
Winchester, Ill. ... D3 58
Winchester, Ind. ... D8 59
Winchester, Ky. ... C5 62
Winchester, Mass. ... g11 65
Winchester, Mo. ... *C7 69
Winchester, Tenn. ... B5 83

Winchester (Independent City),
Va. ... A4 85
Windber, Pa. ... F4 81
Winder, Ga. ... C3 55
Windfall, Ind. ... D6 59
Windgap, Pa. ... E11 81
Windham, Ohio ... A4 78
Windham, co., Conn. ... B8 52
Windham, co., Vt. ... F3 73
Windhoek, Namibia ... E3 24
Wind Lake, Wis. ... F5 88
Windom, Minn. ... G3 67
Windsor, Newf., Can. ... D4 44
Windsor, N.S., Can. ... E5 43
Windsor, Ont., Can. ... E1 41
Windsor, Que., Can. ... D5 42
Windsor, Colo. ... *A6 51
Windsor, Conn. ... B6 52
Windsor, Ill. ... D5 58
Windsor, Mo. ... C4 69
Windsor, N.C. ... B6 76
Windsor, Pa. ... G8 81
Windsor, Vt. ... E3 73
Windsor, co., Vt. ... D2 73
Windsor Heights, Iowa ... e8 60
Windsor Hills, Calif. ... *F4 50
Windsor Locks, Conn. ... B6 52
Windward Islands, see Dominica, Grenada,
St Lucia and St. Vincent, Br. dep., N.A.
Windy Hill, S.C. ... *C8 82
Windy Hills, Ky. ... *H6 62
Winfield, Ala. ... B2 46
Winfield, Ill. ... *B5 58
Winfield, Kans. ... E7 61
Winfield, N.J. ... k7 74
Wingate, N.C. ... C2 76
Wingham, Ont., Can. ... D3 41
Wink, Tex. ... D1 84
Winkelman, Ariz. ... C3 48
Winkler, Man., Can. ... E3 40
Winkler, co., Tex. ... D1 84
Winn, par., La. ... C3 63
Winneba, Ghana ... G4 22
Winnebago, Ill. ... A4 58
Winnebago, Minn. ... G4 67
Winnebago, co., Ill. ... A4 58
Winnebago, co., Iowa ... A4 60
Winnebago, co., Wis. ... H9 88
Winneconne, Wis. ... D5 88
Winnemucca, Nev. ... A3 72
Winner, S.Dak. ... G6 77
Winneshiek, co., Iowa ... A6 60
Winnetka, Ill. ... A6, h9 58
Winnfield, La. ... C3 63
Winnie, Tex. ... *E5 84
Winnipeg, Man., Can. ... E3, h8 40
Winnipeg, lake, Man., Can. ... C2 40
Winnipegosis, Man., Can. ... D2 40
Winnipegosis, lake,
Man. Can. ... C2 40
Winnsboro, La. ... B4 63
Winnsboro, S.C. ... C5 82
Winnsboro, Tex. ... C5 84
Winnsboro Mills, S.C. ... *C5 82
Winona, Minn. ... F7 67
Winona, Miss. ... B4 68
Winona, co., Minn. ... F7 67
Winona Lake, Ind. ... B6 59
Winooski, Vt. ... C1 73
Winschoten, Neth. ... A7 5
Winslow, Ariz. ... B3 48
Winslow, Ind. ... H3 59
Winslow, Maine ... D3 64
Windslow, Wash. ... e10 86
Winsted, Conn. ... B4 52
Winsted, Minn. ... F4 67
Winston, Fla. ... D4 54
Winston, Oreg. ... *D3 80
Winston, co., Ala. ... A2 46
Winston, co., Miss. ... B4 68
Winston-Salem, N.C. ... A2 76
Winter Garden, Fla. ... D5 54
Winter Haven, Fla. ... D5 54
Winter Park, Fla. ... D5 54
Winters, Calif. ... C2 50
Winters, Tex. ... D3 84
Winterset, Iowa ... C4 60
Wintersville, Ohio ... B5 78
Winterthur, Switz. ... E4 6
Winterton, Newf., Can. ... E5 44
Winterville, N.C. ... B5 76
Winthrop, Maine ... D3 64
Winthrop, Mass. ... B6, g12 65
Winthrop, Minn. ... F4 67
Winthrop Harbor, Ill. ... A6, h9 58
Wirt, co., W. Va. ... B3 87

Wisbech, Eng. ... D7 4
Wiscasset, Maine ... D3 64
Wisconsin, state, U.S. ... B8 45
Wisconsin Dells, Wis. ... E4 88
Wisconsin Rapids, Wis. ... D4 88
Wise, Va. ... f9 85
Wise, co., Tex. ... C4 84
Wise, co., Va. ... e9 85
Wishek, N.Dak. ... D6 77
Wisla, riv., Pol. ... B5 7
Wismar, Ger. Dem. Rep. ... B5 6
Wisner, La. ... C4 63
Wisner, Nebr. ... C9 71
Withamsville, Ohio ... C1 78
Witt, Ill. ... D4 58
Wittenberg, Ger. Dem. Rep. ... C6 6
Wittenberge, Ger. Dem. Rep. ... B5 6
Wixom, Mich. ... o14 66
Włocławek, Pol. ... B5 7
Woburn, Mass. ... B5, g11 65
Wolcott, Conn. ... C5 52
Wolcott, N.Y. ... B4 75
Wolfe, co., Que., Can. ... D6 42
Wolfe, co., Ky. ... C6 62
Wolfeboro, N.H. ... D5 73
Wolfe City, Tex. ... C4 84
Wolfenbüttel, Ger., Fed. Rep. of ... B5 6
Wolf Lake, Mich. ... E4 66
Wolf Point, Mont. ... B11 70
Wolfsburg, Ger., Fed. Rep. of ... B5 6
Wolfville, N.S., Can. ... D5 43
Wollongong, Austl. ... F9 25
Wolseley, Sask., Can. ... G4 39
Wolverhampton, Eng. ... D5 4
Wolverine Lake, Mich. ... *F7 66
Wolverton, Eng. ... D6 4
Womelsdrof, Pa. ... F9 81
Wonder Lake, Ill. ... A5, h8 58
Wŏnju, Kor. ... H3 18
Wonsan, Kor. ... G3 18
Wood, co., Ohio ... A2 78
Wood, co., Tex. ... C5 84
Wood, co., W.Va. ... B3 87
Wood, co., Wis. ... D3 88
Woodbine, Iowa ... C2 60
Woodbine, N.J. ... E3 74
Woodbourne, N.Y. ... D6 75
Woodbridge, Conn. ... D4 52
Woodbridge, N.J. ... B4, k7 74
Woodbridge, Va. ... B5 85
Woodburn, Oreg. ... B4, h12 80
Woodbury, Conn. ... C4 52
Woodbury, Ga. ... D2 55
Woodbury, N.J. ... D2 74
Woodbury, N.Y. ... *E7 75
Woodbury, Tenn. ... B5 83
Woodbury, co., Iowa ... B1 60
Woodbury Heights, N.J. ... *D2 74
Woodcliff Lake, N.J. ... g8 74
Woodcroft, Ind. ... *E5 59
Wood Dale, Ill. ... k9 58
Woodford, Eng. ... k13 4
Woodford, co., Ill. ... C4 58
Woodford, co., Ky. ... B5 62
Wood Green, Eng. ... k12 4
Woodland, Calif. ... D4 50
Woodland, Calif. ... C3 50
Woodland, Maine ... C5 64
Woodland, Pa. ... E5 81
Woodland, Wash. ... D3 86
Woodland Beach, Mich. ... *G7 66
Woodlawn, Ky. ... A2 62
Woodlawn, Md. ... *B4 53
Woodlawn, Md. ... *C4 53
Woodlawn, Ohio ... n13 78
Woodlawn Beach, N.Y. ... C2 75
Woodlawn Orchards, Mich. ... *F6 66
Woodley Hills, Va. ... *B5 85
Woodlyn, Pa. ... *B10 81
Wood Lynne, N.J. ... *D2 74
Woodmere, N.Y. ... G2 52
Wood-Ridge, N.J. ... h8 74
Woodridge, N.Y. ... *D6 75
Wood River, Ill. ... E3 58
Woodroffe, mtn., Austl. ... E5 25
Woodruff, S.C. ... B3 82
Woodruff, co., Ark. ... B4 49
Woodruff Place, Ind. ... *E5 59
Woods, co., Okla. ... A3 79
Woodsboro, Tex. ... E4 84
Woods Cross, Utah ... C2 72
Woodsfield, Ohio ... C4 78
Woodside, Calif. ... *D2 50
Woodson, co., Kans. ... E8 61
Woodson Terrace, Mo. ... *C7 69
Woodstock, N.B., Can. ... C2 43

Woodstock, Ont., Can. ... D4 41
Woodstock, Ill. ... A5 58
Woodstock, Vt. ... D2 73
Woodstock, Va. ... B4 85
Woodstown, N.J. ... D2 74
Woodsville, N.H. ... C3 73
Woodville, Calif. ... *D4 50
Woodville, Miss. ... D2 68
Woodville, Ohio ... A2, f7 78
Woodville, Tex. ... D5 84
Woodward, Ala. ... B3, g7 46
Woodward, Iowa ... C4 60
Woodward, Okla. ... A2 79
Woodward, co., Okla. ... A2 79
Woodway, Tex. ... *D4 84
Woolwich, Eng. ... m13 4
Woonsocket, R.I. ... A10 52
Woonsocket, S.Dak. ... F7 77
Wooster, Ohio ... B4 78
Worcester, Eng. ... D5 4
Worcester, Mass. ... B4 65
Worcester, N.Y. ... C6 75
Worcester, S.Afr. ... G3 24
Worchester, co., Eng. ... *D5 4
Worcester, co., Md. ... D7 53
Worcester, co., Mass. ... A3 65
Worden, Ill. ... E4 58
Workington, Eng. ... C5 4
Worland, Wyo. ... B5 89
World ... 2
Wormleysburg, Pa. ... *F8 81
Worms, Ger., Fed. Rep. of ... D4 6
Worth, Ill. ... k9 58
Worth, co., Ga. ... E3 55
Worth, co., Iowa ... A4 60
Worth, co., Mo. ... A3 69
Wortham, Tex. ... D4 84
Worthing, Eng. ... E6 4
Worthington, Ind. ... F4 59
Worthington, Ky. ... B7 62
Worthington, Minn. ... G3 67
Worthington, Ohio ... B2, k10 78
Wrangel, isl., Sov. Un. ... B21 13
Wrangell, Alsk. ... D13, m23 47
Wrangell, mtn., Alsk. ... f19 47
Wray, Colo. ... A8 51
Wrens, Ga. ... C4 55
Wrentham, Mass. ... B5 65
Wrexham, Wales ... D5 4
Wright, co., Iowa ... B4 60
Wright, co., Minn. ... E4 67
Wright, co., Mo. ... D5 69
Wright City, Okla. ... C6 79
Wrightstown, N.J. ... C3 74
Wrightsville, Ga. ... D4 55
Wrightsville, Pa. ... F8 81
Wroclaw (Breslau), Pol. ... C4 7
Wuhan, China ... E7 17
Wuhu, China ... E8 17
Wuppertal, Ger., Fed. Rep. of ... C3 6
Württemberg, reg., Ger.,
Rep. of ... D4 6
Würzburg, Ger., Fed. Rep. of ... D4 6
Wurzen, Ger. Dem. Rep. ... C6 6
Wutongqiao, China ... F5 17
Wuxi, China ... E9 17
Wuxing, China ... E9 17
Wuzhou, China ... G7 17
Wyandanch, N.Y. ... *n15 75
Wyandot, co., Ohio ... B2 78
Wyandotte, Mich. ... F7, p15 66
Wyandotte, co., Kans. ... C9 61
Wyckoff, N.J. ... *A4 74
Wymore, Nebr. ... D9 71
Wyncote, Pa. ... *F11 81
Wyndmoor, Pa. ... *F11 81
Wynne, Ark. ... B5 49
Wynnewood, Okla. ... C4 79
Wynnewood, Pa. ... *F11 81
Wynyard, Austl. ... o15 25
Wynyard, Sask., Can. ... F3, n8 39
Wyoming, Del. ... B6 53
Wyoming, Ill. ... B4 58
Wyoming, Mich. ... F5 66
Wyoming, Minn. ... E6 67
Wyoming, Ohio ... c13 78
Wyoming, Pa. ... n17 81
Wyoming, co., N.Y. ... C2 75
Wyoming, co., Pa. ... D9 81
Wyoming, co., W. Va. ... D3 87
Wyoming, state, U.S. ... 89
Wyomissing, Pa. ... F10 81
Wythe, co., Va. ... D1 85
Wytheville, Va. ... D1 85

X

Xánthi, Grc. B5 14
Xavier, Kans. B8 61
Xenia, Ohio C2 78
Xiamen, China G8 17
Xi'an, China E6 17
Xiangtan, China F7 17

Xianyang, China E6 17
Xichang, China F5 17
Xigazè, China C8 20
Xi Jiang, riv., China G7 17
Xilitla, Mex...................... m14 34
Xingú, riv., Braz. D5 27

Xining, China..................... D5 17
Xinjiang Uygur, auton. reg.
  China F11 13
Xinmin, China C9 17
Xinxiang, China D7 17
Xinyang, China E7 17

Xixabangma, mtn., China C8 20
Xochimilco, Mex. h9 34
Xuanhua, China C8 17
Xuchang, China E7 17
Xuzhou, China E8 17

Y

Ya'an, China F5 17
Yadkin, co., N.C. A2 76
Yadkinville, N.C. A2 76
Yaizu, Jap. o17 18
Yakima, Wash..................... C5 86
Yakima, co., Wash. C5 86
Yakutsk, Sov. Un. C15 13
Yalobusha, co., Miss. A4 68
Yalta, Sov. Un. I10 12
Yalu, China....................... B9 17
Yalvaç, Tur. C8 14
Yamachiche, Que., Can. C5 42
Yamagata, Jap. G10 18
Yamagata, pref.,Jap. *G10 18
Yamaguchi, Jap. I5 18
Yamaguchi, pref., Jap. *I5 18
Yamanashi, pref., Jap. *I9 18
Yamaska, co., Que., Can. C5 42
Yambol, Bul. D8 10
Yamethin, Bur. D10 20
Yamhill, co., Oreg. B3 80
Yamoussoukro, I.C. G3 22
Yanam, India E7 20
Yanbu', Sau. Ar. E2 15
Yancey, co., N.C. f10 76
Yanceyville, N.C. A3 76
Yangquan, China D7 17
Yangtze, riv., China E8 17
Yangzhou, China E8 17
Yankton, S. Dak. H8 77
Yankton, co., S. Dak. G8 77
Yanji, China C10 17
Yanqi, China C2 17
Yantai, China D9 17
Yao, Jap. *I7 18
Yaoundé, Cam. H7 22
Yaracuy, state, Ven. A4 32
Yardley, Pa. F12 81
Yarīm, Yemen G3 15
Yarmouth, N.S., Can. F3 43
Yarmouth, Maine E2, g7 64
Yarmouth, co., N.S., Can. F4 43
Yaroslavl, Sov. Un. C12 12
Yartseveo, Sov. Un. D9 12
Yarumal, Col..................... B2 32

Yasinovataya, Sov. Un. q20 12
Yass, Austl. G7 26
Yates, co., N.Y. C3 75
Yates Center, Kans. E8 61
Yatsushiro, Jap. J5 18
Yauco, P.R....................... *G11 35
Yavapai, co., Ariz. B2 48
Yavorov, Sov. Un. G4 12
Yawatahama, Jap. J6 18
Yazd (Yezd), Iran B8 23
Yazoo, co., Miss. C3 68
Yazoo City, Mis. C3 68
Yeadon, Pa. q20 81
Yeagertown, Pa. E6 81
Yecla, Sp. C5 8
Yefremov, Sov. Un. E12 12
Yegoryevsk, Sov. Un. D12, n19 12
Yelan, Sov. Un. F14 12
Yelets, Sov. Un. E12 12
Yell, co.,Ark. B2 49
Yellow, see Huang He, riv., China
Yellow, sea, China D9 17
Yellowknife, N.W. Ter. Can. D11 36
Yellow Medicine, co., Minn. F2 67
Yellow Springs, Ohio C2 78
Yellowstone, co., Mont. D8 70
Yellowstone, riv., U.S. B2 89
Yellowstone National Park (part),
  co., Wyo. B2 89
Yemen, country, Asia F3 15
Yemen, People's Democratic
  Republic of, country, Asia....... H7 16
Yenakiyevo, Sov. Un. q20 12
Yenangyaung, Bur. *G4 17
Yenisey, riv., Sov. Un. C11 16
Yeniseysk, Sov. Un. D12 13
Yeovil, Eng. E5 4
Yeppoon, Austl. D9 25
Yerevan, Sov. Un. E7 13
Yerupaja, mtn., Peru D2 31
Yessey, Sov. Un. C13 13
Yevpatoriya, Sov. Un. I9 12
Yeysk, Sov. Un. H12 12
Yiannitsá, Grc. *B4 14
Yibin, China F5 17

Yichang, China E7 17
Yichun, China C4 18
Yilan, China B10 17
Yiliang, China G5 17
Yinchuan, China D6 17
Yingkou, China C9 17
Yiyang, China F7 17
Yoakum, Tex...................... E4 84
Yoakum, co., Tex. C1 84
Yogyakarta, Indon., ... G4 9
Yoichi, Jap. E10 18
Yokkaichi, Jap. I8, o15 18
Yokohama, Jap. I9, n18 18
Yokosuka, Jap. I9, n18 18
Yokote, Jap. G10 8
Yolo, co., Calif. C2 50
Yolyn, W. Va. D5 87
Yonago, Jap. I6 18
Yonezawa, Jap. H10 18
Yonghung, Kor. G3 18
Yonkers, N.Y. E7, n15 75
Yonne, dept., Fr. *D5 5
Yorba Linda, Calif. *F5 50
York, Ala. C1 46
York, Ont., Can. *m15 41
York, Eng. D6 4
York, Maine E1 64
York, Nebr. D8 71
York, Pa. G8 81
York, S.C. B5 82
York, co., N.B., Can. C3 43
York, co., Ont., Can. D5 43
York, co., Eng. *D6 4
York, co., Maine E2 64
York, co., Nebr. D8 71
York, co., Pa. G8 81
York, co., S.C. A5 82
York, co., Va. C6 85
Yorkshire, N.Y. C2 75
Yorkton, Sask.,Can. F4, n8 39
Yorktown, Ind. D6 59
Yorktown, N.Y. *D7 75
Yorktown, Tex. E4 84
Yorktown Heights, N.Y. *D7 75
Yorktown Manor, R.I. C11 52

Yorkville, Ill. B5 58
Yorkville, N.Y. B5 75
Yorkville, Ohio B5 78
Yoshkar-Ola, Sov. Un. *D7 13
Yŏsu, Kor. I3 18
Young, Austl. *F8 25
Young, co., Tex. C3 84
Youngstown, N.Y. B2 75
Youngstown, Ohio A5 78
Youngsville, La. D3 63
Youngsville, Pa. C3 81
Youngtown, Ariz. D1 48
Youngwood, Pa. F2 81
Yozgat, Tur. C10 14
Ypacaraí, Par. E4 29
Ypsilanti, Mich. F7, p4 66
Yreka, Calif. B2 50
Ystad, Swe....................... J5 11
Yuanling, China F7 17
Yuba, co., Calif. C3 50
Yuba City, Calif. *C3 50
Yuba City South, Calif. *C3 50
Yūbari, Jap. E10 18
Yucatán, state, Mex. C7 34
Yueyang, China F7 17
Yugoslavia, country, Eur. C3 10
Yukon, Okla. B4 79
Yukon, ter., Can. D6 36
Yukon, riv., N.A. C9 47
Yuma, Ariz. C1 48
Yuma, Colo. A8 51
Yuma, co., Ariz. C2 48
Yuma, co., Colo. A8 51
Yumen, China D4 17
Yumenzhen, China C4 17
Yunnan, prov., China G5 17
Yurécuaro, Mex. m12 34
Yuryevets, Sov. Un. C14 12
Yuryev-Polskiy, Sov. Un. C12 12
Yuty, Par. E4 29
Yuzha, Sov. Un. C13 12
Yuzhno-Sakhalinsk, Sov. Un. E17 13
Yverdon, Switz................... E3 6

Z

Zabkowice, Pol. C4 7
Zabrze, Pol. C5, g9 7
Zacatecas, Mex. C4 34
Zacatecas, state, Mex. C4, m12 34
Zachary, La. D4 63
Zadar, Yugo. C2 10
Zagorsk, Sov. Un. C12 12
Zagreb, Yugo. C2 10
Zāhedān, Iran G9 16
Zaḥlah, Leb. F10 14
Zaire, country, Afr. B4 24
Zaječar, Yugo D6 10
Zákinthos, Grc. D3 14
Zákinthos (Zante), prov., Grc. *D3 14
Zakopane, Pol. D5 7
Zala, co., Hung. *B3 10
Zalaegerszeg, Hung. B3 10
Zalău, Rom. B6 10
Zambales, prov., Phil. *B5 19
Zambezi, riv., Afr. H8 21
Zambia (Northern Rhodesia),
  country, Afr..................... D5 24
Zamboanga, Phil. D6 19
Zamboanga del Norte, prov.,
  Phil. *D6 19
Zamboanga del Sur.,
  prov., Phil. *D6 19
Zamora, Sp. B3 8
Zamora, prov., Sp. *B3 8
Zamora de Hidalgo, Mex. C4, n12 34
Zamosc, Pol. C7 7

Zanesville, Ohio C4 78
Zanjān, Iran A7 23
Zanzibar, Tan. B7 24
Zapata, Tex. F3 84
Zapata, co., Tex. F3 84
Zaporozhye, Sov. Un. H10 12
Zaragoza, Sp. B5 8
Zaragoza, prov., Sp. *B5 8
Zárate, Arg. A5, g7 28
Zaraysk, Sov. Un. D12 12
Zaria, Nig. F6 22
Zashiversk, Sov. Un. C17 13
Žatec, Czech. C2 7
Zavala, co., Tex. E3 84
Zavitaya, Sov. Un. D15 13
Zawiercie, Pol. C5, g10 7
Zaysan, Sov. Un. E11 13
Zdolbunov, Sov. Un. F6 12
Zduńska Wola, Pol. C5 7
Zebulon, N.C. B4 76
Zeeland, Mich. F5 66
Zeeland, prov., Neth. B5 5
Žefat (Safad), Isr. B3, g5 15
Zehdenick, Ger. Dem. Rep. B6 6
Zeigler, Ill. F4 58
Zeist, Neth. A6 5
Zeitz, Ger. Dem Rep. C6 6
Zelienople, Pa. E1 81
Zella-Mehlis, Ger. Dem. Rep. C5 6
Zemetchino, Sov. Un. E14 12
Zenica, Yugo. C3 10

Zephyrhills, Fla. D4 54
Zerbst, Ger. Dem. Rep. C6 6
Zeya, Sov. Un. D15 13
Zgierz, Pol. C5 7
Zhangjiakou, China C7 17
Zhangzhou, China G8 17
Zhanjiang, China G7 17
Zhaoqing, China G7 17
Zhaoxing, China E5 18
Zhaozhou, China D2 18
Zhdanov, Sov. Un. H11 12
Zhejiang, prov., China F9 17
Zhengzhou, China E7 17
Zhenjiang, China E8 17
Zhitomir, Sov. Un. F7 12
Zhizdra, Sov. Un. E10 12
Zhmerinka, Sov. Un. G7 12
Zhongba, China C7 20
Zhuzhou, China F7 17
Zibo, China D8 17
Ziebach, co., S. Dak. F4 77
Zielona Gora, Pol. C3 7
Zigong, China F5 17
Ziguinchor, Sen. F1 22
Zile, Tur. B10 14
Zilwaukee, Mich. E7 66
Zimbabwe, country, Afr........... D6 24
Zimnicea, Rom. D7 10
Zinder, Niger F6 22
Zion, Ill. A6, h9 58

Zionsville, Ind................... E5, k9 59
Zipaquirá, Col. B3 32
Zitácuaro, Mex. n13 34
Zittau, Ger. Dem. Rep. C7 6
Zlatoust, Sov. Un. D8 13
Zlynka, Sov. Un. E8 12
Znamenka, Sov. Un. G9 12
Znojmo, Czech................... D4 7
Zolochev, Sov. Un. G5 12
Zolotonosha, Sov. Un. G9 12
Zomba, Malawi D7 24
Zonguldak, Tur. B8 14
Zrenjanin (Petrovgrad), Yugo. C5 10
Zug, Switz. E4 6
Zug, canton, Switz. *E4 6
Zulia, state, Ven. B3 32
Zumbrota, Minn. F6 67
Zuni, N. Mex. B4 48
Zunyi, China F6 17
Zürich, Switz. *E4 6
Zürich, canton, Switz. *E4 6
Zutphen, Neth. A7 5
Zvenigorodka, Sov. Un. G8 12
Zvolen, Czech. D5 7
Zweibrücken, Ger. Fed. Rep. of .. D3 6
Zwickau, Ger. Dem. Rep. C6 6
Zwolle, La. C2 63
Zwolle, Neth. A7 5
Zyrardów, Pol. B6, m12 7

UNITED STATES GEOGRAPHICAL INFORMATION

GENERAL

ELEVATION

The highest elevation in the United States is Mount McKinley, Alaska, 20,320 feet.

The lowest elevation in the United States is in Death Valley, California, 282 feet below sea level.

The average elevation of the United States is 2,500 feet.

EXTREMITIES

Direction	Location	Latitude	Longitude
North	Point Barrow, Ak.	71° 23'N.	156° 29'W.
South	Ka Lae (point) Hi.	18° 56'N.	155° 41'W.
East	West Quoddy Head, Me.	44° 49'N.	66° 57'W.
West	Cape Wrangell, Ak.	52° 55'N.	172° 27'E.

The two places in the United States separated by the greatest distance are Kure Island, Hawaii, and Elliot Key, Florida. These points are 5,852 miles apart.

LENGTH OF BOUNDARIES

The total length of the Canadian boundary of the United States is 5,525 miles.

The total length of the Mexican boundary of the United States is 1,933 miles.

The total length of the Atlantic coastline of the United States is 2,069 miles.

The total length of the Pacific and Arctic coastline of the United States is 8,683 miles.

The total length of the Gulf of Mexico coastline of the United States is 1,631 miles.

The total length of all coastlines and land boundaries of the United States is 19,841 miles.

The total length of the tidal shoreline and land boundaries of the United States is 96,091 miles.

GEOGRAPHIC CENTERS

The geographic center of the United States (including Alaska and Hawaii) is in Butte County, South Dakota at 44° 58'N., 103° 46'W.

The geographic center of North America is in North Dakota, a few miles west of Devils Lake, at 48° 10'N., 100° 10'W.

EXTREMES OF TEMPERATURE

The highest temperature ever recorded in the United States was 134° F., at Greenland Ranch, Death Valley, California, on July 10, 1913.

The lowest temperature ever recorded in the United States was -80° F., at Prospect Creek, Alaska, on January 23, 1971.

PRECIPITATION

The average annual precipitation for the United States is approximately 29 inches.

Hawaii is the wettest state, with an average annual rainfall of 82 inches. Nevada, with an average annual rainfall of 9 inches, is the driest state.

The greatest local average annual rainfall in the United States is at Mt. Waialeale, Kauai, Hawaii, 460 inches.

The greatest 24-hour rainfall in the United States, 43 inches at Alvin, Texas, July 25-26, 1979.

The lowest local average annual rainfall in the United States is at Death Valley, California, 1.63 inches.

The longest dry period in the United States, 767 days, is at Bagdad, California, October 3, 1912 to November 8, 1914.

Heavy snowfall records include 76 inches in 24 hours at Silver Lake, Colorado, April 14-15, 1921; 189 inches in one storm at Mt. Shasta Ski Bowl, California, February 13-19, 1959.

The greatest seasonal snowfall, 1,122 inches, more than 93 feet, at Paradise Ranger Station, Washington, during the winter of 1971-72.

TERRITORIAL ACQUISITION AND POPULATION MOVEMENT

TERRITORIAL ACQUISITIONS

Accession	Date	Area (sq. mi.)	Cost in Dollars
Original territory of the Thirteen States	1790	888,685	
Purchase of Louisiana Territory, from France	1803	827,192	$11,250,000
By treaty with Spain: Florida	1819	58,560	5,000,000
Other areas	1819	13,443	
Annexation of Texas	1845	390,144	
Oregon Territory, by treaty with Great Britain	1846	285,580	
Mexican Cession	1848	529,017	$15,000,000
Gadsden Purchase, from Mexico	1853	29,640	$10,000,000
Purchase of Alaska, from Russia	1867	586,412	7,200,000
Annexation of Hawaiian Islands	1898	6,450	
Puerto Rico, by treaty with Spain	1899	3,435	
Guam, by treaty with Spain	1899	212	
American Samoa, by treaty with Great Britain and Germany	1900	76	
Virgin Islands, by purchase from Denmark	1917	133	$25,000,000

Note: The Philippines, ceded by Spain in 1898 for $20,000,000 were a territorial possession of the United States from 1898 to 1946. On July 4, 1946 they became the independent Republic of the Philippines.

Note: The Canal Zone, ceded by Panama in 1903 for $10,000,000 was a territory of the United States from 1903 to 1979. As a result of treaties signed in 1977, sovereignty over the Canal Zone reverted to Panama in 1979.

WESTWARD MOVEMENT OF CENTER OF POPULATION

Year	U.S. Population Total at Census	Approximate Location
1790	3,929,214	23 miles east of Baltimore, Md.
1800	5,308,483	18 miles west of Baltimore, Md.
1810	7,239,881	40 miles northwest of Washington, D.C.
1820	9,638,453	16 miles east of Moorefield, W. Va.
1830	12,866,020	19 miles southwest of Moorefield, W. Va.
1840	17,069,453	16 miles south of Clarksburg, W. Va.
1850	23,191,876	23 miles southeast of Parkersburg, W. Va.
1860	31,443,321	20 miles southeast of Chillicothe, Ohio
1870	39,818,449	48 miles northeast of Cincinnati, Ohio
1880	50,155,783	8 miles southwest of Cincinnati, Ohio
1890	62,947,714	20 miles east of Columbus, Ind.
1900	75,994,575	6 miles southeast of Columbus, Ind.
1910	91,972,266	Bloomington, Ind.
1920	105,710,620	8 miles southeast of Spencer, Ind.
1930	122,775,046	3 miles northeast of Linton, Ind.
1940	131,669,275	2 miles southeast of Carlisle, Ind.
1950	150,697,361	8 miles northwest of Olney, Ill.
1960	179,323,175	6 miles northwest of Centralia, Ill.
1970	204,816,296	5 miles southeast of Mascoutah, Ill.
1980	226,549,010	1/4 mile west of DeSoto, Mo.

STATE AREAS AND POPULATIONS

STATE	Land Area square miles	Water Area* square miles	Total Area* square miles	Area Rank land area	1980 Resident Population	1980 Population per square mile	1970 Population	1960 Population	1950 Population	Population Rank 1980	Population Rank 1970	Population Rank 1960
Alabama	50,766	938	51,704	28	3,893,978	77	3,444,165	3,266,740	3,061,743	22	21	19
Alaska	570,833	20,171	591,004	1	401,851	0.7	302,173	226,167	128,643	50	50	50
Arizona	113,510	492	114,002	6	2,718,425	24	1,772,482	1,302,161	749,587	29	33	35
Arkansas	52,082	1,109	53,191	27	2,286,419	44	1,923,295	1,786,272	1,909,511	33	32	31
California	156,297	2,407	158,704	3	23,667,837	151	19,953,134	15,717,204	10,586,223	1	1	2
Colorado	103,598	496	104,094	8	2,889,735	28	2,207,259	1,753,947	1,325,089	28	30	33
Connecticut	4,872	147	5,019	48	3,107,576	638	3,032,217	2,535,234	2,007,280	25	24	25
Delaware	1,933	112	2,045	49	594,317	307	548,104	446,292	318,085	47	46	46
District of Columbia	63	6	69	..	638,432	10,134	756,510	763,956	802,178	..	..	..
Florida	54,157	4,511	58,668	26	9,746,421	180	6,789,443	4,951,560	2,771,305	7	9	10
Georgia	58,060	854	58,914	21	5,463,087	94	4,589,575	3,943,116	3,444,578	13	15	16
Hawaii	6,427	46	6,473	47	964,691	150	769,913	632,772	499,794	39	40	43
Idaho	82,413	1,153	83,566	11	944,038	11	713,008	667,191	588,637	41	42	42
Illinois	55,646	2,226	57,872	24	11,427,414	205	11,113,976	10,081,158	8,712,176	5	5	4
Indiana	35,936	481	36,417	38	5,490,260	153	5,193,669	4,662,498	3,934,224	12	11	11
Iowa	55,965	310	56,275	23	2,913,808	52	2,825,041	2,757,537	2,621,073	27	25	24
Kansas	81,783	499	82,282	13	2,364,236	29	2,249,071	2,178,611	1,905,299	32	28	28
Kentucky	39,674	740	40,414	37	3,660,257	92	3,219,311	3,038,156	2,944,806	23	23	22
Louisiana	44,520	3,230	47,750	33	4,206,098	94	3,643,180	3,257,022	2,683,516	19	20	20
Maine	30,995	2,270	33,265	39	1,125,030	36	993,663	969,265	913,774	38	38	36
Maryland	9,838	623	10,461	42	4,216,941	429	3,922,399	3,100,689	2,343,001	18	18	21
Massachusetts	7,826	460	8,286	45	5,737,081	733	5,689,170	5,148,578	4,690,514	11	10	9
Michigan	56,959	40,148	97,107	22	9,262,070	163	8,875,083	7,823,194	6,371,766	8	7	7
Minnesota	79,548	7,066	86,614	14	4,075,970	51	3,805,069	3,413,864	2,982,483	21	19	18
Mississippi	47,234	457	47,691	31	2,520,631	53	2,216,912	2,178,141	2,178,914	31	29	29
Missouri	68,945	752	69,697	18	4,916,759	71	4,677,399	4,319,813	3,954,653	15	13	13
Montana	145,388	1,657	147,045	4	786,690	5.4	694,409	674,767	591,024	44	43	41
Nebraska	76,639	711	77,350	15	1,569,825	20	1,483,791	1,411,330	1,325,510	35	35	34
Nevada	109,895	667	110,562	7	800,493	7.3	488,738	285,278	160,083	43	47	49
New Hampshire	8,992	286	9,278	44	920,610	102	737,681	606,921	533,242	42	41	45
New Jersey	7,468	319	7,787	46	7,365,011	986	7,168,164	6,066,782	4,835,329	9	8	8
New Mexico	121,336	258	121,594	5	1,303,445	11	1,016,000	951,023	681,187	37	37	37
New York	47,379	5,358	52,737	30	17,558,072	371	18,241,266	16,782,304	14,830,192	2	2	1
North Carolina	48,843	3,826	52,669	29	5,881,385	120	5,082,059	4,556,155	4,061,929	10	12	12
North Dakota	69,299	1,403	70,702	17	652,717	9.4	617,761	632,446	619,636	46	45	44
Ohio	41,004	3,782	44,786	35	10,797,624	263	10,652,017	9,706,397	7,946,627	6	6	5
Oklahoma	68,656	1,301	69,957	19	3,025,495	44	2,559,253	2,328,284	2,233,351	26	27	27
Oregon	96,187	889	97,076	10	2,633,149	27	2,091,385	1,768,687	1,521,341	30	31	32
Pennsylvania	44,892	1,155	46,047	32	11,864,751	264	11,793,909	11,319,366	10,498,012	4	3	3
Rhode Island	1,054	158	1,212	50	947,154	899	949,723	859,488	791,896	40	39	39
South Carolina	30,207	909	31,116	40	3,122,814	103	2,590,516	2,382,594	2,117,027	24	26	26
South Dakota	75,956	1,164	77,120	16	690,768	9.1	666,257	680,514	652,740	45	44	40
Tennessee	41,154	989	42,143	34	4,591,120	112	3,924,164	3,567,089	3,291,718	17	17	17
Texas	262,015	4,790	266,805	2	14,227,574	54	11,196,730	9,579,677	7,711,194	3	4	6
Utah	82,076	2,826	84,902	12	1,461,037	18	1,059,273	890,627	688,862	36	36	38
Vermont	9,273	341	9,614	43	511,456	55	444,732	389,881	377,747	48	48	47
Virginia	39,700	1,063	40,763	36	5,346,797	135	4,648,494	3,966,949	3,318,680	14	14	14
Washington	66,512	1,627	68,139	20	4,132,204	62	3,409,169	2,853,214	2,378,963	20	22	23
West Virginia	24,124	112	24,236	41	1,950,258	81	1,744,237	1,860,421	2,005,552	34	34	30
Wisconsin	54,424	11,789	66,213	25	4,705,642	86	4,417,933	3,951,777	3,434,575	16	16	15
Wyoming	96,988	820	97,808	9	469,557	4.8	332,416	330,066	290,529	49	49	48
United States	3,539,341	139,904	3,679,245	..	226,549,010	64	203,235,298	179,323,175	151,325,798	..	..	..

*Includes the United States area of the Great Lakes.

UNITED STATES GENERAL INFORMATION

STATE	CAPITAL	LARGEST CITY	ENTERED UNION AS STATE Date of Entry	Rank of Entry	GREATEST MEASUREMENT N-S (miles)	E-W (miles)	HIGHEST POINT Location	Altitude (feet)	STATE FLOWER	STATE BIRD	STATE NICKNAME
Alabama	Montgomery	Birmingham	Dec. 14, 1819	22	330	200	Cheaha Mountain	2,407	Camellia	Yellowhammer	Yellowhammer
Alaska	Juneau	Anchorage	Jan. 3, 1959	49	1,332	2,250	Mt. McKinley	20,320	Forget-me-not	Willow Ptarmigan	Last Frontier
Arizona	Phoenix	Phoenix	Feb. 14, 1912	48	390	335	Humphreys Peak	12,633	Saguaro Cactus	Cactus Wren	Grand Canyon
Arkansas	Little Rock	Little Rock	June 15, 1836	25	240	275	Magazine Mtn.	2,753	Apple Blossom	Mockingbird	Land of Opportunity
California	Sacramento	Los Angeles	Sept. 9, 1850	31	800	375	Mt. Whitney	14,494	Golden Poppy	California Valley Quail	Golden
Colorado	Denver	Denver	Aug. 1, 1876	38	270	380	Mt. Elbert	14,433	Rocky Mountain Columbine	Lark Bunting	Centennial
Connecticut*	Hartford	Bridgeport	Jan. 9, 1788	5	75	90	S. slope of Mt. Frissell	2,380	Mountain Laurel	Robin	Constitution
Delaware*	Dover	Wilmington	Dec. 7, 1787	1	95	35	Ebright Road, New Castle Co.	442	Peach Blossom	Blue Hen Chicken	First
District of Columbia	Washington	Washington	March 3, 1791	......	15	15	Tenleytown	410	American Beauty Rose	Wood Thrush	......
Florida	Tallahassee	Jacksonville	March 3, 1845	27	460	400	N. boundary, Walton Co.	345	Orange Blossom	Mockingbird	Sunshine
Georgia*	Atlanta	Atlanta	Jan. 2, 1788	4	315	250	Brasstown Bald	4,784	Cherokee Rose	Brown Thrasher	Peach
Hawaii	Honolulu	Honolulu	Aug. 21, 1959	50	655	1,600	Mauna Kea	13,796	Red Hibiscus	Nene (Hawaiian Goose)	Aloha
Idaho	Boise	Boise	July 3, 1890	43	480	305	Borah Peak	12,662	Syringa	Mountain Bluebird	Gem
Illinois	Springfield	Chicago	Dec. 3, 1818	21	380	205	Charles Mound	1,235	Violet	Cardinal	Prairie
Indiana	Indianapolis	Indianapolis	Dec. 11, 1816	19	265	160	Near Spartanburg	1,257	Peony	Cardinal	Hoosier
Iowa	Des Moines	Des Moines	Dec. 28, 1846	29	205	310	N.W. corner, Osceola Co.	1,670	Wild Rose	Eastern Goldfinch	Hawkeye
Kansas	Topeka	Wichita	Jan. 29, 1861	34	205	410	Mt. Sunflower	4,039	Sunflower	Western Meadowlark	Sunflower
Kentucky	Frankfort	Louisville	June 1, 1792	15	175	350	Black Mountain	4,145	Goldenrod	Kentucky Cardinal	Bluegrass
Louisiana	Baton Rouge	New Orleans	April 30, 1812	18	275	300	Driskill Mountain	535	Magnolia	Pelican	Pelican
Maine	Augusta	Portland	March 15, 1820	23	310	210	Mt. Katahdin	5,268	Pinecone and Tassel	Chickadee	Pine Tree
Maryland*	Annapolis	Baltimore	April 28, 1788	7	120	200	Backbone Mountain	3,360	Black-eyed Susan	Baltimore Oriole	Free
Massachusetts*	Boston	Boston	Feb. 6, 1788	6	110	190	Mt. Greylock	3,491	Mayflower	Chickadee	Bay
Michigan	Lansing	Detroit	Jan. 26, 1837	26	400	310	Mt. Curwood	1,980	Apple Blossom	Robin	Wolverine
Minnesota	St. Paul	Minneapolis	May 11, 1858	32	400	350	Eagle Mountain	2,301	Lady's-slipper	Loon	Gopher
Mississippi	Jackson	Jackson	Dec. 10, 1817	20	340	180	Woodall Mountain	806	Magnolia	Mockingbird	Magnolia
Missouri	Jefferson City	St. Louis	Aug. 10, 1821	24	280	300	Taum Sauk Mountain	1,772	Hawthorn	Bluebird	Show Me
Montana	Helena	Billings	Nov. 8, 1889	41	315	570	Granite Peak	12,799	Bitterroot	Western Meadowlark	Big Sky Country
Nebraska	Lincoln	Omaha	March 1, 1867	37	210	415	S.W. corner, Kimball Co.	5,426	Goldenrod	Western Meadowlark	Cornhusker
Nevada	Carson City	Las Vegas	Oct. 31, 1864	36	485	315	Boundary Peak	13,143	Shrub Sagebrush	Mountain Bluebird	Silver
New Hampshire*	Concord	Manchester	June 21, 1788	9	185	90	Mt. Washington	6,288	Purple Lilac	Purple Finch	Granite
New Jersey*	Trenton	Newark	Dec. 18, 1787	3	166	70	High Point	1,803	Purple Violet	Eastern Goldfinch	Garden
New Mexico	Santa Fe	Albuquerque	Jan. 6, 1912	47	390	350	Wheeler Peak	13,161	Yucca	Roadrunner	Land of Enchantment
New York*	Albany	New York	July 26, 1788	11	310	330	Mt. Marcy	5,344	Rose	Bluebird	Empire
North Carolina*	Raleigh	Charlotte	Nov. 21, 1789	12	200	520	Mt. Mitchell	6,684	Dogwood	Cardinal	Tar Heel
North Dakota	Bismarck	Fargo	Nov. 2, 1889	39	210	360	White Butte	3,506	Wild Prairie Rose	Western Meadowlark	Flickertail
Ohio	Columbus	Cleveland	March 1, 1803	17	230	205	Campbell Hill	1,550	Scarlet Carnation	Cardinal	Buckeye
Oklahoma	Oklahoma City	Oklahoma City	Nov. 16, 1907	46	210	460	Black Mesa	4,973	Mistletoe	Scissor-tailed Flycatcher	Sooner
Oregon	Salem	Portland	Feb. 14, 1859	33	290	375	Mt. Hood	11,235	Oregon Grape	Western Meadowlark	Beaver
Pennsylvania*	Harrisburg	Philadelphia	Dec. 12, 1787	2	180	310	Mt. Davis	3,213	Mountain Laurel	Ruffed Grouse	Keystone
Rhode Island*	Providence	Providence	May 29, 1790	13	50	35	Jerimoth Hill	812	Violet	Rhode Island Red	Little Rhody
South Carolina*	Columbia	Columbia	May 23, 1788	8	215	285	Sassafras Mountain	3,560	Yellow Jessamine	Carolina Wren	Palmetto
South Dakota	Pierre	Sioux Falls	Nov. 2, 1889	40	240	360	Harney Peak	7,242	Pasque	Ring-necked Pheasant	Coyote
Tennessee	Nashville	Memphis	June 1, 1796	16	120	430	Clingmans Dome	6,643	Iris	Mockingbird	Volunteer
Texas	Austin	Houston	Dec. 29, 1845	28	710	760	Guadalupe Peak	8,749	Bluebonnet	Mockingbird	Lone Star
Utah	Salt Lake City	Salt Lake City	Jan. 4, 1896	45	345	275	Kings Peak	13,528	Sego Lily	Sea Gull	Beehive
Vermont*	Montpelier	Burlington	March 4, 1791	14	155	90	Mt. Mansfield	4,393	Red Clover	Hermit Thrush	Green Mountain
Virginia*	Richmond	Norfolk	June 25, 1788	10	205	425	Mt. Rogers	5,729	American Dogwood	Cardinal	Old Dominion
Washington	Olympia	Seattle	Nov. 11, 1889	42	230	340	Mt. Rainier	14,410	Rhododendron	Willow Goldfinch	Evergreen
West Virginia	Charleston	Charleston	June 20, 1863	35	200	225	Spruce Knob	4,862	Rhododendron	Cardinal	Mountain
Wisconsin	Madison	Milwaukee	May 29, 1848	30	300	290	Timms Hill	1,952	Violet	Robin	Badger
Wyoming	Cheyenne	Casper	July 10, 1890	44	275	365	Garnett Peak	13,804	Indian Paintbrush	Meadowlark	Equality
United States	Washington, D.C.	New York	......	......	275	365	Mt. McKinley, Alaska	20,320	......	Bald Eagle	......

*One of the Thirteen Original States

UNITED STATES POPULATION BY STATE OR COLONY, 1650-1980

STATES	1650	1700	1750	1770	1790	1800	1820	1840	1860	1880	1900	1920	1940	1950	1960	1970	1980
Alabama							127,901	590,756	964,201	1,262,505	1,828,697	2,348,174	2,832,961	3,061,743	3,266,740	3,444,165	3,893,978
Alaska											63,592	55,036	72,524	128,643	226,167	302,173	401,851
Arizona										40,440	122,931	334,162	499,261	749,587	1,302,161	1,772,482	2,718,425
Arkansas							14,273	97,574	435,450	802,525	1,311,564	1,752,204	1,949,387	1,909,511	1,786,272	1,923,295	2,286,419
California									379,994	864,694	1,485,053	3,426,861	6,907,387	10,586,223	15,717,204	19,953,134	23,667,837
Colorado									34,277	194,327	539,700	939,629	1,123,296	1,325,089	1,753,947	2,207,259	2,889,735
Connecticut	4,139	25,970	111,280	183,881	237,946	251,002	275,248	309,978	460,147	622,700	908,420	1,380,631	1,709,242	2,007,280	2,535,234	3,032,217	3,107,576
Delaware	185	2,470	28,704	35,496	59,096	64,273	72,749	78,085	112,216	146,608	184,735	223,003	266,505	318,085	446,292	548,104	594,317
District of Columbia						8,144	23,336	33,745	75,080	177,624	278,718	437,571	663,091	802,178	763,956	756,510	638,432
Florida								54,477	140,424	269,493	528,542	968,470	1,897,414	2,771,305	4,951,560	6,789,443	9,746,421
Georgia			5,200	23,375	82,548	162,686	340,989	691,392	1,057,286	1,542,180	2,216,331	2,895,832	3,123,723	3,444,578	3,943,116	4,589,575	5,463,087
Hawaii											154,001	255,881	422,770	499,794	632,772	769,913	964,691
Idaho										32,610	161,772	431,866	524,873	588,637	667,191	713,008	944,038
Illinois							55,211	476,183	1,711,951	3,077,871	4,821,550	6,485,280	7,897,241	8,712,176	10,081,158	11,113,976	11,427,414
Indiana						5,641	147,178	685,866	1,350,428	1,978,301	2,516,462	2,930,390	3,427,796	3,934,224	4,662,498	5,193,669	5,490,260
Iowa								43,112	674,913	1,624,615	2,231,853	2,404,021	2,538,268	2,621,073	2,757,537	2,825,041	2,913,808
Kansas									107,206	996,096	1,470,495	1,769,257	1,801,028	1,905,299	2,178,611	2,249,071	2,364,236
Kentucky				15,700	73,677	220,955	564,317	779,828	1,155,684	1,648,690	2,147,174	2,416,630	2,845,627	2,944,806	3,038,156	3,219,311	3,660,257
Louisiana							153,407	352,411	708,002	939,946	1,381,625	1,798,509	2,363,880	2,683,516	3,257,022	3,643,180	4,206,098
Maine[4]				31,257	96,540	151,719	298,335	501,793	628,279	648,936	694,466	768,014	847,226	913,774	969,265	993,663	1,125,030
Maryland	4,504	29,604	141,073	202,599	319,728	341,548	407,350	470,019	687,049	934,943	1,188,044	1,449,661	1,821,244	2,343,001	3,100,689	3,922,399	4,216,941
Massachusetts[4]	16,603	55,941	188,000	235,308	378,787	422,845	523,287	737,699	1,231,066	1,783,085	2,805,346	3,852,356	4,316,721	4,690,514	5,148,578	5,689,170	5,737,081
Michigan							8,896	212,267	749,113	1,636,937	2,420,982	3,668,412	5,256,106	6,371,766	7,823,194	8,875,083	9,262,070
Minnesota									172,023	780,773	1,751,394	2,387,125	2,792,300	2,982,483	3,413,864	3,805,069	4,075,970
Mississippi						8,850	75,448	375,651	791,305	1,131,597	1,551,270	1,790,618	2,183,796	2,178,914	2,178,141	2,216,912	2,520,631
Missouri							66,586	383,702	1,182,012	2,168,380	3,106,665	3,404,055	3,784,664	3,954,653	4,319,813	4,677,399	4,916,759
Montana										39,159	243,329	548,889	559,456	591,024	674,767	694,409	786,690
Nebraska									28,841	452,402	1,066,300	1,296,372	1,315,834	1,325,510	1,411,330	1,483,791	1,569,825
Nevada									6,857	62,266	42,335	77,407	110,247	160,083	285,278	488,738	800,493
New Hampshire	1,305	4,958	27,505	62,396	141,885	183,858	244,161	284,574	326,073	346,991	411,588	443,083	491,524	533,242	606,921	737,681	920,610
New Jersey		14,010	71,393	117,431	184,139	211,149	277,575	373,306	672,035	1,131,116	1,883,669	3,155,900	4,160,165	4,835,329	6,066,782	7,168,164	7,365,011
New Mexico									93,516	119,565	195,310	360,350	531,818	681,187	951,023	1,016,000	1,303,445
New York		19,107	76,696	162,920	340,120	589,051	1,372,812	2,428,921	3,880,735	5,082,871	7,268,894	10,385,227	13,479,142	14,830,192	16,782,304	18,241,266	17,558,072
North Carolina		10,720	72,984	197,200	393,751	478,103	638,829	753,419	992,622	1,399,750	1,893,810	2,559,123	3,571,623	4,061,929	4,556,155	5,082,059	5,881,385
North Dakota[3]										36,909	319,146	646,872	641,935	619,636	632,446	617,761	652,717
Ohio						45,365	581,434	1,519,467	2,339,511	3,198,062	4,157,545	5,759,394	6,907,612	7,946,627	9,706,397	10,652,017	10,797,624
Oklahoma[5]											790,391	2,028,283	2,336,434	2,233,351	2,328,284	2,559,253	3,025,495
Oregon									52,465	174,768	413,536	783,389	1,089,684	1,521,341	1,768,687	2,091,385	2,633,149
Pennsylvania		17,950	119,666	240,057	434,373	602,365	1,049,458	1,724,033	2,906,215	4,282,891	6,302,115	8,720,017	9,900,180	10,498,012	11,319,366	11,793,909	11,864,751
Rhode Island	785	5,894	33,226	58,196	68,825	69,122	83,059	108,830	174,620	276,531	428,556	604,397	713,346	791,896	859,488	949,723	947,154
South Carolina		5,704	64,000	124,244	249,073	345,591	502,741	594,398	703,708	995,577	1,340,316	1,683,724	1,899,804	2,117,027	2,382,594	2,590,516	3,122,814
South Dakota[3]										98,268	401,570	636,547	642,961	652,740	680,514	666,257	690,768
Tennessee				1,000	35,691	105,602	422,823	829,210	1,109,801	1,542,359	2,020,616	2,337,885	2,915,841	3,291,718	3,567,089	3,924,164	4,591,120
Texas									604,215	1,591,749	3,048,710	4,663,228	6,414,824	7,711,194	9,579,677	11,196,730	14,227,574
Utah									40,273	143,963	276,749	449,396	550,310	688,862	890,627	1,059,273	1,461,037
Vermont				10,000	85,425	154,465	235,981	291,948	315,098	332,286	343,641	352,428	359,231	377,747	389,881	444,732	511,456
Virginia[6]	18,731	58,560	231,033	447,016	691,737	807,557	938,261	1,025,227	1,219,630	1,512,565	1,854,184	2,309,187	2,677,773	3,318,680	3,966,949	4,648,494	5,346,797
Washington									11,594	75,116	518,103	1,356,621	1,736,191	2,378,963	2,853,214	3,409,169	4,132,204
West Virginia[6]					55,873	78,592	136,808	224,537	376,688	618,457	958,800	1,463,701	1,901,974	2,005,552	1,860,421	1,744,237	1,950,258
Wisconsin								30,945	775,881	1,315,497	2,069,042	2,632,067	3,137,587	3,434,575	3,951,777	4,417,933	4,705,642
Wyoming										20,789	92,531	194,402	250,742	290,529	330,066	332,416	469,557
Total[1]	50,368	250,888	1,170,760	2,148,076	3,929,214	5,308,483	9,638,453	17,069,453[2]	31,443,321	50,189,209	76,212,168	106,021,537	132,164,569	151,325,798	179,323,175	203,235,298	226,549,010

[1] All figures prior to 1890 exclude uncivilized Indians. Figures for 1650 through 1770 include only the British colonies that later became the United States. No areas are included prior to their annexation to the United States. However, many of the figures refer to territories prior to their admission as States. U.S. total includes Alaska from 1880 through 1970 and Hawaii from 1900 through 1970.

[2] U.S. total for 1840 includes 6,100 persons on public ships in service of the United States, not credited to any State.

[3] South Dakota figure for 1860 represents entire Dakota Territory. North and South Dakota figures for 1880 are for the parts of Dakota Territory which later constituted the respective States.

[4] Maine figures for 1770 through 1800 are for that area of Massachusetts which later became the State of Maine in 1820. Massachusetts figures exclude Maine from 1770 through 1800, but include it from 1650 through 1750. Massachusetts figure for 1650 also includes population of Plymouth (1,566), a separate colony until 1691.

[5] Oklahoma figure for 1900 includes population of Indian Territory (392,060).

[6] West Virginia figures for 1790 through 1860 are for that area of Virginia which became West Virginia in 1863. These figures are excluded from the figures for Virginia from 1790 through 1860.

UNITED STATES METROPOLITAN AREAS

This table ranks the largest cities of the United States according to their metropolitan area populations. The Ranally Metropolitan Area (RMA) populations reflect Rand McNally's exclusive definition of metropolitan areas. Each RMA includes one or more central cities, as well as socially and economically integrated surrounding areas. The populations of RMAs that are partly in Canada or Mexico are for the United States parts only. The table also indicates central city populations and compares the latest available data to the previous census. Populations are rounded totals. 1980 populations reflect final census data.

1980 Rank	Metropolitan Area	Metropolitan Area Population			City Population	
		Census 4/1/80	Census 4/1/70	% Change 1970–80	Census 4/1/80	% Change 1970–80
1	New York, NY-NJ-CT	16,800,900	17,483,900	−3.9	7,400,800	−10.6
	New York, NY				7,071,600	−10.4
	Newark, NJ				329,200	−13.8
2	Los Angeles, CA	9,763,600	8,672,500	12.6	2,968,600	5.6
3	Chicago, IL-IN-WI	7,717,100	7,577,900	1.8	3,005,100	−10.8
4	Philadelphia-Trenton-Wilmington, PA-NJ-DE-MD	5,208,600	5,322,200	−2.1	1,850,500	−13.3
	Philadelphia, PA				1,688,200	−13.4
	Trenton, NJ				92,100	−12.1
	Wilmington, NJ				70,200	−12.7
5	San Francisco-Oakland-San Jose, CA	4,683,200	4,278,600	9.5	1,647,700	7.2
	San Francisco, CA				679,000	−5.1
	Oakland, CA				339,300	−6.2
	San Jose, CA				629,400	36.9
6	Detroit, MI-CAN	4,445,800	4,526,100	−1.8	1,310,500	−18.8
	Detroit, MI				1,202,500	−20.6
	Ann Arbor, MI				108,000	7.3
7	Boston, MA-NH	3,971,700	3,939,000	.8	899,000	−8.1
	Boston, MA				563,000	−12.2
	Lowell, MA				92,400	−1.9
	Lawrence, MA				63,200	−5.5
	Haverhill, MA				46,900	1.7
	Brockton, MA				95,200	7.0
	Salem, MA				38,300	−5.7
8	Washington, DC-MD-VA	3,221,400	2,992,600	7.6	638,400	−15.6
9	Miami-Ft. Lauderdale, FL	2,827,300	1,973,500	43.3	500,200	5.4
	Miami, FL				346,900	3.6
	Ft. Lauderdale, FL				153,300	9.8
10	Houston, TX	2,755,100	1,903,300	44.8	1,595,100	29.3
11	Dallas-Ft. Worth, TX	2,727,300	2,187,500	24.7	1,289,300	4.1
	Dallas, TX				904,100	7.1
	Ft. Worth, TX				385,200	−2.1
12	Pittsburgh, PA	2,218,800	2,350,300	−5.6	424,000	−18.5
13	Cleveland, OH	2,218,400	2,360,600	−6.0	573,800	−23.6
14	St. Louis, MO-IL	2,203,000	2,285,900	−3.6	452,800	−27.2
15	Seattle-Tacoma, WA	2,077,100	1,823,500	13.9	706,700	−4.3
	Seattle, WA				493,800	−7.0
	Tacoma, WA				158,500	2.7
16	Minneapolis-St. Paul, MN-WI	2,012,400	1,857,500	8.3	641,200	−13.9
	Minneapolis, MN				371,000	−14.6
	St. Paul, MN				270,200	−12.8
17	Atlanta, GA	1,962,500	1,543,200	27.2	425,000	−14.1
18	Baltimore, MD	1,960,400	1,900,300	3.2	786,700	−13.1
19	San Diego, CA-MEX	1,648,500	1,227,700	34.3	875,500	25.5
20	Phoenix, AZ	1,482,400	955,300	55.2	790,000	35.2
21	Cincinnati, OH-KY-IN	1,480,100	1,448,400	2.2	385,500	−15.0
22	Denver, CO	1,405,300	1,083,600	29.7	492,400	−4.3
23	Milwaukee, WI	1,374,700	1,388,900	−1.0	636,300	−11.3
24	Kansas City, MO-KS	1,272,400	1,228,700	3.6	448,000	−11.7
25	Portland, OR-WA	1,227,200	997,100	23.1	368,100	−3.1
26	New Orleans, LA	1,185,000	1,045,300	13.4	557,900	−6.0
27	Buffalo, NY-CAN	1,155,200	1,266,700	−8.8	357,900	−22.7
28	Indianapolis, IN	1,072,500	1,022,500	4.9	700,800	−6.2
29	Hartford-New Britain, CT	1,013,600	999,800	1.4	210,200	−12.9
	Hartford, CT				136,400	−13.7
	New Britain, CT				73,800	−11.5
30	San Antonio, TX	968,200	818,300	18.3	786,000	20.1
31	Columbus, OH	963,600	906,500	6.3	565,000	4.6
32	Providence-Warwick, RI-MA	921,100	910,100	1.3	245,100	−6.7
	Providence, RI				156,800	−12.5
	Warwick, RI				88,300	5.5
33	Louisville, KY-IN	891,400	853,000	4.5	298,700	−17.4
34	Sacramento, CA	866,400	698,100	24.1	275,700	7.2
35	Memphis, TN-AR-MS	852,900	779,200	9.5	646,200	3.6
36	St. Petersburg-Clearwater, FL	852,300	561,800	51.7	324,100	20.8
	St. Petersburg, FL				238,600	10.4
	Clearwater, FL				85,500	64.1
37	Rochester, NY	816,200	811,700	.6	241,700	−18.1
38	Norfolk-Virginia Beach, VA	795,600	725,800	9.6	529,200	10.2
	Norfolk, VA				267,000	−13.3
	Virginia Beach, VA				262,200	52.4
39	Riverside-San Bernardino, CA	768,300	628,800	22.2	289,400	17.2
	Riverside, CA				170,600	21.8
	San Bernardino, CA				118,800	11.1
40	Dayton, OH	768,200	797,200	−3.6	193,500	−20.4
41	Honolulu, HI	762,600	630,500	21.0	365,000	12.3
42	Birmingham, AL	747,400	690,100	8.3	286,800	−4.7
43	Oklahoma City, OK	742,000	627,300	18.3	403,500	9.6
44	Albany-Schenectady-Troy, NY	729,100	717,200	1.7	226,300	−11.8
	Albany, NY				101,700	−12.2
	Schenectady, NY				68,000	−12.8
	Troy, NY				56,600	−10.0
45	Richmond, VA	690,600	621,900	11.0	219,200	−12.1
46	Salt Lake City, UT	682,400	510,200	33.8	163,000	−7.0
47	Jacksonville, FL	635,900	561,700	13.2	540,900	7.3
48	Nashville, TN	633,900	537,800	17.9	455,700	7.0
49	Orlando, FL	619,300	410,900	50.7	128,300	29.6
50	Akron, OH	614,100	635,200	−3.3	237,200	−13.9
51	Toledo, OH-MI	595,500	589,000	1.1	354,600	−7.4
52	Tampa, FL	594,500	454,600	30.8	271,600	−2.2
53	Tulsa, OK	567,100	459,400	23.4	360,900	−9.2
54	Omaha, NE	538,600	512,400	5.1	322,100	−7.1
55	Allentown-Bethlehem, PA-NJ	529,000	499,500	5.9	174,200	−4.1
	Allentown, PA				103,800	−5.6
	Bethlehem, PA				70,400	−3.2
56	Flint, MI	521,200	502,000	3.8	159,600	−17.4
57	Syracuse, NY	518,600	521,200	− .5	170,100	−13.8
58	Grand Rapids, MI	503,800	454,300	10.9	181,800	−8.0
59	New Haven, CT	500,500	488,700	2.4	126,100	−8.4
60	Youngstown-Warren, OH-PA	499,600	507,900	−1.6	172,000	−15.9
	Youngstown, OH				115,400	−18.1
	Warren, OH				56,600	−10.9
61	Tuscon, AZ	495,600	331,000	49.7	336,500	28.0
62	Scranton–Wilkes-Barre, PA	492,700	500,700	−1.6	139,700	−13.6
	Scranton, PA				88,100	−14.2
	Wilkes-Barre, PA				51,600	−12.4
63	Knoxville-Marysville-Oak Ridge, TN	490,000	419,400	16.8	220,200	1.6
	Knoxville, TN				175,000	.2
	Marysville, TN				17,500	26.8
	Oak Ridge, TN				27,700	−2.1
64	Springfield, MA	485,900	498,400	−2.5	152,300	−7.1
65	El Paso, TX-MEX	482,700	360,100	34.0	425,300	32.0
66	Charlotte, NC	479,200	416,800	15.0	315,500	30.7
67	Las Vegas, NV	453,800	267,800	69.5	164,700	30.9
68	Albuquerque, NM	453,200	331,100	36.9	332,300	35.9
69	Bridgeport, CT	438,500	443,700	−1.2	142,500	−8.9
70	Baton Rouge, LA	434,400	328,800	32.1	238,900	44.0
71	Austin, TX	430,200	299,700	43.5	345,900	36.4
72	Worcester, MA	402,900	399,700	.8	161,800	−8.4
73	Harrisburg, PA	396,300	362,900	9.2	53,300	−21.7
74	Greensboro-High Point, NC	392,400	347,800	12.8	219,400	5.8
	Greensboro, NC				155,600	8.0
	High Point, NC				63,800	.9
75	Fresno, CA	389,500	314,100	24.0	235,800	42.3
76	Little Rock, AR	382,000	312,300	22.3	167,700	26.6
77	Columbia, SC	375,900	296,700	26.7	101,200	−10.8
78	Wichita, KS	372,200	353,600	5.3	279,800	1.2
79	Saginaw-Bay City-Midland, MI	362,700	353,600	2.6	156,400	−11.3
	Saginaw, MI				77,500	−15.6
	Bay City, MI				41,600	−15.7
	Midland, MI				37,300	6.0
80	Mobile, AL	361,900	318,300	13.7	200,500	5.5
81	Chattanooga, TN-GA	359,200	316,400	13.5	169,700	41.5
82	West Palm Beach, FL	356,000	233,300	52.6	63,300	10.3
83	Lansing, MI	352,600	319,100	10.5	130,400	− .8
84	Charleston, SC	352,000	274,400	28.3	69,900	4.5
85	Beaumont-Port Arthur, TX	346,300	324,000	6.9	179,400	2.6
	Beaumont, TX				118,100	.5
	Port Arthur, TX				61,300	6.8
86	Greenville, SC	328,500	265,900	23.5	58,200	−5.2
87	Davenport-Rock Island-Moline, IA-IL	320,400	304,000	5.4	196,500	.8
	Davenport, IA				103,300	4.9
	Rock Island, IL				46,800	−6.8
	Moline, IL				46,400	−1.1
88	Peoria, IL	319,700	301,800	5.9	124,200	−2.2
89	Newport News-Hampton, VA	314,600	299,100	5.2	267,500	3.3
	Newport News, VA				194,900	4.8
	Hampton, VA				122,600	1.5
90	Canton-Massillon, OH	311,200	311,100	.3	123,700	−13.3
	Canton, OH				93,100	−15.4
	Massillon, OH				30,600	−5.8
91	Des Moines, IA	308,000	273,800	12.5	191,000	−5.2
92	Jackson, MS	306,900	245,200	25.2	202,900	31.8
93	Spokane, WA-ID	303,200	258,200	17.4	171,300	.5
94	Colorado Springs, CO	301,500	252,300	19.5	214,800	58.5
95	Madison, WI	294,300	263,600	11.6	170,600	− .7
96	Oxnard-Ventura, CA	294,200	222,800	32.0	186,200	44.1
	Oxnard, CA				108,200	52.0
	Ventura, CA				78,000	34.5
97	Shreveport, LA-TX	292,500	260,000	12.5	205,800	13.0
98	Fort Wayne, IN	284,300	270,700	5.0	172,300	−3.4
99	Raleigh, NC	282,800	216,900	30.4	150,300	22.4
100	Sarasota-Bradenton, FL	281,900	187,400	50.4	79,100	29.2
	Sarasota, FL				48,900	21.6
	Bradenton, FL				30,200	43.8
101	Rockford, IL	280,700	281,400	− .3	139,700	−5.2
102	South Bend, IN-MI	279,500	279,600	.0	109,700	−12.7
103	Winston-Salem, NC	278,400	236,700	17.6	138,600	3.7
104	Huntington, WV-KY-OH	273,900	256,600	6.7	63,700	−14.7
105	Corpus Christi, TX	272,000	237,800	14.4	231,100	13.0
106	Lexington, KY	255,600	212,000	20.6	204,200	88.9
107	Augusta, GA-SC	251,100	211,900	18.5	47,500	−20.7
108	New London-Norwich, CT-RI	250,800	242,600	3.4	66,900	−8.7
	New London, CT				28,800	−8.9
	Norwich, CT				38,100	−8.6
109	Pensacola, FL	250,200	210,000	19.1	57,600	−3.2
110	Erie, PA-NY	248,800	235,900	5.5	119,100	−7.9
111	Bakersfield, CA	245,100	198,800	23.3	105,700	52.1
112	Reading, PA	245,100	239,500	2.3	78,700	−10.2
113	Kalamazoo, MI	240,800	222,500	8.2	79,700	−6.9
114	Fayetteville, NC	236,200	202,700	16.5	59,500	11.2
115	Charleston, WV	236,300	244,500	−3.4	64,000	−10.5
116	Columbus, GA-AL	233,400	231,000	1.0	169,400	1.7
117	Binghamton, NY-PA	230,600	238,700	−3.4	55,900	−12.8
118	Melbourne, FL	227,500	155,600	46.2	46,200	15.7
119	Macon, GA	227,400	203,200	11.9	116,900	−4.5
120	Lancaster, PA	227,200	206,600	10.0	54,700	−5.2
121	Montgomery, AL	225,000	182,000	23.6	177,900	33.4
122	Utica-Rome, NY	224,000	246,700	−9.2	119,400	−15.6
	Utica, NY				75,600	−17.3
	Rome, NY				43,800	−12.6
123	Evansville, IN-KY	223,900	209,900	6.7	130,500	−6.0
124	Eugene, OR	218,100	172,100	26.7	105,700	33.8
125	Ogden, UT	217,300	172,000	26.3	64,400	−7.3
126	Roanoke, VA	216,000	196,000	10.2	100,200	8.8
127	Provo, UT	215,200	135,700	58.6	74,100	39.5
128	York, PA	213,300	194,400	9.7	44,600	−11.3
129	Stockton, CA	213,000	182,700	16.6	149,800	36.2
130	Savannah, GA	212,800	194,700	9.3	141,700	19.8
131	McAllen, TX	207,600	127,800	62.4	66,300	76.3
132	Waterbury, CT	205,000	196,100	4.5	103,300	−4.4
133	Durham-Chapel Hill, NC	203,100	170,000	19.5	132,900	9.3
	Durham, NC				100,500	5.3
	Chapel Hill, NC				32,400	23.7
134	Lubbock, TX	198,100	270,700	16.1	174,000	−16.7
135	Biloxi-Gulfport, MS	196,900	164,900	−19.4	89,000	−8.6
	Biloxi, MS				49,300	1.6
	Gulfport, MS				39,700	−18.8
136	Portland, ME	193,800	171,900	12.7	61,600	−5.4
137	Springfield, MO	192,600	157,300	22.4	133,100	10.8
138	Poughkeepsie, NY	191,700	172,000	11.5	29,800	−6.9
139	Huntsville, AL	189,600	178,700	6.1	142,500	2.3
140	Anchorage, AK	184,300	130,000	41.8	174,400	262.6
141	Modesto, CA	183,800	132,700	38.5	107,000	17.3
142	Daytona Beach, FL	178,800	122,700	45.8	54,200	19.6
143	Lincoln, NE	176,500	152,900	15.4	171,900	15.0
144	Reno, NV	176,200	109,900	60.3	100,800	38.3
145	Salem, OR	175,300	129,200	35.7	89,200	29.8
146	Spartanburg, SC	172,100	148,200	16.1	43,800	−1.6
147	Atlantic City, NJ	170,700	156,300	9.2	40,200	−16.1
148	Santa Barbara, CA	170,300	149,900	13.6	74,400	6.0
149	Portsmouth-Dover-Rochester, NH-ME	170,200	144,500	17.8	70,300	9.0
	Portsmouth, NH				26,300	2.3
	Dover, NH				22,400	7.2
	Rochester, NH				21,600	20.7
150	Johnstown, PA	168,400	171,300	−1.7	35,500	−16.5
151	Wheeling, WV, OH	168,200	168,500	− .2	43,100	−10.6

United States Populations and ZIP Codes

The following alphabetical list shows populations for all counties and nearly 10,000 selected cities and towns in the United States. ZIP codes are shown for all of the cities listed in the table. The state abbreviation following each name is that used by the United States Postal Service.

ZIP codes are listed for cities and towns after the state abbreviations. For each city with more than one ZIP code, the range of numbers assigned to the city is shown: For example, the ZIP code range for Chicago is 60601-99, and this indicates that the numbers between 60601 and 60699 are valid Chicago ZIP codes. ZIP code ranges are not listed for counties.

Populations for cities and towns appear as *italics* after the ZIP codes, and populations for counties appear after the state abbreviations. Populations shown for places over 25,000 and selected smaller places, are Dec. 31, 1986 estimates by Market Statistics, S&MM 1987 'Survey of Buying Power'. Other populations are 1980 census figures or estimates by Rand McNally & Company. City populations are for central cities, not metropolitan areas. New England 'town' (or 'township') populations are not included unless the town is considered to be primarily urban and contains only one commonly used place-name.

County names appear in **Boldface** type.

Abbreviations for State Names

AK	Alaska	**HI**	Hawaii	**ME**	Maine	**NJ**	New Jersey	**SD**	South Dakota
AL	Alabama	**IA**	Iowa	**MI**	Michigan	**NM**	New Mexico	**TN**	Tennessee
AR	Arkansas	**ID**	Idaho	**MN**	Minnesota	**NV**	Nevada	**TX**	Texas
AZ	Arizona	**IL**	Illinois	**MO**	Missouri	**NY**	New York	**UT**	Utah
CA	California	**IN**	Indiana	**MS**	Mississippi	**OH**	Ohio	**VA**	Virginia
CO	Colorado	**KS**	Kansas	**MT**	Montana	**OK**	Oklahoma	**VT**	Vermont
CT	Connecticut	**KY**	Kentucky	**NC**	North Carolina	**OR**	Oregon	**WA**	Washington
DC	District of Columbia	**LA**	Louisiana	**ND**	North Dakota	**PA**	Pennsylvania	**WI**	Wisconsin
DE	Delaware	**MA**	Massachusetts	**NE**	Nebraska	**RI**	Rhode Island	**WV**	West Virginia
FL	Florida	**MD**	Maryland	**NH**	New Hampshire	**SC**	South Carolina	**WY**	Wyoming
GA	Georgia								

A

Abbeville, AL 36310 • *3,155*
Abbeville, LA 70510 • *12,391*
Abbeville, SC 29620 • *5,833*
Abbeville, SC • *22,627*
Abbotsford, WI 54405 • *1,901*
Aberdeen, ID 83210 • *1,528*
Aberdeen, MD 21001 • *11,533*
Aberdeen, MS 39730 • *7,184*
Aberdeen, NC 28315 • *1,945*
Aberdeen, OH 45101 • *1,566*
Aberdeen, SD 57401 • *25,800*
Aberdeen, WA 98520 • *16,900*
Aberdeen Township, NJ 07747 • *17,235*
Abernathy, TX 79311 • *2,904*
Abilene, KS 67410 • *6,572*
Abilene, TX 79601-99 • *111,900*
Abingdon, IL 61410 • *4,210*
Abingdon, VA 24210 • *4,318*
Abington, MA 02351 • *13,517*
Abington [Township], PA 19001 • *59,500*
Absecon, NJ 08201 • *6,859*
Academia, OH 43050 • *1,447*
Acadia, LA • *56,427*
Accomack, VA • *31,268*
Ackerman, MS 39735 • *1,598*
Ackley, IA 50601 • *1,900*
Acton, MA 01720 • *2,300*
Acushnet, MA 02743 • *6,030*
Acworth, GA 30101 • *3,648*
Ada, MN 56510 • *1,971*
Ada, OH 45810 • *5,669*
Ada, OK 74820 • *17,200*
Ada, ID • *173,036*
Adair, IA • *9,509*
Adair, KY • *15,233*
Adair, MO • *24,870*
Adair, OK • *18,575*
Adairsville, GA 30103 • *2,137*
Adams, MA 01220 • *10,381*
Adams, NY 13605 • *1,701*
Adams, WI 53910 • *1,744*
Adams, CO • *245,944*
Adams, ID • *3,347*
Adams, IL • *71,622*
Adams, IN • *29,619*
Adams, IA • *5,731*
Adams, MS • *38,035*
Adams, NE • *30,656*
Adams, ND • *3,584*
Adams, OH • *24,328*
Adams, PA • *68,292*
Adams, WA • *13,267*
Adams, WI • *13,457*
Adams Center, NY 13606 • *1,519*
Adams City, CO 80022 • *2,200*
Adamsville, AL 35005 • *4,511*
Adamsville, TN 38310 • *1,453*
Addison, CT 06033 • *2,460*
Addison, IL 60101 • *32,200*
Addison, NY 14801 • *2,028*
Addison, TX 75001 • *7,000*
Addison, VT • *29,406*
Adel, GA 31620 • *5,592*
Adel, IA 50003 • *2,846*
Adelanto, CA 92301 • *2,164*
Adelphi, MD 20783 • *12,530*
Adobe Acres, NM 87105 • *2,400*
Adrian, MI 49221 • *20,800*
Adrian, MO 64720 • *1,484*
Affton, MO 63123 • *23,900*
Afton, MN 55001 • *2,550*
Afton, WY 83110 • *1,481*
Agawam, MA 01001 • *10,190*
Agoura, CA 91301 • *11,399*
Ahoskie, NC 27910 • *4,887*
Aiea, HI 96701 • *15,200*
Aiken, SC 29801 • *17,600*
Aiken, SC • *105,625*
Ainsworth, NE 69210 • *2,256*
Air Park West, NE 68524 • *3,100*
Aitkin, MN 56431 • *1,770*
Aitkin, MN • *13,404*
Ajo, AZ 85321 • *5,189*
Akron, CO 80720 • *1,716*
Akron, IA 51001 • *1,517*
Akron, NY 14001 • *2,971*
Akron, OH 44301-99 • *224,700*
Akron, PA 17501 • *3,471*
Alabaster, AL 35007 • *10,111*
Alachua, FL 32615 • *3,561*
Alachua, FL • *151,348*
Alamance, NC • *99,319*
Alameda, CA 94501 • *75,900*
Alameda, NM 87114 • *5,900*
Alameda, CA • *1,105,379*
Alamo, CA 94507 • *6,700*
Alamo, TN 38001 • *2,615*
Alamo, TX 78516 • *6,644*
Alamogordo, NM 88310-11 • *28,000*
Alamo Heights, TX 78209 • *6,252*
Alamosa, CO 81101 • *6,830*
Alamosa, CO • *11,799*
Albany, CA 94706 • *15,130*
Albany, GA 31701-08 • *85,300*
Albany, IN 47320 • *2,625*
Albany, KY 42602 • *2,083*
Albany, MN 56307 • *1,569*
Albany, MO 64402 • *2,152*
Albany, NY 12201-99 • *100,800*
Albany, OR 97321 • *28,100*
Albany, TX 76430 • *2,450*
Albany, NY • *285,909*
Albany, WY • *29,062*
Albemarle, NC 28001 • *15,110*
Albemarle, VA • *55,783*
Albert Lea, MN 56007 • *18,500*
Albertson, NY 11507 • *5,561*
Albia, IA 52531 • *4,184*
Albion, IL 62806 • *2,285*
Albion, IN 46701 • *1,637*
Albion, MI 49224 • *11,059*
Albion, NE 68620 • *1,997*
Albion, NY 14411 • *4,897*
Albion, PA 16401 • *1,818*
Albion, RI 02802 • *1,600*
Albuquerque, NM 87101-99 • *367,000*
Alcoa, TN 37701 • *7,100*
Alcona, MI • *9,740*
Alcorn, MS • *33,036*
Alden, NY 14004 • *2,488*
Alderwood Manor, WA 98036 • *7,500*
Aledo, IL 61231 • *3,881*
Alexander, IL • *12,264*
Alexander, NC • *24,999*
Alexander City, AL 35010 • *13,807*
Alexandria, IN 46001 • *6,028*
Alexandria, KY 41001 • *4,735*
Alexandria, LA 71301-15 • *54,100*
Alexandria, MN 56308 • *7,608*
Alexandria, VA 22301-99 • *111,800*
Alfalfa, OK • *7,077*
Alfred, NY 14802 • *4,967*
Alger, MI • *9,225*
Algoma, WI 54201 • *3,656*
Algona, IA 50511 • *6,289*
Algona, WA 98002 • *1,467*
Algonac, MI 48001 • *4,412*
Algonquin, IL 60102 • *8,581*
Algood, TN 38501 • *2,406*
Alhambra, CA 91801-99 • *73,000*
Alice, TX 78332 • *21,900*
Aliceville, AL 35442 • *3,207*
Aliquippa, PA 15001 • *17,094*
Allamakee, IA • *15,108*
Allegan, MI 49010 • *4,576*
Allegan, MI • *81,555*
Allegany, NY 14706 • *2,078*
Allegany, MD • *80,548*
Allegany, NY • *51,742*
Alleghany, NC • *9,587*
Alleghany, VA • *14,333*
Allegheny, PA • *1,450,085*
Allen, TX 75002 • *8,314*
Allen, IN • *294,335*
Allen, KS • *1,564*
Allen, KY • *14,128*
Allen, LA • *21,390*
Allen, OH • *112,241*
Allendale, NJ 07401 • *5,901*
Allendale, SC 29810 • *4,400*
Allendale, SC • *10,700*
Allen Park, MI 48101 • *31,400*
Allentown, NJ 08501 • *1,962*
Allentown, PA 18101-99 • *105,600*
Alliance, NE 69301 • *9,920*
Alliance, OH 44601 • *23,600*
Allison Park, PA 15101 • *5,600*
Allouez, WI 54301 • *14,882*
Alma, AR 72921 • *3,009*
Alma, GA 31510 • *3,819*
Alma, MI 48801 • *9,652*
Almont, MI 48003 • *1,857*
Aloha, OR 97007 • *10,000*
Alondra, CA 90249 • *12,096*
Alpena, MI 49707 • *11,400*
Alpena, MI • *32,315*
Alpha, NJ 08865 • *2,644*
Alpharetta, GA 30201 • *3,128*
Alpine, CA 92001 • *5,368*
Alpine, NJ 07620 • *1,549*
Alpine, TX 79830 • *5,465*
Alpine, UT 84003 • *2,649*
Alpine, CA • *1,097*
Alsip, IL 60658 • *17,134*
Alta, IA 51002 • *1,720*
Altadena, CA 91001 • *44,900*
Altamont, IL 62411 • *2,389*
Altamont, OR 97601 • *19,805*
Altamonte Springs, FL 32701 • *26,300*
Altavista, VA 24517 • *3,849*
Alton, IL 62002 • *33,200*
Altoona, IA 50009 • *6,436*
Altoona, PA 16601-03 • *54,800*
Altoona, WI 54720 • *4,393*
Alturas, CA 96101 • *3,025*
Altus, OK 73521 • *23,800*
Alum Rock, CA 95127 • *16,890*
Alva, OK 73717 • *6,416*
Alvarado, TX 76009 • *2,701*
Alvin, TX 77511 • *17,877*
Amador, CA • *19,314*
Amagansett, NY 11930 • *2,188*
Amarillo, TX 79101-99 • *163,700*
Ambler, PA 19002 • *6,628*
Amboy, IL 61310 • *2,377*
Ambridge, PA 15003 • *9,575*
Amelia, LA 70340 • *3,617*
Amelia, VA • *8,405*
American Canyon, CA 94589 • *5,712*
American Falls, ID 83211 • *3,626*
American Fork, UT 84003-04 • *13,459*
Americus, GA 31709 • *16,120*
Amery, WI 54001 • *2,404*
Ames, IA 50010 • *46,100*
Amesbury, MA 01913 • *13,971*
Amherst, MA 01002 • *17,773*
Amherst, NY 14226 • *45,900*
Amherst, OH 44001 • *10,638*
Amherst, VA • *29,122*
Amite, LA 70422 • *4,301*
Amite, MS • *13,369*
Amityville, NY 11701 • *9,076*
Ammon, ID 83401 • *4,669*
Amory, MS 38821 • *7,307*
Amsterdam, NY 12010 • *21,300*
Anaconda, MT 59711 • *12,518*
Anacortes, WA 98221 • *9,013*
Anadarko, OK 73005 • *6,378*
Anaheim, CA 92801-99 • *243,600*
Anahuac, TX 77514 • *1,840*
Anamosa, IA 52205 • *4,958*
Anandale, LA 71301 • *2,000*
Anchorage, AK 99501-40 • *239,500*
Anchorage, KY 40223 • *1,726*
Andalusia, AL 36420 • *10,415*
Anderson, CA 96007 • *7,381*
Anderson, IN 46011-18 • *60,800*
Anderson, SC 29621-24 • *28,600*
Anderson, KS • *8,749*
Anderson, KY • *12,567*
Anderson, SC • *133,235*
Anderson, TN • *67,346*
Anderson, TX • *38,381*
Andover, KS 67002 • *2,801*
Andover, MA 01810 • *8,445*
Andover, MN 55304 • *9,387*
Andrew, MO • *13,980*
Andrews, NC 28901 • *1,621*
Andrews, SC 29510 • *3,129*
Andrews, TX 79714 • *11,061*
Andrews, TX • *13,323*
Androscoggin, ME • *99,657*
Angelina, TX • *64,172*
Angels Camp, CA 95222 • *2,302*
Angier, NC 27501 • *1,709*
Angle Lake, WA 98188 • *5,000*
Angleton, TX 77515 • *13,929*
Angola, IN 46703 • *5,486*
Angola, NY 14006 • *2,292*
Ankeny, IA 50021 • *16,565*
Anna, IL 62906 • *5,408*
Annalee Heights, VA 22042 • *1,750*
Anna Maria, FL 34216 • *1,537*
Annandale, MN 55302 • *1,568*
Annandale, VA 22003 • *34,800*
Annapolis, MD 21401-99 • *34,100*
Ann Arbor, MI 48103-08 • *106,000*
Anne Arundel, MD • *370,775*
Anniston, AL 36201-06 • *30,300*
Annville, PA 17003 • *4,493*
Anoka, MN 55303 • *15,634*
Anoka, MN • *195,998*
Anson, TX 79501 • *2,831*
Anson, NC • *25,649*
Ansonia, CT 06401 • *19,100*
Ansted, WV 25812 • *1,952*
Antelope, NE • *8,675*
Anthony, KS 67003 • *2,661*
Anthony, NM 88021 • *3,285*
Anthony, RI 02816 • *2,980*
Antigo, WI 54409 • *8,500*
Antioch, CA 94509 • *48,800*
Antioch, IL 60002 • *4,419*
Antlers, OK 74523 • *2,989*
Antrim, MI • *16,194*
Antwerp, OH 45813 • *1,765*
Apache, OK 73006 • *1,560*
Apache, AZ • *52,108*
Apache Junction, AZ 85220 • *10,013*
Apalachicola, FL 32320 • *2,565*
Apex, NC 27502 • *2,847*
Apollo, PA 15613 • *2,212*
Apopka, FL 32703-04 • *6,019*
Appalachia, VA 24216 • *2,418*
Appanoose, IA • *15,511*
Appleton, MN 56208 • *1,842*
Appleton, WI 54911-15 • *63,700*
Apple Valley, CA 92307-08 • *14,305*
Apple Valley, MN 55124 • *21,818*
Applewood, CO 80401 • *8,130*
Appling, GA • *15,565*
Appomattox, VA • *11,971*
Aptos, CA 95003 • *7,039*
Arab, AL 35016 • *6,053*
Arabi, LA 70032 • *10,248*
Aransas, TX • *14,260*
Aransas Pass, TX 78336 • *7,173*
Arapahoe, CO • *293,621*
Arcade, CA 95821 • *43,400*
Arcade, NY 14009 • *2,052*
Arcadia, CA 91006 • *49,900*
Arcadia, FL 33821 • *6,002*
Arcadia, IN 46030 • *1,801*
Arcadia, LA 71001 • *3,403*
Arcadia, SC 29320 • *2,088*
Arcadia, WI 54612 • *2,109*
Arcanum, OH 45304 • *2,002*
Arcata, CA 95521 • *14,140*
Archbald, PA 18403 • *6,295*
Archbold, OH 43502 • *3,318*
Archdale, NC 27263 • *5,326*
Archer, TX • *7,266*
Archer City, TX 76351 • *1,862*
Archuleta, CO • *3,664*
Arcola, IL 61910 • *2,714*
Arden, CA 95825 • *56,900*
Arden Hills, MN 55112 • *8,012*
Ardmore, IN 46628 • *2,250*
Ardmore, OK 73401 • *25,000*
Ardsley, NY 10502 • *4,183*
Arenac, MI • *14,706*
Argos, IN 46501 • *1,547*
Arkadelphia, AR 71923 • *10,168*
Arkansas, AR • *24,175*
Arkansas City, KS 67005 • *13,201*
Arkoma, OK 74901 • *2,175*
Arlington, GA 31713 • *1,572*
Arlington, MA 02174 • *45,400*
Arlington, MN 55307 • *1,779*
Arlington, NY 12603 • *11,305*
Arlington, TN 38002 • *1,778*
Arlington, TX 76010-18 • *232,900*
Arlington, VA 22201-99 • *156,400*
Arlington, WA 98223 • *3,282*
Arlington, VA • *152,599*
Arlington Heights, IL 60004-09 • *69,100*
Arma, KS 66712 • *1,676*
Armijo, NM 87105 • *14,600*
Armonk, NY 10504 • *2,238*
Armstrong, PA • *77,768*
Armstrong, TX • *1,994*
Arnaudville, LA 70512 • *1,679*
Arnold, CA 95223 • *2,385*
Arnold, MD 21012 • *12,285*
Arnold, MN 55803 • *1,500*
Arnold, MO 63010 • *19,141*
Arnold, PA 15068 • *6,853*
Aroostook, ME • *91,331*
Arroyo Grande, CA 93420 • *11,290*
Artesia, CA 90701 • *14,301*
Artesia, NM 88210 • *10,385*
Arthur, IL 61911 • *2,122*
Arthur, NE • *513*
Arundel Village, MD 21225 • *5,300*
Arvada, CO 80001-05 • *94,600*
Arvin, CA 93203 • *6,863*
Asbury Park, NJ 07712 • *17,300*
Ascension, LA • *50,068*
Ashaway, RI 02804 • *1,747*
Ashburn, GA 31714 • *4,766*
Ashdown, AR 71822 • *5,282*

Ashe, NC • 22,325
Asheboro, NC 27203 • 16,200
Asherton, TX 78827 • 1,574
Asheville, NC 28801-99 • 59,900
Ashford, AL 36312 • 2,165
Ashland, AL 36251 • 2,052
Ashland, CA 94541 • 13,893
Ashland, KY 41101 • 26,300
Ashland, MA 01721 • 9,165
Ashland, NE 68003 • 2,274
Ashland, NH 03217 • 1,479
Ashland, OH 44805 • 19,700
Ashland, OR 97520 • 14,943
Ashland, PA 17921 • 4,235
Ashland, VA 23005 • 4,640
Ashland, WI 54806 • 9,115
Ashland, OH • 46,178
Ashland, WI • 16,783
Ashland City, TN 37015 • 2,588
Ashley, PA 18706 • 3,512
Ashley, AR • 26,538
Ashtabula, OH 44004 • 23,100
Ashtabula, OH • 104,215
Ashville, AL 35953 • 1,489
Ashville, OH 43103 • 2,046
Ashwaubenon, WI 54304 • 14,486
Asotin, WA • 16,823
Aspen, CO 81611 • 3,678
Aspen Hill, MD 20906 • 9,800
Aspinwall, PA 15215 • 3,284
Assumption, LA • 22,084
Aston, PA 19014 • 14,530
Astoria, OR 97103 • 9,998
Atascadero, CA 93422 • 16,232
Atascosa, TX • 25,055
Atchison, KS 66002 • 11,400
Atchison, KS • 18,397
Atchison, MO • 8,605
Atco, NJ 08004 • 2,020
Athens, AL 35611 • 14,558
Athens, GA 30601-13 • 43,600
Athens, NY 12015 • 1,738
Athens, OH 45701 • 21,000
Athens, PA 18810 • 3,622
Athens, TN 37303 • 12,400
Athens, TX 75751 • 10,197
Athens, OH • 56,399
Atherton, CA 94025 • 7,797
Athol, MA 01331 • 10,634
Atkins, AR 72823 • 3,002
Atkinson, NE 68713 • 1,521
Atkinson, GA • 6,141
Atlanta, GA 30301-99 • 445,000
Atlanta, IL 61723 • 1,807
Atlanta, TX 75551 • 6,272
Atlantic, IA 50022 • 7,789
Atlantic, NJ • 194,119
Atlantic Beach, FL 32233 • 7,847
Atlantic City, NJ 08401-99 • 38,000
Atlantic Highlands, NJ 07716 • 4,950
Atmore, AL 36502 • 8,789
Atoka, OK 74525 • 3,409
Atoka, OK • 12,748
Attala, MS • 19,865
Attalla, AL 35954 • 7,737
Attica, IN 47918 • 3,841
Attica, NY 14011 • 2,659
Attleboro, MA 02703 • 34,800
Atwater, CA 95301 • 17,530
Atwood, IL 61913 • 1,464
Atwood, KS 67730 • 1,665
Auburn, AL 36830 • 28,700
Auburn, CA 95603 • 9,000
Auburn, IL 62615 • 3,616
Auburn, IN 46706 • 8,122
Auburn, KY 42206 • 1,467
Auburn, ME 04210 • 23,100
Auburn, MA 01501 • 14,845
Auburn, MI 48611 • 1,921
Auburn, NE 68305 • 3,482
Auburn, NY 13021 • 33,200
Auburn, WA 98001-03 • 30,400
Auburndale, FL 33823 • 6,501
Auburn Heights, MI 48057 • 15,388
Audrain, MO • 26,458
Audubon, IA 50025 • 2,841
Audubon, NJ 08106 • 9,533
Audubon, PA 19407 • 6,130
Audubon, IA • 8,559
Auglaize, OH • 42,554
August, CA 95201 • 5,445
Augusta, AR 72006 • 3,496
Augusta, GA 30901-99 • 47,400
Augusta, KS 67010 • 6,968
Augusta, KY 41002 • 1,455
Augusta, ME 04330 • 21,900
Augusta, WI 54722 • 1,560
Augusta, VA • 53,732
Aumsville, OR 97325 • 1,432
Aurora, CO 80010-17 • 208,300
Aurora, IL 60504-07 • 90,500
Aurora, IN 47001 • 3,816
Aurora, MN 55705 • 2,670
Aurora, MO 65605 • 6,437
Aurora, NE 68818 • 3,717
Aurora, OH 44202 • 8,177
Aurora, SD • 3,628
Au Sable Forks, NY 12912 • 2,100
Austell, GA 30001 • 3,939
Austin, IN 47102 • 4,857
Austin, MN 55912 • 22,300
Austin, TX 78701-99 • 460,400
Austin, TX • 17,726
Austintown, OH 44512 • 23,700
Autauga, AL • 32,259
Ava, MO 65608 • 2,761
Avalon, CA 90704 • 2,022
Avalon, NJ 08202 • 2,162
Avalon, PA 15202 • 6,240
Avenal, CA 93204 • 4,137
Avenel, MD 20783 • 5,600
Aventura, FL 33180 • 9,698
Avery, NC • 14,409
Avis, PA 17721 • 1,718
Avoca, IA 51521 • 1,650
Avoca, PA 18641 • 3,536
Avocado Heights, CA 91746 • 11,721
Avon, CT 06001 • 1,434
Avon, MA 02322 • 5,026
Avon, NY 14414 • 3,006
Avon, OH 44011 • 7,241
Avon by the Sea, NJ 07717 • 2,337
Avondale, AZ 85323 • 8,168
Avondale, LA 70094 • 6,699
Avondale, OH 45404 • 5,000
Avon Lake, OH 44012 • 13,222
Avon Park, FL 33825 • 8,026
Avoyelles, LA • 41,393
Ayden, NC 28513 • 4,361
Ayer, MA 01432-33 • 6,993
Azalea Park, FL 32807 • 8,301
Azle, TX 76020 • 6,097
Aztec, NM 87410 • 5,512
Azusa, CA 91702 • 35,300

B

Babbitt, MN 55706 • 2,435
Babbitt, NV 89416 • 1,800
Babylon, NY 11702-04 • 12,388
Baca, CO • 5,419
Bacon, GA • 9,379
Bad Axe, MI 48413 • 3,184
Baden, PA 15005 • 5,318
Badin, NC 28009 • 1,514
Bagdad, AZ 86321 • 2,331
Bagdad, FL 32530 • 1,479
Bailey, TX • 8,168
Baileys Crossroads, VA 22041 • 4,600
Bainbridge, GA 31717 • 10,553
Bainbridge, NY 13733 • 1,603
Baird, TX 79504 • 1,696
Baker, LA 70714 • 12,865
Baker, MT 59313 • 2,354
Baker, OR 97814 • 9,471
Baker, FL • 15,289
Baker, GA • 3,808
Baker, OR • 16,134
Bakersfield, CA 93301-99 • 151,800
Balch Springs, TX 75180 • 13,746
Bald Knob, AR 72010 • 2,756
Baldwin, FL 32234 • 1,526
Baldwin, LA 70514 • 2,644
Baldwin, NY 11510 • 31,800
Baldwin, PA 15234 • 23,500
Baldwin, WI 54002 • 1,620
Baldwin, AL • 78,556
Baldwin, GA • 34,686
Baldwin City, KS 66006 • 2,829
Baldwin Park, CA 91706 • 60,800
Baldwinsville, NY 13027 • 6,446
Baldwinville, MA 01436 • 1,709
Baldwyn, MS 38824 • 3,427
Balfour, NC 28706 • 1,772
Ball, LA 71405 • 3,405
Ballard, KY • 8,798
Ballinger, TX 76821 • 4,207
Ballston Spa, NY 12020 • 4,711
Ballwin, MO 63011 • 12,656
Balmville, NY 12550 • 2,919
Baltic, CT 06330 • 2,000
Baltimore, MD 21201-99 • 759,500
Baltimore, OH 43105 • 2,689
Baltimore, MD • 655,615
Baltimore Highlands, MD 21227 • 6,750
Bamberg, SC 29003 • 3,672
Bamberg, SC • 18,118
Bandera, TX • 7,084
Bandon, OR 97411 • 2,311
Bangor, ME 04401 • 30,700
Bangor, MI 49013 • 2,001
Bangor, PA 18013 • 5,006
Bangor Township, MI 48706 • 17,494
Bangs, TX 76823 • 1,716
Banks, GA • 8,702
Banner, NE • 918
Banning, CA 92220 • 14,020
Bannock, ID • 65,421
Baraboo, WI 53913 • 8,081
Baraga, MI • 8,484
Barber, KS • 6,548
Barberton, OH 44203 • 28,100
Barbour, AL • 24,756
Barbour, WV • 16,639
Barboursville, WV 25504 • 3,000
Barbourville, KY 40906 • 3,333
Bardstown, KY 40004 • 6,401
Bargersville, IN 46106 • 1,647
Bar Harbor, ME 04609 • 2,685
Barling, AR 72923 • 3,789
Barnes, ND • 13,960
Barnesboro, PA 15714 • 2,741
Barnesville, GA 30204 • 4,887
Barnesville, MN 56514 • 2,207
Barnesville, OH 43713 • 4,633
Barnsdall, OK 74002 • 1,501
Barnstable, MA 02630 • 2,033
Barnstable, MA • 147,925
Barnwell, SC 29812 • 5,572
Barnwell, SC • 19,868
Barrackville, WV 26559 • 1,815
Barre, VT 05641 • 10,000
Barren, KY • 34,009
Barrington, IL 60010 • 9,029
Barrington, NJ 08007 • 7,418
Barrington, RI 02806 • 16,174
Barron, WI 54812 • 2,595
Barron, WI • 38,730
Barron Lake, MI 49120 • 1,600
Barrow, AK 99723 • 2,267
Barrow, GA • 21,354
Barry, IL 62312 • 1,487
Barry, MI • 45,781
Barry, MO • 24,408
Barstow, CA 92311 • 21,900
Bartholomew, IN • 65,088
Bartlesville, OK 74003-06 • 33,800
Bartlett, IL 60103 • 16,792
Bartlett, TN 38134 • 20,818
Bartlett, TX 76511 • 1,567
Barton, KS • 31,343
Barton, MO • 11,292
Bartonville, IL 61607 • 6,137
Bartow, FL 33830 • 14,780
Bartow, GA • 40,760
Barview, OR 97420 • 1,462
Basehor, KS 66007 • 1,483
Basile, LA 70515 • 2,635
Basking Ridge, NJ 07920 • 3,060
Bassett, VA 24055 • 2,034
Bass Lake, IN 46534 • 1,500
Bastrop, LA 71220 • 15,527
Bastrop, TX 78602 • 3,789
Bastrop, TX • 24,726
Batavia, IL 60510 • 13,758
Batavia, NY 14020 • 16,700
Batavia, OH 45103 • 1,896
Bates, MO • 15,873
Batesburg, SC 29006 • 4,023
Batesville, AR 72501 • 8,840
Batesville, IN 47006 • 4,152
Batesville, MS 38606 • 5,162
Bath, ME 04530 • 10,246
Bath, NY 14810 • 6,042
Bath, PA 18014 • 1,953
Bath, SC 29816 • 2,242
Bath, KY • 10,025
Bath, VA • 5,860
Baton Rouge, LA 70801-99 • 249,100
Battle Creek, MI 49017 • 54,200
Battle Ground, WA 98604 • 2,774
Battle Mountain, NV 89820 • 2,749
Bawcomville, LA 71291 • 2,500
Baxley, GA 31513 • 3,586
Baxter, MN 56401 • 2,625
Baxter, AR • 27,409
Baxter Springs, KS 66713 • 4,730
Bay, AR 72411 • 1,605
Bay, FL • 97,740
Bay, MI • 119,881
Bayard, NE 69334 • 1,435
Bayard, NM 88023 • 3,036
Bayberry, NY 13088 • 6,710
Bay City, MI 48706-08 • 39,000
Bay City, TX 77414 • 20,900
Bayfield, WI • 13,822
Baylor, TX • 4,919
Bay Minette, AL 36507 • 7,455
Bayonet Point, FL 34667 • 16,455
Bayonne, NJ 07002 • 63,900
Bayou Cane, LA 70359 • 15,723
Bayou George, FL 32401 • 1,500
Bayou La Batre, AL 36509 • 2,005
Bay Pines, FL 33504 • 5,757
Bayport, MN 55003 • 2,932
Bayport, NY 11705 • 9,282
Bay Ridge, MD 21403 • 1,989
Bay Saint Louis, MS 39520 • 7,850
Bay Shore, NY 11706 • 32,800
Bayshore Gardens, FL 34207 • 14,945
Bayside, WI 53217 • 4,724
Bay Springs, MS 39422 • 1,884
Baytown, TX 77520-22 • 60,600
Bay Village, OH 44140 • 17,846
Bayville, NY 11709 • 7,034
Beach, IL 60085 • 4,650
Beach Haven, NJ 08008 • 1,714
Beachwood, NJ 08722 • 7,687
Beachwood, OH 44122 • 9,600
Beacon, NY 12508 • 12,937
Beacon Square, FL 34652 • 5,600
Beadle, SD • 19,195
Beardstown, IL 62618 • 6,338
Bear Lake, ID • 6,931
Beatrice, NE 68310 • 12,400
Beaufort, NC 28516 • 3,826
Beaufort, SC 29902 • 8,634
Beaufort, NC • 40,355
Beaufort, SC • 65,364
Beaumont, CA 92223 • 6,840
Beaumont, TX 77701-99 • 123,300
Beauregard, LA • 29,692
Beaver, OK 73932 • 1,939
Beaver, PA 15009 • 5,000
Beaver, UT 84713 • 1,792
Beaver, OK • 6,806
Beaver, PA • 204,441
Beaver, UT • 4,378
Beavercreek, OH 45385 • 33,700
Beaver Dam, KY 42320 • 3,185
Beaver Dam, WI 53916 • 14,000
Beaver Falls, PA 15010 • 12,525
Beaverhead, MT • 8,186
Beaverton, OR 97005-07 • 34,900
Becker, MN • 29,336
Beckham, OK • 19,243
Beckley, WV 25801 • 20,600
Bedford, IN 47421 • 14,100
Bedford, IA 50833 • 1,692
Bedford, MA 01730 • 13,067
Bedford, OH 44146 • 14,700
Bedford, PA 15522 • 3,326
Bedford, TX 76021-22 • 20,821
Bedford, VA 24523 • 6,200
Bedford, PA • 46,784
Bedford, TN • 27,916
Bedford, VA • 34,927
Bedford Heights, OH 44146 • 13,214
Bedford Hills, NY 10507 • 3,140
Bee, TX • 26,030
Beebe, AR 72012 • 3,599
Beecher, IL 60401 • 2,024
Beecher, MI 48505 • 17,178
Beech Grove, IN 46107 • 13,196
Bee Ridge, FL 34233 • 3,313
Beeville, TX 78102 • 14,574
Bel Air, MD 21014 • 8,400
Bel Aire, KS 67220 • 2,395
Belchertown, MA 01007 • 2,531
Belcourt, ND 58316 • 1,803
Belding, MI 48809 • 5,634
Belen, NM 87002 • 5,617
Belfast, ME 04915 • 6,243
Belford, NJ 07718 • 6,300
Belgrade, MT 59714 • 2,336
Belhaven, NC 27810 • 2,430
Belington, WV 26250 • 2,038
Belknap, NH • 42,884
Bell, CA 90201 • 29,300
Bell, KY • 34,330
Bell, TX • 157,820
Bellair, FL 32073 • 5,200
Bellaire, OH 43906 • 8,241
Bellaire, TX 77401 • 14,950
Bella Vista, AR 72712 • 2,589
Bellbrook, OH 45305 • 5,174
Belle, WV 25015 • 1,621
Belleair, FL 34616 • 3,673
Belle Chasse, LA 70037 • 5,412
Bellefontaine, OH 43311 • 12,400
Bellefontaine Neighbors, MO 63137 • 12,082
Bellefonte, PA 16823 • 6,300
Belle Fourche, SD 57717 • 4,692
Belle Glade, FL 33430 • 16,535
Belle Isle, FL 32809 • 2,848
Belle Meade, TN 37205 • 3,182
Belle Plaine, IA 52208 • 2,903
Belle Plaine, KS 67013 • 1,706
Belle Plaine, MN 56011 • 2,754
Belle Vernon, PA 15012 • 1,489
Belleview, FL 32506 • 8,000
Belleview, FL 32620 • 1,913
Belle View, VA 22307 • 3,500
Belleville, IL 62220-25 • 42,200
Belleville, KS 66935 • 2,805
Belleville, MI 48111 • 3,366
Belleville, NJ 07109 • 35,800
Belleville, PA 17004 • 1,689
Bellevue, IA 52031 • 2,450
Bellevue, KY 41073 • 7,678
Bellevue, NE 68005 • 33,100
Bellevue, OH 44811 • 8,187
Bellevue, PA 15202 • 10,128
Bellevue, WA 98004-09 • 81,600
Bellflower, CA 90706 • 59,800
Bell Gardens, CA 90201 • 38,900
Bellingham, MA 02019 • 14,300
Bellingham, WA 98225-27 • 46,500
Bellmawr, NJ 08031 • 13,721
Bellmead, TX 76705 • 7,569
Bellmore, NY 11710 • 18,106
Bellows Falls, VT 05101 • 3,456
Bellport, NY 11713 • 2,809
Bells, TN 38006 • 1,737
Bellville, OH 44813 • 1,714
Bellville, TX 77418 • 2,860
Bellwood, IL 60104 • 19,811
Bellwood, PA 16617 • 2,114
Belmar, NJ 07719 • 6,771
Belmond, IA 50421 • 2,505
Belmont, CA 94002 • 24,700
Belmont, MA 02178 • 25,400
Belmont, NC 28012 • 4,607
Belmont, OH • 82,569
Bel-Nor, MO 63133 • 2,047
Beloit, KS 67420 • 4,367
Beloit, WI 53511 • 34,100
Beloit North, WI 53511 • 5,457
Belpre, OH 45714 • 7,193
Belton, MO 64012 • 12,708
Belton, SC 29627 • 5,312
Belton, TX 76513 • 10,660
Beltrami, MN • 30,982
Beltsville, MD 20705 • 12,760
Belvedere, GA 30032 • 6,100
Belvedere, SC 29841 • 6,859
Belvedere Park, GA 30032 • 17,766
Belvidere, IL 61008 • 15,176
Belvidere, NJ 07823 • 2,475
Belzoni, MS 39038 • 2,982
Bement, IL 61813 • 1,770
Bemidji, MN 56601 • 11,200
Benavides, TX 78341 • 1,978
Benbrook, TX 76126 • 13,579
Bend, OR 97701-09 • 18,900
Benewah, ID • 8,292
Ben Hill, GA • 16,000
Benicia, CA 94510 • 15,376
Benld, IL 62009 • 1,638
Ben Lomond, CA 95005 • 7,238
Bennett, SD • 3,044
Bennettsville, SC 29512 • 9,549
Bennington, VT 05201 • 9,349
Bennington, VT • 33,345
Bensalem, PA 19020 • 57,900
Bensenville, IL 60106 • 16,106
Bensley, VA 23234 • 3,400
Benson, AZ 85602 • 3,737
Benson, MN 56215 • 3,656
Benson, NC 27504 • 2,792
Benson, ND • 7,944
Bent, CO • 5,945
Bentleyville, PA 15314 • 2,525
Benton, AR 72015 • 18,800
Benton, IL 62812 • 7,778
Benton, KY 42025 • 3,700
Benton, LA 71006 • 1,864
Benton, AR • 78,115
Benton, IN • 10,218
Benton, IA • 23,649
Benton, MN • 25,187
Benton, MS • 8,153
Benton, MO • 12,183
Benton, OR • 68,211
Benton, TN • 14,901
Benton, WA • 109,444
Benton City, WA 99320 • 1,980
Benton Harbor, MI 49022 • 14,500
Benton Heights, MI 49022 • 6,787
Bentonville, AR 72712 • 9,920
Benwood, WV 26031 • 1,994
Benzie, MI • 11,205
Berea, KY 40403 • 8,600
Berea, OH 44017 • 19,567
Berea, SC 29611 • 7,500
Beresford, SD 57004 • 1,865
Bergen, NJ • 845,385
Bergenfield, NJ 07621 • 26,300
Berkeley, CA 94701-99 • 109,200
Berkeley, IL 60162 • 5,467
Berkeley, MO 63134 • 15,922
Berkeley, SC • 94,727
Berkeley, WV • 46,775
Berkeley Heights, NJ 07922 • 12,549
Berkley, MI 48072 • 18,637
Berks, PA • 312,509
Berkshire, MA • 145,110
Berlin, MD 21811 • 2,162
Berlin, NH 03570 • 13,084
Berlin, NJ 08009 • 5,786
Berlin, PA 15530 • 1,999
Berlin, WI 54923 • 5,478
Bernalillo, NM 87004 • 3,012
Bernalillo, NM • 419,700
Bernardsville, NJ 07924 • 6,715
Berne, IN 46711 • 3,300
Bernice, LA 71222 • 1,956
Bernie, MO 63822 • 1,975
Berrien, GA • 13,525
Berrien, MI • 171,276
Berrien Springs, MI 49103 • 2,042
Berryville, AR 72616 • 2,966
Berryville, VA 22611 • 1,752
Berthoud, CO 80513 • 2,362
Bertie, NC • 21,024
Bertrand, MI 49120 • 5,000
Berwick, LA 70342 • 4,466
Berwick, ME 03901 • 2,378
Berwick, PA 18603 • 11,850
Berwyn, IL 60402 • 45,500
Berwyn, PA 19312 • 8,150
Bessemer, AL 35020-23 • 31,400
Bessemer, MI 49911 • 2,553
Bessemer City, NC 28016 • 4,787
Bethalto, IL 62010 • 8,630
Bethany, IL 61914 • 1,550
Bethany, MO 64424 • 3,095
Bethany, OK 73008 • 22,300
Bethel, AK 99559 • 3,576
Bethel, CT 06801 • 8,755
Bethel, NC 27812 • 1,825
Bethel, OH 45106 • 2,231
Bethel Acres, OK 74801 • 2,314
Bethel Park, PA 15102 • 33,800
Bethesda, MD 20814-17 • 70,800
Bethlehem, CT 06751 • 1,762
Bethlehem, PA 18015-18 • 71,000
Bethpage, NY 11714 • 16,840
Bettendorf, IA 52722 • 28,900
Beulah, ND 58523 • 2,908
Beverly, MA 01915 • 37,700
Beverly, NJ 08010 • 2,919
Beverly, OH 45715 • 1,471
Beverly Hills, CA 90210-13 • 34,200
Beverly Hills, MI 48009 • 11,598
Bexar, TX • 988,798
Bexley, OH 43209 • 13,405
Bibb, AL • 15,723
Bibb, GA • 150,256
Bicknell, IN 47512 • 4,713
Biddeford, ME 04005 • 21,400
Bienville, LA • 16,387
Big Bear, CA 92315 • 11,151
Big Bear City, CA 92314 • 3,500
Big Flats, NY 14814 • 2,892
Big Horn, MT • 11,096
Big Horn, WY • 11,896
Big Lake, MN 55309 • 2,210
Big Lake, TX 76932 • 3,404
Big Pine, CA 93513 • 1,510
Big Rapids, MI 49307 • 14,361
Big Spring, TX 79720 • 25,700
Big Stone, MN • 7,716
Big Stone Gap, VA 24219 • 4,748
Big Timber, MT 59011 • 1,690
Billerica, MA 01821 • 6,840
Billings, MT 59101-99 • 73,700
Billings, ND • 1,138
Billings Heights, MT 59105 • 8,480
Biloxi, MS 39530-35 • 50,900

Biltmore Forest, NC 28803 • 1,499
Bingham, ID • 36,489
Binghamton, NY 13901-99 • 54,600
Birchwood City, MD 20745 • 8,000
Birchwood Park, DE 19711 • 1,600
Birdsboro, PA 19508 • 3,481
Birmingham, AL 35201-99 • 282,600
Birmingham, MI 48008-12 • 21,000
Bisbee, AZ 85603 • 7,154
Biscayne Gardens, FL 33168 • 13,000
Biscayne Park, FL 33161 • 3,088
Bishop, CA 93514 • 3,333
Bishop, TX 78343 • 3,706
Bishopville, SC 29010 • 3,429
Bismarck, MO 63624 • 1,625
Bismarck, ND 58501 • 50,800
Bixby, OK 74008 • 7,194
Blackfoot, ID 83221 • 10,065
Blackford, IN • 15,570
Black Forest, CO 80908 • 3,372
Black Hawk, SD 57718 • 1,608
Black Hawk, IA • 137,961
Black Jack, MO 63031 • 5,293
Blacklick Estates, OH 43227 • 11,223
Black Mountain, NC 28711 • 4,083
Black Oak, IN 46406 • 10,000
Black River Falls, WI 54615 • 3,434
Blacksburg, SC 29702 • 1,873
Blacksburg, VA 24060-63 • 31,200
Blackshear, GA 31516 • 3,222
Blackstone, MA 01504 • 4,460
Blackstone, VA 23824 • 3,624
Blackville, SC 29817 • 2,840
Blackwell, OK 74631 • 8,400
Blackwood, NJ 08012 • 5,219
Bladen, NC • 30,491
Bladensburg, MD 20710 • 7,691
Blaine, MN 55433 • 35,300
Blaine, WA 98230 • 2,363
Blaine, ID • 9,841
Blaine, MT • 6,999
Blaine, NE • 867
Blaine, OK • 13,443
Blair, NE 68008 • 6,418
Blair, PA • 136,621
Blairsville, PA 15717 • 4,166
Blakely, GA 31723 • 5,880
Blakely, PA 18447 • 7,438
Blanchard, OK 73010 • 1,688
Blanchester, OH 45107 • 3,205
Blanco, TX • 4,681
Bland, VA • 6,349
Blanding, UT 84511 • 3,118
Blasdell, NY 14219 • 3,288
Blauvelt, NY 10913 • 4,470
Blawnox, PA 15238 • 1,653
Bleckley, GA • 10,767
Bledsoe, TN • 9,478
Blennerhassett, WV 26101 • 3,537
Blissfield, MI 49228 • 3,107
Bloomer, WI 54724 • 3,342
Bloomfield, CT 06002 • 7,120
Bloomfield, IN 47424 • 2,705
Bloomfield, IA 52537 • 2,849
Bloomfield, MO 63825 • 1,795
Bloomfield, NJ 07003 • 47,600
Bloomfield, NM 87413 • 4,881
Bloomfield Hills, MI 48013 • 3,985
Bloomfield Township, MI 48013 • 43,500
Bloomingdale, GA 31302 • 1,855
Bloomingdale, IL 60108 • 14,100
Bloomingdale, NJ 07403 • 7,867
Blooming Prairie, MN 55917 • 1,969
Bloomington, CA 92316 • 18,888
Bloomington, IL 61701 • 48,000
Bloomington, IN 47401 • 52,400
Bloomington, MN 55420 • 89,400
Bloomington, TX 77951 • 1,884
Bloomsburg, PA 17815 • 11,400
Blossburg, PA 16912 • 1,757
Blossom, TX 75416 • 1,487
Blount, AL • 36,459
Blount, TN • 77,770
Blountstown, FL 32424 • 2,632
Blountsville, AL 35031 • 1,509
Blountville, TN 37617 • 2,554
Blue Ash, OH 45242 • 9,510
Blue Earth, MN 56013 • 4,132
Blue Earth, MN • 52,314
Bluefield, VA 24605 • 6,024
Bluefield, WV 24701 • 14,700
Blue Hills, CT 06002 • 5,310
Blue Island, IL 60406 • 22,300
Blue Ridge, VA 24064 • 2,347
Blue Ridge Summit, PA 17214 • 1,800
Blue Springs, MO 64015 • 30,800
Bluewell, WV 24701 • 2,752
Bluff Park, AL 35226 • 8,000
Bluffton, IN 46714 • 8,705
Bluffton, OH 45817 • 3,310
Blythe, CA 92225 • 7,502
Blytheville, AR 72315 • 23,700
Boalsburg, PA 16827 • 2,295
Boardman, OH 44512 • 38,300
Boaz, AL 35957 • 7,151
Boca Raton, FL 33431-34 • 60,700
Boerne, TX 78006 • 3,229
Bogalusa, LA 70427 • 16,976
Bogata, TX 75417 • 1,508
Boger City, NC 28092 • 2,252
Bogota, NJ 07603 • 8,344
Bohemia, NY 11716 • 9,308
Boiling Springs, NC 28017 • 2,381
Boiling Springs, PA 17007 • 2,323
Boise, ID 83701-99 • 114,000
Boise, ID • 2,999
Boise City, OK 73933 • 1,761
Bolingbrook, IL 60439 • 41,000
Bolivar, MO 65613 • 5,919
Bolivar, TN 38008 • 6,777
Bolivar, MS • 45,965
Bollinger, MO • 10,301
Bolton Landing, NY 12814 • 1,600
Bon Air, VA 23235 • 16,224
Bonaventure, FL 33317 • 6,000
Bond, IL • 16,224
Bondsville, MA 01009 • 1,906
Bonham, TX 75418 • 7,338
Bon Homme, SD • 8,059
Bonifay, FL 32425 • 2,534
Bonita, CA 92002 • 6,257
Bonita Springs, FL 33923 • 3,400
Bonner, ID • 24,163
Bonners Ferry, ID 83805 • 1,906
Bonner Springs, KS 66012 • 6,266
Bonne Terre, MO 63628 • 3,797
Bonneville, ID • 65,980
Bonney Lake, WA 98390 • 5,328
Bonnie Doone, NC 28303 • 5,950
Boone, IA 50036 • 12,602
Boone, NC 28607 • 10,191
Boone, AR • 26,067
Boone, IL • 28,630
Boone, IN • 36,446
Boone, IA • 26,184
Boone, KY • 45,842
Boone, MO • 100,376
Boone, NE • 7,391
Boone, WV • 30,447
Booneville, AR 72927 • 3,718
Booneville, MS 38829 • 6,199
Boonsboro, MD 21713 • 1,908
Boonton, NJ 07005 • 8,620
Boonville, IN 47601 • 6,300
Boonville, MO 65233 • 6,959
Boonville, NY 13309 • 2,344
Boothbay Harbor, ME 04538 • 2,207
Borden, TX • 859
Bordentown, NJ 08505 • 4,441
Borger, TX 79007 • 16,300
Boron, CA 93516 • 2,040
Boscobel, WI 53805 • 2,662
Bosque, TX • 13,401
Bossert Estates, NJ 08505 • 1,830
Bossier, LA • 80,721
Bossier City, LA 71111-13 • 58,100
Boston, MA 02101-99 • 572,500
Boswell, PA 15531 • 1,480
Botetourt, VA • 23,270
Bothell, WA 98011-12 • 5,345
Bottineau, ND 58318 • 2,829
Bottineau, ND • 9,239
Boulder, CO 80301-99 • 80,200
Boulder, MT 59632 • 1,441
Boulder, CO • 189,625
Boulder City, NV 89005 • 9,590
Boulder Creek, CA 95006 • 5,662
Boulder Hill, IL 60538 • 9,333
Boulevard Heights, MD 20743 • 1,700
Boulevard Park, WA 98188 • 8,382
Boundary, ID • 7,289
Bound Brook, NJ 08805 • 9,710
Bountiful, UT 84010 • 36,400
Bourbon, IN 46504 • 1,522
Bourbon, KS • 15,969
Bourbon, KY • 19,405
Bourbonnais, IL 60914 • 13,280
Bourg, LA 70343 • 2,073
Bovina, TX 79009 • 1,499
Bowdon, GA 30108 • 1,743
Bowie, MD 20715-16 • 34,700
Bowie, TX 76230 • 5,610
Bowie, TX • 75,301
Bowling Green, FL 33834 • 2,310
Bowling Green, KY 42101 • 45,800
Bowling Green, MO 63334 • 3,022
Bowling Green, OH 43402 • 25,100
Bowman, ND 58623 • 2,071
Bowman, ND • 4,229
Box Butte, NE • 13,696
Box Elder, SD 57719 • 3,186
Box Elder, UT • 33,222
Boxford, MA 01921 • 1,841
Boyd, KY • 55,513
Boyd, NE • 3,331
Boyertown, PA 19512 • 3,979
Boyle, KY • 25,066
Boyne City, MI 49712 • 3,348
Boynton Beach, FL 33435-37 • 42,400
Bozeman, MT 59715 • 24,700
Bracken, KY • 7,738
Brackenridge, PA 15014 • 4,297
Brackettville, TX 78832 • 1,676
Braddock, PA 15104 • 5,634
Braddock Heights, MD 21714 • 4,223
Bradenton, FL 34201-10 • 38,000
Bradford, OH 45308 • 2,166
Bradford, PA 16701 • 10,400
Bradford, FL • 20,023
Bradford, PA • 62,919
Bradley, IL 60915 • 11,519
Bradley, WV 25818 • 1,704
Bradley, AR • 13,803
Bradley, TN • 67,547
Bradley Beach, NJ 07720 • 4,772
Brady, TX 76825 • 5,969
Braidwood, IL 60408 • 3,429
Brainerd, MN 56401 • 11,800
Braintree, MA 02184 • 35,600
Branch, MI • 40,188
Branchville, SC 29432 • 1,769
Brandenburg, KY 40108 • 1,831
Brandon, FL 33511 • 33,000
Brandon, MS 39042 • 9,626
Brandon, SC 29611 • 2,170
Brandon, SD 57005 • 2,589
Brandon, VT 05733 • 1,925
Branford, CT 06405 • 5,438
Branford Hills, CT 06405 • 3,460
Branson, MO 65616 • 2,550
Brantley, GA • 8,701
Brant Rock, MA 02020 • 1,850
Bratenahl, OH 44108 • 1,485
Brattleboro, VT 05301 • 8,596
Brawley, CA 92227 • 16,337
Braxton, WV • 13,894
Brazil, IN 47834 • 7,852
Brazoria, TX 77422 • 3,025
Brazoria, TX • 169,587
Brazos, TX • 93,588
Brea, CA 92621 • 33,500
Breathitt, KY • 17,004
Breaux Bridge, LA 70517 • 6,157
Breckenridge, MI 48615 • 1,495
Breckenridge, MN 56520 • 3,909
Breckenridge, TX 76024 • 6,921
Breckenridge Hills, MO 63114 • 5,666
Breckinridge, KY • 16,861
Brecksville, OH 44141 • 10,132
Breese, IL 62230 • 3,581
Bremen, GA 30110 • 3,966
Bremen, IN 46506 • 3,565
Bremen, OH 43107 • 1,432
Bremer, IA • 24,820
Bremerton, WA 98310-15 • 36,200
Brenham, TX 77833 • 10,966
Brent, AL 35034 • 2,862
Brent, FL 32503 • 4,500
Brentwood, CA 94513 • 4,434
Brentwood, MD 20722 • 3,000
Brentwood, MO 63144 • 8,209
Brentwood, NY 11717 • 27,800
Brentwood, OH 45231 • 5,508
Brentwood, PA 15227 • 11,859
Brentwood, SC 29405 • 2,000
Brentwood, TN 37027 • 13,052
Brevard, NC 28712 • 5,323
Brevard, FL • 272,959
Brewer, ME 04412 • 9,017
Brewster, MA 02631 • 1,744
Brewster, NY 10509 • 1,650
Brewster, OH 44613 • 2,321
Brewster, TX • 7,573
Brewton, AL 36426 • 6,680
Briarcliff Manor, NY 10510 • 7,115
Brick [Township], NJ 08723 • 63,400
Bridge City, LA 70094 • 2,500
Bridge City, TX 77611 • 7,667
Bridgehampton, NY 11932 • 1,941
Bridgeport, AL 35740 • 2,974
Bridgeport, CT 06601-99 • 144,100
Bridgeport, IL 62417 • 2,330
Bridgeport, MI 48722 • 3,500
Bridgeport, NE 69336 • 1,668
Bridgeport, OH 43912 • 2,642
Bridgeport, PA 19405 • 4,843
Bridgeport, TX 76026 • 3,737
Bridgeport, WV 26330 • 6,604
Bridgeton, MO 63044 • 18,200
Bridgeton, NJ 08302 • 18,795
Bridgetown, OH 45211 • 11,460
Bridgeview, IL 60455 • 14,155
Bridgeville, PA 15017 • 6,154
Bridgewater, MA 02324 • 6,781
Bridgewater, NJ 08807 • 5,630
Bridgewater, VA 22812 • 3,321
Bridgman, MI 49106 • 2,235
Bridgton, ME 04009 • 1,639
Brielle, NJ 08730 • 4,068
Brigantine, NJ 08203 • 8,318
Brigham City, UT 84302 • 15,596
Brighton, AL 35020 • 5,308
Brighton, CO 80601 • 12,773
Brighton, IL 62012 • 2,364
Brighton, MI 48116 • 5,063
Brighton, NY 14610 • 35,000
Brilliant, OH 43913 • 1,751
Brillion, WI 54110 • 2,907
Brinkley, AR 72021 • 4,909
Briscoe, TX • 2,579
Bristol, CT 06010 • 60,200
Bristol, RI 02809 • 20,128
Bristol, TN 37620 • 24,000
Bristol, VT 05443 • 1,793
Bristol, VA 24201 • 18,400
Bristol, MA • 474,641
Bristol, RI • 46,942
Bristol [Township], PA 19007 • 10,867
Bristow, OK 74010 • 4,702
Britt, IA 50423 • 2,185
Britton, SD 57430 • 1,590
Broadmoor, LA 70501 • 7,051
Broadview, IL 60153 • 8,618
Broadview Heights, OH 44141 • 10,920
Broadview Park, FL 33314 • 6,022
Broadwater, MT • 3,267
Brockport, NY 14420 • 9,776
Brockton, MA 02401-99 • 96,700
Brodhead, WI 53520 • 3,153
Brodheadsville, PA 18322 • 1,500
Broken Arrow, OK 74012-14 • 47,600
Broken Bow, NE 68822 • 3,979
Broken Bow, OK 74728 • 3,965
Bronson, MI 49028 • 2,271
Bronx, NY • 1,168,972
Bronxville, NY 10708 • 6,267
Brooke, WV • 31,117
Brookfield, CT 06804 • 1,500
Brookfield, IL 60513 • 19,395
Brookfield, MO 64628 • 5,555
Brookfield, VA 22021 • 2,600
Brookfield, WI 53005 • 34,100
Brookhaven, MS 39601 • 11,100
Brookhaven, PA 19015 • 7,912
Brookhaven, WV 26505 • 1,661
Brookings, OR 97415 • 3,384
Brookings, SD 57006 • 14,951
Brookings, SD • 24,332
Brooklawn, NJ 08030 • 2,133
Brookline, MA 02146 • 53,400
Brooklyn, IA 52211 • 1,509
Brooklyn, OH 44144 • 12,000
Brooklyn, SC 29720 • 1,800
Brooklyn Center, MN 55429 • 33,200
Brooklyn Park, MD 21225 • 2,800
Brooklyn Park, MN 55443 • 53,000
Brookneal, VA 24528 • 1,454
Brook Park, OH 44142 • 25,000
Brooks, GA • 15,255
Brooks, TX • 8,428
Brookshire, TX 77423 • 2,175
Brookside, DE 19713 • 15,255
Brookston, IN 47923 • 1,701
Brooksville, FL 34601-02 • 5,582
Brookville, IN 47012 • 2,980
Brookville, NY 11545 • 3,290
Brookville, OH 45309 • 4,322
Brookville, PA 15825 • 4,568
Brookwood, NJ 08527 • 5,500
Broomall, PA 19008 • 22,800
Broome, NY • 213,648
Broomfield, CO 80020 • 20,730
Broussard, LA 70518 • 2,923
Broward, FL • 1,018,200
Browardale, FL 33311 • 7,409
Brown, IL • 5,411
Brown, IN • 12,377
Brown, KS • 11,955
Brown, MN • 28,645
Brown, NE • 4,377
Brown, OH • 31,920
Brown, SD • 36,962
Brown, TX • 33,057
Brown, WI • 175,280
Brown Deer, WI 53209 • 12,921
Brownfield, TX 79316 • 10,387
Brownfields, LA 70811 • 1,800
Brownsburg, IN 46112 • 6,242
Browns Mills, NJ 08015 • 10,568
Brownstown, IN 47220 • 2,704
Brownsville, FL 33142 • 18,058
Brownsville, LA 71291 • 3,000
Brownsville, PA 15417 • 4,043
Brownsville, TN 38012 • 10,430
Brownsville, TX 78520-26 • 100,000
Brownwood, TX 76801 • 20,500
Broyhill Park, VA 22042 • 3,600
Bruce, MS 38915 • 2,208
Bruceton, TN 38317 • 1,579
Brule, SD • 5,245
Brundidge, AL 36010 • 3,213
Brunswick, GA 31520 • 19,300
Brunswick, ME 04011 • 10,990
Brunswick, MD 21716 • 4,572
Brunswick, OH 44212 • 29,600
Brunswick, NC • 35,777
Brunswick, VA • 15,632
Brush, CO 80723 • 4,082
Brusly, LA 70719 • 1,762
Bryan, OH 43506 • 7,879
Bryan, TX 77801-06 • 60,900
Bryan, GA • 10,175
Bryan, OK • 30,535
Bryans Road, MD 20616 • 3,739
Bryant, AR 72022 • 3,867
Bryantville, MA 02327 • 1,800
Bryn Mawr, WA 98178 • 1,500
Bryson City, NC 28713 • 1,556
Buchanan, MI 49107 • 5,142
Buchanan, IA • 22,900
Buchanan, MO • 87,888
Buchanan, VA • 37,989
Buckeye, AZ 85326 • 3,434
Buckeye Lake, OH 43008 • 2,521
Buckhannon, WV 26201 • 6,820
Buckingham, VA • 11,751
Buckley, WA 98321 • 3,143
Bucknell Manor, VA 22307 • 2,300
Buckner, MO 64016 • 2,848
Bucks, PA • 479,211
Bucksport, ME 04416 • 2,853
Bucyrus, OH 44820 • 13,433
Buechel, KY 40218 • 6,855
Buena, NJ 08310 • 3,642
Buena Park, CA 90620-24 • 68,100
Buena Vista, CO 81211 • 2,075
Buena Vista, FL 34691 • 3,000
Buena Vista, GA 31803 • 1,544
Buena Vista, VA 24416 • 6,600
Buena Vista, IA • 20,774
Buffalo, IA 52728 • 1,569
Buffalo, MN 55313 • 4,560
Buffalo, MO 65622 • 2,217
Buffalo, NY 14201-99 • 333,900
Buffalo, SC 29321 • 1,641
Buffalo, TX 75831 • 1,507
Buffalo, WY 82834 • 3,799
Buffalo, NE • 34,797
Buffalo, SD • 1,795
Buffalo, WI • 14,309
Buffalo Grove, IL 60089 • 22,230
Buford, GA 30518 • 6,578
Buhl, ID 83316 • 3,629
Buies Creek, NC 27506 • 1,939
Bullhead City, AZ 86430 • 17,091
Bullitt, KY • 43,346
Bulloch, GA • 35,785
Bullock, AL • 10,596
Bull Shoals, AR 72619 • 1,518
Buna, TX 77612 • 1,900
Bunche Park, FL 33054 • 4,000
Buncombe, NC • 160,934
Bunker Hill, IL 62014 • 1,700
Bunker Hill, OR 97420 • 1,555
Bunkie, LA 71322 • 5,364
Bunnell, FL 32010 • 1,816
Buras, LA 70041 • 2,600
Burbank, CA 91501-99 • 91,700
Burbank, IL 60459 • 27,900
Bureau, IL • 39,114
Burgaw, NC 28425 • 1,738
Burgettstown, PA 15021 • 1,867
Burien, WA 98166 • 18,000
Burkburnett, TX 76354 • 10,668
Burke, VA 22015 • 21,000
Burke, GA • 19,349
Burke, NC • 72,504
Burke, ND • 3,822
Burke City, MO 63135 • 1,580
Burkesville, KY 42717 • 2,051
Burleigh, ND • 54,811
Burleson, TX 76028 • 12,884
Burleson, TX • 12,313
Burley, ID 83318 • 8,761
Burlingame, CA 94010 • 26,600
Burlington, CO 80807 • 3,107
Burlington, IA 52601 • 28,600
Burlington, KS 66839 • 2,901
Burlington, MA 01803 • 23,000
Burlington, NJ 08016 • 10,900
Burlington, NC 27215 • 38,400
Burlington, VT 05401-03 • 38,200
Burlington, WA 98233 • 3,894
Burlington, WI 53105 • 8,385
Burlington, NJ • 362,542
Burnet, TX 78611 • 3,410
Burnet, TX • 17,803
Burnett, WI • 12,340
Burney, CA 96013 • 3,187
Burnham, PA 17009 • 2,457
Burns, OR 97720 • 3,579
Burns Flat, OK 73624 • 2,431
Burnsville, MN 55337 • 41,100
Burnsville, NC 28714 • 1,452
Burnt Hills, NY 12027 • 1,550
Burr Ridge, IL 60521 • 5,765
Burt, NE • 8,813
Burton, MI 48509 • 29,600
Bushnell, IL 61422 • 3,811
Butler, AL 36904 • 1,882
Butler, GA 31006 • 1,959
Butler, IN 46721 • 2,509
Butler, MO 64730 • 4,107
Butler, NJ 07405 • 7,616
Butler, PA 16001 • 16,900
Butler, WI 53007 • 2,059
Butler, AL • 21,680
Butler, IA • 17,668
Butler, KS • 44,782
Butler, KY • 11,064
Butler, MO • 37,693
Butler, NE • 9,330
Butler, OH • 258,787
Butler, PA • 147,912
Butner, NC 27509 • 4,240
Butte, MT 59701 • 34,800
Butte, CA • 143,851
Butte, ID • 3,342
Butte, SD • 8,372
Butts, GA • 13,665
Buzzards Bay, MA 02532 • 3,375
Byers, CO 80103 • 1,600
Byesville, OH 43723 • 2,572
Byron, GA 31008 • 1,661
Byron, IL 61010 • 2,035
Byron, MN 55920 • 1,715

C

Cabarrus, NC • 85,895
Cabell, WV • 106,835
Cabin John, MD 20818 • 1,500
Cabool, MO 65689 • 2,090
Cabot, AR 72023 • 6,168
Cache, OK 73527 • 1,661
Cache, UT • 57,176
Caddo, LA • 252,358
Caddo, OK • 30,905
Cadillac, MI 49601 • 10,900
Cadiz, KY 42211 • 1,661
Cadiz, OH 43907 • 4,058
Cahaba Heights, AL 35243 • 4,160
Cahokia, IL 62206 • 18,904

Cairo, GA 31728 • 8,777
Cairo, IL 62914 • 5,931
Calais, ME 04619 • 4,262
Calaveras, CA • 20,710
Calavo Gardens, CA 92041 • 6,100
Calcasieu, LA • 167,223
Caldwell, ID 83605 • 17,699
Caldwell, NJ 07006 • 7,624
Caldwell, OH 43724 • 1,935
Caldwell, TX 77836 • 2,953
Caldwell, KY • 13,473
Caldwell, LA • 10,761
Caldwell, MO • 8,660
Caldwell, NC • 67,746
Caldwell, TX • 23,637
Caledonia, MN 55921 • 2,691
Caledonia, NY 14423 • 2,188
Caledonia, VT • 25,808
Calera, AL 35040 • 2,035
Calexico, CA 92231 • 17,700
Calhoun, GA 30701 • 6,000
Calhoun, AL • 119,761
Calhoun, AR • 6,079
Calhoun, FL • 9,294
Calhoun, GA • 5,717
Calhoun, IL • 5,867
Calhoun, IA • 13,542
Calhoun, MI • 141,557
Calhoun, MS • 15,664
Calhoun, SC • 12,206
Calhoun, TX • 19,574
Calhoun, WV • 8,250
Calhoun City, MS 38916 • 2,033
Calhoun Falls, SC 29628 • 2,491
California, MD 20619 • 5,770
California, MO 65018 • 3,381
California, PA 15419 • 5,703
Calipatria, CA 92233 • 2,636
Calistoga, CA 94515 • 3,879
Callahan, TX • 10,992
Callaway, FL 32401 • 7,440
Callaway, MO • 32,252
Calloway, KY • 30,031
Calumet, WI • 30,867
Calumet City, IL 60409 • 39,800
Calumet Park, IL 60643 • 8,788
Calvert, TX 77837 • 1,732
Calvert, MD • 34,638
Calvert City, KY 42029 • 2,388
Calverton, MD 20705 • 7,649
Calverton Park, MO 63136 • 1,717
Calwa, CA 93725 • 6,640
Camanche, IA 52730 • 4,725
Camarillo, CA 93010 • 45,200
Camas, WA 98607 • 5,681
Camas, ID • 818
Cambria, CA 93428 • 3,061
Cambria, PA • 183,263
Cambrian Park, CA 95124 • 4,000
Cambridge, IL 61238 • 2,217
Cambridge, MD 21613 • 11,703
Cambridge, MA 02138 • 92,300
Cambridge, MN 55008 • 3,287
Cambridge, NY 12816 • 1,820
Cambridge, OH 43725 • 13,000
Cambridge City, IN 47327 • 2,407
Cambridge Springs, PA 16403 • 2,102
Camden, AL 36726 • 2,406
Camden, AR 71701 • 16,800
Camden, DE 19934 • 1,757
Camden, ME 04843 • 3,743
Camden, NJ 08101-99 • 83,200
Camden, NY 13316 • 2,667
Camden, OH 45311 • 1,971
Camden, SC 29020 • 7,462
Camden, TN 38320 • 4,023
Camden, GA • 13,371
Camden, MO • 20,017
Camden, NJ • 471,650
Camden, NC • 5,829
Camdenton, MO 65020 • 2,303
Camelot, WA 98002 • 5,000
Cameron, LA 70631 • 1,736
Cameron, MO 64429 • 4,519
Cameron, TX 76520 • 5,721
Cameron, WV 26033 • 1,474
Cameron, LA • 9,336
Cameron, PA • 6,674
Cameron, TX • 209,727
Cameron Park, CA 95682 • 5,607
Camilla, GA 31730 • 5,414
Camino, CA 95709 • 1,500
Camp, TX • 9,275
Campbell, CA 95008 • 34,800
Campbell, FL 32741 • 2,941
Campbell, MO 63933 • 2,134
Campbell, OH 44405 • 11,619
Campbell, KY • 83,317
Campbell, SD • 2,243
Campbell, TN • 34,923
Campbell, VA • 45,424
Campbell, WY • 24,367
Campbellsport, WI 53010 • 1,740
Campbellsville, KY 42718 • 9,266
Camp Hill, AL 36850 • 1,628
Camp Hill, PA 17011 • 8,100
Camp Springs, MD 20748 • 2,500
Camp Verde, AZ 86322 • 5,850
Canadian, TX 79014 • 3,491
Canadian, OK • 56,452
Canajoharie, NY 13317 • 2,412
Canal Fulton, OH 44614 • 3,481
Canal Winchester, OH 43110 • 2,749
Canandaigua, NY 14424-25 • 10,419
Canastota, NY 13032 • 4,773
Canby, MN 56220 • 2,143

Canby, OR 97013 • 7,673
Candler, GA • 7,518
Candlewood Shores, CT 06804 • 1,620
Cando, ND 58324 • 1,496
Caney, KS 67333 • 2,284
Canfield, OH 44406 • 5,535
Canisteo, NY 14823 • 2,679
Cannelton, IN 47520 • 2,373
Cannon, TN • 10,234
Cannondale, CT 06897 • 1,500
Cannon Falls, MN 55009 • 2,653
Canon City, CO 81212 • 13,037
Canonsburg, PA 15317 • 10,459
Canton, CT 06019 • 1,680
Canton, GA 30114 • 3,601
Canton, IL 61520 • 13,300
Canton, MA 02021 • 18,182
Canton, MI 48187 • 5,000
Canton, MS 39046 • 11,116
Canton, MO 63435 • 2,435
Canton, NY 13617 • 7,055
Canton, NC 28716 • 4,631
Canton, OH 44701-99 • 88,700
Canton, PA 17724 • 1,959
Canton, SD 57013 • 2,886
Canton, TX 75103 • 2,845
Cantonment, FL 32533 • 3,200
Canutillo, TX 79835 • 4,000
Canyon, TX 79015 • 10,724
Canyon, ID • 83,756
Canyon Country, CA 91351 • 15,728
Canyon Lake, TX 78130 • 6,000
Cape Canaveral, FL 32920 • 5,733
Cape Charles, VA 23310 • 1,512
Cape Coral, FL 33904 • 49,000
Cape Elizabeth, ME 04107 • 7,838
Cape Girardeau, MO 63701 • 35,600
Cape Girardeau, MO • 58,837
Cape May, NJ 08204 • 4,853
Cape May, NJ • 82,266
Cape May Court House, NJ 08210 • 3,597
Cape Saint Claire, MD 21401 • 6,022
Capistrano Beach, CA 92624 • 6,168
Capitola, CA 95010 • 9,095
Capitol Heights, MD 20743 • 3,271
Capitol View, SC 29209 • 5,000
Captain Cook, HI 96704 • 2,008
Carbon, MT • 8,099
Carbon, PA • 53,285
Carbon, UT • 22,179
Carbon, WY • 21,896
Carbondale, CO 81623 • 2,084
Carbondale, IL 62901 • 25,400
Carbondale, KS 66414 • 1,518
Carbondale, PA 18407 • 11,255
Carbon Hill, AL 35549 • 2,452
Cardington, OH 43315 • 1,665
Carencro, LA 70520 • 3,712
Carey, OH 43316 • 3,674
Caribou, ME 04736 • 9,916
Caribou, ID • 8,695
Carle Place, NY 11514 • 5,470
Carleton, MI 48117 • 2,786
Carlinville, IL 62626 • 5,439
Carlisle, AR 72024 • 2,567
Carlisle, IA 50047 • 3,073
Carlisle, KY 40311 • 1,757
Carlisle, OH 45005 • 4,556
Carlisle, PA 17013 • 19,700
Carlisle, KY • 5,487
Carl Junction, MO 64834 • 3,937
Carlsbad, CA 92008-09 • 46,600
Carlsbad, NM 88220 • 28,100
Carlstadt, NJ 07072 • 6,166
Carlton, MN • 29,936
Carlyle, IL 62231 • 3,388
Carmel, CA 93923 • 4,707
Carmel, IN 46032 • 23,137
Carmel, NY 10512 • 3,591
Carmi, IL 62821 • 6,641
Carmichael, CA 95608 • 51,300
Carnegie, OK 73015 • 2,016
Carnegie, PA 15106 • 10,099
Carney, MD 21234 • 10,500
Carneys Point, NJ 08069 • 7,574
Carnot, PA 15108 • 4,750
Caro, MI 48723 • 4,317
Carol City, FL 33055 • 50,000
Carolina Beach, NC 28428 • 2,000
Caroline, MD • 23,143
Caroline, VA • 17,904
Carol Stream, IL 60188 • 21,954
Carpentersville, IL 60110 • 25,000
Carpinteria, CA 93013 • 10,835
Carrboro, NC 27510 • 8,039
Carrier Mills, IL 62917 • 2,268
Carrington, ND 58421 • 2,641
Carroll, IA 51401 • 9,705
Carroll, AR • 16,203
Carroll, GA • 56,346
Carroll, IL • 18,779
Carroll, IN • 19,722
Carroll, IA • 22,951
Carroll, KY • 9,270
Carroll, MD • 96,356
Carroll, MS • 9,776
Carroll, MO • 12,131
Carroll, NH • 27,931
Carroll, OH • 25,598
Carroll, TN • 28,285
Carroll, VA • 27,270
Carrollton, GA 30117 • 18,100

Carrollton, IL 62016 • 2,816
Carrollton, KY 41008 • 3,967
Carrollton, MI 48724 • 7,482
Carrollton, MO 64633 • 4,700
Carrollton, OH 44615 • 3,065
Carrollton, TX 75006-08 • 56,600
Carrollwood, FL 33618 • 11,400
Carson, CA 90745 • 89,400
Carson City, NV 89701 • 37,300
Carson, TX • 6,672
Carter, KY • 25,060
Carter, MO • 5,428
Carter, MT • 1,799
Carter, OK • 43,610
Carter, TN • 50,205
Carter Lake, IA 51510 • 3,438
Cartersville, GA 30120 • 9,800
Carterville, IL 62918 • 3,445
Carterville, MO 64835 • 1,973
Carthage, IL 62321 • 2,978
Carthage, MS 39051 • 3,453
Carthage, MO 64836 • 11,104
Carthage, NY 13619 • 3,643
Carthage, TN 37030 • 2,672
Carthage, TX 75633 • 6,447
Caruthersville, MO 63830 • 7,958
Carver, MA 02330 • 1,500
Carver, MN • 37,046
Carver Ranch Estates, FL 33023 • 5,600
Cary, IL 60013 • 6,640
Cary, NC 27511 • 22,315
Caryville, TN 37714 • 2,039
Casa de Oro, CA 92077 • 9,500
Casa Grande, AZ 85222 • 14,971
Casas Adobes, AZ 85704 • 12,155
Cascade, IA 52033 • 1,912
Cascade, MT • 80,696
Cascade Vista, WA 98055 • 7,800
Casey, IL 62420 • 3,026
Casey, KY • 14,818
Cashion, AZ 85329 • 3,014
Cashmere, WA 98815 • 2,240
Casper, WY 82601-15 • 48,300
Cass, IL • 15,084
Cass, IN • 40,936
Cass, IA • 16,932
Cass, MI • 49,499
Cass, MN • 21,050
Cass, MO • 51,029
Cass, NE • 20,297
Cass, ND • 88,247
Cass, TX • 29,430
Cass City, MI 48726 • 2,258
Casselberry, FL 32707-08 • 15,037
Casselton, ND 58012 • 1,661
Cassia, ID • 19,427
Cassopolis, MI 49031 • 1,933
Cassville, MO 65625 • 2,091
Castle Dale, UT 84513 • 1,910
Castle Hills, DE 19720 • 1,950
Castle Park, CA 92011 • 6,300
Castle Point, MO 63136 • 9,800
Castle Rock, CO 80104 • 3,921
Castle Rock, WA 98611 • 2,162
Castle Shannon, PA 15234 • 10,164
Castleton on Hudson, NY 12033 • 1,627
Castlewood, VA 24224 • 2,420
Castro, TX • 10,556
Castro Valley, CA 94546 • 47,300
Castroville, CA 95012 • 4,396
Castroville, TX 78009 • 1,821
Caswell, NC • 20,705
Catahoula, LA • 12,287
Catalina Foothills, AZ 85718 • 1,470
Catasauqua, PA 18032 • 6,711
Cataumet, MA 02534 • 1,500
Catawba, NC • 105,208
Catawissa, PA 17820 • 1,568
Cathedral City, CA 92234 • 11,096
Catlettsburg, KY 41129 • 3,005
Catlin, IL 61817 • 2,226
Catonsville, MD 21228 • 33,900
Catoosa, OK 74015 • 1,561
Catoosa, GA • 36,991
Catron, NM • 2,720
Catskill, NY 12414 • 4,718
Cattaraugus, NY • 72,751
Cavalier, ND 58220 • 1,505
Cavalier, ND • 7,636
Cave City, AR 72521 • 1,634
Cave City, KY 42127 • 2,098
Cave Creek, AZ 85331 • 2,301
Cave Spring, VA 24018 • 15,200
Cavetown, MD 21720 • 1,533
Cayce, SC 29033 • 11,701
Cayuga, NY • 79,894
Cayuga Heights, NY 14850 • 3,170
Cazenovia, NY 13035 • 2,599
Cecil, MD 60,430
Cecil, MD • 60,430
Cedar, IA • 18,635
Cedar, MO • 11,894
Cedar, NE • 11,375
Cedar Bluff, VA 37722 • 2,000
Cedarburg, WI 53012 • 9,005
Cedar City, UT 84720 • 10,972
Cedar Falls, IA 50613 • 33,700
Cedar Grove, NJ 07009 • 12,600
Cedar Grove, WV 25039 • 1,479
Cedar Hill, MO 63016 • 1,512
Cedar Hill, TX 75104 • 6,849
Cedar Hills, OR 97225 • 8,000

Cedarhurst, NY 11516 • 6,162
Cedar Lake, IN 46303 • 8,754
Cedar Rapids, IA 52401-99 • 110,000
Cedar Springs, MI 49319 • 2,615
Cedartown, GA 30125 • 8,619
Cedarville, OH 45314 • 2,799
Celina, OH 45822 • 9,600
Celina, TN 38551 • 1,580
Celina, TX 75009 • 1,520
Center, CO 81125 • 1,630
Center, TX 75935 • 5,827
Centereach, NY 11720 • 31,100
Center Line, MI 48015 • 9,293
Center Moriches, NY 11934 • 5,703
Center Point, AL 35215 • 23,317
Center Point, IA 52213 • 1,591
Centerville, IN 47330 • 2,284
Centerville, IA 52544 • 6,558
Centerville, OH 45459 • 18,886
Centerville, PA 15417 • 4,207
Centerville, TN 37033 • 2,824
Centerville, UT 84014 • 8,069
Central, NM 88026 • 1,968
Central, SC 29630 • 1,914
Central City, IL 62801 • 1,505
Central City, KY 42330 • 5,214
Central City, NE 58826 • 3,083
Central City, PA 15926 • 1,496
Central Falls, RI 02863 • 16,995
Central Heights, AZ 85501 • 1,500
Centralia, IL 62801 • 15,400
Centralia, MO 65240 • 3,537
Centralia, WA 98531 • 11,900
Central Islip, NY 11722 • 42,300
Central Park, WA 98520 • 2,709
Central Point, OR 97502 • 6,499
Central Valley, CA 96019 • 3,424
Central Valley, NY 10917 • 1,705
Central Village, CT 06332 • 1,600
Centre, AL 35960 • 2,351
Centre, PA • 112,760
Centre City, NJ 08051 • 2,070
Centreville, AL 35042 • 2,504
Centreville, IL 62207 • 9,747
Centreville, MD 21617 • 2,018
Centreville, MS 39631 • 1,844
Centreville, VA 22020 • 4,000
Century, FL 32535 • 1,805
Century Village, FL 33409 • 10,619
Ceredo, WV 25507 • 2,255
Ceres, CA 95307 • 13,281
Cerritos, CA 90703 • 58,100
Cerro Gordo, IL 61818 • 1,553
Cerro Gordo, IA • 48,458
Chadbourn, NC 28431 • 1,975
Chadron, NE 69337 • 5,933
Chadwicks, NY 13319 • 2,000
Chaffee, MO 63740 • 3,241
Chaffee, CO • 13,227
Chagrin Falls, OH 44022 • 4,335
Chalfonte, DE 19810 • 2,200
Chalmette, LA 70044 • 36,700
Chamberlain, SD 57325 • 2,258
Chambers, AL • 39,191
Chambers, TX • 18,538
Chambersburg, PA 17201 • 16,600
Chamblee, GA 30341 • 6,700
Champaign, IL 61820-21 • 60,700
Champaign, IL • 168,392
Champaign, OH • 33,649
Champion, OH 44481 • 5,270
Champions, TX 77034 • 14,692
Champlain, NY 12919 • 1,216
Champlin, MN 55316 • 9,006
Chandler, AZ 85224-27 • 64,800
Chandler, IN 47610 • 3,043
Chandler, OK 74834 • 2,926
Chanhassen, MN 55317 • 6,359
Channahon, IL 60410 • 3,788
Channel Lake, IL 60002 • 1,613
Channelview, TX 77530 • 17,471
Chantilly, VA 22021 • 3,600
Chanute, KS 66720 • 10,506
Chapel Hill, NC 27514-16 • 35,900
Chapel Square, VA 22003 • 2,000
Chappaqua, NY 10514 • 6,380
Chardon, OH 44024 • 4,434
Chariton, IA 50049 • 5,116
Chariton, MO • 10,489
Charleroi, PA 15022 • 5,400
Charles, MD • 72,751
Charles City, IA 50616 • 8,778
Charles City, VA • 6,692
Charles Mix, SD • 9,680
Charleston, AR 72933 • 1,748
Charleston, IL 61920 • 19,391
Charleston, MS 38921 • 2,878
Charleston, MO 63834 • 5,230
Charleston, SC 29401-23 • 66,300
Charleston, WV 25301-99 • 58,700
Charleston, SC • 276,974
Charlestown, IN 47111 • 5,596
Charlestown, RI 02813 • 1,500
Charles Town, WV 25414 • 2,857
Charlevoix, MI 49720 • 3,296
Charlevoix, MI • 19,907
Charlotte, MI 48772 • 8,251
Charlotte, NC 28201-99 • 348,000
Charlotte, TN 75011 • 1,443
Charlotte, FL • 58,460
Charlotte, VA • 12,266
Charlotte Harbor, FL 33980 • 2,084
Charlottesville, VA 22901-06 • 40,900

Charlton, GA • 7,343
Charter Oak, CA 91724 • 6,840
Chase, KS • 3,309
Chase, NE • 4,758
Chase City, VA 23924 • 2,749
Chaska, MN 55318 • 8,346
Chatfield, MN 55923 • 2,055
Chatham, IL 62629 • 5,597
Chatham, MA 02633 • 1,922
Chatham, NJ 07928 • 8,537
Chatham, NY 12037 • 2,001
Chatham, GA • 202,226
Chatham, NC • 33,415
Chatsworth, GA 30705 • 2,493
Chattahoochee, FL 32324 • 5,332
Chattahoochee, GA • 21,732
Chattanooga, TN 37401-99 • 166,900
Chattooga, GA • 21,856
Chautauqua, KS • 5,016
Chautauqua, NY • 146,925
Chauvin, LA 70344 • 3,338
Chaves, NM • 51,103
Cheatham, TN • 21,616
Cheboygan, MI 49721 • 5,106
Cheboygan, MI • 20,649
Checotah, OK 74426 • 3,454
Cheektowaga, NY 14225 • 90,300
Chehalis, WA 98532 • 6,000
Chelan, WA 98816 • 2,802
Chelan, WA • 45,061
Chelmsford, MA 01824 • 30,900
Chelsea, MA 02150 • 26,100
Chelsea, MI 48118 • 3,816
Chelsea, OK 74016 • 1,754
Chelsea Estates, DE 19720 • 1,500
Cheltenham Township, PA 19012 • 34,200
Chemung, NY • 97,656
Chenango, NY • 49,344
Chenango Bridge, NY 13745 • 2,890
Cheney, WA 99004 • 7,630
Chenoa, IL 61726 • 1,847
Chenoweth, OR 97058 • 2,820
Cheraw, SC 29520 • 5,654
Cherokee, AL • 18,760
Cherokee, GA • 51,699
Cherokee, IA • 16,238
Cherokee, KS • 22,304
Cherokee, NC • 18,933
Cherokee, OK • 30,684
Cherokee, SC • 40,983
Cherokee, TX • 38,127
Cherokee Village, AR 72525 • 3,200
Cherry, NE • 6,758
Cherry Hill, NJ 08002-03 • 70,200
Cherry Hills Village, CO 80110 • 5,127
Cherryland, CA 94541 • 9,425
Cherryvale, KS 67335 • 2,769
Cherry Valley, CA 92223 • 5,012
Cherryville, NC 28021 • 4,844
Chesaning, MI 48616 • 2,656
Chesapeake, VA 23320-25 • 134,900
Chesapeake, WV 25315 • 2,364
Cheshire, CT 06410 • 5,722
Cheshire, NH • 62,116
Chesilhurst, NJ 08089 • 1,590
Chester, CA 96020 • 1,756
Chester, IL 62233 • 8,401
Chester, NJ 07930 • 1,433
Chester, NY 10918 • 1,910
Chester, PA 19013-16 • 44,400
Chester, SC 29706 • 6,820
Chester, VA 23831 • 11,728
Chester, WV 26034 • 3,297
Chester, PA • 316,660
Chester, SC • 30,148
Chester, TN • 12,727
Chesterfield, SC 29709 • 1,432
Chesterfield, SC • 38,161
Chesterfield, VA • 141,372
Chesterton, IN 46304 • 8,531
Chestertown, MD 21620 • 3,300
Chester Township, PA 19013 • 5,687
Chestnut Hill Estates, DE 19713 • 2,000
Chestnut Ridge, NY 10952 • 8,217
Cheswick, PA 15024 • 2,336
Chetek, WI 54728 • 1,931
Chetopa, KS 67336 • 1,751
Cheverly, MD 20785 • 5,751
Cheviot, OH 45211 • 9,888
Chevy Chase, MD 20815 • 12,232
Chewelah, WA 99109 • 1,888
Cheyenne, WY 82001-09 • 52,000
Cheyenne, CO • 2,153
Cheyenne, KS • 3,678
Cheyenne, NE • 10,057
Chicago, IL 60601-99 • 3,020,300
Chicago Heights, IL 60411 • 35,500
Chicago Ridge, IL 60415 • 13,473
Chickamauga, GA 30707 • 2,232
Chickasaw, AL 36611 • 7,402
Chickasaw, IA • 15,437
Chickasaw, MS • 17,853
Chickasha, OK 73018 • 17,200
Chico, CA 95926-29 • 31,500
Chico North, CA 95926 • 11,733
Chicopee, MA 01013-22 • 56,900
Chicot, AR • 17,793

Chico West, CA 95926 • 6,337
Chiefland, FL 32626 • 1,986
Childersburg, AL 35044 • 5,084
Childress, TX 79201 • 5,817
Childress, TX • 6,950
Chili Center, NY 14624 • 4,360
Chillicothe, IL 61523 • 6,176
Chillicothe, MO 64601 • 9,089
Chillicothe, OH 45601 • 24,200
Chillum, MD 20783 • 14,900
Chilton, WI 53014 • 2,965
Chilton, AL • 30,612
Chimayo, NM 87522 • 1,993
Chincoteague, VA 23336 • 1,607
Chinle, AZ 86503 • 2,815
Chino, CA 91710 • 51,300
Chinook, MT 59523 • 1,660
Chino Valley, AZ 86323 • 3,817
Chipley, FL 32428 • 3,330
Chippewa, MI • 29,029
Chippewa, MN • 14,941
Chippewa, WI • 52,127
Chippewa Falls, WI 54729 • 12,270
Chisago, MN • 25,717
Chisago City, MN 55013 • 1,634
Chisholm, ME 04239 • 1,796
Chisholm, MN 55719 • 5,930
Chittenango, NY 13037 • 4,290
Chittenden, VT • 115,534
Choctaw, OK 73020 • 7,520
Choctaw, AL • 16,839
Choctaw, MS • 8,996
Choctaw, OK • 17,203
Choteau, MT 59422 • 1,798
Chouteau, OK 74337 • 1,559
Chouteau, MT • 6,092
Chowan, NC • 12,558
Chowchilla, CA 93610 • 5,122
Christian, IL • 36,446
Christian, KY • 66,878
Christian, MO • 22,402
Christiansburg, VA 24073 • 10,345
Christopher, IL 62822 • 3,086
Chubbuck, ID 83202 • 7,052
Chula Vista, CA 92010-13 • 128,300
Church Hill, TN 37642 • 4,134
Churchill, OH 44505 • 7,700
Churchill, NV • 13,917
Church Point, LA 70525 • 4,599
Churubusco, IN 46723 • 1,638
Cibola, NM • 30,102
Cicero, IL 60650 • 61,100
Cicero, IN 46034 • 2,557
Cimarron, KS 67835 • 1,491
Cimarron, OK • 3,648
Cimarron Hills, CO 80906 • 6,597
Cincinnati, OH 45201-99 • 372,200
Cinnaminson, NJ 08077 • 16,072
Circle Pines, MN 55014 • 3,321
Circleville, OH 43113 • 11,700
Cisco, TX 76437 • 4,517
Citra, FL 32627 • 1,500
Citronelle, AL 36522 • 2,841
Citrus, CA 91702 • 12,450
Citrus, FL • 54,703
Citrus Heights, CA 95610-11 • 102,100
City of Commerce, CA 90040 • 13,100
City View, SC 29611 • 1,662
Clackamas, OR • 241,911
Clackamas, OR 97015 • 3,250
Claiborne, LA • 17,095
Claiborne, MS • 12,279
Claiborne, TN • 24,595
Clair-Mel City, FL 33619 • 7,000
Clairton, PA 15025 • 12,188
Clallam, WA • 51,648
Clanton, AL 35045 • 7,413
Clara City, MN 56222 • 1,574
Clare, MI 48617 • 3,300
Clare, MI • 23,822
Claremont, CA 91711 • 35,400
Claremont, NH 03743 • 14,300
Claremore, OK 74017 • 12,085
Clarendon, AR 72029 • 2,361
Clarendon, TX 79226 • 2,220
Clarendon, SC • 27,464
Clarendon Hills, IL 60514 • 6,870
Clarinda, IA 51632 • 5,458
Clarion, IA 50525 • 3,060
Clarion, PA 16214 • 6,198
Clarion, PA • 43,362
Clark, NJ 07066 • 16,699
Clark, AR • 23,326
Clark, ID • 798
Clark, IL • 16,913
Clark, IN • 88,838
Clark, KS • 2,599
Clark, KY • 28,322
Clark, MO • 8,493
Clark, NV • 463,087
Clark, OH • 150,236
Clark, SD • 4,894
Clark, WA • 192,227
Clark, WI • 32,910
Clarkdale, AZ 86324 • 1,696
Clarke, AL • 27,702
Clarke, GA • 74,498
Clarke, IA • 8,612
Clarke, MS • 16,945
Clarke, VA • 9,965
Clarksburg, WV 26301 • 20,900
Clarksdale, MS 38614 • 21,500
Clarks Summit, PA 18411 • 5,272

Clarkston, GA 30021 • 4,539
Clarkston, WA 99403 • 6,903
Clarksville, AR 72830 • 5,237
Clarksville, IN 47130 • 15,400
Clarksville, TN 37040-43 • 71,100
Clarksville, TX 75426 • 4,917
Clarksville, VA 23927 • 1,468
Clatskanie, OR 97016 • 1,648
Clatsop, OR • 32,489
Clawson, MI 48017 • 15,103
Claxton, GA 30417 • 2,694
Clay, AL • 13,703
Clay, AR • 20,616
Clay, FL • 67,052
Clay, GA • 3,553
Clay, IL • 15,283
Clay, IN • 24,862
Clay, IA • 19,576
Clay, KS • 9,802
Clay, KY • 22,752
Clay, MN • 49,327
Clay, MS • 21,082
Clay, MO • 136,488
Clay, NE • 8,106
Clay, NC • 6,619
Clay, SD • 13,689
Clay, TN • 7,676
Clay, TX • 9,582
Clay, WV • 11,265
Clay Center, KS 67432 • 4,948
Claymont, DE 19703 • 10,022
Claypool, AZ 85532 • 2,362
Clayton, AL 36016 • 1,589
Clayton, GA 30525 • 1,838
Clayton, MO 63105 • 14,100
Clayton, NJ 08312 • 6,013
Clayton, NM 88415 • 2,968
Clayton, NY 13624 • 1,816
Clayton, NC 27520 • 4,091
Clayton, GA • 150,357
Clayton, IA • 21,098
Clear Creek, CO • 7,308
Clearfield, PA 16830 • 7,500
Clearfield, UT 84015 • 17,982
Clearfield, PA • 83,578
Clearlake, CA 95422 • 8,343
Clear Lake, IA 50428 • 7,458
Clearwater, FL 34615-25 • 100,900
Clearwater, KS 67026 • 1,684
Clearwater, SC 29822 • 3,967
Clearwater, ID • 10,390
Clearwater, MN • 8,761
Cleburne, TX 76031 • 24,200
Cleburne, AL • 12,595
Cleburne, AR • 16,909
Cle Elum, WA 98922 • 1,773
Cleland Heights, DE 19805 • 1,500
Clementon, NJ 08021 • 5,764
Clemmons, NC 27012 • 4,842
Clemson, SC 29631 • 8,366
Cleona, PA 17042 • 2,003
Clermont, FL 32711 • 5,461
Clermont, OH • 128,483
Cleveland, GA 30528 • 1,578
Cleveland, MS 38732 • 14,524
Cleveland, OH 44101-99 • 541,700
Cleveland, OK 74020 • 2,972
Cleveland, TN 37311-12 • 28,600
Cleveland, TX 77327 • 5,977
Cleveland, AR • 7,868
Cleveland, NC • 83,435
Cleveland, OK • 133,173
Cleveland Heights, OH 44118 • 56,300
Cleves, OH 45002 • 2,094
Clewiston, FL 33440 • 5,219
Cliffside Park, NJ 07010 • 21,464
Clifton, AZ 85533 • 4,245
Clifton, CO 81520 • 5,223
Clifton, NJ 07011-15 • 76,600
Clifton, TX 76634 • 3,063
Clifton Forge, VA 24422 • 5,000
Clifton Heights, PA 19018 • 7,320
Clifton Knolls, NY 12065 • 4,265
Clifton Springs, NY 14432 • 2,039
Clinch, GA • 6,660
Clinchco, VA 24226 • 1,500
Clinton, AR 72031 • 2,080
Clinton, CT 06413 • 11,195
Clinton, IL 61727 • 8,014
Clinton, IN 47842 • 5,267
Clinton, IA 52732 • 31,500
Clinton, KY 42031 • 1,720
Clinton, LA 70722 • 1,919
Clinton, MD 20735 • 16,438
Clinton, MA 01510 • 12,771
Clinton, MI 49236 • 2,342
Clinton, MS 39056 • 16,917
Clinton, MO 64735 • 8,366
Clinton, NJ 08809 • 1,910
Clinton, NC 28328 • 7,400
Clinton, OK 73601 • 8,796
Clinton, SC 29325 • 9,969
Clinton, TN 37716 • 8,200
Clinton, UT 84015 • 5,777
Clinton, WA 98236 • 2,000
Clinton, WI 53525 • 1,751
Clinton, IL • 32,617
Clinton, IN • 31,545
Clinton, IA • 57,122
Clinton, KY • 9,321
Clinton, MI • 55,893
Clinton, MO • 15,916
Clinton, NY • 80,750
Clinton, OH • 34,603
Clinton, PA • 38,971

Clinton Township, MI 48043 • 76,400
Clintonville, WI 54929 • 4,567
Clio, MI 48420 • 2,669
Clive, IA 50053 • 6,952
Closter, NJ 07624 • 8,164
Cloud, KS • 12,494
Cloquet, MN 55720 • 11,142
Clover, SC 29710 • 3,451
Cloverdale, CA 95425 • 3,989
Cloverleaf, TX 77015 • 17,317
Cloverport, KY 40111 • 1,585
Clovis, CA 93612 • 40,300
Clovis, NM 88101 • 33,100
Clute, TX 77531 • 9,577
Clyde, NY 14433 • 2,491
Clyde, OH 43410 • 5,489
Clyde, TX 79510 • 2,562
Clymer, PA 15728 • 1,761
Coachella, CA 92236 • 9,129
Coahoma, MS • 36,918
Coal, OK • 6,041
Coal City, IL 60416 • 3,597
Coaldale, PA 18218 • 2,762
Coal Fork, WV 25306 • 2,775
Coalgate, OK 74538 • 2,001
Coal Grove, OH 45638 • 2,602
Coalinga, CA 93210 • 6,593
Coatesville, PA 19320 • 10,698
Cobb, GA • 297,718
Cobleskill, NY 12043 • 5,272
Cochise, AZ • 85,686
Cochituate, MA 01778 • 6,126
Cochran, GA 31014 • 5,121
Cochran, TX • 4,825
Cocke, TN • 28,792
Cockeysville, MD 21030 • 17,013
Cockrell Hill, TX 75211 • 3,262
Cocoa, FL 32922-27 • 21,100
Cocoa Beach, FL 32931 • 10,926
Cocoa West, FL 32922 • 6,432
Coconino, AZ • 75,008
Coconut Creek, FL 33060 • 8,174
Codington, SD • 20,885
Cody, WY 82414 • 8,043
Coeburn, VA 24230 • 2,625
Coeur d'Alene, ID 83814 • 26,700
Coffee, AL • 38,533
Coffee, GA • 26,894
Coffee, TN • 38,311
Coffey, KS • 9,370
Coffeyville, KS 67337 • 14,600
Cohasset, MA 02025 • 6,800
Cohoes, NY 12047 • 18,144
Cokato, MN 55321 • 2,056
Coke, TX • 3,196
Colbert, AL • 54,519
Colby, KS 67701 • 5,544
Colby, WI 54421 • 1,496
Colchester, CT 06415 • 3,190
Colchester, VT 05446 • 1,729
Cold Spring, KY 41076 • 2,117
Cold Spring, MN 56320 • 2,294
Cold Spring Harbor, NY 11724 • 5,336
Coldwater, MI 49036 • 9,461
Coldwater, MS 38618 • 1,505
Coldwater, OH 45828 • 4,220
Cole, MO • 56,663
Coleman, TX 76834 • 5,960
Coleman, TX • 10,439
Coles, IL • 52,260
Colfax, IA 50054 • 2,234
Colfax, LA 71417 • 1,680
Colfax, WA 99111 • 2,780
Colfax, NE • 9,890
Colfax, NM • 13,667
Collegedale, TN 37315 • 4,607
College Park, GA 30337 • 28,100
College Park, MD 20740 • 22,600
College Place, WA 99324 • 5,771
College Station, AR 72053 • 3,800
College Station, TX 77840 • 50,500
Collegeville, PA 19426 • 3,406
Colleton, SC • 31,776
Colleyville, TX 76034 • 6,700
Collier, FL • 85,971
Collier City, FL 33060 • 7,135
Collierville, TN 38017 • 11,584
Collin, TX • 144,576
Collingdale, PA 19023 • 9,539
Collingswood, NJ 08108 • 15,838
Collingsworth, TX • 4,648
Collins, MS 39428 • 2,539
Collins Park, DE 19720 • 2,850
Collinsville, CT 06022 • 2,555
Collinsville, IL 62234 • 19,613
Collinsville, OK 74021 • 3,556
Collinsville, VA 24078 • 7,517
Coloma, MI 49038 • 1,833
Colonial Beach, VA 22443 • 2,474
Colonial Heights, TN 37663 • 6,744
Colonial Heights, VA 23834 • 17,400
Colonial Park, PA 17109 • 10,700
Colonie, NY 12212 • 8,869
Colorado, TX • 18,823
Colorado City, AZ 86021 • 2,099
Colorado City, TX 79512 • 5,405
Colorado Springs, CO 80901-99 • 264,600
Colquitt, GA 31737 • 2,065
Colquitt, GA • 35,376
Colstrip, MT 59323 • 1,476
Colton, CA 92324 • 26,000
Columbia, IL 62236 • 4,269
Columbia, KY 42728 • 3,710
Columbia, MD 21045-46 • 67,200
Columbia, MS 39429 • 7,733

Columbia, MO 65201-05 • 65,600
Columbia, PA 17512 • 10,466
Columbia, SC 29201-99 • 98,700
Columbia, TN 38401 • 27,200
Columbia, AR • 26,644
Columbia, FL • 35,399
Columbia, GA • 40,118
Columbia, NY • 59,487
Columbia, OR • 35,646
Columbia, PA • 61,967
Columbia, WA • 4,057
Columbia, WI • 43,222
Columbia City, IN 46725 • 5,091
Columbia Falls, MT 59912 • 3,112
Columbia Heights, MN 55421 • 20,029
Columbiana, AL 35051 • 2,655
Columbiana, OH 44408 • 4,987
Columbiana, OH • 113,572
Columbine, CO 80120 • 13,300
Columbus, GA 31901-95 • 177,600
Columbus, IN 47201-03 • 31,200
Columbus, KS 66725 • 3,426
Columbus, MS 39701-05 • 29,100
Columbus, MT 59019 • 1,439
Columbus, NE 68601 • 19,000
Columbus, OH 43201-99 • 575,800
Columbus, TX 78934 • 3,923
Columbus, WI 53925 • 4,049
Columbus, NC • 51,037
Columbus Grove, OH 45830 • 2,313
Colusa, CA 95932 • 4,075
Colusa, CA • 12,791
Colville, WA 99114 • 4,510
Comal, TX • 36,446
Comanche, OK 73529 • 1,937
Comanche, TX 76442 • 4,075
Comanche, KS • 2,554
Comanche, OK • 112,456
Comanche, TX • 12,617
Combee Settlement, FL 33801 • 5,400
Combined Locks, WI 54113 • 2,573
Commack, NY 11725 • 35,900
Commerce, GA 30529 • 4,092
Commerce, OK 74339 • 2,556
Commerce, TX 75428 • 8,136
Commerce City, CO 80022 • 16,234
Compton, CA 90221-24 • 93,000
Comstock, MI 49041 • 5,310
Concho, TX • 2,915
Concord, CA 94518-24 • 108,600
Concord, MA 01742 • 4,680
Concord, MO 63128 • 20,896
Concord, NH 03301-03 • 32,700
Concord, NC 28025 • 25,300
Concordia, KS 66901 • 6,847
Concordia, MO 64020 • 2,129
Concordia, LA • 22,981
Conecuh, AL • 15,884
Conejos, CO • 7,794
Conemaugh, PA 15909 • 2,128
Congers, NY 10920 • 7,123
Conklin, NY 13748 • 1,800
Conley, GA 30027 • 6,033
Conneaut, OH 44030 • 13,835
Connell, WA 99326 • 1,981
Connellsville, PA 15425 • 9,800
Connersville, IN 47331 • 17,023
Conover, NC 28613 • 4,245
Conrad, MT 59425 • 3,074
Conroe, TX 77301-05 • 21,300
Conshohocken, PA 19428 • 8,591
Constantine, MI 49042 • 1,680
Contoocook, NH 03229 • 1,499
Contra Costa, CA • 656,380
Converse, TX 78109 • 5,150
Converse, WY • 14,069
Conway, AR 72032 • 23,300
Conway, FL 32809 • 16,000
Conway, NH 03818 • 1,781
Conway, PA 15027 • 2,747
Conway, SC 29526 • 10,240
Conway, AR • 19,505
Conyers, GA 30207-08 • 6,567
Cook, GA • 13,490
Cook, IL • 5,253,655
Cook, MN • 4,092
Cooke, TX • 27,656
Cookeville, TN 38501 • 23,200
Coolidge, AZ 85228 • 6,851
Coon Rapids, IA 50058 • 1,448
Coon Rapids, MN 55433 • 43,400
Cooper, TX 75432 • 2,338
Cooper, MO • 14,643
Cooper City, FL 33328 • 10,140
Cooper Road, LA 71107 • 10,000
Coopersburg, PA 18036 • 2,595
Cooperstown, NY 13326 • 2,342
Coopersville, MI 49404 • 2,889
Coos, NH • 35,147
Coos, OR • 64,047
Coosa, AL • 11,377
Coos Bay, OR 97420 • 14,800
Copiague, NY 11726 • 20,132
Copiah, MS • 26,503
Coplay, PA 18037 • 3,130
Copperas Cove, TX 76522 • 19,469
Coquille, OR 97423 • 4,481
Coral Gables, FL 33134 • 43,000
Coral Hills, MD 20743 • 5,700
Coral Springs, FL 33065 • 58,700
Coral Terrace, FL 33157 • 22,702
Coralville, IA 52241 • 7,687

Coral Way Village, FL 33155 • 9,000
Coram, NY 11727 • 24,752
Coraopolis, PA 15108 • 7,308
Corbin, KY 40701 • 8,800
Corcoran, CA 93212 • 6,454
Corcoran, MN 55340 • 4,252
Cordele, GA 31015 • 11,184
Cordell, OK 73632 • 3,301
Cordova, AL 35550 • 3,123
Cordova, AK 99574 • 1,879
Corinth, MS 38834 • 13,200
Corinth, NY 12822 • 2,702
Cornelia, GA 30531 • 3,203
Cornelius, NC 28031 • 1,921
Cornelius, OR 97113 • 4,896
Cornell, WI 54732 • 1,583
Corning, AR 72422 • 3,650
Corning, CA 96021 • 4,745
Corning, IA 50841 • 1,939
Corning, NY 14830 • 13,300
Cornwall, NY 17016 • 2,653
Cornwall-on-Hudson, NY 12520 • 3,164
Corona, CA 91720 • 47,600
Coronado, CA 92118 • 18,790
Coronado, CO 80229 • 6,890
Corpus Christi, TX 78401-99 • 268,000
Corrigan, TX 75939 • 1,770
Corry, PA 16407 • 7,149
Corsicana, TX 75110 • 24,100
Corson, SD • 5,196
Corte Madera, CA 94925 • 8,429
Cortez, CO 81321 • 7,095
Cortez, FL 34215 • 1,450
Cortland, NY 13045 • 19,400
Cortland, OH 44410 • 5,011
Cortland, NY • 48,820
Corunna, MI 48817 • 3,206
Corvallis, OR 97330-33 • 40,000
Corydon, IN 47112 • 2,724
Corydon, IA 50060 • 1,818
Coryell, TX • 56,767
Coshocton, OH 43812 • 13,300
Coshocton, OH • 36,024
Cosmopolis, WA 98537 • 1,575
Costa Mesa, CA 92626-28 • 89,600
Costilla, CO • 3,071
Cottage Grove, MN 55016 • 18,994
Cottage Grove, OR 97424 • 7,193
Cottle, TX • 2,947
Cotton, OK • 7,338
Cottondale, AL 35453 • 1,960
Cottonport, LA 71327 • 1,911
Cotton Valley, LA 71018 • 1,445
Cottonwood, AZ 86326 • 5,009
Cottonwood, CA 96022 • 1,553
Cottonwood, UT 84121 • 11,554
Cottonwood, MN • 14,854
Cottonwood Heights, UT 84121 • 18,000
Cotuit, MA 02635 • 1,750
Cotulla, TX 78014 • 3,912
Coudersport, PA 16915 • 2,791
Council Bluffs, IA 51501 • 56,800
Council Grove, KS 66846 • 2,381
Country Club Hills, IL 60477 • 14,676
Country Homes, WA 99218 • 4,000
Countryside, IL 60525 • 6,510
Coushatta, LA 71019 • 2,084
Covedale, OH 45238 • 5,830
Covelo, CA 95428 • 1,448
Coventry, CT 06238 • 3,769
Coventry, RI 02816 • 6,980
Covina, CA 91722-24 • 41,900
Covington, GA 30209 • 10,586
Covington, IN 47932 • 2,883
Covington, KY 41011-18 • 47,100
Covington, LA 70433 • 7,892
Covington, OH 45318 • 2,610
Covington, TN 38019 • 6,197
Covington, VA 24426 • 8,000
Covington, AL • 36,850
Covington, MS • 15,927
Cowan, TN 37318 • 1,790
Coweta, OK 74429 • 4,554
Coweta, GA • 39,268
Cowley, KS • 36,824
Cowlitz, WA • 79,548
Cowpens, SC 29330 • 2,023
Coxsackie, NY 12051 • 2,786
Cozad, NE 69130 • 4,453
Crab Orchard, WV 25827 • 3,337
Crafton, PA 15205 • 7,623
Craig, CO 81625 • 9,239
Craig, OK • 15,014
Craig, VA • 3,948
Craighead, AR • 63,239
Craigsville, WV 26205 • 1,562
Cramerton, NC 28032 • 1,869
Crandon, WI 54520 • 1,969
Crane, AZ 85365 • 2,650
Crane, TX 79731 • 3,622
Crane, TX • 4,600
Cranford, NJ 07016 • 24,000
Cranston, RI 02910 • 73,200
Craven, NC • 71,043
Crawford, AR • 36,892
Crawford, GA • 7,684
Crawford, IL • 20,818
Crawford, IN • 9,820
Crawford, IA • 18,935
Crawford, KS • 37,916
Crawford, MI • 9,465
Crawford, MO • 18,300

Crawford, OH • 50,075
Crawford, PA • 88,869
Crawford, WI • 16,556
Crawfordsville, IN 47933 • 13,200
Creedmoor, NC 27522 • 1,641
Creek, OK • 59,016
Creighton, PA 15030 • 1,658
Crenshaw, AL • 14,110
Creola, AL 36525 • 2,066
Cresaptown, MD 21502 • 4,645
Crescent, OK 73028 • 1,651
Crescent City, FL 32012 • 1,722
Crescent Springs, KY 41016 • 1,944
Cresco, IA 52136 • 3,860
Cresskill, NJ 07626 • 7,609
Cresson, PA 16630 • 2,184
Cressona, PA 17929 • 1,810
Cresthaven, FL 33064 • 2,400
Crest Hill, IL 60435 • 9,252
Crestline, CA 92325 • 6,715
Crestline, OH 44827 • 5,406
Creston, IA 50801 • 8,429
Creston, OH 44217 • 1,828
Crestview, FL 32536 • 7,617
Crestwood, IL 60445 • 10,852
Crestwood, MO 63126 • 12,300
Crestwood Village, NJ 08759 • 7,965
Creswell, OR 97426 • 1,872
Crete, IL 60417 • 6,258
Crete, NE 68333 • 4,872
Creve Coeur, IL 61611 • 6,851
Creve Coeur, MO 63141 • 10,800
Crewe, VA 23930 • 2,325
Cricket, NC 28659 • 2,307
Cridersville, OH 45806 • 1,843
Crisfield, MD 21817 • 2,924
Crisp, GA • 19,489
Crittenden, AR • 49,499
Crittenden, KY • 9,207
Crockett, CA 94525 • 2,900
Crockett, TX 75835 • 7,405
Crockett, TN • 14,941
Crockett, TX • 4,608
Crofton, MD 21114 • 12,009
Crook, OR • 13,091
Crook, WY • 5,308
Crookston, MN 56716 • 8,628
Crooksville, OH 43731 • 2,766
Crosby, MN 56441 • 2,218
Crosby, ND 58730 • 1,469
Crosby, TX 77532 • 1,533
Crosby, TX • 8,859
Crosbyton, TX 79322 • 2,289
Cross, AR • 20,434
Cross City, FL 32628 • 2,154
Crossett, AR 71635 • 6,706
Cross Lanes, WV 25313 • 2,130
Cross Plains, WI 53528 • 2,156
Crossville, TN 38555 • 6,405
Croswell, MI 48422 • 2,073
Crothersville, IN 47229 • 1,747
Croton-on-Hudson, NY 10520 • 6,889
Crowell, TX 79227 • 1,509
Crowley, LA 70526 • 16,036
Crowley, TX 76036 • 5,852
Crowley, CO • 2,988
Crown Point, IN 46307 • 16,455
Crow Wing, MN • 41,722
Crozet, VA 22932 • 2,553
Crystal, MN 55428 • 25,300
Crystal Beach, FL 34681 • 1,450
Crystal City, MO 63019 • 3,618
Crystal City, TX 78839 • 8,334
Crystal Falls, MI 49920 • 1,965
Crystal Lake, FL 33803 • 6,827
Crystal Lake, IL 60014 • 20,900
Crystal Lawns, IL 60435 • 1,500
Crystal River, FL 32629 • 2,873
Crystal Springs, MS 39059 • 4,902
Cuba, IL 61427 • 1,648
Cuba, MO 65453 • 2,120
Cuba, NY 14727 • 1,739
Cuba City, WI 53807 • 2,129
Cucamonga, CA 91730 • 72,300
Cudahy, CA 90201 • 18,275
Cudahy, WI 53110 • 19,547
Cuero, TX 77954 • 7,124
Culberson, TX • 3,315
Cullen, LA 71021 • 1,869
Cullman, AL 35055 • 13,200
Cullman, AL • 61,642
Culloden, WV 25510 • 2,931
Cullowhee, NC 28723 • 2,000
Culpeper, VA 22701 • 6,621
Culpeper, VA • 22,620
Culver, IN 46511 • 1,601
Culver City, CA 90230-33 • 40,300
Cumberland, KY 40823 • 3,712
Cumberland, MD 21502 • 23,900
Cumberland, WI 54829 • 1,983
Cumberland, IL • 11,062
Cumberland, KY • 7,289
Cumberland, ME • 215,789
Cumberland, NJ • 132,866
Cumberland, NC • 247,160
Cumberland, PA • 178,541
Cumberland, TN • 28,676
Cumberland, VA • 7,881
Cumberland Center, ME 04021 • 2,015
Cumberland Hill, RI 02864 • 5,421
Cuming, NE • 11,664
Cumming, GA 30130 • 2,094
Cupertino, CA 95014 • 38,700
Currituck, NC • 11,089

Curry, NM • 42,019
Curry, OR • 16,992
Curwensville, PA 16833 • 3,116
Cushing, OK 74023 • 7,720
Custer, SD 57730 • 1,830
Custer, CO • 1,528
Custer, ID • 3,385
Custer, MT • 13,109
Custer, NE • 13,877
Custer, OK • 25,995
Custer, SD • 6,000
Cut Bank, MT 59427 • 3,688
Cutchogue, NY 11935 • 1,730
Cuthbert, GA 31740 • 4,340
Cutler, FL 33157 • 15,593
Cutler Ridge, FL 33157 • 20,886
Cutlerville, MI 49508 • 8,256
Cut Off, LA 70345 • 5,049
Cuyahoga, OH • 1,498,400
Cuyahoga Falls, OH 44221-24 • 42,100
Cynthiana, KY 41031 • 5,881
Cypress, CA 90630 • 43,600
Cypress Lake, FL 33919 • 8,721
Cypress Quarters, FL 34972 • 1,479

D

Dacono, CO 80514 • 2,321
Dacula, GA 30211 • 1,577
Dade, FL • 1,625,781
Dade, GA • 12,318
Dade, MO • 7,383
Dade City, FL 33525 • 5,234
Dadeville, AL 36853 • 3,263
Daggett, UT • 769
Dahlonega, GA 30533 • 2,844
Daingerfield, TX 75638 • 3,030
Dakota, MN • 194,279
Dakota, NE • 16,573
Dakota City, NE 68731 • 1,440
Dale, IN 47523 • 1,693
Dale, AL • 47,821
Dale City, VA 22193 • 39,900
Daleville, AL 36322 • 4,250
Daleville, IN 47334 • 1,749
Dalhart, TX 79022 • 6,854
Dallam, TX • 6,531
Dallas, GA 30132 • 2,508
Dallas, NC 28034 • 3,340
Dallas, OR 97338 • 8,530
Dallas, PA 18612 • 2,679
Dallas, TX 75201-99 • 1,019,900
Dallas, AL • 53,981
Dallas, AR • 10,515
Dallas, IA • 29,513
Dallas, MO • 12,096
Dallas, TX • 1,556,390
Dallastown, PA 17313 • 3,949
Dalton, GA 30720-22 • 21,700
Dalton, MA 01226 • 6,797
Dalton Gardens, ID 83814 • 1,795
Damascus, MD 20872 • 4,129
Dana Point, CA 92629 • 10,602
Danbury, CT 06810-13 • 64,500
Dane, WI • 323,545
Dania, FL 33004 • 11,796
Daniels, MT • 2,835
Danielson, CT 06239 • 4,553
Dannemora, NY 12929 • 3,770
Dansville, NY 14437 • 4,979
Danvers, MA 01923 • 24,200
Danville, AR 72833 • 1,698
Danville, CA 94526 • 28,300
Danville, IL 61832-34 • 37,700
Danville, IN 46122 • 4,220
Danville, KY 40422 • 13,300
Danville, PA 17821 • 5,239
Danville, VA 24540-43 • 45,000
Daphne, AL 36526 • 3,406
Darby, PA 19023 • 11,513
Dardanelle, AR 72834 • 3,621
Dare, NC • 13,377
Darien, CT 06820 • 18,892
Darien, GA 31305 • 1,731
Darien, IL 60559 • 16,427
Darke, OH • 55,096
Darlington, SC 29532 • 7,989
Darlington, WI 53530 • 2,300
Darlington, SC • 62,717
Dauphin, PA • 232,317
Davenport, FL 33837 • 1,509
Davenport, IA 52801-99 • 103,900
Davenport, WA 99122 • 1,559
David City, NE 68632 • 2,514
Davidson, NC 28036 • 3,241
Davidson, NC • 113,162
Davidson, TN • 477,811
Davie, FL 33328 • 35,600
Davie, NC • 24,599
Daviess, IN • 27,836
Daviess, KY • 85,949
Daviess, MO • 8,905
Davis, CA 95616 • 40,800
Davis, OK 73030 • 2,782
Davis, IA • 9,104
Davis, UT • 146,540
Davison, MI 48423 • 6,087
Davison, SD • 17,820
Dawes, NE • 9,609
Dawson, GA 31742 • 5,699
Dawson, MN 56232 • 1,901
Dawson, GA • 4,774
Dawson, MT • 11,805
Dawson, NE • 22,304
Dawson, TX • 16,184
Dawson Springs, KY 42408 • 3,275
Day, SD • 8,133

Dayton, KY 41074 • 6,979
Dayton, OH 45401-99 • 181,200
Dayton, TN 37321 • 5,736
Dayton, TX 77535 • 4,908
Dayton, WA 99328 • 2,565
Daytona Beach, FL 32014-23 • 60,800
Dayville, CT 06241 • 1,500
Deadwood, SD 57732 • 2,035
Deaf Smith, TX • 21,165
Deal, NJ 07723 • 1,952
Deale, MD 20751 • 3,008
Dearborn, MI 48120-26 • 86,700
Dearborn Heights, MI 48127 • 62,700
Dearborn, IN • 34,291
De Baca, NM • 2,454
De Bary, FL 32713 • 4,980
Decatur, AL 35601-03 • 45,200
Decatur, GA 30030-38 • 18,600
Decatur, IL 62521-26 • 91,400
Decatur, IN 46733 • 8,649
Decatur, MI 49045 • 1,915
Decatur, TX 76234 • 4,104
Decatur, GA • 25,495
Decatur, IN • 23,841
Decatur, IA • 9,794
Decatur, KS • 4,509
Decatur, TN • 10,857
Decherd, TN 37324 • 2,233
Decorah, IA 52101 • 8,068
Dedham, MA 02026 • 24,500
Deep River, CT 06417 • 2,495
Deerfield, IL 60015 • 17,432
Deerfield, WI 53531 • 1,466
Deerfield Beach, FL 33441-43 • 45,200
Deer Lodge, MT 59722 • 4,023
Deer Lodge, MT • 12,518
Deer Park, NY 11729 • 31,400
Deer Park, OH 45236 • 6,745
Deer Park, TX 77536 • 22,648
Deer Park, WA 99006 • 2,140
Defiance, OH 43512 • 17,100
Defiance, OH • 39,987
De Forest, WI 53532 • 3,367
De Funiak Springs, FL 32433 • 5,563
De Kalb, IL 60115 • 31,600
De Kalb, TX 75559 • 2,217
De Kalb, AL • 53,658
De Kalb, GA • 483,024
De Kalb, IL • 74,624
De Kalb, IN • 33,606
De Kalb, MO • 8,222
De Kalb, TN • 13,589
Delafield, WI 53018 • 4,550
Del Aire, CA 90250 • 3,900
Delanco, NJ 08075 • 3,730
De Land, FL 32720-24 • 19,900
Delano, CA 93215 • 16,491
Delano, MN 55328 • 2,480
Delavan, IL 61734 • 1,973
Delavan, WI 53115 • 5,684
Delavan Lake, WI 53115 • 2,082
Delaware, OH 43015 • 20,200
Delaware, IN • 128,587
Delaware, IA • 18,933
Delaware, NY • 46,824
Delaware, OH • 53,840
Delaware, OK • 23,946
Delaware, PA • 555,007
Delaware City, DE 19706 • 1,858
Delcambre, LA 70528 • 2,216
Del City, OK 73115 • 27,100
De Leon, TX 76444 • 2,478
De Leon Springs, FL 32028 • 1,669
Delhi, LA 71232 • 3,290
Delhi, NY 13753 • 3,374
Delhi Hills, OH 45238 • 27,400
Dell Rapids, SD 57022 • 2,529
Dellwood, MO 63136 • 6,200
Del Mar, CA 92014 • 5,017
Delmar, NY 12054 • 8,423
Delmar, DE 19940 • 1,709
Del Norte, CA • 18,217
Del Park Manor, DE 19808 • 1,700
Delphi, IN 46923 • 2,781
Delphos, OH 45833 • 7,314
Delran, NJ 08075 • 14,811
Delray Beach, FL 33444-47 • 46,700
Del Rio, FL 33617 • 7,409
Del Rio, TX 78840 • 36,300
Delta, CO 81416 • 3,931
Delta, OH 43515 • 2,831
Delta, UT 84624 • 1,930
Delta, CO • 21,225
Delta, MI • 38,947
Delta, TX • 4,839
Deltona, FL 32725 • 14,000
Demarest, NJ 07627 • 4,963
Deming, NM 88030 • 9,964
Demopolis, AL 36732 • 7,678
Demotte, IN 46310 • 2,559
Denham Springs, LA 70726 • 8,563
Denison, IA 51442 • 6,675
Denison, TX 75020 • 25,000
Denmark, SC 29042 • 4,434
Denmark, WI 54208 • 1,475
Dennis, MA 02638 • 2,500
Dennison, OH 44621 • 3,398
Dennis Port, MA 02639 • 2,570
Denny Terrace, SC 29203 • 1,885
Dent, MO • 14,517
Denton, MD 21629 • 1,927
Denton, TX 76201-06 • 55,400

Denton, TX • 143,126
Dentsville, SC 29204 • 5,000
Denver, CO 80201-99 • 508,000
Denver, IA 50622 • 1,647
Denver, PA 17517 • 2,018
Denver, CO • 492,365
Denver City, TX 79323 • 4,704
Denville, NJ 07834 • 14,380
De Pere, WI 54115 • 14,892
Depew, NY 14043 • 19,500
Deposit, NY 13754 • 1,897
De Queen, AR 71832 • 4,594
De Quincy, LA 70633 • 3,966
Derby, CT 06418 • 12,200
Derby, KS 67037 • 9,786
De Ridder, LA 70634 • 11,287
Dermott, AR 71638 • 4,731
Derry, NH 03038 • 12,248
Derry, PA 15627 • 3,072
Des Allemands, LA 70030 • 2,920
Des Arc, AR 72040 • 2,001
Deschutes, OR • 62,142
Desert Hot Springs, CA 92240 • 5,941
Desha, AR • 19,760
Deshler, OH 43516 • 1,870
Desloge, MO 63601 • 3,581
Des Moines, IA 50301-99 • 193,800
Des Moines, IA • 46,203
Des Moines, WA 98188 • 9,879
De Soto, IL 62924 • 1,589
De Soto, KS 66018 • 2,061
De Soto, MO 63020 • 5,993
De Soto, TX 75115 • 15,538
De Soto, FL • 19,039
De Soto, LA • 25,727
De Soto, MS • 53,930
Despard, WV 26301 • 1,434
Des Peres, MO 63131 • 8,300
Des Plaines, IL 60018 • 57,100
Destin, FL 32541 • 7,189
Destrehan, LA 70047 • 2,382
Detroit, MI 48201-99 • 1,078,900
Detroit Lakes, MN 56501 • 7,106
Deuel, NE • 2,462
Deuel, SD • 5,289
Devils Lake, ND 58301 • 7,442
Devine, TX 78016 • 3,756
Devola, OH 45750 • 2,708
Devon, PA 19333 • 6,620
Devonshire, DE 19810 • 1,800
Dewey, OK 74029 • 3,545
Dewey, OK • 5,922
Dewey, SD • 5,366
De Witt, AR 72042 • 3,928
De Witt, IA 52742 • 4,512
De Witt, MI 48820 • 3,165
De Witt, NY 13214 • 9,024
De Witt, IL • 18,108
De Witt, TX • 18,903
Dexter, ME 04930 • 2,974
Dexter, MI 48130 • 1,524
Dexter, MO 63841 • 7,043
Diamond Bar, CA 91765 • 30,800
Diamond Lake, IL 60060 • 1,500
Diamond Springs, CA 95619 • 2,287
D'Iberville, MS 39532 • 9,000
Diboll, TX 75941 • 5,227
Dickens, TX • 3,539
Dickenson, VA • 19,806
Dickey, ND • 6,107
Dickinson, ND 58601 • 17,700
Dickinson, TX 77539 • 7,505
Dickinson, IA • 15,629
Dickinson, KS • 20,175
Dickinson, MI • 25,341
Dickson, TN 37055 • 7,040
Dickson, TN • 30,037
Dickson City, PA 18519 • 6,699
Dilley, TX 78017 • 2,579
Dillingham, AK 99576 • 1,563
Dillon, MT 59725 • 3,976
Dillon, SC 29536 • 7,065
Dillon, SC • 31,083
Dillsburg, PA 17019 • 1,733
Dilworth, MN 56529 • 2,585
Dimmit, TX • 11,367
Dimmitt, TX 79027 • 5,019
Dinuba, CA 93618 • 9,907
Dinwiddie, VA • 22,602
Dishman, WA 99213 • 10,169
District Heights-Forestville, MD 20747 • 6,799
Divide, ND • 3,494
Dixfield, ME 04224 • 1,725
Dix Hills, NY 11746 • 14,570
Dixie, FL • 7,751
Dixon, CA 95620 • 7,541
Dixon, IL 61021 • 15,710
Dixon, NE • 7,137
Dobbs Ferry, NY 10522 • 10,053
Dock Junction, GA 31520 • 6,189
Doddridge, WV • 7,433
Dodge, GA • 16,955
Dodge, MN • 14,773
Dodge, NE • 35,847
Dodge, WI • 75,064
Dodge Center, MN 55927 • 1,816
Dodge City, KS 67801 • 19,800
Dodge Park, MD 20785 • 5,275
Dodgeville, WI 53533 • 3,458
Dolgeville, NY 13329 • 2,602
Dolomite, AL 35061 • 2,590
Dolores, CO • 1,658
Dolton, IL 60419 • 24,200
Dona Ana, NM • 96,340
Donaldsonville, LA 70346 • 7,901
Donalsonville, GA 31745 • 3,320

Doniphan, MO 63935 • 1,921
Doniphan, KS • 9,268
Donley, TX • 4,075
Donna, TX 78537 • 9,952
Donora, PA 15033 • 7,524
Dooly, GA • 10,826
Door, WI • 25,029
Dora, AL 35062 • 2,327
Doraville, GA 30340 • 7,400
Dorchester, MD • 30,623
Dorchester, SC • 58,761
Dormont, PA 15216 • 11,275
Dorothy Pond, MA 01527 • 1,670
Dothan, AL 36301-04 • 54,500
Dougherty, GA • 100,718
Douglas, AZ 85607 • 13,900
Douglas, GA 31533 • 10,980
Douglas, WY 82633 • 6,030
Douglas, CO • 25,153
Douglas, GA • 54,573
Douglas, IL • 19,774
Douglas, KS • 67,640
Douglas, MN • 27,839
Douglas, MO • 11,594
Douglas, NE • 397,038
Douglas, NV • 19,421
Douglas, OR • 93,748
Douglas, SD • 4,181
Douglas, WA • 22,144
Douglas, WI • 44,421
Douglass, KS 67039 • 1,450
Douglasville, GA 30133-35 • 7,641
Dover, DE 19901 • 23,400
Dover, FL 33527 • 2,354
Dover, MA 02030 • 2,051
Dover, NH 03820 • 23,300
Dover, NJ 07801 • 14,800
Dover, OH 44622 • 11,700
Dover, PA 17315 • 1,910
Dover-Foxcroft, ME 04426 • 2,974
Dover Plains, NY 12522 • 1,753
Dowagiac, MI 49047 • 6,307
Downers Grove, IL 60515-17 • 44,400
Downey, CA 90240-42 • 86,900
Downingtown, PA 19335 • 7,650
Doylestown, OH 44230 • 2,493
Doylestown, PA 18901 • 9,100
Dracut, MA 01826 • 21,249
Draper, UT 84020 • 5,521
Drayton, SC 29333 • 1,443
Drayton Plains, MI 48020 • 18,000
Dreamland Villa, AZ 85205 • 3,400
Dresden, OH 43821 • 1,646
Dresden, TN 38225 • 2,519
Drew, MS 38737 • 2,528
Drew, AR • 17,910
Drexel, OH 45427 • 2,250
Druid Hills, GA 30333 • 9,350
Drumright, OK 74030 • 3,278
Dryden, NY 13053 • 1,761
Duarte, CA 91010 • 16,766
Dublin, CA 94568 • 13,496
Dublin, GA 31021 • 17,100
Dublin, OH 43017 • 3,855
Dublin, PA 18917 • 1,565
Dublin, TX 76446 • 2,723
Dublin, VA 24084 • 2,368
Dubois, IN • 34,238
Du Bois, PA 15801 • 8,900
Dubuque, IA 52001 • 60,100
Dubuque, IA • 86,403
Duchesne, UT 84021 • 1,677
Duchesne, UT • 12,565
Dudley, MA 01570 • 3,700
Dukes, MA • 8,942
Dulce, NM 87528 • 1,648
Duluth, GA 30136 • 2,956
Duluth, MN 55801-99 • 86,000
Dumas, AR 71639 • 6,091
Dumas, TX 79029 • 12,194
Dumfries, VA 22026 • 3,214
Dumont, NJ 07628 • 18,334
Dunaire, GA 30032 • 7,170
Dunbar, WV 25064 • 9,285
Duncan, OK 73533 • 23,000
Duncannon, PA 17020 • 1,645
Duncanville, TX 75116 • 33,600
Dundalk, MD 21222 • 72,800
Dundee, FL 33838 • 2,227
Dundee, IL 60118 • 3,551
Dundee, MI 48131 • 2,575
Dundee, NY 14837 • 1,556
Dundy, NE • 2,861
Dunean, PA 29601 • 5,146
Dunedin, FL 34698 • 32,800
Dunellen, NJ 08812 • 6,593
Dunkirk, IN 47336 • 3,180
Dunkirk, NY 14048 • 15,100
Dunklin, MO • 36,324
Dunlap, IN 46514 • 2,600
Dunlap, TN 37327 • 3,681
Dunleith, DE 19801 • 2,500
Dunmore, PA 18512 • 16,781
Dunn, NC 28334 • 9,300
Dunn, ND • 4,627
Dunn, WI • 34,314
Dunn Loring Woods, VA 22180 • 2,800
Dunsmuir, CA 96025 • 2,253
Dunwoody, GA 30338 • 7,840
Du Page, IL • 658,829
Duplin, NC • 40,952
Dupont, CO 80024 • 5,200
Dupont, PA 18641 • 3,460
Duquesne, PA 15110 • 10,094
Du Quoin, IL 62832 • 6,594
Durand, MI 48429 • 4,206
Durand, WI 54736 • 2,047
Durango, CO 81301 • 13,200
Durant, IA 52747 • 1,583

Durant, MS 39063 • 2,889
Durant, OK 74701 • 11,972
Durham, CA 95938 • 1,500
Durham, CT 06422 • 2,641
Durham, NH 03824 • 8,448
Durham, NC 27701-99 • 108,400
Durham, NC • 152,785
Duryea, PA 18642 • 5,415
Dutchess, NY • 245,055
Duval, FL • 571,003
Duval, TX • 12,517
Duxbury, MA 02332 • 1,685
Dwight, IL 60420 • 4,146
Dyer, IN 46311 • 9,555
Dyer, TN 38330 • 2,442
Dyer, TN • 34,663
Dyersburg, TN 38024 • 15,700
Dyersville, IA 52040 • 3,825

E

Eagan, MN 55121 • 20,700
Eagar, AZ 85925 • 4,002
Eagle, ID 83616 • 2,620
Eagle, CO • 13,320
Eagle Grove, IA 50533 • 4,324
Eagle Lake, MN 56024 • 1,470
Eagle Lake, TX 77434 • 3,921
Eagle Pass, TX 78852 • 26,500
Eagle Point, OR 97524 • 2,845
Eagleton Village, TN 37801 • 3,200
Earle, AR 72331 • 3,517
Earlimart, CA 93219 • 4,578
Earlington, KY 42410 • 2,011
Early, GA • 13,158
Earth, TX 79031 • 1,512
Easley, SC 29640 • 14,264
East Alton, IL 62024 • 7,096
East Aurora, NY 14052 • 6,803
East Baton Rouge, LA • 366,191
East Bernard, TX 77435 • 1,735
East Bethel, MN 55005 • 6,626
East Billerica, MA 01821 • 3,830
East Brewton, AL 36426 • 3,012
East Bridgewater, MA 02333 • 3,270
East Brookfield, MA 01515 • 1,443
East Brunswick, NJ 08816 • 39,900
East Carbon, UT 84520 • 1,942
East Carroll, LA • 11,772
Eastchester, NY 10709 • 20,305
East Chicago, IN 46312 • 37,100
East Chicago Heights, IL 60411 • 5,347
East Cleveland, OH 44112 • 36,200
East Compton, CA 90221 • 6,435
East Dennis, MA 02641 • 1,500
East Detroit, MI 48021 • 36,400
East Douglas, MA 01516 • 1,683
East Dubuque, IL 61025 • 2,194
East Falmouth, MA 02536 • 5,181
East Farmingdale, NY 11735 • 5,522
East Feliciana, LA • 19,015
East Flat Rock, NC 28726 • 3,365
East Gaffney, SC 29340 • 4,092
Eastgate, WA 98004 • 8,341
East Glenville, NY 12302 • 6,537
East Grand Forks, MN 56721 • 8,537
East Grand Rapids, MI 49506 • 10,914
East Greenville, PA 18041 • 2,456
East Greenwich, RI 02818 • 10,211
East Half Hollow Hills, NY 11746 • 7,010
East Hampton, CT 06424 • 2,152
Easthampton, MA 01027 • 15,580
East Hampton, NY 11937 • 1,886
East Hanover, NJ 07936 • 9,319
East Hartford, CT 06108 • 53,000
East Haven, CT 06512 • 25,200
East Helena, MT 59635 • 1,647
East Hemet, CA 92343 • 14,712
East Hills, NY 11576 • 7,160
East Islip, NY 11730 • 13,852
East Jordan, MI 49727 • 2,185
Eastlake, OH 44094 • 22,200
East La Mirada, CA 90638 • 9,688
Eastland, TX 76448 • 3,747
Eastland, TX • 19,480
East Lansing, MI 48823 • 47,300
East Las Vegas, NV 89112 • 6,449
East Liverpool, OH 43920 • 16,000
East Longmeadow, MA 01028 • 12,905
East Los Angeles, CA 90022 • 122,200
Eastman, GA 31023 • 5,330
East Marietta, GA 30062 • 11,900
East Marion, NY 11939 • 1,500
East Meadow, NY 11554 • 39,500
East Midvale, UT 84047 • 6,500
East Millinocket, ME 04430 • 2,361
East Moline, IL 61244 • 20,907
East Naples, FL 33962 • 9,000
East Newark, NJ 07029 • 1,923
East Newnan, GA 30263 • 1,495
East Norriton, PA 19401 • 12,711
East Northport, NY 11731 • 20,187
Easton, MD 21601 • 8,500
Easton, PA 18042 • 26,500
East Orange, NJ 07017-19 • 78,400
East Orleans, MA 02643 • 1,850
East Palatka, FL 32031 • 1,613
East Palestine, OH 44413 • 5,306
East Palo Alto, CA 94303 • 18,106
East Patchogue, NY 11772 • 18,139
East Pea Ridge, WV 25705 • 4,980
East Peoria, IL 61611 • 22,385
East Pepperell, MA 01463 • 2,212
East Petersburg, PA 17520 • 3,600
East Pittsburgh, PA 15112 • 2,493
East Point, GA 30344 • 40,600
Eastport, ME 04631 • 1,982
Eastport, NY 11941 • 1,500
East Porterville, CA 93257 • 5,218
East Porterville, CA 93257 • 5,218
East Prairie, MO 63845 • 3,713
East Providence, RI 02914 • 52,100
East Quogue, NY 11942 • 3,668
East Richmond, CA 94805 • 5,100
East Ridge, TN 37412 • 21,236
East River, CT 06443 • 3,440
East Rochester, NY 14445 • 7,596
East Rockaway, NY 11518 • 10,917
East Rockingham, NC 28379 • 5,190
East Rutherford, NJ 07073 • 7,849
East Saint Louis, IL 62201-08 • 50,900
East Spencer, NC 28039 • 2,150
East Stroudsburg, PA 18301 • 8,039
East Tawas, MI 48730 • 2,584
East Troy, WI 53120 • 2,385
East Tustin, CA 92705 • 10,000
East Vestal, NY 13902 • 6,310
East Walpole, MA 02032 • 3,760
East Wareham, MA 02538 • 1,500
East Washington, PA 15301 • 2,241
East Wenatchee, WA 98801 • 1,640
East Windsor, NJ 08520 • 15,000
Eastwood, MI 49001 • 7,186
Eaton, CO 80615 • 1,932
Eaton, IN 47338 • 1,804
Eaton, OH 45320 • 6,839
Eaton, MI • 88,337
Eaton Rapids, MI 48827 • 4,510
Eatonton, GA 31024 • 4,833
Eatontown, NJ 07724 • 13,800
Eau Claire, WI 54701-03 • 54,700
Eau Claire, WI • 78,805
Ebensburg, PA 15931 • 4,096
Echols, GA • 2,297
Economy, PA 15005 • 9,538
Ecorse, MI 48229 • 14,447
Ector, TX • 115,374
Edcouch, TX 78538 • 3,092
Eddy, NM • 47,855
Eddy, ND • 3,554
Eddystone, PA 19013 • 2,555
Eddyville, KY 42038 • 1,949
Eden, NY 14057 • 3,000
Eden, NC 27288 • 16,100
Eden Prairie, MN 55344 • 24,052
Edenton, NC 27932 • 5,357
Edgar, IL • 21,725
Edgecombe, NC • 55,988
Edgefield, SC 29824 • 2,713
Edgefield, SC • 17,528
Edgemere, MD 21222 • 7,800
Edgemont, CA 92508 • 5,215
Edgemont, SD 57735 • 1,468
Edgemoor, DE 19809 • 7,397
Edgerton, OH 43517 • 1,813
Edgerton, WI 53534 • 4,335
Edgewater, CO 80214 • 4,766
Edgewater, FL 32032 • 6,726
Edgewater, NJ 07020 • 4,628
Edgewater Park, NJ 08010 • 9,273
Edgewood, IN 46011 • 2,215
Edgewood, KY 41017 • 7,243
Edgewood, MD 21040 • 19,455
Edgewood, OH 44004 • 3,099
Edgewood, PA 15218 • 4,382
Edgewood, WA 98371 • 1,800
Edgeworth, PA 15143 • 1,738
Edina, MN 55424 • 48,900
Edina, MO 63537 • 1,520
Edinboro, PA 16412 • 6,324
Edinburg, TX 78539 • 32,200
Edinburgh, IN 46124 • 4,779
Edison, NJ 08817-20 • 78,000
Edmond, OK 73034 • 48,200
Edmonds, WA 98020 • 29,300
Edmondson Heights, MD 21207 • 5,000
Edmonson, KY • 9,962
Edmonton, KY 42129 • 1,448
Edmunds, SD • 5,159
Edna, TX 77957 • 5,650
Edwards, MS 39066 • 1,515
Edwards, IL • 7,961
Edwards, KS • 4,271
Edwards, TX • 2,033
Edwardsville, IL 62025 • 12,480
Edwardsville, KS 66113 • 3,364
Edwardsville, PA 18704 • 5,729
Effingham, IL 62401 • 12,000
Effingham, GA • 18,327
Effingham, IL • 30,944
Egg Harbor City, NJ 08215 • 4,618
Egypt Lake, FL 33614 • 11,932
Ehrenberg, AZ 85334 • 1,500
Elba, AL 36323 • 4,310
Elbert, CO • 6,850
Elbert, GA • 18,758
Elberton, GA 30635 • 5,686
El Cajon, CA 92020-22 • 85,900
El Campo, TX 77437 • 10,462
El Centro, CA 92243 • 28,200
El Cerrito, CA 94530 • 23,700
Eldon, MO 65026 • 4,342
Eldora, IA 50627 • 3,063
El Dorado, AR 71730 • 25,900
Eldorado, IL 62930 • 5,198
El Dorado, KS 67042 • 11,551
Eldorado, TX 76936 • 2,061
El Dorado, CA • 85,812
El Dorado Springs, MO 64744 • 3,868
Eldridge, IA 52748 • 3,279
Electra, TX 76360 • 3,755
El Encanto Heights, CA 93117 • 7,700
Elfers, FL 34680 • 5,000
Elgin, IL 60120-23 • 71,400
Elgin, OR 97827 • 1,701
Elgin, TX 78621 • 4,535
Eliot, ME 03903 • 2,450
Elizabeth, NJ 07201-99 • 107,400
Elizabeth City, NC 27909 • 15,600
Elizabethton, TN 37643 • 12,400
Elizabethtown, KY 42701 • 17,300
Elizabethtown, NC 28337 • 3,551
Elizabethtown, PA 17022 • 8,233
Elizabethville, PA 17023 • 1,531
Elk, KS • 3,918
Elk, PA • 38,338
Elkader, IA 52043 • 1,688
Elk City, OK 73644 • 12,800
Elk Grove, CA 95624 • 10,959
Elk Grove Village, IL 60007 • 30,600
Elkhart, IN 46514-17 • 44,600
Elkhart, KS 67950 • 2,243
Elkhart, IN • 137,330
Elkhorn, WI 53121 • 4,605
Elkhorn City, KY 41522 • 1,446
Elkin, NC 28621 • 2,858
Elkins, WV 26241 • 8,500
Elkland, PA 16920 • 1,974
Elko, NV 89801 • 8,758
Elko, NV • 17,269
Elk Point, SD 57025 • 1,661
Elk Rapids, MI 49629 • 1,504
Elkridge, MD 21227 • 2,100
Elk River, MN 55330 • 6,785
Elkton, KY 42220 • 1,815
Elkton, MD 21921 • 6,468
Elkton, VA 22827 • 1,520
Ellaville, GA 31806 • 1,684
Ellendale, ND 58436 • 1,967
Ellensburg, WA 98926 • 11,752
Ellenton, FL 34222 • 1,561
Ellenville, NY 12428 • 4,405
Ellettsville, IN 47429 • 3,328
Ellicott City, MD 21043 • 4,000
Ellijay, GA 30540 • 1,507
Ellington, CT 06029 • 1,500
Ellinwood, KS 67526 • 2,508
Elliott, KY • 6,908
Ellis, KS 67637 • 2,062
Ellis, KS • 26,098
Ellis, OK • 5,596
Ellis, TX • 59,743
Ellisville, MS 39437 • 4,652
Ellisville, MO 63011 • 6,233
Ellsworth, KS 67439 • 2,465
Ellsworth, ME 04605 • 5,179
Ellsworth, WI 54011 • 2,143
Ellsworth, KS • 6,640
Ellwood City, PA 16117 • 9,998
Elma, WA 98541 • 2,720
Elm City, NC 27822 • 1,561
Elmer, NJ 08318 • 1,569
Elm Grove, WI 53122 • 6,735
Elmhurst, IL 60126 • 45,500
Elmira, NY 14901-99 • 33,800
El Mirage, AZ 85335 • 4,307
Elmira Heights, NY 14903 • 4,279
Elmont, NY 11003 • 27,800
El Monte, CA 91731-34 • 94,400
Elmora, PA 15737 • 1,500
Elmore, AL • 43,390
Elmore, ID • 21,565
Elmwood, IL 61529 • 2,117
Elmwood Park, IL 60635 • 23,400
Elmwood Park, NJ 07407 • 18,377
Elmwood Place, OH 45216 • 2,840
Elon College, NC 27244 • 2,873
Eloy, AZ 85231 • 6,240
El Paso, IL 61738 • 2,676
El Paso, TX 79901-99 • 486,300
El Paso, CO • 309,424
El Paso, TX • 479,899
El Portal, FL 33138 • 2,055
El Reno, OK 73036 • 15,486
El Rio, CA 93030 • 5,674
Elroy, WI 53929 • 1,504
Elsa, TX 78543 • 5,061
El Segundo, CA 90245 • 15,200
Elsmere, DE 19805 • 6,493
Elsmere, KY 41018 • 7,203
Elsmere, NY 12054 • 4,180
El Sobrante, CA 94803 • 10,535
Elton, LA 70532 • 1,450
El Toro, CA 92630 • 41,800
Elvins, MO 63601 • 1,548
Elwood, IN 46036 • 10,867
Elwood, NY 11731 • 11,847
Ely, MN 55731 • 4,820
Ely, NV 89301 • 4,882
Elyria, OH 44035-39 • 57,800
Elysburg, PA 17824 • 1,477
Emanuel, GA • 20,795
Emerson, NJ 07630 • 7,793
Emery, UT • 11,451
Eminence, KY 40019 • 2,260
Emmaus, PA 18049 • 11,001
Emmet, IA • 13,336
Emmet, MI • 22,992
Emmetsburg, IA 50536 • 4,621
Emmett, ID 83617 • 4,605
Emmitsburg, MD 21727 • 1,552
Emmons, ND • 5,877
Emporia, KS 66801 • 26,500
Emporia, VA 23847 • 4,700
Emporium, PA 15834 • 2,837
Emsworth, PA 15202 • 3,074
Encinitas, CA 92024 • 42,000
Endicott, NY 13760 • 14,500
Endwell, NY 13760 • 13,745
Enfield, CT 06082 • 8,151
Enfield, NH 03748 • 1,581
Enfield, NC 27823 • 2,995
England, AR 72046 • 3,186
Engleside, VA 22309 • 24,058
Englewood, CO 80110-12 • 31,900
Englewood, FL 34223-24 • 9,633
Englewood, NJ 07631-32 • 23,600
Englewood, OH 45322 • 11,329
Englewood, TN 37329 • 1,840
Englewood Cliffs, NJ 07632 • 5,698
Enid, OK 73701-06 • 53,100
Enka, NC 28728 • 5,567
Ennis, TX 75119 • 12,110
Enola, PA 17025 • 3,140
Enon, OH 45323 • 2,597
Ensley, FL 32514 • 3,850
Enterprise, AL 36330 • 19,600
Enterprise, OR 97828 • 2,003
Enumclaw, WA 98022 • 5,427
Ephraim, UT 84627 • 2,810
Ephrata, PA 17522 • 11,095
Ephrata, WA 98823 • 5,359
Erath, LA 70533 • 2,259
Erath, TX • 22,560
Erial, NJ 08081 • 2,500
Erie, IL 61250 • 1,725
Erie, PA 16501-99 • 117,100
Erie, NY • 1,015,472
Erie, OH • 79,655
Erie, PA • 279,780
Erin, TN 37061 • 1,614
Erlanger, KY 41018 • 14,466
Errol Heights, OR 97266 • 7,800
Erwin, NC 28339 • 2,828
Erwin, TN 37650 • 4,993
Escalon, CA 95320 • 3,127
Escambia, AL • 38,440
Escambia, FL • 233,794
Escanaba, MI 49829 • 14,000
Escatawpa, MS 39552 • 5,367
Escondido, CA 92025-27 • 81,700
Esmeralda, NV • 777
Esmond, RI 02917 • 4,320
Espanola, NM 87532 • 6,803
Esperance, WA 98043 • 11,120
Espy, PA 17815 • 1,571
Essex, CT 06426 • 2,501
Essex, MD 21221 • 40,400
Essex, MA 01929 • 1,490
Essex, MA • 633,632
Essex, NJ • 851,116
Essex, NY • 36,176
Essex, VT • 6,313
Essex, VA • 8,864
Essex Fells, NJ 07021 • 2,363
Essex Junction, VT 05452 • 7,033
Essexville, MI 48732 • 4,378
Estelle, LA 70072 • 12,724
Estes Park, CO 80517 • 2,703
Estherville, IA 51334 • 7,518
Estill, SC 29918 • 2,308
Estill, KY • 14,495
Etna, PA 15223 • 4,534
Etowah, TN 37331 • 3,977
Etowah, AL • 103,057
Ettrick, VA 23803 • 4,890
Euclid, OH 44117 • 57,100
Eudora, AR 71640 • 3,840
Eudora, KS 66025 • 2,934
Eufaula, AL 36027 • 12,097
Eufaula, OK 74432 • 3,159
Eugene, OR 97401-05 • 105,100
Eulaton, AL 36201 • 1,869
Euless, TX 76039-40 • 29,600
Eunice, LA 70535 • 12,479
Eunice, NM 88231 • 2,970
Eupora, MS 39744 • 2,048
Eureka, CA 95501 • 25,300
Eureka, IL 61530 • 4,306
Eureka, KS 67045 • 3,425
Eureka, MO 63025 • 3,862
Eureka, SC 29706 • 1,627
Eureka, NV • 1,198
Eureka Springs, AR 72632 • 1,989
Eustis, FL 32726 • 9,453
Eutaw, AL 35462 • 2,444
Evangeline, LA • 33,343
Evans, CO 80620 • 5,063
Evans, GA 30809 • 2,000
Evans, GA • 8,428
Evans City, PA 16033 • 2,299
Evansdale, IA 50707 • 4,798
Evanston, IL 60201-99 • 71,800
Evanston, WY 82930 • 6,666
Evansville, IN 47701-99 • 129,500
Evansville, WI 53536 • 2,835
Evansville, WY 82636 • 2,335
Evart, MI 49631 • 1,945
Eveleth, MN 55734 • 5,042
Everett, MA 02149 • 36,500
Everett, PA 15537 • 1,828
Everett, WA 98201-08 • 59,300
Evergreen, AL 36401 • 4,171
Evergreen, CO 80439 • 6,376
Evergreen Park, IL 60642 • 21,200
Everman, TX 76140 • 5,387
Ewa, HI 96706 • 2,637
Ewa Beach, HI 96706-07 • 14,369
Ewing Township, NJ 08618 • 35,700
Excelsior Springs, MO 64024 • 10,424
Exeter, CA 93221 • 5,606
Exeter, NH 03833 • 8,947
Exeter, PA 18643 • 5,493
Experiment, GA 30212 • 2,500

F

Fabens, TX 79838 • 4,285
Fairbanks, AK 99701-03 • 29,800
Fairborn, OH 45324 • 28,500
Fairburn, GA 30213 • 3,466
Fairbury, IL 61739 • 3,544
Fairbury, NE 68352 • 4,885
Fairchance, PA 15436 • 2,106
Fairdale, KY 40118 • 7,315
Fairfax, CA 94930 • 7,391
Fairfax, DE 19803 • 2,000
Fairfax, OK 74637 • 1,949
Fairfax, SC 29827 • 2,154
Fairfax, VA 22030-39 • 20,100
Fairfax, VA • 596,901
Fairfield, AL 35064 • 13,242
Fairfield, CA 94533 • 68,000
Fairfield, CT 06430-32 • 53,900
Fairfield, IL 62837 • 5,944
Fairfield, IA 52556 • 9,428
Fairfield, ME 04937 • 3,169
Fairfield, NJ 07006 • 7,987
Fairfield, OH 45014 • 33,600
Fairfield, TX 75840 • 3,505
Fairfield, CT • 807,143
Fairfield, OH • 93,678
Fairfield, SC • 20,700
Fairfield Bay, AR 72088 • 3,000
Fair Grove, NC 27360 • 1,500
Fairhaven, MA 02719 • 15,759
Fair Haven, NJ 07701 • 5,679
Fair Haven, VT 05743 • 2,819
Fairhope, AL 36532 • 7,286
Fair Lawn, NJ 07410 • 31,300
Fairlawn, OH 44313 • 6,200
Fairlea, WV 24902 • 1,888
Fairmont, IL 60441 • 2,800
Fairmont, MN 56031 • 11,600
Fairmont, NC 28340 • 2,658
Fairmont, WV 26554 • 22,500
Fairmount, IN 46928 • 3,286
Fairmount, NY 13219 • 9,100
Fairmount Heights, MD 20743 • 1,616
Fair Oaks, CA 95628 • 22,602
Fair Oaks, GA 30060 • 8,486
Fairoaks, PA 15003 • 1,854
Fair Plain, MI 49022 • 8,289
Fairport, NY 14450 • 5,970
Fairport Harbor, OH 44077 • 3,357
Fairview, NJ 07022 • 10,519
Fairview, NY 12601 • 5,852
Fairview, OK 73737 • 3,370
Fairview, OR 97024 • 1,804
Fairview, PA 16415 • 1,855
Fairview, TN 37062 • 3,772
Fairview Heights, IL 62208 • 12,000
Fairview Park, IN 47842 • 1,545
Fairview Park, OH 44126 • 19,311
Fairview Shores, FL 32804 • 6,100
Fairway, KS 66205 • 4,619
Fairwood, WA 98055 • 6,000
Fairwood, WA 99218 • 5,337
Falconer, NY 14733 • 2,778
Falcon Heights, MN 55113 • 5,291
Falfurrias, TX 78355 • 6,103
Fallbrook, CA 92028 • 14,041
Fall City, WA 98024 • 1,528
Fallon, NV 89406 • 4,262
Fallon, MT • 3,763
Fall River, MA 02720-26 • 93,500
Fall River, SD • 8,439
Falls, TX • 17,946
Falls Church, VA 22040-48 • 9,400
Falls City, NE 68355 • 5,374
Fallston, MD 21047 • 5,572
Falls Township, PA 19054 • 38,000
Falmouth, KY 41040 • 2,482
Falmouth, ME 04105 • 6,853
Falmouth, MA 02540-41 • 4,800
Falmouth, VA 22401 • 1,500
Fannin, GA • 14,748
Fannin, TX • 24,285
Fanwood, NJ 07023 • 7,767
Fargo, ND 58102-99 • 69,300
Faribault, MN 55021 • 16,241
Faribault, MN • 19,714
Farmer City, IL 61842 • 2,252

Farmers Branch, TX 75234 • 27,700
Farmersville, CA 93223 • 5,544
Farmersville, TX 75031 • 2,360
Farmerville, LA 71241 • 3,768
Farmingdale, ME 04345 • 2,014
Farmingdale, NY 11735 • 7,946
Farmington, CT 06032 • 2,500
Farmington, IL 61531 • 3,118
Farmington, ME 04938 • 3,583
Farmington, MI 48018 • 11,022
Farmington, MN 55024 • 5,140
Farmington, MO 63640 • 8,270
Farmington, NH 03835 • 3,284
Farmington, NM 87401 • 38,500
Farmington, UT 84025 • 4,691
Farmington Hills, MI 48024 • 64,700
Farmingville, NY 11738 • 13,398
Farmland, IN 47340 • 1,560
Farmville, NC 27828 • 4,707
Farmville, VA 23901 • 6,067
Farragut, TN 37922 • 8,316
Farrell, PA 16121 • 8,645
Faulk, SD • 3,327
Faulkland Heights, DE 19808 • 1,650
Faulkner, AR • 46,192
Fauquier, VA • 35,889
Fayette, AL 35555 • 5,287
Fayette, IA 52142 • 1,515
Fayette, MS 39069 • 2,033
Fayette, MO 65248 • 2,983
Fayette, AL • 18,809
Fayette, GA • 29,043
Fayette, IL • 22,167
Fayette, IN • 28,272
Fayette, IA • 25,488
Fayette, KY • 204,165
Fayette, OH • 27,467
Fayette, PA • 159,417
Fayette, TN • 25,305
Fayette, TX • 18,832
Fayette, WV • 57,863
Fayetteville, AR 72701-03 • 39,900
Fayetteville, GA 30214 • 2,715
Fayetteville, NC 28301-09 • 70,200
Fayetteville, PA 17222 • 3,202
Fayetteville, TN 37334 • 8,063
Fayetteville, WV 25840 • 2,366
Federal Heights, CO 80221 • 7,846
Federalsburg, MD 21632 • 1,952
Federal Way, WA 98003 • 16,872
Feeding Hills, MA 01030 • 5,470
Fellowship, NJ 08057 • 4,250
Felton, CA 95018 • 4,000
Fennimore, WI 53809 • 2,212
Fenton, MI 48430 • 8,098
Fentress, TN • 14,826
Ferdinand, IN 47532 • 2,192
Fergus, MT • 13,076
Fergus Falls, MN 56537 • 12,600
Ferguson, MO 63135 • 24,200
Fernandina Beach, FL 32034 • 7,224
Fern Creek, KY 40291 • 16,866
Ferndale, MD 21061 • 2,600
Ferndale, MI 48220 • 25,500
Ferndale, PA 15905 • 2,204
Ferndale, WA 98248 • 3,855
Fern Park, FL 32730 • 8,890
Ferriday, LA 71334 • 4,472
Ferris, TX 75125 • 2,228
Ferron, UT 84523 • 1,718
Ferry, WA • 5,811
Ferry Farms, VA 22401 • 1,600
Festus, MO 63028 • 7,574
Fig Garden, CA 93704 • 9,000
Filer, ID 83328 • 1,645
Fillmore, CA 93015 • 9,602
Fillmore, UT 84631 • 2,083
Fillmore, MN • 21,930
Fillmore, NE • 7,920
Findlay, OH 45840 • 36,200
Finney, KS • 23,825
Fircrest, WA 98466 • 5,477
Firebaugh, CA 93622 • 3,740
Fisher, IL 61843 • 1,572
Fisher, TX • 5,891
Fishers, IN 46038 • 2,008
Fishkill, NY 12524 • 1,555
Fiskdale, MA 01518 • 1,859
Fitchburg, MA 01420 • 40,300
Fitchburg, WI 53575 • 11,965
Fitzgerald, GA 31750 • 10,187
Five Points, NM 87105 • 4,200
Flagler, FL • 10,913
Flagler Beach, FL 32036 • 2,208
Flagstaff, AZ 86001-18 • 40,900
Flanders, NJ 07836 • 3,040
Flandreau, SD 57028 • 2,114
Flathead, MT • 51,966
Flat River, MO 63601 • 4,474
Flat Rock, MI 48134 • 6,853
Flatwoods, KY 41139 • 8,354
Fleetwood, PA 19522 • 3,422
Fleming, KY • 12,323
Flemingsburg, KY 41041 • 2,835
Flemington, NJ 08822 • 4,700
Flint, MI 48501-99 • 150,700
Flomaton, AL 36441 • 1,882
Flora, IL 62839 • 5,379
Flora, IN 46929 • 2,303
Flora, MS 39071 • 1,507
Florala, AL 36442 • 2,165
Floral Park, NY 11001-04 • 16,805
Florence, AL 35630-33 • 37,300
Florence, AZ 85232 • 5,375
Florence, CA 90001 • 41,400
Florence, CO 81226 • 2,987
Florence, KY 41042 • 17,600
Florence, NJ 08518 • 4,203
Florence, OR 97439 • 4,413
Florence, SC 29501-03 • 33,000
Florence, SC • 110,163
Florence, WI • 4,172
Floresville, TX 78114 • 4,381
Florham Park, NJ 07932 • 9,359
Florida, NY 10921 • 1,947
Florida City, FL 33034 • 6,174
Florin, CA 95828 • 16,523
Florissant, MO 63031-34 • 58,100
Flossmoor, IL 60422 • 8,423
Flower Hill, NY 11050 • 4,558
Floyd, GA • 79,800
Floyd, IN • 61,205
Floyd, IA • 19,597
Floyd, KY • 48,764
Floyd, TX • 9,834
Floyd, VA • 11,563
Floydada, TX 79235 • 4,193
Flushing, MI 48433 • 8,624
Fluvanna, VA • 10,244
Foard, TX • 2,158
Folcroft, PA 19032 • 8,231
Foley, AL 36535 • 4,003
Foley, MN 56329 • 1,606
Folkston, GA 31537 • 2,243
Follansbee, WV 26037 • 3,994
Folly Beach, SC 29439 • 1,478
Folsom, CA 95630 • 11,003
Folsom, NJ 08037 • 1,892
Fond du Lac, WI 54935 • 36,200
Fond du Lac, WI • 88,964
Fontana, CA 92335-36 • 52,700
Fontana, WI 53125 • 1,764
Foothill Farms, CA 95841 • 13,700
Ford, IL • 15,265
Ford, KS • 24,315
Ford City, CA 93268 • 3,392
Ford City, PA 16226 • 3,923
Fords Prairie, WA 98531 • 2,582
Fordyce, AR 71742 • 5,175
Forest, MS 39074 • 5,229
Forest, OH 45843 • 1,633
Forest, PA • 5,072
Forest, WI • 9,044
Forest Acres, SC 29206 • 6,276
Forest City, IA 50436 • 4,270
Forest City, NC 28043 • 7,900
Forest City, PA 18421 • 1,924
Forest Grove, OR 97116 • 11,930
Forest Hill, TX 76119 • 11,684
Forest Hills, PA 15221 • 8,198
Forest Knolls, CA 94933 • 2,000
Forest Lake, MN 55025 • 4,596
Forest Park, GA 30050 • 18,782
Forest Park, IL 60130 • 15,177
Forest Park, LA 71291 • 1,500
Forest Park, OH 45240 • 18,566
Forestville, MD 20747 • 16,401
Forked River, NJ 08731 • 1,950
Forks, WA 98331 • 3,060
Forney, TX 75126 • 2,483
Forrest, MS • 66,018
Forrest City, AR 72335 • 13,803
Forsyth, GA 31029 • 4,624
Forsyth, MT 59327 • 2,553
Forsyth, GA • 27,958
Forsyth, NC • 243,683
Fort Atkinson, WI 53538 • 9,785
Fort Bend, TX • 130,846
Fort Benton, MT 59442 • 1,693
Fort Bragg, CA 95437 • 5,263
Fort Branch, IN 47648 • 2,504
Fort Collins, CO 80521-26 • 77,000
Fort Defiance, AZ 86504 • 3,431
Fort Deposit, AL 36032 • 1,519
Fort Dodge, IA 50501 • 27,800
Fort Edward, NY 12828 • 3,561
Fort Fairfield, ME 04742 • 2,282
Fort Gibson, OK 74434 • 2,477
Fort Kent, ME 04743 • 2,375
Fort Lauderdale, FL 33301-99 • 155,800
Fort Lee, NJ 07024 • 32,800
Fort Lupton, CO 80621 • 4,251
Fort Madison, IA 52627 • 13,520
Fort McKinley, OH 45426 • 10,161
Fort Meade, FL 33841 • 5,546
Fort Mill, SC 29715 • 4,162
Fort Mitchell, KY 41017 • 7,294
Fort Morgan, CO 80701 • 8,768
Fort Myers, FL 33901-19 • 41,400
Fort Myers Beach, FL 33931-32 • 5,753
Fort Oglethorpe, GA 30742 • 5,443
Fort Payne, AL 35967 • 11,485
Fort Pierce, FL 34950-54 • 38,600
Fort Pierre, SD 57532 • 1,789
Fort Plain, NY 13339 • 2,555
Fort Scott, KS 66701 • 8,893
Fort Shawnee, OH 45806 • 4,541
Fort Smith, AR 72901-16 • 75,000
Fort Stockton, TX 79735 • 8,688
Fort Thomas, KY 41075 • 16,012
Fortuna, CA 95540 • 7,591
Fort Valley, GA 31030 • 9,000
Fortville, IN 46040 • 2,787
Fort Walton Beach, FL 32548 • 24,400
Fort Washington Forest, MD 20744 • 1,800
Fort Wayne, IN 46801-99 • 170,300
Fort Worth, TX 76101-99 • 447,400
Fort Wright, KY 41011 • 4,481
Forty Fort, PA 18704 • 5,590
Fosston, MN 56542 • 1,599
Foster, ND • 4,611
Foster City, CA 94404 • 23,287
Foster Village, HI 96818 • 3,700
Fostoria, OH 44830 • 15,743
Fountain, CO 80817 • 8,324
Fountain, IN • 19,033
Fountain Hill, PA 18015 • 4,805
Fountain Inn, SC 29644 • 4,226
Fountain Place, LA 70811 • 9,200
Fountain Valley, CA 92708 • 56,100
Four Corners, OR 97301 • 11,331
Fowler, CA 93625 • 2,496
Fowler, IN 47944 • 2,319
Fowlerville, MI 48836 • 2,289
Foxboro, MA 02035 • 5,697
Fox Chapel, PA 15238 • 5,049
Fox Lake, IL 60020 • 7,349
Fox Point, WI 53217 • 7,649
Fox River Grove, IL 60021 • 2,515
Frackville, PA 17931 • 5,308
Framingham, MA 01701 • 64,900
Franconia, VA 22310 • 8,476
Frankenmuth, MI 48734 • 3,753
Frankfort, IL 60423 • 4,357
Frankfort, IN 46041 • 15,221
Frankfort, KY 40601 • 26,700
Frankfort, MI 49635 • 1,603
Frankfort, NY 13340 • 2,995
Franklin, IN 46131 • 12,111
Franklin, KY 42134 • 7,738
Franklin, LA 70538 • 9,584
Franklin, MA 02038 • 18,217
Franklin, NH 03235 • 7,901
Franklin, NJ 07416 • 4,486
Franklin, NC 28734 • 2,640
Franklin, OH 45005 • 10,711
Franklin, PA 16323 • 8,100
Franklin, TN 37064 • 17,111
Franklin, VA 23851 • 7,600
Franklin, WI 53132 • 16,871
Franklin, AL • 28,350
Franklin, AR • 14,705
Franklin, FL • 7,661
Franklin, GA • 15,185
Franklin, ID • 8,895
Franklin, IL • 43,201
Franklin, IN • 19,612
Franklin, IA • 13,036
Franklin, KS • 22,062
Franklin, KY • 41,830
Franklin, LA • 24,141
Franklin, ME • 27,447
Franklin, MA • 64,317
Franklin, MS • 8,208
Franklin, MO • 71,233
Franklin, NE • 4,377
Franklin, NY • 44,929
Franklin, NC • 30,055
Franklin, OH • 869,126
Franklin, PA • 113,629
Franklin, TN • 31,983
Franklin, TX • 6,893
Franklin, VT • 34,788
Franklin, VA • 35,740
Franklin, WA • 35,025
Franklin Lakes, NJ 07417 • 8,769
Franklin Park, IL 60131 • 17,600
Franklin Park, PA 15143 • 6,135
Franklin Square, NY 11010 • 29,200
Franklinton, LA 70438 • 4,119
Franklinville, NY 14737 • 1,887
Frankton, IN 46044 • 2,080
Fraser, MI 48026 • 14,560
Frazier Park, CA 93225 • 1,444
Frederick, MD 21701 • 33,900
Frederick, OK 73542 • 6,153
Frederick, MD • 114,792
Frederick, VA • 34,150
Fredericksburg, TX 78624 • 6,412
Fredericksburg, VA 22401-05 • 18,900
Fredericktown, MO 63645 • 4,036
Fredericktown, OH 43019 • 2,299
Fredonia, KS 66736 • 3,047
Fredonia, NY 14063 • 11,126
Fredonia, WI 53021 • 1,437
Freeborn, MN • 36,329
Freeburg, IL 62243 • 2,989
Freedom, CA 95019 • 6,416
Freedom, PA 15042 • 2,272
Freehold, NJ 07728 • 10,020
Freeland, PA 18224 • 4,285
Freeman, SD 57029 • 1,462
Freemansburg, PA 18017 • 1,879
Freeport, IL 61032 • 26,000
Freeport, ME 04032 • 1,906
Freeport, NY 11520 • 40,100
Freeport, PA 16229 • 2,381
Freeport, TX 77541 • 13,444
Freer, TX 78357 • 3,213
Freestone, TX • 14,830
Fremont, CA 94536-39 • 153,700
Fremont, MI 49412 • 3,672
Fremont, NE 68025 • 24,200
Fremont, NC 27830 • 1,736
Fremont, OH 43420 • 18,000
Fremont, CO • 28,676
Fremont, ID • 10,813
Fremont, IA • 9,401
Fremont, WY • 38,992
French Island, WI 54601 • 4,118
French Lick, IN 47432 • 2,265
Frenchtown, NJ 08825 • 1,573
Fresno, CA 93701-99 • 288,700
Fresno, CA • 514,229
Frewsburg, NY 14738 • 1,908
Fridley, MN 55432 • 30,500
Friendship, NY 14739 • 1,461
Friendswood, TX 77546 • 22,200
Frio, TX • 13,785
Friona, TX 79035 • 3,809
Fritch, TX 79036 • 2,299
Frontenac, KS 66762 • 2,586
Frontier, NE • 3,647
Front Royal, VA 22630 • 11,126
Frostburg, MD 21532 • 7,715
Frostproof, FL 33843 • 2,995
Fruita, CO 81521 • 2,810
Fruit Heights, UT 84037 • 2,728
Fruitland, ID 83619 • 2,559
Fruitland, MD 21826 • 2,694
Fruitland Park, FL 32731 • 2,259
Fruitvale, WA 98902 • 3,967
Fruitville, FL 34232 • 3,070
Fryeburg, ME 04037 • 1,644
Fullerton, CA 92631-35 • 111,700
Fullerton, NE 68638 • 1,506
Fulton, IL 61252 • 3,936
Fulton, KY 42041 • 3,231
Fulton, MS 38843 • 3,238
Fulton, MO 65251 • 11,046
Fulton, NY 13069 • 13,312
Fulton, AR • 9,975
Fulton, GA • 589,904
Fulton, IL • 43,687
Fulton, IN • 19,335
Fulton, KY • 8,971
Fulton, NY • 55,153
Fulton, OH • 37,751
Fulton, PA • 12,842
Fultondale, AL 35068 • 6,217
Fuquay-Varina, NC 27526 • 3,110
Furnas, NE • 6,486

G

Gadsden, AL 35901-05 • 47,300
Gadsden, FL • 41,565
Gaffney, SC 29340 • 13,453
Gage, NE • 24,456
Gahanna, OH 43230 • 18,001
Gaines, TX • 13,150
Gainesville, FL 32601-13 • 85,200
Gainesville, GA 30501-06 • 16,100
Gainesville, TX 76240 • 14,081
Gaithersburg, MD 20877-79 • 31,000
Galax, VA 24333 • 6,700
Galena, IL 61036 • 3,878
Galena, KS 66739 • 3,587
Galena Park, TX 77547 • 9,879
Galesburg, IL 61401 • 33,600
Galesburg, MI 49053 • 1,822
Galeton, PA 16922 • 1,462
Galeville, NY 13088 • 4,695
Galion, OH 44833 • 12,391
Gallatin, MO 64640 • 2,063
Gallatin, TN 37066 • 17,626
Gallatin, IL • 7,590
Gallatin, KY • 4,842
Gallatin, MT • 42,865
Gallia, OH • 30,098
Galliano, LA 70354 • 5,159
Gallipolis, OH 45631 • 5,576
Gallitzin, PA 16641 • 2,315
Gallup, NM 87301 • 24,600
Galt, CA 95632 • 5,514
Galva, IL 61434 • 3,185
Galveston, IN 46932 • 1,822
Galveston, TX 77550-53 • 63,700
Galveston, TX • 195,940
Gambier, OH 43022 • 2,056
Ganado, AZ 86505 • 3,400
Ganado, TX 77962 • 1,770
Gang Mills, NY 14870 • 2,300
Gantt, SC 29605 • 1,600
Garden, NE • 2,802
Gardena, CA 90247-49 • 50,300
Garden City, GA 31408 • 6,895
Garden City, ID 83704 • 4,571
Garden City, KS 67846 • 22,200
Garden City, MI 48135 • 33,000
Garden City, NY 11530 • 22,500
Garden City Park, NY 11040 • 7,712
Gardendale, AL 35071 • 8,562
Garden Grove, CA 92640-45 • 135,200
Garden Home, OR 97223 • 5,500
Gardiner, ME 04345 • 6,485
Gardner, KS 66030 • 2,392
Gardner, MA 01440 • 17,900
Gardnerville, NV 89410 • 2,800
Garfield, NJ 07026 • 26,500
Garfield, CO • 22,514
Garfield, MT • 1,656
Garfield, NE • 2,363
Garfield, OK • 62,820
Garfield, UT • 3,673
Garfield, WA • 2,468
Garfield Heights, OH 44125 • 33,200
Garland, TX 75040-47 • 169,100
Garland, AR • 70,531
Garner, IA 50438 • 2,908
Garner, NC 27529 • 10,396
Garnett, KS 66032 • 3,310
Garrard, KY • 10,853
Garrett, IN 46738 • 4,751
Garrett, MD • 26,498
Garrettsville, OH 44231 • 1,769
Garrison, ND 58540 • 1,830
Garvin, OK • 27,856
Garwood, NJ 07027 • 4,752
Gary, IN 46401-99 • 143,400
Gary, WV 24836 • 2,233
Garysburg, NC 27831 • 1,434
Garyville, LA 70051 • 2,856
Garza, TX • 5,336
Gas City, IN 46933 • 6,370
Gasconade, MO • 13,181
Gaston, NC • 162,568
Gastonia, NC 28052-54 • 55,200
Gate City, VA 24251 • 2,494
Gates, NY 14624 • 30,200
Gates, NC • 8,875
Gatesville, TX 76528 • 6,078
Gatlinburg, TN 37738 • 3,577
Gautier, MS 39553 • 10,392
Gaylord, MI 49735 • 3,011
Gaylord, MN 55334 • 1,933
Geary, OK 73040 • 1,700
Geary, KS • 29,852
Geauga, OH • 74,474
Geistown, PA 15904 • 3,304
Gem, ID • 11,972
Genesee, MI • 450,449
Genesee, NY • 59,400
Geneseo, IL 61254 • 6,373
Geneseo, NY 14454 • 6,746
Geneva, AL 36340 • 4,866
Geneva, IL 60134 • 9,881
Geneva, IN 46740 • 1,430
Geneva, NE 68361 • 2,400
Geneva, NY 14456 • 14,800
Geneva, OH 44041 • 6,655
Geneva, AL • 24,253
Geneva-on-the-Lake, OH 44041 • 1,634
Genoa, IL 60135 • 3,276
Genoa, OH 43430 • 2,213
Gentry, AR 72734 • 1,468
Gentry, MO • 7,887
George, MS • 15,297
Georgetown, CA 95634 • 2,000
Georgetown, CT 06829 • 1,834
Georgetown, DE 19947 • 1,710
Georgetown, IL 61846 • 4,220
Georgetown, IN 47122 • 1,494
Georgetown, KY 40324 • 10,972
Georgetown, MA 01833 • 2,100
Georgetown, OH 45121 • 3,467
Georgetown, SC 29440 • 10,144
Georgetown, TX 78626-28 • 10,090
Georgetown, SC • 42,461
George West, TX 78022 • 2,627
Georgiana, AL 36033 • 1,993
Gering, NE 69341 • 7,760
Germantown, MD 20874 • 9,721
Germantown, OH 45327 • 5,015
Germantown, TN 38138 • 32,600
Germantown, WI 53022 • 10,729
Gettysburg, PA 17325 • 7,194
Gettysburg, SD 57442 • 1,623
Gibbon, NE 68840 • 1,531
Gibbstown, NJ 08027 • 5,404
Gibson, IN • 33,156
Gibson, TN • 49,467
Gibsonburg, OH 43431 • 2,479
Gibson City, IL 60936 • 3,498
Gibsonia, FL 33805 • 5,011
Gibsonia, PA 15044 • 3,500
Gibsonton, FL 33534 • 3,700
Gibsonville, NC 27249 • 2,865
Giddings, TX 78942 • 3,950
Gifford, FL 32960 • 6,240
Gig Harbor, WA 98335 • 2,429
Gila, AZ • 37,080
Gila Bend, AZ 85337 • 1,585
Gilbert, AZ 85234 • 6,674
Gilbert, MN 55741 • 2,721
Gilbert, OR 97266 • 4,000
Gilbertsville, PA 19525 • 3,160
Gilchrist, FL • 5,767
Giles, TN • 24,625
Giles, VA • 17,810
Gilford Park, NJ 08753 • 5,420
Gillespie, IL 62033 • 3,740
Gillespie, TX • 13,532
Gillette, WY 82716 • 21,100
Gilliam, OR • 2,057
Gilman, IL 60938 • 1,913
Gilmer, TX 75644 • 5,167
Gilmer, GA • 11,110
Gilmer, WV • 8,334
Gilpin, CO • 2,441
Gilroy, CA 95020 • 21,641
Girard, IL 62640 • 2,246
Girard, KS 66743 • 2,888
Girard, OH 44420 • 12,517
Girard, PA 16417 • 2,615
Girardville, PA 17935 • 2,268
Glacier, MT • 10,628
Glades, FL • 5,992
Glade Spring, VA 24340 • 1,722
Gladeview, FL 33138 • 18,919
Gladewater, TX 75647 • 6,548
Gladstone, MI 49837 • 4,533
Gladstone, MO 64118 • 28,000
Gladstone, NJ 07934 • 2,038
Gladstone, OR 97027 • 9,500
Gladwin, MI 48624 • 2,479
Gladwin, MI • 19,957
Glascock, GA • 2,382
Glasgow, KY 42141 • 12,500
Glasgow, MT 59230 • 4,455
Glasgow Village, MO 63137 • 5,875
Glassboro, NJ 08028 • 14,574
Glasscock, TX • 1,304
Glassmanor, MD 20745 • 7,751
Glassport, PA 15045 • 6,242
Glastonbury, CT 06033 • 7,049
Glen Allen, VA 23060 • 2,300
Glen Avon, CA 92509 • 8,444

Glen Burnie, MD 21061 • 31,800
Glen Burnie Park, MD 21061 • 6,700
Glen Carbon, IL 62034 • 6,499
Glencoe, AL 35905 • 4,648
Glencoe, IL 60022 • 9,200
Glencoe, MN 55336 • 4,396
Glen Cove, NY 11542 • 24,400
Glendale, AZ 85301-12 • 128,600
Glendale, CA 91201-99 • 156,100
Glendale, CO 80222 • 2,496
Glendale, MO 63122 • 6,035
Glendale, OH 45246 • 2,368
Glen Dale, WV 26038 • 1,875
Glendale, WI 53209 • 14,000
Glendale Heights, IL 60139 • 23,251
Glendive, MT 59330 • 5,978
Glendola, NJ 07719 • 2,340
Glendora, CA 91740 • 42,100
Glendora, NJ 08029 • 5,632
Glen Ellyn, IL 60137 • 25,000
Glenham, NY 12527 • 2,832
Glen Head, NY 11545 • 6,870
Glen Lyon, PA 18617 • 2,352
Glenmora, LA 71433 • 1,479
Glenn, CA • 21,350
Glenn Dale, MD 20769 • 5,106
Glennville, GA 30427 • 4,144
Glenolden, PA 19036 • 7,633
Glenpool, OK 74033 • 2,706
Glen Raven, NC 27215 • 2,755
Glen Ridge, NJ 07028 • 7,855
Glen Rock, NJ 07452 • 11,497
Glen Rock, PA 17327 • 1,662
Glenrock, WY 82637 • 2,736
Glen Rose, TX 76043 • 2,075
Glens Falls, NY 12801 • 16,500
Glenview, IL 60025 • 34,400
Glenville, WV 26351 • 2,155
Glenwood, IL 60425 • 10,538
Glenwood, IA 51534 • 5,280
Glenwood, MN 56334 • 2,523
Glenwood, VA 24541 • 2,276
Glenwood Farms, VA 23223 • 3,300
Glenwood Hills, GA 30032 • 5,240
Glenwood Springs, CO 81601 • 4,890
Globe, AZ 85501 • 6,886
Gloster, MS 39638 • 1,726
Gloucester, MA 01930 • 28,400
Gloucester, NJ • 199,917
Gloucester, VA • 20,107
Gloucester City, NJ 08030 • 13,121
Gloucester Point, VA 23062 • 2,500
Glouster, OH 45732 • 2,211
Gloversville, NY 12078 • 17,600
Gloverville, SC 29828 • 2,619
Glynn, GA • 54,981
Godfrey, IL 62035 • 2,600
Goffstown, NH 03045 • 2,500
Gogebic, MI • 19,686
Gold Beach, OR 97444 • 1,515
Golden, CO 80401-19 • 12,237
Goldendale, WA 98620 • 3,575
Golden Glades, FL 33055 • 23,154
Golden Meadow, LA 70357 • 2,282
Golden Valley, MN 55427 • 23,400
Golden Valley, MT • 1,026
Golden Valley, ND • 2,391
Goldsboro, NC 27530 • 36,900
Goldthwaite, TX 76844 • 1,783
Goleta, CA 93117 • 27,800
Golf Manor, OH 45237 • 4,317
Goliad, TX 77963 • 1,990
Goliad, TX • 5,193
Gonzales, CA 93926 • 2,891
Gonzales, LA 70737 • 7,287
Gonzales, TX 78629 • 7,152
Gonzales, TX • 16,949
Gonzalez, FL 32560 • 6,084
Goochland, VA • 11,761
Goodhue, MN • 38,749
Gooding, ID 83330 • 2,949
Gooding, ID • 11,874
Goodland, KS 67735 • 5,708
Goodlettsville, TN 37072 • 9,581
Goodview, MN 55987 • 2,567
Goodwater, AL 35072 • 1,895
Goodyear, AZ 85323 • 3,137
Goose Creek, SC 29445 • 17,811
Gordo, AL 35466 • 2,112
Gordon, GA 31031 • 2,768
Gordon, NE 69343 • 2,245
Gordon, GA • 30,070
Gordon's Corner, NJ 07728 • 6,320
Gorham, ME 04038 • 4,052
Gorham, NH 03581 • 2,180
Goshen, IN 46526 • 21,000
Goshen, NY 10924 • 4,874
Goshen, WY • 12,040
Gosnell, AR 72319 • 3,755
Gosper, NE • 2,140
Gothenburg, NE 69138 • 3,479
Gould, AR 71643 • 1,671
Goulding, FL 32503 • 5,352
Goulds, FL 33170 • 7,078
Gouverneur, NY 13642 • 4,285
Gove, KS • 3,726
Gowanda, NY 14070 • 2,713
Graceville, FL 32440 • 2,918
Grady, GA • 19,845
Grady, OK • 39,490
Grafton, MA 01519 • 1,520
Grafton, ND 58237 • 5,931
Grafton, OH 44044 • 2,231
Grafton, WV 26354 • 6,845
Grafton, WI 53024 • 8,381
Grafton, NH • 65,806
Graham, CA 90002 • 10,600
Graham, NC 27253 • 8,674
Graham, TX 76046 • 9,170
Graham, AZ • 22,862
Graham, KS • 3,995
Graham, NC • 7,217
Grainger, TN • 16,751
Grambling, LA 71245 • 4,226
Gramercy, LA 70052 • 3,211
Granbury, TX 76048 • 3,332
Granby, MO 64844 • 1,908
Grand, CO • 7,475
Grand, UT • 8,241
Grand Bay, AL 36541 • 3,185
Grand Blanc, MI 48439 • 6,848
Grandfield, OK 73546 • 1,445
Grand Forks, ND 58201 • 45,400
Grand Forks, ND • 66,100
Grand Haven, MI 49417 • 12,300
Grand Island, NE 68801-03 • 40,200
Grand Isle, LA 70358 • 1,982
Grand Isle, VT • 4,613
Grand Junction, CO 81501-06 • 31,900
Grand Ledge, MI 48837 • 6,920
Grand Prairie, TX 75050-53 • 91,300
Grand Rapids, MI 49501-99 • 188,700
Grand Rapids, MN 55744 • 7,934
Grand Saline, TX 75140 • 2,709
Grand Terrace, CA 92324 • 8,498
Grand Traverse, MI • 54,899
Grandview, MO 64030 • 25,700
Grandview, WA 98930 • 5,615
Grandview Heights, OH 43212 • 7,420
Grandville, MI 49418 • 12,412
Granger, IN 46530 • 1,500
Granger, WA 98932 • 1,812
Grangeville, ID 83530 • 3,666
Granite, OK 73547 • 1,617
Granite, MT • 2,700
Granite City, IL 62040 • 35,900
Granite Falls, MN 56241 • 3,451
Granite Falls, NC 28630 • 2,580
Granite Park, UT 84106 • 5,554
Graniteville, VT 05654 • 1,800
Grant, AR • 13,008
Grant, IN • 80,934
Grant, KS • 6,977
Grant, KY • 13,308
Grant, LA • 16,703
Grant, MN • 7,171
Grant, NE • 877
Grant, NM • 26,204
Grant, ND • 4,274
Grant, OK • 6,518
Grant, OR • 8,210
Grant, SD • 9,013
Grant, WA • 48,522
Grant, WV • 10,210
Grant, WI • 51,736
Grants, NM 87020 • 11,439
Grants Pass, OR 97526-27 • 17,800
Grantsville, UT 84029 • 4,419
Granville, IL 61326 • 1,537
Granville, NY 12832 • 2,696
Granville, OH 43023 • 3,851
Granville, NC • 34,043
Grapeland, TX 75844 • 1,634
Grapevine, TX 76051 • 11,801
Grasonville, MD 21638 • 1,910
Grass Lake, IL 60002 • 2,191
Grass Valley, CA 95945-46 • 6,953
Gratiot, MI • 40,448
Graves, KY • 34,049
Gray, GA 31032 • 2,145
Gray, LA 70359 • 4,000
Gray, KS • 5,138
Gray, TX • 26,386
Grayling, MI 49738 • 1,792
Graylyn Crest, DE 19810 • 5,000
Grays Harbor, WA • 66,314
Grayslake, IL 60030 • 5,594
Grayson, KY 41143 • 3,423
Grayson, KY • 20,854
Grayson, TX • 89,796
Grayson, VA • 16,579
Graysville, AL 35073 • 2,642
Grayville, IL 62844 • 2,313
Great Barrington, MA 01230 • 3,150
Great Bend, KS 67530 • 17,500
Great Falls, MT 59401-06 • 58,100
Great Falls, SC 29055 • 2,601
Great Neck, NY 11020-27 • 9,200
Great Neck Estates, NY 11021 • 2,936
Greece, NY 14616 • 65,000
Greeley, CO 80631-39 • 57,400
Greeley, KS • 1,845
Greeley, NE • 3,462
Green, OR 97470 • 3,897
Green, KY • 11,043
Green, WI • 30,012
Greenacres, CA 93308 • 5,381
Greenacres, WA 99016 • 3,900
Greenacres City, FL 33463 • 8,780
Green Bay, WI 54301-99 • 92,400
Greenbelt, MD 20770 • 17,332
Greenbriar, VA 22033 • 6,200
Greenbrier, WV • 37,665
Green Brook, NJ 08812 • 2,380
Greencastle, IN 46135 • 8,403
Greencastle, PA 17225 • 3,679
Green Cove Springs, FL 32043 • 4,154
Greendale, IN 47025 • 3,795
Greendale, WI 53129 • 16,200
Greene, NY 13778 • 1,747
Greene, AL • 11,021
Greene, AR • 30,744
Greene, GA • 11,391
Greene, IL • 16,661
Greene, IN • 30,416
Greene, IA • 12,119
Greene, MS • 9,827
Greene, MO • 185,302
Greene, NY • 40,861
Greene, NC • 16,117
Greene, OH • 129,769
Greene, PA • 40,476
Greene, TN • 54,422
Greene, VA • 7,625
Greeneville, TN 37743 • 14,700
Greenfield, CA 93927 • 4,181
Greenfield, IN 46140 • 11,299
Greenfield, IA 50849 • 2,243
Greenfield, MA 01301 • 14,198
Greenfield, OH 45123 • 5,150
Greenfield, TN 38230 • 2,109
Greenfield, WI 53220 • 32,400
Greenfield Plaza, IA 50315 • 2,200
Green Forest, AR 72638 • 1,609
Green Harbor, MA 02041 • 1,900
Greenhills, OH 45218 • 4,927
Green Island, NY 12183 • 2,696
Green Lake, WI • 18,370
Greenlawn, NY 11740 • 13,869
Greenlee, AZ • 11,406
Greenock, PA 15047 • 2,500
Greenport, NY 11944 • 2,273
Green River, WY 82935 • 12,807
Green Rock, IL 61241 • 3,324
Greensboro, AL 36744 • 3,248
Greensboro, GA 30642 • 2,985
Greensboro, NC 27401-99 • 180,700
Greensburg, IN 47240 • 9,254
Greensburg, KS 67054 • 1,885
Greensburg, KY 42743 • 2,377
Greensburg, PA 15601 • 16,700
Green Springs, OH 44836 • 1,568
Greensville, VA • 10,903
Greentown, IN 46936 • 2,265
Green Tree, PA 15220 • 5,722
Greenup, IL 62428 • 1,655
Greenup, KY • 39,132
Green Valley, AZ 85614 • 7,999
Greenview, SC 29203 • 5,515
Greenville, AL 36037 • 7,807
Greenville, CA 95947 • 1,537
Greenville, IL 62246 • 5,271
Greenville, KY 42345 • 4,631
Greenville, ME 04441 • 1,640
Greenville, MI 48838 • 8,600
Greenville, MS 38701-04 • 40,100
Greenville, NH 03048 • 1,447
Greenville, NY 10583 • 8,706
Greenville, NC 27834-36 • 38,100
Greenville, OH 45331 • 13,200
Greenville, PA 16125 • 7,730
Greenville, RI 02828 • 7,576
Greenville, SC 29601-16 • 59,000
Greenville, TX 75401 • 25,200
Greenville, SC • 287,913
Greenwich, CT 06830-36 • 59,400
Greenwich, NY 12834 • 1,955
Greenwich, OH 44837 • 1,458
Greenwood, AR 72936 • 3,555
Greenwood, IN 46142 • 23,600
Greenwood, MS 38930 • 20,800
Greenwood, PA 16601 • 1,650
Greenwood, SC 29646 • 22,900
Greenwood, KS • 8,764
Greenwood, SC • 57,847
Greenwood Lake, NY 10925 • 2,809
Greenwood Village, CO 80110 • 5,729
Greer, SC 29651 • 10,525
Greer, OK • 7,028
Gregg, TX • 99,495
Gregory, SD 57533 • 1,503
Gregory, SD • 6,015
Grenada, MS 38901 • 11,508
Grenada, MS • 21,043
Gresham, OR 97030 • 37,500
Gresham Park, GA 30316 • 6,232
Gretna, FL 32332 • 1,557
Gretna, LA 70053-54 • 20,300
Gretna, NE 68028 • 1,609
Greybull, WY 82426 • 2,277
Gridley, CA 95948 • 3,982
Griffin, GA 30223 • 22,700
Griffith, IN 46319 • 17,026
Grifton, NC 28530 • 2,179
Griggs, ND • 3,714
Grimes, IA 50111 • 1,973
Grimes, TX • 13,580
Grindall Creek, VA 23234 • 1,900
Grinnell, IA 50112 • 8,868
Groesbeck, OH 45239 • 9,594
Groesbeck, TX 76642 • 3,373
Grosse Ile, MI 48138 • 9,320
Grosse Pointe, MI 48236 • 5,800
Grosse Pointe Farms, MI 48236 • 10,551
Grosse Pointe Park, MI 48236 • 13,562
Grosse Pointe Woods, MI 48236 • 18,886
Grossmont, CA 92041 • 2,600
Groton, CT 06340 • 10,086
Groton, NY 13073 • 2,313
Grove, OK 74344 • 3,378
Grove City, FL 34224 • 1,932
Grove City, OH 43123 • 16,816
Grove City, PA 16127 • 8,162
Grove Hill, AL 36451 • 1,912
Groveland, FL 32736 • 1,992
Groveland, MA 01834 • 3,780
Groveport, OH 43125 • 3,286
Grover City, CA 93433 • 8,827
Groves, TX 77619 • 17,090
Groveton, VA 22306 • 6,300
Groveton Gardens, VA 22303 • 2,600
Grovetown, GA 30813 • 3,384
Groveville, NJ 08620 • 2,900
Gruetli-Laager, TN 37339 • 2,021
Grulla, TX 78548 • 1,442
Grundy, VA 24614 • 1,699
Grundy, IL • 30,582
Grundy, IA • 14,366
Grundy, MO • 11,959
Grundy, TN • 13,787
Grundy Center, IA 50638 • 2,880
Guadalupe, AZ 85283 • 4,506
Guadalupe, CA 93434 • 3,629
Guadalupe, NM • 4,496
Guadalupe, TX • 46,708
Guernsey, WY 82214 • 1,512
Guernsey, OH • 42,024
Gueydan, LA 70542 • 1,695
Guilford, CT 06437 • 2,555
Guilford, NC • 317,154
Guin, AL 35563 • 2,418
Gulf, FL • 10,658
Gulf Breeze, FL 32561 • 5,478
Gulf Gate Estates, FL 34231 • 9,248
Gulfport, FL 33707 • 11,180
Gulfport, MS 39501-07 • 41,700
Gulf Shores, AL 36542 • 2,164
Gunnison, CO 81230 • 5,785
Gunnison, CO • 10,689
Guntersville, AL 35976 • 7,041
Gurdon, AR 71743 • 2,707
Gurnee, IL 60031 • 9,882
Gustine, CA 95322 • 3,142
Guthrie, OK 73044 • 11,382
Guthrie, IA • 11,983
Guthrie Center, IA 50115 • 1,713
Guttenberg, IA 52052 • 2,428
Guttenberg, NJ 07093 • 7,340
Guymon, OK 73942 • 8,492
Gwinnett, GA • 166,903

H

Haakon, SD • 2,794
Habersham, GA • 25,020
Hacienda Heights, CA 91745 • 54,900
Hackensack, NJ 07601-08 • 35,200
Hackettstown, NJ 07840 • 8,850
Haddonfield, NJ 08033 • 12,337
Haddon Heights, NJ 08035 • 8,361
Hadlock, WA 98339 • 1,752
Hagerstown, IN 47346 • 1,950
Hagerstown, MD 21740 • 32,900
Hahira, GA 31632 • 1,534
Hahnville, LA 70057 • 2,947
Hailey, ID 83333 • 2,109
Haines City, FL 33844 • 10,799
Halawa Heights, HI 96701 • 7,000
Hale, AL • 15,604
Hale, TX • 37,592
Hale Center, TX 79041 • 2,297
Haledon, NJ 07508 • 6,607
Haleiwa, HI 96712 • 2,412
Hales Corners, WI 53130 • 7,110
Halethorpe, MD 21227 • 20,163
Haleyville, AL 35565 • 5,306
Half Hollow Hills, NY 11746 • 5,110
Half Moon Bay, CA 94019 • 7,282
Halfway, MD 21740 • 8,659
Halifax, NC • 55,286
Halifax, VA • 30,599
Hall, GA • 75,649
Hall, NE • 47,690
Hall, TX • 5,594
Hallandale, FL 33009 • 39,300
Hallettsville, TX 77964 • 2,865
Hallowell, ME 04347 • 2,502
Halls, TN 37918 • 10,363
Halls, TN 38040 • 2,562
Halls Crossroads, TN 37918 • 1,900
Hallsville, TX 75650 • 1,556
Halstead, KS 67056 • 1,994
Haltom City, TX 76117 • 33,100
Hamblen, TN • 49,300
Hamburg, AR 71646 • 3,394
Hamburg, IA 51640 • 1,597
Hamburg, NJ 07419 • 1,832
Hamburg, NY 14075 • 10,582
Hamburg, PA 19526 • 4,011
Hamden, CT 06514 • 51,100
Hamel, MN 55340 • 2,623
Hamilton, AL 35570 • 5,093
Hamilton, IL 62341 • 3,509
Hamilton, MO 64644 • 1,582
Hamilton, MT 59840 • 2,661
Hamilton, NY 13346 • 3,725
Hamilton, OH 45011-15 • 64,300
Hamilton, TX 76531 • 3,189
Hamilton, FL • 8,761
Hamilton, IL • 9,172
Hamilton, IN • 82,027
Hamilton, IA • 17,862
Hamilton, KS • 2,514
Hamilton, NE • 9,301
Hamilton, NY • 5,034
Hamilton, OH • 873,224
Hamilton, TN • 287,740
Hamilton, TX • 8,297
Hamilton Square, NJ 08690 • 10,970
Ham Lake, MN 55304 • 7,832
Hamlet, NC 28345 • 4,720
Hamlin, TX 79520 • 3,248
Hamlin, SD • 5,261
Hammond, IN 46320-27 • 89,700
Hammond, LA 70401-04 • 20,500
Hammonton, NJ 08037 • 12,298
Hampden, ME 04444 • 2,300
Hampden, MA • 443,018
Hampden Highlands, ME 04444 • 1,540
Hampshire, IL 60140 • 1,735
Hampshire, MA • 138,813
Hampshire, WV • 14,867
Hampton, AR 71744 • 1,627
Hampton, GA 30228 • 2,059
Hampton, IA 50441 • 4,630
Hampton, MD 21204 • 6,203
Hampton, NH 03842 • 6,779
Hampton, NJ 08827 • 1,614
Hampton, SC 29924 • 3,143
Hampton, TN 37658 • 2,236
Hampton, VA 23660-70 • 126,400
Hampton, SC • 18,159
Hampton Bays, NY 11946 • 5,100
Hamtramck, MI 48212 • 21,300
Hanahan, SC 29406 • 13,224
Hanamaulu, HI 96715 • 3,227
Hanceville, AL 35077 • 2,220
Hancock, MD 21750 • 1,887
Hancock, MI 49930 • 5,122
Hancock, NY 13783 • 1,526
Hancock, GA • 9,466
Hancock, IL • 23,877
Hancock, IN • 43,939
Hancock, IA • 13,833
Hancock, KY • 7,742
Hancock, ME • 41,781
Hancock, MS • 24,537
Hancock, OH • 64,581
Hancock, TN • 6,887
Hancock, WV • 41,053
Hand, SD • 4,948
Hanford, CA 93230 • 25,400
Hanna, WY 82327 • 2,288
Hannibal, MO 63401 • 18,800
Hanover, IN 47243 • 4,054
Hanover, MA 02339 • 2,500
Hanover, NH 03755 • 6,861
Hanover, PA 17331 • 15,000
Hanover, VA • 50,398
Hanover Park, IL 60103 • 32,900
Hanover Township, NJ 07981 • 11,846
Hansford, TX • 6,209
Hanson, MA 02341 • 2,120
Hanson, SD • 3,415
Hapeville, GA 30354 • 6,166
Happy Valley, OR 97236 • 1,499
Harahan, LA 70123 • 11,384
Haralson, GA • 18,422
Harbor, OR 97415 • 2,856
Harbor Beach, MI 48441 • 2,000
Harborcreek, PA 16421 • 1,500
Harbor Springs, MI 49740 • 1,567
Hardee, FL • 19,379
Hardeman, TN • 23,873
Hardeman, TX • 6,368
Hardin, MT 59034 • 3,300
Hardin, IL • 5,383
Hardin, IA • 21,776
Hardin, KY • 88,917
Hardin, OH • 32,719
Hardin, TN • 22,280
Hardin, TX • 40,721
Harding, NM • 1,090
Harding, SD • 1,700
Hardinsburg, KY 40143 • 2,211
Hardwick, GA 31034 • 8,800
Hardwick, VT 05843 • 1,476
Hardy, WV • 10,030
Harford, MD • 145,930
Harker Heights, TX 76543 • 7,345
Harkers Island, NC 28531 • 1,901
Harlan, IA 51537 • 5,357
Harlan, KY 40831 • 3,000
Harlan, KY • 41,889
Harlan, NE • 4,292
Harlem, FL 33440 • 2,669
Harlem, GA 30814 • 1,485
Harlingen, TX 78550-52 • 54,400
Harmon, OK • 4,519
Harnett, NC • 59,570
Harney, OR • 8,314
Harper, KS 67058 • 1,823
Harper, KS • 7,778
Harper, OK • 4,715
Harper Woods, MI 48225 • 15,000
Harrah, OK 73045 • 3,398
Harriman, TN 37748 • 8,524
Harrington, DE 19952 • 2,405
Harrington Park, NJ 07640 • 4,532
Harris, GA • 15,464
Harris, TX • 2,409,547
Harrisburg, AR 72432 • 1,921
Harrisburg, IL 62946 • 10,410
Harrisburg, OR 97446 • 1,881
Harrisburg, PA 17101-99 • 52,300

Harris Hill, NY 14221 • 5,087
Harrison, AR 72601 • 11,700
Harrison, MI 48625 • 1,700
Harrison, NJ 07029 • 12,242
Harrison, NY 10528 • 23,046
Harrison, OH 45030 • 5,855
Harrison, TN 37341 • 6,206
Harrison, IN • 27,276
Harrison, IA • 16,348
Harrison, KY • 15,166
Harrison, MS • 157,665
Harrison, MO • 9,890
Harrison, OH • 18,152
Harrison, TX • 52,265
Harrison, WV • 77,710
Harrisonburg, VA 22801 • 27,800
Harrison Township, MI 48043 • 23,464
Harrisonville, MO 64701 • 6,372
Harristown, IL 62537 • 1,456
Harrisville, WV 26362 • 1,673
Harrodsburg, KY 40330 • 7,265
Hart, MI 49420 • 1,888
Hart, GA • 18,585
Hart, KY • 15,402
Hartford, AL 36344 • 2,647
Hartford, CT 06101-99 • 138,400
Hartford, IL 62048 • 1,887
Hartford, KY 42347 • 2,512
Hartford, MI 49057 • 2,493
Hartford, WI 53027 • 7,159
Hartford, CT • 807,766
Hartford City, IN 47348 • 7,622
Hartington, NE 68739 • 1,730
Hartland, WI 53029 • 5,559
Hartley, IA 51346 • 1,700
Hartley, TX • 3,987
Hartsdale, NY 10530 • 10,216
Hartselle, AL 35640 • 8,858
Hartshorne, OK 74547 • 2,380
Hartsville, SC 29550 • 8,939
Hartsville, TN 37074 • 2,674
Hartville, OH 44632 • 1,772
Harvard, IL 60033 • 5,126
Harvey, IL 60426 • 35,300
Harvey, LA 70058 • 15,000
Harvey, ND 58341 • 2,527
Harvey, KS • 30,531
Harwich Port, MA 02646 • 2,300
Harwinton, CT 06791 • 3,293
Harwood Heights, IL 60656 • 8,228
Hasbrouck Heights, NJ 07604 • 12,166
Haskell, OK 74436 • 1,953
Haskell, TX 79521 • 3,782
Haskell, KS • 3,814
Haskell, OK • 11,010
Haskell, TX • 7,725
Haslett, MI 48840 • 7,025
Hastings, MI 49058 • 6,418
Hastings, MN 55033 • 12,827
Hastings, NE 68901 • 22,700
Hastings, PA 16646 • 1,574
Hastings-on-Hudson, NY 10706 • 8,573
Hatboro, PA 19040 • 7,500
Hatfield, PA 19440 • 2,533
Hattiesburg, MS 39401-07 • 42,100
Haughton, LA 71037 • 1,510
Hauppauge, NY 11788 • 20,960
Hauula, HI 96717 • 2,997
Havana, FL 32333 • 2,782
Havana, IL 62644 • 4,277
Havelock, NC 28532 • 17,718
Haverford [Township], PA 19083 • 52,400
Haverhill, MA 01830 • 48,100
Haverstraw, NY 10927 • 8,800
Havre, MT 59501 • 10,900
Havre de Grace, MD 21078 • 8,763
Hawaii, HI • 92,053
Hawaiian Gardens, CA 90716 • 10,548
Hawarden, IA 51023 • 2,722
Hawkins, TN • 43,751
Hawkinsville, GA 31036 • 4,372
Hawley, MN 56549 • 1,634
Haworth, NJ 07641 • 3,509
Haw River, NC 27258 • 1,858
Hawthorne, CA 90250 • 61,400
Hawthorne, NV 89415 • 3,741
Hawthorne, NJ 07506 • 18,200
Hawthorne, NY 10532 • 5,010
Hayden, CO 81639 • 1,720
Hayden, ID 83835 • 2,586
Hayes, NE • 1,356
Hayesville, OR 97303 • 9,213
Hayfield, VA 22310 • 2,300
Hayfork, CA 96041 • 1,788
Haynesville, LA 71038 • 3,454
Hays, KS 67601 • 17,800
Hays, TX • 40,594
Haysville, KS 67060 • 8,006
Hayti, MO 63851 • 3,964
Hayward, CA 94541-46 • 102,800
Hayward, WI 54843 • 1,698
Haywood, NC • 46,495
Haywood, TN • 20,318
Hazard, KY 41701 • 5,371
Hazardville, CT 06082 • 5,436
Hazel Crest, IL 60429 • 13,973
Hazel Dell, WA 98665 • 5,500
Hazel Green, AL 35750 • 1,503
Hazel Park, MI 48030 • 20,914
Hazelwood, MO 63042-45 • 16,155
Hazelwood, NC 28738 • 1,811

Hazen, AR 72064 • 1,636
Hazen, ND 58545 • 2,365
Hazlehurst, GA 31539 • 4,298
Hazlehurst, MS 39083 • 4,437
Hazlet, NJ 07730 • 23,013
Hazleton, PA 18201 • 25,800
Headland, AL 36345 • 3,327
Healdsburg, CA 95448 • 7,217
Healdton, OK 73438 • 3,769
Heard, GA • 6,520
Hearne, TX 77859 • 5,418
Heath, OH 43056 • 6,969
Heavener, OK 74937 • 2,776
Hebbronville, TX 78361 • 4,684
Heber City, UT 84032 • 4,362
Heber Springs, AR 72543 • 4,857
Hebron, IN 46341 • 2,696
Hebron, NE 68370 • 1,906
Hebron, OH 43025 • 2,035
Heeia, HI 96744 • 5,432
Heflin, AL 36264 • 3,014
Helena, AL 35080 • 2,130
Helena, AR 72342 • 9,598
Helena, MT 59601 • 25,800
Hellertown, PA 18055 • 6,025
Helper, UT 84526 • 2,724
Hemet, CA 92343-44 • 30,100
Hemphill, TX • 5,304
Hempstead, NY 11550-54 • 42,300
Hempstead, TX 77445 • 3,456
Hempstead, AR • 23,635
Henderson, KY 42420 • 26,000
Henderson, LA 70517 • 1,560
Henderson, NV 89015 • 24,363
Henderson, NC 27536 • 16,500
Henderson, TN 38340 • 4,632
Henderson, TX 75652 • 11,473
Henderson, IL • 9,114
Henderson, KY • 40,849
Henderson, NC • 58,580
Henderson, TN • 21,390
Henderson, TX • 42,606
Hendersonville, NC 28739 • 8,300
Hendersonville, TN 37075 • 30,400
Hendricks, IN • 69,804
Hendry, FL • 18,599
Hennepin, MN • 941,411
Hennessey, OK 73742 • 2,287
Henniker, NH 03242 • 1,538
Henrico, VA • 180,735
Henrietta, TX 76365 • 3,149
Henry, AL • 15,302
Henry, GA • 36,309
Henry, IL • 57,968
Henry, IN • 53,336
Henry, IA • 18,890
Henry, KY • 12,740
Henry, MO • 19,672
Henry, OH • 28,383
Henry, TN • 28,656
Henry, VA • 57,654
Henryetta, OK 74437 • 6,432
Hephzibah, GA 30815 • 1,452
Heppner, OR 97836 • 1,498
Herculaneum, MO 63048 • 2,293
Hercules, CA 94547 • 5,963
Hereford, TX 79045 • 15,853
Herington, KS 67449 • 2,930
Heritage Village, CT 06488 • 9,700
Herkimer, NY 13350 • 8,383
Herkimer, NY • 66,714
Hermann, MO 65041 • 2,695
Hermantown, MN 55811 • 6,759
Herminie, PA 15637 • 2,000
Hermiston, OR 97838 • 9,642
Hermitage, PA 16148 • 17,300
Hermosa Beach, CA 90254 • 18,070
Hernando, FL 32642 • 1,653
Hernando, MS 38632 • 2,969
Hernando, FL • 44,469
Herndon, VA 22070-71 • 11,449
Herrin, IL 62948 • 10,745
Hershey, PA 17033 • 13,249
Hertford, NC 27944 • 1,941
Hertford, NC • 23,368
Hesperia, CA 92345 • 13,540
Hesston, KS 67062 • 3,013
Hettinger, ND 58639 • 1,739
Hettinger, ND • 4,275
Hewitt, TX 76643 • 5,247
Hewlett, NY 11557 • 6,986
Heyburn, ID 83336 • 2,889
Heyworth, IL 61745 • 1,594
Hialeah, FL 33010-16 • 167,000
Hiawatha, IA 52233 • 4,885
Hiawatha, KS 66434 • 3,702
Hibbing, MN 55746 • 20,200
Hickman, KY 42050 • 2,894
Hickman, KY • 6,065
Hickman, TN • 15,151
Hickory, NC 28601-03 • 25,100
Hickory, MO • 6,367
Hickory Hills, IL 60457 • 13,778
Hicksville, NY 11801-99 • 43,400
Hicksville, OH 43526 • 3,929
Hidalgo, TX 78557 • 2,288
Hidalgo, NM • 6,049
Hidalgo, TX • 283,323
Higganum, CT 06441 • 1,660
Higginsville, MO 64037 • 4,595
High Bridge, NJ 08829 • 3,435
Highland, CA 92346 • 10,400
Highland, IL 62249 • 7,122
Highland, IN 46322 • 24,600
Highland, NY 12528 • 3,967
Highland, OH • 33,477

Highland, VA • 2,937
Highland Falls, NY 10928 • 4,187
Highland Heights, OH 44124 • 5,739
Highland Lakes, NJ 07422 • 2,888
Highland Park, IL 60035 • 32,000
Highland Park, MI 48203 • 25,700
Highland Park, NJ 08904 • 13,396
Highland Park, TX 75205 • 8,909
Highlands, NJ 07732 • 5,187
Highlands, TX 77562 • 6,467
Highlands, FL • 47,526
Highland Springs, VA 23075 • 7,900
High Point, NC 27260-64 • 67,700
High Ridge, MO 63049 • 2,380
High Spire, PA 17034 • 2,959
High Springs, FL 32643 • 2,491
Hightstown, NJ 08520 • 4,581
Highview, KY 40228 • 12,860
Highwood, IL 60430 • 5,455
Hill, MT • 17,985
Hill, TX • 25,024
Hill City, KS 67642 • 2,028
Hillcrest, NY 10977 • 5,733
Hillcrest Center, CA 93306 • 26,900
Hillcrest Heights, MD 20748 • 17,021
Hilliard, FL 32046 • 1,869
Hilliard, OH 43026 • 8,131
Hillsboro, IL 62049 • 4,408
Hillsboro, KS 67063 • 2,717
Hillsboro, MO 63050 • 1,508
Hillsboro, NH 03244 • 1,797
Hillsboro, ND 58045 • 1,600
Hillsboro, OH 45133 • 6,356
Hillsboro, OR 97123-24 • 31,400
Hillsboro, TX 76645 • 7,397
Hillsborough, CA 94010 • 10,372
Hillsborough, NC 27278 • 3,019
Hillsborough, FL • 646,960
Hillsborough, NH • 276,608
Hillsdale, MI 49242 • 7,432
Hillsdale, NJ 07642 • 10,495
Hillsdale, MI • 42,071
Hillside, IL 60162 • 8,279
Hillside, NJ 07205 • 21,300
Hillsville, VA 24343 • 2,123
Hillview, KY 40229 • 7,124
Hilo, HI 96720 • 42,800
Hilton, NY 14468 • 4,151
Hilton Head Island, SC 29928 • 17,622
Hinckley, IL 60520 • 1,447
Hinds, MS • 250,998
Hines, OR 97738 • 1,632
Hinesville, GA 31313 • 11,309
Hingham, MA 02043 • 12,800
Hinsdale, IL 60521 • 17,300
Hinsdale, NH 03451 • 1,546
Hinsdale, CO • 408
Hinton, OK 73047 • 1,432
Hinton, WV 25951 • 4,428
Hitchcock, TX 77563 • 6,103
Hitchcock, NE • 4,079
Hitchcock Lake, CT 06716 • 1,640
Hobart, IN 46342 • 22,700
Hobart, OK 73651 • 4,735
Hobbs, NM 88240 • 34,500
Hobe Sound, FL 33455 • 6,822
Hoboken, NJ 07030 • 41,700
Hocking, OH • 24,304
Hockley, TX • 23,230
Hodgeman, KS • 2,269
Hodgenville, KY 42748 • 2,531
Hoffman Estates, IL 60195 • 40,700
Hogansville, GA 30230 • 3,362
Hohenwald, TN 38462 • 4,008
Ho-Ho-Kus, NJ 07423 • 4,129
Hoisington, KS 67544 • 3,678
Hoke, NC • 20,383
Hokes Bluff, AL 35903 • 3,216
Holbrook, AZ 86025 • 5,785
Holbrook, MA 02343 • 11,140
Holbrook, NY 11741 • 24,342
Holden, MA 01520 • 4,040
Holden, MO 64040 • 2,195
Holden Heights, FL 32805 • 8,000
Holdenville, OK 74848 • 5,469
Holdrege, NE 68949 • 5,624
Holiday, FL 34690 • 15,400
Holiday City at Berkeley, NJ 08757 • 5,750
Holladay, UT 84117 • 25,800
Holland, MI 49423-24 • 29,500
Holland, PA 18966 • 5,250
Hollandale, MS 38748 • 4,336
Holley, NY 14470 • 1,842
Hollidaysburg, PA 16648 • 5,892
Hollins, VA 24019 • 12,295
Hollis, OK 73550 • 2,958
Hollister, CA 95023 • 11,488
Hollister, MO 65672 • 1,439
Holliston, MA 01746 • 12,622
Holly, MI 48442 • 5,237
Holly Hill, FL 32017 • 9,953
Holly Hill, SC 29059 • 1,785
Holly Springs, MS 38635 • 7,285
Hollywood, FL 33020-29 • 127,000
Hollywood, SC 29449 • 2,364
Holmen, WI 54636 • 2,411
Holmes, FL • 14,723
Holmes, MS • 22,970
Holmes, OH • 29,416
Holstein, IA 51025 • 1,477
Holt, AL 35404 • 3,500
Holt, MI 48842 • 10,097
Holt, MO • 6,882

Holt, NE • 13,552
Holton, KS 66436 • 3,132
Holtsville, NY 11742 • 5,000
Holtville, CA 92250 • 4,399
Holyoke, CO 80734 • 2,092
Holyoke, MA 01040 • 43,200
Homedale, ID 83628 • 2,078
Home Gardens, CA 91720 • 5,783
Homeland Park, SC 29621 • 6,720
Homer, AK 99603 • 2,209
Homer, LA 71040 • 4,307
Homer, MI 49245 • 1,791
Homer, NY 13077 • 3,635
Homer City, PA 15748 • 2,248
Homerville, GA 31634 • 3,112
Homestead, FL 33030-35 • 21,900
Homestead, PA 15120 • 5,092
Hometown, IL 60456 • 5,324
Homewood, AL 35209 • 21,300
Homewood, IL 60430 • 18,900
Homewood, OH 45015 • 2,550
Hominy, OK 74035 • 3,130
Honaker, VA 24260 • 1,475
Hondo, TX 78861 • 6,057
Honea Path, SC 29654 • 4,114
Honeoye Falls, NY 14472 • 2,410
Honesdale, PA 18431 • 5,128
Honey Grove, TX 75446 • 1,973
Honokaa, HI 96727 • 1,936
Honolulu, HI 96801-99 • 395,700
Honolulu, HI • 762,565
Hood, TX • 17,714
Hood River, OR 97031 • 4,370
Hood River, OR • 15,835
Hooker, OK 73945 • 1,788
Hooker, NE • 990
Hooksett, NH 03106 • 1,868
Hoopeston, IL 60942 • 6,411
Hoosick Falls, NY 12090 • 3,609
Hoover, AL 35216 • 31,300
Hooverson Heights, WV 26037 • 3,111
Hopatcong, NJ 07843 • 15,531
Hope, AR 71801 • 10,290
Hope, IN 47246 • 2,185
Hopedale, MA 01747 • 3,905
Hope Mills, NC 28348 • 6,298
Hopewell, NJ 08525 • 2,001
Hopewell, VA 23860 • 23,800
Hopewell Junction, NY 12533 • 1,754
Hopkins, MN 55343-45 • 15,336
Hopkins, SC 29061 • 1,600
Hopkins, KY • 46,174
Hopkins, TX • 25,247
Hopkinsville, KY 42240 • 27,600
Hopkinton, MA 01748 • 2,542
Hopwood, PA 15445 • 2,420
Hoquiam, WA 98550 • 9,719
Horicon, WI 53032 • 3,584
Hornell, NY 14843 • 10,000
Horn Lake, MS 38637 • 4,326
Horry, SC • 101,419
Horse Cave, KY 42147 • 2,045
Horseheads, NY 14845 • 7,348
Horsham, PA 19044 • 9,900
Horton, KS 66439 • 2,130
Hortonville, WI 54944 • 2,016
Hot Spring, AR • 26,819
Hot Springs, SD 57747 • 4,742
Hot Springs, WY • 5,710
Hot Springs National Park, AR 71901-14 • 38,000
Houghton, MI 49931 • 6,900
Houghton, NY 14744 • 1,604
Houghton, MI • 37,872
Houghton Lake, MI 48629 • 1,500
Houghton Lake Heights, MI 48630 • 2,449
Houlton, ME 04730 • 5,730
Houma, LA 70360-64 • 34,000
Houston, MS 38851 • 3,745
Houston, MO 65483 • 2,157
Houston, PA 15342 • 1,568
Houston, TX 77001-99 • 1,744,800
Houston, AL • 74,632
Houston, GA • 77,605
Houston, MN • 18,382
Houston, TN • 6,871
Houston, TX • 22,299
Howard, WI 54303 • 8,240
Howard, AR • 13,459
Howard, IN • 86,896
Howard, IA • 11,114
Howard, MD • 118,572
Howard, MO • 10,008
Howard, NE • 6,773
Howard, TX • 33,142
Howards Grove-Millersville, WI 53081 • 1,838
Howell, MI 48843 • 6,976
Howell, MO • 28,807
Howland, ME 04448 • 1,602
Howland, OH 44484 • 7,441
Hoxie, AR 72433 • 2,961
Hoxie, KS 67740 • 1,462
Hoyt Lakes, MN 55750 • 3,186
Huachuca City, AZ 85616 • 1,661
Hubbard, OH 44425 • 9,245
Hubbard, OR 97032 • 1,640
Hubbard, TX 76648 • 1,676
Hubbard, MN • 14,098
Huber Heights, OH 45424 • 43,700
Huber Ridge, OH 43081 • 5,835
Huber South, OH 45439 • 4,800
Hudson, FL 34667 • 5,799
Hudson, IA 50643 • 2,267
Hudson, MA 01749 • 14,156

Hudson, MI 49247 • 2,545
Hudson, NH 03051 • 6,248
Hudson, NY 12534 • 7,986
Hudson, NC 28638 • 2,888
Hudson, OH 44236 • 4,615
Hudson, WI 54016 • 5,434
Hudson, NJ • 556,972
Hudson Falls, NY 12839 • 7,419
Hudsonville, MI 49426 • 4,844
Hudspeth, TX • 2,728
Huerfano, CO • 6,440
Hueytown, AL 35023 • 15,888
Hughes, AR 72348 • 1,919
Hughes, OK • 14,338
Hughes, SD • 14,220
Hughesville, PA 17737 • 2,174
Hugo, MN 55038 • 3,771
Hugo, OK 74743 • 7,172
Hugoton, KS 67951 • 3,165
Huguley, AL 36854 • 2,947
Hull, IA 51239 • 1,714
Hull, MA 02045 • 9,714
Humble, TX 77338-39 • 12,000
Humboldt, IA 50548 • 4,794
Humboldt, KS 66748 • 2,230
Humboldt, TN 38343 • 10,209
Humboldt, CA • 108,514
Humboldt, IA • 12,246
Humboldt, NV • 9,434
Hummels Wharf, PA 17831 • 1,474
Humphreys, MS • 13,931
Humphreys, TN • 15,957
Hunt, TX • 55,248
Hunterdon, NJ • 87,361
Huntingburg, IN 47542 • 5,376
Huntingdon, PA 16652 • 7,042
Huntingdon, TN 38344 • 4,513
Huntingdon, PA • 42,253
Huntington, IN 46750 • 16,202
Huntington, NY 11743 • 21,727
Huntington, TX 75949 • 1,672
Huntington, UT 84528 • 2,316
Huntington, VA 22303 • 5,000
Huntington, WV 25701-99 • 60,800
Huntington, IN • 35,596
Huntington Bay, NY 11743 • 1,783
Huntington Beach, CA 92647-49 • 187,700
Huntington Park, CA 90255 • 52,700
Huntington Station, NY 11746 • 29,900
Huntington Woods, MI 48070 • 6,937
Huntley, IL 60142 • 1,646
Huntsville, AL 35801-99 • 160,000
Huntsville, MO 65259 • 1,657
Huntsville, TX 77340 • 34,300
Hurley, NM 88043 • 1,616
Hurley, NY 12443 • 4,905
Hurley, WI 54534 • 2,015
Hurlock, MD 21643 • 1,690
Huron, OH 44839 • 7,123
Huron, SD 57350 • 12,000
Huron, MI • 36,459
Huron, OH • 54,608
Hurricane, UT 84737 • 2,361
Hurricane, WV 25526 • 3,751
Hurst, TX 76053-54 • 36,300
Hurt, VA 24563 • 1,481
Hutchins, TX 75141 • 2,837
Hutchinson, KS 67501-05 • 41,900
Hutchinson, MN 55350 • 9,244
Hutchinson, SD • 9,350
Hutchinson, TX • 26,304
Huxley, IA 50124 • 1,884
Hyannis, MA 02601 • 9,700
Hyattsville, MD 20780-88 • 12,709
Hybla Valley, VA 22306 • 4,000
Hyde, PA 16843 • 1,791
Hyde, NC • 5,873
Hyde, SD • 2,069
Hyde Park, NY 12538 • 2,550
Hyde Park, UT 84318 • 1,495
Hyrum, UT 84319 • 3,952

I

Iberia, LA • 63,752
Iberville, LA • 32,159
Ida, IA • 8,908
Idabel, OK 74745 • 7,622
Ida Grove, IA 51445 • 2,285
Idaho, ID • 14,769
Idaho Falls, ID 83401-15 • 43,300
Idaho Springs, CO 80452 • 2,077
Idalou, TX 79329 • 2,348
Ilion, NY 13357 • 9,450
Imlay City, MI 48444 • 2,495
Immokalee, FL 33934 • 11,038
Imperial, CA 92251 • 3,451
Imperial, NE 69033 • 1,941
Imperial, PA 15126 • 3,200
Imperial, CA • 92,110
Imperial Beach, CA 92032 • 26,100
Incline Village, NV 89450 • 4,500
Independence, IA 50644 • 6,392
Independence, KS 67301 • 10,598
Independence, KY 41051 • 9,310
Independence, LA 70443 • 1,684
Independence, MO 64050-58 • 115,400
Independence, OH 44131 • 6,607
Independence, OR 97351 • 4,024
Independence, AR • 30,147
Indiana, PA 15701 • 15,300

Indiana, PA • *92,281*
Indianapolis, IN 46201-99 • *722,800*
Indian Harbour Beach, FL 32937 • *5,967*
Indian Heights, IN 46902 • *4,277*
Indian Hills, CO 80454 • *2,000*
Indian Neck, CT 06405 • *2,430*
Indianola, IA 50125 • *10,843*
Indianola, MS 38751 • *9,529*
Indian River, FL • *59,896*
Indian Rocks Beach, FL 34635 • *3,717*
Indiantown, FL 34956 • *3,383*
Indio, CA 92201 • *30,500*
Ingalls Park, IL 60431 • *3,500*
Ingham, MI • *275,520*
Ingleside, TX 78362 • *5,436*
Inglewood, CA 90301-99 • *103,400*
Inglewood, TX 98011 • *6,500*
Ingram, PA 15205 • *4,346*
Inkster, MI 48141 • *32,800*
Inman, SC 29349 • *1,554*
Inniswold, LA 70809 • *1,800*
Inola, OK 74036 • *1,550*
International Falls, MN 56649 • *5,611*
Inver Grove Heights, MN 55075 • *17,171*
Inverness, FL 32650-52 • *4,095*
Inverness, IL 60067 • *5,220*
Inwood, FL 33880 • *6,668*
Inwood, NY 11696 • *8,228*
Inyo, CA • *17,895*
Iola, KS 66749 • *6,938*
Ione, CA 95640 • *2,207*
Ionia, MI 48846 • *5,920*
Ionia, MI • *51,815*
Iosco, MI • *28,349*
Iowa, LA 70647 • *2,437*
Iowa, IA • *15,429*
Iowa, WI • *19,802*
Iowa City, IA 52240 • *52,000*
Iowa Falls, IA 50126 • *6,174*
Iowa Park, TX 76367 • *6,184*
Ipswich, MA 01938 • *4,548*
Iredell, NC • *82,538*
Irion, TX • *1,386*
Irmo, SC 29063 • *3,957*
Iron, MI • *13,635*
Iron, MO • *11,084*
Iron, UT • *17,349*
Iron, WI • *6,730*
Irondale, AL 35210 • *8,670*
Irondequoit, NY 14617 • *56,700*
Iron Mountain, MI 49801 • *8,800*
Iron River, MI 49935 • *2,426*
Ironton, MO 63650 • *1,743*
Ironton, OH 45638 • *14,290*
Ironwood, MI 49938 • *7,200*
Iroquois, IL • *32,976*
Irvine, CA 92714 • *87,400*
Irvine, KY 40336 • *2,889*
Irving, TX 75060-63 • *130,200*
Irvington, NJ 07111 • *62,800*
Irvington, NY 10533 • *5,774*
Irwin, PA 15642 • *4,995*
Irwin, GA • *8,988*
Isabella, MI • *54,110*
Isanti, MN • *23,600*
Ishpeming, MI 49849 • *7,538*
Islamorada, FL 33036 • *1,441*
Island, WA • *44,048*
Island Heights, NJ 08732 • *1,575*
Island Park, NY 11558 • *4,847*
Isla Vista, CA 93117 • *16,700*
Isle of Palms, SC 29451 • *3,421*
Isle of Wight, VA • *21,603*
Islington, MA 02090 • *4,920*
Islip, NY 11751 • *13,438*
Islip Terrace, NY 11752 • *5,588*
Issaquah, WA 98027 • *5,714*
Issaquena, MS • *2,513*
Itasca, IL 60143 • *7,129*
Itasca, TX 76055 • *1,600*
Itasca, MN • *43,069*
Itawamba, MS • *20,518*
Ithaca, MI 48847 • *2,950*
Ithaca, NY 14850-53 • *27,700*
Itta Bena, MS 38941 • *2,904*
Iuka, MS 38852 • *2,888*
Ives Estates, FL 33162 • *6,600*
Ivoryton, CT 06442 • *2,200*
Izard, AR • *10,768*

J

Jacinto City, TX 77029 • *8,953*
Jack, TX • *7,408*
Jacksboro, TN 37757 • *1,729*
Jacksboro, TX 76056 • *4,000*
Jackson, AL 36545 • *6,073*
Jackson, CA 95642 • *2,331*
Jackson, GA 30233 • *4,133*
Jackson, KY 41339 • *2,651*
Jackson, LA 70748 • *3,878*
Jackson, MI 49201-04 • *38,300*
Jackson, MN 56143 • *3,797*
Jackson, MS 39201-99 • *216,400*
Jackson, MO 63755 • *7,827*
Jackson, OH 45640 • *6,675*
Jackson, SC 29831 • *1,771*
Jackson, TN 38301-05 • *49,620*
Jackson, WI 53037 • *1,817*
Jackson, WY 83001 • *4,511*
Jackson, AL • *51,407*
Jackson, AR • *21,646*
Jackson, CO • *1,863*
Jackson, FL • *39,154*
Jackson, GA • *25,343*
Jackson, IL • *61,649*
Jackson, IN • *36,523*
Jackson, IA • *22,503*
Jackson, KS • *11,644*
Jackson, KY • *11,996*
Jackson, LA • *17,321*
Jackson, MI • *151,495*
Jackson, MN • *13,690*
Jackson, MS • *118,015*
Jackson, MO • *629,266*
Jackson, NC • *25,811*
Jackson, OH • *30,592*
Jackson, OK • *30,356*
Jackson, OR • *132,456*
Jackson, SD • *3,437*
Jackson, TN • *9,398*
Jackson, TX • *13,352*
Jackson, WV • *25,794*
Jackson, WI • *16,831*
Jacksonville, AL 36265 • *9,735*
Jacksonville, AR 72076 • *29,000*
Jacksonville, FL 32201-99 • *608,500*
Jacksonville, IL 62650 • *20,700*
Jacksonville, NC 28540-45 • *27,000*
Jacksonville, OR 97530 • *2,030*
Jacksonville, TX 75766 • *13,900*
Jacksonville Beach, FL 32250 • *15,462*
Jaffrey, NH 03452 • *2,684*
Jal, NM 88252 • *2,675*
Jamesburg, NJ 08831 • *4,114*
James City, VA • *22,763*
James Island, SC 29412 • *24,124*
Jamestown, CA 95327 • *2,206*
Jamestown, KY 42629 • *1,441*
Jamestown, NY 14701 • *35,500*
Jamestown, NC 27282 • *2,148*
Jamestown, ND 58401 • *17,000*
Jamestown, OH 45335 • *1,702*
Jamestown, RI 02835 • *4,040*
Jamestown, TN 38556 • *2,364*
Jamul, CA 92035 • *1,826*
Janesville, MN 56048 • *1,897*
Janesville, WI 53545-47 • *51,900*
Jarrettsville, MD 21084 • *1,485*
Jasmine Estates, FL 34668 • *3,500*
Jasonville, IN 47438 • *2,497*
Jasper, AL 35501 • *12,900*
Jasper, FL 32052 • *2,093*
Jasper, GA 30143 • *1,556*
Jasper, IN 47546 • *9,600*
Jasper, TN 37347 • *2,670*
Jasper, TX 75951 • *6,959*
Jasper, GA • *7,553*
Jasper, IL • *11,318*
Jasper, IN • *26,138*
Jasper, IA • *36,425*
Jasper, MS • *17,265*
Jasper, MO • *86,958*
Jasper, SC • *14,504*
Jasper, TX • *30,781*
Jay, OK 74346 • *2,100*
Jay, IN • *23,239*
Jeanerette, LA 70544 • *6,511*
Jeannette, PA 15644 • *13,106*
Jeff Davis, GA • *11,473*
Jeff Davis, TX • *1,647*
Jefferson, GA 30549 • *1,820*
Jefferson, IA 50129 • *4,854*
Jefferson, LA 70121 • *15,550*
Jefferson, OH 44047 • *2,952*
Jefferson, OR 97352 • *1,702*
Jefferson, PA 15025 • *8,643*
Jefferson, TX 75657 • *2,643*
Jefferson, WI 53549 • *5,647*
Jefferson, AL • *671,324*
Jefferson, AR • *90,718*
Jefferson, CO • *371,753*
Jefferson, FL • *10,703*
Jefferson, GA • *18,403*
Jefferson, ID • *15,304*
Jefferson, IL • *36,558*
Jefferson, IN • *30,419*
Jefferson, IA • *16,316*
Jefferson, KS • *15,207*
Jefferson, KY • *684,565*
Jefferson, LA • *454,592*
Jefferson, MS • *9,181*
Jefferson, MO • *146,183*
Jefferson, MT • *7,029*
Jefferson, NE • *9,817*
Jefferson, NY • *88,151*
Jefferson, OH • *91,564*
Jefferson, OK • *8,183*
Jefferson, OR • *11,599*
Jefferson, PA • *48,303*
Jefferson, TN • *31,284*
Jefferson, TX • *250,938*
Jefferson, WA • *15,965*
Jefferson, WV • *30,302*
Jefferson, WI • *66,152*
Jefferson City, MO 65101 • *36,400*
Jefferson City, TN 37760 • *5,775*
Jefferson Davis, LA • *32,168*
Jefferson Davis, MS • *13,846*
Jefferson Farms, DE 19720 • *2,400*
Jefferson Manor, VA 22303 • *2,300*
Jeffersontown, KY 40299 • *19,814*
Jefferson Valley, NY 10535 • *6,420*
Jefferson Village, VA 22042 • *2,500*
Jeffersonville, GA 31044 • *1,473*
Jeffersonville, IN 47130 • *21,700*
Jeffersonville, KY 40337 • *1,528*
Jeffrey City, WY 82310 • *1,882*
Jellico, TN 37762 • *2,798*
Jemez Pueblo, NM 87024 • *1,503*
Jemison, AL 35085 • *1,828*
Jena, LA 71342 • *4,375*
Jenison, MI 49428 • *16,330*
Jenkins, KY 41537 • *3,271*
Jenkins, GA • *8,841*
Jenkintown, PA 19046 • *4,900*
Jenks, OK 74037 • *6,227*
Jennings, LA 70546 • *12,401*
Jennings, MO 63136 • *17,700*
Jennings, IN • *22,854*
Jennings Lodge, OR 97222 • *3,000*
Jensen Beach, FL 34957-58 • *6,639*
Jerauld, SD • *2,929*
Jericho, NY 11753 • *12,739*
Jermyn, PA 18433 • *2,411*
Jerome, ID 83338 • *6,891*
Jerome, ID • *14,840*
Jersey, IL • *20,538*
Jersey City, NJ 07301-99 • *220,600*
Jersey Shore, PA 17740 • *4,631*
Jerseyville, IL 62052 • *7,506*
Jessamine, KY • *26,065*
Jessup, MD 20794 • *4,288*
Jessup, PA 18434 • *4,974*
Jesup, GA 31545 • *9,418*
Jesup, IA 50648 • *2,343*
Jewell, KS • *5,241*
Jewett City, CT 06351 • *3,294*
Jim Hogg, TX • *5,168*
Jim Thorpe, PA 18229 • *5,263*
Jim Wells, TX • *36,498*
Joanna, SC 29351 • *1,839*
Jo Daviess, IL • *23,520*
John Day, OR 97845 • *2,012*
Johnson, AR • *17,423*
Johnson, GA • *8,660*
Johnson, IL • *9,624*
Johnson, IN • *77,240*
Johnson, IA • *81,717*
Johnson, KS • *270,269*
Johnson, KY • *24,432*
Johnson, MO • *39,059*
Johnson, NE • *5,285*
Johnson, TN • *13,745*
Johnson, TX • *67,649*
Johnson, WY • *6,700*
Johnsonburg, PA 15845 • *3,938*
Johnson City, NY 13790 • *17,300*
Johnson City, TN 37601-15 • *44,850*
Johnston, IA 50131 • *3,156*
Johnston, RI 02919 • *25,600*
Johnston, SC 29832 • *2,624*
Johnston, NC • *70,599*
Johnston, OK • *10,356*
Johnston City, IL 62951 • *3,873*
Johnstown, CO 80534 • *1,535*
Johnstown, NY 12095 • *9,360*
Johnstown, OH 43031 • *3,158*
Johnstown, PA 15901-09 • *32,900*
Joliet, IL 60431-36 • *78,600*
Jones, OK 73049 • *2,270*
Jones, GA • *16,579*
Jones, IA • *20,401*
Jones, MS • *61,912*
Jones, NC • *9,705*
Jones, SD • *1,463*
Jones, TX • *17,268*
Jonesboro, AR 72401 • *31,500*
Jonesboro, GA 30236 • *4,132*
Jonesboro, IL 62952 • *1,842*
Jonesboro, IN 46938 • *2,279*
Jonesboro, LA 71251 • *5,061*
Jonesboro, TN 37659 • *2,829*
Jones Creek, TX 77541 • *2,634*
Jonesville, LA 71343 • *2,828*
Jonesville, MI 49250 • *2,172*
Jonesville, NC 28642 • *1,752*
Joplin, MO 64801 • *40,200*
Joppa, MD 21085 • *11,348*
Jordan, MN 55352 • *2,663*
Josephine, OR • *58,855*
Joshua, TX 76058 • *1,470*
Joshua Tree, CA 92252 • *2,083*
Jourdanton, TX 78026 • *2,743*
Juab, UT • *5,530*
Juanita, WA 98033 • *10,500*
Judith Basin, MT • *2,646*
Judsonia, AR 72081 • *2,025*
Julesburg, CO 80737 • *1,528*
Junction, TX 76849 • *2,593*
Junction City, KS 66441 • *21,200*
Junction City, KY 40440 • *2,045*
Junction City, OR 97448 • *3,329*
Juneau, AK 99801 • *26,000*
Juneau, WI 53039 • *2,045*
Juneau, WI • *21,039*
Juniata, PA • *19,188*
Jupiter, FL 33458 • *9,868*
Justice, IL 60458 • *10,345*

K

Kahaluu, HI 96744 • *2,925*
Kahoka, MO 63445 • *2,101*
Kahului, HI 96732 • *14,800*
Kailua, HI 96734 • *39,400*
Kailua Kona, HI 96740 • *4,751*
Kalaheo, HI 96741 • *2,500*
Kalamazoo, MI 49001-09 • *77,700*
Kalamazoo, MI • *212,378*
Kalawao, HI • *144*
Kalispell, MT 59901 • *12,100*
Kalkaska, MI 49646 • *1,654*
Kalkaska, MI • *10,952*
Kalona, IA 52247 • *1,862*
Kamiah, ID 83536 • *1,478*
Kanab, UT 84741 • *2,148*
Kanabec, MN • *12,161*
Kanawha, WV • *231,414*
Kandiyohi, MN • *36,763*
Kane, PA 16735 • *4,916*
Kane, IL • *278,405*
Kane, UT • *4,024*
Kaneohe, HI 96744 • *32,900*
Kankakee, IL 60901 • *29,100*
Kankakee, IL • *102,926*
Kannapolis, NC 28081 • *33,100*
Kansas City, KS 66101-99 • *162,000*
Kansas City, MO 64101-99 • *450,600*
Kapaa, HI 96746 • *4,467*
Kaplan, LA 70548 • *5,016*
Karnes, TX • *13,593*
Karnes City, TX 78118 • *3,296*
Kasson, MN 55944 • *2,827*
Kathleen, FL 33849 • *1,866*
Katy, TX 77449-50 • *5,660*
Kauai, HI • *39,082*
Kaufman, TX 75142 • *4,658*
Kaufman, TX • *39,029*
Kaukauna, WI 54130 • *11,310*
Kaunakakai, HI 96748 • *2,231*
Kay, OK • *49,852*
Kayenta, AZ 86033 • *3,343*
Kaysville, UT 84037 • *10,331*
Keansburg, NJ 07734 • *10,613*
Kearney, MO 64060 • *1,433*
Kearney, NE 68847 • *23,600*
Kearney, NE • *7,053*
Kearns, UT 84118 • *21,353*
Kearny, AZ 85237 • *2,646*
Kearny, NJ 07032 • *35,100*
Kearny, KS • *3,435*
Keego Harbor, MI 48033 • *3,083*
Keene, NH 03431 • *22,400*
Keene, TX 76059 • *3,013*
Keeseville, NY 12944 • *2,025*
Keewatin, MN 55753 • *1,443*
Keith, NE • *9,364*
Keizer, OR 97303 • *19,785*
Kekaha, HI 96752 • *3,260*
Keller, TX 76248 • *5,080*
Kellogg, ID 83837 • *3,417*
Kelseyville, CA 95451 • *1,567*
Kelso, WA 98626 • *11,129*
Kemmerer, WY 83101 • *3,273*
Kemper, MS • *10,148*
Kenai, AK 99611 • *4,324*
Kenbridge, VA 23944 • *1,539*
Ken Caryl, CO 80123 • *10,661*
Kendall, FL 33156 • *50,300*
Kendall, IL • *37,202*
Kendall, TX • *10,635*
Kendall Green, FL 33060 • *6,768*
Kendall Park, NJ 08824 • *7,419*
Kendallville, IN 46755 • *7,299*
Kenedy, TX 78119 • *4,356*
Kenedy, TX • *543*
Kenilworth, IL 60043 • *2,708*
Kenilworth, NJ 07033 • *8,221*
Kenly, NC 27542 • *1,433*
Kenmare, ND 58746 • *1,456*
Kenmore, NY 14217 • *18,474*
Kenmore, WA 98028 • *7,281*
Kennebec, ME • *109,889*
Kennebunk, ME 04043 • *3,294*
Kennebunkport, ME 04046 • *1,685*
Kennedale, TX 76060 • *2,594*
Kennedy Heights, LA 70094 • *2,000*
Kennedy Township, PA 15108 • *7,159*
Kenner, LA 70062-65 • *73,400*
Kennesaw, GA 30144 • *5,098*
Kennett, MO 63857 • *10,145*
Kennett Square, PA 19348 • *4,715*
Kennewick, WA 99336-37 • *37,100*
Kennydale, WA 98055 • *2,000*
Kenosha, WI 53140-42 • *75,600*
Kenosha, WI • *123,137*
Kenova, WV 25530 • *4,454*
Ken Rock, IL 61109 • *5,945*
Kensett, AR 72082 • *1,751*
Kensington, CA 94707 • *5,200*
Kensington, CT 06037 • *7,502*
Kensington, MD 20895 • *1,822*
Kent, OH 44240 • *28,400*
Kent, WA 98031-32 • *27,600*
Kent, DE • *98,219*
Kent, MD • *16,695*
Kent, MI • *444,506*
Kent, RI • *154,163*
Kent, TX • *1,145*
Kentland, IN 47951 • *1,936*
Kenton, OH 43326 • *8,605*
Kenton, TN 38233 • *1,570*
Kenton, KY • *137,058*
Kentwood, LA 70444 • *2,667*
Kentwood, MI 49508 • *35,100*
Kenvil, NJ 07847 • *3,050*
Kenwood, OH 45236 • *9,928*
Kenyon, MN 55946 • *1,529*
Keokuk, IA 52632 • *13,536*
Keokuk, IA • *12,921*
Kerens, TX 75144 • *1,582*
Kerhonkson, NY 12446 • *1,646*
Kermit, TX 79745 • *8,015*
Kern, CA • *403,089*
Kernersville, NC 27284 • *7,828*
Kernville, CA 93238 • *1,660*
Kerr, TX • *28,780*
Kerrville, TX 78028 • *19,600*
Kershaw, SC 29067 • *1,993*
Kershaw, SC • *39,015*
Ketchikan, AK 99901 • *7,600*
Ketchum, ID 83340 • *2,200*
Kettering, MD 20772 • *6,972*
Kettering, OH 45429 • *60,200*
Kewanee, IL 61443 • *14,508*
Kewaskum, WI 53040 • *2,394*
Kewaunee, WI 54216 • *2,801*
Kewaunee, WI • *19,539*
Keweenaw, MI • *1,963*
Keya Paha, NE • *1,301*
Key Biscayne, FL 33149 • *6,313*
Key Largo, FL 33037 • *7,447*
Keyport, NJ 07735 • *7,413*
Keyser, WV 26726 • *6,569*
Key West, FL 33040 • *25,400*
Kidder, ND • *3,833*
Kiel, WI 53042 • *3,083*
Kihei, HI 96753 • *5,644*
Kilgore, TX 75662 • *11,331*
Killearn, FL 32303 • *8,700*
Killeen, TX 76541-44 • *59,600*
Kimball, NE 69145 • *3,120*
Kimball, NE • *4,882*
Kimberly, ID 83341 • *2,307*
Kimberly, WI 54136 • *5,881*
Kimble, TX • *4,063*
Kincaid, IL 62540 • *1,591*
Kinder, LA 70648 • *2,603*
King, NC 27021 • *3,811*
King, TX • *425*
King, WA • *1,269,749*
King and Queen, VA • *5,968*
King City, CA 93930 • *5,495*
Kingfisher, OK 73750 • *4,245*
Kingfisher, OK • *14,187*
King George, VA • *10,543*
Kingman, AZ 86401 • *10,428*
Kingman, KS 67068 • *3,563*
Kingman, KS • *8,960*
Kings, CA • *73,738*
Kings, NY • *2,230,936*
Kingsburg, CA 93631 • *5,115*
Kingsbury, SD • *6,679*
Kingsford, MI 49801 • *5,290*
Kingsgate, WA 98011 • *12,652*
Kings Grant, NC 28405 • *6,562*
Kingsland, GA 31548 • *2,008*
Kingsland, TX 78639 • *2,241*
Kings Mountain, NC 28086 • *9,080*
Kings Park, NY 11754 • *8,360*
Kings Park, VA 22151 • *6,000*
Kings Park West, VA 22030 • *6,000*
Kings Point, FL 33484 • *8,724*
Kings Point, NY 11024 • *5,234*
Kingsport, TN 37660-65 • *32,100*
Kingston, MA 02364 • *4,405*
Kingston, NY 12401 • *24,900*
Kingston, PA 18704 • *15,681*
Kingston, RI 02881 • *5,479*
Kingston, TN 37763 • *4,635*
Kingstree, SC 29556 • *4,147*
Kingsville, MD 21087 • *2,824*
Kingsville, TX 78363 • *29,100*
King William, VA • *9,334*
Kingwood, TX 77339 • *16,261*
Kingwood, WV 26537 • *2,877*
Kinloch, MO 63140 • *4,455*
Kinnelon, NJ 07405 • *7,770*
Kinney, TX • *2,279*
Kinsley, KS 67547 • *2,074*
Kinston, NC 28501 • *25,100*
Kiowa, CO • *1,936*
Kiowa, KS • *4,046*
Kiowa, OK • *12,711*
Kirby, TX 78219 • *6,435*
Kirbyville, TX 75956 • *1,972*
Kirkland, WA 98033-34 • *19,600*
Kirksville, MO 63501 • *16,800*
Kirkwood, MO 63122 • *28,300*
Kirtland, NM 87417 • *2,358*
Kirtland, OH 44094 • *5,969*
Kissimmee, FL 32741-43 • *26,200*
Kit Carson, CO • *7,599*
Kitsap, WA • *147,152*
Kittanning, PA 16201 • *5,432*
Kittery, ME 03904 • *5,465*
Kittitas, WA • *24,877*
Kittson, MN • *6,672*
Klamath, OR • *59,117*
Klamath Falls, OR 97601-03 • *18,200*
Kleberg, TX • *33,358*
Klein, TX 77379 • *9,000*
Klickitat, WA • *15,822*
Knightstown, IN 46148 • *2,325*
Knob Noster, MO 65336 • *2,040*
Knott, KY • *17,940*
Knox, IN 46534 • *3,674*
Knox, IL • *61,607*
Knox, IN • *41,838*
Knox, KY • *30,239*
Knox, ME • *32,941*
Knox, MO • *5,508*
Knox, NE • *11,457*
Knox, OH • *46,304*
Knox, TN • *319,694*
Knox, TX • *5,329*
Knox City, TX 79529 • *1,546*
Knoxville, IL 61448 • *3,432*
Knoxville, IA 50138 • *8,143*
Knoxville, TN 37901-99 • *175,500*
Kodiak, AK 99615 • *4,756*
Kohler, WI 53044 • *1,651*
Kokomo, IN 46901-02 • *46,900*
Koloa, HI 96756 • *1,457*

Konawa, OK 74849 • 1,711
Koochiching, MN • 17,571
Koontz Lake, IN 46574 • 1,436
Kootenai, ID • 59,770
Kosciusko, MS 39090 • 7,415
Kosciusko, IN • 59,555
Kossuth, IA • 21,891
Kotzebue, AK 99752 • 2,090
Kountze, TX 77625 • 2,716
Kouts, IN 46347 • 1,619
Krebs, OK 74554 • 1,754
Kulpmont, PA 17834 • 3,675
Kuna, ID 83634 • 1,767
Kutztown, PA 19530 • 4,040
Kyle, TX 78640 • 2,093

L

Labadieville, LA 70372 • 2,138
La Belle, FL 33935 • 2,287
Labette, KS • 25,682
La Canada Flintridge, CA 91011 • 20,153
Lacey, WA 98503 • 14,709
Lackawanna, NY 14218 • 22,701
Lackawanna, PA • 227,908
Laclede, MO • 24,323
Lacombe, LA 70445 • 5,146
Lacon, IL 61540 • 2,135
Laconia, NH 03246 • 17,100
Lacoochee, FL 33537 • 1,720
Lac qui Parle, MN • 10,592
La Crescent, MN 55947 • 3,674
La Crescenta, CA 91214 • 12,500
La Crosse, KS 67548 • 1,618
La Crosse, WI 54601-03 • 49,000
La Crosse, WI • 91,056
Ladera Heights, CA 90045 • 6,647
Ladson, SC 29456 • 13,246
Ladue, MO 63124 • 9,369
Ladysmith, WI 54848 • 3,826
Lafayette, AL 36862 • 3,647
Lafayette, CA 94549 • 23,280
Lafayette, CO 80026 • 8,985
Lafayette, GA 30728 • 6,517
Lafayette, IN 47901-06 • 43,800
Lafayette, LA 70501-09 • 94,700
Lafayette, NC 28304 • 4,100
Lafayette, TN 37083 • 3,961
Lafayette, AR • 10,213
Lafayette, FL • 4,035
Lafayette, LA • 150,017
Lafayette, MS • 31,030
Lafayette, MO • 29,925
Lafayette, WI • 17,412
Lafayette Southwest, LA 70501 • 5,500
La Feria, TX 78559 • 3,495
La Follette, TN 37766 • 8,342
Lafourche, LA • 82,483
Lagonda, LA 70380 • 5,805
La Grande, OR 97850 • 11,790
La Grange, GA 30240 • 27,000
La Grange, IL 60525 • 15,636
Lagrange, IN 46761 • 2,164
La Grange, KY 40031 • 2,971
La Grange, NC 28551 • 3,147
La Grange, TX 78945 • 3,768
Lagrange, IN • 25,550
La Grange Highlands, IL 60525 • 5,000
La Grange Park, IL 60525 • 13,359
Laguna Beach, CA 92651-54 • 17,858
Laguna Hills, CA 92653 • 16,400
Laguna Niguel, CA 92677 • 12,237
La Habra, CA 90631 • 49,400
Lahaina, HI 96761 • 6,200
La Harpe, IL 61450 • 1,471
Laie, HI 96762 • 4,643
La Junta, CO 81050 • 8,338
Lake, CA • 36,366
Lake, CO • 8,830
Lake, FL • 104,870
Lake, IL • 440,372
Lake, IN • 522,965
Lake, MI • 7,711
Lake, MN • 13,043
Lake, MT • 19,056
Lake, OH • 212,801
Lake, OR • 7,532
Lake, SD • 10,724
Lake, TN • 7,455
Lake Alfred, FL 33850 • 3,134
Lake Arrowhead, CA 92352 • 2,500
Lake Arthur, LA 70549 • 3,615
Lake Barcroft, VA 22041 • 1,800
Lake Bluff, IL 60044 • 4,434
Lake Butler, FL 32054 • 1,830
Lake Carmel, NY 10512 • 7,295
Lake Carroll, FL 33618 • 13,012
Lake Charles, LA 70601-29 • 76,400
Lake City, AR 72437 • 1,842
Lake City, FL 32055 • 9,000
Lake City, IA 51449 • 2,006
Lake City, MN 55041 • 4,505
Lake City, PA 16423 • 2,384
Lake City, SC 29560 • 6,731
Lake City, TN 37769 • 2,378
Lake Crystal, MN 56055 • 2,078
Lake Delta, NY 13440 • 1,980
Lake Elmo, MN 55042 • 5,296
Lake Elsinore, CA 92330 • 5,982
Lake Erie Beach, NY 14006 • 4,625
Lakefield, MN 56150 • 1,845
Lake Forest, FL 33023 • 5,400
Lake Forest, IL 60045 • 15,245
Lake Geneva, WI 53147 • 5,612
Lake Grove, NY 11755 • 9,692
Lake Havasu City, AZ 86403 • 17,749
Lake Helen, FL 32744 • 2,047
Lakehurst, NJ 08733 • 2,908
Lake in the Hills, IL 60102 • 5,651
Lake Jackson, TX 77566 • 22,200
Lake Katrine, NY 12449 • 2,011
Lakeland, FL 33801-09 • 65,500
Lakeland, GA 31635 • 2,647
Lakeland Highlands, FL 33801 • 10,426
Lake Lorraine, FL 32569 • 5,427
Lake Magdalene, FL 33612 • 13,331
Lake Mary, FL 32746 • 2,853
Lake Mills, IA 50450 • 2,281
Lake Mills, WI 53551 • 3,670
Lakemore, OH 44250 • 2,744
Lake Odessa, MI 48849 • 2,171
Lake Of The Woods, MN • 3,764
Lake Orion, MI 48035 • 2,907
Lake Oswego, OR 97034-35 • 22,933
Lake Park, FL 33403 • 7,000
Lake Placid, NY 12946 • 2,490
Lakeport, CA 95453 • 3,675
Lake Providence, LA 71254 • 6,361
Lake Ridge, VA 22191 • 11,072
Lake Ronkonkoma, NY 11779 • 16,000
Lake Shore, MD 21122 • 2,100
Lakeside, CA 92040 • 23,921
Lakeside, FL 32073 • 10,534
Lakeside, OR 97449 • 1,453
Lakeside, VA 23228 • 11,400
Lakeside Park, KY 41017 • 3,062
Lake Station, IN 46405 • 15,083
Lake Stevens, WA 98258 • 1,660
Lakeview, GA 30741 • 5,403
Lake View, NY 14085 • 1,460
Lakeview, NY 11552 • 5,276
Lakeview, OR 97630 • 2,770
Lake Villa, IL 60046 • 1,913
Lake Village, AR 71653 • 3,088
Lakeville, CT 06039 • 1,800
Lakeville, MA 02346 • 1,948
Lakeville, MN 55044 • 14,790
Lake Wales, FL 33853 • 8,466
Lake Wissota, WI 54729 • 1,788
Lakewood, CA 90712-16 • 78,000
Lakewood, CO 80215 • 123,900
Lakewood, IA 50211 • 1,950
Lakewood, NJ 08701 • 22,863
Lakewood, NY 14750 • 3,941
Lakewood, OH 44107 • 59,700
Lakewood Center, WA 98499 • 59,200
Lake Worth, FL 33460-67 • 30,300
Lake Zurich, IL 60047 • 10,574
Lakin, KS 67860 • 1,823
Lamar, CO 81052 • 7,713
Lamar, MO 64759 • 4,053
Lamar, AL • 16,453
Lamar, GA • 12,215
Lamar, MS • 23,821
Lamar, TX • 42,156
La Marque, TX 77568 • 15,372
Lamb, TX • 18,669
Lambert, MS 38643 • 1,624
Lambertville, MI 48144 • 6,341
Lambertville, NJ 08530 • 4,044
La Mesa, CA 92041-44 • 54,000
Lamesa, TX 79331 • 11,790
La Mirada, CA 90638 • 43,100
Lamoille, VT • 16,767
Lamoni, IA 50140 • 2,705
Lamont, CA 93241 • 9,616
La Moure, ND • 6,473
Lampasas, TX 76550 • 6,165
Lampasas, TX • 12,005
Lanai City, HI 96763 • 2,092
Lanark, IL 61046 • 1,483
Lancaster, CA 93534-39 • 58,300
Lancaster, KY 40444 • 3,365
Lancaster, NH 03584 • 2,134
Lancaster, NY 14086 • 13,056
Lancaster, OH 43130 • 35,500
Lancaster, PA 17601-99 • 57,300
Lancaster, SC 29720 • 9,703
Lancaster, TX 75146 • 14,807
Lancaster, WI 53813 • 4,076
Lancaster, NE • 192,884
Lancaster, PA • 362,346
Lancaster, SC • 53,361
Lancaster, VA • 10,129
Lander, WY 82520 • 8,189
Lander, NV • 4,076
Landess, IN 46944 • 1,500
Landis, NC 28088 • 2,092
Landover, MD 20784 • 5,374
Landrum, SC 29356 • 2,141
Lane, KS • 2,472
Lane, OR • 275,226
Lanett, AL 36863 • 5,629
Langdon, ND 58249 • 2,335
Langhorne, PA 19047 • 1,697
Langlade, WI • 19,978
Langley, SC 29834 • 1,714
Langley Park, MD 20787 • 11,100
Lanham, MD 20706 • 7,300
Lanier, GA • 5,654
Lansdale, PA 19446 • 17,700
Lansdowne, MD 21227 • 10,000
Lansdowne, PA 19050 • 11,891
L'Anse, MI 49946 • 2,500
Lansford, PA 18232 • 4,466
Lansing, IL 60438 • 28,400
Lansing, KS 66043 • 5,307
Lansing, MI 48901-99 • 130,700
Lantana, FL 33462 • 8,048
La Palma, CA 90623 • 15,399
La Paz, AZ • 12,557
Lapeer, MI 48446 • 6,198
Lapeer, MI • 70,038
Lapel, IN 46051 • 1,881
La Place, LA 70068 • 16,112
La Plata, MD 20646 • 2,484
La Plata, CO • 27,195
La Porte, IN 46350 • 21,800
La Porte, TX 77571 • 19,226
La Porte, IN • 108,632
La Porte City, IA 50651 • 2,324
La Puente, CA 91744-49 • 33,700
Laramie, WY 82070 • 25,300
Laramie, WY • 68,649
Larchmont, NY 10538 • 6,308
Larchmont North, NY 10538 • 11,240
Laredo, TX 78040-44 • 110,500
Largo, FL 34640-44 • 65,800
Larimer, CO • 149,184
Larimore, ND 58251 • 1,524
La Riviera, CA 95826 • 10,906
Larkspur, CA 94939 • 11,064
Larksville, PA 18704 • 4,410
Larned, KS 67550 • 4,811
Larose, LA 70373 • 5,234
Larue, KY • 11,922
La Salle, CO 80645 • 1,929
La Salle, IL 61301 • 10,000
La Salle, IL • 112,033
La Salle, LA • 17,004
La Salle, TX • 5,514
Las Animas, CO 81054 • 2,818
Las Animas, CO • 14,897
Las Cruces, NM 88001-08 • 54,000
Lassen, CA • 21,661
Las Vegas, NV 89101-99 • 191,900
Las Vegas, NM 87701 • 14,322
Latah, ID • 28,749
Latham, NY 12110 • 11,182
Lathrop, MO 64465 • 1,732
Latimer, OK • 9,840
Latrobe, PA 15650 • 10,000
Latta, SC 29565 • 1,804
Lauderdale, AL • 80,546
Lauderdale, MS • 77,285
Lauderdale, TN • 24,555
Lauderdale Lakes, FL 33313 • 28,400
Lauderhill, FL 33313 • 43,900
Laurel, DE 19956 • 3,052
Laurel, FL 34272 • 1,500
Laurel, MD 20707-08 • 11,900
Laurel, MS 39440 • 21,200
Laurel, MT 59044 • 5,498
Laurel, VA 23060 • 3,000
Laurel, KY • 38,982
Laurel Bay, SC 29902 • 5,238
Laureldale, PA 19605 • 4,047
Laurel Hill, NC 28351 • 2,314
Laurence Harbor, NJ 08879 • 4,000
Laurens, IA 50554 • 1,606
Laurens, SC 29360 • 10,587
Laurens, GA • 36,990
Laurens, SC • 52,214
Laurinburg, NC 28352 • 11,480
Laurium, MI 49913 • 2,678
Lavaca, TX • 19,004
La Vale, MD 21502 • 5,500
Lavallette, NJ 08735 • 2,072
La Vergne, TN 37086 • 6,668
La Verne, CA 91750 • 23,508
Laverne, OK 73848 • 1,563
La Vista, GA 30329 • 4,900
La Vista, NE 68128 • 9,588
Lavonia, GA 30553 • 2,024
Lawndale, CA 90260 • 26,600
Lawnside, NJ 08045 • 3,042
Lawrence, IN 46226 • 26,100
Lawrence, KS 66044-46 • 56,800
Lawrence, MA 01840-45 • 65,400
Lawrence, NY 11559 • 6,175
Lawrence, AL • 30,170
Lawrence, AR • 18,447
Lawrence, IL • 17,807
Lawrence, IN • 42,472
Lawrence, KY • 14,121
Lawrence, MS • 12,518
Lawrence, MO • 28,973
Lawrence, OH • 63,849
Lawrence, PA • 107,150
Lawrence, SD • 18,339
Lawrence, TN • 34,110
Lawrenceburg, IN 47025 • 4,403
Lawrenceburg, KY 40342 • 5,167
Lawrenceburg, TN 38464 • 10,184
Lawrence Park, PA 16511 • 4,584
Lawrenceville, GA 30245 • 13,600
Lawrenceville, IL 62439 • 5,652
Lawrenceville, NJ 08648 • 2,110
Lawrenceville, VA 23868 • 1,484
Lawson, MO 64062 • 1,743
Lawsonia, MD 21817 • 1,687
Lawton, MI 49065 • 1,558
Lawton, OK 73501-07 • 87,800
Layton, UT 84041 • 33,500
Lea, NM • 55,993
Leachville, AR 72438 • 1,882
Lead, SD 57754 • 4,330
Leadville, CO 80461 • 3,879
League City, TX 77573 • 16,578
Leake, MS • 18,790
Lealman, FL 33714 • 19,873
Leavenworth, KS 66048 • 35,800
Leavenworth, WA 98826 • 1,522
Leavenworth, KS • 54,809
Leavittsburg, OH 44430 • 2,220
Leawood, KS 66206 • 13,360
Lebanon, IL 62254 • 3,245
Lebanon, IN 46052 • 11,456
Lebanon, KY 40033 • 6,590
Lebanon, MO 65536 • 9,507
Lebanon, NH 03766 • 11,400
Lebanon, OH 45036 • 9,636
Lebanon, OR 97355 • 10,413
Lebanon, PA 17042 • 26,600
Lebanon, TN 37087 • 14,423
Lebanon, VA 24266 • 3,206
Lebanon, PA • 108,582
Lebanon Junction, KY 40150 • 1,581
Le Center, MN 56057 • 1,967
Le Claire, IA 52753 • 2,899
Lecompte, LA 71346 • 1,661
Lee, MA 01238 • 2,140
Lee, AL • 76,283
Lee, AR • 15,539
Lee, FL • 205,266
Lee, GA • 11,684
Lee, IL • 36,328
Lee, IA • 43,106
Lee, KY • 7,754
Lee, MS • 57,061
Lee, NC • 36,718
Lee, SC • 18,929
Lee, TX • 10,952
Lee, VA • 25,956
Leechburg, PA 15656 • 2,682
Leeds, AL 35094 • 9,378
Leelanau, MI • 14,007
Lee Park, PA 18702 • 3,800
Leesburg, FL 32748-49 • 14,100
Leesburg, VA 22075 • 9,788
Lees Summit, MO 64063 • 33,700
Leesville, LA 71446 • 9,054
Leesville, SC 29070 • 2,296
Leetonia, OH 44431 • 2,121
Leetsdale, PA 15056 • 1,604
Leflore, MS • 41,525
Le Flore, OK • 40,698
Le Grand, CA 95333 • 1,500
Lehi, UT 84043 • 6,848
Lehigh, PA • 272,349
Lehigh Acres, FL 33936 • 9,604
Lehighton, PA 18235 • 5,826
Leicester, MA 01524 • 3,200
Leipsic, OH 45856 • 2,171
Leisure City, FL 33033 • 17,905
Leitchfield, KY 42754 • 4,533
Leland, MS 38756 • 6,667
Le Mars, IA 51031 • 8,276
Lemay, MO 63125 • 36,700
Lemhi, ID • 7,460
Lemmon, SD 57638 • 1,871
Lemmon Valley, NV 89501 • 2,000
Lemon Grove, CA 92045 • 20,780
Lemont, IL 60439 • 5,640
Lemont, PA 16851 • 2,613
Lemoore, CA 93245 • 8,832
Lemoore Station, CA 93245 • 5,888
Lena, IL 61048 • 2,295
Lenawee, MI • 89,948
Lenexa, KS 66215 • 25,400
Lennox, CA 90304 • 18,445
Lennox, SD 57039 • 1,827
Lenoir, NC 28645 • 14,600
Lenoir, NC • 59,819
Lenoir City, TN 37771 • 5,777
Lenox, MA 01240 • 2,668
Leominster, MA 01453 • 35,200
Leon, IA 50144 • 2,094
Leon, FL • 148,655
Leon, TX • 9,594
Leonardo, NJ 07737 • 3,720
Leonardtown, MD 20650 • 1,448
Leonia, NJ 07605 • 8,027
Leon Valley, TX 78238 • 9,088
Leoti, KS 67861 • 1,869
Lepanto, AR 72354 • 1,964
Le Roy, IL 61752 • 2,870
Le Roy, NY 14482 • 4,900
Leslie, MI 49251 • 2,110
Leslie, KY • 14,882
Le Sueur, MN 56058 • 3,763
Le Sueur, MN • 23,434
Letcher, KY • 30,687
Leto, FL 33614 • 9,003
Levelland, TX 79336-38 • 13,809
Levittown, NY 11756 • 57,300
Levittown, PA 19058 • 17,420
Levy, FL • 19,870
Lewes, DE 19958 • 2,197
Lewis, ID • 4,118
Lewis, KY • 14,545
Lewis, MO • 10,901
Lewis, NY • 25,035
Lewis, TN • 9,700
Lewis, WA • 56,025
Lewis, WV • 18,813
Lewis and Clark, MT • 43,039
Lewisburg, OH 45338 • 1,450
Lewisburg, PA 17837 • 5,407
Lewisburg, TN 37091 • 8,760
Lewisburg, WV 24901 • 3,065
Lewisport, KY 42351 • 1,832
Lewiston, ID 83501 • 28,700
Lewiston, ME 04240 • 39,600
Lewiston, NY 14092 • 3,326
Lewiston, UT 84320 • 1,438
Lewistown, IL 61542 • 2,758
Lewistown, MT 59457 • 7,104
Lewistown, PA 17044 • 9,500
Lewisville, AR 71845 • 1,476
Lewisville, TX 75067 • 28,400
Lexington, IL 61753 • 1,806
Lexington, KY 40501-99 • 213,000
Lexington, MA 02173 • 29,000
Lexington, MS 39095 • 2,628
Lexington, MO 64067 • 5,063
Lexington, NE 68850 • 7,040
Lexington, NC 27292 • 16,600
Lexington, OH 44904 • 3,823
Lexington, OK 73051 • 1,731
Lexington, SC 29072 • 2,131
Lexington, TN 38351 • 5,934
Lexington, VA 24450 • 7,292
Lexington, WA 98626 • 1,907
Lexington, SC • 140,353
Lexington Park, MD 20653 • 10,361
Libby, MT 59923 • 2,748
Liberal, KS 67901 • 15,900
Liberty, IN 47353 • 1,844
Liberty, KY 42539 • 2,206
Liberty, MO 64068 • 16,789
Liberty, NY 12754 • 4,293
Liberty, NC 27298 • 1,997
Liberty, SC 29657 • 3,167
Liberty, TX 77575 • 7,945
Liberty, FL • 4,260
Liberty, GA • 37,583
Liberty, MT • 2,329
Liberty, TX • 47,088
Liberty Acres, CA 90250 • 4,700
Liberty Lake, WA 99019 • 1,599
Libertyville, IL 60048 • 17,900
Licking, OH • 120,981
Lighthouse Point, FL 33064 • 11,488
Ligonier, IN 46767 • 3,134
Ligonier, PA 15658 • 1,917
Lihue, HI 96766 • 4,500
Lilbourn, MO 63862 • 1,463
Lilburn, GA 30247 • 3,765
Lillington, NC 27546 • 1,948
Lilly, PA 15938 • 1,462
Lima, NY 14485 • 2,025
Lima, OH 45801-09 • 47,500
Limestone, AL • 46,005
Limestone, TX • 20,224
Limon, CO 80828 • 1,805
Lincoln, AL 35096 • 2,599
Lincoln, CA 95648 • 4,132
Lincoln, IL 62656 • 16,327
Lincoln, KS 67455 • 1,599
Lincoln, ME 04457 • 3,524
Lincoln, MA 01773 • 2,860
Lincoln, NE 68501-99 • 185,300
Lincoln, AR • 13,369
Lincoln, CO • 4,663
Lincoln, GA • 6,716
Lincoln, ID • 3,436
Lincoln, KS • 4,145
Lincoln, KY • 19,053
Lincoln, LA • 39,763
Lincoln, ME • 25,691
Lincoln, MN • 8,207
Lincoln, MS • 30,174
Lincoln, MO • 22,193
Lincoln, MT • 17,752
Lincoln, NE • 36,455
Lincoln, NV • 3,732
Lincoln, NM • 10,997
Lincoln, NC • 42,372
Lincoln, OK • 26,601
Lincoln, OR • 35,264
Lincoln, SD • 13,942
Lincoln, TN • 26,483
Lincoln, WA • 9,604
Lincoln, WV • 23,675
Lincoln, WI • 26,555
Lincoln, WY • 12,177
Lincoln Acres, CA 92047 • 1,800
Lincoln City, OR 97367 • 5,469
Lincoln Heights, OH 45215 • 5,259
Lincoln Park, CO 81212 • 3,426
Lincoln Park, GA 30286 • 1,755
Lincoln Park, MI 48146 • 43,200
Lincoln Park, NJ 07035 • 8,806
Lincolnshire, IL 60069 • 4,151
Lincolnton, NC 28092 • 5,799
Lincoln Village, CA 95207 • 6,476
Lincoln Village, OH 43228 • 10,548
Lincolnwood, IL 60645 • 11,921
Lincroft, NJ 07738 • 4,740
Linda, CA 95901 • 10,225
Lindale, GA 30147 • 2,958
Lindale, TX 75771 • 2,180
Linden, AL 36748 • 2,773
Linden, MI 48451 • 2,174
Linden, NJ 07036 • 37,200
Linden, TX 75563 • 2,443
Lindenhurst, IL 60046 • 7,270
Lindenhurst, NY 11757 • 27,000
Lindenwold, NJ 08021 • 18,196
Lindgren Acres, FL 33177 • 11,986
Lindon, UT 84062 • 2,796
Lindsay, CA 93247 • 6,936
Lindsay, OK 73052 • 3,454
Lindsborg, KS 67456 • 3,155
Lindstrom, MN 55045 • 1,972
Lineville, AL 36266 • 2,257
Linglestown, PA 17112 • 3,700
Linn, IA • 169,775
Linn, KS • 8,234
Linn, MO • 15,495
Linn, OR • 89,495
Lino Lakes, MN 55014 • 5,587
Linthicum Heights, MD 21090 • 7,457

Linton, IN 47441 • 6,315
Linton, ND 58552 • 1,561
Linwood, NJ 08221 • 6,144
Lipscomb, AL 35020 • 3,741
Lipscomb, TX • 3,766
Lisbon, IA 52253 • 1,458
Lisbon, ND 58054 • 2,283
Lisbon, OH 44432 • 3,159
Lisbon Falls, ME 04252 • 4,370
Lisle, IL 60532 • 16,030
Litchfield, CT 06759 • 1,489
Litchfield, IL 62056 • 7,204
Litchfield, MN 55355 • 5,904
Litchfield, CT • 156,769
Litchfield Park, AZ 85340 • 3,708
Lithia Springs, GA 30057 • 9,145
Lithonia, GA 30058 • 2,637
Lititz, PA 17543 • 7,590
Little Canada, MN 55110 • 7,102
Little Chute, WI 54140 • 7,907
Little Falls, MN 56345 • 7,250
Little Falls, NJ 07424 • 11,496
Little Falls, NY 13365 • 6,156
Little Ferry, NJ 07643 • 9,399
Littlefield, TX 79339 • 7,409
Little River, AR • 13,952
Little Rock, AR 72201-99 • 184,500
Little Silver, NJ 07739 • 5,548
Littlestown, PA 17340 • 2,870
Littleton, CO 80120-27 • 33,600
Littleton, MA 01460 • 3,109
Littleton, NH 03561 • 4,480
Live Oak, CA 95062 • 10,000
Live Oak, CA 95953 • 3,103
Live Oak, FL 32060 • 6,732
Live Oak, TX 78233 • 8,183
Live Oak, TX • 9,606
Live Oak Manor, LA 70094 • 1,500
Livermore, CA 94550 • 54,100
Livermore, KY 42352 • 1,672
Livermore Falls, ME 04254 • 2,441
Livingston, AL 35470 • 3,187
Livingston, CA 95334 • 5,326
Livingston, MT 59047 • 6,994
Livingston, NJ 07039 • 28,500
Livingston, TN 38570 • 3,504
Livingston, TX 77351 • 4,928
Livingston, IL • 41,381
Livingston, KY • 9,219
Livingston, LA • 58,806
Livingston, MI • 100,289
Livingston, MO • 15,739
Livingston, NY • 57,006
Livingston Manor, NY 12758 • 1,436
Livonia, MI 48150-54 • 100,100
Llano, TX 78643 • 3,071
Llano, TX • 10,144
Lloyd Harbor, NY 11743 • 3,405
Loch Lomond, VA 22110 • 3,608
Lockhart, FL 32810 • 10,571
Lockhart, TX 78644 • 7,953
Lock Haven, PA 17745 • 9,300
Lockland, OH 45215 • 4,292
Lockney, TX 79241 • 2,334
Lockport, IL 60441 • 9,192
Lockport, LA 70374 • 2,424
Lockport, NY 14094 • 24,500
Lockwood, MT 59101 • 1,600
Locust, NC 28097 • 1,590
Locust Grove, GA 30248 • 1,479
Locust Grove, NY 11791 • 9,670
Lodi, CA 95240 • 43,300
Lodi, NJ 07644 • 23,600
Lodi, OH 44254 • 2,942
Lodi, WI 53555 • 1,959
Logan, IA 51546 • 1,540
Logan, OH 43138 • 6,557
Logan, UT 84321 • 30,000
Logan, WV 25601 • 2,800
Logan, AR • 20,144
Logan, CO • 19,800
Logan, IL • 31,802
Logan, KS • 3,478
Logan, KY • 24,138
Logan, NE • 983
Logan, ND • 3,493
Logan, OH • 39,155
Logan, OK • 26,881
Logan, WV • 50,679
Logansport, IN 46947 • 17,800
Logansport, LA 71049 • 1,565
Loganville, GA 30249 • 1,841
Lolo, MT 59847 • 2,418
Loma Linda, CA 92354 • 10,694
Lombard, IL 60148 • 39,400
Lomira, WI 53048 • 1,446
Lomita, CA 90717 • 18,807
Lompoc, CA 93436 • 30,900
London, KY 40741 • 4,002
London, OH 43140 • 6,958
Londontowne, MD 21037 • 3,500
Lone Grove, OK 73443 • 3,369
Lone Pine, CA 93545 • 1,684
Long, GA • 4,524
Long Beach, CA 90801-99 • 400,000
Long Beach, IN 46360 • 2,262
Long Beach, MS 39560 • 14,199
Long Beach, NY 11561 • 34,200
Longboat Key, FL 34228 • 4,843
Long Branch, NJ 07740 • 30,600
Long Lake, IL 60041 • 2,201
Longmeadow, MA 01106 • 16,301
Longmont, CO 80501 • 50,900
Long Prairie, MN 56347 • 2,859
Long Valley, NJ 07853 • 1,682
Long View, NC 28601 • 3,587
Longview, TX 75601-08 • 75,000
Longview, WA 98632 • 29,400
Longwood, FL 32750 • 10,029
Lonoke, AR 72086 • 4,128
Lonoke, AR • 34,518
Lonsdale, RI 02865 • 3,850
Loogootee, IN 47553 • 3,100
Lookout Mountain, TN 37350 • 1,886
Lorain, OH 44052-55 • 73,100
Lorain, OH • 274,909
Lordsburg, NM 88045 • 3,195
Loretto, TN 38469 • 1,612
Loris, SC 29569 • 2,193
Lorton, VA 22079 • 5,813
Los Alamitos, CA 90720 • 11,529
Los Alamos, NM 87544 • 11,039
Los Alamos, NM • 17,599
Los Altos, CA 94022 • 28,500
Los Altos Hills, CA 94022 • 7,421
Los Angeles, CA 90001-99 • 3,298,200
Los Angeles, CA • 7,477,503
Los Banos, CA 93635 • 10,341
Los Fresnos, TX 78566 • 2,173
Los Gatos, CA 95030 • 28,300
Los Lunas, NM 87031 • 3,525
Los Nietos, CA 90606 • 7,100
Los Osos, CA 93402 • 8,000
Los Padillas, NM 87105 • 2,400
Los Ranchos de Albuquerque, NM 87107 • 2,857
Loudon, TN 37774 • 4,183
Loudon, TN • 28,553
Loudonville, NY 12211 • 11,480
Loudonville, OH 44842 • 2,945
Loudoun, VA • 57,427
Louisa, KY 41230 • 1,832
Louisa, IA • 12,055
Louisa, VA • 17,825
Louisburg, KS 66053 • 1,744
Louisburg, NC 27549 • 3,238
Louisiana, MO 63353 • 4,261
Louisville, CO 80027 • 5,593
Louisville, GA 30434 • 2,823
Louisville, KY 40201-99 • 287,400
Louisville, MS 39339 • 7,323
Louisville, OH 44641 • 7,996
Loup, NE • 859
Love, OK • 7,469
Loveland, CO 80537-39 • 37,000
Loveland, OH 45140 • 9,106
Loveland Park, OH 45140 • 1,653
Lovell, WY 82431 • 2,447
Lovelock, NV 89419 • 1,680
Loves Park, IL 61111 • 13,921
Loving, TX • 91
Lovington, NM 88260 • 9,727
Lowell, IN 46356 • 5,827
Lowell, MA 01850-54 • 93,600
Lowell, MI 49331 • 3,707
Lowell, NC 28098 • 2,917
Lowellville, OH 44436 • 1,558
Lower Burrell, PA 15068 • 13,200
Lower Merion Township, PA 19003 • 60,200
Lower Moreland Township, PA 19006 • 12,472
Lower Paia, HI 96779 • 1,500
Lower Southampton Township, PA 19047 • 18,305
Lowndes, AL • 13,253
Lowndes, GA • 67,972
Lowndes, MS • 57,304
Lowville, NY 13367 • 3,364
Lubbock, TX 79401-99 • 180,200
Lubbock, TX • 211,651
Lucas, IA • 10,313
Lucas, OH • 471,741
Lucasville, OH 45648 • 3,349
Luce, MI • 6,659
Lucedale, MS 39452 • 2,429
Lucerne, CA 95458 • 1,767
Ludington, MI 49431 • 8,937
Ludlow, KY 41016 • 4,959
Ludlow, MA 01056 • 18,150
Lufkin, TX 75901 • 32,700
Lugoff, SC 29078 • 2,939
Luling, LA 70070 • 4,006
Luling, TX 78648 • 5,039
Lumberton, MS 39455 • 2,217
Lumberton, NC 28358 • 19,600
Lumpkin, GA • 10,762
Luna, NM • 15,585
Luna Pier, MI 48157 • 1,443
Lunenburg, MA 01462 • 1,789
Lunenburg, VA • 12,124
Luray, VA 22835 • 3,584
Lusk, WY 82225 • 1,650
Lutcher, LA 70071 • 4,730
Lutherville-Timonium, MD 21093 • 16,871
Lutz, FL 33549 • 5,555
Luverne, AL 36049 • 2,639
Luverne, MN 56156 • 4,568
Luxora, AR 72358 • 1,739
Luzerne, PA 18709 • 3,703
Luzerne, PA • 343,079
Lycoming, PA • 118,416
Lyford, TX 78569 • 1,618
Lykens, PA 17048 • 2,181
Lyman, SC 29365 • 2,194
Lyman, WY 82937 • 2,284
Lyman, SD • 3,864
Lynbrook, NY 11563 • 20,424
Lynch, KY 40855 • 1,614
Lynchburg, VA 24501-15 • 69,100
Lyncourt, NY 13208 • 5,129
Lynden, WA 98264 • 4,022
Lyndhurst, NJ 07071 • 20,326
Lyndhurst, OH 44124 • 18,092
Lyndon, KY 40222 • 4,267
Lyndora, PA 16045 • 3,000
Lynn, MA 01901-08 • 80,400
Lynn, TX • 8,605
Lynne Acres, MD 21207 • 7,700
Lynnfield, MA 01940 • 11,267
Lynn Garden, TN 37665 • 7,213
Lynn Haven, FL 32444 • 6,239
Lynnwood, WA 98036-37 • 24,200
Lynwood, CA 90262 • 55,300
Lyon, IA • 12,896
Lyon, KS • 35,108
Lyon, KY • 6,490
Lyon, MN • 25,207
Lyon, NV • 13,594
Lyons, GA 30436 • 4,203
Lyons, IL 60534 • 9,925
Lyons, KS 67554 • 4,134
Lyons, NY 14489 • 4,160
Lytle, TX 78052 • 1,920

M

Mabank, TX 75147 • 1,443
Mableton, GA 30059 • 21,390
Mabscott, WV 25871 • 1,668
McAdoo, PA 18237 • 2,940
McAlester, OK 74501 • 18,800
McAllen, TX 78501-04 • 83,400
McAlmont, AR 72117 • 1,800
McAlpine, MD 21043 • 2,500
McArthur, OH 45651 • 1,912
McCall, ID 83638 • 2,188
McCamey, TX 79752 • 2,436
McCandless, PA 15237 • 25,300
McClain, OK • 20,291
MacClenny, FL 32063 • 3,851
McCloud, CA 96057 • 1,656
McColl, SC 29570 • 2,677
McComb, MS 39648 • 12,700
McComb, OH 45858 • 1,608
McCone, MT • 2,702
McConnelsville, OH 43756 • 2,018
McCook, NE 69001 • 8,500
McCook, SD • 6,444
McCormick, SC 29835 • 1,725
McCormick, SC • 7,797
McCracken, KY • 61,310
McCreary, KY • 15,634
McCrory, AR 72101 • 1,942
McCulloch, TX • 8,735
McCurtain, OK • 36,151
McDonald, MO • 14,917
McDonough, GA 30253 • 2,778
McDonough, IL • 37,467
McDowell, NC • 35,135
McDowell, WV • 49,899
McDuffie, GA • 18,546
Macedonia, OH 44056 • 6,571
McFarland, CA 93250 • 5,151
McFarland, WI 53558 • 3,783
McGehee, AR 71654 • 5,671
McGregor, TX 76657 • 4,513
McHenry, IL 60050 • 13,536
McHenry, IL • 147,897
McHenry, ND • 7,858
Machesney Park, IL 61111 • 19,514
McIntosh, GA • 8,046
McIntosh, ND • 4,800
McIntosh, OK • 15,562
McKean, PA • 50,635
McKeesport, PA 15130-35 • 28,100
McKees Rocks, PA 15136 • 8,742
McKenzie, TN 38201 • 5,459
McKenzie, ND • 7,132
Mackinac, MI • 10,178
McKinley, NM • 56,536
McKinleyville, CA 95521 • 7,772
McKinney, TX 75069 • 16,256
McLean, VA 22101-06 • 24,000
McLean, IL • 119,149
McLean, KY • 10,090
McLean, ND • 12,383
McLeansboro, IL 62859 • 2,960
McLennan, TX • 170,755
McLeod, MN • 29,657
McLoud, OK 74851 • 4,061
McMechen, WV 26040 • 2,402
McMinn, TN • 41,878
McMinnville, OR 97128 • 14,614
McMinnville, TN 37110 • 11,796
McMullen, TX • 789
McNairy, TN • 22,525
McNulty, OR 97051 • 1,805
Macomb, IL 61455 • 18,900
Macomb, MI • 694,600
Macon, GA 31201-99 • 120,700
Macon, MS 39341 • 2,396
Macon, MO 63552 • 5,680
Macon, AL • 26,829
Macon, GA • 14,003
Macon, IL • 131,375
Macon, MO • 16,313
Macon, NC • 20,178
Macon, TN • 15,700
Macoupin, IL • 49,384
McPherson, KS 67460 • 11,753
McPherson, KS • 26,855
McPherson, NE • 593
McPherson, SD • 4,027
McRae, GA 31055 • 3,409
McSherrystown, PA 17344 • 2,764
Macungie, PA 18062 • 1,899
Madawaska, ME 04756 • 4,165
Madeira, OH 45243 • 9,341
Madelia, MN 56062 • 2,130
Madera, CA 93637-39 • 26,600
Madera, CA • 63,116
Madill, OK 73446 • 3,173
Madison, AL 35758 • 4,057
Madison, CT 06443 • 2,069
Madison, FL 32340 • 3,487
Madison, GA 30650 • 2,954
Madison, IL 62060 • 5,302
Madison, IN 47250 • 12,000
Madison, ME 04950 • 2,788
Madison, MN 56256 • 2,212
Madison, MS 39110 • 2,241
Madison, NE 68748 • 1,950
Madison, NJ 07940 • 15,357
Madison, NC 27025 • 2,806
Madison, OH 44057 • 2,291
Madison, SD 57042 • 6,210
Madison, WV 25130 • 3,228
Madison, WI 53701-99 • 176,400
Madison, AL • 196,966
Madison, AR • 11,373
Madison, FL • 14,894
Madison, GA • 17,747
Madison, ID • 19,480
Madison, IL • 247,661
Madison, IN • 139,336
Madison, IA • 12,597
Madison, KY • 53,352
Madison, LA • 15,975
Madison, MS • 41,613
Madison, MO • 10,725
Madison, MT • 5,448
Madison, NE • 31,382
Madison, NY • 65,150
Madison, NC • 16,827
Madison, OH • 33,004
Madison, TN • 74,546
Madison, TX • 10,649
Madison, VA • 10,232
Madison Heights, MI 48071 • 34,800
Madison Heights, VA 24572 • 14,146
Madisonville, KY 42431 • 17,300
Madisonville, TN 37354 • 2,904
Madisonville, TX 77864 • 3,660
Madras, OR 97741 • 2,323
Madrid, IA 50156 • 2,281
Maeser, UT 84078 • 2,216
Magee, MS 39111 • 3,497
Magna, UT 84044 • 13,138
Magnolia, AR 71753 • 12,000
Magnolia, MS 39652 • 2,461
Magnolia, NJ 08049 • 4,881
Magoffin, KY • 13,515
Mahanoy City, PA 17948 • 6,167
Mahaska, IA • 22,867
Mahnomen, MN • 5,535
Mahomet, IL 61853 • 1,986
Mahoning, OH • 289,487
Mahopac, NY 10541 • 7,681
Mahwah, NJ 07430 • 7,500
Maiden, NC 28650 • 2,574
Maili, HI 96792 • 5,026
Maitland, FL 32751 • 8,763
Major, OK • 8,772
Makaha, HI 96792 • 6,582
Makakilo City, HI 96706 • 7,691
Makawao, HI 96768 • 2,900
Malad City, ID 83252 • 1,915
Malaga, NJ 08328 • 2,140
Malakoff, TX 75148 • 2,082
Malden, MA 02148 • 53,700
Malden, MO 63863 • 6,096
Malheur, OR • 26,896
Malibu, CA 90265 • 10,000
Malone, NY 12953 • 7,668
Malta, MT 59538 • 2,367
Malvern, AR 72104 • 10,163
Malvern, PA 19355 • 2,999
Malverne, NY 11565 • 9,262
Mamaroneck, NY 10543 • 17,616
Mammoth, AZ 85618 • 1,906
Mammoth Lakes, CA 93546 • 3,000
Mamou, LA 70554 • 3,194
Manahawkin, NJ 08050 • 1,469
Manasquan, NJ 08736 • 5,354
Manassas, VA 22110-11 • 19,400
Manassas Park, VA 22111 • 6,524
Manatee, FL • 148,442
Mancelona, MI 49659 • 1,432
Manchester, CT 06040 • 50,100
Manchester, GA 31816 • 4,796
Manchester, IA 52057 • 4,942
Manchester, KY 40962 • 1,838
Manchester, MD 21102 • 1,830
Manchester, MA 01944 • 5,424
Manchester, MI 48158 • 1,686
Manchester, MO 63011 • 6,351
Manchester, NH 03101-99 • 100,700
Manchester, NY 14504 • 1,698
Manchester, OH 45144 • 2,313
Manchester, PA 17345 • 2,027
Manchester, TN 37355 • 7,250
Manchester Center, VT 05255 • 1,719
Mandan, ND 58554 • 15,513
Mandeville, LA 70448 • 6,076
Mangum, OK 73554 • 3,833
Manhasset, NY 11030 • 8,485
Manhattan, KS 66502 • 33,200
Manhattan Beach, CA 90266 • 34,800
Manheim, PA 17545 • 5,015
Manila, AR 72442 • 2,553
Manistee, MI 49660 • 7,665
Manistee, MI • 23,019
Manistique, MI 49854 • 3,962
Manito, IL 61546 • 1,869
Manitou Springs, CO 80829 • 4,475
Manitowoc, WI 54220 • 32,200
Manitowoc, WI • 82,918
Mankato, MN 56001 • 27,800
Manlius, NY 13104 • 5,241
Manly, IA 50456 • 1,496
Mannford, OK 74044 • 1,610
Manning, IA 51455 • 1,609
Manning, SC 29102 • 4,746
Mannington, WV 26582 • 3,036
Manomet, MA 02345 • 1,500
Manorhaven, NY 11050 • 5,384
Mansfield, LA 71052 • 6,485
Mansfield, MA 02048 • 6,786
Mansfield, OH 44901-99 • 52,500
Mansfield, PA 16933 • 3,322
Mansfield, TX 76063 • 8,279
Manson, IA 50563 • 1,924
Mansura, LA 71350 • 2,074
Manteca, CA 95336 • 24,925
Manteno, IL 60950 • 3,155
Manti, UT 84642 • 2,080
Mantua Hills, VA 22030 • 1,600
Manvel, TX 77578 • 3,549
Manville, NJ 08835 • 11,278
Manville, RI 02838 • 3,030
Many, LA 71449 • 3,988
Maple Grove, MN 55369 • 20,525
Maple Heights, OH 44137 • 28,400
Maple Shade, NJ 08052 • 20,525
Mapleton, IA 51034 • 1,495
Mapleton, MN 56065 • 1,516
Mapleton, UT 84663 • 2,726
Maplewood, MN 55109 • 30,100
Maplewood, MO 63143 • 10,960
Maplewood, NJ 07040 • 22,800
Maquoketa, IA 52060 • 6,313
Marana, AZ 85653 • 1,674
Marathon, FL 33050 • 7,568
Marathon, WI 54448 • 1,552
Marathon, WI • 111,270
Marble Falls, TX 78654 • 3,252
Marblehead, MA 01945 • 20,126
Marble Hill, MO 63764 • 1,466
Marceline, MO 64658 • 2,940
Marco, FL 33937 • 4,679
Marcus Hook, PA 19061 • 2,638
Marengo, IL 60152 • 4,380
Marengo, IA 52301 • 2,308
Marengo, AL • 25,047
Marfa, TX 79843 • 2,466
Margate, FL 33063 • 41,300
Margate, MD 21061 • 4,800
Margate City, NJ 08402 • 9,179
Marianna, AR 72360 • 6,220
Marianna, FL 32446 • 7,006
Maricopa, AZ 85239 • 1,600
Maricopa, AZ • 1,509,262
Mariemont, OH 45227 • 3,295
Maries, MO • 7,551
Marietta, GA 30060-67 • 42,400
Marietta, OH 45750 • 16,800
Marietta, OK 73448 • 2,494
Marin, CA • 222,592
Marina, CA 93933 • 20,647
Marina del Rey, CA 90292 • 6,336
Marine City, MI 48039 • 4,414
Marinette, WI 54143 • 11,900
Marinette, WI • 39,314
Marion, AL 36756 • 4,467
Marion, AR 72364 • 3,500
Marion, IL 62959 • 15,300
Marion, IN 46952-53 • 36,000
Marion, IA 52302 • 19,474
Marion, KS 66861 • 1,951
Marion, KY 42064 • 3,392
Marion, MA 02738 • 1,438
Marion, NC 28752 • 3,684
Marion, OH 43302 • 35,600
Marion, SC 29571 • 7,700
Marion, VA 24354 • 7,287
Marion, AL • 30,041
Marion, AR • 11,334
Marion, FL • 122,488
Marion, GA • 5,297
Marion, IL • 43,523
Marion, IN • 765,233
Marion, IA • 29,669
Marion, KS • 13,522
Marion, KY • 17,910
Marion, MS • 25,708
Marion, MO • 28,638
Marion, OH • 67,974
Marion, OR • 204,692
Marion, SC • 34,179
Marion, TN • 24,416
Marion, TX • 10,360
Marion, WV • 65,789
Marionville, MO 65705 • 1,920
Mariposa, CA • 11,108
Marissa, IL 62257 • 2,568
Marked Tree, AR 72365 • 3,201
Markesan, WI 53946 • 1,446
Markham, IL 60426 • 15,172
Markham, TX 77456 • 1,554
Marks, MS 38646 • 2,260
Marksville, LA 71351 • 5,113
Marlboro, NY 12542 • 2,275
Marlboro, SC • 31,634
Marlborough, MA 01752 • 31,700
Marlene Village, OR 97005 • 1,500
Marlette, MI 48453 • 1,761
Marley, MD 21061 • 4,800
Marlin, TX 76661 • 7,099
Marlow, OK 73055 • 5,017
Marlow Heights, MD 20748 • 5,824
Marlton, NJ 08053 • 9,411

Marmet, WV 25315 • 2,196
Maroa, IL 61756 • 1,760
Marquette, MI 49855 • 21,700
Marquette, MI • 74,101
Marquette, WI • 11,672
Marquette Heights, IL 61554
• 3,386
Marrero, LA 70072 • 38,500
Mars, PA 16046 • 1,803
Marseilles, IL 61341 • 5,114
Marshall, AR 72650 • 1,595
Marshall, IL 62441 • 3,379
Marshall, MI 49068 • 7,201
Marshall, MN 56258 • 11,200
Marshall, MO 65340 • 12,781
Marshall, TX 75670 • 24,800
Marshall, WI 53559 • 2,363
Marshall, AL • 65,622
Marshall, IL • 14,479
Marshall, IN • 39,155
Marshall, IA • 41,652
Marshall, KS • 12,787
Marshall, KY • 25,637
Marshall, MN • 13,027
Marshall, MS • 29,296
Marshall, OK • 10,550
Marshall, SD • 5,404
Marshall, TN • 19,698
Marshall, WV • 41,608
Marshallton, DE 19808 • 2,800
Marshalltown, IA 50158 • 26,400
Marshallville, GA 31057 • 1,540
Marshfield, MA 02050 • 4,421
Marshfield, MO 65706 • 3,871
Marshfield, WI 54449 • 20,000
Marshfield Hills, MA 02051
• 2,308
Mars Hill, ME 04758 • 1,500
Mars Hill, NC 28754 • 2,128
Marshville, NC 28103 • 2,011
Mart, TX 76664 • 2,324
Martin, TN 38237 • 8,985
Martin, FL • 64,014
Martin, IN • 11,001
Martin, KY • 13,925
Martin, MN • 24,687
Martin, NC • 25,948
Martin, TX • 4,684
Martinez, CA 94553 • 22,582
Martinez, GA 30907 • 16,472
Martinsburg, PA 16662 • 2,231
Martinsburg, WV 25401 • 13,600
Martins Ferry, OH 43935 • 9,331
Martinsville, IN 46151 • 11,311
Martinsville, VA 24112 • 18,800
Marvell, AR 72366 • 1,724
Maryland City, MD 20707 • 6,250
Maryland Heights, MO 63043
• 27,800
Marysville, CA 95901 • 11,000
Marysville, KS 66508 • 3,670
Marysville, MI 48040 • 7,345
Marysville, OH 43040 • 8,064
Marysville, PA 17053 • 2,452
Marysville, WA 98270 • 6,263
Maryville, MO 64468 • 9,558
Maryville, TN 37801 • 18,200
Mascot, TN 37806 • 2,203
Mascoutah, IL 62258 • 4,962
Mason, MI 48854 • 6,019
Mason, OH 45040 • 8,692
Mason, TX 76856 • 2,153
Mason, WV 25260 • 1,432
Mason, IL • 19,492
Mason, KY • 17,765
Mason, MI • 26,365
Mason, TX • 3,683
Mason, WA • 31,184
Mason, WV • 27,045
Mason City, IL 62664 • 2,719
Mason City, IA 50401 • 30,300
Masontown, PA 15461 • 4,909
Massac, IL • 14,990
Massapequa, NY 11758 • 24,600
Massapequa Park, NY 11762
• 19,779
Massena, NY 13662 • 13,000
Massillon, OH 44646 • 31,500
Mastic, NY 11950 • 10,413
Mastic Beach, NY 11951 • 8,318
Masury, OH 44438 • 1,836
Matagorda, TX • 37,828
Matamoras, PA 18336 • 2,111
Matawan, NJ 07747 • 8,837
Mathews, VA • 7,995
Mathis, TX 78368 • 5,667
Matoaca, VA 23803 • 1,967
Mattapoisett, MA 02739 • 3,159
Matteson, IL 60443 • 11,300
Matthews, NC 28105 • 5,946
Mattituck, NY 11952 • 3,923
Mattoon, IL 61938 • 19,700
Mattydale, NY 13211 • 7,511
Maud, OK 74854 • 1,444
Maugansville, MD 21767 • 1,707
Maui, HI • 70,847
Mauldin, SC 29662 • 8,143
Maumee, OH 43537 • 16,300
Maunawili, HI 96734 • 2,200
Maury, TN • 51,095
Mauston, WI 53948 • 3,284
Maverick, TX • 31,398
Maxton, NC 28364 • 2,711
Mayer, AZ 86333 • 1,800
Mayes, OK • 32,261
Mayfield, KY 42066 • 10,300
Mayfield, PA 18433 • 1,812
Mayfield Heights, OH 44124
• 19,800
Mayflower Village, CA 91016
• 5,017

Maynard, MA 01754 • 9,590
Mayo, MD 21106 • 1,500
Mayodan, NC 27027 • 2,627
Mays Landing, NJ 08330 • 2,054
Maysville, KY 41056 • 7,400
Mayville, NY 14757 • 1,626
Mayville, ND 58257 • 2,255
Mayville, WI 53050 • 4,333
Maywood, CA 90270 • 21,810
Maywood, IL 60153 • 27,300
Maywood, NJ 07607 • 9,895
Mead, WA 99021 • 1,650
Meade, KS 67864 • 1,777
Meade, KS • 4,788
Meade, KY • 22,854
Meade, SD • 20,717
Meadowbrook, TX 32808 • 5,200
Meadowood, DE 19711 • 2,000
Meadville, PA 16335 • 14,800
Meagher, MT • 2,154
Mebane, NC 27302 • 2,782
Mecca, CA 92254 • 1,698
Mechanic Falls, ME 04256 • 2,616
Mechanicsburg, OH 43044 • 1,792
Mechanicsburg, PA 17055
• 10,000
Mechanicsville, VA 23111 • 2,969
Mechanicville, NY 12118 • 5,500
Mecklenburg, NC • 404,270
Mecklenburg, VA • 29,444
Mecosta, MI • 36,961
Medfield, MA 02052 • 6,108
Medford, MA 02155 • 57,300
Medford, NJ 08055 • 1,800
Medford, NY 11763 • 20,418
Medford, OR 97501-04 • 43,700
Medford, WI 54451 • 4,035
Medford Lakes, NJ 08055 • 4,958
Media, PA 19063-65 • 6,119
Mediapolis, IA 52637 • 1,685
Medical Lake, WA 99022 • 3,600
Medicine Lodge, KS 67104
• 2,384
Medina, NY 14103 • 6,392
Medina, OH 44256 • 16,700
Medina, WA 98039 • 3,220
Medina, OH • 113,150
Medina, TX • 23,164
Medway, MA 02053 • 3,890
Meeker, CO 81641 • 2,356
Meeker, MN • 20,594
Mehlville, MO 63129 • 22,900
Meigs, OH • 23,641
Meigs, TN • 7,431
Meiners Oaks, CA 93023 • 5,600
Melbourne, AR 72556 • 1,619
Melbourne, FL 32901-09 • 58,200
Melbourne Beach, FL 32951
• 2,713
Mellette, SD • 2,249
Melrose, FL 32666 • 1,700
Melrose, MA 02176 • 29,000
Melrose, MN 56352 • 2,409
Melrose Park, FL 33312 • 5,672
Melrose Park, IL 60160-65
• 20,600
Melville, LA 71353 • 1,764
Melville, NY 11747 • 8,139
Melvindale, MI 48122 • 12,322
Memphis, FL 34221 • 5,501
Memphis, MO 63555 • 2,105
Memphis, TN 38101-99 • 668,600
Memphis, TX 79245 • 3,352
Mena, AR 71953 • 5,154
Menands, NY 12204 • 4,012
Menard, TX 76859 • 1,697
Menard, IL • 11,700
Menard, TX • 2,346
Menasha, WI 54952 • 14,752
Mendenhall, MS 39114 • 2,533
Mendham, NJ 07945 • 4,899
Mendocino, CA • 66,738
Mendota, CA 93640 • 5,038
Mendota, IL 61342 • 7,134
Mendota Heights, MN 55118
• 7,288
Menifee, KY • 5,117
Menlo Park, CA 94025 • 28,000
Menominee, MI 49858 • 9,600
Menominee, MI • 26,201
Menominee, WI • 3,373
Menomonee Falls, WI 53051
• 27,700
Menomonie, WI 54751 • 12,769
Mentor, OH 44060 • 43,000
Mentor-on-the-Lake, OH 44060
• 7,919
Mequon, WI 53092 • 16,193
Meraux, LA 70075 • 4,100
Merced, CA 95340-44 • 48,300
Merced, CA • 134,558
Mercedes, TX 78570 • 11,851
Mercer, PA 16137 • 2,532
Mercer, IL • 19,286
Mercer, KY • 19,011
Mercer, MO • 4,685
Mercer, NJ • 307,863
Mercer, ND • 9,404
Mercer, OH • 38,334
Mercer, PA • 128,299
Mercer, WV • 64,980
Mercer Island, WA 98040 • 21,522
Mercersburg, PA 17236 • 1,617
Mercerville, NJ 08619 • 15,600
Merchantville, NJ 08109 • 3,972
Meriden, CT 06450 • 58,100
Meridian, ID 83642 • 6,658
Meridian, MS 39301-09 • 48,100
Meridian, PA 16001 • 2,513
Meridian Hills, IN 46260 • 1,801
Meriwether, GA • 21,229

Merkel, TX 79536 • 2,493
Merriam, KS 66203 • 10,794
Merrick, NY 11566 • 24,600
Merrick, NE • 8,945
Merrifield, VA 22116 • 7,525
Merrill, WI 54452 • 9,578
Merrillville, IN 46410 • 27,300
Merrimac, MA 01860 • 2,050
Merrimack, NH • 98,302
Merritt Island, FL 32952-54
• 38,700
Mesa, AZ 85201-16 • 236,900
Mesa, CO • 81,530
Mesilla, NM 88046 • 2,029
Mesquite, TX 75149-50 • 81,600
Metairie, LA 70001-11 • 172,900
Metamora, IL 61548 • 2,482
Metcalfe, KY • 9,484
Methuen, MA 01844 • 38,900
Metropolis, IL 62960 • 7,171
Metter, GA 30439 • 3,531
Metuchen, NJ 08840 • 13,762
Metzger, OR 97223 • 5,544
Mexia, TX 76667 • 7,094
Mexico, ME 04257 • 3,207
Mexico, MO 65265 • 11,900
Mexico, NY 13114 • 1,621
Meyersdale, PA 15552 • 2,581
Miami, AZ 85539 • 2,716
Miami, FL 33101-99 • 385,900
Miami, OK 74354 • 14,600
Miami, IN • 39,820
Miami, KS • 21,618
Miami, OH • 90,381
Miami Beach, FL 33139 • 98,900
Miami Lakes, FL 33014 • 9,809
Miamisburg, OH 45342 • 15,304
Miami Shores, FL 33138 • 9,244
Miami Springs, FL 33166 • 12,350
Micco, FL 32958 • 3,585
Michigan Center, MI 49254
• 5,244
Michigan City, IN 46360 • 36,500
Middleboro, MA 02346 • 7,012
Middleburg, FL 32068 • 2,500
Middleburg Heights, OH 44130
• 15,100
Middlebury, CT 06762 • 4,140
Middlebury, IN 46540 • 1,665
Middlebury, VT 05753 • 5,591
Middlefield, OH 44062 • 1,997
Middle Island, NY 11953 • 5,703
Middleport, NY 14105 • 1,995
Middleport, OH 45760 • 2,971
Middle River, MD 21220 • 27,300
Middlesboro, KY 40965 • 12,000
Middlesex, NJ 08846 • 13,480
Middlesex, CT • 129,017
Middlesex, MA • 1,367,034
Middlesex, NJ • 595,893
Middlesex, VA • 7,719
Middleton, ID 83644 • 1,901
Middleton, MA 01949 • 4,135
Middleton, WI 53562 • 11,851
Middletown, CA 95461 • 2,000
Middletown, CT 06457 • 40,200
Middletown, DE 19709 • 2,946
Middletown, IN 47356 • 2,978
Middletown, KY 40243 • 4,262
Middletown, MD 21769 • 1,748
Middletown, NJ 07748 • 21,300
Middletown, NY 10940 • 23,100
Middletown, OH 45042-44
• 44,300
Middletown, PA 17057 • 10,400
Middletown, RI 02840 • 3,500
Middletown Township, PA 19037
• 10,400
Middleville, MI 49333 • 1,797
Midfield, AL 35228 • 6,182
Midland, MI 48640 • 37,600
Midland, PA 15059 • 4,310
Midland, TX 79701-12 • 103,000
Midland, MI • 73,578
Midland, TX • 82,636
Midland City, AL 36350 • 1,903
Midland Park, NJ 07432 • 7,381
Midlothian, IL 60445 • 14,274
Midlothian, TX 76065 • 3,219
Midvale, UT 84047 • 10,146
Midway, KY 40347 • 1,445
Midway, OR 97233 • 19,000
Midwest City, OK 73110 • 54,200
Mifflin, PA • 46,908
Mifflinburg, PA 17844 • 3,151
Milaca, MN 56353 • 2,104
Milam, TX • 22,732
Milan, IL 61264 • 6,371
Milan, IN 47031 • 1,566
Milan, MI 48160 • 4,182
Milan, MO 63556 • 1,947
Milan, NM 87021 • 3,747
Milan, OH 44846 • 1,569
Milan, TN 38358 • 8,228
Milbank, SD 57252 • 4,120
Miles City, MT 59301 • 9,602
Milford, CT 06460 • 51,600
Milford, DE 19963 • 5,356
Milford, IL 60953 • 1,716
Milford, IA 51351 • 2,076
Milford, ME 04461 • 1,688
Milford, MA 01757 • 24,600
Milford, MI 48042 • 5,041
Milford, NE 68405 • 2,108
Milford, NH 03055 • 6,269
Milford, OH 45150 • 5,679
Mililani Town, HI 96789 • 21,365
Millard, UT • 8,970
Millbrae, CA 94030 • 20,058
Millbrook, AL 36054 • 8,145
Millburn, NJ 07041 • 19,500

Millbury, MA 01527 • 4,940
Mill City, OR 97360 • 1,565
Millcreek, UT 84109 • 28,100
Millcreek Township, PA 16505
• 45,400
Milledgeville, GA 31061 • 13,900
Millen, GA 30442 • 3,988
Miller, SD 57362 • 1,931
Miller, AR • 37,766
Miller, GA • 7,038
Miller, MO • 18,532
Miller Place, NY 11764 • 7,877
Millersburg, OH 44654 • 3,247
Millersburg, PA 17061 • 2,770
Millersville, PA 17551 • 7,668
Mill Hall, PA 17751 • 1,744
Milliken, CO 80543 • 1,506
Millington, TN 38053 • 20,236
Millinocket, ME 04462 • 7,567
Millis, MA 02054 • 3,777
Mills, WY 82644 • 2,139
Mills, IA • 13,406
Mills, TX • 4,477
Millstadt, IL 62260 • 2,736
Milltown, NJ 08850 • 7,136
Mill Valley, CA 94941 • 12,967
Millville, MA 01529 • 1,693
Millville, NJ 08332 • 26,200
Millwood, WA 99212 • 1,717
Milo, ME 04463 • 2,255
Milpitas, CA 95035 • 43,100
Milroy, PA 17063 • 1,594
Milstead, GA 30207 • 1,500
Milton, FL 32570-71 • 7,206
Milton, MA 02186 • 25,900
Milton, PA 17847 • 6,730
Milton, WA 98354 • 3,162
Milton, WV 25541 • 2,178
Milton, WI 53563 • 4,092
Milton-Freewater, OR 97862
• 5,086
Milwaukee, WI 53201-99
• 611,500
Milwaukee, WI • 964,988
Milwaukie, OR 97222 • 18,100
Mimosa Park, LA 70070 • 3,737
Mims, FL 32754 • 7,583
Minco, OK 73059 • 1,489
Minden, LA 71055 • 15,084
Minden, NE 68959 • 2,939
Mine Hill, NJ 07801 • 3,250
Mineola, NY 11501 • 20,700
Mineola, TX 75773 • 4,346
Miner, SD • 3,739
Mineral, CO • 804
Mineral, MT • 3,675
Mineral, NV • 6,217
Mineral, WV • 27,234
Mineral Point, WI 53565 • 2,259
Mineral Wells, TX 76067 • 14,468
Minersville, PA 17954 • 5,635
Minerva, OH 44657 • 4,549
Minetto, NY 13115 • 1,629
Mingo, WV • 37,336
Mingo Junction, OH 43938
• 4,834
Minidoka, ID • 19,718
Minneapolis, KS 67467 • 2,075
Minneapolis, MN 55401-99
• 378,100
Minnehaha, SD • 109,435
Minneota, MN 56264 • 1,470
Minnetonka, MN 55345 • 43,400
Minonk, IL 61760 • 2,039
Minooka, IL 60447 • 1,771
Minot, ND 58701 • 37,200
Minquadale, DE 19720 • 1,700
Minster, OH 45865 • 2,557
Mint Hill, NC 28212 • 9,797
Mio, MI 48647 • 1,500
Mira Loma, CA 91752 • 8,707
Miramar, FL 33023 • 38,200
Mishawaka, IN 46544-45 • 41,500
Mishicot, WI 54228 • 1,503
Missaukee, MI • 10,009
Mission, KS 66205 • 8,643
Mission, TX 78572 • 22,653
Mission Hills, KS 66205 • 3,904
Mission Viejo, CA 92691 • 55,500
Mississippi, AR • 59,517
Mississippi, MO • 15,726
Mississippi State, MS 39762
• 4,600
Missoula, MT 59801-07 • 36,200
Missoula, MT • 76,016
Missouri City, TX 77459 • 24,423
Missouri Valley, IA 51555 • 3,107
Mitchell, IL 62040 • 1,500
Mitchell, IN 47446 • 4,641
Mitchell, NE 69357 • 1,956
Mitchell, SD 57301 • 13,900
Mitchell, GA • 21,114
Mitchell, IA • 12,329
Mitchell, KS • 8,117
Mitchell, NC • 14,428
Mitchell, TX • 9,088
Mitchellville, IA 50169 • 1,530
Moab, UT 84532 • 5,333
Moberly, MO 65270 • 14,200
Mobile, AL 36601-99 • 205,800
Mobile, AL • 364,980
Mobridge, SD 57601 • 4,174
Mocksville, NC 27028 • 2,637
Modesto, CA 95350-56 • 132,300
Modoc, CA • 8,610
Moffat, CO • 13,133
Mogadore, OH 44260 • 4,190
Mohave, AZ • 55,865
Mohawk, NY 13407 • 2,956

Mohnton, PA 19540 • 2,156
Mojave, CA 93501 • 2,886
Mokapu, HI 96863 • 11,615
Mokena, IL 60448 • 4,959
Molalla, OR 97038 • 2,992
Moline, IL 61265 • 45,600
Molino, FL 32577 • 1,456
Momence, IL 60954 • 3,297
Monaca, PA 15061 • 7,661
Monahans, TX 79756 • 8,397
Monarch Mills, SC 29379 • 2,353
Moncks Corner, SC 29461
• 4,179
Mondovi, WI 54755 • 2,545
Monessen, PA 15062 • 10,800
Monett, MO 65708 • 6,148
Monfort Heights, OH 45239
• 9,745
Moniteau, MO • 12,068
Monmouth, IL 61462 • 10,706
Monmouth, OR 97361 • 5,597
Monmouth, NJ • 503,173
Monmouth Beach, NJ 07750
• 3,318
Monmouth Junction, NJ 08852
• 2,579
Mono, CA • 8,577
Monon, IN 47959 • 1,540
Monona, IA 52159 • 1,530
Monona, WI 53716 • 8,809
Monona, IA • 11,692
Monongahela, PA 15063 • 5,950
Monongalia, WV • 75,024
Monroe, GA 30655 • 8,854
Monroe, IA 50170 • 1,875
Monroe, LA 71201-12 • 57,000
Monroe, MI 48161 • 22,500
Monroe, NY 10950 • 5,996
Monroe, NC 28110 • 18,000
Monroe, OH 45050 • 4,256
Monroe, UT 84754 • 1,476
Monroe, WA 98272 • 2,869
Monroe, WI 53566 • 10,027
Monroe, AL • 22,651
Monroe, AR • 14,052
Monroe, FL • 63,188
Monroe, GA • 14,610
Monroe, IL • 20,117
Monroe, IN • 98,785
Monroe, IA • 9,209
Monroe, KY • 12,353
Monroe, MI • 134,659
Monroe, MS • 36,404
Monroe, MO • 9,716
Monroe, NY • 702,238
Monroe, OH • 17,382
Monroe, PA • 69,409
Monroe, TN • 28,700
Monroe, WV • 12,873
Monroe, WI • 35,074
Monroe Center, CT 06468 • 7,900
Monroeville, AL • 36,460 • 5,674
Monroeville, PA 15146 • 29,900
Monrovia, CA 91016 • 33,700
Monsey, NY 10952 • 12,380
Monson, MA 01057 • 2,167
Montague, MI 49437 • 2,332
Montague, TX • 17,410
Mont Alto, PA 17237 • 1,592
Montauk, NY 11954 • 2,828
Mont Belvieu, TX 77580 • 1,730
Montcalm, MI • 47,555
Montclair, CA 91763 • 27,400
Montclair, NJ 07042-44 • 38,500
Mont Clare, PA 19453 • 1,800
Montebello, CA 90640 • 59,400
Montecito, CA 93108 • 9,300
Monterey, CA 93940 • 30,200
Monterey, TN 38574 • 2,629
Monterey, CA • 290,444
Monterey Park, CA 91754
• 61,500
Montesano, WA 98563 • 3,247
Montevallo, AL 35115 • 3,965
Montevideo, MN 56265 • 5,845
Monte Vista, CO 81144 • 3,902
Montezuma, GA 31063 • 4,830
Montezuma, IA 50171 • 1,485
Montezuma, CO • 16,510
Montgomery, AL 36101-99
• 193,800
Montgomery, IL 60538 • 3,630
Montgomery, MN 56069 • 2,349
Montgomery, NY 12549 • 2,316
Montgomery, OH 45242 • 10,084
Montgomery, WV 25136 • 3,104
Montgomery, AL • 197,038
Montgomery, AR • 7,771
Montgomery, GA • 7,011
Montgomery, IL • 31,686
Montgomery, IN • 35,501
Montgomery, IA • 13,413
Montgomery, KS • 42,281
Montgomery, KY • 20,046
Montgomery, MD • 579,053
Montgomery, MS • 13,366
Montgomery, MO • 11,537
Montgomery, NY • 53,439
Montgomery, NC • 22,469
Montgomery, OH • 571,697
Montgomery, PA • 643,621
Montgomery, TN • 83,342
Montgomery, TX • 128,487
Montgomery, VA • 63,516
Montgomery City, MO 63361
• 2,101
Montgomery Village, MD 20879
• 16,600
Monticello, AR 71655 • 8,964

Monticello, FL 32344 • 2,994
Monticello, GA 31064 • 2,382
Monticello, IL 61856 • 4,753
Monticello, IN 47960 • 5,162
Monticello, IA 52310 • 3,641
Monticello, KY 42633 • 5,677
Monticello, MN 55362 • 2,830
Monticello, MS 39654 • 1,834
Monticello, NY 12701 • 6,306
Monticello, UT 84535 • 1,929
Montmorency, MI • 7,492
Montour, PA • 16,675
Montour Falls, NY 14865 • 1,791
Montoursville, PA 17754 • 5,403
Montpelier, ID 83254 • 3,107
Montpelier, IN 47359 • 1,995
Montpelier, OH 43543 • 4,440
Montpelier, VT 05602 • 8,241
Montrose, CO 81401 • 8,722
Montrose, MI 48457 • 1,706
Montrose, PA 18801 • 1,980
Montrose, VA 23231 • 3,400
Montrose, CO • 24,352
Montvale, NJ 07645 • 7,318
Montville, CT 06353 • 1,711
Montville, NJ 07045 • 2,600
Monument Beach, MA 02553 • 1,800
Monument Heights, VA 23226 • 3,100
Moody, SD • 6,692
Moonachie, NJ 07074 • 2,706
Moore, OK 73160 • 43,100
Moore, NC • 50,505
Moore, TN • 4,510
Moore, TX • 16,575
Moorefield, WV 26836 • 2,257
Moorestown, NJ 08057 • 16,400
Mooresville, IN 46158 • 5,493
Mooresville, NC 28115 • 8,575
Moorhead, MN 56560 • 29,400
Moorhead, MS 38761 • 2,358
Moorpark, CA 93021 • 7,798
Moosic, PA 18507 • 6,068
Moosup, CT 06354 • 3,308
Mora, MN 55051 • 2,890
Mora, NM • 4,205
Moraga, CA 94556 • 15,014
Moraine, OH 45439 • 5,325
Moravia, NY 13118 • 1,582
Morehead, KY 40351 • 7,789
Morehead City, NC 28557 • 4,359
Morehouse, LA • 34,803
Morenci, MI 49256 • 2,110
Moreno Valley, CA 92388 • 79,300
Morgan, UT 84050 • 1,896
Morgan, AL • 90,231
Morgan, CO • 22,513
Morgan, GA • 11,572
Morgan, IL • 37,502
Morgan, IN • 51,999
Morgan, KY • 12,103
Morgan, MO • 13,807
Morgan, OH • 14,241
Morgan, TN • 16,604
Morgan, UT • 4,917
Morgan, WV • 10,711
Morgan City, LA 70380 • 16,700
Morganfield, KY 42437 • 3,781
Morgan Hill, CA 95037 • 17,060
Morganton, NC 28655 • 15,400
Morgantown, KY 42261 • 2,000
Morgantown, MS 39120 • 3,288
Morgantown, WV 26505 • 26,700
Morrill, NE • 6,085
Morrilton, AR 72110 • 7,355
Morris, IL 60450 • 8,833
Morris, MN 56267 • 5,367
Morris, KS • 6,419
Morris, NJ • 407,630
Morris, TX • 14,629
Morrison, IL 61270 • 4,605
Morrison, MN • 29,311
Morrison City, TN 37660 • 2,032
Morrisonville, NY 12962 • 1,721
Morris Plains, NJ 07950 • 5,305
Morristown, NJ 07960 • 17,200
Morristown, TN 37814-16 • 22,400
Morrisville, NY 13408 • 2,707
Morrisville, PA 19067 • 9,845
Morrisville, VT 05661 • 2,074
Morro Bay, CA 93442 • 9,064
Morrow, GA 30260 • 4,000
Morrow, OH • 26,480
Morrow, OR • 7,519
Morton, IL 61550 • 14,178
Morton, MS 39117 • 3,303
Morton, TX 79346 • 2,674
Morton, KS • 3,454
Morton, ND • 25,177
Morton Grove, IL 60053 • 23,500
Moscow, ID 83843 • 17,200
Moscow, PA 18444 • 1,536
Moses Lake, WA 98837 • 10,629
Mosheim, TN 37818 • 1,569
Mosinee, WI 54455 • 3,015
Moss Bluff, LA 70611 • 7,004
Moss Point, MS 39563 • 18,998
Motley, TX • 1,950
Moulton, AL 35650 • 3,197
Moultrie, GA 31768 • 15,700
Moultrie, IL • 14,546
Mound, MN 55364 • 9,280
Mound Bayou, MS 38762 • 2,917
Mound City, MO 64470 • 1,447
Moundridge, KS 67107 • 1,453
Mounds, IL 62964 • 1,669
Mounds View, MN 55432 • 12,593
Moundsville, WV 26041 • 12,419

Mountain Brook, AL 35223 • 19,718
Mountain City, TN 37683 • 2,284
Mountain Grove, MO 65711 • 3,976
Mountain Home, AR 72653 • 8,066
Mountain Home, ID 83647 • 7,540
Mountain Iron, MN 55768 • 4,134
Mountain Lake, MN 56159 • 2,277
Mountain Lake Park, MD 21550 • 1,670
Mountain Lakes, NJ 07046 • 4,153
Mountain Park, FL 30087 • 9,425
Mountainside, NJ 07092 • 7,118
Mountain View, AR 72560 • 2,147
Mountain View, CA 94040-43 • 63,600
Mountain View, CO 80521 • 2,100
Mountain View, MO 65548 • 1,664
Mountain View, NM 87105 • 2,300
Mountain View, WY 82601 • 1,500
Mount Airy, MD 21771 • 2,450
Mount Airy, NC 27030 • 7,400
Mount Angel, OR 97362 • 2,876
Mount Arlington, NJ 07856 • 4,251
Mount Ayr, IA 50854 • 1,938
Mount Carmel, IL 62863 • 8,908
Mount Carmel, PA 17851 • 8,190
Mount Carroll, IL 61053 • 1,936
Mount Clemens, MI 48043-46 • 19,200
Mount Dora, FL 32757 • 5,883
Mount Ephraim, NJ 08059 • 4,863
Mount Freedom, NJ 07970 • 1,920
Mount Gilead, OH 43338 • 2,911
Mount Healthy, OH 45231 • 7,562
Mount Holly, NJ 08060 • 10,818
Mount Holly, NC 28120 • 4,530
Mount Holly Springs, PA 17065 • 2,068
Mount Hope, WV 25880 • 1,849
Mount Horeb, WI 53572 • 3,251
Mount Joy, PA 17552 • 5,680
Mount Juliet, TN 37122 • 3,354
Mount Kisco, NY 10549 • 7,800
Mountlake Terrace, WA 98043 • 16,534
Mount Lebanon, PA 15228 • 33,000
Mount Morris, IL 61054 • 2,989
Mount Morris, MI 48458 • 3,246
Mount Morris, NY 14510 • 3,039
Mount Olive, AL 35117 • 2,270
Mount Olive, IL 62069 • 2,357
Mount Olive, NC 28365 • 4,876
Mount Olympus, UT 84117 • 6,068
Mount Orab, OH 45154 • 1,573
Mount Penn, PA 19606 • 3,025
Mount Pleasant, IA 52641 • 7,322
Mount Pleasant, MI 48858 • 22,600
Mount Pleasant, PA 15666 • 5,354
Mount Pleasant, SC 29464 • 17,734
Mount Pleasant, TN 38474 • 3,375
Mount Pleasant, TX 75455 • 12,400
Mount Pleasant, UT 84647 • 2,049
Mount Prospect, IL 60056 • 53,400
Mount Pulaski, IL 62548 • 1,783
Mountrail, ND • 7,679
Mount Rainier, MD 20712 • 7,361
Mount Savage, MD 21545 • 1,640
Mount Shasta, CA 96067 • 2,837
Mount Sinai, NY 11766 • 6,591
Mount Sterling, IL 62353 • 2,186
Mount Sterling, KY 40353 • 5,820
Mount Sterling, OH 43143 • 1,623
Mount Union, PA 17066 • 3,101
Mount Vernon, GA 30445 • 1,737
Mount Vernon, IL 62864 • 18,100
Mount Vernon, IN 47620 • 7,656
Mount Vernon, IA 52314 • 3,325
Mount Vernon, KY 40456 • 2,334
Mount Vernon, MO 65712 • 3,341
Mount Vernon, NY 10550-59 • 66,900
Mount Vernon, OH 43050 • 14,600
Mount Vernon, TX 75457 • 2,025
Mount Vernon, WA 98273 • 14,300
Mount Washington, KY 40047 • 3,997
Mount Wolf, PA 17347 • 1,517
Mount Zion, IL 62549 • 4,563
Moweaqua, IL 62550 • 1,922
Mower, MN • 40,390
Muhlenberg, KY • 32,238
Mukwonago, WI 53149 • 4,014
Mulberry, AR 72947 • 1,444
Mulberry, FL 33860 • 2,932
Muldraugh, KY 40155 • 1,752
Muldrow, OK 74948 • 2,538
Muleshoe, TX 79347 • 4,842
Mullens, WV 25882 • 2,919
Mullins, SC 29574 • 6,068
Multnomah, OR • 562,640
Mulvane, KS 67110 • 4,254
Muncie, IN 47302-07 • 74,200

Muncy, PA 17756 • 2,700
Munday, TX 76371 • 1,738
Mundelein, IL 60060 • 17,053
Munford, TN 38058 • 2,587
Munfordville, KY 42765 • 1,783
Munhall, PA 15120 • 14,535
Munising, MI 49862 • 3,083
Munster, IN 46321 • 20,671
Murfreesboro, AR 71958 • 1,883
Murfreesboro, NC 27855 • 3,007
Murfreesboro, TN 37130 • 40,400
Murphy, MO 63026 • 8,121
Murphy, NC 28906 • 2,070
Murphysboro, IL 62966 • 9,866
Murray, KY 42071 • 15,300
Murray, UT 84107 • 27,200
Murray, GA • 19,685
Murray, MN • 11,507
Murray, OK • 12,147
Murrells Inlet, SC 29576 • 2,410
Murrysville, PA 15668 • 16,036
Muscatine, IA 52761 • 23,800
Muscatine, IA • 40,436
Muscle Shoals, AL 35661 • 8,911
Muscogee, GA • 170,108
Muscoy, CA 92405 • 6,188
Muskego, WI 53150 • 15,277
Muskegon, MI 49440-45 • 39,900
Muskegon, MI • 157,589
Muskegon Heights, MI 49444 • 14,300
Muskingum, OH • 83,340
Muskogee, OK 74401-03 • 42,900
Muskogee, OK • 66,939
Musselshell, MT • 4,428
Mustang, OK 73064 • 7,496
Myers Corner, NY 12590 • 5,180
Myerstown, PA 17067 • 3,131
Myrtle Beach, SC 29577-79 • 27,800
Myrtle Creek, OR 97457 • 3,368
Myrtle Grove, FL 32506 • 14,238
Myrtle Point, OR 97458 • 2,859
Mystic, CT 06355 • 2,333

N

Nabnasset, MA 01886 • 3,600
Nacogdoches, TX 75961 • 28,900
Nacogdoches, TX • 46,786
Nahant, MA 01908 • 3,947
Nampa, ID 83651-53 • 28,300
Nanakuli, HI 96792 • 8,185
Nance, NE • 4,740
Nanticoke, PA 18634 • 13,044
Nantucket, MA 02554 • 3,229
Nantucket, MA • 5,087
Nanty Glo, PA 15943 • 3,936
Nanuet, NY 10954 • 12,578
Napa, CA 94558-59 • 55,800
Napa, CA • 99,199
Naperville, IL 60540 • 57,600
Naples, FL 33940-42 • 21,300
Naples, TX 75568 • 1,908
Naples, UT 84078 • 1,883
Naples Park, FL 33963 • 5,438
Napoleon, OH 43545 • 8,614
Nappanee, IN 46550 • 4,722
Naranja, FL 33032 • 5,000
Narberth, PA 19072 • 4,496
Narragansett, RI 02882 • 3,342
Narrows, VA 24124 • 2,516
Nash, TX 75569 • 2,022
Nash, NC • 67,153
Nashua, IA 50658 • 1,846
Nashua, NH 03060-63 • 77,100
Nashville, AR 71852 • 4,554
Nashville, GA 31639 • 4,831
Nashville, IL 62263 • 3,186
Nashville, MI 49073 • 1,628
Nashville, NC 27856 • 3,033
Nashville, TN 37201-99 • 473,100
Nassau, FL • 32,894
Nassau, NY • 1,321,582
Nassau Shores, NY 11758 • 5,110
Natchez, MS 39120 • 22,500
Natchitoches, LA 71457 • 16,664
Natchitoches, LA • 39,863
Natick, MA 01760 • 30,300
National City, CA 92050 • 58,300
National Park, NJ 08063 • 3,552
Natrona, WY • 71,856
Natrona Heights, PA 15065 • 12,400
Naugatuck, CT 06770 • 29,400
Nautilus Park, CT 06340 • 6,500
Navajo, AZ • 67,629
Navarro, TX • 35,323
Navasota, TX 77868 • 5,971
Nazareth, PA 18064 • 5,443
Nebraska City, NE 68410 • 7,127
Nederland, TX 77627 • 16,855
Nedrow, NY 13120 • 2,980
Needham, MA 02192 • 27,500
Needles, CA 92363 • 4,120
Neenah, WI 54956 • 23,100
Negaunee, MI 49866 • 5,189
Neillsville, WI 54456 • 2,780
Nekoosa, WI 54457 • 2,519
Neligh, NE 68756 • 1,893
Nelson, KY • 27,584
Nelson, ND • 5,233
Nelson, VA • 12,204
Nelsonville, OH 45764 • 4,567
Nemaha, KS • 11,211
Nemaha, NE • 8,367
Neodesha, KS 66757 • 3,414
Neoga, IL 62447 • 1,736
Neosho, MO 64850 • 9,493
Neosho, KS • 18,967
Nephi, UT 84648 • 3,285

Neptune, NJ 07753 • 30,400
Neptune Beach, FL 32233 • 5,248
Neptune City, NJ 07753 • 5,276
Nesconset, NY 11767 • 10,706
Nescopeck, PA 18635 • 1,768
Neshoba, MS • 23,789
Nesquehoning, PA 18240 • 3,346
Ness, KS • 4,498
Ness City, KS 67560 • 1,769
Netcong, NJ 07857 • 3,557
Nether Providence Township, PA 19013 • 12,730
Nettleton, MS 38858 • 1,911
Nevada, IA 50201 • 5,912
Nevada, MO 64772 • 9,044
Nevada, AR • 11,097
Nevada, CA • 51,645
Nevada City, CA 95959 • 2,431
New Albany, IN 47150 • 37,900
New Albany, MS 38652 • 7,072
Newark, CA 94560 • 37,200
Newark, DE 19711-15 • 24,200
Newark, NJ 07101-99 • 320,900
Newark, NY 14513 • 10,017
Newark, OH 43055 • 41,800
New Athens, IL 62264 • 1,937
Newaygo, MI • 34,917
New Baden, IL 62265 • 2,476
New Baltimore, MI 48047 • 5,439
New Bedford, MA 02740-48 • 99,000
Newberg, OR 97132 • 11,030
New Berlin, WI 53151 • 31,100
New Bern, NC 28560 • 16,900
Newbern, TN 38059 • 2,794
Newberry, FL 32669 • 1,826
Newberry, MI 49868 • 2,120
Newberry, SC 29108 • 9,866
Newberry, SC • 31,242
New Bethlehem, PA 16242 • 1,441
New Boston, OH 45662 • 3,188
New Boston, TX 75570 • 4,628
New Braunfels, TX 78130-33 • 22,402
New Bremen, OH 45869 • 2,393
New Brighton, MN 55112 • 23,000
New Brighton, PA 15066 • 7,364
New Britain, CT 06050-53 • 73,900
New Brunswick, NJ 08901-99 • 42,200
New Buffalo, MI 49117 • 2,821
Newburg, KY 40218 • 24,612
Newburg, KY 40218 • 5,827
Newburgh, IN 47630 • 2,906
Newburgh, NY 12550 • 25,000
Newburgh Heights, OH 44105 • 2,678
Newburyport, MA 01950-52 • 15,900
New Canaan, CT 06840 • 17,931
New Carlisle, IN 46552 • 1,439
New Carlisle, OH 45344 • 6,498
New Carrollton, MD 20784 • 12,632
New Cassel, NY 11590 • 9,635
New Castle, DE 19720 • 4,907
New Castle, IN 47362 • 19,000
Newcastle, OK 73065 • 3,076
New Castle, PA 16101-08 • 31,300
Newcastle, WY 82701 • 3,596
New Castle, DE • 398,115
New City, NY 10956 • 37,500
Newcomerstown, OH 43832 • 3,986
New Concord, OH 43762 • 1,860
New Cumberland, PA 17070 • 8,051
New Cumberland, WV 26047 • 1,752
New Egypt, NJ 08533 • 2,111
Newell, WV 26050 • 2,032
New Ellenton, SC 29809 • 2,628
Newellton, LA 71357 • 1,726
New Fairfield, CT 06812 • 4,600
Newfane, NY 14108 • 3,120
Newfield, NJ 08344 • 1,563
New Freedom, PA 17349 • 2,205
New Glarus, WI 53574 • 1,763
Newhall, CA 91321 • 12,029
New Hampton, IA 50659 • 3,940
New Hanover, NC • 103,471
New Haven, CT 06501-99 • 123,900
New Haven, IN 46774 • 7,125
New Haven, MI 48048 • 1,871
New Haven, MO 63068 • 1,581
New Haven, WV 25265 • 1,723
New Haven, CT • 761,337
New Holland, PA 17557 • 4,147
New Holstein, WI 53061 • 3,412
New Hope, AL 35760 • 1,546
New Hope, MN 55428 • 23,900
New Hope, NC 27604 • 6,745
New Hope, PA 18938 • 1,473
New Hyde Park, NY 11040 • 9,801
New Iberia, LA 70560 • 35,600
Newington, CT 06111 • 29,700
Newington, VA 22122 • 2,500
New Johnsonville, TN 37134 • 1,824
New Kensington, PA 15068 • 17,600
New Kent, VA • 8,781
Newkirk, OK 74647 • 2,413
New Lenox, IL 60451 • 5,792
New Lexington, OH 43764 • 5,179

Newllano, LA 71461 • 2,213
New London, CT 06320 • 29,100
New London, IA 52645 • 2,043
New London, OH 44851 • 2,449
New London, WI 54961 • 6,210
New London, CT • 238,409
New Madrid, MO 63869 • 3,204
New Madrid, MO • 22,945
Newman, CA 95360 • 2,785
Newmarket, NH 03857 • 3,749
New Martinsville, WV 26155 • 7,109
New Miami, OH 45011 • 2,980
New Milford, CT 06776 • 5,186
New Milford, NJ 07646 • 16,876
Newnan, GA 30263-65 • 11,449
New Orleans, LA 70101-99 • 565,000
New Oxford, PA 17350 • 1,921
New Paltz, NY 12561 • 4,938
New Paris, OH 45347 • 1,709
New Philadelphia, OH 44663 • 17,200
Newport, AR 72112 • 8,339
Newport, KY 41071-76 • 20,300
Newport, ME 04953 • 1,748
Newport, MN 55055 • 3,323
Newport, NH 03773 • 4,388
Newport, NC 28570 • 1,883
Newport, OR 97365 • 7,519
Newport, PA 17074 • 1,600
Newport, RI 02840 • 30,200
Newport, TN 37821 • 8,031
Newport, VT 05855 • 4,756
Newport, WA 99156 • 1,665
Newport, RI • 81,383
Newport Beach, CA 92660-63 • 68,800
Newport Hills, WA 98006 • 6,000
Newport News, VA 23601-07 • 159,400
New Port Richey, FL 34652-56 • 14,100
New Prague, MN 56071 • 2,952
New Providence, NJ 07974 • 12,426
New Richmond, OH 45157 • 2,769
New Richmond, WI 54017 • 4,306
New River Station, NC 28542 • 5,401
New Roads, LA 70760 • 3,932
New Rochelle, NY 10801-99 • 71,800
New Rockford, ND 58356 • 1,791
New Sarpy, LA 70078 • 2,249
New Smyrna Beach, FL 32069 • 13,557
New Tazwell, TN 37825 • 1,677
Newton, AL 36352 • 1,540
Newton, IL 62448 • 3,186
Newton, IA 50208 • 15,292
Newton, KS 67114 • 16,800
Newton, MA 02158 • 82,300
Newton, MS 39345 • 3,708
Newton, NJ 07860 • 8,100
Newton, NC 28658 • 8,133
Newton, TX 75966 • 1,620
Newton, AR • 7,756
Newton, GA • 34,489
Newton, IN • 14,844
Newton, MS • 19,944
Newton, MO • 40,555
Newton, TX • 13,254
Newton Falls, OH 44444 • 4,960
Newtown, CT 06470 • 2,022
Newtown, OH 45244 • 1,817
Newtown Square, PA 19073 • 11,775
New Ulm, MN 56073 • 13,500
New Washoe City, NV 89701 • 2,543
New Whiteland, IN 46184 • 4,502
New Wilmington, PA 16142 • 2,774
New Windsor, NY 12550 • 7,812
New York, NY 10001-99 • 7,303,300
New York, NY • 1,428,285
Nez Perce, ID • 33,220
Niagara, WI 54151 • 2,079
Niagara, NY • 227,354
Niagara Falls, NY 14301-99 • 65,500
Niagara Town, NY 14302 • 9,648
Niantic, CT 06357 • 3,151
Niceville, FL 32578 • 8,624
Nicholas, KY • 7,157
Nicholas, WV • 28,126
Nicholasville, KY 40356 • 10,319
Nichols Hills, OK 73116 • 4,153
Nicollet, MN • 26,929
Nicoma Park, OK 73066 • 2,588
Niles, IL 60648 • 29,700
Niles, MI 49120 • 13,115
Niles, OH 44446 • 22,600
Ninety Six, SC 29666 • 2,249
Niobrara, WY • 2,924
Nipomo, CA 93444 • 5,247
Niskayuna, NY 12309 • 17,471
Nitro, WV 25143 • 8,074
Niwot, CO 80544 • 1,500
Nixa, MO 65714 • 2,662
Nixon, TX 78140 • 2,008
Noble, OK 73068 • 3,497
Noble, IN • 35,443
Noble, OH • 11,310
Noble, OK • 11,573
Nobles, MN • 21,840
Noblesville, IN 46060 • 12,851
Nocona, TX 76255 • 2,992

Nodaway, MO • 21,996
Nogales, AZ 85621 • 18,600
Nokomis, FL 34275 • 3,108
Nokomis, IL 62075 • 2,656
Nolan, TX • 17,359
Nome, AK 99762 • 2,301
Nora Springs, IA 50458 • 1,572
Norco, CA 91760 • 19,732
Norco, LA 70079 • 4,416
Norcross, GA 30071 • 3,363
Norfolk, CT 06058 • 1,500
Norfolk, NE 68701 • 21,300
Norfolk, NY 13667 • 1,599
Norfolk, VA 23501-99 • 277,900
Norfolk, MA • 606,587
Norland, FL 33169 • 19,471
Normal, IL 61761 • 37,000
Norman, OK 73069-72 • 78,500
Norman, MN • 9,379
Normandy, MO 63121 • 5,174
Norridge, IL 60656 • 15,600
Norris City, IL 62869 • 1,515
Norristown, PA 19401-09 • 34,600
North Adams, MA 01247 • 17,400
North Albany, OR 97321 • 4,499
North Amherst, MA 01059 • 5,616
North Amityville, NY 11701 • 13,140
Northampton, MA 01060 • 29,900
Northampton, PA 18067 • 8,240
Northampton, NC • 22,584
Northampton, PA • 225,418
Northampton, VA • 14,625
North Andover, MA 01845 • 20,129
North Andrews Gardens, FL 33308 • 8,967
North Apollo, PA 15673 • 1,487
North Arlington, NJ 07032 • 16,587
North Atlanta, GA 30319 • 21,340
North Attleboro, MA 02760-63 • 22,600
North Auburn, CA 95603 • 7,619
North Augusta, SC 29841 • 13,593
North Aurora, IL 60542 • 5,205
North Babylon, NY 11703 • 19,019
North Baltimore, OH 45872 • 3,127
North Bay Shore, NY 11706 • 36,300
North Beach, MD 20714 • 1,504
North Bellmore, NY 11710 • 20,360
North Bellport, NY 11713 • 6,100
North Belmont, NC 28012 • 5,000
North Bend, OR 97459 • 9,200
North Bend, WA 98045 • 1,701
North Bennington, VT 05257 • 1,685
North Bergen, NJ 07047 • 47,900
North Berwick, ME 03906 • 1,436
North Billerica, MA 01862 • 5,400
Northborough, MA 01532 • 5,670
North Braddock, PA 15104 • 8,711
North Branch, MN 55056 • 1,597
North Branch, NJ 08876 • 2,620
North Branford, CT 06471 • 6,600
Northbridge, MA 01534 • 3,570
Northbrook, IL 60062 • 31,900
Northbrook, OH 45231 • 8,357
North Brookfield, MA 01535 • 2,543
North Brunswick, NJ 08902 • 25,400
North Caldwell, NJ 07006 • 5,832
North Canton, OH 44720 • 14,228
North Cape May, NJ 08204 • 4,029
North Charleston, SC 29406 • 66,900
North Chicago, IL 60064 • 41,100
North City, WA 98155 • 6,250
North College Hill, OH 45239 • 11,114
North Collins, NY 14111 • 1,496
North Conway, NH 03860 • 2,104
North Crossett, AR 71635 • 3,513
North Dartmouth, MA 02747 • 8,080
North Decatur, GA 30033 • 11,830
North Druid Hills, GA 30033 • 4,900
North East, MD 21901 • 1,469
North East, PA 16428 • 4,568
Northeast Henrietta, NY 14534 • 10,650
North Easton, MA 02356 • 4,420
North Fair Oaks, CA 94025 • 10,308
North Falmouth, MA 02556 • 3,150
Northfield, IL 60093 • 4,887
Northfield, MN 55057 • 12,562
Northfield, NJ 08225 • 7,795
Northfield, OH 44067 • 3,913
Northfield, VT 05663 • 2,033
North Fond du Lac, WI 54935 • 3,844
Northford, CT 06472 • 3,180
North Fort Myers, FL 33903 • 17,200
Northglenn, CO 80233 • 32,100
North Grafton, MA 01536 • 3,050
North Great River, NY 11722 • 11,416
North Grosvenordale, CT 06255 • 1,856
North Gulfport, MS 39501 • 6,660
North Haledon, NJ 07508 • 8,177
North Haven, CT 06473 • 21,900
North Highlands, CA 95660 • 44,800
North Hill, WA 98166 • 10,170
North Houston, TX 77086 • 8,700
North Hudson, WI 54016 • 2,218
North Industry, OH 44707 • 3,250
North Judson, IN 46366 • 1,653
North Kansas City, MO 64116 • 4,300
North Kingstown, RI 02852 • 2,750
North Kingsville, OH 44068 • 2,939
Northlake, IL 60164 • 12,166
North Las Vegas, NV 89030 • 48,700
North Lauderdale, FL 33068 • 18,653
North Liberty, IA 52317 • 2,046
North Lindenhurst, NY 11757 • 11,511
North Little Rock, AR 72114-19 • 66,200
North Logan, UT 84321 • 2,258
North Long Beach, MS 39560 • 7,063
North Madison, OH 44057 • 8,741
North Manchester, IN 46962 • 5,998
North Mankato, MN 56001 • 9,817
North Massapequa, NY 11758 • 21,385
North Merrick, NY 11566 • 12,848
North Merrydale, LA 70812 • 3,500
North Miami, FL 33161 • 44,300
North Miami Beach, FL 33162 • 37,000
North Muskegon, MI 49445 • 4,024
North Myrtle Beach, SC 29582 • 7,404
North Naples, FL 33963 • 7,950
North New Hyde Park, NY 11040 • 15,114
North Ogden, UT 84404 • 9,309
North Olmsted, OH 44070 • 35,600
North Palm Beach, FL 33408 • 11,344
North Park, IL 61111 • 15,806
North Patchogue, NY 11772 • 7,126
North Pembroke, MA 02358 • 2,215
North Plainfield, NJ 07060 • 19,108
North Platte, NE 69101 • 23,100
Northport, AL 35476 • 14,291
North Port, FL 34287 • 6,205
Northport, NY 11768 • 7,651
North Providence, RI 02911 • 30,700
North Reading, MA 01864 • 11,455
North Richland Hills, TX 76118 • 39,300
Northridge, OH 45502 • 5,559
Northridge, OH 45414 • 9,720
North Ridgeville, OH 44039 • 21,522
North Riverside, IL 60546 • 6,400
North Royalton, OH 44133 • 17,671
North Salt Lake, UT 84054 • 5,548
North Scituate, MA 02060 • 4,100
North Sioux City, SD 57049 • 1,992
North Springfield, OR 97477 • 6,140
North Springfield, VA 22151 • 7,000
North St. Paul, MN 55109 • 11,921
North Sudbury, MA 01776 • 2,630
North Syracuse, NY 13212 • 7,970
North Tarrytown, NY 10591 • 7,994
North Terre Haute, IN 47805 • 2,000
North Tonawanda, NY 14120 • 35,000
North Trenholm, SC 29206 • 10,962
Northumberland, PA 17857 • 3,636
Northumberland, PA • 100,381
Northumberland, VA • 9,828
North Uxbridge, MA 01538 • 1,500
Northvale, NJ 07647 • 5,046
North Valley Stream, NY 11580 • 14,530
North Vernon, IN 47265 • 5,768
North Versailles, PA 15137 • 13,294
Northview, MI 49505 • 11,662
Northview, OH 45322 • 9,973
Northville, MI 48167 • 5,698
North Wales, PA 19454 • 3,600
North Wantagh, NY 11793 • 12,677
North Wildwood, NJ 08260 • 4,714
North Wilkesboro, NC 28659 • 3,275
North Windham, ME 04062 • 5,492
Northwood, IA 50459 • 2,193
Northwood, OH 43619 • 5,495
Northwoods, MO 63121 • 5,831
North York, PA 17404 • 1,755
Norton, KS 67654 • 3,400
Norton, MA 02766 • 2,035
Norton, OH 44203 • 12,242
Norton, VA 24273 • 4,600
Norton, KS • 6,689
Norton Shores, MI 49441 • 22,025
Norwalk, CA 90650 • 91,000
Norwalk, CT 06850-56 • 79,300
Norwalk, IA 50211 • 3,298
Norwalk, OH 44857 • 14,358
Norway, ME 04268 • 2,653
Norway, MI 49870 • 2,919
Norwich, CT 06360 • 39,400
Norwich, NY 13815 • 8,082
Norwood, MA 02062 • 29,100
Norwood, NJ 07648 • 4,413
Norwood, NY 13668 • 1,902
Norwood, NC 28128 • 1,818
Norwood, OH 45212 • 25,300
Norwood, PA 19074 • 6,647
Nottoway, VA • 14,666
Novato, CA 94947 • 45,800
Novi, MI 48050 • 25,500
Nowata, OK 74048 • 4,270
Nowata, OK • 11,486
Noxubee, MS • 13,212
Nuckolls, NE • 6,726
Nueces, TX • 268,215
Nutley, NJ 07110 • 29,100
Nutter Fort, WV 26301 • 2,078
Nutting Lake, MA 01865 • 3,180
Nyack, NY 10960 • 6,428
Nye, NV • 9,048
Nyssa, OR 97913 • 2,862

O

Oak Bluffs, MA 02557 • 1,984
Oak Brook, IL 60521 • 7,800
Oak Creek, WI 53154 • 16,932
Oakdale, CA 95361 • 8,474
Oakdale, LA 71463 • 7,155
Oakdale, MN 55119 • 12,123
Oakdale, NY 11769 • 8,090
Oakdale, PA 15071 • 1,955
Oakes, ND 58474 • 2,112
Oakfield, NY 14125 • 1,791
Oak Forest, IL 60452 • 27,000
Oak Grove, KY 42262 • 2,088
Oak Grove, LA 71263 • 2,214
Oak Grove, OR 97267 • 11,640
Oak Grove, SC 29072 • 7,092
Oak Harbor, OH 43449 • 2,678
Oak Harbor, WA 98277 • 12,271
Oak Hill, OH 45656 • 1,713
Oak Hill, WV 25901 • 7,475
Oakhurst, OK 74050 • 2,000
Oakland, CA 94601-99 • 363,500
Oakland, IA 51560 • 1,552
Oakland, ME 04963 • 3,387
Oakland, MD 21550 • 1,994
Oakland, NJ 07436 • 13,443
Oakland, MI • 1,011,793
Oakland City, IN 47660 • 3,301
Oakland Park, FL 33334 • 25,500
Oak Lawn, IL 60453-59 • 58,200
Oaklawn, KS 67216 • 4,200
Oakley, KS 67748 • 2,343
Oaklyn, NJ 08107 • 4,223
Oakmont, PA 15139 • 7,039
Oak Park, CA 91301 • 5,000
Oak Park, IL 60301-99 • 54,900
Oak Park, MI 48237 • 30,800
Oak Ridge, FL 32809 • 15,477
Oakridge, OR 97463 • 3,729
Oak Ridge, TN 37830 • 28,000
Oakton, VA 22124 • 12,500
Oak Valley, NJ 08090 • 5,400
Oakville, CT 06779 • 8,737
Oakville, MO 63129 • 2,970
Oakwood, IL 61858 • 1,627
Oakwood, OH 45419 • 9,372
Oberlin, KS 67749 • 2,387
Oberlin, LA 70655 • 1,764
Oberlin, OH 44074 • 8,660
Obetz, OH 43207 • 3,095
Obion, TN • 32,781
Oblong, IL 62449 • 1,840
O'Brien, IA • 16,972
Ocala, FL 32670-78 • 47,000
Ocean, NJ • 346,038
Oceana, WV 24870 • 2,143
Oceana, MI • 22,002
Ocean Bluff, MA 02065 • 2,500
Ocean City, FL 32548 • 5,582
Ocean City, MD 21842 • 4,946
Ocean City, NJ 08226 • 13,949
Ocean Grove, MA 02777 • 4,560
Ocean Park, WA 98640 • 1,500
Ocean Port, NJ 07757 • 5,888
Oceanside, CA 92054-56 • 97,700
Oceanside, NY 11572 • 33,900
Ocean Springs, MS 39564 • 14,504
Ocean [Township], NJ 07712 • 24,700
Ochiltree, TX • 9,588
Ocilla, GA 31774 • 3,436
Ocoee, FL 32761 • 7,803
Oconee, GA • 12,427
Oconee, SC • 48,611
Oconomowoc, WI 53066 • 9,909
Oconto, WI 54153 • 4,505
Oconto, WI • 28,947
Oconto Falls, WI 54154 • 2,500
Odem, TX 78370 • 2,363
Odenton, MD 21113 • 7,500
Odessa, MO 64076 • 3,088
Odessa, TX 79760-68 • 106,200
Odon, IN 47562 • 1,463
Oelwein, IA 50662 • 7,564
O'Fallon, IL 62269 • 13,225
O'Fallon, MO 63366 • 8,677
Ogallala, NE 69153 • 5,638
Ogden, IA 50212 • 1,953
Ogden, KS 66517 • 1,804
Ogden, UT 84401-99 • 70,500
Ogdensburg, NJ 07439 • 2,737
Ogdensburg, NY 13669 • 12,375
Ogemaw, MI • 16,436
Ogle, IL • 46,338
Oglesby, IL 61348 • 3,979
Oglethorpe, GA • 8,929
Ogunquit, ME 03907 • 1,492
Ohio, IN • 5,114
Ohio, KY • 21,765
Ohio, WV • 61,389
Ohioville, PA 15059 • 4,217
Oil City, PA 16301 • 13,600
Oildale, CA 93308 • 23,382
Ojai, CA 93023 • 6,816
Okaloosa, FL • 109,920
Okanogan, WA 98840 • 2,326
Okanogan, WA • 30,639
Okauchee, WI 53069 • 1,950
Okauchee Lake, WI 53058 • 2,000
Okeechobee, FL 34972-74 • 4,225
Okeechobee, FL • 20,264
Okeene, OK 73763 • 1,601
Okemah, OK 74859 • 3,381
Okemos, MI 48864 • 8,882
Okfuskee, OK • 11,125
Oklahoma, OK • 568,933
Oklahoma City, OK 73101-99 • 451,400
Okmulgee, OK 74447 • 16,263
Okmulgee, OK • 39,169
Okolona, KY 40219 • 20,039
Okolona, MS 38860 • 3,409
Oktibbeha, MS • 36,018
Olathe, KS 66061-62 • 50,800
Olcott, NY 14126 • 1,571
Old Bethpage, NY 11804 • 6,215
Old Bridge, NJ 08857 • 6,090
Old Forge, PA 18518 • 9,304
Oldham, KY • 27,795
Oldham, TX • 2,283
Old Orchard Beach, ME 04064 • 6,291
Old Saybrook, CT 06475 • 1,857
Oldsmar, FL 34677 • 2,608
Old Tappan, NJ 07675 • 4,168
Old Town, ME 04468 • 8,422
Old Village, NY 11023 • 9,168
Olean, NY 14760 • 18,100
Olive Branch, MS 38654 • 2,067
Olive Hill, KY 41164 • 2,539
Olivehurst, CA 95961 • 8,929
Oliver, PA 15472 • 3,777
Oliver, ND • 2,495
Oliver Springs, TN 37840 • 3,659
Olivet, MI 49076 • 1,604
Olivette, MO 63132 • 7,952
Olivia, MN 56277 • 2,802
Olla, LA 71465 • 1,603
Olmos Park, TX 78212 • 2,069
Olmsted, MN • 92,006
Olmsted Falls, OH 44138 • 5,868
Olney, IL 62450 • 9,200
Olney, MD 20832 • 10,000
Olney, TX 76374 • 4,060
Olton, TX 79064 • 2,235
Olympia, WA 98501-07 • 30,800
Olympia Heights, FL 33175 • 35,000
Olyphant, PA 18447 • 5,204
Omaha, NE 68101-99 • 355,000
Omak, WA 98841 • 4,007
Omro, WI 54963 • 2,763
Onalaska, WI 54650 • 9,249
Onancock, VA 23417 • 1,461
Onawa, IA 51040 • 3,283
Oneco, FL 34264 • 6,417
Oneida, NY 13421 • 10,810
Oneida, OH 45042 • 1,650
Oneida, TN 37841 • 4,309
Oneida, ID • 3,258
Oneida, NY • 253,466
Oneida, WI • 31,216
O'Neill, NE 68763 • 4,049
Oneonta, AL 35121 • 4,824
Oneonta, NY 13820 • 14,800
Onondaga, NY • 463,920
Onset, MA 02558 • 1,493
Onslow, NC • 112,784
Ontario, CA 91761-62 • 115,800
Ontario, OH 44862 • 4,100
Ontario, OR 97914 • 9,500
Ontario, NY • 88,909
Ontonagon, MI 49953 • 2,182
Ontonagon, MI • 9,861
Oolitic, IN 47451 • 1,495
Oostburg, WI 53070 • 1,647
Opal Cliffs, CA 95062 • 5,041
Opa-Locka, FL 33054-56 • 14,460
Opelika, AL 36801 • 25,500
Opelousas, LA 70570 • 19,900
Opp, AL 36467 • 7,204
Opportunity, WA 99214 • 21,241
Oquawka, IL 61469 • 1,533
Oracle, AZ 85623 • 2,484
Oradell, NJ 07649 • 8,658
Orange, CA 92667-69 • 101,800
Orange, CT 06477 • 13,000
Orange, MA 01364 • 3,942
Orange, NJ 07050-52 • 31,600
Orange, TX 77630 • 26,000
Orange, VA 22960 • 2,631
Orange, CA • 1,932,709
Orange, FL • 471,016
Orange, IN • 18,677
Orange, NY • 259,603
Orange, NC • 77,055
Orange, TX • 83,838
Orange, VT • 22,739
Orange, VA • 18,063
Orangeburg, SC 29115 • 16,300
Orangeburg, SC • 82,276
Orange City, FL 32763 • 2,795
Orange City, IA 51041 • 4,588
Orange Grove, MS 39501 • 2,700
Orange Park, FL 32073 • 8,766
Orangevale, CA 95662 • 20,585
Orchard City, CO 81410 • 1,914
Orchard Homes, MT 59801 • 4,000
Orchard Mesa, CO 81501 • 4,876
Orchard Park, NY 14127 • 3,671
Orchards, WA 98662 • 4,300
Orchard Valley, WY 82001 • 3,321
Orcutt, CA 93455 • 1,500
Ord, NE 68862 • 2,658
Oregon, IL 61061 • 3,638
Oregon, OH 43616 • 18,675
Oregon, WI 53575 • 3,876
Oregon, MO • 10,238
Oregon City, OR 97045 • 15,000
Orem, UT 84057-58 • 61,800
Orinda, CA 94563 • 16,843
Orion, IL 61273 • 2,013
Oriskany, NY 13424 • 1,680
Orland, CA 95963 • 4,031
Orlando, FL 32801-99 • 149,500
Orland Park, IL 60462 • 30,857
Orleans, IN 47452 • 2,161
Orleans, MA 02653 • 1,811
Orleans, LA • 557,927
Orleans, NY • 38,496
Orleans, VT • 23,440
Orlovista, FL 32811 • 6,474
Ormond Beach, FL 32074-76 • 21,438
Ormond By The Sea, FL 32074 • 7,665
Orofino, ID 83544 • 3,711
Orono, ME 04473 • 10,578
Orono, MN 55323 • 6,845
Oroville, CA 95965-66 • 10,600
Oroville, WA 98844 • 1,483
Orrville, OH 44667 • 7,511
Orting, WA 98360 • 1,787
Ortonville, MN 56278 • 2,550
Orwigsburg, PA 17961 • 2,700
Osage, IA 50461 • 3,718
Osage, KS • 15,319
Osage, MO • 12,014
Osage, OK • 39,327
Osage Beach, MO 65065 • 1,992
Osage City, KS 66523 • 2,667
Osawatomie, KS 66064 • 4,459
Osborne, KS 67473 • 2,120
Osborne, KS • 5,959
Osburn, ID 83849 • 2,220
Osceola, AR 72370 • 8,881
Osceola, IN 46561 • 1,990
Osceola, IA 50213 • 3,750
Osceola, WI 54020 • 1,581
Osceola, FL • 49,287
Osceola, IA • 8,371
Osceola, MI • 18,928
Osceola Mills, PA 16666 • 1,466
Oscoda, MI 48750 • 2,431
Oscoda, MI • 6,858
Osgood, IN 47037 • 1,554
Oshkosh, WI 54901-04 • 51,400
Oskaloosa, IA 52577 • 10,989
Osprey, FL 34229 • 1,660
Osseo, MN 55369 • 2,974
Osseo, WI 54758 • 1,474
Ossian, IN 46777 • 1,945
Ossining, NY 10562 • 20,196
Osterville, MA 02655 • 1,799
Oswego, IL 60543 • 3,021
Oswego, KS 67356 • 2,218
Oswego, NY 13126 • 19,700
Oswego, NY • 113,901
Otay, CA 92010 • 6,400
Oteen, NC 28805 • 2,200
Otero, CO • 22,567
Otero, NM • 44,665
Othello, WA 99344 • 4,454
Otis Orchards, WA 99027 • 4,100
Otoe, NE • 15,183
Otsego, MI 49078 • 3,802
Otsego, MI • 14,993
Otsego, NY • 59,075
Ottawa, IL 61350 • 18,200
Ottawa, KS 66067 • 11,016
Ottawa, OH 45875 • 3,874
Ottawa, KS • 5,971
Ottawa, MI • 157,174
Ottawa, OH • 40,076
Ottawa, OK • 32,870
Ottawa Hills, OH 43606 • 4,065
Otter Tail, MN • 51,937
Ottumwa, IA 52501 • 26,600
Ouachita, AR • 30,541
Ouachita, LA • 139,241
Ouray, CO • 1,925
Outagamie, WI • 128,730
Overland, MO 63114 • 19,620
Overland Park, KS 66204 • 93,700

Overlea, MD 21206 • 6,200
Overlook, OH 45431 • 6,000
Overton, TX 75684 • 2,430
Overton, TN • 17,575
Ovid, MI 48866 • 1,712
Owasso, OK 74055 • 6,486
Owatonna, MN 55060 • 18,800
Owego, NY 13827 • 4,364
Owen, IN • 15,841
Owen, KY • 8,924
Owensboro, KY 42301-03 • 56,000
Owensville, MO 65066 • 2,241
Owings Mills, MD 21117 • 9,526
Owosso, MI 48867 • 16,100
Owsley, KY • 5,709
Owyhee, ID • 8,272
Oxford, AL 36203 • 8,939
Oxford, CT 06483 • 1,600
Oxford, GA 30267 • 1,750
Oxford, MA 01540 • 6,369
Oxford, MI 48051 • 2,746
Oxford, MS 38655 • 9,882
Oxford, NJ 07863 • 1,587
Oxford, NY 13830 • 1,765
Oxford, NC 27565 • 7,787
Oxford, OH 45056 • 17,655
Oxford, PA 19363 • 3,633
Oxford, ME • 48,968
Oxnard, CA 93030-35 • 129,000
Oxon Hill, MD 20745 • 8,100
Oyster Bay, NY 11771 • 6,497
Ozark, AL 36360 • 13,188
Ozark, AR 72949 • 3,486
Ozark, MO 65721 • 2,980
Ozark, MO • 7,961
Ozaukee, WI • 66,981
Ozona, FL 34660 • 1,500
Ozona, TX 76943 • 3,766

P

Pace, FL 32570 • 5,006
Pacific, MO 63069 • 4,410
Pacific, WA 98047 • 2,261
Pacific, WA • 17,237
Pacifica, CA 94044 • 37,100
Pacific City, OR 97135 • 1,500
Pacific Grove, CA 93950 • 15,755
Pacific Palisades, HI 96782 • 9,500
Pacolet, SC 29372 • 1,556
Paddock Lake, WI 53168 • 2,207
Paden City, WV 26159 • 3,671
Paducah, KY 42001-03 • 28,800
Paducah, TX 79248 • 2,216
Page, AZ 86040 • 6,469
Page, IA • 19,063
Page, VA • 19,401
Pageland, SC 29728 • 2,720
Page Manor, OH 45431 • 9,300
Pahala, HI 96777 • 1,619
Pahokee, FL 33476 • 6,346
Paincourtville, LA 70391 • 2,004
Painesville, OH 44077 • 16,900
Painted Post, NY 14870 • 2,196
Paintsville, KY 41240 • 3,815
Palacios, TX 77465 • 4,667
Palatine, IL 60067 • 33,900
Palatka, FL 32077 • 11,100
Palestine, IL 62451 • 1,718
Palestine, TX 75801 • 19,300
Palisade, CO 81526 • 1,551
Palisades Park, NJ 07650 • 13,732
Palma Sola, FL 34209 • 5,297
Palm Bay, FL 32905 • 18,560
Palm Beach, FL 33480 • 11,600
Palm Beach, FL • 576,863
Palm Beach Gardens, FL 33410 • 14,407
Palmdale, CA 93550-51 • 12,928
Palm Desert, CA 92260 • 11,801
Palmer, AK 99645 • 2,141
Palmer, MA 01069 • 3,854
Palmer, MS 39401 • 2,765
Palmer Park, MD 20785 • 7,986
Palmerton, PA 18071 • 5,455
Palmetto, FL 34221 • 8,637
Palmetto, GA 30268 • 2,086
Palmetto Estates, FL 33157 • 5,300
Palm Harbor, FL 34683-85 • 5,215
Palm Springs, CA 92262-64 • 31,300
Palm Springs, FL 33460 • 8,166
Palmyra, MO 63461 • 3,469
Palmyra, NJ 08065 • 7,085
Palmyra, NY 14522 • 3,729
Palmyra, PA 17078 • 7,228
Palmyra, WI 53156 • 1,595
Palo Alto, CA 94301-99 • 57,200
Palo Alto, IA • 12,721
Palo Pinto, TX • 24,062
Palos Heights, IL 60463 • 10,574
Palos Hills, IL 60465 • 16,654
Palos Park, IL 60464 • 3,150
Palos Verdes Estates, CA 90274 • 14,376
Pamlico, NC • 10,398
Pampa, TX 79065 • 21,900
Pana, IL 62557 • 6,040
Panama City, FL 32401-10 • 37,300
Panama City Beach, FL 32407 • 2,148
Panhandle, TX 79068 • 2,226
Panola, MS • 28,164
Panola, TX • 20,724
Panthersville, GA 30032 • 11,366
Paola, KS 66071 • 4,557
Paoli, IN 47454 • 3,637
Paoli, PA 19301 • 5,277
Papaikou, HI 96781 • 1,567
Papillion, NE 68046 • 7,725
Paradise, CA 95969 • 25,500
Paradise, NV 89109 • 87,900
Paradise Hills, NM 87114 • 5,096
Paradise Valley, AZ 85253 • 11,920
Paragould, AR 72450 • 16,300
Paramount, CA 90723 • 42,500
Paramount, MD 21740 • 1,878
Paramus, NJ 07652 • 26,300
Parchment, MI 49004 • 1,817
Pardeeville, WI 53954 • 1,594
Paris, AR 72855 • 3,991
Paris, IL 61944 • 9,885
Paris, KY 40361 • 7,935
Paris, MO 65275 • 1,598
Paris, TN 38242 • 10,834
Paris, TX 75460 • 26,600
Park, CO • 5,333
Park, MT • 12,869
Park, WY • 21,639
Park City, KS 67219 • 4,056
Park City, UT 84060 • 2,823
Parke, IN • 16,372
Parker, AZ 85344 • 2,542
Parker, FL 32401 • 4,298
Parker, TX • 44,609
Parkersburg, IA 50665 • 1,968
Parkersburg, WV 26101-05 • 39,300
Parkesburg, PA 19365 • 2,578
Park Falls, WI 54552 • 3,192
Park Forest, IL 60466 • 26,400
Park Forest South, IL 60466 • 6,245
Park Hills, KY 41015 • 3,500
Parkin, AR 72373 • 2,035
Parkland, WA 98444 • 26,100
Park Layne, OH 45344 • 1,980
Park Rapids, MN 56470 • 2,976
Park Ridge, IL 60068 • 37,400
Park Ridge, NJ 07656 • 8,515
Park River, ND 58270 • 1,844
Parkrose, OR 97230 • 21,108
Parkston, SD 57366 • 1,545
Parkville, MD 21234 • 35,800
Parkville, MO 64152 • 2,091
Parkwater, WA 99211 • 4,850
Parkway, CA 95823 • 12,000
Parkwood, NC 27707 • 3,420
Parlier, CA 93648 • 5,714
Parma, ID 83660 • 1,820
Parma, OH 44129 • 91,000
Parma Heights, OH 44130 • 22,400
Parmer, TX • 11,038
Parowan, UT 84761 • 1,836
Parrish, AL 35580 • 1,583
Parris Island, SC 29905 • 7,752
Parsons, KS 67357 • 13,000
Parsons, TN 38363 • 2,457
Parsons, WV 26287 • 1,937
Pasadena, CA 91101-99 • 131,700
Pasadena, MD 21122 • 3,900
Pasadena, TX 77501-08 • 120,000
Pascagoula, MS 39567 • 31,200
Pasco, WA 99301 • 18,700
Pasco, FL • 193,661
Pascoag, RI 02859 • 3,807
Paso Robles, CA 93446 • 9,163
Pasquotank, NC • 28,462
Passaic, NJ 07055 • 54,900
Passaic, NJ • 447,585
Pass Christian, MS 39571 • 5,014
Pataskala, OH 43062 • 2,284
Patchogue, NY 11772 • 11,900
Paterson, NJ 07501-99 • 139,200
Patrick, VA • 17,647
Patterson, LA 70392 • 4,693
Patton, PA 16668 • 2,441
Paulding, OH 45879 • 2,754
Paulding, GA • 26,110
Paulding, OH • 21,302
Paulsboro, NJ 08066 • 6,944
Pauls Valley, OK 73075 • 5,997
Pawcatuck, CT 06379 • 5,216
Paw Creek, NC 28130 • 1,700
Pawhuska, OK 74056 • 4,771
Pawling, NY 12564 • 1,996
Pawnee, IL 62558 • 2,577
Pawnee, OK 74058 • 1,688
Pawnee, KS • 8,065
Pawnee, NE • 3,937
Pawnee, OK • 15,310
Paw Paw, MI 49079 • 3,211
Pawtucket, RI 02860-65 • 73,400
Paxton, IL 60957 • 4,258
Paxton, MA 01612 • 1,550
Payette, ID 83661 • 5,448
Payette, ID • 15,825
Payne, OK • 62,435
Paynesville, MN 56362 • 2,140
Payson, AZ 85541 • 6,961
Payson, UT 84651 • 8,246
Peabody, KS 66866 • 1,474
Peabody, MA 01960 • 46,500
Peace Dale, RI 02883 • 3,100
Peach, GA • 19,151
Peach Orchard, GA 30906 • 13,800
Peachtree City, GA 30269 • 6,429
Pea Ridge, AR 72751 • 1,488
Pearisburg, VA 24134 • 2,128
Pearl, MS 39208 • 18,602
Pearland, TX 77581 • 13,958
Pearl City, HI 96782 • 31,500
Pearl River, LA 70452 • 1,693
Pearl River, NY 10965 • 15,893
Pearl River, MS • 33,795
Pearsall, TX 78061 • 7,383
Pearson, GA 31642 • 1,827
Pecatonica, IL 61063 • 1,732
Pecos, TX 79772 • 12,855
Pecos, TX • 14,618
Peculiar, MO 64078 • 1,571
Pedricktown, NJ 08067 • 1,500
Peebles, OH 45660 • 1,790
Peekskill, NY 10566 • 19,000
Pekin, IL 61554 • 33,300
Pelahatchie, MS 39145 • 1,445
Pelham, AL 35124 • 7,349
Pelham, GA 31779 • 4,306
Pelham, NY 10803 • 6,848
Pelham Manor, NY 10803 • 6,130
Pelican Rapids, MN 56572 • 1,867
Pella, IA 50219 • 8,349
Pell City, AL 35125 • 6,616
Pell Lake, WI 53157 • 1,826
Pembina, ND • 10,399
Pembroke, MA 02359 • 2,000
Pembroke, NC 28372 • 2,698
Pembroke Park, FL 33009 • 5,326
Pembroke Pines, FL 33024 • 46,500
Pemiscot, MO • 24,987
Pen Argyl, PA 18072 • 3,388
Penbrook, PA 17103 • 3,006
Pender, NC • 22,262
Pendleton, IN 46064 • 2,130
Pendleton, OR 97801 • 14,700
Pendleton, SC 29670 • 3,154
Pendleton, KY • 10,989
Pendleton, WV • 7,910
Pendley Hills, GA 30032 • 5,400
Pend Oreille, WA • 8,580
Penfield, NY 14526 • 6,260
Penn Acres, DE 19720 • 1,950
Penn Hills, PA 15235 • 54,900
Pennington, NJ 08534 • 2,109
Pennington, MN • 15,258
Pennington, SD • 70,361
Pennington Gap, VA 24277 • 1,716
Pennsauken, NJ 08110 • 34,700
Pennsboro, WV 26415 • 1,652
Pennsburg, PA 18073 • 2,339
Penns Grove, NJ 08069 • 5,760
Pennsville, NJ 08070 • 12,467
Penn Yan, NY 14527 • 5,242
Penobscot, ME • 137,015
Pensacola, FL 32501-23 • 65,600
Peoria, AZ 85345 • 12,787
Peoria, IL 61601-99 • 118,800
Peoria, IL • 200,466
Peoria Heights, IL 61614 • 7,453
Peotone, IL 60468 • 2,832
Pepeekeo, HI 96783 • 1,800
Pepin, WI • 7,477
Pepperell, MA 01463 • 2,076
Pepper Pike, OH 44124 • 6,177
Pequannock, NJ 07440 • 13,776
Perham, MN 56573 • 2,086
Perkasie, PA 18944 • 5,241
Perkins, OK 74059 • 1,762
Perkins, NE • 3,637
Perkins, SD • 4,700
Perl-Mack, CO 80221 • 6,002
Perquimans, NC • 9,486
Perrine, FL 33157 • 16,129
Perris, CA 92370 • 6,827
Perry, FL 32347 • 8,254
Perry, GA 31069 • 9,453
Perry, IA 50220 • 7,053
Perry, MI 48872 • 2,051
Perry, NY 14530 • 4,198
Perry, OK 73077 • 5,796
Perry, AL • 15,012
Perry, AR • 7,266
Perry, IL • 21,714
Perry, IN • 19,346
Perry, KY • 33,763
Perry, MS • 9,864
Perry, MO • 16,784
Perry, OH • 31,032
Perry, PA • 35,718
Perry, TN • 6,111
Perry Hall, MD 21128 • 13,455
Perry Heights, OH 44646 • 9,206
Perryman, MD 21130 • 1,819
Perrysburg, OH 43551 • 10,215
Perryton, TX 79070 • 7,991
Perryville, MD 21903 • 2,018
Perryville, MO 63775 • 7,343
Pershing, NV • 3,408
Person, NC • 29,164
Perth Amboy, NJ 08861-63 • 38,800
Peru, IL 61354 • 10,600
Peru, IN 46970 • 13,764
Peru, NY 12972 • 1,716
Peshtigo, WI 54157 • 2,807
Petal, MS 39465 • 8,476
Petaluma, CA 94952 • 39,000
Peterborough, NH 03458 • 2,100
Petersburg, AK 99833 • 2,821
Petersburg, IL 62675 • 2,419
Petersburg, IN 47567 • 2,987
Petersburg, TX 79250 • 1,633
Petersburg, VA 23803-05 • 41,200
Petersburg, WV 26847 • 2,084
Petersville, AL 35633 • 1,730
Petoskey, MI 49770 • 6,300
Petroleum, MT • 655
Pettis, MO • 36,378
Pevely, MO 63070 • 2,732
Pewaukee, WI 53072 • 4,637
Pharr, TX 78577 • 28,600
Phelps, NY 14532 • 2,004
Phelps, MO • 33,633
Phelps, NE • 9,769
Phenix City, AL 36867 • 27,900
Philadelphia, MS 39350 • 6,434
Philadelphia, PA 19101-99 • 1,645,100
Philadelphia, PA • 1,688,210
Phil Campbell, AL 35581 • 1,549
Philippi, WV 26416 • 3,194
Philipsburg, PA 16866 • 3,533
Phillips, TX 79007 • 1,729
Phillips, WI 54555 • 1,522
Phillips, AR • 34,772
Phillips, CO • 4,542
Phillips, KS • 7,406
Phillips, MT • 5,367
Phillipsburg, KS 67661 • 3,229
Phillipsburg, NJ 08865 • 16,647
Philmont, NY 12565 • 1,539
Philomath, OR 97370 • 2,673
Phoenix, AZ 85001-99 • 933,800
Phoenix, IL 60426 • 2,850
Phoenix, NY 13135 • 2,357
Phoenix, OR 97535 • 2,309
Phoenixville, PA 19460 • 14,165
Piatt, IL • 16,581
Picayune, MS 39466 • 10,361
Picher, OK 74360 • 2,180
Pickaway, OH • 43,662
Pickens, SC 29671 • 3,199
Pickens, AL • 21,481
Pickens, GA • 11,652
Pickens, SC • 79,292
Pickerington, OH 43147 • 3,917
Pickett, TN • 4,358
Pico Rivera, CA 90660 • 59,200
Piedmont, AL 36272 • 5,544
Piedmont, CA 94611 • 10,498
Piedmont, MO 63957 • 2,359
Piedmont, OK 73078 • 2,016
Piedmont, SC 29673 • 2,992
Piedmont, WV 26750 • 1,491
Pierce, NE 68767 • 1,535
Pierce, GA • 11,897
Pierce, NE • 8,481
Pierce, ND • 6,166
Pierce, WA • 485,667
Pierce, WI • 31,149
Pierre, SD 57501 • 11,973
Pierre Part, LA 70339 • 3,153
Pigeon Cove, MA 01966 • 1,660
Pigeon Forge, TN 37863 • 2,849
Piggott, AR 72454 • 3,762
Pike, AL • 28,050
Pike, AR • 10,373
Pike, GA • 8,937
Pike, IL • 18,896
Pike, IN • 13,465
Pike, KY • 81,123
Pike, MS • 36,173
Pike, MO • 17,568
Pike, OH • 22,802
Pike, PA • 18,271
Pikesville, MD 21208 • 20,000
Piketon, OH 45661 • 1,726
Pikeville, KY 41501 • 5,800
Pikeville, TN 37367 • 2,100
Pilot Point, TX 76258 • 2,211
Pilot Rock, OR 97868 • 1,630
Pima, AZ 85543 • 1,599
Pima, AZ • 531,443
Pimmit Hills, VA 22043 • 6,658
Pinal, AZ • 90,918
Pinardville, NH 03045 • 4,500
Pinckneyville, IL 62274 • 3,319
Pinconning, MI 48650 • 1,430
Pine, MN • 19,871
Pine Bluff, AR 71601-13 • 69,000
Pine Castle, FL 32809 • 9,992
Pine City, MN 55063 • 2,489
Pine Grove, PA 17963 • 2,244
Pine Hill, NJ 08021 • 8,684
Pine Hills, FL 32808 • 30,800
Pinehurst, MA 01866 • 6,588
Pinehurst, NJ 08201 • 1,850
Pinehurst, NC 28374 • 1,746
Pine Island, MN 55963 • 1,977
Pine Lawn, MO 63120 • 6,570
Pinellas, FL • 728,531
Pinellas Park, FL 34665-66 • 40,700
Pine Ridge, SD 57770 • 3,059
Pinetop, AZ 85935 • 2,339
Pinetops, NC 27864 • 1,465
Pineville, KY 40977 • 2,599
Pineville, LA 71360 • 12,470
Pineville, NC 28134 • 1,525
Pinewald, NJ 08721 • 1,700
Pinewood, FL 33168 • 7,900
Pinewood Park, FL 33168 • 8,300
Pinole, CA 94564 • 14,253
Pinson, AL 35126 • 1,430
Pipestone, MN 56164 • 4,887
Pipestone, MN • 11,690
Piqua, OH 45356 • 20,400
Piscataquis, ME • 17,634
Piscataway, NJ 08854 • 43,400
Pisgah Forest, NC 28768 • 1,899
Pismo Beach, CA 93449 • 5,364
Pitcairn, PA 15140 • 4,175
Pitcher Hill, NY 13212 • 6,063
Pitkin, CO • 10,338
Pitman, NJ 08071 • 9,744
Pitt, NC • 90,146
Pittsburg, CA 94565 • 40,200
Pittsburg, KS 66762 • 18,500
Pittsburg, TX 75686 • 4,245
Pittsburg, OK • 40,524
Pittsburgh, PA 15201-99 • 393,000
Pittsfield, IL 62363 • 4,170
Pittsfield, ME 04967 • 3,117
Pittsfield, MA 01201 • 50,400
Pittsfield, NH 03263 • 1,584
Pittston, PA 18640-44 • 9,930
Pittsylvania, VA • 66,147
Piute, UT • 1,329
Pixley, CA 93256 • 2,488
Placentia, CA 92670 • 39,000
Placer, CA • 117,247
Placerville, CA 95667 • 6,739
Plain City, OH 43064 • 2,102
Plain City, UT 84404 • 2,379
Plainedge, NY 11714 • 9,629
Plainfield, CT 06374 • 2,799
Plainfield, IL 60544 • 3,777
Plainfield, IN 46168 • 9,191
Plainfield, NJ 07060-63 • 46,800
Plainfield Heights, MI 49505 • 5,000
Plains, PA 18705 • 5,455
Plains, TX 79355 • 1,457
Plainsboro, NJ 08536 • 1,560
Plainview, MN 55964 • 2,416
Plainview, NE 68769 • 1,483
Plainview, NY 11803 • 31,500
Plainview, TX 79072 • 22,600
Plainville, CT 06062 • 16,401
Plainville, KS 67663 • 2,458
Plainville, MA 02762 • 5,857
Plainwell, MI 49080 • 3,751
Plaistow, NH 03865 • 1,800
Plano, IL 60545 • 4,875
Plano, TX 75074-75 • 107,000
Plantation, FL 33317 • 55,000
Plant City, FL 33566 • 17,064
Plantsite, AZ 85540 • 1,500
Plantsville, CT 06479 • 7,050
Plaquemine, LA 70764 • 8,906
Plaquemines, LA • 26,049
Platte, MO • 46,341
Platte, NE • 28,852
Platte, WY • 11,975
Platte City, MO 64079 • 2,114
Platteville, CO 80651 • 1,662
Platteville, WI 53818 • 9,580
Plattsburg, MO 64477 • 2,095
Plattsburgh, NY 12901 • 21,100
Plattsmouth, NE 68048 • 6,295
Pleasant Gap, PA 16823 • 1,859
Pleasant Garden, NC 27313 • 1,991
Pleasant Grove, AL 35127 • 7,102
Pleasant Grove, UT 84062 • 10,833
Pleasant Hill, CA 94523 • 28,000
Pleasant Hill, IA 50301 • 3,493
Pleasant Hill, MO 64080 • 3,301
Pleasant Hills, PA 15236 • 9,604
Pleasanton, CA 94566 • 42,000
Pleasanton, TX 78064 • 6,346
Pleasants, WV • 8,236
Pleasant Valley, MO 64068 • 1,545
Pleasant View, CO 80401 • 3,460
Pleasant View, UT 84404 • 3,983
Pleasantville, IA 50225 • 1,531
Pleasantville, NJ 08232 • 14,600
Pleasantville, NY 10570-72 • 6,749
Pleasure Ridge Park, KY 40258 • 18,800
Plentywood, MT 59254 • 2,476
Plover, WI 54467 • 5,310
Plum, PA 15239 • 24,900
Plumas, CA • 17,340
Plymouth, FL 32768 • 2,700
Plymouth, IN 46563 • 7,693
Plymouth, MA 02360 • 7,232
Plymouth, MI 48170 • 9,986
Plymouth, MN 55441 • 43,100
Plymouth, NH 03264 • 3,628
Plymouth, NC 27962 • 4,571
Plymouth, OH 44865 • 1,939
Plymouth, PA 18651 • 7,605
Plymouth, WI 53073 • 6,027
Plymouth, IA • 24,743
Plymouth, MA • 405,437
Plymouth Township, PA 19401 • 17,200
Pocahontas, AR 72455 • 5,995
Pocahontas, IA 50574 • 2,352
Pocahontas, IA • 11,369
Pocahontas, WV • 9,919
Pocasset, MA 02559 • 2,200
Pocatalico, WV 25320 • 2,450
Pocatello, ID 83201-06 • 46,100
Pocola, OK 74902 • 3,268
Pocomoke City, MD 21851 • 3,558
Poinsett, AR • 27,032
Point Clear, AL 36564 • 1,812
Pointe Coupee, LA • 24,045
Point Marion, PA 15474 • 1,642
Point Pleasant, NJ 08742 • 17,747
Point Pleasant, WV 25550 • 5,682
Point Pleasant Beach, NJ 08742 • 5,415
Polk, PA 16342 • 1,884
Polk, AR • 17,007
Polk, FL • 321,652
Polk, GA • 32,386
Polk, IA • 303,170
Polk, MN • 34,844
Polk, MO • 18,822
Polk, NE • 6,320
Polk, NC • 12,984
Polk, OR • 45,203
Polk, TN • 13,602
Polk, TX • 24,407
Polk, WI • 32,351

Polk City, IA 50226 • 1,658
Polo, IL 61064 • 2,643
Polson, MT 59860 • 2,798
Pomeroy, OH 45769 • 2,728
Pomeroy, WA 99347 • 1,716
Pomona, CA 91766-69 • 112,700
Pomona, NJ 08240 • 2,358
Pompano Beach, FL 33060-69 • 69,200
Pompano Beach Highlands, FL 33064 • 9,000
Pompton Lakes, NJ 07442 • 10,660
Ponca City, OK 74601-04 • 28,200
Ponchatoula, LA 70454 • 5,469
Pondera, MT • 6,731
Ponte Vedra Beach, FL 32082 • 1,700
Pontiac, IL 61764 • 11,227
Pontiac, MI 48053-59 • 71,500
Pontotoc, MS 38863 • 4,723
Pontotoc, MS • 20,918
Pontotoc, OK • 32,598
Pooler, GA 31322 • 2,540
Poolesville, MD 20837 • 3,428
Pope, AR • 39,021
Pope, IL • 4,404
Pope, MN • 11,657
Poplar Bluff, MO 63901 • 17,800
Poplarville, MS 39470 • 2,562
Poquonock Bridge, CT 06340 • 2,549
Poquoson, VA 23662 • 8,726
Portage, IN 46368 • 29,300
Portage, MI 49081 • 40,500
Portage, PA 15946 • 3,510
Portage, WI 53901 • 7,896
Portage, OH • 135,856
Portage, WI • 57,420
Portage Lakes, OH 44319 • 11,310
Portageville, MO 63873 • 3,470
Portales, NM 88130 • 9,940
Port Allegany, PA 16743 • 2,593
Port Allen, LA 70767 • 6,114
Port Angeles, WA 98362 • 17,400
Port Aransas, TX 78373 • 1,968
Port Arthur, TX 77640-43 • 63,900
Port Barre, LA 70577 • 2,625
Port Bolivar, TX 77650 • 1,600
Port Carbon, PA 17965 • 2,576
Port Charlotte, FL 33952 • 36,800
Port Chester, NY 10573 • 23,000
Port Clinton, OH 43452 • 7,223
Port Dickinson, NY 13901 • 1,974
Port Edwards, WI 54469 • 2,077
Porter, IN 46304 • 3,441
Porter, TX 77365 • 5,000
Porter, IN • 119,816
Porterdale, GA 30270 • 1,451
Porterville, CA 93257 • 24,600
Port Ewen, NY 12466 • 2,813
Port Gibson, MS 39150 • 2,371
Port Henry, NY 12974 • 1,450
Port Hueneme, CA 93041 • 17,803
Port Huron, MI 48060 • 34,300
Port Isabel, TX 78578 • 3,769
Port Jefferson, NY 11777 • 6,731
Port Jefferson Station, NY 11776 • 9,630
Port Jervis, NY 12771 • 8,699
Portland, CT 06480 • 8,383
Portland, IN 47371 • 7,074
Portland, ME 04101-99 • 63,100
Portland, MI 48875 • 3,963
Portland, OR 97201-99 • 408,900
Portland, TN 37148 • 4,140
Portland, TX 78374 • 12,023
Port Lavaca, TX 77979 • 11,024
Port Monmouth, NJ 07758 • 3,800
Port Neches, TX 77651 • 13,944
Port Norris, NJ 08349 • 1,730
Portola, CA 96122 • 1,885
Port Orange, FL 32019 • 18,756
Port Orchard, WA 98366 • 4,787
Port Richey, FL 34668-69 • 2,165
Port Royal, SC 29935 • 2,977
Port Saint Joe, FL 32456 • 4,027
Port Saint Lucie, FL 34952 • 14,690
Port Salerno, FL 34992 • 4,511
Portsmouth, NH 03801 • 29,800
Portsmouth, OH 45662 • 24,200
Portsmouth, RI 02871 • 3,540
Portsmouth, VA 23701-99 • 111,500
Port Sulphur, LA 70083 • 3,318
Port Townsend, WA 98368 • 6,067
Port Vue, PA 15133 • 5,316
Port Washington, NY 11050 • 14,521
Port Washington, WI 53074 • 8,612
Port Wentworth, GA 31407 • 3,947
Posen, IL 60469 • 4,642
Posey, IN • 26,414
Post, TX 79356 • 3,961
Post Falls, ID 83854 • 5,736
Postville, IA 52162 • 1,475
Poteau, OK 74953 • 7,089
Poteet, TX 78065 • 3,086
Poth, TX 78147 • 1,461
Potomac, MD 20854 • 22,800
Potomac Heights, MD 20640 • 2,456
Potosi, MO 63664 • 2,528
Potsdam, NY 13676 • 10,635
Pottawatomie, KS • 14,782
Pottawatomie, OK • 55,239
Pottawattamie, IA • 86,561
Potter, PA • 17,726
Potter, SD • 3,674
Potter, TX • 98,637
Potter Valley, CA 95469 • 1,500
Pottstown, PA 19464 • 23,500
Pottsville, PA 17901 • 17,500
Poughkeepsie, NY 12601-99 • 30,900
Poulsbo, WA 98370 • 3,453
Poultney, VT 05764 • 1,554
Poway, CA 92064 • 38,600
Powder River, MT • 2,520
Powder Springs, GA 30073 • 3,381
Powell, TN 37849 • 7,220
Powell, WY 82435 • 5,310
Powell, KY • 11,101
Powell, MT • 6,958
Powellhurst, OR 97236 • 9,000
Power, ID • 6,844
Poweshiek, IA • 19,306
Powhatan, VA • 13,062
Powhatan Point, OH 43942 • 2,181
Poydras, LA 70085 • 5,722
Poynette, WI 53955 • 1,447
Prague, OK 74864 • 2,208
Prairie, AR • 10,140
Prairie, MT • 1,836
Prairie du Chien, WI 53821 • 5,859
Prairie du Sac, WI 53578 • 2,145
Prairie Grove, AR 72753 • 1,708
Prairie View, TX 77446 • 3,993
Prairie Village, KS 66208 • 25,500
Pratt, KS 67124 • 6,885
Pratt, KS • 10,275
Prattville, AL 36067 • 18,647
Preble, OH • 38,223
Premont, TX 78375 • 2,984
Prentiss, MS 39474 • 1,465
Prentiss, MS • 24,025
Prescott, AZ 86301 • 22,100
Prescott, AR 71857 • 4,103
Prescott, WI 54021 • 2,654
Presidio, TX 79845 • 1,603
Presidio, TX • 5,188
Presque Isle, ME 04769 • 10,900
Presque Isle, MI • 14,267
Preston, ID 83263 • 3,759
Preston, MN 55965 • 1,478
Preston, WV • 30,460
Prestonsburg, KY 41653 • 4,011
Price, UT 84501 • 9,086
Price, WI • 15,788
Prichard, AL 36610 • 39,800
Prien, LA 70605 • 6,224
Priest River, ID 83856 • 1,639
Prince Edward, VA • 16,456
Prince Frederick, MD 20678 • 1,805
Prince George, VA • 25,733
Prince Georges, MD • 665,071
Princess Anne, MD 21853 • 1,499
Princeton, FL 33032 • 5,300
Princeton, IL 61356 • 7,342
Princeton, IN 47670 • 8,976
Princeton, KY 42445 • 7,073
Princeton, MN 55371 • 3,146
Princeton, NJ 08540-44 • 12,600
Princeton, WV 24740 • 8,323
Princeton, WI 54968 • 1,479
Princeton Junction, NJ 08550 • 2,419
Princeville, IL 61559 • 1,712
Princeville, NC 27886 • 1,508
Prince William, VA • 144,703
Prineville, OR 97754 • 5,276
Prior Lake, MN 55372 • 9,926
Proctor, MN 55810 • 3,180
Proctor, VT 05765 • 1,998
Prophetstown, IL 61277 • 2,141
Prospect, CT 06712 • 6,807
Prospect, KY 40059 • 1,981
Prospect Heights, IL 60070 • 13,262
Prospect Park, NJ 07508 • 5,142
Prospect Park, PA 19076 • 6,593
Prosser, WA 99350 • 3,896
Providence, KY 42450 • 4,434
Providence, RI 02901-40 • 156,000
Providence, UT 84332 • 2,675
Providence, RI • 571,349
Provincetown, MA 02657 • 3,536
Provo, UT 84601-04 • 77,400
Prowers, CO • 13,070
Pryor, OK 74361 • 8,483
Pueblo, CO 81001-19 • 100,200
Pueblo, CO • 125,972
Pukalani, HI 96788 • 3,950
Pulaski, NY 13142 • 2,415
Pulaski, TN 38478 • 7,350
Pulaski, VA 24301 • 10,106
Pulaski, WI 54162 • 1,875
Pulaski, AR • 340,613
Pulaski, GA • 8,950
Pulaski, IL • 8,840
Pulaski, IN • 13,258
Pulaski, KY • 45,803
Pulaski, MO • 42,011
Pulaski, VA • 35,229
Pullman, WA 99163 • 23,500
Pumphrey, MD 21227 • 3,300
Punta Gorda, FL 33950-55 • 6,797
Punxsutawney, PA 15767 • 7,479
Purcell, OK 73080 • 4,638
Purcellville, VA 22132 • 1,567
Purvis, MS 39475 • 2,256
Pushmataha, OK • 11,773
Putnam, CT 06260 • 6,850
Putnam, FL • 50,549
Putnam, GA • 10,295
Putnam, IL • 6,085
Putnam, IN • 29,163
Putnam, MO • 6,092
Putnam, NY • 77,193
Putnam, OH • 32,991
Putnam, TN • 47,690
Putnam, WV • 38,181
Puyallup, WA 98371-74 • 19,300

Q

Quail Oaks, VA 23234 • 2,000
Quaker Hill, CT 06375 • 2,052
Quakertown, PA 18951 • 8,867
Quanah, TX 79252 • 3,890
Quantico Station, VA 22134 • 7,121
Quarryville, PA 17566 • 1,558
Quartz Hill, CA 93534 • 7,421
Quay, NM • 10,577
Queen Annes, MD • 25,508
Queen City, TX 75572 • 1,748
Queen Creek, AZ 85242 • 2,000
Queens, NY • 1,891,325
Queensborough, WA 98011 • 6,500
Quidnessett, RI 02852 • 3,300
Quidnick, RI 02816 • 2,300
Quince Orchard, MD 20877 • 5,107
Quincy, CA 95971 • 2,700
Quincy, FL 32351 • 8,591
Quincy, IL 62301 • 41,200
Quincy, MA 02169 • 83,800
Quincy, MI 49082 • 1,569
Quincy, WA 98848 • 3,525
Quitman, GA 31643 • 5,422
Quitman, MS 39355 • 2,632
Quitman, TX 75783 • 1,893
Quitman, GA • 2,357
Quitman, MS • 12,636
Quonochontaug, RI 02813 • 1,500

R

Rabun, GA • 10,466
Raceland, KY 41169 • 1,970
Raceland, LA 70394 • 6,302
Racine, WI 53401-99 • 83,400
Racine, WI • 173,132
Radcliff, KY 40160 • 14,656
Radford, VA 24141 • 13,456
Radnor Township, PA 19087 • 27,300
Raeford, NC 28376 • 3,630
Ragland, AL 35131 • 1,860
Rahway, NJ 07065-67 • 26,400
Rainbow City, AL 35901 • 6,793
Rainelle, WV 25962 • 1,983
Rainier, OR 97048 • 1,655
Rains, TX • 4,839
Rainsville, AL 35986 • 3,907
Raleigh, NC 27601-99 • 191,600
Raleigh, WV • 86,821
Raleigh Hills, OR 97225 • 6,517
Ralls, TX 79357 • 2,422
Ralls, MO • 8,984
Ralston, NE 68127 • 5,952
Rambleton Acres, DE 19720 • 1,500
Ramblewood, NJ 08054 • 6,475
Ramona, CA 92065 • 8,173
Ramsey, MN 55303 • 10,093
Ramsey, NJ 07446 • 12,899
Ramsey, MN • 459,784
Ramsey, ND • 13,048
Rancho Cordova, CA 95670 • 50,900
Rancho Mirage, CA 92270 • 6,345
Rancho Palos Verdes, CA 90274 • 48,900
Rancho Rinconado, CA 95014 • 5,100
Rancho Santa Fe, CA 92067 • 4,014
Rand, WV 25306 • 2,400
Randall, TX • 75,062
Randallstown, MD 21133 • 20,500
Randleman, NC 27317 • 2,156
Randolph, ME 04345 • 1,834
Randolph, MA 02368 • 28,700
Randolph, VT 05060 • 2,200
Randolph, WI 53956 • 1,691
Randolph, AL • 20,075
Randolph, AR • 16,834
Randolph, GA • 9,599
Randolph, IL • 35,652
Randolph, IN • 29,997
Randolph, MO • 25,460
Randolph, NC • 91,728
Randolph, WV • 28,734
Rangely, CO 81648 • 2,113
Ranger, TX 76470 • 3,142
Rankin, PA 15104 • 2,892
Rankin, MS • 69,427
Ransom, ND • 6,698
Ranson, WV 25438 • 2,471
Rantoul, IL 61866 • 20,641
Rapid City, SD 57701-09 • 54,600
Rapides, LA • 135,282
Rappahannock, VA • 6,093
Raritan, NJ 08869 • 6,128
Raton, NM 87740 • 8,225
Ravalli, MT • 22,493
Raven, VA 24639 • 4,000
Ravena, NY 12143 • 3,091
Ravenel, SC 29470 • 1,655
Ravenna, OH 44266 • 12,000
Ravenswood, WV 26164 • 4,126
Rawlins, WY 82301 • 11,547
Rawlins, KS • 4,105
Ray, MO • 21,378
Raymond, MS 39154 • 1,967
Raymond, WA 98577 • 2,991
Raymondville, TX 78580 • 9,493
Raymore, MO 64083 • 3,154
Rayne, LA 70578 • 9,066
Raynham, MA 02767 • 2,124
Raynham Center, MA 02768 • 3,776
Raytown, MO 64133 • 31,400
Rayville, LA 71269 • 4,610
Reading, MA 01867 • 22,600
Reading, OH 45215 • 12,843
Reading, PA 19601-99 • 78,600
Reagan, TX • 4,135
Real, TX • 2,469
Rector, AR 72461 • 2,336
Red Bank, NJ 07701 • 12,400
Red Bank, TN 37415 • 13,129
Red Bay, AL 35582 • 3,232
Redbird, OH 44057 • 1,600
Red Bluff, CA 96080 • 9,490
Red Bud, IL 62278 • 2,850
Redding, CA 96001-03 • 50,700
Redfield, SD 57469 • 3,027
Redford, MI 48239 • 56,700
Red Hook, NY 12571 • 1,692
Redkey, IN 47373 • 1,537
Red Lake, MN • 5,471
Red Lake Falls, MN 56750 • 1,732
Redlands, CA 92373-74 • 54,200
Red Lion, PA 17356 • 5,824
Red Lodge, MT 59068 • 1,896
Redmond, OR 97756 • 6,452
Redmond, WA 98052-53 • 28,900
Red Oak, GA 30272 • 2,800
Red Oak, IA 51566 • 6,810
Red Oak, TX 75154 • 1,882
Red Oak Mill, NY 12603 • 5,236
Red Oaks, LA 70815 • 2,000
Redondo Beach, CA 90277-78 • 64,400
Red River, LA • 10,433
Red River, TX • 16,101
Red Springs, NC 28377 • 3,607
Red Willow, NE • 12,615
Red Wing, MN 55066 • 13,736
Redwood, UT 84119 • 2,000
Redwood, MN • 19,341
Redwood City, CA 94061-65 • 56,900
Redwood Falls, MN 56283 • 5,210
Reed City, MI 49677 • 2,221
Reedley, CA 93654 • 11,504
Reedsburg, WI 53959 • 5,038
Reedsport, OR 97467 • 4,990
Reedurban, OH 44710 • 6,650
Reese, MI 48757 • 1,645
Reeves, TX • 15,801
Reform, AL 35481 • 2,245
Refugio, TX 78377 • 3,898
Refugio, TX • 9,289
Rehoboth Beach, DE 19971 • 1,730
Reidland, KY 42001 • 3,730
Reidsville, GA 30453 • 2,296
Reidsville, NC 27320 • 12,492
Reinbeck, IA 50669 • 1,808
Reisterstown, MD 21136 • 19,385
Remsen, IA 51050 • 1,592
Reno, NV 89501-99 • 111,700
Reno, KS • 64,983
Renovo, PA 17764 • 1,812
Rensselaer, IN 47978 • 4,944
Rensselaer, NY 12144 • 9,047
Rensselaer, NY • 151,966
Renton, WA 98055-58 • 34,700
Renville, MN 56284 • 1,493
Renville, MN • 20,401
Renville, ND • 3,608
Republic, MO 65738 • 4,485
Republic, KS • 7,569
Reserve, LA 70084 • 7,288
Reston, VA 22090 • 42,800
Revere, MA 02151 • 43,400
Rexburg, ID 83440 • 11,559
Reynolds, MO • 7,230
Reynoldsburg, OH 43068 • 22,800
Reynoldsville, PA 15851 • 3,016
Rhea, TN • 24,235
Rhinebeck, NY 12572 • 2,542
Rhinelander, WI 54501 • 7,800
Rialto, CA 92376 • 49,300
Rice, KS • 11,900
Rice, MN • 46,087
Rice Lake, WI 54868 • 7,691
Rich, UT • 2,100
Richardson, TX 75080-85 • 81,900
Richardson, NE • 11,315
Richardson Park, DE 19804 • 2,200
Richboro, PA 18954 • 5,141
Richfield, MN 55423 • 37,500
Richfield, UT 84701 • 5,482
Richfield Springs, NY 13439 • 1,561
Richford, VT 05476 • 1,471
Rich Hill, MO 64779 • 1,471
Richland, GA 31825 • 1,802
Richland, MO 65556 • 1,922
Richland, WA 99352 • 31,100
Richland, IL • 17,587
Richland, LA • 22,187
Richland, MT • 12,243
Richland, ND • 19,207
Richland, OH • 131,205
Richland, SC • 269,735
Richland, WI • 17,476
Richland Center, WI 53581 • 4,997
Richland Hills, TX 76118 • 7,977
Richlands, VA 24641 • 5,796
Richmond, CA 94801-99 • 79,900
Richmond, IN 47374 • 39,500
Richmond, KY 40475 • 21,900
Richmond, ME 04357 • 1,578
Richmond, MI 48062 • 3,536
Richmond, MO 64085 • 5,499
Richmond, TX 77469 • 10,561
Richmond, UT 84333 • 1,705
Richmond, VA 23201-99 • 216,300
Richmond, GA • 181,629
Richmond, NY • 352,121
Richmond, NC • 45,481
Richmond, VA • 6,952
Richmond Beach, WA 98160 • 6,700
Richmond Heights, FL 33156 • 8,577
Richmond Heights, MO 63117 • 11,100
Richmond Heights, OH 44143 • 9,700
Richmond Highlands, WA 98133 • 26,500
Richton Park, IL 60471 • 10,118
Richwood, OH 43344 • 2,181
Richwood, WV 26261 • 3,568
Ridge, NY 11961 • 7,570
Ridgecrest, CA 93555 • 20,204
Ridgecrest, WA 98155 • 7,300
Ridgefield, CT 06877 • 6,066
Ridgefield, NJ 07657 • 10,294
Ridgefield Park, NJ 07660 • 12,738
Ridgeland, MS 39157 • 5,461
Ridgely, TN 38080 • 1,932
Ridgewood, NJ 07450-52 • 25,100
Ridgway, PA 15853 • 5,604
Ridley Park, PA 19078 • 7,889
Ridley Township, PA 19018 • 33,200
Rifle, CO 81650 • 3,215
Rigby, ID 83442 • 2,624
Riley, KS • 63,505
Rincon, GA 31326 • 1,988
Ringgold, GA 30736 • 1,882
Ringgold, LA 71068 • 1,655
Ringgold, IA • 6,112
Ringling, OK 73456 • 1,561
Ringwood, NJ 07456 • 12,625
Rio Arriba, NM • 29,282
Rio Blanco, CO • 6,255
Rio Dell, CA 95562 • 2,687
Rio Del Mar, CA 95003 • 7,067
Rio Grande, NJ 08242 • 2,016
Rio Grande, CO • 10,511
Rio Grande City, TX 78582 • 8,930
Rio Hondo, TX 78583 • 1,673
Rio Linda, CA 95673 • 7,359
Rio Rancho, NM 87124 • 9,985
Rio Vista, CA 94571 • 3,142
Ripley, MS 38663 • 4,271
Ripley, OH 45167 • 2,174
Ripley, TN 38063 • 6,395
Ripley, WV 25271 • 3,464
Ripley, IN • 24,398
Ripley, MO • 12,458
Ripon, WI 54971 • 7,111
Rising Sun, IN 47040 • 2,478
Ritchie, WV • 11,442
Rittman, OH 44270 • 6,063
Ritzville, WA 99169 • 1,800
Riverbank, CA 95367 • 5,695
Riverdale, CA 93656 • 1,866
Riverdale, GA 30274 • 7,121
Riverdale, IL 60627 • 13,233
Riverdale, MD 20737 • 4,761
Riverdale, NJ 07457 • 2,530
Riverdale, UT 84401 • 6,031
River Edge, NJ 07661 • 11,111
River Falls, WI 54022 • 9,019
River Forest, IL 60305 • 12,392
River Grove, IL 60171 • 10,368
Riverhead, NY 11901 • 6,339
River Hills, WI 53217 • 1,642
River Oaks, TX 76114 • 6,890
River Pines, MA 01821 • 3,620
River Ridge, LA 70123 • 17,146
River Road, OR 97404 • 10,370
River Rouge, MI 48218 • 12,912
Riverside, CA 92501-99 • 202,200
Riverside, IL 60546 • 9,236
Riverside, NJ 08075 • 7,941
Riverside, PA 17868 • 2,266
Riverside, CA • 663,199
Riverton, IL 62561 • 2,783
Riverton, NJ 08077 • 3,068
Riverton, UT 84065 • 7,032
Riverton, WY 82501 • 9,900
Riverton Heights, WA 98188 • 14,182
River Vale, NJ 07675 • 9,489
Riverview, FL 33569 • 3,200
Riverview, MI 48192 • 14,569
Riviera Beach, FL 33404 • 30,000
Riviera Beach, MD 21122 • 5,600
Roane, TN • 48,425
Roane, WV • 15,952

Roanoke, AL 36274 • 5,809
Roanoke, IL 61561 • 2,001
Roanoke, VA 24001-38 • 100,900
Roanoke, VA • 72,945
Roanoke Rapids, NC 27870 • 15,000
Roaring Spring, PA 16673 • 2,962
Robbins, IL 60472 • 8,853
Robbinsdale, MN 55422 • 14,422
Robersonville, NC 27871 • 1,981
Roberts, SD • 10,911
Roberts, TX • 1,187
Robertsdale, AL 36567 • 2,306
Robertson, KY • 2,265
Robertson, TN • 37,021
Robertson, TX • 14,653
Robertsville, NJ 07726 • 6,500
Robeson, NC • 101,610
Robinson, IL 62454 • 7,285
Robinson, TX 76706 • 6,074
Robstown, TX 78380 • 12,100
Rochelle, GA 31079 • 1,626
Rochelle, IL 61068 • 8,982
Rochelle Park, NJ 07662 • 5,603
Rochester, IL 62563 • 2,488
Rochester, IN 46975 • 5,050
Rochester, MI 48063-64 • 7,278
Rochester, MN 55901-04 • 59,100
Rochester, NH 03867 • 23,200
Rochester, NY 14601-99 • 241,500
Rochester, PA 15074 • 4,759
Rochester Hills, MI 48063 • 45,000
Rock, MN • 10,703
Rock, NE • 2,383
Rock, WI • 139,420
Rockaway, NJ 07866 • 6,852
Rockbridge, VA • 17,911
Rockcastle, KY • 13,973
Rockdale, IL 60436 • 1,913
Rockdale, MD 21207 • 4,200
Rockdale, TX 76567 • 5,611
Rockdale, GA • 36,747
Rock Falls, IL 61071 • 10,633
Rockford, IL 61101-99 • 138,400
Rockford, MI 49341 • 3,324
Rockford, MN 55373 • 2,408
Rock Hall, MD 21661 • 1,511
Rock Hill, MO 63124 • 5,702
Rock Hill, SC 29730 • 40,400
Rockingham, NC 28379 • 8,800
Rockingham, NH • 190,345
Rockingham, NC • 83,426
Rockingham, VA • 57,038
Rock Island, IL 61201 • 45,100
Rock Island, IL • 165,968
Rockland, ME 04841 • 7,919
Rockland, MA 02370 • 15,695
Rockland, NY • 259,530
Rockledge, FL 32955 • 11,877
Rockledge, PA 19111 • 2,538
Rocklin, CA 95677 • 7,344
Rockmart, GA 30153 • 3,623
Rockport, IN 47635 • 2,590
Rockport, MA 01966 • 4,690
Rock Port, MO 64482 • 1,511
Rockport, TX 78382 • 3,686
Rock Rapids, IA 51246 • 2,693
Rock Springs, WY 82901 • 21,600
Rockton, IL 61072 • 2,313
Rock Valley, IA 51247 • 2,706
Rockville, IN 47872 • 2,785
Rockville, MD 20850-56 • 48,000
Rockville Centre, NY 11570 • 25,900
Rockwall, TX 75087 • 6,110
Rockwall, TX • 14,528
Rockwell City, IA 50579 • 2,276
Rockwell Park, NC 28213 • 2,600
Rockwood, MI 48173 • 3,346
Rockwood, OR 97233 • 11,000
Rockwood, TN 37854 • 5,855
Rocky Creek, FL 33615 • 7,800
Rocky Ford, CO 81067 • 4,804
Rocky Hill, CT 06067 • 14,559
Rocky Mount, NC 27801-04 • 47,600
Rocky Mount, VA 24151 • 4,198
Rocky Point, NY 11778 • 7,012
Rocky River, OH 44116 • 21,084
Rodeo, CA 94572 • 8,286
Roebling, NJ 08554 • 2,415
Roeland Park, KS 66203 • 7,962
Roessleville, NY 12205 • 11,685
Roger Mills, OK • 4,799
Rogers, AR 72756 • 22,300
Rogers, OK • 46,436
Rogers City, MI 49779 • 3,923
Rogersville, TN 37857 • 4,368
Rohnert Park, CA 94928 • 22,965
Roland, OK 74954 • 1,472
Rolette, ND • 12,177
Rolla, MO 65401 • 13,400
Rolla, ND 58367 • 1,538
Rolling Fork, MS 39159 • 2,590
Rolling Hills Estates, CA 90274 • 7,701
Rolling Meadows, IL 60008 • 20,167
Roma, TX 78584 • 3,384
Rome, GA 30161 • 31,600
Rome, IL 61562 • 2,744
Rome, NY 13440 • 43,600
Romeo, MI 48065 • 3,509
Romeoville, IL 60441 • 15,519
Romney, WV 26757 • 2,094
Romulus, MI 48174 • 23,700
Ronan, MT 59864 • 1,530
Ronceverte, WV 24970 • 2,312
Ronkonkoma, NY 11779 • 20,200
Roodhouse, IL 62082 • 2,364
Rooks, KS • 7,006
Roosevelt, NY 11575 • 14,109
Roosevelt, UT 84066 • 3,842
Roosevelt, MT • 10,467
Roosevelt, NM • 15,695
Roosevelt Park, MI 49441 • 4,015
Rosamond, CA 93560 • 2,869
Roscoe, TX 79545 • 1,628
Roscommon, MI • 16,374
Roseau, MN 56751 • 2,272
Roseau, MN • 12,574
Rosebud, TX 76570 • 2,076
Rosebud, MT • 9,899
Roseburg, OR 97470 • 16,800
Rosedale, MD 21237 • 19,956
Rosedale, MS 38769 • 2,793
Rose Hill, KS 67133 • 1,557
Rose Hill, NC 28458 • 1,508
Rose Hill, VA 22310 • 5,600
Roseland, CA 95407 • 7,915
Roseland, FL 32957 • 1,607
Roseland, NJ 07068 • 5,330
Roseland, OH 44906 • 3,000
Roselle, IL 60172-73 • 19,603
Roselle, NJ 07203 • 20,641
Roselle Park, NJ 07204 • 13,377
Rosemead, CA 91770 • 47,900
Rosemont, CA 95826 • 18,888
Rosemount, MN 55068 • 5,083
Rosenberg, TX 77471 • 21,400
Roseto, PA 18013 • 1,484
Roseville, CA 95678 • 31,300
Roseville, MI 48066 • 52,900
Roseville, MN 55113 • 34,900
Roseville, OH 43777 • 1,915
Rosewood Heights, IL 62024 • 5,085
Rosiclare, IL 62982 • 1,441
Roslyn Heights, NY 11577 • 6,546
Ross, OH 45061 • 2,767
Ross, OH • 65,004
Rossford, OH 43460 • 5,978
Rossmoor, CA 90720 • 10,457
Ross Township, PA 15237 • 33,400
Rossville, GA 30741 • 3,849
Roswell, GA 30075-77 • 35,400
Roswell, NM 88201 • 44,300
Rotan, TX 79546 • 2,284
Rothschild, WI 54474 • 3,338
Rotterdam, NY 12303 • 23,100
Roulette, PA 16746 • 1,500
Round Lake, IL 60073 • 3,175
Round Lake Beach, IL 60073 • 13,829
Round Rock, TX 78664 • 13,092
Roundup, MT 59072 • 2,119
Rouses Point, NY 12979 • 2,266
Routt, CO • 13,404
Rowan, KY • 19,049
Rowan, NC • 99,186
Rowland, NC 28383 • 1,841
Rowland Heights, CA 91748 • 30,800
Rowlett, TX 75088 • 7,522
Roxboro, NC 27573 • 7,532
Roy, UT 84067 • 19,694
Royal Oak, MI 48067-73 • 67,400
Royal Oak, MI 48220 • 5,784
Royal Pines, NC 28704 • 2,000
Royersford, PA 19468 • 4,243
Royse City, TX 75089 • 1,566
Royston, GA 30662 • 2,404
Rubidoux, CA 92509 • 13,200
Rugby, ND 58368 • 3,335
Ruidoso, NM 88345 • 4,260
Ruleville, MS 38771 • 3,332
Rumford, ME 04276 • 6,256
Rumson, NJ 07760 • 7,623
Runnels, TX • 11,872
Runnemede, NJ 08078 • 9,461
Rupert, ID 83350 • 5,476
Rush, IN • 19,604
Rush, KS • 4,516
Rushford, MN 55971 • 1,478
Rush Springs, OK 73082 • 1,451
Rushville, IL 62681 • 3,348
Rushville, IN 46173 • 6,113
Rusk, TX 75785 • 4,681
Rusk, TX • 41,382
Rusk, WI • 15,589
Ruskin, FL 33570 • 5,117
Russell, KS 67665 • 5,427
Russell, KY 41169 • 3,824
Russell, AL • 47,356
Russell, KS • 8,868
Russell, KY • 13,708
Russell, VA • 31,761
Russell Springs, KY 42642 • 1,831
Russellville, AL 35653 • 8,195
Russellville, AR 72801 • 22,500
Russellville, KY 42276 • 7,858
Russellville, OR 97216 • 6,500
Ruston, LA 71270 • 21,900
Rutherford, NJ 07070-75 • 19,068
Rutherford, NC • 53,787
Rutherford, TN • 84,058
Rutherfordton, NC 28139 • 3,434
Rutland, MA 01543 • 2,312
Rutland, VT 05701 • 18,500
Rutland, VT • 58,347
Rye, NY 10580 • 15,083
Rye Brook, NY 10573 • 7,996

S

Sabetha, KS 66534 • 2,297
Sabina, OH 45169 • 2,799
Sabinal, TX 78881 • 1,827
Sabine, LA • 25,280
Sabine, TX • 8,702
Sac, IA • 14,118
Sacaton, AZ 85247 • 1,951
Sac City, IA 50583 • 3,000
Sachse, TX 75040 • 1,640
Saco, ME 04072 • 12,921
Sacramento, CA 95801-99 • 329,500
Sacramento, CA • 783,381
Saddle Brook, NJ 07662 • 14,084
Saddle River, NJ 07458 • 2,763
Safety Harbor, FL 34695 • 6,461
Safford, AZ 85546 • 7,010
Sagadahoc, ME • 28,795
Sagamore Hills, OH 44067 • 4,700
Sag Harbor, NY 11963 • 2,581
Saginaw, MI 48601-08 • 73,800
Saginaw, TX 76179 • 5,736
Saginaw, MI • 228,059
Saguache, CO • 3,935
Saint Albans, VT 05478 • 7,308
Saint Albans, WV 25177 • 12,402
Saint Andrews, SC 29407 • 9,908
Saint Andrews, SC 29210 • 20,245
Saint Ann, MO 63074 • 15,400
Saint Anthony, ID 83445 • 3,212
Saint Anthony, MN 55418 • 7,981
Saint Augustine, FL 32084-86 • 13,400
Saint Bernard, OH 45217 • 5,396
Saint Bernard, LA • 64,097
Saint Charles, IL 60174 • 19,700
Saint Charles, MD 20601 • 13,921
Saint Charles, MI 48655 • 2,276
Saint Charles, MN 55972 • 2,184
Saint Charles, MO 63301-03 • 52,200
Saint Charles, LA • 37,259
Saint Charles, MO • 144,107
Saint Charles Mesa, CO 81006 • 7,050
Saint Clair, MI 48079 • 4,780
Saint Clair, MO 63077 • 3,485
Saint Clair, PA 17970 • 4,037
Saint Clair, AL • 41,205
Saint Clair, IL • 267,531
Saint Clair, MI • 138,802
Saint Clair, MO • 8,622
Saint Clair Shores, MI 48080-82 • 72,800
Saint Clairsville, OH 43950 • 5,700
Saint Cloud, FL 32769 • 7,840
Saint Cloud, MN 56301-04 • 42,900
Saint Croix, WI • 43,262
Saint Croix Falls, WI 54024 • 1,497
Saint David, AZ 85630 • 1,500
Saint Elmo, IL 62458 • 1,611
Saint Francis, KS 67756 • 1,610
Saint Francis, WI 53207 • 10,095
Saint Francis, AR • 30,858
Saint Francisville, LA 70775 • 1,471
Saint Francois, MO • 42,600
Sainte Genevieve, MO 63670 • 4,481
Sainte Genevieve, MO • 15,180
Saint George, SC 29477 • 2,134
Saint George, UT 84770 • 18,900
Saint Helena, CA 94574 • 4,898
Saint Helena, LA • 9,827
Saint Helens, OR 97051 • 7,064
Saint Henry, OH 45883 • 1,596
Saint Ignace, MI 49781 • 2,632
Saint James, MN 56081 • 4,346
Saint James, MO 65559 • 3,328
Saint James, NY 11780 • 12,122
Saint James, LA • 21,495
Saint John, IN 46373 • 3,974
Saint John, KS 67576 • 1,501
Saint Johns, AZ 85936 • 3,368
Saint Johns, MI 48879 • 7,376
Saint Johns, MO 63114 • 7,854
Saint Johns, FL • 51,303
Saint Johnsbury, VT 05819 • 7,150
Saint Johnsville, NY 13452 • 1,974
Saint John the Baptist, LA • 31,924
Saint Joseph, IL 61873 • 1,900
Saint Joseph, LA 71366 • 1,687
Saint Joseph, MI 49085 • 9,500
Saint Joseph, MN 56374 • 2,994
Saint Joseph, MO 64501-99 • 74,700
Saint Joseph, IN • 241,617
Saint Joseph, MI • 56,083
Saint Landry, LA • 84,128
Saint Lawrence, NY • 114,254
Saint Louis, MI 48880 • 4,107
Saint Louis, MO 63101-99 • 428,900
Saint Louis, MN • 222,229
Saint Louis, MO • 973,896
Saint Louis Park, MN 55426 • 44,400
Saint Lucie, FL • 87,182
Saint Maries, ID 83861 • 2,794
Saint Martin, LA • 40,214
Saint Martinville, LA 70582 • 7,965
Saint Mary, LA • 64,253
Saint Marys, GA 31558 • 3,596
Saint Marys, IN 46556 • 1,800
Saint Marys, KS 66536 • 1,598
Saint Marys, OH 45885 • 8,414
Saint Marys, PA 15857 • 6,417
Saint Marys, WV 26170 • 2,219
Saint Marys, MD • 59,895
Saint Matthews, KY 40207 • 13,900
Saint Matthews, SC 29135 • 2,496
Saint Michael, MN 55376 • 1,519
Saint Paris, OH 43072 • 1,742
Saint Paul, MN 55101-99 • 276,500
Saint Paul, NE 68873 • 2,094
Saint Paul Park, MN 55071 • 4,864
Saint Pauls, NC 28384 • 1,639
Saint Peter, MN 56082 • 9,056
Saint Peters, MO 63376 • 17,029
Saint Petersburg, FL 33701-99 • 246,300
Saint Petersburg Beach, FL 33706 • 9,354
Saint Rose, LA 70087 • 2,800
Saint Simons Island, GA 31522 • 6,566
Saint Stephen, SC 29479 • 1,850
Saint Stephens, NC 28601 • 10,797
Saint Tammany, LA • 110,869
Salamanca, NY 14779 • 6,890
Salem, IL 62881 • 7,813
Salem, IN 47167 • 5,290
Salem, MA 01970 • 38,900
Salem, MO 65560 • 4,454
Salem, NH 03079 • 11,500
Salem, NJ 08079 • 6,959
Salem, OH 44460 • 12,500
Salem, OR 97301-09 • 93,800
Salem, SD 57058 • 1,486
Salem, UT 84653 • 2,233
Salem, VA 24153 • 24,500
Salem, WV 26426 • 2,706
Salem, NJ • 64,676
Salida, CO 81201 • 4,870
Salina, KS 67401 • 43,400
Salina, UT 84654 • 1,992
Salinas, CA 93901-15 • 93,400
Saline, MI 48176 • 6,483
Saline, AR • 53,161
Saline, IL • 28,448
Saline, KS • 48,905
Saline, MO • 24,919
Saline, NE • 13,131
Salineville, OH 43945 • 1,629
Salisbury, CT 06068 • 1,600
Salisbury, MD 21801 • 17,800
Salisbury, MA 01952 • 3,265
Salisbury, MO 65281 • 1,975
Salisbury, NC 28144 • 24,200
Sallisaw, OK 74955 • 6,649
Salmon, ID 83467 • 3,308
Salmon Creek, WA 98665 • 1,900
Salt Lake, UT • 619,066
Salt Lake City, UT 84101-99 • 168,400
Salt Springs, FL 32627 • 1,500
Saltville, VA 24370 • 2,376
Saltwater, WA 98188 • 8,000
Saluda, SC 29138 • 2,752
Saluda, SC • 16,150
Samoset, FL 34208 • 5,747
Sampson, NC • 49,687
Samson, AL 36477 • 2,402
Samtown, LA 71301 • 4,125
San Andreas, CA 95249 • 1,912
San Angelo, TX 76901-09 • 86,700
San Anselmo, CA 94960 • 12,067
San Antonio, TX 78201-99 • 933,700
San Augustine, TX 75972 • 2,930
San Augustine, TX • 8,785
San Benito, TX 78586 • 17,988
San Benito, CA • 25,005
San Bernardino, CA 92401-99 • 143,300
San Bernardino, CA • 895,016
Sanborn, SD • 3,213
San Bruno, CA 94066 • 35,300
San Carlos, AZ 85550 • 2,668
San Carlos, CA 94070 • 25,800
San Clemente, CA 92672 • 31,300
Sandalfoot Cove, FL 33433 • 5,299
Sanders, MT • 8,675
Sandersville, GA 31082 • 6,137
Sand Hill, MA 02066 • 1,800
Sandia, NM 87047 • 5,288
San Diego, CA 92101-99 • 1,035,900
San Diego, TX 78384 • 5,225
San Diego, CA • 1,861,846
San Dimas, CA 91773 • 28,700
Sandoval, IL 62882 • 1,734
Sandoval, NM • 34,799
Sandpoint, ID 83864 • 4,460
Sand Springs, OK 74063 • 13,121
Sandston, VA 23150 • 4,500
Sandstone, MN 55072 • 1,594
Sandusky, MI 48471 • 2,216
Sandusky, OH 44870 • 31,100
Sandusky, OH • 63,267
Sandwich, IL 60548 • 5,365
Sandwich, MA 02563 • 1,784
Sandy, OR 97055 • 3,431
Sandy, UT 84070 • 65,000
Sandy Springs, GA 30328 • 21,120
San Elizario, TX 79849 • 1,548
San Felipe Pueblo, NM 87001 • 1,465
San Fernando, CA 91340-46 • 17,731
Sanford, FL 32771-73 • 31,200
Sanford, ME 04073 • 10,268
Sanford, NC 27330 • 17,700
San Francisco, CA 94101-99 • 738,100
San Francisco, CA • 678,974
San Gabriel, CA 91776-78 • 33,100
Sangamon, IL • 176,070
Sanger, CA 93657 • 12,542
Sanger, TX 76266 • 2,574
Sanibel, FL 33957 • 3,363
Sanilac, MI • 40,789
San Jacinto, CA 92383 • 8,427
San Jacinto, TX • 11,434
San Joaquin, CA • 347,342
San Jose, CA 95101-99 • 715,100
San Juan, TX 78589 • 8,651
San Juan, CO • 833
San Juan, NM • 81,433
San Juan, UT • 12,253
San Juan, WA • 7,838
San Juan Capistrano, CA 92675 • 18,959
San Leandro, CA 94577-79 • 68,000
San Lorenzo, CA 94580 • 20,545
San Luis Obispo, CA 93401 • 39,300
San Luis Obispo, CA • 155,435
San Manuel, AZ 85631 • 5,443
San Marcos, CA 92069 • 17,479
San Marcos, TX 78666 • 28,400
San Marino, CA 91108 • 13,307
San Mateo, CA 94401-99 • 82,200
San Mateo, CA • 587,329
San Miguel, CO • 3,192
San Miguel, NM • 22,751
San Pablo, CA 94806 • 22,200
San Patricio, TX • 58,013
Sanpete, UT • 14,620
San Rafael, CA 94901-15 • 45,700
San Ramon, CA 94583 • 20,511
San Remo, NY 11754 • 7,770
San Saba, TX 76877 • 2,850
San Saba, TX • 6,204
Sans Souci, SC 29609 • 8,393
Santa Ana, CA 92701-99 • 232,100
Santa Anna, TX 76878 • 1,535
Santa Barbara, CA 93101-99 • 81,900
Santa Barbara, CA • 298,694
Santa Clara, CA 95050-55 • 91,900
Santa Clara, OR 97401 • 14,288
Santa Clara, CA • 1,295,071
Santa Cruz, CA 95060-66 • 46,700
Santa Cruz, AZ • 20,459
Santa Cruz, CA • 188,141
Santa Fe, NM 87501-09 • 55,300
Santa Fe, TX 77510 • 6,172
Santa Fe, NM • 75,360
Santa Fe Springs, CA 90670 • 15,700
Santa Maria, CA 93454-56 • 50,200
Santa Monica, CA 90401-99 • 96,200
Santa Paula, CA 93060 • 23,400
Santaquin, UT 84655 • 2,175
Santa Rosa, CA 95401-07 • 97,600
Santa Rosa, NM 88435 • 2,469
Santa Rosa, FL • 55,988
Santa Venetia, CA 94901 • 6,000
Santa Ynez, CA 93460 • 3,335
Santee, CA 92071 • 51,600
Santo Domingo Pueblo, NM 87052 • 2,082
Sappington, MO 63126 • 11,388
Sapulpa, OK 74066 • 18,481
Saraland, AL 36571 • 10,308
Saranac Lake, NY 12983 • 5,578
Sarasota, FL 34230-43 • 54,700
Sarasota, FL • 202,251
Saratoga, CA 95070 • 30,200
Saratoga, WY 82331 • 2,410
Saratoga, NY • 153,759
Saratoga Springs, FL 34232 • 13,860
Saratoga Springs, NY 12866 • 24,500
Sardis, MS 38666 • 2,278
Sargent, ND • 5,512
Sarpy, NE • 86,015
Sartell, MN 56377 • 3,427
Satellite Beach, FL 32937 • 9,163
Satsuma, AL 36572 • 3,822
Saugerties, NY 12477 • 3,882
Saugus, CA 91350 • 16,283
Saugus, MA 01906 • 25,500
Sauk, WI • 43,469
Sauk Centre, MN 56378 • 3,709
Sauk City, WI 53583 • 2,703
Sauk Rapids, MN 56379 • 5,793
Sauk Village, IL 60411 • 10,906
Saukville, WI 53080 • 3,494
Sault Sainte Marie, MI 49783 • 13,800
Saunders, NE • 18,716
Sausalito, CA 94965 • 7,338
Savage, MD 20763 • 2,700
Savage, MN 55378 • 5,237
Savanna, IL 61074 • 4,529
Savannah, GA 31401-99 • 149,900
Savannah, MO 64485 • 4,184

Savannah, TN 38372 • 7,084
Savoy, IL 61874 • 2,126
Sawyer, WI • 12,843
Saydel, IA 50313 • 3,500
Saylesville, RI 02865 • 3,510
Saylorsburg, PA 18353 • 1,500
Sayre, OK 73662 • 3,177
Sayre, PA 18840 • 6,951
Sayreville, NJ 08872 • 31,400
Sayville, NY 11782 • 12,013
Scappoose, OR 97056 • 3,213
Scarborough, ME 04074 • 2,280
Scarsdale, NY 10583 • 17,650
Schaumburg, IL 60194 • 57,700
Schenectady, NY 12301-99 • 67,500
Schenectady, NY • 149,946
Schererville, IN 46375 • 13,209
Schertz, TX 78154 • 7,262
Schiller Park, IL 60176 • 11,458
Schleicher, TX • 2,820
Schley, GA • 3,433
Schofield, WI 54476 • 2,226
Schoharie, NY • 29,710
Schoolcraft, MI • 8,575
Schulenburg, TX 78956 • 2,469
Schuyler, NE 68661 • 4,151
Schuyler, IL • 8,365
Schuyler, MO • 4,979
Schuyler, NY • 17,686
Schuylkill, PA • 160,630
Schuylkill Haven, PA 17972 • 5,977
Scioto, OH • 84,545
Scituate, MA 02066 • 5,351
Scotch Plains, NJ 07076 • 20,774
Scotchtown, NY 10940 • 7,352
Scotia, NY 12302 • 7,280
Scotland, MO • 5,415
Scotland, NC • 32,273
Scotland Neck, NC 27874 • 2,834
Scotlandville, LA 70807 • 15,113
Scott, LA 70583 • 2,239
Scott, AR • 9,685
Scott, IL • 6,142
Scott, IN • 20,422
Scott, IA • 160,022
Scott, KS • 5,782
Scott, KY • 21,813
Scott, MN • 43,784
Scott, MS • 24,556
Scott, MO • 39,647
Scott, TN • 19,259
Scott, VA • 25,068
Scott City, KS 67871 • 4,154
Scott City, MO 63780 • 4,630
Scottdale, GA 30079 • 8,770
Scottdale, PA 15683 • 5,833
Scott Lake, FL 33055 • 14,154
Scottsbluff, NE 69361 • 14,100
Scotts Bluff, NE • 38,344
Scottsboro, AL 35768 • 14,758
Scottsburg, IN 47170 • 5,068
Scottsdale, AZ 85251-71 • 113,200
Scotts Valley, CA 95066 • 6,891
Scottsville, KY 42164 • 4,278
Scottsville, NY 14546 • 1,789
Scott Township, PA 15106 • 20,413
Scranton, PA 18501-99 • 83,200
Screven, GA • 14,043
Scurry, TX • 18,192
Sea Bright, NJ 07760 • 1,812
Seabrook, MD 20706 • 7,100
Seabrook, TX 77586 • 4,670
Sea Cliff, NY 11579 • 5,364
Seaford, DE 19973 • 5,256
Seaford, NY 11783 • 16,117
Seaford, VA 23696 • 2,500
Sea Girt, NJ 08750 • 2,650
Seagoville, TX 75159 • 7,304
Seagraves, TX 79359 • 2,596
Sea Isle City, NJ 08243 • 2,644
Seal Beach, CA 90740 • 27,300
Sealy, TX 77474 • 3,875
Searcy, AR 72143 • 14,240
Searcy, AR • 8,847
Seaside, CA 93955 • 39,400
Seaside, OR 97138 • 5,342
Seaside Heights, NJ 08751 • 1,802
Seaside Park, NJ 08752 • 1,795
Seat Pleasant, MD 20743 • 5,217
Seattle, WA 98101-99 • 492,800
Sebastian, FL 32958 • 2,831
Sebastian, AR • 95,172
Sebastopol, CA 95472 • 5,595
Sebewaing, MI 48759 • 2,046
Sebree, KY 42455 • 1,516
Sebring, FL 33870 • 8,736
Sebring, OH 44672 • 5,078
Secaucus, NJ 07094 • 15,100
Security, CO 80911 • 6,660
Sedalia, MO 65301 • 20,700
Sedan, KS 67361 • 1,579
Sedgwick, KS 67135 • 1,471
Sedgwick, CO • 3,266
Sedgwick, KS • 367,088
Sedona, AZ 86336 • 5,368
Sedro Woolley, WA 98284 • 6,110
Seekonk, MA 02771 • 12,269
Seguin, TX 78155 • 17,854
Selah, WA 98942 • 4,500
Selden, NY 11784 • 17,259
Selinsgrove, PA 17870 • 5,227
Sellersburg, IN 47172 • 3,211
Sellersville, PA 18960 • 3,143
Sells, AZ 85634 • 1,864
Selma, AL 36701 • 26,700
Selma, CA 93662 • 11,556

Selma, NC 27576 • 4,762
Selmer, TN 38375 • 3,979
Seminole, OK 74868 • 8,590
Seminole, TX 79360 • 6,080
Seminole, FL • 179,752
Seminole, GA • 9,057
Seminole, OK • 27,473
Seminole Park, FL 34647 • 8,000
Semmes, AL 36575 • 2,250
Senath, MO 63876 • 1,728
Senatobia, MS 38668 • 5,013
Seneca, IL 61360 • 2,098
Seneca, KS 66538 • 2,389
Seneca, MO 64865 • 1,853
Seneca, SC 29678 • 7,588
Seneca, NY • 33,733
Seneca, OH • 59,733
Seneca Falls, NY 13148 • 7,466
Sequatchie, TN • 8,605
Sequim, WA 98382 • 3,013
Sequoyah, OK • 30,749
Sergeant Bluff, IA 51054 • 2,416
Sesser, IL 62884 • 2,238
Seven Hills, OH 44131 • 13,650
Seven Oaks, PA 29210 • 7,000
Severn, MD 21144 • 20,147
Severna Park, MD 21146 • 21,253
Sevier, AR • 14,060
Sevier, TN • 41,418
Sevier, UT • 14,727
Sevierville, TN 37862 • 5,371
Seville, OH 44273 • 1,568
Sewanee, TN 37375 • 2,298
Seward, AK 99664 • 1,843
Seward, NE 68434 • 5,713
Seward, KS • 17,071
Seward, NE • 15,789
Sewell, NJ 08080 • 1,870
Sewickley, PA 15143 • 4,778
Seymour, CT 06483 • 13,434
Seymour, IN 47274 • 15,050
Seymour, MO 65746 • 1,535
Seymour, TX 76380 • 3,657
Seymour, WI 54165 • 2,530
Seymourville, LA 70764 • 2,891
Shackelford, TX • 3,915
Shady Side, MD 20764 • 2,877
Shadyside, OH 43947 • 4,315
Shady Spring, WV 25918 • 1,786
Shafter, CA 93263 • 7,010
Shaker Heights, OH 44120 • 31,000
Shakopee, MN 55379 • 9,941
Shaler Township, PA 15116 • 31,800
Shallowater, TX 79363 • 1,932
Shamokin, PA 17872 • 10,000
Shamokin Dam, PA 17876 • 1,622
Shamrock, TX 79079 • 2,834
Shannon, GA 30172 • 2,040
Shannon, MO • 7,885
Shannon, SD • 11,323
Shannontown, SC 29150 • 7,900
Sharkey, MS • 7,964
Sharon, MA 02067 • 13,601
Sharon, PA 16146 • 16,700
Sharon Hill, PA 19079 • 6,221
Sharonville, OH 45241 • 10,108
Sharp, AR • 14,607
Sharpley, DE 19803 • 1,700
Sharpsburg, PA 15215 • 4,351
Sharpsville, PA 16150 • 5,375
Shasta, CA • 115,715
Shattuck, OK 73858 • 1,759
Shaw, MS 38773 • 2,461
Shawano, WI 54166 • 7,013
Shawano, WI • 35,928
Shawnee, KS 66203 • 31,800
Shawnee, OK 74801 • 29,100
Shawnee, KS • 154,916
Shawneetown, IL 62984 • 1,841
Sheboygan, WI 53081-83 • 47,900
Sheboygan, WI • 100,935
Sheboygan Falls, WI 53085 • 5,253
Sheffield, AL 35660-62 • 11,903
Sheffield, PA 16347 • 1,471
Sheffield Lake, OH 44054 • 10,484
Shelbina, MO 63468 • 2,169
Shelburne Falls, MA 01370 • 2,046
Shelby, MI 49455 • 1,624
Shelby, MS 38774 • 2,540
Shelby, MT 59474 • 3,142
Shelby, NC 28150 • 15,400
Shelby, OH 44875 • 9,703
Shelby, AL • 66,298
Shelby, IL • 23,923
Shelby, IN • 39,887
Shelby, IA • 15,043
Shelby, KY • 23,328
Shelby, MO • 7,826
Shelby, OH • 43,089
Shelby, TN • 777,113
Shelby, TX • 23,084
Shelbyville, IL 62565 • 5,259
Shelbyville, IN 46176 • 14,500
Shelbyville, KY 40065 • 5,329
Shelbyville, TN 37160 • 13,700
Sheldon, IA 51201 • 5,003
Sheldon, TX 77028 • 2,031
Shelley, ID 83274 • 3,300
Shell Rock, IA 50670 • 1,478
Shelton, CT 06484 • 33,900
Shelton, WA 98584 • 7,629
Shenandoah, IA 51601 • 6,274
Shenandoah, PA 17976 • 7,589
Shenandoah, VA 22849 • 1,861
Shenandoah, VA • 27,559
Shepherd, MI 48883 • 1,534

Shepherd, TX 77371 • 1,674
Shepherdstown, WV 25443 • 1,791
Shepherdsville, KY 40165 • 4,454
Sherborn, MA 01770 • 1,490
Sherburne, NY 13460 • 1,561
Sherburne, MN • 29,908
Sheridan, AR 72150 • 3,042
Sheridan, CO 80110 • 5,377
Sheridan, IN 46069 • 2,200
Sheridan, OR 97378 • 2,358
Sheridan, WY 82801 • 16,500
Sheridan, KS • 3,544
Sheridan, MT • 5,414
Sheridan, NE • 7,544
Sheridan, ND • 2,819
Sheridan, WY • 25,048
Sheridan Beach, WA 98155 • 6,873
Sherman, TX 75090 • 32,300
Sherman, KS • 7,759
Sherman, NE • 4,226
Sherman, OR • 2,172
Sherman, TX • 3,174
Sherrelwood, CO 80221 • 10,200
Sherrill, NY 13461 • 2,830
Sherwood, AR 72116 • 11,506
Sherwood, OR 97140 • 2,554
Sherwood Manor, CT 06082 • 6,303
Sherwood Park, DE 19808 • 2,300
Shiawassee, MI • 71,140
Shillington, PA 19607 • 5,601
Shiloh, PA 17404 • 5,315
Shiner, TX 77984 • 2,213
Shinnston, WV 26431 • 3,059
Shippensburg, PA 17257 • 5,261
Shiprock, NM 87420 • 7,237
Shirley, MA 01464 • 1,630
Shirley, NY 11967 • 18,082
Shively, KY 40216 • 16,645
Shoreview, MN 55112 • 17,300
Shorewood, IL 60435 • 5,060
Shorewood, MN 55331 • 4,646
Shorewood, WI 53211 • 14,327
Shorewood Hills, WI 53705 • 1,837
Short Beach, CT 06405 • 2,500
Shortsville, NY 14548 • 1,669
Shoshone, ID • 19,226
Show Low, AZ 85901 • 5,027
Shreve, OH 44676 • 1,608
Shreveport, LA 71101-99 • 223,300
Shrewsbury, MA 01545 • 22,900
Shrewsbury, MO 63119 • 5,077
Shrewsbury, NJ 07701 • 2,962
Shrewsbury, PA 17361 • 2,688
Shullsburg, WI 53586 • 1,484
Sibley, IA 51249 • 3,051
Sibley, MN • 15,448
Sicklerville, NJ 08081 • 1,750
Sidney, MT 59270 • 5,726
Sidney, NE 69162 • 6,010
Sidney, NY 13838 • 4,861
Sidney, OH 45365 • 17,657
Sierra, CA • 3,073
Sierra, NM • 8,454
Sierra Madre, CA 91024 • 10,837
Sierra Vista, AZ 85635 • 31,700
Siesta Key, FL 34242 • 7,010
Signal Hill, CA 90806 • 5,734
Signal Mountain, TN 37377 • 5,818
Sigourney, IA 52591 • 2,330
Sikeston, MO 63801 • 18,300
Siler City, NC 27344 • 4,446
Siloam Springs, AR 72761 • 7,940
Silsbee, TX 77656 • 7,684
Silver Bay, MN 55614 • 2,917
Silver Bow, MT • 38,092
Silver City, NM 88061 • 10,472
Silver Creek, NY 14136 • 3,088
Silverdale, WA 98383 • 1,500
Silver Hill, MD 20746 • 2,400
Silver Lake, MN 01887 • 2,900
Silver Lake, WI 53170 • 1,598
Silver Spring, MD 20901-99 • 69,600
Silverton, NJ 08753 • 7,321
Silverton, OH 45236 • 6,172
Silverton, OR 97381 • 5,168
Silview, DE 19804 • 1,600
Silvis, IL 61282 • 7,130
Simi Valley, CA 93065 • 89,800
Simmesport, LA 71369 • 2,293
Simpson, PA 18407 • 1,670
Simpson, KY • 14,673
Simpson, MS • 23,441
Simpsonville, SC 29681 • 9,037
Simsbury, CT 06070 • 5,488
Sinton, TX 78387 • 6,044
Sioux, IA • 30,813
Sioux, NE • 1,845
Sioux, ND • 3,620
Sioux Center, IA 51250 • 4,588
Sioux City, IA 51101-99 • 80,600
Sioux Falls, SD 57101-99 • 95,700
Siskiyou, CA • 39,732
Sisseton, SD 57262 • 2,789
Sistersville, WV 26175 • 2,367
Sitka, AK 99835 • 7,803
Skagit, WA • 64,138
Skamania, WA • 7,919
Skaneateles, NY 13152 • 2,789
Skiatook, OK 74070 • 3,596
Skokie, IL 60076-77 • 59,600
Skowhegan, ME 04976 • 6,517
Sky Lake, FL 32809 • 6,692

Skyland, NC 28776 • 2,200
Skyway, WA 98178 • 8,500
Slackwood, NJ 08638 • 8,100
Slater, MO 65349 • 2,492
Slatersville, RI 02876 • 2,330
Slatington, PA 18080 • 4,277
Slaton, TX 79364 • 6,804
Slayton, MN 56172 • 2,420
Sleepy Eye, MN 56085 • 3,581
Slidell, LA 70458-61 • 36,600
Slinger, WI 53086 • 1,612
Slippery Rock, PA 16057 • 3,047
Sloan, NY 14225 • 4,529
Sloatsburg, NY 10974 • 3,154
Slocomb, AL 36375 • 2,153
Slope, ND • 1,157
Smackover, AR 71762 • 2,453
Smethport, PA 16749 • 1,797
Smiley, TX 78159 • 5,050
Smith, KS • 5,947
Smith, MS • 15,077
Smith, TN • 14,935
Smith, TX • 128,366
Smith Center, KS 66967 • 2,240
Smithers, WV 25186 • 1,482
Smithfield, NC 27577 • 7,288
Smithfield, UT 84335 • 4,993
Smithfield, VA 23430 • 3,718
Smiths, AL 36877 • 1,700
Smithton, IL 62285 • 1,447
Smithtown, NY 11787 • 23,700
Smithville, MO 64089 • 1,873
Smithville, OH 44677 • 1,467
Smithville, TN 37166 • 3,839
Smithville, TX 78957 • 3,470
Smyrna, DE 19977 • 4,750
Smyrna, GA 30080 • 23,700
Smyrna, TN 37167 • 11,378
Smyth, VA • 33,366
Sneads, FL 32460 • 1,690
Snellville, GA 30278 • 8,514
Snohomish, WA 98290 • 5,294
Snohomish, WA • 337,720
Snowflake, AZ 85937 • 3,656
Snow Hill, MD 21863 • 2,192
Snyder, OK 73566 • 1,848
Snyder, TX 79549 • 12,705
Snyder, PA • 33,584
Social Circle, GA 30279 • 2,591
Socorro, NM 87801 • 7,173
Socorro, NM • 12,566
Soda Springs, ID 83276 • 4,051
Soddy-Daisy, TN 37379 • 8,505
Sodus, NY 14551 • 1,790
Solana Beach, CA 92075 • 12,250
Solano, CA • 235,203
Soldotna, AK 99669 • 2,320
Soledad, CA 93960 • 5,928
Solon, OH 44139 • 14,341
Solvay, NY 13209 • 7,140
Somerdale, NJ 08083 • 5,900
Somers, CT 06071 • 1,643
Somers Point, NJ 08244 • 10,330
Somersworth, NH 03878 • 10,350
Somerton, AZ 85350 • 3,969
Somervell, TX • 4,154
Somerville, MA 02143 • 75,800
Somerville, NJ 08876-77 • 12,200
Somerville, TN 38068 • 2,264
Somerville, TX 77879 • 1,814
Sonoma, CA 95476 • 6,054
Sonoma, CA • 299,681
Sonora, CA 95370 • 3,247
Sonora, TX 76950 • 3,856
Soperton, GA 30457 • 2,981
Soquel, CA 95073 • 6,212
Souderton, PA 18964 • 6,657
Sound Beach, NY 11789 • 8,071
Sourlake, TX 77659 • 1,807
South Acton, NJ 01720 • 3,220
South Amboy, NJ 08879 • 8,322
South Amherst, MA 01002 • 4,861
South Amherst, OH 44001 • 1,848
Southampton, NY 11968 • 4,000
Southampton, VA • 18,731
Southaven, MS 38671 • 16,441
South Bay, FL 33493 • 3,886
South Belmar, NJ 07719 • 1,566
South Beloit, IL 61080 • 4,088
South Bend, IN 46601-99 • 108,600
South Bend, WA 98586 • 1,686
South Berwick, ME 03908 • 2,120
Southborough, MA 01772 • 1,450
South Boston, VA 24592 • 7,500
South Bound Brook, NJ 08880 • 4,331
South Bradenton, FL 34205 • 14,297
South Broadway, WA 98902 • 3,500
South Burlington, VT 05403 • 11,800
Southbury, CT 06488 • 3,000
South Charleston, OH 45368 • 1,682
South Charleston, WV 25303 • 15,968
South Chicago Heights, IL 60411 • 3,757

South Congaree, SC 29169 • 2,113
South Connellsville, PA 15425 • 2,296
South Cottonwood, UT 84120 • 11,117
South Dartmouth, MA 02748 • 9,850
South Daytona, FL 32021 • 11,252
South Decatur, GA 30034 • 19,350
South Deerfield, MA 01373 • 1,926
South Dennis, MA 02660 • 2,500
South Duxbury, MA 02332 • 2,985
South Easton, MA 02375 • 1,530
South Elgin, IL 60177 • 5,970
South El Monte, CA 91733 • 16,623
Southern Pines, NC 28387 • 8,620
South Euclid, OH 44121 • 24,800
South Farmingdale, NY 12779 • 2,196
South Farmingdale, NY 11735 • 16,439
Southfield, MI 48034 • 74,300
South Fulton, TN 38257 • 3,026
South Gastonia, NC 28052 • 2,000
South Gate, CA 90280 • 80,300
Southgate, FL 34239 • 7,322
Southgate, KY 41071 • 2,833
South Gate, MD 21061 • 6,150
Southgate, MI 48195 • 30,600
South Glastonbury, CT 06073 • 1,570
Southglenn, CO 80122 • 5,060
South Glens Falls, NY 12801 • 3,714
South Grafton, MA 01560 • 2,610
South Hackensack, NJ 07606 • 2,229
South Hadley, MA 01075 • 5,340
South Hadley Falls, MA 01075 • 5,100
South Hamilton, MA 01982 • 2,720
South Haven, IN 46383 • 6,679
South Haven, MI 49090 • 5,943
South Hill, NY 14850 • 5,276
South Hill, VA 23970 • 4,347
South Hingham, MA 02043 • 4,080
South Holland, IL 60473 • 23,700
South Houston, TX 77587 • 13,293
South Huntington, NY 11746 • 18,854
South Hutchinson, KS 67505 • 2,226
Southington, CT 06489 • 38,800
South International Falls, MN 56679 • 2,806
South Jacksonville, IL 62650 • 3,382
South Jordan, UT 84065 • 7,492
South Kensington, MD 20895 • 9,344
South Laguna, CA 92677 • 6,013
South Lake Tahoe, CA 95702 • 23,600
South Lancaster, MA 01561 • 2,329
South Laramie, WY 82070 • 1,500
South Laurel, MD 20707 • 8,500
South Lebanon, OH 45065 • 2,700
South Lyon, MI 48178 • 5,214
South Mansfield, LA 71052 • 1,463
South Medford, OR 97501 • 2,898
South Miami, FL 33143 • 10,895
South Miami Heights, FL 33157 • 18,000
South Milwaukee, WI 53172 • 21,069
South Modesto, CA 95350 • 12,492
South Nyack, NY 10960 • 3,602
South Ogden, UT 84403 • 11,366
Southold, NY 11971 • 4,770
South Orange, NJ 07079 • 15,864
South Paris, ME 04281 • 2,128
South Pasadena, CA 91030 • 24,500
South Patrick Shores, FL 32937 • 9,816
South Pittsburg, TN 37380 • 3,723
South Plainfield, NJ 07080 • 20,300
Southport, FL 32409 • 1,992
Southport, IN 46227 • 2,266
Southport, NY 14904 • 8,329
Southport, NC 28461 • 2,824
South Portland, ME 04106 • 23,400
South River, NJ 08882 • 14,361
South Salt Lake, UT 84115 • 10,413
South San Francisco, CA 94080 • 51,900
South San Gabriel, CA 91770 • 5,421
South San Jose Hills, CA 91744 • 16,049
South Setauket, NY 11733 • 5,990
Southside, AL 35901 • 5,141

South Sioux City, NE 68776 • 9,339
South Stony Brook, NY 11790 • 6,120
South St. Paul, MN 55075 • 21,235
South Streator, IL 61364 • 2,334
South Sumter, SC 29150 • 7,096
South Toms River, NJ 08757 • 3,954
South Tucson, AZ 85713 • 6,554
South Valley Stream, NY 11581 • 5,462
South Venice, FL 34293 • 8,075
South Wellfleet, MA 02663 • 2,300
South Westbury, NY 11590 • 9,732
South Whitley, IN 46787 • 1,575
South Whittier, CA 90605 • 48,300
South Williamsport, PA 17701 • 6,581
South Windsor, CT 06074 • 10,800
Southwood, CO 80120 • 2,050
Southwood Acres, CT 06082 • 9,779
South Yarmouth, MA 02664 • 7,525
South Yuba City, CA 95991 • 7,530
South Zanesville, OH 43701 • 1,739
Spalding, GA • 47,899
Spanaway, WA 98387 • 8,868
Spangler, PA 15775 • 2,399
Spanish Fork, UT 84660 • 9,825
Spanish Fort, AL 36527 • 3,415
Spanish Lake, MO 63138 • 20,632
Sparks, NV 89431-33 • 51,300
Sparta, GA 31087 • 1,745
Sparta, IL 62286 • 4,976
Sparta, MI 49345 • 3,373
Sparta, NJ 07871 • 8,498
Sparta, NC 28675 • 1,687
Sparta, TN 38583 • 5,019
Sparta, WI 54656 • 6,934
Spartanburg, SC 29301-18 • 45,700
Spartanburg, SC • 201,861
Spearfish, SD 57783 • 5,251
Spearman, TX 79081 • 3,413
Speedway, IN 46224 • 12,641
Spencer, IN 47460 • 2,732
Spencer, IA 51301 • 11,726
Spencer, MA 01562 • 6,350
Spencer, NC 28159 • 2,938
Spencer, WV 25276 • 2,799
Spencer, WI 54479 • 1,754
Spencer, IN • 19,361
Spencer, KY • 5,929
Spencerport, NY 14559 • 3,424
Spencerville, OH 45887 • 2,184
Spindale, NC 28160 • 4,246
Spink, SD • 9,201
Spirit Lake, IA 51360 • 3,976
Spiro, OK 74959 • 2,221
Spokane, WA 99201-99 • 175,800
Spokane, WA • 341,835
Spooner, WI 54801 • 2,365
Spotswood, NJ 08884 • 7,840
Spotsylvania, VA • 34,435
Sprague, WV 25926 • 2,090
Spring, TX 77373 • 3,000
Spring Arbor, MI 49283 • 2,101
Springboro, OH 45066 • 5,420
Spring City, PA 19475 • 3,389
Spring City, TN 37381 • 2,232
Springdale, AR 72764 • 25,900
Springdale, OH 45246 • 10,900
Springdale, PA 15144 • 4,418
Springdale, SC 29169 • 2,985
Springer, NM 87747 • 1,657
Springerville, AZ 85938 • 1,878
Springfield, CO 81073 • 1,657
Springfield, FL 32401 • 7,220
Springfield, IL 62701-99 • 104,400
Springfield, KY 40069 • 3,179
Springfield, MA 01101-99 • 151,000
Springfield, MI 49015 • 5,917
Springfield, MN 56087 • 2,303
Springfield, MO 65801-99 • 142,300
Springfield, NJ 07081 • 13,955
Springfield, OH 45501-99 • 69,200
Springfield, OR 97477-78 • 40,000
Springfield, PA 19064 • 24,800
Springfield, TN 37172 • 10,950
Springfield, VT 05156 • 5,603
Springfield, VA 22150-61 • 12,500
Springfield Township, PA 19118 • 20,344
Spring Garden, PA 17403 • 11,127
Spring Grove, PA 17362 • 1,832
Spring Hill, FL 34606 • 6,468
Spring Hill, KS 66083 • 2,005
Springhill, LA 71075 • 6,516
Spring Lake, MI 49456 • 2,731
Spring Lake, NJ 07762 • 4,215
Spring Lake, NC 28390 • 6,485
Spring Lake Heights, NJ 07762 • 5,424
Spring Lake Park, MN 55432 • 6,477
Springvale, ME 04083 • 2,940
Spring Valley, CA 92077-78 • 49,000
Spring Valley, IL 61362 • 5,822
Spring Valley, MN 55975 • 2,616
Spring Valley, NY 10977 • 22,200
Springville, AL 35146 • 1,476
Springville, NY 14141 • 4,285
Springville, UT 84663-64 • 12,101
Spruce Pine, NC 28777 • 2,282
Spur, TX 79370 • 1,690
Stafford, KS • 5,694
Stafford, VA • 40,470
Stafford Springs, CT 06076 • 3,392
Stambaugh, MI 49964 • 1,442
Stamford, CT 06901-99 • 103,200
Stamford, TX 79553 • 4,542
Stamps, AR 71860 • 2,859
Stanaford, WV 25927 • 2,016
Stanfield, AZ 85272 • 1,700
Stanfield, OR 97875 • 1,623
Stanford, CA 94305 • 11,045
Stanford, KY 40484 • 2,764
Stanhope, NJ 07874 • 3,638
Stanislaus, CA • 265,900
Stanley, NC 28164 • 2,341
Stanley, ND 58784 • 1,631
Stanley, WI 54768 • 2,095
Stanley, SD • 2,533
Stanleytown, VA 24168 • 1,761
Stanleyville, NC 27045 • 5,039
Stanly, NC • 48,517
Stanton, CA 90680 • 28,700
Stanton, KY 40380 • 2,691
Stanton, NE 68779 • 1,603
Stanton, TX 79782 • 2,314
Stanton, KS • 2,339
Stanton, NE • 6,549
Stanwood, WA 98292 • 1,646
Staples, MN 56479 • 2,887
Star City, AR 71667 • 2,066
Star City, WV 26505 • 1,464
Stark, IL • 7,389
Stark, ND • 23,697
Stark, OH • 378,823
Starke, FL 32091 • 5,306
Starke, IN • 21,997
Starkville, MS 39759 • 16,700
Starr, TX • 27,266
State College, PA 16801-05 • 34,600
Stateline, NV 89449 • 1,500
Statesboro, GA 30458 • 15,100
Statesville, NC 28677 • 19,600
Staunton, IL 62088 • 4,744
Staunton, VA 24401 • 21,500
Stayton, OR 97383 • 4,396
Steamboat Springs, CO 80487 • 5,098
Stearns, KY 42647 • 1,557
Stearns, MN • 108,161
Steele, MO 63877 • 2,419
Steele, MN • 30,328
Steele, ND • 3,106
Steeleville, IL 62288 • 2,240
Steelton, PA 17113 • 6,484
Steelville, MO 65565 • 1,470
Steger, IL 60475 • 9,269
Steilacoom, WA 98388 • 4,886
Stephens, GA • 21,763
Stephens, OK • 43,419
Stephens, TX • 9,926
Stephenson, IL • 49,536
Stephenville, TX 76401 • 11,881
Sterling, CO 80751 • 11,600
Sterling, IL 61081 • 15,900
Sterling, KS 67579 • 2,312
Sterling, VA 22170 • 16,080
Sterling, TX • 1,206
Sterling Heights, MI 48077 • 112,100
Steuben, IN • 24,694
Steuben, NY • 99,217
Steubenville, OH 43952 • 23,900
Stevens, KS • 4,736
Stevens, MN • 11,322
Stevens, WA • 28,979
Stevenson, AL 35772 • 2,568
Stevens Point, WI 54481 • 22,900
Stewart, GA • 5,896
Stewart, TN • 8,665
Stewartville, MN 55976 • 3,925
Stickney, IL 60402 • 5,893
Stigler, OK 74462 • 2,630
Stillwater, MN 55082 • 12,290
Stillwater, NY 12170 • 1,572
Stillwater, OK 74074-76 • 38,300
Stillwater, MT • 5,598
Stilwell, OK 74960 • 2,369
Stinnett, TX 79083 • 2,222
Stirling, NJ 07980 • 1,800
Stockbridge, GA 30281 • 2,103
Stockton, CA 95201-13 • 187,700
Stockton, IL 61085 • 1,872
Stockton, KS 67669 • 1,825
Stockton, MO 65785 • 1,432
Stoddard, MO • 29,009
Stokes, NC • 33,086
Stone, AR • 9,022
Stone, MS • 9,716
Stone, MO • 15,587
Stoneham, MA 02180 • 22,600
Stone Mountain, GA 30083 • 4,867
Stonewall, TX • 2,406
Stonewood, WV 26301 • 2,058
Stony Brook, NY 11790 • 6,880
Stony Point, NY 10980 • 8,686
Storey, NV • 1,503
Storm Lake, IA 50588 • 8,814
Storrs, CT 06268 • 11,394
Story, IA • 72,326
Story City, IA 50248 • 2,762
Stoughton, MA 02072 • 27,400
Stoughton, WI 53589 • 7,589
Stow, OH 44224 • 25,700
Stowe, PA 19464 • 3,860
Stowe Township, PA 15136 • 9,202
Strafford, NH • 85,408
Strasburg, OH 44680 • 2,091
Strasburg, PA 17579 • 1,999
Strasburg, VA 22657 • 2,311
Stratford, CT 06497 • 51,000
Stratford, DE 19720 • 2,100
Stratford, NJ 08084 • 8,005
Stratford, OK 74872 • 1,459
Stratford, TX 79084 • 1,917
Stratford Landing, VA 22308 • 2,800
Strathmore, CA 93267 • 1,955
Strawberry Point, IA 52076 • 1,463
Streamwood, IL 60103 • 26,800
Streator, IL 61364 • 15,100
Streetsboro, OH 44241 • 9,055
Strongsville, OH 44136 • 31,100
Stroud, OK 74079 • 3,148
Stroudsburg, PA 18360 • 5,500
Struthers, OH 44471 • 13,624
Stuart, FL 34994-97 • 11,300
Stuart, IA 50250 • 1,650
Stuarts Draft, VA 24477 • 1,776
Sturbridge, MA 01566 • 1,891
Sturgeon Bay, WI 54235 • 8,847
Sturgis, KY 42459 • 2,293
Sturgis, MI 49091 • 9,468
Sturgis, SD 57785 • 5,184
Sturtevant, WI 53177 • 4,130
Stutsman, ND • 24,154
Stuttgart, AR 72160 • 10,983
Sublette, WY • 4,548
Succasunna, NJ 07876 • 7,750
Sudbury, MA 01776 • 1,860
Sudbury Center, MA 01776 • 2,590
Suffern, NY 10901 • 10,794
Suffolk, VA 23434-38 • 51,400
Suffolk, MA • 650,142
Suffolk, NY • 1,284,231
Sugar Creek, MO 64054 • 4,305
Sugarcreek, PA 16323 • 5,954
Sugar Hill, GA 30518 • 2,473
Sugar Land, TX 77478-79 • 11,599
Sugarland Run, VA 22170 • 6,258
Sugar Loaf, VA 24018 • 6,500
Suisun City, CA 94585 • 11,087
Suitland, MD 20746 • 33,700
Sulligent, AL 35586 • 2,130
Sullivan, IL 61951 • 4,526
Sullivan, IN 47882 • 4,774
Sullivan, MO 63080 • 5,461
Sullivan, IN • 21,107
Sullivan, MO • 7,434
Sullivan, NH • 36,063
Sullivan, NY • 65,155
Sullivan, PA • 6,349
Sullivan, TN • 143,968
Sullivans Island, SC 29482 • 1,867
Sully, SD • 1,990
Sulphur, LA 70663 • 19,709
Sulphur, OK 73086 • 5,516
Sulphur Springs, TX 75482 • 12,804
Sultan, WA 98294 • 1,578
Sumiton, AL 35148 • 2,815
Summerfield, NC 27358 • 1,680
Summers, WV • 15,875
Summersville, WV 26651 • 2,972
Summerville, GA 30747 • 4,878
Summerville, SC 29483 • 12,009
Summit, IL 60501 • 10,110
Summit, MS 39666 • 1,753
Summit, NJ 07901 • 20,900
Summit, TN 37363 • 1,500
Summit, CO • 8,848
Summit, OH • 524,472
Summit, UT • 10,198
Summit Hill, PA 18250 • 3,418
Sumner, IA 50674 • 2,335
Sumner, WA 98390 • 4,936
Sumner, KS • 24,928
Sumner, TN • 85,790
Sumter, SC 29150-54 • 28,000
Sumter, AL • 16,908
Sumter, FL • 24,272
Sumter, GA • 29,360
Sumter, SC • 88,243
Sunbury, OH 43074 • 2,101
Sunbury, PA 17801 • 12,200
Sun City, AZ 85351 • 51,800
Sun City, CA 92381 • 6,500
Sun City Center, FL 33570 • 5,605
Suncook, NH 03275 • 4,698
Sundown, TX 79372 • 1,511
Sunflower, MS • 34,844
Sunland Park, NM 88063 • 4,313
Sunny Isles, FL 33160 • 12,564
Sunnymead, CA 92388 • 11,554
Sunnyside, CA 93727 • 5,000
Sunnyside, WA 98944 • 9,225
Sunnyvale, CA 94086-89 • 113,400
Sun Prairie, WI 53590 • 12,931
Sunray, TX 79086 • 1,952
Sunrise, FL 33313 • 50,600
Sunrise Manor, NV 89110 • 55,500
Sunset, FL 33143 • 13,531
Sunset, LA 70584 • 2,300
Sunset, UT 84015 • 5,733
Sun Valley, NV 89433 • 8,822
Superior, AZ 85273 • 4,600
Superior, NE 68978 • 2,502
Superior, WI 54880 • 27,500
Suquamish, WA 98392 • 1,498
Surf City, NJ 08008 • 1,571
Surfside, FL 33154 • 3,763
Surfside Beach, SC 29577 • 2,522
Surgoinsville, TN 37873 • 1,559
Surprise, AZ 85345 • 3,723
Surry, NC • 59,449
Surry, VA • 6,046
Susanville, CA 96130 • 6,520
Susquehanna, PA 18847 • 1,994
Susquehanna, PA • 37,876
Sussex, NJ 07461 • 2,418
Sussex, WI 53089 • 3,699
Sussex, DE • 97,983
Sussex, NJ • 116,119
Sussex, VA • 10,874
Sutherlin, OR 97479 • 4,560
Sutter, CA • 52,246
Sutter Creek, CA 95685 • 1,705
Sutton, TX • 5,130
Suwannee, FL • 22,287
Swain, NC • 10,283
Swainsboro, GA 30401 • 7,602
Swampscott, MA 01907 • 13,837
Swannanoa, NC 28778 • 5,586
Swansea, IL 62221 • 5,529
Swanton, OH 43558 • 3,424
Swanton, VT 05488 • 2,520
Swanwyck Estates, DE 19720 • 1,700
Swarthmore, PA 19081 • 5,950
Swartz Creek, MI 48473 • 5,013
Swatara Township, PA 17111 • 19,300
Swedesboro, NJ 08085 • 2,031
Sweeny, TX 77480 • 3,538
Sweet Grass, MT • 3,216
Sweet Home, OR 97386 • 6,921
Sweet Springs, MO 65351 • 1,694
Sweetwater, FL 33152 • 8,251
Sweetwater, TN 37874 • 5,310
Sweetwater, TX 79556 • 12,242
Sweetwater, WY • 41,723
Sweetwater Creek, FL 33614 • 18,000
Swift, MN • 12,920
Swisher, TX • 9,723
Swissvale, PA 15218 • 11,345
Switzerland, FL 32043 • 2,400
Switzerland, IN • 7,153
Swoyerville, PA 18704 • 5,795
Sycamore, IL 60178 • 9,219
Sykesville, MD 21784 • 1,712
Sykesville, PA 15865 • 1,537
Sylacauga, AL 35150 • 12,708
Sylva, NC 28779 • 1,699
Sylvania, GA 30467 • 3,352
Sylvania, OH 43560 • 15,527
Sylvan Lake, MI 48053 • 1,949
Sylvester, GA 31791 • 5,874
Syosset, NY 11791 • 9,818
Syracuse, IN 46567 • 2,579
Syracuse, KS 67878 • 1,654
Syracuse, NE 68446 • 1,638
Syracuse, NY 13201-99 • 164,700
Syracuse, UT 84041 • 3,702

T

Tabor City, NC 28463 • 2,710
Tacoma, WA 98401-99 • 163,000
Taft, CA 93268 • 5,316
Taft, TX 78390 • 3,686
Tahlequah, OK 74464 • 9,708
Tahoka, TX 79373 • 3,262
Takoma Park, MD 20912 • 16,231
Talbot, GA • 6,536
Talbot, MD • 25,604
Talent, OR 97540 • 2,577
Taliaferro, GA • 2,032
Talladega, AL 35160 • 19,800
Talladega, AL • 73,826
Tallahassee, FL 32301-17 • 121,200
Tallahatchie, MS • 17,157
Tallapoosa, GA 30176 • 2,647
Tallapoosa, AL • 38,676
Tallassee, AL 36078 • 5,583
Talleyville, DE 19803 • 6,880
Tallmadge, OH 44278 • 14,200
Tallulah, LA 71282 • 11,341
Tama, IA 52339 • 2,968
Tama, IA • 19,533
Tamalpais Valley, CA 94941 • 5,000
Tamaqua, PA 18252 • 8,843
Tamarac, FL 33321 • 34,200
Tamiami, FL 33165 • 17,607
Tampa, FL 33601-99 • 290,000
Taney, MO • 20,467
Taneytown, MD 21787 • 2,618
Tangipahoa, LA • 80,698
Tanglewood, FL 33907 • 8,229
Taos, NM 87571 • 3,369
Taos, NM • 19,456
Tappahannock, VA 22560 • 1,821
Tappan, NY 10983 • 8,267
Tara Hills, CA 94564 • 6,000
Tarboro, NC 27886 • 10,279
Tarentum, PA 15084 • 6,419
Tarkio, MO 64491 • 2,375
Tarpey, CA 93727 • 4,000
Tarpon Springs, FL 34689-91 • 13,251
Tarrant, TX • 860,880
Tarrant City, AL 35217 • 8,148
Tarrytown, NY 10591 • 10,648
Tate, MS • 20,119
Tattnall, GA • 18,134
Taunton, MA 02780 • 46,800
Tavares, FL 32778 • 4,398
Tavernier, FL 33070 • 1,834
Tawas City, MI 48763 • 1,967
Taylor, AZ 85939 • 2,006
Taylor, MI 48180 • 72,900
Taylor, PA 18517 • 7,246
Taylor, TX 76574 • 10,619
Taylor, FL • 16,532
Taylor, GA • 7,902
Taylor, IA • 8,353
Taylor, KY • 21,178
Taylor, TX • 110,932
Taylor, WV • 16,584
Taylor, WI • 18,817
Taylor Mill, KY 41015 • 4,509
Taylors, SC 29687 • 12,100
Taylorsville, UT 84107 • 17,448
Taylorville, IL 62568 • 11,386
Tazewell, TN 37879 • 2,105
Tazewell, VA 24651 • 4,468
Tazewell, IL • 132,078
Tazewell, VA • 50,511
Tchula, MS 39169 • 1,931
Teague, TX 75860 • 3,390
Teaneck, NJ 07666 • 38,400
Teaticket, MA 02536 • 2,600
Tecumseh, MI 49286 • 7,320
Tecumseh, NE 68450 • 1,926
Tecumseh, OK 74873 • 5,123
Tehachapi, CA 93561 • 4,126
Tehama, CA • 38,888
Tekamah, NE 68061 • 1,886
Telfair, GA • 11,445
Telford, PA 18969 • 3,507
Tell City, IN 47586 • 8,704
Teller, CO • 8,034
Temecula, CA 92390 • 1,783
Tempe, AZ 85281-89 • 134,800
Temperance, MI 48182 • 3,500
Temple, GA 30179 • 1,520
Temple, PA 19560 • 1,486
Temple, TX 76501-03 • 47,400
Temple City, CA 91780 • 31,800
Temple Terrace, FL 33617 • 11,097
Tenafly, NJ 07670 • 13,552
Tennille, GA 31089 • 1,709
Tensas, LA • 8,525
Terra Alta, WV 26764 • 1,946
Terrebonne, LA • 94,393
Terre Haute, IN 47801-08 • 57,500
Terrell, TX 75160 • 13,269
Terrell, GA • 12,017
Terrell, TX • 1,595
Terrell Hills, TX 78209 • 4,644
Terry, TX • 14,581
Terrytown, LA 70053 • 23,548
Terryville, CT 06786 • 5,234
Terryville, NY 11776 • 7,380
Teton, ID • 2,897
Teton, MT • 6,491
Teton, WY • 9,355
Tewksbury, MA 01876 • 10,540
Texarkana, AR 75502 • 22,300
Texarkana, TX 75501-05 • 34,300
Texas, MO • 21,070
Texas, OK • 17,727
Texas City, TX 77590-92 • 44,100
Thatcher, AZ 85552 • 3,374
Thayer, MO 65791 • 2,211
Thayer, NE • 7,582
The Colony, TX 75056 • 11,586
The Dalles, OR 97058 • 10,600
Theodore, AL 36582 • 6,392
The Plains, OH 45780 • 2,044
Thermopolis, WY 82443 • 4,000
The Village, OK 73120 • 11,114
The Village of India, OH 45243 • 5,521
The Woodlands, TX 77380 • 8,443
Thibodaux, LA 70301-02 • 17,200
Thief River Falls, MN 56701 • 9,105
Thiensville, WI 53092 • 3,341
Thomas, OK 73669 • 1,515
Thomas, GA • 38,098
Thomas, KS • 8,451
Thomas, NE • 973
Thomaston, CT 06787 • 3,590
Thomaston, GA 30286 • 9,682
Thomaston, ME 04861 • 2,348
Thomasville, AL 36784 • 4,387
Thomasville, GA 31792 • 18,400
Thomasville, NC 27360 • 16,300
Thompson Falls, MT 59873 • 1,478
Thomson, GA 30824 • 7,001
Thonotosassa, FL 33592 • 1,500
Thornton, CO 80229 • 48,500
Thorntown, IN 46071 • 1,468
Thorofare, NJ 08086 • 1,800
Thorp, WI 54771 • 1,635
Thousand Oaks, CA 91360-63 • 98,100
Three Oaks, MI 49128 • 1,774
Three Rivers, MA 01080 • 3,322
Three Rivers, MI 49093 • 7,015
Three Rivers, TX 78071 • 2,133
Throckmorton, TX • 2,053
Throop, PA 18512 • 4,166
Thunderbolt, GA 31404 • 2,165
Thurmont, MD 21788 • 2,934
Thurston, NE • 7,186
Thurston, WA • 124,264
Tiburon, CA 94920 • 7,680
Tice, FL 33905 • 6,645
Ticonderoga, NY 12883 • 2,938

Tiffin, OH 44883 • 19,800
Tift, GA • 32,862
Tifton, GA 31794 • 14,400
Tigard, OR 97223 • 18,364
Tillamook, OR 97141 • 4,115
Tillamook, OR • 21,164
Tillman, OK • 12,398
Tillmans Corner, AL 36619
• 5,000
Tillson, NY 12486 • 1,529
Tilton, IL 61833 • 2,405
Tiltonsville, OH 43963 • 1,750
Timberlake, VA 24502 • 8,700
Timberville, VA 22853 • 1,510
Timmonsville, SC 29161 • 2,112
Tinley Park, IL 60477 • 29,100
Tinton Falls, NJ 07724 • 7,740
Tioga, ND 58852 • 1,597
Tioga, NY • 49,812
Tioga, PA • 40,973
Tippah, MS • 18,739
Tipp City, OH 45371 • 5,595
Tippecanoe, IN • 121,702
Tipton, IN 46072 • 5,004
Tipton, IA 52772 • 3,055
Tipton, MO 65081 • 2,155
Tipton, OK 73570 • 1,475
Tipton, IN • 16,819
Tipton, TN • 32,930
Tiptonville, TN 38079 • 2,438
Tishomingo, MS • 18,434
Tishomingo, OK 73460 • 3,212
Titus, TX • 21,442
Titusville, FL 32780-83 • 41,600
Titusville, PA 16354 • 6,884
Tiverton, RI 02878 • 7,653
Toast, NC 27049 • 2,339
Toccoa, GA 30577 • 8,869
Todd, KY • 11,874
Todd, MN • 24,991
Todd, SD • 7,328
Todd Estates, DE 19713 • 3,000
Toledo, IA 52342 • 2,445
Toledo, OH 43601-99 • 342,400
Toledo, OR 97391 • 3,221
Tolland, CT • 114,823
Tolleson, AZ 85353 • 4,433
Tolono, IL 61880 • 2,434
Toluca, IL 61369 • 1,471
Tomah, WI 54660 • 7,204
Tomahawk, WI 54487 • 3,527
Tomball, TX 77375 • 3,996
Tombstone, AZ 85638 • 1,632
Tom Green, TX • 84,784
Tompkins, NY • 87,085
Tompkinsville, KY 42167 • 3,077
Toms River, NJ 08753-57 • 7,465
Tonawanda, NY 14150 • 18,693
Tonganoxie, KS 66086 • 1,864
Tonkawa, OK 74653 • 3,524
Tonopah, NV 89049 • 1,952
Tooele, UT 84074 • 14,335
Tooele, UT • 26,033
Toole, MT • 5,559
Toombs, GA • 22,592
Topeka, KS 66601-99 • 119,900
Toppenish, WA 98948 • 6,517
Topsfield, MA 01983 • 2,647
Topsham, ME 04086 • 4,657
Topton, PA 19562 • 1,818
Toronto, OH 43964 • 6,934
Torrance, CA 90501-99 • 141,400
Torrance, NM • 7,491
Torrington, CT 06790 • 32,300
Torrington, WY 82240 • 5,441
Totowa, NJ 07512 • 11,448
Touisset, MA 02777 • 1,520
Towanda, PA 18848 • 3,526
Tower City, PA 17980 • 1,667
Town and Country, WA 99210
• 5,578
Towner, ND • 4,052
Town 'n Country, FL 33615
• 11,400
Town of Tonawanda, NY 14223
• 67,500
Towns, GA • 5,638
Townsend, MT 59644 • 1,587
Towson, MD 21204 • 52,200
Tracy, CA 95376 • 18,428
Tracy, MN 56175 • 2,478
Tracy City, TN 37387 • 1,536
Tracyton, WA 98393 • 2,304
Traer, IA 50675 • 1,703
Trafford, PA 15085 • 3,662
Trail Creek, IN 46360 • 2,581
Traill, ND • 9,624
Transylvania, NC • 23,417
Travelers Rest, SC 29690 • 3,017
Traverse, MN • 5,542
Traverse City, MI 49684 • 16,100
Travis, TX • 419,573
Treasure, MT • 981
Treasure Island, FL 33706 • 6,316
Trego, KS • 4,165
Tremont, IL 61568 • 2,096
Tremont, PA 17981 • 1,796
Tremonton, UT 84337 • 3,464
Trempealeau, WI • 26,158
Trenton, GA 30752 • 1,682
Trenton, IL 62293 • 2,424
Trenton, MI 48183 • 22,762
Trenton, MO 64683 • 6,811
Trenton, NJ 08601-99 • 93,500
Trenton, OH 45067 • 6,401
Trenton, TN 38382 • 4,601
Treutlen, GA • 6,087
Trevorton, PA 17881 • 2,192
Triadelphia, WV 26059 • 1,461
Triangle, VA 22172 • 4,770
Tri City, OR 97457 • 3,439

Trigg, KY • 9,384
Trimble, KY • 6,253
Trinidad, CO 81082 • 9,663
Trinity, NC 27370 • 6,878
Trinity, TX 75862 • 2,620
Trinity, CA • 11,858
Trinity, TX • 9,450
Trion, GA 30753 • 1,732
Triumph, LA 70041 • 1,600
Trooper, PA 19401 • 7,370
Trotwood, OH 45426 • 8,300
Troup, TX 75789 • 1,911
Troup, GA • 50,003
Trousdale, TN • 6,137
Troutdale, OR 97060 • 5,908
Troy, AL 36081 • 13,124
Troy, IL 62294 • 5,131
Troy, MI 48084 • 68,500
Troy, MO 63379 • 2,624
Troy, NY 12180-83 • 55,400
Troy, NC 27331 • 2,702
Troy, OH 45373 • 19,800
Truckee, CA 95734 • 2,389
Trumann, AR 72472 • 6,395
Trumansburg, NY 14886 • 1,722
Trumbull, CT 06611 • 33,700
Trumbull, OH • 241,863
Trussville, AL 35173 • 3,507
Truth or Consequences (Hot
Springs), NM 87901 • 5,219
Tryon, NC 28782 • 1,796
Tualatin, OR 97062 • 11,800
Tuba City, AZ 86045 • 5,045
Tuckahoe, NY 10707 • 6,076
Tucker, GA 30084 • 22,250
Tucker, WV • 8,675
Tuckerman, AR 72473 • 2,078
Tuckerton, NJ 08087 • 2,472
Tucson, AZ 85701-99 • 377,900
Tucumcari, NM 88401 • 6,765
Tukwila, WA 98188 • 5,100
Tulare, CA 93274 • 27,200
Tulare, CA • 245,738
Tularosa, NM 88352 • 2,536
Tulia, TX 79088 • 5,033
Tullahoma, TN 37388 • 15,800
Tulsa, OK 74101-99 • 378,600
Tulsa, OK • 470,593
Tumwater, WA 98502 • 6,705
Tunica, MS • 9,652
Tunkhannock, PA 18657 • 2,144
Tuolumne, CA 95379 • 1,708
Tuolumne, CA • 33,928
Tupelo, MS 38801 • 27,100
Tupper Lake, NY 12986 • 4,478
Turley, OK 74156 • 6,336
Turlock, CA 95380 • 33,600
Turner, GA • 9,510
Turner, SD • 9,255
Turners Falls, MA 01376 • 4,711
Turtle Creek, PA 15145 • 6,959
Tuscaloosa, AL 35401-06
• 75,600
Tuscaloosa, AL • 137,541
Tuscarawas, OH • 84,614
Tuscola, IL 61953 • 4,327
Tuscola, MI • 56,961
Tuscumbia, AL 35674 • 9,137
Tuskegee, AL 36083 • 13,327
Tustin, CA 92680 • 43,500
Tuttle, OK 73089 • 3,051
Twentynine Palms, CA 92277
• 7,465
Twentynine Palms Base, CA
92278 • 7,079
Twiggs, GA • 9,354
Twin Falls, ID 83301 • 28,300
Twin Falls, ID • 52,927
Twin Knolls, AZ 85207 • 5,210
Twin Lakes, WI 53181 • 3,474
Twin Rivers, NJ 08520 • 7,742
Twinsburg, OH 44087 • 7,632
Two Harbors, MN 55616 • 4,039
Two Rivers, WI 54241 • 13,354
Tybee Island, GA 31328 • 2,240
Tyler, TX 75701-13 • 78,200
Tyler, TX • 16,223
Tyler, WV • 11,320
Tyler Heights, WV 25312 • 4,070
Tylertown, MS 39667 • 1,976
Tyrone, PA 16686 • 6,346
Tyrrell, NC • 3,975
Tysons Corner, VA 22101 • 7,500

U

Uhrichsville, OH 44683 • 6,130
Uinta, WY • 13,021
Uintah, UT • 20,506
Ukiah, CA 95482 • 13,600
Uleta, FL 33162 • 10,000
Ulster, NY • 158,158
Ulysses, KS 67880 • 4,946
Umatilla, FL 32784 • 1,872
Umatilla, OR 97882 • 3,199
Umatilla, OR • 58,861
Unadilla, GA 31091 • 1,566
Uncasville, CT 06382 • 1,597
Underwood, AL 35630 • 1,950
Unicoi, TN • 16,362
Union, MS 39365 • 1,931
Union, MO 63084 • 5,506
Union, NJ 07083 • 50,600
Union, OH 45322 • 5,219
Union, OR 97883 • 2,062
Union, SC 29379 • 10,523
Union, UT 84047 • 3,100
Union, AR • 48,573
Union, FL • 10,166
Union, GA • 9,390

Union, IL • 17,765
Union, IN • 6,860
Union, IA • 13,858
Union, KY • 17,821
Union, LA • 21,167
Union, MS • 21,741
Union, NJ • 504,094
Union, NM • 4,725
Union, NC • 70,380
Union, OH • 29,536
Union, OR • 23,921
Union, PA • 32,870
Union, SC • 30,764
Union, SD • 10,938
Union, TN • 11,707
Union Beach, NJ 07735 • 6,354
Union City, CA 94587 • 49,600
Union City, GA 30291 • 5,700
Union City, IN 47390 • 3,908
Union City, MI 49094 • 1,667
Union City, NJ 07087 • 56,900
Union City, OH 45390 • 1,985
Union City, PA 16438 • 3,623
Union City, TN 38261 • 10,800
Uniondale, NY 11553 • 20,016
Union Gap, WA 98903 • 3,184
Union Grove, WI 53182 • 3,517
Union Lake, MI 48085 • 12,000
Union Park, FL 32817 • 19,175
Union Point, GA 30669 • 1,750
Union Springs, AL 36089 • 4,431
Uniontown, AL 36786 • 2,112
Uniontown, OH 44685 • 1,500
Uniontown, PA 15401 • 13,600
Union Village, RI 02895 • 2,150
Unionville, CT 06085 • 3,500
Unionville, MO 63565 • 2,178
Universal City, TX 78148 • 10,720
University City, MO 63130
• 43,600
University Gardens, NY 11020
• 4,600
University Heights, OH 44118
• 15,401
University Park, NM 88003
• 4,353
University Park, TX 75205
• 23,800
University Place, WA 98465
• 20,381
Upland, CA 91786 • 57,300
Upland, IN 46989 • 3,335
Upper Arlington, OH 43221
• 36,500
Upper Chinchester Township, PA
19061 • 14,377
Upper Darby, PA 19082-84
• 84,500
Upper Dublin Township, PA 19002
• 22,800
Upper Greenwood Lake, NJ 07421
• 2,734
Upper Merion Township, PA 19406
• 26,400
Upper Moreland Township, PA
19090 • 25,600
Upper Providence Township, PA
19063 • 9,477
Upper Saddle River, NJ 07458
• 7,958
Upper Saint Clair, PA 15241
• 18,700
Upper Sandusky, OH 43351
• 5,967
Upper Southampton Township, PA
19006 • 15,806
Upshur, TX • 28,595
Upshur, WV • 23,427
Upson, GA • 25,998
Upton, MA 01568 • 1,500
Upton, TX • 4,619
Urbana, IL 61801 • 34,100
Urbana, OH 43078 • 10,762
Urbandale, IA 50322 • 19,422
Utah, UT • 218,106
Utica, MI 48077-78 • 5,282
Utica, NY 13501-99 • 72,600
Utica, OH 43080 • 2,238
Uvalde, TX 78801 • 15,247
Uvalde, TX • 22,441
Uxbridge, MA 01569 • 3,340

V

Vacaville, CA 95688 • 51,500
Vacherie, LA 70090 • 2,169
Vadnais Heights, MN 55110
• 5,111
Vail, CO 81657 • 3,555
Valatie, NY 12184 • 1,620
Valdese, NC 28690 • 3,364
Valdez, AK 99686 • 3,079
Valdosta, GA 31601-05 • 40,100
Vale, OR 97918 • 1,500
Valencia, CA 91355 • 12,163
Valencia, NM • 31,013
Valencia Heights, SC 29205
• 4,786
Valentine, NE 69201 • 2,829
Valhalla, NY 10595 • 6,200
Valinda, CA 91744 • 18,700
Vallejo, CA 94590-92 • 92,900
Valle Vista, CA 92343 • 5,474
Valley, AL 36854 • 8,946
Valley, NE 68064 • 1,716
Valley, ID • 5,604
Valley, MT • 10,250
Valley, NE • 5,633
Valley Center, KS 67147 • 3,300
Valley City, ND 58072 • 7,774

Valley Cottage, NY 10989 • 8,214
Valley Falls, RI 02864 • 10,892
Valley Forge, PA 19481 • 1,500
Valley Park, MO 63088 • 3,232
Valley Ridge, WA 98188 • 6,500
Valley Station, KY 40272 • 20,000
Valley Stream, NY 11580-82
• 35,000
Valley View, PA 17983 • 1,722
Valparaiso, FL 32580 • 6,142
Valparaiso, IN 46383 • 23,200
Val Verde, UT 84010 • 6,422
Val Verde, TX • 35,910
Van, TX 75790 • 1,881
Van Alstyne, TX 75095 • 1,860
Van Buren, AR 72956 • 12,620
Van Buren, ME 04785 • 3,282
Van Buren, AR • 13,357
Van Buren, IA • 8,626
Van Buren, MI • 66,814
Van Buren, TN • 4,728
Vance, NC • 36,748
Vanceburg, KY 41179 • 1,939
Vancouver, WA 98660-68
• 44,000
Vandalia, IL 62471 • 6,111
Vandalia, MO 63382 • 3,170
Vandalia, OH 45377 • 13,161
Vandenberg Village, CA 93436
• 5,839
Vander, NC 28301 • 1,671
Vanderburgh, IN • 167,515
Vandercook Lake, MI 49203
• 4,975
Vandergrift, PA 15690 • 6,823
Van Horn, TX 79855 • 2,772
Van Lear, KY 41265 • 2,035
Vansant, VA 24656 • 2,708
Van Wert, OH 45891 • 11,035
Van Wert, OH • 30,458
Van Zandt, TX • 31,426
Varina, VA 23231 • 2,000
Varnville, SC 29944 • 1,948
Vassar, MI 48768 • 2,727
Vaughn, MT 59487 • 2,270
Veazie, ME 04401 • 1,610
Veedersburg, IN 47987 • 2,261
Velda Rose Estates, AZ 85205
• 2,330
Venango, PA • 64,444
Veneta, OR 97487 • 2,449
Venice, FL 34292-93 • 14,200
Venice, IL 62090 • 3,480
Venice Gardens, FL 34293
• 6,568
Ventnor City, NJ 08406 • 11,704
Ventura (San Buenaventura), CA
93001-06 • 88,300
Ventura, CA • 529,174
Veradale, WA 99037 • 7,526
Vergennes, VT 05491 • 2,273
Vermilion, OH 44089 • 11,012
Vermilion, IL • 95,222
Vermilion, LA • 48,458
Vermillion, SD 57069 • 10,136
Vermillion, IN • 18,229
Vernal, UT 84078 • 7,181
Vernon, AL 35592 • 2,609
Vernon, CT 06066 • 30,100
Vernon, TX 76384 • 12,695
Vernon, LA • 53,475
Vernon, MO • 19,806
Vernon, WI • 25,642
Vernon Hills, IL 60061 • 12,400
Vernonia, OR 97064 • 1,785
Vero Beach, FL 32960-65
• 18,300
Verona, MS 38879 • 2,497
Verona, NJ 07044 • 14,166
Verona, PA 15147 • 3,179
Verona, WI 53593 • 3,336
Versailles, IN 47042 • 1,560
Versailles, KY 40383 • 6,427
Versailles, MO 65084 • 2,406
Versailles, OH 45380 • 2,384
Vestal, NY 13850 • 5,530
Vestavia Hills, AL 35216 • 17,192
Vian, OK 74962 • 1,521
Vicksburg, MI 49097 • 2,224
Vicksburg, MS 39180 • 27,100
Victor, NY 14564 • 2,370
Victoria, TX 77901-05 • 58,100
Victoria, VA 23974 • 2,004
Victoria, TX • 68,807
Victorville, CA 92392 • 21,800
Vidalia, GA 30474 • 10,393
Vidalia, LA 71373 • 5,936
Vidor, TX 77662 • 12,464
Vienna, GA 31092 • 2,886
Vienna, VA 22180 • 15,469
Vienna, WV 26105 • 11,500
View Park, CA 90043 • 5,900
Vigo, IN • 112,385
Vilas, WI • 16,535
Villa Grove, IL 61956 • 2,707
Villa Hills, KY 41016 • 5,616
Villa Park, CA 92667 • 7,187
Villa Park, IL 60181 • 23,500
Villa Rica, GA 30180 • 3,420
Villas, NJ 08251 • 5,909
Ville Platte, LA 70586 • 9,201
Villisca, IA 50864 • 1,434
Vincennes, IN 47591 • 20,800
Vincent, AL 35178 • 1,652
Vine Grove, KY 40175 • 3,648
Vineland, NJ 08360 • 55,100
Vineyard Haven, MA 02568
• 1,704
Vinita, OK 74301 • 6,740
Vinton, IA 52349 • 5,040
Vinton, LA 70668 • 3,631

Vinton, VA 24179 • 8,027
Vinton, OH • 11,584
Viola, NY 10952 • 5,340
Violet, LA 70092 • 6,000
Virden, IL 62690 • 3,899
Virginia, IL 62691 • 1,825
Virginia, MN 55792 • 9,900
Virginia Beach, VA 23450-64
• 328,400
Viroqua, WI 54665 • 3,716
Visalia, CA 93277-79 • 61,100
Vista, CA 92083-84 • 46,600
Vivian, LA 71082 • 4,225
Volusia, FL • 258,762

W

Wabash, IN 46992 • 12,985
Wabash, IL • 13,713
Wabash, IN • 36,640
Wabasha, MN 55981 • 2,372
Wabasha, MN • 19,335
Wabasso, FL 32970 • 2,157
Wabaunsee, KS • 6,867
Waco, TX 76701-99 • 108,500
Waconia, MN 55387 • 2,638
Wade Hampton, SC 29607
• 20,180
Wadena, MN 56482 • 4,699
Wadena, MN • 14,192
Wadesboro, NC 28170 • 4,206
Wadley, GA 30477 • 2,438
Wadsworth, IL 60083 • 1,475
Wadsworth, OH 44281 • 15,166
Wagner, SD 57380 • 1,453
Wagoner, OK 74467 • 6,191
Wagoner, OK • 41,801
Wahiawa, HI 96786 • 16,911
Wahkiakum, WA • 3,832
Wahoo, NE 68066 • 3,555
Wahpeton, ND 58075 • 9,889
Waialua, HI 96791 • 4,051
Waianae, HI 96792 • 5,000
Wailua, HI 96746 • 1,587
Wailuku, HI 96793 • 10,500
Waimanalo, HI 96795 • 3,562
Waimea, HI 96796 • 1,569
Waipahu, HI 96797 • 31,800
Waipio Acres, HI 96786 • 4,091
Waite Park, MN 56387 • 3,496
Wake, NC • 301,321
Wa Keeney, KS 67672 • 2,388
Wakefield, MA 01880 • 25,200
Wakefield, MI 49968 • 2,591
Wakefield, RI 02879-83 • 3,450
Wake Forest, NC 27587 • 3,780
Wakulla, FL • 10,887
Walbridge, OH 43465 • 2,900
Walden, NY 12586 • 5,659
Waldo, ME • 28,414
Waldorf, MD 20601 • 9,782
Waldport, OR 97394 • 1,549
Waldron, AR 72958 • 2,642
Waldwick, NJ 07463 • 10,802
Walhalla, SC 29691 • 3,977
Walker, LA 70785 • 2,957
Walker, MI 49504 • 16,000
Walker, AL • 68,660
Walker, GA • 56,470
Walker, TX • 41,789
Walker Mill, MD 20747 • 10,651
Walkersville, MD 21793 • 2,212
Walkerton, IN 46574 • 2,051
Wallace, ID 83873 • 1,736
Wallace, NC 28466 • 2,903
Wallace, KS • 2,045
Walla Walla, WA 99362 • 25,800
Walla Walla, WA • 47,435
Walled Lake, MI 48088 • 4,748
Waller, TX • 19,798
Wallingford, CT 06492 • 38,000
Wallington, NJ 07057 • 10,741
Wallkill, NY 12589 • 2,064
Wallowa, OR • 7,273
Walnut, CA 91789 • 12,478
Walnut, IL 61376 • 1,513
Walnut Creek, CA 94595-98
• 61,000
Walnut Creek West, CA 94598
• 5,893
Walnut Park, CA 90255 • 11,811
Walnutport, PA 18088 • 2,007
Walnut Ridge, AR 72476 • 4,152
Walpole, MA 02081 • 5,274
Walsenburg, CO 81089 • 3,945
Walsh, ND • 15,371
Walterboro, SC 29488 • 6,485
Walters, OK 73572 • 2,778
Walthall, MS • 13,761
Waltham, MA 02154 • 57,700
Walton, KY 41094 • 1,651
Walton, NY 13856 • 3,329
Walton, FL • 21,300
Walton, GA • 31,211
Walworth, WI 53184 • 1,607
Walworth, SD • 7,011
Walworth, WI • 71,507
Wamac, IL 62801 • 1,665
Wamego, KS 66547 • 3,159
Wamesit, MA 01876 • 2,700
Wanaque, NJ 07465 • 10,025
Wando Woods, SC 29405 • 5,253
Wantagh, NY 11793 • 19,817
Wapakoneta, OH 45895 • 8,402
Wapato, WA 98951 • 3,307
Wapello, IA • 40,241
Wappingers Falls, NY 12590
• 5,110
War, WV 24892 • 2,158

Ward, ND · 58,392
Ward, TX · 13,976
Warden, WA 98857 · 1,479
Ware, MA 01082 · 6,806
Warehouse Point, CT 06088 · 1,880
Ware Shoals, SC 29692 · 2,370
Warminster, PA 18974 · 36,700
Warner Robins, GA 31093 · 45,300
Warr Acres, OK 73132 · 9,940
Warren, AR 71671 · 7,646
Warren, IL 61087 · 1,595
Warren, MA 01083 · 1,548
Warren, MI 48093-99 · 154,600
Warren, MN 56762 · 2,105
Warren, OH 44481-85 · 53,700
Warren, PA 16365 · 11,500
Warren, RI 02885 · 10,640
Warren, GA · 6,583
Warren, IL · 21,943
Warren, IN · 8,976
Warren, IA · 34,878
Warren, KY · 71,828
Warren, MS · 51,627
Warren, MO · 14,900
Warren, NJ · 84,429
Warren, NY · 54,854
Warren, NC · 16,232
Warren, OH · 99,276
Warren, PA · 47,449
Warren, TN · 32,653
Warren, VA · 21,200
Warren Park, IN 46219 · 1,803
Warrensburg, MO 64093 · 13,807
Warrensburg, NY 12885 · 2,834
Warrensville Heights, OH 44122 · 16,565
Warrenton, GA 30828 · 2,172
Warrenton, MO 63383 · 3,219
Warrenton, OR 97146 · 2,493
Warrenton, VA 22186 · 3,907
Warrenville, IL 60555 · 9,287
Warrick, IN · 41,474
Warrington, FL 32507 · 15,792
Warrington, PA 18976 · 6,980
Warrior, AL 35180 · 3,260
Warsaw, IL 62379 · 1,842
Warsaw, IN 46580 · 11,400
Warsaw, MO 65355 · 1,494
Warsaw, NY 14569 · 3,619
Warsaw, NC 28398 · 2,910
Warwick, NY 10990 · 4,320
Warwick, RI 02886-89 · 89,700
Wasatch, UT · 8,523
Wasco, CA 93280 · 9,613
Wasco, OR · 21,732
Waseca, MN 56093 · 8,219
Waseca, MN · 18,448
Washakie, WY · 9,496
Washburn, ND 58577 · 1,767
Washburn, WI 54891 · 2,080
Washburn, WI · 13,174
Washington, DC 20001-99 · 620,000
Washington, GA 30673 · 4,662
Washington, IL 61571 · 10,364
Washington, IN 47501 · 11,400
Washington, IA 52353 · 6,776
Washington, KS 66968 · 1,488
Washington, MO 63090 · 9,251
Washington, NJ 07882 · 6,429
Washington, NC 27889 · 9,600
Washington, PA 15301 · 18,200
Washington, UT 84780 · 3,092
Washington, AL · 16,821
Washington, AR · 100,494
Washington, CO · 5,304
Washington, FL · 14,509
Washington, GA · 18,842
Washington, ID · 8,803
Washington, IL · 15,472
Washington, IN · 21,932
Washington, IA · 20,141
Washington, KS · 8,543
Washington, KY · 10,764
Washington, LA · 44,207
Washington, ME · 34,963
Washington, MD · 113,086
Washington, MN · 113,571
Washington, MS · 72,344
Washington, MO · 17,983
Washington, NE · 15,508
Washington, NY · 54,795
Washington, NC · 14,801
Washington, OH · 64,266
Washington, OK · 48,113
Washington, OR · 245,860
Washington, PA · 217,074
Washington, RI · 93,317
Washington, TN · 88,755
Washington, TX · 21,998
Washington, UT · 26,065
Washington, VT · 52,393
Washington, VA · 46,487
Washington, WI · 84,848
Washington Court House, OH 43160 · 12,682
Washington Park, FL 33314 · 7,240
Washington Park, IL 62204 · 8,223
Washington Terrace, UT 84403 · 8,212
Washington Township, NJ 07675 · 9,550
Washita, OK · 13,798
Washoe, NV · 193,623
Washougal, WA 98671 · 3,834

Washtenaw, MI · 264,748
Wasilla, AK 99687 · 1,559
Waskom, TX 75692 · 1,821
Watauga, TX 76137 · 10,284
Watauga, NC · 31,666
Watchung, NJ 07060 · 5,400
Waterbury, CT 06701-26 · 103,200
Waterbury, VT 05676 · 1,892
Waterford, CT 06385 · 2,736
Waterford, MI 48095 · 64,300
Waterford, NY 12188 · 2,405
Waterford, PA 16441 · 1,568
Waterford, WI 53185 · 2,051
Waterloo, IL 62298 · 4,646
Waterloo, IN 46793 · 1,951
Waterloo, IA 50701-99 · 70,700
Waterloo, NY 13165 · 5,303
Waterloo, WI 53594 · 2,393
Watertown, CT 06795 · 5,920
Watertown, MA 02172 · 33,400
Watertown, NY 13601 · 28,400
Watertown, SD 57201 · 16,700
Watertown, WI 53094 · 18,500
Water Valley, MS 38965 · 4,146
Waterville, ME 04901 · 18,200
Waterville, MN 56096 · 1,717
Waterville, NY 13480 · 1,672
Waterville, OH 43566 · 3,884
Watervliet, MI 49098 · 1,867
Watervliet, NY 12189 · 11,354
Watford City, ND 58854 · 2,384
Watkins Glen, NY 14891 · 2,440
Watonga, OK 73772 · 4,139
Watonwan, MN · 12,361
Watseka, IL 60970 · 5,543
Watsontown, PA 17777 · 2,366
Watsonville, CA 95076 · 27,800
Wauchula, FL 33873 · 3,296
Wauconda, IL 60084 · 5,688
Waukee, IA 50263 · 2,227
Waukegan, IL 60085-87 · 72,700
Waukesha, WI 53186-88 · 52,100
Waukesha, WI · 280,080
Waukomis, OK 73773 · 1,551
Waukon, IA 52172 · 3,983
Waunakee, WI 53597 · 3,866
Waupaca, WI 54981 · 4,472
Waupaca, WI · 42,831
Waupun, WI 53963 · 8,132
Waurika, OK 73573 · 2,369
Wausau, WI 54401 · 32,400
Wauseon, OH 43567 · 6,173
Waushara, WI · 18,526
Wautoma, WI 54982 · 1,629
Wauwatosa, WI 53213 · 50,100
Waveland, MS 39576 · 4,186
Waverly, IL 62692 · 1,537
Waverly, IA 50677 · 8,444
Waverly, MI 48917 · 6,700
Waverly, NE 68462 · 1,726
Waverly, NY 14892 · 4,738
Waverly, OH 45690 · 4,603
Waverly, TN 37185 · 4,405
Waverly, VA 23890 · 2,284
Waxahachie, TX 75165 · 14,624
Waycross, GA 31501 · 19,400
Wayland, MA 01778 · 2,550
Wayland, MI 49348 · 2,023
Wayland, NY 14572 · 1,846
Waylyn, SC 29405 · 2,400
Wayne, MI 48184-88 · 21,159
Wayne, NE 68787 · 5,240
Wayne, NJ 07470 · 48,700
Wayne, WV 25570 · 1,495
Wayne, GA · 20,750
Wayne, IL · 18,059
Wayne, IN · 76,058
Wayne, IA · 8,199
Wayne, KY · 17,022
Wayne, MI · 2,337,891
Wayne, MS · 19,135
Wayne, MO · 11,277
Wayne, NE · 9,858
Wayne, NY · 84,581
Wayne, NC · 97,054
Wayne, OH · 97,408
Wayne, PA · 35,237
Wayne, TN · 13,946
Wayne, UT · 1,911
Wayne, WV · 46,021
Waynesboro, GA 30830 · 5,760
Waynesboro, MS 39367 · 5,349
Waynesboro, PA 17268 · 10,100
Waynesboro, TN 38485 · 2,109
Waynesboro, VA 22980 · 18,500
Waynesburg, PA 15370 · 4,482
Waynesville, MO 65583 · 2,879
Waynesville, NC 28786 · 6,944
Waynesville, OH 45068 · 1,796
Waynewood, VA 22308 · 5,000
Wayzata, MN 55391 · 3,621
Weakley, TN · 32,896
Weatherford, OK 73096 · 9,640
Weatherford, TX 76086 · 12,614
Weatherly, PA 18255 · 2,891
Weatogue, CT 06089 · 2,249
Weaver, AL 36277 · 2,765
Weaverville, CA 96093 · 2,787
Weaverville, NC 28787 · 1,495
Webb, TX · 99,258
Webb City, MO 64870 · 7,309
Webberville, MI 48892 · 1,535
Weber, UT · 144,616
Weber City, VA 24251 · 1,543
Webster, MA 01570 · 14,480
Webster, NY 14580 · 5,499
Webster, SD 57274 · 2,417
Webster, TX 77598 · 2,405
Webster, GA · 2,341
Webster, IA · 45,953

Webster, KY · 14,832
Webster, LA · 43,631
Webster, MS · 10,300
Webster, MO · 20,414
Webster, NE · 4,858
Webster, WV · 12,245
Webster City, IA 50595 · 8,572
Webster Groves, MO 63119 · 23,500
Wedgewood, MO 63031 · 6,700
Weed, CA 96094 · 2,879
Weedsport, NY 13166 · 1,952
Weehawken, NJ 07087 · 13,168
Weigelstown, PA 17315 · 5,213
Weimar, TX 78962 · 2,128
Weirsdale, FL 32695 · 1,500
Weirton, WV 26062 · 23,600
Weiser, ID 83672 · 4,771
Wekiva Springs, FL 32750 · 5,000
Welch, WV 24801 · 3,885
Welcome, SC 29611 · 6,922
Weld, CO · 123,438
Weldon, NC 27890 · 1,844
Wellesley, MA 02181 · 26,900
Wellford, SC 29385 · 2,143
Wellington, KS 67152 · 8,212
Wellington, OH 44090 · 4,146
Wellington, TX 79095 · 3,043
Wells, MN 56097 · 2,777
Wells, IN · 25,401
Wells, ND · 6,979
Wellsboro, PA 16901 · 3,805
Wellsburg, WV 26070 · 3,963
Wellston, OH 45692 · 6,016
Wellsville, KS 66092 · 1,612
Wellsville, MO 63384 · 1,546
Wellsville, NY 14895 · 5,769
Wellsville, OH 43968 · 5,095
Wellsville, UT 84339 · 1,952
Welsh, LA 70591 · 3,515
Wenatchee, WA 98801 · 18,200
Wendell, ID 83355 · 1,974
Wendell, NC 27591 · 2,222
Wenham, MA 01984 · 3,897
Wenonah, NJ 08090 · 2,303
Wentzville, MO 63385 · 3,193
Weslaco, TX 78596 · 24,200
Wesleyville, PA 16510 · 3,998
West, TX 76691 · 2,485
West Acton, MA 01720 · 5,230
West Allis, WI 53214 · 64,600
West Amityville, NY 11758 · 6,623
West Andover, MA 01810 · 1,970
West Athens, CA 90247 · 8,531
West Babylon, NY 11704 · 43,200
West Baton Rouge, LA · 19,086
West Bay Shore, NY 11706 · 5,118
West Bend, WI 53095 · 22,800
West Berlin, NJ 08091 · 2,970
West Billerica, MA 01862 · 1,920
West Bloomfield Township, MI 48033 · 45,200
Westborough, MA 01581 · 13,619
West Bountiful, UT 84087 · 3,556
West Boylston, MA 01583 · 3,130
West Bradenton, FL 34205 · 8,767
West Branch, IA 52358 · 1,867
West Branch, MI 48661 · 1,785
West Bridgewater, MA 02379 · 2,140
Westbrook, CT 06498 · 2,035
Westbrook, ME 04092 · 14,976
West Burlington, IA 52655 · 3,371
Westbury, NY 11590 · 13,871
Westby, WI 54667 · 1,797
West Caldwell, NJ 07006 · 11,407
West Carroll, LA · 12,922
West Carrollton, OH 45449 · 13,148
West Carson, CA 90502 · 17,997
West Carthage, NY 13619 · 1,824
Westchester, FL 33144 · 20,000
Westchester, IL 60153 · 17,730
West Chester, PA 19380-82 · 18,700
Westchester, NY · 866,599
West Chicago, IL 60185 · 12,550
West Columbia, SC 29169 · 11,044
West Columbia, TX 77486 · 4,109
West Compton, CA 90220 · 5,907
West Concord, MA 01742 · 5,331
West Concord, NC 28025 · 3,200
West Covina, CA 91790-93 · 94,800
West Crossett, AR 71635 · 1,466
West Dennis, MA 02670 · 2,030
West Des Moines, IA 50265 · 23,400
West Elmira, NY 14905 · 5,485
Westerly, RI 02891 · 15,600
Westernport, MD 21562 · 2,706
Western Springs, IL 60558 · 12,876
Westerville, OH 43081 · 23,414
West Falmouth, MA 02574 · 1,600
West Fargo, ND 58078 · 11,044
West Feliciana, LA · 12,186
Westfield, IN 46074 · 2,783
Westfield, MA 01085 · 37,100
Westfield, NJ 07090-92 · 30,200
Westfield, NY 14787 · 3,446
West Fork, AR 72774 · 1,526
West Frankfort, IL 62896 · 9,543
West Freehold, NJ 07728 · 9,929
Westgate, FL 33401 · 2,100
West Gate, VA 22110 · 7,119

West Gate of Lomond, VA 22110 · 5,400
West Glens Falls, NY 12801 · 5,331
West Grove, PA 19390 · 1,820
Westham, VA 23229 · 3,600
West Hanover, MA 02339 · 1,700
West Hartford, CT 06107 · 61,400
West Haven, CT 06516 · 53,400
West Haven, OR 97225 · 3,400
West Haverstraw, NY 10993 · 9,181
West Hazleton, PA 18201 · 4,871
West Helena, AR 72390 · 11,367
West Hempstead, NY 11552 · 18,536
West Hollywood, CA 90069 · 39,100
West Islip, NY 11795 · 30,500
West Jefferson, OH 43162 · 4,448
West Jordan, UT 84084 · 40,800
West Lafayette, IN 47906 · 21,247
West Lafayette, OH 43845 · 2,225
Westlake, LA 70669 · 5,246
Westlake, OH 44145 · 19,483
Westlake Village, CA 91361 · 6,130
Westland, MI 48185 · 80,900
West Laramie, WY 82070 · 2,000
West Lawn, PA 19609 · 1,686
West Liberty, IA 52776 · 2,723
West Liberty, WV 26074 · 1,653
West Linn, OR 97068 · 12,405
West Long Branch, NJ 07764 · 7,380
West Marion, NC 28752 · 1,596
West Medway, MA 02053 · 1,940
West Melbourne, FL 32901 · 5,078
West Memphis, AR 72301 · 27,800
Westmere, NY 12203 · 6,881
West Miami, FL 33174 · 6,076
West Mifflin, PA 15122 · 24,800
West Milford, NJ 07480 · 1,700
West Milton, OH 45383 · 4,119
West Milwaukee, WI 53214 · 3,535
Westminster, CA 92683 · 76,000
Westminster, CO 80030 · 63,200
Westminster, MD 21157 · 8,808
Westminster, SC 29693 · 3,114
West Modesto, CA 95351 · 6,135
West Monroe, LA 71291 · 16,500
Westmont, CA 90044 · 29,300
Westmont, IL 60559 · 20,404
Westmont, NJ 08108 · 5,630
Westmont, PA 15905 · 6,113
Westmoreland, TN 37186 · 1,754
Westmoreland, PA · 392,294
Westmoreland, VA · 14,041
Westmorland, CA 92281 · 1,590
West Mystic, CT 06388 · 3,364
West Newton, PA 15089 · 3,387
West New York, NJ 07093 · 41,500
West Norriton, PA 19401 · 14,034
West Nyack, NY 10994 · 5,770
Weston, MA 02193 · 11,169
Weston, MO 64098 · 1,440
Weston, OH 43569 · 1,708
Weston, WV 26452 · 6,250
Weston, WI 54476 · 8,775
Weston, WY · 7,106
West Orange, NJ 07052 · 40,500
Westover, WV 26505 · 4,884
West Palm Beach, FL 33401-18 · 71,700
West Pasco, WA 99301 · 5,729
West Paterson, NJ 07424 · 11,293
West Pensacola, FL 32505 · 28,700
West Peoria, IL 61604 · 5,219
West Pittston, PA 18643 · 5,980
West Plains, MO 65775 · 8,100
West Point, CA 95255 · 1,500
West Point, GA 31833 · 4,305
West Point, MS 39773 · 9,123
West Point, NE 68788 · 3,609
West Point, NY 10996 · 8,105
West Point, UT 84015 · 2,170
West Point, VA 23181 · 2,726
Westport, CT 06880 · 25,800
Westport, IN 47283 · 1,450
Westport, WA 98595 · 1,954
West Portsmouth, OH 45662 · 4,095
West Puente Valley, CA 91744 · 20,445
West Reading, PA 19611 · 4,507
West Rutland, VT 05777 · 2,351
West Sacramento, CA 95691 · 25,100
West Saint Paul, MN 55118 · 19,400
West Salem, WI 54669 · 3,276
West Sayville, NY 11796 · 8,185
West Seneca, NY 14224 · 49,000
West Simsbury, CT 06092 · 2,140
West Slope, OR 97225 · 5,364
West Springfield, MA 01089 · 27,100
West Springfield, VA 22152 · 18,000
West Terre Haute, IN 47885 · 2,806

West Union, IA 52175 · 2,783
West Union, OH 45693 · 2,791
West Unity, OH 43570 · 1,639
West University Place, TX 77005 · 12,010
Westvale, NY 13219 · 6,169
West Valley City, UT 84120 · 91,600
Westview, FL 33168 · 9,102
West View, PA 15229 · 7,648
Westville, IL 61883 · 3,573
Westville, IN 46391 · 2,887
Westville, NJ 08093 · 4,786
West Wareham, MA 02576 · 1,837
West Warwick, RI 02893 · 28,900
West Webster, NY 14580 · 8,690
Westwego, LA 70094 · 12,663
West Whittier, CA 90606 · 13,800
West Willow, MI 48197 · 5,400
Westwood, CA 96137 · 2,081
Westwood, KS 66205 · 1,783
Westwood, KY 41101 · 5,973
Westwood, MA 02090 · 6,500
Westwood, MI 49007 · 8,519
Westwood, NJ 07675 · 10,714
Westwood Lakes, FL 33165 · 11,478
West Wyoming, PA 18644 · 3,288
West Yarmouth, MA 02673 · 3,882
West York, PA 17404 · 4,526
Wethersfield, CT 06109 · 26,200
Wetumka, OK 74883 · 1,725
Wetumpka, AL 36092 · 4,341
Wetzel, WV · 21,874
Wewahitchka, FL 32465 · 1,742
Wewoka, OK 74884 · 6,280
Wexford, MI · 25,102
Weyauwega, WI 54983 · 1,549
Weymouth, MA 02188 · 54,500
Wharton, NJ 07885 · 5,485
Wharton, TX 77488 · 9,033
Wharton, TX · 40,242
Whatcom, WA · 106,701
Wheatland, CA 95692 · 1,474
Wheatland, WY 82201 · 5,816
Wheatland, MT · 2,359
Wheaton, IL 60187-89 · 51,000
Wheaton, MD 20902 · 53,300
Wheaton, MN 56296 · 1,969
Wheat Ridge, CO 80033 · 31,600
Wheeler, TX 79096 · 1,584
Wheeler, GA · 5,155
Wheeler, NE · 1,060
Wheeler, OR · 1,513
Wheeler, TX · 7,137
Wheelersburg, OH 45694 · 4,796
Wheeling, IL 60090 · 23,266
Wheeling, WV 26003 · 40,800
Whitacres, CT 06082 · 2,410
White, AR · 50,835
White, GA · 10,120
White, IL · 17,864
White, IN · 23,867
White, TN · 19,567
White Bear Lake, MN 55110 · 23,800
White Bluff, TN 37187 · 2,095
White Castle, LA 70788 · 2,160
White Center, WA 98126 · 18,000
White City, OR 97503 · 5,445
White City, UT 84070 · 7,267
Whitefish, MT 59937 · 3,703
Whitefish Bay, WI 53217 · 14,930
White Hall, AR 71602 · 3,070
White Hall, IL 62092 · 2,935
Whitehall, MI 49461 · 2,856
Whitehall, NY 12887 · 3,241
Whitehall, OH 43213 · 23,200
Whitehall, PA 15227 · 15,143
Whitehall, PA 18052 · 8,055
Whitehall, WI 54773 · 1,530
White Horse, NJ 08610 · 10,098
Whitehouse, OH 43571 · 2,137
White House, TN 37188 · 2,795
White Island Shores, MA 02538 · 2,000
Whitemarsh Township, PA 19428 · 14,985
White Meadow Lake, NJ 07866 · 8,429
White Oak, OH 45239 · 9,563
White Oak, PA 15131 · 9,480
White Pigeon, MI 49099 · 1,478
White Pine, TN 37890 · 2,040
White Pine, NV · 8,167
White Plains, MD 20695 · 5,167
White Plains, NY 10601-99 · 45,600
Whiteriver, AZ 85941 · 1,600
White River Junction, VT 05001 · 2,582
White Rock, NM 87544 · 6,560
White Salmon, WA 98672 · 1,853
Whitesboro, NY 13492 · 4,460
Whitesboro, TX 76273 · 3,197
Whitesburg, KY 41858 · 1,525
White Settlement, TX 76108 · 13,508
Whiteside, IL · 65,970
White Sulphur Springs, WV 24986 · 3,371
Whiteville, NC 28472 · 5,565
Whitewater, WI 53190 · 11,520
Whitewright, TX 75491 · 1,760
Whitfield, GA · 65,789
Whitfield Estates, FL 34243 · 3,000
Whiting, IN 46394 · 5,630
Whiting, WI 54481 · 2,050

Whitinsville, MA 01588 • 5,379
Whitley, IN • 26,215
Whitley, KY • 33,396
Whitley City, KY 42653 • 1,683
Whitman, MA 02382 • 13,534
Whitman, WV 25652 • 1,651
Whitman, WA • 40,103
Whitman Square, NJ 08012
• 3,490
Whitmire, SC 29178 • 2,038
Whitmore Lake, MI 48189 • 2,920
Whitmore Village, HI 96786
• 2,318
Whitney, SC 29303 • 1,800
Whitney, TX 76692 • 1,631
Whittier, CA 90601-10 • 73,500
Whitwell, TN 37397 • 1,783
Wibaux, MT • 1,476
Wichita, KS 67201-99 • 289,600
Wichita, KS • 3,041
Wichita, TX • 121,082
Wichita Falls, TX 76301-11
• 99,500
Wickenburg, AZ 85358 • 3,535
Wickliffe, OH 44092 • 16,790
Wickliffe, OH 44515 • 7,240
Wicomico, MD • 64,540
Widefield, CO 80911 • 12,112
Wiggins, MS 39577 • 3,205
Wilbarger, TX • 15,931
Wilber, NE 68465 • 1,624
Wilberforce, OH 45384 • 2,512
Wilbraham, MA 01095 • 3,379
Wilburton, OK 74578 • 2,996
Wilcox, AL • 14,755
Wilcox, GA • 7,682
Wilder, VT 05088 • 1,461
Wildwood, FL 32785 • 2,665
Wildwood, NJ 08260 • 4,913
Wildwood Crest, NJ 08260
• 4,149
Wilkes, GA • 10,951
Wilkes, NC • 58,657
Wilkes-Barre, PA 18701-99
• 48,700
Wilkesboro, NC 28697 • 2,335
Wilkin, MN • 8,454
Wilkinsburg, PA 15221 • 22,200
Wilkinson, GA • 10,368
Wilkinson, MS • 10,021
Wilkins Township, PA 15145
• 8,472
Will, IL • 324,460
Willacy, TX • 17,495
Willamina, OR 97396 • 1,749
Willard, MO 65781 • 1,799
Willard, OH 44890 • 5,720
Willcox, AZ 85643 • 3,243
Williams, CA 95987 • 1,655
Williams, ND • 22,237
Williams, OH • 36,369
Williams Bay, WI 53191 • 1,763
Williamsburg, IA 52361 • 2,033
Williamsburg, KY 40769 • 5,560
Williamsburg, OH 45176 • 1,952
Williamsburg, VA 23185 • 11,200
Williamsburg, SC • 38,226
Williamson, NY 14589 • 1,768
Williamson, WV 25661 • 5,300
Williamson, IL • 56,538
Williamson, TN • 58,108
Williamson, TX • 76,507
Williamsport, IN 47993 • 1,747
Williamsport, MD 21795 • 2,153
Williamsport, PA 17701 • 32,400
Williamston, MI 48895 • 2,981
Williamston, NC 27892 • 6,159
Williamston, SC 29697 • 4,310
Williamstown, KY 41097 • 2,502
Williamstown, MA 01267 • 4,798
Williamstown, NJ 08094 • 5,768
Williamstown, PA 17098 • 1,664
Williamstown, WV 26187 • 3,095
Williamsville, NY 14221 • 6,017
Willingboro, NJ 08046 • 40,100
Willis, TX 77378 • 1,674
Williston, FL 32696 • 2,240
Williston, ND 58801 • 17,100
Williston, SC 29853 • 3,173
Williston Park, NY 11596 • 8,216
Willits, CA 95490 • 4,008

Willmar, MN 56201 • 16,300
Willoughby, OH 44094 • 19,800
Willoughby Hills, OH 44092
• 8,612
Willow Brook, CA 90222 • 34,000
Willowbrook, IL 60521 • 6,254
Willowick, OH 44094 • 17,834
Willow Run, DE 19805 • 1,950
Willow Run, MI 48197 • 6,400
Willows, CA 95988 • 4,777
Willow Springs, IL 60480 • 4,147
Willow Springs, MO 65793 • 2,215
Willston, VA 22044 • 2,800
Wilmer, TX 75172 • 2,367
Wilmerding, PA 15148 • 2,421
Wilmette, IL 60091 • 27,100
Wilmington, DE 19801-99
• 70,400
Wilmington, IL 60481 • 4,424
Wilmington, MA 01887 • 17,471
Wilmington, NC 28401-07
• 49,200
Wilmington, OH 45177 • 10,431
Wilmington Island, GA 31410
• 7,546
Wilmington Manor, DE 19720
• 2,000
Wilmington Manor Gardens, DE
19720 • 1,600
Wilmore, KY 40390 • 3,787
Wilson, NC 27893 • 35,700
Wilson, OK 73463 • 1,585
Wilson, PA 18042 • 7,564
Wilson, KS • 12,128
Wilson, NC • 63,132
Wilson, TN • 56,064
Wilson, TX • 16,756
Wilsonville, OR 97070 • 2,920
Wilton, CT 06897 • 7,200
Wilton, IA 52778 • 2,502
Wilton, ME 04294 • 2,262
Wilton Manors, FL 33334 • 12,742
Wimauma, FL 33598 • 1,477
Winamac, IN 46996 • 2,370
Winchendon, MA 01475 • 4,030
Winchester, IL 62694 • 1,716
Winchester, IN 47394 • 5,659
Winchester, KY 40391 • 15,216
Winchester, MA 01890 • 20,701
Winchester, NH 89101 • 19,728
Winchester, NH 03470 • 1,732
Winchester, TN 37398 • 6,195
Winchester, VA 22601 • 21,100
Windber, PA 15963 • 5,585
Windcrest, TX 78239 • 5,332
Winder, GA 30680 • 6,705
Windgap, PA 18091 • 2,651
Windham, OH 44288 • 3,721
Windham, CT • 92,312
Windham, VT • 36,933
Wind Lake, WI 53185 • 2,400
Windom, MN 56101 • 4,666
Window Rock, AZ 86515 • 2,230
Wind Point, WI 53402 • 1,695
Windsor, CO 80550 • 4,277
Windsor, CT 06095 • 17,517
Windsor, MO 65360 • 3,058
Windsor, NC 27983 • 2,126
Windsor, VT 05089 • 4,084
Windsor, VT • 51,030
Windsor Heights, IA 50311
• 5,474
Windsor Hills, CA 90052 • 6,200
Windsor Locks, CT 06096
• 12,190
Windy Hill, SC 29501 • 1,622
Winfield, AL 35594 • 3,781
Winfield, KS 67156 • 11,866
Winfield, NJ 07036 • 1,785
Wingate, NC 28174 • 2,615
Winkler, TX • 9,944
Winn, LA • 17,253
Winnebago, IL 61088 • 1,644
Winnebago, MN 56098 • 1,869
Winnebago, WI 54985 • 1,433
Winnebago, IL • 250,884
Winnebago, IA • 13,010
Winnebago, WI • 131,772
Winneconne, WI 54986 • 1,935
Winnemucca, NV 89445 • 4,140
Winner, SD 57580 • 3,472
Winneshiek, IA • 21,876

Winnetka, IL 60093 • 12,772
Winnfield, LA 71483 • 7,311
Winnsboro, LA 71295 • 5,921
Winnsboro, SC 29180 • 2,919
Winnsboro, TX 75494 • 3,458
Winnsboro Mills, SC 29180
• 1,890
Winona, MN 55987 • 24,400
Winona, MS 38967 • 6,177
Winona, MN • 46,256
Winona Lake, IN 46590 • 2,827
Winooski, VT 05404 • 6,318
Winslow, AZ 86047 • 7,921
Winslow, ME 04901 • 5,903
Winslow, WA 98110 • 2,196
Winsted, CT 06098 • 8,092
Winsted, MN 55395 • 1,522
Winston, FL 33803 • 5,500
Winston, OR 97496 • 3,415
Winston, AL • 21,953
Winston, MS • 19,474
Winston-Salem, NC 27101-17
• 146,500
Winter Garden, FL 32787 • 6,789
Winter Haven, FL 33880-83
• 23,000
Winter Park, FL 32789-93
• 24,200
Winter Park, NC 28401 • 4,504
Winters, CA 95694 • 2,652
Winters, TX 79567 • 3,061
Winterset, IA 50273 • 4,021
Winter Springs, FL 32708
• 10,475
Wintersville, OH 43952 • 4,724
Winterville, NC 28590 • 2,052
Winthrop, ME 04364 • 3,264
Winthrop, MA 02152 • 19,294
Winthrop Harbor, IL 60096
• 5,427
Wirt, WV • 4,922
Wisconsin Dells, WI 53965 • 2,521
Wisconsin Rapids, WI 54494
• 19,600
Wise, VA 24293 • 3,894
Wise, TX • 26,575
Wise, VA • 43,863
Withamsville, OH 45245 • 5,000
Wixom, MI 48096 • 6,705
Woburn, MA 01801 • 37,400
Wolcott, CT 06716 • 6,070
Wolcott, NY 14590 • 1,496
Wolfe, KY • 6,698
Wolfeboro, NH 03894 • 1,800
Wolfe City, TX 75496 • 1,594
Wolf Lake, MI 49442 • 3,876
Wolf Point, MT 59201 • 3,074
Wolf Trap, VA 22090 • 9,875
Womelsdorf, PA 19567 • 1,827
Wood, OH • 107,372
Wood, TX • 24,697
Wood, WV • 93,648
Wood, WI • 72,799
Woodbine, IA 51579 • 1,463
Woodbine, NJ 08270 • 2,809
Woodbourne, OH 45459 • 6,000
Woodbridge, CT 06525 • 7,700
Woodbridge, VA 22191-99
• 28,800
Woodbridge [Township], NJ 07095
• 95,100
Woodburn, OR 97071 • 11,196
Woodbury, GA 30293 • 1,738
Woodbury, MN 55119 • 14,726
Woodbury, NJ 08096 • 10,700
Woodbury, NY 11797 • 7,043
Woodbury, TN 37190 • 2,385
Woodbury, IA • 100,884
Woodcliff Lake, NJ 07675 • 5,644
Wood Dale, IL 60191 • 11,251
Woodfield, SC 29206 • 9,588
Woodford, IL • 33,320
Woodford, KY • 17,778
Woodhaven, MI 48183 • 10,902
Woodlake, CA 93286 • 4,343
Woodland, CA 95695 • 34,800
Woodland, WA 98901-09 • 2,341
Woodland Park, CO 80863
• 2,634
Woodlawn, KY 42001 • 1,600
Woodlawn, MD 21207 • 8,000
Woodlawn, MD 20784 • 5,306

Woodlawn, OH 45215 • 2,715
Woodlawn, VA 24381 • 1,689
Woodlynne, NJ 08107 • 2,578
Woodmere, NY 11598 • 17,205
Woodmont, CT 06460 • 1,797
Woodmoor, MD 21207 • 7,600
Woodridge, IL 60517 • 25,300
Wood-Ridge, NJ 07075 • 7,929
Wood River, IL 62095 • 12,446
Woodruff, SC 29388 • 5,171
Woodruff, AR • 11,222
Woods, OK • 10,923
Woodsboro, TX 78393 • 1,974
Woods Cross, UT 84087 • 4,263
Woodsfield, OH 43793 • 3,145
Woodside, CA 94062 • 5,291
Woodson, KS • 4,600
Woodstock, GA 30188 • 2,699
Woodstock, IL 60098 • 13,200
Woodstock, NY 12498 • 2,280
Woodstock, VA 22664 • 2,627
Woodstown, NJ 08098 • 3,250
Woodville, FL 32362 • 1,768
Woodville, MS 39669 • 1,512
Woodville, OH 43469 • 2,050
Woodville, TX 75979 • 2,821
Woodward, OK 73801 • 15,300
Woodward, OK • 21,172
Woodway, TX 76710 • 7,091
Woonsocket, RI 02895 • 45,400
Wooster, OH 44691 • 20,000
Worcester, MA 01601-99
• 162,100
Worcester, MD • 30,889
Worcester, MA • 646,352
Worland, WY 82401 • 6,391
Worth, IL 60482 • 11,592
Worth, GA • 18,064
Worth, IA • 9,075
Worth, MO • 3,008
Worthington, IN 47471 • 1,574
Worthington, KY 41183 • 1,948
Worthington, MN 56187 • 9,700
Worthington, OH 43085 • 15,016
Wrangell, AK 99929 • 2,184
Wray, CO 80758 • 2,131
Wrens, GA 30833 • 2,415
Wrentham, MA 02093 • 2,110
Wright, FL 32548 • 13,011
Wright, IA • 16,319
Wright, MN • 58,681
Wright, MO • 16,188
Wrightsboro, NJ 08562 • 3,031
Wrightsville, GA 31096 • 2,526
Wrightsville, PA 17368 • 2,365
Wrightsville Beach, NC 28480
• 2,910
Wrightwood, CA 92397 • 2,511
Wyandanch, NY 11798 • 13,215
Wyandot, OH • 22,651
Wyandotte, MI 48192 • 31,700
Wyandotte, KS • 172,335
Wyckoff, NJ 07481 • 15,500
Wymore, NE 68466 • 1,841
Wynne, AR 72396 • 7,822
Wynnewood, OK 73098 • 2,615
Wyoming, IL 61491 • 1,614
Wyoming, MI 49509 • 62,800
Wyoming, MN 55092 • 1,559
Wyoming, OH 45215 • 8,282
Wyoming, PA 18644 • 3,655
Wyoming, NY • 39,895
Wyoming, PA • 26,433
Wyoming, WV • 35,993
Wyomissing, PA 19610 • 6,700
Wythe, VA • 25,522
Wytheville, VA 24382 • 7,135

X

Xenia, OH 45385 • 24,000

Y

Yadkin, NC • 28,439
Yadkinville, NC 27055 • 2,216
Yakima, WA 98901-09 • 49,900
Yakima, WA • 172,508
Yale, MI 48097 • 1,814
Yale, OK 74085 • 1,652
Yalobusha, MS • 13,139
Yamhill, OR • 55,332

Yancey, NC • 14,934
Yanceyville, NC 27379 • 1,869
Yankton, SD 57078 • 12,100
Yankton, SD • 18,952
Yaphank, NY 11980 • 5,000
Yardley, PA 19067 • 2,533
Yardville, NJ 08620 • 6,190
Yarmouth, ME 04096 • 2,981
Yarmouth Port, MA 02675 • 2,490
Yarnell, AZ 85362 • 1,500
Yates, NY • 21,459
Yates Center, KS 66783 • 1,998
Yavapai, AZ • 68,145
Yazoo, MS • 27,349
Yazoo City, MS 39194 • 13,147
Yeadon, PA 19050 • 11,727
Yell, AR • 17,026
Yellow Medicine, MN • 13,653
Yellow Springs, OH 45387 • 4,077
Yellowstone, MT • 108,035
Yellowstone National Park, MT
• 275
Yerington, NV 89447 • 2,021
Yoakum, TX 77995 • 6,148
Yoakum, TX • 8,299
Yolo, CA • 113,374
Yonkers, NY 10701-99 • 191,300
Yorba Linda, CA 92686 • 36,500
York, AL 36925 • 3,392
York, ME 03909 • 3,130
York, NE 68467 • 7,723
York, PA 17401-99 • 44,000
York, SC 29745 • 6,412
York, ME • 139,666
York, NE • 14,798
York, PA • 312,963
York, SC • 106,720
York, VA • 35,463
Yorketown, NJ 07726 • 5,330
Yorktown, IN 47396 • 3,945
Yorktown, NY 10598 • 5,270
Yorktown, TX 78164 • 2,498
Yorktown Heights, NY 10598
• 6,300
Yorktown Manor, RI 02852
• 2,520
Yorkville, IL 60560 • 3,422
Yorkville, NY 13495 • 3,115
Yorkville, OH 43971 • 1,447
Young, TX • 19,083
Youngstown, NY 14174 • 2,191
Youngstown, OH 44501-99
• 107,300
Youngsville, PA 16371 • 2,006
Youngtown, AZ 85363 • 2,254
Youngwood, PA 15697 • 3,749
Ypsilanti, MI 48197-98 • 24,100
Yreka, CA 96097 • 5,916
Yuba, CA • 49,733
Yuba City, CA 95991 • 20,900
Yucaipa, CA 92399 • 20,000
Yucca Valley, CA 92284 • 8,294
Yukon, OK 73099 • 17,112
Yulee, FL 32097 • 3,168
Yuma, AZ 85364-69 • 45,800
Yuma, CO 80759 • 2,824
Yuma, AZ • 78,054
Yuma, CO • 9,682

Z

Zachary, LA 70791 • 7,747
Zanesville, OH 43701 • 28,500
Zapata, TX 78076 • 3,831
Zapata, TX • 6,628
Zavala, TX • 11,666
Zebulon, NC 27597 • 2,055
Zeeland, MI 49464 • 4,764
Zeigler, IL 62999 • 1,858
Zelienople, PA 16063 • 3,502
Zephyrhills, FL 34248-49 • 6,137
Ziebach, SD • 2,308
Zillah, WA 98953 • 1,599
Zilwaukee, MI 48604 • 2,201
Zion, IL 60099 • 17,865
Zionsville, IN 46077 • 3,948
Zolfo Springs, FL 33890 • 1,495
Zumbrota, MN 55992 • 2,129
Zuni, NM 87327 • 5,551
Zwolle, LA 71486 • 2,602

WORLD POPULATIONS

This table includes every urban center of 50,000 or more population in the world (excluding the United States), as well as many other important or well-known cities and towns. The table also lists major political subdivisions (states, provinces, etc.) of many countries.

The population figures are all from recent censuses (designated C) or official estimates (designated E), except for a few cities for which only unofficial estimates are available (designated UE). The date of the census or estimate is specified for each country. Individual exceptions are dated in parentheses.

For many cities, a second population figure is given accompanied by a star (★). The starred population refers to the city's entire metropolitan area, including suburbs. These metropolitan areas have been defined by Rand McNally & Company, following consistent rules to facilitate comparisons among the urban centers of various countries. Where a place is part of the metropolitan area of another city, that city's name is specified in parentheses preceded by (★). Some important places that are considered to be secondary central cities of their areas are designated by (★★) preceding the name of the metropolitan area's main city. A population preceded by a triangle (▲) refers to an entire municipality, commune, or other district, which includes rural areas in addition to the urban center itself. The names of capital cities appear in CAPITALS; the largest city in each country is designated by the symbol (•).

For more recent population totals for countries, see the Rand McNally population estimates in the World Political Information table. For lists of the largest metropolitan areas, see the World Metropolitan Areas and United States Metropolitan Areas tables.

AFGHANISTAN / Afghānestān

1979 C	13,051,358

Cities and Towns

Andkhvoy (1975 E)	46,000
Baghlān (1973 E)	29,000
Chārīkār (1973 E)	19,000
Ghaznī (1973 E)	24,000
Herāt	140,323
Jalālābād	53,915
• KĀBUL	913,164
Kandahār (Qandahār)	178,409
Khānābād (1973 E)	18,000
Kholm (1973 E)	22,000
Mazār-e Sharīf	103,372
Meymaneh (1975 E)	29,000
Pol-e Khomrī (1973 E)	25,000
Qondūz	53,251
Sheberghān (1973 E)	17,000

ALBANIA / Shqipëri

1983 E	2,841,300

Cities and Towns

Berati (Berat)	36,600
Durrësi (Durrës)	72,400
Elbasani (Elbasan)	69,900
Fieri (Fier)	37,000
Gjirokastra (Gjirokastër)	21,400
Kavaja (Kavajë)	22,500
Korça (Korçë)	57,100
Lushnja (Lushnje)	24,200
Shkodra (Scutari)	71,200
Stalin (Kuçovë) (1971 E)	14,300
• TIRANA (TIRANË)	206,100
Vlora (Valona)	61,100

ALGERIA / Djazaïr

1977 C	16,948,000

Cities and Towns

Aïn Benian (★ Algiers) (1966 C)	17,653
Aïn el Beïda (▲ 44,275)	42,578
Aïn Sefra (▲ 26,234) (1974 E)	13,100
Aïn Témouchent (▲ 41,987)	29,844
• ALGIERS (EL DJAZAÏR) (★ 1,724,705)	1,523,000
Annaba (Bône) (▲ 255,938)	222,607
Barika (▲ 40,957) (1966 C)	13,689
Batna (▲ 112,095)	102,756
Béchar (Colomb-Béchar) (▲ 72,790)	56,563
Bejaïa (Bougie) (▲ 89,530)	73,960
Beni Saf (▲ 23,368) (1966 C)	18,507
Beskra (Biskra) (▲ 90,471)	76,988
Bordj Bou Arreridj (▲ 65,007)	54,505
Bordj Menaïel (▲ 87,736) (1974 E)	38,700
Boufarik (▲ 50,006)	33,561
Bouïra (▲ 50,007)	26,800
Bou Saâda (▲ 50,104)	46,760
Cherchell (▲ 40,308) (1974 E)	17,100
Constantine (Qacentina) (▲ 355,059)	344,454
Djidjelli (▲ 49,794)	35,065
Douéra (1974 E)	55,993
Ech Cheliff (Orléansville) (▲ 114,327)	80,500
El Affroun (▲ 67,566) (1974 E)	47,500
El Beyyadh (▲ 33,743) (1974 E)	21,200
El Boulaïda (Blida) (▲ 160,893)	136,033
El Djelfa (▲ 50,953)	47,435
El Eulma (▲ 49,946)	41,564
El Ghazawet (▲ 29,592) (1974 E)	16,600
El Qoll (▲ 40,860) (1974 E)	14,100
El Wad (▲ 72,065)	47,173
Frenda (▲ 23,349)	16,400
Ghardaïa (▲ 70,508)	57,153
Ghilizane	55,450
Guelma (▲ 60,059)	56,106
Hadjout (▲ 32,334) (1974 E)	27,100
Khemis Miliana (▲ 57,769)	37,252
Khenchla (▲ 50,297)	44,223
Koléa (▲ 48,133) (1974 E)	35,900
Laghouat (▲ 59,157)	40,156
Lakhdaria (▲ 53,780) (1974 E)	30,800
Lemdiyya (Médéa) (▲ 72,251)	57,828
Maghnia (▲ 44,777) (1974 E)	31,000
Mechriyya (1974 E)	23,681
Melyana (▲ 46,217) (1974 E)	27,200
Mestghanem (Mostaganem) (▲ 101,639)	85,059
Mohammadia (▲ 49,730) (1974 E)	30,000
Mouaskar (Mascara) (▲ 62,301)	49,370
Oran (Wahran) (▲ 491,901)	409,788
Oued Zenati (▲ 81,036) (1974 E)	31,900
Qasr el Boukhari (▲ 36,986) (1974 E)	18,400
Rouiba (▲ 87,540) (1974 E)	20,300
Saïda (▲ 62,064)	55,855
Sidi bel Abbès (▲ 115,961)	112,988
Sig (▲ 41,725) (1974 E)	33,900
Skikda (Philippeville) (▲ 107,717)	91,395
Sougueur (▲ 20,809)	18,300
Souk Ahras (▲ 60,059)	52,144
Sour el Ghozlane (▲ 67,205) (1974 E)	32,100
Stif (Sétif) (▲ 144,221)	129,754
Tbessa (▲ 67,194)	61,063
Tihert (▲ 62,915)	53,277
Tilimsen (▲ 109,408)	88,505
Tissemsilt (▲ 22,770) (1974 E)	17,300
Tizi-Ouzou (▲ 73,120)	38,979
Touggourt (▲ 75,554)	42,519
Wargla (Ouargla) (▲ 77,354)	42,098

AMERICAN SAMOA / Amerika Samoa

1980 C	32,279

Cities and Towns

• PAGO PAGO	3,075

ANDORRA

1982 C	38,051

Cities and Towns

• ANDORRA	14,928

ANGOLA

1982 E	8,140,000

Cities and Towns

Benguela (1974 E)	60,000
Cabinda (1970 C)	21,124
Huambo (Nova Lisboa) (1974 E)	65,000
Lobito (1974 E)	120,000
• LUANDA	1,200,000
Lubango (1970 C)	31,674
Malanje (1970 C)	31,599

ANGUILLA

1974 C	6,519

Cities and Towns

• South Hill	774
THE VALLEY	760

ANTIGUA AND BARBUDA

1977 E	72,000

Cities and Towns

• SAINT JOHNS	24,359

ARGENTINA

1980 C	27,947,446

Cities and Towns

Almirante Brown (★ Buenos Aires)	326,856
Alta Gracia	30,668
Avellaneda (★ Buenos Aires)	330,654
Azul	44,062
Bahía Blanca	223,818
Balcarce	29,406
Bell Ville	26,494
Berazategui (★ Buenos Aires)	197,187
Berisso (★ Buenos Aires)	64,255
Bragado	27,406
• BUENOS AIRES (★ 10,700,000)	2,922,829
Campana (★ Buenos Aires)	53,994
Cañada de Gómez	24,569
Caseros (Tres de Febrero) (★ Buenos Aires)	343,004
Casilda	23,074
Chacabuco	26,860
Chivilcoy	44,579
Cipolletti	40,268
Comodoro Rivadavia	96,865
Concepción	29,355
Concepción del Uruguay	46,247
Concordia	94,222
Córdoba (★ 1,070,000)	993,055
Coronel Rosales	56,620
Corrientes	180,612
Cruz del Eje	23,255
Curuzú Cuatiá	24,962
Cutral-Có	25,911
Ensenada (★ Buenos Aires)	41,202
Esquel	17,277
Esteban Echeverría (★ Buenos Aires)	183,908
Florencio Varela (★ Buenos Aires)	165,842
Formosa	93,603
General Pico	30,173
General Roca	3,841
General San Martín (★ Buenos Aires)	384,306
General Sarmiento (San Miguel) (★ Buenos Aires)	499,648
Godoy Cruz (★ Mendoza)	141,553
Goya	47,395
Gualeguay	25,075
Gualeguaychú	51,400
Guaymallén (★ Mendoza)	157,334
Junín	62,458
La Banda (★★ Santiago del Estero)	46,837
Lanús (★ Buenos Aires)	465,691
La Plata (★★ Buenos Aires)	454,884
La Rioja	67,043
Las Heras (★ Mendoza)	96,545
Lomas de Zamora (★ Buenos Aires)	508,620
Luján (★ Buenos Aires)	48,377
Maipú	7,289
Mar del Plata	414,696
Mendoza (★ 690,000)	118,427
Mercedes	50,992
Mercedes (★ Buenos Aires)	41,484
Merlo (★ Buenos Aires)	293,059
Moreno (★ Buenos Aires)	188,524
Morón (★ Buenos Aires)	596,769
Necochea	51,069
Neuquén	90,089
Olavarría	64,374
Paraná	161,638
Pergamino	68,612
Pilar (★ Buenos Aires)	74,629
Posadas	143,889
Presidencia Roque Sáenz Peña	49,341
Quilmes (★ Buenos Aires)	445,662
Rafaela	53,273
Reconquista	33,106
Resistencia	220,104
Río Cuarto	110,254
Río Tercero	34,745
Rosario (★ 1,045,000)	938,120
Salta	260,744
San Carlos de Bariloche	48,980
San Carlos de Bolívar	16,382
San Fernando (★ Buenos Aires)	128,939
San Fernando del Valle de Catamarca (★ 90,000)	77,931
San Francisco (★ 58,536)	51,932
San Isidro (★ Buenos Aires)	287,048
San Juan (★ 310,000)	117,731
San Justo (★ Buenos Aires)	941,499
San Lorenzo (★ Rosario)	78,983
San Luis	70,999
San Miguel de Tucumán (★ 525,000)	392,751
San Nicolás [de los Arroyos]	98,495
San Pedro	27,386
San Pedro [de Jujuy]	37,101
San Rafael	70,959
San Ramón de la Nueva Orán	32,910
San Salvador de Jujuy	124,950
Santa Fe	291,966
Santiago del Estero (★ 200,000)	148,758
Santo Tomé	35,840
Tafí Viejo	26,660
Tandil	79,429
Tartagal	31,556
Tigre (★ Buenos Aires)	199,366
Trelew	52,372
Tres Arroyos	41,265
Ushuaia	11,029
Venado Tuerto	47,501
Vicente López (★ Buenos Aires)	289,815
Victoria	18,894
Viedma	24,346
Villa Ángela	25,744
Villa Carlos Paz	29,655
Villa Constitución	36,425
Villa Krause (★ San Juan)	66,506
Villa María	67,560
Zárate	67,143

Provinces

Buenos Aires	10,865,408
Catamarca	207,717
Chaco	701,392
Chubut	263,116
Córdoba	2,407,754
Corrientes	661,454
Distrito Federal	2,922,829
Entre Ríos	908,313
Formosa	295,887
Jujuy	410,008
La Pampa	208,260
La Rioja	164,217
Mendoza	1,196,228
Misiones	588,977
Neuquén	243,850
Río Negro	383,354
Salta	662,870
San Juan	465,976
San Luis	214,416
Santa Cruz	114,941
Santa Fe	2,465,546
Santiago del Estero	594,920
Tierra del Fuego, Antártida e Islas del Atlántico Sur (Ter.)	27,358
Tucumán	972,655

ARUBA

1986 E	64,763

Cities and Towns

• ORANJESTAD	19,800

AUSTRALIA

1984 E	15,544,500

Cities and Towns

Adelaide (★ 983,200)	12,040
Albany	13,990
Albury (★ 57,440) (1981 C)	53,214
Alice Springs	22,000
Altona (★ Melbourne) (1981 C)	30,909
Armidale	19,600
Ashfield (★ Sydney)	41,350
Auburn (★ Sydney)	46,900
Ballarat (★ 71,930) (1981 C)	35,681
Bankstown (★ Sydney)	153,600
Bathurst	24,900
Bendigo (★ 58,818) (1981 C)	31,841
Blacktown (★ Sydney)	192,200
Blue Mountains (★ Sydney)	62,200
Botany (★ Sydney)	35,100
Box Hill (★ Melbourne) (1981 C)	47,579
Brighton (★ Melbourne) (1981 C)	33,697
Brisbane (★ 1,146,610)	734,750
Brisbane Water (★ Sydney) (1981 C)	71,984
Broadmeadows (★ Melbourne) (1981 C)	103,540
Broken Hill	27,200
Brunswick (★ Melbourne) (1981 C)	44,464
Bunbury	23,940
Bundaberg (★ 42,050)	32,880
Burnside (★ Adelaide)	38,210
Burwood (★ Sydney)	28,950
Cairns (★ 64,840)	38,700
Camberwell (★ Melbourne) (1981 C)	85,883
Campbelltown (★ Sydney)	112,000
Campbelltown (★ Adelaide)	45,490
CANBERRA (★ 264,450)	243,450
Canning (★ Perth)	60,940
Canterbury (★ Sydney)	128,000
Caulfield (★ Melbourne) (1981 C)	69,922
Cessnock (★★ Newcastle)	42,100
Chelsea (★ Melbourne) (1981 C)	26,034
Coburg (★ Melbourne) (1981 C)	55,035
Croydon (★ Melbourne) (1981 C)	36,210
Dandenong (★ Melbourne) (1981 C)	54,962
Darwin (★ 68,500) (1985 E)	65,200
Devonport (1981 C)	21,424
Doncaster and Templestowe (★ Melbourne) (1981 C)	90,660
Drummoyne (★ Sydney)	31,700
Dubbo	30,500
Elizabeth (★ Adelaide)	32,340
Enfield (★ Adelaide)	66,750
Essendon (★ Melbourne) (1981 C)	56,380
Fairfield (★ Sydney)	143,500
Footscray (★ Melbourne) (1981 C)	49,756
Frankston (★ Melbourne) (1981 C)	78,808
Fremantle (★ Perth)	23,480
Gawler (★ 9,600)	6,860
Geelong (★ 137,173) (1981 C)	14,471
Geraldton	19,840
Glenorchy (★ Hobart) (1981 C)	41,019
Gosnells (★ Perth)	59,150
Goulburn (1981 C)	21,755
Grafton	17,350
Hawthorn (★ Melbourne) (1981 C)	30,689
Heidelberg (★ Melbourne) (1981 C)	64,757
Hobart (★ 168,359) (1981 C)	47,920
Holroyd (★ Sydney)	81,050
Horsham (1981 C)	12,034
Hurstville (★ Sydney)	66,000
Ipswich (★ Brisbane)	73,680
Kalgoorlie (★ 21,000)	10,100
Keilor (★ Melbourne) (1981 C)	81,762
Knox (★ Melbourne) (1981 C)	88,902
Kogarah (★ Sydney)	47,450
Lake Macquarie (★ Newcastle)	161,000
Launceston (★ 84,784) (1981 C)	31,273
Leichhardt (★ Sydney)	57,400
Lismore	37,050
Liverpool (★ Sydney)	94,700
Mackay (★ 48,760)	22,550
Maitland (★ Newcastle)	44,550
Malvern (★ Melbourne) (1981 C)	43,211
Manly (★ Sydney)	37,150
Marion (★ Adelaide)	70,910
Marrickville (★ Sydney)	83,650
Maryborough	22,400
Melbourne (★ 2,722,817) (1981 C)	63,388
Melville (★ Perth)	66,510
Mitcham (★ Adelaide)	61,950
Moe (1981 C)	16,649

C Census. E Official estimate. UE Unofficial estimate.
• Largest city in country.

★ Population or designation of metropolitan area, including suburbs (see headnote).
▲Population of an entire municipality, commune, or district, including rural area.

Moorabbin (★ Melbourne)
(1981 C) ...97,810
Mordialloc (★ Melbourne)
(1981 C) ...27,869
Morwell (1981 C) ...16,491
Mosman (★ Sydney) ...26,700
Mount Gambier (★ 21,200) ...19,260
Mount Isa ...25,020
Murray Bridge (1981 C) ...8,664
Newcastle (★ 419,100) ...138,800
Noarlunga (★ Adelaide) ...69,850
Northcote (★ Melbourne)
(1981 C) ...51,235
North Sydney (★ Sydney) ...49,600
Nunawading (★ Melbourne)
(1981 C) ...97,052
Oakleigh (★ Melbourne)
(1981 C) ...55,612
Orange ...32,200
Parramatta (★ Sydney) ...131,800
Penrith (★ Sydney) ...131,000
Perth (★ 898,918) ...82,600
Port Adelaide (★ Adelaide) ...37,310
Port Augusta ...16,340
Port Lincoln ...12,350
Port Pirie ...15,750
Prahran (★ Melbourne)
(1981 C) ...45,018
Preston (★ Melbourne)
(1981 C) ...84,519
Queanbeyan (★ Canberra) ...21,000
Randwick (★ Sydney) ...116,600
Redcliffe (★ Brisbane) ...44,950
Richmond (★ Melbourne)
(1981 C) ...24,506
Ringwood (★ Melbourne)
(1981 C) ...38,665
Rockdale (★ Sydney) ...84,650
Rockhampton (★ 56,520) ...54,630
Ryde (★ Sydney) ...90,600
Saint Kilda (★ Melbourne)
(1981 C) ...49,366
Sale (1981 C) ...12,968
Salisbury (★ Adelaide) ...92,270
Sandringham (★ Melbourne)
(1981 C) ...31,175
Shellharbour (★ Wollongong) ...46,000
Shepparton (★ 34,695)
(1981 C) ...23,579
Shoalhaven ...56,600
South Barwon (★ Geelong)
(1981 C) ...35,307
South Perth (★ Perth) ...32,700
Southport (Gold Coast)
(★ 198,330) ...116,540
Springvale (★ Melbourne)
(1981 C) ...80,186
Stirling (★ Perth) ...169,840
Sunshine (★ Melbourne)
(1981 C) ...94,419
• Sydney (★ 3,358,550) ...79,400
Tamworth (1981 C) ...31,779
Tea Tree Gully (★ Adelaide) ...73,500
Toowoomba ...74,360
Townsville (★ 100,530) ...82,140
Unley (★ Adelaide) ...36,670
Wagga Wagga ...49,650
Wangaratta (1981 C) ...16,202
Warrnambool (1981 C) ...21,414
Waverley (★ Melbourne)
(1981 C) ...122,471
Waverley (★ Sydney) ...62,900
West Torrens (★ Adelaide) ...45,810
Whyalla (★ 31,460) ...30,590
Willoughby (★ Sydney) ...52,950
Wollongong (★ 235,900) ...176,500
Woodville (★ Adelaide) ...80,560
Woollahra (★ Sydney) ...53,150

States

Australian Capital Territory
(Ter.) ...245,600
New South Wales ...5,405,100
Northern Territory (Ter.) ...139,900
Queensland ...2,505,100
South Australia ...1,353,000
Tasmania ...437,300
Victoria ...4,075,900
Western Australia ...1,382,600

AUSTRIA / Österreich

1981 C ...7,555,338

Cities and Towns

Amstetten ...21,989
Baden [bei Wien] (★ Vienna) ...23,140
Bad Ischl ...12,970
Braunau [am Inn] ...16,318
Bregenz ...24,561
Bruck [ah der Mur] (★ 49,000) ...15,068
Dornbirn ...38,641
Feldkirch ...23,745
Gmunden ...12,653
Graz (★ 270,000) ...243,166
Hallein ...15,377
Innsbruck (★ 150,000) ...117,287

Kapfenberg (★★ Bruck an
der Mur) ...25,716
Kitzbühel ...7,840
Klagenfurt (★ 97,000) ...87,321
Klosterneuburg (★ Vienna) ...22,975
Knittelfeld ...14,136
Krems [an der Donau] ...23,056
Kufstein ...13,118
Leoben (★ 46,000) ...31,989
Leonding (★ Linz) ...19,389
Lienz ...11,661
Linz (★ 285,000) ...199,910
Lustenau ...17,401
Mödling (★ Vienna) ...19,276
Mürzzuschlag ...10,751
Salzburg (★ 170,000) ...139,426
Sankt Pölten ...50,419
Sankt Veit [an der Glan] ...12,007
Solbad Hall [in Tirol] ...12,614
Spittal ...14,736
Steyr (★ 55,000) ...38,942
Stockerau (★ Vienna) ...12,679
Ternitz ...16,120
Traun (★ Linz) ...21,464
• VIENNA (WIEN) (★ 1,875,000)
(1982 E) ...1,524,510
Villach ...52,692
Wels (★ 64,000) ...51,060
Wiener Neustadt (★ 43,000) ...35,006
Wolfsberg ...28,097

States

1982 ESTIMATE

Burgenland ...270,083
Kärnten (Carinthia) ...537,137
Niederösterreich (Lower
Austria) ...1,431,400
Oberösterreich (Upper
Austria) ...1,276,807
Salzburg ...446,981
Steiermark (Styria) ...1,188,878
Tirol (Tyrol) ...591,069
Vorarlberg ...307,220
Wien (Vienna) ...1,524,510

BAHAMAS

1982 E ...218,000

Cities and Towns

Freeport ...25,000
Matthew Town (1963 C) ...1,258
• NASSAU ...135,000
West End (1963 C) ...1,942

BAHRAIN / Al Baḥrayn

1981 C ...350,798

Cities and Towns

Al Muḥarraq (★ Manama) ...46,061
• MANAMA (★ 224,643) ...108,684

BANGLADESH

1981 C ...87,052,000

Cities and Towns

Barisāl ...159,298
Bhairab Bāzār ...63,749
Bogra ...68,237
Brāhmanbāria ...88,635
Chāndpur ...72,638
Chittagong (★ 1,388,476) ...980,000
Chuādānga ...47,815
Comilla ...126,130
• DACCA (DHAKA)
(★ 3,458,602) ...1,850,000
Dinājpur ...96,343
Farīdpur ...66,911
Gopālpur ...30,970
Jamālpur ...89,847
Jessore (★ 157,000) ...149,426
Jhenida ...49,355
Khulna ...623,184
Kishorganj ...52,081
Kurīgrām ...46,132
Kushtia ...70,243
Mādārīpur ...58,645
Mymensingh (Nasirābād)
(★ 225,000) ...107,863
Naogaon ...51,791
Nārāyanganj (★★ Dacca) ...196,139
Narsingdi ...70,006
Nawābganj ...65,286
Netrakona ...39,116
Noākhāli ...46,572
Pābna ...101,080
Pārbatipur ...18,993
Patuākhāli ...45,818
Rājshāhi (Rampur Boalia)
(★ 171,600) ...142,117

Rangpur ...155,964
Saidpur ...128,085
Sātkhira ...58,311
Sherpur ...51,854
Sirājganj ...104,522
Sitakunda (★ Chittagong) ...237,520
Sylhet ...166,847
Tangail ...77,748
Tongi (★ Dacca) ...94,154

BARBADOS

1980 C ...248,983

Cities and Towns

• BRIDGETOWN (★ 115,000) ...7,466

BELGIUM / Belgique / België

1983 E ...9,858,017

Cities and Towns

Aalst (Alost) (★ Brussels) ...78,068
Anderlecht (★ Brussels) ...92,912
Antwerp (Antwerpen) (Anvers)
(★ 1,100,000) ...490,524
Arlon (▲ 22,201) ...16,600
Ath (Aat) (▲ 24,022) ...14,300
Auderghem (★ Brussels) ...30,038
Bastogne (▲ 11,567) ...6,800
Berchem-Sainte-Agathe
(Sint-Agatha-Berchem)
(★ Brussels) ...18,621
Binche ...33,298
Braine-l'Alleud (★ Brussels) ...30,549
Brasschaat (★ Antwerp) ...32,736
Brugge (Bruges) (★ 220,000) ...118,218
• BRUSSELS (BRUXELLES)
(BRUSSEL) (★ 2,395,000) ...137,738
Charleroi (★ 490,000) ...216,144
Châtelet (★ Charleroi) ...38,316
Dendermonde (▲ 42,470) ...22,800
Edegem (★ Antwerp) ...23,731
Eeklo ...19,483
Ekeren (★ Antwerp) ...30,367
Etterbeek (★ Brussels) ...44,101
Eupen ...16,974
Evere (★ Brussels) ...30,264
Forest (Vorst) (★ Brussels) ...50,260
Ganshoren (★ Brussels) ...21,349
Geel (▲ 31,463) ...17,300
Genk (★★ Hasselt) ...61,808
Gent (Ghent) (Gand)
(★ 465,000) ...236,540
Geraardsbergen (Grammont)
(▲ 30,381) ...14,900
Halle (Hal) (★ Brussels) ...32,416
Hamme ...22,737
Harelbeke (★ Kortrijk) ...25,402
Hasselt (★ 285,000) ...65,437
Herentals ...24,001
Herstal (★ Liège) ...38,010
Huy (▲ 17,544) ...12,600
Ieper (Ypres) (▲ 34,758) ...21,200
Ixelles (Elseue) (★ Brussels) ...76,146
Izegem ...26,582
Jette (★ Brussels) ...39,590
Knokke [-Heist] ...29,402
Kortrijk (Courtrai) (★ 201,000) ...75,587
La Louvière (★ 148,000) ...76,534
Leuven (Louvain) (★ 170,000) ...85,068
Liège (Luik) (★ 755,000) ...207,496
Lier (Lierre) (★ Antwerp) ...31,296
Lokeren ...33,741
Maasmechelen (Mechelen) ...33,693
Mechelen (Malines)
(★ 121,000) ...77,010
Menen (★ 29,875) ...32,978
Mol (▲ 29,875) ...16,800
Molenbeek Saint-Jean (Sint-Jans-
Molenbeek) (★ Brussels) ...71,891
Mons (Bergen) (★ 245,000) ...91,868
Mortsel (★ Antwerp) ...26,625
Mouscron (Moeskroen)
(★ Lille, France) ...54,402
Namur (Namen) (★ 145,000) ...101,860
Nivelles (Nijvel) (▲ 21,665) ...16,600
Oostende (Ostende)
(★ 121,000) ...69,129
Oudenaarde (Audenarde)
(▲ 27,233) ...13,600
Roeselare (Roulers) ...51,649
Ronse (Renaix-Gleiche) ...24,217
Saint-Gilles (Sint-Gillis)
(★ Brussels) ...44,193
Schaerbeek (Schaarbeek)
(★ Brussels) ...105,672
Schoten (★ Antwerp) ...30,973
Seraing (★ Liège) ...63,001
Sint-Niklaas (Saint-Nicolas) ...68,157
Sint-Truiden (Saint-Trond)
(▲ 36,698) ...17,300
Soignies (Zinnik) (▲ 23,419) ...11,600
Spa ...9,716
Tienen (Tirlemont) ...32,506

Tongeren (Tongres) (▲ 29,704) ...18,600
Tournai (Doornik) (▲ 67,379) ...45,000
Turnhout ...37,461
Uccle (Ukkel) (★ Brussels) ...75,675
Verviers (★ 102,000) ...54,294
Veurne (Furnes) (▲ 11,256) ...7,500
Vilvoorde (★ Brussels) ...32,868
Waregem ...33,469
Waterloo (★ Brussels) ...24,933
Woluwe-Saint-Lambert (Sint-
Lambrechts-Woluwe)
(★ Brussels) ...49,250
Woluwe-Saint-Pierre (Sint-Pieters-
Woluwe) (★ Brussels) ...40,368
Zottegem (▲ 24,885) ...12,800

Provinces

Antwerp (Antwerpen)
(Anvers) ...1,577,246
Brabant ...2,221,383
East Flanders (Oost-Vlaanderen)
(Flandre Orientale) ...1,332,265
Hainaut (Henegouwen) ...1,291,610
Liège (Luik) ...995,576
Limburg (Limbourg) ...724,032
Luxembourg (Luxemburg) ...222,784
Namur (Namen) ...408,741
West Flanders (West-Vlaanderen)
(Flandre Occidentale) ...1,084,380

BELIZE

1980 C ...145,353

Cities and Towns

• Belize City ...39,771
BELMOPAN ...2,935
Corozal ...6,899
Orange Walk ...8,439
Punta Gorda ...2,396
San Ignacio ...5,616
Stann Creek ...6,661

BENIN / Bénin

1980 E ...3,567,000

Cities and Towns

• Cotonou ...215,000
PORTO-NOVO ...123,000

BERMUDA

1985 E ...56,000

Cities and Towns

• HAMILTON (★ 15,000) ...1,676
Saint George ...1,707

BHUTAN / Druk-Yul

1977 E ...1,232,000

Cities and Towns

• THIMBU ...8,982

BOLIVIA

1985 E ...6,429,226

Cities and Towns

Cobija ...4,989
Cochabamba ...317,251
• LA PAZ ...992,592
Oruro ...178,393
Potosí ...113,380
Santa Cruz ...441,717
SUCRE ...86,609
Tarija ...60,621
Trinidad ...40,288

Departments

Beni ...239,810
Chuquisaca ...462,904
Cochabamba ...979,171
La Paz ...2,091,429
Oruro ...412,756
Pando ...46,933
Potosí ...878,232
Santa Cruz ...1,047,964
Tarija ...270,027

BOPHUTHATSWANA

1982 E ...1,347,000

Cities and Towns

• Ga-Rankuwa (1980 C) ...48,300
Mabopane (1970 C) ...22,559
MMABATHO (★ Mafikeng, S. Afr.)
(1977 E) ...9,062

BOTSWANA

1982 E ...973,000

Cities and Towns

Francistown ...32,000
• GABORONE (GABERONES)
(1983 E) ...72,200
Kanye ...22,000
Lobatse ...20,000
Mahalatswe ...19,000
Mochudi ...20,000
Molepolole ...19,000
Seiebi Phikwe ...29,000

BRAZIL / Brasil

1980 C ...119,002,706

Cities and Towns

Alagoinhas ...76,331
Alegrete ...54,746
Alvorada ...90,339
Americana ...121,743
Anápolis ...160,571
Andradina ...42,036
Apucarana ...63,678
Aracaju ...287,934
Araçatuba ...113,925
Araguari ...73,307
Arapiraca ...83,963
Araraquara ...77,186
Araras ...54,214
Araxá ...51,311
Assis ...57,184
Bagé ...66,720
Barbacena ...69,566
Barra do Piraí ...51,191
Barra Mansa (★★ Volta
Redonda) ...123,335
Barretos ...65,318
Bauru ...180,093
Bayeux (★ João Pessoa) ...58,474
Belém (★ 1,000,000) ...933,287
Belford Roxo (★ Rio de
Janeiro) ...282,695
Belo Horizonte
(★ 2,450,000) ...1,780,855
Betim (★ Belo Horizonte) ...76,801
Blumenau ...144,785
Boa Vista ...43,131
Botucatu ...56,752
Bragança Paulista ...60,976
BRASÍLIA ...1,176,935
Cachoeira do Sul ...59,977
Cachoeirinha (★ Porto Alegre) ...62,751
Cachoeiro de Itapemirim ...85,024
Campina Grande ...222,102
Campinas (★ 875,000) ...566,627
Campo Grande ...282,857
Campos ...178,457
Campos Elyseos (★ Rio
de Janeiro) ...162,997
Canoas (★ Porto Alegre) ...213,999
Carapicuíba (★ São Paulo) ...185,816
Cariacica (★ Vitória) ...57,702
Caruaru ...137,502
Cascavel ...100,329
Castanhal ...51,729
Catanduva ...64,755
Caucaia (★ Fortaleza) ...68,033
Cavaleiro (★ Recife) ...85,961
Caxias ...56,668
Caxias do Sul ...198,683
Chapecó ...53,181
Coelho da Rocha (★ Rio
de Janeiro) ...140,028
Colatina ...61,120
Colombo (★ Curitiba) ...54,979
Conselheiro Lafaiete ...66,229
Contagem (★ Belo
Horizonte) ...111,545
Corumbá ...66,077
Criciúma ...74,018
Cruz Alta ...53,659
Cruzeiro ...55,182
Cubatão (★ Santos) ...78,303
Cuiabá ...167,880
Curitiba (★ 1,300,000) ...1,024,975
Diadema (★ São Paulo) ...228,660
Divinópolis ...108,279
Dourados ...76,783
Duque de Caxias (★ Rio
de Janeiro) ...306,243
Embu (★ São Paulo) ...95,800
Esteio (★ Porto Alegre) ...50,208
Feira de Santana ...227,004

C Census. E Official estimate. UE Unofficial estimate.
• Largest city in country.

★ Population or designation of metropolitan area, including suburbs (see headnote).
▲Population of an entire municipality, commune, or district, including rural area.

Ferraz de Vasconcelos
(★ São Paulo) 54,810
Florianópolis (★ 240,000) 153,652
Fortaleza (★ 1,490,000) 1,307,611
Foz do Iguaçu 93,506
Franca 144,117
Garanhuns 64,823
Goiânia (★ 760,000) 702,858
Governador Valadares 173,624
Guaratinguetá 72,961
Guarujá (★ Santos) 67,708
Guarulhos (★ São Paulo) 426,693
Ijuí 52,520
Ilhéus 71,376
Imperatriz 111,705
Ipatinga (★ 200,000) 105,030
Ipiíba (★ Rio de Janeiro) 98,069
Itabira 57,649
Itabuna 130,163
Itajaí 78,779
Itajubá 53,433
Itapecerica da Serra
(★ São Paulo) 52,346
Itapetininga 61,298
Itapevi (★ São Paulo) 53,441
Itaquaquecetuba (★ São Paulo) 73,064
Itaquari (★ Vitória) 127,659
Itu 62,267
Ituiutaba 65,153
Itumbiara 56,573
Jaboatão (★ Recife) 66,890
Jacareí 104,241
Jandira 36,017
Jaú 59,561
Jequié 84,708
João Pessoa (Paraíba)
(★ 475,000) 290,247
Joinville 216,986
Juazeiro (★★ Petrolina) 60,811
Juazeiro do Norte 125,191
Juiz de Fora 299,432
Jundiaí 221,888
Lajes 108,727
Limeira 137,809
Linhares 53,507
Londrina 257,899
Lorena 51,300
Luziânia 67,297
Macapá 88,930
Maceió 375,771
Manaus 611,763
Marília 103,815
Maringá 158,091
Mauá (★ São Paulo) 205,740
Mesquita (★ Rio de Janeiro) 125,314
Mogi das Cruzes
(★ São Paulo) 122,434
Mogi-Guaçu 65,421
Monjolo (★ Rio de Janeiro) 96,165
Montes Claros 151,713
Mossoró 117,971
Muriaé 50,058
Muribeca dos Guararapes
(★ Recife) 137,903
Natal 376,446
Neves (★ Rio de Janeiro) 138,130
Nilópolis (★ Rio de Janeiro) 102,959
Niterói (★ Rio de Janeiro) 382,736
Nova Friburgo 88,872
Nova Iguaçu (★ Rio de
Janeiro) 491,766
Novo Hamburgo
(★ Porto Alegre) 133,221
Olinda (★ Recife) 266,751
Osasco (★ São Paulo) 474,543
Ourinhos 52,671
Paranaguá 71,107
Paranavaí 52,593
Parnaíba 79,321
Parque Industrial (★ Belo
Horizonte) 166,626
Passo Fundo 103,064
Passos 56,956
Patos 58,705
Patos de Minas 59,849
Paulo Afonso 61,978
Pelotas 196,919
Petrolina (★ 175,000) 73,580
Petrópolis (★ Rio de Janeiro) 150,249
Pindamonhangaba 51,147
Pinheirinho (★ Curitiba) 41,248
Piracicaba 179,380
Poá (★ São Paulo) 52,512
Poços de Caldas 81,440
Ponta Grossa 171,810
Porto Alegre (★ 2,225,000) 1,125,477
Porto Velho 101,162
Pouso Alegre 50,553
Praia Grande (★ Santos) 54,038
Presidente Prudente 127,903
Queimados (★ Rio de Janeiro) 94,303
Recife (★ 2,300,000) 1,203,899
Ribeirão Preto 300,828
Rio Branco 87,449
Rio Claro 103,119
Rio de Janeiro
(★ 8,975,000) 5,090,700
Rio Grande 130,149
Rondonópolis 52,315
Salvador (★ 1,725,000) 1,501,981
Santa Bárbara d'Oeste 71,880
Santa Cruz [do Sul] 52,096
Santa Maria 151,156
Santana do Livramento 58,072
Santarém 102,181
Santo André (★ São Paulo) 549,556
Santo Ângelo 50,173
Santos (★ 900,000) 410,933
São Bernardo [do Campo]
(★ São Paulo) 381,097
São Caetano do Sul
(★ São Paulo) 163,082
São Carlos 109,167
São Gonçalo (★ Rio de
Janeiro) 221,591
São João del Rei 53,341
São João de Meriti (★ Rio
de Janeiro) 210,574
São José do Rio Preto 172,127
São José dos Campos 268,034
São José dos Pinhais
(★ Curitiba) 55,332
São Leopoldo (★ Porto Alegre) 94,868
São Lourenco da Mata
(★ Recife) 58,843
São Luís (★ 475,000) 182,258
• São Paulo (★ 12,525,000) 8,493,226
São Vicente (★ Santos) 192,858
Sapucaia do Sul (★ Porto
Alegre) 78,849
Sete Lagoas 94,432
Sete Pontes (★ Rio de
Janeiro) 61,046
Sobral 69,208
Sorocaba 254,672
Suzano (★ São Paulo) 95,167
Taboão da Serra
(★ São Paulo) 97,655
Taubaté 155,376
Teófilo Otoni 83,084
Teresina (★ 410,000) 339,042
Teresópolis 78,753
Timon (★ Teresina) 55,266
Tubarão 64,508
Uberaba 180,228
Uberlândia 230,185
Uruguaiana 79,077
Varginha 57,774
Vicente de Carvalho
(★ Santos) 83,368
Vila Velha (Espírito Santo)
(★ Vitória) 74,154
Vitória (★ 600,000) 165,090
Vitória da Conquista 125,516
Vitória de Santo Antão 62,870
Volta Redonda (★ 325,000) 180,126

States

Acre 301,303
Alagoas 1,982,591
Amapá (Ter.) 175,257
Amazonas 1,430,089
Bahia 9,454,346
Ceará 5,288,253
Distrito Federal 1,176,935
Espírito Santo 2,023,340
Fernando de Noronha
(Ter.) 1,279
Goiás 3,859,602
Maranhão 3,996,404
Mato Grosso 1,138,691
Mato Grosso do Sul 1,369,567
Minas Gerais 13,378,553
Pará 3,403,391
Paraíba 2,770,176
Paraná 7,629,392
Pernambuco 6,141,993
Piauí 2,139,021
Rio de Janeiro 11,291,520
Rio Grande do Norte 1,898,172
Rio Grande do Sul 7,773,837
Rondônia 491,069
Roraima (Ter.) 79,159
Santa Catarina 3,627,933
São Paulo 25,040,712
Sergipe 1,140,121

BRUNEI

1981 C 191,765

Cities and Towns

• BANDAR SERI BEGAWAN
(BRUNEI) 63,868
Seria 23,511

BULGARIA / Bâlgarija

1984 E 8,960,679

Cities and Towns

Blagoevgrad (Gorna
Dzhumaya) 70,000
Burgas 188,000
Dimitrovgrad 54,000
Gabrovo 84,000
Kazanlŭk 62,000
Khaskovo 91,000
Kŭrdzhali 60,000
Kyustendil 56,000
Lovech 51,000
Mikhaylovgrad 58,000
Pazardzhik 81,000
Pernik (Dimitrovo) 98,000
Pleven 144,000
Plovdiv 378,000
Razgrad 56,000
Ruse 185,000
Shumen (Kolarovgrad) 107,000
Silistra 60,000
Sliven 104,000
• SOFIA (SOFIYA)
(★ 1,182,900) 1,102,000
Stara Zagora 152,000
Tolbukhin (Dobrich) 105,000
Varna 297,000
Veliko Tŭrnovo (Tŭrnovo) 65,000
Vidin 64,000
Vratsa 77,000
Yambol 91,000

Provinces

1980 ESTIMATE

Blagoevgrad 335,352
Burgas 432,721
Gabrovo 176,910
Khaskovo 294,933
Kŭrdzhali 283,178
Kyustendil 199,292
Lovech 212,089
Mikhaylovgrad 234,697
Pazardzhik 321,011
Pernik 175,089
Pleven 373,655
Plovdiv 748,239
Razgrad 191,929
Ruse 295,184
Shumen 250,912
Silistra 173,888
Sliven 234,526
Smolyan 172,683
Sofiya (Sofia) (City) 1,142,582
Sofiya 310,379
Stara Zagora 409,468
Tolbukhin 251,548
Tŭrgovishte 172,326
Varna 465,897
Veliko Tŭrnovo 349,144
Vidin 170,815
Vratsa 292,323
Yambol 205,882

BURKINA FASO

1984 E 6,965,886

Cities and Towns

Bobo Dioulasso 194,396
Koudougou (1977 E) 38,000
• OUAGADOUGOU 345,150
Ouahigouya (1977 E) 27,000

BURMA / Myanmā

1983 C 35,313,905

Cities and Towns

Bassein 144,092
Chauk (1953 C) 24,466
Henzada (1970 E) 85,000
Insein (★ Rangoon) (1973 C) 143,625
Kanbe (★ Rangoon)
(1973 C) 253,600
Mandalay 532,895
Meiktila (1953 C) 25,180
Mergui (1953 C) 33,697
Monywa 106,873
Moulmein 219,991
Myaungmya (1953 C) 24,532
Myingyan (1970 E) 65,000
Myitkyinā (1953 C) 12,833
Pakokku (1953 C) 30,943
Pegu 150,447
Prome (Pyè) (1970 E) 65,000
• RANGOON (★ 3,000,000) 2,458,712
Sagaing (1953 C) 15,439
Sittwe (Akyab) 107,607
Taunggyi 107,907
Tavoy (1970 E) 53,000
Thaton (1953 C) 38,047
Thingangyun (★ Rangoon)
(1973 C) 141,210
Toungoo (1953 C) 31,589
Yenangyaung (1953 C) 24,416

BURUNDI

1983 E 4,523,513

Cities and Towns

• BUJUMBURA 229,980
Bururi (1979 E) 7,800
Gitega (1979 E) 19,500
Muyinga (1982 E) 5,400

CAMEROON / Cameroun

1984 E 9,542,400

Cities and Towns

Bafoussam 88,000
Bamenda 69,000
• Douala 841,000
Foumban 48,000
Garoua 92,000
Kumba 64,000
Limbe (Victoria) (1976 C) 27,016
Maroua 95,000
Ngaoundéré 58,000
Nkongsamba 101,000
YAOUNDE 561,000

CANADA

1981 C 24,343,181

Cities and Towns

ALBERTA 2,237,724
Banff 4,208
Calgary 592,743
Camrose 12,570
Edmonton (★ 657,057) 532,246
Fort McMurray 31,000
Fort Saskatchewan
(★ Edmonton) 12,169
Grande Prairie 24,263
Jasper 3,269
Leduc 12,471
Lethbridge 54,072
Lloydminster, Alta. and
Sask. prov. 15,031
Medicine Hat (★ 49,645) 40,380
Red Deer 46,393
Saint Albert (★ Edmonton) 31,996
Sherwood Park
(★ Edmonton) 29,285
Spruce Grove 10,326

BRITISH COLUMBIA 2,744,467
Burnaby (★ Vancouver) 136,494
Campbell River 15,370
Chilliwack 40,642
Courtenay (★ 35,218) 8,992
Cranbrook 15,915
Dawson Creek 11,373
Esquimalt (★ Victoria) 15,870
Fort Saint John 13,891
Kamloops (★ 64,997) 64,048
Kelowna (★ 77,468) 59,196
Kitimat (★ Terrace) 12,462
Langley (★ Vancouver) 15,124
Nanaimo (★ 57,694) 47,069
New Westminster
(★ Vancouver) 38,550
North Vancouver
(★ Vancouver) 33,952
Oak Bay (★ Victoria) 16,990
Penticton 23,181
Port Alberni (★ 32,558) 19,892
Port Coquitlam (★ Vancouver) 27,535
Port Moody (★ Vancouver) 14,917
Powell River (★ 19,364) 13,423
Prince George 67,559
Prince Rupert (★ 18,402) 16,197
Richmond (★ Vancouver) 96,154
Terrace (★ 32,486) 10,914
Trail (★ 22,939) 9,599
Vancouver (★ 1,268,183) 414,281
Vernon (★ 42,158) 19,987
Victoria (★ 233,481) 64,379
West Vancouver
(★ Vancouver) 35,728
White Rock (★ Vancouver) 13,550

MANITOBA 1,026,241
Brandon 36,242
Churchill 1,186
Flin Flon, Man. and Sask. prov.
(★ 9,897) 8,261
Portage la Prairie (★ 20,709) 13,086
Selkirk 10,037
Thompson (★ 14,319) 14,288
Winnipeg (★ 584,842) 564,473

NEW BRUNSWICK 696,403
Bathurst (★ 24,267) 15,705
Campbellton (★ 15,508) 9,818
Edmundston (★ 21,901) 12,044
Fredericton (★ 64,439) 43,723
Moncton (★ 98,354) 54,743
Oromocto (★ 13,648) 9,064
Riverview (★ Moncton) 14,907
Saint John (★ 114,048) 80,521

NEWFOUNDLAND 567,681
Carbonear (★ 12,983) 5,335
Channel-Port-aux-Basques 5,988
Conception Bay South
(★ Saint John's) 10,856
Corner Brook (★ 32,269) 24,339
Gander 10,404
Grand Falls (★ 14,512) 8,765
Happy Valley-Goose Bay 7,103
Kilbride (★ Saint John's) 5,014
Labrador City (★ 14,693) 11,538
Marystown 6,299
Mount Pearl (★ Saint John's) 11,543
Saint John's (★ 154,820) 83,770
Saint John's Metropolitan Area
(★ Saint John's) 24,485
Stephenville 8,876
Windsor (★ Grand Falls) 5,747

NORTHWEST TERRITORIES 45,741
Eskimo Point 1,022
Fort Smith 2,298
Frobisher Bay 2,333
Hay River 2,863
Inuvik 3,147
Pine Point 1,861
Rae 1,378
Rankin Inlet 1,109
Yellowknife 9,483

NOVA SCOTIA 847,442
Dartmouth (★ Halifax) 62,277
Glace Bay (★★ Sydney) 21,466
Halifax (★ 277,727) 114,594
Kentville (★ 20,920) 4,974
Louisbourg 1,410
New Glasgow (★ 39,412) 10,464
Sydney (★ 87,489) 29,444
Sydney Mines (★ 35,348) 8,501
Truro (★ 39,751) 12,552

ONTARIO 8,625,107
Ajax (★ Toronto) 25,475
Ancaster (★ Hamilton) 14,428
Aurora (★ Toronto) 16,267
Barrie (★ 61,271) 38,423
Belleville (★ 46,370) 34,881
Brampton (★ Toronto) 149,030
Brantford (★ 88,330) 74,315
Brockville (★ 35,659) 19,896
Burlington (★ Hamilton) 114,853
Caledon (★ Toronto) 26,645
Cambridge (Galt)
(★★ Kitchener) 77,183
Chatham (★ 47,182) 40,952
Cobourg (★ 20,194) 11,385
Collingwood 12,064
Cornwall (★ 53,405) 46,144
Dundas (★ Hamilton) 19,586
Dunnville 11,353
East Gwillimbury 12,565
East York (★ Toronto) 101,974
Elliot Lake 16,723
Etobicoke (★ Toronto) 298,713
Fergus (★ 12,125) 6,064
Fort Erie 24,096
Gloucester (★ Ottawa) 72,859
Grimsby (★ Hamilton) 15,797
Guelph (★ 78,456) 71,207
Haileybury (★ 13,220) 4,925
Haldimand 16,866
Halton Hills 35,190
Hamilton (★ 542,095) 306,434
Hawkesbury (★ 11,294) 9,877
Huntsville 11,467
Kanata (★ Ottawa) 19,728
Kapuskasing 12,014
Kenora (★ 15,737) 9,817
Kingston (★ 114,982) 52,616
Kirkland Lake 12,219
Kitchener (★ 287,801) 139,734
Leamington (★ 21,369) 12,528
Lincoln 14,196
Lindsay (★ 16,836) 13,596
London (★ 283,668) 254,280
Markham (★ Toronto) 77,037
Midland (★ 33,925) 12,132
Milton 28,067
Mississauga (★ Toronto) 315,056
Nanticoke 19,816
Nepean (★ Ottawa) 84,361
Newcastle 32,229
Newmarket (★ Toronto) 29,753
Niagara Falls (★★ Saint
Catharines) 70,960
Niagara-on-the-Lake (★ Saint
Catharines) 12,186
Nickel Centre (★ Sudbury) 12,318
North Bay (★ 57,137) 51,268
North York (★ Toronto) 559,521
Oakville (★ Toronto) 75,773
Orangeville 13,740
Orillia (★ 30,860) 23,955
Oshawa (★ 154,217) 117,519
OTTAWA (★ 717,978) 295,163

C Census. E Official estimate. UE Unofficial estimate.
• Largest city in country.
★ Population or designation of metropolitan area, including suburbs (see headnote).
▲Population of an entire municipality, commune, or district, including rural area.

Owen Sound (★ 27,295) 19,883
Pelham (★ Saint Catharines) 11,104
Pembroke (★ 22,187) 14,026
Petawawa (★ 13,240) 5,520
Peterborough (★ 85,701) 60,620
Pickering (★ Toronto) 37,754
Port Colborne (★ Saint Catharines) 19,225
Rayside-Balfour (★ Sudbury) 15,017
Richmond Hill (★ Toronto) 37,778
Saint Catharines (★ 304,353) 124,018
Saint Thomas 28,165
Sarnia (★ 83,951) 50,892
Sault Sainte Marie (★ 86,962) 82,697
Scarborough (★ Toronto) 443,353
Simcoe 14,326
Smiths Falls (★ 15,045) 8,831
Stoney Creek (★ Hamilton) 36,762
Stratford (★ 28,064) 26,262
Sudbury (★ 149,923) 91,829
Thorold (★ Saint Catharines) 15,412
Thunder Bay (★ 121,379) 112,486
Tillsonburg 10,487
Timmins 46,114
• Toronto (★ 2,998,947) 599,217
Trenton (★ 39,106) 15,085
Valley East (★ Sudbury) 20,433
Vanier (Eastview) (★ Ottawa) 18,792
Vaughan (Woodbridge) (★ Toronto) 29,674
Walden (★ Sudbury) 10,139
Wallaceburg 11,506
Waterloo (★ Kitchener) 49,428
Welland (★★ Saint Catharines) 45,448
Whitby (★ Oshawa) 36,698
Whitchurch-Stouffville (★ Toronto) 13,557
Windsor (★ 246,110) 192,083
Woodstock 26,603
York (★ Toronto) 134,617

PRINCE EDWARD ISLAND 122,506
Charlottetown (★ 44,999) 15,282
Summerside (★ 14,950) 7,828

QUEBEC / QUÉBEC 6,438,403
Alma 26,322
Ancienne-Lorette (Notre-Dame-de-Lorette) (★ Québec) 12,935
Anjou (★ Montréal) 37,346
Asbestos (★ 14,229) 7,967
Aylmer East (★ Ottawa) 26,695
Baie-Comeau (★ 29,490) 12,866
Beaconsfield (★ Montréal) 19,613
Beauport (★ Québec) 60,447
Bécancour 10,247
Beloeil (★ Montréal) 17,540
Blainville (★ Montréal) 14,682
Boisbriand (★ Montréal) 13,471
Boucherville (★ Montréal) 29,704
Brossard (★ Montréal) 52,232
Cap-de-la-Madeleine (★ Trois-Rivières) 32,626
Chambly (★ Montréal) 12,190
Charlesbourg (★ Québec) 68,326
Châteauguay (★ Montréal) 36,928
Chibougamau 10,732
Chicoutimi (★ 135,172) 60,064
Côte-Saint-Luc (★ Montréal) 27,531
Cowansville 12,240
Dolbeau (★ 15,448) 8,766
Dollard-des-Ormeaux (★ Montréal) 39,940
Dorval (★ Montréal) 17,722
Drummondville (★ 54,679) 27,374
Gaspé 17,261
Gatineau (★ Ottawa) 74,988
Granby (★ 45,667) 38,069
Grand'Mère (★ Shawinigan) 15,442
Greenfield Park (★ Montréal) 18,527
Hauterive (★ Baie-Comeau) 13,995
Hull (★ Ottawa) 56,225
Joliette (★ 34,463) 16,987
Jonquière (★★ Chicoutimi) 60,354
Kirkland (★ Montréal) 10,476
La Baie 20,935
Lachine (★ Montréal) 37,521
Lachute (★ 18,135) 11,729
La Prairie (★ Montréal) 10,627
LaSalle (★ Montréal) 76,299
La Tuque (★ 13,589) 11,556
Lauzon (★ Québec) 13,362
Laval (★ Montréal) 268,335
Lévis (★ Québec) 17,895
Longueuil (★ Montréal) 124,320
Loretteville (★ Québec) 15,060
Magog (★ 18,149) 13,604
Mascouche (★ Montréal) 20,345
Matane 13,612
Mirabel 14,080
Montmagny 12,405
Montréal (★ 2,828,349) 980,354
Montréal-Nord (★ Montréal) 94,914
Mont-Royal (★ Montréal) 19,247
Mont-Saint-Hilaire (★ Montréal) 10,066
Outremont (★ Montréal) 24,338
Pierrefonds (★ Montréal) 38,390
Pointe-aux-Trembles (★ Montréal) 36,270
Pointe-Claire (★ Montréal) 24,571
Québec (★ 576,075) 166,474
Repentigny (★ Montréal) 34,419
Rimouski (★ 37,458) 29,120
Rivière-du-Loup (★ 20,521) 13,459
Roberval 11,429
Rouyn (★ 28,648) 17,224
Saint-Bruno (★ Montréal) 22,880
Saint-Eustache (★ Montréal) 29,716
Sainte-Foy (★ Québec) 68,883
Saint-Hubert (★ Montréal) 60,573
Saint-Hyacinthe (★ 47,440) 38,246
Saint-Jean (★ 60,710) 35,640
Saint-Jérôme (★ 43,786) 25,123
Sainte-Julie (★ Montréal) 14,243
Saint-Lambert (★ Montréal) 20,557
Saint-Laurent (★ Montréal) 65,900
Saint-Léonard (★ Montréal) 79,429
Sainte-Thérèse-de-Blainville (★ Montréal) 18,750
Sept-Îles (Seven Islands) (★ 30,057) 29,262
Shawinigan (★ 62,699) 23,011
Shawinigan-Sud (★ Shawinigan) 11,325
Sherbrooke (★ 117,324) 74,075
Sillery (★ Québec) 12,825
Sorel (★ 47,030) 20,347
Terrebonne (★ Montréal) 11,769
Thetford Mines (★ 34,698) 19,965
Tracy (★ Sorel) 12,843
Trois-Rivières (★ 111,453) 50,466
Trois-Rivières-Ouest (★ Trois-Rivières) 13,107
Val-Bélair (★ Québec) 12,695
Val-d'Or (★ 23,495) 21,371
Valleyfield (★ 39,491) 29,574
Vanier (Québec-Ouest) (★ Québec) 10,725
Verdun (★ Montréal) 61,287
Victoriaville (★ 35,920) 21,838
Ville-Saint-Georges (★ 18,778) 10,342
Westmount (★ Montréal) 20,480

SASKATCHEWAN 968,313
Lloydminster, Sask. and Alta. prov. 15,031
Moose Jaw (★ 36,057) 33,941
North Battleford (★ 18,702) 14,030
Prince Albert (★ 38,331) 31,380
Regina (★ 164,313) 162,613
Saskatoon 154,210
Swift Current (★ 16,574) 14,747
Yorkton 15,339

YUKON 23,153
Dawson 697
Faro 1,652
Whitehorse 14,814

CAPE VERDE / Cabo Verde

1980 C 296,093

Cities and Towns

Mindelo 36,265
• PRAIA 37,480

CAYMAN ISLANDS

1979 C 16,677

Cities and Towns

• GEORGETOWN 7,617

CENTRAL AFRICAN REPUBLIC / République centrafricaine

1982 E 2,395,000

Cities and Towns

Bambari 35,000
• BANGUI 340,000
Bouar 48,000

CHAD / Tchad

1979 E 4,405,000

Cities and Towns

Abéché 54,000
Kélo 27,000
Koumra 27,000
Moundou 66,000
• N'DJAMENA (FORT-LAMY) 303,000
Sarh (Fort-Archambault) 65,000

CHILE

1982 C 11,329,736

Cities and Towns

Angol 31,005
Antofagasta 185,486
Apoquindo (★ Santiago) (1970 C) 90,722
Arica 139,320
Calama 81,684
Cauquenes 23,908
Chillán 118,163
Chuquicamata 16,891
Concepción (★ 535,000) 267,891
Conchalí (★ Santiago) (1970 C) 246,046
Copiapó 69,045
Coquimbo 62,186
Coronel 65,918
Curicó 60,550
Iquique 110,153
La Calera 38,322
La Cisterna (★ Santiago) (1970 C) 246,537
La Granja (★ Santiago) (1970 C) 163,882
La Serena 83,283
Las Rejas (★ Santiago) (1970 C) 44,681
La Unión 16,925
Lebu 16,952
Limache 22,711
Linares 46,433
Lo Prado Arriba (★ Santiago) (1970 C) 112,548
Los Andes 34,613
Los Ángeles 70,529
Lota 47,133
Melipilla 33,654
Ñuñoa (★ Santiago) (1970 C) 280,733
Osorno 95,286
Ovalle 43,023
Parral 21,221
Penco (★ Concepción) 30,939
Providencia (★ Santiago) (1970 C) 85,678
Puente Alto (★ Santiago) 109,239
Puerto Aisén 9,176
Puerto Montt 84,410
Puerto Natales 14,250
Punta Arenas 95,332
Quillota 44,824
Quilpué (★ Valparaíso) 84,136
Quinta Normal (★ Santiago) (1970 C) 138,007
Rancagua 139,925
Renca (★ Santiago) (1970 C) 68,440
San Antonio 61,486
San Bernardo (★ Santiago) 117,132
San Carlos 21,919
San Felipe 31,656
San Fernando 32,432
San Miguel (★ Santiago) (1970 C) 320,883
• SANTIAGO (★ 4,025,000) 425,924
Talca 128,544
Talcahuano (★★ Concepción) 202,368
Temuco 157,297
Tocopilla 21,883
Tomé 34,107
Valdivia 100,046
Vallenar 38,375
Valparaíso (★ 700,000) 265,355
Victoria 19,743
Villa Alemana 55,766
Viña del Mar (★ Valparaíso) 244,899

Regions

1984 ESTIMATE

Aisén del General Carlos Ibáñez del Campo 71,369
Antofagasta 338,219
Atacama 214,718
Biobío 1,569,431
Coquimbo 439,938
La Araucanía 677,951
Libertador General Bernardo O'Higgins 589,347
Los Lagos 904,557
Magallanes y Antártica Chilena 117,401
Maule 739,329
Metropolitana 4,722,528
Tarapacá 266,428
Valparaíso (1982 E) 1,326,834

CHINA / Zhongguo

1982 C 1,008,175,288

Cities and Towns

Abagnar Qi (Xilin Hot) 61,629
Acheng 95,148
Aihui (Heihe) (▲ 66,163) 60,000
Aksu 87,989
Anci (Langfang) (▲ 171,972) 75,000
Anda 135,922
Ankang 97,318
Anlu 42,662
Anqing (▲ 418,773) 160,000
Anqiu 59,374
Anshan (1985 E) 1,280,000
Anshun (▲ 207,886) 100,000
Anyang (▲ 504,311) 250,000
Arxan 46,961
Baicheng (▲ 266,420) 150,000
Baiquan 57,539
Baiyin (1975 UE) 50,000
Baoding (▲ 502,407) 400,000
Baoji (▲ 338,754) 275,000
Baoqing 47,024
Baotou (▲ 1,063,600) (1984 E) 866,200
Baoying 53,498
Bayan 43,230
Bei'an 123,119
Beihai (▲ 168,442) 125,000
Beipiao 131,829
Bengbu (▲ 558,677) 425,000
Benxi (Xiaoshi) 43,869
Benxi (▲ 810,500) (1984 E) 678,500
Bijie 113,977
Binhai (Dongkan) 48,731
Binxian (Beizhen) 127,326
Binxian (Binzhou) 43,335
Bo'ai (Qinghua) 46,142
Boli 76,028
Bose 76,185
Boshan (1975 UE) 100,000
Boxian (Bozhou) 63,982
Boxing 57,554
Boyang 58,812
Bozhen 54,376
Butha Qi 55,000
Cangshan (Bianzhuang) 79,334
Cangzhou (▲ 266,384) 120,000
Canton (Guangzhou) (▲ 3,290,000) (1985 E) 2,570,000
Chaihe 40,328
Changchun (Hsinking) (▲ 1,860,000) (1985 E) 1,480,000
Changde (▲ 204,125) 175,000
Changge 67,002
Changji 44,465
Changle 43,092
Changli 41,583
Changqing 65,094
Changsha (1984 E) 1,123,900
Changshou 54,832
Changshu (Yushan) 78,058
Changtu 51,920
Changyi 64,513
Changzhi (▲ 436,149) 300,000
Changzhou (▲ 500,740) 425,000
Chao'an (▲ 164,099) 130,000
Chaoxian 72,936
Chaoyang (Miancheng), Guangdong prov. 94,195
Chaoyang, Liaoning prov. (▲ 213,606) 125,000
Chengde (▲ 316,398) 150,000
Chengdu (Chengtu) (▲ 2,580,000) (1985 E) 1,590,000
Chenghai 75,080
Chengwu 43,244
Chenxian (Chenzhou) (▲ 167,089) 85,000
Chifeng (▲ 297,929) 100,000
Chiping 44,036
Chongqing (Chungking) (▲ 2,780,000) (1985 E) 2,080,000
Chuxian 85,661
Chuxiong (Lucheng) 52,596
Da'an (Dalai) 78,275
Dachangzhen (1975 UE) 50,000
Dandong (Antung) (▲ 537,745) 400,000
Danyang 47,754
Daqing (Anda) (▲ 764,046) 150,000
Dashiqiao 77,774
Dashitou 63,426
Datong (Qiaotou) 60,584
Datong (▲ 981,000) (1984 E) 688,200
Dawa 164,928
Daxian (▲ 189,117) 100,000
Daxing (Huangcun) 55,110
Dehui 65,386
Dengfeng 49,746
Dengxian 42,121
Deqing 48,726
Deyang 86,696
Dezhou (▲ 260,724) 125,000
Didao (1975 UE) 50,000
Dinghai 50,792
Dingshuzhen 46,114
Dingtao 44,955
Dingxian 59,918
Dongfeng 47,850
Dongguan (Guancheng) 82,108
Dongjingcheng 42,888
Donglong 58,557
Dongming 44,660
Dongning 46,224
Dongshan 41,942
Dongsheng 47,010
Dongtai 70,875
Dorbod (Taikang) 42,394
Dukou (▲ 517,559) 200,000
Dunhua 118,770
Duyun 97,620
Echeng (▲ 124,255) 60,000
Enshi (▲ 98,712) 50,000
Erenhot 7,246
Ergun Zuoqi (Genhe) 56,050
Fanjiatun (1984 C) 40,354
Feixian 73,246
Fengcheng, Jiangxi prov. 44,609
Fengcheng, Liaoning prov. 66,412
Fengzhen 44,393
Fenyang 41,479
Foshan (▲ 285,547) 200,000
Fu'an 42,325
Fujin 66,140
Fuling 93,652
Fushan 43,685
Fushun (1985 E) 1,240,000
Fuxian (Wafangdian) 130,881
Fuxin (▲ 653,200) (1984 E) 551,300
Fuxin 42,176
Fuyang (▲ 169,893) 90,000
Fuyu, Heilongjiang prov. 53,490
Fuyu, Jilin prov. 106,514
Fuzhou (▲ 161,512) 80,000
Fuzhou (Fuchou) (▲ 1,164,800) (1984 E) 754,500
Gaixian (Gaizhou) 62,762
Ganhe 48,917
Gannan 41,174
Ganzhou (Kanchow) (▲ 328,423) 180,000
Gaomi 86,217
Gaoqing (Tianzhen) 70,411
Gaoyou 63,268
Gaozhou 40,866
Gejiu (▲ 327,929) 250,000
Golmud (▲ 57,202) 40,000
Gongchangling 49,281
Gongxi 48,001
Gongxian (Xiaoyi) 54,505
Guanghan (Luocheng) 47,456
Guangyuan (Jialing) 101,318
Guanxian 49,782
Guanxian (Guankou) 65,891
Gucheng 57,781
Guichi (Chizhou) 45,477
Guilin (Kweilin) (▲ 429,988) 325,000
Guixian (Guicheng) 58,016
Guiyang (▲ 1,352,700) (1984 E) 871,000
Gushi 50,380
Haicheng 124,426
Haifeng (Haicheng) 50,853
Haikang (Leizhou) 46,965
Haikou 266,302
Hailar (▲ 163,549) 90,000
Hailin 66,360
Hailong (Meihekou) 81,951
Hailun 88,986
Haimen 66,009
Haining (Xiashi) 40,669
Haiyang (Dongcun) 77,098
Hami (▲ 94,878) 60,000
Handan (▲ 954,300) (1984 E) 727,500
Hangu (1975 UE) 100,000
Hangzhou (Hangchou) (1985 E) 1,250,000
Hanzhong (▲ 396,795) 200,000
Harbin (Haerhpin) (1985 E) 2,630,000
Hebi (▲ 351,869) 200,000
Hechi (Jinchengjiang) 63,958
Hechuan 63,119
Hefei (▲ 853,100) (1984 E) 594,200
Hegang (▲ 576,159) 325,000
Heishan 45,431
Helong 65,082
Hengshui (▲ 102,879) 50,000
Hengyang (▲ 527,105) 350,000
Hepu (Lianzhou) 44,769
Heshan (▲ 101,694) 40,000
Hexian (Babu) 42,157
Heyuan (Yuancheng) 40,272
Heze (Caozhou) 141,174
Hohhot (Kweisui) (▲ 778,000) (1984 E) 542,800
Honghu (Xindi) 52,969
Hongjiang (▲ 67,283) 30,000
Horqin Youyi Qianqi (Ulan Hot) (▲ 172,542) 100,000
Hotan 73,541
Houma (▲ 148,569) 60,000
Huadian 83,507
Huai'an (Huaicheng) 83,420
Huaibei (▲ 442,946) 150,000
Huaide (Gongzhuling) 113,864
Huaihua (▲ 96,908) 50,000
Huainan (Hwainan) (▲ 1,063,000) (1984 E) 603,200
Huaiyang (Huizu) 44,833
Huanan 51,080

C Census. E Official estimate. UE Unofficial estimate.
• Largest city in country.
★ Population or designation of metropolitan area, including suburbs (see headnote).
▲ Population of an entire municipality, commune, or district, including rural area.

Huangchuan 48,259
Huanggang (Huangzhou) 65,961
Huangnihe 51,898
Huangshi (▲ 431,713) 200,000
Huangyan 50,262
Huanren 50,377
Huantai (Suozhen) 44,903
Huilai (Huicheng) 58,771
Huinan (Chaoyang) 54,644
Huixian 45,965
Huizhou (▲ 166,543) 100,000
Hulan 83,787
Hunjiang (▲ 681,290) 125,000
Huzhou (▲ 945,616) 135,000
Jiading 53,692
Jiamusi (▲ 529,830) 350,000
Ji'an (▲ 174,204) 115,000
Jiangdu 44,320
Jiangjin 41,747
Jiangling (Jingzhou) 85,813
Jiangmen (▲ 216,097) 175,000
Jiangyin (Chengjiang) 69,133
Jiangyou (Zhongba) 78,762
Jian'ou 56,416
Jianping (Yebaishou) 45,410
Jianyang (Jiancheng) 48,026
Jiaohe 49,021
Jiaojiang (▲ 154,559) 75,000
Jiaoxian 55,639
Jiaozuo (▲ 487,643) 350,000
Jiawang (1975 UE) 50,000
Jiaxing (▲ 670,041) 175,000
Jiayuguan 81,378
Jiazi 91,976
Jidong 72,734
Jieshi 71,067
Jiexiu 46,254
Jieyang (Rongcheng) 110,277
Jilin (Kirin) (▲ 1,114,100) (1984 E) 882,700
Jimo 68,443
Jinan (Tsinan) (1985 E) 1,430,000
Jinchang (Baijiazui) (▲ 111,477) 50,000
Jincheng 52,755
Jingdezhen (▲ 506,960) 400,000
Jinghong (Yunjinghong) 41,218
Jingmen (▲ 112,738) 50,000
Jinhua (▲ 842,904) 125,000
Jining, Inner Mongolia prov. (▲ 156,800) 125,000
Jining, Shandong prov. (▲ 211,232) 150,000
Jinshi 84,215
Jinxi 152,203
Jinxian (Jinzhou) 94,613
Jinzhou (▲ 748,700) (1984 E) 584,800
Jishou 49,225
Jishu 84,540
Jiujiang (▲ 364,687) 150,000
Jiuquan (Suzhou) 43,418
Jiutai 69,601
Jixi (Chihsi) (▲ 798,900) (1984 E) 626,300
Jixian (Fulitun) 56,318
Jixian 59,389
Juancheng 54,110
Junan (Shizilu) 90,222
Junxian (Danjiang) 60,774
Juxian 51,666
Kaifeng (▲ 604,219) 450,000
Kaili 99,158
Kaiping (Sanbu) 40,873
Kaiyuan (▲ 204,951) 100,000
Karamay (▲ 168,868) 90,000
Kashi (Kaxgar) (▲ 274,130) 150,000
Keshan 72,472
Korla (▲ 121,991) 50,000
Kunming (Yünnanfu) (▲ 1,490,000) (1985 E) 1,080,000
Kunshan (Yushan) 47,735
Kuqa 43,750
Kuytun (▲ 223,968) 75,000
Laixi (Shuiji) 41,117
Laiyang 52,387
Langxiang 70,731
Lanxi 49,337
Lanxi 47,053
Lanzhou (Lanchou) (▲ 1,350,000) (1985 E) 1,060,000
Laohekou (Guanghua) (▲ 101,439) 50,000
Lechang 71,815
Leiyang (1980 C) 77,044
Lengshuijiang(▲ 255,763) 150,000
Lengshuitan 41,424
Leping 48,288
Leshan (▲ 954,382) 150,000
Lhasa 105,897
Lianxian (Lianzhou) 40,360
Lianyungang (▲ 395,730) 275,000
Liaocheng 129,337
Liaoyang (▲ 448,807) 275,000
Liaoyuan (▲ 759,577) 300,000
Lihu 60,174
Lijiang Naxi (Dayan) 42,129
Liling 72,106
Linfen (▲ 190,626) 75,000
Lingling (Yongzhou) 81,202
Lingxian 40,617
Linhai 66,699
Linhe 77,199
Linkou 55,444
Linqing 70,616
Linqu 84,196
Linru 51,744
Linxia 65,204
Linyi 42,760
Linying 44,516
Lishi 51,316
Lishu 41,000
Lishui 55,508
Liuhe 46,009
Liujiachang 40,208
Liupanshui (Shuicheng) (▲ 2,089,552) 75,000
Liuzhou (▲ 585,387) 375,000
Liyang (Licheng) 42,396
Liyujiang (1975 UE) 50,000
Longhai (Shima) 40,193
Longjiang 78,403
Longyan (▲ 356,243) 75,000
Loudi (▲ 102,182) 50,000
Lu'an (▲ 145,597) 70,000
Luanchuan 40,297
Lüda (Dairen) (Dalian) (▲ 1,630,000) (1985 E) 1,380,000
Lufeng (Donghai) 86,688
Luhe (Lucheng) 52,569
Lujiang 42,660
Luohe (▲ 152,105) 90,000
Luoyang (▲ 1,023,900) (1984 E) 624,000
Lushan 40,752
Lüshun (1975 UE) 40,000
Luzhou (Luchou) (▲ 303,403) 250,000
Ma'anshan (▲ 350,513) 275,000
Manzhouli (▲ 107,875) 70,000
Maoming (▲ 409,744) 250,000
Meixian (Meizhou) (▲ 109,647) 65,000
Mengjin 41,706
Mengxian 45,599
Mengyin 70,602
Mianduhe 46,629
Mianyang (Xiantao), Hubei prov. (▲ 768,500) 52,525
Mianyang, Sichuan prov. (▲ 776,165) 100,000
Mingshui 45,466
Minhang (1975 UE) 60,000
Minquan 52,591
Mishan 56,772
Mixian 64,776
Mudanjiang (▲ 580,982) 400,000
Muling 49,856
Muling (Bamiantong) 42,616
Muping 50,126
Naizishan 66,955
Nancha (1975 UE) 50,000
Nanchang (Liantang) 42,115
Nanchang (1984 E) 1,088,800
Nanchong 220,531
Nanjing (Nanking) (1985 E) 2,250,000
Nanning (▲ 902,900) (1984 E) 564,900
Nanpiao 67,274
Nanping (▲ 405,174) 100,000
Nantong (▲ 380,988) 300,000
Nanxiong 41,099
Nanyang (▲ 271,872) 100,000
Nanzhang 44,846
Nehe 60,211
Neihuang 56,039
Neijiang (▲ 278,592) 225,000
Nenjiang 74,647
Ning'an 57,888
Ningbo (▲ 468,232) 350,000
Ningde 41,828
Ningyang 55,424
Nong'an 44,855
Orogen Zizhiqi (Alihe) 52,142
Orqohan 44,875
Panshan 86,109
Panshi 63,015
Panyu (Shiqiao) 46,474
PEKING (BEIJING) (★ 6,450,000) (1985 E) 5,860,000
Penglai 46,826
Pengxian (Tianpeng) 42,212
Pingding 47,620
Pingdingshan (▲ 475,950) 350,000
Pingdu 46,308
Pingliang 71,290
Pingnan 40,140
Pingxiang, Guangxi Zhuangzu prov. (▲ 78,300) 50,000
Pingxiang, Jiangxi prov. (▲ 1,224,762) 150,000
Pingyi 89,373
Pingyin 62,827
Puqi 63,197
Putuo (Shenjiamen) 62,298
Puyang 42,062
Qian Gorlos (Qianguozhen) 72,307
Qianyang (Anjiang) 44,905
Qihe (Yancheng) 43,556
Qilimiao 45,724
Qing'an 47,825
Qingdao (Tsingtao) (1985 E) 1,250,000
Qinggang 49,861
Qingjiang (Zhangshu), Jiangxi prov. 49,377
Qingjiang, Jiangsu prov. (▲ 246,617) 150,000
Qingyuan (Qingcheng) 63,197
Qinhuangdao (▲ 403,701) 300,000
Qinzhou 51,452
Qiqihar (Tsitsihar) (▲ 1,246,000) (1984 E) 955,200
Qitaihe (▲ 259,857) 125,000
Qixia 54,158
Qixian 53,041
Qizhou 48,010
Quanyang 43,436
Quanzhou (▲ 410,229) 175,000
Qujing 75,132
Quzhou (▲ 971,787) 120,000
Raoping (Huanggang) 60,177
Rizhao 78,489
Roncheng (Yatou) 52,878
Rugao (Rucheng) 50,780
Rui'an 57,261
Rushan (Xiacun) 65,903
Sandu 47,437
Sanmenxia (▲ 140,410) 90,000
Sanming (▲ 204,307) 80,000
Shache (Yarkant) 44,641
Shahe (Dalian) 83,870
• Shanghai (★ 9,300,000) (1985 E) 6,980,000
Shangqui (Shangkiu) (▲ 183,431) 150,000
Shangrao (▲ 136,924) 90,000
Shangshui 50,191
Shangzhi 56,186
Shanhetun 50,746
Shantou (Swatow) (▲ 722,805) 400,000
Shanwei 60,505
Shanxian 74,820
Shaoguan (▲ 344,892) 160,000
Shaowu 58,733
Shaoxing (▲ 1,107,176) 225,000
Shaoyang (▲ 399,257) 250,000
Shashi (▲ 243,792) 175,000
Shengfang 45,999
Shenqiu (Huaidian) 43,271
Shenxian 50,208
Shenyang (Mukden) (▲ 4,200,000) (1985 E) 3,250,000
Shenzhen (▲ 113,616) 60,000
Shiguaigou (1975 UE) 50,000
Shihezi (▲ 549,426) 75,000
Shijiazhuang (1984 E) 1,127,800
Shijiusuo 43,976
Shilong 40,473
Shiyan (▲ 301,420) 150,000
Shizuishan (▲ 304,228) 135,000
Shouguang 83,400
Shuangcheng 102,677
Shuangfeng 52,209
Shuangliao 73,874
Shuangyashan (▲ 397,525) 200,000
Shulan 52,924
Shunde (Daliang) 47,564
Shuyang (Shucheng) 52,247
Simao 40,953
Siping (▲ 344,390) 200,000
Sishui 82,990
Siyang (Zhongxing) 41,437
Songjiang 68,052
Songjianghe 55,989
Suifenhe 19,842
Suihua 167,997
Suileng 66,643
Suining 90,632
Suixian (Suizhou) (▲ 132,814) 60,000
Suqian (Sucheng) 53,600
Suxian (Suzhou) (▲ 193,253) 90,000
Suzhou (Soochow) (1984 E) 695,500
Tai'an (▲ 1,274,770) 125,000
Tailai 58,541
Taishan (Taicheng) 45,600
Taixian (Jiangyan) 46,877
Taixing 47,339
Taiyuan (▲ 1,880,000) (1985 E) 1,390,000
Taizhou (▲ 161,549) 150,000
Tancheng 61,857
Tangshan (▲ 1,366,100) (1984 E) 921,100
Tao'an (Taonan) 72,021
Tengxian 61,404
Tianjin (Tientsin) (1985 E) 5,380,000
Tianmen 52,066
Tianshui (Beidaobu) 43,104
Tianshui (▲ 186,460) 125,000
Tiefa (▲ 146,367) 60,000
Tieli 108,654
Tieling (▲ 210,754) 100,000
Tongchuan (▲ 377,710) 200,000
Tonghua (▲ 354,843) 200,000
Tongliao (▲ 225,432) 80,000
Tongling (▲ 202,578) 100,000
Tongren 54,269
Tongxian (Tongzhou) 90,056
Tongyu (Kaitong) 43,350
Tumen (▲ 93,197) 50,000
Tunxi (▲ 99,794) 80,000
Ürümqi (Urumchi) (▲ 1,147,300) (1984 E) 947,000
Wangkui 62,638
Wangqing 66,055
Wanxian (▲ 269,757) 160,000
Weifang (▲ 371,993) 275,000
Weihai (▲ 210,415) 75,000
Weihe 47,494
Weinan 88,492
Weishan (Xiazhen) 57,932
Weixian (Hanting) 50,180
Wendeng 57,189
Wenling 43,823
Wenxian 44,781
Wenzhou (▲ 508,613) 325,000
Wuchang (1980 C) 68,202
Wuchuan (Meilü) 61,348
Wuhai (▲ 219,616) 60,000
Wuhan (Hankow) (1985 E) 3,400,000
Wuhu (▲ 456,222) 360,000
Wulian (Hongning) 51,718
Wuqing (Yangcun) 40,656
Wusong 64,017
Wuwei (Liangzhou) 84,713
Wuxi (▲ 825,100) (1984 E) 696,300
Wuzhou (Wuchou) (1980 C) 251,145
Xiaguan (▲ 119,877) 60,000
Xiamen (Amoy) (▲ 510,656) 350,000
Xi'an (Sian) (▲ 2,330,000) (1985 E) 1,730,000
Xiangfan (▲ 316,007) 175,000
Xiangtan (Siangtan) (▲ 482,953) 350,000
Xiangxiang 67,253
Xiangyin 45,880
Xianyang (Sienyang) (▲ 497,432) 200,000
Xiaogan (1980 C) 69,479
Xiaoshan 61,332
Xichang 149,566
Xifeng 42,113
Xihua (1985 C) 40,022
Xin'an 46,823
Xinghua (Xinxing) 74,360
Xinglongzhen 52,961
Xingning (Xingcheng) 46,309
Xingtai (▲ 335,804) 150,000
Xingyi 41,729
Xinhua 42,565
Xinhui (Huicheng) 78,447
Xining (▲ 571,546) 400,000
Xinjin (Pulandian) 40,562
Xinmin 48,028
Xintai 104,251
Xinwen (Suncun) (1975 UE) 50,000
Xinxian 76,595
Xinxiang (▲ 508,609) 325,000
Xinyang (▲ 220,470) 125,000
Xinyu 70,604
Xiuyan 51,362
Xuancheng 62,805
Xuanhua (1975 UE) 140,000
Xuanwei 70,081
Xuchang (▲ 227,678) 135,000
Xuguit Qi (Yakeshi) 114,164
Xuzhou (1984 E) 806,400
Ya'an 78,677
Yan'an (▲ 250,847) 150,000
Yancheng 150,030
Yangcheng 57,255
Yanggu 45,839
Yangjiang (Jiangcheng) 88,527
Yangjiazhangzi 44,152
Yangquan (▲ 466,563) 325,000
Yangzhou (Yangchou) (▲ 304,959) 225,000
Yanji (▲ 175,957) 100,000
Yanji (Longjing) 59,970
Yanling 52,679
Yanshou 40,385
Yantai (▲ 384,336) 200,000
Yanzhou 55,919
Yexian 54,086
Yi'an 60,633
Yibin 245,064
Yichang (Ichang) (▲ 363,578) 175,000
Yichuan 58,914
Yichun (▲ 814,300) (1984 E) 758,200
Yidu 78,040
Yilan 56,440
Yima (▲ 78,153) 50,000
Yimianpo 47,469
Yinan (Jiehu) 67,803
Yinchuan (▲ 363,508) 200,000
Yingcheng 66,844
Yingkou (▲ 419,640) 200,000
Yingtan (▲ 102,485) 50,000
Yining (Gulja) (▲ 225,024) 160,000
Yishan (Qingyuan) 54,148
Yishui 88,149
Yiyang (▲ 163,240) 125,000
Yiyuan (Nanma) 53,800
Yong'an 85,717
Yongchuan 69,940
Yuci (▲ 268,204) 120,000
Yueyang (▲ 980,945) 125,000
Yulin, Guangxi Zhuangzu prov. 99,082
Yulin, Shaanxi prov. 56,906
Yumen (Laojunmiao) (▲ 178,893) 150,000
Yuncheng, Shandong prov. 54,262
Yuncheng, Shansi prov. 82,158
Yunxiao 43,548
Yunyang 54,903
Yushu 62,270
Yutai (Guting) 41,990
Yuxian 64,521
Yuyao 52,823
Zaoyang 44,401
Zaozhuang (▲ 1,238,256) 150,000
Zhangjiakou (▲ 605,911) 350,000
Zhangzhou (Changchou) (▲ 295,382) 160,000
Zhanhua (Fuguo) 48,193
Zhanjiang (▲ 867,062) 300,000
Zhao'an 50,979
Zhaodong 118,423
Zhaoqing (▲ 169,799) 100,000
Zhaotong (▲ 115,897) 60,000
Zhaoyuan 56,389
Zhaoyuan 49,179
Zhaozhou 43,634
Zhengzhou (Chengchou) (▲ 1,590,000) (1985 E) 1,000,000
Zhenjiang (Chinkiang) (▲ 346,024) 250,000
Zhenlai 42,520
Zhongshan (Shiqizhen) 98,307
Zhoucun (1975 UE) 50,000
Zhoukou (▲ 206,570) 150,000
Zhuanghe 41,236
Zhucheng 103,869
Zhuhai (▲ 133,211) 65,000
Zhumadian (▲ 141,973) 65,000
Zhuoxian (Zhouzhou) 49,046
Zhuzhou (▲ 385,660) 275,000
Zibo (Zhangdian) (▲ 2,280,500) (1984 E) 762,500
Zigong (▲ 875,339) 450,000
Ziyang 52,590
Zouping 49,274
Zouxian 90,333
Zunyi (▲ 341,959) 275,000

Political Divisions

1985 ESTIMATE

Anhui 51,560,000
Beijing (Peking) (Auton. City) 9,600,000
Fujian 27,130,000
Gansu 20,410,000
Guangdong 62,530,000
Guangxi Zhuangzu (Auton. Region) 38,730,000
Guizhou (Kweichow) 29,680,000
Hebei 55,480,000
Heilongjiang 33,110,000
Henan (Honan) 77,130,000
Hubei (Hupeh) 49,310,000
Hunan 56,220,000
Inner Mongolia (Nei Mongol) 20,070,000
Jiangsu (Kiangsu) 62,130,000
Jiangxi 34,600,000
Jilin 22,980,000
Liaoning 36,860,000
Ningxia Huizu (Ningsia Hui) (Auton. Region) 4,150,000
Qinghai 4,070,000
Shaanxi (Shensi) 30,020,000
Shandong 76,950,000
Shanghai (Municipality) 12,170,000
Shanxi 26,270,000
Sichuan 101,880,000
Tianjin (Tientsin) (Municipality) 8,080,000
Xinjiang Uygur 13,610,000
Xizang (Tibet) (Auton. Region) 1,990,000
Yunnan 34,060,000
Zhejiang (Chekiang) 40,300,000

CISKEI

1981 E 645,000

Cities and Towns

BISHO (1970 E) 4,800
• Mdantsane (★ East London, S. Afr.) (1980 C) 159,360
Zwelitsha (★ King William's Town, S. Afr.) (1980 C) 29,260

COLOMBIA

1985 C 26,525,670

Cities and Towns

Apartadó 29,053

C Census. E Official estimate. UE Unofficial estimate.
• Largest city in country.

★ Population or designation of metropolitan area, including suburbs (see headnote).
▲ Population of an entire municipality, commune, or district, including rural area.

Armenia ... 179,727
Armero ... 20,962
Barrancabermeja ... 139,708
Barranquilla (★ 1,125,000) ... 891,545
Bello (★ Medellín) ... 198,183
• BOGOTÁ (★ 4,250,000) ... 3,967,988
Bucaramanga (★ 495,000) ... 342,169
Buenaventura ... 157,528
Buga ... 82,766
Caldas ... 35,906
Cali (★ 1,400,000) ... 1,347,810
Cartagena ... 495,028
Cartago ... 92,231
Ciénaga ... 53,436
Cúcuta (★ 440,000) ... 355,828
Duitama ... 55,357
Envigado (★ Medellín) ... 84,944
Espinal ... 34,980
Facatativá ... 43,675
Florencia ... 66,025
Florida ... 29,680
Floridablanca (★ Bucaramanga) ... 137,868
Girardot ... 65,281
Ibagué ... 265,598
Ipiales ... 45,592
Itagüí (★ Medellín) ... 133,444
La Dorada ... 43,053
Líbano ... 23,664
Lorica ... 23,557
Magangué ... 49,450
Maicao ... 47,508
Malambo (★ Barranquilla) ... 50,295
Manizales (★ 325,000) ... 275,220
Medellín (★ 2,070,000) ... 1,473,351
Montería ... 158,064
Neiva ... 179,609
Ocaña ... 51,922
Palmira ... 174,425
Pamplona ... 33,137
Pasto ... 196,800
Pereira (★ 390,000) ... 232,311
Piedecuesta ... 34,538
Planeta Rica ... 24,817
Popayán ... 140,839
Puerto Berrío ... 21,191
Quibdó ... 47,898
Ríohacha ... 46,572
Rionegro ... 32,804
Sabanalarga ... 35,617
Santa Marta ... 193,160
Santa Rosa de Cabal (★ Pereira) ... 36,646
Sevilla ... 31,274
Sincelejo ... 118,559
Soacha (★ Bogotá) (1981 C) ... 99,953
Sogamoso ... 64,398
Soledad (★ Barranquilla) ... 156,846
Sonsón ... 14,393
Tuluá ... 99,134
Tumaco ... 44,721
Tunja ... 87,334
Valledupar ... 140,481
Villavicencio ... 159,808
Yumbo ... 43,738
Zipaquirá ... 45,477

Departments

Amazonas (Comisaría) (1980 E) ... 23,300
Antioquia ... 3,720,025
Arauca (Intendencia) (1980 E) ... 92,200
Atlántico ... 1,406,545
Bolívar ... 1,199,437
Boyacá ... 1,089,387
Caldas ... 789,730
Caquetá ... 177,259
Casanare (Intendencia) (1973 C) ... 83,500
Cauca ... 674,824
Cesar ... 584,152
Chocó ... 68,506
Córdoba ... 878,738
Cundinamarca ... 1,358,978
Distrito Especial (Bogotá) ... 3,967,988
Guainía (Comisaría) (1980 E) ... 12,900
Guajira ... 245,284
Guaviare (Comisaría) ...
Huila ... 636,642
Magdalena ... 760,611
Meta ... 321,563
Nariño ... 848,618
Norte de Santander ... 871,966
Putumayo (Intendencia) (1980 E) ... 81,900
Quindío ... 375,762
Risaralda ... 623,756
San Andrés y Providencia (Intendencia) ... 36,515
Santander ... 1,427,110
Sucre ... 523,525
Tolima ... 1,028,239
Valle del Cauca ... 2,833,940
Vaupés (Comisaría) (1980 E) ... 38,800
Vichada (Comisaría) (1980 E) ... 15,800

COMOROS / Comores / Al Qumur

1980 C ... 346,992

Cities and Towns

• MORONI ... 20,112
Mutsamudu ... 14,000

CONGO (PEOPLE'S REPUBLIC OF THE CONGO)

1984 C ... 1,912,429

Cities and Towns

• BRAZZAVILLE ... 595,102
Jacob ... 35,628
Loubomo ... 49,458
Pointe-Noire ... 195,398

COOK ISLANDS

1981 C ... 17,753

Cities and Towns

• AVARUA ... 9,525

COSTA RICA

1984 E ... 2,534,000

Cities and Towns

Alajuela ... 43,400
Cartago ... 28,600
Desamparados (★ San José) (1982 E) ... 39,485
Guadalupe (★ San José) (1982 E) ... 35,503
Heredia ... 30,300
Limón (▲ 55,400) ... 44,600
Puntarenas ... 36,400
• SAN JOSÉ (★ 620,000) ... 277,800
San Juan (★ San José) (1982 E) ... 23,709
San Pedro (★ San José) (1982 E) ... 29,750
San Vicente (★ San José) (1982 E) ... 19,625

CUBA

1981 C ... 9,723,605

Cities and Towns

Amancio Rodríguez ... 21,097
Artemisa ... 33,907
Banes ... 31,237
Baracoa ... 35,754
Bayamo ... 99,967
Cabaiguán ... 26,460
Caibarién ... 31,872
Camagüey ... 244,091
Cárdenas ... 59,352
Ciego de Ávila ... 73,820
Cienfuegos ... 102,297
Colón ... 34,744
Contramaestre ... 22,168
Florida ... 39,482
Guanajay ... 20,548
Guantánamo ... 166,558
Güines ... 41,591
Güira de Melena ... 21,088
• HAVANA (LA HABANA) (★ 1,975,000) ... 1,914,466
Holguín ... 186,236
Jobabo ... 14,895
Jovellanos ... 20,635
Manzanillo ... 87,830
Matanzas ... 100,367
Mayarí ... 21,076
Moa ... 26,893
Morón ... 39,779
Nueva Gerona ... 30,212
Nuevitas ... 34,869
Palma Soriano ... 55,851
Pinar del Río ... 96,149
Placetas ... 37,310
Puerto Padre ... 23,310
Ranchuelo (▲ 60,829) ... 14,700
Remedios (▲ 47,347) ... 16,200
Sagua de Tánamo ... 15,435
Sagua la Grande ... 42,291
San Antonio de los Baños ... 27,488
Sancti-Spíritus ... 71,430
San José de las Lajas ... 26,917
San Luis ... 24,347
Santa Clara ... 172,652
Santiago de Cuba ... 349,444
Trinidad ... 32,935
Vertientes ... 22,432
Victoria de las Tunas ... 84,735

CYPRUS / Kípros / Kıbrıs

1982 E ... 642,731

Cities and Towns

Ammókhostos (Famagusta) (1980 E) ... 50,000
Lárnax (Larnaca) (★ 48,330) ... 35,823
Lemesós (Limassol) (★ 107,161) ... 74,782
• NICOSIA (LEVKOSÍA) (★ 149,071) ... 48,221
Páfos (★ 20,824) ... 13,124

CZECHOSLOVAKIA / Československo

1985 E ... 15,479,642

Cities and Towns

Banská Bystrica ... 75,980
Beroun ... 23,790
Bratislava ... 409,100
Břeclav ... 25,495
Brno ... 383,443
České Budějovice (Budweis) ... 93,520
Cheb ... 31,345
Chomutov ... 58,105
Děčín ... 55,284
Frýdek-Místek (★ Ostrava) ... 63,143
Gottwaldov (Zlín) ... 85,383
Havířov (★ Ostrava) ... 90,013
Havlíčkův Brod ... 25,182
Hlohovec ... 22,781
Hodonín ... 26,584
Hradec Králové ... 98,476
Humenné ... 30,987
Jablonec [nad Nisou] ... 45,459
Jihlava ... 53,074
Karlovy Vary (Carlsbad) ... 58,541
Karviná (★★ Ostrava) ... 76,428
Kladno (★ 87,000) ... 72,548
Kolín ... 30,879
Komárno ... 36,140
Košice ... 218,238
Krnov ... 26,055
Kroměříž ... 25,851
Levice ... 29,127
Liberec ... 100,048
Liptovský Mikuláš ... 27,745
Litvínov ... 21,452
Lučenec ... 28,028
Mariánské Lázně (Marienbad) ... 18,510
Martin ... 61,045
Michalovce ... 34,142
Mladá Boleslav ... 48,325
Most ... 63,634
Náchod ... 20,242
Nitra ... 83,338
Nové Zámky ... 38,870
Nový Jičín ... 32,495
Olomouc ... 105,516
Opava ... 61,545
Orlová (★ Ostrava) ... 33,658
Ostrava (★ 745,000) ... 325,431
Ostrov ... 19,591
Pardubice ... 93,822
Piešťany ... 31,909
Písek ... 29,068
Plzeň (Pilsen) ... 174,555
Poprad ... 45,822
Považská Bystrica ... 35,726
• PRAGUE (PRAHA) (★ 1,270,000) ... 1,189,828
Přerov ... 50,355
Prešov ... 80,515
Příbram ... 39,145
Prievidza ... 45,457
Prostějov ... 51,081
Ružomberok ... 28,404
Sokolov ... 28,646
Spišská Nová Ves ... 35,628
Šumperk ... 33,301
Tábor ... 33,956
Teplice ... 53,928
Topol'čany ... 35,009
Třebíč ... 36,130
Trenčín ... 51,515
Třinec ... 44,685
Trnava ... 68,721
Trutnov ... 30,440
Uherské Hradiště ... 37,329
Ústí nad Labem (★ 106,000) ... 90,520
Valašské Meziříčí ... 26,998
Vsetín ... 31,074
Žilina ... 89,847
Znojmo ... 37,983
Zvolen ... 39,063

Republics

Česká Socialistická Republika ... 10,336,459
Slovenská Socialistická Republika ... 5,143,183

Regions

Bratislava (City) ... 409,100
Jihočeský ... 694,642
Jihomoravský ... 2,055,908
Praha (Prague) (City) ... 1,189,828
Severočeský ... 1,180,269
Severomoravský ... 1,953,649
Středočeský ... 1,141,163
Stredoslovenský ... 1,570,456
Východočeský ... 1,245,964
Východoslovenský ... 1,451,716
Západočeský ... 875,036
Západoslovenský ... 1,711,911

Historic Provinces

Bohemia (Čechy) ... 6,326,902
Moravia (Morava) ... 4,009,557
Sloviakia (Slovensko) ... 5,143,183

DENMARK / Danmark

1984 E ... 5,112,130

Cities and Towns

Åbenrå (▲ 21,182) ... 15,400
Albertslund (★ Copenhagen) ... 29,591
Ålborg ... 154,840
Århus ... 250,404
Ballerup [-Måløv] (★ Copenhagen) ... 47,443
Brøndby (★ Copenhagen) ... 36,186
• COPENHAGEN (KØBENHAVN) (★ 1,470,000) ... 482,937
Esbjerg ... 80,534
Fredericia ... 45,896
Frederiksberg (★ Copenhagen) ... 88,114
Frederikshavn ... 35,518
Gentofte (★ Copenhagen) ... 67,112
Gladsakse (★ Copenhagen) ... 62,845
Glostrup (★ Copenhagen) ... 19,542
Greve (★ Copenhagen) ... 42,851
Haderslev (▲ 29,985) ... 9,200
Helsingør (Elsinore) ... 56,161
Herlev (★ Copenhagen) ... 27,874
Herning (▲ 55,923) ... 29,300
Hillerød ... 33,278
Hjørring (▲ 34,304) ... 23,700
Høje Tåstrup (★ Copenhagen) ... 43,675
Holbæk (▲ 29,795) ... 20,900
Holstebro (▲ 37,405) ... 28,600
Horsens ... 54,717
Hvidovre (★ Copenhagen) ... 50,583
Køge (▲ 35,102) ... 25,400
Kolding ... 56,519
Lyngby (Kongens Lyngby) [-Tårbæk] (★ Copenhagen) ... 50,696
Middelfart ... 18,094
Næstved (▲ 45,071) ... 38,300
Nakskov ... 16,813
Nykøbing Falster (▲ 25,431) ... 18,734
Odense ... 170,961
Randers ... 61,410
Ringsted (▲ 28,138) ... 16,600
Rødovre (★ Copenhagen) ... 36,869
Rønne ... 15,320
Roskilde ... 49,110
Silkeborg (▲ 47,164) ... 33,600
Skagen ... 13,877
Skive (▲ 26,726) ... 19,200
Slagelse (▲ 33,401) ... 28,400
Søllerød (★ Copenhagen) ... 31,484
Sønderborg ... 27,785
Svendborg (▲ 39,162) ... 24,700
Tårnby (★ Copenhagen) ... 40,577
Thisted (▲ 29,816) ... 12,400
Vejle ... 49,602
Viborg (▲ 39,144) ... 29,000
Vordingborg (▲ 19,697) ... 8,500

Counties

Århus ... 579,839
Bornholm ... 47,243
Frederiksberg (City) ... 88,114
Frederiksborg ... 332,852
Fyn ... 453,291
København ... 616,210
København (City) ... 482,937
Nordjylland ... 482,108
Ribe ... 215,247
Ringkøbing ... 264,071
Roskilde ... 207,059
Sønderjylland ... 249,762
Storstrøm ... 257,585
Vejle ... 326,725
Vestsjælland ... 277,839
Viborg ... 230,618

DJIBOUTI

1976 E ... 226,000

Cities and Towns

• DJIBOUTI ... 120,000

DOMINICA

1984 E ... 77,000

Cities and Towns

• ROSEAU ... 9,348

DOMINICAN REPUBLIC / República Dominicana

1981 C ... 5,647,977

Cities and Towns

Azua ... 31,481
Bajos de Haina ... 33,135
Baní ... 36,705
Barahona ... 49,334
Bonao ... 44,486
La Romana ... 91,571
La Vega ... 52,432
Mao (Valverde) ... 33,527
Moca ... 31,176
Puerto Plata ... 45,348
Salvaleón de Higüey ... 33,501
San Cristóbal ... 58,520
San Francisco de Macorís ... 64,906
San Juan [de la Maguana] ... 49,764
San Pedro de Macorís ... 78,562
Santiago [de los Caballeros] ... 278,638
• SANTO DOMINGO ... 1,313,172

ECUADOR

1982 C ... 8,050,630

Cities and Towns

Alfaro (★ Guayaquil) ... 49,660
Ambato ... 100,454
Azogues ... 14,548
Babahoyo ... 42,266
Chone (1974 C) ... 23,647
Cuenca ... 157,213
Esmeraldas ... 91,382
Guaranda ... 13,685
Guayaquil (★ 1,255,000) ... 1,204,532
Ibarra ... 53,428
Jipijapa (1974 C) ... 19,719
Latacunga ... 28,764
Loja ... 71,652
Machala ... 108,156
Manta ... 99,222
Milagro ... 77,010
Pasaje ... 26,224
Portoviejo ... 102,628
Quevedo (1974 C) ... 43,123
QUITO (★ 1,050,000) ... 890,355
Riobamba ... 75,455
Santo Domingo de los Colorados ... 69,235
Tulcán ... 30,985

Provinces

Azuay ... 443,044
Bolívar ... 141,566
Cañar ... 174,674
Carchi ... 125,452
Chimborazo ... 320,268
Cotopaxi ... 279,765
El Oro ... 337,818
Esmeraldas ... 247,311
Galápagos (Ter.) ... 6,119
Guayas ... 2,047,001
Imbabura ... 245,745
Loja ... 358,952
Los Ríos ... 457,065
Manabí ... 858,780
Morona-Santiago ... 70,217
Napo ... 115,110
Pastaza ... 31,779
Pichincha ... 1,376,831
Tungurahua ... 324,286
Zamora-Chinchipe ... 46,691
Zones in dispute with Peru ... 42,156

EGYPT / Mişr

1985 E ... 48,503,000

Cities and Towns

Abnūb (1966 C) ... 31,195
Abū Kabīr (1966 C) ... 41,789
Abū Tīj (1966 C) ... 28,161
Akhmīm (1966 C) ... 44,829
Al 'Arīsh (1966 C) ... 40,338
Al Badārī (1966 C) ... 26,531
Alexandria (Al Iskandarīyah) (★ 3,350,000) ... 2,821,000
Al Fashn (1966 C) ... 27,746
Al Fayyūm ... 218,500
Al Hawāmidīyah (★ Cairo) (1966 C) ... 36,227

C Census.   E Official estimate.   UE Unofficial estimate.
• Largest city in country

★ Population or designation of metropolitan area, including suburbs (see headnote).
▲ Population of an entire municipality, commune, or district, including rural area.

Al Madīnah al Fikrīyah (1966 C) ... 21,504
Al Maḩallah al Kubrá ... 362,700
Al Manshāh (1966 C) ... 25,027
Al Manşūrah (El Mansura) (★ 375,000) ... 328,700
Al Manzilah (1966 C) ... 33,298
Al Maţarīyah (1966 C) ... 41,105
Al Minyā ... 191,800
Al Qanāţir al Khayrīyah (1966 C) ... 22,447
Al Qaşr (1966 C) ... 3,321
Al Quşayr (1966 C) ... 5,525
Al Qūşīyah (1966 C) ... 25,991
Armant (1966 C) ... 38,308
Ashmūn (1966 C) ... 32,168
Ash Shuhadā' (1966 C) ... 21,947
As Sallūm (1966 C) ... 2,483
As Sinbillāwayn (1966 C) ... 40,686
Aswān ... 182,700
Asyūţ ... 274,400
At Ţaţālīyah (1966 C) ... 20,438
Az Zaqāzīq ... 266,800
Bahtīm (★ Cairo) (1966 C) ... 32,510
Banhā ... 115,500
Banī Mazār (1966 C) ... 34,053
Banī Suwayf ... 151,200
Bibā (1966 C) ... 22,871
Bilbays (1966 C) ... 58,070
Bilqās Qism Awwal (1966 C) ... 41,067
Biyalā (1966 C) ... 33,008
Būlāq ad Dakrūr (★ Cairo) (1966 C) ... 75,130
Būsh (1966 C) ... 21,174
• CAIRO (AL QĀHIRAH) (★ 9,300,000) ... 6,205,000
Damanhūr ... 221,500
Dayr Mawās (1966 C) ... 16,947
Dayrūţ (1966 C) ... 27,646
Dishnā (1966 C) ... 21,857
Disūq (1966 C) ... 45,580
Dumyāţ (Damietta) ... 118,100
Fāqūs (1966 C) ... 40,561
Fuwah (1966 C) ... 30,654
Giheina al Gharbiya (1966 C) ... 24,203
Giza (Al Jīzah) (★ Cairo) ... 1,608,400
Ḩawsh 'Īsā (1966 C) ... 30,006
Hihyā (1966 C) ... 17,696
Idfū (1966 C) ... 27,326
Idkū (1966 C) ... 42,239
Ismailia (Al Ismā'īlīyah) (★ 235,000) ... 191,700
Isnā (1966 C) ... 27,383
Jirjā (1966 C) ... 44,150
Kafr ad Dawwār (★ Alexandria) (1983 E) ... 160,554
Kafr ash Shaykh (1966 C) ... 51,544
Kafr az Zayyāt (1966 C) ... 34,084
Kafr Salīm (★ Alexandria) (1966 C) ... 40,381
Kawm Umbū (1966 C) ... 27,227
Luxor (Al Uqşur) ... 137,300
Maghāghah (1966 C) ... 33,211
Mallawī (1966 C) ... 59,938
Manfalūţ (1966 C) ... 34,132
Minūf (1966 C) ... 48,256
Minyā al Qamḩ (1966 C) ... 31,533
Mīt Ghamr (★ 82,000) (1966 C) ... 43,665
Nafīshah (★ Al Ismā'īlīyah) (1966 C) ... 29,483
Port Said (Būr Sa'īd) ... 374,000
Qalyūb (1966 C) ... 49,303
Qinā ... 137,100
Qūş (1966 C) ... 27,462
Rashīd (Rosetta) (1966 C) ... 36,711
Samālūţ (1966 C) ... 37,861
Samannūd (1966 C) ... 29,749
Sāqiyat Makkī (1966 C) ... 22,967
Sawhāj ... 131,300
Shibīn al Kawm ... 129,600
Shibīn al Qanāţir (1966 C) ... 20,618
Shirbīn (1966 C) ... 25,089
Shubrā al Khaymah (★ Cairo) ... 515,500
Sīdī Sālim (1966 C) ... 21,096
Sinnūris (1966 C) ... 34,855
Sīwah (1966 C) ... 3,569
Suez (As Suways) ... 254,000
Ţahţā (1966 C) ... 38,915
Ţalā (1966 C) ... 25,448
Ţalkhā (★ Al Manşūrah) (1966 C) ... 23,742
Ţanţā ... 364,700
Ţimā (1966 C) ... 29,293
Warrāq al 'Arab (★ Cairo) (1966 C) ... 31,263
Ziftā (★★ Mīt Ghamr) (1966 C) ... 37,883

EL SALVADOR

1983 E ... 4,949,000

Cities and Towns

Ahuachapán ... 19,900
Chalchuapa (▲ 54,508) (1979 E) ... 23,086
Cojutepeque ... 30,100
Cuscatancingo ... 26,400
Ilopango ... 28,800
La Unión (▲ 46,346) (1979 E) ... 23,142
Mejicanos (★ San Salvador) ... 86,500
Nueva San Salvador ... 51,000
Quezaltepeque (▲ 38,578) (1979 E) ... 16,143
San Marcos ... 35,000
San Miguel ... 85,000
• SAN SALVADOR (★ 800,000) ... 445,100
Santa Ana ... 132,200
San Vicente ... 25,700
Sonsonate ... 46,700
Soyapango (★ San Salvador) (1979 E) ... 38,583
Usulután ... 30,600
Villa Delgado (★ San Salvador) ... 64,600
Zacatecoluca ... 24,700

EQUATORIAL GUINEA / Guinea Ecuatorial

1983 C ... 300,000

Cities and Towns

Bata ... 24,100
• MALABO ... 30,710

ETHIOPIA / Ityopiya

1982 E ... 32,775,000

Cities and Towns

• ADDIS ABABA ... 1,408,068
Adwa (1978 E) ... 21,107
Akaki Beseka (1978 E) ... 30,870
Akordat (1978 E) ... 25,861
Asela (1978 E) ... 30,694
Asmara ... 474,241
Bahir Dar ... 58,299
Debre Birhan (1978 E) ... 21,842
Debre Markos (1978 E) ... 35,818
Debre Zeyit ... 57,251
Dese ... 83,288
Dire Dawa ... 91,629
Gonder ... 85,941
Harer ... 70,289
Jima ... 71,311
Keren (1978 E) ... 33,368
Massawa (Mitsiwa) ... 36,839
Mekele ... 52,332
Nazret ... 80,702

FAEROE ISLANDS / Føroyar

1984 E ... 44,805

Cities and Towns

• TÓRSHAVN ... 14,443

FALKLAND ISLANDS

1980 C ... 1,813

Cities and Towns

• STANLEY ... 1,050

FIJI

1984 E ... 686,000

Cities and Towns

Lautoka (★ 37,000) ... 27,000
• SUVA (★ 150,000) ... 74,000

FINLAND / Suomi

1984 E ... 4,893,748

Cities and Towns

Borgå (Porvoo) ... 19,505
Espoo (Esbo) (★ Helsinki) ... 152,929
Hämeenlinna ... 42,461
• HELSINKI (HELSINGFORS) (★ 900,000) ... 484,263
Hyvinkää ... 38,432
Iisalmi ... 23,409
Imatra ... 35,412
Jakobstad (Pietarsaari) ... 20,563
Joensuu ... 46,354
Jyväskylä (★ 89,000) ... 64,834
Kajaani ... 35,913
Kemi ... 26,544
Kerava (★ Helsinki) ... 25,878
Kokkola (Gamlakarleby) ... 34,461
Kotka ... 59,474
Kouvola (★ 55,000) ... 31,644
Kuopio ... 77,371
Kuusankoski (★★ Kouvola) ... 22,301
Lahti (★ 109,000) ... 94,347
Lappeenranta ... 53,966
Mariehamn (Maarianhamina) ... 9,824
Mikkeli ... 29,345
Nokia (★ Tampere) ... 24,150
Oulu (★ 112,000) ... 96,525
Pori ... 78,933
Rauma ... 30,964
Riihimäki ... 24,292
Rovaniemi ... 32,369
Savonlinna ... 28,575
Tampere (★ 241,000) ... 168,150
Turku (Åbo) (★ 221,000) ... 162,282
Vaasa (Vasa) ... 54,497
Vantaa (Vanda) (★ Helsinki) ... 141,991
Varkaus ... 24,743

Provinces

Ahvenanmaa (Åland) ... 23,595
Häme ... 675,127
Keski-Suomi ... 247,351
Kuopio ... 255,740
Kymi ... 341,709
Lappi ... 200,879
Mikkeli ... 209,256
Oulu (Uleåborg) ... 430,903
Pohjois-Karjala ... 177,633
Turku-Pori ... 712,439
Uusimaa (Nyland) ... 1,175,373
Vaasa (Vasa) ... 443,743

FRANCE

1982 C ... 54,334,871

Cities and Towns

Abbeville ... 24,915
Agen (★ 58,288) ... 31,593
Aigues-Mortes ... 4,472
Aix-en-Provence ... 121,327
Aix-les-Bains (★ 31,680) ... 23,451
Ajaccio ... 54,089
Albi (★ 60,181) ... 45,947
Alençon (★ 43,101) ... 31,608
Alès (★ 70,180) ... 43,268
Alfortville (★ Paris) ... 36,231
Amiens (★ 154,498) ... 131,332
Angers (★ 195,859) ... 136,038
Angoulême (★ 103,552) ... 46,197
Annecy (★ 112,632) ... 49,965
Antibes (★★ Cannes) ... 62,859
Antony (★ Paris) ... 54,610
Arcachon (★ 39,931) ... 13,293
Argenteuil (★ Paris) ... 95,347
Arles (★ 52,547) ... 37,571
Armentières (★ 57,000) ... 24,834
Arras (★ 80,447) ... 41,736
Asnières [-sur-Seine] (★ Paris) ... 71,077
Athis-Mons (★ Paris) ... 28,496
Aubervilliers (★ Paris) ... 67,719
Auch (▲ 23,258) ... 20,273
Aulnay-sous-Bois (★ Paris) ... 75,996
Aurillac (★ 35,829) ... 30,963
Autun ... 20,587
Auxerre (★ 42,126) ... 38,741
Avignon (★ 174,264) ... 89,132
Avranches (★ 14,889) ... 9,468
Bagneux (★ Paris) ... 40,385
Bagnolet (★ Paris) ... 32,557
Barentin (★ 19,499) ... 12,364
Bar-le-Duc ... 18,471
Bastia (★ 50,596) ... 44,020
Bayeux ... 14,721
Bayonne (★ 127,477) ... 41,381
Beauvais ... 52,365
Belfort (★ 76,221) ... 51,206
Besançon (★ 120,772) ... 113,283
Béthune (★ 147,000) ... 25,508
Béziers (★ 81,347) ... 76,647
Biarritz (★★ Bayonne) ... 26,598
Blois (★ 61,049) ... 47,243
Bobigny (★ Paris) ... 42,723
Bois-Colombes (★ Paris) ... 23,780
Bondy (★ Paris) ... 44,301
Bordeaux (★ 640,012) ... 208,159
Boulogne-Billancourt (★ Paris) ... 102,582
Boulogne-sur-Mer (★ 98,566) ... 47,653
Bourg [-en-Bresse] (★ 53,463) ... 41,098
Bourges (★ 92,202) ... 76,432
Brest (★ 201,145) ... 156,060
Briançon (★ 13,123) ... 9,710
Brive [-la-Gaillarde] (★ 64,301) ... 51,511
Bron (★ Lyon) ... 40,638
Bruay [-en-Artois] (★ 110,000) ... 22,893
Caen (★ 183,526) ... 114,068
Cagnes-sur-Mer (★ Nice) ... 35,214
Cahors ... 19,707
Calais (★ 100,823) ... 76,527
Caluire [-et-Cuire] (★ Lyon) ... 41,931
Cambrai (★ 49,581) ... 35,272
Cannes (★ 245,000) ... 72,259
Carcassonne ... 41,153
Carmaux (★ 19,422) ... 12,113
Castres ... 45,578
Châlons-sur-Marne (★ 63,061) ... 51,137
Chalon-sur-Saône (★ 78,064) ... 56,194
Chambéry (★ 96,163) ... 53,427
Chamonix [-Mont-Blanc] (★ 10,512) ... 7,406
Champigny-sur-Marne (★ Paris) ... 76,176
Chantilly (★ 28,128) ... 10,065
Charleville-Mézières (★ 67,694) ... 58,667
Chartres (★ 77,795) ... 37,119
Châteauroux (★ 66,851) ... 51,942
Château-Thierry (★ 22,696) ... 14,557
Châtellerault (★ 68,000) ... 35,838
Châtenay-Malabry (★ Paris) ... 28,580
Châtillon (★ Paris) ... 24,834
Chatou (★ Paris) ... 28,437
Chaumont ... 27,554
Chauny (★ 20,078) ... 13,435
Chelles (★ Paris) ... 41,838
Cherbourg (★ 85,485) ... 28,442
Chinon (▲ 8,622) ... 6,032
Choisy-le-Roi (★ Paris) ... 35,476
Cholet ... 55,524
Clamart (★ Paris) ... 48,353
Clermont-Ferrand (★ 256,189) ... 147,361
Clichy (★ Paris) ... 46,895
Cognac (★ 31,189) ... 20,660
Colmar (★ 82,468) ... 62,483
Colombes (★ Paris) ... 78,777
Compiègne (★ 62,778) ... 40,384
Concarneau (★ 23,893) ... 15,747
Corbeil [-Essonnes] (★ Paris) ... 37,846
Courbevoie (★ Paris) ... 59,830
Coutances ... 9,930
Creil (★ 82,505) ... 34,709
Créteil (★ Paris) ... 71,693
Dax (★ 29,000) ... 18,648
Deauville ... 4,682
Decazeville (★ 21,925) ... 8,804
Denain (★★ Valenciennes) ... 21,825
Dieppe (★ 41,812) ... 35,957
Dijon (★ 215,865) ... 140,942
Dinard (★ 15,838) ... 9,590
Dives-sur-Mer (★ 11,204) ... 5,508
Dôle (★ 31,546) ... 26,889
Douai (★ 202,366) ... 42,576
Douarnenez ... 17,653
Drancy (★ Paris) ... 60,183
Dreux (★ 44,706) ... 33,379
Dunkerque (★ 195,705) ... 73,120
Elbeuf (★ 51,083) ... 17,224
Épernay (★ 34,355) ... 27,668
Épinal (★ 53,000) ... 37,818
Épinay [-sur-Seine] (★ Paris) ... 50,314
Étaples (★ 22,701) ... 11,292
Eu (★ 20,506) ... 8,588
Évreux (★ 54,654) ... 46,045
Évry (★ Paris) ... 29,471
Falaise ... 8,597
Fécamp ... 21,436
Foix ... 9,282
Fontaine (★ Grenoble) ... 22,827
Fontainebleau (★ 40,000) ... 15,679
Fontenay [-sous-Bois] (★ Paris) ... 52,627
Forbach (★ 66,000) ... 27,187
Fougères ... 24,362
Fréjus (★ 60,289) ... 31,662
Gagny (★ Paris) ... 34,861
Gap (▲ 30,676) ... 21,874
Garges-lès-Gonesse (★ Paris) ... 40,182
Gennevilliers (★ Paris) ... 45,396
Givors (★ 33,000) ... 20,544
Granville (★ 17,890) ... 13,546
Grasse (▲ 37,673) ... 24,553
Grenoble (★ 392,021) ... 156,637
Guebwiller (★ 25,427) ... 10,689
Guéret ... 15,720
Haguenau (★ 32,403) ... 26,629
Hayange (★ 70,000) ... 17,848
Hendaye ... 10,572
Hénin-Beaumont (Hénin-Liétard) (★★ Lens) ... 26,037
Houilles (★ Paris) ... 29,537
Hyères (★★ Toulon) ... 32,191
Issy [-les-Moulineaux] (★ Paris) ... 45,772
Ivry-sur-Seine (★ Paris) ... 55,699
Jœuf (★ 28,000) ... 9,016
La Baule-Escoublac (★ Saint-Nazaire) ... 14,553
La Ciotat (★ 39,956) ... 31,727
La Courneuve (★ Paris) ... 33,537
La Garenne-Colombes (★ Paris) ... 20,990
La Grand'Combe (★ 15,000) ... 8,329
Lambersart (★ Lille) ... 28,520
Laon ... 26,682
La Rochelle (★ 102,143) ... 75,840
La Roche-sur-Yon ... 45,098
La Seyne [-sur-Mer] (★ Toulon) ... 57,659
Laval ... 50,360
Le Blanc-Mesnil (★ Paris) ... 47,037
Le Creusot (★ 44,389) ... 32,149
Le Grand-Quevilly (★ Rouen) ... 31,650
Le Havre (★ 254,595) ... 199,388
Le Mans (★ 191,080) ... 147,697
Lens (★ 327,383) ... 38,244
Le Perreux-sur-Marne (★ Paris) ... 27,647
Le Puy [-en-Velay] (★ 42,382) ... 24,064
Les Sables-d'Olonne (★ 32,436) ... 16,100
Levallois-Perret (★ Paris) ... 53,500
Le Vésinet (★ Paris) ... 17,272
L'Haÿ-les-Roses (★ Paris) ... 29,568
Libourne (★ 26,992) ... 22,119
Liévin (★ Lens) ... 33,096
Lille (★ 1,020,000) ... 168,424
Limoges (★ 171,689) ... 140,400
Lisieux (★ 29,063) ... 24,940
Livry-Gargan (★ Paris) ... 32,778
Loches (▲ 6,772) ... 5,847
Lomme (★ Lille) ... 28,281
Longwy (★ 80,000) ... 17,338
Lons-le-Saunier (★ 26,410) ... 20,105
Lorient (★ 104,025) ... 62,554
Lourdes ... 17,425
Lunéville ... 21,468
Lyon (★ 1,220,844) ... 413,095
Mâcon (★ 47,274) ... 38,404
Maisons-Alfort (★ Paris) ... 51,065
Maisons-Laffitte (★ Paris) ... 22,595
Malakoff (★ Paris) ... 32,553
Mantes [-la-Jolie] (★ 170,265) ... 43,564
Marcq-en-Baroeul (★ Lille) ... 35,278
Marignane (★ Marseille) ... 31,109
Marseille (★ 1,110,511) ... 874,436
Martigues (★ 72,316) ... 31,157
Massy (★ Paris) ... 40,135
Maubeuge (★ 109,000) ... 36,061
Mazamet (★ 26,676) ... 12,840
Meaux (★ 55,797) ... 45,005
Melun (★ 82,479) ... 35,005
Mende ... 10,929
Menton (★ 35,000) ... 25,072
Mérignac (★ Bordeaux) ... 51,306
Metz (★ 186,437) ... 114,232
Meudon (★ Paris) ... 48,450
Millau ... 21,695
Montargis (★ 51,954) ... 16,110
Montauban (▲ 50,682) ... 36,758
Montbéliard (★ 128,194) ... 31,836
Montceau-les-Mines (★ 51,290) ... 26,925
Mont-de-Marsan (★ 33,616) ... 27,326
Montélimar (★ 38,292) ... 29,161
Montereau [-faut-Yonne] (★ 26,663) ... 19,413
Montigny [-lès-Metz] (★ Metz) ... 22,114
Montluçon (★ 70,000) ... 49,912
Montmorency (★ Paris) ... 20,798
Montpellier (★ 221,307) ... 197,231
Montreuil [-sous-Bois] (★ Paris) ... 93,368
Montrouge (★ Paris) ... 38,517
Morlaix (★ 27,829) ... 15,558
Moulins (★ 43,082) ... 25,159
Moyeuvre [-Grande] (★ 70,000) ... 10,287
Mulhouse (★ 220,613) ... 112,157
Nancy (★ 306,982) ... 96,317
Nanterre (★ Paris) ... 88,578
Nantes (★ 468,857) ... 240,539
Narbonne ... 41,565
Neuilly [-sur-Seine] (★ Paris) ... 64,170
Nevers (★ 59,274) ... 43,013
Nice (★ 449,496) ... 337,085
Nîmes (★ 132,343) ... 124,220
Niort (★ 61,959) ... 58,203
Nogent [-sur-Marne] (★ Paris) ... 24,630
Noisy-le-Grande (★ Paris) ... 40,585
Noisy-le-Sec (★ Paris) ... 36,880
Noyon ... 14,041
Orange (▲ 26,499) ... 18,727
Orléans (★ 220,478) ... 102,710
Orly (★ Paris) ... 23,766
Oullins (★ Lyon) ... 27,168
Oyonnax (★ 28,107) ... 22,739
Palaiseau (★ Paris) ... 28,369
Pantin (★ Paris) ... 43,553
Paray-le-Monial ... 10,639
• PARIS (★ 9,775,000) (1984 E) ... 2,149,900
Pau (★ 131,265) ... 83,790
Périgueux (★ 59,716) ... 32,916
Perpignan (★ 137,915) ... 111,669
Pessac (★ Bordeaux) ... 50,267
Poissy (★ Paris) ... 36,389
Poitiers (★ 103,204) ... 79,350
Pont-à-Mousson (★ 22,661) ... 14,942
Pontoise (★ Paris) ... 28,434
Port-de-Bouc ... 20,106
Privas (★ 14,108) ... 10,345
Puteaux (★ Paris) ... 36,117
Quimper ... 56,907
Reims (★ 199,388) ... 194,656
Rennes (★ 234,418) ... 117,234
Rezé (★ Nantes) ... 33,562
Riom (★ 23,316) ... 18,346
Rive-de-Gier (★ 37,000) ... 15,806
Roanne (★ 81,786) ... 48,705
Rochefort (★ 35,122) ... 26,167
Rodez (★ 37,953) ... 24,368
Romans [-sur-Isère] (★ 47,083) ... 33,152
Rosny-sous-Bois (★ Paris) ... 36,970
Roubaix (★★ Lille) ... 101,602

C Census. E Official estimate. UE Unofficial estimate.
• Largest city in country.
★ Population or designation of metropolitan area, including suburbs (see headnote).
▲ Population of an entire municipality, commune, or district, including rural area.

Rouen (★ 379,879) ... 101,945
Royan (★ 28,327) ... 17,540
Rueil-Malmaison (★ Paris) ... 63,412
Saint-Avold (★ 26,543) ... 12,389
Saint-Brieuc (★ 83,900) ... 48,563
Saint-Chamond (★ 82,059) ... 40,267
Saint-Cyr-l'École (★ Paris) ... 14,996
Saint-Denis (★ Paris) ... 90,829
Saint-Dié (★ 27,708) ... 23,759
Saint-Dizier ... 35,189
Saint-Étienne (★ 317,228) ... 204,955
Saint-Étienne-du-Rouvray (★ Rouen) ... 32,444
Saint-Germain-en-Laye (★ Paris) ... 38,499
Saint-Jean-de-Luz (★ 23,868) ... 12,769
Saint-Lô (★ 27,656) ... 23,212
Saint-Malo ... 46,347
Saint-Martin-d'Hères (★ Grenoble) ... 35,188
Saint-Maur-des-Fossés (★ Paris) ... 80,811
Saint-Nazaire (★ 130,271) ... 68,348
Saint-Omer (★ 29,000) ... 15,415
Saint-Ouen (★ Paris) ... 43,606
Saint-Quentin (★ 71,887) ... 63,567
Saintes ... 25,471
Saint-Tropez (▲ 6,213) ... 4,961
Salon-de-Provence (★ 41,091) ... 34,846
Sarcelles (★ Paris) ... 53,630
Sarreguemines ... 24,763
Sartrouville (★ Paris) ... 46,197
Saumur ... 32,149
Savigny-sur-Orge (★ Paris) ... 32,502
Schiltigheim (★ Strasbourg) ... 29,574
Sedan (★ 30,871) ... 23,477
Senlis ... 14,514
Sens (★ 35,178) ... 26,602
Sète (★ 58,865) ... 39,545
Sèvres (★ Paris) ... 20,208
Soissons (★ 47,305) ... 30,213
Sotteville-lès-Rouen (★ Rouen) ... 30,558
Stains (★ Paris) ... 36,079
Strasbourg (★ 400,000) ... 248,712
Suresnes (★ Paris) ... 35,187
Tarbes (★ 80,000) ... 51,422
Thann (★ 28,406) ... 7,788
Thionville (★ 138,034) ... 40,573
Thonon-les-Bains (★ 45,372) ... 27,161
Toul (★ 22,878) ... 17,406
Toulon (★ 410,393) ... 179,423
Toulouse (★ 541,271) ... 347,995
Tourcoing (★★ Lille) ... 96,908
Tours (★ 262,786) ... 132,209
Trouville [-sur-Mer] (★ 18,533) ... 6,008
Troyes (★ 125,240) ... 63,581
Tulle ... 18,880
Valence (★ 106,041) ... 66,356
Valenciennes (★ 349,505) ... 40,275
Vannes ... 42,178
Vanves (★ Paris) ... 22,868
Vénissieux (★ Lyon) ... 64,804
Verdun (★ 26,944) ... 21,516
Versailles (★ Paris) ... 91,494
Vesoul (★ 26,592) ... 18,412
Vichy (★ 63,501) ... 30,527
Vienne (★ 41,019) ... 28,294
Vierzon ... 34,209
Villefranche-sur-Mer (★ Nice) ... 7,363
Villefranche [-sur-Saône] (★ 43,000) ... 28,881
Villejuif (★ Paris) ... 52,448
Villemomble (★ Paris) ... 27,571
Villeneuve-d'Ascq (★ Lille) ... 59,527
Villeneuve-Saint-Georges (★ Paris) ... 28,119
Villeurbanne (★ Lyon) ... 115,960
Vincennes (★ Paris) ... 42,870
Viry-Châtillon (★ Paris) ... 30,224
Vitry-le-François (★ 21,192) ... 18,261
Vitry-sur-Seine (★ Paris) ... 85,263
Voiron (★ 33,492) ... 18,911
Wattrelos (★ Lille) ... 44,626

Departments

1984 ESTIMATE

AIN ... 431,800
Aisne ... 533,800
Allier ... 367,800
Alpes-de-Haute-Provence (Basses-Alpes) ... 121,100
Alpes-Maritimes ... 893,500
Ardèche ... 271,300
Ardennes ... 300,800
Ariège ... 135,300
Aube ... 290,500
Aude ... 283,200
Aveyron ... 278,300
Bas-Rhin ... 926,800
Belfort, Territoire de ... 133,300
Bouches-du-Rhône ... 1,739,600
Calvados ... 596,200
Cantal ... 162,000
Charente ... 339,400
Charente-Maritime ... 518,000
Cher ... 321,400
Corrèze ... 242,100
Corse-du-Sud ... 110,900
Côte-d'Or ... 477,900
Côtes-du-Nord ... 539,100
Creuse ... 138,600
Deux-Sèvres ... 343,700
Dordogne ... 379,100
Doubs ... 477,700
Drôme ... 398,800
Essonne ... 1,006,300
Eure ... 473,700
Eure-et-Loir ... 370,400
Finistère ... 836,200
Gard ... 540,200
Gers ... 173,700
Gironde ... 1,147,200
Haute-Corse ... 133,700
Haute-Garonne ... 837,500
Haute-Loire ... 206,900
Haute-Marne ... 210,600
Hautes-Alpes ... 106,700
Haute-Saône ... 234,900
Haute-Savoie ... 509,100
Hautes-Pyrénées ... 228,200
Haute-Vienne ... 357,000
Haut-Rhin ... 656,200
Hauts-de-Seine ... 1,373,800
Hérault ... 721,900
Ille-et-Vilaine ... 762,400
Indre ... 241,300
Indre-et-Loire ... 513,400
Isère ... 960,300
Jura ... 244,500
Landes ... 300,200
Loire ... 739,400
Loire-Atlantique ... 1,012,300
Loiret ... 548,300
Loir-et-Cher ... 299,000
Lot ... 155,600
Lot-et-Garonne ... 300,600
Lozère ... 74,100
Maine-et-Loire ... 687,900
Manche ... 469,300
Marne ... 547,000
Mayenne ... 274,200
Meurthe-et-Moselle ... 715,300
Meuse ... 199,700
Morbihan ... 600,200
Moselle ... 1,008,100
Nièvre ... 238,000
Nord ... 2,522,200
Oise ... 678,800
Orne ... 295,700
Paris ... 2,149,900
Pas-de-Calais ... 1,419,100
Puy-de-Dôme ... 598,500
Pyrénées-Atlantiques (Basses Pyrénées) ... 561,200
Pyrénées-Orientales ... 343,800
Rhône ... 1,450,500
Saône-et-Loire ... 571,700
Sarthe ... 508,100
Savoie ... 329,600
Seine-et-Marne ... 929,000
Seine-Maritime ... 1,198,200
Seine-Saint-Denis ... 1,326,800
Somme ... 546,300
Tarn ... 339,400
Tarn-et-Garonne ... 192,200
Val-de-Marne ... 1,186,600
Val-d'Oise ... 945,000
Var ... 732,500
Vaucluse ... 435,500
Vendée ... 490,300
Vienne ... 374,600
Vosges ... 395,400
Yonne ... 313,800
Yvelines ... 1,230,000

Historic Regions

1984 ESTIMATE

Alsace ... 1,583,000
Aquitaine ... 2,688,300
Auvergne ... 1,335,200
Basse-Normandie ... 1,361,200
Bourgogne ... 1,601,400
Bretagne ... 2,737,900
Centre ... 2,293,800
Champagne-Ardenne ... 1,348,900
Corse (Corsica) ... 244,600
Franche-Comté ... 1,090,400
Haute-Normandie ... 1,671,900
Île-de-France ... 10,147,400
Languedoc-Roussillon ... 1,963,200
Limousin ... 737,700
Lorraine ... 2,318,500
Midi-Pyrénées ... 2,340,200
Nord ... 3,941,300
Pays de la Loire ... 2,972,800
Picardie ... 1,758,900
Poitou-Charentes ... 1,575,700
Provence-Alpes-Côte D'Azur ... 4,028,900
Rhône-Alpes ... 5,090,800

FRENCH GUIANA / Guyane française

1982 C ... 72,012

Cities and Towns

• CAYENNE ... 38,093
Kourou ... 7,061
Saint-Laurent [-du-Maroni] (▲ 6,971) ... 4,500

FRENCH POLYNESIA / Polynésie française

1983 C ... 166,753

Cities and Towns

• PAPEETE (★ 80,000) ... 23,496

GABON

1985 E ... 1,312,000

Cities and Towns

Franceville ... 58,800
Lambaréné ... 49,500
• LIBREVILLE ... 235,700
Port-Gentil ... 124,400

GAMBIA

1983 C ... 696,000

Cities and Towns

• BANJUL (BATHURST) (★ 109,486) ... 44,536

GERMAN DEMOCRATIC REPUBLIC (EAST GERMANY) / Deutsche Demokratische Republik

1983 E ... 16,701,487

Cities and Towns

Altenburg ... 54,999
Annaberg-Buchholz ... 26,514
Apolda ... 28,911
Arnstadt ... 29,916
Aschersleben ... 34,303
Aue ... 28,793
Bautzen ... 50,502
• BERLIN (EAST) (★★ Berlin) ... 1,185,533
Bernburg ... 41,006
Bitterfeld (★ 105,000) ... 21,768
Blankenburg ... 18,763
Borna ... 23,221
Brandenburg ... 95,133
Burg bei Magdeburg ... 28,216
Coswig (★ Dresden) ... 28,696
Cottbus ... 120,723
Crimmitschau ... 25,539
Delitzsch ... 27,856
Dessau (★ 135,000) ... 103,738
Döbeln ... 26,751
Dresden (★ 640,000) ... 522,532
Eberswald[-Finow] ... 53,473
Eilenburg ... 21,724
Eisenach ... 50,895
Eisenhüttenstadt ... 49,491
Eisleben ... 27,346
Erfurt ... 214,231
Falkensee (★ Berlin) ... 23,794
Finsterwalde ... 24,082
Forst [Lausitz] ... 26,709
Frankfurt [an der Oder] ... 84,072
Freiberg ... 51,290
Freital (★ Dresden) ... 45,199
Fürstenwalde [Spree] ... 35,240
Gera ... 129,891
Glauchau ... 29,697
Görlitz ... 80,216
Gotha ... 57,662
Greifswald ... 62,991
Greiz ... 35,228
Güstrow ... 38,931
Halberstadt ... 47,115
Halle (★ 480,000) ... 236,139
Halle-Neustadt (★ Halle) ... 91,510
Heidenau (★ Dresden) ... 19,270
Henningsdorf bei Berlin (★ Berlin) ... 27,334
Hettstedt ... 22,112
Hoyerswerda ... 70,698
Ilmenau ... 29,470
Jena ... 106,555
Karl-Marx-Stadt (Chemnitz) (★ 460,000) ... 318,917
Köthen ... 34,728
Lauchhammer ... 24,438
Leipzig (★ 710,000) ... 558,994
Limbach-Oberfrohna (★ Karl-Marx-Stadt) ... 22,573
Lübbenau ... 21,401
Luckenwalde ... 27,039
Ludwigsfelde ... 20,970
Magdeburg (★ 395,000) ... 289,075
Markkleeberg (★ Leipzig) ... 20,095
Meerane ... 21,677
Meiningen ... 25,907
Meissen ... 38,710
Merseburg (★★ Halle) ... 49,219
Mühlhausen (Thomas-Müntzer-Stadt) ... 43,656
Naumburg [an der Saale] ... 32,913
Neubrandenburg ... 82,450
Neuruppin ... 26,294
Neustrelitz ... 27,028
Nordhausen ... 47,203
Oranienburg (★ Berlin) ... 28,121
Parchim ... 23,374
Pirna ... 48,253
Plauen ... 78,797
Potsdam (★ Berlin) ... 135,922
Prenzlau ... 23,702
Quedlinburg ... 29,167
Radebeul (★ Dresden) ... 34,928
Rathenow ... 31,896
Reichenbach ... 25,446
Riesa ... 51,285
Rostock ... 241,146
Rudolstadt ... 31,913
Saalfeld ... 34,141
Salzwedel ... 22,850
Sangerhausen ... 33,604
Sassnitz ... 14,813
Schmalkalden ... 17,440
Schneeberg ... 21,689
Schönebeck ... 44,876
Schwedt ... 51,881
Schwerin ... 124,975
Senftenberg ... 31,796
Sömmerda ... 23,251
Sondershausen ... 23,667
Sonneberg ... 28,827
Spremberg ... 24,166
Stassfurt ... 27,249
Stendal (1982 E) ... 45,792
Stralsund ... 75,335
Strausberg (★ Berlin) ... 25,576
Suhl ... 51,731
Tangermünde ... 11,814
Torgau ... 21,291
Waren ... 24,101
Weimar ... 64,007
Weissenfels ... 39,044
Weisswasser ... 34,624
Werdau ... 19,986
Wernigerode ... 36,166
Wilhelm-Pieck-Stadt Guben ... 34,726
Wismar ... 57,874
Wittenberge ... 31,053
Wittenberg [Lutherstadt] ... 54,306
Wolfen (★★ Bitterfeld) ... 41,299
Wurzen ... 19,120
Zeitz ... 43,716
Zerbst ... 18,912
Zittau ... 40,554
Zwickau (★ 170,000) ... 120,486

Districts

Berlin, [East] (City) ... 1,185,533
Cottbus ... 883,924
Dresden ... 1,796,347
Erfurt ... 1,238,628
Frankfurt ... 708,958
Gera ... 743,115
Halle ... 1,810,022
Karl-Marx-Stadt ... 1,902,973
Leipzig ... 1,392,558
Magdeburg ... 1,258,977
Neubrandenburg ... 620,979
Potsdam ... 1,121,900
Rostock ... 895,909
Schwerin ... 591,979
Suhl ... 549,685

GERMANY, FEDERAL REPUBLIC OF (WEST GERMANY) / Bundesrepublik Deutschland

1984 E ... 61,049,256

Cities and Towns

Aachen (★ 545,000) ... 239,801
Aalen (★ 80,000) ... 62,861
Achern ... 20,648
Achim (★ Bremen) ... 27,564
Ahaus ... 28,897
Ahlen ... 52,537
Ahrensburg (★ Hamburg) ... 26,908
Albstadt ... 46,226
Alfeld (Leine) ... 22,939
Alsdorf (★ Aachen) ... 46,031
Altena ... 22,595
Amberg ... 43,669
Andernach (★★ Neuwied) ... 26,697
Ansbach ... 37,591
Arnsberg ... 75,135
Aschaffenburg (★ 145,000) ... 59,088
Augsburg (★ 400,000) ... 244,400
Aurich ... 34,976
Backnang ... 28,999
Baden-Baden ... 48,622
Bad Harzburg (★ Goslar) ... 23,913
Bad Hersfeld ... 28,032
Bad Homburg vor der Höhe (★ Frankfurt am Main) ... 50,647
Bad Honnef am Rhein (★ Bonn) ... 20,468
Bad Kissingen ... 21,452
Bad Kreuznach ... 39,957
Bad Nauheim (★ Frankfurt am Main) ... 26,540
Bad Neuenahr-Ahrweiler ... 25,306
Bad Oeynhausen ... 43,235
Bad Oldesloe ... 20,787
Bad Reichenhall ... 17,581
Bad Salzuflen (★★ Herford) ... 50,494
Bad Vilbel (★ Frankfurt am Main) ... 25,063
Balingen ... 29,614
Bamberg (★ 120,000) ... 69,990
Barsinghausen (★ Hannover) ... 32,745
Bayreuth (★ 90,000) ... 71,811
Beckum ... 36,861
Bensheim ... 33,215
Berchtesgaden ... 8,126
Bergheim (Erft) (★ Cologne) ... 53,882
Bergisch Gladbach (★ Cologne) ... 100,749
Bergkamen (★ Essen) ... 47,665
Berlin (West) (★ 3,790,000) ... 1,848,585
Biberach [an der Riss] ... 27,662
Bielefeld (★ 525,000) ... 301,460
Bietigheim-Bissingen (★ Stuttgart) ... 34,944
Bingen ... 22,545
Böblingen (★ Stuttgart) ... 40,489
Bocholt ... 65,710
Bochum (★★ Essen) ... 384,774
BONN (★ 570,000) ... 291,291
Borken ... 33,127
Bornheim (★ Bonn) ... 35,614
Bottrop (★ Essen) ... 112,353
Brake ... 17,069
Bramsche ... 23,391
Braunschweig (Brunswick) (★ 330,000) ... 253,057
Bremen (★ 800,000) ... 530,520
Bremerhaven (★ 190,000) ... 135,095
Bretten ... 23,200
Brilon ... 24,482
Bruchsal ... 36,548
Brühl (★ Cologne) ... 41,252
Buchholz in der Nordheide (★ Hamburg) ... 30,460
Bückeburg ... 20,477
Bünde ... 38,816
Burgdorf (★ Hannover) ... 28,668
Butzbach ... 21,172
Buxtehude (★ Hamburg) ... 32,512
Calw ... 22,240
Castrop-Rauxel (★ Essen) ... 76,428
Celle ... 70,754
Cloppenburg ... 21,798
Coburg ... 44,239
Coesfeld ... 31,367
Cologne (Köln) (★ 1,810,000) ... 922,286
Crailsheim ... 25,065
Cuxhaven ... 56,977
Dachau (★ Munich) ... 33,141
Darmstadt (★ 310,000) ... 134,718
Datteln (★ Essen) ... 36,605
Deggendorf ... 30,363
Delmenhorst (★★ Bremen) ... 70,671
Detmold ... 66,282
Dillingen (★ Saarlouis) ... 20,341
Dinkelsbühl ... 10,504
Dinslaken (★ Essen) ... 60,430
Ditzingen (★ Stuttgart) ... 21,929
Dormagen (★ Cologne) ... 56,985
Dorsten (★ Essen) ... 72,020
Dortmund (★★ Essen) ... 579,697
Dreieich (★ Frankfurt am Main) ... 38,028
Duderstadt ... 22,696
Duisburg (★★ Essen) ... 522,829
Dülmen ... 39,720
Düren (★ 110,000) ... 84,631
Düsseldorf (★ 1,215,000) ... 565,843
Eckernförde ... 23,840
Einbeck ... 27,819
Elmshorn ... 41,169
Emden ... 50,164
Emmendingen ... 24,922
Emmerich ... 29,268
Emsdetten ... 30,926
Ennepetal (★ Essen) ... 33,725
Erftstadt (★ Cologne) ... 44,306
Erkelenz ... 36,358
Erkrath (★ Düsseldorf) ... 44,267
Erlangen (★★ Nürnberg) ... 100,523
Eschwege ... 23,125
Eschweiler (★★ Aachen) ... 52,869
Espelkamp ... 22,020
• Essen (★ 5,050,000) ... 625,705
Esslingen (★ Stuttgart) ... 86,996
Ettlingen (★ Karlsruhe) ... 37,005
Euskirchen ... 44,986
Fellbach (★ Stuttgart) ... 39,602

C Census. E Official estimate. UE Unofficial estimate.
• Largest city in country.
★ Population or designation of metropolitan area, including suburbs (see headnote).
▲ Population of an entire municipality, commune, or district, including rural area.

Filderstadt (★ Stuttgart) ... 36,772
Flensburg (★ 103,000) ... 86,873
Forchheim ... 28,629
Frankenthal (★ Mannheim) ... 43,865
Frankfurt [am Main] (★ 1,880,000) ... 599,634
Frechen (★ Cologne) ... 42,719
Freiburg [im Breisgau] (★ 225,000) ... 181,304
Freising ... 35,841
Friedrichshafen ... 51,094
Fulda (★ 79,000) ... 55,441
Fürstenfeldbruck (★ Munich) ... 32,050
Fürth (★★ Nürnberg) ... 97,623
Gaggenau ... 27,944
Ganderkesee (★ Bremen) ... 25,965
Garbsen (★ Hannover) ... 57,292
Garmisch-Partenkirchen ... 28,049
Geesthacht (★ Hamburg) ... 25,257
Geislingen (★ Göppingen) ... 26,158
Geldern ... 27,024
Gelsenkirchen (★★ Essen) ... 287,956
Georgsmarienhütte (★ Osnabrück) ... 30,737
Germering (★ Munich) ... 35,189
Gevelsberg (★ Essen) ... 30,442
Giessen (★ 160,000) ... 70,743
Gifhorn ... 33,831
Gladbeck (★ Essen) ... 76,812
Goch ... 28,761
Göppingen (★ 155,000) ... 51,713
Goslar (★ 84,000) ... 50,516
Göttingen ... 132,454
Greven ... 28,595
Grevenbroich (★ Düsseldorf) ... 56,580
Gronau (★ Enschede, Netherlands) ... 39,712
Gummersbach ... 48,277
Gütersloh (★★ Bielefeld) ... 78,414
Haan (★ Wuppertal) ... 27,745
Hagen (★★ Essen) ... 207,636
Haltern (★ Essen) ... 31,582
Hamburg (★ 2,250,000) ... 1,592,447
Hameln (★ 72,000) ... 55,992
Hamm ... 166,641
Hanau [am Main] (★★ Frankfurt am Main) ... 84,373
Hannover (★ 1,005,000) ... 514,010
Hattingen (★ Essen) ... 54,887
Heide ... 21,012
Heidelberg (★★ Mannheim) ... 133,693
Heidenheim (★ 89,000) ... 47,352
Heilbronn (★ 230,000) ... 110,666
Heiligenhaus (★ Essen) ... 28,678
Heinsberg ... 36,055
Helmstedt ... 25,882
Hemer ... 31,854
Hennef (★ Siegburg) ... 29,943
Heppenheim (★ Mannheim) ... 24,006
Herdecke (★ Essen) ... 24,223
Herford (★ 120,000) ... 59,941
Herne (★ Essen) ... 173,226
Herrenberg (★ Stuttgart) ... 25,437
Herten (★ Essen) ... 68,423
Herzogenrath (★ Aachen) ... 43,050
Hilden (★ Düsseldorf) ... 53,297
Hildesheim (★ 140,000) ... 101,017
Hof ... 51,183
Hofheim am Taunus (★ Frankfurt am Main) ... 33,695
Holzminden ... 21,370
Homburg (★★ Zweibrücken) ... 41,600
Höxter ... 31,867
Hückelhoven ... 35,463
Hürth (★ Cologne) ... 50,437
Husum ... 24,317
Ibbenbüren ... 42,404
Idar-Oberstein ... 34,527
Ingolstadt (★ 138,000) ... 90,763
Iserlohn ... 89,951
Itzehoe ... 32,394
Jüchen (★ Mönchengladbach) ... 20,700
Jülich ... 30,181
Kaarst (★ Düsseldorf) ... 39,042
Kaiserslautern (★ 138,000) ... 98,212
Kamen (★ Essen) ... 44,324
Kamp-Lintfort (★ Essen) ... 36,724
Karlsruhe (★ 490,000) ... 269,638
Kassel (★ 370,000) ... 184,997
Kaufbeuren ... 41,545
Kehl (★ Strasbourg, France) ... 28,902
Kempen (★ Essen) ... 31,090
Kempten [in Allgäu] ... 56,691
Kerpen (★ Cologne) ... 54,909
Kiel (★ 335,000) ... 245,751
Kirchheim unter Teck (★ Stuttgart) ... 32,904
Kleve (Cleves) ... 44,223
Koblenz (★ 180,000) ... 111,235
Königswinter (★ Bonn) ... 33,971
Konstanz ... 68,605
Korbach ... 22,298
Kornwestheim (★ Stuttgart) ... 26,124
Korschenbroich (★ Düsseldorf) ... 26,843
Krefeld (★★ Essen) ... 217,276
Kreuztal (★ Siegen) ... 29,071
Kulmbach ... 27,535
Laatzen (★ Hannover) ... 36,005
Lage ... 31,787
Lahnstein (★ Koblenz) ... 18,516
Lahr ... 34,671
Lampertheim (★ Mannheim) ... 30,508
Landau in der Pfalz ... 35,568
Landshut ... 56,230
Langen (★ Frankfurt am Main) ... 28,440
Langenfeld (★ Düsseldorf) ... 48,096
Langenhagen (★ Hannover) ... 46,323
Leer ... 30,436
Lehrte (★ Hannover) ... 38,931
Leinfelden-Echterdingen (★ Stuttgart) ... 34,892
Lemgo ... 39,124
Lengerich ... 20,345
Leonberg (★ Stuttgart) ... 39,109
Leverkusen (★ Cologne) ... 155,411
Limburg [an der Lahn] ... 28,778
Lindau ... 23,510
Lingen ... 45,099
Lippstadt ... 60,106
Löhne ... 36,265
Lörrach (★ Basel, Switzerland) ... 40,734
Lübeck (★ 260,000) ... 211,707
Lüdenscheid ... 73,496
Ludwigsburg (★ Stuttgart) ... 77,054
Ludwigshafen am Rhein (★★ Mannheim) ... 155,311
Lüneburg ... 60,194
Lünen (★ Essen) ... 84,084
Maintal (★ Frankfurt am Main) ... 36,730
Mainz (★★ Wiesbaden) ... 187,447
Mannheim (★ 1,410,000) ... 295,178
Marburg [an der Lahn] ... 76,260
Marl (★ Essen) ... 87,231
Meerbusch (★ Düsseldorf) ... 48,817
Melle ... 40,201
Memmingen ... 37,623
Menden ... 51,959
Meppen ... 28,783
Merzig ... 29,173
Meschede ... 29,695
Mettmann (★ Düsseldorf) ... 35,797
Minden (★ 125,000) ... 75,419
Moers (★ Essen) ... 97,753
Mönchengladbach (★ 410,000) ... 255,085
Monheim (★ Düsseldorf) ... 40,426
Mülheim [am der Ruhr] (★ Essen) ... 173,190
Münden ... 23,928
Munich (München) (★ 1,955,000) ... 1,267,451
Münster ... 272,626
Neckarsulm (★ Heilbronn) ... 21,982
Nettetal ... 36,961
Neuburg [an der Donau] ... 24,323
Neu-Isenburg (★ Frankfurt am Main) ... 34,889
Neumarkt [in der Oberpfalz] ... 31,497
Neumünster ... 78,743
Neunkirchen [Saar] (★ 135,000) ... 50,382
Neuss (★ Düsseldorf) ... 143,762
Neustadt am Rübenberge (★ Hannover) ... 37,996
Neustadt [an der Weinstrasse] ... 48,958
Neu-Ulm (★ Ulm) ... 46,441
Neuwied (★ 150,000) ... 58,795
Nienburg ... 29,600
Norden ... 24,069
Nordenham (★★ Bremerhaven) ... 29,177
Norderstedt (★ Hamburg) ... 66,680
Nordhorn ... 47,788
Nördlingen ... 18,340
Northeim ... 31,196
Nürnberg (Nuremberg) (★ 1,040,000) ... 468,352
Nürtingen (★ Stuttgart) ... 35,500
Oberammergau ... 4,772
Oberhausen (★★ Essen) ... 223,265
Oberursel (★ Frankfurt am Main) ... 38,689
Oelde ... 27,101
Oer-Erkenschwick (★ Essen) ... 27,033
Offenbach (★ Frankfurt am Main) ... 107,378
Offenburg ... 50,048
Oldenburg ... 138,469
Olpe ... 22,138
Osnabrück (★ 270,000) ... 153,587
Osterode am Harz ... 27,284
Overath (★ Cologne) ... 22,818
Paderborn ... 109,514
Papenburg ... 28,497
Passau ... 52,356
Peine ... 45,886
Pforzheim (★ 220,000) ... 104,023
Pinneberg (★ Hamburg) ... 35,459
Pirmasens ... 46,930
Plettenberg ... 27,555
Porta Westfalica (★ Minden) ... 33,721
Pulheim (★ Cologne) ... 47,121
Rastatt ... 37,319
Ratingen (★ Düsseldorf) ... 87,710
Ravensburg (★ 75,000) ... 42,794
Recklinghausen (★ Essen) ... 117,989
Regensburg (★ 205,000) ... 126,681
Reinbek (★ Hamburg) ... 25,196
Remagen (★ Bonn) ... 14,112
Remscheid (★★ Wuppertal) ... 121,830
Rendsburg ... 31,109
Reutlingen (★ 160,000) ... 96,337
Rheda-Wiedenbrück (★ Bielefeld) ... 37,564
Rheinberg (★ Essen) ... 26,087
Rheine ... 70,685
Rheinfelden ... 27,166
Rietberg ... 23,322
Rinteln ... 25,693
Rodgau (★ Frankfurt am Main) ... 36,697
Rosenheim ... 52,112
Rösrath (★ Cologne) ... 21,360
Rothenburg [ob der Tauber] ... 11,285
Rottenburg am Neckar ... 32,634
Rottweil ... 23,249
Rüsselsheim (★★ Wiesbaden) ... 58,167
Saarbrücken (★ 385,000) ... 188,763
Saarlouis (★ 115,000) ... 37,625
Salzgitter ... 107,023
Sankt Augustin (★ Bonn) ... 50,208
Sankt Ingbert ... 41,015
Sankt Wendel ... 26,463
Schleswig ... 28,960
Schmallenberg ... 24,445
Schorndorf (★ Stuttgart) ... 33,925
Schwabach (★ Nürnberg) ... 35,245
Schwäbisch Gmünd ... 56,073
Schwäbisch Hall ... 30,728
Schweinfurt (★ 110,000) ... 51,059
Schwelm (★ Wuppertal) ... 30,021
Schwerte (★ Essen) ... 47,684
Seelze (★ Hannover) ... 29,596
Seesen ... 21,955
Seevetal (★ Hamburg) ... 37,121
Selb ... 20,506
Selm (★ Essen) ... 25,502
Siegburg (★ 165,000) ... 34,352
Siegen (★ 200,000) ... 107,774
Sindelfingen (★ Stuttgart) ... 55,362
Singen (Hohentwiel) ... 41,908
Sinsheim ... 27,220
Soest ... 41,362
Solingen (★★ Wuppertal) ... 158,418
Speyer ... 43,748
Springe ... 29,339
Stade ... 42,915
Stadthagen ... 22,388
Steinfurt ... 31,460
Stolberg (★★ Aachen) ... 56,550
Straubing ... 41,883
Stuttgart (★ 1,935,000) ... 561,567
Sulzbach-Rosenberg ... 17,678
Sulzbach [Saar] (★ Saarbrücken) ... 19,980
Sundern [Sauerland] ... 25,274
Taunusstein (★ Wiesbaden) ... 26,034
Trier (★ 125,000) ... 94,190
Troisdorf (★★ Siegburg) ... 60,267
Tübingen ... 75,333
Tuttlingen ... 30,894
Uelzen ... 35,781
Ulm (★ 210,000) ... 98,604
Unna (★ Essen) ... 57,569
Vaihingen an der Enz (★ Stuttgart) ... 22,508
Varel ... 23,878
Vechta ... 23,905
Velbert (★ Essen) ... 89,261
Verden ... 24,231
Viernheim (★ Mannheim) ... 29,166
Viersen (★★ Mönchengladbach) ... 78,784
Villingen-Schwenningen ... 76,600
Voerde (★ Essen) ... 32,705
Völklingen (★★ Saarbrücken) ... 43,781
Waiblingen (★ Stuttgart) ... 44,522
Walsrode ... 22,531
Waltrop (★ Essen) ... 27,555
Warburg ... 21,742
Warendorf ... 33,283
Warstein ... 27,613
Wedel (★ Hamburg) ... 30,166
Wegberg (★ Mönchengladbach) ... 24,462
Weiden [in der Oberpfalz] ... 42,224
Weil am Rhein (★ Basel, Switzerland) ... 25,914
Weingarten (★ Ravensburg) ... 22,302
Weinheim (★ Mannheim) ... 40,989
Werdohl ... 20,088
Werl ... 25,836
Wermelskirchen (★ Wuppertal) ... 33,905
Werne an der Lippe (★ Essen) ... 27,808
Wesel ... 54,895
Wetter (★ Essen) ... 28,611
Wetzlar (★ 105,000) ... 49,731
Wiesbaden (★ 800,000) ... 267,467
Wilhelmshaven (★ 135,000) ... 97,495
Willich (★ Essen) ... 39,625
Witten (★ Essen) ... 102,195
Wolfenbüttel (★★ Braunschweig) ... 48,976
Wolfsburg ... 122,099
Worms (★★ Mannheim) ... 72,610
Wunstorf (★ Hannover) ... 37,480
Wuppertal (★ 855,000) ... 379,393
Würselen (★ Aachen) ... 33,826
Würzburg (★ 210,000) ... 129,995
Zweibrücken (★ 105,000) ... 33,341

States

Baden-Württemberg ... 9,241,083
Bayern (Bavaria) ... 10,957,544
Berlin, [West] (City) ... 1,848,585
Bremen ... 665,615
Hamburg ... 1,592,447
Hessen (Hesse) ... 5,535,185
Niedersachsen (Lower Saxony) ... 7,216,304
Nordrhein-Westfalen (North Rhinewestphalia) ... 16,703,875
Rheinland-Pfalz (Rhineland-Palatinate) ... 3,623,985
Saarland ... 1,050,837
Schleswig-Holstein ... 2,613,796

Districts

Arnsberg ... 3,577,394
Berlin, [West] (City) ... 1,848,585
Braunschweig ... 1,604,173
Bremen ... 665,615
Darmstadt ... 3,395,976
Detmold ... 1,786,688
Düsseldorf ... 5,057,569
Freiburg ... 1,873,762
Giessen ... 963,382
Hamburg ... 1,592,447
Hannover ... 2,022,840
Karlsruhe ... 2,396,234
Kassel ... 1,175,827
Koblenz ... 1,352,896
Köln ... 3,879,568
Lüneburg ... 1,468,108
Mittelfranken ... 1,515,309
Münster ... 2,402,656
Niederbayern ... 1,010,896
Oberbayern ... 3,687,742
Oberfranken ... 1,039,947
Oberpfalz ... 963,467
Rheinhessen-Pfalz ... 1,800,658
Saarland ... 1,050,837
Schleswig-Holstein ... 2,613,796
Schwaben ... 1,540,912
Stuttgart ... 3,453,655
Trier ... 470,431
Tübingen ... 1,517,432
Unterfranken ... 1,199,271
Weser-Ems ... 2,121,183

GHANA

1984 C ... 12,205,574

Cities and Towns

• ACCRA (★ 1,250,000) ... 859,640
Ashiaman (★ Accra) ... 49,427
Bawku ... 33,900
Bolgatanga ... 31,500
Cape Coast ... 86,620
Ho ... 37,200
Keta ... 12,700
Koforidua ... 54,400
Kumasi (★ 600,000) ... 348,880
Nkawkaw ... 34,100
Nsawam ... 31,900
Obuasi ... 60,100
Oda ... 24,400
Sekondi (★ 175,352) ... 32,355
Tafo (★ Kumasi) ... 50,432
Takoradi (★★ Sekondi) ... 61,527
Tamale (★ 168,091) ... 136,828
Tarkwa ... 22,000
Tema (★★ Accra) ... 99,608
Teshie (★ Accra) ... 62,954
Wa ... 36,000
Winneba ... 26,200
Yendi ... 30,700

GIBRALTAR

1981 C ... 29,648

Cities and Towns

• GIBRALTAR ... 29,648

GREECE / Ellás

1981 C ... 9,740,417

Cities and Towns

Agrínion (★ 45,087) ... 35,774
Aiyáleo (★ Athens) ... 81,906
Aíyion (Aegion) (★ 25,723) ... 20,955
Akharnaí (Acharnae) ... 40,185
Alexandroúpolis ... 34,535
Amaliás ... 14,698
Amaroúsion (★ Athens) ... 48,151
Ampelókipoi (★ Thessaloníki) ... 40,033
Árgos ... 20,702
Árta ... 18,283
• ATHENS (ATHÍNAI) (★ 3,027,331) ... 885,737
Ayía Paraskeví (★ Athens) ... 32,904
Ayía Varvára (★ Athens) ... 29,259
Áyioi Anáryiroi (★ Athens) ... 30,320
Áyios Dhimítrios (★ Athens) ... 51,421
Dháfni (★ Athens) ... 26,887
Dráma ... 36,109
Édhessa (Edessa) ... 16,054
Elevsís (Eleusis) ... 20,320
Ermoúpolis (Syros) (★ 16,595) ... 13,876
Flórina (Phlorina) ... 12,562
Galátsion (★ Athens) ... 50,096
Glifádha (★ Athens) ... 44,018
Ilioúpolis (★ Athens) ... 69,560
Ioánnina ... 44,829
Iráklion (★ Athens) ... 37,833
Iráklion (Candia) (★ 110,958) ... 102,398
Kaisarianí (★ Athens) ... 28,972
Kalámai (★ 43,235) ... 42,075
Kalamariá (★ Thessaloníki) ... 51,676
Kallithéa (★ Athens) ... 117,319
Kardhítsa ... 27,291
Kastoría ... 17,133
Kateríni (★ 39,895) ... 38,404
Kavála ... 56,375
Keratsínion (★ Athens) ... 74,179
Kérkira (Corfu) ... 33,561
Khaïdhárion (★ Athens) ... 47,396
Khalándrion (★ Athens) ... 54,320
Khalkís (Chalcis) ... 44,867
Khaniá (Canea) (★ 61,976) ... 47,451
Khíos (Chios) (★ 29,742) ... 24,070
Kholargós (★ Athens) ... 31,703
Kifisiá (★ Athens) ... 31,876
Komotiní ... 34,051
Koridhallós (★ Athens) ... 61,313
Kórinthos (Corinth) ... 22,658
Kozáni ... 30,994
Lamía ... 41,667
Lárisa ... 102,048
Levádhia (Lebadea) ... 16,864
Mégara ... 17,719
Mitilíni (Mytilene) ... 24,115
Návplion (Nauplia) ... 10,609
Néa Ionía (★ Athens) ... 59,202
Néa Liósia (★ Athens) ... 72,427
Neápolis (★ Thessaloníki) ... 31,464
Néa Smírni (★ Athens) ... 67,408
Níkaia (★ Athens) ... 90,368
Palaión Fáliron (★ Athens) ... 53,273
Pátrai (Patras) (★ 154,596) ... 142,163
Peristérion (★ Athens) ... 140,858
Piraiévs (Piraeus) (★★ Athens) ... 196,389
Pírgos (Pyrgos) ... 21,958
Ródhos (Rhodes) ... 40,392
Salamís ... 20,437
Sérrai ... 45,213
Spárti (Sparta) (★ 14,388) ... 12,975
Thessaloníki (Salonika) (★ 706,180) ... 406,413
Thívai (Thebes) ... 18,712
Tríkala ... 40,857
Trípolis (Tripolitza) ... 21,311
Véroia ... 37,087
Víron (★ Athens) ... 57,880
Vólos (★ 107,407) ... 71,378
Xánthi ... 31,541
Zográfos (★ Athens) ... 84,548

GREENLAND / Kalaallit Nunaat / Gronland

1984 E ... 52,347

Cities and Towns

Angmagssalik ... 1,343
Egedesminde ... 3,245
Godhavn ... 976
• GODTHÅB (NUUK) ... 10,559
Holsteinsborg ... 4,524
Julianehåb ... 2,777
Sukkertoppen ... 3,122
Thule ... 449

GRENADA

1979 E ... 110,100

Cities and Towns

• SAINT GEORGE'S (★ 25,000) ... 7,500

GUADELOUPE

1982 C ... 328,400

Cities and Towns

BASSE-TERRE (★ 26,600) ... 13,656
Capesterre (▲ 17,472) ... 7,572
Les Abymes (★ Pointe-à-Pitre) ... 56,165
• Pointe-à-Pitre (★ 83,000) ... 25,310

C Census. E Official estimate. UE Unofficial estimate.
• Largest city in country.

★ Population or designation of metropolitan area, including suburbs (see headnote).
▲ Population of an entire municipality, commune, or district, including rural area.

GUAM

1980 C 105,979

Cities and Towns

• AGANA (★ 44,000) 896
Tamuning 8,862

GUATEMALA

1981 C 6,054,227

Cities and Towns

Amatitlán 20,407
Antigua Guatemala 15,801
Chimaltenango 14,967
Chiquimula 18,965
Coatepeque 19,307
Cobán 14,152
Escuintla 36,931
• GUATEMALA (★ 1,100,000) 754,243
Huehuetenango 12,422
Mazatenango 20,918
Puerto Barrios 24,235
Quezaltenango 62,719
Retalhuleu 22,001
Tiquisate 12,096
Zacapa 12,482

GUERNSEY

1986 C 55,482

Cities and Towns

• SAINT PETER PORT (★ 36,000) 16,085

GUINEA / Guinée

1980 E 4,830,000

Cities and Towns

• CONAKRY (1979 E) 600,000
Kankan 229,000
Kindia (1979 E) 80,000
Labé 253,000
Mamou (1967 E) 18,000
Nzérékoré (1972 E) 23,000
Siguiri (1967 E) 15,000

GUINEA-BISSAU / Guiné-Bissau

1979 C 777,214

Cities and Towns

• BISSAU 109,486

GUYANA

1983 E 918,000

Cities and Towns

• GEORGETOWN (★ 188,000) 78,500
Linden (1980 C) 30,043
Mackenzie (1982 E) 30,000
New Amsterdam (1982 E) 20,000

HAITI / Haïti

1982 C 5,053,791

Cities and Towns

Cap-Haïtien 64,406
Gonaïves 34,209
Jacmel 13,730
Jérémie 18,493
Les Cayes 34,090
Pétionville (★ Port-au-Prince) 35,333
• PORT-AU-PRINCE (★ 760,000) 684,284
Port-de-Paix 15,540
Saint-Marc 24,165

HONDURAS

1983 E 4,092,000

Cities and Towns

Choluteca 53,800
Comayagua 28,100
Danlí 18,000
El Progreso 53,000
Juticalpa 14,100
La Ceiba 61,400
La Lima (1974 C) 14,631
Puerto Cortés 40,200
San Pedro Sula 344,500
• TEGUCIGALPA 532,500
Tela 27,300

HONG KONG

1981 C 5,021,066

Cities and Towns

Kowloon (★★ Victoria) 799,123
New Kowloon (Xinjiulong) (★★ Victoria) 1,651,064
Sha Tin (★ Victoria) 109,471
Sheung Shui 49,595
Tai Po 39,891
Tsun Wan (★ Victoria) 599,011
Tuen Mun (★ Victoria) 89,901
• VICTORIA (HONG KONG) (XIANGGANG) (★ 4,515,000) 1,183,621
Yuen Long 51,392

HUNGARY / Magyarország

1985 E 10,657,000

Cities and Towns

Ajka 33,937
Baja 40,199
Békés (▲ 22,188) 18,100
Békéscsaba (▲ 70,203) 61,000
• BUDAPEST (★ 2,540,000) 2,071,484
Cegléd (▲ 40,270) 32,800
Csongrád (▲ 21,419) 18,700
Debrecen 208,891
Dunaújváros 61,932
Eger 64,702
Érd (★ Budapest) 44,904
Esztergom 31,901
Gödöllő (★ Budapest) 29,373
Gyöngyös 37,349
Győr 128,252
Gyula (▲ 35,324) 30,400
Hajdúböszörmény (▲ 31,546) 28,200
Hajdúszoboszló 24,177
Hatvan 25,089
Hódmezővásárhely (▲ 54,551) 45,600
Jászberény (▲ 30,983) 24,900
Kaposvár 73,715
Karcag 24,889
Kazincbarcika 38,653
Kecskemét (▲ 101,800) 81,300
Kiskunfélegyháza (▲ 35,735) 27,100
Kiskunhalas (▲ 31,287) 22,800
Komló 30,653
Makó 29,439
Miskolc 211,645
Mohács (▲ 21,473) 18,100
Mosonmagyaróvár 29,939
Nagykanizsa 55,175
Nagykőrös (▲ 27,153) 21,200
Nyíregyháza (▲ 116,414) 90,200
Orosháza (▲ 36,667) 32,100
Ózd 47,577
Pápa 34,573
Pécs 175,477
Salgótarján 49,542
Sopron 56,421
Szeged 178,591
Székesfehérvár 110,203
Szekszárd 38,166
Szentes (▲ 35,778) 31,400
Szolnok 79,619
Szombathely 85,830
Tata 25,658
Tatabánya 76,823
Törökszentmiklós (▲ 24,723) 21,500
Vác 35,777
Várpalota 28,531
Veszprém 63,058
Zalaegerszeg 60,691

Counties

Bács-Kiskun 561,000
Baranya 256,500
Békés 425,000
Borsod-Abaúj-Zemplén 583,400
Budapest (Independent City) 2,072,000
Csongrád 276,400
Debrecen (City) 208,900
Fejér 424,000
Győr (City) 128,300
Győr-Sopron 300,700
Hajdú-Bihar 342,100
Heves 344,000
Komárom 322,000
Miskolc (City) 211,600
Nógrád 235,000
Pécs (City) 175,500
Pest 985,000
Somogy 355,000
Szabolcs-Szatmár 582,000
Szeged (City) 178,600
Szolnok 438,000
Tolna 267,000
Vas 282,000
Veszprém 389,000
Zala 314,000

ICELAND / Ísland

1984 E 240,443

Cities and Towns

Akureyri 13,711
Hafnarfjörður (★ Reykjavík) 12,979
Keflavík 6,907
Kópavogur (★ Reykjavík) 14,546
• REYKJAVÍK (★ 130,722) 88,745

INDIA / Bhārat

1981 C 685,184,692

Cities and Towns

Abohar 86,334
Achalpur (Ellichpur) 81,186
Ādilābād 53,482
Adītyapur (★ Jamshedpur) 53,421
Ādoni 108,939
Agartala 132,186
Āgra (★ 747,318) 694,191
Ahmadābād (★ 2,400,000) 2,059,725
Ahmadnagar (★ 181,210) 143,937
Aijal 74,493
Ajmer 375,593
Akola 225,412
Akot 51,936
Alandur (★ Madras) 97,449
Alīgarh 320,861
Alīpur Duār (★ 71,573) 45,324
Allahābād (★ 650,070) 616,051
Alleppey 169,940
Almora (★ 22,705) 20,758
Alwar 145,795
Amalner 67,516
Ambāla (★ 233,110) 104,565
Ambāla Sadar (★ Ambāla) 80,741
Ambarnāth (★ Bombay) 96,347
Ambāsamudram (★ 52,591) 29,761
Ambattur (★ Madras) 115,901
Āmbūr 66,042
Amrāvati (Amraoti) 261,404
Amreli (★ 58,241) 56,598
Amritsar 594,844
Amroha 112,682
Anakāpalle 73,179
Ānand 83,936
Anantapur 119,531
Arcot (★ 94,363) 38,836
Arkonam 59,405
Arni 49,365
Arrah 125,111
Aruppukkottai 72,245
Asansol (★ 1,050,000) 183,375
Ashoknagar-Kalyangarh (★ Hābra) 55,176
Āttūr 50,517
Aurangābād (★ 316,421) 284,607
Avadi (★ Madras) 124,701
Azamgarh 66,523
Badagara 64,174
Bāgalkot 67,858
Bahraich 99,889
Baidyabāti (★ Calcutta) 70,573
Bālāghāt (★ 53,183) 49,564
Balāngīr 54,943
Balasore 65,779
Ballarpur 61,398
Ballia 61,704
Bālly 147,735
Balrāmpur 46,058
Bālurghāt (★ 112,621) 104,646
Bal'y 54,859
Bānda 72,379
Bangalore (★ 2,950,000) 2,476,355
Bangaon 69,885
Bānkura 94,954
Bānsbāria (★ Calcutta) 77,020
Bānswāra (★ 48,070) 46,749
Bāpatla 55,347
Baranagar (★ Calcutta) 170,343
Bārāsat (★ Calcutta) 66,504
Barauni 56,366
Baraut 46,292
Bareilly (★ 449,425) 386,734
Baripāda (★ 52,989) 40,314
Barmer 55,554
Baroda (Vadodara) (★ 744,881) 734,473
Barrackpore (★ Calcutta) 115,253
Bārsi 72,537
Basīrhāt 81,040
Basti 69,357
Batāla (★ 101,966) 87,135
Beāwar 89,998
Begusarai (★ 68,305) 56,633
Behāla (South Suburban) (★ Calcutta) 378,765
Bela (Pratapgarh) 49,932
Belgaum (★ 300,372) 274,430
Bellary 201,579
Berhampore (★ 102,311) 92,889
Berhampur 162,550
Bettiah 72,167
Betūl 46,293
Bhadrakh 60,600
Bhadrāvati (★ 130,606) 53,551
Bhadrāvati New Town (★★ Bhadrāvati) 77,055
Bhadreswar (★ Calcutta) 58,858
Bhāgalpur 225,062
Bhandāra 56,025
Bharatpur 105,274
Bhatinda (★ 127,363) 124,453
Bhātpāra (★ Calcutta) 260,761
Bhaunagar (★ 308,642) 307,121
Bhavāni (★ 80,472) 28,898
Bhilai (Bhilainagar) (★ 490,214) 290,090
Bhīlwāra 122,625
Bhīmavaram 101,894
Bhind 74,515
Bhiwandi (★ Bombay) 115,298
Bhiwāni 101,277
Bhopāl 671,018
Bhubaneswar 219,211
Bhuj (★ 70,211) 69,693
Bhusāwal (★ 132,142) 123,133
Bīdar 78,856
Bihār 151,343
Bījāpur 147,313
Bijnor 56,713
Bīkaner (★ 287,712) 253,174
Bilāspur (★ 187,104) 147,218
Bīr (Bhir) 80,287
Birlapur (★ 50,831) 20,470
Birnagar (★ 67,066) 14,581
Bishnupur 47,529
Bodhan 50,807
Bodināyakkanūr 59,168
Bokāro Steel City (★ 264,480) 224,099
Bombay (★ 9,950,000) 8,243,405
Botād 50,274
Brajrajnagar 54,033
Broach (Bharuch) (★ 120,524) 110,070
Budaun 93,004
Budge Budge (★ Calcutta) 66,424
Bulandshahr 103,436
Būndi (★ 48,027) 47,736
Burdwān 167,364
Burhānpur 140,896
• Calcutta (★ 11,100,000) 3,305,006
Calicut (Kozhikode) (★ 546,058) 394,447
Cambay 68,791
Cannanore (★ 157,797) 60,904
Chākdaha 59,308
Chakradharpur (★ 44,532) 29,272
Chālisgaon 59,342
Champdāni (★ Calcutta) 76,138
Chandannagar (Chandernagore) (★ Calcutta) 101,925
Chandausi 66,970
Chandīgarh (★ 422,841) 373,789
Chandrapur 115,777
Changanācheri 51,955
Channapatna 50,725
Chāpra 111,564
Chhatarpur 51,959
Chhindwāra 75,178
Chidambaram (★ 62,543) 55,920
Chikmagalūr 60,582
Chilakalūrupet 61,645
Chīrāla 72,040
Chitradurga 74,580
Chittaranjan (★ 61,045) 50,748
Chittoor 86,230
Churu (★ 62,070) 61,811
Cochin (★ 685,836) 513,249
Coimbatore (★ 965,000) 704,514
Cooch Behār (★ 80,101) 62,127
Coonoor (★ 92,242) 44,750
Cuddalore 127,625
Cuddapah 103,125
Cumbum 50,340
Cuttack (★ 327,412) 269,950
Dabgram 76,402
Dabhoi 44,357
Dabra 33,421
Dalhousie (★ 4,189) 2,936
Daltonganj 51,952
Damān 21,003
Damoh (★ 76,758) 75,573
Dānāpur (★ Patna) 58,684
Darbhanga 176,301
Darjeeling 57,603
Datia 49,386
Dāvangere 196,621
Dehra Dūn (★ 293,010) 211,416
Dehra Dūn Cantonment (★ Dehra Dūn) 43,566
Dehri 90,409
Delhi (★ 7,200,000) 4,884,234
Delhi Cantonment (★ Delhi) 85,166
Deoband 51,270
Deoghar (★ 59,120) 52,904
Deolāli (★★ Nāsik) 77,666
Deolāli Cantonment (★ Nāsik) 57,745
Deoria 55,720
Dewās 83,465
Dhamtari 55,797
Dhānbād (★ 825,000) 120,221
Dhār 48,870
Dharmapuri 51,223
Dharmavaram 50,969
Dhorāji (★ 77,716) 76,556
Dhrāngadhra 51,280
Dhubri (★ 45,580) (1971 C) 36,503
Dhule 210,759
Dibrugarh (1971 C) 80,348
Digboi (★ 32,388) (1971 C) 16,538
Dindigul 164,103
Dohad (★ 82,256) 55,256
Dombivli (★ Bombay) 103,222
Dum-Dum (★ Calcutta) 33,604
Durg (★★ Bhilai) 114,637
Durgāpur 311,798
Dwārka 21,375
Elūru (Ellore) 168,154
English Bāzār 79,010
Erode (★ 275,999) 142,252
Etah 53,784
Etāwah 112,174
Faizābād (Fyzabad) (★ 143,167) 101,873
Farīdābād New Township (★ Delhi) 330,864
Farrukhābād (★ 160,796) 145,793
Fatehpur, Rājasthān state 51,084
Fatehpur, Uttar Pradesh state 84,831
Fatehpur Sīkri 17,908
Fīrozābād 202,338
Fīrozpur (Ferozepore) (★ 105,840) 61,162
Gadag 117,368
Gandhidham (★ 61,489) 61,415
Gandhinagar 62,443
Gangāvathi 58,735
Garden Reach (★ Calcutta) 191,107
Gārulia (★ Calcutta) 57,061
Gauhāti (★ 200,377) (1971 C) 123,783
Gaya 247,075
Ghāziābād (★ 287,170) 271,730
Ghāzīpur 60,725
Giridih 65,444
Godhra (★ 86,228) 85,784
Gonda 70,847
Gondal (★ 66,818) 66,096
Gondia 100,423
Gorakhpur (★ 307,501) 290,814
Gudivāda 80,198
Gudiyāttam (★ 80,674) 75,044
Gulbarga 221,325
Guna (★ 64,659) 60,255
Guntakal 84,599
Guntūr 367,699
Gurgaon (★ 100,877) 89,115
Guruvayur (★ 59,467) 17,858
Gwalior (★ 555,862) 539,015
Hābra (★ 129,610) 74,434
Hājīpur 62,520
Haldwāni 77,300
Hālisahar (★ Calcutta) 95,579
Hānsi 50,365
Hanumāngarh 60,071
Hāpur 102,837
Hardoi 67,259
Hardwār (★ 145,946) 114,180
Harihar 52,334
Hassan 71,534
Hāthras 92,962
Hazāribāgh 80,155
Hindupur 55,901
Hinganghāt 59,075
Hisār (★ 137,369) 131,309
Hooghly-Chinsura (★ Calcutta) 125,193
Hoshiārpur 85,648
Hospet (★ 115,351) 90,572
Howrah (★ Calcutta) 744,429
Hubli [-Dhārwār] 527,108
Hyderābād (★ 2,750,000) 2,187,262
Ichalkaranji 133,751
Imphāl 156,622
Indore (★ 850,000) 829,327
Itārsi (★ 69,619) 62,499
Jabalpur (★ 757,303) 614,162
Jabalpur Cantonment (★ Jabalpur) 61,026
Jadabpur (★ Calcutta) 251,968
Jagādhri (★★ Yamunānagar) 43,102
Jagdalpur (★ 63,632) 51,286
Jagtiāl 53,213
Jaipur (★ 1,025,000) 977,165
Jālgaon 145,335
Jālna 122,276
Jalpaiguri 61,743
Jamālpur 78,356
Jammu (★ 223,361) 206,135
Jāmnagar (Navanagar) (★ 317,362) 277,615

C Census. E Official estimate. UE Unofficial estimate.
• Largest city in country.
★ Population or designation of metropolitan area, including suburbs (see headnote).
▲ Population of an entire municipality, commune, or district, including rural area.

Jamshedpur (★ 669,580) 438,385
Jangaon 70,727
Jaora (★ 47,548) 47,129
Jaridih Bazar (★ 101,946) 46,477
Jaunpur 105,140
Jetpur (★ 63,074) 62,806
Jeypore 53,981
Jhānsi (★ 284,141) 246,172
Jharia (★★ Dhanbād) 57,496
Jhārsuguda 54,859
Jīnd 56,748
Jodhpur 506,345
Jorhāt (★ 70,674) (1971 C) 30,247
Jullundur (★ 441,552) 408,186
Junāgadh (★ 120,416) 118,646
Kadaiyanallūr 60,306
Kadiri 52,774
Kaithal 58,385
Kākināda (Cocanada) 226,409
Kālol (★ Ahmadābād) 69,946
Kalyān (★ Bombay) 136,052
Kāmārhāti (★ Calcutta) 234,951
Kambam 50,340
Kamptee (★ Nāgpur) 67,364
Kānchipuram (Conjeeveram)
(★ 145,254) 130,926
Kānchrāpāra (★ Calcutta) 88,798
Kānpur (★ 1,875,000) 1,481,789
Kānpur Cantonment
(★ Kānpur) 90,311
Kapūrthala 50,300
Karād 54,364
Kāraikkudi (★ 100,141) 66,993
Karīmnagar 86,125
Karnāl 132,107
Karūr (★ 93,810) 72,692
Kāsganj 61,402
Kashīpur 51,773
Katihār (★ 122,005) 104,781
Kātwa (★ 44,430) 32,890
Kāvali 48,119
Kayankulam (Kayamkulam) 61,327
Kerkend (★ Dhānbād) 75,186
Khadki (Kirkee) (★ Pune) 80,797
Khāmgaon 61,992
Khammam 98,757
Khandwa 114,725
Khanna 53,761
Kharagpur (★ 232,575) 150,475
Kharagpur Railway Settlement
(★ Kharagpur) 82,100
Khargone 52,749
Khurja 67,119
Kirkee Cantonment 80,835
Kishanganj 51,790
Kishangarh 62,032
Kohīma 34,340
Kolār 65,834
Kolār Gold Fields (★ 144,385) 77,679
Kolhāpur (★ 351,392) 340,625
Konnagar (★ Calcutta) 51,211
Korba 83,387
Kota 358,241
Kot Kapūra 47,550
Kottagūdem 94,894
Kottayam 64,431
Kovilpatti 63,964
Krishnagiri 48,335
Krishnanagar 98,141
Kulti (★★ Asansol) 41,323
Kumbakonam (★ 141,794) 132,832
Kundla (★ 51,431) 49,740
Kurasia (★ 53,015) 12,963
Kurichi (★ Coimbatore) 48,936
Kurnool 206,362
Lakhīmpur 61,003
Lalitpur 55,756
Lātūr 111,986
Leh 8,718
Lucknow (★ 1,060,000) 895,721
Lucknow Cantonment
(★ Lucknow) 59,614
Ludhiāna 607,052
Machilīpatnam (Bandar) 138,530
Madanapalle 54,938
Madgaon (Margao) (★ 64,858) 53,076
Madras (★ 4,475,000) 3,276,622
Madurai (★ 960,000) 820,891
Mahbūbnagar 87,503
Mahuva (★ 56,072) 53,625
Mainpuri 58,928
Mālegaon 245,883
Māler Kotla 65,756
Malkajgiri (★ Hyderābād) 65,776
Mandasor 77,603
Mandya 100,285
Mangalore (★ 306,078) 172,252
Mango (★ Jamshedpur) 67,284
Manjeri 53,959
Manmād 51,439
Mannārgudi 51,738
Mathura (Muttra) (★ 160,995) 147,493
Maunath Bhanjan 86,326
Māyūram 67,675
Meerut (★ 536,615) 417,395
Meerut Cantonment
(★ Meerut) 94,210
Mehsāna (Mahesāna)
(★ 73,024) 72,872
Melappālaiyam (★ Tirunelveli) 57,683
Mettuppālaiyam 59,537
Mhow Cantonment (★ 76,037) 70,130
Midnapore 86,118
Miraj (★★ Sāngli) 105,455
Mirzāpur 127,787
Modinagar (★ 87,665) 78,243
Moga 80,272
Mokameh 51,047
Monghyr 129,260
Morādābād (★ 345,350) 330,051
Morena 69,864
Mormugão 69,684
Morvi 73,327
Motīhāri (★ 63,212) 57,911
Muktsar 50,941
Murwāra (Katni) (★ 123,017) 77,862
Mussoorie (★ 18,233) 16,323
Muzaffarnagar 171,816
Muzaffarpur 190,416
Mysore (★ 479,081) 441,754
Nabadwīp (★ 129,800) 109,108
Nadiād 142,689
Nāgappattinam (★ 90,650) 82,828
Nāgaur 48,005
Nāgda 56,602
Nāgercoil 171,648
Nagīna 50,405
Nāgpur (★ 1,302,066) 1,219,461
Naihāti (★ Calcutta) 114,607
Naini Tāl (★ 26,093) 24,835
Najībābād 55,109
Nalgonda 62,458
Nānded 191,269
Nandurbār 65,394
Nandyāl 88,185
Nangi (★ Calcutta) 54,035
Narasapur 46,033
Narasaraopet 67,032
Nāsik (★ 429,034) 262,428
Navsāri (★ 129,266) 106,793
Nawābganj (★ 62,216) 51,518
Neemuch (★ 68,853) 65,860
Nellore 237,065
NEW DELHI (★★ Delhi) 273,036
Neyveli (★ 98,866) 88,000
Nizāmābād 183,061
North Barrackpore (★ Calcutta) 81,758
North Dum-Dum (★ Calcutta) 96,418
Nowgong (1971 C) 56,537
Ongole 85,302
Ootacamund 78,277
Orai 66,397
Outer Burnpur (★ Asansol) 86,803
Pālakollu 46,146
Pālanpur 61,262
Pālayankottai (★★ Tirunelveli) 87,302
Pālghāt (★ 117,986) 111,245
Pāli 91,568
Pallavaram (★ Madras) 83,901
Palni (★ 68,389) 64,444
Palwal 47,328
Panaji (Panjim) (Nova Goa)
(★ 77,226) 43,165
Pānchur (★ Calcutta) 51,223
Pandharpur 64,380
Pānihāti (★ Calcutta) 205,718
Pānīpat 137,927
Panruti 43,042
Paramagudi 61,149
Parbhani 109,364
Parli 48,946
Pātan 79,196
Pathānkot 110,039
Patiāla (★ 206,254) 205,141
Patna (★ 1,025,000) 776,371
Pattukkottai 49,484
Periyakulam 44,310
Petlād 47,020
Phagwāra (★ 75,961) 72,499
Pīlibhīt 88,548
Pimpri-Chinchwad (★ Pune) 220,966
Pollāchi (★ 114,971) 82,354
Pondicherry (★ 251,420) 162,636
Ponmalai (★ Tiruchchirāppalli) 55,995
Ponnāni 43,226
Ponnur 50,206
Porbandar (★ 133,307) 115,182
Port Blair 49,634
Proddatūr 107,070
Pudukkottai 87,952
Pune (Poona)
(★ 1,775,000) 1,203,351
Pune Cantonment (★ Pune) 85,986
Puri 100,942
Purnea (★ 109,875) 91,144
Purūlia 73,904
Quilon (★ 167,598) 137,943
Rabkavi Banhatti 51,693
Rāe Bareli 89,697
Rāichūr 124,762
Raiganj (★ 66,705) 60,343
Raigarh (★ 69,791) 68,060
Raipur 338,245
Rājahmundry (★ 268,370) 203,358
Rājapālaiyam 101,640
Rajhara-Jharandalli 55,307
Rājkot 445,076
Rāj-Nāndgaon 86,367
Rājpur (★ 60,734) 43,985
Rājpura 58,645
Rāmanāthapuram 45,719
Ramgarh [Cantonment]
(★ 65,268) 41,257
Rāmpur 204,610
Rānāghāt (★ 83,744) 58,356
Rānchī (★ 502,771) 489,626
Rānībennur 58,118
Rānīganj (★ 119,101) 48,702
Ratlām (★ 155,578) 142,319
Ratnāgiri 47,036
Raurkela (★ 322,610) 206,821
Raurkela Civil Township
(★ Raurkela) 96,000
Rewa 100,641
Rewāri 51,562
Rishra (★ Calcutta) 81,001
Robertson Pet (★ Kolār
Gold Fields) 61,099
Rohtak 166,767
Roorkee (★ 79,076) 61,851
Sāgar (★ 207,479) 160,392
Sahāranpur 295,355
Saharsa 57,580
Sahijpur Bogha
(★ Ahmadābād) 65,327
Salem (★ 518,615) 361,394
Sambalpur (★ 162,214) 110,282
Sambhal 108,232
Sāngli (★ 268,988) 152,339
Sāntipur 82,980
Sardarnagar (★ Ahmadābād) 50,128
Sardārshahr (★ 56,388) 55,473
Sasarām 73,457
Sātāra 83,336
Satna (★ 96,667) 90,476
Saunda (★ 99,990) 70,780
Sawai Mādhopur (★ 59,083) 28,139
Secunderābād Cantonment
(★ Hyderābād) 135,994
Sehore 52,190
Seoni 54,017
Serampore (★ Calcutta) 127,304
Shahdol (★ 49,631) 44,342
Shāhjahānpur (★ 205,095) 185,396
Shāmli 51,850
Shikohābād 47,083
Shillong (★ 174,703) 109,244
Shimoga 151,783
Shivpuri 75,738
Sholāpur (★ 514,860) 511,103
Shrirampur 55,491
Sidhpur (★ 52,706) 51,953
Sīkar 102,970
Silchar (1971 C) 52,596
Silīguri 154,378
Simla 70,604
Sindri (★★ Dhānbād) 70,645
Sirsa 89,068
Sītāpur 101,210
Sivakāsi (★ 83,072) 59,827
Siwān 51,284
Sonīpat 109,369
South Dum-Dum (★ Calcutta) 230,266
Sri Gangānagar
(Gangānagar) 123,692
Srīkākulam 68,145
Srikalahasti 51,306
Srīnagar (★ 606,002) 594,775
Srīrangam (★ Tiruchchirāppalli) 64,241
Srīvilliputtūr 61,458
Sūjāngarh 55,546
Sultānpur 48,782
Surat (★ 913,806) 776,583
Surendranagar (★ 130,602) 89,619
Tādepallegūdem 62,574
Tādpatri 53,920
Tāmbaram (★ Madras) 86,923
Tānda 54,474
Tanuku 53,618
Tellicherry (★ 98,704) 75,561
Tenāli 119,257
Tenkāsi 49,214
Thāna (★ Bombay) 309,897
Thānesar 49,052
Thanjāvūr (Tanjore) 184,015
Theni-Allinagaram 53,018
Tindivanam 56,520
Tinsukia (1971 C) 54,911
Tiruchchirāppalli (Trichinopoly)
(★ 609,548) 362,045
Tiruchendūr (★ 68,884) 24,233
Tiruchengodu 53,941
Tirunelveli (Tinnevelly)
(★ 323,344) 128,850
Tirupati 115,292
Tiruppattūr 52,422
Tiruppur (★ 215,859) 165,223
Tiruvannāmalai 89,462
Tiruvottiyūr (★ Madras) 134,014
Titāgarh (★ Calcutta) 104,534
Tonk 77,653
Trichūr (★ 170,122) 77,923
Trivandrum (★ 520,125) 483,086
Tumkūr 108,670
Tuticorin (★ 250,677) 192,949
Udaipur 232,588
Udamalpet 54,852
Udgīr 50,564
Ujjain (★ 282,203) 278,454
Ulhāsnagar (★ Bombay) 273,668
Unnāo 75,983
Upleta 54,907
Uttarpara-Kotrung (★ Calcutta) 79,598
Valparai 115,452
Valsad (Bulsar) (★ Bombay) 54,017
Vāniyambādi (★ 75,042) 59,107
Vārānasi (Benares)
(★ 925,000) 708,647
Vasai (Bassein) (★ 52,398) 34,940
Vellore (★ 274,041) 174,247
Verāval (★ 105,307) 85,048
Vidisha 65,521
Vijayawāda (Bezwada)
(★ 543,008) 454,577
Vikramasingapuram 49,319
Villupuram 77,091
Viramgām 48,275
Virudunagar 68,047
Vishākhapatnam (Vizagapatam)
(★ 603,630) 565,321
Visnagar 46,631
Vizianagaram 114,806
Warangal 335,150
Wardha 88,495
Yamunānagar (★ 160,424) 109,304
Yavatmāl 89,071
Yemmiganur 50,701

States

Andaman and Nicobar
Islands (Ter.) 188,741
Andhra Pradesh 53,549,673
Arunachal Pradesh (Ter.) 631,839
Assam 19,896,843
Bihār 69,914,734
Chandīgarh (Ter.) 451,610
Dādra and Nagar
Haveli (Ter.) 103,676
Delhi (Ter.) 6,220,406
Goa [, Damān and Diu]
(Ter.) 1,086,730
Gujarat 34,085,799
Haryana 12,922,618
Himachal Pradesh 4,280,818
Jammu and Kashmir 5,987,389
Karnataka (Mysore) 37,135,714
Kerala 25,453,680
Lakshadweep (Ter.) 40,249
Madhya Pradesh 52,178,844
Mahārāshtra 62,784,171
Manipur 1,420,953
Meghalaya 1,335,819
Mizoram (Ter.) 493,757
Nāgāland 774,930
Orissa 26,370,271
Pondicherry (Ter.) 604,471
Punjab 16,788,915
Rājasthān 34,261,862
Sikkim 316,385
Tamil Nadu (Madras) 48,408,077
Tripura 2,053,058
Uttar Pradesh 110,862,013
West Bengal 54,580,647

INDONESIA

1980 C 147,490,298

Cities and Towns

Amahai (1961 C) 18,256
Ambon (Amboina)
(▲ 208,898) 111,910
Amuntai (1961 C) 27,383
Balikpapan (▲ 280,675) 208,040
Banda Aceh (Kuturaja) 72,090
Bandung (★ 1,800,000) 1,462,637
Bangil (1961 C) 28,275
Bangkalan (1961 C) 22,514
Banjarmasin 381,286
Bantul (1961 C) 30,572
Banyuwangi (1961 C) 89,303
Baubau (1961 C) 21,060
Bekasi (★ Jakarta) 144,290
Bengkulu 64,783
Binjai 76,464
Blitar 78,503
Blora (1971 C) 53,504
Bogor (★ 560,000) 247,409
Bojonegoro (1971 C) 52,597
Bondowoso (1961 C) 35,760
Brebes (1971 C) 44,456
Bukittinggi 70,771
Ciamis (1961 C) 35,189
Cianjur 105,660
Cilacap 127,020
Cimahi (1971 C) 72,367
Cirebon (★ 275,000) 223,776
Denpasar 159,230
Depok (★ Jakarta) 126,690
Dili (▲ 67,039) 6,890
Ende (1961 C) 26,843
Garut 145,620
Gorontalo 97,628
Gresik (1971 C) 48,561
Indramayu (1961 C) 25,710
• JAKARTA (★ 7,000,000) 6,503,449
Jambi (▲ 230,373) 155,760
Jayapura (Sukarnapura)
(1976 E) 61,054
Jember 171,280
Jepara (1961 C) 18,921
Jombang (1971 C) 45,450
Kandangan (1961 C) 26,112
Kebumen (1961 C) 25,125
Kediri 221,830
Kendari (1961 C) 11,672
Klaten 117,360
Kotabumi (1961 C) 37,496
Krawang (1971 C) 61,361
Kualakapuas (1961 C) 18,573
Kudus 154,480
Kuningan (1961 C) 21,542
Kupang (1971 C) 52,698
Lahat (1971 C) 41,030
Langsa (1971 C) 55,016
Lawang (1961 C) 35,852
Lhokseumawe (1961 C) 28,386
Lumajang (1971 C) 48,995
Madiun (★ 180,000) 150,562
Magelang (★ 160,000) 123,484
Magetan (1961 C) 26,818
Majalengka (1961 C) 14,361
Majene (1961 C) 24,259
Makale (1961 C) 32,578
Malang 511,780
Manado 217,159
Martapura (1971 C) 69,729
Mataram 210,490
Medan (★ 1,450,000) 1,378,955
Mojokerto 68,849
Nganjuk (1961 C) 23,499
Ngawi (1961 C) 29,220
Padang (▲ 480,922) 296,680
Padangpanjang 34,517
Padangsidempuan (1971 C) 49,090
Pakanbaru (1971 C) 186,262
Palangkaraya 60,447
Palembang 787,187
Palopo (1961 C) 29,724
Palu (1961 C) 16,977
Pamekasan (1971 C) 41,416
Pangkalpinang 90,096
Parepare 86,450
Pasuruan (★ 125,000) 95,864
Pati (1971 C) 46,037
Payakumbuh 78,836
Pekalongan (★ 260,000) 132,558
Pemalang (1971 C) 77,672
Pematangsiantar 150,376
Perabumulih (1961 C) 41,951
Pinrang (1961 C) 23,818
Ponorogo (1971 C) 67,711
Pontianak 304,778
Praya (1961 C) 26,729
Probolinggo 100,296
Purbolinggo (1961 C) 22,698
Purwakarta (1971 C) 49,703
Purwokerto 143,790
Purworejo (1971 C) 52,956
Raba (1961 C) 29,881
Rangkasbitung (1961 C) 30,822
Rantauprapat (1961 C) 25,707
Rembang (1961 C) 22,985
Salatiga 85,849
Samarinda (▲ 264,718) 182,470
Sampit (1961 C) 24,876
Semarang (★ 1,050,000) 1,026,671
Serang (1971 C) 56,263
Sibolga 59,897
Sidoarjo (1971 C) 41,254
Singaraja (1971 C) 42,289
Singkawang (1961 C) 35,169
Situbondo (1971 C) 55,348
Solok 31,724
Sragen (1961 C) 25,685
Subang (1971 C) 42,437
Sukabumi (★ 225,000) 109,994
Sumedang (1961 C) 27,891
Sungaipenuh (1961 C) 36,766
Surabaya (★ 2,150,000) 2,027,913
Surakarta (★ 550,000) 469,888
Tangerang (1971 C) 50,893
Tanjungbalai (1981 C) 41,894
Tanjungkarang-Telukbetung
(★ 375,000) 284,275
Tanjungpandan (1961 C) 29,412
Tanjungpinang (1961 C) 37,638
Tarutung (1961 C) 24,998
Tasikmalaya 192,270
Tebingtinggi 92,087
Tegal (★ 340,000) 131,728
Tual (1961 C) 38,403
Tuban (1961 C) 38,575
Tulungagung (1971 C) 68,899
Ujung Pandang (Makasar) 709,038
Watampone (1971 C) 54,720
Yogyakarta (★ 480,000) 398,727

Provinces

Aceh 2,611,271
Bali 2,469,930
Bengkulu 768,064
Irian Jaya 1,173,875

C Census. E Official estimate. UE Unofficial estimate.
• Largest city in country.
★ Population or designation of metropolitan area, including suburbs (see headnote).
▲Population of an entire municipality, commune, or district, including rural area.

Jakarta Raya (Greater Jakarta) 6,503,449
Jambi 1,445,994
Jawa Barat (West Java) 27,453,525
Jawa Tengah (Central Java) 25,372,889
Jawa Timur (East Java) 29,188,852
Kalimantan Barat (West Borneo) 2,486,068
Kalimantan Selatan (South Borneo) 2,064,649
Kalimantan Tengah (Central Borneo) 954,353
Kalimantan Timur (East Borneo) 1,218,016
Lampung 4,624,785
Maluku (Moluccas) 1,411,006
Nusa Tenggara Barat (West Nusa Tenggara) 2,724,664
Nusa Tenggara Timur (East Nusa Tenggara) 2,737,166
Riau 2,168,535
Sulawesi Selatan (South Celebes) 6,062,212
Sulawesi Tengah (Central Celebes) 1,289,635
Sulawesi Tenggara (Tenggara Celebes) 942,302
Sulawesi Utara (North Celebes) 2,115,384
Sumatera Barat (West Sumatra) 3,406,816
Sumatera Selatan (South Sumatra) 4,629,801
Sumatera Utara (North Sumatra) 8,360,894
Timor Timur 555,350
Yogyakarta 2,750,813

IRAN / Īrān

1982 E 40,777,000

Cities and Towns

Ābādān (1976 C) 296,081
Ābādeh 45,000
Āghā Jārī 64,000
Ahar 52,000
Ahar 31,000
Ahvāz 471,000
Āmol 100,000
Andīmeshk 53,000
Arāk 210,000
Ardabīl 222,000
Bābol 96,000
Bakhtarān (Kermānshāh) 532,000
Bam 46,000
Bandar 'Abbās 175,000
Bandar-e Anzalī (Bandar-e Pahlavī) 83,000
Bandar-e Khomeynī (Bandar-e Shāhpūr) 47,000
Bandar-e Māhshahr 88,000
Behbehān 84,000
Behshahr 45,000
Bīrjand 68,000
Bojnūrd 82,000
Borāzjān 53,000
Borūjerd 178,000
Būshehr 121,000
Dezfūl 141,000
Do Gonbadān 47,000
Dow Rūd 52,000
Emāmshahr (Shāhrūd) 68,000
Eşfahān (Isfahan) 927,000
Eslāmābād 71,000
Eslamshahr (★ Tehrān) 108,000
Fasā 67,000
Gonbad-e Qābūs 75,000
Gorgān 114,000
Hamadān 234,000
Īlām 75,000
Jahrom 68,000
Karaj (★ Tehrān) 526,272
Kāshān 110,000
Kāshmar (Turshīz) 40,000
Kāzerūn 63,000
Kermān 239,000
Khomeynishahr (Homāyūnshahr) 98,000
Khorramābād 200,000
Khorramshahr (1976 C) 146,709
Khvoy 103,000
Lāhījān 35,000
Mahābād 63,000
Malāyer 84,000
Marāgheh 90,000
Marand 59,000
Marv Dasht 72,000
Mashhad (Meshed) 1,130,000
Masjed Soleymān 116,000
Mīāndowāb 52,000
Mīāneh 57,000
Nahāvand 45,000
Najafābād 114,000
Neyshābūr 95,000
Orūmīyeh (Reẕā'īyeh) 263,000
Qā'emshahr (Shāhī) 92,000
Qazvīn 244,000
Qom 424,000
Qomsheh 67,000
Qūchān 61,000
Rafsanjān 61,000
Rāmhormoz 53,000
Rasht 260,000
Robāţ Karīm 40,000
Sabzevār 108,000
Salmās (Dīlmān) 44,000
Sanandaj 172,000
Saqqez 76,000
Sārī 125,000
Sāveh 46,000
Semnān 54,000
Shahr Kord 63,000
Shīrāz 800,000
Sīrjān 67,000
Tabrīz 852,000
• TEHRĀN (★ 6,400,000) 5,734,199
Torbat-e Ḩeydarīyeh 62,000
Varāmīn 51,000
Yazd 193,000
Zābol 58,000
Zāhedān 165,000
Zanjān 175,000
Zarrīn Shahr 69,000

IRAQ / Al 'Irāq

1985 E 15,584,987

Cities and Towns

Ad Dīwānīyah (1970 E) 62,300
Al 'Amārah 131,758
Al Fallūjah (1965 C) 38,072
Al Ḩillah (Hilla) 215,249
Al Kūfah (1965 C) 30,862
Al Kūt (Kūt al Imāra) (1965 C) 42,116
An Najaf 242,603
An Nāşirīyah 138,842
Ar Ramādī 137,388
As Samāwah (1965 C) 33,473
As Sulaymānīyah 279,424
Az Zubayr (1965 C) 41,408
• BAGHDĀD (★ 4,000,000) 2,200,000
Ba'qūbah 114,516
Basra (Al Başrah) 616,700
Irbīl 333,903
Karbalā' 184,574
Kirkūk (1970 E) 207,900
Mosul (Al Mawşil) 570,926
Sāmarrā' (1965 C) 24,746
Tall 'Afar (1965 C) 36,837

IRELAND / Éire

1981 C 3,443,405

Cities and Towns

An Uaimh (Navan) (★ 11,136) 4,124
Arklow (Inbhear Mór) 8,646
Athlone (Áth Luain) (★ 14,426) 9,444
Balbriggan (★ 6,708) 5,582
Bray (Brí Chualann) (★ Dublin) 22,853
Carlow (Ceatharlach) (★ 13,164) 11,722
Castlebar (Caisleán an Bharraigh) (★ 7,423) 6,409
Clonmel (Cluain Meala) (★ 14,808) 12,407
Cobh (★ 8,439) 6,587
Cork (Corcaigh) (★ 185,000) 136,344
Drogheda (DroicheadÁtha) (★ 23,615) 23,247
Droichead Nua(★ 10,716) 5,780
• DUBLIN (BAILE ÁTHA CLIATH) (★ 1,140,000) 525,882
Dundalk (Dún Dealgan) (★ 29,135) 25,663
Dún Laoghaire (★ Dublin) 54,496
Ennis (Inis) (★ 14,640) 6,223
Enniscorthy (Inis Coirthe) (★ 7,261) 5,014
Galway (Gaillimh) (★ 41,861) 37,835
Kilkenny (Cill Choinnigh) (★ 16,886) 9,466
Killarney (Cill Áirne) (★ 9,083) 7,693
Letterkenny (★ 7,992) 6,444
Limerick (Luimneach) (★ 82,000) 60,736
Lucan (★ Dublin) 11,763
Mallow (Mala) (★ 7,482) 6,572
Monaghan (Muineachán) (★ 6,275) 6,177
Mullingar (Muileann Cearr) (★ 11,703) 7,854
Naas (Nás na Ríogh) (★ Dublin) 8,345
Nenagh (Aonach Urmhumhan) (★ 5,871) 5,717
Portlaoise (Portlaoghise) (★ 7,756) 4,049
Shannon 7,998
Sligo (Sligeach) (★ 18,002) 17,232
Swords (★ Dublin) 11,138
Thurles (Durlas Éile) (★ 7,644) 7,352
Tipperary (Tiobrad Árann) (★ 5,169) 4,984
Tralee (Tráighlí) (★ 17,035) 16,495
Tuam (Tuaim) (★ 6,093) 4,366
Tullamore (Tulach Mhór) (★ 8,724) 7,901
Waterford (Port Láirge) (★ 39,636) 38,473
Wexford (Loch Garman) (★ 15,364) 11,417

Counties

Carlow 39,820
Cavan 53,855
Clare 87,567
Cork 402,465
Donegal 125,112
Dublin 1,003,164
Galway 172,018
Kerry 122,770
Kildare 104,122
Kilkenny 70,806
Laoighis 51,171
Leitrim 27,609
Limerick 161,661
Longford 31,140
Louth 88,514
Mayo 114,766
Meath 95,419
Monaghan 51,192
Offaly 58,312
Roscommon 54,543
Sligo 55,474
Tipperary 135,261
Waterford 88,591
Westmeath 61,523
Wexford 99,081
Wicklow 87,449

Historic Provinces

Connacht 424,410
Leinster 1,790,521
Munster 998,315
Ulster 230,159

ISLE OF MAN

1986 C 64,282

Cities and Towns

Castletown 3,019
• DOUGLAS (★ 28,500) 20,368
Peel 3,660
Ramsey 5,778

ISRAEL / Yisra'el / Isrā'īl

1984 E 4,141,400

Cities and Towns

'Afula 22,700
'Akko (★ Haifa) 37,700
Ashdod 68,900
Ashqelon 54,700
Bat Yam (★ Tel Aviv-Yafo) 131,200
Be'er Sheva' (Beersheba) 114,300
Bene Beraq (★ Tel Aviv-Yafo) 100,400
Dimona 26,600
Elat (Elath) 18,800
Giv'atayim (★ Tel Aviv-Yafo) 46,600
Ḩadera 40,000
Haifa (Ḩefa) (★ 435,000) 224,700
Herzliyya (★ Tel Aviv-Yafo) 66,100
Hod HaSharon (★ Tel Aviv-Yafo) 22,100
Ḩolon (★ Tel Aviv-Yafo) 137,800
JERUSALEM (YERUSHALAYIM) (AL-QUDS)(★ 475,000) 446,500
Karmi'el (Carmiel) 18,000
Kefar Sava (★ Tel Aviv-Yafo) 47,500
Lod (Lydda) (★ Tel Aviv-Yafo) 41,400
Nahariyya 28,600
Nazareth (Naẕerat) (★ 73,000) 46,300
Naẕerat 'Illit (★ Nazareth) 25,100
Nes Ẕiyyona (★ Tel Aviv-Yafo) 16,000
Netanya (★ Tel Aviv-Yafo) 107,200
Or Yehuda (★ Tel Aviv-Yafo) 19,800
Petaḩ Tiqwa (★ Tel Aviv-Yafo) 128,300
Qiryat Atta (★ Haifa) 34,200
Qiryat Bialik (★ Haifa) 31,800
Qiryat Gat 26,800
Qiryat Motzkin (★ Haifa) 28,100
Qiryat Ono (★ Tel Aviv-Yafo) 22,000
Qiryat Shemona 15,700
Qiryat Yam (★ Haifa) 30,600
Ra'ananna (★ Tel Aviv-Yafo) 42,500
Ramat Gan (★ Tel Aviv-Yafo) 116,500
Ramat HaSharon (★ Tel Aviv-Yafo) 34,100
Ramla (★ Tel Aviv-Yafo) 43,200
Reḩovot (★ Tel Aviv-Yafo) 70,000
Rishon leẔiyyon (★ Tel Aviv-Yafo) 109,600
Taiyibe 18,100
• Tel Aviv-Yafo (Tel Aviv-Jaffa) (★ 1,650,000) 323,400
Tiberias (Teverya) 29,500
Tirat Karmel (★ Haifa) 15,600
Umm el Faḩm 21,300
Yavne (★ Tel Aviv-Yafo) 17,500

Districts

Central 871,700
Haifa 588,600
Jerusalem 495,000
Northern 670,200
Southern 501,700
Tel Aviv 1,014,200

ISRAELI OCCUPIED TERRITORIES

1984 E 1,361,500

Cities and Towns

Bethlehem (Bayt Laḩm) (1971 E) 25,000
• Gaza (Ghazzah) (1967 C) 118,272
Hebron (Al Khalīl) (1971 E) 43,000
Jabālyah (1967 C) 43,604
Janīn (1971 E) 20,000
Jericho (Arīḩā) (1967 C) 6,829
Jerusalem (Al-Quds) (★ Jerusalem, Israel) (1976 E) 90,000
Khān Yūnis (1967 C) 52,997
Nābulus (1971 E) 64,000
Rafaḩ (1967 C) 49,812

Territories

Gaza Strip 511,500
Golan Heights 21,400
West Bank 828,600

ITALY / Italia

1981 C 56,243,935

Cities and Towns

Abano Terme 16,320
Acerra (★ Naples) 31,700
Acireale (▲ 47,888) 29,400
Adrano 33,393
Afragola (★ Naples) 57,564
Agrigento 51,931
Alassio 13,130
Alba 31,050
Albano Laziale (★ Rome) 22,100
Alberobello 9,778
Alcamo 42,059
Alessandria 100,518
Alghero (▲ 36,383) 30,400
Altamura 51,328
Amalfi 6,052
Ancona 106,421
Andria 83,319
Anzio 27,094
Aosta 37,682
Arezzo 91,535
Ascoli Piceno 54,193
Assisi (▲ 24,440) 19,000
Asti 76,950
Augusta 38,900
Avellino 56,120
Aversa (★ Naples) 50,525
Avezzano (▲ 33,509) 29,100
Avola 29,173
Bagheria 39,867
Barcellona [Pozzo di Gotto] (▲ 36,869) 25,400
Bari (★ 450,000) 370,781
Barletta 83,719
Bassano del Grappa 38,262
Battipaglia (▲ 40,470) 32,100
Belluno 36,513
Benevento (▲ 61,443) 51,900
Bergamo (★ 340,000) 121,846
Biella 53,572
Bisceglie 45,899
Bitonto 49,616
Bollate (★ Milan) 42,159
Bologna (★ 530,000) 455,853
Bolzano (Bozen) 104,606
Bordighera (▲ 11,896) 9,500
Brescia 206,460
Bressanone (Brixen) (▲ 16,109) 12,200
Bresso (★ Milan) 32,644
Brindisi 88,947
Busto Arsizio (★ Milan) 79,769
Cagliari (★ 300,000) 232,785
Caltagirone 35,682
Caltanissetta (▲ 60,713) 54,000
Camaiore (▲ 30,293) 22,100
Campobasso 48,291
Canicattì 31,952
Canosa [di Puglia] 30,363
Cantù 36,754
Capannoli (▲ 42,552) 35,700
Capua 18,053
Carbonia 32,130
Carpi (▲ 60,507) 52,400
Carrara (★★ Massa) 68,460
Casale Monferrato 40,871
Cascina 35,511
Caserta 66,754
Casoria (★ Naples) 68,355
Cassino (▲ 31,139) 26,300
Castel Gandolfo (★ Rome) 3,600
Castellammare di Stabia (★ Naples) 70,317
Castelvetrano 30,577
Catania (★ 515,000) 378,521
Catanzaro 100,637
Cattolica 15,522
Cava de'Tirreni (★ Salerno) 44,600
Cefalù (▲ 13,073) 11,100
Cerignola (▲ 50,682) 44,700
Cesano Maderno (★ Milan) 31,727
Cesena (▲ 89,640) 67,600
Cesenatico (▲ 20,056) 15,800
Chiavari 29,632
Chieri (▲ 30,905) 26,300
Chieti 55,207
Chioggia (▲ 53,566) 38,200
Chivasso 26,430
Ciampino (★ Rome) 31,471
Cinisello Balsamo (★ Milan) 80,323
Cittadella (▲ 17,215) 7,000
Città di Castello (▲ 37,242) 28,400
Civitanova Marche (▲ 36,052) 31,500
Civitavecchia 45,836
Collegno (★ Turin) 46,408
Cologno Monzese (★ Milan) 52,305
Como (★ 160,000) 95,183
Conegliano (▲ 35,846) 29,400
Corato 41,138
Corsico (★ Milan) 42,807
Cortina d'Ampezzo 7,806
Cortona (▲ 22,281) 2,900
Cosenza (★ 140,000) 105,806
Crema 34,610
Cremona 80,758
Crotone 58,281
Cuneo 55,385
Desio (★ Milan) 32,664
Domodossola 20,069
Eboli 30,787
Empoli 44,961
Enna 27,705
Ercolano (Resina) (★ Naples) 57,495
Erice 25,274
Este 18,052
Faenza (▲ 55,003) 39,700
Fano (▲ 52,255) 43,200
Fasano (▲ 35,310) 22,600
Favara 32,793
Fermo (▲ 34,337) 26,300
Ferrara (▲ 150,265) 123,200
Fiesole (★ Florence) 14,774
Florence (Firenze) (★ 650,000) 453,293
Foggia 157,126
Foligno (▲ 52,484) 46,200
Forlì (▲ 109,815) 91,900
Francavilla Fontana 32,588
Frascati (★ Rome) 18,728
Frattamaggiore (★ Naples) 38,103
Frosinone 44,688
Gaeta 22,605
Gallarate (★ Milan) 46,915
Gela 74,789
Genoa (Genova) (★ 830,000) 760,300
Giugliano in Campania (★ Naples) 43,471
Gorizia 41,325
Gravina [in Puglia] 36,097
Grosseto (▲ 69,556) 61,500
Grottaglie 27,888
Grugliasco (★ Turin) 34,473
Gubbio (▲ 31,986) 9,800
Guidonia [Montecelio] (★ Rome) 50,990
Iesi (Jesi) (▲ 41,097) 34,900
Iglesias 30,117
Imola (▲ 60,010) 47,800
Imperia 41,838
Isernia (▲ 18,794) 14,300
Ivrea 27,694
L'Aquila 63,465
La Spezia (★ 188,000) 115,215
Latina (▲ 92,674) 81,000
Lecce 91,265
Lecco 51,349
Legnago 27,051
Legnano (★ Milan) 49,308
Lentini 31,330
Licata 40,050
Limbiate (★ Milan) 32,724
Lissone (★ Milan) 30,019
Livorno (Leghorn) 175,371
Lodi 42,873
Loreto (▲ 10,622) 5,900
Lucca 91,097

C Census. E Official estimate. UE Unofficial estimate.
• Largest city in country.

★ Population or designation of metropolitan area, including suburbs (see headnote).
▲ Population of an entire municipality, commune, or district, including rural area.

Lucera (▲ 33,221) 28,400
Lugo (▲ 34,042) 20,000
Macerata (▲ 43,847) 37,200
Maddaloni (▲ 32,994) 25,900
Magenta 23,694
Manduria 29,675
Manfredonia (▲ 52,674) 45,500
Mantova 60,932
Marino (★ Rome) 29,762
Marsala (▲ 79,093) 46,300
Martina [Franca] (▲ 42,790) 31,500
Massa (★ 145,000) 65,726
Matera 51,000
Mazara del Vallo 43,636
Merano (Meran) 33,508
Messina 255,890
• Milan (Milano) (★ 3,775,000) 1,634,638
Milazzo (▲ 30,399) 20,300
Modena 179,933
Modica (▲ 45,769) 30,100
Molfetta 65,951
Moncalieri (★ Turin) 61,740
Monfalcone 30,277
Monopoli (▲ 43,424) 29,400
Monreale 24,054
Montecatini Terme 21,505
Montepulciano (▲ 14,087) 9,400
Monte Sant'Angelo 16,500
Monza (★ Milan) 122,103
Naples (Napoli) (★ 2,765,000) 1,210,503
Nardò (▲ 28,433) 22,300
Nettuno (▲ 28,872) 24,900
Nicastro (Lamezia Terme) (▲ 63,990) 30,700
Nichelino (★ Turin) 44,218
Nocera Inferiore (▲ 47,698) 40,100
Nola (▲ 30,979) 23,700
Novara 101,635
Novi Ligure 30,835
Nuoro 35,903
Oristano 29,085
Orvieto (▲ 22,509) 16,800
Otranto 4,811
Paderno Dugnano (★ Milan) 39,140
Padova (★ 270,000) 231,337
Pagani 31,584
Palermo 699,691
Parma 176,750
Partinico 27,805
Paternò 45,144
Pavia 85,056
Perugia 142,522
Pesaro 90,147
Pescara 131,345
Piacenza 108,177
Piazza Armerina 20,990
Pietrasanta 25,139
Pinerolo 35,862
Piombino 39,389
Pisa 104,334
Pistoia (▲ 93,516) 83,600
Poggibonsi 26,539
Pompei (★ Naples) 13,500
Pontedera 28,043
Pordenone 51,369
Portici (★ Naples) 79,259
Portoferraio 10,755
Portofino 742
Potenza 65,388
Pozzuoli (★ Naples) 61,300
Prato (★ 202,000) 158,797
Ragusa (▲ 63,898) 53,000
Rapallo 28,318
Ravello (▲ 2,314) 1,400
Ravenna (▲ 137,597) 101,000
Reggio di Calabria 171,324
Reggio nell'Emilia 129,893
Rho (★ Milan) 50,740
Riccione 31,271
Rieti (▲ 43,045) 38,500
Rimini 126,949
Riva [del Garda] 13,011
Rivoli (★ Turin) 49,146
ROME (ROMA) (★ 3,115,000) 2,830,569
Rosignano Marittimo 29,671
Rovereto 33,042
Rovigo 51,708
Salerno (★ 235,000) 157,243
Salsomaggiore Terme 17,750
San Benedetto del Tronto 44,464
San Donà di Piave (▲ 31,825) 22,300
San Gimignano (▲ 7,377) 2,700
San Giorgio a Cremano (★ Naples) 61,721
San Remo (▲ 60,787) 50,200
San Severo 54,273
Santa Maria [Capua Vetere] 32,252
Sarno (▲ 30,583) 20,700
Saronno 36,747
Sassari 118,158
Sassuolo 39,931
Savona (★ 115,000) 75,069
Scandicci (★ Florence) 53,974
Schio 35,596
Sciacca (▲ 34,294) 30,600
Senigallia (▲ 40,108) 34,100
Seregno (★ Milan) 37,653
Sesto [Fiorentino] (★ Florence) 44,869
Sesto San Giovanni (★ Milan) 94,738
Sestri Levante 21,416
Settimo Torinese (★ Turin) 44,024
Siena 61,888
Siracusa 117,689
Sondrio 22,775
Sora (▲ 27,390) 15,500
Sorrento (▲ 42,900) 17,301
Spoleto (▲ 36,839) 31,600
Sulmona (▲ 24,212) 21,600
Taormina 10,085
Taranto 242,774
Taurianova (▲ 16,372) 12,400
Teramo (▲ 50,864) 40,300
Termini Imerese 25,680
Terni 111,401
Terracina (▲ 37,328) 28,000
Tivoli (★ Rome) 50,969
Todi (▲ 16,905) 3,800
Torre Annunziata (★ Naples) 57,097
Torre del Greco (★ Naples) 102,890
Torremaggiore 17,112
Tortona 28,806
Trani 44,235
Trapani (▲ 71,430) 61,900
Trento 98,833
Treviglio 25,741
Treviso 87,069
Trieste 251,380
Turin (Torino) (★ 1,600,000) 1,103,520
Udine (★ 126,000) 101,264
Urbino (▲ 15,918) 12,800
Varese 90,285
Velletri (▲ 41,114) 26,800
Venice (Venezia) (★ 415,000) 332,775
Verbania 32,589
Vercelli 51,975
Verona 261,208
Viareggio 58,136
Vibo Valentia (▲ 30,751) 24,700
Vicenza 113,931
Vigevano 65,228
Villa San Giovanni (▲ 12,558) 9,300
Viterbo (▲ 57,830) 49,400
Vittoria 50,220
Vittorio Veneto 30,028
Voghera 42,639

Regions

1984 ESTIMATE

Abruzzi 1,244,403
Basilicata (Lucania) 617,265
Calabria 2,116,749
Campania 5,607,718
Emilia-Romagna 3,947,140
Friuli-Venezia-Giulia 1,224,221
Lazio (Latium) 5,080,060
Liguria 1,778,024
Lombardia (Lombardy) 8,885,224
Marche (Marches) 1,424,378
Molise 332,667
Piemonte (Piedmont) 4,411,921
Puglia (Apulia) 3,978,058
Sardegna (Sardinia) 1,628,690
Sicilia (Sicily) 5,051,413
Toscana (Tuscany) 3,580,589
Trentino-Alto Adige 877,205
Umbria 814,942
Valle d'Aosta 113,587
Veneto (Venetia) 4,366,244

Provinces

1984 ESTIMATE

Agrigento 483,989
Alessandria 457,815
Ancona 437,604
Aosta 113,587
Arezzo 313,537
Ascoli Piceno 357,094
Asti 212,613
Avellino 443,426
Bari 1,498,529
Belluno 218,504
Benevento 294,250
Bergamo 906,399
Bologna 922,423
Bolzano 433,229
Brescia 1,026,918
Brindisi 402,508
Cagliari 749,942
Caltanissetta 292,849
Campobasso 239,642
Caserta 788,100
Catania 1,042,832
Catanzaro 764,527
Chieti 379,426
Como 781,629
Cosenza 766,219
Cremona 330,646
Cuneo 548,363
Enna 195,875
Ferrara 376,561
Firenze (Florence) 1,199,988
Foggia 695,047
Forlì 606,444
Frosinone 473,834
Genova (Genoa) 1,019,140
Gorizia 143,006
Grosseto 220,672
Imperia 223,854
Isernia 93,025
L'Aquila 296,866
La Spezia 238,896
Latina 453,028
Lecce 793,749
Livorno 347,108
Lucca 384,428
Macerata 294,176
Mantova 375,054
Massa-Carrara 205,503
Matera 206,464
Messina 681,719
Milano (Milan) 3,991,521
Modena 596,505
Napoli (Naples) 3,041,808
Novara 504,769
Nuoro 276,758
Oristano 158,339
Padova 814,820
Palermo 1,234,091
Parma 398,938
Pavia 506,599
Perugia 588,353
Pesaro e Urbino 335,504
Pescara 291,883
Piacenza 276,063
Pisa 389,422
Pistoia 265,493
Pordenone 276,691
Potenza 410,801
Ragusa 284,238
Ravenna 355,530
Reggio di Calabria 586,003
Reggio nell'Emilia 414,676
Rieti 144,607
Roma (Rome) 3,735,020
Rovigo 252,145
Salerno 1,040,134
Sassari 443,651
Savona 296,134
Siena 254,438
Siracusa 403,559
Sondrio 175,708
Taranto 588,225
Teramo 276,228
Terni 226,589
Torino (Turin) 2,298,841
Trapani 432,261
Trento 443,976
Treviso 728,262
Trieste 274,673
Udine 529,851
Varese 790,750
Venezia (Venice) 839,088
Vercelli 389,520
Verona 780,195
Vicenza 733,230
Viterbo 273,571

IVORY COAST / Côte d'Ivoire

1979 E 7,920,000

Cities and Towns

Abengourou (1975 C) 31,239
• ABIDJAN (1980 E) 1,500,000
Agboville (1975 C) 27,192
Bouaké 230,000
Daloa 100,000
Danané (1975 C) 19,872
Dimbokro (1975 C) 30,986
Divo (1975 C) 37,896
Gagnoa (1975 C) 42,362
Grand-Bassam (1975 C) 25,808
Korhogo (1975 C) 47,657
Man 100,000
YAMOUSSOUKRO (1975 C) 35,585

JAMAICA

1982 C 2,190,357

Cities and Towns

• KINGSTON (★ 740,000) 586,930
Mandeville 34,502
May Pen 40,962
Montego Bay 70,265
Ocho Rios 6,094
Port Antonio 12,285
Portmore (★ Kingston) 66,976
Savanna-la-Mar 14,912
Spanish Town (★ Kingston) 89,097

JAPAN / Nihon

1985 C 121,047,196

Cities and Towns

Abashiri 44,285
Abiko (★ Tōkyō) 111,661
Ageo (★ Tōkyō) 178,589
Aioi 39,868
Aizu-wakamatsu 118,144
Akashi (★ Ōsaka) 263,365
Akigawa (★ Tōkyō) 45,762
Akishima (★ Tōkyō) 97,544
Akita 296,381
Akō 52,376
Amagasaki (★ Ōsaka) 509,115
Amagi (▲ 43,575) 31,600
Anan (▲ 60,752) 48,100
Anjō 133,061
Annaka (▲ 44,601) 34,500
Aomori 294,050
Arao (★ Ōmuta) 62,570
Arida (▲ 35,401) 29,600
Asahikawa 363,630
Asaka (★ Tōkyō) 94,432
Ashibetsu (▲ 30,017) 25,500
Ashikaga 167,656
Ashiya (★ Ōsaka) 87,127
Atami 49,374
Atsugi (★ Tōkyō) 175,596
Ayabe (▲ 41,906) 31,800
Ayase (★ Tōkyō) 71,146
Beppu 134,782
Bibai (▲ 37,411) 29,400
Bisai (★ Nagoya) 56,234
Chiba (★ Tōkyō) 788,920
Chichibu 61,013
Chigasaki (★ Tōkyō) 185,029
Chikugo (▲ 43,359) 35,600
Chikushino (★ Fukuoka) 63,242
Chino (▲ 47,275) 26,800
Chiryū (★ Nagoya) 50,506
Chita (★ Nagoya) 70,013
Chitose 73,610
Chōfu (★ Tōkyō) 191,076
Chōshi (▲ 87,884) 77,900
Daitō (★ Ōsaka) 122,440
Dazaifu (★ Fukuoka) 57,737
Ebetsu (★ Sapporo) 90,328
Ebina (★ Tōkyō) 93,160
Eniwa (▲ 48,305) 33,800
Fuchū (★ Tōkyō) 201,972
Fuchū 47,751
Fuji (★ 370,000) 214,451
Fujieda (★ Shizuoka) 111,987
Fujiidera (★ Ōsaka) 65,257
Fujimi (★ Tōkyō) 85,698
Fujinomiya (★★ Fuji) 112,642
Fujioka (▲ 57,083) 46,900
Fujisawa (★ Tōkyō) 328,387
Fuji-yoshida 54,796
Fukaya (▲ 89,123) 71,600
Fukuchiyama (▲ 65,995) 56,200
Fukui 250,261
Fukuoka (★ 1,750,000) 1,160,402
Fukuroi (▲ 49,480) 40,700
Fukushima 270,752
Fukuyama 360,264
Funabashi (★ Tōkyō) 506,967
Furukawa (▲ 60,718) 48,400
Fussa (★ Tōkyō) 51,481
Futtsu (▲ 56,777) 48,200
Gamagōri 85,580
Gifu 411,740
Ginowan 69,206
Gobō (▲ 30,446) 24,800
Gose (★ Ōsaka) 32,900
Gosen (▲ 40,260) 27,900
Goshogawara (▲ 49,538) 34,500
Gotemba 74,882
Gushikawa (▲ 51,354) 44,900
Gyōda 79,359
Habikino (★ Ōsaka) 111,396
Hachinohe 241,428
Hachiōji (★ Tōkyō) 426,650
Hadano (★ Tōkyō) 141,806
Hagi 52,741
Hakodate 319,190
Hamada 51,070
Hamakita (▲ 77,227) 68,000
Hamamatsu 514,118
Hanamaki (▲ 69,885) 54,500
Handa (★ Nagoya) 92,883
Hannō (★ Tōkyō) 66,550
Haramachi (▲ 48,413) 40,300
Hashima 59,760
Hasuda (★ Tōkyō) 34,800
Hatogaya (★ Tōkyō) 55,424
Hatsukaichi (★ Hiroshima) 52,020
Hekinan 63,778
Higashihiroshima (★ Hiroshima) 84,718
Higashikurume (★ Tōkyō) 110,079
Higashimatsuyama 70,425
Higashimurayama (★ Tōkyō) 123,794
Higashiōsaka (★ Ōsaka) 522,798
Higashiyamato (★ Tōkyō) 69,879
Hikari (★ Tokuyama) 49,245
Hikone 94,205
Himeji (★ 660,000) 452,916
Himi (▲ 62,110) 52,300
Hino (★ Tōkyō) 156,006
Hirakata (★ Ōsaka) 382,257
Hiratsuka (★ Tōkyō) 229,976
Hirosaki (▲ 176,082) 134,800
Hiroshima (★ 1,575,000) 1,044,129
Hisai (▲ 39,143) 34,900
Hita (▲ 65,730) 57,900
Hitachi 206,075
Hitoyoshi (▲ 42,292) 35,600
Hōfu 118,074
Honjō, Saitama pref. (▲ 56,492) 49,200
Hōya (★ Tōkyō) 91,563
Hyūga 59,159
Ibara (▲ 37,212) 26,700
Ibaraki (★ Ōsaka) 250,468
Ichihara (★ Tōkyō) 237,618
Ichikawa (★ Tōkyō) 397,806
Ichinomiya (★★ Nagoya) 257,392
Ichinoseki (▲ 60,942) 49,200
Iida (▲ 92,402) 73,200
Iizuka (★ 110,000) 81,868
Ikeda (★ Ōsaka) 101,682
Ikoma (★ Ōsaka) 86,296
Imabari 125,116
Imaichi (▲ 53,113) 44,000
Imari (▲ 62,044) 50,700
Ina (▲ 59,010) 48,600
Inagi (★ Tōkyō) 50,749
Inazawa (★ Nagoya) 83,200
Innoshima (▲ 37,239) 32,100
Inuyama (★ Nagoya) 68,723
Iruma (★ Tōkyō) 118,603
Isahaya (▲ 88,374) 76,600
Ise (Uji-yamada) 105,455
Isehara (★ Tōkyō) 77,765
Isesaki 112,458
Ishigaki (▲ 41,181) 27,300
Ishinomaki 122,674
Ishioka (▲ 49,055) 41,300
Itami (★ Ōsaka) 182,731
Itō 70,195
Itoigawa (▲ 35,797) 27,700
Iwai (▲ 42,177) 29,100
Iwaki (Taira) (1984 C) 350,566
Iwakuni 111,831
Iwakura (★ Nagoya) 42,507
Iwamizawa (▲ 81,665) 73,100
Iwata 80,811
Iwatsuki (★ Tōkyō) 100,904
Iyo-mishima 38,603
Izumi (▲ 40,085) 30,500
Izumi (★ Ōsaka) 137,633
Izumi (★ Sendai) 124,216
Izumi-ōtsu (★ Ōsaka) 67,757
Izumi-sano (★ Ōsaka) 91,563
Izumo (▲ 80,748) 68,000
Joetsu 130,659
Jōyō (★ Ōsaka) 81,849
Kadoma (★ Ōsaka) 140,545
Kaga 68,631
Kagoshima 530,496
Kainan (★ Wakayama) 50,779
Kaizuka (★ Ōsaka) 79,591
Kakamigahara 124,464
Kakegawa (▲ 68,723) 55,600
Kakogawa (★ Ōsaka) 227,312
Kamagaya (★ Tōkyō) 85,705
Kamaishi 60,005
Kamakura (★ Tōkyō) 175,490
Kameoka (▲ 76,206) 66,500
Kameyama 35,510
Kamifukuoka (★ Tōkyō) 57,641
Kamo (★ 35,959) 28,500
Kanazawa 430,480
Kani (★ Nagoya) 6,910
Kanonji (▲ 45,571) 38,300
Kanoya (▲ 76,031) 60,200
Kanuma (▲ 88,079) 73,200
Karatsu (▲ 78,746) 70,100
Kariya (★ Nagoya) 112,402
Karuizawa 15,050
Kasai 52,107
Kasaoka (▲ 60,594) 53,500
Kashihara (★ Ōsaka) 112,881
Kashiwa (★ Tōkyō) 273,130
Kashiwara (★ Ōsaka) 73,251
Kashiwazaki (▲ 86,020) 73,350
Kasuga (★ Fukuoka) 75,554
Kasugai (★ Nagoya) 256,991
Kasukabe (★ Tōkyō) 171,889
Katano (★ Ōsaka) 64,205
Katsuta 102,768
Kawachi-nagano (★ Ōsaka) 91,261
Kawagoe (★ Tōkyō) 285,435
Kawaguchi (★ Tōkyō) 403,012
Kawanishi (★ Ōsaka) 136,376
Kawanoe 38,538
Kawasaki (★ Tōkyō) 1,088,611
Kazo (▲ 50,538) 41,200
Kazuno 44,499
Kesennuma 68,139
Kimitsu (▲ 84,311) 71,900
Kiryū 131,268
Kisarazu 120,201
Kishiwada (★ Ōsaka) 185,735
Kita-ibaraki (▲ 51,034) 45,700
Kitakami (▲ 56,741) 46,200
Kitakyūshū (★ 1,525,000) 1,056,400
Kitami 107,280
Kitamoto (★ Tōkyō) 58,114
Kiyose (★ Tōkyō) 65,067

C Census. E Official estimate. UE Unofficial estimate.
• Largest city in country.
★ Population or designation of metropolitan area, including suburbs (see headnote).
▲Population of an entire municipality, commune, or district, including rural area.

Kobayashi (▲ 40,976) ... 27,300
Kōbe (★★ Ōsaka) ... 1,410,843
Kōchi ... 312,253
Kodaira (★ Tōkyō) ... 158,673
Kōfu ... 202,405
Koga (★ Tōkyō) ... 57,539
Koganei (★ Tōkyō) ... 104,684
Kokubu ... 40,934
Kokubunji (★ Tōkyō) ... 95,469
Komae (★ Tōkyō) ... 73,646
Komaki (★ Nagoya) ... 113,284
Komatsu ... 106,047
Komatsushima (▲ 44,000) ... 38,300
Komoro (▲ 43,704) ... 26,200
Kōnan (★ Nagoya) ... 92,048
Kōnosu (★ Tōkyō) ... 60,565
Kōriyama ... 301,672
Kosai (▲ 41,372) ... 27,700
Koshigaya (★ Tōkyō) ... 253,483
Kudamatsu (★★ Tokuyama) ... 54,446
Kuki (★ Tōkyō) ... 58,635
Kumagaya ... 143,496
Kumamoto ... 555,722
Kunitachi (★ Tōkyō) ... 64,881
Kurashiki ... 413,644
Kurayoshi (▲ 52,349) ... 43,000
Kure (★★ Hiroshima) ... 226,489
Kurobe (▲ 36,135) ... 24,900
Kuroiso ... 49,742
Kurume ... 222,848
Kusatsu (★ Ōsaka) ... 87,543
Kushiro ... 214,545
Kuwana (★ Nagoya) ... 94,730
Kyōto (★★ Ōsaka) ... 1,479,125
Machida (★ Tōkyō) ... 321,182
Maebashi ... 277,319
Maizuru ... 98,779
Marugame ... 74,273
Masuda (▲ 54,050) ... 46,200
Matsubara (★ Ōsaka) ... 136,455
Matsudo (★ Tōkyō) ... 427,479
Matsue ... 140,000
Matsumoto ... 197,348
Matsuyama ... 426,646
Matsuzaka (▲ 116,886) ... 104,200
Mihara ... 85,975
Miki (★ Ōsaka) ... 74,527
Minamata (▲ 36,520) ... 31,700
Minamiashigara ... 41,706
Minō (★ Ōsaka) ... 114,770
Minokamo (▲ 41,701) ... 37,200
Misato (★ Tōkyō) ... 107,963
Misawa (▲ 41,426) ... 34,500
Mishima (★★ Numazu) ... 99,600
Mitaka (★ Tōkyō) ... 166,175
Mito ... 228,987
Mitsuke (▲ 42,545) ... 37,400
Miura (★ Tōkyō) ... 44,300
Miyako ... 61,654
Miyakonojō (▲ 132,099) ... 107,600
Miyazaki ... 279,118
Mizunami (▲ 40,078) ... 32,500
Mizusawa (▲ 57,256) ... 47,800
Mobara (▲ 76,931) ... 66,500
Mombetsu ... 32,163
Mooka (▲ 57,261) ... 43,500
Moriguchi (★ Ōsaka) ... 159,402
Morioka ... 235,469
Moriyama (▲ 53,053) ... 47,300
Mukō (★ Ōsaka) ... 52,216
Munakata ... 60,972
Murakami ... 33,325
Muroran (★ 195,000) ... 136,209
Musashi-murayama (★ Tōkyō) ... 60,930
Musashino (★ Tōkyō) ... 138,810
Mutsu ... 49,292
Nabari ... 56,474
Nagahama ... 55,532
Nagano ... 336,967
Nagaoka ... 183,756
Nagaokakyō (★ Ōsaka) ... 75,242
Nagareyama (★ Tōkyō) ... 124,682
Nagasaki ... 449,382
Nagoya (★ 4,800,000) ... 2,116,350
Naha ... 303,680
Nakama (★ Kitakyūshū) ... 50,294
Nakatsu (▲ 66,258) ... 58,000
Nakatsugawa (▲ 53,277) ... 46,900
Nanao ... 50,581
Nankoku (▲ 47,553) ... 36,000
Nara (★ Ōsaka) ... 327,702
Narashino (★ Tōkyō) ... 136,365
Narita ... 77,178
Naruto (▲ 64,330) ... 56,600
Natori (★ Sendai) ... 43,200
Naze ... 49,764
Nemuro ... 40,675
Neyagawa (★ Ōsaka) ... 258,230
Nichinan (▲ 51,967) ... 45,000
Niigata ... 475,633
Niihama ... 132,192
Niitsu (▲ 63,846) ... 55,600
Niiza (★ Tōkyō) ... 129,284
Nikkō ... 21,705
Nishinomiya (★ Ōsaka) ... 421,267
Nishio (▲ 91,930) ... 81,900
Nishiwaki ... 38,770
Nobeoka ... 136,381
Noboribetsu (★ Muroran) ... 58,372
Noda (★ Tōkyō) ... 105,937
Nōgata ... 64,479
Noshiro (▲ 59,167) ... 50,500
Numata (▲ 47,177) ... 38,400
Numazu (★ 495,000) ... 210,484
Obihiro ... 162,930
Ōbu (★ Nagoya) ... 66,696
Ōda (▲ 38,239) ... 29,400
Ōdate (▲ 71,794) ... 60,900
Odawara ... 185,947
Ōfunato ... 39,300
Oga (▲ 36,950) ... 30,900
Ōgaki ... 145,909
Ōita ... 390,105
Ojiya (▲ 44,204) ... 35,200
Ōkawa ... 47,837
Okaya ... 61,750
Okayama ... 572,423
Okazaki ... 284,996
Okegawa (★ Tōkyō) ... 61,499
Okinawa ... 101,205
Ōmagari (▲ 41,543) ... 32,500
Ōme (★ Tōkyō) ... 110,830
Ōmi-hachiman (★ Ōsaka) ... 63,794
Ōmiya (★ Tōkyō) ... 373,015
Ōmura (▲ 69,472) ... 60,800
Ōmuta (★ 225,000) ... 159,423
Ōno (▲ 41,927) ... 33,500
Ono ... 45,686
Onoda (★ Ube) ... 46,364
Ōnojō (★ Fukuoka) ... 69,431
Onomichi ... 100,642
Ōsaka (★ 16,450,000) ... 2,636,260
Ōta ... 133,670
Ōtake ... 34,760
Otaru (★★ Sapporo) ... 172,490
Ōtawara (▲ 49,540) ... 37,100
Ōtsu (★ Ōsaka) ... 234,547
Ōtsuki ... 34,915
Owari-asahi (★ Nagoya) ... 57,415
Oyama (▲ 134,242) ... 113,100
Rumoi ... 35,542
Ryōtsu (▲ 20,412) ... 14,700
Ryūgasaki (▲ 48,857) ... 40,300
Sabae ... 61,452
Saga ... 168,254
Sagamihara (★ Tōkyō) ... 482,778
Saijō (▲ 56,515) ... 50,400
Saiki ... 54,709
Sakado (★ Tōkyō) ... 87,586
Sakai (★ Ōsaka) ... 818,368
Sakaide ... 66,082
Sakaiminato ... 37,351
Sakata (▲ 101,392) ... 85,800
Saku (▲ 59,975) ... 48,400
Sakura (★ Tōkyō) ... 109,000
Sakurai ... 59,011
Sanda (★ Ōsaka) ... 34,400
Sanjō ... 86,325
Sano ... 80,753
Sapporo (★ 1,900,000) ... 1,542,979
Sasebo ... 250,635
Satte (▲ 51,462) ... 45,800
Sawara (▲ 49,780) ... 36,800
Sayama (★ Tōkyō) ... 144,366
Seki ... 64,148
Sendai, Kagoshima pref. (▲ 71,441) ... 57,800
Sendai, Miyagi pref. (★ 1,175,000) ... 700,248
Sennan (★ Ōsaka) ... 60,062
Seto ... 124,625
Settsu (★ Ōsaka) ... 86,332
Shibata (▲ 77,219) ... 62,800
Shibukawa (1981 C) ... 47,814
Shijōnawate (★ Ōsaka) ... 50,354
Shiki (★ Tōkyō) ... 58,935
Shimabara (▲ 46,061) ... 39,500
Shimada (▲ 72,388) ... 63,200
Shimizu (★★ Shizuoka) ... 242,166
Shimminato (★ Takaoka) ... 41,707
Shimodate (▲ 63,957) ... 52,400
Shimonoseki (★★ Kitakyūshū) ... 269,167
Shingū ... 38,230
Shinjō (▲ 43,033) ... 33,500
Shiogama (★ Sendai) ... 61,825
Shiojiri (▲ 55,956) ... 44,500
Shirakawa (▲ 44,679) ... 39,100
Shiroishi (▲ 42,262) ... 34,300
Shizuoka (★ 975,000) ... 468,362
Sōja (▲ 51,238) ... 43,500
Sōka (★ Tōkyō) ... 194,204
Suita (★ Ōsaka) ... 348,946
Sukagawa (▲ 58,785) ... 44,100
Sukumo (▲ 26,255) ... 21,500
Sumoto (▲ 44,563) ... 38,500
Susono (★ Numazu) ... 45,149
Suwa ... 52,330
Suzaka (▲ 53,610) ... 44,500
Suzuka ... 164,937
Tachikawa (★ Tōkyō) ... 146,531
Tagajō (★ Sendai) ... 54,436
Tagawa ... 59,730
Tajimi (★ Nagoya) ... 84,829
Takaishi (★ Ōsaka) ... 66,974
Takamatsu ... 327,001
Takaoka (★ 220,000) ... 175,780
Takarazuka (★ Ōsaka) ... 194,273
Takasago (★ Ōsaka) ... 91,434
Takasaki ... 231,764
Takatsuki (★ Ōsaka) ... 348,783
Takayama ... 65,033
Takefu ... 69,148
Takehara (▲ 36,286) ... 32,000
Takikawa (▲ 52,005) ... 46,400
Tama (★ Tōkyō) ... 122,131
Tamana (▲ 46,114) ... 35,900
Tamano ... 76,957
Tanabe (▲ 70,827) ... 59,800
Tanashi (★ Tōkyō) ... 71,333
Tatebayashi (▲ 75,141) ... 65,500
Tateyama (▲ 56,035) ... 47,100
Tatsuno (★ Himeji) ... 41,157
Tendō (▲ 55,123) ... 42,800
Tenri (▲ 69,130) ... 59,700
Tenryū (▲ 25,008) ... 21,900
Toba ... 28,363
Tochigi ... 86,289
Toda (★ Tōkyō) ... 76,960
Tōkai (★ Nagoya) ... 95,278
Tōkamachi (▲ 48,005) ... 39,700
Toki ... 65,308
Tokoname (★ Nagoya) ... 53,077
Tokorozawa (★ Tōkyō) ... 275,165
Tokushima ... 257,886
Tokuyama (★ 250,000) ... 112,638
• TŌKYŌ (★ 27,700,000) ... 8,353,674
Tomakomai ... 158,058
Tomioka (▲ 48,552) ... 37,300
Tondabayashi (★ Ōsaka) ... 102,610
Toride (★ Tōkyō) ... 78,609
Tosa-shimizu (▲ 23,015) ... 20,600
Tosu ... 55,788
Tottori ... 137,060
Towada (▲ 61,294) ... 46,000
Toyama ... 314,111
Toyoake (★ Nagoya) ... 57,969
Toyohashi (▲ 322,142) ... 287,700
Toyokawa ... 107,430
Toyonaka (★ Ōsaka) ... 413,219
Toyooka ... 47,711
Toyota ... 308,106
Tsu ... 150,692
Tsubame ... 44,650
Tsuchiura ... 120,175
Tsuruga ... 65,670
Tsuruoka (▲ 100,199) ... 87,900
Tsushima (★ Nagoya) ... 58,728
Tsuyama (▲ 86,835) ... 77,000
Ube (★ 230,000) ... 174,854
Ueda (▲ 116,178) ... 102,300
Ueno (▲ 60,811) ... 51,800
Uji (★ Ōsaka) ... 165,411
Uozu ... 49,824
Urasoe ... 81,612
Urawa (★ Tōkyō) ... 377,233
Urayasu (★ Tōkyō) ... 93,756
Usa (▲ 52,216) ... 39,500
Usuki (▲ 39,719) ... 34,200
Utsunomiya ... 405,384
Uwajima ... 71,379
Wakayama (★ 495,000) ... 401,357
Wakkanai ... 51,854
Wakō (★ Tōkyō) ... 55,212
Warabi (★ Tōkyō) ... 70,407
Yachiyo (★ Tōkyō) ... 142,188
Yaizu (★ Shizuoka) ... 108,557
Yamagata ... 245,159
Yamaguchi (▲ 124,213) ... 107,400
Yamato (★ Tōkyō) ... 177,669
Yamato-kōriyama (★ Ōsaka) ... 89,624
Yamato-takada (★ Ōsaka) ... 65,223
Yame (▲ 40,286) ... 33,000
Yanai (▲ 37,413) ... 25,300
Yao (★ Ōsaka) ... 276,397
Yashio (★ Tōkyō) ... 67,635
Yatsushiro (▲ 108,790) ... 88,700
Yawata (★ Ōsaka) ... 72,338
Yawatahama (▲ 41,600) ... 33,000
Yōkaichi ... 39,741
Yokkaichi ... 263,003
Yokohama (★★ Tōkyō) ... 2,992,644
Yokosuka (★ Tōkyō) ... 427,087
Yokote (▲ 43,266) ... 34,800
Yonago ... 131,794
Yonezawa (▲ 93,725) ... 82,800
Yono (★ Tōkyō) ... 71,598
Yotsukaidō (★ Tōkyō) ... 67,007
Yūbari ... 31,665
Yūki (▲ 52,286) ... 30,500
Yukuhashi (▲ 65,527) ... 58,900
Yuzawa (▲ 37,078) ... 22,000
Zama (★ Tōkyō) ... 99,994
Zentsūji (▲ 38,630) ... 28,500
Zushi (★ Tōkyō) ... 57,656

Prefectures

Aichi ... 6,455,121
Akita ... 1,254,010
Aomori ... 1,524,442
Chiba ... 5,148,150
Ehime ... 1,529,978
Fukui ... 817,639
Fukuoka ... 4,719,225
Fukushima ... 2,080,293
Gifu ... 2,028,534
Gumma ... 1,921,271
Hiroshima ... 2,819,177
Hokkaidō ... 5,679,432
Hyōgo ... 5,278,062
Ibaraki ... 2,725,004
Ishikawa ... 1,152,326
Iwate ... 1,433,606
Kagawa ... 1,022,567
Kagoshima ... 1,819,258
Kanagawa ... 7,431,621
Kōchi ... 839,800
Kumamoto ... 1,837,750
Kyōto ... 2,586,455
Mie ... 1,747,314
Miyagi ... 2,176,290
Miyazaki ... 1,175,547
Nagano ... 2,136,921
Nagasaki ... 1,593,966
Nara ... 1,304,965
Niigata ... 2,478,463
Ōita ... 1,250,217
Okayama ... 1,916,839
Okinawa ... 1,179,115
Ōsaka ... 8,668,114
Saga ... 880,018
Saitama ... 5,863,669
Shiga ... 1,155,843
Shimane ... 794,585
Shizuoka ... 3,574,677
Tochigi ... 1,866,065
Tokushima ... 834,906
Tōkyō ... 11,828,262
Tottori ... 616,025
Toyama ... 1,118,364
Wakayama ... 1,087,191
Yamagata ... 1,261,666
Yamaguchi ... 1,601,629
Yamanashi ... 832,824

JERSEY

1981 C ... 72,970

Cities and Towns

• SAINT HELIER (★ 45,000) ... 24,941

JORDAN / Al Urdunn

1984 E ... 2,595,100

Cities and Towns

Al 'Aqabah ... 33,500
Al Karak (1979 C) ... 11,805
Al Mafraq ... 25,200
• 'AMMĀN (★ 1,250,000) ... 777,500
Ar Ramthā ... 32,400
Ar Ruṣayfah (★ 'Ammān) ... 61,300
As Salṭ ... 39,400
Az Zarqā' ... 265,700
Irbid ... 136,200
Ma'ān (1979 C) ... 11,308
Ma'dabā ... 33,700

KAMPUCHEA / Kâmpŭchéa Prâchéathipâtéyy

1981 E ... 5,756,141

Cities and Towns

Batdambang (1962 C) ... 38,780
Kampong Cham (1962 C) ... 28,532
• PHNOM PENH ... 400,000

KENYA

1979 C ... 15,327,061

Cities and Towns

Eldoret ... 50,503
Kakamega ... 32,025
Kisumu ... 152,643
Machakos ... 84,320
Meru ... 72,049
Mombasa ... 341,148
• NAIROBI ... 827,775
Nakuru ... 92,851
Nyeri ... 35,753
Thika ... 41,324

KIRIBATI

1978 C ... 56,213

Cities and Towns

BAIRIKI ... 1,956
• Bikenibeu ... 3,971

KOREA, NORTH / Chosŏn-minjujuŭi-inmin-konghwaguk

1981 E ... 18,317,000

Cities and Towns

Aoji-ri (1944 C) ... 39,616
Chŏngjin ... 490,000
Haeju (1967 E) ... 115,000
Hamhŭng (1970 E) ... 150,000
Hŭngnam (1976 E) ... 260,000
Kaesŏng (1976 E) ... 240,000
Kilchu (1944 C) ... 30,026
Kimchaek (Sŏngjin) (1967 E) ... 265,000
Najin (1944 C) ... 34,338
Nampo (Chinnampo) (1967 E) ... 130,000
Ongjin (1949 C) ... 32,965
Pukchŏng (1944 C) ... 30,709
• PYŎNGYANG (★ 1,600,000) (1980 E) ... 1,283,000
Sariwŏn (1944 C) ... 42,957
Sinŭiju (1970 E) ... 300,000
Songnim (1944 C) ... 53,035
Tanchŏn (1944 C) ... 32,761
Wŏnsan (1970 E) ... 350,000

Provinces

1972 ESTIMATE

Chagang-do (Jagang) ... 759,000
Hamgyŏng-namdo (South Hamgyeong) ... 1,923,000
Hamgyŏng-pukto (North Hamgyeong) ... 1,545,000
Hwanghae-namdo (South Hwanghae) ... 1,489,000
Hwanghae-pukto (North Hwanghae) ... 1,111,000
Kaesŏng (Gaeseong) (City) ... 235,000
Kangwŏn-do (Gangweon) ... 1,220,000
P'yŏngan-namdo (South Pyeongan) ... 2,222,000
P'yŏngan-pukto (North Pyeongan) ... 1,761,000
P'yŏngyang (Pyeongyang) ... 1,843,000
Yanggang-do ... 460,000

KOREA, SOUTH / Taehan-min'guk

1983 E ... 39,951,000

Cities and Towns

Andong (▲ 111,152) (1982 E) ... 93,000
Anyang (★ Seoul) (1982 E) ... 274,093
Bucheon (★ Seoul) ... 340,000
Changwŏn (1982 E) ... 130,862
Chechŏn (▲ 96,343) (1982 E) ... 66,700
Cheju (▲ 182,005) (1982 E) ... 99,200
Chinhae (1982 E) ... 122,864
Chinju ... 219,000
Chŏnan (▲ 137,143) (1982 E) ... 96,300
Chŏngju (1982 E) ... 76,082
Chŏngŭp (▲ 66,009) (1980 C) ... 45,200
Chŏnju ... 305,000
Chunchŏn (1982 E) ... 162,373
Chungju (▲ 119,563) (1982 E) ... 83,100
Chungmu (1982 E) ... 81,010
Inchŏn (★★ Seoul) (1985 C) ... 1,387,000
Iri (▲ 177,770) (1982 E) ... 147,600
Kangnŭng (▲ 123,159) (1982 E) ... 80,900
Kimchŏn (▲ 78,542) (1982 E) ... 59,400
Kimhae (1982 E) ... 72,741
Kumi (1982 E) ... 118,593
Kŭmsŏng (1982 E) ... 60,251
Kunsan (1982 E) ... 175,700
Kwangju ... 843,000
Kwangmyŏng (★ Seoul) (1982 E) ... 191,431
Kyŏngju (▲ 127,948) (1982 E) ... 76,500
Masan ... 424,000
Mokpo ... 228,000
Namwŏn (▲ 59,660) (1982 E) ... 41,200
Pohang (▲ 245,000) ... 200,500
Pusan (1985 C) ... 3,517,000
Pyŏngtaek (1980 C) ... 60,842
Samchŏnpo (▲ 72,741) (1982 E) ... 43,700
Sangju (▲ 48,979) (1980 C) ... 26,200
Seongnam (★ Seoul) ... 417,000
• SEOUL (SŎUL) (★ 13,400,000) (1985 C) ... 9,646,000
Sŏgwipo (1982 E) ... 79,260
Sŏkcho (1982 E) ... 71,083
Songjŏng (▲ 50,800) (1980 C) ... 32,300
Songtan (1982 E) ... 64,470
Sunchŏn (▲ 116,323) (1982 E) ... 78,100
Suwŏn (★ Seoul) ... 374,000
Taebaek (1982 E) ... 115,008
Taegu (1985 C) ... 2,031,000
Taejŏn ... 800,000
Tongduchŏn (1982 E) ... 67,763
Tonghae (1982 E) ... 101,746

C Census. E Official estimate. UE Unofficial estimate.
• Largest city in country.

★ Population or designation of metropolitan area, including suburbs (see headnote).
▲ Population of an entire municipality, commune, or district, including rural area.

Ŭijŏngbu (★ Seoul) (1982 E) .. 141,147
Ulsan (▲ 510,000) 345,700
Wŏnju (1982 E) 143,546
Yongchan (1982 E) 55,280
Yŏngju (▲ 84,769) (1982 E).....60,800
Yŏsu (1982 E) 172,681

Provinces

Cheju Do (Jeju) 478,000
Chŏlla Namdo (South Jeonia)................... 3,818,000
Chŏlla Pukto (North Jeonia).. 2,303,000
Ch'ungch'ŏng Namdo (South Chungcheong)............ 3,038,000
Ch'ungch'ŏng Pukto (North Chungcheong)............ 1,425,000
Inchŏn (City) 1,220,000
Kangwŏn Do (Gangweon) ... 1,825,000
Kyŏnggi Do (Gyeonggi) 4,358,000
Kyŏngsang Namdo (South Gyeongsang) 3,518,000
Kyŏngsang Pukto (North Gyeongsang) 3,129,000
Pusan (Busan) (City)......... 3,395,000
Sŏul (Seoul) (City)........... 9,204,000
Taegu (City).................. 1,959,000

KUWAIT / Al Kuwayt

1980 C 1,355,827

Cities and Towns

Abraq Khīṭān (★ Kuwait).........48,138
Al Farwānīyah (★ Kuwait)........57,716
Al Jahrah (★ Kuwait)............66,977
As-Sālimīyah (★ Kuwait) 145,729
Ḩawallī (★ Kuwait) 152,270
• Kuwait (Al Kuwayt) (★ 1,085,000)................60,365

LAOS / Lao

1981 E 3,811,000

Cities and Towns

Louangphrabang (1973 E).......43,000
Pakxe (1973 E) 44,860
Savannakhet (1973 E) 50,691
• VIANGCHAN (VIENTIANE)..... 210,000

LEBANON / Al Lubnān

1982 E 2,637,000

Cities and Towns

Ba'labakk (Baalbek)..............24,000
• BEIRUT (BAYRŪT) (★ 1,675,000)............... 509,000
Jūniyah..........................29,000
Ṣaydā (Sidon).................. 105,000
Tripoli (Ṭarābulus)............. 198,000
Tyre (Ṣūr) (1970 E) 12,500
Zaḩlah 45,000

LESOTHO

1976 C 1,213,960

Cities and Towns

• MASERU.........................14,686

LIBERIA

1981 E 1,911,000

Cities and Towns

Buchanan (1974 C) 23,994
• MONROVIA.................... 243,243

LIBYA / Lībīya

1981 E 3,096,000

Cities and Towns

Benghazi (Banghāzī) 367,600
Darnah (1973 E) 21,000
Misrātah 116,900
• TRIPOLI (ṬARĀBULUS) 858,500
Ṭubruq (Tobruk) 71,800
Zāwiyat al Bayḑā' (Beida)........96,300

LIECHTENSTEIN

1985 E 27,076

Cities and Towns

• VADUZ 4,927

LUXEMBOURG

1981 C 364,606

Cities and Towns

Differdange (★ Esch-sur-Alzette) 8,588
Dudelange 14,074
Esch-sur-Alzette (★ 96,000) 25,142
• LUXEMBOURG (★ 112,000).....78,924

MACAO / Macau

1984 E 350,000

Cities and Towns

• MACAO 350,000

MADAGASCAR / Madagasikara

1982 E 9,230,000

Cities and Towns

• ANTANANARIVO 700,000
Antsirabe (▲ 91,000).............48,000
Antsiranana 100,000
Fianarantsoa 120,000
Mahajanga 85,000
Manakara (1975 C) 20,037
Marovoay (1975 C) 16,303
Toamasina 100,000
Toliara 55,000

MALAWI / Malaŵi

1981 E 6,123,000

Cities and Towns

• Blantyre 229,000
LILONGWE 103,000
Mzuzu 20,000
Zomba 25,000

MALAYSIA

1980 C 13,486,433

Cities and Towns

Alor Setar 71,682
Ayer Itam (★ George Town) 36,538
Batu Pahat 66,022
Bukit Mertajam 28,408
Butterworth (★★ George Town)..........................76,651
George Town (Pinang) (★ 525,000)................. 250,578
Ipoh 300,325
Johor Baharu (★ Singapore) ... 249,880
Kajang 30,012
Kampar 24,978
Kelang 196,209
Keluang 51,778
Kota Baharu 170,559
Kota Kinabalu (Jesselton)........59,500
• KUALA LUMPUR (★ 1,250,000)............... 937,817
Kuala Terengganu 186,608
Kuantan 136,625
Kuching 74,229
Kulim 27,067
Melaka (Malacca) 88,073
Miri 53,799
Muar (Bandar Maharani) 65,775
Petaling Jaya (★ Kuala Lumpur) 218,331
Port Dickson 24,035
Sandakan 73,144
Segamat 34,493
Seremban 136,252
Sibu 86,860
Sungai Petani 45,987
Taiping 149,292
Tawau 45,249
Telok Anson (Teluk Intan) 49,711

States

Johor 1,600,946
Kedah 1,102,639
Kelantan 888,831
Melaka 453,163
Negeri Sembilan 563,799
Pahang 790,537
Perak 1,773,644
Perlis 147,376
Pinang 911,668
Sabah (North Borneo) 1,003,487
Sarawak 1,294,846
Selangor 1,475,400
Terengganu 542,280
Wilayah Persekutuan (Federal Territory) 937,817

MALDIVES

1985 C 181,453

Cities and Towns

• MALE 46,334

MALI

1980 E 6,982,000

Cities and Towns

• BAMAKO 502,000
Djénné (1976 C) 10,275
Gao 36,000
Goundam (1976 C) 10,468
Kati (1976 C)....................24,831
Kayes 51,000
Kita (1976 C)....................17,491
Koulikoro (1976 C)...............16,134
Koutiala (1976 C) 27,156
Mopti 63,000
Nioro du Sahel (1976 C).........11,717
San (1976 C).....................23,378
Ségou 77,000
Sikasso 56,000
Tombouctou (Timbuktu) (1976 C) 19,166

MALTA

1984 E 331,997

Cities and Towns

Birkirkara (★ Valletta) 18,041
Ħamrun (★ Valletta)..............14,087
Qormi (★ Valletta)...............17,130
Rabat (Victoria), Gozo I. 5,522
Sliema (★ Valletta) 20,071
• VALLETTA (★ 215,000) 14,013

MARTINIQUE

1982 C 328,566

Cities and Towns

• FORT-DE-FRANCE (★ 116,017)....................99,844
Le Lamentin (▲ 26,367) 7,207
Saint-Pierre 5,438
Schœlcher (★ Fort-de-France) ... 18,094

MAURITANIA / Mauritanie / Mūrītāniyā

1982 C 1,727,000

Cities and Towns

Aleg (1962 C)..................... 1,360
Atar 19,000
'Ayoûn el 'Atroûs (1962 C) 4,877
Fdérik (1976 C)...................18,000
Kaédi (1979 E)...................22,000
Kiffa (1976 C)....................17,000
Néma (1962 C) 3,893
Nouadhibou 24,400
• NOUAKCHOTT 150,000
Rosso 18,500
Zouîrât 22,000

MAURITIUS

1984 E 1,023,934

Cities and Towns

Beau Bassin-Rose Hill (★ Port Louis) 93,684
Curepipe (★ Port Louis)..........64,370
• PORT LOUIS (★ 415,000) 136,812
Quatre Bornes (★ Port Louis) ...65,699
Vacoas-Phoenix (★ Port Louis)...55,456

MAYOTTE

1978 C 47,246

Cities and Towns

• DZAOUDZI (★ 6,979) 4,147

MEXICO / México

1980 C 67,395,826

Cities and Towns

Acámbaro 38,224
Acaponeta 15,272
Acapulco [de Juárez] 301,902
Acayucan 32,398
Actopan 16,215
Agua Dulce 27,242
Agua Prieta 28,862
Aguascalientes................ 293,152
Alvarado 22,633
Ameca 25,946
Amecameca [de Juárez] 23,508
Apatzingán 55,522
Apizaco 30,498
Arandas 19,835
Arriaga 17,848
Atlixco 53,207
Atotonilco el Alto 21,276
Autlán de Navarro 27,926
Caborca 33,696
Cadereyta Jiménez 26,539
Campeche 128,434
Cananea 19,551
Cancún 33,273
Cárdenas, Michoacán state 26,217
Cárdenas, Tabasco state 34,078
Celaya 141,675
Cerro Azul 29,082
Chetumal 56,709
Chihuahua 385,603
Chilpancingo [de los Bravos] 67,498
Cholula [de Rivadabia] (★ Puebla de Zaragoza) 26,748
Ciudad Acuña 38,898
Ciudad Camargo 29,433
Ciudad del Carmen 72,489
Ciudad de Naucalpan de Juárez (★ Mexico City)............. 723,723
Ciudad de Valles 65,609
Ciudad Guzmán 60,938
Ciudad Hidalgo 32,311
Ciudad Ixtepec 13,302
Ciudad Jiménez 23,786
Ciudad Juárez (★★ El Paso, Tex., U.S.A.)................. 544,496
Ciudad Lerdo (★ Torreón) 33,470
Ciudad Madero (★ Tampico)... 132,444
Ciudad Mante 70,647
Ciudad Melchor Múzquiz 22,115
Ciudad Mendoza (★ Orizaba) 25,330
Ciudad Obregón 165,572
Ciudad Serdán 12,824
Ciudad Victoria 140,161
Coatepec 28,499
Coatzacoalcos 127,170
Colima 86,044
Comalcalco 25,021
Comitán [de Domínguez] 27,374
Córdoba 99,972
Cortazar 35,330
Cosamaloapan [de Carpio] 29,457
Cuauhtémoc 43,546
Cuautla 24,153
Cuernavaca 192,770
Culiacán 304,826
Delicias 65,504
Dolores Hidalgo 23,143
Durango 257,915
Ecatepec de Morelos (★ Mexico City)............. 741,821
El Grullo 16,595
Empalme 31,555
Encarnación de Díaz 14,795
Ensenada 120,483
Escuinapa [de Hidalgo] 20,247
Etzatlán 10,309
Fortín de las Flores 14,046
Fresnillo [de González Echeverría] 56,066
Garza García (★ Monterrey) 81,974
Gómez Palacio (★★ Torreón) .. 116,967
Guadalajara (★ 2,325,000)... 1,626,152
Guadalupe 25,395
Guadalupe (★ Monterrey)...... 370,524
Guamúchil 36,308
Guanajuato 48,981
Guasave (1970 C) 26,080
Guaymas 54,826
Hermosillo 297,175
Heroica Nogales 65,603
Hidalgo del Parral 75,590
Huajuapan de León 16,743
Huamantla 21,944
Huatabampo 22,635
Huauchinango 25,776
Huixtla 21,578
Iguala 66,005
Irapuato 170,138
Izúcar de Matamoros 27,714
Jacona de Plancarte 29,955
Jalapa Enríquez 204,594
Jalostotitlán 13,031
Jerez de García Salinas 28,629
Jiquilpan de Juárez 22,149
Jojutla 21,243
Juchitán [de Zaragoza] 38,801
La Barca 20,889
Lagos de Moreno 44,223
La Paz 91,453
La Piedad [Cavadas] 47,441
Las Choapas 35,807
León [de los Aldamas] 593,002
Linares 33,012
Loma Bonita 24,344
Los Mochis 122,531
Los Reyes [de Salgado] 23,633
Magdalena 13,618
Manzanillo 39,088
Martínez de la Torre 25,837
Matamoros (★★ Brownsville, Tex., U.S.A.)................. 188,745
Matamoros [de la Laguna] (★ Torreón) 28,175
Matehuala 41,550
Matías Romero 15,092
Mazatlán 199,830
Meoqui 14,859
Mérida 400,142
Mexicali (★ 365,000)........... 341,559
• MEXICO CITY (CIUDAD DE MÉXICO)(★ 14,100,000)... 8,831,079
Minatitlán 106,765
Mineral del Monte 8,605
Monclova 115,786
Montemorelos 28,342
Monterrey (★ 2,015,000)..... 1,090,009
Morelia 297,544
Moroleón 37,500
Motul [de Felipe Carrillo Puerto] 15,919
Múgica 21,239
Navojoa 62,901
Netzahualcóyotl (★ Mexico City)........... 1,341,230
Nogales (★ Orizaba) 22,499
Nueva Casas Grandes 28,514
Nueva Rosita 33,121
Nuevo Laredo (★★ Laredo, Tex., U.S.A.)................. 201,731
Oaxaca [de Juárez]............ 154,223
Ocotlán 48,931
Ojinaga 18,162
Orizaba (★ 215,000) 114,848
Pachuca [de Soto] 110,351
Pánuco 26,652
Papantla [de Olarte] 43,935
Parras de la Fuente 23,453
Pátzcuaro 32,902
Pénjamo 17,307
Piedras Negras 67,455
Poza Rica de Hidalgo 166,799
Progreso 24,257
Puebla [de Zaragoza] (★ 1,055,000)............... 835,759
Puerto Vallarta 38,645
Puruándiro 17,535
Querétaro 215,976
Reynosa 194,693
Río Bravo 55,236
Ríoverde 30,267
Romita 14,492
Rosario 12,171
Sabinas 27,413
Sabinas Hidalgo 23,187
Sahuayo [de Díaz] 43,258
Salamanca 96,703
Salina Cruz 40,010
Saltillo 284,937
Salvatierra 28,878
San Andrés Tuxtla 40,412
San Cristóbal de las Casas 42,026
San Francisco del Oro 10,813
San Francisco del Rincón 40,943
San Juan de los Lagos 26,204
San Juan del Río 27,204
San Juan Teotihuacán (★ Mexico City)................ 6,815
San Luis de la Paz 19,306
San Luis Potosí (★ 470,000)... 362,371
San Luis Río Colorado 76,684
San Martín Texmelucan 36,712
San Miguel de Allende 30,003
San Miguel el Alto 13,949
San Nicolás de los Garzas (★ Monterrey)............... 280,696
San Pedro de las Colonias 35,879
Santa Ana Chiautempan 13,204
Santa Bárbara 14,894
Santa Catarina (★ Monterrey) ...87,673
Santa Cruz de Juventino Rosas 20,436
Santa Inés Zacatelco (★ Puebla de Zaragoza) 19,421
Santa Rosalía 8,221
Santiago Ixcuintla 17,516
Sayula 17,809
Silao 32,248
Soledad Díez Gutiérrez (★ San Luis Potosí)............49,173
Sombrerete 13,562
Tala 19,680
Tamazula de Gordiano 14,080
Tamazunchale 12,863
Tampico (★ 435,000) 267,957

C Census. E Official estimate. UE Unofficial estimate.
• Largest city in country.

★ Population or designation of metropolitan area, including suburbs (see headnote).
▲ Population of an entire municipality, commune, or district, including rural area.

Tangancícuaro [de Arista] 14,433
Tantoyuca 19,552
Tapachula 85,766
Taxco de Alarcón 36,315
Tecate 23,909
Tecomán 46,371
Tecuala 14,755
Tehuacán 79,547
Tehuantepec 22,019
Teocaltiche 16,559
Tepatitlán [de Morelos] 41,813
Tepic 145,741
Tequila 15,514
Texcoco [de Mora]
(★ Mexico City) 30,593
Teziutlán 25,119
Ticul 18,255
Tierra Blanca 31,653
Tijuana (★★ San Diego, Calif., U.S.A.) 429,500
Tizimín 26,305
Tlalnepantla [de Comonfort] (★ Mexico City) 778,173
Tlapacoyan 14,000
Tlaquepaque (★ Guadalajara) 133,500
Tlaxcala [de Xicohténcatl] 14,437
Toluca [de Lerdo] 199,778
Tonalá 19,013
Torreón (★ 575,000) 328,086
Tula de Allende 18,744
Tulancingo 53,400
Tuxpan 24,476
Tuxpan de Rodríguez Cano 56,037
Tuxtepec 29,060
Tuxtla Gutiérrez 131,096
Umán 10,273
Unión de Tula 7,670
Uriangato 19,845
Uruapan [del Progreso] 122,828
Valladolid 28,201
Valle de Santiago 37,645
Valle Hermoso 27,966
Venustiano Carranza 8,546
Veracruz [Llave] (★ 385,000) 284,822
Vicente Guerrero (★ Orizaba) (1970 C) 11,688
Vicente Guerrero (★ Puebla de Zaragoza) 27,589
Villa Flores 20,313
Villa Frontera 32,568
Villahermosa 158,216
Xicotepec de Juárez 18,473
Yautepec 17,899
Yurécuaro 16,123
Yuriria 14,960
Zaachila 8,474
Zacapu 39,570
Zacatecas 80,088
Zacatepec 18,042
Zacoalco [de Torres] 13,105
Zamora de Hidalgo 86,998
Zapopan (★ Guadalajara) 345,390
Zapotiltic 14,552
Zihuatanejo (1970 C) 4,879
Zitácuaro 47,520
Zumpango 19,389

States

Aguascalientes 519,439
Baja California Norte 1,177,886
Baja California Sur 215,139
Campeche 420,553
Chiapas 2,084,717
Chihuahua 2,005,477
Coahuila 1,557,265
Colima 346,293
Distrito Federal (Federal District) 8,831,079
Durango 1,182,320
Guanajuato 3,006,110
Guerrero 2,109,513
Hidalgo 1,547,493
Jalisco 4,371,998
México 7,564,335
Michoacán 2,868,824
Morelos 947,089
Nayarit 726,120
Nuevo León 2,513,044
Oaxaca 2,369,076
Puebla 3,347,685
Querétaro 739,605
Quintana Roo 225,985
San Luis Potosí 1,673,893
Sinaloa 1,849,879
Sonora 1,513,731
Tabasco 1,062,961
Tamaulipas 1,924,484
Tlaxcala 556,597
Veracruz 5,387,680
Yucatán 1,063,733
Zacatecas 1,136,830

MONACO

1982 C 27,063

Cities and Towns

• MONACO (★ 50,000) 27,063

MONGOLIA / Mongol Ard Uls

1985 E 1,866,300

Cities and Towns

Choybalsan (1979 C) 29,800
Darhan 69,800
Erdene 42,900
• ULAN BATOR (ULAANBAATAR) 488,200

MONTSERRAT

1980 C 11,606

Cities and Towns

• PLYMOUTH 1,568

MOROCCO / Al Maghrib

1982 C 20,419,555

Cities and Towns

Agadir 110,479
Al Hoceima (1971 C) 18,686
Beni Mellal (1971 C) 53,826
Berkane (1971 C) 39,015
Berrechid (1971 C) 20,113
• Casablanca (Dar el Beida) (★ 2,250,000) 2,139,204
El Jadida (Mazagan) (1971 C) 55,501
Essaouira (Mogador) (1971 C) 30,061
Fès (Fez) 448,823
Fkih Ben Salah (1971 C) 26,918
Jerada (1971 C) 30,633
Kenitra 188,194
Khemisset (1971 C) 21,811
Khenifra (1971 C) 25,526
Khouribga 127,181
Ksar el Kebir (1971 C) 48,262
Ksar es Souk (1971 C) 16,775
Larache (1971 C) 45,710
Marrakech 439,728
Meknès 319,783
Mohammedia (Fedala) 105,120
Nador (1971 C) 32,490
Ouarzazate (1971 C) 11,142
Oued Zem (1971 C) 33,323
Ouezzane (1971 C) 33,267
Oujda 260,082
RABAT (★ 850,000) 518,616
Safi 197,309
Salé (★★ Rabat) 289,391
Sefrou (1971 C) 28,607
Settat (1971 C) 42,325
Sidi Ifni (1971 C) 13,650
Sidi Kacem (1971 C) 26,831
Sidi Slimane (1971 C) 20,398
Tangier (Tanger) 266,346
Taroudant (1971 C) 22,272
Taza (1971 C) 55,157
Tétouan 199,615
Youssoufia (1971 C) 22,435

MOZAMBIQUE / Moçambique

1980 C 12,130,000

Cities and Towns

Beira 230,744
Chimoio (Vila Pery) 74,372
Inhambane 54,990
Lichinga 39,487
• MAPUTO (LOURENÇO MARQUES) 755,300
Nacala 80,426
Nampula 156,185
Pemba 42,962
Quelimane 62,174
Tete 48,064
Xai-Xai (João Belo) 44,164

NAMIBIA

1981 C 1,099,000

Cities and Towns

Gobabis (1970 C) 4,428
Keetmanshoop (1978 E) 11,400
Lüderitz (1978 E) 6,460
Mariental (1970 C) 4,629
Otjiwarongo (1978 E) 9,925
Rehoboth (1970 C) 5,363
Swakopmund (1970 C) 5,681
Tsumeb (1978 E) 10,928
• WINDHOEK 88,700

NAURU / Naoero

1984 E 8,000

NEPAL / Nepāl

1981 C 15,022,839

Cities and Towns

Bhaktapur 48,472
Birātnagar 93,544
Bīrganj 43,642
Dharān Bāzār 42,146
• KATHMANDU (★ 320,000) 235,160
Lalitpur (★ Kathmandu) 79,875
Mahendranagar 43,834
Nepālganj 34,015
Pokhara 46,642

NETHERLANDS / Nederland

1984 E 14,394,600

Cities and Towns

Aalsmeer 20,379
Alkmaar (★ 120,000) 83,892
Almelo 62,941
Alphen aan den Rijn 54,560
Amersfoort (★ 130,000) 86,896
Amstelveen (★ Amsterdam) 68,518
• AMSTERDAM (★ 1,825,000) 676,439
Apeldoorn 144,108
Arnhem (★ 290,746) (1982 E) 128,598
Assen 46,745
Bergen op Zoom 45,568
Beverwijk (★ Amsterdam) 34,947
Breda (★ 153,517) 118,662
Brunssum (★ Heerlen) 29,595
Bussum (★ Amsterdam) 33,401
Capelle aan den IJssel (▲ 53,444) 40,000
Castricum (★ Amsterdam) 22,726
De Bilt (★ Utrecht) 31,834
Delft (★ The Hague) 86,733
Delfzijl 24,953
Den Helder 63,826
Deventer 64,823
Doetinchem (▲ 39,755) 29,900
Dordrecht (★ 199,156) 107,475
Drachten (Smallingerland) (▲ 50,724) 40,500
Edam [-Volendam] (★ Amsterdam) 24,019
Ede (▲ 86,816) 45,600
Eindhoven (★ 374,109) 192,854
Emmen (▲ 91,010) 36,100
Enschede (★ 248,200) 144,938
Geldrop (★ Eindhoven) 26,568
Geleen (★ 177,410) 34,828
Goes 31,155
Gorinchem 27,538
Gouda 60,026
Groningen (★ 206,611) 167,866
Haarlem (★ Amsterdam) 152,511
Haarlemmermeer (▲ 83,428) 11,400
Harderwijk 32,505
Harlingen (1983 E) 15,752
Heemstede (★ Amsterdam) 25,730
Heerenveen (▲ 37,407) 20,800
Heerlen (★ 266,095) 93,283
Helmond 60,582
Hengelo (★★ Enschede) 76,855
Hilversum (★ Amsterdam) 88,417
Hoogeveen (▲ 45,031) 34,000
Hoorn 50,473
IJmuiden (Velsen) (★ Amsterdam) 58,287
Kampen 31,944
Katwijk aan Zee 38,659
Kerkrade (★ Heerlen) 53,231
Leeuwarden 85,435
Leiden (★ 176,360) 104,261
Lelystad (▲ 55,141) 14,400
Maassluis (★ Rotterdam) 33,107
Maastricht (★ 157,329) 113,277
Meppel 22,752
Middelburg 38,854
Nieuwegein 53,601
Nijmegen (★ 233,992) 147,102
Oldenzaal 28,827
Oss 50,086
Papendrecht (★ Dordrecht) 25,787
Purmerend (★ Amsterdam) 45,829
Renkum (★ Arnhem) 12,500
Ridderkerk (★ Rotterdam) 47,124
Rijswijk (★ The Hague) 49,790
Roermond 38,209
Roosendaal 56,519
Rotterdam (★ 1,095,000) 555,349
Schiedam (★ Rotterdam) 69,849
's-Hertogenbosch (★ 186,946) 89,059
Sittard (★★ Geleen) 43,889
Sliedrecht 22,746
Sneek 29,473
Soest (★ Armersfoort) 40,355
Spijkenisse (★ Rotterdam) 54,381
Tegelen (★ Venlo) (1983 E) 18,096
Terneuzen (▲ 35,339) 22,200
THE HAGUE ('S-GRAVENHAGE) (★ 775,000) 445,213
Tiel 29,849
Tilburg (★ 221,684) 154,094
Utrecht (★ 501,357) 230,414
Veendam 28,532
Veenendaal 43,228
Veldhoven (★ Eindhoven) 35,519
Venlo (★ 87,000) 62,935
Vlaardingen (★ Rotterdam) 76,466
Vlissingen (Flushing) (▲ 46,150) 26,500
Voorburg (★ The Hague) 41,945
Vught (★ 's-Hertogenbosch) 23,205
Waalwijk 28,808
Wageningen 32,083
Wassenaar (★ The Hague) 26,950
Weert (▲ 39,402) 28,600
Winschoten 20,660
Woerden 25,629
Zaandam (Zaanstad) (★ Amsterdam) 128,413
Zeist (★ Utrecht) 60,478
Zoetermeer (★ The Hague) 77,632
Zutphen 31,683
Zwijndrecht (★★ Dordrecht) 39,862
Zwolle 87,340

Provinces

Almere 33,000
Drenthe 427,300
Dronten 22,200
Friesland 597,200
Gelderland 1,735,800
Groningen 561,500
Lelystad 55,100
Limburg 1,083,600
North Brabant (Noord-Brabant) 2,103,000
North Holland (Noord-Holland) 2,307,400
Overijssel 1,042,100
South Holland (Zuid-Holland) 3,139,200
Utrecht 929,400
Zeeland 355,500
Zeewolde 800

NETHERLANDS ANTILLES / Nederlandse Antillen

1981 E 192,056

Cities and Towns

Kralendijk (1953 E) 600
• WILLEMSTAD (★ 94,133) (1960 C) 43,547

Political Divisions

Bonaire 9,222
Curacao 164,579
Saba 1,011
Sint Eustatius 1,325
Sint Maarten 15,919

NEW CALEDONIA / Nouvelle-Calédonie

1983 C 145,368

Cities and Towns

• NOUMEA (★ 83,000) 60,112

NEW ZEALAND

1985 E 3,265,300

Cities and Towns

• Auckland (★ 860,000) 143,600
Birkenhead (★ Auckland) 23,300
Blenheim (★ 23,200) 18,750
Christchurch (★ 305,000) 161,700
Dunedin (★ 107,000) 74,500
East Coast Bays (★ Auckland) 35,100
Gisborne (★ 32,600) 30,500
Hamilton (★ 103,800) 96,700
Hastings (★★ Napier) 38,200
Invercargill (★ 54,100) 49,700
Kapiti (★ 21,400) 16,200
Lower Hutt (★ Wellington) 62,900
Manukau (★ Auckland) 182,800
Masterton (★ 20,000) 18,400
Mount Albert (★ Auckland) 26,100
Mount Eden (★ Auckland) 18,000
Mount Roskill (★ Auckland) 33,500
Mount Wellington (★ Auckland) 19,250
Napier (★ 112,700) 50,500
Nelson (★ 44,400) 34,300
New Plymouth (★ 46,400) 37,000
Palmerston North (★ 69,700) 62,700
Papakura (★ Auckland) 24,100
Papatoetoe (★ Auckland) 22,000
Porirua (★ Wellington) 40,600
Rotorua (★ 52,100) 39,200
Takapuna (★ Auckland) 72,500
Tauranga (★ 60,300) 42,100
Timaru (★ 28,700) 27,900
Tokoroa (★ 19,450) 18,850
Upper Hutt (★ Wellington) 32,000
Wainuiomata (★ Wellington) 19,150
Waitemata (★ Auckland) 99,000
Wanganui (★ 39,800) 37,100
WELLINGTON (★ 342,500) 133,200
Whangarei (★ 43,500) 39,400

NICARAGUA

1981 E 2,823,979

Cities and Towns

Bluefields 20,608
Chinandega 51,684
Granada 64,642
León 92,764
• MANAGUA 644,588
Masaya 54,708
Matagalpa 29,906
Rivas 18,360

NIGER

1983 E 5,772,000

Cities and Towns

Agadez 30,800
Maradi 65,100
• NIAMEY 399,100
Tahoua 41,900
Zinder 82,800

NIGERIA

1982 E 89,117,500

Cities and Towns

Aba 210,700
Abakaliki 50,130
Abeokuta 301,000
Ado-Ekiti 253,300
Akure 114,400
Awka 78,360
Bauchi 60,730
Benin City 161,700
Bida (1963 C) 55,007
Birnin Kebbi 42,580
Calabar 122,800
Deba (1963 C) 60,679
Ede 216,400
Effon-Alaiye 107,900
Enugu 222,600
Epe 71,090
Gombe 76,000
Gusau 111,400
Ibadan 1,009,400
Idah 44,610
Ife 209,100
Igboho (1963 C) 46,776
Ijebu Ode 110,300
Ikare 99,220
Ikerre 172,400
Ikire (1963 C) 54,022
Ikirun (1963 C) 79,516
Ikorodu (1963 C) 81,024
Ikot Ekpene 61,280
Ila (1975 E) 155,000
Ilawe-Ekiti (1963 C) 80,833
Ilesha 266,700
Ilobu 140,100
Ilorin 335,400
Inisa (1963 C) 52,482
Ise-Ekiti (1963 C) 45,323
Iseyin 153,100
Iwo 255,100
Jos 145,400
Kaduna (1975 E) 202,000
Kano 475,000
Katsina 145,500
Kaura Namoda 46,700
Keffi 50,990
Kishi (1963 C) 42,374
Kumo (1963 C) 64,878
Lafia 86,320
Lafiagi 50,820
• LAGOS (★ 3,500,000) 1,404,000
Maiduguri 225,100
Makurdi 86,800
Minna 96,470

C Census. E Official estimate. UE Unofficial estimate.
• Largest city in country.

★ Population or designation of metropolitan area, including suburbs (see headnote).
▲ Population of an entire municipality, commune, or district, including rural area.

Mubi	45,170
Mushin (★ Lagos)	234,500
Nguru	69,520
Offa	138,800
Ogbomosho	514,400
Oka	100,900
Ondo	119,500
Onitsha	262,100
Oron	54,940
Oshogbo	336,000
Owerri	52,670
Owo (1963 C)	89,693
Oyo	180,700
Port Harcourt	288,900
Sapele	98,110
Shagamu	82,600
Shaki	122,700
Shomolu (★ Lagos)	104,100
Sokoto	144,300
Ugep (1963 C)	44,945
Umuahia	46,370
Uyo	53,390
Warri	88,840
Zaria	267,300

NIUE

1979 E 3,578

Cities and Towns

• ALOFI	960

NORWAY / Norge

1983 E 4,122,707

Cities and Towns

Ålesund	34,909
Arendal (★ 22,500)	11,743
Bergen (★ 239,000)	207,232
Bodø	33,646
Drammen (★ 73,000)	50,605
Fredrikstad (★ 52,000)	27,618
Gjøvik	26,077
Halden	26,223
Hamar (★ 28,000)	15,837
Hammerfest	7,208
Harstad	21,765
Haugesund (★ 31,000)	27,043
Kongsberg	20,629
Kristiansand	61,834
Kristiansund	17,895
Larvik (★ 19,000)	8,226
Lillehammer	21,954
Molde	21,057
Moss (★ 30,000)	24,967
Narvik	19,080
• OSLO (★ 720,000)	448,747
Porsgrunn (★★ Skien)	31,247
Ringerike	26,839
Sandefjord	35,158
Sandnes (★ Stavanger)	38,079
Sarpsborg (★ 41,500)	12,143
Skien (★ 77,981)	46,734
Stavanger (★ 132,000)	92,012
Steinkjer	20,694
Tønsberg (★ 37,500)	8,921
Tromsø	47,322
Trondheim	134,652
Vadsø	5,995

Counties

Akershus	376,129
Aust-Agder	92,751
Buskerud	217,402
Finnmark	77,394
Hedmark	187,784
Hordaland	394,545
Møre og Romsdal	237,315
Nordland	245,017
Nord-Trøndelag	126,713
Oppland	182,108
Oslo	448,747
Østfold	234,751
Rogaland	312,576
Sogn og Fjordane	106,175
Sør-Trøndelag	246,200
Telemark	161,944
Troms	147,709
Vest-Agder	138,745
Vestfold	188,702

OMAN / 'Umān

1980 E 891,000

Cities and Towns

Maṭraḥ (1971 E)	14,000
• MUSCAT (MASQAṬ)	30,000
Nazwá	25,000
Ṣuḥār	20,000
• Ṣūr	30,000

PACIFIC ISLANDS, TRUST TERRITORY OF THE

1980 C 132,929

Cities and Towns

Garapan	2,063
Jarej-Uliga-Delap	8,583
Kolonia	5,549
Koror	6,222

Political Divisions

Federated States of Micronesia	73,160
Marshall Islands	30,873
Northern Mariana Islands	16,780
Palau (Belau)	12,116

PAKISTAN / Pākistān

1981 C 83,782,000

Cities and Towns

Abbottābād (★ 66,000)	32,000
Ahmadpur East	57,000
Bahāwalnagar	74,000
Bahāwalpur (★ 178,000)	150,000
Bannu (★ 43,000)	35,000
Campbellpore (★ 40,000)	26,000
Chārsadda	62,000
Chīchāwatni	50,000
Chiniot	106,000
Chishtiān Mandi	62,000
Dādu	39,000
Daska	56,000
Dera Ghāzi Khān	103,000
Dera Ismāīl Khān (★ 68,000)	64,000
Drigh Road Cantonment (★ Karāchi)	57,000
Faisalabad (Lyallpur)	1,092,000
Gojra	68,000
Gujrānwāla (★ 654,000)	597,000
Gujrānwāla Cantonment (★ Gujrānwāla)	71,000
Gujrāt	154,000
Gwādar	17,000
Hāfizābād	83,000
Hyderābād (★ 833,000)	745,000
Hyderābād Cantonment (★ Hyderābād)	50,000
ISLĀMĀBĀD (★★ Rāwalpindi)	201,000
Jacobābād	80,000
Jarānwāla	70,000
Jhang Sadar	195,000
Jhelum (★ 106,000)	92,000
Kamālia	61,000
Kāmoke	71,000
• Karāchi (★ 5,150,000)	4,776,000
Karāchi Cantonment (★ Karāchi)	203,000
Kasūr	155,000
Khairpur	62,000
Khānewāl	89,000
Khānpur	71,000
Khāriān (★ 52,000)	16,000
Khushāb (★ 75,000)	56,000
Kohāt (★ 78,000)	55,000
Lahore (★ 2,975,000)	2,685,000
Lahore Cantonment (★ Lahore)	237,000
Lārkāna	123,000
Leiah	52,000
Mandi Būrewāla	86,000
Mardān (★ 148,000)	142,000
Miānwāli	59,000
Mingāora	88,000
Mīrpur Khās	124,000
Multān (★ 730,000)	694,000
Muzaffargarh	53,000
Nawābshāh	102,000
Nowshera (★ 75,000)	39,000
Okāra (★ 154,000)	128,000
Pākpattan	70,000
Peshāwar (★ 575,000)	500,000
Peshāwar Cantonment (★ Peshāwar)	55,000
Quetta (★ 285,000)	243,000
Rahīmyār Khān (★ 132,000)	119,000
Rāwalpindi (★ 1,040,000)	452,000
Rāwalpindi Cantonment (★ Rāwalpindi)	354,000
Sādiqābad	64,000
Sāhīwāl (Montgomery)	152,000
Sargodha (★ 294,000)	235,000
Sargodha Cantonment (★ Sargodha)	59,000
Shekhūpura	141,000
Shikārpur	88,000
Siālkot (★ 296,000)	252,000
Sibi	23,000
Sukkur	193,000
Tando Ādam	63,000
Turbat	52,000
Vihāri	53,000
Wāh Cantonment	122,000
Wazīrābād	63,000

PANAMA / Panamá

1980 C 1,795,012

Cities and Towns

Balboa (★ Panamá)	1,904
Colón (★ 88,000)	59,840
David	49,472
La Chorrera	37,566
La Concepción	10,823
• PANAMÁ (★ 625,000)	389,172
Puerto Armuelles	12,562
San Miguelito (★ Panamá)	156,611
Santiago	24,205

PAPUA NEW GUINEA

1980 C 3,010,727

Cities and Towns

Lae	61,617
Madang	21,335
• PORT MORESBY	123,624
Rabaul	14,954
Wewak	19,890

PARAGUAY

1982 C 3,026,165

Cities and Towns

• ASUNCIÓN (★ 700,000)	455,517
Caacupé (1972 C)	7,278
Concepción	22,866
Coronel Oviedo	21,782
Encarnación	27,632
Fernando de la Mora (★ Asunción)	66,810
Lambaré (★ Asunción)	61,722
Luque (★ Asunción) (1972 C)	13,921
Paraguarí (1972 C)	5,036
Pedro Juan Caballero	37,331
Pilar	13,135
Puerto Presidente Stroessner	39,676
San Lorenzo (★ Asunción)	74,632
Villa Hayes (1972 C)	4,749
Villarrica	21,203

Departments

Alto Paraguay	8,918
Alto Paraná	192,518
Amambay	68,534
Asunción (Distrito Federal)	455,517
Boquerón	14,611
Caaguazú	299,227
Caazapá	109,530
Canendiyu	66,296
Central	494,264
Chaco	286
Concepción	135,204
Cordillera	194,668
Guairá	143,452
Itapúa	263,021
Misiones	79,278
Ñeembucú	70,689
Nueva Asunción	231
Paraguarí	205,160
Presidente Hayes	32,949
San Pedro	191,812

PERU / Perú

1981 C 17,031,221

Cities and Towns

Abancay	19,863
Arequipa (★ 446,942)	108,023
Ayacucho (★ 69,533)	57,432
Barranco (★ Lima)	46,478
Barrio Obrero Industrial (★ Lima)	404,856
Breña (★ Lima)	112,398
Cajamarca	62,259
Callao (★★ Lima)	264,133
Cerro de Pasco (★ 66,373)	55,597
Chachapoyas	11,853
Chiclayo (★ 279,527)	213,095
Chimbote	223,341
Chincha Alta	41,369
Chorrillos (★ Lima)	141,881
Chosica	65,139
Chulucanas (▲ 63,163)	35,000
Cuzco (★ 184,550)	89,563
Huacho	43,398
Huancavelica	21,137
Huancayo (★ 164,954)	84,845
Huanuco	61,812
Huaraz	44,814
Ica	114,786
Iquitos	178,738
Jesús María (★ Lima)	83,179
Juliaca	87,651
Lambayeque (▲ 30,784)	24,000
La Oroya	34,940
La Victoria (★ Lima)	270,778
• LIMA (★ 4,608,010)	371,122
Lince (★ Lima)	80,456
Magdalena del Mar (★ Lima)	55,535
Miraflores (★ Lima)	103,453
Moyobamba	14,376
Pisco	55,604
Piura (★ 207,934)	144,609
Pucallpa	112,263
Pueblo Libre (★ Lima)	83,985
Puerto Maldonado	12,693
Puno	67,397
Rímac (★ Lima)	184,484
San Isidro (★ Lima)	71,203
Sullana	89,037
Surco (★ Lima)	146,636
Surquillo (★ Lima)	134,158
Tacna	97,173
Talara	57,351
Trujillo (★ 354,301)	202,469
Tumbes	47,936
Vitarte (★ Lima)	145,504

Departments

Amazonas	254,560
Ancash	818,289
Apurímac	323,346
Arequipa	706,580
Ayacucho	503,392
Cajamarca	1,045,569
Callao (Province)	443,413
Cuzco (Cusco)	832,504
Huancavelica	346,797
Huánuco	484,780
Ica	433,897
Junín	852,238
La Libertad	962,949
Lambayeque	674,442
Lima	4,745,877
Loreto	445,368
Madre de Dios	33,007
Moquegua	101,610
Pasco	213,125
Piura	1,125,865
Puno	890,258
San Martín	319,751
Tacna	143,085
Tumbes	103,839
Ucayali	200,669

PHILIPPINES / Pilipinas

1980 C 48,098,460

Cities and Towns

Angeles	188,834
Angono	26,571
Antipolo (▲ 68,912)	60,000
Bacolod	262,415
Bacoor (★ Manila)	90,364
Baguio	119,009
Bais (▲ 49,301)	9,400
Balagtas	28,654
Baliuag	70,555
Basilan (Isabela) (▲ 49,891)	13,200
Basista	17,191
Batangas (▲ 143,570)	21,300
Binalbagan (▲ 49,428)	21,000
Biñan (★ Manila)	83,684
Binangonan	80,989
Bislig (▲ 81,615)	40,000
Bocaue	49,693
Bulan (▲ 60,911)	16,200
Butuan (▲ 172,489)	69,600
Cabanatuan (▲ 138,298)	38,400
Cadiz (▲ 129,632)	27,000
Cagayan de Oro (▲ 227,312)	51,300
Cainta (★ Manila)	59,025
Calamba (▲ 121,175)	41,400
Calapan (▲ 67,370)	17,000
Calbayog (▲ 106,719)	11,300
Caloocan (★ Manila)	467,816
Calumpit	45,454
Carmona (★ Manila)	65,014
Catarman (▲ 59,021)	16,600
Catbalogan (▲ 58,737)	19,300
Cavite (★ 175,000)	87,666
Cebu (★ 600,000)	490,281
Cordoba	16,455
Cotabato (▲ 83,871)	61,600
Daet (▲ 54,789)	29,900
Dagupan	98,344
Davao (▲ 610,375)	270,600
Digos (▲ 70,065)	26,000
Dinagat	36,726
Dipolog (▲ 61,919)	26,100
Dumaguete	83,411
Escalante (▲ 71,293)	8,900
General Santos (Dadiangas) (▲ 149,396)	58,900
Gingoog (▲ 79,937)	19,900
Guagua	72,609
Guiguinto	27,751
Ilagan (▲ 79,336)	13,900
Iligan (▲ 167,358)	14,600
Iloilo	244,827
Iriga (▲ 66,113)	12,100
Jolo	52,429
Kawit (★ Cavite)	35,365
Koronadal (▲ 80,566)	19,300
La Carlota (▲ 45,812)	22,700
Laoag (▲ 69,648)	32,900
Lapu-Lapu	98,723
Las Piñas (★ Manila)	136,514
Legazpi (▲ 99,766)	42,600
Lingayen (▲ 65,187)	17,800
Lipa (▲ 121,166)	21,000
Lucena	107,880
Maasin (▲ 59,731)	13,500
Macabebe	45,830
Makati (★ Manila)	372,631
Malabon (★ Manila)	191,001
Malaybalay (▲ 60,779)	9,500
Malolos	95,699
Manaoag	36,742
Mandaluyong (★ Manila)	205,366
Mandaue (★ Cebu)	110,590
Mangaldan	50,434
• MANILA (★ 6,800,000)	1,630,485
Marawi	53,812
Marikina (★ Manila)	211,613
Mati (▲ 78,178)	19,400
Meycauayan (★ Manila)	83,579
Muntinglupa (★ Manila)	136,679
Naga	90,712
Navotas (★ Manila)	126,146
Noveleta (★ Cavite)	14,460
Olongapo	156,430
Ormoc (▲ 104,978)	15,300
Ozamiz (▲ 77,832)	18,900
Pagadian (▲ 80,861)	35,000
Parañaque (★ Manila)	208,552
Pasay (★ Manila)	287,770
Pasig (★ Manila)	268,570
Puerto Princesa (▲ 60,234)	24,400
Pulilan	38,110
Quezon City (★ Manila)	1,165,865
Rosario (★ Cavite)	33,312
Roxas (Capiz) (▲ 81,183)	21,500
Sagay (▲ 99,118)	33,700
San Carlos (▲ 91,627)	24,200
San Fernando	110,891
San Juan del Monte (★ Manila)	130,088
San Pablo (▲ 131,655)	48,000
San Pedro	74,556
Santa Cruz	60,620
Santa Rosa (★ Manila)	64,325
Santo Tomas, Pampanga prov.	24,951
Santo Tomas, Pangasinan prov.	8,946
Silay (▲ 111,131)	31,400
Surigao (▲ 79,745)	30,700
Tacloban	102,523
Tagaytay (▲ 16,322)	2,500
Tagbilaran	42,683
Tagig (★ Manila)	134,137
Tagum (▲ 86,201)	33,400
Talisay (▲ 53,624)	27,200
Tarlac (▲ 175,691)	30,800
Taytay (▲ 75,328))	23,200
Toledo (▲ 91,668)	11,000
Trece Martires (▲ 8,579)	1,400
Tuguegarao (▲ 73,507)	16,500
Valenzuela (★ Manila)	212,363
Victorias (▲ 55,959)	29,000
Vigan	33,483
Zamboanga (▲ 343,722)	69,600

PITCAIRN

1986 C 70

Cities and Towns

• ADAMSTOWN	64

POLAND / Polska

1984 E 37,063,000

Cities and Towns

Augustów	26,300
Będzin (★ Katowice)	77,100
Bełchatów	45,400
Biała Podlaska	45,600
Białogard	23,500
Białystok	245,400
Bielawa (★★ Dzierżoniów)	33,400
Bielsko-Biała	174,100
Bochnia	26,700
Bolesławiec (Bunzlau)	42,000
Brzeg (Brieg)	37,200
Bydgoszcz	361,400
Bytom (★★ Katowice)	239,200
Chełm	59,400
Chojnice	34,900
Chorzów (★★ Katowice)	144,200
Chrzanów	38,400
Ciechanów	38,400
Cieszyn	35,400
Czechowice-Dziedzice	34,200
Czeladź (★ Katowice)	37,500

C Census. E Official estimate. UE Unofficial estimate.
• Largest city in country.

★ Population or designation of metropolitan area, including suburbs (see headnote).
▲ Population of an entire municipality, commune, or district, including rural area.

Częstochowa 246,600
Dąbrowa Górnicza (★ Katowice) 136,800
Dębica 39,000
Dzierżoniów (Reichenbach) (★ 88,000) 37,900
Elbląg (Elbing) 117,000
Ełk (Lyck) 42,700
Gdańsk (Danzig) (★ 890,000) 467,200
Gdynia (★★ Gdańsk) 243,100
Giżycko 26,800
Gliwice (Gleiwitz) (★★ Katowice) 212,500
Głogów 64,200
Gniezno 67,400
Gorzów [Wielkopolski] 115,100
Grodzisk Mazowiecki (★ Warsaw) 24,600
Grudziądz 93,900
Inowrocław 70,900
Jarosław 39,600
Jasło 33,600
Jastrzębie-Zdrój 101,000
Jaworzno (★ Katowice) 95,200
Jelenia Góra (Hirschberg) 90,400
Kalisz 103,500
Kamienna Góra (Landeshut) 22,900
• Katowice (★ 2,750,000) 363,300
Kędzierzyn-Koźle 71,700
Kętrzyn 27,900
Kielce 200,500
Kłodzko (Glatz) 29,300
Knurów (★ Katowice) 44,600
Kołobrzeg (Kolberg) 40,800
Konin 74,400
Kościan 22,300
Koszalin (Köslin) 99,500
Kraków (★ 820,000) 740,300
Kraśnik 34,300
Krosno 44,100
Krotoszyn 25,700
Kutno 45,200
Kwidzyn (Marienwerder) 34,800
Lębork 31,400
Legionowo (★ Warsaw) 45,500
Legnica (Liegnitz) 97,700
Leszno 53,900
Łódź (★ 1,050,000) 849,400
Łomża 49,300
Łowicz 27,700
Lubań 22,500
Lubin 72,500
Lublin (★ 380,000) 324,100
Lubliniec 23,500
Łuków 27,600
Malbork (Marienburg) 37,500
Mielec 48,700
Mikołów (★ Katowice) 35,300
Mińsk Mazowiecki 31,000
Mława 25,600
Mysłowice (★ Katowice) 86,500
Myszków 31,300
Nowa Ruda 26,200
Nowa Sól 41,100
Nowy Sącz 69,700
Nowy Targ 30,100
Nysa (Neisse) 44,000
Oława 30,800
Oleśnica 35,500
Olkusz 33,000
Olsztyn (Allenstein) 147,100
Opole (Oppeln) 124,000
Ostróda (Osterode) 30,700
Ostrołęka 43,100
Ostrowiec [Świętokrzyski] 71,300
Ostrów Wielkopolski 67,100
Oświęcim 45,700
Otwock (★ Warsaw) 45,400
Pabianice (★ Łódź) 72,600
Piaseczno (★ Warsaw) 24,300
Piekary Śląskie (★ Katowice) 67,800
Piła (Schneidemühl) 66,300
Piotrków [Trybunalski] 78,200
Płock 114,500
Poznań (★ 660,000) 574,100
Prudnik 23,700
Pruszków (★ Warsaw) 52,600
Przemyśl 64,900
Pszczyna 37,400
Puławy 49,300
Racibórz (Ratibor) 59,800
Radom 213,500
Radomsko 42,300
Ruda Śląska (★ Katowice) 164,600
Rumia (★ Gdańsk) 33,400
Rybnik 135,500
Rzeszów 138,000
Sanok 34,800
Siedlce 62,900
Siemianowice Śląskie (★ Katowice) 80,900
Sieradz 35,600
Skarżysko-Kamienna 47,600
Skierniewice 36,200
Słupsk (Stolp) 91,800
Sochaczew 34,700
Sopot (Zoppot) (★ Gdańsk) 51,500
Sosnowiec (★★ Katowice) 255,000
Stalowa Wola 62,900
Starachowice 54,300
Stargard [Szczeciński] 64,600
Starogard [Gdański] 45,000
Suwałki 48,800
Świdnica (Schweidnitz) 60,300
Świdnik (★ Lublin) 36,900
Świecie 24,800
Świętochłowice (★ Katowice) 61,000
Świnoujście (Swinemünde) 43,900
Szczecin (Stettin) (★ 440,000) 390,800
Szczecinek 37,500
Szczytno (Ortelsburg) 24,700
Tarnobrzeg 41,600
Tarnów 113,200
Tarnowskie Góry (★ Katowice) 72,200
Tczew 57,500
Tomaszów Mazowiecki 66,100
Toruń 186,200
Trzebinia 21,100
Turek 26,400
Tychy (★ Katowice) 181,800
Wałbrzych (Waldenburg) (★ 205,000) 138,000
Wałcz 25,100
WARSAW (WARSZAWA) (★ 2,175,000) 1,649,000
Wejherowo 45,600
Włocławek 115,300
Wodzisław Śląski 107,700
Wołomin (★ Warsaw) 33,100
Wrocław (Breslau) 636,000
Września 25,200
Zabrze (Hindenburg) (★★ Katowice) 198,000
Żagań (Sagan) 25,800
Zakopane 29,900
Zamość 54,800
Żary (Sorau) 37,700
Zawiercie 55,700
Zduńska Wola 41,800
Zgierz (★ Łódź) 54,900
Zgorzelec 34,600
Zielona Góra (Grünberg) 109,400
Żory 61,900
Żyrardów (★ Warsaw) 38,900
Żywiec 29,500

Voivodships

Biała Podlaska 296,000
Białystok 666,000
Bielsko-Biała 865,000
Bydgoszcz 1,074,000
Chełm 239,000
Ciechanów 416,000
Częstochowa 763,000
Elbląg 463,000
Gdańsk 1,387,000
Gorzów Wielkopolski 479,000
Jelenia Góra 507,000
Kalisz 691,000
Katowice 3,895,000
Kielce 1,101,000
Konin 455,000
Koszalin 484,000
Kraków 1,205,000
Krosno 470,000
Legnica 485,000
Leszno 373,000
Łódź 1,149,000
Łomża 337,000
Lublin 977,000
Nowy Sącz 659,000
Olsztyn 717,000
Opole 1,006,000
Ostrołęka 382,000
Piła 460,000
Piotrków Trybunalski 628,000
Płock 507,000
Poznań 1,289,000
Przemyśl 392,000
Radom 725,000
Rzeszów 683,000
Siedlce 633,000
Sieradz 399,000
Skierniewice 408,000
Słupsk 391,000
Suwałki 443,000
Szczecin 933,000
Tarnobrzeg 577,000
Tarnów 239,000
Toruń 634,000
Wałbrzych 732,000
Warszawa 2,396,000
Włocławek 424,000
Wrocław 1,109,000
Zamość 486,000
Zielona Góra 639,000

PORTUGAL

1981 C 9,833,014

Cities and Towns

Agualva-Cacém (★ Lisbon) 34,341
Águas Santas (★ Porto) 26,523
Algés (★ Lisbon) 20,377
Algueirão-Mem Martins (★ Lisbon) 28,154
Almada (★ Lisbon) 42,607
Amadora (★ Lisbon) 95,518
Angra do Heroísmo, Azores Is. 12,292
Aveiro 28,625
Baixa da Banheira (★ Lisbon) 21,358
Barreiro (★ Lisbon) 50,863
Beja 19,600
Braga 63,033
Bragança 14,181
Castelo Branco 21,256
Coimbra 74,616
Cova da Piedade (★ Lisbon) 28,251
Covilhã 21,807
Damaia (★ Lisbon) 23,261
Évora 34,851
Faro 27,974
Funchal, Madeira Is. 44,111
Guimarães 21,947
Horta, Azores Is. 5,749
Laranjeiro (★ Lisbon) 20,374
• LISBON (LISBOA) (★ 2,250,000) 807,167
Matosinhos (★ Porto) 26,404
Montijo (★ Lisbon) 23,017
Moscavide (★ Lisbon) 17,797
Odivelas (★ Lisbon) 38,322
Oeiras (★ Lisbon) 32,529
Olhão 20,080
Ponta Delgada, Azores Is. 21,187
Portimão 19,605
Porto (Oporto) (★ 1,225,000) 327,368
Póvoa de Varzim 23,729
Queluz (★ Lisbon) 42,241
Sacavém (★ Lisbon) 24,116
Santarém 19,761
Setúbal 77,885
Sintra (★ Lisbon) 9,322
Vila do Conde 20,613
Vila Nova de Gaia (★ Porto) 62,469
Viseu 20,070

Districts

Açores (Azores) (Auton. Region) 243,410
Aveiro 622,988
Beja 188,420
Braga 708,924
Bragança 184,252
Castelo Branco 234,230
Coimbra 436,324
Évora 180,277
Faro 323,534
Guarda 205,631
Leiria 420,229
Lisboa (Lisbon) 2,069,467
Madeira (Auton. Region) 252,844
Portalegre 142,905
Porto 1,562,287
Santarém 454,123
Setúbal 658,326
Viana do Castelo 256,814
Vila Real 264,381
Viseu 423,648

PUERTO RICO

1980 C 3,196,520

Cities and Towns

Adjuntas (▲ 18,786) 5,239
Aguadilla (★ 152,793) 22,039
Aibonito (▲ 22,167) 9,331
Arecibo (★ 160,336) 48,779
Bayamón (★ San Juan) 185,087
Caguas (★ San Juan) 87,214
Carolina (★ San Juan) 147,835
Cataño (★ San Juan) 26,243
Cayey (▲ 41,099) 23,305
Coamo (▲ 30,822) 12,851
Corozal (★ San Juan) 5,889
Fajardo (▲ 32,087) 26,928
Guánica (▲ 18,799) 9,628
Guayama (▲ 40,183) 21,097
Guayanilla (▲ 21,050) 6,163
Guaynabo (★ San Juan) 65,075
Humacao (★ San Juan) 19,147
Isabela (★ Aguadilla) 12,087
Manatí (★ San Juan) 17,347
Mayagüez (★ 200,464) 82,968
Ponce (★ 232,551) 161,739
San Germán (★ Mayagüez) 13,054
• SAN JUAN (★ 1,775,260) 424,600
San Sebastián (▲ 35,690) 10,619
Trujillo Alto (★ San Juan) 41,141
Utuado (▲ 34,505) 11,113
Vega Alta (★ San Juan) 10,582
Vega Baja (★ San Juan) 18,233
Yabucoa (▲ 31,425) 6,797
Yauco (▲ 37,742) 14,594

QATAR / Qaṭar

1981 E 220,000

Cities and Towns

• DOHA (AD DAWHAH) 190,000

REUNION / Réunion

1982 C 515,798

Cities and Towns

Le Port (▲ 30,131) 26,000
• SAINT-DENIS (▲ 109,072) 84,400
Saint-Pierre (▲ 50,082) 24,000

ROMANIA / România

1983 E 22,533,074

Cities and Towns

Aiud 28,334
Alba Iulia 59,369
Alexandria 47,730
Arad 183,774
Bacău 165,655
Baia-Mare 129,719
Bîrlad 66,476
Bistrița 67,311
Blaj 22,812
Borșa 27,539
Botoșani 94,536
Brăila 224,998
Brașov 331,240
• BUCHAREST (BUCUREȘTI) (★ 2,250,000) 1,995,156
Buzău 126,780
Călărași 63,005
Caracal 34,337
Caransebeș 31,198
Carei 26,933
Cîmpia Turzii 26,592
Cîmpina 37,089
Cîmpulung 39,777
Cluj-Napoca 301,244
Codlea 23,416
Constanța 315,662
Craiova 260,422
Cugir 29,650
Curtea-de-Argeș 28,016
Dej 38,229
Deva 75,161
Dorohoi 27,495
Drobeta-Turnu-Severin 92,235
Făgăraș 39,666
Fetești 29,874
Focșani 77,391
Galați 285,077
Gheorghe Gheorghiu-Dej 49,330
Giurgiu 62,710
Hunedoara 87,001
Huși 26,789
Iași 305,598
Lugoj 51,763
Lupeni 30,603
Mangalia 37,167
Medgidia 46,668
Mediaș 70,933
Miercurea Ciuc 43,578
Moinești 22,194
Odorheiu Secuiesc 38,410
Oltenița 27,837
Oradea 206,206
Pașcani 33,176
Petrila (★ Petroșani) 25,885
Petroșani (★ 74,000) 47,289
Piatra-Neamț 102,584
Pitești 149,684
Ploiești (★ 300,000) 229,915
Rădăuți 26,989
Reghin 34,816
Reșița 101,902
Rîmnicu-Sărat 34,160
Rîmnicu-Vîlcea 86,615
Roman 67,962
Roșiorii de Vede 33,223
Săcele 33,841
Satu Mare 124,691
Sebeș 29,619
Sfîntu Gheorghe 62,355
Sibiu 172,117
Sighetu Marmației 42,118
Sighișoara 36,437
Slatina 68,525
Slobozia 42,248
Suceava 85,250
Tecuci 42,449
Timișoara 303,499
Tîrgoviște 82,034
Tîrgu-Jiu 81,488
Tîrgu Mureș 154,506
Tîrnăveni 28,634
Tulcea 79,290
Turda 59,695
Turnu-Măgurele 33,451
Vaslui 57,571
Vulcan 32,125
Zalău 50,108
Zărnesti 26,191

RWANDA

1981 E 5,109,000

Cities and Towns

Butare 26,100
• KIGALI 156,700

SAINT CHRISTOPHER-NEVIS

1980 C 44,404

Cities and Towns

• BASSETERRE 14,725
Charlestown 1,771

SAINT HELENA

1976 C 5,147

Cities and Towns

• JAMESTOWN 1,516

SAINT LUCIA

1984 E 134,006

Cities and Towns

• CASTRIES 50,798

SAINT PIERRE AND MIQUELON / Saint-Pierre-et-Miquelon

1982 C 6,041

Cities and Towns

• SAINT-PIERRE 5,371

SAINT VINCENT AND THE GRENADINES

1984 E 108,748

Cities and Towns

• KINGSTOWN (★ 27,948) 18,378

SAN MARINO

1980 E 21,537

Cities and Towns

• SAN MARINO 4,623

SAO TOME AND PRINCIPE / São Tomé e Príncipe

1970 C 73,631

Cities and Towns

• SÃO TOMÉ 17,380

SAUDI ARABIA / Al 'Arabīyah as Su'ūdīyah

1981 E 9,320,000

Cities and Towns

Abhā (1974 C) 30,150
Ad Dammām (1980 E) 200,000
Al Hufūf (Hofuf) (1974 C) 101,271
Al Khubar (1974 C) 48,817
Al Mubarraz (1974 C) 54,325
Aṭ Ṭā'if (1980 E) 300,000
Aẓ Ẓahrān (Dhahran) (1974 UE) 25,000
Buraydah (1974 C) 69,940
Ḥā'il (1974 C) 40,502
• Jiddah 1,300,000
Khamīs Mushayṭ (1974 C) 49,581
Mecca (Makkah) (1980 E) 550,000
Medina (Al Madīnah) (1980 E) 290,000
Najran (1974 C) 47,501
Qīzān (1974 C) 32,812
RIYADH (AR RIYĀḌ) 1,250,000
Tabūk (1974 C) 74,825

C Census. E Official estimate. UE Unofficial estimate.
• Largest city in country.
★ Population or designation of metropolitan area, including suburbs (see headnote).
▲ Population of an entire municipality, commune, or district, including rural area.

Senegal / Sénégal

1982 E ... 6,038,000

Cities and Towns

• DAKAR ... 1,341,000
Diourbel ... 64,913
Kaolack ... 125,776
Saint-Louis ... 107,072
Tambacounda ... 31,078
Thiès ... 139,170
Ziguinchor ... 84,104

SEYCHELLES

1984 E ... 64,718

Cities and Towns

• VICTORIA ... 23,000

SIERRA LEONE

1979 C ... 3,381,000

Cities and Towns

Bo ... 32,900
• FREETOWN (★ 375,000) ... 300,000
Kenema ... 31,300
Koindu (1974 C) ... 75,800
Lunsar ... 18,000
Makeni ... 26,500
Port Loko (1974 C) ... 10,500

SINGAPORE

1984 E ... 2,529,100

Cities and Towns

• SINGAPORE (★ 2,760,000) .. 2,529,100

SOLOMON ISLANDS

1978 E ... 212,868

Cities and Towns

• HONIARA ... 16,125

SOMALIA / Soomaaliya

1980 E ... 3,645,000

Cities and Towns

Berbera ... 65,000
Hargeysa (1976 E) ... 90,000
Kismaayo ... 70,000
Marka (1976 E) ... 65,000
• MOGADISHU (MUQDISHO) ... 400,000

SOUTH AFRICA / Suid-Afrika

1980 C ... 24,208,140

Cities and Towns

Alberton (★ Johannesburg) ... 46,920
Alexandra (★ Johannesburg) ... 56,460
Aliwal North ... 5,160
Atteridgeville-Saulsville (★ Pretoria) ... 89,980
Beaufort West (★ 19,920) ... 16,560
Bellville (★ Cape Town) ... 65,720
Benoni (★ Johannesburg) ... 68,500
Bethal (★ 27,480) ... 9,420
Bethlehem (★ 39,920) ... 12,080
Bloemfontein (★ 235,000) ... 102,600
Bloemfontein (Black Township) (★ Bloemfontein) ... 91,020
Boksburg (★ Johannesburg) ... 108,680
Brakpan (★ Johannesburg) ... 38,560
CAPE TOWN (KAAPSTAD) (★ 1,790,000) ... 859,940
Carletonville (★ 122,740) ... 100,220
Clermont (★ Durban) ... 34,180
Constantia (★ Cape Town) ... 23,100
Cradock (★ 26,260) ... 11,320
Daveyton (★ Johannesburg) ... 91,640
De Aar (★ 21,620) ... 14,940
Duduza (★ Johannesburg) ... 27,380
Duncanvillage (★ East London) .. 28,500
Dundee ... 9,000
Durban (★ 1,550,000) ... 677,760
East London (Oos-Londen) (★ 320,000) ... 77,060
Edendale (★ Pietermaritzburg) ... 47,560
Edenvale (★ Johannesburg) ... 31,600
Elsies River (★ Cape Town) ... 75,240
Empumalanga (★ Durban) ... 50,660
Ermelo (★ 31,400) ... 10,860
Evaton (★ Vereeniging) ... 57,440
Ezakheni ... 25,440
Galeshewe (★ Kimberley) ... 70,540
George (★ 43,260) ... 34,940
Germiston (★★ Johannesburg) ... 113,000
Goodwood (★ Cape Town) ... 32,480
Graaff-Reinet (★ 22,840) ... 14,700
Grahamstown (★ 51,040) ... 25,120
Guguleto (★ Cape Town) ... 74,760
Harrismith ... 5,280
Ikageng (★ Potchefstroom) ... 38,640
Imbali Township (★ Pietermaritzburg) ... 28,140
• Johannesburg (★ 3,650,000) .. 703,980
Jouberton (★ Klerksdorp) ... 31,420
Kagiso (★ Johannesburg) ... 43,380
Katlehong (★ Johannesburg) .. 157,300
Kempton Park (★ Johannesburg) ... 75,880
Kimberley (★ 145,000) ... 70,920
King William's Town (★ 48,300) ... 14,260
Klerksdorp (★ 205,000) ... 44,000
Kraaifontein (★ Cape Town) ... 28,000
Kroonstad (★ 62,440) ... 20,900
Krugersdorp (★ Johannesburg) .. 70,040
Kwa Mashu (★ Durban) ... 117,680
Kwanobuhle (★ Port Elizabeth) .. 33,700
Kwatema (★ Johannesburg) ... 91,200
Kwazakele (★ Port Elizabeth) ... 99,180
Ladysmith (★ 31,300) ... 21,880
Langa (★ Cape Town) ... 33,320
Madadeni (★ Newcastle) ... 60,940
Mafikeng (★ 16,000) ... 6,500
Mamelodi (★ Pretoria) ... 144,000
Mariannhill (★ Durban) ... 27,940
Middelburg (★ 38,120) ... 18,600
Mohlakeng (★ Johannesburg) ... 30,800
Mosselbaai (★ 22,180) ... 17,600
Nelspruit (★ 40,300) ... 14,660
New Brighton (★ Port Elizabeth) ... 62,600
Newcastle (★ 155,000) ... 34,120
Nigel (★ Johannesburg) ... 24,520
Ntuzuma (★ Durban) ... 28,620
Nyamasan (★ Nelspruit) ... 25,640
Odendaalsrus (★★ Welkom) ... 7,280
Orkney (★★ Klerksdorp) ... 18,500
Oudtshoorn (★ 35,980) ... 33,480
Ozisweni (★ Newcastle) ... 55,840
Paarl (★★ Cape Town) ... 59,140
Parow (★ Cape Town) ... 68,760
Parys (★ 20,880) ... 6,540
Phalaborwa (★ 29,740) ... 9,700
Pietermaritzburg (★ 230,000) .. 126,300
Pietersburg (★ 57,080) ... 25,500
Pinetown (★ Durban) ... 29,180
Port Elizabeth (★ 690,000) ... 281,600
Potchefstroom (★ 77,560) ... 38,920
Potgietersrus (★ 22,140) ... 7,640
PRETORIA (★ 960,000) ... 435,100
Queenstown (★ 35,640) ... 15,060
Randburg (★ Johannesburg) ... 65,840
Randfontein (★ Johannesburg) .. 49,040
Roodepoort-Maraisburg (★ Johannesburg) ... 129,700
Rustenburg ... 30,420
Sandton (★ Johannesburg) ... 70,540
Sasolburg (★★ Vereeniging) ... 26,020
Sebokeng (★ Vereeniging) ... 165,080
Seshego (★ Pietersburg) ... 28,880
Shapeville (★ Vereeniging) ... 50,640
Soshanguve (★ Pretoria) ... 63,220
Soweto (★ Johannesburg) ... 868,580
Springs (★ Johannesburg) ... 78,700
Standerton (★ 33,700) ... 11,960
Stellenbosch (★★ Cape Town) .. 37,680
Stilfontein (★★ Klerksdorp) ... 13,280
Strand (★ Cape Town) ... 25,260
Tembisa (★ Johannesburg) ... 195,080
Thabong (★ Welkom) ... 49,520
Tokoza (★ Johannesburg) ... 42,280
Tsakane (★ Johannesburg) ... 31,780
Uitenhage (★★ Port Elizabeth) ... 49,840
Umlazi (★ Durban) ... 190,120
Upington (★ 31,940) ... 25,880
Vanderbijlpark (★★ Vereeniging) ... 61,240
Vereeniging (★ 525,000) ... 60,680
Verwoerdburg (★ Pretoria) ... 39,980
Virginia (★ 65,000) ... 14,060
Vosloosrus (★ Johannesburg) ... 48,100
Vredenburg-Saldanha ... 27,480
Vryburg (★ 23,700) ... 8,980
Vryheid (★ 19,480) ... 11,260
Walvisbaai (Walvis Bay) (★ 20,440) ... 11,600
Welkom (★ 215,000) ... 48,380
Westonaria (★ Johannesburg) ... 54,560
Westville (★ Durban) ... 26,260
Witbank (Black Township) (★ Witbank) ... 44,080
Witbank (★ 82,680) ... 38,600
Worcester (★ 50,080) ... 41,880
Zwide (★ Port Elizabeth) ... 81,580

Provinces

Cape ... 5,091,360
Natal ... 6,098,480
Orange Free State ... 2,089,480
Transvaal ... 10,928,820

SOVIET UNION / Sovetskiy Soyuz

1985 E ... 276,290,000

Cities and Towns

Abakan ... 147,000
Abay (1974 E) ... 41,000
Abdulino (1974 E) ... 25,000
Achinsk ... 120,000
Agryz (1974 E) ... 19,000
Akhtubinsk ... 52,000
Akhtyrka (1974 E) ... 43,000
Aktyubinsk ... 231,000
Alapayevsk ... 51,000
Alatyr (1974 E) ... 46,000
Aleksandriya ... 93,000
Aleksandrov ... 65,000
Aleksin ... 70,000
Aleysk (1974 E) ... 37,000
Ali-Bayramly (1974 E) ... 38,000
Alma-Ata (★ 1,130,000) ... 1,068,000
Almalyk ... 114,000
Almetyevsk ... 123,000
Alytus ... 68,000
Amursk ... 51,000
Anapa (1974 E) ... 30,000
Andizhan ... 275,000
Andropov (Rybinsk) ... 251,000
Angarsk ... 256,000
Angren ... 122,000
Antratsit (★★ Krasnyy Luch) ... 68,000
Anzhero-Sudzhensk ... 110,000
Apatity ... 76,000
Apsheronsk (1974 E) ... 33,000
Araisk (1974 E) ... 39,000
Arkalyk ... 66,000
Arkhangelsk ... 408,000
Armavir ... 168,000
Arsenyev ... 65,000
Artem ... 72,000
Artemovsk ... 91,000
Artemovskiy (1974 E) ... 38,000
Arzamas ... 105,000
Asbest ... 82,000
Asha (1974 E) ... 38,000
Ashkhabad ... 356,000
Asino (1974 E) ... 31,000
Astrakhan ... 493,000
Atbasar (1974 E) ... 39,000
Atkarsk (1974 E) ... 30,000
Avdeyevka (★ Donetsk) (1974 E) ... 33,000
Ayaguz (1974 E) ... 40,000
Azov ... 79,000
Baku (★ 1,935,000) ... 1,104,000
Balakhna (★ Gorkiy) (1974 E) ... 37,000
Balakleya (1974 E) ... 31,000
Balakovo ... 180,000
Balashikha (★ Moscow) ... 128,000
Balashov ... 97,000
Balkhash ... 82,000
Barabinsk (1974 E) ... 37,000
Baranovichi ... 149,000
Barnaul (★ 635,000) ... 578,000
Bataysk (★ Rostov-na-Donu) ... 96,000
Batumi ... 132,000
Bayram-Ali (1974 E) ... 36,000
Bekabad (Begovat) ... 77,000
Belaya Kalitva (1974 E) ... 35,000
Belaya Tserkov ... 181,000
Belebey (1974 E) ... 39,000
Belgorod ... 280,000
Belgorod-Dnestrovskiy ... 52,000
Belogorsk ... 70,000
Belorechensk (1974 E) ... 38,000
Beloretsk ... 73,000
Belovo ... 117,000
Beltsy ... 147,000
Bendery ... 122,000
Berdichev ... 86,000
Berdsk (★ Novosibirsk) ... 75,000
Berdyansk ... 130,000
Berezniki ... 195,000
Berezovskiy (1974 E) ... 39,000
Bezhetsk (1974 E) ... 30,000
Birobidzan ... 78,000
Biysk ... 226,000
Blagoveshchensk ... 195,000
Bobruysk ... 223,000
Bogoroditsk (1974 E) ... 32,000
Bogorodsk (★ Gorkiy) (1974 E) ... 37,000
Bologoye (1974 E) ... 34,000
Bor (★ Gorkiy) ... 64,000
Borislav (1974 E) ... 36,000
Borisoglebsk ... 68,000
Borisov ... 132,000
Borispol (1974 E) ... 36,000
Borovichi ... 63,000
Boyarka (★ Kiev) (1974 E) ... 31,000
Bratsk ... 240,000
Brest ... 222,000
Brezhnev (Naberezhnyye Chelny) (1984 E) ... ▲414,000
Brovary (★ Kiev) ... 67,000
Bryanka (★ Stakhanov) ... 64,000
Bryansk ... 430,000
Budennovsk ... 51,000
Bugulma ... 86,000
Buguruslan ... 53,000
Bukhara ... 209,000
Buy (1974 E) ... 28,000
Buynaksk ... 51,000
Buzuluk ... 80,000
Chapayevsk ... 86,000
Chardzhou ... 157,000
Chaykovskij ... 78,000
Chebarkul (1974 E) ... 42,000
Cheboksary ... 389,000
Chekhov ... 56,000
Chelyabinsk (★ 1,275,000) ... 1,096,000
Cheremkhovo ... 73,000
Cherepovets ... 299,000
Cherkassy ... 273,000
Cherkessk ... 102,000
Chernigov ... 278,000
Chernogorsk ... 78,000
Chernovtsy ... 244,000
Chernyakhovsk (Insterburg) (1974 E) ... 34,000
Chervonograd ... 67,000
Chimkent ... 369,000
Chirchik (★ Tashkent) ... 153,000
Chistopol ... 65,000
Chita ... 336,000
Chu (1974 E) ... 35,000
Chusovoy ... 58,000
Chust (1974 E) ... 31,000
Daugavpils ... 124,000
Debaltsevo (1983 E) ... 37,000
Derbent ... 80,000
Dimitrov (★★ Krasnoarmeysk) ... 62,000
Dimitrovgrad (Melekess) ... 116,000
Dmitrov ... 63,000
Dneprodzerzhinsk (★★ Dnepropetrovsk) ... 271,000
Dnepropetrovsk (★ 1,560,000) ... 1,153,000
Dobropolye (1974 E) ... 31,000
Dolgoprudnyy (★ Moscow) ... 69,000
Domodedovo (★ Moscow) ... 50,000
Donetsk, Donetsk oblast (★ 2,185,000) ... 1,073,000
Donetsk, Rostov oblast (1974 E) ... 42,000
Donskoy (★ Novomoskovsk) (1974 E) ... 34,000
Drogobych ... 74,000
Druzhkovka (★ Kramatorsk) ... 69,000
Dubna ... 61,000
Dushanbe ... 552,000
Dzerzhinsk (★ Gorlovka) (1974 E) ... 46,000
Dzerzhinsk (★ Gorkiy) ... 274,000
Dzhalal-Abad ... 70,000
Dzhambul ... 303,000
Dzhankoy ... 50,000
Dzhetygara (1974 E) ... 39,000
Dzhezkazgan ... 102,000
Dzhizak ... 85,000
Echmiadzin (★ Yerevan) ... 51,000
Ekibastuz ... 119,000
Elektrostal ... 148,000
Elista ... 81,000
Engels (★★ Saratov) ... 177,000
Fastov ... 54,000
Feodosiya ... 82,000
Fergana ... 195,000
Frolovo (1974 E) ... 38,000
Frunze ... 604,000
Fryazino (★ Moscow) ... 50,000
Furmanov (1974 E) ... 41,000
Gatchina (★ Leningrad) ... 79,000
Gelendzhik (1974 E) ... 31,000
Geokchay (1974 E) ... 30,000
Georgiu-Dez (Liski) ... 53,000
Georgiyevsk ... 60,000
Glazov ... 94,000
Glukhov (1974 E) ... 30,000
Gomel ... 465,000
Gori ... 61,000
Gorkiy (Gorki) (★ 1,965,000) ... 1,399,000
Gorlovka (★ 710,000) ... 342,000
Gorno-Altaysk (1974 E) ... 39,000
Gorodets (1974 E) ... 35,000
Grodno ... 247,000
Groznyy ... 393,000
Gryazi (1974 E) ... 42,000
Gubakha (1974 E) ... 32,000
Gubkin ... 71,000
Gudermes (1974 E) ... 34,000
Gukovo ... 72,000
Gulistan (1975 E) ... 39,000
Guryev ... 145,000
Gus-Khrustalnyy ... 75,000
Ilichevsk (★ Odessa) ... 50,000
Ingulets (1974 E) ... 35,000
Inta ... 56,000
Irbit ... 52,000
Irkutsk ... 597,000
Ishim ... 64,000
Ishimbay ... 64,000
Iskitim ... 67,000
Ivano-Frankovsk ... 210,000
Ivanovo ... 474,000
Ivanteyevka (★ Moscow) ... 51,000
Izmail ... 89,000
Izyum ... 62,000
Jelgava ... 70,000
Jurmala (★ Rīga) ... 60,000
Kachkanar (1974 E) ... 38,000
Kafan (1974 E) ... 31,000
Kagan (1974 E) ... 38,000
Kagul (1974 E) ... 31,000
Kakhovka (1974 E) ... 35,000
Kalinin ... 438,000
Kaliningrad (★ Moscow) ... 143,000
Kaliningrad (Königsberg) ... 385,000
Kaluga ... 297,000
Kalush ... 65,000
Kamenets-Podolskiy ... 97,000
Kamenka (1974 E) ... 32,000
Kamen-na-Obi (1974 E) ... 40,000
Kamensk-Shakhtinskiy ... 75,000
Kamensk-Uralskiy ... 200,000
Kamyshin ... 116,000
Kamyshlov (1974 E) ... 31,000
Kanash ... 50,000
Kandalaksha (1974 E) ... 43,000
Kansk ... 105,000
Kapsukas (1974 E) ... 33,000
Kara-Balty ... 53,000
Karaganda ... 617,000
Karpinsk (1974 E) ... 37,000
Karshi ... 133,000
Kartaly (1974 E) ... 44,000
Kashira (1974 E) ... 42,000
Kasimov (1974 E) ... 34,000
Kaspiysk ... 58,000
Kattakurgan ... 60,000
Kaunas ... 405,000
Kazan (★ 1,100,000) ... 1,047,000
Kemerovo ... 507,000
Kentau ... 58,000
Kerch ... 168,000
Khabarovsk ... 576,000
Khanty-Mansiysk (1974 E) ... 26,000
Kharkov (★ 1,865,000) ... 1,554,000
Khartsyzsk (★ Donetsk) ... 66,000
Khasavyurt ... 73,000
Kherson ... 346,000
Khimki (★ Moscow) ... 125,000
Khmelnitskiy ... 217,000
Khodzheyli ... 52,000
Kholmsk ... 50,000
Kiev (Kiyev) (★ 2,740,000) ... 2,448,000
Kimovsk (1974 E) ... 44,000
Kimry ... 60,000
Kinel (1974 E) ... 40,000
Kineshma ... 104,000
Kirishi (1974 E) ... 34,000
Kirov ... 411,000
Kirovabad ... 261,000
Kirovakan ... 165,000
Kirovo-Chepetsk ... 85,000
Kirovograd ... 263,000
Kirovsk (1974 E) ... 40,000
Kirovsk (★ Stakhanov) (1974 E) ... 40,000
Kiselevsk (★★ Prokopyevsk) ... 126,000
Kishinev ... 624,000
Kislovodsk ... 108,000
Kizel (1974 E) ... 42,000
Klaipėda (Memel) ... 195,000
Klimovsk (★ Moscow) ... 56,000
Klin ... 94,000
Klintsy ... 71,000
Kohtla-Järve ... 77,000
Kokand ... 166,000
Kokchetav ... 120,000
Kolchugino (1974 E) ... 43,000
Kolomna ... 156,000
Kolomyya ... 60,000
Kolpino (★ Leningrad) ... 130,000
Kommunarsk (★ Stakhanov) ... 124,000
Komsomolsk-na-Amure ... 300,000
Konakovo (1974 E) ... 33,000
Kondopoga (1974 E) ... 32,000
Konotop ... 90,000
Konstantinovka ... 114,000
Kopeysk (★ Chelyabinsk) ... 100,000
Korkino (1981 E) ... 63,000
Korosten (1986 E) ... 71,000
Korsakov (1974 E) ... 40,000
Kostroma ... 269,000
Kotelnich (1974 E) ... 31,000
Kotlas ... 68,000
Kotovsk (1974 E) ... 39,000
Kovel ... 63,000
Kovrov ... 153,000
Kramatorsk (★ 465,000) ... 192,000
Krasnoarmeysk (★ 170,000) ... 67,000
Krasnodar ... 609,000
Krasnodon ... 50,000
Krasnogorsk (★ Moscow) ... 86,000
Krasnokamensk ... 65,000
Krasnokamsk ... 57,000
Krasnoturinsk ... 64,000
Krasnoufimsk (1974 E) ... 40,000

C Census. E Official estimate: UE Unofficial estimate.
• Largest city in country.

★ Population or designation of metropolitan area, including suburbs (see headnote).
▲Population of an entire municipality, commune, or district, including rural area.

Krasnouralsk (1974 E) 40,000
Krasnovodsk 57,000
Krasnoyarsk 872,000
Krasnyy Luch (★ 235,000) 111,000
Krasnyy Sulin (1974 E) 43,000
Kremenchug 224,000
Krivoy Rog 684,000
Kronshtadt (★ Leningrad) (1970 C) 39,477
Kropotkin 72,000
Krymsk (Krymskaya) (1983 E) 50,000
Kstovo (★ Gorkiy) 63,000
Kuba (1974 E) 19,000
Kulebaki (1974 E) 46,000
Kulyab 66,000
Kumertau 59,000
Kungur 82,000
Kupyansk (1974 E) 34,000
Kurgan 343,000
Kurganinsk (1974 E) 38,000
Kurgan-Tyube 51,000
Kursk 420,000
Kushva (1974 E) 43,000
Kustanay 199,000
Kutaisi 214,000
Kuybyshev (1974 E) 44,000
Kuybyshev (★ 1,480,000) 1,257,000
Kuznetsk 97,000
Kyshtym (1974 E) 39,000
Kyzyl 75,000
Kyzyl-Kiya (1974 E) 33,000
Kzyl-Orda 183,000
Labinsk 57,000
Leninabad 150,000
Leninakan 223,000
Leningrad (★ 5,650,000) 4,329,000
Leninogorsk, Tatarskaya Auton. S. S. R. 59,000
Leninogorsk, Vostochno-Kazakhstanskaya oblast' 68,000
Leninsk (1974 E) 31,000
Leninsk-Kuznetskiy 138,000
Lenkoran (1974 E) 38,000
Lesozavodsk (1974 E) 38,000
Lida 75,000
Liepāja 112,000
Lipetsk 447,000
Lisichansk (★ 385,000) 122,000
Livny (1974 E) 42,000
Lobnya (★ Moscow) 58,000
Lomonosov (★ Leningrad) (1974 E) 43,000
Lozovaya 64,000
Lubny 57,000
Luga (1974 E) 35,000
Lutsk 172,000
Lvov 742,000
Lysva 76,000
Lytkarino (★ Moscow) 50,000
Lyubertsy (★ Moscow) 161,000
Lyubotin (1974 E) 33,000
Lyudinovo (1974 E) 36,000
Magadan 142,000
Magnitogorsk 422,000
Makeyevka (★★ Donetsk) 451,000
Makhachkala 301,000
Marganets 54,000
Margilan 123,000
Mariinsk (1974 E) 40,000
Mary 85,000
Maykop 140,000
Mednogorsk (1974 E) 36,000
Melitopol 170,000
Mezhdurechensk 101,000
Miass 160,000
Michurinsk 102,000
Mikhaylovka 57,000
Millerovo (1974 E) 37,000
Mineralnyye Vody 74,000
Mingechaur 74,000
Minsk (★ 1,525,000) 1,472,000
Minusinsk 69,000
Mogilev 343,000
Molodechno 84,000
Monchegorsk 61,000
Morshansk (1977 E) 50,000
• MOSCOW (MOSKVA) (★ 12,650,000) 8,408,000
Mozdok (1974 E) 33,000
Mozhga (1974 E) 41,000
Mozyr 93,000
Mtsensk (1974 E) 34,000
Mukachevo 84,000
Murmansk 419,000
Murom 121,000
Myski (1974 E) 38,000
Mytishchi (★ Moscow) 151,000
Nakhichevan (1974 E) 37,000
Nakhodka 150,000
Nalchik 227,000
Namangan 275,000
Naro-Fominsk 58,000
Narva 79,000
Navoy 99,000
Nazarovo 60,000
Nebit-Dag 81,000
Neftekamsk 90,000
Nefteyugansk 78,000
Neryungri 57,000
Nevinnomyssk 114,000
Nevyansk (1974 E) 31,000
Nezhin 79,000
Nikolayev 486,000
Nikolayevsk [-na-Amure] (1974 E) 33,000
Nikolskiy 60,000
Nikopol 155,000
Nizhnekamsk 170,000
Nizhneudinsk (1974 E) 42,000
Nizhnevartovsk 190,000
Nizhniy Tagil 419,000
Noginsk 121,000
Norilsk 180,000
Novaya Kakhovka 51,000
Novgorod 220,000
Novoaltaysk (★ Barnaul) 50,000
Novocheboksarsk 103,000
Novocherkassk 186,000
Novodvinsk 50,000
Novoekonomicheskoye (★★ Krasnoarmeysk) (1970 C) 31,214
Novograd-Volynskiy 51,000
Novokazalinsk (1970 C) 34,815
Novokuybyshevsk (★ Kuybyshev) 110,000
Novokuznetsk 577,000
Novomoskovsk, Dnepropetrovsk oblast 74,000
Novomoskovsk, Tula oblast (★ 365,000) 147,000
Novopolotsk 84,000
Novorossiysk 175,000
Novoshakhtinsk 106,000
Novosibirsk (★ 1,545,000) 1,393,000
Novotroitsk 103,000
Novovolynsk 52,000
Novozybkov (1974 E) 39,000
Novyy Urengoy 61,000
Noyabrsk 60,000
Nukus 139,000
Obninsk 91,000
Odessa (★ 1,190,000) 1,126,000
Odintsovo (★ Moscow) 116,000
Okha (1974 E) 31,000
Oktyabr'sk (1974 E) 33,000
Oktyabrskiy 102,000
Omsk (★ 1,130,000) 1,108,000
Ordzhonikidze 303,000
Orekhovo-Zuyevo (★ 205,000) 136,000
Orel 328,000
Orenburg 519,000
Orsha 119,000
Orsk 266,000
Osh 199,000
Osinniki 63,000
Otradnyy (1974 E) 46,000
Panevėžys 116,000
Pärnu 53,000
Partizansk (Suchan) (1974 E) 49,000
Pavlodar 315,000
Pavlograd 119,000
Pavlovo 71,000
Pavlovskiy Posad 71,000
Pechora 62,000
Penza 527,000
Pereslavl-Zalesskiy (1974 E) 33,000
Perevalsk (★ Stakhanov) (1974 E) 32,000
Perm (★ 1,125,000) 1,056,000
Pervomaysk 77,000
Pervomaysk (★ Stakhanov) (1974 E) 46,000
Pervouralsk 136,000
Petrodvorets (★ Leningrad) 77,000
Petropavlovsk 226,000
Petropavlovsk [-Kamchatskiy] 245,000
Petrovsk (1974 E) 34,000
Petrozavodsk 255,000
Pinsk 109,000
Podolsk (★ Moscow) 208,000
Polevskoy 69,000
Polotsk 79,000
Poltava 302,000
Poti (1977 E) 54,000
Priluki 71,000
Prokhladnyy 52,000
Prokopyevsk (★ 410,000) 274,000
Przhevalsk 60,000
Pskov 194,000
Pugachev (1974 E) 35,000
Pushkin (★ Leningrad) 91,000
Pushkino 74,000
Pyatigorsk 118,000
Ramenskoye (★ Moscow) 85,000
Rasskazovo (1974 E) 40,000
Razdan 52,000
Rechitsa 69,000
Reutov (★ Moscow) 66,000
Revda 65,000
Rēzekne (1974 E) 34,000
Rezh (1974 E) 34,000
Rīga (★ 970,000) 883,000
Rodniki (1974 E) 30,000
Romny 53,000
Roslavl 60,000
Rossosh 52,000
Rostov (1974 E) 31,000
Rostov-na-Donu (★ 1,125,000) 986,000
Rovenki 67,000
Rovno 221,000
Rtishchevo (1974 E) 41,000
Rubezhnoye (★★ Lisichansk) 69,000
Rubtsovsk 165,000
Rudnyy 116,000
Rustavi (★ Tbilisi) 143,000
Ruzayevka 52,000
Ryazan 494,000
Rybachye (1974 E) 33,000
Rybnitsa 53,000
Rzhev 70,000
Safonovo 55,000
Salavat 149,000
Salsk 61,000
Samarkand 371,000
Saran 62,000
Saransk 307,000
Sarapul 110,000
Saratov (★ 1,145,000) 899,000
Satka (1974 E) 44,000
Segezha (1974 E) 33,000
Semipalatinsk 317,000
Serdobsk (1974 E) 37,000
Serov 102,000
Serpukhov 142,000
Sevastopol 341,000
Severodonetsk (★★ Lisichansk) 124,000
Severodvinsk (Molotovsk) 230,000
Severomorsk 54,000
Shadrinsk 86,000
Shakhtersk (★★ Torez) 72,000
Shakhtinsk 59,000
Shakhty 221,000
Shchekino 70,000
Shchelkovo (★ Moscow) 106,000
Shchuchinsk 52,000
Shebekino (1974 E) 36,000
Sheki (Nukha) 53,000
Shepetovka (1974 E) 42,000
Shevchenko 147,000
Shostka 85,000
Shumerlya (1974 E) 35,000
Shuya 72,000
Šiauliai 134,000
Sibay (1974 E) 40,000
Simferopol 331,000
Slantsy (1974 E) 42,000
Slavyansk (★★ Kramatorsk) 143,000
Slavyansk-na-Kubani 56,000
Slobodskoy (1974 E) 36,000
Slutsk 53,000
Smela 71,000
Smolensk 331,000
Snezhnoye (★ Torez) 67,000
Sochi 310,000
Sokol (1974 E) 48,000
Soligorsk 85,000
Solikamsk 106,000
Solnechnogorsk (★ Moscow) 52,000
Solntsevo (★ Moscow) (1984 E) 62,000
Sosnovyy Bor 53,000
Sovetsk (Tilsit) (1974 E) 40,000
Spassk-Dalniy 58,000
Stakhanov (Kadiyevka) (★ 600,000) 110,000
Staraya Russa (1974 E) 37,000
Staryy Oskol 154,000
Stavropol 293,000
Sterlitamak 240,000
Stryy 61,000
Stupino 73,000
Sukhumi 126,000
Sumgait (★ Baku) 223,000
Sumy 256,000
Surgut 203,000
Suzdal (1959 C) 9,000
Sverdlovsk 81,000
Sverdlovsk (★ 1,540,000) 1,300,000
Svetlogorsk 65,000
Svetlovodsk (Kremges) 53,000
Svobodnyy 77,000
Syktyvkar 213,000
Syzran 173,000
Taganrog 289,000
Taldy-Kurgan 106,000
Talgar (1974 E) 35,000
Tallinn 464,000
Tambov 296,000
Tartu 111,000
Tashauz 103,000
Tashkent (★ 2,260,000) 2,030,000
Tatarsk (1974 E) 31,000
Tavda (1974 E) 47,000
Tayshet (1974 E) 35,000
Tbilisi (★ 1,335,000) 1,158,000
Temirtau 225,000
Termez 66,000
Ternopol 182,000
Teykovo (1974 E) 42,000
Tikhoretsk 66,000
Tikhvin 67,000
Tiraspol 162,000
Tobolsk 75,000
Tokmak 68,000
Tokmak (1974 E) 39,000
Tolyatti (Stavropol) 594,000
Tomsk 475,000
Topki (1974 E) 30,000
Torez (Chistyakovo) (★ 285,000) 88,000
Torzhok (1977 E) 50,000
Troitsk 91,000
Tselinograd (Akmolinsk) 262,000
Tskhinvali (1975 E) 34,000
Tuapse 63,000
Tula (★ 630,000) 532,000
Tulun 54,000
Turkestan 76,000
Tuymazy 51,000
Tynda 56,000
Tyumen 425,000
Ufa (★ 1,080,000) 1,064,000
Uglich (1974 E) 37,000
Ukhta 100,000
Ulan-Ude 335,000
Ulyanovsk 544,000
Uman 86,000
Uralsk 192,000
Ura-Tyube (1974 E) 36,000
Urgench 116,000
Uryupinsk (1974 E) 39,000
Usolye-Sibirskoye 107,000
Ussuriysk 156,000
Ust-Ilimsk 97,000
Ustinov (Izhevsk) 611,000
Ust-Kamenogorsk 307,000
Ust-Kut 56,000
Ust'-Labinsk (1974 E) 38,000
Uzhgorod 107,000
Uzlovaya (★★ Novomoskovsk) 64,000
Valuyki (1974 E) 30,000
Velikiye Luki 110,000
Velikiy Ustyug (1974 E) 38,000
Ventspils 51,000
Verkhniy Ufaley (1974 E) 38,000
Verkhnyaya Pyshma (★ Sverdlovsk) (1974 E) 40,000
Verkhnyaya Salda 56,000
Vichuga 51,000
Vidnoye (1974 E) 40,000
Vilnius 544,000
Vinnitsa 367,000
Vitebsk 335,000
Vladimir 331,000
Vladivostok 600,000
Volgodonsk 165,000
Volgograd (Stalingrad) (★ 1,305,000) 974,000
Volkhov 50,000
Vologda 269,000
Volsk 66,000
Volzhsk 58,000
Volzhskiy (★ Volgograd) 245,000
Vorkuta 108,000
Voronezh 850,000
Voroshilovgrad (Lugansk) 497,000
Voskresensk 79,000
Votkinsk 99,000
Voznesensk (1974 E) 39,000
Vyatskiye Polyany (1974 E) 35,000
Vyazma 55,000
Vyazniki (1974 E) 44,000
Vyborg 80,000
Vyksa 59,000
Vyshniy Volochek 71,000
Yakutsk 180,000
Yalta 86,000
Yangiyul 69,000
Yaroslavl 626,000
Yartsevo (1974 E) 39,000
Yasinovataya (1974 E) 39,000
Yefremov 57,000
Yegoryevsk 73,000
Yelabuga (1974 E) 35,000
Yelets 116,000
Yemanzhelinsk (1974 E) 34,000
Yenakiyevo (★★ Gorlovka) 117,000
Yerevan (★ 1,240,000) 1,133,000
Yermak (1974 E) 40,000
Yessentuki 83,000
Yevpatoriya 103,000
Yeysk 76,000
Yoshkar-Ola 231,000
Yurga 89,000
Yuzhno-Sakhalinsk 158,000
Yuzhno-Uralsk (1974 E) 37,000
Zagorsk 112,000
Zaporozhye 852,000
Zavolzhye (1974 E) 38,000
Zelenodolsk 89,000
Zelenograd (★ Moscow) 142,000
Zhdanov 522,000
Zheleznodorozhnyy (★ Moscow) 86,000
Zheleznogorsk 77,000
Zheltyye Vody 59,000
Zhigulevsk (1977 E) 50,000
Zhitomir 275,000
Zhmerinka (1974 E) 38,000
Zhukovskiy 98,000
Zima (1977 E) 51,000
Zlatoust 204,000
Zugdidi (1974 E) 41,000
Zyryanovsk 54,000

Republics

Armenia 3,317,000
Azerbaijan S.S.R. 6,614,000
Byelorussia (White Russia) 9,942,000
Estonia 1,530,000
Georgia 5,201,000
Kazakh S.S.R. 15,842,000
Kirghiz S.S.R. 3,967,000
Latvia 2,604,000
Lithuania 3,570,000
Moldavia 4,111,000
Russian Soviet Federative Socialist Republic 143,090,000
Tajik S.S.R. 4,499,000
Turkmen S.S.R. 3,189,000
Ukraine 50,840,000
Uzbek S.S.R. 17,974,000

SPAIN / España

1984 E 38,872,389

Cities and Towns

Águilas (▲ 20,595) (1981 C) 18,400
Albacete 121,909
Alcalá [de Guadaira] (▲ 45,352) (1981 C) 38,400
Alcalá de Henares (★ Madrid) 146,994
Alcalá la Real (▲ 20,049) (1981 C) 9,200
Alcantarilla (1981 C) 24,406
Alcázar de San Juan (1981 C) 25,185
Alcira (1981 C) 37,446
Alcobendas (★ Madrid) 66,249
Alcorcón (★ Madrid) 144,478
Alcoy 67,431
Algeciras 92,474
Algemesí (1981 C) 24,552
Algorta (Guecho) (▲ 74,236) 36,000
Alicante 253,722
Almadén (1981 C) 9,521
Almendralejo (1981 C) 23,628
Almería 149,310
Andújar (▲ 34,946) (1981 C) 28,800
Antequera (▲ 35,171) (1981 C) 24,100
Aranjuez (1981 C) 35,936
Arcos de la Frontera (▲ 24,902) (1981 C) 15,500
Arizgoiti (Basauri) (★ Bilbao) 45,000
Arrecife, Canary Is. (1981 C) 29,502
Ávila 42,165
Avilés (★ 131,000) 89,992
Badajoz (▲ 116,790) 92,800
Badalona (★ Barcelona) 229,281
Baracaldo (★ Bilbao) 118,692
Barcelona (★ 4,040,000) 1,770,296
Baza (▲ 20,609) (1981 C) 14,800
Bilbao (★ 985,000) 397,541
Burgos 155,849
Burjasot (★ Valencia) (1981 C) 35,583
Burriana (1981 C) 25,003
Cabra (▲ 19,819) (1981 C) 15,600
Cáceres 69,734
Cádiz (★ 240,000) 160,839
Camas (★ Sevilla) (1981 C) 25,327
Carmona (1981 C) 22,779
Cartagena (▲ 174,195) 142,300
Castellón de la Plana 129,518
Cerdanyola de Vallés (★ Barcelona) 52,337
Chiclana [de la Frontera] (1981 C) 36,203
Cieza (1981 C) 29,932
Ciudad Real 53,546
Córdoba 291,370
Cornellá (★ Barcelona) 90,270
Coslada (★ Madrid) 60,297
Cuenca 40,888
Daimiel (1981 C) 16,260
Don Benito (1981 C) 28,418
Dos Hermanas 60,563
Écija (▲ 34,619) (1981 C) 26,200
Éibar (1981 C) 36,494
Elche (▲ 175,073) 144,600
Elda 55,322
El Ferrol [del Caudillo] (★ 129,000) 90,410
El Puerto de Santa María 59,844
Esplugas Llobregat (★ Barcelona) (1981 C) 45,834
Figueras (1981 C) 30,532
Fuenlabrada (★ Madrid) 107,283
Gandía (▲ 51,611) 40,500
Gavá (★ Barcelona) (1981 C) 33,456
Gerona 67,259
Getafe (★ Madrid) 128,522
Gijón 262,395
Granada 256,191
Granollers (★ Barcelona) (1981 C) 45,300
Guadalajara 58,436

C Census. E Official estimate. UE Unofficial estimate.
• Largest city in country.

★ Population or designation of metropolitan area, including suburbs (see headnote).
▲ Population of an entire municipality, commune, or district, including rural area.

Guadix (▲ 19,860) (1981 C) 15,400
Guernica y Luno (▲ 17,836) (1981 C) 12,100
Hellín (▲ 22,651) (1981 C) 16,300
Hospitalet (★ Barcelona) 288,290
Huelva 137,453
Huesca 42,337
Ibiza (1981 C) 25,489
Igualada (1981 C) 31,451
Irún 54,877
Jaén 102,262
Játiva (1981 C) 23,755
Jerez de la Frontera (▲ 184,905) 138,700
La Coruña 240,463
La Línea 58,945
La Orotava, Canary Is. (▲ 31,394) (1981 C) 9,700
Las Palmas de Gran Canaria, Canary Is. 377,353
Leganés (★ Madrid) 168,984
León (★ 159,000) 133,658
Lérida (▲ 110,293) 87,800
Linares (▲ 58,149) 51,800
Logroño 113,576
Loja (▲ 19,465) (1981 C) 10,400
Lorca (▲ 65,162) 27,100
Lucena (1981 C) 29,717
Lugo (▲ 74,389) 62,300
• MADRID (★ 4,650,000) 3,200,234
Mahón (1981 C) 22,926
Málaga 537,619
Manacor (1981 C) 24,153
Manresa 66,951
Marbella (▲ 65,568) 39,000
Martos (▲ 21,672) (1981 C) 16,500
Mataró 99,126
Mérida (1981 C) 41,783
Mieres (▲ 59,942) 21,200
Miranda de Ebro (1981 C) 36,812
Mislata (★ Valencia) (1981 C) 33,384
Morón de la Frontera (▲ 27,311) (1981 C) 23,800
Móstoles (★ Madrid) 164,304
Motril (▲ 39,784) (1981 C) 31,500
Murcia (▲ 305,221) 200,300
Olot (1981 C) 24,892
Onteniente (1981 C) 28,123
Orense (▲ 98,649) 85,500
Orihuela (▲ 52,237) 20,400
Oviedo 189,376
Palencia 74,311
Palma [de Mallorca] 311,197
Pamplona 181,668
Parla (★ Madrid) 62,694
Peñarroya-Pueblonuevo (1981 C) 13,219
Plasencia (1981 C) 32,178
Ponferrada 56,710
Pontevedra (▲ 67,027) 34,700
Portugalete (★ Bilbao) 59,307
Prat de Llobregat (★ Barcelona) 63,433
Priego [de Córdoba] (▲ 19,485) (1981 C) 11,700
Puente-Genil (▲ 25,615) (1981 C) 22,200
Puerto de la Cruz, Canary Is. (▲ 39,241) (1981 C) 29,000
Puertollano 51,845
Rentería (★ San Sebastián) (1981 C) 45,789
Reus 82,354
Ronda (▲ 31,383) (1981 C) 23,000
Rota (1981 C) 25,291
Rubí (★ Barcelona) (1981 C) 43,532
Sabadell (★ Barcelona) 189,775
Sagunto 57,380
Salamanca 159,336
Sama [de Langreo] (▲ 57,407) 9,700
San Adrián de Besós (★ Barcelona) (1981 C) 36,052
San Baudilio de Llobregat (★ Barcelona) 74,783
San Cristóbal de la Laguna, Canary Is. (▲ 107,735) (1982 E) 23,500
San Fernando (★★ Cádiz) 76,101
Sanlúcar [de Barrameda] (▲ 52,327) 37,600
San Sebastián (★ 285,000) 178,906
Santa Coloma [de Gramanet] (★ Barcelona) 140,274
Santa Cruz de Tenerife, Canary Is. (1981 C) 185,899
Santander 187,057
Santiago [de Compostela] (▲ 85,197) 62,300
Santurce-Antiguo (★ Bilbao) 54,036
Segovia 53,005
Sestao (★ Bilbao) (1981 C) 39,933
Sevilla (Seville) (★ 945,000) 672,435
Soria 31,405
Sueca (1981 C) 24,195
Talavera de la Reina 67,216
Tarragona 113,075
Tarrasa (★ Barcelona) 165,233
Telde, Canary Is. (▲ 68,684) 20,400
Teruel 26,750
Toledo 57,778
Tolosa (▲ 18,894) (1981 C) 15,300
Tomelloso (1981 C) 26,655
Torrejón de Ardoz (★ Madrid) 81,639
Torrelavega (▲ 58,088) 27,000
Torrente (★ Valencia) 55,028
Tortosa (▲ 31,445) (1981 C) 13,600
Totana (▲ 18,394) (1981 C) 14,500
Úbeda (1981 C) 28,717
Utrera (▲ 37,877) (1981 C) 30,000
Valdepeñas (1981 C) 24,946
Valencia (★ 1,270,000) 785,273
Valladolid 331,404
Vall de Uxó (1981 C) 26,145
Vélez-Málaga (▲ 41,776) (1981 C) 20,400
Vich (1981 C) 30,057
Vigo 277,460
Villanueva y Geltrú (1981 C) 43,560
Villarreal [de los Infantes] (▲ 38,385) (1981 C) 34,100
Villarrobledo (1981 C) 19,655
Villena (1981 C) 28,279
Vitoria 199,239
Zamora 61,151
Zaragoza (Saragossa) 601,235

Regions

Andalusia 6,773,737
Aragón 1,229,611
Asturias 1,150,664
Baleares 705,609
Canarias (Canary Is.) 1,426,422
Cantabria 527,603
Castilla-La Mancha 1,693,801
Castilla-León 2,641,882
Cataluña 6,077,114
Extremadura 1,098,422
Galicia 2,899,586
La Rioja 260,251
Madrid 4,865,334
Murcia 1,011,098
Navarra 520,413
País Vasco 2,184,176
Palencia 192,682
Valencia 3,806,666

Provinces

Alava 268,884
Albacete 349,751
Alicante 1,205,977
Almería 438,132
Asturias 1,150,664
Ávila 186,864
Badajoz 663,727
Baleares 705,609
Barcelona 4,697,745
Burgos 368,171
Cáceres 434,695
Cádiz 1,043,801
Cantabria (Santander) 527,603
Castellón 446,367
Ciudad Real 489,509
Córdoba 747,841
Cuenca 218,769
Gerona 489,298
Granada 793,909
Guadalajara 147,618
Guipúzcoa 708,456
Huelva 439,142
Huesca 216,532
Jaén 663,564
La Coruña 1,128,309
La Rioja 260,251
Las Palmas 754,949
León 539,041
Lérida 358,059
Lugo 411,818
Madrid 4,865,334
Málaga 1,099,494
Murcia 1,011,098
Navarra 520,413
Orense 441,186
Pontevedra 918,273
Salamanca 371,959
Santa Cruz de Tenerife (1983 E) 671,473
Segovia 152,818
Sevilla 1,547,854
Soria 101,271
Tarragona 532,012
Teruel 153,673
Toledo 488,154
Valencia 2,154,322
Valladolid 497,974
Vizcaya 1,206,836
Zamora 231,102
Zaragosa 859,406

SPANISH NORTH AFRICA / Plazas de Soberanía en el Norte de África

1984 E 125,069

Cities and Towns

• Ceuta 68,822
Melilla 56,247

SRI LANKA

1981 C 14,848,364

Cities and Towns

Anuradhapura 36,000
Badulla 33,000
Battaramulla (★ Colombo) 56,535
Batticaloa 43,000
• COLOMBO (★ 1,975,000) 587,647
Dalugama (★ Colombo) 47,723
Dehiwala-Mount Lavinia (★ Colombo) 173,529
Galle 77,183
Jaffna 118,215
Kalutara 31,503
Kandy 97,872
Kegalla 15,000
Kelaniya (★ Colombo) 36,738
Kolonnawa (★ Colombo) 41,005
Kotikawatta (★ Colombo) 48,262
Kotte (★ Colombo) 101,039
Kurunegala 27,000
Maharagama (★ Colombo) 49,765
Matale 30,000
Matara 39,000
Moratuwa (★ Colombo) 134,826
Negombo 60,762
Puttalam 21,000
Ratnapura 37,000
Trincomalee 45,000

SUDAN / As Sūdān

1983 C 20,564,364

Cities and Towns

Al Junaynah (1973 C) 35,424
Al Qaḑārif (1973 C) 66,465
An Nuhūd (1973 C) 26,002
'Aṭbarah 73,000
Barbar (1973 C) 11,303
El Fasher (1973 C) 51,932
El Obeid (Al Ubayyiḑ) 140,000
Jūbā (1973 C) 56,737
Kassalā 143,000
• KHARTOUM (AL KHARṬŪM) (★ 1,550,000) 476,218
Khartoum North (Al Kharṭūm Baḩrī) (★ Khartoum) 341,146
Kūstī (1973 C) 65,257
Malakāl (1973 C) 34,898
Nyala (1973 C) 59,852
Omdurman (Umm Durmān) (★★ Khartoum) 526,287
Port Sudan (Būr Sūdān) 206,727
Sannār (1973 C) 28,546
Sinjah (1973 C) 19,452
Ṭawkar (1973 C) 13,394
Umm Ruwābah (1973 C) 19,713
Wad Madanī 141,000
Wāw (1973 C) 52,752

SURINAME

1980 C 354,860

Cities and Towns

• PARAMARIBO (★ 192,810) 67,905

SWAZILAND

1982 E 585,000

Cities and Towns

Manzini (★ 30,000) 14,000
• MBABANE 33,000

SWEDEN / Sverige

1984 E 8,342,621

Cities and Towns

Alingsås (▲ 31,074) 20,300
Ängelholm (▲ 31,071) 17,800
Arvika (▲ 26,616) 13,600
Avesta (▲ 25,317) 17,500
Boden (▲ 29,113) 18,700
Bollnäs (▲ 28,059) 13,100
Borås 99,945
Borlänge 46,181
Enköping (▲ 32,808) 18,700
Eskilstuna 88,664
Eslöv (▲ 26,356) 13,800
Falkenberg (▲ 35,523) 15,900
Falun (▲ 51,443) 33,000
Gällivare (▲ 23,717) 7,800
Gävle (▲ 87,817) 67,300
Göteborg (Gothenburg) (★ 699,151) 424,085
Halmstad (▲ 76,971) 49,400
Härnösand (▲ 27,556) 19,300
Hässleholm (▲ 48,600) 16,000
Helsingborg 104,689
Huddinge (★ Stockholm) 69,581
Hudiksvall (▲ 37,723) 14,800
Järfälla (★ Stockholm) 55,776
Jönköping 107,031
Kalmar (▲ 53,747) 30,300
Karlshamn (▲ 31,678) 17,700
Karlskoga 35,170
Karlskrona (▲ 59,660) 31,900
Karlstad 74,324
Katrineholm (▲ 31,883) 21,500
Kiruna 27,220
Köping (▲ 26,503) 19,200
Kristianstad (▲ 69,581) 30,900
Kristinehamn (▲ 26,356) 19,800
Kungsbacka (▲ 47,700) 13,600
Landskrona 35,350
Lidingö (★ Stockholm) 37,987
Lidköping (▲ 35,229) 21,400
Lindesberg (▲ 24,870) 8,400
Linköping 115,600
Ljungby (▲ 27,360) 13,600
Ludvika (▲ 30,281) 16,700
Luleå 66,811
Lund 81,199
Malmö (★ 305,000) 229,107
Mariestad (▲ 24,178) 15,500
Mjölby (▲ 25,769) 12,300
Mölndal (★ Göteborg) 49,063
Motala (▲ 41,364) 29,300
Nacka (★ Stockholm) 59,009
Nässjö (▲ 30,900) 17,000
Norrköping 118,451
Norrtälje (▲ 42,101) 13,400
Nyköping (▲ 64,686) 28,300
Örebro 117,569
Örnsköldsvik (▲ 59,918) 29,700
Oskarshamn (▲ 27,788) 18,700
Österhaninge (★ Stockholm) 33,000
Östersund (▲ 56,407) 40,800
Partille (★ Göteborg) 28,681
Piteå (▲ 38,797) 16,200
Ronneby (▲ 29,684) 11,800
Sandviken 40,778
Skellefteå (▲ 74,329) 30,000
Skövde (▲ 46,273) 29,900
Söderhamn (▲ 30,525) 13,700
Södertälje (★ Stockholm) 79,429
Sollefteå (▲ 25,515) 9,200
Sollentuna (★ Stockholm) 47,587
Solna (★ Stockholm) 48,828
• STOCKHOLM (★ 1,420,198) 653,455
Sundbyberg (★ Stockholm) 27,444
Sundsvall (▲ 93,569) 50,600
Täby (★ Stockholm) 52,771
Trelleborg (▲ 34,071) 22,000
Trollhättan 48,922
Tumba (Botkyrka) (★ Stockholm) 65,927
Uddevalla (▲ 45,703) 30,100
Umeå (▲ 84,192) 54,900
Upplands Väsby (★ Stockholm) 33,477
Uppsala 152,579
Vänersborg (▲ 35,540) 20,400
Varberg (▲ 45,828) 20,500
Värnamo (▲ 30,495) 23,500
Västerås 117,658
Västervik (▲ 40,395) 21,000
Växjö (▲ 66,173) 43,700
Vetlanda (▲ 28,190) 12,200
Visby (Gotland) (▲ 56,203) 20,100

Counties

Älvsborg 426,325
Blekinge 151,652
Gävleborg 290,533
Göteborg och Bohus 712,078
Gotland 56,203
Halland 238,347
Jämtland 134,731
Jönköping 300,924
Kalmar 239,380
Kopparberg 285,113
Kristianstad 280,330
Kronoberg 174,265
Malmöhus 747,140
Norrbotten 263,684
Örebro 270,961
Östergötland 392,887
Skaraborg 270,382
Södermanland 250,515
Stockholm 1,562,490
Uppsala 249,712
Värmland 280,499
Västerbotten 245,181
Västernorrland 263,598
Västmanland 255,691

Historic Provinces

Ångermanland 158,091
Blekinge 151,652
Bohuslän 233,501
Dalarna 285,697
Dalsland 56,223
Gästrikland 146,975
Gotland 56,203
Halland 242,009
Hälsingland 144,509
Härjedalen 11,726
Jämtland 116,473
Lappland 117,490
Medelpad 125,108
Närke 172,361
Norrbotten 193,625
Öland 23,988
Östergötland 389,878
Skåne 1,025,804
Småland 700,383
Södermanland 967,937
Uppland 1,116,385
Värmland 326,308
Västerbotten 183,146
Västergötland 1,111,174
Västmanland 285,975

SWITZERLAND / Schweiz / Suisse / Svizzera

1985 E 6,455,900

Cities and Towns

Aarau (★ 51,300) 15,800
Adliswil (★ Zürich) 16,200
Allschwil (★ Basel) 18,200
Altdorf 8,200
Appenzell 4,800
Arbon (★ 40,800) 12,400
Arosa (1980 C) 2,782
Baar (★ Zug) 15,200
Baden (★ 70,800) 14,000
Basel (Bâle) (★ 580,000) 176,200
Bellinzona (★ 35,800) 16,800
BERN (BERNE) (★ 300,500) 140,600
Biel (Bienne) (★ 82,800) 52,600
Bülach 13,000
Burgdorf (★ 18,200) 15,300
Château d'Oex (1980 C) 2,872
Chiasso (1980 C) 8,583
Chur (Coire) (★ 42,400) 31,000
Davos 10,200
Delémont 11,300
Einsiedeln (1980 C) 9,629
Emmen (★ Luzern) 22,900
Frauenfeld 19,000
Fribourg (Freiburg) (★ 55,800) 35,000
Geneva (Genève) (★ 435,000) 159,500
Glarus 5,600
Grenchen (★ 24,000) 15,900
Grindelwald (1980 C) 3,555
Herisau 14,600
Illnau [-Effretikon] (★ Zürich) 14,800
Interlaken (1980 C) 4,852
Köniz (★ Bern) 35,500
Kreuzlingen (★ 22,100) 16,200
Kriens (★ Luzern) 20,800
La Chaux-de-Fonds 35,800
Langenthal (★ 21,500) 13,800
Lausanne (★ 256,400) 126,200
Lauterbrunnen (1980 C) 3,077
Le Locle 11,000
Liestal (★ Basel) 12,000
Locarno (★ 41,600) 14,300
Lugano (★ 93,000) 27,800
Luzern (Lucerne) (★ 158,400) 61,000
Martigny 12,200
Meiringen (1980 C) 4,072
Monthey 11,500
Montreux (★★ Vevey) 18,800
Morges (★ 18,800) 13,200
Neuchâtel (Neuenburg) (★ 57,600) 32,700
Nyon 13,400
Olten (★ 44,200) 18,200
Riehen (★ Basel) 20,100
Rorschach (★★ Arbon) (1980 C) 9,878
Sankt Gallen (Saint-Gall) (★ 114,000) 73,500
Sankt Moritz (1980 C) 5,900
Sarnen 7,800
Schaffhausen (★ 53,300) 34,100
Schwyz 12,400
Sierre 13,100
Sion (Sitten) 22,900
Solothurn (Soleure) (★ 34,400) 15,400
Stans 5,800
Thun (Thoune) (★ 66,000) 36,800
Uster 24,700
Vernier (★ Genève) 27,800
Vevey (★ 59,800) 15,400
Wädenswil 19,000
Wettingen (★ Baden) 18,100
Wil (★ 22,800) 16,000
Winterthur (★ 106,800) 84,600
Wohlen (★ 15,500) 11,400
Yverdon (Iferten) 20,900
Zermatt (1980 C) 3,548
Zug (Zoug) (★ 52,300) 21,300
• Zürich (★ 780,000) 354,500

C Census. E Official estimate. UE Unofficial estimate.
• Largest city in country.
★ Population or designation of metropolitan area, including suburbs (see headnote).
▲ Population of an entire municipality, commune, or district, including rural area.

Cantons

Aargau 464,600
Appenzell-Ausser Rhoden 48,800
Appenzell-Inner Rhoden 13,000
Basel-Land 223,500
Basel-Stadt 197,500
Bern (Berne) 921,500
Fribourg (Freiburg) 190,400
Genève 360,500
Glarus 36,400
Graubünden (Grisons) 164,800
Jura 64,400
Luzern (Lucerne) 302,200
Neuchâtel 154,700
Nidwalden 30,200
Obwalden 27,000
Sankt Gallen 398,600
Schaffhausen 69,600
Schwyz 100,900
Solothurn 218,200
Thurgau 189,200
Ticino (Tessin) 273,500
Uri 33,600
Valais (Wallis) 227,300
Vaud (Waadt) 539,600
Zug 79,000
Zürich 1,126,900

SYRIA / As Sūrīyah

1981 C 9,052,628

Cities and Towns

Aleppo (Ḥalab) (★ 1,035,000) 985,413
Al Ḥasakah 73,426
Al Qāmishlī 92,990
Ar Raqqah 87,138
As Suwaydā' 43,414
• DAMASCUS (DIMASHQ) (★ 1,850,000) (1986 E) 1,259,000
Dar'ā 49,534
Dayr az Zawr 92,091
Dūmā (★ Damascus) 51,337
Ḥamāh 177,208
Ḥimṣ (Homs) 346,871
Idlib 51,682
Jaramānah (★ Damascus) 64,305
Latakia (Al Lādhiqīyah) 96,791
Ṭarṭūs 52,589

TAIWAN / T'aiwan

1982 E 18,457,923

Cities and Towns

Changhua (▲ 182,804) (1980 C) 140,100
Chiai 252,376
Chilung (Keelung) 349,686
Chungho (★ T'aipei) (1980 C) 285,365
Chungli (Chunli) (1980 C) 210,024
Chutung (1980 C) 69,598
Fengshan (Kaohsiunghsien) (★ Kaohsiung) (1980 C) 222,817
Fengyüan (T'aichunghsien) (▲ 127,563) (1980 C) 101,700
Hsichih (★ T'aipei) (1980 C) 70,031
Hsinchu 288,880
Hsinchuang (★ T'aipei) (1980 C) 182,623
Hsintien (★ T'aipei) (1980 C) 176,663
Hualien (1980 C) 101,953
Ilan (▲ 81,751) (1980 C) 70,900
Kangshan (1980 C) 78,049
Kaohsiung (★ 1,675,000) 1,248,175
Lotung (1980 C) 57,925
Lukang (Luchiang) (1980 C) 72,019
Makung (▲ 55,678) (1980 C) 23,000
Miaoli (1980 C) 81,500
Nant'ou (1980 C) 84,038
Panch'iao (T'aipeihsien) (★ T'aipei) (1980 C) 414,556
P'ingchen (★ T'aipei) (1980 C) 98,054
P'ingtung (▲ 186,655) (1980 C) 152,400
Quemoy (Chinmen) (▲ 51,958) (1980 C) 14,000
Sanch'ung (★ T'aipei) (1980 C) 350,383
Shulin (★ T'aipei) (1980 C) 75,700
Tach'i (1980 C) 67,209
T'aichung 621,566
T'ainan 609,934
• T'AIPEI (★ 5,265,000) 2,327,641
T'aitung (▲ 110,352) (1980 C) 79,100
Tanshui (★ T'aipei) (1980 C) 28,000
T'aoyüan (1980 C) 182,884
T'oufen (1980 C) 66,536
T'uch'eng (★ T'aipei) (1980 C) 34,834
Yangmei (1980 C) 84,353
Yungho (★ T'aipei) (1980 C) 213,630

TANZANIA

1978 C 17,557,000

Cities and Towns

Arusha 55,000
• DAR ES SALAAM 757,346
Dodoma 46,000
Iringa 57,000
Kigoma 50,000
Mbeya 77,000
Morogoro 62,000
Moshi 52,000
Mtwara 49,000
Mwanza 111,000
Tabora 67,000
Tanga 103,000
Ujiji (1967 C) 21,369
Zanzibar 110,669

THAILAND / Prathet Thai

1983 E 49,515,074

Cities and Towns

• BANGKOK (KRUNG THEP) (★ 5,900,000) (1984 E) 5,174,682
Ban Phai 34,664
Ban Pong 24,333
Buriram 27,103
Chachoengsao 38,588
Chanthaburi 28,856
Chiang Mai 150,499
Chiang Rai 37,071
Chon Buri 46,792
Hat Yai (Ban Hat Yai) 113,964
Hua Hin 32,017
Kalasin 29,758
Kanchanaburi 31,643
Khon Kaen 115,515
Lampang 45,598
Lop Buri 36,678
Maha Sarakham 36,043
Nakhon Pathom 45,187
Nakhon Phanom 32,415
Nakhon Ratchasima 190,762
Nakhon Sawan 95,128
Nakhon Si Thammarat 69,834
Narathiwat 34,804
Nong Khai 24,833
Nonthaburi (★ Bangkok) 38,873
Pattani 34,342
Pattaya 40,475
Phatthalung 32,279
Phayao 24,230
Phet Buri 34,327
Phetchabun 28,208
Phitsanulok 72,052
Phra Nakhon Si Ayutthaya 55,319
Phuket 45,917
Rat Buri 44,976
Rayong 38,435
Roi Et 32,502
Sakon Nakhon 23,690
Samut Prakan (★ Bangkok) 65,155
Samut Sakhon 48,903
Samut Songkhram 32,872
Sara Buri 48,669
Songkhla 79,725
Suphan Buri 23,505
Surat Thani (Ban Don) 40,288
Surin 35,044
Trang 45,349
Ubon Ratchathani 100,255
Udon Thani 82,483
Uttaradit 31,698
Warin Chamrap 30,143
Yala 55,947

TOGO

1981 C 2,702,945

Cities and Towns

Atakpamé 24,377
Lama-Kara 28,480
• LOMÉ 369,926
Palimé 27,669
Sokodé 48,098
Tsévié 20,247

TOKELAU

1981 C 1,572

TONGA

1984 C 96,592

Cities and Towns

• NUKU'ALOFA 21,745

TRANSKEI

1982 E 2,400,000

Cities and Towns

• UMTATA (1978 E) 30,000

TRINIDAD AND TOBAGO

1980 C 1,059,825

Cities and Towns

Arima 11,390
Barataria 14,983
Chaguanas 6,122
Morvant 25,416
Point Fortin 6,538
• PORT OF SPAIN (★ 425,000) 65,906
Princes Town 8,288
San Fernando 33,490
Sangre Grande 8,948
Scarborough 6,057
Tunapuna (★ Port of Spain) 10,251

TUNISIA / Tunisie / Tunis

1975 C 5,588,209

Cities and Towns

Ariana (★ Tunis) 47,833
Bardo (★ Tunis) 49,367
Béja 39,226
Bizerte 62,856
El Kairouan 54,546
El Kasserine 22,594
El Kef 27,939
Gabès 40,585
Gafsa 42,225
Hammam Lif (★ Tunis) 35,634
Jendouba (Souk el Arba) 18,127
Kalaa Kebira 23,508
La Goulette (★ Tunis) 41,912
Manouba (★ Tunis) 23,167
Menzel Bourguiba 42,111
Monastir 26,759
Msaken 33,559
Nabeul 30,476
Sfax (★ 260,000) 171,297
Sousse 69,530
• TUNIS (★ 915,000) 550,404

TURKEY / Türkiye

1980 C 44,736,957

Cities and Towns

Adana 574,515
Adapazarı 130,977
Adıyaman 53,219
Afyonkarahisar 74,562
Ağri (Karaköse) 40,532
Akhisar 61,491
Aksaray 62,927
Akşehir 40,312
Alaşehir 25,611
Alibeyköy (★ İstanbul) 45,532
Amasya 48,066
ANKARA (★ 1,975,000) 1,877,755
Antakya (Antioch) 94,942
Antalya 173,501
Artvin 14,307
Aydın 74,021
Bafra 50,213
Balıkesir 124,051
Bandırma 53,497
Batman 86,172
Bayburt 22,578
Bayrampaşa (★ İstanbul) 165,723
Bergama 34,716
Bingöl (Çapakçur) 28,146
Bitlis 27,137
Bolu 38,283
Bolvadin 30,599
Bornova (★ İzmir) 60,397
Buca (★ İzmir) 103,105
Burdur 44,630
Bursa 445,113
Çamdibi (★ İzmir) 50,523
Çanakkale 39,979
Çankırı 34,933
Çarşamba 28,422
Ceyhan 57,307
Çorlu 47,086
Çorum 75,726
Denizli 135,373
Diyarbakır 235,617
Düzce 37,858
Edirne 71,914
Elâzığ 142,983
Ereğli, Konya prov. 56,931
Ereğli, Zonguldak prov. 50,105
Erzincan 70,982
Erzurum 190,241
Esenler (★ İstanbul) 68,509
Eskişehir 309,431
Gaziantep 374,290
Gebze (★ İzmit) 58,318
Gelibolu (Gallipoli) 14,721
Giresun 45,690
Gölcük 45,950
Gültepe (★ İzmir) 48,240
Güngören (★ İstanbul) 74,761
İnegöl 45,237
İskenderun (Alexandretta) 124,824
Isparta 86,475
• İstanbul (★ 4,650,000) 2,772,708
İzmir (Smyrna) (★ 1,200,000) 757,854
İzmit (Kocaeli) 190,423
Kadirli 40,643
Kâğıthane (★ İstanbul) 175,540
Karabük 84,137
Karaman 51,208
Kars 58,799
Kartal (★ İstanbul) 68,291
Kastamonu 35,464
Kayseri 281,320
Kilis 58,335
Kırıkhan 49,891
Kırıkkale 178,401
Kırklareli 36,296
Kırşehir 49,913
Kocasinan (★ İstanbul) 96,312
Konya 329,139
Kozan 42,462
Küçükçekmece (★ İstanbul) 81,503
Küçükköy (★ İstanbul) 100,406
Küçükyalı (★ İstanbul) 46,640
Kütahya 99,436
Lüleburgaz 35,689
Malatya 179,074
Maltepe (★ İstanbul) 90,439
Manisa 94,167
Maraş 178,557
Mardin 39,137
Mersin 216,308
Muş 40,977
Nazilli 60,003
Nevşehir 37,161
Niğde 39,835
Nizip 38,967
Ödemiş 40,736
Ordu 52,785
Osmaniye 84,212
Pendik (★ İstanbul) 48,219
Polatlı 43,530
Rize 43,407
Safrakköyü 83,560
Salihli 51,826
Samsun 198,749
Siirt 42,291
Silvan (Miyafarkin) 43,624
Sinop 18,328
Sivas 172,864
Söke 37,413
Tarsus 121,074
Tatvan 40,296
Tekirdağ 52,093
Tire 32,291
Tokat 60,855
Trabzon 108,403
Turgutlu 55,396
Turhal 46,864
Ümraniye (★ İstanbul) 71,954
Urfa 147,488
Uşak 71,469
Van 92,801
Viranşehir 40,820
Yeşilbağ (★ İstanbul) 53,594
Yozgat 36,349
Zile 30,637
Zonguldak (★ 195,000) 109,044

TURKS AND CAICOS ISLANDS

1980 C 7,436

Cities and Towns

• GRAND TURK 3,146

TUVALU

1979 C 7,349

Cities and Towns

• FUNAFUTI 2,191

UGANDA

1980 C 12,636,179

Cities and Towns

Bugembe (1969 C) 46,884
Entebbe 21,289
Fort Portal (Kabarole) 26,806
Gulu 14,958
Jinja 45,060
• KAMPALA 458,503
Masaka 29,123
Mbale 28,039
Mbarara 23,255
Tororo 16,707

UNITED ARAB EMIRATES / Al Imārāt al 'Arabīyeh al Muttaḥidah

1980 C 980,000

Cities and Towns

ABU DHABI (ABŪ ẒABY) 242,975
'Ajmān (1968 C) 3,725
Al 'Ayn 101,663
Al Fujayrah (1968 C) 2,001
Ash Shāriqah 125,149
• Dubai (Dubayy) 265,702
Ra's al Khaymah (1968 C) 8,764
Umm al Qaywayn (1968 C) 2,928

UNITED KINGDOM

1981 C 55,648,994

Political Divisions

ENGLAND 46,220,955
NORTHERN IRELAND 1,488,077
SCOTLAND 5,149,500
WALES 2,790,462

Cities and Towns

ENGLAND 46,220,955
Abingdon (★ Oxford) 22,686
Accrington (Hyndburn) (★★ Blackburn) 79,200
Adur (Shoreham-by-Sea) (★ Brighton) 58,800
Aldershot (Rushmoor) (★ London) 80,800
Andover 31,006
Ashford 40,500
Ashton-under-Lyne (Tameside) (★★ Manchester) 218,800
Aycliffe 24,720
Aylesbury 48,400
Banbury 35,796
Banstead see Reigate [and Banstead]
Barnsley 225,800
Barnstaple 19,025
Barrow-in-Furness 72,800
Basildon (★ London) 153,200
Basingstoke 67,300
Bath 84,100
Batley (★ Leeds) 42,572
Battle (1971 C) 4,987
Bedford (North Bedfordshire) 74,500
Bedlington 15,072
Beeston and Stapleford (Broxtowe) (★ Nottingham) 65,400
Benfleet (Castle Point) (★ London) 86,000
Berkhamsted (★ London) 15,461
Berwick-upon-Tweed 12,200
Bexhill-on-Sea 35,529
Birkenhead (Wirral) (★ Liverpool) 341,000
Birmingham (★ 2,675,000) 1,022,300
Bishop Auckland 32,572
Bishop's Stortford (★ London) 22,807
Blackburn (★ 221,900) 141,700
Blackpool (★ 280,000) 148,700
Blyth (Blyth Valley) 78,200
Bodmin 12,148
Bognor Regis 39,536
Bolton (★★ Manchester) 263,000
Bootle 62,463
Boston 26,200
Bournemouth (★ 315,000) 143,000
Bracknell (★ London) 50,100
Bradford (★★ Leeds) 464,100
Bradford-on-Avon 8,752
Braintree 30,400
Brentwood (★ London) 72,700
Bridgwater 26,132
Bridlington 29,329
Brighton (★ 420,000) 150,200
Bristol (★ 630,000) 400,300
Bromsgrove (★ Birmingham) 43,600
Broxbourne see Cheshunt
Broxtowe see Beeston and Stapleford
Burgess Hill (★ London) 23,542
Burnham-on-Sea 14,920
Burnley (★ 160,000) 93,700
Burton-on-Trent (East Staffordshire) 48,500
Bury (★★ Manchester) 177,600
Bury Saint Edmunds 28,914
Buxton 20,797
Calderdale see Halifax
Camberley see Frimley and Camberley
Camborne [-Redruth] (Kerrier) 46,700
Cambridge 100,200

C Census. E Official estimate. UE Unofficial estimate.
• Largest city in country.

★ Population or designation of metropolitan area, including suburbs (see headnote).
▲ Population of an entire municipality, commune, or district, including rural area.

Cannock (Cannock Chase) (★ Birmingham) 84,900
Canterbury 36,000
Carlisle 71,200
Carlton (Gedling) (★ Nottingham) 104,300
Castleford (★ Leeds) 36,032
Caterham and Warlingham (Tandridge) (★ London) 33,900
Chalfont Saint Giles (1971 C) 7,118
Chatham (Medway) (★ London) 142,800
Chelmsford (★ London) 58,500
Cheltenham 86,100
Chertsey (Runnymede) (★ London) 73,100
Chesham (★ London) 20,655
Cheshunt (Broxbourne) (★ London) 79,700
Chester 58,100
Chesterfield (★ 127,000) 96,300
Chester-le-Street (★ Newcastle) 51,800
Chichester 24,300
Chigwell (★ London) 51,290
Chippenham 19,290
Chorley (★★ Preston) 54,700
Christchurch (★ Bournemouth) 38,200
Cirencester 15,622
Clacton-on-Sea 44,000
Cleethorpes (★ Grimsby) 35,500
Clevedon 17,915
Coalville 30,832
Colchester 83,900
Consett (★ Newcastle) 33,433
Corby 52,400
Coventry (★ 645,000) 318,600
Cowes 19,663
Crawley (★ London) 72,700
Crewe 47,800
Crosby (★ Liverpool) 53,660
Darlington 97,800
Dartford (★ London) 77,900
Dartmouth 6,298
Deal 25,989
Derby (★ 27,500) 216,500
Dewsbury (★★ Leeds) 48,339
Doncaster 81,900
Dorchester 14,049
Dorking (★ London) 22,369
Dover 33,700
Dronfield (★ Sheffield) 23,304
Dudley (★★ Birmingham) 300,700
Dunstable (★ Luton) 30,912
Durham 27,200
Eastbourne 77,300
East Grinstead (★ London) 22,263
Eastleigh (★ Southampton) 92,400
East Retford 19,348
Ellesmere Port (★ Liverpool) 82,500
Elmbridge see Walton and Weybridge
Ely 10,268
Epsom [and Ewell] (★ London) 69,000
Eton (★ London) 3,523
Evesham 15,271
Ewell see Epsom [and Ewell]
Exeter 99,200
Exmouth 28,787
Falmouth 18,525
Fareham (★ Portsmouth) 88,100
Farnham (★ London) 35,289
Faversham 16,098
Felixstowe 20,858
Fleet (★ London) 26,004
Fleetwood (★★ Blackpool) 28,467
Folkestone 44,200
Formby (Shepway) (★ Liverpool) 25,798
Frimley and Camberley (Surrey Heath) (★ London) 52,600
Frome 14,527
Gainsborough 18,691
Gateshead (★ Newcastle) 214,100
Gillingham (★ London) 95,900
Glastonbury 6,773
Glossop (★ Manchester) 25,339
Gloucester (★ 115,000) 91,600
Godmanchester see Huntingdon [and Godmanchester]
Goole 17,127
Gosport (★ Portsmouth) 77,400
Grantham 30,084
Gravesend (Gravesham) (★ London) 96,300
Great Yarmouth 48,700
Grimsby (Great Grimsby) (★ 145,000) 91,800
Guildford (★ London) 58,600
Halifax (Calderdale) 192,500
Haltemprice (★ Hull) 53,633
Harlow (★ London) 79,400
Harrogate 67,000
Hartlepool (★★ Middlesbrough) 94,600
Harwich 15,078
Haslemere (★ London) 13,900
Hastings 75,900
Hatfield 25,160
Havant (★ Portsmouth) 114,800
Haverhill 17,146
Heanor 24,655
Hemel Hempstead (Dacorum) (★ London) 80,900
Hemsworth 14,138
Henley-on-Thames 10,976
Hereford 48,000
Herne Bay 27,528
Hertford (★ London) 21,412
Hertsmere (★ London) 88,600
Hexham 9,630
High Wycombe (Wycombe) (▲ 156,800) 68,900
Hinckley (★★ Coventry) 55,600
Hitchin 30,317
Horsham (★ London) 25,438
Hove (★ Brighton) 88,500
Hucknall (★ Nottingham) 28,142
Huddersfield (Kirklees) (▲ 377,400) 125,800
Hull (Kingston-upon-Hull) (★ 350,000) 272,500
Huntingdon [and Godmanchester] 17,467
Huyton-with-Roby (★ Liverpool) 174,100
Hythe 12,723
Ilkeston (★ Nottingham) 33,031
Ipswich 119,700
Kendal 23,411
Kenilworth (★ Coventry) 19,315
Kerrier see Camborne [-Redruth]
Keswick 5,635
Kettering 45,400
Kidderminster (Wyre Forest) 91,600
King's Lynn 33,340
Kingswood (★ Bristol) 84,200
Lancaster 47,900
Leamington (Royal Leamington Spa) (★★ Coventry) 42,953
Leatherhead (Mole Valley) (★ London) 40,800
Leeds (★ 1,540,000) 718,100
Leek 19,739
Leicester (★ 495,000) 283,000
Letchworth 31,835
Lewes 14,000
Leyland (South Ribble) (★ Preston) 97,700
Lichfield 25,800
Lincoln 75,900
Littlehampton 22,181
Liverpool (★ 1,525,000) 518,900
• LONDON (★ 11,100,000) 6,851,400
Long Eaton (★ Nottingham) 32,895
Loughborough (Charnwood) 49,700
Lowestoft (Waveney) 55,800
Ludlow 7,596
Luton (★ 220,000) 164,200
Lymington 38,698
Lytham Saint Anne's (Fylde) (★ Blackpool) 40,300
Macclesfield 47,000
Maidenhead (★ London) 49,038
Maidstone 72,500
Malvern 31,400
Manchester (★ 2,775,000) 464,200
Mansfield (★ 198,000) 99,900
Margate (Thanet) 121,900
Market Harborough 15,934
Marlborough 5,771
Matlock 20,750
Melton Mowbray 23,554
Middlesbrough (Teesside) (★ 580,000) 150,600
Milton Keynes 126,500
Morecambe [and Heysham] (★★ Lancaster) 41,187
Nelson (★★ Burnley) 30,435
Newark [-upon-Trent] 24,100
Newbury 27,000
Newcastle-upon-Tyne (★ 1,300,000) 285,300
Newcastle-under-Lyme (★★ Stoke-on-Trent) 74,200
Newmarket 16,235
Newport 23,570
Newton Abbot 20,927
Newtown 9,348
Northampton 158,900
Northwich 17,126
Norwich (★ 230,000) 125,900
Nottingham (★ 655,000) 277,500
Nuneaton (★★ Coventry) 113,200
Oadby and Wigston (★ Leicester) 53,000
Oakham 7,996
Oldham (★★ Manchester) 221,800
Ormskirk (★ Liverpool) 27,753
Oxford (★ 230,000) 114,400
Penrith 12,205
Penzance 19,521
Peterborough 116,200
Peterlee 22,756
Plymouth (★ 290,000) 250,300
Poole (★★ Bournemouth) 120,000
Portsmouth (★ 485,000) 187,900
Preston (★ 250,000) 125,800
Queenborough [-In-Sheppey] 33,362
Ramsgate (Thanet) 39,642
Rawtenstall 22,231
Rayleigh (★ London) 29,146
Reading (★ 200,000) 136,200
Redcar (★ Middlesbrough) 85,600
Redditch (★ Birmingham) 67,400
Redruth see Camborne[-Redruth]
Reigate [and Banstead] (★ London) 116,700
Rickmansworth (★ London) 29,408
Ripon 11,952
Rochdale (★★ Manchester) 228,400
Rotherham (★★ Sheffield) 251,900
Rugby 59,564
Rushden 22,253
Ryde 24,346
Rye 4,293
Saint Albans (★ London) 125,400
Saint Austell [with Fowey] 36,639
Saint Helens 190,000
Salford (★ Manchester) 247,400
Salisbury 35,700
Sandwich 4,227
Scarborough 43,300
Scunthorpe 65,900
Seaford 17,785
Seaham (★ Newcastle) 21,130
Selby 10,726
Sevenoaks (★ London) 17,070
Sheffield (★ 710,000) 547,600
Shrewsbury 60,400
Sittingbourne and Milton 33,645
Skelmersdale [and Holland] (West Lancashire) (★ Manchester) 43,700
Slough (★ London) 96,900
Smethwick (Sandwell) (Warley) (★ Birmingham) 309,900
Solihull (★ Birmingham) 198,500
Southampton (★ 415,000) 208,800
Southend-on-Sea (★ London) 157,500
Southport (Sefton) (★★ Liverpool) 90,000
South Shields (South Tyneside) (★★ Newcastle) 162,500
Spalding 18,223
Spenborough (★ Leeds) 42,371
Spennymoor 20,630
Stafford 55,100
Staines (Spelthorne) (★ London) 92,800
Stamford 16,153
Stanley (★ Newcastle) 41,210
Stapleford see Beeston and Stapleford
Stevenage 74,500
Stockport (★ Manchester) 291,000
Stockton-on-Tees (★★ Middlesbrough) 172,600
Stoke-on-Trent (★ 440,000) 250,700
Stratford-on-Avon 20,800
Stretford (Trafford) (★ Manchester) 222,200
Stroud 20,930
Sudbury 9,883
Sunderland (★★ Newcastle) 299,100
Surrey Heath see Frimley and Camberley
Sutton-in-Ashfield (Ashfield) (★★ Mansfield) 41,300
Swadlincote 23,388
Swindon (Thamesdown) 151,600
Tamworth 65,100
Tandridge see Caterham and Warlingham
Taunton 35,326
Telford (The Wrekin) 123,525
Tewkesbury 9,554
Thetford 19,591
Thornton Cleveleys (★ Blackpool) 26,139
Thurrock (★ London) 126,800
Tiverton 16,539
Todmorden 14,665
Tonbridge (★ London) 30,800
Torquay (Torbay) 112,400
Trowbridge 22,984
Truro 16,277
Tunbridge Wells 46,000
Tynemouth (North Tyneside) (★ Newcastle) 200,100
Ulverston 11,963
Wakefield (★★ Leeds) 60,800
Walsall (★★ Birmingham) 267,500
Walton and Weybridge (Elmbridge) (★ London) 113,000
Warlingham see Caterham and Warlingham
Warrington 168,600
Warwick (★★ Coventry) 22,100
Watford (★ London) 74,700
Wellingborough 44,300
Wells 8,374
Welwyn Garden City (★ London) 41,300
West Bridgford (★ Nottingham) 28,073
Weston-super-Mare 57,900
Weybridge see Walton and Weybridge
Weymouth [and Portland] 57,400
Whitby 13,763
Whitehaven 26,714
Whitstable 27,896
Widnes (Halton) 122,500
Wigan (★★ Manchester) 310,000
Wilmslow (★ Manchester) 30,207
Winchester 32,100
Windermere 8,575
Windsor (New Windsor) (★ London) 28,700
Winsford 26,915
Woking (★ London) 81,800
Wokingham 24,800
Wolverhampton (★★ Birmingham) 256,500
Worcester 75,700
Workington 27,581
Worksop 36,893
Worthing (★★ Brighton) 92,600
Yeovil 27,900
York (★ 145,000) 101,600

Counties

Avon 909,408
Bedfordshire 504,986
Berkshire 675,153
Buckinghamshire 565,992
Cambridgeshire 575,177
Cheshire 926,293
Cleveland 565,775
Cornwall and Isles of Scilly 430,506
Cumbria 483,427
Derby 906,929
Devon 952,000
Dorset 591,990
Durham 604,728
East Sussex 652,568
Essex 1,469,065
Gloucestershire 499,351
Greater London 6,696,008
Greater Manchester 2,594,778
Hampshire 1,456,367
Hereford and Worcester 630,218
Hertfordshire 954,535
Humberside 847,666
Isle of Wight 118,192
Kent 1,463,055
Lancashire 1,372,118
Leicestershire 842,577
Lincolnshire 547,560
Merseyside 1,513,070
Norfolk 693,490
Northamptonshire 527,532
Northumberland 299,905
North Yorkshire 666,610
Nottinghamshire 982,631
Oxfordshire 515,079
Shropshire 375,610
Somerset 424,988
South Yorkshire 1,301,813
Staffordshire 1,012,320
Suffolk 596,354
Surrey 999,393
Tyne and Wear 1,143,245
Warwickshire 473,620
West Midlands 2,644,634
West Sussex 658,562
West Yorkshire 2,037,510
Wiltshire 518,167

NORTHERN IRELAND 1,488,077

Antrim 22,342
Armagh 12,700
Ballymena 28,166
Bangor (North Down) (★ Belfast) (1984 E) 67,600
Belfast (★ 685,000) (1984 E) 318,600
Castlereagh (★ Belfast) (1984 E) 59,400
Enniskillen 10,429
Larne 18,224
Lisburn (★ Belfast) 40,391
Londonderry (Derry) (★ 97,200) (1984 E) 68,000
Lurgan (★ 63,000) 20,991
Newry 19,426
Newtownabbey (★ Belfast) (1984 E) 72,400
Newtownards 20,531
Omagh 14,627
Portadown (★★ Lurgan) 21,333

SCOTLAND 5,149,500

Aberdeen 212,542
Airdrie (★ Glasgow) 45,500
Alloa 26,500
Arbroath 23,913
Ardrossan (★★ Irvine) 11,337
Ayr (★ 100,000) 48,600
Bearsden [and Milngavie] (★ Glasgow) 40,122
Clydebank (★ Glasgow) 52,385
Coatbridge 50,700
Cumbernauld (★ Glasgow) 48,100
Dumbarton (★ Glasgow) 23,080
Dumfries 31,800
Dundee 185,616
Dunfermline (★ 125,817) 53,800
East Kilbride (★ Glasgow) 70,600
Edinburgh (★ 630,000) 446,361
Elgin 18,501
Falkirk (★ 148,171) 37,800
Forfar 12,501
Glasgow (★ 1,800,000) 767,456
Glenrothes (★★ Kirkcaldy) 35,000
Grangemouth (★★ Falkirk) 21,871
Greenock (★ 101,000) 56,194
Hamilton (★ Glasgow) 51,900
Hawick 16,033
Helensburgh (★ Glasgow) 16,259
Inverness 39,700
Irvine (★ 94,000) 54,600
Johnstone (★ Glasgow) 43,400
Kilmarnock (★ 84,000) 51,800
Kirkcaldy (★ 148,171) 48,400
Kirkintilloch (★ Glasgow) 33,200
Kirkwall 5,713
Lerwick 6,333
Livingston 36,700
Montrose 11,990
Motherwell (★ Glasgow) 149,900
Oban 7,211
Paisley (★ Glasgow) 86,100
Perth 42,000
Peterhead 16,504
Port Glasgow 21,681
Prestwick (★ Ayr) 13,174
Saint Andrews 10,358
Stirling (★ 61,000) 38,400
Stonehouse 5,038
Stranraer 10,665
Thurso 8,700
Wick 7,754

Regions

Borders 99,248
Central 273,078
Dumfries and Galloway 145,078
Fife 326,480
Grampian 470,596
Highland 200,030
Lothian 735,892
Orkney (Island Area) 18,906
Shetland (Island Area) 26,716
Strathclyde 2,397,827
Tayside 391,529
Western Isles (Island Area) 31,766

WALES 2,790,462

Aberdare (Cynon Valley) 36,800
Aberystwyth 8,666
Bangor 12,174
Barry (Vale of Glamorgan) (★ Cardiff) 43,200
Brecon 7,422
Bridgend 15,699
Caernarfon 9,506
Caerphilly (Rhymney Valley) (★ Cardiff) 42,400
Cardiff (★ 625,000) 281,300
Carmarthen 12,302
Colwyn Bay 26,278
Ebbw Vale (Blaenau Gwent) 24,400
Flint 16,454
Islwyn (★ Newport) 64,800
Llandudno 18,991
Llanelli 24,100
Merthyr Tydfil 60,200
Milford Haven 13,934
Monmouth 7,509
Neath (★★ Swansea) 26,500
Newport (★ 310,000) 134,200
Pembroke 15,618
Pontypool (Torfaen) (★★ Newport) 90,300
Pontypridd (Taff-Ely) (★ Cardiff) 33,200
Port Talbot (Afan) (★ 130,000) 54,600
Prestatyn 16,439
Rhondda (★★ Cardiff) 81,700
Rhyl (Rhuddlan) 22,700
Swansea (★ 275,000) 188,500
Wrexham 40,600

Counties

Clwyd 390,173
Dyfed 329,977
Gwent 439,684
Gwynedd 230,468
Mid Glamorgan 537,866
Powys 110,467
South Glamorgan 384,633
West Glamorgan 367,194

URUGUAY

1975 C 2,788,429

Cities and Towns

Artigas 29,211
Canelones 15,988
Durazno 25,981
Florida 25,374
Fray Bentos 19,407
La Paz (★ Montevideo) 14,653
Las Piedras (★ Montevideo) 53,331
Maldonado 22,762
Melo 38,487
Mercedes 34,512

C Census. E Official estimate. UE Unofficial estimate.
• Largest city in country.
★ Population or designation of metropolitan area, including suburbs (see headnote).
▲ Population of an entire municipality, commune, or district, including rural area.

Minas ... 35,225
• MONTEVIDEO (★ 1,450,000) ... 1,237,227
Paysandú ... 62,199
Punta del Este ... 7,197
Rivera ... 48,780
Rocha ... 21,502
Salto ... 73,897
San Carlos ... 16,925
San José de Mayo ... 28,554
Santa Lucía ... 14,079
Tacuarembó ... 37,692
Treinta y Tres ... 23,448
Trinidad ... 17,597

Departments

Artigas ... 57,947
Canelones ... 325,594
Cerro Largo ... 74,027
Colonia ... 111,832
Durazno ... 55,699
Flores ... 24,745
Florida ... 67,129
Lavalleja ... 65,180
Maldonado ... 76,211
Montevideo ... 1,237,227
Paysandú ... 98,508
Río Negro ... 50,123
Rivera ... 82,043
Rocha ... 60,258
Salto ... 103,074
San José ... 88,000
Soriano ... 80,614
Tacuarembó ... 84,535
Treinta y Tres ... 45,683

VANUATU

1986 E ... 138,000

Cities and Towns

• PORT-VILA (★ 18,000) ... 13,067

VATICAN CITY / Città del Vaticano

1982 E ... 736

VENDA

1982 E ... 374,000

Cities and Towns

Makeareda (1976 E) ... 1,972
• THOHOYANDOU (1977 E) ... 2,366

VENEZUELA

1981 C ... 14,515,885

Cities and Towns

Acarigua ... 80,200
Altagracia de Orituco (1971 C) ... 18,717
Anaco (1971 C) ... 29,003
Araure (1971 C) ... 22,466
Bachaquero (1971 C) ... 17,896
Barcelona (1971 C) ... 78,201
Barinas ... 90,000
Barquisimeto ... 504,000
Baruta (★ Caracas) ... 200,063
Boconó (1971 C) ... 15,915
Cabimas ... 183,000
Cagua (1971 C) ... 29,601
Calabozo ... 51,000
• CARACAS (★ 3,600,000) ... 3,041,000
Caripito (1971 C) ... 19,053
Carora (1971 C) ... 36,115
Carúpano ... 82,000
Catia La Mar (★ Caracas) (1971 C) ... 62,200
Chacao (★ Caracas) ... 72,703
Chivacoa (1971 C) ... 19,210
Ciudad Bolívar ... 151,000
Ciudad Guayana (Santo Tomé de Guayana) ... 212,000
Ciudad Ojeda ... 129,000
Coro ... 95,000
Cumaná ... 173,000
El Tigre ... 93,000
El Tocuyo (1971 C) ... 19,351
El Vigía (1971 C) ... 20,970
Guacara (1971 C) ... 38,793
Guanare (1971 C) ... 34,148
Guarenas (★ Caracas) ... 101,742
Güigüe (1971 C) ... 18,067
La Guaira (★ Caracas) (1971 C) ... 20,344
La Victoria ... 56,000
Los Dos Caminos (★ Caracas) ... 63,346
Los Teques (★ Caracas) ... 112,857
Machiques (1971 C) ... 18,898
Maiquetía (★ Caracas) (1971 C) ... 59,238
Maracaibo ... 929,000
Maracay ... 355,000
Mariara (1971 C) ... 24,284
Maturín ... 181,000
Mérida ... 99,000
Morón (1971 C) ... 19,451
Ocumare del Tuy ... 40,666
Palo Negro (1971 C) ... 19,173
Petare (★ Caracas) ... 395,715
Porlamar (1971 C) ... 31,985
Pozuelos ... 69,200
Puerto Cabello ... 94,000
Puerto la Cruz ... 81,800
Punto Fijo ... 123,000
San Antonio del Táchira (1971 C) ... 20,342
San Carlos (1971 C) ... 21,029
San Carlos del Zulia (1971 C) ... 26,762
San Cristóbal ... 280,000
San Felipe ... 56,000
San Fernando de Apure (1971 C) ... 38,960
San José de Guanipa (El Tigrito) (1971 C) ... 22,530
San Juan de los Morros (1971 C) ... 38,265
San Mateo (1971 C) ... 17,389
Trujillo (1971 C) ... 25,921
Tucupita (1971 C) ... 21,417
Turmero (1971 C) ... 43,832
Upata (1971 C) ... 22,793
Valencia ... 523,000
Valera ... 115,000
Valle de la Pascua (1971 C) ... 36,809
Villa de Cura (1971 C) ... 27,832
Yaritagua (1971 C) ... 21,363

States

Amazonas (Ter.) ... 45,667
Anzoátegui ... 683,717
Apure ... 188,187
Aragua ... 891,623
Barinas ... 326,166
Bolívar ... 668,340
Carabobo ... 1,062,268
Cojedes ... 133,991
Delta Amacuro (Ter.) ... 56,720
Distrito Federal (Federal District) ... 2,070,742
Falcón ... 503,896
Guárico ... 393,467
Lara ... 945,064
Mérida ... 459,361
Miranda ... 1,421,442
Monagas ... 388,536
Nueva Esparta ... 197,198
Portuguesa ... 424,984
Sucre ... 585,698
Táchira ... 660,234
Trujillo ... 433,735
Yaracuy ... 300,597
Zulia ... 1,674,252

VIETNAM / Viet Nam

1979 C ... 52,741,766

Cities and Towns

Bac Lieu (1967 E) ... 41,700
Bac Ninh (1960 C) ... 22,520
Bien Hoa ... 190,086
Buon Me Thuot (1967 E) ... 37,500
Cam Pha (1971 E) ... 90,000
Cam Ranh (1973 E) ... 118,111
Can Tho ... 182,856
Chau Phu (1971 E) ... 40,400
Da Lat (1973 E) ... 105,072
Da Nang ... 318,655
Gia Dinh (1968 E) ... 151,100
Ha Dong (1960 C) ... 25,001
Hai Duong (1960 C) ... 24,752
Haiphong (▲ 1,279,067) ... 330,755
HANOI (★ 1,500,000) ... 819,913
• Ho Chi Minh City (Thanh Pho Ho Chi Minh) (★ 3,100,000) ... 2,441,185
Hon Gay ... 115,312
Hue ... 165,865
Khanh Hung (1967 E) ... 40,300
Kontum (1967 E) ... 18,700
Long Xuyen ... 112,488
My Tho ... 101,496
Nam Dinh ... 161,180
Nha Trang ... 172,663
Phan Rang (1967 E) ... 21,900
Phan Thiet (1967 E) ... 58,300
Phu Cuong (1971 E) ... 34,400
Phu Vinh (1971 E) ... 51,500
Pleiku (1967 E) ... 23,700
Quan Long (1967 E) ... 33,500
Qui Nhon ... 130,534
Rach Gia (1971 E) ... 104,161
Sa Dec (1967 E) ... 34,800
Tam Ky (1971 E) ... 18,100
Tan An (1967 E) ... 20,800
Thai Nguyen ... 138,023
Thanh Hoa ... 103,981
Truc Giang (1967 E) ... 45,200
Tuy Hoa (1967 E) ... 24,300
Vinh ... 154,040
Vinh Long (1971 E) ... 35,300
Vung Tau (1971 E) ... 108,436

VIRGIN ISLANDS, BRITISH

1980 C ... 12,034

Cities and Towns

• ROAD TOWN ... 2,479

VIRGIN ISLANDS OF THE UNITED STATES

1980 C ... 96,569

Cities and Towns

• CHARLOTTE AMALIE (★ 32,000) ... 11,842

WALLIS AND FUTUNA / Wallis et Futuna

1976 C ... 9,113

Cities and Towns

MATA-UTU ... 558
• Ono ... 624

WESTERN SAHARA

1974 E ... 108,000

Cities and Towns

• EL AAIÚN (LA'YOUN) ... 20,000

WESTERN SAMOA / Samoa i Sisifo

1981 C ... 156,349

Cities and Towns

• APIA ... 33,170

YEMEN / Al Yaman

1980 C ... 7,162,000

Cities and Towns

Dhamār ... 39,900
Hodeida (Al Ḥudaydah) ... 126,400
• ṢAN'Ā' ... 277,800
Ta'izz ... 119,600

YEMEN, PEOPLE'S DEMOCRATIC REPUBLIC OF / Jumhūrīyat al Yaman ad Dīmuqrāṭīyah ash Sha'bīyah

1977 E ... 1,797,000

Cities and Towns

• ADEN ('ADAN) ... 271,600
Al Mukallā ... 50,000
Madīnat ash Sha'b (Al Ittiḥad) (1973 E) ... 10,000

YUGOSLAVIA / Jugoslavija

1981 C ... 22,427,595

Cities and Towns

Banja Luka (▲ 183,618) ... 104,000
Bečej (1971 C) ... 26,470
• BELGRADE (BEOGRAD) (★ 1,400,000) ... 936,200
Bihać (1971 C) ... 24,026
Bijeljina (1971 C) ... 24,722
Bitola (▲ 137,835) ... 72,900
Bor (1971 C) ... 29,039
Brčko (1971 C) ... 25,422
Čačak (1971 C) ... 38,170
Celje (1971 C) ... 31,788
Cetinje (1971 C) ... 11,892
Đakovica (1971 C) ... 29,638
Dubrovnik (1971 C) ... 31,106
Karlovac (1971 C) ... 47,532
Kikinda (1971 C) ... 37,487
Kosovska Mitrovica (1971 C) ... 42,241
Kragujevac (▲ 164,823) ... 89,900
Kraljevo (1971 C) ... 27,817
Kranj (1971 C) ... 27,209
Kruševac (1971 C) ... 29,469
Kumanovo (1971 C) ... 46,406
Leskovac (1971 C) ... 44,255
Ljubljana (▲ 305,211) ... 205,600
Maribor (▲ 185,699) ... 105,100
Mostar (1971 C) ... 47,606
Nikšić (1971 C) ... 28,547
Niš (▲ 230,711) ... 151,600
Novi Pazar (1971 C) ... 29,072
Novi Sad (▲ 257,685) ... 170,800
Ohrid (1971 C) ... 26,370
Osijek (▲ 158,790) ... 103,600
Pančevo (★ Belgrade) ... 60,600
Peć (1971 C) ... 42,113
Pirot (1971 C) ... 29,228
Požarevac (1971 C) ... 33,121
Prilep (1971 C) ... 48,242
Priština (▲ 211,156) ... 96,100
Prizren (1971 C) ... 41,661
Pula (1971 C) ... 47,414
Rijeka (▲ 193,044) ... 160,300
Šabac (1971 C) ... 42,307
Sarajevo (▲ 448,500) ... 374,500
Šibenik (1971 C) ... 30,090
Sisak (1971 C) ... 38,421
Skopje (▲ 506,547) ... 406,400
Slavonski Brod (1971 C) ... 38,762
Smederevo (1971 C) ... 40,289
Sombor (1971 C) ... 43,971
Split (▲ 235,922) ... 193,600
Sremska Mitrovica (1971 C) ... 31,921
Štip (1971 C) ... 27,289
Subotica (▲ 154,611) ... 93,500
Svetozarevo (1971 C) ... 27,542
Tetovo (1971 C) ... 35,792
Titograd (▲ 132,290) ... 73,000
Titovo Užice (1971 C) ... 34,312
Titov Veles (1971 C) ... 36,026
Tuzla (▲ 121,717) ... 61,100
Valjevo (1971 C) ... 26,367
Varaždin (1971 C) ... 34,270
Vinkovci (1971 C) ... 29,072
Vranje (1971 C) ... 25,685
Vršac (1971 C) ... 34,231
Vukovar (1971 C) ... 30,149
Zadar (1971 C) ... 43,187
Zagreb ... 768,700
Zenica (▲ 132,733) ... 60,500
Zrenjanin (▲ 139,300) ... 63,900

Republics

Bosnia-Hercegovina (Bosna i Hercegovina) ... 4,124,008
Croatia (Hrvatska) ... 4,601,469
Macedonia (Makedonija) ... 1,912,267
Montenegro (Crna Gora) ... 584,310
Serbia (Srbija) ... 9,313,677
Slovenia (Slovenija) ... 1,891,864

ZAIRE / Zaïre

1984 C ... 29,671,407

Cities and Towns

Bandundu ... 63,189
Beni ... 73,319
Boma ... 88,556
Bukavu ... 171,064
Bumba ... 46,823
Bunia ... 46,224
Butembo ... 78,633
Gandajika ... 60,263
Gemena ... 62,641
Goma ... 76,745
Ilebo ... 48,831
Isiro ... 78,871
Kabalo ... 38,787
Kabinda ... 81,752
Kalemie (Albertville) ... 70,694
Kalima ... 22,716
Kamina ... 5,970
Kananga (Luluabourg) ... 290,898
Kikwit ... 146,784
Kindu ... 68,044
• KINSHASA (LÉOPOLDVILLE) ... 2,653,558
Kisangani (Stanleyville) ... 282,650
Kolwezi ... 201,382
Likasi (Jadotville) ... 194,465
Lisala ... 40,471
Lubumbashi (Élisabethville) ... 543,268
Matadi ... 144,742
Mbandaka (Coquilhatville) ... 125,263
Mbanza-Ngungu ... 43,900
Mbuji-Mayi (Bakwanga) ... 423,363
Mwene-Ditu ... 72,567
Tshikapa ... 105,484
Yangambi ... 53,726

ZAMBIA

1980 C ... 5,661,801

Cities and Towns

Chililabombwe (Bancroft) (★ 56,582) ... 25,900
Chingola ... 130,872
Kabwe (Broken Hill) ... 127,420
Kalulushi ... 53,383
Kitwe (★ 283,962) ... 207,500
Livingstone ... 61,296
Luanshya (★ 113,422) ... 61,600
• LUSAKA ... 535,830
Mufulira (★ 138,824) ... 77,100
Ndola ... 250,490

ZIMBABWE

1982 C ... 7,539,000

Cities and Towns

Bulawayo ... 413,814
Chinhoyi ... 24,322
Chitungwiza (★ Harare) ... 172,556
Gweru ... 78,918
• HARARE (SALISBURY) (★ 890,000) ... 656,011
Hwange ... 39,202
Kadoma ... 44,613
Kwekwe ... 47,607
Masvingo (Nyanda) ... 30,642
Mutare ... 69,621
Zvishavane ... 26,758

C Census. E Official estimate. UE Unofficial estimate.
• Largest city in country.

★ Population or designation of metropolitan area, including suburbs (see headnote).
▲ Population of an entire municipality, commune, or district, including rural area.